CENSUS OF INDIA 1891

Owing to the antiquity and rarity of this book, certain pages are regrettably absent, and readability is compromised due to the blurring of the original text. If you possess any insights regarding the availability of these missing sections, kindly inform us. Your assistance is crucial in ensuring the completion of this significant work for the benefit of future generations.

CENSUS OF INDIA, 1891

BOOK-32: VOLUME XXIII

HIS HIGHNESS THE NIZAM'S DOMINIONS

PART III
IMPERIAL AND SUPPLEMENTRY TABLES AND CASTE INDEX

MIRZA MEHDY KHAN

GYAN

Published by

Gyan Publishing House
5, Ansari Road
Daryaganj, New Delhi-110002
Phone: 011-47034999, 9811692060
E-mail: books@gyanbooks.com

Distribution Network
gyanbooks.com
India, USA, Canada, UK, Australia

ISBN: 978-81-212-7129-5 (Set) 28 Vols. In 49 Bindings
978-81-212-6927-8 (PB) Book-32, Vol. XXIII, Pt. III

First Published, 1893

2nd Impression 2024

Printed at: Gyan Press, Delhi.

CENSUS OF INDIA 1891

CENSUS OF INDIA, 1891.

VOLUME XXIII.

HIS HIGHNESS THE NIZAM'S DOMINIONS.

PART III.

IMPERIAL AND SUPPLEMENTARY TABLES,

AND

CASTE INDEX.

BY

MIRZA MEHDY KHAN, A.R.S.M., F.G.S., M.R.A.S., &c.,
Provincial Superintendent of Census Operations.

BOMBAY:
PRINTED FOR HIS HIGHNESS THE NIZAM'S GOVERNMENT
BY MESSRS. JEHANGIR B. MARZBAN & CO. AT THE "ADVOCATE OF INDIA" STEAM PRESS.
1893.

BOMBAY: PRINTED AT THE ADVOCATE OF INDIA STEAM PRESS.

CENSUS OF INDIA, 1891.

VOLUME XXIII.

H. H. THE NIZAM'S DOMINIONS.

PART III.

IMPERIAL AND SUPPLEMENTARY TABLES.

TABLE OF CONTENTS.

ADDENDA ET CORRIGENDA.

Table No.	Table Title.	Number of Sub-page.	Name of District, &c.	Number of column.	For	Read
I.	Area, Houses and Population ...	2	Elgandal	13	536,408	536,621
			Do.	16	504,473	504,260
			Total Districts	13	5,315,845	5,316,058
			Do.	16	5,131,066	5,130,853
			Do. Including Hyderabad ...	13	5,315,845	5,316,058
			Do. ...	16	5,131,066	5,130,853
			Grand Total	13	5,320,081	5,320,294
			Do.	16	5,133,420	5,133,207
VI.	Religions	2	City	10	38,609	38,600
			Total City and Suburbs ...		48,402	84,402
VII.	Age by Religion	2	Bedar	7	11,505	11,465
			Parbhani		9,939	9,979
			Bedar	9	16,020	15,979
			Parbhani		14,150	14,191
		12	Aurangabad	19	2	3
			Birh		3	2
XVI.	Castes and Sub-divisions	34	Total Unspecified	6	827,262	827,254
			Do. Total		969,357	969,349
			Do. Unspecified	7	421,232	421,228
			Do. Total		494,719	494,715
			Do. Unspecified	8	406,030	406,026
			Do. Total		474,638	474,634
		36	Naldrug Unspecified	42	175,158	175,150
			Do. Total		200,926	200,918
			Do. Unspecified	43	89,124	89,120
			Do. Total		102,255	102,251
			Do. Unspecified	44	86,034	86,030
			Do. Total		98,671	98,667
		110	Total Unspecified	6	121,156	121,449
			Do. Total		415,208	415,501
			Do. Unspecified	7	62,945	63,122
			Do. Total		213,154	213,331
			Do. Unspecified	8	58,211	58,327
			Do. Total		202,054	202,170
			Hyderabad Unspecified... ...	9	3,837	3,978
			Do. Total		5,091	5,232
			Do. Unspecified ...	10	2,240	2,332
			Do. Total		3,030	3,122
			Do. Unspecified ...	11	1,597	1,646
			Do. Total		2,061	2,110
			Bidar Unspecified	45	25,971	26,123
			Do. Total		141,209	141,361
			Do. Unspecified	46	13,114	13,199
			Do. Total		71,643	71,728
			Do. Unspecified	47	12,857	12,924
			Do. Total		69,566	69,633
XVIIA.	Occupations by age	11	Total Order VI.	6	65,629	651,629
		13	Total Serial No. 91.	36	84	87
XVIIB.	Occupations by district	2	Grand Total Order No. I. ...	6	51,110	541,110
			Do. Order No. II. ...	7	8,426	37,926
C.	Literate by Language known ...	65	Total Group 28	7	3	...
	Caste Index	XIV	Erkala	3	11,915	11,955

TABLE I.

AREA, HOUSES AND POPULATION.

TABLE I.

Area, Houses and Population.

District or State.	Area	Number of		Occupied Houses.			Population.								
							Total.			Males.			Females.		
	In square miles.	Towns.	Villages.	Total.	Towns.	Villages.	Total.	Towns.	Villages.	Total.	Towns.	Villages.	Total.	Towns.	Villages.
1	2	3	4	5	6	7	8	9	10	11	12	13	14	15	16
Telingana. Hyderabad City...	2·50	1	...	21,008	21,008	...	124,057	124,057	...	62,748	62,748	..	61,309	61,309	..
Suburbs including Secunderabad	23·50		...	75,660	75,660	...	290,982	290,982	...	153,576	153,576	..	137,406	137,406	..
Total	26	1	...	96,668	96,668	...	415,039	415,039	...	216,824	216,324	..	198,715	198,715	...
Atraf-i-Balda District ...	3,802	...	850	75,877	...	75,877	889,784	...	889,784	198,258	...	198,258	191,526	...	191,526
Mahabubnagar (Nagar Karnul)	6,497	2	1,353	131,171	3,501	127,670	674,649	18,110	656,539	341,601	9,152	332,449	333,048	8,958	324,090
Nalgonda	4,131	1	960	108,848	1,028	107,820	624,617	5,906	618,711	319,823	2,960	316,863	304,794	2,946	301,848
Warangal (Khamam) ...	9,779	2	1,517	156,403	1,898	154,505	853,129	16,596	836,533	438,635	8,571	430,064	414,494	8,025	406,469
Elgandal	7,207	8	1,543	196,987	10,476	186,511	1,094,601	53,720	1,040,881	563,845	27,224	536,408	530,756	26,496	504,473
Indur	4,822	6	1,113	128,461	9,476	118,985	639,598	47,830	591,768	319,237	23,102	296,135	320,361	24,728	295,633
Medak	2,017	2	632	74,939	3,372	71,567	364,735	14,906	349,829	183,908	7,278	176,630	180,827	7,628	173,199
Mahratwara. Aurangabad.	6,176	5	1,831	163,940	15,267	148,673	828,975	78,616	750,359	421,018	39,893	381,125	407,957	38,723	369,234
Birh...	4,430	5	1,008	128,614	11,977	116,637	642,722	51,586	591,136	328,530	26,204	302,326	314,192	25,382	288,810
Nander	3,343	5	1,169	144,107	8,860	135,247	632,529	41,099	591,430	320,136	20,417	299,719	312,393	20,682	291,711
Naldrug	4,010	7	855	130,229	11,881	118,348	649,272	51,786	597,486	331,747	26,614	305,133	317,525	25,172	292,353
Bidar.	4,180	7	1,437	180,290	11,727	168,563	901,984	55,872	846,112	457,088	27,499	429,589	444,896	28,373	416,528
Parbhani	5,087	8	1,502	160,228	16,094	144,134	805,335	71,046	734,289	410,499	36,246	374,253	394,836	34,800	360,036
Sirpur Tandur	5,029	1	945	41,597	1,265	40,332	231,754	6,084	225,670	116,955	2,862	114,093	114,799	3,222	111,577
Karnatic or Kanada. Gulbarga	4,064	5	1,104	136,469	12,176	124,293	649,258	57,887	591,371	329,678	29,551	300,127	319,580	28,336	291,244
Raichur	3,661	6	919	102,392	12,216	90,176	512,455	62,497	449,958	260,217	31,729	228,488	252,238	30,768	221,470
Lingasugur	4,907	5	1,273	124,994	7,544	117,450	620,014	34,959	585,055	311,394	17,209	294,185	308,620	17,750	290,870
Total Districts ..	82,672	75	20,011	2,185,546	138,758	20,46,788	11,115,411	668,500	10,446,911	5,652,569	336,511	5,315,845	54,62,842	331,989	5,131,066
Total Districts including Hyderabad	82,698	76	20,011	2,282·214	235,426	20,46,788	11,530,450	1,083,539	10,446,911	5,868,893	552,835	5,315,845	5,661,557	530,704	5,131,066
Railways	.....	...	...	1,573	...	1,573	6,590	...	6,590	4,236	..	4,236	2,354	...	2,354
Grand Total...	82,698	76	20,011	2,283,787	235,426	20,48,361	11,537,040	1,083,539	10,453,501	5,873,129	552,835	5,320,081	5,663,911	530,704	5,133,420

TABLE II.

VARIATION IN THE ENUMERATED POPULATION SINCE LAST CENSUS.

TABLE II.
Variation in Population.

TABLE II.

Variation in the enumerated population since last Census.

District or State.	Total. 1891.	Total. 1881.	Total. Variation.	Males. 1891.	Males. 1881.	Males. Variation.	Females. 1891.	Females. 1881.	Females. Variation.
1	2	3	4	5	6	7	8	9	10
Hyderabad: City ...	124,057	128,675	882	62,748	61,031	1,717	61,309	62,644	−1,335
Hyderabad: Suburbs including Secunderabad...	290,982	243,742	47,240	153,576	126,846	26,730	137,406	116,896	20,510
Total ...	415,039	367,417	47,622	216,324	187,877	28,447	198,715	179,540	19,175
Telingana: Atraf-i Balda District ...	389,784	355,787	33,997	198,258	179,943	18,315	191,526	175,844	15,682
Mahabubnagar (Nagar Karnul) ...	674,649	547,694	126,955	341,601	275,680	65,921	333,048	272,014	61,034
Nalgonda ...	624,617	494,190	130,427	319,823	251,419	68,404	304,794	242,771	62,023
Warangal (Khamam) ...	858,129	675,746	177,383	438,635	344,807	93,828	414,494	330,939	83,555
Elgandal ...	1,094,601	939,539	155,062	563,845	478,410	85,435	530,756	461,129	69,627
Indur ...	639,598	577,264	62,334	319,237	288,652	30,585	320,361	288,612	31,749
Medak ...	364,735	326,720	38,015	183,908	163,735	20,173	180,827	162,985	17,842
Mahratwara: Aurangabad ...	828,975	730,380	98,595	421,018	373,084	47,934	407,957	357,296	50,661
Birh ...	642,722	558,745	83,977	328,530	286,170	42,360	314,192	272,575	41,617
Nander ...	632,529	636,023	−3,494	320,136	323,402	−3,266	312,393	312,621	−228
Naldrug ...	649,272	543,402	105,870	331,747	278,276	53,471	317,525	265,126	52,399
Bidar ...	901,984	788,827	113,157	457,088	401,517	55,571	444,896	387,310	57,586
Parbhani ...	805,335	685,099	120,236	410,499	351,559	58,940	394,836	333,540	61,296
Sirpur Tandur ...	231,754	214,674	17,080	116,955	108,489	8,516	114,799	106,285	8,564
Karnatic or Kanada: Gulbarga ...	649,258	523,838	125,420	329,678	264,641	65,037	319,580	259,197	60,388
Raichur ...	512,455	398,782	113,673	260,217	202,738	57,479	252,238	196,044	56,194
Lingasugur ...	620,014	480,715	139,299	311,394	241,347	70,047	308,620	239,368	69,252
Total Districts ...	11,115,411	9,477,425	1,637,986	5,652,569	4,818,819	833,750	5,462,842	4,668,606	799,236
Total Districts including Hyderabad...	11,530,450	9,844,842	1,685,608	5,868,893	5,001,696	867,197	5,661,557	4,848,146	818,411
Railways ...	6,590	752	5,838	4,236	441	3,795	2,354	311	2,043
Grand Total ...	11,537,040	9,845,594	1,691,446	5,873,129	5,002,137	870,992	5,663,911	4,843,457	820,454

TABLE III.

TOWNS AND VILLAGES CLASSIFIED BY POPULATION

TABLE III.

Towns and Villages classified by Population.

District or State.	Total No. of Towns and Villages.	Total Population.	1—199		200—499		500—999		1,000—1,999		2,000—2,999		3,000—4,999		5,000 9,999		10,000—14,999		15,000—19,999		20,000—49,999		50,000 and over.	
			No.	Population.	No.	Population	No.	Population.	No.	Population.	No.	Population.	No.	Population.	No.	Population	No.	Population.	No.	Population.	No.	Population.	No.	Population.
1	2	3	4	5	6	7	8	9	10	11	12	13	14	15	16	17	18	19	20	21	22	23	24	25
Hyderabad { City...	...	124,057	...	...	...	...	...	...	...	...	...	...	...	...	...	...	...	...	...	...	...	...	...	124,057
Hyderabad { Suburbs including Secunderabad...	1	290,982	...	...	...	...	...	...	...	...	...	...	...	...	...	...	...	...	...	...	...	...	1	290,982
Total......	1	415,039	...	...	...	...	...	...	...	...	...	...	...	...	...	...	...	...	...	...	...	...	1	415,039
Telingana { Atraf-i-Balda District	850	889,784	323	32,041	259	83,817	169	116,808	82	112,833	14	34,171	3	10,614	...	...	...	...	...	...	...	...	...	...
Mahabubnagar (Nagar Karnul) ...	1,355	674,649	418	42,682	468	153,263	316	222,400	125	168,453	19	43,544	7	26,247	1	6,222	1	11,888	...	...	...	...	...	...
Nalgonda	961	624,617	172	19,168	314	111,805	283	202,756	164	217,484	24	55,553	3	11,945	1	5,906	...	...	...	...	...	...	...	...
Warangal (Khamam)	1,519	853,129	460	44,629	448	152,486	382	278,329	185	251,083	36	86,289	6	23,717	1	5,112	1	11,484	...	...	...	...	...	...
Elgandal	1,551	1,094,601	348	36,856	404	138,094	455	329,966	277	379,509	43	99,661	16	56,795	8	53,720	...	...	...	...	...	...	...	...
Indur	1,119	639,598	343	38,549	386	141,655	237	169,065	116	145,082	22	62,834	9	34,583	4	25,416	2	22,414	...	...	...	...	...	...
Medak...	634	364,735	141	15,627	252	86,228	160	109,583	59	79,933	12	28,976	8	29,482	2	14,906	...	...	...	...	...	...	...	...
Mahratwara { Aurangabad	1,836	828,975	632	65,958	706	227,910	364	256,440	105	136,091	17	37,779	7	26,181	3	21,376	...	...	...	...	2	57,240	...	...
Birh	1,013	642,722	182	24,147	400	133,735	301	204,842	88	115,365	23	58,407	14	54,640	3	18,669	1	13,923	1	18,994	...	...	...	...
Nander	1,174	632,529	299	35,877	463	157,637	283	193,743	96	128,931	21	50,589	7	24,653	4	27,994	1	13,105	...	...	...	...	...	...
Naldrug	862	649,272	119	14,717	278	95,969	289	201,650	132	181,674	27	68,326	10	35,150	6	41,275	1	10,511	...	...	...	...	...	...
Bidar	1,444	901,984	232	29,938	585	195,904	423	295,333	153	201,270	29	72,643	15	51,024	5	31,531	2	24,341	...	...	...	...	...	...
Parbhani	1,510	805,335	425	49,838	577	193,423	358	243,984	104	139,380	27	64,391	11	43,823	4	26,705	4	44,341	...	...	...	...	...	...
Sirpur Tandur	946	231,754	606	52,171	216	67,640	90	62,542	31	38,424	2	4,893	...	...	1	6,084	...	...	...	...	...	...	...	...
Karnatic or Kanada { Gulbarga	1,109	649,258	272	31,295	450	153,717	241	159,560	100	138,657	30	69,226	11	38,916	4	29,687	...	...	...	...	1	28,200	...	...
Raichur	925	512,455	237	28,677	377	128,598	218	147,903	69	92,422	11	25,903	7	26,455	4	24,651	1	14,672	...	...	1	23,174	...	...
Lingasugur...	1,278	620,014	388	45,166	547	181,154	231	159,762	75	103,124	18	43,806	14	52,043	5	34,959	...	...	...	...	...	...	...	...
Total Districts......	20,086	11,115,411	5,597	607,286	7,130	2,402,535	4,800	3,354,616	1,961	2,629,715	375	906,991	148	545,768	56	374,218	14	166,679	1	18,994	4	108,614	...	...
Total Districts including Hyderabad ...	20,087	11,530,450	5,597	607,286	7,130	2,402,585	4,800	3,354,616	1,961	2,629,715	375	906,991	148	545,768	56	374,218	14	166,679	1	18,994	4	108,614	1	415,039
Railways......	...	6,590	...	...	...	...	...	...	...	...	...	...	...	...	...	...	...	...	...	...	...	...	...	...
Grand Total......	20,087	11,537,040	5,597	607,286	7,130	2,402,585	4,800	3,354,616	1,961	2,629,715	375	906,991	148	545,768	56	374,218	14	166,679	1	18,994	4	108,614	1	415,039

N. B.—As the Statement showing population of Railways was sent in from the Berar Office shown only by sections and not by Stations the population of each of the different Stations cannot be, and has not been amalgamated with that of the district or town in which it is situated, and only the total population is given collectively in the second column. Thus the details not being shown the totals of town and village population in the grand total columns will not agree with the grand total of total population until 6590, the total population of Railways, be deducted from the grand total of total population, which is obvious.

TABLE IV.

TOWNS BY POPULATION.

NOTE.—In this Table, towns marked with an asterisk, were merely villages during the Census of 1881, but since then their populations have increased and they have been classed as towns in this Census. The populations of those towns italicized as well as marked with an asterisk owing to the destruction of the records of the preceding Census cannot be ascertained and are consequently not stated.

Rajura and Selu in the Bedar and Parbhani districts, respectively, were in last Census, classified as Towns, having contained over 5,000 inhabitants, but the number having fallen, they have been excluded from the list of Towns, thus :—

		Population 1891.				Population 1881.		
		Total.	M.	F.		Total.	M.	F.
Rajura......	Bedar district	4,539	2,237	2,302	....	5,064	2,653	2,411
Selu.........	Parbhani district ...	3,979	2,061	1,918	....	5,055	2,571	2,484

Bolarum, was shown as a Town, in the Atraf-i-Balda district, in 1881, with a total population of 13,207—(males 6,789—females 6,418) but in 1891, it was included in the Secunderabad Cantonment. Its total population at the recent Census being 12,123 (males 6,551, females 5,572) hence its not appearing in the list of Towns.

TABLE IV.

Towns according to Population compared with the preceding Census.

Towns.	District.	Muny. or Cant.	Both sexes.			Males.			Females.		
			1891.	1881.	Difference.	1891.	1881.	Difference.	1891.	1881.	Difference.
1	2	3	4	5	6	7	8	9	10	11	12
Hyderabad. City	......	M. ...	124,057	123,675	382	62,748	61,031	1,717	61,309	62,644	− 1,335
Hyderabad. Suburbs including Secunderabad ...	......	C. & M.	290,982	243,742	47,240	153,576	126,846	26,730	137,406	116,896	20,510
Aurangabad	Aurangabad.	M. & C.	33,887	30,219	3,668	17,186	15,546	1,640	16,701	14,673	2,028
Gulbarga	Gulbarga ...	M. ...	28,200	22,834	5,366	14,747	11,898	2,849	13,453	10,936	2,517
Raichur	Raichur ...	M. & C.	23,174	15,387	7,787	11,836	7,817	4,019	11,338	7,570	3,768
Jalnapur	Aurangabad.	M. & C.	19,128	16,199	2,929	10,196	7,912	2,284	8,932	8,287	645
Birh	Birh ...	M. ...	18,994	17,398	1,596	9,533	8,639	894	9,461	8,759	702
Gudwal	Raichur ...	...	14,672	12,207	2,465	7,917	6,461	1,456	6,755	5,746	1,009
Ambajogai	Birh ...	M. & C.	13,923	12,052	1,871	7,135	5,982	1,153	6,788	6,070	718
Nander	Nander ...	M. ...	13,105	14,091	− 986	6,488	6,996	− 508	6,617	7,095	− 478
Kalyani	Bidar ...	...	13,026	11,092	1,934	6,458	5,561	897	6,568	5,531	1,037
Hingoli	Parbhani ...	M. & C.	11,966	14,804	− 2,838	6,283	7,623	− 1,340	5,683	7,181	− 1,498
Narainpett	Mahbubnagar ...	M. ...	11,888	11,290	598	5,880	5,471	409	6,008	5,819	189
Warangal	Warangal ...	M. ...	11,484	8,545	2,939	6,027	4,413	1,614	5,457	4,132	1,325
Indur	Indur ...	M. ...	11,482	10,264	1,218	5,671	5,053	618	5,811	5,211	600
Kadrabad	Aurangabad.	M. & C.	11,402	9,876	1,526	5,463	4,768	695	5,939	5,108	831
Basmat	Parbhani ...	...	11,361	11,022	339	5,614	5,686	−72	5,747	5,336	411
Bidar	Bidar ...	M. ...	11,315	9,730	1,585	5,643	4,918	725	5,672	4,812	860
Nirmal	Indur ...	...	10,932	10,577	355	5,188	4,910	278	5,744	5,667	77
Manwat	Parbhani ...	...	10,912	8,767	2,145	5,683	4,422	1,261	5,229	4,345	884
Dharasco	Naldrug ...	M. ...	10,511	8,801	1,710	5,512	4,600	912	4,999	4,201	798
Parbhani	Parbhani ...	M. ...	10,102	7,996	2,106	5,233	4,147	1,086	4,869	3,849	1,020
Shorapur	Lingsugur ...	...	9,754	9,900	− 146	4,635	4,777	− 142	5,119	5,123	− 4
Jagtial	Elgandal ...	...	9,538	7,302	2,236	4,899	3,719	1,180	4,639	3,583	1,056
Aland	Gulbarga ...	...	9,538	6,201	3,337	4,887	3,113	1,774	4,651	3,088	1,563
Lathur	Naldrug ...	...	9,063	8,648	415	4,730	4,345	385	4,333	4,303	30
Paithain	Aurangabad.	...	8,788	10,874	—2,086	4,318	6,074	− 1,756	4,470	4,800	− 330
Kosgi	Gulbarga ...	...	8,418	7,946	472	4,105	3,829	276	4,313	4,117	196
Sonepett	Parbhani ...	...	8,090	6,407	1,683	4,075	3,014	1,061	4,015	3,393	622
Thair*	Naldrug ...	...	8,015	3,984	4,031	4,077	2,000	2,077	3,938	1,984	1,954
Homnabad	Bidar ...	...	7,736	7,199	537	3,728	3,613	115	4,008	3,586	422
Khandar*	Nander ...	...	7,709	4,074	3,635	3,858	2,067	1,791	3,851	2,007	1,844
Bhysa	Do. ...	...	7,688	6,701	987	3,785	3,326	459	3,903	3,375	528
Siddipett	Elgandal ...	...	7,671	7,002	669	3,899	3,468	431	3,772	3,534	238
Parli	Birh ...	...	7,659	7,090	569	3,966	3,462	504	3,693	3,628	65
Medak	Medak ...	...	7,556	7,026	530	3,575	3,264	311	3,981	3,762	219
Sadaseopett	Do. ...	...	7,350	8,775	− 1,425	3,703	4,210	− 507	3,647	4,565	− 918
Deodrug*	Raichur ...	...	7,213	4,587	2,626	3,524	2,260	1,264	3,689	2,327	1,362

TABLE IV.

Towns according to Population compared with the preceding Census—*continued.*

Towns.	District.	Muny. or Cant.	Both Sexes.			Males.			Females.		
			1891.	1881	Difference.	1891.	1881.	Difference.	1891.	1881.	Difference.
1	2	3	4	5	6	7	8	9	10	11	12
Armur	Indur	...	7,015	5,530	1,485	3,409	2,750	659	3,606	2,780	826
Kopal	Lingasugur	...	6,991	5,083	1,908	3,553	2,500	1,053	3,438	2,583	855
Tuljapur	Naldrug	...	6,862	5,938	924	3,519	2,912	607	3,343	3,026	317
*Yadgir**	Raichur	...	6,767	...	...	3,159	...	...	3,608	...	...
Pathri	Parbhani	...	6,726	6,572	154	3,358	3,189	169	3,368	3,383	− 15
Udgir	Bidar	...	6,722	7,141	− 419	3,362	3,524	− 162	3,360	3,617	− 257
Gangakhair	Parbhani	...	6,653	5,517	1,136	3,364	2,861	503	3,289	2,656	633
Mudgal	Lingasugur	...	6,641	5,064	1,577	3,258	2,461	797	3,383	2,603	780
Mudhole	Indur	...	6,624	6,177	447	3,153	3,008	145	3,471	3,169	302
Deglur	Nander	...	6,578	6,808	− 230	3,282	3,372	− 90	3,296	3,436	− 140
Kohir	Bidar	...	6,557	7,027	− 470	3,118	3,549	− 431	3,439	3,478	− 39
Wemalwada	Elgandal	...	6,511	6,097	414	3,279	3,055	224	3,232	3,042	190
Chithapur*	Gulbarga	...	6,435	4,025	2,410	3,245	1,980	1,265	3,190	2,045	1,145
Karimnagar	Elgandal	M.	6,348	5,436	912	3,479	2,989	490	2,869	2,447	422
Mahabubnagar*	Mahbubnagar	M.	6,222	4,680	1,542	3,272	2,408	864	2,950	2,272	678
*Gungawati**	Lingasugur	...	6,188	...	...	3,086	...	...	3,102	...	...
Owsa	Naldrug	...	6,091	5,640	451	3,056	2,909	147	3,035	2,731	304
Edlabad	Sirpur Tandur	M.	6,084	5,522	562	2,862	2,594	268	3,222	2,928	294
Manthani	Elgandal	...	6,046	5,794	252	2,897	2,779	118	3,149	3,015	134
Mukhair	Nander	...	6,019	5,795	224	3,004	3,036	− 32	3,015	2,759	256
Peddapalli	Elgandal	...	5,995	6,158	− 163	2,948	3,020	− 72	3,047	3,138	− 91
Kondalwadi	Indur	...	5,936	7,570	−1,634	2,890	3,848	− 958	3,046	3,722	− 676
Nalgonda	Nalgonda	M.	5,906	5,283	623	2,960	2,830	130	2,946	2,453	493
Koratla	Elgandal	...	5,892	5,522	370	2,944	2,705	239	2,948	2,817	131
Moorum*	Naldrug	...	5,874	4,079	1,795	3,028	2,090	938	2,846	1,989	857
Bodhan	Indur	...	5,841	5,898	− 57	2,791	2,795	− 4	3,050	3,103	− 53
Chinnur	Elgandal	...	5,719	5,721	− 2	2,879	2,772	107	2,840	2,949	− 109
*Manvi**	Raichur	...	5,669	...	...	2,803	...	...	2,866	...	...
*Majalgaon**	Birh	...	5,556	...	...	2,778	...	...	2,778	...	...
*Dharur**	do.	...	5,454	...	...	2,792	...	...	2,662	...	...
*Sugar**	Lingasugur	...	5,435	...	...	2,727	...	...	2,708	...	...
Baizapur	Aurangabad	...	5,411	5,300	111	2,730	2,629	101	2,681	2,671	10
Bhalki	Bidar	...	5,383	5,163	220	2,663	2,533	130	2,720	2,630	90
Wasi*	Naldrug	...	5,370	4,086	1,284	2,692	2,047	645	2,678	2,039	639
Kodangal*	Gulbarga	...	5,296	2,457	2,839	2,567	1,161	1,406	2,729	1,296	1,433
Wulur	Parbhani	...	5,236	5,980	− 744	2,636	3,029	− 393	2,600	2,951	− 351
*Akeli**	Bidar	...	5,133	...	...	2,527	...	...	2,606	...	...
*Matwada**	Warangal	...	5,112	...	...	2,544	...	...	2,568	...	...
*Jalhalli**	Raichur	...	5,002	...	...	2,490	...	...	2,512	...	...

TABLE V.

TOWNS ARRANGED TERRITORIALLY, WITH POPULATION BY RELIGION.

TABLE V.

Towns arranged territorially, with Population by Religion.

DISTRICT.	TOWN.	Total Population. Total.	Total Population. Males.	Total Population. Females.	Hindu. Total.	Hindu. Males.	Hindu. Females.	Mahomedan. Total.	Mahomedan. Males.	Mahomedan. Females.	Christian. Total.	Christian. Males.	Christian. Females.	Sikh. Total.	Sikh. Males.	Sikh. Females.	Parsi. Total.	Parsi. Males.	Parsi. Females.	Jain. Total.	Jain. Males.	Jain. Females.	Jew. Total.	Jew. Males.	Jew. Females.
City	....	124,057	62,748	61,309	48,868	25,728	22,685	75,498	36,898	38,600	44	27	17	59	29	30	1	1	...	92	65	27	...	...	...
Suburbs including Secunderabad... ...	....	290,982	153,576	137,406	178,477	93,064	85,413	97,363	51,561	45,802	13,785	8,129	5,656	610	369	241	615	371	244	111	75	36	21	7	14
Total ..	....	415,039	216,324	198,715	226,840	118,792	108,048	172,861	88,459	84,402	13,829	8,156	5,673	669	398	271	616	372	244	203	140	63	21	7	14
Mahabubnagar ...	Narainpett ..	11,888	5,880	6,008	9,102	4,454	4,648	2,781	1,422	1,359	...	...	...	4	3	1	...	...	...	1	1	...	...	...	...
Do. ..	Mahabubnagar	6,222	3,272	2,950	4,351	2,227	2,124	1,814	1,019	795	57	26	31	..	...	...	...	...	...	...	...	...	...	...	...
Total ..	....	18,110	9,152	8,958	13,453	6,681	6,772	4,595	2,441	2,154	57	26	31	4	3	1	...	...	...	1	1	...	...	...	...
Nalgonda	Nalgonda ..	5,906	2,960	2,946	3,184	1,606	1,578	2,621	1,291	1,330	22	17	5	72	44	28	7	2	5	...	...	...	...	...	...
Warangal	Warangal ..	11,484	6,027	5,457	8,354	4,337	4,017	2,762	1,485	1,277	104	50	54	252	147	105	12	8	4	...	...	...	...	...	...
Do.	Matwada ..	5,112	2,544	2,568	3,438	1,746	1,692	1,674	798	876	...	..	..	...	...	...	...	...	...	...	...	...	...	...	...
Total ...	....	16,596	8,571	8,025	11,792	6,083	5,709	4,436	2,283	2,153	104	50	54	252	147	105	12	8	4	...	...	...	...	...	...
Elgandal	Jagtial ...	9,538	4,899	4,639	8,239	4,225	4,014	1,298	673	625	...	...	...	...	...	...	1	1	...	...	...	...	...	...	...
Do.	Sidipett ..	7,671	3,899	3,772	6,434	3,328	3,106	1,213	557	656	24	14	10	...	...	..	...	...	...	...	...	...	...	...	...
Do.	Wemalwada ..	6,511	3,279	3,232	6,227	3,131	3,096	284	148	136	...	...	...	...	...	..	...	...	...	...	...	...	...	...	...
Do.	Karimnagar...	6,848	3,479	3,369	4,418	2,375	2,043	1,542	874	668	102	73	29	286	157	129	...	...	...	...	...	...	...	...	...
Do.	Manthani ...	6,046	2,897	3,149	5,814	2,744	3,070	232	153	79	...	...	...	...	...	...	...	...	...	...	...	...	...	...	...
Do.	Peddapalli ..	5,995	2,948	3,047	4,910	2,414	2,496	1,085	534	551	...	...	...	...	...	...	...	...	...	...	...	...	...	...	...
Do.	Koratla ...	5,892	2,944	2,948	4,645	2,342	2,303	1,247	602	645	..	...	...	...	..	...	...	...	...	...	...	...	...	...	...
Do.	Chinnur ...	5,719	2,879	2,840	5,131	2,561	2,570	583	315	268	5	3	2	..	..	...	...	...	...	...	...	...	...	...	...
Total ...	....	53,720	27,224	26,496	45,818	23,120	22,698	7,484	3,856	3,628	131	90	41	286	157	129	1	1	...	...	...	...	...	...	...
Indur	Indur ...	11,482	5,671	5,811	8,081	3,927	4,154	3,096	1,597	1,499	9	3	6	290	143	147	6	1	5	...	...	...	...	...	...
Do.	Nirmal	10,932	5,188	5,744	8,532	4,072	4,460	2,392	1,112	1,280	...	..	...	5	2	3	1	1	...	2	1	1	...	...	...
Do.	Armur .	7,015	3,409	3,606	6,192	3,032	3,160	810	372	438	...	..	..	...	...	...	...	...	...	13	5	8	...	...	...
Do.	Mudhole ...	6,624	3,153	3,471	4,298	2,088	2,210	2,294	1,049	1,245	...	...	...	32	16	16	...	...	...	...	...	...	...	...	...
Do.	Kundalwadi...	5,936	2,890	3,046	4,916	2,371	2,545	1,014	517	497	...	...	..	...	..	...	...	...	...	6	2	4	...	...	...
Do.	Bodhan ...	5,841	2,791	3,050	4,465	2,137	2,328	1,371	650	721	3	2	1	..	...	...	...	...	...	2	2	...	...	...	...
Total ...	....	47,830	23,102	24,728	36,484	17,627	18,857	10,977	5,297	5,680	12	5	7	327	161	166	7	2	5	23	10	13	...	...	...

TABLE V.

Towns arranged territorially, with Population by Religion.—*Continued.*

DISTRICT.	TOWN.	TOTAL POPULATION. Total.	Males.	Females.	HINDU. Total.	Males.	Females.	MAHOMEDAN. Total.	Males.	Females.	CHRISTIAN. Total.	Males.	Females.	SIKH. Total.	Males.	Females.	PARSI. Total.	Males.	Females.	JAIN. Total.	Males.	Females.	JEW. Total.	Males.	Females.
Medak	Medak ...	7,556	3,575	3,981	5,296	2,570	2,726	2,075	913	1,162	28	15	13	157	77	80	...	...	...	...	...	...	...	...	...
Do.	Sadasopett ...	7,350	3,703	3,647	6,284	3,117	3,167	1,064	586	478	...	...	...	...	...	...	...	...	...	2	...	2	...	...	...
Total ...	......	14,906	7,278	7,628	11,580	5,687	5,893	3,139	1,499	1,640	28	15	13	157	77	80	...	...	...	2	...	2	...	...	...
Aurangabad ...	Aurangabad ...	33,887	17,186	16,701	18,907	9,687	9,220	14,041	6,961	7,080	316	168	148	52	29	23	60	36	24	511	305	206	...	...	...
Do.	Jaluapur ...	19,128	10,196	8,932	13,282	7,139	6,143	5,519	2,878	2,641	143	81	62	1	1	...	18	9	9	165	88	77	...	...	...
Do.	Paithan ...	8,788	4,318	4,470	6,351	3,133	3,218	2,338	1,137	1,201	2	1	1	...	...	...	1	1	...	96	46	50	...	...	...
Do.	Kadrabad ...	11,402	5,463	5,939	7,401	3,584	3,817	3,586	1,652	1,934	45	19	26	...	...	...	35	13	22	335	195	140	...	...	...
Do.	Baizapur ...	5,411	2,730	2,681	4,154	2,094	2,060	1,161	584	577	...	...	...	...	...	...	7	3	4	89	49	40	...	...	...
Total ...	......	78,616	39,893	38,723	50,095	25,637	24,458	26,645	13,212	13,433	506	269	237	53	30	23	121	62	59	1,196	683	513	...	...	...
Birh	Birh	18,994	9,533	9,461	13,016	6,536	6,480	5,510	2,746	2,764	24	12	12	195	102	93	8	3	5	241	134	107	...	...	...
Do.	Ambajogai or Mominabad	13,923	7,135	6,788	9,336	4,746	4,590	4,277	2,224	2,053	95	52	43	34	19	15	7	4	3	174	90	84	...	...	...
Do.	Parli ...	7,659	3,966	3,693	6,353	3,295	3,058	1,054	535	519	5	4	1	...	...	...	2	2	...	245	130	115	...	...	...
Do.	Mazalgaon ...	5,556	2,778	2,778	4,319	2,162	2,157	1,166	580	586	8	6	2	...	...	...	...	...	...	63	30	33	...	...	...
Do.	Dharur ...	5,454	2,792	2,662	4,108	2,100	2,008	1,284	659	625	...	...	...	...	...	...	...	...	...	62	33	29	...	...	...
Total ...	......	51,586	26,204	25,382	37,132	18,839	18,293	13,291	6,744	6,547	132	74	58	229	121	108	17	9	8	785	417	368	...	...	...
Nander	Nandor ...	13,105	6,488	6,617	7,304	3,733	3,571	5,068	2,377	2,691	...	...	...	659	344	315	7	6	1	67	28	39	...	...	...
Do.	Khandar ...	7,709	3,858	3,851	5,790	2,910	2,880	1,856	920	936	...	...	...	...	...	...	...	...	...	63	28	35	...	...	...
Do.	Bhysa ...	7,688	3,785	3,903	5,141	2,537	2,604	2,547	1,248	1,299	...	...	...	...	...	...	...	...	...	...	...	...	...	...	...
Do.	Deglur ...	6,578	3,282	3,296	4,961	2,505	2,456	1,529	740	789	...	...	...	55	19	36	...	...	...	33	18	15	...	...	...
Do.	Mukhair ...	6,019	3,004	3,015	4,670	2,341	2,329	1,272	627	645	...	...	...	18	11	7	...	...	...	59	25	34	...	...	...
Total ...	......	41,099	20,417	20,682	27,866	14,026	13,840	12,272	5,912	6,360	...	...	...	732	374	358	7	6	1	222	99	123	...	...	...
Naldrug	Dharaseo ...	10,511	5,512	4,999	7,504	3,919	3,585	2,623	1,399	1,224	18	12	6	...	...	...	2	2	...	364	180	184	...	...	...
Do.	Lathur ...	9,063	4,730	4,333	6,694	3,534	3,160	2,166	1,096	1,070	6	2	4	...	...	...	...	...	...	197	98	99	...	...	...
Do.	Thair ...	8,015	4,077	3,938	7,225	3,679	3,546	779	390	389	...	...	...	...	...	...	...	...	...	11	8	3	...	...	...
Do.	Tuljapur ...	6,862	3,519	3,343	6,212	3,176	3,036	551	285	266	...	...	...	...	...	...	...	...	...	99	58	41	...	...	...
Do.	Owsa ...	6,091	3,056	3,035	4,220	2,105	2,115	1,842	935	907	...	...	...	...	...	...	...	...	...	29	16	13	...	...	...
Do.	Moorum ...	5,874	3,028	2,846	4,855	2,478	2,377	952	510	442	...	...	...	...	...	...	...	...	...	67	40	27	...	...	...
Do.	Wasi ...	5,370	2,692	2,678	4,724	2,352	2,372	608	318	290	...	...	...	...	...	...	...	...	...	38	22	16	...	...	...
Total ...	......	51,786	26,614	25,172	41,434	21,243	20,191	9,521	4,938	4,588	24	14	10	...	...	...	2	2	...	805	422	383	...	...	...

TABLE V.

Towns arranged territorially, with Population by Religion.—*Continued.*

District.	Town.	Total Population.			Hindu.			Mahomedan.			Christian.			Sikh.			Parsi.			Jain.			Jew.		
		Total.	Males.	Females.	Total.	Males.	Females.	Total.	Males.	Females.	Total.	Males.	Females.	Total.	Males.	Females.	Total.	Males.	Females.	Total.	Males.	Females.	Total.	Males.	Females.
Bidar	Kalyani ...	13,026	6,458	6,568	7,364	3,666	3,698	5,625	2,773	2,852	...	...	...	3	2	1	...	...	...	34	17	17	...	...	...
Do.	Bidar ...	11,315	5,643	5,672	5,475	2,792	2,683	5,745	2,807	2,938	9	6	3	4	3	1	...	...	...	82	35	47	...	...	...
Do.	Homnabad ...	7,736	3,728	4,008	5,752	2,733	3,019	1,874	945	929	4	1	3	...	...	...	...	...	...	106	49	57	...	...	...
Do.	Udgir ...	6,722	3,362	3,360	4,331	2,205	2,126	2,308	1,107	1,201	...	...	...	...	...	...	3	2	1	80	48	32	...	...	...
Do.	Kohir ...	6,557	3,118	3,439	3,384	1,598	1,786	3,170	1,518	1,652	...	...	...	...	...	...	...	...	...	3	2	1	...	...	...
Do.	Bhalki ...	5,383	2,663	2,720	4,281	2,126	2,155	1,079	526	553	...	...	...	...	...	...	...	...	...	23	11	12	...	...	...
Do.	Akeli ...	5,133	2,527	2,606	3,528	1,768	1,760	1,597	755	842	...	...	...	...	...	...	...	...	...	8	4	4	...	...	...
Total ...	......	55,872	27,499	28,373	34,115	16,888	17,227	21,398	10,431	10,967	13	7	6	7	5	2	3	2	1	336	166	170	...	...	...
Parbhani	Hingoli ...	11,966	6,283	5,683	7,526	3,888	3,638	3,993	2,087	1,906	65	39	26	267	205	62	9	2	7	106	62	44	...	...	...
Do.	Basmath ...	11,361	5,614	5,747	8,228	4,091	4,137	3,018	1,468	1,550	1	1	...	...	...	...	2	2	...	112	52	60	...	...	...
Do.	Manwat ...	10,912	5,683	5,229	8,848	4,584	4,264	1,564	830	734	...	...	...	...	...	...	...	...	...	500	269	231	...	...	...
Do.	Parbhani ...	10,102	5,233	4,869	6,319	3,358	2,961	3,571	1,763	1,808	...	...	...	1	1	...	1	1	...	210	110	100	...	...	...
Do.	Sonepett ...	8,090	4,075	4,015	6,562	3,312	3,250	1,825	658	667	..	...	...	24	11	13	...	...	...	179	94	85	...	...	...
Do.	Pathri ...	6,726	3,358	3,368	3,941	1,963	1,978	2,693	1,355	1,338	...	...	...	...	...	...	...	...	...	92	40	52	...	...	...
Do.	Gungakhair ...	6,653	3,364	3,289	5,352	2,696	2,656	1,233	631	602	...	...	...	3	...	3	...	...	...	65	37	28	...	...	...
Do.	Wulur ...	5,236	2,636	2,600	3,773	1,923	1,850	1,082	526	556	...	...	...	...	...	...	...	...	...	381	187	194	...	...	...
Total ...	......	71,046	36,246	34,800	50,549	25,815	24,734	18,479	9,318	9,161	66	40	26	295	217	78	12	5	7	1,645	851	794	...	...	...
Sirpur Tandur... ...	Yedlabad ...	6,084	2,862	3,222	4,759	2,206	2,553	1,318	656	662	...	...	...	...	...	...	...	...	...	7	...	7	...	...	...
Gulbarga	Gulbarga ...	28,200	14,747	13,453	15,211	8,027	7,184	12,668	6,547	6,121	175	88	87	...	...	...	5	4	1	141	81	60	...	...	...
Do.	Aland ...	9,538	4,887	4,651	4,458	2,311	2,147	4,478	2,267	2,211	...	...	...	...	...	...	1	1	...	601	308	293	...	...	...
Do.	Kosgi ...	8,418	4,105	4,313	6,999	3,463	3,536	1,418	642	776	...	...	...	...	...	...	...	...	...	1	...	1	...	...	...
Do.	Chithapur ...	6,435	3,245	3,190	4,394	2,213	2,181	2,008	1,016	992	1	1	...	...	...	...	7	4	3	25	11	14	...	...	...
Do.	Kodangal ...	5,296	2,567	2,729	4,281	2,093	2,188	1,015	474	541	...	...	...	...	...	...	...	...	...	...	...	...	...	...	...
Total ...	......	57,887	29,551	28,336	35,343	18,107	17,236	21,587	10,946	10,641	176	89	87	...	...	...	13	9	4	768	400	368	...	...	...
Raichur	Raichur ...	23,174	11,836	11,338	16,892	8,552	8,340	5,821	3,023	2,798	304	155	149	4	3	1	33	19	14	120	84	36	...	...	...
Do.	Gudwall ...	14,672	7,917	6,755	11,235	5,951	5,284	3,435	1,964	1,471	1	1	...	...	...	...	1	1	...	...	...	...	...	...	...
Do.	Deodrug ...	7,213	3,524	3,689	5,579	2,684	2,895	1,634	840	794	...	...	...	...	...	...	...	...	...	...	...	...	...	...	...
Do.	Yadgir ...	6,767	3,159	3,608	3,439	1,648	1,791	3,290	1,494	1,796	1	...	1	...	...	...	...	...	...	37	17	20	...	...	...
Do.	Manvi ...	5,669	2,803	2,866	4,218	2,060	2,158	1,450	742	708	...	...	...	...	...	...	...	...	...	1	1	...	...	...	...
Do.	Jalhalli ...	5,002	2,490	2,512	4,490	2,221	2,269	512	269	243	...	...	...	...	...	...	...	...	...	...	...	...	...	...	...
Total ...	......	62,497	31,729	30,768	45,858	23,116	22,737	16,142	8,332	7,810	306	156	150	4	3	1	34	20	14	158	102	56	...	...	...
Lingasugur	Shorapur ...	9,754	4,635	5,119	6,969	3,291	3,678	2,690	1,280	1,410	9	5	4	...	...	...	...	...	...	86	59	27	...	...	...
Do.	Kopal ...	6,991	3,553	3,438	4,798	2,385	2,413	2,113	1,114	999	17	9	8	...	...	...	3	2	1	60	43	17	...	...	...
Do.	Mudgal ...	6,641	3,258	3,383	4,252	2,085	2,167	2,163	1,061	1,102	201	94	107	...	...	...	...	...	...	25	18	7	...	...	...
Do.	Gungawati ...	6,138	3,036	3,102	4,718	2,320	2,398	1,418	715	703	...	...	...	...	...	...	...	...	...	2	1	1	...	...	...
Do.	Sagar... ...	5,435	2,727	2,708	4,132	2,076	2,056	1,303	651	652	...	...	...	...	...	...	...	...	...	...	...	...	...	...	...
Total ...	......	34,959	17,209	17,750	24,869	12,157	12,712	9,687	4,821	4,866	227	108	119	...	...	...	3	2	1	173	121	52	...	...	...
Grand Total ...	......	1,083,589	552,885	530,704	701,166	357,630	343,536	356,453	180,431	176,022	15,633	9,116	6,517	3,637	1,787	1,850	855	502	353	6,824	3,412	2,912	21	7	14

TABLE VI.

RELIGIONS.

TABLE VI.

Religions.

District or State.	Total Population.			Hindu.			Mussulman.		
	Total.	Males.	Females.	Total.	Males.	Females.	Total.	Males.	Females.
Telingana.									
Hyderabad. City...	124,057	62,748	61,309	48,363	25,728	22,635	75,498	36,898	38,609
Hyderabad. Suburbs including Secunderabad	290,982	153,576	137,406	178,477	93,064	85,413	97,363	51,561	45,802
Total......	415,039	216,324	198,715	226,840	118,792	108,048	172,861	88,459	48,402
Atraf i-Balda District	389,784	198,258	191,526	346,357	175,815	170,542	42,626	22,033	20,593
Mahabubnagar (Nagar Karnul)	674,649	341,601	333,048	618,889	313,686	305,158	55,610	27,796	27,814
Nalgonda	624,617	319,823	304,794	593,449	303,850	289,599	30,909	15,833	15,076
Warangal	853,129	438,635	414,494	808,440	415,393	393,047	42,882	22,257	20,625
Elgandal	1,094,601	563,845	530,756	1,050,045	540,939	509,106	44,013	22,593	21,420
Indur	639,598	319,237	320,361	588,138	293,699	294,439	50,193	24,894	25,299
Medak	364,735	183,908	180,827	326,267	164,560	161,707	38,047	19,126	18,921
Mahratwara.									
Aurangabad	828,975	421,018	407,957	724,876	367,815	357,061	94,217	47,952	46,265
Birh	642,722	328,530	314,192	586,349	299,236	287,113	51,812	26,831	24,981
Nander	632,529	320,136	312,393	574,320	290,302	284,018	56,018	28,707	27,311
Naldrug	649,272	331,747	317,525	586,540	299,462	287,078	58,034	29,799	28,235
Bidar	901,984	457,088	444,896	785,543	397,793	387,750	114,743	58,885	56,858
Parbhani	805,335	410,499	394,836	732,737	373,246	359,491	66,696	34,098	32,598
Sirpur Tandur	231,754	116,955	114,799	192,869	97,144	95,725	10,006	5,065	4,941
Karnatic or Kanada.									
Gulbarga	649,258	329,678	319,580	552,137	279,964	272,173	95,179	48,685	46,494
Raichur	512,455	260,217	252,238	460,011	233,282	226,729	51,877	26,607	25,270
Lingasugur	620,014	311,894	308,620	556,975	279,077	277,898	61,624	31,491	30,133
Total Districts......	11,115,411	5,652,569	5,462,842	10,083,892	5,125,263	4,958,629	964,486	492,152	472,334
Total Districts including Hyderabad	11,530,450	5,868,893	5,661,557	10,310,732	5,244,055	5,066,677	1,137,347	580,611	556,736
Railways	6,590	4,236	2,354	4,517	2,916	1,601	1,319	885	434
Grand Total......	11,537,040	5,873,129	5,663,911	10,315,249	5,246,971	5,068,278	1,138,666	581,496	557,170

TABLE VI.
Religions.

Christian.			Sikh.			Parsi.			Jain.			Gond.			Bhil.			Jew.		
Total.	Males.	Females.	Total.	Males.	Females.	Total.	Males.	Females.	Total.	Males.	Females.	Total.	Males.	Females.	Total.	Males.	Females.	Total.	Males.	Females.
44	27	17	59	29	30	1	1	...	92	65	27	......	...	...	...	...	...	...	...	...
13,785	8,129	5,656	610	369	241	615	371	244	111	75	36	......	...	...	...	...	...	21	7	14
13,829	8,156	5,673	669	398	271	616	372	244	208	140	68	......	...	...	...	...	...	21	7	14
450	216	234	254	143	111	3	2	1	94	49	45	......	...	...	...	...	...	...	...	...
121	67	54	75	48	27	...	...	...	4	4	...	......	...	...	...	...	...	...	...	...
135	73	62	111	63	48	13	4	9	...	...	...	......	...	...	...	...	...	...	...	...
1,484	794	690	281	161	120	40	28	12	2	2	...	......	...	...	...	...	...	...	...	...
193	122	71	335	182	153	3	2	1	12	7	5	......	...	...	...	...	...	...	...	...
40	22	18	553	286	267	7	2	5	129	61	68	538	273	265	...	...	...	...	...	...
106	53	53	213	121	92	...	...	...	102	48	54	......	...	...	...	...	...	...	...	...
1,929	960	969	275	119	156	130	68	62	7,548	4,104	3,444	......	...	...	...	...	...	...	...	...
148	86	62	245	130	115	19	11	8	4,149	2,236	1,913	......	...	...	...	...	...	...	...	...
2	2	...	1,130	581	549	7	6	1	1,046	534	512	6	4	2	...	...	...	...	...	...
214	107	107	5	4	1	10	10	...	4,469	2,365	2,104	......	...	...	...	...	...	...	...	...
21	12	9	57	30	27	3	2	1	1,617	866	751	......	...	...	...	...	...	...	...	...
67	41	26	362	255	107	24	12	12	5,449	2,847	2,602	......	...	...	...	...	...	...	...	...
...	...	...	44	22	22	1	1	...	248	128	120	28,116	14,360	13,756	470	235	235	...	...	...
287	150	137	14	5	9	66	43	23	1,575	831	744	......	...	...	...	...	...	...	...	...
335	177	158	4	3	1	34	20	14	194	128	66	......	...	...	...	...	...	...	...	...
398	203	195	5	3	2	13	8	5	999	612	387	......	...	...	...	...	...	...	...	...
5,930	3,085	2,845	3,963	2,156	1,807	373	219	154	27,637	14,822	12,815	28,660	14,637	14,023	470	235	235	...	...	...
19,759	11,241	8,518	4,632	2,554	2,078	989	591	398	27,840	14,962	12,878	28,660	14,637	14,023	470	235	235	21	7	14
670	389	281	5	2	3	69	37	32	5	4	1	......	...	...	...	...	...	5	3	2
20,429	11,630	8,799	4,637	2,556	2,081	1,058	628	430	27,845	14,966	12,879	28,660	14,637	14,023	470	235	235	26	10	16

TABLE VII.

AGES BY RELIGIONS.

TABLE VII.

Age by Religion Part (A)—All Religions.

	District or State.	Total Population.			Age Period.															
					Under 1 year.		1 year.		2 years.		3 years.		4 years.		Total 0—4		5—9		10—14	
		Total.	Males.	Females.	Males.	Females.	Males.	Females.	Males.	Females.	Males.	Females.	Males.	Females.	Males.	Females.	Males.	Females.	Males.	Females.
	1	2	3	4	5	6	7	8	9	10	11	12	13	14	15	16	17	18	19	20
Telingana. Hyderabad.	City	124,057	62,748	61,309	1,466	1,462	697	692	1,058	1,081	984	951	1,026	1,082	5,281	5,268	4,751	4,824	4,961	4,570
	Suburbs including Secunderabad	290,982	153,576	137,406	3,655	3,670	1,910	2,027	3,207	3,298	3,010	3,195	2,948	2,905	14,730	15,095	14,967	14,930	13,998	12,389
	Total	415,039	216,324	198,715	5,121	5,132	2,607	2,719	4,265	4,379	3,994	4,146	3,974	3,987	19,961	20,363	19,718	19,754	18,959	16,959
	Atraf-i-Balda District	389,784	198,258	191,526	4,750	5,206	4,013	4,481	5,693	6,349	5,731	6,279	5,455	5,450	25,642	27,765	25,271	24,168	20,876	16,647
	Mahabubnagar (Nagar Karnul)	674,649	341,601	333,048	8,246	9,126	7,567	8,615	11,543	12,764	11,476	12,801	11,204	11,846	50,036	54,652	46,648	48,728	34,547	27,526
	Nalgonda	624,617	319,823	304,794	10,330	11,256	4,790	5,588	11,278	12,297	12,359	13,404	11,408	11,584	50,165	54,074	46,240	45,418	38,275	30,437
	Warangal (Khamam)	858,129	438,635	414,494	10,166	10,959	8,736	9,918	14,092	15,532	15,889	17,267	14,421	15,060	63,254	68,781	63,401	60,503	54,332	43,217
	Elgandal	1,094,601	563,845	530,756	13,613	14,418	13,149	14,552	19,654	20,738	18,364	19,985	18,843	19,248	83,623	88,886	82,727	77,476	76,996	58,312
	Indur	689,598	319,237	320,361	7,767	8,111	7,589	7,910	8,781	9,183	8,518	9,819	9,127	9,089	41,782	43,612	43,493	40,677	38,264	30,539
	Medak	364,735	183,908	180,827	3,904	4,049	4,183	4,715	4,918	5,085	4,790	5,074	4,787	4,797	22,577	23,670	23,283	22,468	19,648	16,046
Mahratwara.	Aurangabad	828,975	421,018	407,957	11,957	12,700	8,783	9,778	13,197	15,186	11,554	13,839	11,248	12,114	56,739	63,617	55,685	54,714	45,787	38,049
	Birh	642,722	328,530	314,192	9,273	10,032	7,164	8,000	11,453	12,402	9,171	10,824	9,868	9,824	46,429	50,582	42,228	39,916	34,182	26,388
	Nander	632,529	320,136	312,393	8,675	9,288	7,468	7,998	11,328	12,012	8,151	9,213	10,251	10,320	45,868	48,826	42,480	39,882	36,479	28,297
	Naldrug	649,272	331,747	317,525	10,806	11,539	7,324	8,242	12,397	13,589	9,153	10,203	10,489	10,255	50,169	58,828	41,257	39,581	33,287	25,248
	Bidar	901,984	457,088	444,896	11,939	12,970	11,505	12,182	16,020	16,856	10,627	11,679	13,832	14,055	63,842	67,742	56,714	54,380	48,728	39,372
	Parbhani	805,335	410,499	394,836	10,749	12,133	9,939	11,418	14,150	16,298	11,178	13,112	12,680	12,887	58,777	65,848	52,887	50,452	42,983	34,236
	Sirpur Tandur	231,754	116,955	114,799	2,605	2,692	3,043	3,343	3,525	4,125	3,680	4,334	4,020	4,609	16,873	19,103	18,362	17,799	15,642	12,541
Karnatic or Kanada.	Gulbarga	649,258	329,678	319,580	8,820	9,235	8,862	9,590	11,282	11,912	9,789	10,393	10,748	10,496	49,501	51,626	40,762	39,003	27,664	21,916
	Raichur	512,455	260,217	252,238	8,613	9,206	5,499	5,959	9,477	10,046	10,038	10,742	9,220	9,134	42,847	45,087	37,189	36,102	20,985	16,528
	Lingasugur	620,014	311,394	308,620	9,781	10,239	6,516	7,090	11,646	12,375	10,630	11,059	11,442	11,259	50,015	52,022	42,733	42,398	25,354	20,892
	Total Districts	11,115,411	5,652,569	5,462,842	151,994	1,63,159	126,130	139,314	190,424	206,694	171,048	188,977	178,548	181,587	818,139	879,671	761,800	728,655	613,479	486,141
	Total Districts including Hyderabad	11,530,450	5,868,893	5,661,557	157,115	1,68,291	128,737	142,033	194,689	211,073	175,042	193,128	182,517	185,514	838,100	900,034	781,018	748,409	632,438	508,100
	Railways	6,590	4,236	2,354	70	51	84	71	80	85	75	80	77	77	386	364	304	298	153	156
	Grand Total	11,537,040	5,873,129	5,663,911	157,185	1,68,342	128,821	142,104	194,769	211,158	175,117	193,208	182,594	185,591	838,486	900,398	781,322	748,707	632,591	503,256

TABLE VII.

Age by Religion Part (A)—All Religions.—*Continued.*

District or State.	Age Period. 15–19		20–24		25–29		30–34		35–39		40–44		45–49		50–54		55–59		60 and over.		Unspecified.	
	Males.	Females.	Males.	Females.	Males.	Females.	Males.	Females.	Males.	Females.	Males.	Females.	Males.	Females.	Males.	Females.	Males.	Females.	Males.	Females.	Males.	Females.
	21	22	23	24	25	26	27	28	29	30	31	32	33	34	35	36	37	38	39	40	41	42
Telingana. Hyderabad.																						
City...	5,670	6,788	7,050	8,138	7,140	6,071	7,146	5,696	3,909	2,668	5,614	5,176	2,080	1,423	3,899	3,854	983	735	4,298	4,670	16	1,438
Suburbs including Secunderabad	12,951	14,409	17,653	16,523	17,199	12,815	16,256	13,055	9,187	5,747	12,199	10,400	4,781	3,059	8,164	7,514	2,191	1,512	9,371	9,682	29	276
Total......	18,621	21,192	24,603	24,661	24,339	18,886	23,402	18,751	13,096	8,410	17,813	15,576	6,861	4,482	12,063	11,368	3,174	2,247	13,669	14,352	45	1,714
Atraf-i-Balda District... ...	15,207	15,515	16,583	18,818	27,952	16,652	17,762	17,876	11,094	8,055	25,356	14,096	6,528	4,529	10,981	10,977	2,567	1,829	12,864	14,346	80	258
Mahabubnagar (Nagar Karnul)	25,528	26,368	29,795	33,644	31,746	29,300	30,283	31,132	19,986	14,208	25,374	23,102	11,311	7,716	15,478	16,563	3,618	3,041	17,062	21,735	209	338
Nalgonda	27,020	26,454	26,775	29,336	26,202	23,679	24,826	25,045	15,154	10,527	20,559	18,814	8,600	5,475	14,862	18,555	3,243	2,177	17,811	19,587	91	216
Warangal (Khamam)	35,751	34,458	36,687	41,047	36,999	33,794	37,696	36,519	19,395	13,646	31,741	27,464	10,592	6,790	21,319	19,791	3,492	2,484	23,727	25,752	249	348
Elgandal	45,581	45,867	45,825	51,087	46,686	43,929	44,825	44,069	27,041	19,904	35,380	33,037	14,872	10,308	26,242	24,199	5,600	4,028	28,277	29,146	220	508
Indur	23,475	25,911	24,810	30,356	31,267	29,577	29,352	30,626	17,614	14,236	28,428	23,277	10,124	7,917	15,846	17,541	3,478	2,908	16,204	22,474	100	710
Medak	13,671	14,361	14,878	17,447	17,158	16,283	16,094	16,807	10,211	7,738	14,042	13,705	6,176	4,316	10,778	10,667	2,582	1,995	12,787	14,071	78	1,258
Mahratwara.																						
Aurangabad	30,388	33,318	30,605	38,930	42,914	37,553	39,032	36,517	25,546	20,151	29,677	27,567	14,909	10,797	20,524	18,009	5,794	3,957	23,168	24,364	250	414
Birh	22,045	23,501	24,155	32,152	34,345	30,170	31,022	29,902	19,562	16,246	24,587	21,934	11,381	8,441	16,603	14,770	4,282	2,970	17,448	17,884	266	386
Nander	19,611	21,745	22,801	28,746	33,242	30,467	31,105	30,027	17,870	14,298	24,735	23,761	10,360	7,877	17,086	16,517	3,756	2,897	14,522	18,431	271	627
Naldrug...	21,730	23,472	24,922	31,701	35,370	31,189	31,227	30,557	19,141	15,603	25,212	22,878	11,878	8,249	16,748	14,742	4,344	3,107	16,332	17,194	185	176
Bidar	30,286	31,051	34,506	41,225	46,548	42,472	42,364	43,109	25,131	20,114	35,618	34,307	16,440	12,025	24,959	24,040	6,485	4,844	25,299	29,840	168	375
Parbhani	24,981	27,487	29,372	37,049	42,865	38,077	40,669	37,845	24,690	19,241	32,478	28,470	13,788	9,894	22,121	19,528	4,806	3,468	19,896	22,962	186	289
Sirpur Tandur	7,818	8,221	8,406	9,927	10,024	9,871	10,879	10,259	5,845	4,479	8,417	7,733	3,084	2,241	5,448	5,397	1,085	921	5,046	6,267	31	40
Karnatic or Kanada.																						
Gulbarga	22,714	22,510	25,960	30,720	34,725	32,312	32,648	33,340	20,579	15,465	26,933	23,569	12,415	8,393	16,067	16,374	4,101	3,320	15,497	20,887	112	145
Raichur	17,300	17,060	24,450	27,614	25,534	23,838	23,612	23,942	16,248	11,720	18,836	16,739	9,806	6,406	10,883	11,175	3,216	2,742	9,832	13,287	29	48
Lingasugur	22,887	22,284	27,925	32,254	30,916	29,860	29,459	30,827	18,871	15,278	22,961	20,917	10,871	7,801	13,404	14,541	4,041	3,284	11,883	16,141	74	121
Total Districts......	405,938	419,583	448,455	531,053	544,493	499,023	512,855	508,399	318,978	240,904	415,334	381,370	182,625	129,175	279,289	268,381	66,485	49,917	287,655	334,318	2,544	6,252
Total Districts including Hyderabad	424,559	440,775	473,058	555,714	568,832	517,909	536,257	527,150	327,074	249,314	438,147	396,946	189,486	183,657	291,352	279,749	69,659	52,164	301,324	348,670	2,589	7,966
Railways......	194	208	548	335	732	308	605	224	463	91	368	125	170	64	159	88	62	20	92	73	...	...
Grand Total......	424,753	440,983	473,606	556,049	569,564	518,217	536,862	527,374	327,537	249,405	438,515	397,071	189,656	183,721	291,511	279,837	69,721	52,184	301,416	348,743	2,589	7,966

TABLE VII.

Age by Religion Part (B)—Hindus.

District or State.		Total Hindus. Total.	Males.	Females.	Age period. Under 1 year. Males.	Females.	1 year. Males.	Females.	2 years. Males.	Females.	3 years. Males.	Females.	4 years. Males.	Females.	Total. 0–4 Males.	Females.	5–9 Males.	Females.	10–14 Males.	Females.
1		2	3	4	5	6	7	8	9	10	11	12	13	14	15	16	17	18	19	20
Telingana. Hyderabad.	City	48,363	25,728	22,635	549	568	266	288	407	436	489	409	371	380	2,082	2,081	1,931	1,974	1,956	1,751
	Suburbs including Secunderabad	178,477	93,064	85,413	2,224	2,264	1,145	1,294	1,980	2,012	1,995	2,052	1,786	1,718	9,130	9,340	9,289	9,856	8,638	7,722
	Total......	226,840	118,792	108,048	2,773	2,832	1,411	1,582	2,387	2,448	2,484	2,461	2,157	2,098	11,162	11,421	11,170	11,830	10,594	9,473
	Atraf-i-Balda District	346,357	175,815	170,542	4,262	4,695	3,585	4,041	5,078	5,703	5,207	5,664	4,891	4,828	23,023	24,931	22,536	21,456	18,165	14,874
	Mahabubnagar (Nagar Karnul) ...	618,839	313,686	305,153	7,542	8,418	7,001	8,023	10,615	11,778	10,603	11,866	10,373	10,473	46,134	50,558	42,650	39,850	31,670	25,249
	Nalgonda	593,449	303,850	289,599	9,886	10,728	4,583	5,292	10,848	11,772	11,862	12,828	10,902	11,075	48,081	51,695	44,045	43,175	36,361	28,921
	Warangal (Khamam)	808,440	415,393	393,047	9,636	10,456	8,367	9,451	13,441	14,778	15,146	16,527	13,761	14,382	60,351	65,594	60,169	57,358	51,572	41,109
	Elgandal	1,050,045	540,939	509,106	13,165	13,937	12,712	14,092	18,953	19,966	17,790	19,252	18,105	18,494	80,725	85,741	79,398	74,207	73,953	55,963
	Indur	588,138	293,699	294,439	7,228	7,625	7,060	7,394	8,062	8,482	7,882	8,665	8,339	8,281	38,571	40,447	40,013	37,413	35,188	28,224
	Medak...	326,267	164,560	161,707	3,495	3,708	3,768	4,264	4,359	4,492	4,325	4,577	4,279	4,272	20,226	21,313	20,636	20,103	17,507	14,472
Mahratwara.	Aurangabad	724,876	367,815	357,061	10,543	11,140	7,788	8,662	11,658	13,480	10,156	12,216	9,872	10,598	50,017	56,096	48,810	47,874	40,009	33,392
	Birh	586,349	299,236	287,113	8,475	9,261	6,535	7,311	10,534	11,397	8,424	9,454	8,519	8,923	42,487	46,346	38,595	36,468	31,096	24,259
	Nander	574,320	290,302	284,018	7,928	8,559	6,788	7,323	10,397	10,950	7,410	8,379	9,336	9,402	41,859	44,613	38,645	36,158	33,085	25,852
	Naldrug	586,540	299,462	287,078	9,864	10,478	6,629	7,500	11,234	12,382	8,366	9,329	9,504	9,260	45,597	48,949	37,221	35,650	30,156	22,815
	Bidar	785,543	397,793	387,750	10,412	11,284	10,086	10,785	13,984	14,746	9,194	10,123	11,980	12,161	55,656	59,099	49,141	47,283	42,402	34,433
	Parbhani	732,737	373,246	359,491	9,911	11,220	9,147	10,547	13,013	14,909	10,249	11,964	11,600	11,748	53,920	60,388	48,096	45,973	38,998	31,240
	Sirpur Tandur	192,869	97,144	95,725	2,227	2,265	2,541	2,810	2,938	3,384	3,026	3,657	3,280	3,709	14,012	15,825	15,357	15,040	13,200	10,526
Karnatic or Kanada.	Gulbarga	552,137	279,964	272,173	7,565	7,910	7,513	8,140	9,619	10,133	8,428	8,910	9,087	8,865	42,212	43,958	34,321	32,916	23,608	18,573
	Raichur	460,011	233,282	226,729	7,728	8,305	4,948	5,377	8,499	9,024	9,181	9,740	8,275	8,245	38,631	40,691	33,331	32,375	18,815	14,845
	Lingasugur.	556,975	279,077	277,898	8,813	9,229	5,830	6,384	10,495	11,135	9,625	9,977	10,270	10,139	45,033	46,864	38,248	38,058	22,774	18,914
	Total Districts......	10,083,892	5,125,263	4,958,629	138,685	149,263	114,881	127,346	173,727	188,511	156,874	173,128	162,873	164,855	746,540	803,103	691,207	661,892	558,554	448,661
Total Districts including Hyderabad ...		10,310,732	5,244,055	5,066,677	141,458	152,095	116,292	128,928	176,114	190,959	159,358	175,589	164,580	166,953	757,702	814,524	702,377	672,722	569,148	458,134
	Railways......	4,517	2,916	1,601	45	87	65	50	58	57	46	57	57	56	271	257	192	191	97	88
	Grand Total......	10,315,249	5,246,971	5,068,278	141,503	152,182	116,357	128,978	176,172	191,016	159,854	175,646	164,587	167,009	757,973	814,781	702,569	672,913	569,245	458,222

TABLE VII.

Age by Religion. Part (B)—Hindus.—*Continued.*

District or State.	15—19 Males.	15—19 Females.	20—24 Males.	20—24 Females.	25—29 Males.	25—29 Females.	30—34 Males.	30—34 Females.	35—39 Males.	35—39 Females.	40—44 Males.	40—44 Females.	45—49 Males.	45—49 Females.	50—54 Males.	50—54 Females.	55—59 Males.	55—59 Females.	60 and over. Males.	60 and over. Females.	Unspecified. Males.	Unspecified. Females.
	21	22	23	24	25	26	27	28	29	30	31	32	33	34	35	36	37	38	39	40	41	42
Tellingana. Hyderabad. City	2,123	2,099	2,772	2,605	3,071	2,260	3,264	2,281	1,716	1,028	2,485	2,047	853	542	1,565	1,513	364	257	1,591	1,844	5	353
Suburbs including Secunderabad	7,863	8,733	9,983	10,184	10,125	7,880	10,363	8,356	5,587	3,590	7,592	6,559	2,814	1,909	4,964	4,868	1,194	892	5,555	6,058	17	16
Total......	9,986	10,832	12,755	12,789	13,196	10,140	13,627	10,637	7,303	4,618	10,077	8,606	3,667	2,451	6,529	6,381	1,558	1,149	7,146	7,902	22	369
Atraf-i-Balda District	13,548	13,862	14,727	16,689	15,915	14,768	15,657	15,851	9,847	7,214	13,448	12,582	5,749	4,082	9,610	9,782	2,242	1,625	11,295	12,777	58	49
Mahabubnagar (Nagar Karnul) ..	23,441	24,279	27,488	30,710	29,263	26,801	27,893	28,512	18,412	13,085	23,228	21,113	10,896	7,074	14,160	15,058	3,296	2,798	15,473	19,816	187	215
Nalgonda	25,641	25,228	25,470	27,825	24,729	22,454	23,517	23,791	14,282	9,951	19,489	17,796	8,141	5,173	14,067	12,878	3,067	2,059	16,871	18,529	89	124
Warangal (Khamam)	33,785	32,681	34,628	38,876	34,769	31,982	35,586	34,609	18,290	12,951	30,106	25,923	10,061	6,431	20,131	18,697	3,259	2,305	22,441	24,258	245	272
Elgandal	48,629	44,170	44,008	48,945	44,763	42,170	42,924	42,183	25,928	19,117	38,777	31,532	14,281	9,985	25,086	23,071	5,349	3,891	27,011	27,818	212	362
Indur...	21,625	23,886	22,908	27,817	28,781	27,195	26,944	28,078	16,213	13,159	21,511	21,212	9,317	7,348	14,525	16,064	3,197	2,708	14,820	20,792	86	96
Medak	12,298	12,991	13,348	15,631	15,416	14,616	14,471	15,072	9,143	7,015	12,559	12,305	5,586	3,956	9,648	9,647	2,319	1,798	11,410	12,722	48	66
Mahratwara. Aurangabad	26,353	29,230	26,412	34,043	37,828	33,083	34,148	31,916	22,477	17,750	25,817	28,900	13,097	9,583	17,646	15,568	5,081	3,538	19,909	20,892	216	246
Birh...	20,020	21,491	21,958	28,425	31,416	27,620	28,244	27,219	17,802	14,922	22,309	20,018	10,418	7,702	15,084	13,464	3,917	2,689	15,697	16,206	248	284
Nander	17,589	19,742	20,512	26,088	30,152	27,799	28,277	27,342	16,151	13,115	22,559	21,583	9,402	7,210	15,477	15,014	3,411	2,612	12,941	16,619	242	271
Naldrug	19,562	21,337	22,423	28,729	32,064	28,250	28,160	27,589	17,298	14,137	22,655	20,597	10,676	7,491	14,984	13,249	3,900	2,850	14,642	15,361	124	124
Bidar	26,126	26,885	29,982	35,897	40,770	37,229	37,007	37,607	22,077	17,703	31,050	29,828	14,413	10,578	21,692	20,926	5,650	4,281	21,685	25,814	142	187
Parbhani	22,548	24,947	26,537	33,708	38,999	34,806	37,069	34,378	22,564	17,546	29,505	25,836	12,594	9,045	20,057	17,655	4,383	3,175	17,804	20,587	172	207
Sirpur Tandur	6,602	6,919	6,991	8,185	8,384	8,218	8,859	8,450	4,853	3,762	6,826	6,368	2,580	1,911	4,455	4,463	915	784	4,087	5,241	23	33
Karnatic or Kanada. Gulbarga	19,880	19,192	21,955	26,089	29,607	27,580	27,845	28,451	17,654	13,319	22,798	20,002	10,520	7,223	13,563	14,101	3,502	2,900	12,914	17,788	90	86
Raichur	15,493	15,385	21,998	24,869	22,943	21,344	21,168	21,452	14,613	10,645	16,787	14,986	8,846	5,809	9,638	10,032	2,861	2,497	8,629	11,758	29	41
Lingasugur	20,562	20,204	25,018	28,990	27,734	26,888	26,828	27,636	16,868	13,837	20,531	18,814	9,779	7,094	11,914	13,109	3,681	3,024	10,560	14,872	52	94
Total Districts......	368,197	382,429	406,363	481,516	493,533	452,803	464,087	460,086	284,467	219,228	374,945	344,402	165,256	117,595	251,637	242,778	60,030	45,534	258,189	301,845	2,258	2,757
Total Districts including Hyderabad.	378,183	393,261	419,118	494,255	506,729	462,943	477,714	470,723	291,770	223,846	385,022	353,008	168,923	120,046	258,166	249,159	61,588	46,683	265,335	309,747	2,280	3,126
Railways......	110	130	367	226	516	225	438	172	323	66	270	84	125	39	102	55	42	18	63	50	...	...
Grand Total......	378,293	393,391	419,485	494,481	507,245	463,168	478,152	470,895	292,093	223,912	385,292	353,092	169,048	120,085	258,268	249,214	61,630	46,701	265,398	309,797	2,280	3,126

TABLE VII.

Age by Religion. Part (C)—Mussulmans.

District or State.	Total Mussulmans.			Age Period.															
				Under 1 Year.		1 year.		2 years.		3 years.		4 years.		Total 0—4.		5—9		10—14	
	Total.	Males.	Females.	Males.	Females.	Males.	Females.	Males.	Females.	Males.	Females.	Males.	Females.	Males.	Females.	Males.	Females.	Males.	Females.
1	2	3	4	5	6	7	8	9	10	11	12	13	14	15	16	17	18	19	20
Telingana. Hyderabad. City	75,498	36,898	38,600	916	890	430	404	651	643	543	542	654	700	3,194	3,179	2,812	2,844	2,998	2,818
Telingana. Hyderabad. Suburbs including Secunderabad	97,363	51,561	45,802	1,254	1,203	650	605	1,048	1,123	850	992	1,005	1,006	4,802	4,929	4,871	4,738	4,687	3,942
Total......	172,861	88,459	84,402	2,170	2,093	1,080	1,009	1,694	1,766	1,393	1,534	1,659	1,706	7,996	8,108	7,683	7,582	7,685	6,755
Telingana. Atraf-i-Balda District	42,626	22,033	20,593	476	496	424	433	603	642	517	605	556	603	2,576	2,779	2,676	2,670	2,170	1,742
Telingana. Mahabubnagar (Nagar Karnul) ...	55,610	27,796	27,814	702	710	563	591	925	981	868	934	827	873	3,885	4,089	3,977	3,819	2,865	2,278
Telingana. Nalgonda	30,909	15,833	15,076	443	521	205	287	427	523	494	569	502	502	2,071	2,352	2,177	2,225	1,901	1,509
Telingana. Warangal (Khamam)	42,882	22,257	20,625	501	485	352	447	609	725	666	709	630	639	2,758	3,005	3,106	3,049	2,659	2,028
Telingana. Elgandal	44,013	22,593	21,420	445	479	426	449	694	758	564	679	780	747	2,859	3,112	3,289	3,230	3,008	2,384
Telingana. Indur	50,193	24,894	25,299	531	475	512	500	709	688	624	639	771	789	3147	3,086	3,395	3,182	3,010	2,257
Telingana. Medak...	38,047	19,126	18,921	398	335	412	444	551	537	461	491	504	522	2,326	2,329	2,578	2,340	2,128	1,566
Mahratwara. Aurangabad	94,217	47,952	46,265	1,281	1,389	895	996	1,422	1,564	1,267	1,478	1,257	1,399	6,122	6,826	6,307	6,234	5,205	4,203
Mahratwara. Birh	51,812	26,831	24,981	720	705	585	634	860	924	692	814	800	843	3,657	3,920	3,329	3,212	2,830	1,880
Mahratwara. Nander	56,018	28,707	27,311	721	701	648	639	899	1,035	727	805	886	898	3,881	4,078	3,730	3,597	3,263	2,355
Mahratwara. Naldrug	58,084	29,799	28,285	859	984	647	690	1,087	1,120	729	817	919	931	4,241	4,542	3,773	3,676	2,886	2,223
Mahratwara. Bidar	114,743	58,385	56,358	1,508	1,616	1,362	1,427	1,973	2,092	1,412	1,534	1,830	1,864	8,085	8,533	7,488	7,019	6,241	4,870
Mahratwara. Parbhani	66,696	34,098	32,598	772	839	771	816	1,111	1,298	871	1,074	1,026	1,085	4,551	5,112	4,496	4,182	3,664	2,739
Mahratwara. Sirpur Tandur	10,006	5,065	4,941	103	127	98	109	136	161	150	150	167	198	654	745	735	707	683	547
Karnatic or Kanada. Gulbarga	95,179	48,685	46,494	1,230	1,308	1,334	1,432	1,638	17,53	1,333	1,450	1,633	1,609	7,168	7,547	6,331	5,981	3,975	3,269
Karnatic or Kanada. Raichur	51,877	26,607	25,270	879	891	547	578	974	1,016	850	998	938	883	4,188	4,366	3,822	3,701	2,089	1,653
Karnatic or Kanada. Lingasugur	61,624	31,491	30,133	949	990	678	693	1,132	1,222	991	1,062	1,157	1,106	4,907	5,073	4,397	4,252	2,495	1,937
Total Districts......	964,486	492,152	472,334	12,518	13,046	10,459	11,115	15,750	17,034	13,216	14,808	15,133	15,486	67,076	71,489	65,601	63,076	51,062	39,385
Total Districts including Hyderabad ...	1,137,347	580,611	556,736	14,688	15,139	11,539	12,124	17,444	18,800	14,609	16,342	16,792	17,192	75,072	79,597	73,284	70,658	58,747	46,140
Railways......	1,319	885	434	8	6	7	15	14	13	16	14	11	13	56	61	59	54	34	34
Grand Total......	1,138,666	581,496	557,170	14,696	15,145	11,546	12,139	17,458	18,813	14,625	16,356	16,803	17,205	75,128	79,658	73,343	70,712	58,781	46,174

TABLE VII.

Age by Religion. Part (C)—Mussulmans.—*Continued.*

District or State.	Age Period. 15—19 Males.	15—19 Females.	20—24 Males.	20—24 Females.	25—29 Males.	25—29 Females.	30—34 Males.	30—34 Females.	35—39 Males.	35—39 Females.	40—44 Males.	40—44 Females.	45—49 Males.	45—49 Females.	50—54 Males.	50—54 Females.	55—59 Males.	55—59 Females.	60 and over. Males.	60 and over. Females.	Unspecified. Males.	Unspecified. Females.
	21	22	23	24	25	26	27	28	29	30	31	32	33	34	35	36	37	38	39	40	41	42
Telingana. Hyderabad. City	3,534	4,676	4,259	5,524	4,053	3,798	3,872	3,410	2,185	1,628	3,116	3,125	1,224	879	2,826	2,389	617	478	2,697	2,822	11	1,085
Suburbs including Secunderabad	4,447	4,962	5,500	5,737	5,579	4,329	5,202	4,223	3,173	1,844	4,204	3,511	1,729	966	2,938	2,484	890	551	3,528	3,377	11	259
Total......	7,981	9,638	9,759	11,261	9,632	8,127	9,074	7,633	5,358	3,472	7,320	6,636	2,953	1,845	5,264	4,773	1,507	1,029	6,225	6,199	22	1,344
Atraf-i-Balda District	1,630	1,625	1,827	2,076	2,010	1,839	2,071	1,990	1,226	831	1,861	1,489	767	441	1,344	1,170	320	200	1,533	1,587	22	204
Mahabubnagar (Nagar Karnul).	2,075	2,079	2,298	2,925	2,471	2,492	2,381	2,612	1,564	1,119	2,140	1,981	907	641	1,307	1,502	317	242	1,587	1,917	22	128
Nalgonda	1,372	1,221	1,289	1,494	1,462	1,213	1,791	1,245	856	572	1,057	1,012	452	301	798	672	174	118	936	1,050	2	92
Warangal Khamam	1,889	1,693	1,959	2,054	2,130	1,730	2,008	1,847	1,054	677	1,565	1,484	516	349	1,140	1,057	227	124	1,242	1,452	4	76
Elgandal	1,872	1,671	1,788	2,108	1,897	1,741	1,882	1,874	1,091	774	1,586	1,491	628	368	11,92	1,119	249	187	1,250	1,315	7	146
Indur	1,802	1,973	1,847	2,479	2,429	2,324	2,341	2,489	1,359	1,047	1,863	2,020	785	549	1,288	1,441	270	190	1,345	1,649	13	613
Medak	1,367	1,355	1,502	1,794	1,721	1,640	1,606	1,722	1,053	714	1,463	1,387	630	357	1,116	1,002	257	191	1,364	1,832	25	1,192
Mahratwara. Aurangabad	3,634	3,698	3,769	4,427	4,559	4,069	4,394	4,199	2,708	2,132	3,504	3,354	1,578	1,129	2,575	2,236	607	377	2,956	3,216	34	165
Birh...	1,854	1,836	1,980	2,479	2,697	2,372	2,533	2,480	1,604	1,220	2,101	1,787	852	681	1,430	1,202	318	256	1,623	1,555	23	102
Nander	1,944	1,933	2,196	2,542	2,978	2,576	2,709	2,587	1,643	1,137	2,093	2,082	922	635	1,498	1,436	327	269	1,495	1,734	28	355
Naldrug	1,960	1,959	2,279	2,746	3,064	2,738	2,841	2,831	1,692	1,333	2,383	2,135	1,088	695	1,630	1,386	393	230	1,558	1,689	11	52
Bidar	4,101	4,111	4,439	5,257	5,682	5,169	5,265	5,423	2,995	2,368	4,492	4,418	1,983	1,419	3,208	3,076	819	550	3,561	3,957	26	188
Parbhani	2,221	2,311	2,522	3,080	3,479	3,010	3,302	3,199	1,907	1,526	2,702	2,432	1,057	769	1,897	1,726	361	250	1,925	2,181	14	81
Sirpur Tandur	357	356	399	449	492	422	544	454	281	193	389	366	120	95	226	257	47	33	184	315	4	2
Karnatic or Kanada. Gulbarga	3,265	3,245	3,902	4,542	5,006	4,627	4,694	4,806	2,861	2,098	4,046	3,501	1,843	1,140	2,448	2,227	585	412	2,589	3,040	22	59
Raichur	1,779	1,642	2,407	2,719	2,555	2,470	2,417	2,472	1,606	1,069	2,027	1,735	947	591	1,236	1,137	347	243	1,187	1,465	...	7
Lingsugur	2,246	2,025	2,812	3,186	3,065	2,917	3,055	3,143	1,951	1,417	2,380	2,074	1,071	692	1,453	1,401	348	257	1,289	1,732	22	27
Total Districts......	35,368	34,733	39,215	46,357	47,697	43,349	45,334	45,373	27,451	20,227	37,602	34,748	16,146	10,852	25,781	24,047	5,966	4,079	27,574	31,136	279	3,483
Total Districts including Hyderabad ..	43,349	44,371	48,974	57,618	57,329	51,476	54,408	53,006	32,809	23,699	44,922	41,384	19,099	12,697	31,045	28,820	7,473	5,108	33,799	37,335	301	4,827
Railways......	43	48	120	67	150	51	135	29	98	12	79	30	38	11	45	22	7	1	21	14	...	...
Grand Total......	43,392	44,419	49,094	57,685	57,479	51,527	54,543	53,035	32,907	23,711	45,001	41,414	19,137	12,708	31,090	28,842	7,480	5,109	33,820	37,349	301	4,827

TABLE VII.

Age by Religion. Part (D)—Christians.

District or State.		Total Christians.		Age Period.															
				Under 1 year.		1 year		2 years.		3 years.		4 years.		Total. 0—4		5—9		10—14	
	Total.	Males.	Females.	Males.	Females.	Males.	Females	Males	Females.	Males.	Females.	Males.	Females.	Males.	Females.	Males.	Females	Males.	Females.
1	2	3	4	5	6	7	8	9	10	11	12	13	14	15	16	17	18	19	20
Telingana. Hyderabad. City	44	27	17	...	...	1	...	...	...	1	...	...	1	2	1	4	...	1	1
Telingana. Hyderabad. Suburbs including Secunderabad...	13,785	8,129	5,656	157	191	108	114	176	153	160	137	151	168	752	768	796	785	606	674
Total......	13,829	8,156	5,673	157	191	109	114	176	158	161	137	151	169	754	764	800	785	607	675
Atraf-i-Balda District...	450	216	234	8	12	2	7	7	2	6	5	4	14	27	40	41	32	24	24
Mahabubnagar (Nagar Karnul)	121	67	54	2	2	2	1	2	4	4	1	3	...	13	8	9	13	8	3
Nalgonda	135	73	62	1	3	1	3	1	1	2	5	3	7	8	19	9	10	7	4
Warangal (Khamam)...	1,484	794	690	24	17	17	15	33	24	25	26	29	37	128	119	104	90	89	70
Elgandal...	193	122	71	2	2	5	2	1	2	5	2	4	3	17	11	20	13	22	1
Indur	40	22	18	2	...	1	1	1	...	...	1	...	2	4	4	4	3	1	...
Medak	106	53	53	2	1	2	5	...	1	2	1	2	...	8	8	9	6	...	1
Mahratwara. Aurangabad	1,929	960	969	31	42	26	32	30	39	33	35	31	30	151	178	130	160	97	109
Birh	148	86	62	4	2	1	4	3	1	4	1	...	2	12	10	12	8	7	8
Nander	2	2	......	...	...	...	...	...	...	...	...	...	...	...	...	...	...	...	...
Naldrug	214	107	107	5	6	1	4	3	5	5	4	5	7	19	26	22	6	4	14
Bidar	21	12	9	...	...	...	1	...	...	1	...	...	1	1	2	1	1	2	...
Parbhani	67	41	26	1	...	2	...	...	1	...	2	...	...	3	3	3	3	3	3
Karnatic or Kanada. Gulbarga	287	150	137	4	7	5	1	5	4	5	8	6	6	25	26	19	18	10	14
Raichur	335	177	158	4	7	3	4	1	4	5	3	5	4	18	22	25	16	14	23
Lingasugur...	398	203	195	5	5	3	7	6	6	6	5	4	3	24	26	30	37	16	17
Total Districts......	5,930	3,085	2,845	95	106	71	87	93	94	103	99	96	116	458	502	438	416	304	291
Total Districts including Hyderabad......	19,759	11,241	8,518	252	297	180	201	269	247	264	236	247	285	1,212	1,266	1,238	1,201	911	966
Railways......	670	389	281	14	7	10	6	6	13	13	8	7	7	50	41	49	44	20	31
Grand Total......	20,429	11,630	8,799	266	304	190	207	275	260	277	244	254	292	1,262	1,307	1,287	1,245	931	997

Age by Religion. Part (E)—Bhils.

District or State.	Total.	Males.	Females.	Males.	Females.	Males.	Females	Males	Females.	Males.	Females.	Males.	Females.	Males.	Females.	Males.	Females	Males.	Females.
Sirpur Tandur	470	235	235	6	6	9	8	10	13	5	7	12	11	42	45	49	27	24	32
Total Districts......	470	235	235	6	6	9	8	10	13	5	7	12	11	42	45	49	27	24	32
Total Districts including Hyderabad ...	470	235	235	6	6	9	8	10	13	5	7	12	11	42	45	49	27	24	32
Grand Total......	470	235	235	6	6	9	8	10	13	5	7	12	11	42	45	49	27	24	32

TABLE VII.

Age by Religion Part (D) Christians.—*Continued.*

District or State.	Age Period. 15—19 Males.	15—19 Females.	20—24 Males.	20—24 Females.	25—29 Males.	25—29 Females.	30—34 Males.	30—34 Females.	35—39 Males.	35—39 Females.	40—44 Males.	40—44 Females.	45—49 Males.	45—49 Females.	50—54 Males.	50—54 Females.	55—59 Males.	55—59 Females.	60 and over. Males.	60 and over. Females.	Unspecified. Males.	Unspecified. Females.
	21	22	23	24	25	26	27	28	29	30	31	32	33	34	35	36	37	38	39	40	41	42
Telingana. Hyderabad. City	4	1	4	3	1	1	1	3	3	3	2	1	2	...	3	1	...	...	...	2	...	...
Suburbs including Secunderabad ...	562	659	1,962	590	1,394	552	602	424	380	291	317	292	216	166	201	184	92	57	249	218	...	1
Total......	566	660	1,966	593	1,395	553	603	427	383	294	319	293	218	166	204	185	92	57	249	220	...	1
Atraf-i Balda District...	15	14	12	28	15	25	19	24	10	9	24	10	2	2	5	12	2	1	20	13	...	...
Mahabubnagar (Nagar Karnul)	4	6	7	3	4	5	5	4	3	4	6	4	4	1	4	2	...	1	...	...	...	...
Nalgonda	2	2	9	7	6	6	13	3	5	1	7	3	3	1	...	2	2	...	2	4	...	...
Warangal (Khamam)	56	74	86	100	81	68	84	50	36	15	54	35	11	8	32	27	4	3	29	31	...	...
Elgandal	11	13	10	16	11	5	7	4	5	3	6	3	6	...	3	2	1	...	2	...	1	...
Indur	1	2	1	1	3	2	1	2	2	1	...	1	...	1	...	...	2	...	2	1	1	...
Medak	3	7	7	4	8	9	2	4	3	4	8	2	2	...	2	2	1	...	...	6	...	...
Mahratwara. Aurangabad	62	69	64	92	103	87	91	70	58	40	53	62	36	21	61	37	12	6	42	38	...	...
Birh	1	9	9	8	9	7	12	4	8	3	6	3	3	...	4	1	...	...	3	1	...	...
Nander	...	...	...	...	...	...	...	...	2	...	...	...	...	...	...	...	...	...	...	...	...	...
Naldrug...	3	8	7	7	10	9	9	14	5	3	10	6	5	5	7	3	...	1	6	5	...	...
Bidar	1	...	...	1	3	3	...	1	1	...	2	...	1	...	...	...	...	1	...	...	...	...
Parbhani	2	4	6	3	7	3	3	3	3	...	5	2	2	...	1	...	...	1	3	1	...	...
Karnatic or Kanada. Gulbarga	9	17	20	12	26	17	12	7	9	3	6	12	3	2	6	1	1	...	4	8	...	...
Raichur	10	20	24	17	21	15	15	12	16	3	10	12	9	3	2	4	5	2	8	9	...	...
Lingasugur...	17	23	19	24	35	17	20	19	11	5	9	13	7	1	7	7	1	...	7	6	...	...
Total Districts......	197	268	281	323	342	278	293	221	177	94	206	168	94	45	134	100	31	16	128	123	2	...
Total Districts including Hyderabad	763	928	2,247	916	1,737	831	896	648	560	388	525	461	312	211	338	285	123	73	377	343	2	1
Railways......	38	28	58	39	58	27	30	22	36	11	17	10	6	12	11	7	10	1	6	8	...	...
Grand Total......	801	956	2,305	955	1,795	858	926	670	596	399	542	471	318	223	349	292	133	74	383	351	2	1

Age by Religion Part (I) Bhils.—*Continued.*

District or State.	15—19 Males.	15—19 Females.	20—24 Males.	20—24 Females.	25—29 Males.	25—29 Females.	30—34 Males.	30—34 Females.	35—39 Males.	35—39 Females.	40—44 Males.	40—44 Females.	45—49 Males.	45—49 Females.	50—54 Males.	50—54 Females.	55—59 Males.	55—59 Females.	60 and over. Males.	60 and over. Females.	Unspecified. Males.	Unspecified. Females.
Sirpur Tandur	14	28	19	25	27	12	11	18	12	6	13	21	3	2	9	13	2	...	10	6	...	...
Total Districts......	14	28	19	25	27	12	11	18	12	6	13	21	3	2	9	13	2	...	10	6	...	...
Total Districts including Hyderabad......	14	28	19	25	27	12	11	18	12	6	13	21	3	2	9	13	2	...	10	6	...	...
Grand Total......	14	28	19	25	27	12	11	18	12	6	13	21	3	2	9	13	2	...	10	6	...	...

TABLE VII.

Age by Religion Part (E) Sikhs.

District or State.	Total Sikhs.			Age Period.															
				Under 1 year.		1 year.		2 years.		3 years.		4 years.		Total 0–4.		5–9		10–14	
	Total.	Males.	Females.	Males.	Females.	Males.	Females.	Males.	Females.	Males.	Females.	Males.	Females.	Males.	Females.	Males.	Females.	Males.	Females.
1	2	3	4	5	6	7	8	9	10	11	12	13	14	15	16	17	18	19	20
Tellingana. Hyderabad. City	59	29	30	1	1	...	...	...	1	...	...	1	1	2	3	3	3	...	3
Suburbs including Secunderabad. ...	610	369	241	4	3	2	5	1	4	1	3	3	6	11	21	21	15	26	21
Total......	669	398	271	5	4	2	5	1	5	1	3	4	7	13	24	24	18	26	24
Atraf-i-Balda District	254	143	111	4	3	1	...	3	2	...	3	2	3	10	11	14	6	9	3
Mahabubnagar (Nagar Karnul)	75	48	27	...	1	1	...	1	1	1	...	1	...	4	2	7	1	4	1
Nalgonda	111	63	48	...	4	1	1	2	1	1	2	1	...	5	8	8	3	6	2
Warangal (Khamam)...	281	161	120	4	1	...	...	8	4	2	5	1	2	15	12	20	11	12	9
Elgandal...	335	182	153	1	...	6	9	6	5	5	2	4	4	22	20	23	26	18	14
Indur	553	286	267	3	6	5	2	4	9	4	4	5	2	21	23	26	27	29	28
Medak	213	121	92	4	2	1	3	2	4	1	4	1	2	9	14	10	8	8	4
Mahratwara. Aurangabad	275	119	156	1	2	4	6	4	6	4	8	3	6	16	28	18	18	12	14
Birh	245	130	115	2	2	2	2	4	5	...	1	5	2	13	12	17	13	14	10
Nander	1,130	581	549	9	12	16	17	18	12	4	19	16	8	63	68	61	71	68	50
Naldrug	5	4	1	...	...	...	...	...	...	...	...	...	...	...	...	...	...	...	...
Bidar	57	30	27	1	2	1	...	...	...	2	...	1	...	5	2	4	...	8	2
Parbhani...	362	255	107	10	3	3	3	4	3	1	2	1	2	19	13	8	15	15	9
Sirpur Tandur	44	22	22	1	...	2	3	...	...	...	...	1	...	4	3	1	7	4	1
Karnatic or Kanada. Gulbarga	14	5	9	1	...	...	...	...	...	...	...	...	...	1	...	...	3	...	...
Raichur	4	3	1	...	...	1	...	...	...	...	...	...	...	1	...	...	...	...	...
Lingasugur...	5	3	2	...	...	...	...	...	...	...	...	...	...	...	...	...	2	1	...
Total Districts......	3,963	2,156	1,807	41	38	44	45	56	52	25	50	42	31	208	216	217	211	208	147
Total Districts including Hyderabad	4,632	2,554	2,078	46	42	46	50	57	57	26	53	46	38	221	240	241	229	229	171
Railways......	5	2	3	...	...	...	...	...	...	...	...	...	...	...	...	...	...	...	...
Grand Total......	4,637	2,556	2,081	46	42	46	50	57	57	26	53	46	38	221	240	241	229	229	171

TABLE VII.

Age by Religion Part (E) Sikhs.—*Continued.*

District or State.	Age Period. 15—19 Males.	15—19 Females.	20—24 Males.	20—24 Females.	25—29 Males.	25—29 Females.	30—34 Males.	30—34 Females.	35—39 Males.	35—39 Females.	40—44 Males.	40—44 Females.	45—49 Males.	45—49 Females.	50—54 Males.	50—54 Females.	55—59 Males.	55—59 Females.	60 and over. Males.	60 and over. Females.	Unspecified. Males.	Unspecified. Females.
	21	22	23	24	25	26	27	28	29	30	31	32	33	34	35	36	37	38	39	40	41	42
Tellingana. Hyderabad. City...	...	4	3	3	5	6	4	2	...	3	5	1	1	...	1	...	2	...	3	2	...	...
Suburbs including Secunderabad ...	40	27	60	24	58	26	34	28	17	12	48	23	8	8	32	17	3	5	16	14	...	...
Total......	40	31	63	27	58	32	38	30	17	15	53	24	9	8	33	17	5	5	19	16	...	...
Atraf-i-Balda District ...	9	9	14	18	9	16	10	9	9	1	23	10	5	...	14	11	3	1	14	16	...	...
Mahabubnagar (Nagar Karnul) ...	3	4	2	6	6	2	3	4	6	...	5	4	4	...	2	1	...	...	2	2	...	...
Nalgonda ...	5	3	7	10	5	6	5	4	9	3	5	3	4	...	2	3	...	...	2	3	...	...
Warangal (Khamam)...	19	8	13	15	12	11	10	11	13	3	13	16	3	1	15	10	2	2	14	11	...	...
Elgandal ...	18	12	18	17	13	12	12	7	15	10	10	10	7	5	11	7	1	...	14	13	...	...
Indur ...	25	20	34	27	28	27	25	26	15	12	30	27	6	4	20	21	5	4	22	20	...	1
Medak ...	6	5	18	8	11	11	18	5	6	4	9	8	5	2	9	11	5	3	12	9	...	...
Mahratwara. Aurangabad ...	6	16	4	14	10	10	14	14	10	11	7	14	3	...	8	7	2	2	9	8	...	...
Birh ...	12	6	11	11	5	5	11	17	6	7	12	9	7	1	8	8	2	4	12	12	...	...
Nander ...	42	36	43	55	51	42	55	53	32	18	51	61	19	9	35	40	10	4	50	42	1	...
Naldrug...	1	...	1	...	...	...	1	1	1	...	...	...	...	...	...	...	...	...	...	...	...	...
Bidar ...	3	7	2	2	3	...	3	1	1	3	3	4	...	1	1	2	1	...	1	3	...	...
Parbhani ...	17	8	83	14	45	16	32	9	11	7	9	6	5	1	7	4	1	...	3	5	...	...
Sirpur Tandur ...	1	1	...	3	5	1	2	1	...	1	2	3	1	1	...	...	1	...	1	...	...	...
Karnatic or Kanada. Gulbarga ...	...	...	...	...	...	1	1	1	...	...	1	...	...	...	1	2	...	...	1	2	...	...
Raichur ...	...	1	...	...	...	...	...	...	2	...	...	...	...	...	...	...	...	...	...	...	...	...
Lingasugur ...	...	...	1	...	...	...	...	...	...	...	...	...	...	...	1	...	...	...	...	...	...	...
Total Districts......	167	136	251	200	203	160	197	163	136	80	180	175	69	25	134	127	33	20	157	146	1	1
Total Districts including Hyderabad ...	207	167	314	227	261	192	235	193	153	95	233	199	78	33	167	144	38	25	176	162	1	1
Railways......	...	1	...	...	...	1	...	...	1	...	...	...	...	...	...	1	...	...	1	...	...	...
Grand Total......	207	168	314	227	261	193	235	193	154	95	233	199	78	33	167	145	38	25	177	162	1	1

TABLE VII.

Age by Religion Part (F) Parsis.

District or State.		Total Parsis.			Age Period.															
					Under 1 year.		1 year.		2 years.		3 years.		4 years.		Total 0—4		5—9		10—14	
		Total.	Males.	Females.	Males.	Females.	Males.	Females.	Males.	Females.	Males.	Females.	Males.	Females.	Males.	Females.	Males.	Females.	Males.	Females.
1		2	3	4	5	6	7	8	9	10	11	12	13	14	15	16	17	18	19	20
Telingana: Hyderabad	City	1	1	...	...	...	...	...	...	...	...	...	...	...	...	...	...	...	...	...
	Suburbs including Secunderabad	615	371	244	14	7	5	8	7	5	4	9	3	7	33	36	38	28	35	27
	Total	616	372	244	14	7	5	8	7	5	4	9	3	7	33	36	38	28	35	27
Telingana	Atraf-i-Balda District	3	2	1	...	...	...	...	...	...	...	...	...	...	...	...	...	...	1	...
	Mahabubnagar (Nagar Karnul)	...	...	...	...	...	...	...	...	...	...	...	...	...	...	...	...	...	...	...
	Nalgonda	13	4	9	...	...	...	...	...	...	...	...	...	...	...	...	1	5	...	1
	Warangal (Khamam)	40	28	12	1	...	...	...	1	1	...	...	...	...	2	1	2	...	...	1
	Elgandal	3	2	1	...	...	...	...	...	...	...	...	...	...	...	...	...	...	...	...
	Indur	7	2	5	...	...	...	...	...	...	...	1	...	...	...	1	...	2	...	...
	Medak	...	...	...	...	...	...	...	...	...	...	...	...	...	...	...	...	...	...	...
Mahratwara	Aurangabad	130	68	62	...	2	2	1	1	2	3	...	1	1	7	6	10	9	2	6
	Birh	19	11	8	...	...	...	...	...	...	...	...	...	...	...	...	...	2	3	1
	Nander	7	6	1	...	...	...	...	...	...	...	...	...	...	...	...	...	...	1	...
	Naldrug	10	10	...	...	...	...	...	...	...	...	...	...	...	...	...	...	...	1	...
	Bidar	3	2	1	...	...	...	...	...	...	...	...	...	...	...	...	1	...	...	...
	Parbhani	24	12	12	...	...	...	...	...	1	1	...	...	2	1	3	2	1	2	2
	Sirpur Tandur	1	1	...	...	...	...	...	...	...	...	...	...	...	...	...	...	...	...	...
Karnatic or Kanada	Gulbarga	66	43	23	1	...	2	1	1	1	4	...	...	2	8	4	1	6	1	...
	Raichur	34	20	14	...	1	...	...	1	...	1	...	2	...	4	1	3	3	3	3
	Lingasugur	13	8	5	...	...	...	...	2	...	...	1	...	...	2	1	1	1	...	...
	Total Districts	373	219	154	2	3	4	2	6	5	9	2	3	5	24	17	21	29	14	14
	Total Districts including Hyderabad	989	591	398	16	10	9	10	13	10	13	11	6	12	57	53	59	57	49	41
	Railways	69	37	32	3	...	2	...	1	2	...	1	2	1	8	4	4	9	1	3
	Grand Total	1,058	628	430	19	10	11	10	14	12	13	12	8	13	65	57	63	66	50	44

TABLE VII.

Age by Religion Part (F) Parsis—*Continued.*

District or State.	15—19 Males.	15—19 Females.	20—24 Males.	20—24 Females.	25—29 Males.	25—29 Females.	30—34 Males.	30—34 Females.	35—39 Males.	35—39 Females.	40—44 Males.	40—44 Females.	45—49 Males.	45—49 Females.	50—54 Males.	50—54 Females.	55—59 Males.	55—59 Females.	60 and over. Males.	60 and over. Females.	Unspecified. Males.	Unspecified. Females.
	21	22	23	24	25	26	27	28	29	30	31	32	33	34	35	36	37	38	39	40	41	42
Telingana. Hyderabad. City	...	...	...	...	...	...	...	...	...	...	...	...	...	...	...	...	...	...	1	...	...	...
Telingana. Hyderabad. Suburbs including Secunderabad	25	21	34	31	41	23	45	23	26	10	31	10	10	9	23	7	9	7	20	12	1	...
Total	25	21	34	31	41	23	45	23	26	10	31	10	10	9	23	7	9	7	21	12	1	...
Telingana. Atraf i-Balda District	...	...	...	...	...	...	...	...	...	...	...	...	...	...	1	1	...	...	...	...	...	...
Mahabubnagar (Nagar Karnul)	...	...	...	...	...	...	...	...	...	...	...	...	...	...	...	...	...	...	...	...	...	...
Nalgonda	...	...	...	...	...	...	...	2	2	...	1	...	...	...	...	...	...	...	...	1	...	...
Warangal (Khamam)	1	2	1	2	6	3	8	2	2	...	3	...	1	1	1	...	...	...	1	...	...	...
Elgandal	...	...	...	...	1	1	...	...	1	...	...	...	...	...	...	...	...	...	...	...	...	...
Indur	...	1	...	1	1	...	...	...	...	...	...	...	1	...	...	...	...	...	...	...	...	...
Medak	...	...	...	...	...	...	...	...	...	...	...	...	...	...	...	...	...	...	...	...	...	...
Mahratwara. Aurangabad	8	7	8	9	4	7	6	3	7	3	2	5	4	1	3	...	1	3	5	3	...	...
Birh	2	1	3	2	...	...	...	...	...	1	...	1	...	...	3	...	...	...	1	...	...	...
Nander	1	...	...	1	3	...	...	...	...	...	...	...	1	...	...	...	...	...	...	...	...	...
Naldrug	2	...	2	...	...	...	2	...	...	...	1	...	...	...	1	...	1	...	...	...	...	...
Bidar	...	...	...	...	...	...	...	1	...	...	1	...	...	...	...	...	...	...	...	...	...	...
Parbhani	...	2	...	...	2	...	1	2	4	1	...	...	...	...	...	...	...	...	...	1	...	...
Sirpur Tandur	...	...	...	...	...	...	...	...	...	...	...	...	...	...	1	...	...	...	...	...	...	...
Karnatic or Kanada. Gulbarga	3	2	4	3	6	2	4	...	3	...	6	4	3	2	3	...	1	...	...	...	...	...
Raichur	...	1	1	...	...	...	2	3	1	1	4	1	...	1	1	...	...	...	1	...	...	...
Lingasugur	1	...	...	1	2	1	1	...	...	...	...	...	...	...	...	1	1	...	...	...	...	...
Total Districts	18	16	19	19	25	14	24	13	20	6	18	11	10	5	14	2	4	3	8	5	...	...
Total Districts including Hyderabad	43	37	53	50	66	37	69	36	46	16	49	21	20	14	37	9	13	10	29	17	1	...
Railways	2	...	2	2	6	4	2	1	4	2	2	1	1	2	1	3	3	...	1	1	...	...
Grand Total	45	37	55	52	72	41	71	37	50	18	51	22	21	16	38	12	16	10	30	18	1	...

TABLE VII.

Age by Religion Part (G) Jains.

District or State.		Total Jains.			Age Period.															
					Under 1 year.		1 year.		2 years.		3 years.		4 years.		Total 0—4		5—9		10—14	
		Total.	Males.	Females.	Males.	Females.	Males.	Females.	Males.	Females.	Males.	Females.	Males.	Females.	Males.	Females.	Males.	Females.	Males.	Females.
1		2	3	4	5	6	7	8	9	10	11	12	13	14	15	16	17	18	19	20
Telingana. Hyderabad	City	92	65	27	...	3	...	...	...	1	1	...	...	...	1	4	1	3	6	2
	Suburbs including Secunderabad	111	75	36	2	1	...	...	...	...	...	1	...	...	2	2	2	4	5	3
	Total	208	140	63	2	4	...	...	...	1	1	1	...	...	3	6	3	7	11	5
	Atraf-i-Balda District	94	49	45	...	...	1	...	2	...	1	2	2	2	6	4	4	4	7	4
	Mahabubnagar (Nagar Karnul)	4	4	...	...	...	...	...	...	...	...	...	...	...	...	...	...	...	...	...
	Nalgonda	...	...	...	...	...	...	...	...	...	...	...	...	...	...	...	...	...	...	...
	Warangal (Khamam)	2	2	...	...	...	...	...	...	...	...	...	...	...	...	...	...	...	...	...
	Elgandal	12	7	5	...	...	...	...	...	2	...	...	...	...	...	2	2	...	...	...
	Indur	129	61	68	...	2	...	1	...	...	...	1	...	1	...	5	8	8	6	10
	Medak	102	48	54	5	3	...	...	1	1	1	1	1	1	8	6	5	6	10	8
Mahratwara.	Aurangabad	7,548	4,104	3,444	101	125	68	81	82	95	91	102	84	80	426	483	410	419	461	325
	Birh	4,149	2,236	1,913	72	62	41	49	52	75	51	54	44	54	260	294	270	213	233	180
	Nander	1,046	534	512	17	16	16	14	9	14	10	10	12	17	64	71	44	56	61	40
	Naldrug	4,469	2,365	2,104	78	71	47	48	73	82	53	58	61	57	312	311	241	249	240	196
	Bidar	1,617	866	751	18	18	16	19	22	18	18	22	21	29	95	106	79	77	80	67
	Parbhani	5,449	2,847	2,602	55	71	56	52	63	86	56	70	53	50	283	329	282	278	301	243
	Sirpur Tandur	248	128	120	3	3	2	6	...	5	3	4	3	3	11	21	26	12	17	17
Karnatic or Kanada.	Gulbarga	1,575	831	744	19	15	8	16	19	21	19	25	22	14	87	91	90	79	75	60
	Raichur	194	128	66	2	2	...	...	2	2	1	1	...	2	5	7	8	7	14	4
	Lingasugur	999	612	387	9	15	5	6	11	12	8	14	11	11	44	58	57	48	68	24
Total Districts		27,687	14,822	12,815	379	403	260	292	336	413	312	359	314	321	1,601	1,788	1,526	1,456	1,578	1,178
Total Districts including Hyderabad		27,840	14,962	12,878	381	407	260	292	336	414	313	360	314	321	1,604	1,794	1,529	1,463	1,584	1,178
Railways		5	4	1	...	...	...	...	...	...	...	...	...	...	...	...	...	...	1	...
Grand Total		27,845	14,966	12,879	381	407	260	292	336	414	313	360	314	321	1,604	1,794	1,529	1,463	1,585	1,178

TABLE VII.

Age by Religion Part (G) Jains.—*Continued.*

	District or State.	15–19 Males.	15–19 Females.	20–24 Males.	20–24 Females.	25–29 Males.	25–29 Females.	30–34 Males.	30–34 Females.	35–39 Males.	35–39 Females.	40–44 Males.	40–44 Females.	45–49 Males.	45–49 Females.	50–54 Males.	50–54 Females.	55–59 Males.	55–59 Females.	60 and over. Males.	60 and over. Females.	Unspecified. Males.	Unspecified. Females.
		21	22	23	24	25	26	27	28	29	30	31	32	33	34	35	36	37	38	39	40	41	42
Telingana. Hyderabad.	City...	9	3	12	3	10	6	5	...	5	1	6	2	...	2	4	1	...	...	6	...	...	...
	Suburbs including Secunderabad	14	6	12	5	5	4	8	1	4	...	7	4	4	...	6	4	3	...	3	3	...	...
	Total......	23	9	24	8	15	10	13	1	9	1	13	6	4	2	10	5	3	...	9	3	...	...
Telingana.	Atraf i-Balda District...	5	5	3	7	3	4	5	2	2	...	5	5	...	4	7	1	...	2	2	3	...	...
	Mahabubnagar (Nagar Karnul)	...	...	...	...	2	...	1	...	1	...	...	...	...	...	...	...	...	...	...	...	...	...
	Nalgonda	...	...	...	...	...	...	...	...	...	...	...	...	...	...	...	...	...	...	...	...	...	...
	Warangal (Khamam) ...	1	...	...	...	1	...	...	...	...	...	...	...	...	...	...	...	...	...	...	...	...	...
	Elgandal	1	1	1	1	1	...	...	1	1	...	1	...	...	...	...	...	...	...	...	...	...	...
	Indur ...	6	7	2	5	5	5	9	7	8	3	4	4	4	3	5	5	1	3	3	3	...	...
	Medak ...	2	3	3	10	2	7	2	4	6	1	3	3	3	1	3	5	...	3	1	2	...	...
Mahratwara.	Aurangabad	325	298	348	345	410	297	384	315	286	215	294	282	191	113	231	161	91	31	247	207	...	3
	Birh ...	156	158	194	227	218	166	222	182	142	93	159	116	101	57	124	95	45	21	112	110	...	1
	Nander ...	34	34	50	60	58	50	64	45	42	28	32	34	16	28	25	27	8	12	36	36	...	1
	Naldrug...	202	168	210	219	232	192	214	172	145	130	163	140	104	58	126	104	50	26	126	189	...	...
	Bidar ...	55	48	83	68	90	71	89	76	57	40	70	57	48	27	58	36	15	12	52	66	...	...
	Parbhani	193	215	224	244	333	242	262	254	201	161	257	194	180	79	159	138	61	37	161	187	...	1
	Sirpur Tandur ...	11	9	9	9	9	11	10	6	5	8	9	26	5	4	8	3	...	...	8	4	...	...
Karnatic or Kanada.	Gulbarga ...	57	54	79	74	80	85	92	75	52	45	76	50	46	26	46	43	12	8	39	54	...	...
	Raichur ...	18	11	20	9	15	9	10	3	10	2	8	5	4	2	6	2	3	...	7	5	...	...
	Lingasugur...	61	32	75	53	80	37	60	29	46	19	41	16	14	14	29	23	10	3	27	31	...	...
	Total Districts......	1,127	1,043	1,301	1,331	1,539	1,176	1,424	1,171	1,004	740	1,122	872	661	411	827	643	296	158	821	847	...	6
	Total Districts including Hyderabad...	1,150	1,052	1,325	1,339	1,554	1,186	1,437	1,172	1,013	741	1,135	878	665	413	837	648	299	158	830	850	...	6
	Railways......	1	1	1	...	...	...	...	...	1	...	...	...	...	...	...	...	...	...	...	...	...	...
	Grand Total......	1,151	1,053	1,326	1,339	1,554	1,186	1,437	1,172	1,014	741	1,135	878	665	413	837	648	299	158	830	850	...	6

TABLE VII.

Age by Religion Part (H) Gonds.

District or State.	Total Gonds.			Age Period.															
				Under 1 year.		1 year.		2 years.		3 years.		4 years.		Total 0—4		5—9		10—14	
	Total.	Males.	Females.	Males.	Females.	Males.	Females.	Males.	Females.	Males.	Females.	Males.	Females.	Males.	Females.	Males.	Females.	Males.	Females.
1	2	3	4	5	6	7	8	9	10	11	12	13	14	15	16	17	18	19	20
Indur	538	273	265	3	3	11	12	5	9	8	8	12	14	89	46	47	42	30	20
Nander	6	4	2	...	...	...	...	...	1	...	...	1	...	1	1	...	...	1	...
Sirpur Tandur	28,116	14,360	13,756	265	291	391	407	441	562	496	516	557	688	2,150	2,464	2,194	2,006	1,714	1,418
Total Districts......	28,660	14,637	14,023	268	294	402	419	446	572	504	524	570	702	2,190	2,511	2,241	2,048	1,745	1,438
Total Districts including Hyderabad	28,660	14,637	14,023	268	294	402	419	446	572	504	524	570	702	2,190	2,511	2,241	2,048	1,745	1,438
Grand Total......	28,660	14,637	14,023	268	294	402	419	446	572	504	524	570	702	2,190	2,511	2,241	2,048	1,745	1,438

Age by Religion Part (J) Jews.

	Total Jews.																		
Suburbs including Secunderabad	21	7	14	...	1	...	1	...	1	...	1	...	...	...	4	...	4	1	...
Total......	21	7	14	...	1	...	1	...	1	...	1	...	...	...	4	...	4	1	...
Total Districts including Hyderabad	21	7	14	...	1	...	1	...	1	...	1	...	...	...	4	...	4	1	...
Railways......	5	3	2	...	1	...	...	1	...	...	...	...	...	1	1	...	...	...	...
Grand Total......	26	10	16	...	2	...	1	1	1	...	1	...	...	1	5	...	4	1	...

TABLE VII.

Age by Religion Part (H) Gonds.—*Continued.*

District or State.	15–19 Males.	15–19 Females.	20–24 Males.	20–24 Females.	25–29 Males.	25–29 Females.	30–34 Males.	30–34 Females.	35–39 Males.	35–39 Females.	40–44 Males.	40–44 Females.	45–49 Males.	45–49 Females.	50–54 Males.	50–54 Females.	55–59 Males.	55–59 Females.	60 and over. Males.	60 and over. Females.	Unspecified. Males.	Unspecified. Females.
	21	22	23	24	25	26	27	28	29	30	31	32	33	34	35	36	37	38	39	40	41	42
Indur ...	16	22	18	26	20	24	32	24	17	14	20	13	11	12	8	10	8	8	12	9	...	...
Nander ...	1	...	...	...	...	...	...	...	...	...	...	1	...	...	1	...	...	...	...	...	...	...
Sirpur Tandur ...	833	908	988	1,256	1,107	1,207	1,453	1,330	694	509	1,228	959	375	228	744	661	120	104	756	701	4	5
Total Districts......	850	930	1,006	1,282	1,127	1,231	1,485	1,354	711	523	1,248	973	386	240	753	671	123	107	768	710	4	5
Total Districts including Hyderabad ...	850	930	1,006	1,282	1,127	1,231	1,485	1,354	711	523	1,248	973	386	240	753	671	123	107	768	710	4	5
Grand Total	850	930	1,006	1,282	1,127	1,231	1,485	1,354	711	523	1,248	973	386	240	753	671	123	107	768	710	4	5

Age by Religion Part (J) Jews.—*Continued.*

District or State.	15–19 Males.	15–19 Females.	20–24 Males.	20–24 Females.	25–29 Males.	25–29 Females.	30–34 Males.	30–34 Females.	35–39 Males.	35–39 Females.	40–44 Males.	40–44 Females.	45–49 Males.	45–49 Females.	50–54 Males.	50–54 Females.	55–59 Males.	55–59 Females.	60 and over. Males.	60 and over. Females.	Unspecified. Males.	Unspecified. Females.
Suburbs including Secunderabad...	...	1	2	2	2	1	2	...	...	...	...	1	...	1	...	...	...	...	...	...	...	...
Total......	...	1	2	2	2	1	2	...	...	...	...	1	...	1	...	...	...	...	...	...	...	...
Total Districts including Hyderabad ...	...	1	2	2	2	1	2	...	...	...	...	1	...	1	...	...	...	...	...	...	...	...
Railways......	...	...	...	1	2	...	...	...	...	...	...	...	...	...	...	...	...	...	...	...	...	...
Grand Total....	...	1	2	3	4	1	2	...	...	...	...	1	...	1	...	...	...	...	...	...	...	...

TABLE VIII.

CIVIL CONDITION BY RELIGION AND AGE.

TABLE VIII.

Civil Condition by Religion and Age. Part (A)—All Religions.

(1) UNMARRIED.

District or State.	Unmarried Total.			Age Period. 0–4		5–9		10–14		15–19		20–24		25–29	
	Total.	Males.	Females.	Males.	Females.	Males.	Females.	Males.	Females.	Males.	Females.	Males.	Females.	Males.	Females.
1	2	3	4	5	6	7	8	9	10	11	12	13	14	15	16
Telingana. Hyderabad. City	43,844	25,663	18,181	5,251	5,268	4,672	4,514	4,566	2,812	4,269	2,127	3,080	1,190	1,727	469
Suburbs including Secunderabad	108,974	68,509	40,465	14,680	15,027	14,749	13,668	12,975	6,361	9,273	2,850	8,279	1,264	4,255	647
Total......	152,818	94,172	58,646	19,911	20,295	19,421	18,182	17,541	9,173	18,542	4,477	11,359	2,454	5,982	1,116
Atraf-i Bal'a District	142,584	89,517	53,067	25,444	27,384	24,791	19,288	18,372	3,586	9,902	707	5,356	553	2,518	418
Mahabubnagar (Nagar Kurnul) ...	257,327	158,908	98,419	49,772	53,759	45,672	33,751	29,833	5,998	15,662	1,208	9,302	926	4,251	633
Nalgonda	275,851	166,194	109,657	49,979	53,728	45,886	41,507	86,577	10,722	19,605	1,241	8,629	625	2,985	350
Warangal (Khamam)	369,512	222,403	1,471,09	62,909	68,109	62,785	54,586	51,015	17,697	24,966	2,672	12,177	1,191	4,455	629
Elgandal	444,427	269,210	175,217	83,014	87,716	81,188	64,785	67,069	15,964	28,684	2,427	8,603	1,247	2,647	687
Indur	206,447	128,140	78,307	41,468	42,106	40,845	26,304	27,433	5,463	9,445	1,252	4,091	776	2,075	586
Medak	127,602	81,295	46,307	22,431	23,300	22,864	17,169	17,581	2,986	8,580	675	4,690	517	2,280	855
Mahratwara. Aurangabad	292,338	175,230	117,158	56,430	62,804	53,893	42,271	36,470	8,776	14,276	1,145	6,485	521	8,354	841
Birh	219,685	133,783	85,902	46,096	49,422	40,451	28,865	26,435	5,316	10,012	648	4,922	338	2,518	273
Nander	207,587	127,107	80,480	45,418	47,287	39,856	25,476	25,141	4,572	7,517	728	3,808	528	2,190	459
Naldrug	229,482	139,098	90,384	49,879	52,707	39,813	29,561	26,623	5,844	10,757	670	5,8,34	384	2,943	282
Bidar	302,402	186,600	115,802	63,460	65,841	54,267	88,005	88,075	7,652	14,937	1,135	7,407	679	3,675	527
Parbhani	262,357	156,527	105,830	58,126	63,637	49,048	32,632	28,350	5,911	8,626	967	4,747	590	3,020	520
Sirpur Tandar	89,733	51,761	37,972	16,722	18,592	17,194	13,514	11,394	4,646	8,184	575	1,610	212	745	108
Karnatic or Kanada. Gulbarga	218,725	135,547	83,178	49,130	49,427	38,885	25,674	21,264	4,670	11,262	942	6,738	623	3,927	468
Raichur	199,676	119,417	80,259	42,525	48,749	35,705	27,420	16,823	4,757	9,646	1,049	7,683	977	3,527	604
Lingasugur	231,647	136,848	94,799	49,081	49,221	39,925	30,010	19,116	6,331	11,770	1,900	7,981	1,809	4,117	1,540
Total Districts......	4,077,432	2,477,585	1,599,847	811,884	858,739	733,068	550,818	497,571	120,891	218,831	19,941	110,013	12,496	51,177	8,775
Total Districts including Hyderabad ...	4,230,250	2,571,757	1,658,493	831,795	879,034	752,489	569,000	515,112	130,064	227,378	24,418	121,372	14,950	57,159	9,891
Railways......	2,242	1,479	763	382	857	300	266	141	86	150	27	250	11	165	10
Grand Total......	4,232,492	2,573,236	1,659,256	8,32177	879,391	752,789	569,266	515,253	180,150	227,523	24,445	121,622	14,961	57,324	9,901

TABLE VIII.

Civil Condition by Religion and Age. Part (A)—All Religions—*Continued.*

(1) UNMARRIED.—*Continued.*

Age Period.—*Continued.*

	District or State.	30—34		35—39		40—44		45—49		50—54		55—59		60 and over.		Unspecified.	
		Males.	Females.	Males.	Females.	Males.	Females.	Males.	Females.	Males.	Females.	Males.	Females.	Males.	Females.	Males.	Females.
		17	18	19	20	21	22	23	24	25	26	27	28	29	30	31	32
Telingana. Hyderabad.	City	896	275	333	107	387	162	111	83	162	73	47	13	179	80	3	1,058
	Suburbs including Secunderabad	1,870	416	727	189	720	202	255	40	306	110	82	28	333	145	5	18
	Total......	2,766	691	1,060	296	1,107	364	366	73	468	183	129	41	512	225	8	1,076
	Atraf-i-Balda District	1,202	314	461	135	600	213	194	58	280	183	52	26	298	177	47	80
	Mahabubnagar (Nagar Kurnul) ...	1,837	599	687	270	743	431	256	126	350	253	72	51	362	293	109	121
	Nalgonda	1,094	370	375	168	401	257	130	82	223	199	88	38	268	292	54	78
	Warangal (Khamam)	1,794	588	505	210	690	400	174	117	320	277	65	31	388	411	160	191
	Elgandal	1,124	603	409	235	473	419	171	147	311	326	64	44	312	380	141	237
	Indur...	1,114	519	421	224	486	319	175	97	255	201	44	26	242	222	46	212
	Medak...	990	305	427	120	550	210	175	59	296	126	69	17	380	117	82	351
Mahratwara.	Aurangabad	1,504	307	683	160	722	241	293	68	423	124	97	35	460	197	140	168
	Birh	1,219	271	490	110	567	177	226	62	288	90	72	17	321	126	166	187
	Nander	1,090	357	428	140	581	308	208	86	312	154	59	85	350	171	149	229
	Naldrug	1,188	259	496	122	585	173	222	44	303	88	83	26	274	128	98	96
	Bidar	1,606	504	651	210	845	399	357	106	518	248	118	50	583	289	101	157
	Parbhani	1,596	440	694	194	856	294	309	85	479	174	100	26	491	262	85	98
	Sirpur Tandur	380	112	117	37	161	61	56	11	71	41	19	4	88	37	20	22
Karnatic or Kanada.	Gulbarga	1,718	410	650	198	751	266	293	86	384	145	81	26	385	162	79	81
	Raichur	1,576	545	594	217	542	367	211	144	252	173	76	48	242	186	15	28
	Lingasugur	2,073	1,337	865	598	807	784	326	265	396	505	102	111	327	365	12	28
	Total Districts......	23,105	7,840	8,953	8,348	10,360	5,319	8,776	1,643	5,461	8,257	1,211	611	5,721	8,815	1,454	2,354
	Total Districts including Hyderabad ...	25,871	8,531	10,013	8,644	11,467	5,683	4,142	1,716	5,929	8,440	1,840	652	6,288	4,040	1,462	8,430
	Railways......	48	4	23	1	12	1	4	......	2	...	1	...	1	......	......	......
	Grand Total......	25,919	8,535	10,036	8,645	11,479	5,684	4,146	1,716	5,931	8,440	1,841	652	6,234	4,040	1,462	8,430

TABLE VIII.

Civil Condition by Religion and Age. Part (A)—All Religions—*Continued.*

District or State.	Married.														
	Total Married.			Age Period.											
				0—4		5—9		10—14		15—19		20—24		25—29	
	Total.	Males.	Females.	Males.	Females.	Males.	Females.	Males.	Females.	Males.	Females.	Males.	Females.	Males.	Females.
1	2	3	4	5	6	7	8	9	10	11	12	13	14	15	16
Telingana. Hyderabad. City	61,827	33,129	28,198	...	...	77	290	388	1,715	1,360	4,468	8,838	6,364	5,125	4,816
Telingana. Hyderabad. Suburbs including Secunderabad	143,443	77,008	66,435	44	56	207	1,223	989	5,885	3,583	11,543	8,949	13,966	12,390	10,354
Total......	204,770	110,137	94,633	44	56	284	1,513	1,377	7,600	4,943	16,011	12,787	20,330	17,515	15,170
Telingana. Atraf-i-Balda Districts	196,727	99,819	96,908	181	340	459	4,781	1,959	12,756	5,230	14,280	11,011	16,956	15,053	14,314
Mahabubnagar (Nagar Kurnul) ...	335,530	169,179	166,351	218	799	926	9,774	4,618	21,064	9,716	24,264	20,116	30,499	26,743	25,360
Nalgonda	289,759	144,647	145,112	151	290	331	3,778	1,671	19,190	7,335	24,230	17,938	26,808	22,895	21,020
Warangal (Khamam)	402,078	203,561	198,512	802	546	589	5,752	3,258	24,740	10,656	30,496	24,147	37,214	31,971	29,866
Elgandal	552,233	279,049	273,184	561	1,089	1,499	12,380	9,822	41,089	21,648	41,826	36,836	46,578	43,411	39,166
Indur	351,282	176 687	174,595	287	1,445	2,555	14,024	10,641	24,353	13,822	23,700	20,347	27,633	28,496	25,749
Medak	188,797	93,973	94,824	131	323	341	5,187	2,024	12,806	5,006	13,168	10,008	15,709	14,589	18,991
Mahratwara. Aurangabad	455,518	228,418	227,100	270	759	1,708	12,219	9,053	28,701	15,813	31,530	23,633	37,118	38,509	34,848
Birh	360,452	180,810	179,642	289	1,100	1,688	10,844	7,523	20,604	11,767	22,325	18,833	29,761	31,030	27,991
Nander	352,449	177,536	174,913	400	1,530	2,465	14,084	10,860	23,131	11,686	20,513	18,428	27,077	29,964	27,765
Naldrug	355,822	179,279	176,543	277	1,076	1,365	9,790	6,440	19,044	10,677	22,339	18,651	30,130	31,591	28 885
Bidar	493,949	249,542	244,407	854	1,661	2,323	15,913	10,233	30,960	14,867	29,190	26,352	38,949	41,537	38,717
Parbhani	461,374	235,103	226,271	609	2,145	3,660	17,437	14,136	27,708	15,919	25,912	23,918	35,119	38,552	35,154
Sirpur Tandur	120,340	61,157	59,183	137	487	1,125	4,135	4,123	7,632	4,554	7,398	6,659	9,271	9,046	9,049
Karnatic or Kanada. Gulbarga	346,291	176,283	170,008	848	2,126	1,748	13,037	6,043	16,758	10,985	20,858	18,493	28,502	29,654	28,861
Raichur	253.471	129,268	124,203	800	1,291	1,426	8,504	3,976	11,523	7,449	15,549	16,336	25,179	21,351	20,983
Lingasugur	313,560	158,267	155,293	897	2,718	2,635	12,049	5,937	14,109	10,733	19,643	19,345	28,668	25,778	25,542
Total Districts......	5,829,577	2,942,528	2,887,049	5,712	19,725	26,843	173,688	112,817	356,168	187,863	387,216	331,041	491,171	480,120	447,261
Total Districts including Hyderabad ...	6,084,347	3,052,665	2,981,682	5,756	19,781	27,127	175,201	113,694	363,768	192,806	403,227	343,828	511,501	497,685	462,431
Railways......	3,913	2,601	1,312	4	7	4	81	12	70	43	176	294	313	555	289
Grand Total......	6,088,260	3,055,266	2,982,994	5,760	19,788	27,131	175 282	113,706	363,838	192,849	403,403	344,122	511,814	498,190	462,720

TABLE VIII.

Civil Condition by Religion and Age. Part (A)—All Religions—*Continued.*

District or State.	MARRIED—*Continued.* Age Period—*Continued.* 30—34 Males.	30—34 Females.	35—39 Males.	35—39 Females.	40—44 Males.	40—44 Females.	45—49 Males.	45—49 Females.	50—54 Males.	50—54 Females.	55—59 Males.	55—59 Females.	60 and over. Males.	60 and over. Females.	Unspecified. Males.	Unspecified. Females.
	17	18	19	20	21	22	23	24	25	26	27	28	19	30	31	32
Telingana. Hyderabad. City	5,877	4,094	3,315	1,688	4,699	2,397	1,725	594	8,048	989	725	200	2,945	566	7	17
Suburbs including Secunderabad	18,643	9,580	7,938	3,736	10,386	5,140	4,028	1,356	6,628	1,987	1,686	896	6,527	1,184	15	29
Total......	19,520	13,674	11,253	5,424	15,085	7,537	5,748	1,950	9,676	2,976	2,411	596	9,472	1,750	22	46
Atraf-i-Balda District	15,929	13,850	10,116	5,472	13,687	7,413	5,748	1,911	9,156	3,028	2,105	411	9,235	1,377	5	84
Mahabubnagar (Nagar Karnul) ...	27,305	24,045	18,356	9,519	22,869	11,394	10,026	2,932	13,027	4,146	2,952	658	12,281	1,828	26	74
Nalgonda	23,132	20,170	14,349	7,756	19,240	11,180	7,950	2,817	13,191	4,720	2,818	651	13,629	2,419	22	88
Warangal (Khamam)	34,927	29,336	18,322	10,721	29,445	16,047	9,750	3,521	18,866	6,701	2,997	791	18,306	3,221	25	60
Elgandal	42,609	35,729	25,865	15,071	32,972	20,183	13,690	5,679	23,090	8,816	4,798	1,810	22,228	4,119	25	149
Indur	27,083	23,814	16,254	9,822	20,914	12,331	8,866	3,588	13,017	4,791	2,884	756	11,494	2,298	27	296
Medak	14,546	13,032	9,299	5,429	12,400	7,430	5,431	1,900	8,964	3,285	2,108	435	9,163	1,562	18	567
Mahratwara. Aurangabad	36,215	31,639	23,745	15,857	26,974	17,633	13,378	5,721	17,593	6,485	4,795	1,270	16,687	3,182	45	138
Birh	28,672	25,950	18,198	12,975	22,340	14,320	10,237	4,729	14,274	5,601	3,537	1,067	12,867	2,282	55	93
Nander	28,565	25,078	16,394	10,763	22,045	13,802	9,074	3,679	14,264	4,839	3,027	760	10,315	1,648	49	244
Naldrug	28,999	26,377	17,804	12,263	23,021	14,280	10,615	4,285	14,420	5,018	3,573	975	11,819	2,088	27	48
Bidar	39,037	36,191	23,289	15,141	32,167	20,277	14,541	5,866	21,143	7,312	5,334	1,195	18,328	2,911	37	124
Parbhani	37,399	32,804	22,701	15,183	29,204	18,275	12,178	5,419	18,718	6,878	3,853	1,163	14,205	2,947	61	132
Sirpur Taandr	10,088	8,619	5,452	3,460	7,703	4,783	2,794	1,238	4,691	1,929	908	331	3,871	848	6	8
Karnatic or Kanada. Gulbarga	29,325	26,923	18,613	10,821	23,615	12,197	10,698	3,330	13,098	4,186	3,228	654	10,420	1,771	20	34
Raichur	21,049	18,645	14,741	7,826	16,752	7,974	8,095	2,447	8,841	2,709	2,499	496	6,452	1,074	1	8
Lingasugur	25,983	23,482	16,811	10,184	19,879	10,163	9,249	3,017	10,482	3,499	3,033	747	7,499	1,444	6	29
Total Districts......	470,863	415,684	290,309	177,762	375,177	219,682	162,315	62,079	236,830	83,878	54,389	13,670	208,294	36,899	456	2,166
Total Districts including Hyderabadad..	490,383	429,358	301,562	183,186	390,262	227,219	168,063	64,029	246,506	86,854	56,800	14,266	217,766	38,649	477	2,212
Railways......	540	200	410	75	328	76	148	25	137	33	52	5	74	12	...	...
Grand Total......	490,923	429,558	301,972	183,261	390,590	227,295	168,211	64,054	246,643	86,887	56,852	14,271	217,840	38,661	477	2,212

TABLE VIII.

Civil Condition by Religion and Age. Part (A)—All Religons—*Continued.*

(3) WIDOWED.

District or State.		Total Widowed.			Age Period. 0—4		5—9		10—14		15—19		20—24		25—29	
		Total.	Males.	Females.	Males.	Females.	Males.	Females.	Males.	Females.	Males.	Females.	Males.	Females.	Males.	Females.
1		2	3	4	5	6	7	8	9	10	11	12	13	14	15	16
Telingana. Hyderabad.	City	18,494	3,934	14,560	......	...	2	20	6	39	41	188	132	580	286	786
	Suburbs including Secunderabad	38,246	7,994	30,252	3	7	6	37	31	139	93	511	318	1,290	545	1,813
	Total......	56,740	11,928	44,812	3	7	8	57	37	178	134	699	450	1,870	831	2,599
	Atraf i Balda District	50,300	8,865	41,435	15	36	20	99	44	805	73	524	214	1,308	874	1,922
	Mahabubnagar (Nagar Karnul) ...	81,297	13,324	67,973	18	38	38	180	88	452	138	884	370	2,201	742	3,290
	Nalgonda	58,676	8,851	49,825	9	25	17	114	22	505	69	968	204	1,888	862	2,298
	Warangal (Khamam)	81,179	12,508	68,671	13	49	18	146	50	772	121	1,287	352	2,633	569	3,287
	Elgandal	97,411	15,367	82,044	16	53	22	293	87	1,227	185	1,588	870	3,230	618	4,051
	Indur...	81,580	14,355	67,225	20	51	84	334	182	703	203	943	865	1,932	684	3,227
	Medak	47,995	8,546	39,449	11	37	23	98	33	246	78	511	176	1,210	327	1,927
Mahratwara.	Aurangabad	80,585	17,133	63,452	21	32	66	207	245	553	284	620	467	1,276	1,039	2,354
	Birh	62,110	13,729	48,381	24	42	67	177	212	405	255	510	383	1,037	781	1,883
	Nander	72,015	15,253	56,762	27	42	144	309	467	587	397	494	544	1,125	1,069	2,220
	Naldrug	63,734	13,264	50,470	6	38	70	219	219	849	289	457	426	1,176	821	2,015
	Bidar...	105,350	20,822	84,528	22	233	117	453	410	752	473	721	736	1,582	1,331	3,217
	Parbhani	81,050	18,608	62,442	31	58	170	867	479	590	422	574	701	1,307	1,261	2,382
	Sirpur Tandur	21,615	4,007	17,608	11	23	42	144	123	261	78	251	132	444	232	718
Karnatic or Kanada.	Gulbarga	84,060	17,765	66,295	22	66	122	284	350	486	464	708	719	1,581	1,138	2,971
	Raichur	59,207	11,497	47,710	19	40	56	172	132	248	203	461	428	1,453	655	2,245
	Lingasugur	74,571	16,173	58,398	31	78	169	335	297	450	380	735	643	1,766	1,017	2,774
Total Districts......		1,202,735	230,067	972,668	316	941	1,240	3,931	3,440	8,891	4,112	12,231	7,230	27,144	18,020	42,776
Total Districts including Hyderabad ...		1,259,475	241,995	1,017,480	319	948	1,248	3,988	3,477	9,069	4,246	12,930	7,680	29,014	18,851	45,375
Railways......		435	156	279	......	...	......	1	......	...	1	5	4	11	12	9
Grand Total......		1,259,910	242,151	1,017,759	319	948	1,248	3,989	3,477	9,069	4,247	12,935	7,684	29,025	18,863	45,384

TABLE VIII.

Civil Condition by Religion and Age. Part (A)—All Religions—*Continued.*

District or State.	(3) WIDOWED—*Continued.* Age Period.—*Continued.* 30—34 Males.	30—34 Females.	35—39 Males.	35—39 Females.	40—44 Males.	40—44 Females.	45—49 Males.	45—49 Females.	50—54 Males.	50—54 Females.	55—59 Males.	55—59 Females.	60 & over. Males.	60 & over. Females.	Unspecified. Males.	Unspecified. Females.
	17	18	19	20	21	22	23	24	25	26	27	28	29	30	31	32
Telingana. Hyderabad. City	869	1,324	261	868	528	2,616	244	796	687	2,791	211	522	1,172	4,024	...	6
Suburbs including Secunderabad	730	3,058	517	1,819	1,087	5,057	500	1,668	1,228	5,415	421	1,087	2,509	8,346	6	15
Total......	1,099	4,377	778	2,687	1,610	7,673	744	2,459	1,915	8,206	682	1,609	3,681	12,370	6	21
Atraf-i-Balda District	628	3,708	515	2,446	1,119	6,465	585	2,559	1,548	7,816	410	1,391	8,824	12,838	1	23
Mahabubnagar (Nagar Karnul) ...	1,129	6,467	937	4,412	1,752	11,262	1,022	4,651	2,089	12,155	589	2,828	4,402	19,604	15	49
Nalgonda	596	4,498	425	2,598	906	7,364	515	2,574	1,486	8,628	887	1,486	8,899	16,850	4	89
Warangal (Khamam)	966	6,579	565	3,211	1,597	11,006	667	8,151	2,130	12,804	430	1,611	5,018	22,092	12	43
Elgandal	1,077	7,720	762	4,592	1,929	12,416	1,008	4,475	2,830	15,042	784	2,674	5,723	24,624	6	59
Indur	1,149	6,279	934	4,182	2,022	10,618	1,080	4,228	2,570	12,589	599	2,119	4,458	19,989	5	136
Medak	547	8,466	479	2,187	1,091	6,054	567	2,855	1,517	7,241	409	1,548	8,286	12,384	2	190
Mahratwara. Aurangabad	1,301	4,556	1,107	4,128	1,971	9,684	1,285	5,001	2,498	11,889	900	2,652	5,992	20,972	12	28
Bish	1,118	3,665	865	8,153	1,661	7,424	914	3,645	2,027	9,071	670	1,886	4,788	15,454	14	29
Nander	1,429	4,568	1,041	8,379	2,094	9,630	1,073	4,110	2,449	11,516	667	2,098	3,840	16,600	12	84
Naldrug	1,034	3,907	838	3,212	1,594	8,419	1,029	8,915	2,020	9,631	684	2,102	4,232	15,015	2	15
Bidar	1,709	6,405	1,179	4,754	2,596	13,618	1,587	6,051	3,291	16,471	1,030	3,597	6,881	26,626	10	48
Parbhani	1,646	4,575	1,278	3,844	2,388	9,879	1,296	4,382	2,904	12,458	851	2,270	5,174	19,727	7	34
Sirpur Tandur	408	1,527	275	979	551	2,887	233	991	677	8,427	158	586	1,086	5,871	1	4
Karnatic or Kanada. Gulbarga	1,595	6,008	1,310	4,442	2,562	11,097	1,418	4,972	2,576	12,086	796	2,689	4,687	18,945	6	20
Raichur	986	4,748	912	3,673	1,586	8,397	999	3,813	1,790	8,286	641	2,197	3,134	11,970	6	7
Lingasugur	1,398	6,001	1,194	4,491	2,269	9,966	1,294	4,514	2,521	10,528	904	2,425	4,050	14,326	6	9
Total Districts......	18,716	84,667	14,616	59,683	29,638	156,181	16,472	65,387	36,863	181,078	10,859	35,604	73,424	293,337	121	817
Total Districts including Hyderabad ...	19,815	89,044	15,394	62,370	31,248	163,854	17,216	67,846	38,778	189,284	11,491	37,213	77,105	305,707	127	838
Railways......	17	20	30	15	28	48	18	39	20	55	9	15	17	61	...	...
Grand Total......	19,832	89,064	15,424	62,385	31,276	163,902	17,234	67,885	38,798	189,339	11,500	37,228	77,122	305,768	127	838

TABLE VIII.

Civil Condition by Religion and Age. Part (A)—All Religions:—*Continued.*

District or State.	Total Unspecified. Total.	Males.	Females.	0—4 Males.	0—4 Females.	5—9 Males.	5—9 Females.	10—14 Males.	10—14 Females.	15—19 Males.	15—19 Females.	20—24 Males.	20—24 Females.	25—29 Males.	25—29 Females.	30—34 Males.	30—34 Females.	35—39 Males.	35—39 Females.	40—44 Males.	40—44 Females.	45—49 Males.	45—49 Females.	50—54 Males.	50—54 Females.	55—59 Males.	55—59 Females.	60 and over. Males.	60 and over. Females.	Unspecified. Males.	Unspecified. Females.
1	2	3	4	5	6	7	8	9	10	11	12	13	14	15	16	17	18	19	20	21	22	23	24	25	26	27	28	29	30	31	32
Telingana. Hyderabad. City ...	892	22	370	...	...	...	...	1	4	...	...	...	4	2	...	4	3	...	...	5	1	...	...	2	1	...	...	2	...	6	357
Suburbs including Secunderabad ...	819	65	254	8	5	5	2	3	4	2	5	7	8	9	1	13	6	5	8	6	1	8	...	2	2	2	1	2	7	8	214
Total......	711	87	624	3	5	5	2	4	8	2	5	7	7	11	1	17	9	5	8	11	2	8	...	4	8	2	1	4	7	9	571
Atraf-i-Balda District ...	178	57	116	2	5	1	...	1	...	2	4	2	6	7	8	3	4	2	2	...	5	1	1	2	5	...	1	7	14	27	66
Mahabubnagar (Nagar Karnul) ...	495	190	305	28	56	12	18	8	22	7	12	7	18	10	17	12	21	6	7	10	15	7	7	7	9	...	4	17	15	59	94
Nalgonda ...	331	131	200	26	31	6	19	5	20	11	15	9	15	10	11	4	12	5	5	12	13	5	2	12	13	...	2	15	26	11	16
Warangal ...	365	163	202	30	27	9	19	9	8	8	8	11	9	4	12	9	16	8	4	9	11	1	1	8	9	...	1	15	28	52	54
Elgandal ...	530	219	311	32	28	18	18	18	32	14	26	16	32	10	25	15	17	5	6	6	19	3	7	11	15	4	...	19	28	48	63
Indur... ...	339	105	234	7	10	9	15	8	20	5	16	7	15	12	15	6	14	5	8	6	14	3	4	4	10	1	7	10	20	22	66
Medak ...	341	94	247	4	10	5	9	10	8	7	7	4	11	12	10	11	4	6	2	1	11	3	2	1	15	1	...	8	8	21	150
Mahratwara. Aurangabad ...	484	237	247	18	22	18	17	19	19	15	23	20	15	12	10	12	15	11	6	10	9	3	7	15	11	2	...	29	18	53	80
Birh ...	475	208	267	20	18	17	30	12	13	11	18	17	16	16	28	18	16	9	8	19	13	4	5	14	8	3	...	22	22	31	77
Nander ...	478	240	238	23	17	15	13	11	7	11	10	21	16	19	23	21	24	7	11	15	21	5	2	11	8	3	4	17	12	61	70
Naldrug ...	234	106	128	7	7	9	11	5	11	7	6	11	11	15	7	6	14	3	6	12	6	7	5	5	20	4	4	7	13	8	17
Bidar ...	283	124	159	6	7	7	9	10	8	9	5	11	15	5	11	12	9	12	9	10	18	5	2	7	9	3	2	7	14	20	46
Parbhani ...	554	261	293	11	8	9	16	18	27	14	34	11	33	32	21	28	26	17	20	30	22	5	8	25	23	2	4	26	26	33	25
Sirpur Tandur ...	66	30	36	3	1	1	6	2	2	2	2	5	...	1	1	3	1	1	3	2	2	1	1	4	...	...	...	1	11	4	6
Karnatic or Kanada. Gulbarga ...	182	83	99	1	7	7	8	7	2	3	7	10	14	6	12	10	4	6	4	5	9	6	5	9	7	1	1	5	9	7	10
Raichur ...	101	35	66	3	7	2	6	4	...	2	1	3	5	1	6	1	4	1	4	6	1	1	2	...	7	...	1	4	7	7	15
Lingasugur ...	236	106	130	6	5	4	4	4	2	4	6	6	11	4	4	5	7	1	6	6	4	2	5	5	9	2	1	7	6	50	60
Total Districts......	5,667	2,389	3,278	227	266	149	218	151	191	182	195	171	242	176	211	171	208	100	111	159	188	62	66	135	168	26	32	216	267	514	915
Total Districts including Hyderabad ...	6,378	2,476	3,902	280	271	154	220	155	199	184	200	178	249	187	212	188	217	105	114	170	190	65	66	189	171	28	33	220	274	523	1486
Railways......	...	...	...	...	...	...	...	...	...	...	...	...	...	...	...	...	...	...	...	...	...	...	...	...	...	...	...	...	...	...	...
Grand Total......	6,378	2,476	3,902	280	271	154	220	155	199	184	200	178	249	187	212	188	217	105	114	170	190	65	66	189	171	28	33	220	274	523	1486

TABLE VIII.

Civil Condition by Religion and Age Part (B) Hindus.

District or State.	(1) Unmarried.														
	Total Unmarried.			Age Period.											
				0—4		5—9		10—14		15—19		20—24		25—29	
	Total.	Males.	Females.	Males.	Females.	Males.	Females.	Males.	Females.	Males.	Females.	Males.	Females.	Males.	Females.
1	2	3	4	5	6	7	8	9	10	11	12	13	14	15	16
Telingana. Hyderabad. City	14,156	8,806	5,350	2,032	2,081	1,887	1,739	1,703	579	1,288	244	752	156	496	95
Telingana. Hyderabad. Suburbs including Secunderabad	61,081	38,021	23,060	9,094	9,288	9,083	8,209	7,785	2,856	4,898	964	3,284	624	1,621	386
Total......	75,237	46,827	28,410	11,126	11,364	10,970	9,948	9,488	3,435	6,186	1,208	4,036	780	2,117	481
Atraf-i-Balda District	124,257	78,292	45,965	22,852	24,603	22,100	16,714	16,253	2,471	8,477	463	4,234	485	1,929	337
Mahabubnagar (Nagar Karnul) ...	283,447	144,415	89,032	45,911	49,707	41,727	30,170	27,180	4,748	13,957	979	8,107	834	3,672	590
Nalgonda.	260,928	157,268	103,660	47,923	51,379	43,720	39,315	84,707	9,601	18,348	1,077	7,782	566	2,494	383
Warangal (Khamam)	348,496	209,652	138,844	60,027	65,019	59,581	51,501	48,314	16,135	23,171	2,402	10,902	1,104	3,904	591
Elgandal	423,556	256,812	166,744	80,141	84,614	77,894	61,615	64,154	14,287	22,047	2,158	7,613	1,160	2,249	648
Indur	185,892	115,649	70,243	38,300	38,998	37,442	23,316	24,602	4,192	8,035	1,018	8,304	668	1,644	539
Medak	111,579	71,352	40,227	20,095	20,992	20,293	14,954	15,518	2,100	7,411	516	3,831	458	1,840	317
Mahratwara. Aurangabad	249,072	149,420	99,652	49,754	55,351	47,143	35,892	31,141	6,183	11,309	702	4,600	357	2,385	250
Birh	196,787	119,840	769,47	42,186	45,237	36,894	25,766	23,607	4,251	8,516	445	3,952	251	1,954	200
Nander	184,062	112,900	711,62	41,442	43,069	36,113	22,129	22,079	3,343	6,075	541	2,844	439	1,695	407
Naldrug	204,479	124,032	80,447	45,338	47,888	35,867	26,110	23,810	4,785	9,239	480	4,749	286	23,29	222
Bidar	255,077	157,978	97,099	55,318	57,329	46,843	31,567	32,297	5,226	11,782	664	5,394	467	2,659	389
Parbhani	232,792	139,028	93,764	53,327	58,268	44,378	28,593	24,819	4,319	6,882	650	3,546	410	2,242	379
Sirpur Tandur	74,031	42,782	31,249	13,911	15,388	14,348	11,207	9,464	3,689	2,573	459	1,235	166	551	86
Karnatic or Kanada. Gulbarga	179,789	112,174	67,615	41,903	41,873	32,635	20,286	17,600	3,003	8,817	612	4,966	463	2,860	360
Raichur	177,691	106,407	71,284	38,346	39,427	31,952	24,063	14,926	3,874	8,374	894	6,634	886	3,052	544
Lingasugur	206,029	121,546	84,483	44,190	44,210	35,612	26,339	16,883	5,413	10,218	1,661	6,772	1,662	3,589	1,431
Total Districts......	3,647,964	2,219,547	1,428,417	740,964	783,352	664,542	489,537	447,304	97,570	185,281	15,721	90,465	10,607	40,948	7,623
Total Districts including Hyderabad ...	3,723,201	2,266,374	1,456,827	752,090	794,716	675,512	499,485	456,792	101,005	191,367	16,929	94,501	11,387	43,065	8,104
Railways......	1,382	914	468	268	251	189	162	86	83	75	9	133	4	101	4
Grand Total......	3,724,583	2,267,288	1,457,295	752,358	794,967	675,701	499,647	456,878	101,088	191,442	16,938	94,634	11,391	43,166	8,108

TABLE VIII.

Civil Condition by Religon and Age Part (B) Hindus—*Continued.*

District or State.	(1) Unmarried.—*Continued.* Age Period. 30—34 Males.	30—34 Females.	35—39 Males.	35—39 Females.	40—44 Males.	40—44 Females.	45—49 Males.	45—49 Females.	50—54 Males.	50—54 Females.	55—59 Males.	55—59 Females.	60 and over. Males.	60 and over. Females.	Unspecified. Males.	Unspecified. Females.
	17	18	19	20	21	22	28	24	25	26	27	28	29	30	31	32
Telingana. Hyderabad City	265	75	112	24	135	45	42	8	58	21	20	...	66	16	...	267
Suburbs including Secunderabad	905	279	869	121	402	137	140	31	186	69	52	12	201	87	1	2
Total......	1,170	854	481	145	537	182	182	39	244	90	72	12	267	108	1	269
Atraf i-Balda District	882	273	362	118	486	188	165	54	226	117	41	28	242	148	42	26
Mahabubnagar (Nagar Karnal) ...	1,625	564	609	252	646	414	285	120	309	240	68	50	320	280	99	84
Nalgonda	956	852	825	159	873	248	115	74	193	193	88	87	246	281	53	49
Warangal (Khamam)	1,615	555	467	197	632	369	159	108	298	259	62	31	364	400	156	178
Elgandal	993	582	370	231	433	403	154	138	281	319	62	41	288	364	133	184
Indur...	901	464	355	197	420	302	156	93	209	185	84	25	208	215	39	36
Medak	774	275	351	109	467	192	145	57	259	116	62	14	285	103	21	24
Mahratwara. Aurangabad	1,064	231	496	105	524	163	210	49	299	83	75	26	352	181	118	129
Birh	974	202	389	82	450	133	190	48	235	71	62	12	275	90	156	159
Nander	875	819	356	123	491	266	180	71	267	143	52	81	297	152	184	129
Naldrug	953	214	416	93	498	134	183	33	253	65	70	21	236	94	91	72
Bidar	1,177	364	490	156	667	294	299	76	404	201	100	35	464	237	84	94
Parbhani	1,278	331	574	131	729	204	274	60	401	121	79	19	421	201	78	78
Sirpur Tandur	279	80	89	33	128	51	41	10	58	33	15	3	75	26	15	18
Karnatic or Kanada. Gulbarga	1,303	324	499	151	592	195	237	61	302	104	71	15	321	107	68	61
Raichur	1,384	510	534	211	493	346	187	130	230	160	67	47	213	174	15	18
Lingasugur	1,794	1,273	771	565	712	740	288	241	366	483	90	106	301	338	10	21
Total Districts......	18,827	6,914	7,453	2,908	8,741	4,637	8,218	1,423	4,590	2,893	1,044	536	4,908	3,341	1,812	1,355
Total Districts including Hyderabad ...	19,997	7,268	7,934	3,053	9,278	4,819	3,400	1,462	4,834	2 983	1,116	548	5,175	3,444	1,813	1,624
Railways......	34	4	14	1	8	...	3	...	1	...	1	...	1	...	...	...
Grand Total......	20,081	7,272	7,948	3,054	9,286	4,819	3,403	1,462	4,835	2,983	1,117	548	5,176	3,444	1,813	1,624

TABLE VIII.

Civil Condition by Religion and Age Part (B) Hindus.

District or State.		(2) Married. Total Married.			Age Period. 0—4		5—9		10—14		15—19		20—24		25—29	
		Total.	Males.	Females.	Males.	Females.	Males.	Females.	Males.	Females.	Males.	Females.	Males.	Females.	Males.	Females.
1		2	3	4	5	6	7	8	9	10	11	12	13	14	15	16
Telingana.	Hyderabad { City	26,002	15,140	10,862	...	...	42	221	252	1,148	863	1,747	1,940	2,178	2,444	1,754
	Hyderabad { Suburbs including Secunderabad	91,990	49,792	42,198	35	50	152	1,120	840	4,747	2,903	7,389	6,468	8,555	8,137	6,211
	Total......	117,992	64,932	53,060	85	50	194	1,341	1,092	5,895	3,766	9,136	8,408	10,733	10,581	7,965
	Atraf-i-Balda District	176,797	89,505	87,292	164	301	423	4,653	1,872	12,115	5,004	12,919	10,297	15,077	13,639	12,685
	Mahabubnagar (Nagar Karnul) ...	310,150	156,673	153,477	184	767	882	9,537	4,451	20,063	9,342	22,460	19,023	27,831	24,881	23,189
	Nalgonda	276,616	138,048	138,568	129	268	304	3,739	1,631	18,806	7,215	23,[illegible]11	17,482	25,445	21,883	19,934
	Warangal (Khamam)	382,861	193,676	189,185	282	508	565	5,692	3,203	24,206	10,492	29,043	23,374	35,255	30,314	28,266
	Elgandal	532,830	269,161	263,669	545	1,055	1,462	12,294	9,700	40,447	21,331	40,452	36,029	44,669	41,908	37,620
	Indur	326,825	164,516	162,309	256	1,411	2,485	13,772	10,403	23,338	13,384	21,984	19,244	25,375	26,485	28,686
	Medak...	170,981	85,243	85,738	122	286	319	5,052	1,954	12,129	4,804	12,000	9,350	14,045	18,256	12,559
Maharatwara.	Aurangabad	405,667	208,239	20[illegible],428	286	705	1,590	11,775	8,630	26,676	14,771	27,963	21,872	32,618	34,559	30,814
	Birh	332,443	166,669	165,774	268	1,059	1,623	10,510	7,276	19,611	11,251	20,566	17,639	27,223	28,782	25,693
	Nander	324,157	163,062	161,095	378	1,492	2,382	13,717	10,544	21,929	11,127	18,737	17,134	24,624	27,436	25,370
	Naldrug	324,192	163,252	160,940	251	1,027	1,278	9,329	6,134	17,744	10,041	20,422	17,261	27,351	28,956	26,210
	Bidar	437,433	220,904	216,529	317	1,562	2,187	15,290	9,703	28,481	13,877	25,588	23,883	34,043	36,878	34,038
	Parbhani	425,850	216,830	209,020	563	2,064	3,549	17,015	13,708	26,333	15,252	23,736	22,335	32,113	35,549	32,260
	Sirpur Tandur	100,355	51,005	49,350	97	419	979	3,704	3,631	6,598	3,963	6,234	5,644	7,641	7,636	7,500
Karnatic or Kanada.	Gulbarga	299,162	152,183	146,979	800	2,028	1,576	12,352	5,664	15,120	10,118	17,951	16,313	24,233	25,722	24,631
	Raichur....	228,671	116,475	112,196	267	1,223	1,330	8,143	3,760	10,729	6,927	14,060	14,971	22,637	19,302	18,718
	Lingasugur	283,280	142,787	140,493	825	2,589	2,493	11,409	5,607	13,072	9,986	17,833	17,642	25,695	23,251	23,937
Total Districts......		5,338,270	2,693,228	2,645,042	5,179	18,764	25,427	167,983	107,871	337,297	178,945	355,159	308,993	445,870	440,387	406,110
Total Districts including Hyderabad ...		5,456,262	2,758,160	2,698,102	5,214	18,814	25,621	169,324	108,963	343,292	182,711	364,295	317,401	456,603	450,968	414,075
Railways......		2,818	1,880	938	3	6	3	28	11	55	34	119	231	214	405	215
Grand Total......		5,459,080	2,760,040	2,699,040	5,217	18,820	25,624	169,352	108,974	343,347	182,745	364,414	317,632	456,817	451,373	414,290

TABLE VIII.

Civil Condition & Age

Hindus.

TABLE VIII.

Civil Condition by Religion and Age Part (B) Hindus.—*Continued.*

District or State	(2) MARRIED—*Continued.* Age Period. 30—34 Males.	30—34 Females.	35—39 Males.	35—39 Females.	40—44 Males.	40—44 Females.	45—49 Males.	45—49 Females.	50—54 Males.	50—54 Females.	55—59 Males.	55—59 Females.	60 and over. Males.	60 and over. Females.	Unspecified. Males.	Unspecified. Females.
	17	18	19	20	21	22	23	24	25	26	27	28	29	30	31	32
Telingana. Hyderabad. City	2,820	1,545	1,485	598	2,117	862	703	193	1,197	370	251	56	1,024	189	2	1
Hyderabad. Suburbs including Secunderabad	8,949	5,860	4,867	2,201	6,446	3,051	2,333	818	3,951	1,261	897	237	3,805	692	9	6
Total......	11,769	7,405	6,352	2,799	8,563	3,913	3,036	1,011	5,148	1,631	1,148	293	4,829	881	11	7
Atraf-i-Balda District	14,201	12,226	9,018	4,866	11,946	6,571	5,054	1,694	7,974	2,676	1,828	864	8,081	1,136	4	9
Mahabubnagar (Nagar Karnul) ...	25,192	21,922	16,929	8,690	20,934	10,361	9,194	2,663	11,878	3,720	2,675	592	11,086	1,659	22	28
Nalgonda	21,992	19,156	13,552	7,337	18,242	10,579	7,529	2,669	12,497	4,495	2,658	619	12,912	2,273	22	37
Warangal (Khamam)	33,053	27,814	17,283	9,717	27,940	15,148	9,258	3,344	17,806	6,349	2,791	758	17,290	3,061	25	29
Elgandal	40,883	34,197	24,826	14,465	31,482	19,271	13,087	5,507	22,028	8,395	4,588	1,270	21,207	3,985	25	92
Indur	24,971	21,899	14,968	9,102	19,196	11,188	8,140	3,320	11,885	4,398	2,607	712	10,468	2,096	24	23
Medak...	13,179	11,640	8,334	4,897	11,070	6,657	4,865	1,734	7,979	2,952	1,879	888	8,116	1,385	16	14
Maharatwara. Aurangabad	31,918	27,744	20,991	13,999	23,564	15,406	11,796	5,086	15,148	5,677	4,238	1,151	14,341	2,754	40	65
Birh	26,239	23,666	16,614	11,930	20,314	13,033	9,375	4,303	12,944	5,115	3,234	969	11,113	2,039	47	57
Nander	26,048	22,864	14,818	9,866	20,096	12,521	8,220	3,877	12,929	4,373	2,780	682	9,182	1,467	43	76
Naldrug	26,250	23,781	16,115	11,104	20,680	12,836	9,560	3,881	12,910	4,485	3,208	905	10,590	1,886	23	29
Bidar	34,259	31,559	20,504	13,354	28,022	17,612	12,730	5,118	18,334	6,337	4,617	1,062	15,562	2,444	31	41
Parbhani	34,236	29,916	20,781	13,902	26,533	16,670	11,109	5,001	16,972	6,213	3,512	1,077	12,677	2,642	54	78
Sirpur Tandur	8,245	7,025	4,524	2,858	6,236	3,851	2,343	1,026	3,808	1,551	761	266	3,188	672	5	5
Karnatic or Kanada. Gulbarga	25,132	22,920	16,010	9,221	19,965	10,195	9,040	2,836	11,009	8,492	2,732	550	8,592	1,487	10	13
Raichur...	18,889	16,608	13,236	7,035	14,887	7,030	7,262	2,204	7,799	2,425	2,213	454	5,631	934	1	1
Lingasugur	23,266	20,951	14,996	9,158	17,756	9,081	8,304	2,714	9,278	3,113	2,764	692	6,614	1,289	5	10
Total Districts......	427,953	375,888	263,499	161,501	338,863	198,010	146,866	56,477	213,228	75,766	49,025	12,506	186,595	33,009	397	607
Total Districts including Hyderabad ...	439,722	383,288	269,851	164,300	347,426	201,928	149,902	57,488	218,376	77,397	50,173	12,799	191,424	33,890	408	614
Railways......	392	151	287	53	240	52	108	14	86	19	32	4	48	8	...	...
Grand Total......	440,114	383,439	270,138	164,353	347,666	201,975	150,010	57,502	218,462	77,416	50,205	12,803	191,472	33,898	408	614

TABLE VIII.

Civil Condition by Religion and Age Part (B) Hindus.

District or State.	(3) Widowed. Total Widowed. Total.	Males.	Females.	Age Period. 0–4 Males.	0–4 Females.	5–9 Males.	5–9 Females.	10–14 Males.	10–14 Females.	15–19 Males.	15–19 Females.	20–24 Males.	20–24 Females.	25–29 Males.	25–29 Females.
1	2	3	4	5	6	7	8	9	10	11	12	13	14	15	16
Telingana — Hyderabad — City	8,112	1,778	6,334	...	...	2	14	1	28	22	108	80	270	131	411
Telingana — Hyderabad — Suburbs including Secunderabad	25,874	5,287	20,187	...	7	2	27	13	118	62	879	231	955	364	1,282
Total......	33,486	7,015	26,471	...	7	4	41	14	141	84	487	311	1,225	495	1,693
Atraf-i-Balda District	45,226	7,985	37,241	5	28	12	89	39	288	65	476	194	1,171	342	1,748
Mahabubnagar (Nagar Karnul) ...	74,815	12,430	62,385	13	26	31	168	82	427	135	828	352	2,028	701	3,008
Nalgonda	55,611	8,414	47,197	4	21	16	102	20	494	68	925	197	1,799	348	2,177
Warangal (Khamam)	76,748	11,910	64,838	12	42	15	141	47	761	116	1,233	348	2,509	547	3,114
Elgandal	93,192	14,762	78,430	12	45	20	282	82	1,202	178	1,589	351	3,088	598	3,879
Indur	75,193	13,436	61,757	8	31	77	316	175	678	201	871	354	1,764	640	2,959
Medak	43,548	7,906	35,642	5	31	21	91	29	235	75	469	163	1,118	308	1,732
Mahratwara — Aurangabad	69,771	14,962	54,809	9	28	62	194	224	515	361	546	427	1,060	924	2,009
Birh	56,732	12,544	44,188	15	34	63	164	208	388	244	464	354	986	715	1,704
Nander	65,692	14,130	51,562	22	36	137	299	452	578	378	454	516	1,013	1,008	2,000
Naldrug	57,668	12,082	45,586	2	27	67	201	207	326	275	429	402	1,081	765	1,811
Bidar	92,805	18,808	73,997	15	208	105	417	392	719	460	628	697	1,375	1,229	2,792
Parbhani	73,603	17,159	56,444	21	48	161	349	456	562	402	529	645	1,157	1,180	2,148
Sirpur Tandur	18,482	3,380	15,102	1	17	29	124	103	238	65	224	108	878	196	631
Karnatic or Kanada — Gulbarga	73,026	15,528	57,498	8	50	103	270	332	448	442	628	666	1,382	1,019	2,579
Raichur	53,563	10,369	43,194	16	34	47	163	125	242	191	430	390	1,341	589	2,078
Lingasugur	67,467	14,665	52,802	19	60	189	307	280	428	354	704	599	1,623	941	2,516
Total Districts...	10,93,087	210,420	882,667	187	751	1,105	3,677	3,248	8,524	3,910	11,372	6,757	24,822	12,040	38,880
Total Districts including Hyderabad ...	11,26,578	217,435	909,138	187	758	1,109	3,718	3,262	8,665	3,994	11,859	7,068	26,047	12,535	40,573
Railways......	317	122	195	...	...	...	1	...	...	1	2	3	8	10	6
Grand Total	11,26,890	217,557	909,333	187	758	1,109	3,719	3,262	8,665	3,995	11,861	7,071	26,055	12,545	40,579

TABLE VIII.

Civil Condition by Religion and Age Part (B) Hindus.—*Continued.*

District or State.	(3) WIDOWED.—*Continued.* Age Period. 30—34 Males.	30—34 Females.	35—39 Males.	35—39 Females.	40—44 Males.	40—44 Females.	45—49 Males.	45—49 Females.	50—54 Males.	50—54 Females.	55—59 Males.	55—59 Females.	60 & over. Males.	60 & over. Females.	Unspecified. Males.	Unspecified. Females.
	17	18	19	20	21	22	23	24	25	26	27	28	29	30	31	32
Telingana. Hyderabad City ...	179	658	119	406	282	1,140	108	341	810	1,122	93	201	501	1,689	...	1
Suburbs including Secunderabad ...	507	2,214	351	1,268	742	3,371	339	1,060	826	3,536	245	643	1,549	5,272	6	5
Total	686	2,872	470	1,674	974	4,511	447	1,401	1,186	4,658	338	844	2,050	6,911	6	6
Atraf-i-Balda District ...	572	3,352	465	2,233	1,011	5,818	530	2,333	1,408	6,985	872	1,238	2,970	11,487	...	5
Mahabubnagar (Nagar Karnul) ...	1,066	6,007	868	4,136	1,635	10,325	961	4,284	1,969	11,092	553	2,153	4,052	17,870	12	33
Nalgonda ...	567	4,270	400	2,450	863	6,965	492	2,429	1,365	8,179	376	1,402	3,700	15,957	3	27
Warangal (Khamam) ...	909	6,226	537	3,033	1,526	10,402	643	2,978	2,024	12,080	406	1,520	4,774	20,770	12	24
Elgandal ...	1,034	7,890	728	4,418	1,857	11,841	987	4,283	2,716	14,342	695	2,580	5,498	23,499	6	43
Indur ...	1,066	5,708	885	8,854	1,890	9,711	1,019	8,932	2,427	11,473	555	1,966	4,185	18,470	4	24
Medak ...	512	8,158	456	2,007	1,021	5,446	524	2,163	1,409	6,565	377	1,396	8,005	11,230	1	6
Mahratwara. Aurangabad ...	1,152	3,930	982	3,640	1,720	8,323	1,088	4,392	2,137	9,800	771	2,361	5,196	17,995	9	21
Birh ...	1,020	3,341	791	2,903	1,528	6,842	849	3,348	1,848	8,274	618	1,708	4,289	14,062	12	20
Nander ...	1,335	4,137	970	3,115	1,959	8,777	997	3,762	2,272	10,490	626	1,897	3,453	14,993	10	16
Naldrug ...	952	3,534	765	2,936	1,467	7,622	928	3,574	1,816	8,690	623	1,922	3,811	13,423	2	10
Bidar ...	1,561	5,677	1,073	4,186	2,353	11,909	1,380	5,382	2,948	14,380	931	3,182	5,655	23,125	9	22
Parbhani ...	1,532	4,105	1,194	3,495	2,215	8,941	1,207	3,980	2,662	11,304	790	2,078	4,687	17,722	7	36
Sirpur Tandur ...	882	1,845	239	868	460	2,464	195	874	585	2,879	139	515	878	4,541	...	4
Karnatic or Kanada. Gulbarga ...	1,400	5,204	1,141	3,944	2,237	9,604	1,237	4,321	2,243	10,501	698	2,335	3,997	16,231	5	6
Raichur ...	894	4,335	842	3,895	1,401	7,609	896	3,474	1,609	7,444	581	1,995	2,782	10,647	6	7
Lingasugur ...	1,258	5,405	1,096	4,108	2,058	8,989	1,185	4,135	2,266	9,506	826	2,225	3,638	12,790	6	7
Total Districts......	17,162	77,119	18,432	54,721	27,201	1,41,588	15,118	59,644	33,699	1,63,984	9,937	82,473	66,520	2,64,812	104	300
Total Districts including Hyderabad...	17,848	79,991	18,902	56,395	28,175	1,46,099	15,565	61,045	34,835	1,68,642	10,275	88,317	68,570	2,71,728	110	306
Railways......	12	17	22	12	22	32	14	25	15	36	9	14	14	42	...	...
Grand Total......	17,860	80,008	18,924	56,407	28,197	1,46,131	15,579	61,070	34,850	1,68,678	10,284	83,331	68,584	2,71,765	110	306

TABLE VIII.

Civil Condition by Religion and Age Part (B) Hindus.

District or State.		(4) Unspecified. Total Unspecified. Total.	Males.	Females.	Age Period. 0—4 Males.	0—4 Females.	5—9 Males.	5—9 Females.	10—14 Males.	10—14 Females.	15—19 Males.	15—19 Females.	20—24 Males.	20—24 Females.	25—29 Males.	25—29 Females.	30—34 Males.	30—34 Females.	35—39 Males.	35—39 Females.	40—44 Males.	40—44 Females.	45—49 Males.	45—49 Females.	50—54 Males.	50—54 Females.	55—59 Males.	55—59 Females.	60 and over. Males.	60 and over. Females.	Unspecified. Males.	Unspecified. Females.
1		2	3	4	5	6	7	8	9	10	11	12	13	14	15	16	17	18	19	20	21	22	23	24	25	26	27	28	29	30	31	32
Telingana. Hyderabad.	City	93	4	89	...	...	...	...	...	1	...	..	...	1	...	..	...	3	...	...	1	...	...	...	...	...	...	...	...	...	3	84
	Suburbs including Secunderabad	82	14	18	1	...	2	...	...	1	...	1	...	...	3	1	2	3	...	...	2	...	2	...	1	2	...	...	...	7	1	3
	Total......	125	18	107	1	...	2	...	...	2	...	1	...	1	3	1	2	6	...	...	3	...	2	...	1	2	...	...	...	7	4	87
	Atraf-i-Balda District	77	33	44	2	4	1	...	1	...	2	4	2	6	5	3	2	...	2	2	...	5	...	1	2	4	...	...	2	6	12	9
	Mahabubnagar (Nagar Karnul) ...	427	168	259	26	53	10	15	7	11	7	12	6	17	9	14	10	19	6	7	8	13	6	7	4	6	...	3	15	7	54	75
	Nalgonda	294	120	174	25	27	5	19	3	20	10	15	9	15	9	10	2	12	5	5	11	9	5	1	12	11	...	1	13	18	11	11
	Warangal (Khamam)...	340	155	185	30	25	8	19	8	7	6	3	10	8	4	11	9	14	3	4	8	10	1	1	3	9	...	1	13	27	52	46
	Elgandal...	467	204	263	27	27	17	16	17	27	13	21	15	28	8	23	14	14	4	3	5	18	3	7	11	15	4	...	18	20	48	44
	Indur	228	98	130	7	7	9	9	8	16	5	13	6	15	12	11	6	7	5	6	5	11	2	3	4	8	1	5	9	11	19	8
	Medak	159	59	100	4	4	3	6	6	8	3	6	4	10	12	8	6	4	2	2	1	10	2	2	1	14	1		4	4	10	22
Mahratwara.	Aurangabad	866	194	172	18	17	15	13	14	18	12	19	13	13	10	10	9	11	8	6	9	8	3	6	12	8	2	...	20	12	49	31
	Birh	387	183	204	18	16	15	23	10	9	9	16	13	15	15	23	11	10	8	7	17	10	4	8	12	4	3	..	20	15	28	48
	Nander	409	210	199	22	16	13	13	10	7	9	10	18	12	18	22	19	22	7	11	13	19	5	...	9	8	3	2	9	7	55	50
	Naldrug	201	96	105	6	7	9	10	5	10	7	6	11	11	14	7	5	10	2	4	10	5	5	3	5	9	4	2	5	8	8	13
	Bidar	228	103	125	6	5	6	9	10	7	7	5	8	12	4	10	10	7	10	7	8	13	4	2	6	8	2	2	4	8	18	30
	Parbhani	492	229	263	9	8	8	16	15	26	12	32	11	28	28	19	23	26	15	18	28	21	4	4	22	17	2	1	19	22	33	25
	Sirpur Tandur	51	27	24	3	1	1	5	2	1	1	2	4	...	1	1	3	...	1	3	2	2	1	1	4	...	...	...	1	2	3	6
Karnatic or Kanada.	Gulbarga	160	79	81	1	7	7	8	7	2	3	6	10	11	6	10	10	8	4	3	4	8	6	5	9	4	1	...	4	3	7	6
	Raichur	86	31	55	2	7	2	6	4	...	1	1	3	5	..	4	1	4	1	4	6	1	1	1	...	3	...	1	3	3	7	15
	Lingasugur...	199	79	120	4	5	4	3	4	1	4	6	5	11	3	4	5	7	...	6	5	4	2	4	4	7	1	1	7	5	31	56
	Total Districts......	4,571	2,068	2,503	210	236	133	195	131	170	111	177	148	217	158	190	145	170	83	98	140	167	54	51	120	135	24	19	166	183	445	495
Total Districts including Hyderabad ...		4,696	2,086	2,610	211	236	135	195	131	172	111	178	148	218	161	191	147	176	83	98	143	167	56	51	121	137	24	19	166	190	449	582
	Railways......	...	...	...	...	...	...	...	...	...	...	..	...	..	..	...	...	...	...	...	...	...	...	...	...	...	...	...	...	..	...	...
	Grand Total......	4,696	2,086	2,610	211	236	135	195	131	172	111	178	148	218	161	191	147	176	83	98	143	167	56	51	121	137	24	19	166	190	449	582

TABLE VIII.

Civil Condition by Religion and Age. Part (C)—Mussulmans.

District or State.	(1) UNMARRIED.														
	Unmarried Total.			Age Period.											
				0–4		5–9		10–14		15–19		20–24		25–29	
	Total.	Males.	Females.	Males.	Females.	Males.	Females.	Males.	Females.	Males.	Females.	Males.	Females.	Males.	Females.
1	2	3	4	5	6	7	8	9	10	11	12	13	14	15	16
Telingana. Hyderabad. City	29,624	16,815	12,809	3,194	3,179	2,777	2,770	2,860	2,230	3,023	1,882	2,318	1,082	1,229	373
Suburbs including Secunderabad	38,829	24,371	14,458	4,790	4,920	4,820	4,634	4,534	2,850	3,809	1,035	3,146	503	1,603	201
Total......	68,453	41,186	27,267	7,984	8,099	7,597	7,404	7,894	5,080	6,832	2,917	5,464	1,585	2,832	574
Atraf-i-Balda District	18,012	11,040	6,972	2,550	2,730	2,634	2,584	2,079	1,092	1,408	285	1,107	115	585	74
Mahabubnagar (Nagar Karnul) ...	23,781	14,426	9,355	3,845	4,042	3,929	3,567	2,691	1,247	1,700	227	1,193	91	575	42
Nalgonda	14,815	8,865	5,950	2,043	2,322	2,150	2,175	1,857	1,118	1,251	164	839	59	440	17
Warangal (Khamam)	20,210	12,253	7,957	2,738	2,962	3,080	2,988	2,608	1,509	1,728	259	1,240	84	530	36
Elgandal	20,615	12,225	8,390	2,836	3,069	3,250	3,182	2,876	1,669	1,610	265	978	87	394	39
Indur	20,111	12,228	7,883	3,105	3,030	3,324	2,914	2,782	1,252	1,380	280	774	113	421	46
Medak	15,865	9,839	6,026	2,311	2,280	2,547	2,196	2,045	883	1,158	158	845	57	435	38
Mahratwara. Aurangabad	39,510	23,447	16,063	6,081	6,770	6,194	5,846	4,821	2,417	2,721	420	1,723	156	910	86
Birh	21,127	12,790	8,337	3,628	3,878	3,263	2,899	2,600	982	1,380	193	896	83	519	71
Nander	22,805	13,738	9,067	3,851	4,033	3,643	3,256	2,964	1,210	1,406	184	936	88	481	51
Naldrug	23,833	13,994	9,839	4,214	4,489	3,691	3,256	2,603	1,046	1,401	189	1,020	92	576	60
Bidar	46,791	28,269	18,522	8,042	8,405	7,339	6,385	5,711	2,413	3,121	471	1,984	211	1,004	137
Parbhani	27,827	16,392	11,435	4,499	5,029	4,393	3,835	3,316	1,586	1,656	308	1,124	176	718	139
Sirpur Tandur	4,555	2,686	1,869	647	725	729	678	618	871	288	50	193	14	116	10
Karnatic or Kanada. Gulbarga	38,272	22,953	15,819	7,107	7,436	6,149	5,301	3,595	1,640	2,402	328	1,729	159	1,047	105
Raichur...	21,731	12,852	8,879	4,151	4,292	3,718	3,332	1,868	856	1,248	150	1,027	87	462	58
Lingasugur	25,020	14,918	10,107	4,822	4,928	4,229	3,598	2,158	898	1,496	283	1,114	186	543	109
Total Districts......	404,380	242,910	161,470	66,470	70,420	64,262	57,882	47,187	22,134	27,844	4,064	18,722	1,808	9,756	1,118
Total Districts including Hyderabad ...	472,833	284,096	188,737	74,454	78,519	71,859	65,286	54,581	27,214	34,176	6,981	24,186	3,343	12,588	1,692
Railways......	454	314	140	56	60	59	51	33	21	38	3	65	3	42	1
Grand Total......	473,287	284,410	188,877	74,510	78,579	71,918	65,337	54,614	27,235	34,214	6,984	24,251	3,346	12,630	1,693

TABLE VIII.

Civil Condition by Religion and Age Part (C)—Mussulmans—*Continued.*

(1) UNMARRIED—*Continued.*

District or State		Age Period. 30—34 Males.	30—34 Females.	35—39 Males.	35—39 Females.	40—44 Males.	40—44 Females.	45—49 Males.	45—49 Females.	50—54 Males.	50—54 Females.	55—59 Males.	55—59 Females.	60 & over. Males.	60 & over. Females.	Unspecified. Males.	Unspecified. Females.
		17	18	19	20	21	22	23	24	25	26	27	28	29	30	31	32
Tellingana. Hyderabad	City	629	200	219	82	251	117	68	25	104	52	27	18	118	68	8	791
	Suburbs including Secunderabad	745	111	299	48	274	57	100	5	104	26	25	11	119	46	8	16
	Total......	1,374	311	518	125	525	174	168	80	208	78	52	24	232	109	6	807
	Atraf-i-Balda District	819	40	99	22	113	24	28	4	58	16	10	8	55	29	5	54
	Mahabubnagar (Nagar Karnul) ...	209	84	74	18	93	17	21	6	40	13	4	1	42	13	10	87
	Nalgonda	137	17	49	9	27	14	14	8	30	6	5	1	22	11	1	29
	Warangal (Khamam)	172	30	88	10	57	28	15	7	21	15	3	..	24	11	4	18
	Elgandal	127	21	88	4	39	16	15	9	29	7	2	8	24	16	7	58
	Indur	204	53	63	27	63	16	19	8	44	15	10	1	32	7	7	176
	Medak	213	29	76	11	81	18	80	2	86	10	7	3	44	14	11	327
Mahratwara.	Aurangabad	876	74	145	53	172	75	71	18	101	40	18	9	92	61	22	88
	Birh	199	66	87	26	95	43	25	13	40	19	7	5	41	32	10	27
	Nander	192	88	65	17	77	42	26	15	88	11	5	4	40	19	14	99
	Naldrug	209	45	73	28	82	37	86	11	88	23	10	5	84	84	7	24
	Bidar	419	137	157	53	173	105	56	30	111	46	18	15	117	51	17	63
	Parbhani	289	106	104	60	107	86	32	24	69	51	18	7	60	59	7	19
	Sirpur Tandur	49	14	16	...	14	2	7	1	7	8	2	..	3	4	2	2
Karnatic or Kanada.	Gulbarga	408	82	148	47	150	71	54	25	81	41	10	11	62	59	11	20
	Raichur	191	34	58	6	47	20	23	14	22	13	9	1	28	11	...	5
	Lingasugur	266	63	92	82	90	43	37	23	29	22	9	4	26	26	2	2
	Total Districts......	8,979	888	1,382	428	1,480	657	509	213	789	851	147	73	746	451	187	993
Total Districts including Hyderabad ...		5,353	1,194	1,900	548	2,005	831	677	243	997	429	199	97	978	560	143	1,800
	Railways......	10	...	6	..	4	1	1	...	...	...	...	..	...	...	...	...
	Grand Total......	5,363	1,194	1,906	548	2,009	832	678	243	997	429	199	97	978	560	143	1,800

TABLE VIII.

Civil Condition by Religion and Age. Part (C)—Mussulmans.

District or State.	(2) Married. Total Married. Total.	Males.	Females.	Age Period. 0—4 Males.	0—4 Females.	5—9 Males.	5—9 Females.	10—14 Males.	10—14 Females.	15—19 Males.	15—19 Females.	20—24 Males.	20—24 Females.	25—29 Males.	25—29 Females.
1	2	3	4	5	6	7	8	9	10	11	12	13	14	15	16
Telingana. Hyderabad. City	35,224	17,921	17,303	...	...	85	68	132	564	492	2,715	1,889	4,180	2,669	3,054
Suburbs including Secunderabad	46,435	24,648	21,787	9	6	46	95	134	1,070	618	3,803	2,264	4,922	3,801	3,644
Total......	81,659	42,569	39,090	9	6	81	163	266	1,634	1,110	6,518	4,153	9,102	6,470	6,698
Atraf-i-Balda District	19,554	10,117	9,437	17	85	34	127	86	633	219	1,347	701	1,884	1,392	1,593
Mahabubnagar (Nagar Karnul) ...	25,291	12,457	12,834	33	32	44	237	167	1,000	872	1,797	1,086	2,661	1,854	2,165
Nalgonda	18,021	6,527	6,494	22	22	25	39	40	380	120	1,015	443	1,347	1,002	1,074
Warangal (Khamam)	18,334	9,422	8,912	19	35	22	56	52	507	155	1,382	708	1,848	1,580	1,522
Elgandal	19,160	9,757	9,403	14	34	36	86	121	635	254	1,353	792	1,877	1,482	1,528
Indur	23,740	11,771	11,969	30	33	64	245	221	977	420	1,669	1,062	2,205	1,966	2,015
Medak	17,617	8,622	8,995	9	37	22	134	70	673	202	1,155	644	1,647	1,267	1,409
Mahratwara. Aurangabad	44,925	22,660	22,265	30	43	107	873	364	1,754	888	3,213	2,005	4,079	3,555	3,674
Birh	25,733	12,979	12,754	19	34	60	299	219	880	463	1,600	1,052	2,311	2,122	2,139
Nander	27,150	13,898	13,252	24	38	78	338	287	1,133	519	1,710	1,282	2,843	2,436	2,314
Naldrug	29,121	14,760	14,361	24	42	79	402	273	1,153	550	1,746	1,237	2,567	2,441	2 482
Bidar	55,607	28,152	27,455	36	97	136	599	513	2,423	966	3,552	2,414	4,889	4,580	4,614
Parbhani	32,101	16,464	15,637	40	73	94	332	828	1,177	551	1,962	1,861	2,761	2,697	2,649
Sirpur Tandur	4,283	2,220	2,063	3	17	5	28	59	172	73	292	201	399	367	367
Karnatic or Kanada. Gulbarga	46,133	23,568	22,565	48	95	165	668	363	1,598	842	2,828	2,128	4,189	3,845	4,144
Raichur	24,538	12,640	11,898	33	68	95	360	214	791	519	1,463	1,343	2,524	2,027	2,244
Lingasugur	29,628	15,094	14,534	71	127	138	630	320	1,022	727	1,765	1,655	2,909	2,448	2,556
Total Districts......	455,936	231,108	224,828	472	857	1,204	4,948	3,697	16,903	7,840	29,859	20,059	42,840	37,061	38,489
Total Districts including Hyderabad ...	537,595	273,677	263,918	481	863	1,285	5,111	3,963	18,537	8,950	36,377	24,212	51,442	43,531	45,187
Railways......	788	547	241	..	1	...	3	1	13	5	43	54	62	107	48
Grand Total......	538,383	274,224	264,159	481	864	1,285	5,114	3,964	18,550	8,955	36,420	24,266	51,504	43,638	45,235

TABLE VIII.

Civil Condition by Religion and Age. Part (C)—Mussulmans—*Continued.*

(2) MARRIED—*Continued.*

District or State.	30—34 Males.	30—34 Females.	35—39 Males.	35—39 Females.	40—44 Males.	40—44 Females.	45—49 Males.	45—49 Females.	50—54 Males.	50—54 Females.	55—59 Males.	55—59 Females.	60 and over. Males.	60 and over. Females.	Unspecified. Males.	Unspecified. Females.
	17	18	19	20	21	22	23	24	25	26	27	28	29	30	31	32
Telingana. Hyderabad. City	3,049	2,544	1,826	1,088	2,574	1,534	1,020	401	1,844	618	472	144	1,914	377	5	16
Suburbs including Secunderabad	4,245	3,344	2,728	1,321	3,630	1,874	1,483	443	2,464	651	706	137	2,514	455	6	22
Total......	7,294	5,888	4,554	2,409	6,204	3,408	2,503	844	4,308	1,269	1,178	281	4,428	832	11	38
Atraf-i-Balda District	1,698	1,596	1,079	599	1,643	827	683	213	1,162	337	272	46	1,130	175	1	75
Mahabubnagar (Nagar Karnul) ...	2,107	2,116	1,421	825	1,928	1,027	825	268	1,144	426	277	66	1,195	163	4	51
Nalgonda	1,124	1,008	783	418	987	598	416	147	692	225	158	82	715	148	...	46
Warangal (Khamam)	1,782	1,469	991	492	1,441	869	480	173	1,016	840	200	84	976	154	...	31
Elgandal	1,711	1,524	1,019	597	1,475	904	592	171	1,049	416	208	40	1,004	181	...	57
Indur	2,055	1,864	1,248	692	1,673	1,123	705	256	1,108	387	219	41	997	194	3	268
Medak	1,354	1,881	951	525	1,314	767	559	164	974	330	219	46	1,035	174	2	558
Mahratwara. Aurangabad	3,901	3,564	2,455	1,649	3,120	2,025	1,397	567	2,176	746	484	108	2,173	398	5	72
Birh	2,242	2,113	1,458	970	1,881	1,209	779	393	1,229	448	271	94	1,176	228	8	36
Nander	2,432	2,135	1,509	871	1,886	1,225	825	287	1,292	450	284	72	1,088	178	6	168
Naldrug	2,556	2,432	1,557	1,061	2,182	1,359	965	870	1,415	483	385	63	1,142	182	4	19
Bidar	4,703	4,569	2,734	1,759	4,085	2,635	1,774	733	2,762	967	705	129	2,738	456	6	83
Parbhani	2,914	2,655	1,731	1,149	2,447	1,481	949	374	1,618	614	304	74	1,423	282	7	54
Sirpur Tandur	474	343	250	135	303	172	104	43	200	54	41	7	140	84	...	...
Karnatic or Kanada. Gulbarga	4,099	3,942	2,549	1,565	3,579	1,963	1,614	482	2,048	635	482	102	1,801	328	10	21
Raichur	2,135	2,026	1,478	787	1,850	934	824	239	1,034	280	279	40	809	140	...	2
Lingasugur	2,653	2,499	1,765	1,008	2,084	1,072	928	297	1,177	378	264	55	863	197	1	19
Total Districts......	39,940	37,286	24,978	15,102	33,878	20,190	14,419	5,177	22,096	7,516	5,002	1,049	20,405	3,607	57	1,555
Total Districts including Hyderabad ...	47,234	43,124	29,532	17,511	40,082	23,598	16,922	6,021	26,404	8,785	6,180	1,330	24,833	4,439	68	1,593
Railways......	121	26	88	11	70	18	34	3	40	9	7	1	20	3	...	...
Grand Total......	47,355	43,150	29,620	17,522	40,152	23,616	16,956	6,024	26,444	8,794	6,187	1,331	24,853	4,442	68	1,593

TABLE VIII.

Civil Condition by Religion and Age. Part (C)—Mussulmans.

District or State.	(3) WIDOWED. Total Widowed. Total.	Total Widowed. Males.	Total Widowed. Females.	0—4 Males.	0—4 Females.	5—9 Males.	5—9 Females.	10—14 Males.	10—14 Females.	15—19 Males.	15—19 Females.	20—24 Males.	20—24 Females.	25—29 Males.	25—29 Females.
1	2	3	4	5	6	7	8	9	10	11	12	13	14	15	16
Telingana. Hyderabad { City	10,851	2,144	8,207	......	...	...	6	5	16	19	79	52	809	153	371
Telingana. Hyderabad { Suburbs including Secunderabad	11,818	2,494	9,824	8	...	3	8	16	19	18	120	88	809	169	484
Total......	22,169	4,688	17,531	8	...	3	14	21	85	37	199	185	618	322	855
Atraf-i-Balda District	4,966	854	4,112	9	13	8	9	5	17	8	43	19	127	81	172
Mahabubnagar (Nagar Karnul) ...	6,470	891	5,579	5	12	2	12	6	25	8	55	18	172	41	282
Nalgonda	3,088	430	2,606	5	4	1	11	2	11	—	42	7	88	19	121
Warangal (Khamam)	4,813	574	3,739	1	6	8	5	8	11	4	52	10	121	20	171
Elgandal	4,175	596	3,579	4	8	2	10	5	25	7	48	17	140	19	172
Indur...	6,235	890	5,345	12	20	7	17	7	24	2	71	11	161	42	259
Medak	4,883	630	3,753	6	6	2	7	4	10	8	41	13	89	19	191
Mahratwara. Aurangabad	9,666	1,802	7,864	11	8	3	11	15	82	22	61	84	190	92	809
Birh	4,864	1,037	3,827	8	6	4	12	9	14	9	41	28	84	55	162
Nander	5,996	1,043	4,953	5	6	7	8	11	12	17	89	26	107	60	210
Naldrug	5,547	1,035	4,512	2	11	8	17	10	23	9	24	22	87	46	196
Bidar...	12,292	1,945	10,347	7	29	12	85	17	83	12	88	88	204	97	417
Parbhani	6,708	1,212	5,496	10	10	8	15	17	25	12	89	87	138	60	220
Sirpur Tandur	1,167	158	1,009	4	8	1	6	6	4	1	14	5	86	9	45
Karnatic or Kanada. Gulbarga	10,752	2,160	8,592	13	16	17	12	17	86	21	78	50	191	114	876
Raichur	5,593	1,111	4,482	3	6	9	9	7	6	11	29	87	108	65	166
Lingasugur	6,939	1,457	5,482	12	18	80	28	17	21	28	27	42	141	78	252
Total Districts......	103,102	17,825	85,277	117	182	119	224	158	829	164	792	414	2,184	862	3,721
Total Districts including Hyderabad ...	125,271	22,463	102,808	120	182	122	238	179	864	201	991	549	2,802	1,184	4,576
Railways......	77	24	53	......	...	......	...	......	...	...	2	1	2	1	2
Grand Total......	125,348	22,487	102,861	120	182	122	288	179	864	201	993	550	2,804	1,185	4,578

TABLE VIII.

Civil Condition by Religion and Age. Part (C)—Mussulmans.—*Continued.*

District or State.	(3) WIDOWED.—*Continued.* Age Period. 30—34 Males.	30—34 Females.	35—39 Males.	35—39 Females.	40—44 Males.	40—44 Females.	45—49 Males.	45—49 Females.	50—54 Males.	50—54 Females.	55—59 Males.	55—59 Females.	60 and over. Males.	60 and over. Females.	Unspecified. Males.	Unspecified. Females.
	17	18	19	20	21	22	23	24	25	26	27	28	29	30	31	32
Telingana. Hyderabad. City	190	666	140	458	287	1,473	136	458	376	1,668	118	321	668	2,382	...	5
Suburbs including Secunderabad	201	765	141	477	296	1,579	145	518	369	1,757	157	402	893	2,876	...	10
Total......	391	1,431	281	935	588	3,052	281	971	745	3,425	275	723	1,561	5,258	...	15
Atraf-i-Balda District	54	850	48	210	105	638	55	224	129	816	38	150	344	1,325	1	18
Mahabubnagar (Nagar Karnul) ...	63	460	69	276	117	935	60	367	120	1,060	36	174	348	1,733	3	16
Nalgonda	28	220	24	145	42	396	22	145	71	439	11	84	197	888	1	12
Warangal (Khamam)	54	846	25	175	66	586	21	169	103	702	24	90	240	1,286	...	19
Elgandal	43	326	33	170	71	570	21	188	114	696	39	94	221	1,115	...	17
Indur...	82	565	48	326	126	878	60	289	136	1,037	41	146	815	1,440	1	112
Medak...	84	812	22	178	68	601	40	191	106	661	31	142	281	1,140	1	184
Mahratwara. Aurangabad	114	557	105	430	211	1,253	110	543	295	1,447	105	260	682	2,756	3	7
Birh	90	295	58	223	123	532	48	273	159	731	40	157	404	1,288	2	9
Nander	83	412	69	249	128	813	71	331	166	975	38	191	360	1,532	2	68
Naldrug	75	350	61	242	117	738	85	312	177	879	48	160	380	1,468	...	5
Bidar	141	715	102	554	233	1,678	152	656	334	2,062	95	406	704	3,444	1	26
Parbhani	94	438	71	315	147	864	75	367	207	1,055	39	166	435	1,836	...	8
Sirpur Tandur	21	97	15	58	22	192	9	51	19	200	4	26	41	277	1	...
Karnatic or Kanada. Gulbarga	187	781	162	485	316	1,466	175	633	319	1,548	93	298	675	2,658	1	14
Raichur	91	412	70	276	130	781	100	337	180	840	59	202	349	1,310	...	...
Lingasugur	186	581	93	377	205	959	106	371	246	999	74	198	400	1,508	...	2
Total Districts......	1,390	7,217	1,075	4,689	2,227	13,880	1,210	5,447	2,881	16,147	815	2,944	6,376	27,004	17	517
Total Districts including Hyderabad ...	1,781	8,648	1,356	5,624	2,810	16,932	1,491	6,418	3,626	19,572	1,090	3,667	7,937	32,262	17	532
Railways......	4	3	4	1	5	11	3	8	5	13	...	...	1	11	...	...
Grand Total......	1,785	8,651	1,360	5,625	2,815	16,943	1,494	6,426	3,631	19,585	1,090	3,667	7,938	32,273	17	532

TABLE VIII.

Civil Condition by Religion and Age. Part (C)—Mussulmans.

District or State.	(4) UNSPECIFIED. Total Unspecified. Total.	Males.	Females.	Age Period. 0—4 Males.	0—4 Females.	5—9 Males.	5—9 Females.	10—14 Males.	10—14 Females.	15—19 Males.	15—19 Females.	20—24 Males.	20—24 Females.	25—29 Males.	25—29 Females.	30—34 Males.	30—34 Females.	35—39 Males.	35—39 Females.	40—44 Males.	40—44 Females.	45—49 Males.	45—49 Females.	50—54 Males.	50—54 Females.	55—59 Males.	55—59 Females.	60 and over. Males.	60 and over. Females.	Unspecified. Males.	Unspecified. Females.
1	2	3	4	5	6	7	8	9	10	11	12	13	14	15	16	17	18	19	20	21	22	23	24	25	26	27	28	29	30	31	32
Telingana. Hyderabad. City	299	18	281	...	...	...	...	1	3	...	...	...	3	2	...	4	...	...	...	4	1	...	...	2	1	...	...	2	...	3	273
Suburbs including Secunderabad	281	48	233	...	3	2	1	3	3	2	4	7	3	6	...	11	3	5	3	4	1	1	...	1	...	2	1	2	...	2	211
Total......	580	66	514	...	3	2	1	4	6	2	4	7	6	8	...	15	3	5	3	8	2	1	...	3	1	2	1	4	...	5	484
Atraf-i-Balda District	94	22	72	...	1	...	...	...	...	...	...	...	...	2	...	...	4	...	...	...	...	1	...	...	1	...	1	4	8	15	57
Mahabubnagar (Nagar Karnul) ...	68	22	46	2	3	2	3	1	1	...	...	1	1	1	3	2	2	...	...	2	2	1	...	3	3	...	1	2	8	5	19
Nalgonda	37	11	26	1	4	1	...	2	...	1	...	...	...	1	1	2	...	...	...	1	4	...	1	...	2	...	1	2	8	...	5
Warangal (Khamam)	25	8	17	...	2	1	...	1	1	2	...	1	1	...	1	...	2	...	...	1	1	...	...	...	...	...	...	2	1	...	8
Elgandal	63	15	48	5	1	1	2	1	5	1	5	1	4	2	2	1	3	1	3	1	1	...	...	...	...	...	...	1	8	...	19
Indur...	107	5	102	...	3	...	6	...	4	...	3	...	...	...	4	...	7	...	2	1	3	1	1	...	2	...	2	1	8	2	57
Medak	182	35	147	...	6	2	3	4	...	4	1	...	1	...	2	5	...	4	...	...	1	1	...	...	1	...	...	4	4	11	128
Mahratwara. Aurangabad	116	43	73	...	5	3	4	5	...	3	4	7	2	2	...	3	4	3	...	1	1	...	1	3	3	...	...	9	1	4	48
Birh	88	25	63	2	2	2	2	2	4	2	2	4	1	1	...	2	6	1	1	2	3	...	2	2	4	...	...	2	7	3	29
Nander	67	28	39	1	1	2	...	1	...	2	...	2	4	1	1	2	2	...	...	2	2	...	2	2	...	...	2	7	5	6	20
Naldrug	33	10	23	1	...	...	1	...	1	...	...	...	...	1	...	1	4	1	2	2	1	2	2	...	1	...	2	2	5	...	4
Bidar	53	19	34	...	2	1	...	...	1	2	...	3	3	1	1	2	2	2	2	1	...	1	...	1	1	1	...	2	6	2	16
Parbhani	60	30	30	2	...	1	...	3	1	2	2	...	5	4	2	5	...	1	2	1	1	1	4	3	6	...	3	7	4	...	...
Sirpur Tandur	1	1	...	...	...	...	...	...	...	...	...	...	...	...	...	...	...	...	...	...	...	...	...	...	...	...	...	...	...	1	...
Karnatic or Kanada. Gulbarga	22	4	18	...	...	...	...	...	...	...	1	...	3	...	2	...	1	2	1	1	1	...	...	...	3	...	1	1	1	...	4
Raichur	15	4	11	1	...	...	...	...	...	1	...	...	...	1	2	...	...	...	...	...	...	...	1	...	4	...	...	1	4	...	...
Lingasugur	37	27	10	2	...	...	1	...	1	...	...	1	...	1	...	...	...	1	...	1	...	...	1	1	2	1	...	...	1	19	4
Total Districts......	1,068	309	759	17	30	16	22	20	19	20	18	20	25	18	21	25	37	16	13	17	21	8	15	15	33	2	13	47	74	68	418
Total Districts including Hyderabad ...	1,648	875	1,273	17	33	18	23	24	25	22	22	27	31	26	21	40	40	21	16	25	23	9	15	18	34	4	14	51	74	73	902
Railways......	...	...	...	...	...	...	...	...	...	...	...	...	...	...	...	...	...	...	...	...	...	...	...	...	...	...	...	...	...	...	...
Grand Total......	1,648	875	1,273	17	33	18	23	24	25	22	22	27	31	26	21	40	40	21	16	25	23	9	15	18	34	4	14	51	74	73	902

TABLE VIII.

Civil Condition by Religion and Age. Part (D)—Christians.

(1) UNMARRIED.

District or State.	Total Unmarried.			Age Period. 0—4		5—9		10—14		15—19		20—24		25—29	
	Total.	Males.	Females.	Males.	Females.	Males.	Females.	Males.	Females.	Males.	Females.	Males.	Females.	Males.	Females.
1	2	3	4	5	6	7	8	9	10	11	12	13	14	15	16
Telingana — Hyderabad — City	25	18	7	2	1	4	...	1	1	4	...	3	2	1	1
Telingana — Hyderabad — Suburbs including Secunderabad	8,521	5,755	2,766	750	761	787	775	594	624	512	338	1,787	129	996	57
Total......	8,546	5,773	2,778	752	762	791	775	595	625	516	338	1,790	131	997	58
Atraf-i-Balda District	212	108	104	26	86	89	82	28	22	12	8	6	3	2	1
Mahabubnagar (Nagar Karnul) ...	68	41	27	13	8	9	13	8	8	3	1	1	...	1	1
Nalgonda	62	31	31	8	19	7	10	7	2	2	...	5	...	...	...
Warangal (Khamam)	689	412	277	127	115	108	86	86	46	49	11	29	3	14	2
Elgandal	100	73	27	15	11	19	12	22	1	10	3	2	...	2	...
Indur..	19	11	8	4	4	4	8	1	...	1	1	...	...	1	...
Medak	46	27	19	8	8	9	6	...	1	8	1	3	2	2	...
Mahratwara — Aurangabad	817	485	332	150	174	125	148	81	44	85	9	17	5	12	5
Birh	71	43	28	12	10	12	7	7	6	1	3	2	...	4	1
Nander	...	...	...	...	...	...	...	...	...	...	...	...	...	...	...
Naldrug	87	50	37	19	26	21	6	4	5	2	...	2	...	2	...
Bidar	9	5	4	1	2	1	1	2	...	1	...	...	1	...	...
Parbhani	85	22	13	3	8	8	3	3	8	2	8	6	1	4	...
Sirpur Tandur	...	...	...	...	...	...	...	...	...	...	...	...	...	...	...
Karnatic or Kanada — Gulbarga	182	75	57	25	24	18	15	8	9	8	1	8	1	4	3
Raichur	168	96	72	18	22	24	15	14	22	9	5	16	4	10	1
Lingasugur	187	102	85	24	26	29	87	15	10	15	5	8	6	7	..
Total Districts......	2,702	1,531	1,171	453	488	428	889	281	174	158	51	105	26	65	14
Total Districts including Hyderabad...	11,248	7,304	3,944	1,205	1,250	1,214	1,164	876	799	669	389	1,895	157	1,062	72
Railways......	370	232	138	49	41	48	44	70	80	85	15	51	8	22	5
Grand Total......	11,618	7,536	4,082	1,254	1,291	1,262	1,208	896	829	704	404	1,946	160	1,084	77

TABLE VIII.

Civil Condition by Religion and Age. Part (D)—Christians.—*Continued.*

District or State.	(1) UNMARRIED.—*Continued.* Age Period. 30—34 Males.	30—34 Females.	35—39 Males.	35—39 Females.	40—44 Males.	40—44 Females.	45—49 Males.	45—49 Females.	50—54 Males.	50—54 Females.	55—59 Males.	55—59 Females.	60 & over. Males.	60 & over. Females.	Unspecified. Males.	Unspecified. Females.
	17	18	19	20	21	22	23	24	25	26	27	28	29	30	31	32
Telingana. Hyderabad. City ...	...	...	1	1	1	...	1	...	...	...	...	...	...	1	...	...
Suburbs including Secunderabad ...	208	26	51	22	33	7	12	4	11	9	4	8	10	11	...	...
Total......	208	26	52	23	34	7	13	4	11	9	4	8	10	12	...	...
Atraf-i-Balda District ...	...	1	...	...	...	1	...	...	...	...	...	...	...	...	...	...
Mahabubnagar (Nagar Karnul) ...	1	1	1	...	3	...	...	...	1	...	...	...	...	...	...	...
Nalgonda ...	1	...	...	...	1	...	...	...	...	...	...	...	...	...	...	...
Warangal (Khamam) ...	3	3	...	3	1	3	...	2	...	3	...	...	...	...	...	...
Elgandal ...	2	...	...	...	...	...	...	...	...	...	...	...	...	...	1	...
Indur ...	...	...	...	...	...	...	...	...	...	...	...	...	...	...	...	...
Medak ...	1	1	...	...	1	...	...	...	...	...	...	...	...	...	...	...
Mahratwara. Aurangabad ...	3	...	4	1	2	...	1	1	2	...	...	...	3	...	...	...
Birh ...	3	...	...	...	1	...	...	...	1	...	...	...	...	1	...	...
Nander ...	...	...	...	...	...	...	...	...	...	...	...	...	...	...	...	...
Naldrug ...	...	...	...	...	...	...	...	...	...	...	...	...	...	...	...	...
Bidar ...	...	...	...	...	...	...	...	...	...	...	...	...	...	...	...	...
Parbhani ...	...	...	1	...	...	...	...	...	...	...	...	...	...	...	...	...
Sirpur Tandar ...	...	...	...	...	...	...	...	...	...	...	...	...	...	...	...	...
Karnatic or Kannada. Gulbarga ...	2	3	1	...	1	...	...	...	...	...	...	...	...	1	...	...
Raichur ...	1	1	2	...	1	1	1	...	...	...	...	...	...	1	...	...
Lingasugur ...	3	...	1	...	...	1	...	...	...	...	...	...	...	...	...	...
Total Districts......	20	10	10	4	11	6	2	3	4	3	...	...	3	3	1	...
Total Districts including Hyderabad ...	228	36	62	27	45	13	15	7	15	12	4	8	13	15	1	...
Railways......	4	...	2	...	...	...	...	...	1	...	...	...	...	...	...	...
Grand Total......	232	36	64	27	45	13	15	7	16	12	4	8	13	15	1	...

TABLE VIII.

Civil Condition by Religion and Age. Part (D)—Christians.

District or State.	Total Married. Total.	Total Married. Males.	Total Married. Females.	0—4 Males.	0—4 Females.	5—9 Males.	5—9 Females.	10—14 Males.	10—14 Females.	15—19 Males.	15—19 Females.	20—24 Males.	20—24 Females.	25—29 Males.	25—29 Females.
1	2	3	4	5	6	7	8	9	10	11	12	13	14	15	16
(2) MARRIED.															
Telingana.															
Hyderabad. City ...	10	5	5	...	...	...	...	...	...	...	1	1	...	...	...
Hyderabad. Suburbs including Secunderabad ...	4,328	2,152	2,176	...	...	7	7	10	49	89	310	171	438	387	453
Total......	4,338	2,157	2,181	...	...	7	7	10	49	89	311	172	438	387	453
Atraf-i-Balda District ...	199	94	105	...	4	2	...	1	2	8	4	6	23	18	22
Mahabubnagar (Nagar Karnul) ...	48	26	22	...	...	...	...	...	...	1	4	6	3	8	4
Nalgonda ...	63	40	23	...	...	2	...	...	2	...	1	4	7	6	6
Warangal (Khamam) ...	717	371	346	1	8	1	4	8	24	7	62	57	94	66	65
Elgandal ...	87	46	41	2	...	1	...	...	...	1	10	6	16	9	5
Indur ...	17	8	9	...	...	...	...	...	...	...	1	...	1	2	2
Medak ...	49	26	23	...	...	...	...	...	...	...	6	4	2	6	8
Maharatwara.															
Aurangabad ...	997	499	498	1	4	5	17	16	65	27	60	47	87	89	78
Birh ...	74	41	33	...	...	...	1	...	2	...	6	7	8	5	6
Nander ...	2	2	...	...	...	...	...	...	...	...	...	...	...	...	...
Naldrug ...	115	56	59	...	...	1	...	...	9	1	8	5	7	7	9
Bidar ...	9	5	4	...	...	...	...	...	...	...	...	...	...	8	3
Parbhani ...	29	18	11	...	...	...	...	...	...	...	1	...	2	8	8
Sirpur Tandur ...	...	...	...	...	...	...	...	...	...	...	...	...	...	...	...
Karnatic or Kanada.															
Gulbarga ...	129	69	60	...	2	1	3	1	5	1	16	11	11	21	9
Raichur ...	146	79	67	...	...	1	1	...	1	...	18	8	10	11	14
Lingasugur ...	168	88	80	...	...	1	...	1	7	2	17	11	18	27	14
Total Districts......	2,849	1,468	1,381	4	13	15	26	22	117	43	209	172	289	271	248
Total Districts including Hyderabad ...	7,187	3,625	3,562	4	13	22	33	32	166	82	520	344	727	658	701
Railways......	260	147	113	1	...	1	...	...	1	3	12	7	35	35	21
Grand Total......	7,447	3,772	3,675	5	13	23	33	32	167	85	532	351	762	693	722

TABLE VIII.

Civil Condition by Religion and Age. Part (D)—Christians.—*Continued.*

District or State.	(2) Married.—*Continued.* Age Period. 30—34 Males.	30—34 Females.	35—39 Males.	35—39 Females.	40—44 Males.	40—44 Females.	45—49 Males.	45—49 Females.	50—54 Males.	50—54 Females.	55—59 Males.	55—59 Females.	60 & over. Males.	60 & over. Females.	Unspecified. Males.	Unspecified. Females.
	17	18	19	20	21	22	23	24	25	26	27	28	29	30	31	32
Telingana. Hyderabad. City ...	1	3	...	...	...	...	1	...	2	1	...	...	...	...	...	...
Suburbs including Secunderabad ...	376	383	305	197	257	187	189	83	163	67	70	18	178	33	...	1
Total......	377	386	305	197	257	187	190	83	165	68	70	18	178	33	...	1
Atraf-i-Balda District ...	17	20	9	7	21	6	2	2	4	9	2	1	14	5	...	...
Mahabubnagar (Nagar Karnul) ...	4	3	2	4	3	3	4	1	3	...	...	...	...	...	...	...
Nalgonda ...	12	1	5	1	6	1	2	1	...	...	2	...	1	3	...	...
Warangal (Khamam) ...	80	41	34	11	51	22	9	3	31	8	4	3	27	6	...	...
Elgandal ...	5	4	5	2	5	2	6	...	3	2	1	...	2	...	...	...
Indur ...	1	2	2	1	...	1	...	1	...	...	1	...	2	...	...	...
Medak ...	1	3	3	3	7	1	2	...	2	...	1	...	...	...	...	...
Mahratwara. Aurangabad ...	84	69	51	36	50	51	34	16	54	12	11	1	30	2	...	...
Birh ...	9	4	8	3	5	3	3	...	2	...	...	...	2	...	...	...
Nander ...	...	...	2	...	...	...	...	...	...	...	...	...	...	...	...	...
Naldrug ...	9	13	5	3	10	6	5	2	7	1	...	1	6	...	...	...
Bidar ...	...	1	1	...	...	...	1	...	...	...	...	...	...	...	...	...
Parbani ...	3	3	2	...	4	1	2	...	1	...	...	1	3	...	...	...
Sirpur Tandur ...	...	...	...	...	...	...	...	...	...	...	...	...	...	...	...	...
Karnatic or Kanada. Gulbarga ...	8	3	8	1	5	7	3	1	6	1	1	...	3	1	...	...
Raichur ...	14	11	14	1	9	7	7	3	2	4	5	2	8	...	...	...
Lingasugur ...	15	11	8	3	8	4	5	1	6	3	1	...	3	2	...	...
Total Districts......	262	189	159	76	184	115	85	31	121	40	29	9	101	19	...	...
Total Districts including Hyderabad ...	639	525	464	273	441	302	275	114	286	108	99	27	279	52	...	1
Railways......	25	22	30	9	16	5	5	6	10	1	10	...	4	1	...	...
Grand Total......	664	547	494	282	457	307	280	120	296	109	109	27	283	53	...	1

TABLE VIII.

Civil Condition by Religion and Age. Part (D)—Christians.

(3) WIDOWED.

District or State.	Total Widowed. Total.	Total Widowed. Males.	Total Widowed. Females.	0—4 Males.	0—4 Females.	5—9 Males.	5—9 Females.	10—14 Males.	10—14 Females.	15—19 Males.	15—19 Females.	20—24 Males.	20—24 Females.	25—29 Males.	25—29 Females.
1	2	3	4	5	6	7	8	9	10	11	12	13	14	15	16
Telingana. Hyderabad. City	9	4	5	...	...	...	...	...	...	...	...	...	1	...	...
Telingana. Hyderabad. Suburbs including Secunderabad	930	219	711	...	...	1	2	2	1	11	11	4	23	11	42
Total......	939	223	716	...	...	1	2	2	1	11	11	4	24	11	42
Atraf-i-Balda District	89	14	25	1	...	...	...	...	...	...	2	...	2	...	2
Mahabubnagar (Nagar Karnul) ...	5	...	5	...	...	...	...	...	...	...	1	...	...	...	...
Nalgonda	10	2	8	...	...	...	...	...	...	...	1	...	...	...	...
Warangal (Khamam)	78	11	67	...	1	...	...	...	...	...	1	...	3	1	1
Elgandal	6	3	3	...	...	...	1	...	...	...	...	2	...	...	...
Indur	2	1	1	...	...	...	...	...	...	...	...	...	...	...	...
Medak...	11	...	11	...	...	...	...	...	...	...	...	...	...	...	1
Mahratwara. Aurangabad	115	26	89	...	...	...	...	...	...	...	...	...	...	2	4
Birh	8	2	1	...	...	...	...	...	...	...	...	...	...	...	...
Nander	...	...	...	...	...	...	...	...	...	...	...	...	...	...	...
Naldrug	12	1	11	...	...	...	...	...	...	...	...	...	...	1	...
Bidar	8	2	1	...	...	...	...	...	...	...	...	...	...	...	...
Parbhani	8	1	2	...	...	...	...	...	...	...	...	...	...	...	...
Sirpur Tandur	...	...	...	...	...	...	...	...	...	...	...	...	...	...	...
Karnatic or Kanada. Gulbarga	26	6	20	...	...	...	...	1	...	...	...	1	...	1	5
Raichur	21	2	19	...	...	...	...	...	...	1	2	...	3	...	...
Lingasugur	43	18	30	...	...	...	...	...	...	...	1	...	...	1	3
Total Districts......	877	84	298	1	1	...	1	1	...	1	8	3	8	6	16
Total Districts including Hyderabad...	1,316	307	1,009	1	1	1	3	3	1	12	19	7	32	17	58
Railways......	40	10	30	...	...	...	...	...	...	...	1	...	1	1	1
Grand Total......	1,356	317	1,039	1	1	... 1	3	3	1	12	20	7	33	18	59

TABLE VIII.

Civil Condition by Religion and Age. Part (D)—Christians.—*Continued.*

District or State.	(3) WIDOWED.—*Continued.* Age Period. 30—34 Males.	30—34 Females.	35—39 Males.	35—39 Females.	40—44 Males.	40—44 Females.	45—49 Males.	45—49 Females.	50—54 Males.	50—54 Females.	55—59 Males.	55—59 Females.	60 & over. Males.	60 & over. Females.	Unspecified. Males.	Unspecified. Females.
	17	18	19	20	21	22	23	24	25	26	27	28	29	30	31	32
Telingana. Hyderabad. City	...	...	2	2	1	1	...	...	1	...	...	...	...	1	...	...
Suburbs including Secunderabad	18	65	24	72	27	98	15	79	27	108	18	86	61	174	...	...
Total......	18	65	26	74	28	99	15	79	28	108	18	86	61	175	...	...
Atraf-i-Balda District	2	8	1	2	8	8	...	...	1	8	...	...	6	8	...	...
Mahabubnagar (Nagar Karnul) ...	...	...	...	...	...	1	...	...	...	2	...	1	...	...	...	...
Nalgonda	...	2	...	...	...	2	1	...	...	2	...	...	1	1	...	...
Warangal (Khamam)	1	6	2	1	2	10	2	8	1	16	...	...	2	25	...	...
Elgandal	...	...	...	1	1	1	...	...	...	...	...	...	...	...	...	...
Indur...	...	...	...	...	...	...	...	...	...	...	1	...	...	1	...	...
Medak	...	...	...	1	...	1	...	...	...	2	...	...	...	6	...	...
Mahratwara. Aurangabad	4	1	8	8	1	11	1	4	5	25	1	5	9	86	...	..
Birh	...	...	...	...	...	...	...	...	1	1	...	...	1	...	...	...
Nander	...	...	...	...	...	...	...	...	...	...	...	...	...	...	...	...
Naldrug	...	1	...	...	...	...	...	8	...	2	...	...	...	5	..	...
Bidar	...	...	...	...	2	...	...	...	...	...	...	1	...	...	...	...
Parbhani	...	...	...	...	1	1	...	...	...	...	...	...	...	1	...	...
Sirpur Tandur	...	...	...	...	...	...	...	...	...	...	...	...	...	...	...	...
Karnatic or Kanada. Gulbarga...	2	1	...	2	...	5	...	1	...	...	...	...	1	6	...	...
Raichur	...	...	...	2	...	4	1	...	...	...	...	...	...	8	...	...
Lingasugur	2	8	2	2	1	8	2	...	1	4	...	...	4	4	...	..
Total Districts......	11	22	8	14	11	47	7	11	9	57	2	7	24	101	...	...
Total Districts including Hyderabad ...	29	87	34	88	39	146	22	90	87	165	20	48	85	276	...	...
Railways......	1	...	4	2	1	5	1	6	...	6	...	1	2	7	...	...
Grand Total......	30	87	38	90	40	151	23	96	87	171	20	44	87	283	...	...

TABLE VIII.

Civil Condition by Religion and Age. Part (D)—Christians.

(4) UNSPECIFIED.

District or State.	Total Unspecified. Total.	Total Unspecified. Males.	Total Unspecified. Females.	0—4 Males.	0—4 Females.	5—9 Males.	5—9 Females.	10—14 Males.	10—14 Females.	15—19 Males.	15—19 Females.	20—24 Males.	20—24 Females.	25—29 Males.	25—29 Females.	30—34 Males.	30—34 Females.	35—39 Males.	35—39 Females.	40—44 Males.	40—44 Females.	45—49 Males.	45—49 Females.	50—54 Males.	50—54 Females.	55—59 Males.	55—59 Females.	60 and over. Males.	60 and over. Females.	Unspecified. Males.	Unspecified. Females.
1	2	3	4	5	6	7	8	9	10	11	12	13	14	15	16	17	18	19	20	21	22	23	24	25	26	27	28	29	30	31	32
Telingana. Hyderabad. City	...	...	...	...	...	...	...	...	...	...	...	...	...	...	...	...	...	...	...	...	...	...	...	...	...	...	...	...	...	...	...
Suburbs including Secunderabad	6	3	3	2	2	1	1	...	...	...	...	...	...	...	...	...	...	...	...	...	...	...	...	...	...	...	...	...	...	...	...
Total......	6	3	3	2	2	1	1	...	...	...	...	...	...	...	...	...	...	...	...	...	...	...	...	...	...	...	...	...	...	...	...
Atraf-i-Balda District	...	...	...	...	...	...	...	...	...	...	...	...	...	...	...	...	...	...	...	...	...	...	...	...	...	...	...	...	...	...	...
Mahabubnagar (Nagar Karnul) ...	...	...	...	...	...	...	...	...	...	...	...	...	...	...	...	...	...	...	...	...	...	...	...	...	...	...	...	...	...	...	...
Nalgonda	...	...	...	...	...	...	...	...	...	...	...	...	...	...	...	...	...	...	...	...	...	...	...	...	...	...	...	...	...	...	...
Warangal (Khamam)	...	...	...	...	...	...	...	...	...	...	...	...	...	...	...	...	...	...	...	...	...	...	...	...	...	...	...	...	...	...	...
Elgandal	...	...	...	...	...	...	...	...	...	...	...	...	...	...	...	...	...	...	...	...	...	...	...	...	...	...	...	...	...	...	...
Indur	2	2	...	...	...	...	...	...	...	...	...	1	...	...	...	...	...	...	...	...	...	...	...	...	...	...	...	...	...	1	...
Medak	...	...	...	...	...	...	...	...	...	...	...	...	...	...	...	...	...	...	...	...	...	...	...	...	...	...	...	...	...	...	...
Mahratwara. Aurangabad	...	...	...	...	...	...	...	...	...	...	...	...	...	...	...	...	...	...	...	...	...	...	...	...	...	...	...	...	...	...	...
Birh	...	...	...	...	...	...	...	...	...	...	...	...	...	...	...	...	...	...	...	...	...	...	...	...	...	...	...	...	...	...	...
Nander	...	...	...	...	...	...	...	...	...	...	...	...	...	...	...	...	...	...	...	...	...	...	...	...	...	...	...	...	...	...	...
Naldrug	...	...	...	...	...	...	...	...	...	...	...	...	...	...	...	...	...	...	...	...	...	...	...	...	...	...	...	...	...	...	...
Bidar	...	...	...	...	...	...	...	...	...	...	...	...	...	...	...	...	...	...	...	...	...	...	...	...	...	...	...	...	...	...	...
Parbhani	...	...	...	...	...	...	...	...	...	...	...	...	...	...	...	...	...	...	...	...	...	...	...	...	...	...	...	...	...	...	...
Sirpur Tandur	...	...	...	...	...	...	...	...	...	...	...	...	...	...	...	...	...	...	...	...	...	...	...	...	...	...	...	...	...	...	...
Karnatic or Kanada. Gulbarga	...	...	...	...	...	...	...	...	...	...	...	...	...	...	...	...	...	...	...	...	...	...	...	...	...	...	...	...	...	...	...
Raichur	...	...	...	...	...	...	...	...	...	...	...	...	...	...	...	...	...	...	...	...	...	...	...	...	...	...	...	...	...	...	...
Lingasugur	...	...	...	...	...	...	...	...	...	...	...	...	...	...	...	...	...	...	...	...	...	...	...	...	...	...	...	...	...	...	...
Total Districts......	2	2	...	...	...	...	...	...	...	...	...	1	...	...	...	...	...	...	...	...	...	...	...	...	...	...	...	...	...	1	...
Total Districts including Hyderabad ...	8	5	3	2	2	1	1	...	...	...	...	1	...	...	...	...	...	...	...	...	...	...	...	...	...	...	...	...	...	1	...
Railways......	...	...	...	...	...	...	...	...	...	...	...	...	...	...	...	...	...	...	...	...	...	...	...	...	...	...	...	...	...	...	...
Grand Total......	8	5	3	2	2	1	1	...	...	...	...	1	...	...	...	...	...	...	...	...	...	...	...	...	...	...	...	...	...	1	...

TABLE VIII.

Civil Condition by Religion and Age Part (E)—Sikhs.

District or State.	(1) Unmarried. Total Unmarried. Total.	Males.	Females.	Age Period. 0—4 Males.	0—4 Females.	5—9 Males.	5—9 Females.	10—14 Males.	10—14 Females.	15—19 Males.	15—19 Females.	20—24 Males.	20—24 Females.	25—29 Males.	25—29 Females.	30—34 Males.	30—34 Females.	35—39 Males.	35—39 Females.	40—44 Males.	40—44 Females.	45—49 Males.	45—49 Females.	50—45 Males.	50—45 Females.	55—59 Males.	55—59 Females.	60 and over. Males.	60 and over. Females.	Unspecified. Males.	Unspecified. Females.
1	2	3	4	5	6	7	8	9	10	11	12	13	14	15	16	17	18	19	20	21	22	23	24	25	26	27	28	29	30	31	32
Tellingana. Hyderabad. City	16	9	7	2	3	3	2	...	1	...	1	1	...	1	...	2	...	...	...	...	...	...	...	...	...	...	...	...	...	...	...
Suburbs including Secunderabad	227	169	58	11	21	19	15	25	3	23	2	36	4	25	3	8	...	6	3	8	1	2	...	5	4	...	1	1	1	...	...
Total......	243	178	65	13	24	22	17	25	4	23	3	37	4	26	3	10	...	6	3	8	1	2	...	5	4	...	1	1	1	...	...
Atraf-i-Balda District	74	56	18	10	11	14	4	9	1	8	1	8	...	2	1	1	...	...	...	1	...	1	...	1	...	...	...	1	...	...	...
Mahabubnagar (Nagar Karnul)	80	25	5	3	2	7	1	4	...	2	1	1	1	2	...	2	...	3	...	1	...	...	...	...	...	...	...	...	...	...	...
Nalgonda	39	29	10	5	8	8	2	6	...	4	...	3	...	1	...	...	...	1	...	...	...	1	...	...	...	...	...	...	...	...	...
Warangal (Khamam)	105	76	29	15	12	19	11	12	6	17	...	5	...	3	...	4	...	...	...	...	...	...	...	1	...	...	...	...	...	...	...
Elgandal	149	95	54	22	20	23	26	17	7	16	1	9	...	1	...	2	...	1	...	1	...	2	...	1	...	...	...	...	...	...	...
Indur	188	125	63	21	23	26	26	27	10	20	1	12	...	9	1	6	...	...	...	2	1	...	1	1	...	...	...	1	...	...	...
Medak	70	48	22	9	14	10	7	8	1	6	...	10	...	2	...	2	...	...	...	...	...	...	...	...	...	...		1	...	...	...
Mahratwara. Aurangabad	106	57	49	16	28	18	15	9	5	2	1	4	...	2	...	2	...	...	...	2	...	1	...	...	...	...	...	1	...	...	...
Birh	89	60	29	12	12	17	12	14	3	8	...	4	...	1	...	3	...	...	...	...	1	...	...	1	...	...	...	...	1	...	...
Nander	404	267	137	61	67	60	55	56	12	20	1	14	1	8	1	10	...	4	...	11	...	2	...	5	...	2	...	13	...	1	...
Naldrug	1	1	...	...	...	...	...	...	...	1	...	...	...	...	...	...	...	...	...	...	...	...	...	...	...	...	...	...	...	...	...
Bidar	20	14	6	5	2	4	...	3	2	1	...	...	...	...	...	...	...	...	...	1	...	...	...	...	1	...	...	...	1	...	...
Parbhani	120	87	33	18	13	8	12	15	6	6	...	23	...	10	...	4	...	2	...	1	1	...	...	...	1	...	...	...	...	...	...
Sirpur Tandur	19	8	11	4	3	1	7	3	...	...	...	...	...	...	...	...	...	...	1	...	...	...	...	...	...	...	...	...	...	...	...
Karnatic or Kanada. Gulbarga	5	2	3	1	...	...	3	...	...	...	...	...	...	...	...	...	...	...	...	...	...	...	...	...	...	...	...	1	...	...	...
Raichur	1	1	...	1	...	...	...	...	...	...	...	...	...	...	...	...	...	...	...	...	...	...	...	...	...	...	...	...	...	...	...
Lingasugur	5	3	2	...	...	...	2	1	...	...	...	1	...	...	...	...	...	...	...	...	...	...	...	1	...	...	...	...	...	...	...
Total Districts......	1,425	954	471	203	215	215	183	184	53	111	6	94	2	41	3	36	...	11	1	20	3	7	1	11	2	2	...	18	2	1	...
Total Districts including Hyderabad	1,668	1,132	536	216	239	237	200	209	57	134	9	131	6	67	6	46	...	17	4	28	4	9	1	16	6	2	1	19	3	1	...
Railways......	...	...	...	...	...	...	...	...	...	...	...	...	...	...	...	...	...	...	...	...	...	...	...	...	...	...	...	...	...	...	...
Grand Total......	1,668	1,132	536	216	239	237	200	209	57	134	9	131	6	67	6	46	...	17	4	28	4	9	1	16	6	2	1	19	3	1	...

TABLE VIII.

Civil Condition by Religion and Age. Part (E)—Sikhs.

District or State.	(2) Married. Total Married. Total.	Males.	Females.	Age Period. 0—4 Males.	0—4 Females.	5—9 Males.	5—9 Females.	10—14 Males.	10—14 Females.	15—19 Males.	15—19 Females.	20—24 Males.	20—24 Females.	25—29 Males.	25—29 Females.	30—34 Males.	30—34 Females.	35—39 Males.	35—39 Females.	40—44 Males.	40—44 Females.	45—49 Males.	45—49 Females.	50—54 Males.	50—54 Females.	55—59 Males.	55—59 Females.	60 and over. Males.	60 and over. Females.	Unspecified. Males.	Unspecified. Females.
1	2	3	4	5	6	7	8	9	10	11	12	13	14	15	16	17	18	19	20	21	22	23	24	25	26	27	28	29	30	31	32
Telingana. Hyderabad. City	34	19	15	...	...	...	1	...	2	...	2	2	3	4	3	2	2	...	1	4	1	1	...	1	...	2	...	3	...	...	...
Suburbs including Secunderabad	305	173	132	...	...	2	...	1	17	17	25	24	18	28	22	25	22	11	8	21	18	6	4	23	2	8	1	12	...	...	...
Total......	339	192	147	...	...	2	1	1	19	17	27	26	21	32	25	27	24	11	9	25	14	7	4	24	2	5	1	15	...	...	...
Atraf-i-Balda District	126	76	50	...	...	...	1	...	2	1	7	6	15	6	11	8	7	8	...	22	6	4	...	10	1	3	...	8	...	...	...
Mahabubnagar (Nagar Karnul) ...	38	20	18	1	...	...	...	...	1	1	3	1	4	4	2	1	4	3	...	4	3	3	...	2	...	...	...	...	1	...	...
Nalgonda	54	29	25	...	...	...	...	...	2	...	3	4	9	4	6	4	8	7	...	4	2	3	...	2	...	...	...	1	...	...	...
Warangal (Khamam)	134	74	60	...	...	1	...	...	3	2	8	8	15	8	10	5	10	12	1	10	8	2	...	12	4	2	1	12	...	...	...
Elgandal	150	82	68	...	...	...	...	1	7	2	10	9	15	11	12	10	4	14	7	9	6	5	1	10	3	1	...	10	3	...	...
Indur	277	144	133	...	...	...	1	2	17	5	18	22	23	18	21	19	24	14	10	24	11	6	2	14	3	3	1	17	2	...	...
Medak	114	67	47	...	...	...	1	...	2	...	4	8	8	9	10	10	5	6	4	8	5	4	2	7	2	4	1	11	3	...	...
Mahratwara. Aurangabad	181	51	80	...	...	...	3	3	9	4	14	...	14	7	10	12	13	8	9	4	6	1	...	8	1	...	1	4	...	...	...
Birh	138	66	67	1	...	...	1	—	7	4	6	7	11	4	4	8	15	6	7	12	6	7	...	7	6	1	1	9	3	...	...
Nander	579	289	290	2	1	1	16	11	87	22	85	29	51	42	87	42	42	28	13	87	39	16	4	24	12	7	1	28	2	...	...
Naldrug	4	3	1	...	...	...	...	...	...	...	...	1	...	...	...	1	1	1	...	...	...	...	...	...	...	...	...	...	...	...	...
Bidar	30	15	15	...	...	...	...	...	...	2	7	2	2	3	...	3	1	1	2	2	1	...	1	1	1	1	...	...	...	...	...
Parbhani	210	148	62	1	...	...	3	...	8	9	8	52	14	33	15	26	8	7	5	7	4	5	...	5	...	1	...	2	2	...	...
Sirpur Tandur	24	14	10	...	...	...	...	1	1	1	1	...	3	5	1	2	1	...	...	2	2	1	1	...	...	1	...	1	...	...	...
Karnatic or Kanada. Gulbarga	5	3	2	...	...	...	...	...	...	...	...	...	...	...	1	1	1	...	...	1	...	...	...	1	...	...	...	...	...	...	...
Raichur	8	2	1	...	...	...	...	...	...	...	1	...	...	...	...	...	...	2	...	...	...	...	...	...	...	...	...	...	...	...	...
Lingasugur	...	...	...	...	...	...	...	...	...	...	...	...	...	...	...	...	...	...	...	...	...	...	...	...	...	...	...	...	...	...	...
Total Districts......	2,012	1,083	929	5	1	2	26	18	91	53	125	149	184	154	140	152	139	117	58	146	99	57	11	103	33	24	6	103	16	...	...
Total Districts including Hyderabad ...	2,351	1,275	1,076	5	1	4	27	19	110	70	152	175	205	186	165	179	163	128	67	171	113	64	15	127	35	29	7	118	16	...	...
Railways......	5	2	3	...	...	...	...	...	...	...	1	...	...	...	1	...	...	1	...	...	...	...	...	...	1	...	...	1	...	...	...
Grand Total......	2,356	1,277	1,079	5	1	4	27	19	110	70	153	175	205	186	166	179	163	129	67	171	113	64	15	127	36	29	7	119	16	...	...

TABLE VIII.

Civil Condition by Religion and Age. Part (E)—Sikhs.

District or State.	(3) Widowed. Total Widowed. Total.	Males.	Females.	Age Period. 0—4 Males.	0—4 Females.	5—9 Males.	5—9 Females.	10—14 Males.	10—14 Females.	15—19 Males.	15—19 Females.	20—24 Males.	20—24 Females.	25—29 Males.	25—29 Females.	30—34 Males.	30—34 Females.	35—39 Males.	35—39 Females.	40—44 Males.	40—44 Females.	45—49 Males.	45—49 Females.	50—54 Males.	50—54 Females.	55—59 Males.	55—59 Females.	60 and over. Males.	60 and over. Females.	Unspecified. Males.	Unspecified. Females.
1	2	3	4	5	6	7	8	9	10	11	12	13	14	15	16	17	18	19	20	21	22	23	24	25	26	27	28	29	30	31	32
Tellingana. Hyderabad. City	9	1	8	...	...	...	...	...	...	...	1	...	...	...	3	...	...	..	2	1	...	...	...	...	...	...	...	...	2	...	...
Suburbs including Secunderabad	78	27	51	...	...	...	...	...	1	...	...	...	2	...	1	1	6	...	1	19	9	...	4	4	11	...	3	3	13	...	...
Total......	87	28	59	...	...	...	...	...	1	...	1	...	2	...	4	1	6	...	3	20	9	...	4	4	11	...	3	3	15	...	...
Atraf-i Balda District	52	9	43	...	...	...	1	...	...	...	1	...	3	1	4	...	2	1	1	...	4	...	...	3	10	...	1	4	16	...	...
Mahabubnagar (Nagar Karnul) ...	7	3	4	...	...	...	...	...	...	...	...	...	1	...	...	...	...	...	...	...	1	1	...	...	1	...	...	2	1	...	...
Nalgonda	18	5	13	...	...	...	1	...	...	1	...	...	1	...	...	1	1	1	3	1	1	...	...	...	3	...	..	1	3	...	...
Warangal (Khamam)	42	11	31	...	...	...	...	...	...	...	...	...	...	1	1	1	1	1	2	3	8	1	1	2	6	...	1	2	11	...	...
Elgandal	36	5	31	...	...	...	...	...	...	...	1	...	2	1	...	...	3	...	3	...	4	...	4	...	4	...	...	4	10	...	..
Indur	87	17	70	...	...	...	...	...	1	...	1	...	4	1	5	...	2	1	2	4	15	...	1	5	18	2	3	4	18	...	...
Medak	29	6	23	...	...	...	...	...	1	...	1	...	...	...	1	1	...	...	...	1	3	1	...	2	9	1	2	...	6	...	..
Mahratwara. Aurangabad	38	11	27	...	...	...	...	...	...	...	1	...	...	1	...	...	1	2	2	1	8	1	...	...	6	2	1	4	8	...	...
Birh	23	4	19	...	...	...	...	...	...	...	...	...	...	...	1	...	2	...	...	...	2	...	1	...	2	1	3	3	8	...	...
Nander	146	24	122	...	...	...	...	1	1	...	...	...	3	1	4	3	11	...	5	3	22	1	5	6	28	1	3	8	40	...	..
Naldrug	...	...	...	...	...	...	...	...	...	...	...	...	...	...	...	...	...	...	...	...	...	...	..	...	...	...	...	...	...	...	...
Bidar	6	...	6	...	...	...	...	...	...	...	...	...	...	...	...	...	...	...	1	..	3	...	..	...	...	...	...	...	2	...	...
Parbhani	32	20	12	...	...	...	...	...	...	2	...	8	...	2	1	2	1	2	2	1	1	...	1	2	3	...	...	1	3	...	...
Sirpur Tandur	1	...	1	...	...	...	...	...	...	...	...	...	...	...	...	...	...	...	...	...	1	...	...	...	...	...	...	...	...	...	...
Karnatic or Kanada. Gulbarga	4	...	4	...	...	...	...	...	...	...	...	...	...	...	...	...	...	...	...	...	...	...	..	...	2	...	...	...	2	...	...
Raichur	...	...	...	...	...	...	...	...	...	...	...	...	...	...	...	...	...	...	...	...	...	...	...	...	...	..	...	...	...	...	...
Lingasugur	...	...	...	...	...	...	...	...	...	...	...	...	...	...	...	...	...	...	...	...	...	...	...	...	...	...	...	...	...	...	...
Total Districts......	521	115	406	...	...	...	2	1	3	3	5	8	14	8	17	8	24	8	21	14	73	5	13	20	92	7	14	33	128	...	...
Total Districts including Hyderabad ...	608	143	465	...	...	...	2	1	4	3	6	8	16	8	21	9	30	8	24	34	82	5	17	24	103	7	17	36	143	...	...
Railways......	...	...	...	...	...	...	...	...	...	...	...	...	...	...	...	...	...	...	...	...	...	...	...	...	..	...	...	...	...	...	...
Grand Total......	608	143	465	...	...	...	2	1	4	3	6	8	16	8	21	9	30	8	24	34	82	5	17	24	103	7	17	36	143	...	...

TABLE VIII.

Civil Condition by Religion and Age. Part (E)—Sikhs.

(4) UNSPECIFIED.

District or State.	Total Unspecified.			Age Period.																											
				0—4		5—9		10—11		15—19		20—24		25—29		30—34		35—39		40—44		45—49		50—54		55—59		60 and over.		Unspecified.	
	Total.	Males.	Females.	Males.	Females.	Males.	Females.	Males.	Females.	Males.	Females.	Males.	Females.	Males.	Females.	Males.	Females.	Males.	Females.	Males.	Females.	Males.	Females.	Males.	Females.	Males.	Females.	Males.	Females.	Males.	Females.
1	2	3	4	5	6	7	8	9	10	11	12	13	14	15	16	17	18	19	20	21	22	23	24	25	26	27	28	29	30	31	32
Telingana. Hyderabad. City	...	...	...	...	...	...	...	...	...	...	...	...	...	...	...	...	...	...	...	...	...	...	...	...	...	...	...	...	...	...	...
Suburbs including Secunderabad	...	...	...	...	...	...	...	...	...	...	...	...	...	...	...	...	...	...	...	...	...	...	...	...	...	...	...	...	...	...	...
Total......	...	...	...	...	...	...	...	...	...	...	...	...	...	...	...	...	...	...	...	...	...	...	...	...	...	...	...	...	...	...	...
Atraf-i-Balda District	2	2	...	...	...	...	...	...	...	...	...	...	...	...	...	1	...	...	...	...	...	...	...	...	...	...	...	1	...	...	...
Mahabubnagar (Nagar Karnul) ...	...	...	...	...	...	...	...	...	...	...	...	...	...	...	...	...	...	...	...	...	...	...	...	...	...	...	...	...	...	...	...
Nalgonda.	...	...	...	...	...	...	...	...	...	...	...	...	...	...	...	...	...	...	...	...	...	...	...	...	...	...	...	...	...	...	...
Warangal (Khamam)	...	...	...	...	...	...	...	...	...	...	...	...	...	...	...	...	...	...	...	...	...	...	...	...	...	...	...	...	...	...	...
Elgandal	...	...	...	...	...	...	...	...	...	...	...	...	...	...	...	...	...	...	...	...	...	...	...	...	...	...	...	...	...	...	...
Indur	1	...	1	...	...	...	...	...	...	...	...	...	...	...	...	...	...	...	...	...	...	...	...	...	...	...	...	...	...	...	1
Medak	...	...	...	...	...	...	...	...	...	...	...	...	...	...	...	...	...	...	...	...	...	...	...	...	...	...	...	...	...	...	...
Mahratwara. Aurangabad	...	...	...	...	...	...	...	...	...	...	...	...	...	...	...	...	...	...	...	...	...	...	...	...	...	...	...	...	...	...	...
Birh	...	...	...	...	...	...	...	...	...	...	...	...	...	...	...	...	...	...	...	...	...	...	...	...	...	...	...	...	...	...	...
Nander	1	1	...	...	...	...	...	...	...	...	...	...	...	...	...	...	...	...	...	...	...	...	...	...	...	...	...	1	...	...	...
Naldrug	...	...	...	...	...	...	...	...	...	...	...	...	...	...	...	...	...	...	...	...	...	...	...	...	...	...	...	...	...	...	...
Bidar	1	1	...	...	...	...	...	...	...	...	...	...	...	...	...	...	...	...	...	...	...	...	...	...	...	...	...	1	...	...	...
Parbhani	...	...	...	...	...	...	...	...	...	...	...	...	...	...	...	...	...	...	...	...	...	...	...	...	...	...	...	...	...	...	...
Sirpur Tandur	...	...	...	...	...	...	...	...	...	...	...	...	...	...	...	...	...	...	...	...	...	...	...	...	...	...	...	...	...	...	...
Karnatic or Kanada. Gulbarga	...	...	...	...	...	...	...	...	...	...	...	...	...	...	...	...	...	...	...	...	...	...	...	...	...	...	...	...	...	...	...
Raichur	...	...	...	...	...	...	...	...	...	...	...	...	...	...	...	...	...	...	...	...	...	...	...	...	...	...	...	...	...	...	...
Lingasugur	...	...	...	...	...	...	...	...	...	...	...	...	...	...	...	...	...	...	...	...	...	...	...	...	...	...	...	...	...	...	...
Total Districts......	5	4	1	...	...	...	...	...	...	...	...	...	...	...	...	1	...	...	...	...	...	...	...	...	...	...	...	3	...	...	1
Total Districts including Hyderabad ...	5	4	1	...	...	...	...	...	...	...	...	...	...	...	...	1	...	...	...	...	...	...	...	...	...	...	...	3	...	...	1
Railways......	...	...	...	...	...	...	...	...	...	...	...	...	...	...	...	...	...	...	...	...	...	...	...	...	...	...	...	...	...	...	...
Grand Total......	5	4	1	...	...	...	...	...	...	...	...	...	...	...	...	1	...	...	...	...	...	...	...	...	...	...	...	3	...	...	1

TABLE VIII.

Civil Condition by Religion and Age. Part (F)—Parsis.

District or State.	(1) Unmarried.																													
	Total Unmarried.			Age Period.																										
				0–4		5–9		10–14		15–19		20–24		25–29		30–34		35–39		40–44		45–49		50–54		55–59		60 and over.		Unspecified.	
	Total.	Males.	Females.	Males.	Females.	Males.	Females.	Males.	Females.	Males.	Females.	Males.	Females.	Males.	Females.	Males.	Females.	Males.	Females.	Males.	Females.	Males.	Females.	Males.	Females.	Males.	Females.	Males.	Females.	Males.	Females.
1	2	3	4	5	6	7	8	9	10	11	12	13	14	15	16	17	18	19	20	21	22	23	24	25	26	27	28	29	30	31	32
Telingana. Hyderabad. City	...	...	...	...	...	...	...	...	...	...	...	...	...	...	...	...	...	...	...	...	...	...	...	...	...	...	...	...	...	...	...
Suburbs including Secunderabad	260	157	103	33	36	38	27	31	25	21	10	19	4	6	...	4	...	2	...	2	...	...	...	...	...	...	1	...	...	1	...
Total......	260	157	103	33	36	38	27	31	25	21	10	19	4	6	...	4	...	2	...	2	...	...	...	...	...	...	1	...	...	1	...
Atraf-i-Balda District	1	1	...	...	...	...	...	1	...	...	...	...	...	...	...	...	...	...	...	...	...	...	...	...	...	...	...	...	...	...	...
Mahabubnagar (Nagar Karnul) ...	...	...	...	...	...	...	...	...	...	...	...	...	...	...	...	...	...	...	...	...	...	...	...	...	...	...	...	...	...	...	...
Nalgonda	7	1	6	...	...	1	5	...	1	...	...	...	...	...	...	...	...	...	...	...	...	...	...	...	...	...	...	...	...	...	...
Warangal (Khamam)	12	10	2	2	1	2	...	...	1	1	...	1	...	4	...	...	...	...	...	...	...	...	...	...	...	...	...	...	...	...	...
Elgandal	1	1	...	...	...	...	...	...	...	...	...	...	...	1	...	...	...	...	...	...	...	...	...	...	...	...	...	...	...	...	...
Indur	8	...	8	...	1	...	2	...	...	...	...	...	...	...	...	...	...	...	...	...	...	...	...	...	...	...	...	...	...	...	...
Medak...	...	...	...	...	...	...	...	...	...	...	...	...	...	...	...	...	...	...	...	...	...	...	...	...	...	...	...	...	...	...	...
Mahratwara. Aurangabad	55	33	22	7	6	9	8	3	3	7	4	4	1	1	...	1	...	...	...	...	...	...	...	...	...	1	...	...	...	...	...
Birh	9	5	4	...	...	...	2	2	1	2	1	1	...	...	...	...	...	...	...	...	...	...	...	...	...	...	...	...	...	...	...
Nander	8	3	...	...	...	...	...	1	...	1	...	...	...	1	...	...	...	...	...	...	...	...	...	...	...	...	...	...	...	...	...
Naldrug	8	3	...	...	...	...	...	1	...	1	...	...	...	...	...	...	...	...	...	...	...	...	...	...	...	1	...	...	...	...	...
Bidar	1	1	...	...	...	1	...	...	...	...	...	...	...	...	...	...	...	...	...	...	...	...	...	...	...	...	...	...	...	...	...
Parbhani	11	5	6	1	3	2	1	2	2	...	...	...	...	...	...	...	...	...	...	...	...	...	...	...	...	...	...	...	...	...	...
Sirpur Tandur	...	...	...	...	...	...	...	...	...	...	...	...	...	...	...	...	...	...	...	...	...	...	...	...	...	...	...	...	...	...	...
Karnatic or Kanada. Gulbarga	30	21	9	8	3	1	6	1	...	2	...	4	...	3	...	1	...	...	...	1	...	...	...	...	...	...	...	...	...	...	...
Raichur	17	10	7	4	1	3	3	3	3	...	...	...	...	...	...	...	...	...	...	...	...	...	...	...	...	...	...	...	...	...	...
Lingasugur	5	3	2	2	1	...	1	...	...	1	...	...	...	...	...	...	...	...	...	...	...	...	...	...	...	...	...	...	...	...	...
Total Districts......	158	97	61	24	16	19	28	14	11	15	5	10	1	10	...	2	...	...	...	1	...	...	...	...	...	2	...	...	...	...	...
Total Districts including Hyderabad...	418	254	164	57	52	57	55	45	36	36	15	29	5	16	...	6	...	2	...	3	...	...	...	...	...	2	1	...	...	1	...
Railways......	33	17	16	8	4	4	9	1	2	2	...	1	1	...	...	...	...	1	...	...	...	...	...	...	...	...	...	...	...	...	...
Grand Total......	451	271	180	65	56	61	64	46	38	38	15	30	6	16	...	6	...	3	...	3	...	...	...	...	...	2	1	...	...	1	...

TABLE VIII.

Civil Condition by Religion and Age. Part (F)—Parsis.

(2) MARRIED.

District or State.	Total Married: Total.	Total Married: Males.	Total Married: Females.	0—4 Males.	0—4 Females.	5—9 Males.	5—9 Females.	10—14 Males.	10—14 Females.	15—19 Males.	15—19 Females.	20—24 Males.	20—24 Females.	25—29 Males.	25—29 Females.	30—34 Males.	30—34 Females.	35—39 Males.	35—39 Females.	40—44 Males.	40—44 Females.	45—49 Males.	45—49 Females.	50—54 Males.	50—54 Females.	55—59 Males.	55—59 Females.	50 and over Males.	50 and over Females.	Unspecified Males.	Unspecified Females.
1	2	3	4	5	6	7	8	9	10	11	12	13	14	15	16	17	18	19	20	21	22	23	24	25	26	27	28	29	30	31	32
Telingana. Hyderabad. City ...	1	1	...	...	...	...	...	...	...	...	...	...	...	...	...	...	...	...	...	...	...	...	...	...	...	...	...	1	...	...	...
Suburbs including Secunderabad ...	323	204	119	...	...	...	1	4	2	4	11	15	27	34	20	39	20	23	9	28	10	9	8	22	4	8	3	18	4	...	...
Total......	324	205	119	...	...	...	1	4	2	4	11	15	27	34	20	39	20	23	9	28	10	9	8	22	4	8	3	19	4	...	...
Atraf-i-Balda District ...	1	1	...	...	...	...	...	...	...	...	...	...	...	...	...	...	...	...	...	...	...	...	...	1	...	...	...	...	...	...	...
Mahabubnagar (Nagar Karnul) ...	...	...	...	...	...	...	...	...	...	...	...	...	...	...	...	...	...	...	...	...	...	...	...	...	...	...	...	...	...	...	...
Nalgonda ...	5	3	2	...	...	...	...	...	...	...	...	...	...	...	...	...	2	2	...	1	...	...	...	...	...	...	...	...	...	...	...
Warangal (Khamam) ...	26	17	9	...	...	...	...	...	...	...	1	...	2	2	3	7	2	2	...	3	...	1	1	1	...	...	...	1	...	...	...
Elgandal ...	2	1	1	...	...	...	...	...	...	...	...	...	...	...	1	...	...	1	...	...	...	...	...	...	...	...	...	...	...	...	...
Indur ...	4	2	2	...	...	...	...	...	...	...	1	...	1	1	...	...	...	...	...	...	...	1	...	...	...	...	...	...	...	...	...
Medak ...	...	...	...	...	...	...	...	...	...	...	...	...	...	...	...	...	...	...	...	...	...	...	...	...	...	...	...	...	...	...	...
Mahratwara. Aurangabad ...	67	34	33	...	...	1	1	...	3	1	2	4	8	3	6	5	2	7	3	2	5	4	1	3	...	...	1	4	1	...	...
Birh ...	9	5	4	...	...	...	...	...	...	...	...	2	2	...	...	...	...	...	1	...	1	...	...	2	...	...	...	1	...	...	...
Nander ...	4	3	1	...	...	...	...	...	...	...	...	...	1	2	...	...	...	...	...	...	...	1	...	...	...	...	...	...	...	...	...
Naldrug ...	7	7	...	...	...	...	...	...	...	1	...	2	...	...	...	2	...	...	...	1	...	...	...	1	...	...	...	...	...	...	...
Bidar... ...	2	1	1	...	...	...	...	...	...	...	...	...	...	...	...	...	1	...	...	1	...	...	...	...	...	...	...	...	...	...	...
Parbhani ...	18	7	6	...	...	...	...	...	...	...	2	...	...	2	...	1	2	4	1	...	...	...	...	...	...	...	...	...	1	...	...
Sirpur Tandur ...	1	1	...	...	...	...	...	...	...	...	...	...	...	...	...	...	...	...	...	...	...	...	...	1	...	...	...	...	...	...	...
Karnatic or Kanada. Gulbarga ...	35	21	14	...	1	...	...	...	...	1	2	...	3	3	2	3	...	3	...	4	4	3	2	3	...	1	...	...	...	...	...
Raichur ...	14	8	6	...	...	...	...	...	...	...	1	1	...	...	...	2	3	1	1	2	1	...	...	1	...	...	...	1	...	...	...
Lingasugur ...	8	5	3	...	...	1	...	...	...	...	...	...	1	2	1	1	...	...	...	...	...	...	...	...	1	1	...	...	...	...	...
Total Districts......	198	116	82	...	1	2	1	...	3	3	9	9	18	15	13	21	12	20	6	14	11	10	4	13	1	2	1	7	2	...	...
Total Districts including Hyderabad	522	321	201	...	1	2	2	4	5	7	20	24	45	49	33	60	32	43	15	42	21	19	12	35	5	10	4	26	6	...	...
Railways......	35	20	15	...	...	...	...	...	1	...	...	1	1	6	4	2	1	3	2	2	1	1	2	1	3	3	...	1	...	...	...
Grand Total......	557	341	216	...	1	2	2	4	6	7	20	25	46	55	37	62	33	46	17	44	22	20	14	36	8	13	4	27	6	...	...

TABLE VIII.

Civil Condition by Religion and Age. Part (F)—Parsis.

(3) WIDOWED.

District or State.	Total Widowed.			Age Period, 0—4		5—9		10—14		15—19		20—24		25—29		30—34		35—39		40—44		45—49		50—54		55—59		60 and over.		Unspecified.	
	Total.	Males.	Females.	Males.	Females.	Males.	Females.	Males.	Females.	Males.	Females.	Males.	Females.	Males.	Females.	Males.	Females.	Males.	Females.	Males.	Females.	Males.	Females.	Males.	Females.	Males.	Females.	Males.	Females.	Males.	Females.
1	2	3	4	5	6	7	8	9	10	11	12	13	14	15	16	17	18	19	20	21	22	23	24	25	26	27	28	29	30	31	32
Suburbs including Secunderabad ...	32	10	22	...	...	...	...	...	...	...	...	...	...	1	3	2	3	1	1	1	...	1	1	1	3	1	3	2	8	...	...
Total......	32	10	22	...	...	...	...	...	...	...	...	...	...	1	3	2	3	1	1	1	...	1	1	1	3	1	3	2	8	...	...
Atraf-i-Balda District	1	...	1	...	...	...	...	...	...	...	...	...	...	...	...	...	...	...	...	...	...	...	...	...	1	...	...	...	...	...	...
Nalgonda	1	...	1	...	...	...	...	...	...	...	...	...	...	...	...	...	...	...	...	...	...	...	...	...	...	...	...	...	...	...	...
Warangal (Khamam)	2	1	1	...	...	...	...	...	...	...	1	...	...	...	...	1	...	...	...	...	...	...	...	...	...	...	...	...	1	...	...
Aurangabad	8	1	7	...	...	...	...	...	...	...	1	...	...	...	1	...	1	...	...	...	...	...	...	...	...	...	2	1	2	...	...
Birh...	1	1	...	...	...	...	...	...	...	...	...	...	...	...	...	...	...	...	...	...	...	...	...	1	...	...	...	...	...	...	...
Gulbarga	1	1	...	...	...	...	...	...	...	...	...	...	...	...	...	...	...	...	...	1	...	...	...	...	...	...	...	...	...	...	...
Raichur...	3	2	1	...	...	...	...	...	...	...	...	...	...	...	...	...	...	...	...	2	...	...	1	...	...	...	...	...	...	...	...
Total Districts......	17	6	11	...	...	...	...	...	...	...	2	...	...	...	1	1	1	...	...	3	...	...	1	1	1	...	2	1	3	...	...
Total Districts including Hyderabad ...	49	16	33	...	...	...	...	...	...	...	2	...	...	1	4	3	4	1	1	4	...	1	2	2	4	1	5	3	11	...	...
Railways......	1	...	1	...	...	...	...	...	...	...	...	...	...	...	...	...	...	...	...	...	...	...	...	...	...	...	...	...	1	...	...
Grand Total......	50	16	34	...	...	...	...	...	...	...	2	...	...	1	4	3	4	1	1	4	...	1	2	2	4	1	5	3	12	...	...

(4) UNSPECIFIED.

District or State.	Total Unspecified.			Age Period, 0—4		5—9		10—14		15—19		20—24		25—29		30—34		35—39		40—44		45—49		50—54		55—59		60 and over,		Unspecified.	
	Total.	Males	Females	Males.	Females.	Males.	Females.	Males.	Females	Males.	Females.	Males.	Females.	Males.	Females.	Males.	Females.	Males.	Females.	Males.	Females.	Males.	Females.	Males.	Females.	Males.	Females,	Males.	Females.	Males,	Females,
1	2	3	4	5	6	7	8	9	10	11	12	13	14	15	16	17	18	19	20	21	22	23	24	25	26	27	28	29	30	31	32
——	...	...	...	...	...	...	...	...	...	...	...	...	...	...	...	...	...	...	...	...	...	...	...	...	...	...	...	...	...	...	...
Grand Total......	...	...	...	...	...	...	...	...	...	...	...	...	...	...	...	...	...	...	...	...	...	...	...	...	...	...	...	...	...	...	...

TABLE VIII.

Civil Condition by Religion and Age. – Part (G)—Jains.

(1) UNMARRIED.

District or State.	Total Unmarried. Total.	Total Unmarried. Males.	Total Unmarried. Females.	0–4 Males.	0–4 Females.	5–9 Males.	5–9 Females.	10–14 Males.	10–14 Females.	15–19 Males.	15–19 Females.	20–24 Males.	20–24 Females.	25–29 Males.	25–29 Females.	30–34 Males.	30–34 Females.	35–39 Males.	35–39 Females.	40–44 Males.	40–44 Females.	45–49 Males.	45–49 Females.	50–54 Males.	50–54 Females.	55–59 Males.	55–59 Females.	60 and over. Males.	60 and over. Females.	Unspecified. Males.	Unspecified. Females.
1	2	3	4	5	6	7	8	9	10	11	12	13	14	15	16	17	18	19	20	21	22	23	24	25	26	27	28	29	30	31	32
Telingana. Hyderabad. City...	28	15	8	1	4	1	3	2	1	4	...	6	...	...	...	...	...	1	...	...	...	...	...	...	...	...	...	...	...	...	...
Suburbs including Secunderabad	43	32	11	2	2	2	4	5	3	10	...	5	...	3	...	...	...	...	...	1	...	1	...	...	2	1	...	2	...	...	...
Total......	66	47	19	3	6	3	7	7	4	14	...	11	...	3	...	...	...	1	...	1	...	1	...	...	2	1	...	2	...	...	...
Atraf-i Balda District	28	20	8	6	4	4	4	7	...	2	...	1	...	...	...	...	...	...	...	...	...	...	...	...	...	...	...	...	...	...	...
Mahabubnagar (Nagar Karnul)	1	1	...	...	...	...	...	...	...	...	...	...	...	1	...	...	...	...	...	...	...	...	...	...	...	...	...	...	...	...	...
Nalgonda	...	...	...	...	...	...	...	...	...	...	...	...	...	...	...	...	...	...	...	...	...	...	...	...	...	...	...	...	...	...	...
Warangal (Khamam)	...	...	...	...	...	...	...	...	...	...	...	...	...	...	...	...	...	...	...	...	...	...	...	...	...	...	...	...	...	...	...
Elgandal	6	4	2	...	2	2	...	...	...	1	...	1	...	...	...	...	...	...	...	...	...	...	...	...	...	...	...	...	...	...	...
Indur	37	21	16	...	5	7	5	3	5	3	...	1	...	...	...	2	1	2	...	1	...	...	...	1	...	...	...	1	...	...	...
Medak	42	29	13	8	6	5	6	10	1	2	...	1	...	1	...	...	...	...	...	1	...	...	...	1	...	...	...	...	...	...	...
Mahratwara. Aurangabad	2,828	1,838	990	422	475	404	367	415	124	202	9	137	2	94	...	58	2	38	1	22	3	10	...	21	1	3	...	12	5	...	1
Birh	1,602	1,045	557	258	285	265	179	205	73	105	6	67	4	40	1	40	3	14	2	21	...	11	1	11	...	3	...	5	2	...	1
Nander	811	198	113	63	67	40	36	41	7	15	2	14	...	5	...	13	...	3	...	2	...	...	...	2	...	...	...	...	...	...	1
Naldrug	1,579	1,018	561	308	304	234	189	205	58	113	1	63	6	36	...	26	...	7	1	5	2	3	...	12	...	2	...	4	...	...	...
Bidar	504	333	171	94	103	79	52	62	11	32	...	29	...	12	1	10	3	4	1	4	...	2	...	3	...	...	...	2	...	...	...
Parbhani	1,572	993	579	278	321	264	188	195	45	80	6	48	3	46	2	25	3	13	3	19	3	3	1	9	1	3	...	10	2	...	1
Sirpur Tandur	81	47	34	10	21	23	5	8	4	2	1	1	1	...	...	...	2	1	...	...	...	...	...	1	...	...	...	1	...	...	...
Karnatic or Kanada. Gulbarga	497	322	175	86	91	82	63	60	18	33	1	31	...	13	...	4	1	2	...	7	...	2	...	1	...	...	...	1	1	...	...
Raichur	68	51	17	5	7	8	7	12	2	15	...	6	...	3	1	...	...	...	...	1	...	...	...	...	...	...	...	1	...	...	...
Lingasugur.	401	281	120	43	56	55	38	59	15	40	1	36	5	28	...	10	1	1	1	5	...	1	1	...	...	3	1	...	1	...	...
Total Districts......	9,557	6,201	3,356	1,581	1,747	1,472	1,139	1,282	363	645	27	436	21	279	5	188	16	85	9	88	8	32	3	62	2	14	1	37	11	...	4
Total Districts including Hyderabad.	9,623	6,248	3,375	1,584	1,753	1,475	1,146	1,289	367	659	27	447	21	282	5	188	16	86	9	89	8	33	3	62	4	15	1	39	11	...	4
Railways......	1	1	...	...	...	...	...	1	...	...	...	...	...	...	...	...	...	...	...	...	...	...	...	...	...	...	...	...	...	...	...
Grand Total......	9,624	6,249	3,375	1,584	1,753	1,475	1,146	1,290	367	659	27	447	21	282	5	188	16	86	9	89	8	33	3	62	4	15	1	39	11	...	4

TABLE VIII.

Civil Condition by Religion and Age. Part (G)—Jains.

District or State.	(2) MARRIED. Total Married. Total.	Males.	Females.	Age Period. 0–4 Males.	0–4 Females.	5–9 Males.	5–9 Females.	10–14 Males.	10–14 Females.	15–19 Males.	15–19 Females.	20–24 Males.	20–24 Females.	25–29 Males.	25–29 Females.	30–34 Males.	30–34 Females.	35–39 Males.	35–39 Females.	40–44 Males.	40–44 Females.	45–49 Males.	45–49 Females.	50–54 Males.	50–54 Females.	55–59 Males.	55–59 Females.	60 and over. Males.	60 and over. Females.	Unspecified. Males.	Unspecified. Females.
1	2	3	4	5	6	7	8	9	10	11	12	13	14	15	16	17	18	19	20	21	22	23	24	25	26	27	28	29	30	31	32
Telingana. Hyderabad. City	58	43	13	...	...	...	...	4	1	5	3	6	3	8	5	5	...	4	1	4	...	...	...	4	...	...	...	3	...	...	...
Suburbs including Secunderabad	55	36	19	...	...	...	...	...	...	2	5	7	4	2	3	7	1	4	...	4	4	3	...	5	2	2	...	...	...	...	...
Total......	111	79	32	...	...	...	...	4	1	7	8	13	7	10	8	12	1	8	1	8	4	3	...	9	2	2	...	8	...	...	...
Atraf-i-Balda District	50	26	24	...	...	...	...	...	4	3	3	1	7	3	8	5	1	2	...	5	3	...	2	5	...	...	...	2	1	...	...
Mahabubnagar (Nagar Karnul).	8	3	...	...	...	...	...	...	...	...	...	...	...	1	...	1	...	1	...	...	...	...	...	...	...	...	...	...	...	...	...
Nalgonda	...	...	...	...	...	...	...	...	...	...	...	...	...	...	...	...	...	...	...	...	...	...	...	...	...	...	...	...	...	...	...
Warangal (Khamam)	1	1	...	...	...	...	...	...	...	...	...	...	...	1	...	...	...	...	...	...	...	...	...	...	...	...	...	...	...	...	...
Elgandal	4	2	2	...	...	...	...	...	...	...	1	...	1	1	...	...	...	...	...	1	...	...	...	...	...	...	...	...	...	...	...
Indur	66	34	32	...	...	1	3	3	5	3	7	1	5	4	2	7	3	6	3	2	1	3	1	2	1	1	1	1	...	...	...
Medak	36	15	21	...	...	...	...	...	2	...	3	2	7	1	5	2	3	5	...	1	...	1	...	2	1	...	...	1	...	...	...
Mahratwara. Aurangabad	3,781	1,935	1,796	3	7	5	50	40	194	122	278	205	317	296	266	295	247	233	161	284	140	146	51	154	49	67	8	185	27	...	1
Birh	2,060	1,050	1,010	1	7	5	33	28	104	49	147	126	206	167	149	174	152	112	64	128	68	73	33	90	82	81	3	66	12	...	...
Nander	553	279	274	1	4	4	18	17	32	17	31	33	58	48	44	43	37	37	13	26	16	12	11	18	4	6	5	17	1	...	...
Naldrug	2,383	1,201	1,182	2	7	7	59	33	138	84	163	145	205	187	184	181	150	126	95	148	79	85	32	87	44	35	6	81	20	...	...
Bidar	868	465	403	1	2	...	24	17	56	22	43	53	65	73	62	72	60	49	26	57	29	36	14	46	7	11	4	28	11	...	...
Parbhani	3,171	1,636	1,535	5	8	17	87	100	195	107	203	165	229	268	227	219	220	176	126	213	119	113	44	117	46	36	11	100	20	...	...
Sirpur Tandur	140	73	67	1	...	3	6	9	13	9	8	7	7	9	11	10	4	4	6	7	8	2	1	7	2	...	...	5	1	...	...
Karnatic or Kanada. Gulbarga	827	439	388	...	...	6	14	15	40	23	51	46	66	63	74	82	57	43	84	61	28	38	9	81	8	7	2	24	5	...	...
Raichur	99	64	35	...	...	...	...	2	2	3	11	13	8	11	7	9	2	10	2	4	2	2	1	5	...	2	...	3	...	...	...
Lingasugur	476	293	183	1	2	2	10	9	8	18	28	37	45	50	84	48	21	42	14	31	6	12	5	21	4	3	...	19	6	...	...
Total Districts......	14,468	7,516	6,952	15	37	50	304	273	798	460	977	834	1,226	1,183	1,068	1,148	957	846	544	918	499	523	204	585	198	199	40	482	104	...	1
Total Districts including Hyderabad.	14,579	7,595	6,984	15	37	50	304	277	794	467	985	847	1,233	1,193	1,076	1,160	958	854	545	926	503	526	204	594	200	201	40	485	104	...	1
Railways......	4	3	1	...	...	...	...	...	...	1	1	1	...	...	...	...	...	1	...	...	...	...	...	...	...	...	...	...	...	...	...
Grand Total......	14,583	7,598	6,985	15	37	50	304	277	794	468	986	848	1,238	1,198	1,076	1,160	958	855	545	926	503	526	204	594	200	201	40	485	104	...	1

TABLE VIII.

Civil Condition by Religion and Age. Part (G)—Jains.

District or State.	(3) Widowed. Total Widowed.			Age Period. 0—4		5—9		10—14		15—19		20—24		25—29		30—34		35—39		40—44		45—49		50—54		55—59		60 and over.		Unspecified.	
	Total.	Males.	Females.	Males.	Females.	Males.	Females.	Males.	Females.	Males.	Females.	Males.	Females.	Males.	Females.	Males.	Females.	Males.	Females.	Males.	Females.	Males.	Females.	Males.	Females.	Males.	Females.	Males.	Females.	Males.	Females.
1	2	3	4	5	6	7	8	9	10	11	12	13	14	15	16	17	18	19	20	21	22	23	24	25	26	27	28	29	30	31	32
Telingana. Hyderabad. City	13	7	6	...	...	...	...	...	...	...	...	...	...	2	1	...	...	...	...	2	2	...	2	...	1	...	...	3	...	...	...
Suburbs including Secunderabad	13	7	6	...	...	...	...	...	...	2	1	...	1	...	1	1	...	...	...	2	...	...	...	1	...	...	...	1	3	...	...
Total	26	14	12	...	...	...	...	...	...	2	1	...	1	2	2	1	...	...	...	4	2	...	2	1	1	...	...	4	3	...	...
Atraf-i-Balda District	16	3	13	...	...	...	...	...	...	...	2	1	...	...	1	...	1	...	...	...	2	...	2	2	1	...	2	...	2	...	...
Mahabubnagar (Nagar Karnul)...	...	...	...	...	...	...	...	...	...	...	...	...	...	...	...	...	...	...	...	...	...	...	...	...	...	...	...	...	...	...	...
Nalgonda	...	...	...	...	...	...	...	...	...	...	...	...	...	...	...	...	...	...	...	...	...	...	...	...	...	...	...	...	...	...	...
Warangal (Khamam)	1	1	...	...	...	...	...	...	...	1	...	...	...	...	...	...	...	...	...	...	...	...	...	...	...	...	...	...	...	...	...
Elgandal	2	1	1	...	...	...	...	...	...	...	...	...	...	...	...	...	1	1	...	...	...	...	...	...	...	...	...	...	...	...	...
Indur	25	6	19	...	...	...	...	...	...	...	...	...	...	1	3	...	3	...	...	1	3	1	2	2	4	...	2	1	2	...	...
Medak...	24	4	20	...	...	...	...	...	...	...	...	...	3	...	2	...	1	1	1	1	3	2	1	...	4	...	3	...	2	...	...
Mahratwara. Aurangabad	987	331	656	1	1	1	2	6	6	1	11	6	26	20	31	31	66	15	53	38	89	35	62	56	111	21	23	100	175	...	...
Birh......	487	141	346	1	2	...	1	...	8	2	5	1	17	11	16	8	27	16	27	10	48	17	23	23	63	11	18	41	96	...	...
Nander	181	56	125	...	...	...	2	3	1	2	1	2	2	5	6	8	8	2	10	4	18	4	12	5	23	2	7	19	35	...	...
Naldrug	507	146	361	2	...	...	1	2	...	5	4	2	8	9	8	7	22	12	34	10	59	16	26	27	60	13	20	41	119	...	...
Bidar	244	67	177	...	1	...	1	1	...	1	5	1	3	5	8	7	13	4	13	8	28	5	13	9	29	4	8	22	55	...	...
Parbhani	704	216	488	...	...	1	3	6	3	6	6	11	12	19	13	18	31	11	32	24	72	14	34	33	91	22	26	51	165	...	...
Sirpur Tandur	27	8	19	...	...	...	1	...	...	...	...	1	1	...	...	...	...	...	2	2	8	3	3	...	1	...	...	2	3	...	...
Karnatic or Kanada. Gulbarga	251	70	181	1	...	2	2	...	2	1	2	2	8	4	11	6	17	7	11	8	22	6	17	14	35	5	6	14	48	...	...
Raichur	27	13	14	...	...	...	...	...	...	...	...	1	1	1	1	1	1	...	...	3	3	2	1	1	2	1	...	3	5	...	...
Lingasugur	122	38	84	...	...	...	...	...	1	3	3	2	3	2	3	2	7	3	4	5	10	1	8	8	19	4	2	8	24	...	...
Total Districts......	3,605	1,101	2,504	5	4	4	13	18	16	22	39	30	84	77	108	88	198	72	187	114	365	106	204	180	443	83	117	302	781	...	...
Total Districts including Hyderabad ...	3,631	1,115	2,516	5	4	4	13	18	16	24	40	30	85	79	105	89	198	72	187	118	367	106	206	181	444	83	117	306	784	...	...
Railways......	...	...	...	...	...	...	...	...	...	...	...	...	...	...	...	...	...	...	...	...	...	...	...	...	...	...	...	...	...	...	...
Grand Total......	3,631	1,115	2,516	5	4	4	13	18	16	24	40	30	85	79	105	89	198	72	187	118	367	106	206	181	444	83	117	306	734	...	...

TABLE VIII.

Civil Condition by Religion and Age. Part (G)—Jains.

District or State.	(4) UNSPECIFIED. Total Unspecified. Total.	Males.	Females.	Age Period. 0—4 Males.	0—4 Females.	5—9 Males.	5—9 Females.	10—14 Males.	10—14 Females.	15—19 Males.	15—19 Females.	20—24 Males.	20—24 Females.	25—29 Males.	25—29 Females.	30—34 Males.	30—34 Females.	35—39 Males.	35—39 Females.	40—44 Males.	40—44 Females.	45—49 Males.	45—49 Females.	50—54 Males.	50—54 Females.	55—59 Males.	55—59 Females.	60 and over. Males.	60 and over. Females.	Unspecified. Males.	Unspecified. Females.
1	2	3	4	5	6	7	8	9	10	11	12	13	14	15	16	17	18	19	20	21	22	23	24	25	26	27	28	29	30	31	32
Telingana. Hyderabad. City	...	...	...	...	...	...	...	...	...	...	...	...	...	...	...	...	...	...	...	...	...	...	...	...	...	...	...	...	...	...	...
Suburbs including Secunderabad	...	...	...	...	...	...	...	...	...	...	...	...	...	...	...	...	...	...	...	...	...	...	...	...	...	...	...	...	...	...	...
Total......	...	...	...	...	...	...	...	...	...	...	...	...	...	...	...	...	...	...	...	...	...	...	...	...	...	...	...	...	...	...	...
Atraf-i-Balda District	...	...	...	...	...	...	...	...	...	...	...	...	...	...	...	...	...	...	...	...	...	...	...	...	...	...	...	...	...	...	...
Mahabubnagar (Nagar Karnul) ...	...	...	...	...	...	...	...	...	...	...	...	...	...	...	...	...	...	...	...	...	...	...	...	...	...	...	...	...	...	...	...
Nalgonda	...	...	...	...	...	...	...	...	...	...	...	...	...	...	...	...	...	...	...	...	...	...	...	...	...	...	...	...	...	...	...
Warangal (Khamam)	...	...	...	...	...	...	...	...	...	...	...	...	...	...	...	...	...	...	...	...	...	...	...	...	...	...	...	...	...	...	...
Elgandal	...	...	...	...	...	...	...	...	...	...	...	...	...	...	...	...	...	...	...	...	...	...	...	...	...	...	...	...	...	...	...
Indur	1	...	1	...	...	...	...	...	...	...	...	...	...	...	...	...	...	...	...	...	...	...	...	...	...	...	...	...	1	...	...
Medak...	...	...	...	...	...	...	...	...	...	...	...	...	...	...	...	...	...	...	...	...	...	...	...	...	...	...	...	...	...	...	...
Mahratwara. Aurangabad	2	...	2	...	...	...	...	...	1	...	...	...	...	...	...	...	...	...	...	...	...	...	...	...	...	...	...	...	...	...	
Birh	...	...	...	...	...	...	...	...	...	...	...	...	...	...	...	...	...	...	...	...	...	...	...	...	...	...	...	...	...	...	...
Nander	1	1	...	...	...	...	...	...	...	...	...	1	...	...	...	...	...	...	...	...	...	...	...	...	...	...	...	...	...	...	...
Naldrug	...	...	...	...	...	...	...	...	...	...	...	...	...	...	...	...	...	...	...	...	...	...	...	...	...	...	...	...	...	...	...
Bidar	1	1	...	...	...	...	...	...	...	...	...	...	...	...	...	...	...	...	...	1	...	...	...	...	...	...	...	...	...	...	...
Parbhani	2	2	...	...	...	...	...	...	...	...	...	...	...	...	...	...	...	1	...	1	...	...	...	...	...	...	...	...	...	...	...
Sirpur Tandur	...	...	...	...	...	...	...	...	...	...	...	...	...	...	...	...	...	...	...	...	...	...	...	...	...	...	...	...	...	...	...
Karnatic or Kanada. Gulbarga	...	...	...	...	...	...	...	...	...	...	...	...	...	...	...	...	...	...	...	...	...	...	...	...	...	...	...	...	...	...	...
Raichur	...	...	...	...	...	...	...	...	...	...	...	...	...	...	...	...	...	...	...	...	...	...	...	...	...	...	...	...	...	...	...
Lingasugur	...	...	...	...	...	...	...	...	...	...	...	...	...	...	...	...	...	...	...	...	...	...	...	...	...	...	...	...	...	...	...
Total Districts......	7	4	3	...	...	...	...	...	1	...	...	1	...	...	...	...	...	1	...	2	...	...	...	...	...	...	...	...	1	...	1
Total Districts including Hyderabad ...	7	4	3	...	...	...	...	...	1	...	...	1	...	...	...	...	...	1	...	2	...	...	...	...	...	...	...	...	1	...	1
Railways......	...	...	...	...	...	...	...	...	...	...	...	...	...	...	...	...	...	...	...	...	...	...	...	...	...	...	...	...	...	...	...
Grand Total......	7	4	3	...	...	...	...	...	1	...	...	1	...	...	...	...	...	1	...	2	...	...	...	...	...	...	...	...	1	...	1

TABLE VIII.

Civil Condition by Religion and Age. Part (H)—Gonds.

(1) UNMARRIED.

District or State.	Total Unmarried.			Age Period. 0—4		5—9		10—14		15—19		20—24		25—29		30—34		35—39		40—44		45—49		50—54		55—59		60 and over.		Unspecified.	
	Total.	Males.	Females.	Males.	Females.	Males.	Females.	Males.	Females.	Males.	Females.	Males.	Females.	Males.	Females.	Males.	Females.	Males.	Females.	Males.	Females.	Males.	Females.	Males.	Females.	Males.	Females.	Males.	Females.	Males.	Females.
1	2	3	4	5	6	7	8	9	10	11	12	13	14	15	16	17	18	19	20	21	22	23	24	25	26	27	28	29	30	31	32
Indur	197	106	91	38	45	42	88	18	4	6	2	...	...	...	...	1	1	1	...	...	...	...	...	...	1	...	...	...	...	...	...
Nander	2	1	1	1	1	...	...	...	...	...	...	...	...	...	...	...	...	...	...	...	...	...	...	...	...	...	...	...	...	...	...
Sirpur Tandur	10,838	6,120	4,718	2,108	2,411	2,047	1,598	1,282	571	823	59	174	28	78	12	52	15	11	2	19	8	8	...	5	5	2	1	8	6	3	2
Total Districts......	11,037	6,227	4,810	2,147	2,457	2,089	1,636	1,300	575	829	61	174	28	78	12	53	16	12	2	19	8	8	...	5	6	2	1	8	6	3	2
Total Districts including Hyderabad ...	11,037	6,227	4,810	2,147	2,457	2,089	1,636	1,300	575	829	61	174	28	78	12	53	16	12	2	19	8	8	...	5	6	2	1	8	6	3	2
Grand Total......	11,037	6,227	4,810	2,147	2,457	2,089	1,636	1,300	575	829	61	174	28	78	12	53	16	12	2	19	8	8	...	5	6	2	1	8	6	3	2

(2) MARRIED.

District or State.	Total Married.			Age Period. 0—4		5—9		10—14		15—19		20—24		25—29		30—34		35—39		40—44		45—49		50—54		55—59		60 and over.		Unspecified.	
	Total.	Males.	Females.	Males.	Females.	Males.	Females.	Males.	Females.	Males.	Females.	Males.	Females.	Males.	Females.	Males.	Females.	Males.	Females.	Males.	Females.	Males.	Females.	Males.	Females.	Males.	Females.	Males.	Females.	Males.	Females.
1	2	3	4	5	6	7	8	9	10	11	12	13	14	15	16	17	18	19	20	21	22	23	24	25	26	27	28	29	30	31	32
Indur	803	162	141	1	1	5	3	12	16	10	20	18	23	20	23	30	22	16	14	19	7	11	8	8	2	3	1	9	1	...	...
Nander	4	3	1	...	...	...	...	1	...	1	...	...	...	...	...	...	...	...	...	...	1	...	...	1	...	...	...	...	...	...	...
Sirpur Tandur	15,801	7,729	7,572	36	50	135	394	418	827	497	836	796	1,199	1,002	1,161	1,346	1,231	662	457	1,142	735	341	167	666	315	103	58	584	139	1	3
Total Districts......	15,608	7,894	7,714	37	51	140	397	431	843	508	856	814	1,222	1,022	1,184	1,376	1,253	678	471	1,161	743	352	175	675	317	106	59	593	140	1	3
Total Districts including Hyderabad ...	15,608	7,894	7,714	37	51	140	397	431	843	508	856	814	1,222	1,022	1,184	1,376	1,253	678	471	1,161	743	352	175	675	317	106	59	593	140	1	3
Grand Total......	15,608	7,894	7,714	37	51	140	397	431	843	508	856	814	1,222	1,022	1,184	1,376	1,253	678	471	1,161	743	352	175	675	317	106	59	593	140	1	3

TABLE VIII.

Civil Condition by Religion and Age. Part (H)—Gonds.

(3) WIDOWED.

District or State.	Total Widowed.			Age Period.																											
				0—4		5—9		10—14		15—19		20—24		25—29		30—34		35—39		40—44		45—49		50—54		55—59		60 and over.		Unspecified.	
	Total.	Males.	Females.	Males.	Females.	Males.	Females.	Males.	Females.	Males.	Females.	Males.	Females.	Males.	Females.	Males.	Females.	Males.	Females.	Males.	Females.	Males.	Females.	Males.	Females.	Males.	Females.	Males.	Females.	Males.	Females.
1	2	3	4	5	6	7	8	9	10	11	12	13	14	15	16	17	18	19	20	21	22	23	24	25	26	27	28	29	30	31	32
Indur	88	5	33	...	...	...	1	...	...	...	...	...	8	...	1	1	1	...	...	1	6	...	4	...	7	...	2	3	8	...	...
Sirpur Tandur	1,963	509	1,454	6	3	12	13	14	19	12	13	17	29	27	34	55	83	21	50	67	216	26	61	73	341	15	45	164	547	...	...
Total Districts......	2,001	514	1,487	6	3	12	14	14	19	12	13	17	32	27	35	56	84	21	50	68	222	26	65	73	348	15	47	167	555	...	...
Total Districts including Hyderabad ...	2,001	514	1,487	6	3	12	14	14	19	12	13	17	32	27	35	56	84	21	50	68	222	26	65	73	348	15	47	167	555	...	...
Grand Total......	2,001	514	1,487	6	3	12	14	14	19	12	13	17	32	27	35	56	84	21	50	68	222	26	65	73	348	15	47	167	555	...	...

(4) UNSPECIFIED.

District or State.	Total Unspecified.			Age Period.																											
				0—4		5—9		10—14		15—19		20—24		25—29		30—34		35—39		40—44		45—49		50—54		55—59		60 and over.		Unspecified.	
	Total.	Males.	Females.	Males.	Females.	Males.	Females.	Males.	Females.	Males.	Females.	Males.	Females.	Males.	Females.	Males.	Females.	Males.	Females.	Males.	Females.	Males.	Females.	Males.	Females.	Males.	Females.	Males.	Females.	Males.	Females.
1	2	3	4	5	6	7	8	9	10	11	12	13	14	15	16	17	18	19	20	21	22	23	24	25	26	27	28	29	30	31	32
Sirpur Tandur	14	2	12	...	...	...	1	...	1	1	...	1	...	...	...	...	1	...	...	...	...	...	...	...	...	...	...	...	9	...	...
Total Districts......	14	2	12	...	...	...	1	...	1	1	...	1	...	...	...	...	1	...	...	...	...	...	...	...	...	...	...	...	9	...	...
Total Districts including Hyderabad ...	14	2	12	...	...	...	1	...	1	1	...	1	...	...	...	...	1	...	...	...	...	...	...	...	...	...	...	...	9	...	...
Grand Total......	14	2	12	...	...	...	1	...	1	1	...	1	...	...	...	...	1	...	...	...	...	...	...	...	...	...	...	...	9	...	...

TABLE VIII.

Civil Condition by Religion and Age. Part (I)—Bhils.

(1) UNMARRIED.

District or State.	Total Unmarried.			Age Period. 0—4		5—9		10—14		15—19		20—24		25—29		30—34		35—39		40—44		45—49		50—54		55—59		60 and over.		Unspecified.	
	Total.	Males.	Females.	Males.	Females.	Males.	Females.	Males.	Females.	Males.	Females.	Males.	Females.	Males.	Females.	Males.	Females.	Males.	Females.	Males.	Females.	Males.	Females.	Males.	Females.	Males.	Females.	Males.	Females.	Males.	Females.
1	2	3	4	5	6	7	8	9	10	11	12	13	14	15	16	17	18	19	20	21	22	23	24	25	26	27	28	29	30	31	32
Sirpur Tandur	209	118	91	42	44	46	24	19	11	3	6	7	8	...	...	...	1	...	1	...	...	...	...	...	...	...	...	1	1	...	...
Total Districts......	209	118	91	42	44	46	24	19	11	8	6	7	3	...	...	...	1	...	1	...	...	...	...	...	...	...	...	1	1	...	...
Total Districts including Hyderabad ...	209	118	91	42	44	46	24	19	11	8	6	7	8	...	...	...	1	...	1	...	...	...	...	...	...	...	...	1	1	...	...
Grand Total......	209	118	91	42	44	46	24	19	11	3	6	7	8	...	...	...	1	...	1	...	...	...	...	...	...	...	...	1	1	...	...

(2) MARRIED.

District or State.	Total Married.			Age Period. 0—4		5—9		10—14		15—19		20—24		25—29		30—34		35—39		40—44		45—49		50—54		55—59		60 and over.		Unspecified.	
	Total.	Males.	Females.	Males.	Females.	Males.	Females.	Males.	Females.	Males.	Females.	Males.	Females.	Males.	Females.	Males.	Females.	Males.	Females.	Males.	Females.	Males.	Females.	Males.	Females.	Males.	Females.	Males.	Females.	Males.	Females.
1	2	3	4	5	6	7	8	9	10	11	12	13	14	15	16	17	18	19	20	21	22	23	24	25	26	27	28	29	30	31	32
Sirpur Tandur	286	115	121	...	1	3	8	5	21	11	22	11	22	27	9	11	15	12	4	13	15	8	...	9	7	2	...	8	2	...	...
Total Districts......	286	115	121	...	1	3	8	5	21	11	22	11	22	27	9	11	15	12	4	13	15	3	...	9	7	2	...	8	2	...	...
Total Districts including Hyderabad ...	286	115	121	...	1	3	3	5	21	11	22	11	22	27	9	11	15	12	4	13	15	3	...	9	7	2	...	8	2	...	...
Grand Total......	286	115	121	...	1	3	8	5	21	11	22	11	22	27	9	11	15	12	4	13	15	8	...	9	7	2	...	8	2	...	...

TABLE VIII.

Civil Condition by Religion and Age. Part (I)—Bhils.

(3) WIDOWED.

District or State.	Total Widowed.			Age Period. 0—4		5—9		10—14		15—19		20—24		25—29		30—34		35—39		40—44		45—49		50—54		55—59		60 and over.		Unspecified.	
	Total.	Males.	Females.	Males.	Females.	Males.	Females.	Males.	Females.	Males.	Females.	Males.	Females.	Males.	Females.	Males.	Females.	Males.	Females.	Males.	Females.	Males.	Females.	Males.	Females.	Males.	Females.	Males.	Females.	Males.	Females.
1	2	3	4	5	6	7	8	9	10	11	12	13	14	15	16	17	18	19	20	21	22	23	24	25	26	27	28	29	30	31	32
Sirpur Tandur	25	2	23	...	...	...	...	...	...	...	...	1	...	...	3	...	2	...	1	...	6	...	2	...	6	...	...	1	3	...	...
Total Districts......	25	2	23	...	...	...	...	...	...	...	...	1	...	...	3	...	2	...	1	...	6	...	2	...	6	...	...	1	3	...	...
Total Districts including Hyderabad ...	25	2	23	...	...	...	...	...	...	...	...	1	...	...	3	...	2	...	1	...	6	...	2	...	6	...	...	1	3	...	...
Grand Total......	25	2	23	...	...	...	...	...	...	...	...	1	...	...	3	...	2	...	1	...	6	...	2	...	6	...	...	1	3	...	...

(4) UNSPECIFIED.

District or State.	Total Unspecified.			Age Period. 0—4		5—9		10—14		15—19		20—24		25—29		30—34		35—39		40—44		45—49		50—54		55—59		60 and over.		Unspecified.	
	Total.	Males.	Females.	Males.	Females.	Males.	Females.	Males.	Females.	Males.	Females.	Males.	Females.	Males.	Females.	Males.	Females.	Males.	Females.	Males.	Females.	Males.	Females.	Males.	Females.	Males.	Females.	Males.	Females.	Males.	Females.
1	2	3	4	5	6	7	8	9	10	11	12	13	14	15	16	17	18	19	20	21	22	23	24	25	26	27	28	29	30	31	32
——	...	...	...	...	...	...	...	...	...	...	...	...	...	...	...	...	...	...	...	...	...	...	...	...	...	...	...	...	...	...	...
Grand Total......	...	...	...	...	...	...	...	...	...	...	...	...	...	...	...	...	...	...	...	...	...	...	...	...	...	...	...	...	...	...	...

TABLE VIII.

Civil Condition by Religion and Age. Part (J)—Jews.

(1) UNMARRIED.

District or State.	Total Unmarried. Total.	Total Unmarried. Males.	Total Unmarried. Females.	0—4 Males.	0—4 Females.	5—9 Males.	5—9 Females.	10—14 Males.	10—14 Females.	15—19 Males.	15—19 Females.	20—24 Males.	20—24 Females.	25—29 Males.	25—29 Females.	30—34 Males.	30—34 Females.	35—39 Males.	35—39 Females.	40—44 Males.	40—44 Females.	45—49 Males.	45—49 Females.	50—54 Males.	50—54 Females.	55—59 Males.	55—59 Females.	60 and over. Males.	60 and over. Females.	Unspecified. Males.	Unspecified. Females.
1	2	3	4	5	6	7	8	9	10	11	12	13	14	15	16	17	18	19	20	21	22	23	24	25	26	27	28	29	30	31	32
Suburbs including Secunderabad ...	18	4	9	...	4	...	4	1	...	...	1	2	...	1	...	...	...	...	...	...	...	...	...	...	...	...	...	...	...	...	...
Total......	13	4	9	...	4	...	4	1	...	...	1	2	...	1	...	...	...	...	...	...	...	...	...	...	...	...	...	...	...	...	...
Total Districts including Hyderabad ...	13	4	9	...	4	...	4	1	...	...	1	2	...	1	...	...	...	...	...	...	...	...	...	...	...	...	...	...	...	...	...
Railways......	2	1	1	1	1	...	...	...	...	...	...	...	...	...	...	...	...	...	...	...	...	...	...	...	...	...	...	...	...	...	...
Grand Total......	15	5	10	1	5	...	4	1	...	...	1	2	...	1	...	...	...	...	...	...	...	...	...	...	...	...	...	...	...	...	...

(2) MARRIED.

District or State.	Total Married. Total.	Total Married. Males.	Total Married. Females.	0—4 Males.	0—4 Females.	5—9 Males.	5—9 Females.	10—14 Males.	10—14 Females.	15—19 Males.	15—19 Females.	20—24 Males.	20—24 Females.	25—29 Males.	25—29 Females.	30—34 Males.	30—34 Females.	35—39 Males.	35—39 Females.	40—44 Males.	40—44 Females.	45—49 Males.	45—49 Females.	50—54 Males.	50—54 Females.	55—59 Males.	55—59 Females.	60 and over. Males.	60 and over. Females.	Unspecified. Males.	Unspecified. Females.
1	2	3	4	5	6	7	8	9	10	11	12	13	14	15	16	17	18	19	20	21	22	23	24	25	26	27	28	29	30	31	32
Suburbs including Secunderabad ...	7	3	4	...	...	...	...	...	...	...	...	...	2	1	1	2	...	...	...	...	1	...	...	...	...	...	...	...	...	...	...
Total......	7	3	4	...	...	...	...	...	...	...	...	...	2	1	1	2	...	...	...	...	1	...	...	...	...	...	...	...	...	...	...
Total Districts including Hyderabad ...	7	3	4	...	...	...	...	...	...	...	...	...	2	1	1	2	...	...	...	...	1	...	...	...	...	...	...	...	...	...	...
Railways......	3	2	1	...	...	...	...	...	...	...	...	...	1	2	...	...	...	...	...	...	...	...	...	...	...	...	...	...	...	...	...
Grand Total......	10	5	5	...	...	...	...	...	...	...	...	...	3	3	1	2	...	...	...	...	1	...	...	...	...	...	...	...	...	...	...

TABLE VIII.

Civil Condition by Religion and Age. Part (J)—Jews.

(3) WIDOWED.

District or State.	Total Widowed.			Age Period. 0—4		5—9		10—14		15—19		20—24		25—29		30—34		35—39		40—44		45—49		50—54		55—59		60 and over.		Unspecified.	
	Total.	Males.	Females.	Males.	Females.	Males	Females.	Males.	Females.	Males.	Females.	Males.	Females.	Males.	Females.	Males.	Females.	Males.	Females.	Males.	Females.	Males.	Females.	Males.	Females.	Males.	Females.	Males.	Females.	Males.	Females.
1	2	3	4	5	6	7	8	9	10	11	12	13	14	15	16	17	18	19	20	21	22	23	24	25	26	27	28	29	30	31	32
Suburbs including Secunderabad ...	1	...	1	...	...	...	...	...	...	...	...	...	...	...	...	...	...	...	...	...	...	...	1	...	...	...	...	...	...	...	...
Total......	1	...	1	...	...	...	...	...	...	...	...	...	...	...	...	...	...	...	...	...	...	...	1	...	...	...	...	...	...	...	...
Total Districts including Hyderabad ...	1	...	1	...	...	...	...	...	...	...	...	...	...	...	...	...	...	...	...	...	...	...	1	...	...	...	...	...	...	...	...
Railways......	...	...	...	...	...	...	...	...	...	...	...	...	...	...	...	...	...	...	...	...	...	...	...	...	...	...	...	...	...	...	...
Grand Total......	1	...	1	...	...	...	...	...	...	...	...	...	...	...	...	...	...	...	...	...	...	...	1	...	...	...	...	...	...	...	...

(4) UNSPECIFIED.

District or State.	Total Unspecified.			Age Period. 0—4		5—9		10—14		15—19		20—24		25—29		30—34		35—39		40—44		45—49		50—54		55—59		60 and over.		Unspecified.	
	Total.	Males.	Females.	Males.	Females.	Males.	Females.	Males.	Females.	Males.	Females.	Males.	Females.	Males.	Females.	Males.	Females.	Males.	Females.	Males.	Females.	Males.	Females.	Males.	Females.	Males.	Females.	Males.	Females.	Males.	Females.
1	2	3	4	5	6	7	8	9	10	11	12	13	14	15	16	17	18	19	20	21	22	23	24	25	26	27	28	29	30	31	32
——	...	...	...	...	...	...	...	...	...	...	...	...	...	...	...	...	...	...	...	...	...	...	...	...	...	...	...	...	...	...	...
Grand Total......	...	...	...	...	...	...	...	...	...	...	...	...	...	...	...	...	...	...	...	...	...	...	...	...	...	...	...	...	...	...	...

TABLE IX.

EDUCATION BY RELIGION AND AGE.

In each part of this Table only those districts are shown which contain followers of the religion to which the part relates.

TABLE IX.

Education by Religion and Age. Part (A)—All Religions.

District or State.	Total Population.			Total by Education.								Age Period.			
				Learning.		Literate.		Illiterate.		Unspecified.		0—14			
												Total.		Learning.	
	Total.	Males.	Females.	Males.	Females.	Males.	Females.	Males.	Females.	Males.	Females.	Males.	Females.	Males.	Females.
1	2	3	4	5	6	7	8	9	10	11	12	13	14	15	16
Telingana. Hyderabad. City ...	124,057	62,748	61,309	8,377	307	12,058	731	47,307	58,897	6	1,374	14,943	14,662	2,587	242
Suburbs including Secunderabad ...	290,982	153,576	137,406	7,423	1,481	33,270	4,861	112,880	130,981	3	83	43,695	42,414	5,816	1,307
Total......	415,039	216,324	198,715	10,800	1,788	45,328	5,592	160,187	189,878	9	1,457	58,638	57,076	8,403	1,549
Atraf-i-Balda District ...	389,784	198,258	191,526	2,524	33	14,059	817	181,662	191,053	18	123	71,289	68,580	2,228	80
Mahabubnagar (Nagar Karnul) ...	674,649	341,601	333,048	4,462	167	21,926	674	315,161	332,155	52	52	131,226	125,901	3,982	141
Nalgonda ...	624,617	319,823	304,794	3,079	72	16,362	348	300,366	304,356	16	18	134,680	129,929	2,754	59
Warangal (Khamam) ...	853,129	438,635	414,494	4,540	207	24,389	684	409,695	413,603	11	...	180,987	172,451	4,056	193
Elgandal ...	1,094,601	563,845	530,756	4,525	71	28,535	633	530,699	529,938	86	114	243,346	224,674	4,078	60
Indur ...	639,598	319,237	320,361	3,907	42	16,863	207	298,388	320,080	79	32	123,539	114,828	3,489	34
Medak ...	364,735	183,908	180,827	3,216	63	15,101	251	165,566	180,482	25	31	65,458	62,179	2,884	45
Mahratwara. Aurangabad ...	828,975	421,018	407,957	6,188	143	22,523	437	392,222	407,331	85	46	158,211	156,380	5,031	124
Birh ...	642,722	328,530	314,192	3,655	53	15,659	208	308,911	313,723	805	208	122,834	116,836	3,021	47
Nander ...	632,529	320,136	312,393	3,015	32	12,722	220	303,595	311,621	804	520	124,827	117,005	2,584	18
Naldrug ...	649,272	331,747	317,525	4,657	41	16,067	113	310,896	317,321	127	50	124,713	118,657	3,989	34
Bidar ...	901,984	457,088	444,896	5,548	118	20,940	162	430,445	444,509	155	107	169,284	161,494	4,719	110
Parbhani ...	805,335	410,499	394,836	3,734	19	17,065	136	389,633	394,639	67	42	154,647	150,536	3,136	15
Sirpur Tandur ...	231,754	116,955	114,799	639	1	2,821	17	113,490	114,777	5	4	50,877	49,443	551	1
Karnatic or Kanada. Gulbarga ...	649,258	329,678	319,580	4,297	72	17,393	182	307,972	319,311	16	15	117,927	112,545	3,752	66
Raichur ...	512,455	260,217	252,238	2,940	104	15,728	397	241,529	251,720	20	17	100,971	97,717	2,470	87
Lingasugur ...	620,014	311,394	308,620	4,683	160	18,988	293	287,664	308,082	59	85	118,102	115,312	4,027	149
Total Districts......	11,115,411	5,652,569	5,462,842	65,609	1,398	297,141	5,279	5,287,894	5,454,701	1,925	1,464	2,192,918	2,094,467	56,651	1,213
Total Districts including Hyderabad ...	11,530,450	5,868,893	5,661,557	76,409	8,186	342,469	10,871	5,448,081	5,644,579	1,934	2,921	2,251,556	2,151,548	65,054	2,762
Railways......	6,590	4,236	2,354	90	51	972	192	3,174	2,111	...	...	843	818	72	48
Grand Total......	11,537,040	5,873,129	5,663,911	76,499	3,237	343,441	11,063	5,451,255	5,646,690	1,934	2,921	2,252,399	2,152,361	65,126	2,810

TABLE IX.

Education by Religion and Age. Part (A)—All Religions.—*Continued.*

District or State.	Age Period.—contd. 0—14—contd. Literate. Males.	Literate. Females.	Illiterate. Males.	Illiterate. Females.	Unspecified. Males.	Unspecified. Females.	15—24 Total. Males.	Total. Females.	Learning. Males.	Learning. Females.	Literate. Males.	Literate. Females.	Illiterate. Males.	Illiterate. Females.	Unspecified. Males.	Unspecified. Females.
	17	18	19	20	21	22	23	24	25	26	27	28	29	30	31	32
Telingana. Hyderabad. City ...	844	56	12,012	14,364	...	...	12,720	14,921	672	42	2,654	226	9,394	14,653	...	...
Suburbs including Secunderabad ...	1,805	1,591	36,073	39,513	1	8	80,504	80,932	1,342	119	9,088	1,275	20,079	29,537	...	1
Total......	2,149	1,647	48,085	53,877	1	8	43,224	45,853	2,014	161	11,737	1,501	29,478	44,190	...	1
Atraf-i-Balda District ...	994	50	68,066	68,500	1	...	81,790	34,333	238	2	8,200	96	28,350	84,233	2	2
Mahabubnagar (Nagar Karnul) ...	1,585	90	125,688	125,655	21	15	55,318	60,012	410	11	5,245	171	49,660	59,823	3	7
Nalgonda ...	1,322	47	130,599	129,817	5	6	53,795	55,790	256	8	8,978	108	49,560	55,678	1	1
Warangal (Khamam) ...	1,995	109	174,936	172,149	...	...	72,438	75,505	406	7	5,953	194	66,079	75,304	...	...
Elgandal ...	2,555	98	236,697	224,483	16	33	91,356	96,954	843	5	6,925	165	84,081	96,775	7	9
Indur ...	1,162	31	118,862	114,753	26	10	48,285	56,267	367	3	8,554	54	44,850	56,206	14	4
Medak ...	1,235	31	61,329	62,093	10	10	28,549	81,808	258	6	3,580	68	24,710	81,733	1	1
Mahratwara. Aurangabad ...	1,100	58	152,055	156,182	25	16	60,993	72,248	983	4	4,598	134	55,396	72,105	16	5
Birh ...	941	25	118,769	116,688	103	76	46,200	54,653	553	3	3,000	68	42,603	54,561	44	21
Nander ...	797	29	121,177	116,781	269	177	42,412	50,491	338	1	2,543	38	89,435	50,372	96	80
Naldrug ...	621	13	120,116	118,596	37	14	46,652	55,173	650	8	8,272	27	42,720	55,127	10	16
Bidar ...	1,184	19	163,325	161,336	56	29	64,792	72,276	703	3	4,208	31	59,860	72,227	21	15
Parbhani ...	989	21	150,506	150,485	16	15	54,353	64,536	508	3	8,262	29	50,575	64,497	8	7
Sirpur Tandur ...	201	3	50,124	49,439	1	...	16,224	18,148	71	...	624	7	15,529	18,141	...	...
Karnatic or Kanada. Gulbarga ...	757	22	113,415	112,452	3	5	48,674	53,230	509	2	3,517	48	44,646	53,176	2	4
Raichur ...	580	54	97,918	97,570	3	6	41,750	44,674	396	8	3,625	120	37,729	44,535	...	1
Lingasugur ...	830	34	113,234	115,116	11	13	50,812	54,538	483	6	3,894	90	46,430	54,484	5	8
Total Districts...	18,848	734	2,116,816	2,092,095	603	425	854,393	950,686	7,472	70	64,978	1,458	781,713	948,927	230	181
Total Districts including Hyderabad ...	20,997	2,381	2,164,901	2,145,972	604	428	897,617	996,489	9,486	231	76,715	2,959	811,186	993,117	230	182
Railways......	52	88	719	732	...	...	742	543	9	8	282	58	451	482	...	...
Grand Total......	21,049	2,419	2,165,620	2,146,704	604	428	898,359	997,032	9,495	234	76,997	3,017	811,637	993,599	230	182

TABLE IX.

Education by Religion and Age. Part (A)—All Religions.—*Continued.*

	District or State.	Age Period.—con'd.																			
		25 and over.										Unspecified.									
		Total.		Learning.		Literate.		Illiterate.		Unspecified.		Total.		Learning.		Literate.		Illiterate.		Unspecified.	
		Males.	Females.	Males.	Females.	Males.	Females.	Males.	Females.	Males.	Females.	Males.	Females.	Males.	Females.	Males.	Females.	Males.	Females.	Males.	Females.
		33	34	35	36	37	38	39	40	41	42	43	44	45	46	47	48	49	50	51	52
Telingana. Hyderabad.	City	35,069	30,288	118	19	9,060	447	25,888	29,822	8	...	16	1,438	...	4	...	2	13	58	8	1,374
	Suburbs including Secunderabad	79,348	63,784	265	52	22,380	1,971	56,701	61,759	2	2	29	276	...	8	2	24	27	172	...	77
	Total......	114,417	94,072	383	71	81,440	2,418	82,589	91,581	5	2	45	1,714	...	7	2	26	40	280	8	1,451
	Atraf-i-Balda District	95,099	88,860	58	1	9,864	171	85,171	88,186	6	2	80	253	...	...	1	...	75	184	4	119
	Mahabubnagar (Nagar Karnul) ...	154,848	146,797	118	12	15,091	402	139,616	146,868	23	20	209	888	2	8	5	11	197	814	5	10
	Nalgonda	131,257	118,859	69	10	11,062	192	120,121	118,652	5	5	91	216	...	...	...	1	86	209	5	6
	Warangal (Khamam)	184,961	166,190	78	7	16,438	880	168,437	165,803	8	...	249	848	...	...	3	1	248	347	3	...
	Elgandal	228,923	208,620	103	6	19,048	867	209,757	208,228	15	19	220	508	1	...	7	8	164	452	48	53
	Indur...	147,813	148,556	51	4	12,145	121	135,086	148,420	31	11	100	710	...	1	2	1	90	701	8	7
	Medak	89,828	85,582	73	4	10,285	145	79,458	85,428	12	10	78	1,258	1	8	1	7	69	1,288	2	10
Mahratwara.	Aurangabad	201,564	178,915	173	15	16,814	245	1,84,533	178,682	44	23	250	414	1	...	11	...	238	412	...	2
	Birh	159,230	142,317	81	3	11,712	115	147,286	142,100	151	99	266	886	...	...	6	...	258	374	7	12
	Nander	152,626	144,270	93	13	9,373	153	142,785	143,882	425	222	271	627	...	...	9	...	248	586	14	41
	Naldrug	160,247	143,519	67	4	12,173	73	147,929	143,422	78	20	135	176	1	...	1	...	131	176	2	...
	Bidar...	222,844	210,751	124	5	15,548	112	207,108	210,596	64	88	168	375	2	...	...	...	152	850	14	25
	Parbhani	201,313	179,475	89	1	12,811	86	188,372	179,376	41	12	186	289	1	...	8	...	180	281	2	8
	Sirpur Tandur	49,828	47,168	17	...	1,995	7	47,808	47,160	8	1	31	40	...	...	1	...	29	87	1	8
Karnatic or Kanada.	Gulbarga	162,965	153,660	85	4	18,114	112	149,805	153,538	11	6	112	145	1	...	5	...	106	145	...	...
	Raichur	117,467	109,799	74	9	11,523	208	105,862	109,579	8	8	29	48	...	...	...	5	20	86	9	7
	Lingasugur	142,406	138,649	178	5	14,264	169	127,950	138,460	19	15	74	121	...	...	...	...	50	72	24	49
	Total Districts......	2,602,714	2,411,487	1,476	103	213,260	8,058	2,387,084	2,407,820	944	506	2,544	6,252	10	12	55	29	2,381	5,859	148	852
	Total Districts including Hyderabad ...	2,717,131	2,505,559	1,859	174	244,700	5,476	2,469,623	2,499,401	949	508	2,589	7,966	10	19	57	55	2,371	6,089	151	1,803
	Railways......	2,651	993	9	...	638	96	2,004	897	...	...	...	...	...	...	...	...	...	...	...	...
	Grand Total......	2,719,782	2,506,552	1,868	174	245,338	5,572	2,471,627	2,500,298	949	508	2,589	7,966	10	19	57	55	2,371	6,089	151	1,803

TABLE IX.

Education by Religion and Age. Part (B)—Hindus.

District or State.	Total Hindus.			Total by Education.								Age Period. 0—14			
				Learning.		Literate.		Illiterate.		Unspecified.		Total.		Learning.	
	Total.	Males.	Females.	Males.	Females.	Males.	Females.	Males.	Females.	Males.	Females.	Males.	Females.	Males.	Females.
1	2	3	4	5	6	7	8	9	10	11	12	13	14	15	16
Telingana. Hyderabad. City	48,363	25,728	22,635	837	16	4,817	69	20,074	22,209	...	341	5,919	5,806	667	12
Suburbs including Secunderabad	178,477	93,064	85,413	3,075	278	16,777	738	73,210	84,394	2	8	27,007	26,418	2,422	250
Total......	226,840	118,792	108,048	3,912	289	21,594	807	93,284	106,603	2	349	32,926	32,224	3,089	262
Atraf-i-Balda District	346,357	175,815	170,542	2,008	15	12,110	288	161,687	170,233	10	6	63,724	61,261	1,801	18
Mahabubnagar (Nagar Karnul) ...	618,839	313,686	305,153	3,598	95	19,860	572	290,186	304,450	42	36	120,454	115,692	3,199	79
Nalgonda	598,449	308,850	289,599	2,512	29	14,824	295	286,498	289,259	16	16	128,487	123,791	2,297	23
Warangal (Khamam)	808,440	415,393	393,047	3,644	55	22,021	454	389,728	392,538	5	...	172,092	164,056	3,288	50
Elgandal	1,050,045	540,939	509,106	3,906	58	26,437	529	510,511	508,408	85	111	234,071	215,911	3,565	47
Indur...	588,138	293,699	294,439	3,181	22	15,098	158	275,354	294,227	66	32	118,772	106,084	2,868	20
Medak...	326,267	164,560	161,707	2,345	15	13,235	163	148,957	161,507	23	22	58,369	55,888	2,156	13
Mahratwara. Aurangabad	724,876	367,815	357,061	4,596	35	17,230	156	345,918	356,826	71	44	138,836	137,362	3,777	30
Birh	586,349	299,236	287,113	2,957	19	13,246	100	282,763	286,809	270	185	112,178	107,078	2,458	14
Nander	574,320	290,302	284,018	2,520	14	11,254	121	275,876	283,468	652	415	113,589	106,623	2,188	10
Naldrug	586,540	299,462	287,078	3,880	18	14,097	68	281,381	286,951	104	41	112,974	107,414	3,811	16
Bidar	785,543	397,793	387,750	4,468	85	18,477	96	374,706	387,535	142	84	147,199	140,815	3,824	31
Parbhani	732,737	373,246	359,491	3,014	7	14,692	84	355,479	359,368	61	32	141,014	137,601	2,579	7
Sirpur Tandur	192,869	97,144	95,725	515	1	2,549	13	94,077	95,711	8	...	42,569	41,391	450	1
Karnatic or Kanada. Gulbarga	552,137	279,964	272,173	3,381	19	15,144	88	261,432	272,054	7	12	100,186	95,447	3,000	18
Raichur	460,011	233,282	226,729	2,361	59	13,929	265	216,975	226,389	17	16	90,777	87,911	1,994	48
Lingasugur	556,975	279,077	277,898	4,031	107	17,020	192	257,976	277,521	50	78	106,060	103,886	2,501	104
Total Districts......	10,088,892	5,125,263	4,958,629	52,917	603	261,223	3,592	4,809,499	4,953,304	1,624	1,130	1,996,301	1,908,156	46,851	524
Total Districts including Hyderabad ...	10,310,732	5,244,055	5,066,677	56,829	892	282,817	4,399	4,902,783	5,059,507	1,626	1,479	2,029,227	1,940,380	49,940	786
Railways......	4,517	2,916	1,601	23	2	489	24	2,404	1,575	...	...	560	536	17	2
Grand Total......	10,315,249	5,246,971	5,068,278	56,852	894	283,306	4,423	4,905,187	5,061,482	1,626	1,479	2,029,787	1,940,916	49,957	788

TABLE IX.

Education by Religion and Age. Part (B)—Hindus.—*Continued.*

District or State.	Age Period.—*contd.* 0—14—*contd.* Literate. Males.	Literate. Females.	Illiterate. Males.	Illiterate. Females.	Unspecified. Males.	Unspecified. Females.	15—24 Total. Males.	Total. Females.	Learning. Males.	Learning. Females.	Literate. Males.	Literate. Females.	Illiterate. Males.	Illiterate. Females.	Unspecified. Males.	Unspecified. Females.
	17	18	19	20	21	22	23	24	25	26	27	28	29	30	31	32
Telingana. Hyderabad. City	160	7	5,092	5,787	...	...	4,895	4,704	142	2	1,064	18	3,689	4,684	...	...
Suburbs including Secunderabad	924	152	23,660	26,018	1	8	17,846	18,867	531	11	4,401	265	12,914	18,590	...	1
Total......	1,084	159	28,752	31,800	1	8	22,741	23,571	673	13	5,465	283	16,603	23,274	...	1
Atraf-i-Balda District	889	38	61,033	61,210	1	...	28,275	30,551	162	1	2,782	74	25,329	30,474	2	2
Mahabubnagar (Nagar Karnul) ...	1,413	68	115,822	115,533	20	12	50,929	54,989	307	5	4,757	148	45,863	54,834	2	2
Nalgonda	1,227	42	124,958	128,720	5	6	51,111	53,053	168	2	3,588	86	47,354	52,964	1	1
Warangal (Khamam)	1,837	69	166,972	163,937	...	...	68,413	71,557	295	2	5,333	119	62,785	71,436	...	...
Elgandal	2,389	74	228,101	215,757	16	33	87,637	93,115	258	5	6,376	180	81,001	92,971	7	9
Indur	1,082	24	109,802	106,030	20	10	44,533	51,703	268	...	3,215	38	41,037	51,661	13	4
Medak	1,074	20	55,129	55,846	10	9	25,641	28,622	183	2	3,154	48	22,358	28,576	1	1
Mahratwara. Aurangabad	812	17	134,225	137,299	22	16	52,765	63,273	708	...	3,437	31	48,609	63,237	16	5
Birh	258	12	108,873	106,979	89	68	41,978	49,916	434	3	2,553	24	38,951	49,869	40	20
Nander	679	25	110,495	106,438	227	150	38,101	45,830	277	1	2,229	24	35,521	45,736	74	69
Naldrug	532	10	109,100	107,376	31	12	41,985	50,066	528	1	2,846	16	38,602	50,036	9	13
Bidar	1,041	10	142,281	140,748	53	26	56,108	62,782	544	1	3,723	18	51,821	62,753	20	10
Parbhani	835	11	137,586	137,569	14	14	49,085	58,655	873	...	2,767	13	45,938	58,636	7	6
Sirpur Tandur	181	2	41,937	41,388	1	...	13,593	15,104	57	...	573	4	12,963	15,100	...	...
Karnatic or Kanada. Gulbarga	657	8	96,477	95,418	2	3	41,385	45,281	358	...	3,028	18	37,958	45,259	1	4
Raichur	503	25	88,277	87,832	8	6	37,491	40,254	306	2	3,219	85	33,966	40,166	...	1
Lingasugur	714	24	101,834	103,697	11	11	45,580	49,194	392	2	3,460	50	41,725	49,137	3	5
Total Districts...	16,623	479	1,932,902	1,906,777	525	376	774,560	863,945	5,558	27	57,085	921	711,771	862,845	196	152
Total Districts including Hyderabad ...	17,707	638	1,961,654	1,938,577	526	379	797,301	887,516	6,231	40	62,500	1,204	728,374	886,119	196	153
Railways......	17	7	526	527	...	..	477	356	2	...	141	9	334	347	...	...
Grand Total......	17,724	645	1,962,180	1,939,104	526	379	797,778	887,872	6,233	40	62,641	1,213	728,708	886,466	196	153

TABLE IX.

Education by Religion and Age. Part (B)—Hindus.—*Continued.*

District or State.	Age Period.—contd. 25 & over. Total. Males.	Total. Females.	Learning. Males.	Learning. Females.	Literate. Males.	Literate. Females.	Illiterate. Males.	Illiterate. Females.	Unspecified. Males.	Unspecified. Females.	Unspecified. Total. Males.	Total. Females.	Learning. Males.	Learning. Females.	Literate. Males.	Literate. Females.	Illiterate. Males.	Illiterate. Females.	Unspecified. Males.	Unspecified. Females.
	33	34	35	36	37	38	39	40	41	42	43	44	45	46	47	48	49	50	51	52
Telingana. Hyderabad. City	14,909	11,772	28	2	3,593	44	11,288	11,726	...	...	5	853	...	...	...	...	5	12	...	841
Suburbs including Secunderabad	48,194	40,112	122	12	11,451	321	36,620	39,777	1	2	17	16	...	...	1	...	16	14	...	2
Total......	63,108	51,884	150	14	15,044	365	47,908	51,503	1	2	22	869	...	...	1	...	21	26	...	843
Atraf-i-Balda District	83,758	78,681	45	1	8,488	126	75,270	78,552	5	2	58	49	...	...	1	...	55	47	2	2
Mahabubnagar (Nagar Karnul) ...	142,116	134,257	90	8	13,685	345	128,326	133,886	15	18	187	215	2	3	5	11	175	197	5	4
Nalgonda	124,163	112,681	47	4	10,009	167	114,102	112,455	5	5	89	124	...	...	...	...	84	120	5	4
Warangal (Khamam)	174,643	157,162	66	3	14,848	266	159,727	156,893	2	...	245	272	...	...	3	...	229	272	3	...
Elgandal	219,019	199,718	87	6	17,665	324	201,252	199,369	15	19	212	362	1	...	7	1	157	311	47	50
Indur...	135,308	136,556	45	2	10,800	95	124,436	136,448	27	11	86	96	...	...	1	1	79	88	6	7
Medak	80,502	77,131	55	...	9,006	100	71,430	77,022	11	9	48	66	1	...	1	...	45	68	1	3
Mahratwara. Aurangabad	175,998	156,180	115	5	12,971	108	162,879	156,044	38	28	216	246	1	...	10	...	205	246	...	...
Birh	144,837	129,840	65	2	9,929	64	134,708	129,685	135	89	248	284	...	...	6	...	231	276	6	8
Nander	138,870	131,294	55	3	8,337	72	129,639	131,037	339	182	242	271	...	...	9	...	221	257	12	14
Naldrug	144,379	129,474	41	1	10,718	42	133,558	129,415	62	16	124	124	...	...	1	...	121	124	2	...
Bidar	194,344	183,966	99	3	13,713	68	180,477	183,866	55	29	142	187	1	...	...	...	137	168	14	19
Parbhani	182,975	163,028	61	...	11,088	60	171,788	162,957	38	11	172	207	1	...	2	...	167	206	2	1
Sirpur Tandur	40,959	89,197	8	...	1,794	7	39,155	89,190	2	...	28	88	...	...	1	...	22	38	...	...
Karnatic or Kanada. Gulbarga	138,408	131,859	22	1	11,461	62	126,916	131,291	4	5	90	86	1	...	3	...	86	86	...	...
Raichur	104,985	98,523	61	9	10,207	150	94,712	98,362	5	2	29	41	...	...	...	5	20	29	9	7
Lingasugur	127,385	124,774	138	1	12,846	118	114,389	124,642	12	18	52	94	...	...	...	...	28	45	24	49
Total Districts......	2,352,144	2,183,771	1,100	49	187,515	2,174	2,162,764	2,181,114	765	484	2,258	2,757	8	3	50	18	2,062	2,568	138	168
Total Districts including Hyderabad ...	2,415,247	2,235,655	1,250	63	202,559	2,539	2,210,672	2,232,617	766	436	2,280	3,126	8	3	51	18	2,083	2,594	138	511
Railways......	1,879	709	4	...	331	8	1,544	701	...	...	...	...	...	...	...	...	...	...	...	...
Grand Total......	2,417,126	2,236,364	1,254	63	202,890	2,547	2,212,216	2,233,318	766	436	2,280	3,126	8	3	51	18	2,083	2,594	138	511

TABLE IX.

Education by Religion and Age. Part (C)—Mussulmans.

District or State.	Total Mussulmans.			Total by Education.								Age Period. 0–14			
				Learning.		Literate.		Illiterate.		Unspecified.		Total.		Learning.	
	Total.	Males.	Females.	Males.	Females.	Males.	Females.	Males.	Females.	Males.	Females.	Males.	Females.	Males.	Females.
1	2	3	4	5	6	7	8	9	10	11	12	13	14	15	16
Telingana. Hyderabad. City	75,498	36,898	38,600	2,583	290	7,178	658	27,186	36,624	6	1,038	9,004	8,836	1,915	229
Telingana. Hyderabad. Suburbs including Secunderabad	97,368	51,561	45,802	3,548	598	10,980	1,542	37,082	43,587	1	75	14,360	13,609	2,734	505
Total......	172,861	88,459	84,402	6,081	888	18,108	2,195	64,268	80,211	7	1,108	23,364	22,445	4,649	784
Telingana. Atraf-i-Balda District	42,628	22,038	20,593	509	18	1,840	66	19,681	20,892	8	117	7,432	7,191	421	17
Mahabubnagar (Nagar Karnul) ...	55,610	27,796	27,814	849	58	2,026	91	24,911	27,649	10	16	10,727	10,181	721	50
Nalgonda	30,909	15,833	15,076	559	40	1,492	47	13,782	14,987	...	2	6,149	6,086	451	38
Warangal (Khamam)	42,882	22,257	20,625	852	145	2,126	171	19,273	20,309	6	...	8,523	8,082	734	138
Elgandal	44,018	22,598	21,420	568	9	1,999	74	20,025	21,884	1	8	9,151	8,676	467	9
Indur	50,198	24,894	25,299	697	17	1,600	89	22,584	25,248	18	...	9,552	8,525	596	11
Medak...	38,047	19,126	18,921	853	47	1,755	75	16,516	18,790	2	9	7,022	6,235	718	32
Mahratwara. Aurangabad	94,217	47,952	46,265	1,180	69	3,327	159	43,487	46,085	8	2	17,634	17,268	902	57
Birh	51,812	26,831	24,981	476	28	1,387	87	24,985	24,853	38	18	9,816	9,012	375	23
Nander	56,018	28,707	27,311	438	18	1,127	98	27,002	27,090	140	105	10,874	10,025	345	8
Naldrug	58,084	29,799	28,285	559	21	1,137	86	28,083	28,170	20	8	10,900	10,441	440	16
Bidar	114,748	58,385	56,858	1,028	82	2,202	62	55,143	56,191	12	23	21,814	20,422	847	78
Parbhani	66,696	34,098	32,598	579	11	1,515	31	31,998	32,547	6	9	12,711	12,083	436	7
Sirpur Tandur	10,006	5,065	4,941	114	...	259	8	4,691	4,936	1	2	2,072	1,999	97	...
Karnatic or Kanada. Gulbarga	95,179	48,685	46,494	856	50	1,938	66	45,891	46,375	5	8	17,474	16,797	697	45
Raichur	51,877	26,607	25,270	552	81	1,611	66	24,441	25,172	8	1	10,099	9,720	454	25
Lingasugur	61,624	31,491	30,133	604	47	1,600	78	29,279	30,001	8	7	11,799	11,262	488	40
Total Districts......	964,486	492,152	472,334	11,278	686	28,986	1,249	451,672	470,074	271	325	183,739	173,950	9,179	589
Total Districts including Hyderabad...	1,137,347	580,611	556,786	17,354	1,574	47,089	3,444	515,940	550,285	278	1,433	207,103	196,395	13,828	1,323
Railways......	1,319	885	434	28	8	199	16	658	415	...	...	149	149	19	2
Grand Total......	1,138,666	581,496	557,170	17,382	1,577	47,288	3,460	516,598	550,700	278	1,433	207,252	196,544	13,847	1,325

TABLE IX.

Education & Age. Mussulmans.

TABLE IX.

Education by Religion and Age. Part (C)—Mussulmans.—*Continued.*

District or State.	Age Period.—contd.															
	0—14—contd.						15—24									
	Literate.		Illiterate.		Unspecified.		Total.		Learning.		Literate.		Illiterate.		Unspecified.	
	Males.	Females.	Males.	Females.	Males.	Females.	Males.	Females.	Males.	Females.	Males.	Females.	Males.	Females.	Males.	Females.
	17	18	19	20	21	22	23	24	25	26	27	28	29	30	31	32
Telingana. — Hyderabad: City	181	47	6,908	8,560	...	...	7,793	10,200	528	40	1,566	206	5,699	9,954	...	...
Hyderabad: Suburbs including Secunderabad	556	304	11,070	12,800	...	...	9,947	10,699	686	56	2,498	489	6,763	10,154	...	...
Total......	737	351	17,978	21,360	...	...	17,740	20,899	1,214	96	4,064	695	12,462	20,108	...	...
Atraf-i-Balda District	90	12	6,911	7,162	...	...	3,457	3,701	75	1	394	17	2,988	3,683	...	...
Mahabubnagar (Nagar Karnul) ...	171	22	9,834	10,106	1	3	4,373	5,004	101	5	479	19	3,792	4,975	1	5
Nalgonda	94	5	5,604	6,048	...	...	2,661	2,715	87	1	379	19	2,195	2,695	...	...
Warangal (Khamam)	139	30	7,650	7,914	...	...	3,848	3,747	107	3	550	53	3,191	3,691	...	...
Elgandal	158	20	8,526	8,647	...	...	3,660	3,779	86	...	520	18	3,054	3,761	...	...
Indur...	70	6	8,880	8,508	6	...	3,649	4,452	95	3	301	11	3,252	4,438	1	...
Medak	154	11	6,155	6,191	...	1	2,869	3,149	123	4	399	19	2,347	3,126	...	...
Mahratwara. — Aurangabad	154	25	16,576	17,181	2	...	7,403	8,125	228	4	748	64	6,427	8,057	...	...
Birh	104	11	9,324	8,974	13	4	3,834	4,315	88	...	259	33	3,488	4,281	4	1
Nander	90	4	10,399	9,986	40	27	4,140	4,475	57	...	250	13	3,813	4,451	20	11
Naldrug	54	3	10,401	10,420	5	2	4,239	4,705	95	2	232	9	3,911	4,692	1	2
Bidar	127	9	20,837	20,332	3	3	8,540	9,368	155	2	489	13	7,945	9,348	1	5
Parbhani	95	6	12,178	12,019	2	1	4,743	5,391	120	3	330	12	4,292	5,376	1	...
Sirpur Tandur	19	...	1,956	1,999	...	...	756	805	12	...	47	3	697	802	...	...
Karnatic or Kanada. — Gulbarga...	89	10	16,687	16,740	1	2	7,167	7,787	147	2	434	28	6,585	7,762	1	...
Raichur	60	12	9,585	9,683	...	...	4,186	4,361	86	6	349	26	3,751	4,329	...	...
Lingasugur	92	6	11,224	11,214	...	2	5,058	5,211	88	3	330	27	4,638	5,178	2	3
Total Districts......	1,760	192	172,727	173,124	73	45	74,583	81,090	1,750	39	6,440	379	66,361	80,645	32	27
Total Districts including Hyderabad ...	2,497	543	190,705	194,484	73	45	92,323	101,989	2,964	135	10,504	1,074	78,823	100,753	32	27
Railways......	8	3	122	144	...	...	163	115	5	1	53	6	105	108	...	...
Grand Total......	2,505	546	190,827	194,628	73	45	92,486	102,104	2,969	136	10,557	1,080	78,928	100,861	32	27

TABLE IX.

Education by Religion and Age. Part (C)—Mussulmans.—*Concluded.*

District or State.	Age Period.—*contd.*																			
	25 and over.										Unspecified.									
	Total.		Learning.		Literate.		Illiterate.		Unspecified.		Total.		Learning.		Literate.		Illiterate		Unspecified.	
	Males.	Females.	Males.	Females.	Males.	Females.	Males.	Females.	Males.	Females.	Males.	Females.	Males.	Females.	Males.	Females.	Males.	Females.	Males.	Females.
	33	34	35	36	37	38	39	40	41	42	43	44	45	46	47	48	49	50	51	52
Telingana. Hyderabad { City	20,090	18,479	90	17	5,426	898	14,571	18,064	3	...	11	1,085	...	4	...	2	8	46	8	1,033
Suburbs including Secunderabad	27,243	21,235	128	34	7,876	725	19,238	20,476	1	...	11	259	...	3	...	24	11	157	...	75
Total......	47,333	39,714	218	51	13,302	1,123	33,809	38,540	4	...	22	1,344	...	7	...	26	19	203	8	1,108
Atraf-i-Balda District	11,132	9,497	13	...	1,356	37	9,762	9,460	1	...	22	204	...	...	...	...	20	87	2	117
Mahabubnagar (Nagar Karnul) ...	12,674	12,506	27	3	1,376	50	11,263	12,451	8	2	22	123	...	...	...	...	22	117	...	6
Nalgonda	7,021	6,183	21	6	1,019	22	5,981	6,155	...	...	2	92	...	...	...	1	2	89	...	2
Warangal (Khamam)	9,882	8,720	11	4	1,487	87	8,428	8,629	6	...	4	76	...	...	...	1	4	75	...	...
Elgandal	9,775	8,819	15	...	1,821	34	8,489	8,785	...	...	7	146	...	...	...	2	6	141	1	3
Indur	11,680	11,709	6	2	1,229	22	10,441	11,685	4	...	18	613	...	1	...	...	11	612	2	...
Medak	9,210	8,345	17	3	1,202	38	7,990	8,303	1	1	25	1,192	...	8	...	7	24	1,170	1	7
Mahratwara. { Aurangabad	22,881	20,712	50	8	2,424	70	20,401	20,634	6	...	34	165	...	...	1	...	38	163	...	2
Birh	13,158	11,553	13	...	1,024	43	12,106	11,501	15	9	23	101	...	...	...	...	22	97	1	4
Nander	13,665	12,456	36	10	787	81	12,764	12,325	78	40	28	355	...	...	...	...	26	328	2	27
Naldrug	14,649	13,037	23	3	851	24	13,761	13,006	14	4	11	52	1	...	...	...	10	52	...	...
Bidar	28,005	26,380	25	2	1,636	40	26,336	26,329	8	9	26	188	1	...	...	...	25	182	...	6
Parbhani	16,680	15,093	23	1	1,089	18	15,515	15,078	3	1	14	81	...	...	1	...	13	74	...	7
Sirpur Tandur	2,283	2,135	5	...	193	...	2,034	2,134	1	1	4	2	...	...	...	...	4	1	...	1
Karnatic or Kanada. { Gulbarga...	24,022	21,851	12	3	1,408	33	22,599	21,814	3	1	22	59	...	...	2	...	20	59	...	...
Raichur	12,322	11,182	12	...	1,202	28	11,105	11,153	3	1	...	7	...	...	...	...	...	7	...	...
Lingasugur	14,612	13,633	33	4	1,178	45	13,395	13,582	6	2	22	27	...	...	...	...	22	27	...	...
Total Districts......	233,551	213,811	342	49	20,732	667	21[illegible],320	218,024	157	71	279	3,483	2	9	4	11	264	3,281	9	182
Total Districts including Hyderabad ...	280,884	253,525	560	100	34,084	1,790	246,129	251,564	161	71	301	4,827	2	16	4	37	283	3,484	12	1,290
Railways......	573	170	4	...	188	7	431	163	...	...	...	...	...	...	...	...	...	...	...	...
Grand Total......	281,457	253,695	564	100	34,172	1,797	246,560	251,727	161	71	301	4,827	2	16	4	37	283	3,484	12	1,290

TABLE IX.

Education by Religion and Age. Part (D)—Christians.

District or State.	Total Christians.			Total by Education.								Age Period.											
				Learning.		Literate.		Illiterate.		Unspecified.		0—14										15—24	
												Total.		Learning.		Literate.		Illiterate.		Unspecified.		Total.	
	Total.	Males.	Females.	Males.	Females.	Males.	Females.	Males.	Females.	Males.	Females.	Males.	Females.	Males.	Females.	Males.	Females.	Males.	Females.	Males.	Females.	Males.	Females.
1	2	3	4	5	6	7	8	9	10	11	12	13	14	15	16	17	18	19	20	21	22	23	24
Telingana. Hyderabad. City	44	27	17	1	...	15	4	11	13	...	...	7	2	...	...	1	1	6	1	...	...	8	4
Hyderabad. Suburbs including Secunderabad	13,785	8,129	5,656	703	587	5,102	2,458	2,324	2,611	...	...	2,154	2,222	596	580	300	1,119	1,258	573	...	...	2,524	1,249
Total......	13,829	8,156	5,673	704	587	5,117	2,462	2,335	2,624	...	...	2,161	2,224	596	580	301	1,120	1,264	574	...	...	2,532	1,253
Atraf-i-Balda District	450	216	234	3	...	24	11	189	223	...	...	92	96	2	...	3	...	87	96	...	...	27	42
Mahabubnagar (Nagar Karnul) ...	121	67	54	14	14	20	11	33	29	...	...	80	24	11	12	1	...	18	12	...	...	11	9
Nalgonda	135	73	62	5	1	17	4	51	57	...	...	24	33	8	1	1	...	20	32	...	...	11	9
Warangal (Khamam)	1,484	794	690	28	7	143	51	623	682	...	...	321	279	25	5	13	10	283	264	...	...	142	174
Elgandal	193	122	71	49	4	46	27	27	40	...	...	59	25	44	4	1	4	14	17	...	...	21	29
Indur...	40	22	18	2	1	12	6	8	11	...	...	9	7	2	1	1	1	6	5	...	...	2	3
Medak...	106	53	53	7	1	24	11	22	41	...	...	17	15	4	...	...	...	13	15	...	...	10	11
Mahratwara. Aurangabad	1,929	960	969	62	87	216	80	678	852	4	...	378	447	57	36	17	9	304	402	...	...	126	161
Birh	148	86	62	11	9	35	10	40	43	...	...	31	26	8	8	2	...	21	18	...	...	10	17
Nander	2	2	...	...	...	2	...	...	...	...	...	...	...	...	...	...	...	...	...	...	...	...	...
Naldrug	214	107	107	5	...	11	4	91	102	...	1	45	46	5	...	...	...	40	46	...	...	10	15
Bidar	21	12	9	...	...	6	3	6	6	...	...	4	3	...	...	1	...	3	3	...	...	1	1
Parbhani	67	41	26	3	1	24	4	14	21	...	...	9	9	1	1	1	1	7	7	...	...	8	7
Sirpur Tandur	...	...	...	...	...	...	...	...	...	...	...	...	...	...	...	...	...	...	...	...	...	...	...
Karnatic or Kanada. Gulbarga	287	150	137	7	3	50	20	93	114	...	...	54	58	5	3	1	2	48	53	...	...	29	29
Raichur	335	177	158	11	8	100	61	66	89	...	...	57	61	11	8	9	17	37	36	...	...	34	37
Lingasugur	398	203	195	10	5	55	21	138	169	...	...	70	80	5	4	1	4	64	72	...	...	36	47
Total Districts......	5,930	3,085	2,845	217	91	785	324	2,079	2,429	4	1	1,200	1,209	183	83	52	48	965	1,078	...	...	478	591
Total Districts including Hyderabad ...	19,759	11,241	8,518	921	678	5,902	2,786	4,414	5,058	4	1	3,361	3,433	779	613	853	1,168	2,229	1,652	...	...	3,010	1,844
Railways......	670	389	281	36	42	256	134	97	105	...	...	119	116	33	40	26	24	60	52	...	...	96	67
Grand Total......	20,429	11,630	8,799	957	720	6,158	2,920	4,511	5,158	4	1	3,480	3,549	812	653	879	1,192	2,289	1,704	...	...	3,106	1,911

TABLE IX.

Education by Religion and Age. Part (D)—Christians.—*contd.*

District or State.	Age Period.—*contd.* 15—24—*contd.* Learning. Males.	Learning. Females.	Literate. Males.	Literate. Females.	Illiterate. Males.	Illiterate. Females.	Unspecified. Males.	Unspecified. Females.	25 and over. Total. Males.	Total. Females.	Learning. Males.	Learning. Females.	Literate. Males.	Literate. Females.	Illiterate. Males.	Illiterate. Females.	Unspecified. Males.	Unspecified. Females.	Unspecified. Total. Males.	Total. Females.	Learning. Males.	Learning. Females.	Literate. Males.	Literate. Females.	Illiterate. Males.	Illiterate. Females.	Unspecified. Males.	Unspecified. Females.
	25	26	27	28	29	30	31	32	33	34	35	36	37	38	39	40	41	42	43	44	45	46	47	48	49	50	51	52
Telingana. Hyderabad. City ...	1	...	7	1	...	3	...	...	12	11	...	...	7	2	5	9	...	...	...	...	...	...	...	...	...	...	...	...
Suburbs including Secunderabad ...	100	51	2,060	479	364	719	...	...	3,451	2,184	7	6	2,742	860	702	1,318	...	...	...	1	...	...	...	...	...	1	...	...
Total	101	51	2,067	480	364	722	...	...	3,463	2,195	7	6	2,749	862	707	1,327	...	...	...	1	...	...	...	...	...	1	...	...
Atraf-i-Balda District ...	1	...	5	4	21	38	...	...	97	96	...	...	16	7	81	89	...	...	...	...	...	...	...	...	...	...	...	...
Mahabubnagar (Nagar Karnul) ...	2	1	6	4	3	4	...	...	26	21	1	1	13	7	12	13	...	...	...	...	...	...	...	...	...	...	...	...
Nalgonda ...	1	...	3	2	7	7	...	...	38	20	1	...	13	2	24	18	...	...	...	...	...	...	...	...	...	...	...	...
Warangal (Khamam) ...	3	2	52	19	87	153	...	...	331	237	...	...	78	22	253	215	...	...	...	...	...	...	...	...	...	...	...	...
Elgandal ...	4	...	17	17	...	12	...	...	41	17	1	...	28	6	12	11	...	...	1	...	...	...	...	...	1	...	...	...
Indur ...	...	...	2	2	...	1	...	...	10	8	...	...	8	3	2	5	...	...	1	...	...	...	1	...	...	...	...	...
Medak ...	2	...	7	5	1	6	...	...	26	27	1	1	17	6	8	20	...	...	...	...	...	...	...	...	...	...	...	...
Mahratwara. Aurangabad ...	3	...	42	29	81	132	...	...	456	361	2	1	157	42	293	318	4	...	...	...	...	...	...	...	...	...		...
Birh ...	2	...	6	5	2	12	...	...	45	19	1	1	27	5	17	13	...	...	...	...	...	...	...	...	...	...	...	...
Nander ...	...	...	...	...	...	...	...	...	2	...	...	...	2	...	...	...	...	...	...	...	...	...	...	...	...	...	...	...
Naldrug ...	...	...	1	1	9	13	...	1	52	46	...	...	10	3	42	43	...	...	...	...	...	...	...	...	...	...	...	...
Bidar ...	...	...	1	...	...	1	...	...	7	5	...	...	4	3	3	2	...	...	...	...	...	...	...	...	...	...	...	...
Parbhani ...	1	...	5	1	2	6	...	...	24	10	1	...	18	2	5	8	...	...	...	...	...	...	...	...	...	...	...	...
Sirpur Tandur ...	...	...	...	...	...	...	...	...	...	...	...	...	...	...	...	...	...	...	...	...	...	...	...	...	...	...	...	...
Karnatic or Kanada. Gulbarga ...	1	...	11	5	17	24	...	...	67	50	1	...	38	13	28	37	...	...	...	...	...	...	...	...	...	...	...	...
Raichur ...	...	...	28	18	6	19	...	...	86	60	...	...	63	26	23	34	...	...	...	...	...	...	...	...	...	...	...	...
Lingasugur ...	3	1	9	12	24	34	...	...	97	68	2	...	45	5	50	63	...	...	...	...	...	...	...	...	...	...	...	...
Total Districts......	23	4	195	124	260	462	...	1	1,405	1,045	11	4	537	152	853	889	4	...	2	...	...	...	1	...	1	...	...	...
Total Districts including Hyderabad ...	124	55	2,262	604	624	1,184	...	1	4,868	3,240	18	10	3,286	1,014	1,560	2,216	4	...	2	1	...	...	1	...	1	1	...	...
Railways......	2	2	83	41	11	24	...	...	174	98	1	...	147	69	26	29	...	...	...	...	...	...	...	...	...	...	...	...
Grand Total......	126	57	2,345	645	635	1,208	...	1	5,042	3,338	19	10	3,433	1,088	1,586	2,245	4	...	2	1	...	...	1	...	1	1	...	...

TABLE IX.

Education by Religion and Age. Part (E) Sikhs.

District or State.	Total Sikhs.			Total by Education. Learning.		Literate.		Illiterate.		Unspecified.		Age Period. 0–14. Total.		Learning.		Literate.		Illiterate.		Unspecified.		15–24. Total.	
	Total.	Males.	Females.	Males.	Females.	Males.	Females.	Males.	Females.	Males.	Females.	Males.	Females.	Males.	Females.	Males.	Females.	Males.	Females.	Males.	Females.	Males.	Females.
1	2	3	4	5	6	7	8	9	10	11	12	13	14	15	16	17	18	19	20	21	22	23	24
Telingana. Hyderabad. City	59	29	30	1	...	12	4	16	26	...	...	5	9	1	...	...	1	4	8	...	...	3	7
Suburbs including Secunderabad	610	869	241	36	...	152	3	181	238	...	...	58	57	12	...	7	...	39	57	...	...	100	51
Total......	669	898	271	37	...	164	7	197	264	...	...	63	66	13	...	7	1	43	65	...	...	102	58
Atraf-i-Balda District...	254	143	111	1	...	57	2	85	109	...	...	33	20	1	...	9	...	23	20	...	...	23	27
Mahabubnagar (Nagar Karnul) ...	75	48	27	1	...	18	...	29	27	...	...	15	4	1	...	...	...	14	4	...	...	5	10
Nalgonda	111	63	48	3	1	26	1	34	46	...	...	19	13	8	1	...	...	16	12	...	...	12	13
Warangal (Khamam)	281	161	120	14	...	77	...	70	120	...	...	47	32	13	...	6	...	28	32	...	...	32	23
Elgandal	335	182	153	2	...	50	2	130	151	...	...	63	60	2	...	7	...	54	60	...	...	86	29
Indur	553	286	267	17	...	111	2	158	265	...	...	76	78	14	...	3	...	59	78	...	...	59	47
Medak...	218	121	92	6	...	64	2	51	90	...	...	27	26	6	...	8	...	18	26	...	...	24	13
Mahratwara. Aurangabad	275	119	156	14	...	35	...	70	156	...	...	46	60	13	...	5	...	28	60	...	...	10	30
Birh	245	130	115	8	...	19	...	103	115	...	...	44	35	4	...	1	...	39	35	...	...	23	17
Nander	1,130	581	549	22	...	131	...	423	549	5	...	192	189	20	...	13	...	157	189	2	...	85	91
Naldrug	5	4	1	...	...	4	...	...	1	...	...	...	...	...	...	...	...	...	...	...	...	2	...
Bidar	57	30	27	1	...	4	...	25	27	...	...	12	4	1	...	...	...	11	4	...	...	5	9
Parbhani	362	255	107	5	...	81	1	169	106	...	...	42	37	8	...	1	...	38	37	...	...	100	22
Sirpur Tandur	44	22	22	...	...	...	...	22	22	...	...	9	11	...	...	...	...	9	11	...	...	1	4
Karnatic or Kanada. Gulbarga	14	5	9	...	...	1	...	4	9	...	...	1	3	...	...	...	...	1	3	...	...	...	...
Raichur	4	3	1	...	...	...	...	3	1	...	...	1	...	...	...	...	...	1	...	...	...	...	1
Lingasugur	5	3	2	...	...	1	...	2	2	...	...	1	2	...	...	...	...	1	2	...	...	1	...
Total Districts......	3,963	2,156	1,807	94	1	679	10	1,378	1,796	5	...	628	574	81	1	48	...	497	573	2	...	418	386
Total Districts including Hyderabad...	4,632	2,554	2,078	131	1	843	17	1,575	2,060	5	...	691	640	94	1	55	1	540	638	2	...	521	894
Railways......	5	2	3	...	...	...	...	2	3	...	...	...	...	...	...	...	...	...	...	...	...	...	1
Grand Total......	4,637	2,556	2,081	131	1	843	17	1,577	2,063	5	...	691	640	94	1	55	1	540	638	2	...	521	895

TABLE IX.

Education by Religion and Age. Part (E) Sikhs.—*Continued.*

Age Period.—*contd.*

District or State.	15—24—*contd.* Learning. Males.	Learning. Females.	Literate. Males.	Literate. Females.	Illiterate. Males.	Illiterate. Females.	Unspecified. Males.	Unspecified. Females.	25 and over. Total. Males.	Total. Females.	Learning. Males.	Learning. Females.	Literate. Males.	Literate. Females.	Illiterate. Males.	Illiterate. Females.	Unspecified. Males.	Unspecified. Females.	Unspecified. Total. Males.	Total. Females.	Learning. Males.	Learning. Females.	Literate. Males.	Literate. Females.	Illiterate. Males.	Illiterate. Females.	Unspecified. Males.	Unspecified. Females.
	25	26	27	28	29	30	31	32	33	34	35	36	37	38	39	40	41	42	43	44	45	46	47	48	49	50	51	52
Telingana. Hyderabad. City	...	...	3	1	...	6	...	...	21	14	...	...	9	2	12	12	...	...	...	...	...	...	...	...	...	...	...	...
Suburbs including Secunderabad	16	...	48	1	36	50	...	...	211	133	8	...	97	2	106	131	...	...	...	...	...	...	...	...	...	...	...	...
Total......	16	...	51	2	36	56	...	...	232	147	8	...	106	4	118	143	...	...	...	...	...	...	...	...	...	...	...	...
Atraf-i-Balda District	...	...	11	1	12	26	...	...	87	64	...	...	37	1	50	63	...	...	...	...	...	...	...	...	...	...	...	...
Mahabubnagar (Nagar Karnul)	...	...	3	...	2	10	...	...	28	13	...	...	15	...	13	13	...	...	...	...	...	...	...	...	...	...	...	...
Nalgonda	...	...	8	1	4	12	...	...	32	22	...	...	18	...	14	22	...	...	...	...	...	...	...	...	...	...	...	...
Warangal (Khamam)	1	...	15	...	16	23	...	...	82	65	...	...	56	...	26	65	...	...	...	...	...	...	...	...	...	...	...	...
Elgandal	...	...	12	...	24	29	...	...	83	64	...	...	31	2	52	62	...	...	...	...	...	...	...	...	...	...	...	...
Indur	3	...	32	1	24	46	...	...	151	141	...	...	76	1	75	140	...	...	...	1	...	...	...	...	...	1	...	...
Medak	...	...	16	1	8	12	...	...	70	53	...	...	45	1	25	52	...	...	...	...	...	...	...	...	...	...	...	...
Mahratwara. Aurangabad	1	...	5	...	4	30	...	...	63	66	...	...	25	...	38	66	...	...	...	...	...	...	...	...	...	...	...	...
Birh	4	...	3	...	16	17	...	...	63	63	...	...	15	...	48	63	...	...	...	...	...	...	...	...	...	...	...	...
Nander	1	...	16	...	66	91	2	...	303	269	1	...	102	...	199	269	1	...	1	...	...	...	...	...	1	...	...	...
Naldrug	...	...	2	...	...	...	...	...	2	1	...	...	2	...	...	1	...	...	...	...	...	...	...	...	...	...	...	...
Bidar	...	...	1	...	4	9	...	...	13	14	...	...	3	...	10	14	...	...	...	...	...	...	...	...	...	...	...	...
Parbhani	1	...	34	...	65	22	...	...	113	48	1	...	46	1	66	47	...	...	...	...	...	...	...	...	...	...	...	...
Sirpur Tandur	...	...	...	...	1	4	...	...	12	7	...	...	...	...	12	7	...	...	...	...	...	...	...	...	...	...	...	...
Karnatic or Kanada. Gulbarga	...	...	...	...	...	...	...	...	4	6	...	...	1	...	3	6	...	...	...	...	...	...	...	...	...	...	...	...
Raichur	...	...	...	...	...	1	...	...	2	...	...	...	...	...	2	...	...	...	...	...	...	...	...	...	...	...	...	...
Lingasugur	...	...	...	...	1	...	...	...	1	...	...	...	1	...	...	...	...	...	...	...	...	...	...	...	...	...	...	...
Total Districts......	11	...	158	4	247	332	2	...	1,109	896	2	...	473	6	633	890	1	...	1	1	...	...	...	...	1	1	...	...
Total Districts including Hyderabad...	27	...	209	6	283	388	2	...	1,341	1,043	10	...	579	10	751	1,033	1	...	1	1	...	...	...	...	1	1	...	...
Railways......	...	...	...	...	...	1	...	...	2	2	...	...	...	...	2	2	...	...	...	...	...	...	...	...	...	...	...	...
Grand Total......	27	...	209	6	283	389	2	...	1,343	1,045	10	...	579	10	753	1,085	1	...	1	1	...	...	...	...	1	1	...	...

TABLE IX.

Education by Religion and Age. Part (F) Parsis.

District or State.	Total Parsis.			Total by Education. Learning.		Literate.		Illiterate.		Unspecified.		Age Period. 0—14 Total.		Learning.		Literate.		Illiterate.		Unspecified.		15—24 Total.	
	Total.	Males.	Females.	Males.	Females.	Males.	Females.	Males.	Females.	Males.	Females.	Males.	Females.	Males.	Females.	Males.	Females.	Males.	Females.	Males.	Females.	Males.	Females.
1	2	3	4	5	6	7	8	9	10	11	12	13	14	15	16	17	18	19	20	21	22	23	24
Tolingana. Hyderabad. City	1	1	...	...	...	1	...	...	...	...	...	...	...	...	...	...	...	...	...	...	...	...	...
Suburbs including Secunderabad	615	371	244	57	22	244	119	70	103	...	...	106	91	48	21	16	16	42	54	...	...	59	52
Total......	616	372	244	57	22	245	119	70	103	...	...	106	91	48	21	16	16	42	54	...	...	59	52
Atraf-i-Balda District	3	2	1	...	...	...	...	2	1	...	...	1	...	...	...	...	...	1	...	...	...	...	...
Mahabubnagar (Nagar Karnul) ...	...	...	...	...	...	...	...	...	...	...	...	...	...	...	...	...	...	...	...	...	...	...	...
Nalgonda	13	4	9	...	1	3	1	1	7	...	...	1	6	...	1	...	...	1	5	...	...	...	...
Warangal (Khamam)	40	28	12	2	...	20	8	6	4	...	...	4	2	1	...	...	...	3	2	...	...	2	4
Elgandal	3	2	1	...	...	2	1	...	...	...	...	...	...	...	...	...	...	...	...	...	...	...	...
Indur	7	2	5	...	2	2	2	...	1	...	...	...	3	...	2	...	...	...	1	...	...	...	2
Medak	...	...	...	...	...	...	...	...	...	...	...	...	...	...	...	...	...	...	...	...	...	...	...
Mahratwara. Aurangabad	130	68	62	9	2	43	35	16	25	...	...	20	21	4	1	4	7	12	13	...	...	16	16
Birh	19	11	8	3	2	7	3	1	3	...	...	2	3	1	2	1	...	...	1	...	...	5	3
Nander	7	6	1	1	...	5	1	...	...	...	...	1	...	...	...	1	...	...	...	...	...	1	1
Naldrug	10	10	...	...	...	10	...	...	...	...	...	1	...	...	...	1	...	...	...	...	...	4	...
Bidar	3	2	1	1	...	1	1	...	...	...	...	1	...	1	...	...	...	...	...	...	...	...	...
Parbhani	24	12	12	2	...	3	6	7	6	...	...	5	6	2	...	1	2	2	4	...	...	...	2
Sirpur Tandur	1	1	...	...	...	...	...	1	...	...	...	...	...	...	...	...	...	...	...	...	...	...	...
Karnatic or Kanada. Gulbarga	66	43	23	1	...	22	4	20	19	...	...	10	10	1	...	...	...	9	10	...	...	7	5
Raichur	34	20	14	6	6	7	4	7	4	...	...	10	7	6	6	...	...	4	1	...	...	1	1
Lingasugur	13	8	5	1	1	4	2	3	2	...	...	3	2	1	1	...	...	2	1	...	...	1	1
Total Districts......	373	219	154	26	14	129	68	64	72	...	...	59	60	17	13	8	9	34	38	...	...	37	35
Total Districts including Hyderabad ...	989	591	398	83	36	374	187	134	175	...	...	165	151	65	34	24	25	76	92	...	...	96	87
Railways......	69	37	32	3	4	24	18	10	10	...	...	13	16	3	4	1	4	9	8	...	...	4	2
Grand Total......	1,058	628	430	86	40	398	205	144	185	...	...	178	167	68	38	25	29	85	100	...	...	100	89

TABLE IX.

Education by Religion and Age. Part (F) Parsis.—*Continued.*

District or State.	Age Period.—Contd.																											
	15—24—contd.								25 and over.										Unspecified.									
	Learning.		Literate.		Illiterate.		Unspecified.		Total.		Learning.		Literate.		Illiterate.		Unspecified.		Total.		Learning.		Literate.		Illiterate.		Unspecified.	
	Males.	Females.	Males.	Females.	Males.	Females.	Males.	Females.	Males.	Females.	Males.	Females.	Males.	Females.	Males.	Females.	Males.	Females.	Males.	Females.	Males.	Females.	Males.	Females.	Males.	Females.	Males.	Females.
	25	26	27	28	29	30	31	32	33	34	35	36	37	38	39	40	41	42	43	44	45	46	47	48	49	50	51	52
Telingana. Hyderabad. City	...	...	...	...	...	...	...	...	1	...	...	...	1	...	...	...	...	...	...	...	...	...	...	...	...	...	...	...
Suburbs including Secunderabad	9	1	48	41	2	10	...	...	205	101	...	...	179	62	26	89	...	...	1	...	...	...	1	...	...	...	...	...
Total......	9	1	48	41	2	10	...	...	206	101	...	...	180	62	26	89	...	...	1	...	...	...	1	...	...	...	...	...
Atraf-i-Balda District...	...	...	...	...	...	...	...	...	1	1	...	...	...	...	1	1	...	...	...	...	...	...	...	...	...	...	...	...
Mahabubnagar (Nagar Karnul) ...	...	...	...	...	...	...	...	...	...	...	...	...	...	...	...	...	...	...	...	...	...	...	...	...	...	...	...	...
Nalgonda	...	...	...	...	...	...	...	...	3	3	...	...	8	1	...	2	...	...	...	...	...	...	...	...	...	...	...	...
Warangal (Khamam)	...	...	2	3	...	1	...	...	22	6	1	...	18	5	3	1	...	...	...	...	...	...	...	...	...	...	...	...
Elgandal	...	...	...	...	...	...	...	...	2	1	...	...	2	1	...	...	...	...	...	...	...	...	...	...	...	...	...	...
Indur	...	...	...	2	...	...	...	...	2	...	...	...	2	...	...	...	...	...	...	...	...	...	...	...	...	...	...	...
Medak	...	...	...	...	...	...	...	...	...	...	...	...	...	...	...	...	...	...	...	...	...	...	...	...	...	...	...	...
Mahratwara. Aurangabad	4	...	11	10	1	6	...	...	82	25	1	1	28	18	3	6	...	...	...	...	...	...	...	...	...	...	...	...
Birh	2	...	2	2	1	1	...	...	4	2	...	...	4	1	...	1	...	...	...	...	...	...	...	...	...	...	...	...
Nander	1	...	...	1	...	...	...	...	4	...	...	...	4	...	...	...	...	...	...	...	...	...	...	...	...	...	...	...
Naldrug	...	...	4	...	...	...	...	...	4	...	...	...	5	...	...	...	...	...	...	...	...	...	...	...	...	...	...	...
Bidar	...	...	...	...	...	...	...	...	1	1	...	...	1	1	...	...	...	...	...	...	...	...	...	...	...	...	...	...
Parbhani	...	...	...	2	...	...	...	...	7	4	...	...	2	2	5	2	...	...	...	...	...	...	...	...	...	...	...	...
Sirpur Tandur	...	...	...	...	...	...	...	...	1	...	...	...	...	...	1	...	...	...	...	...	...	...	...	...	...	...	...	...
Karnatic or Kanada. Gulbarga	...	...	3	2	4	3	...	...	26	8	...	...	19	2	7	6	...	...	...	...	...	...	...	...	...	...	...	...
Raichur	...	...	1	...	...	1	...	...	9	6	...	...	6	4	3	2	...	...	...	...	...	...	...	...	...	...	...	...
Lingasugur	...	...	1	1	...	...	...	...	4	2	...	...	3	1	1	1	...	...	...	...	...	...	...	...	...	...	...	...
Total Districts......	7	...	24	23	6	12	...	...	123	59	2	1	97	36	24	22	...	...	...	...	...	...	...	...	...	...	...	...
Total Districts including Hyderabad ...	16	1	72	64	8	22	...	...	329	160	2	1	277	98	50	61	...	...	1	...	...	...	1	...	...	...	...	...
Railways......	...	...	4	2	...	...	...	...	20	14	...	...	19	12	1	2	...	...	...	...	...	...	...	...	...	...	...	...
Grand Total......	16	1	76	66	8	22	...	...	349	174	2	1	296	110	51	63	...	...	1	...	...	...	1	...	...	...	...	...

TABLE IX.

Education by Religion and Age. Part (G) Jains.

District or State.	Total Jains. Total.	Total Jains. Males.	Total Jains. Females.	Total by Education. Learning. Males.	Learning. Females.	Literate. Males.	Literate. Females.	Illiterate. Males.	Illiterate. Females.	Unspecified. Males.	Unspecified. Females.	Age Period. 0—14. Total. Males.	0—14 Total. Females.	0—14 Learning. Males.	0—14 Learning. Females.	0—14 Literate. Males.	0—14 Literate. Females.	0—14 Illiterate. Males.	0—14 Illiterate. Females.	0—14 Unspecified. Males.	0—14 Unspecified. Females.	15—24 Total. Males.	15—24 Total. Females.
1	2	3	4	5	6	7	8	9	10	11	12	13	14	15	16	17	18	19	20	21	22	23	24
Telingana. Hyderabad. City	92	65	27	5	1	40	1	20	25	...	...	8	9	4	1	2	...	2	8	...	...	21	6
Suburbs including Secunderabad	111	75	36	3	...	61	1	11	35	...	...	9	9	3	...	2	...	4	9	...	...	26	11
Total......	203	140	63	8	1	101	2	31	60	...	...	17	18	7	1	4	...	6	17	...	...	47	17
Atraf-i-Balda District	94	49	45	3	...	28	...	18	45	...	...	17	12	3	...	3	...	11	12	...	...	8	12
Mahabubnagar (Nagar Karnul) ...	4	4	...	...	...	2	...	2	...	...	...	...	...	...	...	...	...	...	...	...	...	...	...
Nalgonda	...	...	...	...	...	...	...	...	...	...	...	...	...	...	...	...	...	...	...	...	...	...	...
Warangal (Khamam)	2	2	...	...	...	2	...	...	...	...	...	...	...	...	...	...	...	...	...	...	...	1	...
Elgandal	12	7	5	...	...	1	...	6	5	...	...	2	2	...	...	...	...	2	2	...	...	2	2
Indur...	129	61	68	2	...	35	...	24	68	...	...	14	23	2	...	6	...	6	23	...	...	8	12
Medak...	102	48	54	5	...	23	...	20	54	...	...	23	15	5	...	4	...	14	15	...	...	5	13
Mahratwara. Aurangabad	7,548	4,104	3,444	327	...	1,672	7	2,103	3,437	2	...	1,297	1,227	278	...	108	...	910	1,227	1	...	673	643
Birh	4,149	2,236	1,913	200	...	965	8	1,069	1,900	2	5	763	687	175	...	75	2	512	681	1	4	350	385
Nander	1,046	534	512	34	...	203	...	290	512	7	...	169	167	31	...	14	...	124	167	...	...	84	94
Naldrug	4,469	2,365	2,104	213	2	808	5	1,341	2,097	3	...	793	756	183	2	34	...	575	754	1	...	412	387
Bidar	1,617	866	751	50	1	250	...	565	750	1	...	254	250	46	1	15	...	193	249	...	...	138	116
Parbhani	5,449	2,847	2,602	131	...	750	10	1,966	2,591	...	1	866	850	115	...	56	1	695	849	...	...	417	459
Sirpur Tandur	248	128	120	3	...	7	...	118	120	...	...	54	50	2	...	...	...	52	50	...	...	20	18
Karnatic or Kanada. Gulbarga	1,575	831	744	52	...	243	4	532	740	4	...	252	230	49	...	10	2	193	228	...	...	136	128
Raichur	194	128	66	10	...	81	1	37	65	...	...	27	18	5	...	8	...	14	18	...	...	38	20
Lingasugur	999	612	387	37	...	308	...	266	387	1	...	169	130	37	...	23	...	109	130	...	...	186	85
Total Districts......	27,637	14,822	12,815	1,067	3	5,378	35	8,357	12,771	20	6	4,700	4,417	931	3	356	5	8,410	4,405	8	4	2,428	2,374
Total Districts including Hyderabad ...	27,840	14,962	12,878	1,075	4	5,479	37	8,388	12,831	20	6	4,717	4,435	938	4	360	5	8,416	4,422	8	4	2,475	2,391
Railways......	5	4	1	...	...	2	...	2	1	...	...	1	...	...	...	...	...	1	...	...	...	2	1
Grand Total......	27,845	14,966	12,879	1,075	4	5,481	37	8,390	12,832	20	6	4,718	4,435	938	4	360	5	8,417	4,422	8	4	2,477	2,392

TABLE IX.

Education by Religion and Age. Part (G) Jains.—*Continued.*

District or State.	Age Period.—*Contd.* 15—24—*contd.* Learning. Males.	Learning. Females.	Literate. Males.	Literate. Females.	Illiterate. Males.	Illiterate. Females.	Unspecified. Males.	Unspecified. Females.	25 and over. Total. Males.	Total. Females.	Learning. Males.	Learning. Females.	Literate. Males.	Literate. Females.	Illiterate. Males.	Illiterate. Females.	Unspecified. Males.	Unspecified. Females.	Unspecified. Total. Males.	Total. Females.	Learning. Males.	Learning. Females.	Literate. Males.	Literate. Females.	Illiterate. Males.	Illiterate. Females.	Unspecified. Males.	Unspecified. Females.
	25	26	27	28	29	30	31	32	33	34	35	36	37	38	39	40	41	42	43	44	45	46	47	48	49	50	51	52
Telingana. Hyderabad. City ...	1	...	14	...	6	6	...	...	86	12	...	...	24	1	12	11	...	...	...	...	...	...	...	...	...	...	...	...
Suburbs including Secunderabad ...	...	...	26	...	...	11	...	...	40	16	...	...	33	1	7	15	...	...	...	...	...	...	...	...	...	...	...	...
Total......	1	...	40	...	6	17	...	...	76	28	...	...	57	2	19	26	...	...	...	...	...	...	...	...	...	...	...	...
Atraf-i-Balda District ...	...	...	8	...	...	12	...	...	24	21	...	...	17	...	7	21	...	...	...	...	...	...	...	...	...	...	...	...
Mahabubnagar (Nagar Karnul) ...	...	...	...	...	...	...	...	...	4	...	...	...	2	...	2	...	...	...	...	...	...	...	...	...	...	...	...	...
Nalgonda ...	...	...	...	...	...	...	...	...	...	...	...	...	...	...	...	...	...	...	...	...	...	...	...	...	...	...	...	...
Warangal (Khamam) ...	...	...	1	...	...	...	...	...	1	...	...	...	1	...	...	...	...	...	...	...	...	...	...	...	...	...	...	...
Elgandal ...	...	...	...	...	2	2	...	...	3	1	...	...	1	...	2	1	...	...	...	...	...	...	...	...	...	...	...	...
Indur ...	...	...	4	...	4	12	...	...	39	33	...	...	25	...	14	33	...	...	...	...	...	...	...	...	...	...	...	...
Medak... ...	...	...	4	...	1	13	...	...	20	26	...	...	15	...	5	26	...	...	...	...	...	...	...	...	...	...	...	...
Mahratwara. Aurangabad ...	44	...	355	...	274	643	...	...	2,134	1,571	5	...	1,209	7	919	1,564	1	...	...	3	...	...	...	...	...	3	...	...
Birh ...	23	...	177	4	150	381	...	...	1,123	840	2	...	713	2	407	837	1	1	...	1	...	...	...	...	...	1	...	...
Nander ...	2	...	48	...	34	94	...	...	281	250	1	...	141	...	132	250	7	...	...	1	...	...	...	...	...	1	...	...
Naldrug ...	27	...	187	1	198	386	...	...	1,160	961	3	...	587	4	568	957	2	...	...	...	...	...	...	...	...	...	...	...
Bidar ...	4	...	44	...	90	116	...	...	474	385	...	...	191	...	282	385	1	...	...	...	...	...	...	...	...	...	...	...
Parbhani ...	13	...	126	1	278	457	...	1	1,564	1,292	3	...	568	8	993	1,284	...	...	...	1	...	...	...	...	...	1	...	...
Sirpur Tandur ...	1	...	1	...	18	18	...	...	54	52	...	...	6	...	48	52	...	...	...	...	...	...	...	...	...	...	...	...
Karnatic or Kanada. Gulbarga ...	3	...	46	...	87	128	...	...	443	386	...	...	187	2	252	384	4	...	...	...	...	...	...	...	...	...	...	...
Raichur ...	4	...	28	1	6	19	...	...	63	28	1	...	45	...	17	28	...	...	...	...	...	...	...	...	...	...	...	...
Lingasugur ...	...	...	94	...	42	85	...	...	307	172	...	...	191	...	115	172	1	...	...	...	...	...	...	...	...	...	...	...
Total Districts......	121	...	1,123	7	1,184	2,366	...	1	7,694	6,018	15	...	3,899	23	3,768	5,994	17	1	...	6	...	...	...	...	...	6	...	...
Total Districts including Hyderabad ...	122	...	1,163	7	1,190	2,383	...	1	7,770	6,046	15	...	3,956	25	3,782	6,020	17	1	...	6	...	...	...	...	...	6	...	...
Railways......	...	...	1	...	1	1	...	...	1	...	...	...	1	...	...	...	...	...	...	...	...	...	...	...	...	...	...	...
Grand Total......	122	...	1,164	7	1,191	2,384	...	1	7,771	6,046	15	...	3,957	25	3,782	6,020	17	1	...	6	...	...	...	...	...	6	...	...

TABLE IX.

Education by Religion and Age. Part (H)—Gonds.

District or State.	Total Gonds.			Total by Education.								Age Period.											
				Learning.		Literate.		Illiterate.		Unspecified.		0—14										15—24	
												Total.		Learning.		Literate.		Illiterate.		Unspecified.		Total.	
	Total.	Males.	Females.	Males.	Females.	Males.	Females.	Males.	Females.	Males.	Females.	Males.	Females.	Males.	Females.	Males.	Females.	Males.	Females.	Males	Females.	Males.	Females.
1	2	3	4	5	6	7	8	9	10	11	12	18	14	15	16	17	18	19	20	21	22	23	24
Telingana. Hyderabad. City	...	...	...	...	...	...	...	...	...	...	...	...	...	...	...	...	...	...	...	...	...	...	...
Suburbs including Secunderabad	...	...	...	...	...	...	...	...	...	...	...	...	...	...	...	...	...	...	...	...	...	...	...
Total	...	...	...	...	...	...	...	...	...	...	...	...	...	...	...	...	...	...	...	...	...	...	...
Atraf-i-Balda District	...	...	...	...	...	...	...	...	...	...	...	...	...	...	...	...	...	...	...	...	...	...	...
Mahabubnagar (Nagar Karnul)	...	...	...	...	...	...	...	...	...	...	...	...	...	...	...	...	...	...	...	...	...	...	...
Nalgonda	...	...	...	...	...	...	...	...	...	...	...	...	...	...	...	...	...	...	...	...	...	...	...
Warangal (Khamam)	...	...	...	...	...	...	...	...	...	...	...	...	...	...	...	...	...	...	...	...	...	...	...
Elgandal	...	...	...	...	...	...	...	...	...	...	...	...	...	...	...	...	...	...	...	...	...	...	...
Indur	538	273	265	8	...	5	...	260	265	...	...	116	108	7	...	...	...	109	108	...	...	84	48
Medak	...	...	...	...	...	...	...	...	...	...	...	...	...	...	...	...	...	...	...	...	...	...	...
Mahratwara. Aurangabad	...	...	...	...	...	...	...	...	...	...	...	...	...	...	...	...	...	...	...	...	...	...	...
Birh	...	...	...	...	...	...	...	...	...	...	...	...	...	...	...	...	...	...	...	...	...	...	...
Nander	6	4	2	...	...	...	...	4	2	...	...	2	1	...	...	...	...	2	1	...	...	1	...
Naldrug	...	...	...	...	...	...	...	...	...	...	...	...	...	...	...	...	...	...	...	...	...	...	...
Bidar	...	...	...	...	...	...	...	...	...	...	...	...	...	...	...	...	...	...	...	...	...	...	...
Parbhani	...	...	...	...	...	...	...	...	...	...	...	...	...	...	...	...	...	...	...	...	...	...	...
Sirpur Tandur	28,116	14,360	13,756	7	...	6	1	14,346	13,753	1	2	6,058	5,888	2	...	1	1	6,055	5,887	...	...	1,821	2,164
Karnatic or Kanada. Gulbarga	...	...	...	...	...	...	...	...	...	...	...	...	...	...	...	...	...	...	...	...	...	...	...
Raichur	...	...	...	...	...	...	...	...	...	...	...	...	...	...	...	...	...	...	...	...	...	...	...
Lingasugur	...	...	...	...	...	...	...	...	...	...	...	...	...	...	...	...	...	...	...	...	...	...	...
Total Districts	28,660	14,637	14,023	15	...	11	1	14,610	14,020	1	2	6,176	5,997	9	...	1	1	6,166	5,996	...	...	1,856	2,212
Total Districts including Hyderabad	28,660	14,637	14,023	15	...	11	1	14,610	14,020	1	2	6,176	5,997	9	...	1	1	6,166	5,996	...	...	1,856	2,212
Railways	...	...	...	...	...	...	...	...	...	...	...	...	...	...	...	...	...	...	...	...	...	...	...
Grand Total	28,660	14,637	14,023	15	...	11	1	14,610	14,020	1	2	6,176	5,997	9	...	1	1	6,166	5,996	...	...	1,856	2,212

TABLE IX.

Education by Religion and Age. Part (H) Gonds.—*Continued.*

District or State.	Age Period.—*contd.* 15-24—*contd.* Learning. Males.	Learning. Females.	Literate. Males.	Literate. Females.	Illiterate. Males.	Illiterate. Females.	Unspecified. Males.	Unspecified. Females.	25 and over. Total. Males.	Total. Females.	Learning. Males.	Learning. Females.	Literate. Males.	Literate. Females.	Illiterate. Males.	Illiterate. Females.	Unspecified. Males.	Unspecified. Females.	Unspecified. Total. Males.	Total. Females.	Learning. Males.	Learning. Females.	Literate. Males.	Literate. Females.	Illiterate. Males.	Illiterate. Females.	Unspecified. Males.	Unspecified. Females.
	25	26	27	28	29	30	31	32	33	34	35	36	37	38	39	40	41	42	43	44	45	46	47	48	49	50	51	52
Telingana. Hyderabad. City	...	...	...	...	...	...	...	...	...	...	...	...	...	...	...	...	...	...	...	...	...	...	...	...	...	...	...	...
Suburbs including Secunderabad	...	...	...	...	...	...	...	...	...	...	...	...	...	...	...	...	...	...	...	...	...	...	...	...	...	...	...	...
Total......	...	...	...	...	...	...	...	...	...	...	...	...	...	...	...	...	...	...	...	...	...	...	...	...	...	...	...	...
Atraf-i-Balda District	...	...	...	...	...	...	...	...	...	...	...	...	...	...	...	...	...	...	...	...	...	...	...	...	...	...	...	...
Mahabubnagar (Nagar Karnul) ...	...	...	...	...	...	...	...	...	...	...	...	...	...	...	...	...	...	...	...	...	...	...	...	...	...	...	...	...
Nalgonda	...	...	...	...	...	...	...	...	...	...	...	...	...	...	...	...	...	...	...	...	...	...	...	...	...	...	...	...
Warangal (Khamam)	...	...	...	...	...	...	...	...	...	...	...	...	...	...	...	...	...	...	...	...	...	...	...	...	...	...	...	...
Elgandal	...	...	...	...	...	...	...	...	...	...	...	...	...	...	...	...	...	...	...	...	...	...	...	...	...	...	...	...
Indur	1	...	...	...	33	48	...	...	123	109	...	...	5	...	118	109	...	...	...	...	...	...	...	...	...	...	...	...
Medak...	...	...	...	...	...	...	...	...	...	...	...	...	...	...	...	...	...	...	...	...	...	...	...	...	...	...	...	...
Mahratwara. Aurangabad	...	...	...	...	...	...	...	...	...	...	...	...	...	...	...	...	...	...	...	...	...	...	...	...	...	...	...	...
Birh	...	...	...	...	...	...	...	...	...	...	...	...	...	...	...	...	...	...	...	...	...	...	...	...	...	...	...	...
Nander	...	...	...	...	1	...	...	...	1	1	...	...	...	...	1	1	...	...	...	...	...	...	...	...	...	...	...	...
Naldrug	...	...	...	...	...	...	...	...	...	...	...	...	...	...	...	...	...	...	...	...	...	...	...	...	...	...	...	...
Bidar	...	...	...	...	...	...	...	...	...	...	...	...	...	...	...	...	...	...	...	...	...	...	...	...	...	...	...	...
Parbhani	...	...	...	...	...	...	...	...	...	...	...	...	...	...	...	...	...	...	...	...	...	...	...	...	...	...	...	...
Sirpur Tandur	1	...	3	...	1,817	2,164	...	...	6,477	5,699	4	...	2	...	6,471	5,699	...	...	4	5	...	...	...	...	3	3	1	2
Karnatic or Kanada. Gulbarga	...	...	...	...	...	...	...	...	...	...	...	...	...	...	...	...	...	...	...	...	...	...	...	...	...	...	...	...
Raichur	...	...	...	...	...	...	...	...	...	...	...	...	...	...	...	...	...	...	...	...	...	...	...	...	...	...	...	...
Lingasugur	...	...	...	...	...	...	...	...	...	...	...	...	...	...	...	...	...	...	...	...	...	...	...	...	...	...	...	...
Total Districts......	2	...	3	...	1,851	2,212	...	...	6,601	5,809	4	...	7	...	6,590	5,809	...	...	4	5	...	...	...	...	3	3	1	2
Total Districts including Hyderabad...	2	...	3	...	1,851	2,212	...	...	6,601	5,809	4	...	7	...	6,590	5,809	...	...	4	5	...	...	...	...	3	3	1	2
Railways......	...	...	...	...	...	...	...	...	...	...	...	...	...	...	...	...	...	...	...	...	...	...	...	...	...	...	...	...
Grand Total......	2	...	3	...	1,851	2,212	...	...	6,601	5,809	4	...	7	...	6,590	5,809	...	...	4	5	...	...	...	...	3	3	1	2

TABLE IX.

Education by Religion and Age. Part (I)—Bhils.

District or State.	Total Bhils.			Total by Education. Learning.		Literate.		Illiterate.		Unspecified.		Age Period. 0–14 Total.		Learning.		Literate.		Illiterate.		Unspecified.		15–24 Total.	
	Total.	Males.	Females.	Males.	Females.	Males.	Females.	Males.	Females.	Males.	Females.	Males.	Females.	Males.	Females.	Males.	Females.	Males.	Females.	Males.	Females.	Males.	Females.
1	2	3	4	5	6	7	8	9	10	11	12	13	14	15	16	17	18	19	20	21	22	23	24
Telingana. Hyderabad. City	...	...	...	...	...	...	...	...	...	...	...	...	...	...	...	...	...	...	...	...	...	...	...
Suburbs including Secunderabad	...	...	...	...	...	...	...	...	...	...	...	...	...	...	...	...	...	...	...	...	...	...	...
Total......	...	...	...	...	...	...	...	...	...	...	...	...	...	...	...	...	...	...	...	...	...	...	...
Atraf-i-Balda District	...	...	...	...	...	...	...	...	...	...	...	...	...	...	...	...	...	...	...	...	...	...	...
Mahabubnagar (Nagar Karnul)	...	...	...	...	...	...	...	...	...	...	...	...	...	...	...	...	...	...	...	...	...	...	...
Nalgonda	...	...	...	...	...	...	...	...	...	...	...	...	...	...	...	...	...	...	...	...	...	...	...
Warangal (Khamam)	...	...	...	...	...	...	...	...	...	...	...	...	...	...	...	...	...	...	...	...	...	...	...
Elgandal	...	...	...	...	...	...	...	...	...	...	...	...	...	...	...	...	...	...	...	...	...	...	...
Indur	...	...	...	...	...	...	...	...	...	...	...	...	...	...	...	...	...	...	...	...	...	...	...
Medak	...	...	...	...	...	...	...	...	...	...	...	...	...	...	...	...	...	...	...	...	...	...	...
Mahratwara. Aurangabad	...	...	...	...	...	...	...	...	...	...	...	...	...	...	...	...	...	...	...	...	...	...	...
Birh	...	...	...	...	...	...	...	...	...	...	...	...	...	...	...	...	...	...	...	...	...	...	...
Nander	...	...	...	...	...	...	...	...	...	...	...	...	...	...	...	...	...	...	...	...	...	...	...
Naldrug	...	...	...	...	...	...	...	...	...	...	...	...	...	...	...	...	...	...	...	...	...	...	...
Bidar	...	...	...	...	...	...	...	...	...	...	...	...	...	...	...	...	...	...	...	...	...	...	...
Parbhani	...	...	...	...	...	...	...	...	...	...	...	...	...	...	...	...	...	...	...	...	...	...	...
Sirpur Tandur	470	285	285	...	...	...	...	285	285	...	...	115	104	...	...	...	...	115	104	...	...	33	53
Karnatic or Kanada. Gulbarga	...	...	...	...	...	...	...	...	...	...	...	...	...	...	...	...	...	...	...	...	...	...	...
Raichur	...	...	...	...	...	...	...	...	...	...	...	...	...	...	...	...	...	...	...	...	...	...	...
Lingsugur	...	...	...	...	...	...	...	...	...	...	...	...	...	...	...	...	...	...	...	...	...	...	...
Total Districts......	470	285	285	...	...	...	...	285	285	...	...	115	104	...	...	...	...	115	104	...	...	33	53
Total Districts including Hyderabad ...	470	285	285	...	...	...	...	285	285	...	...	115	104	...	...	...	...	115	104	...	...	33	53
Railways......	...	...	...	...	...	...	...	...	...	...	...	...	...	...	...	...	...	...	...	...	...	...	...
Grand Total......	470	285	285	...	...	...	...	285	285	...	...	115	104	...	...	...	...	115	104	...	...	33	53

TABLE IX.

Education by Religion and Age. Part (I)—Bhils—*Continued.*

District or State.	Age Period.—*contd.*																											
	15—24—*contd.*								25 and over.										Unspecified.									
	Learning.		Literate.		Illiterate.		Unspecified.		Total.		Learning.		Literate.		Illiterate.		Unspecified.		Total.		Learning.		Literate.		Illiterate.		Unspecified.	
	Males.	Females.	Males.	Females.	Males.	Females.	Males.	Females.	Males.	Females.	Males.	Females.	Males.	Females.	Males.	Females.	Males.	Females.	Males.	Females.	Males.	Females.	Males.	Females.	Males.	Females.	Males.	Females.
	25	26	27	28	29	30	31	32	33	34	35	36	37	38	39	40	41	42	43	44	45	46	47	48	49	50	51	52
Telingana. Hyderabad. City ...	...	...	...	...	...	...	...	...	...	...	...	...	...	...	...	...	...	...	...	...	...	...	...	...	...	...	...	...
Suburbs including Secunderabad ...	...	...	...	...	...	...	...	...	...	...	...	...	...	...	...	...	...	...	...	...	...	...	...	...	...	...	...	...
Total......	...	...	...	...	...	...	...	...	...	...	...	...	...	...	...	...	...	...	...	...	...	...	...	...	...	...	...	...
Atraf-i-Balda District ...	...	...	...	...	...	...	...	...	...	...	...	...	...	...	...	...	...	...	...	...	...	...	...	...	...	...	...	...
Mahabubnagar (Nagar Karnul) ...	...	...	...	...	...	...	...	...	...	...	...	...	...	...	...	...	...	...	...	...	...	...	...	...	...	...	...	...
Nalgonda ...	...	...	...	...	...	...	...	...	...	...	...	...	...	...	...	...	...	...	...	...	...	...	...	...	...	...	...	...
Warangal (Khamam) ...	...	...	...	...	...	...	...	...	...	...	...	...	...	...	...	...	...	...	...	...	...	...	...	...	...	...	...	...
Elgandal ...	...	...	...	...	...	...	...	...	...	...	...	...	...	...	...	...	...	...	...	...	...	...	...	...	...	...	...	...
Indur.. ...	...	...	...	...	...	...	...	...	...	...	...	...	...	...	...	...	...	...	...	...	...	...	...	...	...	...	...	...
Medak ...	...	...	...	...	...	...	...	...	...	...	...	...	...	...	...	...	...	...	...	...	...	...	...	...	...	...	...	...
Mahratwara. Aurangabad ...	...	...	...	...	...	...	...	...	...	...	...	...	...	...	...	...	...	...	...	...	...	...	...	...	...	...	...	...
Birh ...	...	...	...	...	...	...	...	...	...	...	...	...	...	...	...	...	...	...	...	...	...	...	...	...	...	...	...	...
Nander ...	...	...	...	...	...	...	...	...	...	...	...	...	...	...	...	...	...	...	...	...	...	...	...	...	...	...	...	...
Naldrug ...	...	...	...	...	...	...	...	...	...	...	...	...	...	...	...	...	...	...	...	...	...	...	...	...	...	...	...	...
Bidar ...	...	...	...	...	...	...	...	...	...	...	...	...	...	...	...	...	...	...	...	...	...	...	...	...	...	...	...	...
Parbhani ...	...	...	...	...	...	...	...	...	...	...	...	...	...	...	...	...	...	...	...	...	...	...	...	...	...	...	...	...
Sirpur Tandur ...	...	...	...	...	33	53	...	...	87	78	...	...	...	...	87	78	...	...	...	...	...	...	...	...	...	...	...	...
Karnatic or Kanada. Gulbarga ...	...	...	...	...	...	...	...	...	...	...	...	...	...	...	...	...	...	...	...	...	...	...	...	...	...	...	...	...
Raichur ...	...	...	...	...	...	...	...	...	...	...	...	...	...	...	...	...	...	...	...	...	...	...	...	...	...	...	...	...
Lingasugur ...	...	...	...	...	...	...	...	...	...	...	...	...	...	...	...	...	...	...	...	...	...	...	...	...	...	...	...	...
Total Districts......	...	...	...	...	33	53	...	...	87	78	...	...	...	...	87	78	...	...	...	...	...	...	...	...	...	...	...	...
Total Districts including Hyderabad...	...	...	...	...	33	53	...	...	87	78	...	...	...	...	87	78	...	...	...	...	...	...	...	...	...	...	...	...
Railways......	...	...	...	...	...	...	...	...	...	...	...	...	...	...	...	...	...	...	...	...	...	...	...	...	...	...	...	...
Grand Total......	...	...	...	...	83	58	...	...	87	78	...	...	...	...	87	78	...	...	...	...	...	...	...	...	...	...	...	...

TABLE IX.

Education by Religion and Age. Part (J)—Jews.

District or State.	Total Jews.			Total by Education. Learning.		Literate.		Illiterate.		Unspecified.		Age Period. 0—14 Total.		Learning.		Literate.		Illiterate.		Unspecified.		Total. 15—24	
	Total.	Males.	Females.	Males.	Females.	Males.	Females.	Males.	Females.	Males.	Females.	Males.	Females.	Males.	Females.	Males.	Females.	Males.	Females.	Males.	Females.	Males.	Females.
1	2	3	4	5	6	7	8	9	10	11	12	13	14	15	16	17	18	19	20	21	22	23	24
Telingana — Hyderabad — City	...	...	...	...	...	...	...	...	...	...	...	...	...	...	...	...	...	...	...	...	...	...	...
Telingana — Hyderabad — Suburbs including Secunderabad	21	7	14	1	1	4	...	2	13	...	...	1	8	1	1	...	...	...	7	...	...	2	3
Total......	21	7	14	1	1	4	...	2	13	...	...	1	8	1	1	...	...	...	7	...	...	2	3
Atraf-i Balda District	...	...	...	...	...	...	...	...	...	...	...	...	...	...	...	...	...	...	...	...	...	...	...
Mahabubnagar (Nagar Karnul)	...	...	...	...	...	...	...	...	...	...	...	...	...	...	...	...	...	...	...	...	...	...	...
Nalgonda	...	...	...	...	...	...	...	...	...	...	...	...	...	...	...	...	...	...	...	...	...	...	...
Warangal (Khamam)	...	...	...	...	...	...	...	...	...	...	...	...	...	...	...	...	...	...	...	...	...	...	...
Elgandal	...	...	...	...	...	...	...	...	...	...	...	...	...	...	...	...	...	...	...	...	...	...	...
Indur	...	...	...	...	...	...	...	...	...	...	...	...	...	...	...	...	...	...	...	...	...	...	...
Medak	...	...	...	...	...	...	...	...	...	...	...	...	...	...	...	...	...	...	...	...	...	...	...
Mahratwara — Aurangabad	...	...	...	...	...	...	...	...	...	...	...	...	...	...	...	...	...	...	...	...	...	...	...
Birh	...	...	...	...	...	...	...	...	...	...	...	...	...	...	...	...	...	...	...	...	...	...	...
Nander	...	...	...	...	...	...	...	...	...	...	...	...	...	...	...	...	...	...	...	...	...	...	...
Naldrug	...	...	...	...	...	...	...	...	...	...	...	...	...	...	...	...	...	...	...	...	...	...	...
Bidar	...	...	...	...	...	...	...	...	...	...	...	...	...	...	...	...	...	...	...	...	...	...	...
Parbhani	...	...	...	...	...	...	...	...	...	...	...	...	...	...	...	...	...	...	...	...	...	...	...
Sirpur Tandur	...	...	...	...	...	...	...	...	...	...	...	...	...	...	...	...	...	...	...	...	...	...	...
Karnatic or Kanada — Gulbarga	...	...	...	...	...	...	...	...	...	...	...	...	...	...	...	...	...	...	...	...	...	...	...
Raichur	...	...	...	...	...	...	...	...	...	...	...	...	...	...	...	...	...	...	...	...	...	...	...
Lingasugur	...	...	...	...	...	...	...	...	...	...	...	...	...	...	...	...	...	...	...	...	...	...	...
Total Districts......	...	...	...	...	...	...	...	...	...	...	...	...	...	...	...	...	...	...	...	...	...	...	...
Total Districts including Hyderabad ...	21	7	14	1	1	4	...	2	13	...	...	1	8	1	1	...	...	...	7	...	...	2	3
Railways......	5	3	2	...	...	2	...	1	2	...	...	1	1	...	...	...	...	1	1	...	...	...	1
Grand Total......	26	10	16	1	1	6	...	3	15	...	...	2	9	1	1	...	...	1	8	...	...	2	4

TABLE IX.

Education by Religion and Age. Part (J) Jews.—*Continued.*

District or State.	Age Period.—*Contd.* 15—24—*Contd.* Learning. Males.	Learning. Females.	Literate. Males.	Literate. Females.	Illiterate. Males.	Illiterate. Females.	Unspecified. Males.	Unspecified. Females.	25 and over. Total. Males.	Total. Females.	Learning. Males.	Learning. Females.	Literate. Males.	Literate. Females.	Illiterate. Males.	Illiterate. Females.	Unspecified. Males.	Unspecified. Females.	Unspecified. Total. Males.	Total. Females.	Learning. Males.	Learning. Females.	Literate. Males.	Literate. Females.	Illiterate. Males.	Illiterate. Females.	Unspecified. Males.	Unspecified. Females.
	25	26	27	28	29	30	31	32	33	34	35	36	37	38	39	40	41	42	43	44	45	46	47	48	49	50	51	52
Telingana. Hyderabad. City	...	...	...	...	...	...	...	...	...	...	...	...	...	...	...	...	...	...	...	...	...	...	...	...	...	...	...	...
Suburbs including Secunderabad	...	...	2	...	...	3	...	...	4	3	...	...	2	...	2	3	...	...	...	...	...	...	...	...	...	...	...	...
Total......	...	...	2	...	...	3	...	...	4	3	...	...	2	...	2	3	...	...	...	...	...	...	...	...	...	...	...	...
Atraf-i-Balda District	...	...	...	...	...	...	...	...	...	...	...	...	...	...	...	...	...	...	...	...	...	...	...	...	...	...	...	...
Mahabubnagar (Nagar Karnul) ...	...	...	...	...	...	...	...	...	...	...	...	...	...	...	...	...	...	...	...	...	...	...	...	...	...	...	...	...
Nalgonda	...	...	...	...	...	...	...	...	...	...	...	...	...	...	...	...	...	...	...	...	...	...	...	...	...	...	...	...
Warangal (Khamam)	...	...	...	...	...	...	...	...	...	...	...	...	...	...	...	...	...	...	...	...	...	...	...	...	...	...	...	...
Elgandal	...	...	...	...	...	...	...	...	...	...	...	...	...	...	...	...	...	...	...	...	...	...	...	...	...	...	...	...
Indur	...	...	...	...	...	...	...	...	...	...	...	...	...	...	...	...	...	...	...	...	...	...	...	...	...	...	...	...
Medak	...	...	...	...	...	...	...	...	...	...	...	...	...	...	...	...	...	...	...		...	...	...	...	...	...	...	...
Mahratwara. Aurangabad	...	...	...	...	...	...	...	...	...	...	...	...	...	...	...	...	...	...	...	...	...	...	...	...	...	...	...	...
Birh	...	...	...	...	...	...	...	...	...	...	...	...	...	...	...	...	...	...	...	...	...	...	...	...	...	...	...	...
Nander	...	...	...	...	...	...	...	...	...	...	...	...	...	...	...	...	...	...	...	...	...	...	...	...	...	...	...	...
Naldrug	...	...	...	...	...	...	...	...	...	...	...	...	...	...	...	...	...	...	...	...	...	...	...	...	...	...	...	...
Bidar	...	...	...	...	...	...	...	...	...	...	...	...	...	...	...	...	...	...	...	...	...	...	...	...	...	...	...	...
Parbhani	...	...	...	...	...	...	...	...	...	...	...	...	...	...	...	...	...	...	...	...	...	...	...	...	...	...	...	...
Sirpur Tandur	...	...	...	...	...	...	...	...	...	...	...	...	...	...	...	...	...	...	...	...	...	...	...	...	...	...	...	...
Karnatic or Kanada. Gulbarga...	...	...	...	...	...	...	...	...	...	...	...	...	...	...	...	...	...	...	...	...	...	...	...	...	...	...	...	...
Raichur	...	...	...	...	...	...	...	...	...	...	...	...	...	...	...	...	...	...	...	...	...	...	...	...	...	...	...	...
Lingasugur	...	...	...	...	...	...	...	...	...	...	...	...	...	...	...	...	...	...	...	...	...	...	...	...	...	...	...	...
Total Districts......	...	...	...	...	...	...	...	...	...	...	...	...	...	...	...	...	...	...	...	...	...	...	...	...	...	...	...	...
Total Districts including Hyderabad ...	...	...	2	...	...	3	...	...	4	3	...	...	2	...	2	3	...	...	...	...	...	...	...	...	...	...	...	...
Railways......	...	...	...	...	...	1	...	...	2	...	...	...	2	...	...	...	...	...	...	...	...	...	...	...	...	...	...	...
Grand Total......	...	...	2	...	...	4	...	...	6	3	...	...	4	...	2	3	...	...	...	...	...	...	...	...	...	...	...	...

TABLE X.

PARENT TONGUE.

TABLE X.

Parent Tongue.

District or State.		Total Population: Total.	Total Population: Males.	Total Population: Females.	A—Vernaculars of India. Languages of the Province of Hyderabad. Canarese: Total.	Canarese: Males.	Canarese: Females.	Marathi: Total.	Marathi: Males.	Marathi: Females.	Telugu: Total.	Telugu: Males.	Telugu: Females
1		2	3	4	5	6	7	8	9	10	11	12	13
Hyderabad.	City	124,057	62,748	61,309	741	362	379	6,156	8,195	2,961	29,576	15,130	14,446
	Suburbs including Secunderabad	290,982	153,576	137,406	1,456	818	638	10,431	5,747	4,684	129,313	65,055	64,258
	Total......	415,039	216,324	198,715	2,197	1,180	1,017	16,587	8,942	7,645	158,889	80,185	78,704
Telingana.	Atraf-i-Balda District	389,784	198,258	191,526	829	482	347	1,955	1,065	890	337,354	170,678	166,676
	Mahbubnagar Nagar Karnul) ...	674,649	341,601	333,048	28,510	14,493	14,017	6,975	8,609	3,366	570,382	288,298	282,084
	Nalgonda	624,617	319,823	304,794	80	47	33	1,397	691	706	567,563	289,152	278,411
	Warangal (Khamam)	853,129	438,635	414,494	353	190	163	12,659	6,682	5,977	751,825	385,258	366,572
	Elgandal	1,094,601	563,845	530,756	342	193	149	15,996	8,352	7,644	1,018,773	524,382	494,391
	Indur	639,598	319,237	320,361	23,620	11,880	11,740	51,135	25,874	25,261	498,083	247,573	250,510
	Medak	364,735	183,908	180,827	1,470	772	698	3,067	1,645	1,422	316,636	159,189	157,447
	Aurangabad	828,975	421,018	407,957	1,151	583	568	663,713	834,951	328,762	8,896	4,429	4,467
	Birh	642,722	328,530	314,192	2,133	1,107	1,026	569,092	290,012	279,080	2,918	1,544	1,374
	Nander	632,529	320,136	312,393	29,734	15,025	14,709	435,174	220,203	214,971	95,221	47,512	47,709
	Naldrug	649,272	331,747	317,525	26,305	13,597	12,708	550,298	280,628	269,670	5,312	2,760	2,552
	Bidar	901,984	457,088	444,896	288,334	145,486	142,848	342,729	174,967	167,762	143,041	71,018	72,023
	Parbhani	805,335	410,499	394,836	985	331	654	697,766	354,352	343,414	10,274	5,213	5,061
	Sirpur Tandur	231,754	116,955	114,799	543	280	263	73,113	37,320	35,793	100,324	49,815	50,509
Kanada or	Gulbarga...	649,258	329,678	319,580	340,832	171,992	168,840	33,229	17,315	15,914	159,475	80,497	78,978
	Raichur	512,455	260,217	252,238	184,839	92,146	92,693	8,193	4,268	3,925	260,126	133,120	127,006
	Lingasugur	620,014	311,394	308,620	518,136	258,719	259,417	9,467	4,985	4,482	24,003	12,336	11,667
	Total Districts......	11,115,411	5,652,569	5,462,842	1,448,196	727,323	720,873	3,475,958	1,766,919	1,709,039	4,870,206	2,472,769	2,397,437
	Total Districts including Hyderabad ...	11,530,450	5,868,893	5,661,557	1,450,393	728,503	721,890	3,492,545	1,775,861	1,716,684	5,029,095	2,552,954	2,476,141
	Railways......	6,590	4,236	2,354	653	411	242	1,313	727	586	1,974	1,382	592
	Grand Total......	11,537,040	5,873,129	5,663,911	1,451,046	728,914	722,132	3,493,858	1,776,588	1,717,270	5,031,069	2,554,336	2,476,733

TABLE X.

Parent Tongue.—*Continued.*

A.—VERNACULARS OF INDIA.—*contd.*

District or State.	Languages of the Province of Hyderabad.—*concluded.*						Other Indian Languages.								
	Urdu.			Total.			Hindi.			Hindi Gypsy.			Tamil.		
	Total.	Males.	Females.	Total.	Males.	Females.	Total.	Males.	Females.	Total.	Males.	Females.	Total.	Males.	Females.
	14	15	16	17	18	19	20	21	22	23	24	25	26	27	28
Telingana. Hyderabad. City	81,055	39,547	41,508	117,528	58,234	59,294	2,771	1,748	1,023	......	......	......	80	43	37
Suburbs including Secunderabad	113,875	60,749	53,126	255,075	132,369	122,706	5,532	3,486	2,046	142	114	28	15,346	7,850	7,496
Total.....	194,930	100,296	94,634	372,603	190,603	182,000	8,303	5,234	3,069	142	114	28	15,426	7,898	7,533
Atraf-i-Balda District	4,4135	22,877	21,258	384,273	195,102	189,171	417	192	225	8,098	1,835	1,263	1,342	666	676
Mahabubnagar (Nagar Karnul) ...	57,664	28,808	28,856	663,531	335,208	328,323	176	115	61	8,217	4,830	3,387	1,604	822	782
Nalgonda	27,049	13,743	13,306	596,089	303,633	292,456	212	107	105	25,943	14,801	11,142	2,047	1,064	983
Warangal (Khamam)	38,325	19,976	18,349	803,162	412,101	391,061	539	396	143	29,110	15,745	13,365	3,729	1,983	1,746
Elgandal	40,415	20,789	19,626	10,75,526	553,716	521,810	137	82	55	8,919	4,885	4,034	1,161	575	586
Indur	51,647	25,639	26,008	624,485	310,966	313,519	2,058	1,172	886	10,636	5,776	4,860	226	140	86
Medak...	38,368	19,285	19,083	359,541	180,891	178,650	279	153	126	8,280	1,954	1,326	645	328	317
Mahratwara. Aurangabad	12,029	64,431	60,598	798,789	404,394	394,395	16,507	9,171	7,336	8,997	4,901	4,096	250	138	112
Birh	54,061	27,902	26,159	628,204	320,565	307,639	8,770	4,920	3,850	4,351	2,255	2,096	34	21	13
Nander	59,273	30,311	28,962	619,402	313,051	306,351	8,058	1,932	1,126	8,817	4,544	4,273	56	32	24
Naldrug	59,436	30,391	29,045	641,351	327,376	313,975	5,285	2,898	2,387	1,396	784	612	......	......	......
Bidar	118,279	60,865	57,914	892,383	451,836	440,547	2,984	1,717	1,267	5,168	2,771	2,397	68	36	32
Parbhani	69,260	35,664	33,596	778,285	395,560	382,725	10,845	6,506	4,339	13,091	6,877	6,214	88	19	19
Sirpur Tandur	10,580	5,314	5,266	184,560	92,729	91,831	13,813	7,011	6,802	5,498	2,900	2,598	17	10	7
Karnatic or Kanada. Gulbarga	98,355	50,245	48,110	631,891	320,049	311,842	2,734	1,535	1,199	9,342	5,239	4,103	147	67	80
Raichur	52,313	26,869	25,444	505,471	256,403	249,068	519	293	226	4,093	2,249	1,844	1,317	667	650
Lingasugur	57,784	29,649	28,135	609,390	305,689	303,701	857	539	318	5,946	3,186	2,760	892	446	446
Total Districts.....	1,001,973	512,258	489,715	10,796,333	5,479,269	5,317,064	69,190	38,739	30,451	155,902	85,532	70,370	13,573	7,014	6,559
Total Districts including Hyderabad ...	1,196,903	612,554	584,349	11,168,936	5,669,872	5,499,064	77,493	43,973	33,520	156,044	85,646	70,398	28,999	14,907	14,092
Railways.....	1,479	990	489	5,419	3,510	1,909	65	42	23	149	97	52	267	156	111
Grand Total.....	1,198,382	613,544	584,838	11,174,355	5,673,382	5,500,973	77,558	44,015	33,543	156,193	85,743	70,450	29,266	15,063	14,203

TABLE X.

Parent Tongue.

TABLE X.

Parent Tongue.—*Continued.*

District or State.	A—VERNACULARS OF INDIA.—*contd.*																	
	Other Indian Languages.—*contd.*																	
	Gond.			Gujarati.			Panjabi.			Uriya (Jaganathi.)			Sindhi.			Bengali.		
	Total.	Males.	Females.	Total.	Males.	Females.	Total.	Males.	Females.	Total.	Males.	Females.	Total.	Males.	Females.	Total.	Males.	Females.
	29	30	31	32	33	34	35	36	37	38	39	40	41	42	43	44	45	46
Telingana. Hyderabad. City	......	......	......	265	170	95	43	30	13	...	...	...	21	21	...	4	4	...
Telingana. Hyderabad. Suburbs including Secunderabad	6	3	3	1,453	847	606	85	55	30	55	24	31	26	21	5	26	17	9
Total......	6	3	3	1,718	1,017	701	128	85	43	55	24	31	47	42	5	30	21	9
Atraf-i-Balda District	....	......	......	52	36	16	38	16	22	...	...	...	...	...	...	...	...	...
Mahabubnagar (Nagar Karnul) ...	....	......	......	599	289	310	13	9	4	4	2	2	...	...	...	...	...	...
Nalgonda	......	......	......	54	31	23	94	67	27	...	...	...	...	...	...	...	...	...
Warangal (Khamam)	3,165	1,591	1,574	12,457	6,260	6,197	311	185	126	6	3	3	...	...	...	...	...	...
Elgandal	8,267	4,243	4,024	97	53	44	81	17	14	...	...	...	...	...	...	...	...	...
Indur	1,266	658	608	130	70	60	135	71	64	4	4	...	...	...	...	...	...	...
Medak	3	3	......	172	100	72	68	45	23	87	37	50	...	...	...	...	...	...
Mahratwara. Aurangabad	......	......	......	2,830	1,473	1,357	210	148	62	...	...	...	...	...	...	...	...	...
Birh	......	......	......	686	379	307	23	13	10	...	...	...	...	...	...	...	...	...
Nander	27	14	13	192	107	85	366	106	260	...	...	...	5	5	...	...	...	...
Naldrug	......	......	......	826	426	400	15	15	...	...	...	...	...	...	...	...	...	...
Bidar...	20	9	11	585	320	265	62	27	35	...	...	...	...	...	...	...	...	...
Parbhani	......	......	......	1,387	696	691	674	415	259	...	...	...	...	...	...	...	...	...
Sirpur Tandur	23,847	11,952	11,895	144	75	69	157	92	65	...	...	...	...	...	...	...	...	...
Karnatic or Kanada. Gulbarga	......	......	......	3,422	1,883	1,539	98	40	58	8	7	1	...	...	...	...	...	...
Raichur	49	27	22	235	135	100	11	6	5	...	...	...	...	...	...	1	1	...
Lingasugur	......	......	......	1,278	678	600	...	...	...	16	8	8	10	2	8	...	...	...
Total Districts.....	36,144	18,497	17,647	25,146	13,011	12,135	2,306	1,272	1,034	125	61	64	15	7	8	1	1	...
Total Districts including Hyderabad...	36,150	18,500	17,650	26,864	14,028	12,836	2,434	1,357	1,077	180	85	95	62	49	13	31	22	9
Railways.....	7	7	......	130	88	42	5	5	...	...	...	...	...	...	...	7	5	2
Grand Total.....	36,157	18,507	17,650	26,994	14,116	12,878	2,439	1,362	1,077	180	85	95	62	49	13	38	27	11

TABLE X.

Parent Tongue.—*Continued.*

A—VERNACULARS OF INDIA.—*concluded.*

OTHER INDIAN LANGUAGES.—*concluded.*

District or State.	Chenchu. Total.	Chenchu. Males.	Chenchu. Females.	Kur. Total.	Kur. Males.	Kur. Females.	Kashmiri. Total.	Kashmiri. Males.	Kashmiri. Females.	Malayalam. Total.	Malayalam. Males.	Malayalam. Females.	Total. Total.	Total. Males.	Total. Females.
	47	48	49	50	51	52	53	54	55	56	57	58	59	60	61
Telingana.															
Hyderabad. City	...	...	...	...	...	...	6	4	2	...	...	...	8,190	2,020	1,170
Hyderabad. Suburbs including Secunderabad	23	13	10	...	...	...	15	9	6	16	11	5	22,725	12,450	10,275
Total......	23	13	10	...	...	...	21	13	8	16	11	5	25,915	14,470	11,445
Atraf-i-Balda District	3	...	8	...	...	...	...	...	...	...	...	...	4,950	2,745	2,205
Mahabubnagar (Nagar Karnul)	1	...	1	103	51	52	...	...	...	...	...	...	10,717	6,118	4,599
Nalgonda	25	15	10	...	...	...	...	...	...	1	1	...	28,376	16,086	12,290
Warangal (Khamam)	353	176	177	...	...	...	...	...	...	...	...	...	49,670	26,339	23,331
Elgandal	...	...	...	41	14	27	...	...	...	...	...	...	18,653	9,869	8,784
Indur	...	...	...	...	...	...	...	...	...	...	...	...	14,455	7,891	6,564
Medak	16	9	7	...	...	...	...	...	...	...	...	...	4,550	2,629	1,921
Mahratwara.															
Aurangabad	...	...	...	29	14	15	...	...	...	...	...	...	28,823	15,845	12,978
Birh	...	...	...	96	30	66	...	...	...	12	12	...	13,972	7,630	6,342
Nander	...	...	...	...	...	...	...	...	...	...	...	...	12,521	6,740	5,781
Naldrug	...	...	...	2	1	1	...	...	...	1	1	...	7,525	4,125	3,400
Bidar	...	...	...	61	37	24	...	...	...	...	...	...	8,948	4,917	4,031
Parbhani	...	...	...	9	...	9	...	...	...	...	...	...	26,044	14,513	11,531
Sirpur Tandur	...	...	...	2,878	1,434	1,444	...	...	...	1,212	659	553	47,066	24,133	22,933
Karnatic or Kanada.															
Gulbarga	...	...	...	812	430	382	...	...	...	...	...	...	16,563	9,201	7,362
Raichur	...	...	...	392	204	188	...	...	...	...	...	...	6,617	3,582	3,035
Lingasugur	...	...	...	1,331	684	647	...	...	...	...	...	...	10,330	5,543	4,787
Total Districts......	398	200	198	5,754	2,899	2,855	...	...	...	1,226	673	553	309,780	167,906	141,874
Total Districts including Hyderabad	421	213	208	5,754	2,899	2,855	21	13	8	1,242	684	558	335,695	182,376	153,319
Railways......	...	...	...	...	...	...	...	...	...	1	...	1	631	400	231
Grand Total......	421	213	208	5,754	2,899	2,855	21	13	8	1,243	684	559	336,326	182,776	153,550

TABLE X.

Parent Tongue.—*Continued.*

B—VERNACULARS OF ASIATIC COUNTRIES BEYOND INDIA.

District or State.	Arabic.			Armenian.			Baloch.			Chinese.			Persian.			Pashtu.			Turki (Chagatai.)		
	Total.	Males.	Females	Total.	Males.	Females.	Total.	Males.	Females.	Total.	Males.	Females.	Total.	Males.	Females.	Total.	Males.	Females.	Total.	Males.	Females.
	62	63	64	65	66	67	68	69	70	71	72	73	74	75	76	77	78	79	80	81	82
Telingana. Hyderabad. City	2,378	2,004	374	...	...	...	7	7	...	...	...	...	184	121	63	328	299	29	9	9	...
Suburbs including Secunderabad	4,523	2,787	1,736	3	3	...	6	6	...	2	2	...	525	302	223	631	498	133	6	5	1
Total......	6,901	4,791	2,110	3	3	...	13	13	...	2	2	...	709	423	286	959	797	162	15	14	1
Atraf-i-Balda District	261	213	48	...	...	...	...	...	...	...	...	...	...	...	...	148	122	26	13	5	8
Mahabubnagar (Nagar Karnul) ...	227	230	97	...	...	...	...	...	...	...	...	...	...	...	...	45	27	18	2	2	...
Nalgonda	117	81	36	...	...	...	...	...	...	...	...	...	...	...	...	18	13	5	...	...	...
Warangal (Khamam)	142	91	51	...	...	...	...	...	...	...	...	...	...	...	...	20	18	2	...	...	...
Elgandal	246	140	106	...	...	...	...	...	...	...	...	...	...	...	...	40	21	19	11	6	5
Indur	472	268	204	...	...	...	...	...	...	...	...	...	1	1	...	135	88	47	...	...	...
Medak	495	292	203	...	...	...	...	...	...	...	...	...	...	...	...	114	71	43	9	7	2
Mahratwara. Aurangabad	609	314	295	...	...	...	...	...	...	...	...	...	26	2	24	555	364	191	...	...	...
Birh	371	223	148	...	...	...	...	...	...	...	...	...	15	9	6	96	66	30	...	...	...
Nander	477	272	205	...	...	...	...	...	...	...	...	...	3	3	...	105	56	49	...	...	...
Naldrug	284	180	104	...	...	...	...	...	...	...	...	...	2	2	...	94	54	40	...	...	...
Bidar...	466	200	266	...	...	...	...	...	...	...	...	...	3	3	...	131	106	25	...	...	...
Parbhani	713	272	441	...	...	...	...	...	...	...	...	...	...	...	...	267	134	133	...	...	...
Sirpur Tandur	98	78	20	...	...	...	...	...	...	...	...	...	...	...	...	30	15	15	...	...	...
Karnatic or Kanada. Gulbarga	556	291	265	...	...	...	...	...	...	...	...	...	3	2	1	148	83	65	...	...	...
Raichur...	152	115	37	...	...	...	...	...	...	...	...	...	29	17	12	2	2	...	...	...	...
Lingasugur	164	105	59	...	...	...	...	...	...	...	...	...	6	4	2	11	11	...	20	...	20
Total Districts......	5,950	3,365	2,585	...	...	...	...	...	...	...	...	...	88	43	45	1,959	1,251	708	55	20	35
Total Districts including Hyderabad...	12,851	8,156	4,695	3	3	...	13	13	...	2	2	...	797	466	331	2,918	2,048	870	70	34	36
Railways......	18	11	7	2	2	...	...	...	...	...	...	...	18	16	2	1	1	...	...	...	...
Grand Total......	12,869	8,167	4,702	5	5	...	13	13	...	2	2	...	815	482	333	2,919	2,049	870	70	34	36

TABLE X.

Parent Tongue.—*Continued.*

District or State.	B—Vernaculars of Asiatic Countries beyond India—concld. Total.			C—Languages of European Countries. Bohemian.			Dutch.			English.			French.			German.			Italian.		
	Total.	Males.	Females.	Total.	Males.	Females.	Total.	Males.	Females.	Total.	Males.	Females.	Total.	Males.	Females.	Total.	Males.	Females.	Total.	Males.	Females.
	83	84	85	86	87	88	89	90	91	92	93	94	95	96	97	98	99	100	101	102	103
Hyderabad. City	2,906	2,440	466	...	...	...	...	...	...	76	45	31	...	...	...	...	...	...	...	...	...
Hyderabad. Suburbs including Secunderabad	5,696	3,603	2,093	1	...	1	2	2	...	7,302	5,028	2,274	7	1	6	17	10	7	17	3	14
Total......	8,602	6,043	2,559	1	...	1	2	2	...	7,378	5,078	2,305	7	1	6	17	10	7	17	3	14
Telingana. Atraf-i-Balda District	422	340	82	...	...	...	...	...	...	125	57	68	...	...	...	...	...	...	...	...	...
Mahabubnagar (Nagar Karnul) ...	374	259	115	...	...	...	...	...	...	23	12	11	...	...	...	...	...	...	...	...	...
Nalgonda	135	94	41	...	...	...	...	...	...	11	7	4	...	...	...	...	...	...	...	...	...
Warangal (Khamam)	162	109	53	...	...	...	...	...	...	135	86	49	...	...	...	...	...	...	...	...	...
Elgandal	297	167	130	...	...	...	...	...	...	62	37	25	...	...	...	...	...	...	...	...	...
Indur	608	357	251	...	...	...	...	...	...	28	14	14	...	...	...	...	...	...	...	...	...
Medak...	613	370	248	...	...	...	...	...	...	26	18	8	...	...	...	...	...	...	...	...	...
Mahratwara. Aurangabad	1,190	680	510	...	...	...	...	...	...	164	93	71	...	...	...	...	...	...	...	...	...
Birh	482	298	184	...	...	...	...	...	...	64	37	27	...	...	...	...	...	...	...	...	...
Nander	585	331	254	...	...	...	...	...	...	2	2	...	...	...	...	...	...	...	...	...	...
Naldrug	380	236	144	...	...	...	...	...	...	10	6	4	...	...	...	...	...	...	...	...	...
Bidar	600	309	291	...	...	...	...	...	...	17	10	7	...	...	...	...	...	...	...	...	...
Parbhani	980	406	574	...	...	...	...	...	...	24	19	5	...	...	...	...	...	...	...	...	...
Sirpur Tandur	128	93	35	...	...	...	...	...	...	...	...	...	...	...	...	...	...	...	...	...	...
Karnatic or Kanada. Gulbarga	707	376	331	...	...	...	...	...	...	93	50	43	...	...	...	...	...	...	...	...	...
Raichur	183	134	49	...	...	...	...	...	...	170	89	81	...	...	...	...	...	...	1	1	...
Lingasugur	201	120	81	...	...	...	...	...	...	72	42	30	...	...	...	...	...	...	...	...	...
Total Districts......	8,052	4,679	3,373	...	...	...	...	...	...	1,026	579	447	...	...	...	...	...	...	1	1	...
Total Districts including Hyderabad ...	16,654	10,722	5,932	1	...	1	2	2	...	8,404	5,652	2,752	7	1	6	17	10	7	18	4	14
Railways......	39	30	9	...	...	...	...	...	...	481	280	201	1	1	...	3	2	1	...	...	...
Grand Total......	16,693	10,752	5,941	1	...	1	2	2	...	8,885	5,932	2,953	8	2	6	20	12	8	18	4	14

TABLE X.

Parent Tongue.—*Continued.*

District or State.	C—Languages of European Countries. Polish. Total.	Polish. Males.	Polish. Females.	Portuguese. Total.	Portuguese. Males.	Portuguese. Females.	Turki (Osmanli.) Total.	Turki (Osmanli.) Males.	Turki (Osmanli.) Females.	Danish. Total.	Danish. Males.	Danish. Females.	Total. Total.	Total. Males.	Total. Females.	D—Others. Abyssinian. Total.	Abyssinian. Males.	Abyssinian. Females.	Unspecified. Total.	Unspecified. Males.	Unspecified. Females.
	104	105	106	107	108	109	110	111	112	113	114	115	116	117	118	119	120	121	122	123	124
Telingana. — Hyderabad. City	...	...	...	5	4	1	2	1	1	...	...	...	83	50	33	1	1	...	349	3	346
Suburbs including Secunderabad	1	1	...	71	57	14	5	3	2	...	...	...	7,428	5,105	2,318	52	42	10	11	7	4
Total......	1	1	...	76	61	15	7	4	3	...	...	...	7,506	5,155	2,351	53	43	10	360	10	350
Atraf-i-Balda District	...	...	...	...	...	...	...	...	...	...	...	...	125	57	68	13	13	...	1	1	...
Mahabubnagar (Nagar Karnul) ...	...	...	...	...	...	...	...	...	...	1	1	...	24	13	11	1	1	...	2	2	...
Nalgonda	...	...	...	...	...	...	...	...	...	...	...	...	11	7	4	...	...	...	6	3	3
Warangal (Khamam)	...	...	...	...	...	...	...	...	...	...	...	...	135	86	49	...	...	...	...	...	...
Elgandal	...	...	...	...	...	...	...	...	...	...	...	...	62	37	25	...	...	...	63	56	7
Indur	...	...	...	...	...	...	17	4	13	...	...	...	45	18	27	...	...	...	5	5	...
Medak	...	...	...	...	...	...	...	...	...	...	...	...	26	18	8	...	...	...	...	...	...
Mahratwara. Aurangabad	...	...	...	...	...	...	...	...	...	...	...	...	164	93	71	...	...	...	9	6	3
Birh	...	...	...	...	...	...	...	...	...	...	...	...	64	37	27	...	...	...	...	...	...
Nander	...	...	...	...	...	...	...	...	...	...	...	...	2	2	...	7	4	3	12	8	4
Naldrug	...	...	...	...	...	...	...	...	...	...	...	...	10	6	4	...	...	...	6	4	2
Bidar	...	...	...	...	...	...	...	...	...	...	...	...	17	10	7	...	...	...	36	16	20
Parbhani	...	...	...	...	...	...	...	...	...	...	...	...	24	19	5	...	...	...	2	1	1
Sirpur Tandur	...	...	...	...	...	...	...	...	...	...	...	...	...	...	...	...	...	...	...	...	...
Karnatic or Kanada. Gulbarga	...	...	...	...	...	...	...	...	...	...	...	...	93	50	43	...	...	...	4	2	2
Raichur	...	...	...	13	8	5	...	...	...	...	...	...	184	98	86	...	...	...	...	...	...
Lingasugur	...	...	...	...	...	...	...	...	...	...	...	...	72	42	30	...	...	...	21	...	21
Total Districts......	...	...	...	13	8	5	17	4	13	1	1	...	1,058	593	465	21	18	3	167	104	63
Total Districts including Hyderabad ...	1	1	...	89	69	20	24	8	16	1	1	...	8,564	5,748	2,816	74	61	13	527	114	413
Railways......	...	...	...	16	13	3	...	...	...	...	...	...	501	296	205	...	...	...	...	...	...
Grand Total......	1	1	...	105	82	23	24	8	16	1	1	...	9,065	6,044	3,021	74	61	13	527	114	413

TABLE XI.

BIRTH PLACE.

TABLE XI.

Birth Places.

District or State.		Grand Total.			A—Provinces and States in India. His Highness the Nizam's Dominions. Hyderabad.			Atraf-i-Balda.			Medak.		
		Total.	Males.	Females.	Total.	Males.	Females.	Total.	Males.	Females.	Total.	Males.	Females.
1		2	3	4	5	6	7	8	9	10	11	12	13
Telingana. Hyderabad.	City	124,057	62,748	61,309	88,215	40,612	47,603	2,501	1,308	1,193	2,805	1,643	1,162
	Suburbs including Secunderabad	290,982	153,576	137,406	204,337	101,354	102,983	5,179	2,702	2,477	3,889	2,280	1,609
	Total......	415,039	216,324	198,715	292,552	141,966	150,586	7,680	4,010	3,670	6,694	3,923	2,771
Telingana.	Atraf-i-Balda District	389,784	198,258	191,526	18,726	9,276	9,450	301,234	157,299	143,935	22,547	10,549	11,998
	Mahabubnagar (Nagar Karnul) ..	674,649	341,601	333,048	2,429	1,114	1,315	12,253	5,829	6,924	555	298	257
	Nalgonda	624,617	319,823	304,794	2,363	1,218	1,145	7,413	3,639	3,774	445	289	156
	Warangal (Khamam)	853,129	438,635	414,494	2,656	1,464	1,192	617	331	286	575	290	285
	Elgandal	1,094,601	563,845	530,756	1,031	606	425	1,025	451	574	2,491	1,038	1,453
	Indur	639,598	319,237	320,361	914	471	443	105	64	41	6,435	2,445	3,990
	Medak...	364,735	183,908	180,827	2,914	1,344	1,570	7,293	3,174	4,119	327,575	167,078	160,497
Mahratwara.	Aurangabad	828,975	421,018	407,957	4,434	1,974	2,460	61	23	38	22	16	6
	Birh	642,722	328,530	314,192	844	512	332	174	87	87	14	11	3
	Nander	632,529	320,136	312,393	743	427	316	4	3	1	248	123	125
	Naldrug	649,272	331,747	317,525	4,181	2,232	1,949	......	......	......	79	50	29
	Bidar	901,984	457,088	444,896	2,269	1,080	1,189	977	417	560	3,991	1,664	2,327
	Parbhani	805,335	410,499	394,836	3,421	1,713	1,708	27	13	14	61	42	19
	Sirpur Tandur	231,754	116,955	114,799	234	146	88	2	2	......	30	12	18
Karnatic or Kanada.	Gulbarga	649,258	329,678	319,580	7,842	3,880	3,962	670	284	386	660	349	311
	Raichur	512,455	260,217	252,238	2,046	1,102	944	28	20	8	57	27	30
	Lingasugur	620,014	311,394	308,620	2,223	1,284	939	......	......	......	92	56	36
Total Districts......		11,115,411	5,652,569	5,462,842	59,270	29,843	29,427	331,883	171,136	160,747	365,877	184,337	181,540
Total Districts including Hyderabad ...		11,530,450	5,868,893	5,661,557	351,822	171,809	180,013	339,563	175,146	164,417	372,571	188,260	184,311
Railways......		6,590	4,236	2,354	2,098	1,342	756	......	......	......	10	7	3
Grand Total......		11,537,040	5,873,129	5,663,911	353,920	173,151	180,769	339,563	175,146	164,417	372,581	188,267	184,314

TABLE XI.

Birth Places.—*Continued.*

A—PROVINCES AND STATES IN INDIA.—*contd.*

HIS HIGHNESS THE NIZAM'S DOMINIONS.—*contd.*

DISTRICT OR STATE.	Elgandal.			Bidar.			Warangal.			Mahabubnagar.			Nalgonda.		
	Total.	Males.	Females.	Total.	Males.	Females.	Total.	Males.	Females.	Total.	Males.	Females.	Total.	Males.	Females.
	14	15	16	17	18	19	20	21	22	23	24	25	26	27	28
Telingana. Hyderabad. City	1,204	834	870	2,730	1,560	1,171	764	472	292	2,835	1,398	937	765	461	304
Suburbs including Secunderabad	1,827	1,167	660	2,104	1,296	808	873	497	876	2,374	1,374	1,000	1,333	761	572
Total......	3,031	2,001	1,030	4,835	2,856	1,979	1,637	969	668	4,709	2,772	1,987	2,098	1,222	876
Atraf-i-Balda District	5,472	2,414	3,058	4,130	1,798	2,332	1,272	543	729	10,934	4,963	5,971	17,310	7,196	10,114
Mahabubnagar (Nagar Karnul) ...	380	223	157	337	183	154	1,212	549	663	633,620	322,983	310,637	4,486	1,868	2,628
Nalgonda	1,566	835	731	94	57	37	14,728	7,146	7,582	3,462	1,702	1,760	584,608	299,649	284,959
Warangal (Khamam)	13,895	6,228	7,667	305	72	233	783,865	404,446	379,419	1,133	607	526	16,603	7,933	8,670
Elgandal	1,071,888	552,786	519,102	154	91	63	8,390	3,683	4,707	807	422	385	773	354	419
Indur...	4,266	1,815	2,451	4,186	1,771	2,415	155	76	79	124	70	54	45	28	17
Medak	6,224	2,524	3,700	8,589	1,623	1,966	500	337	163	882	411	471	1,189	596	593
Mahratwara. Aurangabad	20	14	6	442	264	178	11	7	4	16	11	5	6	4	2
Birh	3	2	1	3,094	1,140	1,954	4	2	2	7	7	...	17	13	4
Nander	141	82	59	23,315	10,645	12,670	58	29	29	20	12	8	14	7	7
Naldrug	9	6	3	13,005	5,641	7,364	4	3	1	11	6	5	11	2	9
Bidar	378	239	139	864,125	439,383	424,742	39	10	29	73	38	35	44	39	5
Parbhani	73	61	12	6,238	2,959	3,279	11	3	8	10	7	3	3	3	...
Sirpur Tandur	3,244	1,684	1,560	177	105	72	4	1	3	1	...	1	65	45	20
Karnatic or Kanada. Gulbarga	43	32	11	9,083	4,688	4,395	41	22	19	5,391	2,104	3,287	54	31	23
Raichur	633	355	278	199	111	88	28	17	11	10,274	4,259	6,015	9	8	1
Lingasugur	61	51	10	70	39	31	43	29	14	1,646	728	918	6	2	4
Total Districts......	1,108,296	569,351	538,945	932,543	470,570	461,973	810,365	416,903	393,462	668,411	338,330	330,081	625,243	317,773	307,470
Total Districts including Hyderabad ...	1,111,327	571,352	539,975	937,378	473,426	463,952	812,002	417,872	394,130	673,120	341,102	332,018	627,341	318,995	308,346
Railways......	......	...	...	31	23	8	...	...	...	2	2	...	...	...	...
Grand Total......	1,111,327	571,352	539,975	937,409	473,449	463,960	812,002	417,872	394,130	673,122	341,104	332,018	627,341	318,995	308,346

TABLE XI.

Birth Places.—*Continued.*

A—PROVINCES AND STATES IN INDIA.—*contd.*

HIS HIGHNESS THE NIZAM'S DOMINIONS.—*contd.*

District or State.	Aurangabad. Total.	Aurangabad. Males.	Aurangabad. Females.	Nander. Total.	Nander. Males.	Nander. Females.	Birh. Total.	Birh. Males.	Birh. Females.	Parbhani. Total.	Parbhani. Males.	Parbhani. Females.	Gulbarga. Total.	Gulbarga. Males.	Gulbarga. Females.
	29	30	31	32	33	34	35	36	37	38	39	40	41	42	43
Telingana. Hyderabad. City	965	556	409	690	411	279	448	256	192	239	146	93	1,442	830	612
Telingana. Hyderabad. Suburbs including Secunderabad	3,299	1,878	1,421	727	466	261	856	402	454	437	300	137	1,878	1,122	756
Total......	4,264	2,434	1,830	1,417	877	540	1,304	658	646	676	446	230	3,320	1,952	1,368
Telingana. Atraf-i-Balda District...	299	121	178	77	54	23	1	...	1	14	7	7	1,757	781	976
Mahabubnagar (Nagar Karnul) ...	61	41	20	95	49	46	6	5	1	29	15	14	8,287	3,883	4,404
Nalgonda	65	47	18	78	44	34	7	4	3	2	...	2	76	43	33
Warangal (Khamam)	89	58	31	192	101	91	106	95	11	10	7	3	186	113	73
Elgandal	45	33	12	99	57	42	29	23	6	5	3	2	104	66	38
Indur	216	132	84	12,106	5,490	6,616	1,097	563	534	446	197	249	195	138	57
Medak...	201	125	76	3,394	1,725	1,669	11	5	6	16	14	2	313	142	171
Mahratwara. Aurangabad	737,841	377,409	360,432	723	383	340	13,689	6,188	7,501	7,055	3,123	3,932	194	119	75
Birh	13,915	6,433	7,482	792	492	300	580,566	303,264	277,802	4,967	1,817	3,150	228	112	116
Nander	522	316	206	560,162	287,226	272,936	1,367	1,150	217	12,965	5,155	7,810	265	155	110
Naldrug	812	396	416	854	435	419	16,746	6,363	10,383	788	421	367	1,264	562	702
Bidar	362	190	172	6,223	2,979	3,244	2,677	1,201	1,476	1,547	642	905	5,894	2,511	3,383
Parbhani	12,232	5,443	6,789	20,166	8,484	11,682	18,756	8,328	10,428	711,875	366,484	345,391	1,012	499	513
Sirpur Tandur	79	43	36	1,123	626	497	261	144	117	778	410	368	12	11	1
Karnatic or Kanada. Gulbarga...	898	229	669	260	173	87	233	129	104	1,582	820	762	585,781	298,918	286,863
Raichur	699	371	328	33	21	12	59	36	23	170	83	87	5,993	2,769	3,224
Lingasugur	190	116	74	46	31	15	69	38	31	46	15	31	4,267	1,907	2,360
Total Districts......	768,026	391,503	376,523	606,423	308,370	298,053	635,680	327,536	308,144	742,295	379,213	363,082	615,828	312,729	303,099
Total Districts including Hyderabad ...	772,290	393,937	378,353	607,840	309,247	298,593	636,984	328,194	308,790	742,971	379,659	363,312	619,148	314,681	304,467
Railways......	78	56	22	4	2	2	4	4	...	1	...	1	384	219	165
Grand Total......	772,368	393,993	378,375	607,844	309,249	298,595	636,988	328,198	308,790	742,972	379,659	363,313	619,532	314,900	304,632

TABLE XI.

Birth Places.—*Continued.*

District or State.		Raichur. Total.	Raichur. Males.	Raichur. Females.	Naldrug. Total.	Naldrug. Males.	Naldrug. Females.	Lingasugur. Total.	Lingasugur. Males.	Lingasugur. Females.	Indur. Total.	Indur. Males.	Indur. Females.	Sirpur Tandur. Total.	Sirpur Tandur. Males.	Sirpur Tandur. Females.
		A—PROVINCES AND STATES IN INDIA.—*contd.* His Highness the Nizam's Dominions.—*contd.*														
		44	45	46	47	48	49	50	51	52	53	54	55	56	57	58
Telingana. Hyderabad.	City	619	360	259	199	116	83	178	98	80	2,559	1,965	594	...	...	...
	Suburbs including Secunderabad	704	382	322	394	216	178	554	828	226	2,798	1,774	1,024	...	...	...
	Total......	1,323	742	581	593	332	261	732	426	306	5,357	3,739	1,618	...	...	...
Telingana.	Atraf-i-Balda District	164	108	56	16	10	6	28	17	11	950	533	417	39	18	21
	Mahabubnagar (Nagar Karnul) ...	6,134	2,478	3,656	29	22	7	909	400	509	237	146	91	11	1	10
	Nalgonda	52	42	10	2	2	...	15	4	11	155	101	54	...	...	...
	Warangal (Khamam)	189	109	80	1	...	1	28	16	12	632	428	204	5	1	4
	Elgandal	1,417	762	655	9	7	2	37	22	15	4,238	2,242	1,996	102	38	64
	Indur	20	11	9	69	55	14	16	10	6	606,365	304,099	302,266	832	194	138
	Medak...	72	34	38	1	1	...	23	14	9	7,433	3,061	4,372	18	13	5
Mahratwara.	Aurangabad	58	37	21	417	226	191	262	149	113	155	93	62	5	3	2
	Birh	34	18	16	7,828	2,690	5,138	34	18	16	161	100	61	2	2	...
	Nander	24	17	7	590	294	296	22	13	9	21,750	9,521	12,229	67	27	40
	Naldrug	80	32	48	568,897	299,033	269,864	81	45	86	158	78	80	4	4	...
	Bidar	61	27	34	3,331	1,435	1,896	74	42	82	3,875	1,720	2,155	...	...	...
	Parbhani	85	42	43	1,493	721	772	100	55	45	851	482	369	27	17	10
	Sirpur Tandur	22	20	2	47	31	16	7	4	3	2,087	1,140	947	206,521	103,986	102,535
Karnatic or Kanada.	Gulbarga	2,796	1,271	1,525	1,969	945	1,024	5,576	2,642	2,934	278	202	76	36	33	3
	Raichur	465,411	237,756	227,655	128	82	46	10,792	5,017	5,775	66	43	23	...	...	...
	Lingasugur	12,200	5,225	6,975	132	86	46	561,756	284,531	277,225	268	117	151	...	...	...
	Total Districts......	488,819	247,989	240,830	584,959	305,640	279,319	579,760	292,999	286,761	649,659	324,106	325,553	207,169	104,337	102,832
Total Districts including Hyderabad ...		490,142	248,731	241,411	585,552	305,972	279,580	580,492	293,425	287,067	655,016	327,845	327,171	207,169	104,337	102,832
	Railways......	139	84	55	1	...	1	9	8	1	1	...	1	...	...	...
	Grand Total......	490,281	248,815	241,466	585,553	305,972	279,581	580,501	293,433	287,068	655,017	327,845	327,172	207,169	104,337	102,832

TABLE XI.
Birth Places.

TABLE XI.

Birth Places.—*Continued.*

District or State.	A—Provinces and States in India.—*contd.*																	
	His Highness the Nizam's Dominions.—*concld.*						I—British Territory.											
	Unspecified—H. H. the Nizam's Dominions.			Total—H. H. the Nizam's Dominions.			Assam.			Bengal.			Berar.			Bombay.		
	Total.	Males.	Females.	Total.	Males.	Females.	Total.	Males.	Females.	Total.	Males.	Females.	Total.	Males.	Females.	Total.	Males.	Females.
	59	60	61	62	63	64	65	66	67	68	69	70	71	72	73	74	75	76
Telingana. Hyderabad. City	2,263	522	1,741	110,922	53,548	57,374	1	1	...	78	65	13	199	122	77	574	369	205
Telingana. Hyderabad. Suburbs including Secunderabad	2,045	1,034	1,011	235,608	119,333	116,275	2	...	2	765	516	249	835	486	349	3,289	1,892	1,397
Total......	4,308	1,556	2,752	346,530	172,881	173,649	3	1	2	843	581	262	1,034	608	426	3,863	2,261	1,602
Atraf-i-Balda District	1,271	600	671	386,241	196,287	189,954	...	...	...	30	22	8	50	41	9	570	305	265
Mahabubnagar (Nagar Karnul) ...	251	111	140	671,321	339,693	331,628	...	...	...	8	7	1	12	6	6	845	200	145
Nalgonda	4	3	1	615,135	314,825	300,310	...	...	...	5	5	...	4	4	...	86	47	39
Warangal (Khamam)	303	187	116	821,390	422,486	398,904	...	...	...	10	10	...	29	18	11	437	261	176
Elgandal	73	53	20	1,092,717	562,737	529,980	...	...	...	2	2	...	8	7	1	146	66	80
Indur	624	342	282	637,716	317,971	319,745	...	...	...	...	...	...	203	113	90	482	292	190
Medak...	472	219	253	362,120	182,440	179,680	...	...	...	...	...	...	76	44	32	187	113	74
Mahratwara. Aurangabad	1,542	817	725	766,953	390,860	376,093	...	...	...	71	59	12	11,082	4,909	6,173	39,450	17,867	21,583
Birh	848	407	441	613,532	317,127	296,405	...	...	...	12	9	3	584	310	274	25,541	9,138	16,403
Nander	1,119	514	605	623,396	315,716	307,680	...	...	...	2	2	...	5,581	2,070	3,511	1,363	814	549
Naldrug	1,583	727	856	608,567	316,036	292,531	...	...	...	26	21	5	417	220	197	37,738	13,908	23,830
Bidar	2,480	1,246	1,234	898,420	454,863	443,557	...	...	...	4	2	2	60	38	22	1,976	1,154	822
Parbhani	2,569	1,418	1,151	779,010	396,774	382,236	...	...	...	39	25	14	14,991	6,440	8,551	3,661	2,142	1,519
Sirpur Tandur	2,361	1,248	1,113	217,055	109,658	107,397	...	...	...	...	...	...	9,357	4,622	4,735	1,012	364	648
Karnatic or Kanada. Gulbarga	4,608	2,183	2,425	627,301	318,935	308,366	...	...	...	17	15	2	78	34	44	18,352	8,593	9,759
Raichur...	496	233	263	497,121	252,310	244,811	...	...	...	31	25	6	197	118	79	2,414	1,217	1,197
Lingasugur	714	352	362	583,829	294,607	289,222	...	...	...	92	75	17	32	17	15	20,783	9,715	11,068
Total Districts......	21,318	10,660	10,658	10,801,824	5,503,325	5,298,499	...	...	...	349	279	70	42,761	19,011	23,750	154,543	66,196	88,347
Total Districts including Hyderabad ...	25,626	12,216	13,410	11,148,354	5,676,206	5,472,148	3	1	2	1,192	860	332	43,795	19,619	24,176	158,406	68,457	89,949
Railways......	651	481	170	3,413	2,228	1,185	...	...	...	89	28	11	49	31	18	1,322	793	529
Grand Total......	26,277	12,697	13,580	11,151,767	5,678,434	5,473,333	3	1	2	1,281	888	343	43,844	19,650	24,194	159,728	69,250	90,478

TABLE XI.

Birth Places.—*Continued.*

A—PROVINCES AND STATES IN INDIA.—*contd.*

I—BRITISH TERRITORY.—*contd.*

District or State.	Burma. Total.	Burma. Males.	Burma. Females.	Central Provinces. Total.	Central Provinces. Males.	Central Provinces. Females.	Coorg. Total.	Coorg. Males.	Coorg. Females.	Madras. Total.	Madras. Males.	Madras. Females.	Nort-West Provinces. Total.	Nort-West Provinces. Males.	Nort-West Provinces. Females.	Oudh. Total.	Oudh. Males.	Oudh. Females.
	77	78	79	80	81	82	83	84	85	86	87	88	89	90	91	92	93	94
Telingana. Hyderabad. City	4	2	2	...	...	...	...	...	...	1,704	1,010	694	1,243	876	367	1,205	766	439
Suburbs including Secunderabad	120	55	65	2,549	1,858	1,191	11	5	6	19,876	11,188	8,688	3,381	2,475	906	1,662	1,165	497
Total......	124	57	67	2,549	1,858	1,191	11	5	6	21,580	12,198	9,382	4,624	3,351	1,273	2,867	1,981	936
Atraf-i-Balda District	...	...	...	52	38	14	...	...	...	1,168	595	578	88	68	20	11	9	2
Mahabubnagar (Nagar Karnul) ...	...	...	...	15	13	2	...	...	...	1,908	997	906	57	39	18	...	...	...
Nalgonda	...	...	...	5	5	...	...	...	...	8,307	4,315	3,992	24	19	5	8	8	...
Warangal (Khamam)	...	...	...	164	102	62	...	...	...	28,966	14,409	14,557	35	21	14	231	199	32
Elgandal	...	...	...	125	66	59	...	...	...	794	474	320	189	178	11	12	11	1
Indur	...	...	...	58	40	18	...	...	...	357	225	132	31	22	9	...	...	...
Medak	...	...	...	90	51	39	...	...	...	731	899	832	72	41	31	...	...	...
Mahratwara. Aurangabad	2	2	...	1,162	619	543	...	...	...	348	211	137	1,806	1,424	382	...	...	...
Birh	...	...	...	305	188	117	...	...	...	157	101	56	159	107	52	...	...	...
Nander	...	...	...	119	72	47	...	...	...	40	25	15	141	112	29	...	...	...
Naldrug	...	...	...	25	...	25	...	...	...	56	38	18	95	83	12	...	...	...
Bidar	...	...	...	100	65	35	...	...	...	96	67	29	136	76	60	...	...	...
Parbhani	2	1	1	311	166	145	...	...	...	61	35	26	1,294	946	348	...	...	...
Sirpur Tandur	...	...	...	1,372	844	528	...	...	...	27	13	14	46	31	15	...	...	...
Karnatic or Kanada. Gulbarga	...	...	...	122	54	68	...	...	...	748	428	320	127	113	14	...	...	...
Raichur	...	...	...	33	16	17	...	...	...	11,258	5,569	5,689	410	346	64	...	...	...
Lingasugur	...	...	...	14	8	6	...	...	...	14,096	6,222	7,874	54	39	15	...	...	...
Total Districts......	4	3	1	4,072	2,347	1725	...	...	...	69,113	34,123	34,990	4,764	3,665	1,099	257	222	35
Total Districts including Hyderabad...	128	60	68	6,621	3,705	2,916	11	5	6	90,693	46,321	44,372	9,388	7,016	2,372	3,124	2,153	971
Railways......	6	1	5	161	104	57	1	...	1	497	321	176	148	97	51	7	3	4
Grand Total......	134	61	73	6,782	3,809	2,973	12	5	7	91,190	46,642	44,548	9,536	7,113	2,423	3,131	2,156	975

TABLE XI.

Birth Places.—*Continued.*

District or State.	A—PROVINCES AND STATES IN INDIA.—*contd.*																				
	I.—British Territory.—*concld.*									II.—Feudatory States.											
	Punjab.			Andamans.			Total British Territory.			Baroda.			Mysore.			Kashmir.			Rajputana States.		
	Total.	Males.	Females.	Total.	Males.	Females.	Total.	Males.	Females.	Total.	Males.	Females.	Total.	Males.	Females.	Total.	Males.	Females.	Total.	Males.	Females.
	95	96	97	98	99	100	101	102	103	104	105	106	107	108	109	110	111	112	113	114	115
Telingana. Hyderabad. City	1,256	938	318	...	...	...	6,264	4,149	2,115	...	...	...	70	51	19	24	21	3	1,987	1,342	645
Suburbs including Secunderabad	1,050	814	236	3	2	1	33,543	19,956	13,587	...	...	...	4,041	2,139	1,902	29	9	20	4,186	2,809	1,377
Total......	2,306	1,752	554	3	2	1	39,807	24,105	15,702	...	...	...	4,111	2,190	1,921	53	30	23	6,173	4,151	2,022
Atraf-i-Balda District	84	70	14	...	...	...	2,053	1,148	905	...	...	...	41	25	16	...	...	...	117	74	43
Mahabubnagar (Nagar Karnul) ...	47	40	7	...	...	...	2,387	1,302	1,085	...	...	...	17	12	5	...	...	...	66	52	14
Nalgonda	30	22	8	...	...	...	8,464	4,420	4,044	...	...	...	1	1	...	...	...	...	21	12	9
Warangal (Khamam)	66	52	14	...	...	...	29,938	15,072	14,866	...	...	...	11	4	7	1	...	1	67	49	18
Elgandal	21	15	6	...	...	...	1,297	819	478	...	...	...	22	9	13	...	...	...	257	64	193
Indur	76	61	15	...	...	...	1,207	753	454	...	...	...	1	1	...	...	...	...	152	117	35
Medak...	70	60	10	...	...	...	1,226	708	518	...	...	...	17	15	2	...	...	...	89	28	11
Mahratwara. Aurangabad	382	293	89	...	...	...	54,303	25,384	28,919	...	...	...	...	...	...	...	...	...	2,240	1,517	723
Birh	70	50	20	...	...	...	26,828	9,903	16,925	...	...	...	...	...	...	...	...	...	1,895	1,236	659
Nander	186	127	59	...	...	...	7,432	3,222	4,210	...	...	...	...	...	...	...	...	...	1,026	723	303
Naldrug	60	51	9	...	...	...	38,417	14,321	24,096	...	...	...	...	...	...	1	1	...	1,336	838	498
Bidar	103	70	33	...	...	...	2,475	1,472	1,003	...	...	...	...	...	...	...	...	...	721	459	262
Parbhani	332	261	71	...	...	...	20,691	10,016	10,675	67	32	35	34	18	16	...	...	...	3,896	2,640	1,256
Sirpur Tandur	11	10	1	...	...	...	11,825	5,884	5,941	...	...	...	...	...	...	...	...	...	34	24	10
Karnatic or Kanada. Gulbarga	53	39	14	...	...	...	19,497	9,276	10,221	...	...	...	...	...	...	...	...	...	315	211	104
Raichur...	6	1	5	...	...	...	14,349	7,292	7,057	...	...	...	77	59	18	...	...	...	328	220	108
Lingasugur	25	18	7	...	...	...	35,096	16,094	19,002	...	...	...	127	76	51	2	2	...	361	278	83
Total Districts......	1,622	1,240	382	...	...	...	277,485	127,086	150,399	67	32	35	348	220	128	4	3	1	12,871	8,542	4,329
Total Districts including Hyderabad...	3,928	2,992	936	3	2	1	317,292	151,191	166,101	67	32	35	4,459	2,410	2,049	57	33	24	19,044	12,698	6,351
Railways......	16	14	2	...	...	...	2,246	1,392	854	5	5	...	96	54	42	1	1	...	...	...	...
Grand Total......	3,944	3,006	938	3	2	1	319,538	152,583	166,955	72	37	35	4,555	2,464	2,091	58	34	24	19,044	12,698	6,351

TABLE XI.

Birth Places.—*Continued.*

District or State.		A—Provinces and States in India,—*concld.* II.—Feudatory States.—*concld.* Central India States. Total.	Males.	Females.	Madras States. Total.	Males.	Females.	French Settlements. (Pondicherry.) Total.	Males.	Females.	Portuguese Settlements. (Goa.) Total.	Males.	Females.	India *Unspecified.* Total.	Males.	Females.	Total Feudatory States. Total.	Males.	Females.	Total A. Provinces and States in India. Total.	Males.	Females.
		116	117	118	119	120	121	122	123	124	125	126	127	128	129	130	131	132	133	134	135	136
Telingana. Hyderabad.	City	191	105	86	...	...	...	...	...	...	...	...	...	2,611	1,765	846	4,883	3,284	1,599	122,069	60,981	61,088
	Suburbs including Secunderabad	754	459	295	...	...	...	...	...	...	65	49	16	6,916	3,776	3,140	15,991	9,241	6,750	285,142	1,48,530	136,612
	Total......	945	564	881	...	...	...	...	...	...	65	49	16	9,527	5,541	3,986	20,874	12,525	8,349	407,211	2,09,511	197,700
	Atraf-i-Balda District	...	...	...	...	...	...	...	...	...	...	...	...	1,138	570	568	1,296	669	627	889,590	1,98,104	191,486
	Mahabubnagar (Nagar Karnul) ...	...	...	...	...	...	...	...	...	...	...	...	...	663	390	273	746	454	292	674,454	3,41,449	333,005
	Nalgonda	...	...	...	...	...	...	...	...	...	...	...	...	988	506	427	955	519	436	624,554	3,19,764	304,790
	Warangal (Khamam)	...	...	...	...	...	...	...	...	...	...	...	...	1,679	996	683	1,758	1,049	709	853,086	4,38,607	414,479
	Elgandal	...	...	...	2	2	...	...	...	...	...	...	...	115	64	51	396	139	257	1,094,410	5,68,695	530,715
	Indur	...	...	...	...	...	...	...	...	...	...	...	...	190	140	50	843	258	85	639,266	3,18,982	320,284
	Medak	...	...	...	...	...	...	...	...	...	...	...	...	1,089	516	573	1,145	559	586	364,491	1,83,707	180,784
Mahratwara.	Aurangabad	...	...	...	...	...	...	2	2	...	10	8	2	5,009	2,894	2,115	7,261	4,421	2,840	828,517	4,20,665	407,852
	Birh	...	...	...	...	...	...	...	...	...	...	...	...	326	161	165	2,221	1,397	824	642,581	3,28,427	314,154
	Nander	...	...	...	...	...	...	...	...	...	...	...	...	421	291	130	1,447	1,014	433	632,275	3,19,952	312,323
	Naldrug	30	30	...	...	...	...	...	...	...	...	...	...	740	370	370	2,107	1,239	868	649,091	3,31,596	317,495
	Bidar	...	...	...	...	...	...	...	...	...	...	...	...	156	117	39	877	576	301	901,772	4,56,911	444,861
	Parbhani	...	...	...	...	...	...	...	...	...	3	3	...	1,387	804	583	5,887	3,497	1,890	805,088	4,10,287	394,801
	Sirpur Tandur	...	...	...	...	...	...	...	...	...	...	...	...	2,758	1,319	1,439	2,792	1,343	1,449	231,672	1,16,885	114,787
Karnatic or Kanada.	Gulbarga	...	...	...	...	...	...	...	...	...	2	2	...	1,624	818	806	1,941	1,031	910	648,739	3,29,242	319,497
	Raichur...	69	58	11	...	...	...	...	...	...	...	...	...	133	77	56	607	414	193	512,077	2,60,016	252,061
	Lingasugur	20	17	3	...	...	...	...	...	...	2	1	1	316	153	163	828	527	301	619,753	3,11,228	308,525
	Total Districts......	119	105	14	2	2	...	2	2	...	17	14	3	18,677	10,186	8,491	32,107	19,106	13,001	11,111,416	5,649,517	5,461,899
	Total Districts including Hyderabad...	1,064	669	395	2	2	...	2	2	...	82	63	19	28,204	15,727	12,477	52,981	31,631	21,350	11,518,627	58,59,028	5,659,599
	Railways......	...	...	...	...	...	...	4	2	2	18	17	1	740	487	253	864	566	298	6,523	4,186	2,337
	Grand Total......	1,064	669	395	2	2	...	6	4	2	100	80	20	28,944	16,214	12,730	53,845	32,197	21,648	11,525,150	58,63,214	5,661,936

TABLE XI.

Birth Places.—*Continued.*

District or State.	B—Asia beyond India. I—Adjacent to India. Baluchistan.			Afghanistan.			Yaghestan.			Turkistan.			Nipal.			China.			Straits Settlements and Malaya.			Ceylon.			Total Countries adjoining India.		
	Total.	Males.	Females.	Total.	Males.	Females.	Total.	Males.	Females.	Total.	Males.	Females.	Total.	Males.	Females.	Total.	Males.	Females.	Total.	Males.	Females.	Total.	Males.	Females.	Total.	Males.	Females.
	137	138	139	140	141	142	143	144	145	146	147	148	149	150	151	152	153	154	155	156	157	158	159	160	161	162	163
Telingana. Hyderabad. City	8	7	1	149	129	20	...	...	...	22	17	5	2	2	...	26	21	5	...	...	...	...	...	...	207	176	31
Suburbs including Secunderabad	13	10	3	164	144	20	...	...	...	10	7	3	1	...	1	5	4	1	2	1	1	2	2	...	197	168	29
Total......	21	17	4	313	273	40	...	...	...	32	24	8	3	2	1	31	25	6	2	1	1	2	2	...	404	344	60
Atraf-i-Balda District	...	...	...	21	21	...	...	...	...	...	...	...	...	...	...	...	...	...	...	...	...	...	...	...	21	21	...
Mahabubnagar (Nagar Karnul)	9	5	4	14	13	1	...	...	...	...	...	...	...	...	...	1	1	...	...	...	...	...	...	...	24	19	5
Nalgonda	...	...	...	2	1	1	...	...	...	...	...	...	...	...	...	5	5	...	...	...	...	...	...	...	7	6	1
Warangal (Khamam)	...	...	...	2	2	...	...	...	...	...	...	...	...	...	...	...	...	...	...	...	...	...	...	...	2	2	...
Elgandal	...	...	...	5	5	...	...	...	...	...	...	...	...	...	...	...	...	...	...	...	...	1	...	1	6	5	1
Indur	...	...	...	45	31	14	...	...	...	...	...	...	30	15	15	1	1	...	...	...	...	...	...	...	76	47	29
Medak	...	...	...	14	13	1	...	...	...	...	...	...	...	...	...	...	...	...	...	...	...	...	...	...	14	13	1
Mahratwara. Aurangabad	...	...	...	238	180	58	...	...	...	...	...	...	6	4	2	2	1	1	...	...	...	...	...	...	246	185	61
Birh	1	1	...	81	60	21	...	...	...	...	...	...	...	...	...	2	1	1	...	...	...	...	...	...	84	62	22
Nander	...	...	...	65	56	9	...	...	...	...	...	...	2	2	...	...	...	...	...	...	...	...	...	...	67	58	9
Naldrug	...	...	...	56	54	2	...	...	...	...	...	...	...	...	...	...	...	...	...	...	...	1	1	...	57	55	2
Bidar	...	...	...	87	73	14	5	4	1	...	...	...	...	...	...	1	1	...	...	...	...	...	...	...	93	78	15
Parbhani	...	...	...	126	110	16	...	...	...	...	...	...	...	...	...	...	...	...	...	...	...	...	...	...	126	110	16
Sirpur Tandur	...	...	...	10	6	4	...	...	...	...	...	...	...	...	...	...	...	...	...	...	...	...	...	...	10	6	4
Karnatic or Kanada. Gulbarga	...	...	...	331	292	39	...	...	...	3	3	...	11	8	3	...	...	...	...	...	...	1	1	...	346	304	42
Raichur	...	...	...	13	13	...	...	...	...	...	...	...	...	...	...	...	...	...	1	1	...	9	...	9	23	14	9
Lingasugur	...	...	...	9	8	1	...	...	...	18	16	2	4	4	...	...	...	...	...	...	...	...	...	...	31	28	3
Total Districts......	10	6	4	1,119	938	181	5	4	1	21	19	2	53	33	20	12	10	2	1	1	...	12	2	10	1,233	1,013	220
Total Districts including Hyderabad ...	31	23	8	1,432	1,211	221	5	4	1	53	43	10	56	85	21	48	35	8	3	2	1	14	4	10	1,637	1,857	280
Railways......	...	...	...	5	1	4	...	...	...	...	...	...	...	...	...	2	1	1	...	...	...	7	3	4	14	5	9
Grand Total......	31	23	8	1,437	1,212	225	5	4	1	53	43	10	56	85	21	45	36	9	3	2	1	21	7	14	1,651	1,362	289

TABLE XI.

Birth Places.—*Continued.*

District or State.	B—Asia beyond India.—*concld.* II—Remote from India. Persia. Total.	Males.	Females.	Arabia. Total.	Males.	Females.	Chinese Tartary. Total.	Males.	Females.	Asia *Unspecified.* Total.	Males.	Females.	Total Asia remote from India. Total.	Males.	Females.	Total B—Asia beyond India. Total.	Males.	Females.	Europe. England. Total.	Males.	Females.
	164	165	166	167	168	169	170	171	172	173	174	175	176	177	178	179	180	181	182	183	184
Telingana. Hyderabad. City	102	84	18	1,625	1,466	159	...	...	...	...	...	...	1,727	1,550	177	1,934	1,726	208	2	1	1
Suburbs including Secunderabad	51	39	12	1,080	975	105	4	1	3	1	...	1	1,136	1,015	121	1,333	1,183	150	2,220	2,047	173
Total	153	123	30	2,705	2,441	264	4	1	3	1	...	1	2,863	2,565	298	3,267	2,909	358	2,222	2,048	174
Atraf-i-Balda District	21	20	1	147	110	37	...	...	...	...	...	...	168	130	38	189	151	38	4	2	2
Mahabubnagar (Nagar Karnul)...	...	...	...	164	129	35	...	...	...	...	...	...	164	129	35	188	148	40	1	1	...
Nalgonda	1	1	...	53	51	2	...	...	...	...	...	...	54	52	2	61	58	3	...	...	...
Warangal (Khamam)	...	...	...	18	11	7	...	...	...	...	...	...	18	11	7	20	13	7	17	11	6
Elgandal	...	...	...	175	140	35	...	...	...	...	...	...	175	140	35	181	145	36	10	5	5
Indur	1	1	...	253	205	48	...	...	...	...	...	...	254	206	48	330	253	77	2	2	...
Medak...	2	2	...	220	179	41	...	...	...	...	...	...	222	181	41	236	194	42	5	4	1
Mahratwara. Aurangabad	...	...	...	190	152	38	...	...	...	...	...	...	190	152	38	436	337	99	16	10	6
Birh......	...	...	...	49	33	16	...	...	...	...	...	...	49	33	16	133	95	38	...	...	...
Nander	...	...	...	184	123	61	...	...	...	...	...	...	184	123	61	251	181	70	2	2	...
Naldrug	...	...	...	101	88	13	...	...	...	...	...	...	101	88	13	158	143	15	...	...	...
Bidar	...	...	...	113	93	20	...	...	...	...	...	...	113	93	20	206	171	35	...	...	...
Parbhani	...	...	...	116	98	18	...	...	...	...	...	...	116	98	18	242	208	34	...	...	...
Sirpur Tandur	...	...	...	72	64	8	...	...	...	...	...	...	72	64	8	82	70	12	...	...	...
Karnatic or Kanada. Gulbarga	...	...	...	173	132	41	...	...	...	...	...	...	173	132	41	519	436	83	...	...	...
Raichur	...	...	...	61	57	4	...	...	...	...	...	...	61	57	4	84	71	13	10	8	2
Lingasugur	1	1	...	16	14	2	...	...	...	...	...	...	17	15	2	48	43	5	5	4	1
Total Districts......	26	25	1	2,105	1,679	426	...	...	...	...	...	...	2,131	1,704	427	3,364	2,717	647	72	49	23
Total Districts including Hyderabad ...	179	148	31	4,810	4,120	690	4	1	3	1	...	1	4,994	4,269	725	6,631	5,626	1,005	2,294	2,097	197
Railways......	7	7	...	...	...	...	...	...	...	...	...	...	7	7	...	21	12	9	35	29	6
Grand Total......	186	155	31	4,810	4,120	690	4	1	3	1	...	1	5,001	4,276	725	6,652	5,638	1,014	2,329	2,126	203

TABLE XI.

Birth Places.—*Continued.*

District or State.		C—Europe.—*contd.* Scotland. Total.	Scotland. Males.	Scotland. Females.	Ireland. Total.	Ireland. Males.	Ireland. Females.	Malta. Total.	Malta. Males.	Malta. Females.	France. Total.	France. Males.	France. Females.	Belgium. Total.	Belgium. Males.	Belgium. Females.	Holland. Total.	Holland. Males.	Holland. Females.	Denmark. Total.	Denmark. Males.	Denmark. Females.	Austria. Total.	Austria. Males.	Austria. Females.
		185	186	187	188	189	190	191	192	193	194	195	196	197	198	199	200	201	202	203	204	205	206	207	208
Tellingana. Hyderabad.	City	...	...	...	...	...	...	...	...	...	1	1	...	...	...	...	...	...	...	...	...	...	...	...	...
	Suburbs including Secunderabad	90	83	7	990	897	93	10	5	5	11	6	5	7	4	3	1	1	...	2	1	1	2	2	...
	Total......	90	83	7	990	897	93	10	5	5	12	7	5	7	4	3	1	1	...	2	1	1	2	2	...
	Atraf-i-Balda District	1	1	...	...	...	...	...	...	...	...	...	...	...	...	...	...	...	...	...	...	...	...	...	...
	Mahabubnagar (Nagar Karnul) ...	...	...	...	...	...	...	...	...	...	...	...	...	...	...	...	...	...	...	1	1	...	...	...	...
	Nalgonda	...	...	...	...	...	...	...	...	...	...	...	...	...	...	...	...	...	...	...	...	...	...	...	...
	Warangal (Khamam)	2	2	...	...	...	...	...	...	...	...	...	...	...	...	...	...	...	...	...	...	...	1	1	...
	Elgandal	...	...	...	...	...	...	...	...	...	...	...	...	...	...	...	...	...	...	...	...	...	...	...	...
	Indur	...	...	...	...	...	...	...	...	...	...	...	...	...	...	...	...	...	...	...	...	...	...	...	...
	Medak...	1	1	...	...	...	...	...	...	...	...	...	...	...	...	...	...	...	...	...	...	...	...	...	...
Mahratwara.	Aurangabad	3	3	...	2	2	...	...	...	...	...	...	...	...	...	...	...	...	...	...	...	...	...	...	...
	Birh	2	2	...	2	2	...	...	...	...	...	...	...	...	...	...	...	...	...	...	...	...	...	...	...
	Nander	...	...	...	...	...	...	...	...	...	...	...	...	...	...	...	...	...	...	...	...	...	...	...	...
	Naldrug	...	...	...	...	...	...	...	...	...	...	...	...	...	...	...	...	...	...	...	...	...	...	...	...
	Bidar	...	...	...	...	...	...	...	...	...	...	...	...	...	...	...	...	...	...	...	...	...	...	...	...
	Parbhani	...	...	...	1	1	...	...	...	...	...	...	...	...	...	...	...	...	...	...	...	...	...	...	...
	Sirpur Tandur	...	...	...	...	...	...	...	...	...	...	...	...	...	...	...	...	...	...	...	...	...	...	...	...
Karnatic or Kanada.	Gulbarga	...	...	...	...	...	...	...	...	...	...	...	...	...	...	...	...	...	...	...	...	...	...	...	...
	Raichur	...	...	...	...	...	...	...	...	...	...	...	...	...	...	...	...	...	...	...	...	...	...	...	...
	Lingasugur	...	...	...	...	...	...	...	...	...	...	...	...	...	...	...	...	...	...	...	...	...	...	...	...
	Total Districts......	9	9	...	5	5	...	...	...	...	...	...	...	...	...	...	...	...	...	1	1	...	1	1	...
	Total Districts including Hyderabad ...	99	92	7	995	902	93	10	5	5	12	7	5	7	4	3	1	1	...	3	2	1	3	3	...
	Railways......	6	6	...	3	2	1	...	...	...	...	...	...	...	...	...	...	...	...	...	...	...	...	...	...
	Grand Total......	105	98	7	998	904	94	10	5	5	12	7	5	7	4	3	1	1	...	3	2	1	3	3	...

TABLE XI.
Birth Places.—*Continued.*

District or State.	C—Europe,—contd. Italy. Total.	Italy. Males.	Italy. Females.	Spain. Total.	Spain. Males.	Spain. Females.	Portugal. Total.	Portugal. Males.	Portugal. Females.	Germany. Total.	Germany. Males.	Germany. Females.	Turkey in Europe. Total.	Turkey in Europe. Males.	Turkey in Europe. Females.	Europe Unspecified, Total.	Europe Unspecified, Males.	Europe Unspecified, Females.	Total C—Europe. Total.	Total C—Europe. Males.	Total C—Europe. Females.	D—Africa. Egypt. Total.	Egypt. Males.	Egypt. Females.
	209	210	211	212	213	214	215	216	217	218	219	220	221	222	223	224	225	226	227	228	229	230	231	232
Telingana. Hyderabad. City	...	...	...	...	...	...	4	3	1	...	...	...	...	...	...	...	...	...	7	5	2	...	...	...
Suburbs including Secunderabad	8	7	1	2	2	...	1	1	...	18	12	6	1	1	...	...	...	...	8,363	8,069	294	1	1	...
Total......	8	7	1	2	2	...	5	4	1	18	12	6	1	1	...	...	...	...	8,370	8,074	296	1	1	...
Atraf-i-Balda District	...	...	...	...	...	...	...	...	...	...	...	...	...	...	...	...	...	...	5	8	2	...	...	...
Mahabubnagar (Nagar Karnul) ...	...	...	...	...	...	...	...	...	...	...	...	...	...	...	...	...	...	...	2	2	...	...	...	...
Nalgonda	...	...	...	...	...	...	...	...	...	2	1	1	...	...	...	...	...	...	2	1	1	...	...	...
Warangal (Khamam)	...	...	...	...	...	...	...	...	...	...	...	...	...	...	...	...	...	...	20	14	6	...	...	...
Elgandal	...	...	...	...	...	...	...	...	...	...	...	...	...	...	...	...	...	...	10	5	5	...	...	...
Indur	...	...	...	...	...	...	...	...	...	...	...	...	...	...	...	...	...	...	2	2	...	...	...	...
Medak...	...	...	...	...	...	...	...	...	...	...	...	...	...	...	...	...	...	...	6	5	1	...	...	...
Mahratwara. Aurangabad	...	...	...	...	...	...	...	...	...	...	...	...	...	...	...	...	...	...	21	15	6	...	...	...
Birh	...	...	...	...	...	...	...	...	...	...	...	...	...	...	...	...	...	...	4	4	...	...	...	...
Nander	...	...	...	...	...	...	...	...	...	...	...	...	1	1	...	...	...	...	8	8	...	...	...	...
Naldrug	...	...	...	...	...	...	...	...	...	...	...	...	...	...	...	...	...	...	...	...	...	...	...	...
Bidar	6	6	...	...	...	...	...	...	...	...	...	...	...	...	...	...	...	...	6	6	...	...	...	...
Parbhani	...	...	...	...	...	...	...	...	...	...	...	...	...	...	...	4	3	1	5	4	1	...	...	...
Sirpur Tandur	...	...	...	...	...	...	...	...	...	...	...	...	...	...	...	...	...	...	...	...	...	...	...	...
Karnatic or Kanada. Gulbarga	...	...	...	...	...	...	...	...	...	...	...	...	...	...	...	...	...	...	...	...	...	...	...	...
Raichur	1	1	...	...	...	...	...	...	...	1	1	...	...	...	...	...	...	...	12	10	2	...	...	...
Lingasugur	...	...	...	...	...	...	...	...	...	1	1	...	...	...	...	...	...	...	6	5	1	...	...	...
Total Districts......	7	7	...	...	...	...	...	...	...	4	3	1	1	1	...	4	3	1	104	79	25	...	...	...
Total Districts including Hyderabad...	15	14	1	2	2	...	5	4	1	22	15	7	2	2	...	4	3	1	3,474	3,153	321	1	1	...
Railways......	...	...	...	...	...	...	...	...	...	...	...	...	...	...	...	...	...	...	44	37	7	...	...	...
Grand Total......	15	14	1	2	2	...	5	4	1	22	15	7	2	2	...	4	3	1	3,518	3,190	328	1	1	...

TABLE XI.

Birth Places.—*Continued.*

District or State.	D—AFRICA.—*concld.* Abyssinia (Habsan) &c. Total.	Males.	Females.	Africa *Unspecified.* Total.	Males.	Females.	D—Total Africa. Total.	Males.	Females.	E.—AMERICA. E—America *Unspecified.* Total.	Males.	Females.	F.—AUSTRALASIA. F—Australia *Unspecified.* Total.	Males.	Females.	H—*Unspecified* of the World. Total.	Males.	Females.
	233	234	235	236	237	238	239	240	241	242	243	244	245	246	247	248	249	250
Telingana. Hyderabad. City	9	8	1	38	28	10	47	36	11	...	...	...	...	...	...	...	...	...
Suburbs including Secunderabad.	23	19	4	23	21	2	47	41	6	18	13	5	7	5	2	1,072	735	337
Total......	32	27	5	61	49	12	94	77	17	18	13	5	7	5	2	1,072	735	337
Atraf-i-Balda District	...	...	...	...	...	...	...	...	...	...	...	...	...	...	...	...	...	...
Mahabubnagar (Nagar Karnul) ...	...	...	...	1	1	...	1	1	...	4	1	3	...	...	...	...	...	...
Nalgonda	...	...	...	...	...	...	...	...	...	...	...	...	...	...	...	...	...	...
Warangal (Khamam) ...	...	...	...	...	...	...	...	...	...	3	1	2	...	...	...	...	...	...
Elgandal	...	...	...	...	...	...	...	...	...	...	...	...	...	...	...	...	...	...
Indur	...	...	...	...	...	...	...	...	...	...	...	...	...	...	...	...	...	...
Medak	...	...	...	...	...	...	...	...	...	...	...	...	...	...	...	2	2	...
Mahratwara. Aurangabad	...	...	...	...	...	...	...	...	...	1	1	...	...	...	...	...	...	...
Birh	4	4	...	...	...	...	4	4	...	...	...	...	...	...	...	...	...	...
Nander	...	...	...	...	...	...	...	...	...	...	...	...	...	...	...	...	...	...
Naldrug	...	...	...	...	...	...	...	...	...	23	8	15	...	...	...	...	...	...
Bidar	...	...	...	...	...	...	...	...	...	...	...	...	...	...	...	...	...	...
Parbhani	...	...	...	...	...	...	...	...	...	...	...	...	...	...	...	...	...	...
Sirpur Tandur	...	...	...	...	...	...	...	...	...	...	...	...	...	...	...	...	...	...
Karnatic or Kanadi. Gulbarga	...	...	...	...	...	...	...	...	...	...	...	...	...	...	...	...	...	...
Raichur	...	...	...	...	...	...	...	...	...	1	1	...	...	...	...	281	119	162
Lingasugur	...	...	...	...	...	...	...	...	...	2	1	1	...	...	...	205	117	88
Total Districts......	4	4	...	1	1	...	5	5	...	34	13	21	...	...	...	488	238	250
Total Districts including Hyderabad ...	36	31	5	62	50	12	99	82	17	52	26	26	7	5	2	1,560	973	587
Railways......	...	...	...	...	...	...	...	...	...	2	1	1	...	...	...	...	...	...
Grand Total......	36	31	5	62	50	12	99	82	17	54	27	27	7	5	2	1,560	973	587

TABLE XII.

PERSONS OF UNSOUND MIND BY AGE.

TABLE XII.

Persons of Unsound Mind by Age.

District or State.	Total Insane.			Distribution by Age.																											
				0—4		5—9		10—14		15—19		20—24		25—29		30—34		35—39		40—44		45—49		50—54		55—59		60 and over.		Unspecified.	
	Total.	Males.	Females.	Males.	Females.	Males.	Females.	Males.	Females.	Males.	Females.	Males.	Females.	Males.	Females.	Males.	Females.	Males.	Females.	Males.	Females.	Males.	Females.	Males.	Females.	Males.	Females.	Males.	Females.	Males.	Females.
1	2	3	4	5	6	7	8	9	10	11	12	13	14	15	16	17	18	19	20	21	22	23	24	25	26	27	28	29	30	31	32
Telingana. Hyderabad. City	28	19	9	3	...	...	...	...	2	2	1	1	...	2	1	3	...	...	1	2	2	...	1	4	...	1	...	1	1	...	...
Suburbs including Secunderabad	85	73	12	2	1	3	1	1	3	2	2	7	...	12	...	12	1	11	1	8	...	6	...	4	1	2	...	3	2	...	...
Total......	113	92	21	5	1	3	1	1	5	4	3	8	...	14	1	15	1	11	2	10	2	6	1	8	1	3	...	4	3	...	...
Atraf-i-Balda District	83	49	34	2	2	2	4	3	1	4	5	5	4	5	5	11	2	5	1	6	3	2	...	2	3	1	1	1	3	..	...
Mahabubnagar (Nagar Karnul) ...	82	43	39	...	1	5	3	5	5	5	6	5	4	4	2	8	4	2	...	1	3	1	2	2	2	1	...	4	7	...	...
Nalgonda	118	76	42	5	...	6	4	12	4	7	6	11	8	5	5	10	6	2	1	5	5	1	...	7	2	...	1	3	...	2	...
Warangal (Khamam)	177	106	71	1	6	8	7	10	7	14	13	12	9	12	6	15	11	10	3	11	3	1	1	6	1	1	...	5	4	...	...
Elgandal	181	111	70	2	2	12	7	12	7	11	15	14	9	11	8	17	6	8	1	10	5	2	4	4	6	...	...	8	4	...	1
Indur...	128	78	50	3	4	15	4	11	8	6	4	7	8	14	3	9	5	1	2	4	2	...	3	1	2	1	1	6	3	...	...
Medak	86	58	28	2	1	6	2	4	2	13	4	7	5	7	2	4	3	1	1	1	3	2	...	6	2	1	...	4	3	...	...
Mahratwara. Aurangabad	92	72	20	4	1	4	3	3	6	9	3	8	2	7	3	8	...	7	...	7	1	3	1	6	...	3	...	3	...	...	...
Birh	53	32	21	1	...	4	...	8	5	2	2	5	3	2	4	4	2	1	...	4	2	...	1	1	...	...	...	...	2	...	...
Nander	63	41	22	2	2	4	2	5	3	...	1	6	3	2	4	5	...	3	...	4	5	3	...	4	1	...	...	3	1	...	...
Naldrug	50	38	12	2	2	3	...	6	1	8	2	6	2	3	2	3	...	1	1	3	2	1	...	1	...	1	...	...	...	...	...
Bidar...	116	75	41	...	3	4	1	6	6	7	2	10	4	13	4	9	10	7	2	5	1	2	4	4	3	...	...	8	1	...	...
Parbhani	73	55	18	...	1	2	2	9	...	7	2	6	4	5	...	8	1	2	1	5	2	2	1	4	3	1	...	3	1	1	...
Sirpur Tandur	45	29	16	1	1	4	6	10	1	1	1	4	1	2	1	2	1	1	...	2	1	1	...	1	3	...	...	...	...	...	...
Karnatic or Kanada. Gulbarga	46	29	17	...	1	...	1	6	2	4	4	4	1	3	4	3	2	3	...	...	1	1	1	4	...	1	...	...	...	...	...
Raichur	39	25	14	2	2	4	4	4	2	2	1	2	1	4	1	...	...	2	...	1	...	1	1	1	1	..	1	2	...	...	...
Lingasugur	39	27	12	...	...	2	3	4	...	3	1	8	3	1	2	1	...	3	1	2	...	1	1	1	...	...	1	1	...	...	...
Total Districts......	1,471	944	527	27	29	85	53	118	60	103	72	120	71	100	52	117	53	59	14	71	39	24	20	55	29	11	5	51	29	3	1
Total Districts including Hyderabad ...	1,584	1,036	548	32	30	88	54	119	65	107	75	128	71	114	53	132	54	70	16	81	41	30	21	63	30	14	5	55	32	3	1
Railways......	...	...	...	...	...	...	...	...	...	...	...	...	...	...	...	...	...	...	...	...	...	...	...	...	...	...	...	...	...	...	...
Grand Total......	1,584	1,036	548	32	30	88	54	119	65	107	75	128	71	114	53	132	54	70	16	81	41	30	21	63	30	14	5	55	32	3	1

TABLE XII. A.

PERSONS OF UNSOUND MIND BY CASTE, TRIBE OR RACE.

TABLE XII A.

Persons of Unsound Mind by Caste, Tribe or Race.

Class.	Group.	Castes.	City and suburbs including Secunderabad.			Atraf-i-Balda.			Mahabubnagar (Nagar Karnul.)			Nalgonda.			Warangal. (Khamam).			Elgandal.			Indur.			Medak.			Aurangabad.			Birh.		
			Total.	Males.	Females.	Total.	Males.	Females.	Total.	Males.	Females.	Total.	Males.	Females.	Total.	Males.	Females.	Total.	Males.	Females.	Total.	Males.	Females.	Total.	Males.	Females.	Total.	Males.	Females.	Total.	Males.	Females.
1	2	3	4	5	6	7	8	9	10	11	12	13	14	15	16	17	18	19	20	21	22	23	24	25	26	27	28	29	30	31	32	33
A. Agricultural.	1	Elma	...	...	...	...	...	...	1	1	...	...	...	...	2	1	1	1	1	...	3	1	2	...	...	...	...	...	...	...	...	...
	"	Mahratta	...	...	...	1	...	1	...	...	...	...	...	...	1	...	1	3	2	1	1	1	...	1	1	...	10	8	2	12	8	4
	"	Rajput	...	...	...	1	1	...	...	...	...	...	...	...	1	1	...	1	1	...	...	...	...	1	1	...	...	...	...	1	1	...
	"	Parbhu	1	...	1	...	...	...	...	...	...	...	...	...	...	...	...	...	...	...	...	...	...	...	...	...	...	...	...	...	...	...
		Total......	1	...	1	2	1	1	1	1	...	...	...	...	4	2	2	5	4	1	4	2	2	2	2	...	10	8	2	13	9	4
	2 a.	Gujar	...	...	...	...	...	...	...	...	...	...	...	...	...	...	...	...	...	...	...	...	...	...	...	...	...	...	...	1	1	...
	"	Kunbi	2	1	1	9	5	4	12	7	5	7	7	...	11	8	3	14	11	3	21	18	3	9	7	2	19	16	3	6	4	2
	"	Mali	...	...	...	...	...	...	...	...	...	...	...	...	...	...	...	...	...	...	...	...	...	...	...	...	6	5	1	1	...	1
	"	Munurwad	2	1	1	...	...	...	1	...	1	...	...	...	2	1	1	12	8	4	7	3	4	2	1	1	...	...	...	...	...	...
	"	Pichakuntla	...	...	...	1	1	...	1	...	1	...	...	...	...	...	...	...	...	...	...	...	...	...	...	...	...	...	...	...	...	...
	"	Satani	...	...	...	...	...	...	1	1	...	...	...	...	2	2	...	1	1	...	...	...	...	...	...	...	...	...	...	...	...	...
	"	Mutrasi	1	1	...	9	4	5	4	1	3	6	2	4	6	2	4	6	3	3	...	...	...	11	8	3	...	...	...	...	...	...
		Total......	5	3	2	19	10	9	19	9	10	13	9	4	21	13	8	33	23	10	28	21	7	22	16	6	25	21	4	8	5	3
	2 b.	Koli	...	...	...	...	...	...	...	...	...	...	...	...	...	...	...	...	...	...	12	7	5	...	...	...	1	1	...	...	...	...
		Total......	...	...	...	...	...	...	...	...	...	...	...	...	...	...	...	...	...	...	12	7	5	...	...	...	1	1	...	...	...	...
	2 c.	Dher	5	4	1	6	2	4	17	9	8	33	22	11	22	10	12	27	14	13	11	7	4	5	2	3	7	4	3	4	2	2
	"	Mang	3	3	...	1	1	...	...	...	...	...	...	...	13	5	8	...	...	...	11	7	4	8	4	4	1	1	...	1	...	1
		Total......	8	7	1	7	3	4	17	9	8	33	22	11	35	15	20	27	14	13	22	14	8	13	6	7	8	5	3	5	2	3
	4	Gond	...	...	...	...	...	...	...	...	...	...	...	...	...	...	...	...	...	...	...	...	...	...	...	...	1	...	1	...	...	...
	"	Chenchwad	...	...	...	...	...	...	1	...	1	1	...	1	...	...	...	...	...	...	...	...	...	...	...	...	...	...	...	...	...	...
	"	Koya	...	...	...	...	...	...	...	...	...	...	...	...	5	4	1	1	1	...	...	...	...	...	...	...	...	...	...	...	...	...
		Total......	...	...	...	...	...	...	1	...	1	1	...	1	5	4	1	1	1	...	...	...	...	...	...	...	1	...	1	...	...	...

TABLE XII A.

Persons of Unsound Mind by Caste, Tribe or Race.—*Continued.*

Class.	Group.	Castes.	Nander. Total.	Nander. Males.	Nander. Females.	Naldrug. Total.	Naldrug. Males.	Naldrug. Females.	Bidar. Total.	Bidar. Males.	Bidar. Females.	Parbhani. Total.	Parbhani. Males.	Parbhani. Females.	Sirpur Tandur. Total.	Sirpur Tandur. Males.	Sirpur Tandur. Females.	Gulbarga. Total.	Gulbarga. Males.	Gulbarga. Females.	Raichur. Total.	Raichur. Males.	Raichur. Females.	Lingasugur. Total.	Lingasugur. Males.	Lingasugur. Females.	Railways. Total.	Railways. Males.	Railways. Females.	Total. Total.	Total. Males.	Total. Females.
			34	35	36	37	38	39	40	41	42	43	44	45	46	47	48	49	50	51	52	53	54	55	56	57	58	59	60	61	62	63
A. Agricultural.	1 ...	Elma	...	...	...	4	...	4	3	1	2	...	...	...	1	...	1	...	...	...	...	...	...	...	...	...	...	...	...	15	5	10
	" ...	Mahratta	12	4	8	15	12	3	9	4	5	24	14	10	...	...	...	...	...	...	2	2	...	1	1	...		...	...	92	57	35
	" ...	Rajput	...	...	...	1	1	...	3	3	...	...	...	...	...	...	...	...	...	...	...	...	...	...	...	...	...	...	...	9	9	...
	" ...	Parbhu	...	...	...	...	...	...	...	...	...	...	...	...	...	...	...	...	...	...	...	...	...	...	...	...	...	...	...	1	...	1
		Total......	12	4	8	20	13	7	15	8	7	24	14	10	1	...	1	...	...	...	2	2	...	1	1	...	...	...	...	117	71	46
	2 a. ...	Gujar	...	...	...	...	...	...	...	...	...	...	...	...	...	...	...	...	...	...	...	...	...	...	...	...	...	...	...	1	1	...
	" ...	Kunbi	...	...	...	3	2	1	2	1	1	...	...	...	6	2	4	2	1	1	3	2	1	2	1	1	...	...	...	128	93	35
	" ...	Mali	...	...	...	2	1	1	3	3	...	2	1	1	...	...	...	...	...	...	...	...	...	...	...	...	...	...	...	14	10	4
	" ...	Munurwad...	4	2	2	...	...	...	1	1	...	...	...	...	1	1	...	1	1	...	...	...	...	1	1	...	...	...	...	34	20	14
	" ...	Pichakuntla	...	...	...	...	...	...	...	...	...	...	...	...	...	...	...	...	...	...	...	...	...	...	...	...	...	...	...	2	1	1
	" ...	Satani	...	...	...	...	...	...	...	...	...	...	...	...	...	...	...	...	...	...	...	...	...	...	...	...	...	...	...	4	4	...
	" ...	Mutrasi	...	...	...	...	...	...	...	...	...	...	...	...	...	...	...	...	...	...	...	...	...	...	...	...	...	...	...	43	21	22
		Total......	4	2	2	5	3	2	6	5	1	2	1	1	7	3	4	3	2	1	3	2	1	3	2	1	...	...	...	226	150	76
	2 b. ...	Koli	3	2	1	...	...	...	7	4	3	...	...	...	1	1	...	2	...	2	3	1	2	3	1	2	...	...	...	32	17	15
		Total......	3	2	1	...	...	...	7	4	3	...	...	...	1	1	...	2	...	2	3	1	2	3	1	2	...	...	...	32	17	15
	2 c. ...	Dher	8	5	3	1	1	...	8	7	1	11	9	2	8	6	2	1	1	...	1	1	...		...	...	...	...	...	175	106	69
	" ...	Mang	5	3	2	1	1	...	7	4	3	4	3	1	5	3	2	3	1	2	...	...	...	...	...	...	...	...	...	63	36	27
		Total......	13	8	5	2	2	...	15	11	4	15	12	3	13	9	4	4	2	2	1	1	...	...	...	...	...	...	...	238	142	96
	4 ...	Gond	...	...	...	...	...	...	...	...	...	...	...	...	...	...	...	...	...	...	...	...	...	...	...	...	...	...	...	1	...	1
	" ...	Chenchwad	...	...	...	...	...	...	...	...	...	...	...	...	...	...	...	...	...	...	...	...	...	...	...	...	...	...	...	2	...	2
	" ...	Koya	...	...	...	...	...	...	...	...	...	...	...	...	...	...	...	...	...	...	...	...	...	...	...	...	...	...	...	6	5	1
		Total......	...	...	...	...	...	...	...	...	...	...	...	...	...	...	...	...	...	...	...	...	...	...	...	...	...	...	...	9	5	4

TABLE XII A.
Persons of Unsound Mind.

TABLE XII A.

Persons of Unsound Mind by Caste, Tribe or Race.—*Continued.*

Class.	Group.	Castes.	City and suburbs including Secunderabad. Total.	Males.	Females.	Atraf-i-Balda. Total.	Males.	Females.	Mahabubnagar (Nagar Karnul.) Total.	Males.	Females.	Nalgonda. Total.	Males.	Females.	Warangal. (Khamam.) Total.	Males.	Females.	Elgandal. Total.	Males.	Females.	Indur. Total.	Males.	Females.	Medak. Total.	Males.	Females.	Aurangabad. Total.	Males.	Females.	Birh. Total.	Males.	Females.
1	2	3	4	5	6	7	8	9	10	11	12	13	14	15	16	17	18	19	20	21	22	23	24	25	26	27	28	29	30	31	32	33
B. Professional.	5	Brahmin	7	6	1	1	1	...	4	2	2	1	1	...	6	6	...	8	6	2	3	3	...	...	...	...	4	3	1	4	3	1
	"	Jangam	...	...	...	2	2	...	1	...	1	...	...	...	1	1	...	1	1	...	...	...	...	1	...	1	...	...	...	2	2	...
		Total......	7	6	1	3	3	...	5	2	3	1	1	...	7	7	...	9	7	2	3	3	...	1	...	1	4	3	1	6	5	1
	6	Gosain	...	...	...	...	...	...	...	...	...	...	...	...	...	...	...	...	...	...	...	...	...	...	...	...	...	...	...	...	...	...
		Total......	...	...	...	...	...	...	...	...	...	...	...	...	...	...	...	...	...	...	...	...	...	...	...	...	...	...	...	...	...	...	...	...
	7	Gurao	...	...	...	...	...	...	...	...	...	...	...	...	...	...	...	...	...	...	...	...	...	...	...	...	...	...	...	...	...	...
		Total	...	...	...	...	...	...	...	...	...	...	...	...	...	...	...	...	...	...	...	...	...	...	...	...	...	...	...	...	...	...
	8	Bhat	...	...	...	...	...	...	1	1	...	...	...	...	...	...	...	2	2	...	...	...	...	...	...	...	...	...	...	...	...	...
		Total......	...	...	...	...	...	...	1	1	...	...	...	...	...	...	...	2	2	...	...	...	...	...	...	...	...	...	...	...	...	...
	9	Kayesth	2	2	...	...	...	...	...	...	...	...	...	...	1	...	1	...	...	...	...	...	...	...	...	...	...	...	...	...	...	...
		Total......	2	2	...	...	...	...	...	...	...	...	...	...	1	...	1	...	...	...	...	...	...	...	...	...	...	...	...	...	...	...
C. Commercial.	14	Bablija	...	...	...	5	2	3	...	...	...	2	2	...	3	2	1	2	2	...	...	...	...	2	1	1	...	...	...	...	...	...
	"	Komti	1	1	...	8	6	2	5	3	2	6	5	1	8	8	...	...	...	...	4	1	3	5	3	2	...	...	...	...	...	...
	"	Wani	2	1	1	...	...	...	1	...	1	...	...	...	...	...	...	18	9	9	2	2	...	...	...	...	5	5	...	...	...	...
		Total......	3	2	1	13	8	5	6	3	3	8	7	1	11	10	1	20	11	9	6	3	3	7	4	3	5	5	...	...	...	...

TABLE XII A.

Persons of Unsound Mind by Caste, Tribe or Race.—*Continued*.

Class.	Group.	Castes.	Nander.			Naldrug.			Bidar.			Parbhani.			Sirpur Tandur.			Gulbarga.			Raichur.			Lingasugur.			Railways.			Total.		
			Total.	Males.	Females.	Total.	Males.	Females.	Total.	Males.	Females.	Total.	Males.	Females.	Total.	Males.	Females.	Total.	Males.	Females.	Total.	Males.	Females.	Total.	Males.	Females.	Total.	Males.	Females.	Total.	Males.	Females.
			34	35	36	37	38	39	40	41	42	43	44	45	46	47	48	49	50	51	52	53	54	55	56	57	58	59	60	61	62	63
B. Professional.	5	Brahmin	2	2	...	...	...	...	6	2	4	6	6	...	1	1	...	3	2	1	...	...	...	...	...	...	...	...	...	56	44	12
	"	Jangam	...	...	...	...	...	...	...	...	...	...	...	...	1	1	...	...	...	...	...	...	...	1	...	1	...	...	...	10	7	3
		Total	2	2	...	...	...	...	6	2	4	6	6	...	2	2	...	3	2	1	...	...	...	1	...	1	...	...	...	66	51	15
	6	Gosain	...	...	...	1	1	...	...	...	...	1	1	...	...	...	...	...	...	...	...	...	...	...	...	...	...	...	...	2	2	...
		Total	...	...	...	1	1	...	...	...	...	1	1	...	...	...	...	...	...	...	...	...	...	...	...	...	...	...	...	2	2	...
	7	Gurao	3	3	...	...	...	...	1	...	1	1	1	...	2	2	...	...	...	...	...	...	...	...	...	...	...	...	...	7	6	1
		Total	3	3	...	...	...	...	1	...	1	1	1	...	2	2	...	...	...	...	...	...	...	...	...	...	...	...	...	7	6	1
	8	Bhat	...	...	...	...	...	...	...	...	...	...	...	...	...	...	...	...	...	...	...	...	...	...	...	...	...	...	...	3	3	...
		Total	...	...	...	...	...	...	...	...	...	...	...	...	...	...	...	...	...	...	...	...	...	...	...	...	...	...	...	3	3	...
	9	Kayesth	...	...	...	...	...	...	...	...	...	...	...	...	...	...	...	...	...	...	...	...	...	...	...	...	...	...	...	3	2	1
		Total	...	...	...	...	...	...	...	...	...	...	...	...	...	...	...	...	...	...	...	...	...	...	...	...	...	...	...	3	2	1
C. Commercial.	14	Bablija	...	...	...	...	...	...	1	...	1	...	...	...	...	...	...	...	...	...	3	3	...	...	...	...	...	...	...	18	12	6
	"	Komti	2	2	...	...	...	...	2	2	...	...	...	...	...	...	...	2	2	...	...	...	...	...	...	...	...	...	...	43	33	10
	"	Wani	5	3	2	4	3	1	22	16	6	1	1	...	1	1	...	8	2	6	...	...	...	8	7	1	...	...	...	77	50	27
		Total	7	5	2	4	3	1	25	18	7	1	1	...	1	1	...	10	4	6	3	3	...	8	7	1	...	...	...	138	95	43

TABLE XII A.

Persons of Unsound Mind by Caste, Tribe or Race.—*Continued.*

Class.	Group.	Castes.	City and suburbs including Secunderabad. Total.	Males.	Females.	Atraf-i-Balda. Total.	Males.	Females.	Mahabubnagar (Nagar Karnul.) Total.	Males.	Females.	Nalgonda. Total.	Males.	Females.	Warangal. (Khamam.) Total.	Males.	Females.	Elgandal. Total.	Males.	Females.	Indur. Total.	Males.	Females.	Medak. Total.	Males.	Females.	Aurangabad. Total.	Males.	Females.	Birh. Total.	Males.	Females.
1	2	3	4	5	6	7	8	9	10	11	12	13	14	15	16	17	18	19	20	21	22	23	24	25	26	27	28	29	30	31	32	33
C. Commercial.	16	Banjara	1	...	1	...	...	...	...	...	...	...	...	...	...	...	...	...	...	...	...	...	...	...	...	...	...	...	...	...	...	...
	"	Lad...	...	...	...	...	...	...	...	...	...	...	...	...	...	...	...	...	...	...	...	...	...	...	...	...	...	...	...	...	...	...
	"	Lambani	...	...	...	1	...	1	...	...	...	4	4	...	5	4	1	...	...	...	...	...	...	...	...	...	1	1	...	...	...	...
		Total......	1	...	1	1	...	1	...	...	...	4	4	...	5	4	1	...	...	...	...	...	...	...	...	...	1	1	...	...	...	...
D. Artisan and Village Menial.	17	Panchal	...	...	...	1	1	...	...	...	...	...	...	...	...	...	...	...	...	...	...	...	...	...	...	...	...	...	...	...	...	...
	"	Sonar	1	1	...	...	...	...	...	...	...	3	2	1	2	...	2	2	1	1	1	1	...	4	2	2	1	1	...	4	3	1
		Total....	1	1	...	1	1	...	...	...	...	3	2	1	2	...	2	2	1	1	1	1	...	4	2	2	1	1	...	4	3	1
	18	Hajjam	...	...	...	...	...	...	1	1	..	...	...	...	2	1	1	3	2	1	5	2	3	1	...	1	1	1	...	1	...	1
		Total......	...	...	...	...	...	...	1	1	...	...	...	...	2	1	1	3	2	1	5	2	3	1	...	1	1	1	...	1	...	1
	19	Lohar	...	...	...	...	[illegible]	...	...	...	...	...	...	...	...	...	...	1	...	1	3	3	...	...	...	...	...	...	...	...	...	...
		Total......	...	...	...	...	...	...	...	...	...	...	...	...	...	...	...	1	...	1	3	3	...	...	...	...	...	...	...	...	...	...
	20	Barhai, (Sutar)	1	...	1	1	...	1	1	1	...	...	...	...	2	2	...	...	...	...	...	...	...	...	...	...	...	...	...	...	...	...
	"	Od or Gaondi	...	...	...	...	...	...	1	...	1	...	...	...	...	...	...	3	...	3	...	...	...	...	...	...	...	...	...	...	...	...
	"	Hanigaru ...	...	...	...	...	...	...	...	...	...	...	...	...	...	...	...	...	...	...	...	...	...	...	...	...	...	...	...	...	...	...
		Total......	1	...	1	1	...	1	2	1	1	...	...	...	2	2	...	3	...	3	...	...	...	...	...	...	...	...	...	...	...	...
	21	Kasar	...	...	...	...	...	...	...	...	...	...	...	...	...	...	...	...	...	...	1	1	...	...	...	...	...	...	...	1	1	...
		Total......	...	...	...	...	...	...	...	...	...	...	...	...	...	...	...	...	...	...	1	1		...	...	...	...	...	...	1	1	...
	22	Darzi	...	...	...	...	...	...	...	...	...	...	...	...	...	...	...	1	1	...	...	...	...	...	...	...	...	...	...	...	...	...
	"	Zingar	...	...	...	...	...	...	...	...	...	...	...	...	...	...	...	...	...	...	...	...	...	...	...	...	...	...	...	...	...	...
		Total......	...	...	...	...	...	...	...	...	...	...	...	...	...	...	...	1	1	...	...	...	...	...	...	...	...	...	...	...	...	...

TABLE XII A.

Persons of Unsound Mind by Caste, Tribe or Race.—*Continued.*

Class.	Group.	Castes.	Nander.			Naldrug.			Bidar.			Parbhani.			Sirpur Tandur.			Gulbarga.			Raichur.			Lingasugur.			Railways.			Total.		
			Total.	Males.	Females.	Total.	Males.	Females.	Total.	Males.	Females.	Total.	Males.	Females.	Total.	Males.	Females.	Total.	Males.	Females.	Total.	Males.	Females.	Total.	Males.	Females.	Total.	Males.	Females.	Total.	Males.	Females.
			34	35	36	37	38	39	40	41	42	43	44	45	46	47	48	49	50	51	52	53	54	55	56	57	58	59	60	61	62	63
C. Commercial.	16	Banjara	...	...	...	...	...	...	...	...	...	...	...	...	...	...	...	...	...	...	...	...	...	...	...	...	...	...	...	1	...	1
	"	Lad	...	...	...	...	...	...	1	1	...	...	...	...	...	...	...	...	...	...	...	...	...	...	...	...	...	...	...	1	1	...
	"	Lambani	...	...	...	...	...	...	...	...	...	1	1	...	1	...	1	4	3	1	...	...	...	...	...	...	...	...	...	17	13	4
		Total......	...	...	...	...	...	...	1	1	...	1	1	...	1	...	1	4	3	1	...	...	...	...	...	...	...	...	...	19	14	5
D. Artisan and Village Menial.	17	Panchal	1	1	...	...	...	...	1	...	1	...	...	...	...	...	...	1	...	1	2	2	...	...	...	...	...	...	...	6	4	2
	"	Sonar	...	...	...	...	...	...	2	1	1	3	2	1	...	...	...	1	1	...	...	...	...	...	...	...	...	...	...	24	15	9
		Total......	1	1	...	...	...	...	3	1	2	3	2	1	...	...	...	2	1	1	2	2	...	...	...	...	...	...	...	30	19	11
	18	Hajjam	...	...	...	...	...	...	...	...	...	1	...	1	...	...	...	...	...	...	...	...	...	1	...	1	...	...	...	16	7	9
		Total......	...	...	...	...	...	...	...	...	...	1	...	1	...	...	...	...	...	...	...	...	...	1	...	1	...	...	...	16	7	9
	19	Lohar	1	1	...	...	...	...	1	1	...	1	...	1	...	...	...	...	...	...	...	...	...	...	...	...	...	...	...	7	5	2
		Total......	1	1	...	...	...	...	1	1	...	1	...	1	...	...	...	...	...	...	...	...	...	...	...	...	...	...	...	7	5	2
	20	Barhai, (Sutar)	1	1	...	...	...	...	4	1	3	...	...	...	1	1	...	...	...	...	...	...	...	...	...	...	...	...	...	11	6	5
	"	Od or Gaondi	...	...	...	...	...	...	...	...	...	...	...	...	...	...	...	1	1	...	...	...	...	...	...	...	...	...	...	5	1	4
	"	Hanigaru	...	...	...	...	...	...	...	...	...	...	...	...	...	...	...	...	...	...	...	...	...	3	3	...	...	...	...	3	3	...
		Total......	1	1	...	...	...	...	4	1	3	...	...	...	1	1	...	1	1	...	...	...	...	3	3	...	...	...	...	19	10	9
	21	Kasar	...	...	...	1	1	...	1	...	1	...	...	...	...	...	...	...	...	...	...	...	...	...	...	...	...	...	...	4	3	1
		Total......	...	...	...	1	1	...	1	...	1	...	...	...	...	...	...	...	...	...	...	...	...	...	...	...	...	...	...	4	3	1
	22	Darzi	...	...	...	...	...	...	...	...	...	...	...	...	...	...	...	...	...	...	...	...	...	1	1	...	...	...	...	2	2	...
	"	Zingar	...	...	...	...	...	...	...	...	...	...	...	...	...	...	...	2	2	...	1	...	1	...	...	...	...	...	...	3	2	1
		Total......	...	...	...	...	...	...	...	...	...	...	...	...	...	...	...	2	2	...	1	...	1	1	1	...	...	...	...	5	4	1

TABLE XII A.

Persons of Unsound Mind by Caste, Tribe or Race.—*Continued.*

Class.	Group.	Castes.	City and suburbs including Secunderabad.			Atraf-i-Balda.			Mahabubnagar. (Nagar Karnul.)			Nalgonda.			Warangal. (Khamam.)			Elgandal.			Indur.			Medak.			Aurangabad.			Birh.		
			Total.	Males.	Females.	Total.	Males.	Females.	Total.	Males.	Females.	Total.	Males.	Females.	Total.	Males.	Females.	Total.	Males.	Females.	Total.	Males.	Females.	Total.	Males.	Females.	Total.	Males.	Females.	Total.	Males.	Females.
1	2	3	4	5	6	7	8	9	10	11	12	13	14	15	16	17	18	19	20	21	22	23	24	25	26	27	28	29	30	31	32	33
D. Artizan and Village Menial.	23	Khatri	1	1	...	...	...	...	...	...	...	...	...	...	...	...	...	...	...	...	2	1	1	...	...	...	1	1	...	...	...	...
	"	Rangari or Rangrez	...	...	...	...	...	...	...	...	...	...	...	...	...	...	...	...	...	...	2	1	1	...	...	...	...	...	...	...	...	...
	"	Sali or Julaha	...	...	...	4	1	3	...	...	...	2	1	1	3	2	1	16	10	6	6	5	1	4	3	1	...	...	...	1	...	1
		Total......	1	1	...	4	1	3	...	...	...	2	1	1	3	2	1	16	10	6	10	7	3	4	3	1	1	1	...	1	...	1
	24	Dhobi	1	1	...	...	...	...	1	1	...	2	1	1	6	3	3	3	...	3	3	1	2	1	1	...	2	2	...	...	...	...
		Total......	1	1	...	...	...	...	1	1	...	2	1	1	6	3	3	3	...	3	3	1	2	1	1	...	2	2	...	...	...	...
	25	Pinjari	...	...	...	...	...	...	...	...	...	1	...	1	...	...	...	1	1	...	...	...	...	...	...	...	...	...	...	...	...	...
		Total......	...	...	...	...	...	...	...	...	...	1	...	1	...	...	...	1	1	...	...	...	...	...	...	...	...	...	...	...	...	...
	26	Dhangar	...	...	...	5	2	3	3	3	...	17	8	9	18	12	6	18	9	9	10	5	5	9	7	2	4	4	...	9	5	4
		Total......	...	...	...	5	2	3	3	3	...	17	8	9	18	12	6	18	9	9	10	5	5	9	7	2	4	4	...	9	5	4
	27	Teli	...	...	...	...	...	...	...	...	...	2	1	1	...	...	...	...	...	...	...	...	...	...	...	...	2	1	1	...	...	...
		Total......	...	...	...	...	...	...	...	...	...	2	1	1	...	...	...	...	...	...	...	...	...	...	...	...	2	1	1	...	...	...
	28	Kumhar	...	...	...	...	...	...	1	1	...	3	2	1	8	4	4	2	1	1	...	...	...	...	...	...	3	3	...	...	...	...
		Total......	...	...	...	...	...	...	1	1	...	3	2	1	8	4	4	2	1	1	...	...	...	...	...	...	3	3	...	...	...	...

TABLE XII A.

Persons of Unsound Mind by Caste, Tribe or Race.—*Continued.*

Class.	Group.	Castes.	Nander. Total.	Nander. Males.	Nander. Females.	Naldrug. Total.	Naldrug. Males.	Naldrug. Females.	Bidar. Total.	Bidar. Males.	Bidar. Females.	Parbhani. Total.	Parbhani. Males.	Parbhani. Females.	Sirpur Tandur. Total.	Sirpur Tandur. Males.	Sirpur Tandur. Females.	Gulbarga. Total.	Gulbarga. Males.	Gulbarga. Females.	Raichur. Total.	Raichur. Males.	Raichur. Females.	Lingasugur. Total.	Lingasugur. Males.	Lingasugur. Females.	Railways. Total.	Railways. Males.	Railways. Females.	Total. Total.	Total. Males.	Total. Females.
			34	35	36	37	38	39	40	41	42	43	44	45	46	47	48	49	50	51	52	53	54	55	56	57	58	59	60	61	62	63
D. Artisan and Village Menial.	23	Khatri	...	...	...	...	...	...	...	...	...	...	...	...	2	...	2	...	...	...	...	...	...	...	...	...	...	...	...	6	3	3
	"	Rangari or Rangrez ...	...	...	...	...	...	...	...	...	...	...	...	...	...	...	...	1	1	...	...	...	...	...	...	...	...	...	...	3	2	1
	"	Sali or Julaha	1	1	...	...	...	...	...	...	...	...	...	...	4	2	2	1	1	...	1	1	...	...	...	...	...	...	...	43	27	16
		Total......	1	1	...	...	...	...	...	...	...	...	...	...	6	2	4	2	2	...	1	1	...	...	...	...	...	...	...	52	32	20
	24	Dhobi	...	...	...	...	...	...	2	1	1	...	...	...	1	1	...	...	...	...	...	...	...	4	2	2	...	...	...	26	14	12
		Total......	...	...	...	...	...	...	2	1	1	...	...	...	1	1	...	...	...	...	...	...	...	4	2	2	...	...	...	26	14	12
	25	Pinjari	...	...	...	...	...	...	...	...	...	...	...	...	...	...	...	...	...	...	...	...	...	...	...	...	...	...	...	2	1	1
		Total......	...	...	...	...	...	...	...	...	...	...	...	...	...	...	...	...	...	...	...	...	...	...	...	...	...	...	...	2	1	1
	26	Dhangar	4	3	1	4	4	...	8	6	2	5	5	...	2	2	...	4	4	...	5	4	1	5	4	1	...	...	...	130	87	43
		Total......	4	3	1	4	4	...	8	6	2	5	5	...	2	2	...	4	4	...	5	4	1	5	4	1	...	...	...	130	87	43
	27	Teli...	...	...	...	1	1	...	...	...	...	...	...	...	...	...	...	...	...	...	1	1	...	1	1	...	...	...	...	7	5	2
		Total......	...	...	...	1	1	...	...	...	...	...	...	...	...	...	...	...	...	...	1	1	...	1	1	...	...	...	...	7	5	2
	28	Kumhar	...	...	...	1	1	...	...	...	...	1	1	...	3	3	...	...	...	...	...	...	...	...	...	...	...	...	...	22	16	6
		Total......	...	...	...	1	1	...	...	...	...	1	1	...	3	3	...	...	...	...	...	...	...	...	...	...	...	...	...	22	16	6

TABLE XII A.

Persons of Unsound Mind by Caste, Tribe or Race—*Continued.*

Class.	Group.	Castes.	City and suburbs including Secunderabad.			Atraf-i-Balda.			Mahabubnagar. (Nagar Karnul.)			Nalgonda.			Warangal. (Khamam.)			Elgandal.			Indur.			Medak.			Aurangabad.			Birh.		
			Total.	Males.	Females.	Total.	Males.	Females.	Total.	Males.	Females.	Total.	Males.	Females.	Total.	Males.	Females.	Total.	Males.	Females.	Total.	Males.	Females.	Total.	Males.	Females.	Total.	Males.	Females.	Total.	Males.	Females.
1	2	3	4	5	6	7	8	9	10	11	12	13	14	15	16	17	18	19	20	21	22	23	24	25	26	27	28	29	30	31	32	33
D. Artisan and Village Menial.	35 ..	Bhoi	2	1	1	...	...	...	...	...	...	...	...	...	...	...	...	...	...	...	13	4	9	...	...	...	...	...	...	...	...	...
		Besta	...	...	...	...	...	...	2	1	1	...	...	...	1	1	...	6	2	4	...	...	...	1	1	...	...	...	...	...	...	...
		Total......	2	1	1	...	...	...	2	1	1	...	...	...	1	1	...	6	2	4	13	4	9	1	1	...	...	...	...	...	...	...
	36 ...	Goundla	1	1	...	6	4	2	3	2	1	4	3	1	9	5	4	7	7	...	1	...	1	4	2	2	...	...	...	...	...	...
		Kalal	...	...	...	...	...	...	...	...	...	...	...	...	...	...	...	...	...	...	...	...	...	...	...	...	...	...	...	...	...	...
		Total......	1	1	...	6	4	2	3	2	1	4	3	1	9	5	4	7	7	...	1	...	1	4	2	2	...	...	...	...	...	...
	37 ...	Kasai	...	...	...	...	...	...	2	2	...	...	...	...	...	...	...	1	1	...	...	...	...	...	...	...	...	...	...	...	...	...
		Total......	...	...	...	...	...	...	2	2	...	...	...	...	...	...	...	1	1	...	...	...	...	...	...	...	...	...	...	...	...	...
	38 ...	Chamar	2	2	...	...	...	...	...	...	...	...	...	...	...	...	...	...	...	...	...	...	...	...	...	...	1	...	1	...	...	...
	" ...	Dhoro	...	...	...	...	...	...	...	...	...	...	...	...	...	...	...	...	...	...	...	...	...	...	...	...	2	2	...	...	...	...
		Total	2	2	...	...	...	...	...	...	...	...	...	...	...	...	...	...	...	...	...	...	...	...	...	...	3	2	1	...	...	...
E. Vagrant minor artisans and performers, &c.	38 a. ..	Bedar	...	...	...	...	...	...	...	...	...	...	...	...	...	...	...	...	...	...	...	...	...	...	...	...	...	...	...	...	...	...
		Naik	...	...	...	...	...	...	...	...	...	...	...	...	1	1	...	...	...	...	1	...	1	...	...	...	...	...	...	...	...	...
		Total......	...	...	...	...	...	...	...	...	...	...	...	...	1	1	...	...	...	...	1	...	1	...	...	...	...	...	...	...	...	...
	40 ...	Waddewar	...	...	...	1	...	1	...	...	...	3	1	2	4	4	...	...	...	...	...	...	...	...	...	...	1	...	1	...	...	...
		Total......	...	...	...	1	...	1	...	...	...	3	1	2	4	4	...	...	...	...	...	...	...	...	...	...	1	...	1	...	...	...

TABLE XII A.

Persons of Unsound Mind by Casto, Tribe or Race.—*Continued.*

Class.	Group.	Castes.	Nander. Total.	Nander. Males.	Nander. Females.	Naldrug. Total.	Naldrug. Males.	Naldrug. Females.	Bidar. Total.	Bidar. Males.	Bidar. Females.	Parbhani. Total.	Parbhani. Males.	Parbhani. Females.	Sirpur Tandur. Total.	Sirpur Tandur. Males	Sirpur Tandur. Females.	Gulbarga. Total.	Gulbarga. Males.	Gulbarga. Females.	Raichur. Total.	Raichur. Males.	Raichur. Females.	Lingasugur. Total.	Lingasugur. Males.	Lingasugur. Females.	Railways. Total.	Railways. Males.	Railways. Females.	Total. Total.	Total. Males.	Total. Females.
			34	35	36	37	38	39	40	41	42	43	44	45	46	47	48	49	50	51	52	53	54	55	56	57	58	59	60	61	62	63
D. Artisan and Village Menial.	35 ...	Bhoi	1	1	...	...	...	...	...	...	...	...	...	...	1	...	1	...	...	...	...	...	...	...	...	...	...	...	...	17	6	11
		Besta	...	...	...	...	...	...	...	...	...	...	...	...	...	...	...	...	...	...	1	...	1	...	...	...	...	...	...	11	5	6
		Total......	1	1	...	...	...	...	...	...	...	...	...	...	1	...	1	...	...	...	1	...	1	...	...	...	...	...	...	28	11	17
	36 ...	Goundla	...	...	...	...	...	...	2	2	...	...	...	...	...	...	...	1	1	...	1	1	...	...	...	...	...	...	...	39	28	11
		Kalal	...	...	...	...	...	...	...	...	...	...	...	...	1	...	1	...	...	...	...	...	...	...	...	...	...	...	...	1	...	1
		Total......	...	...	...	...	...	...	2	2	...	...	...	...	1	...	1	1	1	...	1	1	...	...	...	...	...	...	...	40	28	12
	37 ...	Kasai	...	...	...	...	...	...	...	...	...	...	...	...	...	...	...	...	...	...	...	...	...	...	...	...	...	...	...	3	3	...
		Total......	...	...	...	...	...	...	...	...	...	...	...	...	...	...	...	...	...	...	...	...	...	...	...	...	...	...	...	3	3	...
	38 ...	Chamar	1	1	...	...	...	...	1	...	1	...	...	...	...	...	...	1	1	...	...	...	...	...	...	...	...	...	...	6	4	2
	" ...	Dhore	...	...	...	...	...	...	...	...	...	...	...	...	...	...	...	...	...	...	...	...	...	...	...	...	...	...	...	2	2	...
		Total......	1	1	...	...	...	...	1	...	1	...	...	...	...	...	...	1	1	...	...	...	...	...	...	...	...	...	...	8	6	2
E. Vagrant minor artisans and performers, &c.	38 a. ...	Bedar	...	...	...	...	...	...	...	...	...	...	...	...	...	...	...	...	...	...	8	3	5	1	1	...	...	...	...	9	4	5
		Naik	...	...	...	...	...	...	...	...	...	...	...	...	...	...	...	...	...	...	...	...	...	...	...	...	...	...	...	2	1	1
		Total......	...	...	...	...	...	...	...	...	...	...	...	...	...	...	...	...	...	...	8	3	5	1	1	...	...	...	...	11	5	6
	40 ...	Waddewar...	1	1	...	1	...	1	1	1	...	...	...	...	...	...	...	...	...	...	3	1	2	1	...	1	...	...	...	16	8	8
		Total......	1	1	...	1	...	1	1	1	...	...	...	...	...	...	...	...	...	...	3	1	2	1	...	1	...	...	...	16	8	8

TABLE XII A.

Persons of Unsound Mind by Caste, Tribe or Race.—*Continued.*

Class.	Group.	Castes.	City and suburbs including Secunderabad. Total.	Males.	Females.	Atraf-i-Balda. Total.	Males.	Females.	Mahabubnagar. (Nagar Karnul.) Total.	Males.	Females.	Nalgonda. Total.	Males.	Females.	Warangal. (Khamam.) Total.	Males.	Females.	Elgandal. Total.	Males.	Females.	Indur. Total.	Males.	Females.	Medak. Total.	Males.	Females.	Aurangabad. Total.	Males.	Females.	Bīrh. Total.	Males.	Females.
1	2	3	4	5	6	7	8	9	10	11	12	13	14	15	16	17	18	19	20	21	22	23	24	25	26	27	28	29	30	31	32	33
E. Vagrant minor artisans and performers, &c.	43 ...	Burud	...	...	...	...	...	...	1	1	...	...	...	...	...	...	...	1	1	...	...	...	...	...	...	...	...	...	...	...	...	...
		Kaikadi	...	...	...	...	...	...	...	...	...	...	...	...	...	...	...	...	...	...	...	...	...	...	...	...	1	1	...	...	...	...
		Total......	...	...	...	...	...	...	1	1	...	...	...	...	...	...	...	1	1	...	...	...	...	...	...	...	1	1	...	...	...	...
	44 ...	Erkulwad	...	...	...	1	...	1	...	...	...	2	1	1	5	4	1	...	...	...	...	...	...	...	...	...	...	...	...	...	...	...
		Total......	...	...	...	1	...	1	...	...	...	2	1	1	5	4	1	...	...	...	...	...	...	...	...	...	...	...	...	...	...	...
	46 ...	Domari	...	...	...	...	...	...	...	...	...	...	...	...	1	...	1	...	...	...	...	...	...	...	...	...	...	...	...	...	...	...
		Total......	...	...	...	...	...	...	...	...	...	...	...	...	1	...	1	...	...	...	...	...	...	...	...	...	...	...	...	...	...	...
F. Races and Nationalities.	48 ..	Mughal	...	...	...	...	...	...	...	...	...	...	...	...	...	...	...	...	...	...	...	...	...	...	...	...	1	1	...	...	...	...
		Sheikh	44	37	7	11	10	1	3	...	3	2	2	...	1	...	1	...	...	...	2	2	...	13	10	3	...	...	...	1	1	...
		Syed	6	6	...	2	2	...	1	1	...	...	...	...	1	1	...	...	...	...	...	...	...	1	1	...	9	8	1	...	...	...
		Pathan	7	6	1	1	...	1	2	1	1	...	...	...	...	...	...	...	...	...	2	2	...	...	...	...	2	...	2	1	1	...
		Other Mussulmans... ...	2	2	...	1	1	...	...	...	...	2	2	...	9	3	6	6	4	2	1	...	1	...	...	...	3	3	...	2	...	2
		Total	59	51	8	15	13	2	6	2	4	4	4	...	11	4	7	6	4	2	5	4	1	14	11	3	15	12	3	4	2	2
	49 b. ...	Dasri	...	...	...	...	...	...	...	...	...	...	...	...	...	...	...	1	...	1	...	...	...	1	1	...	...	...	...	...	...	...
		Jain	...	...	...	...	...	...	...	...	...	...	...	...	...	...	...	...	...	...	...	...	...	...	...	...	...	...	...	...	...	...
		Perika	...	...	...	...	...	...	...	...	...	2	1	1	...	...	...	1	1	...	...	...	...	...	...	...	...	...	...	...	...	...
		Telinga	2	1	1	4	3	1	10	3	7	9	6	3	13	7	6	11	8	3	...	...	...	2	2	...	...	...	...	...	...	...
		Other Hindus	15	12	3	...	...	...	...	...	...	4	2	2	2	1	1	...	...	...	...	...	...	...	...	...	3	...	3	1	...	1
		Total......	17	13	4	4	3	1	10	3	7	15	9	6	15	8	7	13	9	4	...	...	...	3	3	...	3	...	3	1	...	1
	52 ...	Christians (Native) ...	1	1	...	...	...	...	...	...	...	...	...	...	...	...	...	...	...	...	...	...	...	...	...	...	...	...	...	...	...	...
		Total......	1	1	...	...	...	...	...	...	...	...	...	...	...	...	...	...	...	...	...	...	...	...	...	...	...	...	...	...	...	...
		Grand Total......	113	92	21	83	49	34	82	43	39	118	76	42	177	106	71	181	111	70	128	78	50	86	58	28	92	72	20	53	32	21

TABLE XII A.

Persons of Unsound Mind by Caste, Tribe or Race.—*Continued.*

Class.	Group.	Castes.	Nander.			Naldrug.			Bidar.			Parbhani.			Sirpur Tandur.			Gulbarga.			Raichur.			Lingasugur.			Railways.			Total.		
			Total.	Males.	Females.	Total.	Males.	Females.	Total.	Males.	Females.	Total.	Males.	Females.	Total.	Males.	Females.	Total.	Males.	Females.	Total.	Males.	Females.	Total.	Males.	Females.	Total.	Males.	Females.	Total.	Males.	Females.
			34	35	36	37	38	39	40	41	42	43	44	45	46	47	48	49	50	51	52	53	54	55	56	57	58	59	60	61	62	63
E. Vagrant minor artisans and performers, &c.	43	Burud	...	...	...	...	...	...	...	...	...	...	...	...	...	...	...	...	...	...	...	...	...	...	...	...	...	...	...	2	2	...
		Kaikadi	...	...	...	...	...	...	...	...	...	...	...	...	...	...	...	...	...	...	...		...	...	...	...	...	...	...	1	1	...
		Total	...	...	...	...	...	...	...	...	...	...	...	...	...	...	...	...	...	...	...	...	...	...	...	...	...	...	...	3	3	...
	44	Erkulwad	...	...	...	...	...	...	...	...	...	...	...	...	...	...	...	...	...	...	...	...	...	...	...	...	...	...	...	8	5	3
		Total	...	...	...	...	...	...	...	...	...	...	...	...	...	...	...	...	...	...	...	...	..	...	...	...	...	...	...	8	5	3
	46	Domari	...	...	...	...	...	...	...	...	...	...	...	...	...	...	...	...	...	...	...	...	...	...	...	...	...	...	...	1	...	1
		Total	...	...	...	...	...	...	...	...	...	...	...	...	...	...	...	...	...	...	...	...	...	...	...	...	...	...	...	1	...	1
F. Races and Nationalities.	48	Mughal	...	...	...	...	...	...	...	...	...	...	...	...	...	...	...	...	...	...	...	...	...	...	...	...	...	...	...	1	1	...
		Sheikh	...	...	...	4	4	...	4	2	2	7	6	1	...	...	...	1	...	1	...	...	...	...	...	...	...	...	...	93	74	19
		Syed	...	...	...	...	...	...	...	...	...	...	...	...	...	...	...	...	...	...	...	...	...	...	...	...	...	...	...	20	19	1
		Pathan	...	...	...	3	3	...	...	...	...	...	...	...	...	...	...	...	...	...	...	...	...	...	...	...	...	...	...	18	13	5
		Other Mussulmans	5	2	3	...	...	...	11	9	2	3	3	...	...	...	...	5	4	1	4	3	1	3	2	1	...	...	...	57	38	19
		Total	5	2	3	7	7	...	15	11	4	10	9	1		...	...	6	4	2	4	3	1	3	2	1	...	...	...	189	145	44
	49 b.	Dasri	...	...	...	...	...	...	...	...	...	...	...	...	...	...	...	...	...	...	...	...	...	...	...	...	...	...	...	2	1	1
		Jains	...	...	...	1	...	1	1	1	...	...	...	...	...	...	...	...	...	...	...	...	...	...	...	...	...	...	...	2	1	1
		Perika	...	...	...	...	...	...	...	...	...	...	...	...	...	...	...	...	...	...	...	...	...	...	...	...	...	...	...	3	2	1
		Telinga	...	...	...	...	...	...	...	...	...	...	...	...	...	...	...	...	...	...	...	...	...	...	...	...	...	...	...	51	30	21
		Other Hindus	3	3	...	2	2	...	1	1	...	1	1	...	2	2	...	1	...	1	...	...	...	3	2	1	...	...	...	38	26	12
		Total	3	3	...	3	2	1	2	2	...	1	1	...	2	2	...	1	...	1	...	...	...	3	2	1	...	...	...	96	60	36
	52	Christians (Native)	...	...	...	...	...	...	...	...	...	...	...	...	...	...	...	...	...	...	...	...	...	...	...	...	...	...	...	1	1	...
		Total	...	...	...	...	...	...	...	...	...	...	...	...	...	...	...	...	...	...	...	...	...	...	...	...	...	...	...	1	1	...
		Grand Total	63	41	22	50	38	12	116	75	41	73	55	18	45	29	16	46	29	17	39	25	14	39	27	12	...	...	...	1,584	1,036	548

TABLE XIII.

DEAF-MUTES BY AGE.

TABLE XIII.

Deaf-Mutes by Age.

District or State.	Total Deaf Mutes.			Distribution by Age.																											
				0—4		5—9		10—14		15—19		20—24		25—29		30—34		35—39		40—44		45—49		50—54		55—59		60 and over.		Unspecified.	
	Total.	Males.	Females.	Males.	Females.	Males.	Females.	Males.	Females.	Males.	Females.	Males.	Females.	Males.	Females.	Males.	Females.	Males.	Females.	Males.	Females.	Males.	Females.	Males.	Females.	Males.	Females.	Males.	Females.	Males.	Females.
1	2	3	4	5	6	7	8	9	10	11	12	13	14	15	16	17	18	19	20	21	22	23	24	25	26	27	28	29	30	31	32
Telingana. Hyderabad. City	83	22	11	...	1	2	1	8	8	2	2	2	...	5	1	...	...	2	1	4	2	1	...	...	...	...	...	1	...	...	...
Suburbs including Secunderabad	110	61	49	1	1	4	5	9	4	7	9	3	6	7	...	7	2	4	3	4	3	3	2	3	3	4	...	5	10	...	1
Total......	148	88	60	1	2	6	6	12	7	9	11	5	6	12	1	7	2	6	4	8	5	4	2	3	3	4	...	6	10	...	1
Atraf-i-Balda District	199	122	77	8	2	16	6	8	7	7	9	11	5	14	7	6	7	7	5	12	6	7	3	8	9	2	2	21	9	...	...
Mahabubnagar (Nagar Karnul) ...	382	235	147	9	14	29	20	38	19	25	13	30	18	25	12	12	9	10	2	17	11	14	6	11	6	5	1	10	16	...	...
Nalgonda	318	203	115	11	8	24	18	22	13	25	13	25	19	27	17	15	9	8	4	11	2	8	2	8	8	8	...	16	7	...	...
Warangal (Khamam)	485	309	176	11	10	30	17	37	20	27	22	52	17	19	10	24	24	15	9	29	9	7	5	18	6	9	2	31	25	...	...
Elgandal	477	293	184	11	11	42	33	48	29	40	18	30	19	21	15	22	14	9	6	15	7	5	4	17	11	5	4	28	13	...	...
Indur	136	86	50	6	1	8	4	7	6	11	2	12	5	7	9	12	6	5	1	8	5	...	1	4	3	3	...	8	7	...	...
Medak	254	144	110	4	4	16	6	13	8	12	8	12	12	7	10	17	9	8	6	8	8	5	10	14	5	7	5	20	19	1	...
Mahratwara. Aurangabad	272	178	94	6	4	20	11	15	9	15	10	10	9	15	10	24	4	12	9	14	4	9	3	12	5	6	1	20	12	...	3
Birh	222	142	80	5	3	12	14	9	6	9	7	18	6	11	2	21	10	9	2	13	6	4	8	10	5	1	3	20	8	...	...
Nander	224	128	96	5	8	11	10	21	13	13	10	6	9	13	5	16	9	6	5	12	11	4	4	14	4	2	2	5	11	...	...
Naldrug	180	111	69	2	...	8	4	10	8	12	8	12	12	17	9	19	6	7	4	7	6	9	5	2	5	...	1	6	6	...	...
Bidar	337	226	111	5	2	20	12	29	10	20	11	17	5	28	9	18	15	13	6	18	20	12	4	18	5	5	3	22	9	1	...
Parbhani	216	130	86	4	5	13	16	16	7	8	6	10	5	19	8	16	12	9	6	11	8	8	3	9	2	2	...	10	7	...	1
Sirpur Tandur	72	39	33	1	...	9	5	5	5	2	1	3	...	...	8	5	2	1	2	3	3	2	2	3	...	2	...	3	5	...	...
Karnatic or Kanada. Gulbarga	180	111	69	5	2	12	16	14	8	11	5	7	7	16	9	10	6	10	6	7	3	8	...	5	5	1	...	5	7	...	...
Raichur	146	86	60	6	5	9	9	13	8	8	3	12	8	5	12	9	3	6	3	5	3	4	1	4	...	1	2	4	3	...	...
Lingasugur	175	102	73	3	2	11	12	16	6	5	10	21	11	12	9	10	9	5	1	6	6	1	...	4	1	2	2	6	4	...	...
Total Districts......	4,275	2,645	1,630	97	76	290	213	321	172	250	156	288	167	256	161	256	154	140	77	196	118	102	61	161	75	56	28	230	168	2	4
Total Districts including Hyderabad ...	4,418	2,728	1,690	98	78	296	219	333	179	259	167	293	173	268	162	263	156	146	81	204	123	106	68	164	78	60	28	236	178	2	5
Railways......	1	1	...	...	...	...	...	...	...	1	...	...	...	...	...	...	...	...	...	...	...	...	...	...	...	...	...	...	...	...	...
Grand Total......	4,419	2,729	1,690	98	78	296	219	333	179	260	167	293	173	268	162	263	156	146	81	204	123	106	68	164	78	60	28	236	178	2	5

TABLE XIII A.

DEAF-MUTES BY CASTE, TRIBE OR RACE.

TABLE XIII A.

Deaf-Mutes by Caste, Tribe or Race.

Class.	Group.	Castes.	City and suburbs including Secunderabad.			Atraf-i-Balda.			Mahabubnagar. (Nagar Karnul.)			Nalgonda.			Warangal. (Khamam.)			Elgandal.			Indur.			Medak.			Aurangabad.			Birh.		
			Total.	Males.	Females.	Total.	Males.	Females.	Total.	Males.	Females.	Total.	Males.	Females.	Total.	Males.	Females.	Total.	Males.	Females.	Total.	Males.	Females.	Total.	Males.	Females.	Total.	Males.	Females.	Total.	Males.	Females.
1	2	3	4	5	6	7	8	9	10	11	12	13	14	15	16	17	18	19	20	21	22	23	24	25	26	27	28	29	30	31	32	33
A. Agricultural.	1 ...	Elma ...	...	...	...	...	...	...	2	2	...	3	2	1	4	2	2	15	13	2	...	...	...	2	1	1	...	...	...	3	1	2
		Lodhi ...	...	...	...	...	...	...	1	1	...	...	...	...	...	...	...	...	...	...	...	...	...	...	...	...	...	...	...	...	...	...
		Mahratta ...	...	...	...	...	...	...	5	4	1	...	...	...	3	1	2	6	4	2	3	2	1	3	3	...	20	13	7	54	32	22
		Rajput ...	1	...	1	...	...	...	...	...	...	1	1	...	3	2	1	...	...	...	...	...	...	...	...	...	1	...	1	2	1	1
		Rathore ...	...	...	...	...	...	...	...	...	...	...	...	...	...	...	...	...	...	...	...	...	...	...	...	...	...	...	...	...	...	...
		Total......	1	...	1	...	...	...	8	7	1	4	3	1	10	5	5	21	17	4	3	2	1	5	4	1	21	13	8	59	34	25
	2a. ...	Andh ...	...	...	...	...	...	...	...	...	...	...	...	...	...	...	...	...	...	...	...	...	...	...	...	...	...	...	...	...	...	...
		Aryan ...	...	...	...	...	...	...	...	...	...	...	...	...	1	1	...	...	...	...	...	...	...	...	...	...	...	...	...	...	...	...
		Kunbi ...	6	3	3	32	21	11	53	32	21	25	17	8	41	26	15	47	28	19	20	8	12	26	14	12	77	51	26	21	15	6
		Mali ...	...	...	...	...	...	...	...	...	...	...	...	...	...	...	...	...	...	...	...	...	...	...	...	...	7	4	3	7	4	3
		Munurwad	5	4	1	3	1	2	7	3	4	2	...	2	8	6	2	19	12	7	6	2	4	2	1	1	...	...	...	...	...	...
		Mutrasi ...	...	...	...	19	14	5	10	7	3	21	12	9	20	13	7	17	12	5	...	...	...	46	29	17	...	...	...	...	...	...
		Satani ...	...	...	...	1	1	...	...	...	...	2	2	...	1	...	1	...	...	...	...	...	...	3	2	1	...	...	...	...	...	...
		Vanjari ...	...	...	...	1	1	...	...	...	...	...	...	...	...	...	...	...	...	...	...	...	...	...	...	...	...	...	...	...	...	...
		Total......	11	7	4	56	38	18	70	42	28	50	31	19	71	46	25	83	52	31	26	10	16	77	46	31	84	55	29	28	19	9
	2b. ...	Gaoli ...	1	1	...	...	...	...	3	3	...	...	...	...	...	...	...	...	...	...	16	14	2	...	...	...	8	2	6	1	1	...
		Total......	1	1	...	...	...	...	3	3	...	...	...	...	...	...	...	...	...	...	16	14	2	...	...	...	8	2	6	1	1	...
	2c. ...	Dher ...	13	7	6	23	16	7	61	38	23	40	26	14	96	59	37	47	35	12	11	11	...	23	14	9	24	15	9	19	16	3
		Mang ...	5	2	3	9	6	3	...	...	...	...	...	...	...	...	...	...	...	...	8	8	...	...	...	...	8	7	1	11	7	4
		Total......	18	9	9	32	22	10	61	38	23	40	26	14	96	59	37	47	35	12	19	19	...	23	14	9	32	22	10	30	23	7
	4 ...	Chenchwad	...	...	...	...	...	...	1	...	1	...	...	...	...	...	...	...	...	...	...	...	...	...	...	...	...	...	...	...	...	...
		Gond ...	...	...	...	...	...	...	...	...	...	...	...	...	...	...	...	...	...	...	...	...	...	...	...	...	...	...	...	...	...	...
		Gond H ...	...	...	...	...	...	...	...	...	...	...	...	...	...	...	...	...	...	...	...	...	...	...	...	...	2	...	2	...	...	...
		Koya ...	...	...	...	...	...	...	...	...	...	...	...	...	...	...	...	2	1	1	...	...	...	...	...	...	...	...	...	...	...	...
		Total......	...	...	...	...	...	...	1	...	1	...	...	...	...	...	...	2	1	1	...	...	...	...	...	...	2	...	2	...	...	...

TABLE XIII A.

Deaf-Mutes by Caste, Tribe or Race.—*Continued.*

Class.	Group.	Castes.	Nander.			Naldrug.			Bidar.			Parbhani.			Sirpur Tandur.			Gulbarga.			Raichur.			Lingasugur.			Railways.			Total.		
			Total.	Males.	Females.	Total.	Males.	Females.	Total.	Males.	Females.	Total.	Males.	Females.	Total.	Males.	Females.	Total.	Males.	Females.	Total.	Males.	Females.	Total.	Males.	Females.	Total.	Males.	Females.	Total.	Males.	Females.
			34	35	36	37	38	39	40	41	42	43	44	45	46	47	48	49	50	51	52	53	54	55	56	57	58	59	60	61	62	63
A. Agricultural.	1	Elma	...	...	...	...	...	...	15	13	2	1	...	1	...	...	...	...	...	...	...	...	...	...	...	...	...	...	...	45	34	11
		Lodhi	...	...	...	...	...	...	...	...	...	...	...	...	...	...	...	...	...	...	...	...	...	...	...	...	...	...	...	1	1	...
		Mahratta	54	33	21	37	21	16	66	45	21	59	39	20	9	5	4	1	...	1	...	...	...	...	...	...	...	...	...	320	202	118
		Rajput	2	2	...	...	...	...	1	...	1	...	...	...	1	1	...	1	...	1	1	...	1	2	2	...	...	...	...	16	9	7
		Rathore	...	...	...	...	...	...	...	...	...	...	...	...	...	...	...	1	1	...	...	...	...	...	...	...	...	...	...	1	1	...
		Total	56	35	21	37	21	16	82	58	24	60	39	21	10	6	4	3	1	2	1	...	1	2	2	...	...	...	...	383	247	136
	2a.	Andh	4	4	...	...	...	...	...	...	...	...	...	...	...	...	...	...	...	...	...	...	...	...	...	...	...	...	...	4	4	...
		Aryan	...	...	...	...	...	...	...	...	...	...	...	...	...	...	...	...	...	...	...	...	...	...	...	...	...	...	...	1	1	...
		Kunbi	3	2	1	22	14	8	4	3	1	1	1	...	8	3	5	12	7	5	13	12	1	3	2	1	...	...	...	414	259	155
		Mali	...	...	...	5	5	...	...	...	...	6	2	4	...	...	...	...	...	...	...	...	...	...	...	...	...	...	...	25	15	10
		Munurwad	2	...	2	...	...	...	...	...	...	...	...	...	1	1	...	1	1	...	4	1	3	1	...	1	...	...	...	61	32	29
		Mutrasi	...	...	...	...	...	...	2	1	1	...	...	...	...	...	...	...	...	...	...	...	...	...	...	...	...	...	...	135	88	47
		Satani	...	...	...	...	...	...	...	...	...	...	...	...	...	...	...	...	...	...	...	...	...	...	...	...	...	...	...	7	5	2
		Vanjari	...	...	...	...	...	...	...	...	...	...	...	...	...	...	...	...	...	...	...	...	...	...	...	...	...	...	...	1	1	...
		Total	9	6	3	27	19	8	6	4	2	7	3	4	9	4	5	13	8	5	17	13	4	4	2	2	...	...	...	648	405	243
	2b.	Gaoli	12	7	5	...	...	...	19	15	4	1	1	...	1	1	...	17	11	6	9	5	4	11	7	4	...	...	...	99	68	31
		Total	12	7	5	...	...	...	19	15	4	1	1	...	1	1	...	17	11	6	9	5	4	11	7	4	...	...	...	99	68	31
	2c.	Dher	22	15	7	15	11	4	39	24	15	47	32	15	2	1	1	19	16	3	13	8	5	21	9	12	...	...	...	535	353	182
		Mang	23	11	12	15	10	5	20	12	8	4	1	3	1	...	1	16	6	10	...	...	...	...	...	...	...	...	...	120	70	50
		Total	45	26	19	30	21	9	59	36	23	51	33	18	3	1	2	35	22	13	13	8	5	21	9	12	...	...	...	655	423	232
	4	Chenchwad	...	...	...	...	...	...	...	...	...	...	...	...	...	...	...	...	...	...	...	...	...	...	...	...	...	...	...	1	...	1
		Gond	...	...	...	...	...	...	...	...	...	...	...	...	9	4	5	...	...	...	...	...	...	...	...	...	...	...	...	9	4	5
		Gond H	...	...	...	...	...	...	...	...	...	...	...	...	...	...	...	...	...	...	...	...	...	...	...	...	...	...	...	2	...	2
		Koya	...	...	...	...	...	...	...	...	...	...	...	...	...	...	...	...	...	...	...	...	...	...	...	...	...	...	...	2	1	1
		Total	...	...	...	...	...	...	...	...	...	...	...	...	9	4	5	...	...	...	...	...	...	...	...	...	...	...	...	14	5	9

TABLE XIII A.

Deaf-Mutes by Caste, Tribe or Race.—*Continued.*

Class.	Group.	Castes.	City and suburbs including Secunderabad.			Atraf-i-Balda.			Mahabubnagar. (Nagar Karnul.)			Nalgonda.			Warangal. (Khamam.)			Elgandal.			Indur.			Medak.			Aurangabad.			Birh.		
			Total.	Males.	Females.	Total.	Males.	Females.	Total.	Males.	Females.	Total.	Males.	Females.	Total.	Males.	Females.	Total.	Males.	Females.	Total.	Males.	Females.	Total.	Males.	Females.	Total.	Males.	Females.	Total.	Males.	Females.
1	2	3	4	5	6	7	8	9	10	11	12	13	14	15	16	17	18	19	20	21	22	23	24	25	26	27	28	29	30	31	32	33
B. Professional.	5 ...	Brahmin	6	3	3	3	2	1	5	3	2	8	6	2	17	10	7	10	7	3	3	2	1	5	2	3	8	6	2	12	3	9
		Jangam	...	...	...	1	1	...	2	2	...	1	1	...	...	...	...	...	...	...	2	1	1	2	...	2	3	3	...	...	...	...
		Total......	6	3	3	4	3	1	7	5	2	9	7	2	17	10	7	10	7	3	5	3	2	7	2	5	11	9	2	12	3	9
	6 ...	Gosain	...	...	...	...	...	...	...	...	...	...	...	...	...	...	...	...	...	...	...	...	...	...	...	...	1	1	...	6	3	3
		Total......	...	...	...	...	...	...	...	...	...	...	...	...	...	...	...	...	...	...	...	...	...	...	...	...	1	1	...	6	3	3
	7 ...	Gurao	...	...	...	...	...	...	...	...	...	...	...	...	...	...	...	...	...	...	...	...	...	...	...	...	...	...	...	1	1	...
		Total......	...	...	...	...	...	...	...	...	...	...	...	...	...	...	...	...	...	...	...	...	...	...	...	...	...	...	...	1	1	...
	8 ...	Bhat	...	...	...	...	...	...	...	...	...	1	1	...	...	...	...	...	...	...	...	...	...	...	...	...	...	...	...	...	...	...
		Total......	...	...	...	...	...	...	...	...	...	1	1	...	...	...	...	...	...	...	...	...	...	...	...	...	...	...	...	...	...	...
	9 ...	Mudelliar	2	1	1	...	...	...	...	...	...	...	...	...	...	...	...	3	1	2	...	...	...	...	...	...	...	...	...	...	...	...
		Total......	2	1	1	...	...	...	...	...	...	...	...	...	...	...	...	3	1	2	...	...	...	...	...	...	...	...	...	...	...	...
	12 ...	Kanchani	...	...	...	...	...	...	1	1	...	...	...	...	...	...	...	1	...	1	...	...	...	...	...	...	...	...	...	...	...	...
		Total......	...	...	...	...	...	...	1	1	...	...	...	...	...	...	...	1	...	1	...	...	...	...	...	...	...	...	...	...	...	...
C. Commercial.	14 ...	Balija	...	...	...	4	3	1	13	8	5	5	3	2	6	5	1	...	...	...	...	...	...	6	...	6	1	1	...	...	...	...
		Komti	5	3	2	13	10	3	17	11	6	15	12	3	26	13	13	28	14	9	2	...	2	11	5	6	1	1	...	...	...	...
		Wani	6	3	3	2	...	2	6	1	5	...	...	...	...	...	...	...	...	...	8	3	5	1	...	1	12	5	7	3	1	2
		Total......	11	6	5	19	13	6	36	20	16	20	15	5	32	18	14	28	14	9	10	3	7	18	5	13	14	7	7	3	1	2

TABLE XIII A.

Deaf-Mutes by Caste, Tribe or Race.—*Continued.*

Class.	Group.	Castes.	Nander.			Naldrug.			Bidar.			Parbhani.			Sirpur Tandur.			Gulbarga.			Raichur.			Lingasugur.			Railways.			Total.		
			Total.	Males.	Females.	Total.	Males.	Females.	Total.	Males.	Females.	Total.	Males.	Females.	Total.	Males.	Females.	Total.	Males.	Females.	Total.	Males.	Females.	Total.	Males.	Females.	Total.	Males.	Females.	Total.	Males.	Females.
			34	35	36	37	38	39	40	41	42	43	44	45	46	47	48	49	50	51	52	53	54	55	56	57	58	59	60	61	62	63
B. Professional.	5 ...	Brahmin	1	1	...	7	5	2	9	7	2	10	5	5	...	...	...	4	2	2	4	4	...	11	7	4	...	...	...	123	75	48
		Jangam	4	4	...	...	...	...	2	1	1	4	2	2	...	...	...	3	2	1	...	...	...	...	...	...	...	...	...	24	17	7
		Total......	5	5	...	7	5	2	11	8	3	14	7	7	...	...	...	7	4	3	4	4	...	11	7	4	...	...	...	147	92	55
	6 ...	Gosain	1	1	...	...	...	...	...	...	...	...	...	...	...	...	...	...	...	...	...	...	...	...	...	...	...	...	...	8	5	3
		Total......	1	1	...	...	...	...	...	...	...	...	...		...	...	...	...	...	...	...	...	...	...	...	...	...	...	...	8	5	3
	7 ...	Gurao	3	1	2	...	...	...	...	...	...	1	1	...	...	...	...	...	...	...	...	...	...	...	...	...	.	...	...	5	3	2
		Total......	3	1	2	...	...	...	...	...	...	1	1	...	...	...	...	...	...	...	...	...	...	...	...	...	...	...	...	5	3	2
	8 ...	Bhat	...	...	...	...	...	...	...	...	...	.	...	...	1	1	...	...	...	...	1	1	...	2	2	...	...	...	...	5	5	...
		Total......	...	...	...	...	...	...	...	...	...	...	...	...	1	1	...	...	...	...	1	1	...	2	2	...	...	...	...	5	5	...
	9 ...	Mudelliar	...	...	...	...	.	...	...	...	...	...	...	...	...	...	...	...	...	...	...	...	...	...	...	...	...	...	...	5	2	3
		Total......	...	...	...	...	.	...	...	...	...	...	...	...	...	...	...	...	...	...	...	...	...	...	...		...	...	...	5	2	3
	12 ...	Kanchani	...	...	...	...	...	...	...	...	...	...	...	...	...	...	...	...	...	...	...	...	...	...	...	...	...	...	...	2	1	1
		Total......	...	...	...	...	...	...	...	...	...	...	...	...		...	...	...	...	...	...	...	...	...	...	...	...	...	...	2	1	1
C. Commercial.	14 ...	Balija	...	...	...	...	...	...	...	...	...	...	...	...	...	...	...	...	...	...	20	12	8	...	...	...	...	...	...	55	32	23
		Komti	9	8	1	...	...	...	4	2	2	...	...	...	3	1	2	3	2	1	5	2	3	1	1	...	...	...	...	138	85	53
		Wani	24	8	16	10	3	7	57	39	18	7	5	2	...	...	...	35	25	10	...	...	...	33	20	13	...	...	...	204	113	91
		Total......	33	16	17	10	3	7	61	41	20	7	5	2	3	1	2	38	27	11	25	14	11	34	21	13	...	...	...	397	230	167

TABLE XIII A.

Deaf-Mutes by Caste, Tribe or Race.—*Continued.*

Class.	Group.	Castes.	City and suburbs including Secunderabad. Total.	Males.	Females.	Atraf-i-Balda. Total.	Males.	Females.	Mahabubnagar. (Nagar Karnul.) Total.	Males.	Females.	Nalgonda. Total.	Males.	Females.	Warangal. (Khamam.) Total.	Males.	Females.	Elgandal. Total.	Males.	Females.	Indur. Total.	Males.	Females.	Medak. Total.	Males.	Females.	Aurangabad. Total.	Males.	Females.	Birh. Total.	Males.	Females.
1	2	3	4	5	6	7	8	9	10	11	12	13	14	15	16	17	18	19	20	21	22	23	24	25	26	27	28	29	30	31	32	33
C. Commercial.	16 ...	Banjara	6	3	3	...	...	...	...	...	...	...	...	...	...	...	...	5	5	...	...	...	...	...	...	...	...	...	...	...	...	...
		Lad	...	...	...	...	...	...	...	...	...	...	...	...	...	...	...	...	...	...	...	...	...	...	...	...	...	...	...	...	...	...
		Lambani	...	...	...	1	...	1	...	...	...	5	5	...	3	3	...	...	...	...	1	...	1	...	...	...	4	3	1	8	3	5
		Total......	6	3	3	1	...	1	...	...	...	5	5	...	3	3	...	5	5	...	1	...	1	...	...	...	4	3	1	8	3	5
D. Artisan and Village Menial.	17 ...	Panchal	...	...	...	...	...	...	...	...	...	1	...	1	...	...	...	...	...	...	1	1	...	1	1	...	...	...	...	1	1	...
		Sonar	1	1	...	4	4	...	11	7	4	2	1	1	8	4	4	5	5	...	1	1	...	4	4	...	1	1	...	5	3	2
		Total......	1	1	...	4	4	...	11	7	4	3	1	2	8	4	4	5	5	...	2	2	...	5	5	...	1	1	...	6	4	2
	18 ...	Hajjam	2	1	1	...	...	...	3	2	1	4	3	1	11	6	5	5	2	3	1	1	...	9	6	3	2	2	...	1	1	...
		Total......	2	1	1	...	...	...	3	2	1	4	3	1	11	6	5	5	2	3	1	1	...	9	6	3	2	2	...	1	1	...
	19 ...	Lohar	...	...	...	...	...	...	1	1	...	...	...	...	...	...	...	...	...	...	3	3	...	...	...	..	4	3	1	...	...	...
		Total......	...	...	...	...	...	...	1	1	...	...	...	...	...	...	...	...	...	...	3	3	...	...	...	.	4	3	1	...	...	...
	20 ...	Sutar (or Barhai)	1	...	1	5	3	2	8	6	2	3	2	1	1	1	...	18	12	6	...	...	...	...	...	...	4	3	1	4	3	1
		Gaondi	...	...	...	...	...	...	1	...	1	...	...	...	1	1	...	3	3	...	...	...	...	...	...	...	...	...	...	2	1	1
		Total......	1	...	1	5	3	2	9	6	3	3	2	1	2	2	...	21	15	6	...	...	...	...	...	...	4	3	1	6	4	2
	21 ...	Kasar	...	...	...	...	...	...	...	...	...	2	2	...	4	2	2	1	...	1	...	...	...	...	...	...	...	...	...	1	...	1
		Total......	...	...	...	...	...	...	...	...	...	2	2	...	4	2	2	1	...	1	...	...	...	...	...	...	...	...	...	1	...	1
	22 ...	Darzi	...	...	...	...	...	...	...	...	...	...	...	...	1	1	...	1	...	1	...	...	...	1	1		...	...	...	...	...	...
		Total......	...	...	...	...	...	...	...	...	...	...	...	...	1	1	...	1	...	1	...	...	...	1	1	...	...	...	...	...	...	...

TABLE XIII A.

Deaf-Mutes by Caste, Tribe or Race.—*Continued.*

Class.	Group.	Castes.	Nander. Total.	Nander. Males.	Nander. Females.	Naldrug. Total.	Naldrug. Males.	Naldrug. Females.	Bidar. Total.	Bidar. Males.	Bidar. Females.	Parbhani. Total.	Parbhani. Males.	Parbhani. Females.	Sirpur Tandur. Total.	Sirpur Tandur. Males.	Sirpur Tandur. Females.	Gulbarga. Total.	Gulbarga. Males.	Gulbarga. Females.	Raichur. Total.	Raichur. Males.	Raichur. Females.	Lingasugur. Total.	Lingasugur. Males.	Lingasugur. Females.	Railways. Total.	Railways. Males.	Railways. Females.	Total. Total.	Total. Males.	Total. Females.
			34	35	36	37	38	39	40	41	42	43	44	45	46	47	48	49	50	51	52	53	54	55	56	57	58	59	60	61	62	63
C. Commercial.	16	Banjara	...	...	...	...	...	...	...	...	...	...	...	...	...	...	...	...	...	...	...	...	...	...	...	...	...	...	...	11	8	3
		Lad	...	...	...	...	...	...	...	...	...	...	...	...	...	...	...	1	1	...	...	...	...	...	...	...	...	...	...	1	1	...
		Lambani	4	4	...	6	3	3	17	12	5	4	3	1	6	8	3	3	3	...	...	...	...	1	1	...	...	...	...	63	43	20
		Total	4	4	...	6	3	3	17	12	5	4	3	1	6	3	8	4	4	...	...	...	...	1	1	...	...	...	...	75	52	23
D. Artisan and Village Menial.	17	Panchal	...	...	...	...	...	...	5	3	2	...	...	...	...	...	...	1	...	1	3	2	1	2	2	...	...	...	...	15	10	5
		Sonar	2	1	1	1	...	1	...	...	...	...	...	...	1	1	...	1	1	...	...	...	...	...	.	...	...	...	...	47	34	13
		Total	2	1	1	1	...	1	5	3	2	...	...	...	1	1	...	2	1	1	3	2	1	2	2	...	...	...	...	62	44	18
	18	Hajjam	5	2	3	3	2	1	...	...	...	...	...	...	...	...	...	...	...	...	2	1	1	1	1	...	...	...	...	49	30	19
		Total	5	2	3	3	2	1	...	...	...	...	...	...	...	...	...	...	...	...	2	1	1	1	1	...	...	...	...	49	30	19
	19	Lôhar	1	1	...	...	...	...	...	...	...	3	2	1	1	1	...	...	...	...	...	...	...	...	...	...	...	...	...	13	11	2
		Total	1	1	...	...	...	...	...	...	...	3	2	1	1	1	...	...	...	...	...	...	...	...	...	...	...	...	...	13	11	2
	20	Sutar (or Barhai)	2	2	...	1	1	...	9	6	3	1	...	1	1	...	1	1	1	...	...	...	...		...	...	...	...	...	59	40	19
		Gaondi	2	1	1	...	...	...	...	...	...	...	...	...	...	...	...	3	1	2	2	1	1	...	...	...	...	...	...	14	8	6
		Total	4	3	1	1	1	...	9	6	3	1	...	1	1	...	1	4	2	2	2	1	1	...	...	...	...	...	...	78	48	25
	21	Kasar	1	...	1	2	1	1	...	...	...	1	1	...	1	1	...	1	...	1	...	...	...	...	...	...	...	...	...	14	7	7
		Total	1	...	1	2	1	1	...	...	...	1	1	...	1	1	...	1	...	1	...	...	...	...	...	...	...	...	...	14	7	7
	22	Darzi	1	1	...	...	...	...	...	...	...	...	...	...	...	...	...	...	...	...	...	...	...	1	...	1	...	...	...	5	3	2
		Total	1	1	...	...	...	...	...	...	...	...	...	...	...	...	...	...	...	...	...	...	...	1	...	1	...	...	...	5	3	2

TABLE XIII A.

Deaf-Mutes by Caste, Tribe or Race.—*Continued.*

Class.	Group.	Castes.	City and suburbs including Secunderabad.			Atraf-i-Balda.			Mahabubnagar. (Nagar Karnul.)			Nalgonda.			Warangal. (Khamam.)			Elgandal.			Indur.			Medak.			Aurangabad.			Birh.		
			Total.	Males.	Females.	Total.	Males.	Females.	Total.	Males.	Females.	Total.	Males.	Females.	Total.	Males.	Females.	Total.	Males.	Females.	Total.	Males.	Females.	Total.	Males.	Females.	Total.	Males.	Females.	Total.	Males.	Females.
1	2	3	4	5	6	7	8	9	10	11	12	13	14	15	16	17	18	19	20	21	22	23	24	25	26	27	28	29	30	31	32	33
D. Artisan and Village Menial.	23 ...	Khatri	5	3	2	...	...	...	...	...	...	...	...	...	...	...	...	...	...	...	...	...	...	...	...	...	...	...	...	...	...	...
		Rangari or Rangrez ...	...	...	...	...	...	...	...	...	...	...	...	...	...	...	...	...	...	...	2	...	2	...	...	...	1	1	...	1	1	...
		Julaha	5	2	3	10	8	2	12	9	3	10	7	3	17	11	6	56	32	24	16	10	6	19	13	6	1	...	1	4	2	2
		Total......	10	5	5	10	8	2	12	9	3	10	7	3	17	11	6	56	32	24	18	10	8	19	13	6	2	1	1	5	3	2
	24 ...	Dhobi	8	4	4	...	...	...	6	3	3	13	8	5	12	10	2	9	3	6	3	2	1	2	1	1	5	4	1	1	1	...
		Total......	8	4	4	...	...	...	6	3	3	13	8	5	12	10	2	9	3	6	3	2	1	2	1	1	5	4	1	1	1	..
	25 ...	Pinjari	...	...	...	...	...	...	...	...	...	...	...	...	...	...	...	1	1	...	...	...	...	...	...	...	...	...	...	...	...	...
		Total......	...	...	...	...	...	.	...	...	...	...	...	...	...	...	...	1	1	...	...	...	...	...	...	...	...	...	...	.	...	...
	26 ...	Dhangar	...	...	...	13	6	7	41	21	20	47	36	11	42	26	16	45	27	18	7	3	4	8	3	5	15	9	6	5	3	2
		Kurma	...	...	...	...	...	...	7	4	3	...	...	...	...	...	...	...	...	...	...	...	...	...	...	...	...	...	...	...	...	...
		Total......	...	...	...	13	6	7	48	25	23	47	36	11	42	26	16	45	27	18	7	3	4	8	3	5	15	9	6	5	3	2
	27 ...	Teli...	...	...	...	...	...	...	...	...	...	...	...	...	...	...	...	7	3	4	...	—	...	...	...	...	1	1	...	5	4	1
		Total......	...	...	...	...	...	...	...	...	...	...	...	...	...	...	...	7	3	4	...	...	...	...	...	...	1	1	...	5	4	1
	28 ..	Kumbar	...	...	...	14	8	6	4	2	2	12	8	4	25	12	13	11	7	4	3	...	3	6	4	2	...	...	...	...	...	...
		Total......	...	...	...	14	8	6	4	2	2	12	8	4	25	12	13	11	7	4	3	...	3	6	4	2	...	...	.	...	...	...
	35 ...	Besta	...	...	...	1	1	...	13	9	4	1	1	...	5	3	2	7	4	3	...	...	...	...	...	...	...	...	..	...	...	...
		Bhoi	2	...	2	...	...	...	...	...		...	...	...	...	...	...	...	...	...	10	7	3	...	...	...	1	1	...	...	...	...
		Total......	2	...	2	1	1	...	13	9	4	1	1	...	5	3	2	7	4	3	10	7	3	...	...	...	1	1	...	...	...	...

TABLE XIII A.

Deaf-Mutes by Caste, Tribe or Race.—*Continued.*

Class.	Group.	Castes.	Nander. Total.	Nander. Males.	Nander. Females.	Naldrug. Total.	Naldrug. Males.	Naldrug. Females.	Bidar. Total.	Bidar. Males.	Bidar. Females.	Parbhani. Total.	Parbhani. Males.	Parbhani. Females.	Sirpur Tandur. Total.	Sirpur Tandur. Males.	Sirpur Tandur. Females.	Gulbarga. Total.	Gulbarga. Males.	Gulbarga. Females.	Raichur. Total.	Raichur. Males.	Raichur. Females.	Lingasugur. Total.	Lingasugur. Males.	Lingasugur. Females.	Railways. Total.	Railways. Males.	Railways. Females.	Total. Total.	Total. Males.	Total. Females.
			34	35	36	37	38	39	40	41	42	43	44	45	46	47	48	49	50	51	52	53	54	55	56	57	58	59	60	61	62	63
D. Artisan and Village Menial.	23	Khatri	1	1	...	...	...	...	...	...	...	2	1	1	...	...	...	2	1	1	3	2	1	1	1	...	...	...	...	14	9	5
		Rangari or Rangrez	...	...	...	1	1	...	...	...	...	4	3	1	...	...	...	1	1	...	...	...	...	...	...	...	...	...	...	10	7	3
		Julaha	...	...	...	1	...	1	7	5	2	1	1	...	1	1	...	1	1	...	...	...	...	2	...	2	...	...	...	163	102	61
		Total......	1	1	...	2	1	1	7	5	2	7	5	2	1	1	...	4	3	1	3	2	1	3	1	2	...	...	...	187	118	69
	24	Dhobi	...	...	...	...	...	...	...	...	...	...	...	...	2	1	1	...	...	...	6	4	2	...	...	...	...	...	...	67	41	26
		Total......	...	...	...	...	...	...	...	...	...	...	...	...	2	1	1	...	...	...	6	4	2	...	...	...	...	...	...	67	41	26
	25	Pinjari	...	...	...	...	...	...	...	...	...	...	...	...	...	...	...	...	...	...	...	...	...	...	...	...	...	...	...	1	1	...
		Total......	...	...	...	...	...	...	...	...	...	...	...	...	...	...	...	...	...	...	...	...	...	...	...	...	...	...	...	1	1	...
	26	Dhangar	12	3	9	9	4	5	22	10	12	17	8	9	3	2	1	18	8	5	20	10	10	30	14	16	...	...	...	349	193	156
		Kurma	...	...	...	...	...	...	...	...	...	...	...	...	...	...	...	...	...	...	...	...	...	...	...	...	...	...	...	7	4	3
		Total......	12	3	9	9	4	5	22	10	12	17	8	9	3	2	1	18	8	5	20	10	10	30	14	16	...	...	...	356	197	159
	27	Teli	3	3	...	3	2	1	2	...	2	...	...	...	1	...	1	1	1	...	...	...	...	...	...	...	...	...	...	23	14	9
		Total......	3	3	...	3	2	1	2	...	2	...	...	...	1	...	1	1	1	...	...	...	...	...	...	...	...	...	...	23	14	9
	28	Kumhar	3	2	1	...	...	...	...	...	...	2	2	...	10	8	2	1	...	1	6	1	5	1	1	...	...	...	...	98	55	43
		Total......	3	2	1	...	...	...	...	...	...	2	2	...	10	8	2	1	...	1	6	1	5	1	1	...	...	...	...	98	55	43
	35	Besta	...	...	...	...	...	...	...	...	...	...	...	...	...	...	...	...	...	...	1	1	...	...	...	...	...	...		28	19	9
		Bhoi	4	...	4	...	...	...	...	...	...	2	1	1	1	...	1	...	...	...	...	...	...	...	...	...	...	...	...	20	9	11
		Total......	4	...	4	...	...	...	...	...	...	2	1	1	1	...	1	...	...	...	1	1	...	...	...	...	...	...	...	48	28	20

TABLE XIII A.

Deaf-Mutes by Caste, Tribe or Race.—*Continued.*

Class.	Group.	Castes.	City and suburbs including Secunderabad.			Atraf-i-Balda.			Mahabubnagar. (Nagar Karnul.)			Nalgonda.			Warangal. (Khamam.)			Elgandal.			Indur.			Medak.			Aurangabad.			Birh.		
			Total.	Males.	Females.	Total.	Males.	Females.	Total.	Males.	Females.	Total.	Males.	Females.	Total.	Males.	Females.	Total.	Males.	Females.	Total.	Males.	Females.	Total.	Males.	Females.	Total.	Males.	Females.	Total.	Males.	Females.
1	2	3	4	5	6	7	8	9	10	11	12	13	14	15	16	17	18	19	20	21	22	23	24	25	26	27	28	29	30	31	32	33
D. Artisan and Village Menial.	36 ...	Goundla	2	1	1	13	6	7	13	7	6	17	8	9	31	22	9	28	14	14	...	...	...	12	6	6	...	...	...	...	...	...
		Total......	2	1	1	13	6	7	13	7	6	17	8	9	31	22	9	28	14	14	...	...	...	12	6	6	...	...	...	...	...	...
	37 ...	Kasai	...	...	...	...	...	...	1	1	...	...	...	...	...	...	...	...	...	...	...	...	...	...	...	...	...	...	...	...	...	...
		Total......	...	...	...	...	...	...	1	1	...	...	...	...	...	...	...	...	...	...	...	...	...	...	...	...	...	...	...	...	...	...
	38 ...	Chamar	3	2	1	...	...	...	...	...	...	...	...	...	...	...	...	...	...	...	...	...	...	21	11	10	6	3	3	3	2	1
		Dhore	...	...	...	...	...	...	...	...	...	...	...	...	...	...	...	...	...	...	...	...	...	...	...	...	...	...	...	1	...	1
		Mochi	...	...	...	...	...	...	...	...	...	14	7	7	...	...	...	41	22	19	...	...	...	...	...	...	...	...	...	...	...	...
		Total......	3	2	1	...	...	...	...	...	...	14	7	7	...	...	...	41	22	19	...	...	...	21	11	10	6	3	3	4	2	2
	38 A. ...	Bedar	...	...	...	...	...	...	1	...	1	...	...	...	...	...	...	...	...	...	...	...	...	...	...	...	...	...	...	1	1	...
		Total......	...	...	...	...	...	...	1	...	1	...	...	...	...	...	...	...	...	...	...	...	...	...	...	...	...	...	...	1	1	...
E. Vagrant Minor Artisans and Performers.	40 ...	Waddowar	...	...	...	1	1	...	5	4	1	8	5	3	6	6	...	1	...	1	...	...	...	1	...	1	5	4	1	...	...	...
		Total......	...	...	...	1	1	...	5	4	1	8	5	3	6	6	...	1	...	1	...	...	...	1	...	1	5	4	1	...	...	...
	41 ...	Beldar	...	...	...	...	...	...	...	...	...	...	...	...	...	...	...	...	...	...	...	...	...	...	...	...	1	1	...	...	...	...
		Total......	...	...	...	...	...	...	...	...	...	...	...	...	...	...	...	...	...	...	...	...	...	...	...	...	1	1	...	...	...	...
	43 ...	Burud	...	...	...	...	...	...	...	...	...	...	...	...	1	1	...	1	1	...	...	...	...	...	...	...	...	...	...	...	...	...
		Kaikadi	...	...	...	...	...	...	...	...	...	...	...	...	...	...	...	...	...	...	...	...	...	...	...	...	...	...	...	1	...	1
		Total......	...	...	...	...	...	...	...	...	...	...	...	...	1	1	...	1	1	...	...	...	...	...	...	...	...	...	...	1	...	1

TABLE XIII A.

Deaf-Mutes by Caste, Tribe or Race.—*Continued.*

Class.	Group.	Castes.	Nander. Total.	Nander. Males.	Nander. Females.	Naldrug. Total.	Naldrug. Males.	Naldrug. Females.	Bidar. Total.	Bidar. Males.	Bidar. Females.	Parbhani. Total.	Parbhani. Males.	Parbhani. Females.	Sirpur Tandur. Total.	Sirpur Tandur. Males.	Sirpur Tandur. Females.	Gulbarga. Total.	Gulbarga. Males.	Gulbarga. Females.	Raichur. Total.	Raichur. Males.	Raichur. Females.	Lingasugur. Total.	Lingasugur. Males.	Lingasugur. Females.	Railways. Total.	Railways. Males.	Railways. Females.	Total. Total.	Total. Males.	Total. Females.
			34	35	36	37	38	39	40	41	42	43	44	45	46	47	48	49	50	51	52	53	54	55	56	57	58	59	60	61	62	63
D. Artisan and Village Menial.	36 ...	Goundla	...	...	...	...	...	...	1	1	...	...	...	...	...	...	...	1	...	1	1	1	...	3	8	...	...	...	...	122	69	53
		Total......	...	...	...	...	...	...	1	1	...	...	...	...	...	...	...	1	...	1	1	1	...	8	3	...	...	...	...	122	69	53
	37 ...	Kasai	...	...	...	...	...	...	...	...	...	...	...	...	...	...	...	...	...	...	...	...	...	...	...	...	...	...	...	1	1	...
		Total......	...	...	...	...	...	...	...	...	...	...	...	...	...	...	...	...	...	...	...	...	...	...	...	...	...	...	...	1	1	...
	38 ...	Chamar	1	1	...	7	4	3	1	1	...	5	3	2	...	...	...	2	1	1	...	...	...	...	...	...	...	...	...	49	28	21
		Dhore	...	...	...	1	1	...	...	...	...	...	...	...	...	...	...	...	...	...	...	...	...	...	...	...	...	...	...	2	1	1
		Mochi	...	...	...	...	...	...	...	...	...	...	...	...	...	...	...	...	...	...	...	...	...	...	...	...	...	...	...	55	29	26
		Total......	1	1	...	8	5	3	1	1	...	5	3	2	...	...	...	2	1	1	...	...	...	...	...	...	...	...	...	106	58	48
	38 A. ...	Bedar	...	...	...	...	...	...	...	...	...	...	...	...	...	...	...	1	1	...	17	12	5	22	16	6	...	...	...	42	30	12
		Total......	...	...	...	...	...	...	...	...	...	...	...	...	...	...	...	1	1	...	17	12	5	22	16	6	...	...	...	42	30	12
E. Vagrant Minor Artisans and Performers.	40 ...	Waddewar...	...	...	...	1	...	1	1	...	1	3	2	1	1	...	1	5	4	1	1	1	...	3	2	1	...	...	...	42	29	13
		Total......	...	...	...	1	...	1	1	...	1	3	2	1	1	...	1	5	4	1	1	1	...	3	2	1	...	...	...	42	29	13
	41 ...	Beldar	...	...	...	...	...	...	...	...	...	...	...	...	...	...	...	...	...	...	...	...	...	...	...	...	...	...	...	1	1	...
		Total......	...	...	...	...	...	...	...	...	...	...	...	...	...	...	...	...	...	...	...	...	...	...	...	...	...	...	...	1	1	...
	43 ...	Burud	...	...	...	...	...	...	...	...	...	...	...	...	...	...	...	1	1	...	...	...	...	1	...	1	...	...	...	4	3	1
		Kaikadi	...	...	...	...	...	...	1	...	1	1	1	...	...	...	...	...	...	...	...	...	...	...	...	...	...	...	...	3	1	2
		Total......	...	...	...	...	...	...	1	...	1	1	1	..	...	...	...	1	1	...	...	...	...	1	...	1	...	...	...	7	4	3

TABLE XIII A.

Deaf-Mutes by Caste, Tribe or Race.—*Continued.*

Class.	Group.	Castes.	City and suburbs including Secunderabad.			Atraf-i-Balda.			Mahabubnagar. (Nagar Karnul.)			Nalgonda.			Warangal. (Khamam.)			Elgandal.			Indur.			Medak.			Aurangabad.			Birh.		
			Total.	Males.	Females.	Total.	Males.	Females.	Total.	Males.	Females.	Total.	Males.	Females.	Total.	Males.	Females.	Total.	Males.	Females.	Total.	Males.	Females.	Total.	Males.	Females.	Total.	Males.	Females.	Total.	Males.	Females.
1	2	3	4	5	6	7	8	9	10	11	12	13	14	15	16	17	18	19	20	21	22	23	24	25	26	27	28	29	30	31	32	33
E. Vagrant Minor Artisans & Performers.	44 ...	Erkulwad	...	...	...	2	2	...	1	1	...	4	2	2	...	...	...	1	1	...	...	...	...	...	...	...	...	...	...	...	...	...
		Total......	...	...	...	2	2	...	1	1	...	4	2	2	...	...	...	1	1	...	...	...	...	...	...	...	...	...	...	...	...	...
F. Races and Nationalities.	48 ...	Mughal	...	...	...	...	...	...	...	...	...	2	...	2	...	...	...	...	...	...	...	...	...	...	...	...	...	...	...	...	...	...
		Other Mussulmans... ...	10	6	4	...	...	...	15	10	5	9	6	3	26	15	11	11	6	5	7	5	2	1	1	...	27	21	6	20	14	6
		Parsi	...	...	...	...	...	...	...	...	...	...	...	...	1	1	...	...	...	...	...	...	...	...	...	...	...	...	...	...	...	...
		Pathan	...	...	...	2	1	1	...	...	...	...	...	...	1	1	...	2	1	1	...	...	...	3	3	...	...	...	...	...	...	...
		Sheikh	29	22	7	4	1	3	10	7	3	6	4	2	3	3	...	...	...	...	2	2	...	14	8	6	8	3	5	17	16	1
		Syed	7	3	4	3	...	3	4	3	1	...	...	...	...	...	...	...	...	...	...	...	...	1	...	1	...	...	...	...	...	...
		Total......	46	31	15	9	2	7	29	20	9	17	10	7	31	20	11	13	7	6	9	7	2	19	12	7	35	24	11	37	30	7
	49 ...	Dasri	...	...	...	...	...	...	...	...	...	...	...	...	1	1	...	...	...	...	...	...	...	2	1	1	...	...	...	...	...	...
		Jain	...	...	...	...	...	...	...	...	...	...	...	...	...	...	...	...	...	...	...	...	...	...	...	...	4	3	1	...	...	...
		Other Hindus	9	6	3	8	3	5	7	2	5	18	6	12	18	11	7	1	...	1	...	...	...	1	1	...	7	5	2	1	1	...
		Perika	...	...	...	...	...	...	...	...	...	2	2	...	8	8	...	...	...	...	...	...	...	...	...	...	...	...	...	...	...	...
		Sikh	...	...	...	...	...	...	...	...	...	...	...	...	...	...	...	...	...	...	...	...	...	...	...	...	1	1	...	...	...	...
		Telinga	...	...	...	7	2	5	31	20	11	14	7	7	32	21	11	27	17	10	...	...	...	18	9	9	...	...	...	...	...	...
		Total......	9	6	3	15	5	10	38	22	16	34	15	19	59	41	18	28	17	11	...	...	...	21	11	10	12	9	3	1	1	...
	52 ...	Christian (Native)... ...	3	2	1	...	...	...	...	...	...	...	...	...	1	1	...	...	...	...	...	...	...	...	...	...	1	...	1	...	...	...
		Total......	3	2	1	...	...	...	...	...	...	...	...	...	1	1	...	...	...	...	...	...	...	...	...	...	1	...	1	...	...	...
		Grand Total......	143	83	60	199	122	77	382	235	147	318	203	115	485	309	176	477	293	184	136	86	50	254	144	110	272	178	94	222	142	80

TABLE XIII A.

Deaf-Mutes by Caste, Tribe or Race.—*Continued.*

Class.	Group.	Castes.	Nander. Total.	Nander. Males.	Nander. Females.	Naldrug. Total.	Naldrug. Males.	Naldrug. Females.	Bidar. Total.	Bidar. Males.	Bidar. Females.	Parbhani. Total.	Parbhani. Males.	Parbhani. Females.	Sirpur Tandur. Total.	Sirpur Tandur. Males.	Sirpur Tandur. Females.	Gulbarga. Total.	Gulbarga. Males.	Gulbarga. Females.	Raichur. Total.	Raichur. Males.	Raichur. Females.	Lingasugur. Total.	Lingasugur. Males.	Lingasugur. Females.	Railways. Total.	Railways. Males.	Railways. Females.	Total. Total.	Total. Males.	Total. Females.
			34	35	36	37	38	39	40	41	42	43	44	45	46	47	48	49	50	51	52	53	54	55	56	57	58	59	60	61	62	63
E. Vagrant Minor Artisans & Performers.	44 ...	Erkulwad	...	...	...	...	...	...	...	...	...	...	...	...	...	...	...	...	...	...	...	...	...	...	...	...	...	...	...	8	6	2
		Total......	...	...	...	...	...	...	...	...	...	...	...	...	...	...	...	...	...	...	...	...	...	...	...	...	...	...	...	8	6	2
F. Races and Nationalities.	48 ...	Mughal	...	...	...	...	...	...	...	...	...	...	...	...	...	...	...	...	...	...	1	...	1	...	...	...	...	...	...	3	...	3
		Other Mussulmans... ...	8	3	5	2	1	1	26	19	7	11	6	5	...	...	...	22	9	13	12	5	7	13	5	8	...	...	...	220	182	88
		Parsi	...	...	...	2	2	...	...	...	...	...	...	...	...	...	...	...	...	...	...	...	...	...	...	...	...	...	...	3	3	...
		Pathan	...	...	...	...	...	...	...	...	...	2	1	1	...	...	...	...	...	...	...	...	...	...	...	...	...	...	...	10	7	3
		Sheikh	...	...	...	23	17	6	5	5	...	6	3	3	5	2	3	...	...	...	...	...	...	...	...	...	...	...	...	132	98	39
		Syed	...	...	...	...	...	...	...	...	...	...	...	...	...	...	...	...	...	...	...	...	...	...	...	...	...	...	...	15	6	9
		Total......	8	3	5	27	20	7	31	24	7	19	10	9	5	2	3	22	9	13	13	5	8	13	5	8	...	...	...	383	241	142
	49 ...	Dasri	...	...	...	...	...	...	...	...	...	...	...	...	...	...	...	...	...	...	...	...	...	1	1	...	...	...	...	4	3	1
		Jain	2	1	1	3	2	1	...	...	...	3	1	2	...	...	...	1	...	1	...	...	...	...	...	...	...	...	...	13	7	6
		Other Hindus	5	4	1	3	1	2	2	2	...	7	2	5	2	1	1	3	2	1	1	...	1	8	5	3	1	1	...	102	53	49
		Perika	...	...	...	...	...	...	...	...	...	...	...	...	...	...	...	...	...	...	...	...	...	...	...	...	...	...	...	10	10	...
		Sikh	1	...	1	...	...	...	...	...	...	...	...	...	...	...	...	...	...	...	...	...	...	...	...	...	...	...	...	2	1	1
		Telinga	2	1	1	...	...	...	...	...	...	...	...	...	...	...	...	1	1	...	...	...	...	...	...	...	.	...	...	132	78	54
		Total......	10	6	4	6	3	3	2	2	...	10	3	7	2	1	1	5	3	2	1	...	1	9	6	3	1	1	...	263	152	111
	52 ...	Christian (Native) ...	...	...	...	...	...	...	...	...	...	...	...	...	...	...	...	...	...	...	...	...	...	...	...	...	...	...	...	5	3	2
		Total......	...	...	...	...	...	...	...	...	...	...	...	...	...	...	...	...	...	...	...	...	...	...	...	...	...	...	...	5	3	2
		Grand Total.....	224	128	96	180	111	69	337	226	111	216	130	86	72	39	33	180	111	69	146	86	60	175	102	73	1	1	...	4,419	2,729	1,690

TABLE XIV.

BLIND BY AGE.

TABLE XIV.

Blind by Age.

District or State.	Total Blind.			Distribution by Age.																											
				0—4		5—9		10—14		15—19		20—24		25—29		30—34		35—39		40—44		45—49		50—54		55—59		60 and over.		Unspecified.	
	Total.	Males.	Females.	Males.	Females.	Males.	Females.	Males.	Females.	Males.	Females.	Males.	Females.	Males.	Females.	Males.	Females.	Males.	Females.	Males.	Females.	Males.	Females.	Males.	Females.	Males.	Females.	Males.	Females.	Males.	Females.
1	2	3	4	5	6	7	8	9	10	11	12	13	14	15	16	17	18	19	20	21	22	23	24	25	26	27	28	29	30	31	32
Tellingana. Hyderabad. City	56	34	22	1	1	1	1	1	2	2	1	2	1	3	1	3	1	3	...	2	2	2	1	2	1	2	1	10	8	...	1
Suburbs including Secunderabad	207	115	92	...	1	5	2	5	5	10	6	8	4	10	3	9	8	3	5	12	9	6	1	9	10	1	3	37	34	...	1
Total......	263	149	114	1	2	6	3	6	7	12	7	10	5	13	4	12	9	6	5	14	11	8	2	11	11	3	4	47	42	...	2
Atraf-i-Balda District	430	229	201	13	8	24	14	15	13	15	16	27	15	23	17	16	16	7	11	13	22	11	6	12	16	5	5	48	41	...	..
Mahabubnagar (Nagar Karnul) ...	703	373	330	27	25	50	25	50	24	29	17	36	26	29	24	26	21	19	10	25	30	15	9	16	29	6	13	45	70	...	7
Nalgonda	530	292	238	29	17	34	20	21	15	26	16	30	32	25	22	24	17	3	12	17	19	12	5	18	13	7	3	46	47	...	...
Warangal (Khamam)	601	338	263	15	11	36	17	28	13	23	17	19	19	17	15	23	13	14	7	24	22	11	8	30	26	9	4	89	91	...	...
Elgandal	601	356	245	17	18	29	16	38	18	18	17	30	11	24	8	27	16	11	8	26	20	12	8	32	24	5	9	85	72	2	...
Indur	284	162	122	6	4	11	9	16	7	12	11	9	8	17	4	17	5	20	5	11	9	5	7	7	14	4	3	26	33	1	3
Medak...	530	306	224	9	9	25	10	17	10	15	11	28	19	21	11	28	19	17	13	23	20	10	7	36	22	9	7	68	64	...	2
Mahratwara. Aurangabad	1,121	687	484	39	21	60	42	67	38	47	26	45	41	71	45	50	38	36	27	38	42	28	17	49	37	13	14	91	93	3	3
Birh	845	459	386	20	16	51	35	46	31	38	25	44	22	48	27	45	39	22	31	37	43	19	16	26	21	6	3	60	76	2	1
Nander	715	371	344	29	19	39	23	35	24	27	16	25	21	31	30	31	16	21	25	34	30	16	18	28	32	11	9	44	80	...	1
Naldrug	670	389	281	22	8	35	30	54	31	26	11	32	21	40	24	43	25	26	21	28	26	11	9	14	22	10	12	48	38	...	3
Bidar	1,244	679	565	26	33	67	61	70	32	47	28	63	36	63	46	62	45	36	29	52	54	34	17	50	57	21	11	87	115	1	1
Parbhani	1,009	551	458	29	17	56	42	65	23	25	20	48	32	46	45	47	52	39	30	40	49	25	11	52	57	8	13	70	66	1	1
Sirpur Tandur	140	75	65	2	3	10	5	9	6	4	5	8	3	5	5	7	1	2	1	8	7	4	3	4	5	1	2	16	19	...	...
Karnatic or Kanada. Gulbarga	445	256	189	10	15	41	25	19	9	18	7	24	14	24	14	20	16	18	9	18	16	18	9	19	13	8	6	21	36	3	...
Raichur	222	117	105	9	12	12	9	10	8	12	8	13	9	13	5	8	8	8	6	6	8	7	4	5	5	5	8	9	20	...	...
Lingasugur	277	151	126	12	5	15	13	19	7	11	8	18	14	15	12	14	12	5	7	10	12	7	8	8	9	6	3	10	21	1	...
Total Districts......	10,367	5,741	4,626	314	241	595	396	579	309	393	259	499	348	507	354	488	359	304	252	405	480	240	157	406	402	134	120	863	982	14	22
Total Districts including Hyderabad ...	10,630	5,890	4,740	315	243	601	399	585	316	405	266	509	348	520	358	500	368	310	257	419	441	248	159	417	418	137	124	910	1,024	14	24
Railways......	2	2	...	...	...	...	...	...	...	...	...	...	...	...	...	1	...	1	...	...	...	...	...	...	...	...	...	...	...	...	...
Grand Total......	10,632	5,892	4,740	315	243	601	399	585	316	405	266	509	348	520	358	501	368	311	257	419	441	248	159	417	418	137	124	910	1,024	14	24

TABLE XIV A.

BLIND BY CASTE, TRIBE OR RACE.

TABLE XIV A.

Blind by Caste, Tribe or Race.

Class.	Group.	Castes.	City and suburbs including Secunderabad.			Atraf-i-Balda.			Mahabubnagar. (Nagar Karnul.)			Nalgonda.			Warangal. (Khamam.)			Elgandal.			Indur.			Medak.			Aurangabad.			Birh.		
			Total.	Males.	Females.	Total.	Males.	Females.	Total.	Males.	Females.	Total.	Males.	Females.	Total.	Males.	Females.	Total.	Males.	Females.	Total.	Males.	Females.	Total.	Males.	Females.	Total.	Males.	Females.	Total.	Males.	Females.
1	2	3	4	5	6	7	8	9	10	11	12	13	14	15	16	17	18	19	20	21	22	23	24	25	26	27	28	29	30	31	32	33
A. Agricultural.	1	Elma	...	...	...	1	1	...	5	3	2	2	1	1	5	1	4	10	8	2	...	...	...	...	...	...	...	...	...	6	2	4
		Lodhi	5	2	3	...	...	...	...	...	...	...	...	...	...	...	...	...	...	...	...	...	...	...	...	...	...	...	...	...	...	...
		Mahratta	2	...	2	5	4	1	3	2	1	1	1	...	12	6	6	9	6	3	32	27	5	7	2	5	87	55	32	275	150	125
		Rajput	12	8	4	...	...	...	3	3	...	...	...	...	2	2	...	...	...	...	...	...	...	...	...	...	30	24	6	3	1	2
		Total......	19	10	9	6	5	1	11	8	3	3	2	1	19	9	10	19	14	5	32	27	5	7	2	5	117	79	38	284	153	131
	2a	Andh	...	...	...	...	...	...	...	...	...	...	...	...	...	...	...	...	...	...	...	...	...	...	...	...	...	...	...	...	...	...
		Anjani	...	...	...	...	...	...	...	...	...	...	...	...	...	...	...	...	...	...	...	...	...	...	...	...	...	...	...	...	...	...
		Aryan	...	...	...	...	...	...	...	...	...	...	...	...	...	...	...	...	...	...	1	...	1	...	...	...	...	...	...	1	...	1
		Kachi	3	3	...	...	...	...	...	...	...	...	...	...	...	...	...	...	...	...	...	...	...	...	...	...	...	...	...	...	...	...
		Kunbi	5	3	2	44	25	19	96	49	47	49	29	20	52	30	22	62	33	29	11	4	7	46	23	23	399	218	181	89	51	38
		Mali	10	4	6	...	...	...	...	...	...	...	...	...	...	...	...	...	...	...	...	...	...	...	...	...	56	38	18	14	9	5
		Munurwad	4	2	2	15	8	7	16	6	10	4	1	3	6	4	2	31	16	15	23	15	8	9	6	3	1	...	1	...	...	...
		Mutrasi	1	1	...	29	10	19	38	19	19	24	11	13	49	31	18	19	9	10	...	...	...	78	40	38	1	1	...	...	...	...
		Pichakuntla	...	...	...	...	...	...	2	1	1	1	1	...	...	...	...	...	...	...	...	...	...	...	...	...	...	...	...	...	...	...
		Satani	...	...	...	...	...	...	...	...	...	...	...	...	3	1	2	3	...	3	...	...	...	...	...	...	...	...	...	...	...	...
		Vanjari	...	...	...	...	...	...	...	...	...	...	...	...	1	...	1	2	1	1	...	...	...	...	...	...	...	...	...	...	...	...
		Total......	23	13	10	88	43	45	152	75	77	78	42	36	111	66	45	117	59	58	35	19	16	133	69	64	457	257	200	104	60	44
	2b	Ahir	4	2	2	...	...	...	...	...	...	...	...	...	...	...	...	...	...	...	...	...	...	...	...	...	...	...	...	4	3	1
		Koli	...	...	...	...	...	...	...	...	...	...	...	...	...	...	...	...	...	...	20	5	15	1	1	...	...	...	...	17	7	10
		Total	4	2	2	...	...	...	...	...	...	...	...	...	...	...	...	...	...	...	20	5	15	1	1	...	...	...	...	21	10	11
	2c	Dher	40	18	22	53	30	23	101	59	42	84	52	32	62	44	18	51	31	20	33	18	15	59	38	26	110	55	55	62	27	35
		Mang	7	3	4	23	9	14	...	...	...	...	...	...	21	11	10	...	...	...	21	14	7	50	30	20	25	13	12	24	11	13
		Total......	47	21	26	76	39	37	101	59	42	84	52	32	83	55	28	51	31	20	54	32	22	109	68	46	135	68	67	86	38	48
	4	Gond	...	...	...	...	...	...	...	...	...	...	...	...	...	...	...	...	...	...	1	...	1	...	...	...	...	...	...	...	...	...
		Gond H	...	...	...	...	...	...	...	...	...	...	...	...	...	...	...	...	...	...	...	...	...	...	...	...	5	4	1	3	1	2
		Koya	...	...	...	...	...	...	...	...	...	...	...	...	11	6	5	...	...	...	...	...	...	...	...	...	...	...	...	...	...	...
		Total......	...	...	...	...	...	...	...	...	...	...	...	...	11	6	5	...	...	...	1	...	1	...	...	...	5	4	1	3	1	2

TABLE XIV A.

Blind by Caste, Tribe or Race.—*Continued.*

Class.	Group.	Castes.	Nander. Total.	Nander. Males.	Nander. Females.	Naldrug. Total.	Naldrug. Males.	Naldrug. Females.	Bidar. Total.	Bidar. Males.	Bidar. Females.	Parbhani. Total.	Parbhani. Males.	Parbhani. Females.	Sirpur Tandur. Total.	Sirpur Tandur. Males.	Sirpur Tandur. Females.	Gulbarga. Total.	Gulbarga. Males.	Gulbarga. Females.	Raichur. Total.	Raichur. Males.	Raichur. Females.	Lingasugur. Total.	Lingasugur. Males.	Lingasugur. Females.	Railways. Total.	Railways. Males.	Railways. Females.	Total. Total.	Total. Males.	Total. Females.
			34	35	36	37	38	39	40	41	42	43	44	45	46	47	48	49	50	51	52	53	54	55	56	57	58	59	60	61	62	63
A. Agricultural.	1	Elma	2	...	2	3	3	...	67	44	23	1	...	1	...	...	...	2	1	1	...	...	...	...	...	...	...	...	...	104	64	40
		Lodhi	...	...	...	2	...	2	...	...	...	1	1	...	...	...	...	...	...	...	...	...	...	...	...	...	...	...	...	8	3	5
		Mahratta	199	103	96	208	126	82	184	95	89	374	200	174	14	7	7	11	5	6	1	1	...	12	8	4	...	...	...	1,436	798	688
		Rajput	6	4	2	2	1	1	4	1	3	3	2	1	...	...	...	2	2	...	1	1	...	...	...	...	...	...	...	68	49	19
		Total......	207	107	100	215	130	85	255	140	115	379	203	176	14	7	7	15	8	7	2	2	...	12	8	4	...	...	...	1,616	914	702
	2a	Andh	5	8	2	...	...	...	...	...	...	9	3	6	...	...	...	...	...	...	...	...	...	...	...	...	...	...	...	14	6	8
		Anjani	...	...	...	...	...	...	...	...	...	...	...	...	1	1	...	...	...	...	...	...	...	...	...	...	...	...	...	1	1	...
		Aryan	...	...	...	...	...	...	...	...	...	...	...	...	...	...	...	...	...	...	...	...	...	...	...	...	...	...	...	2	...	2
		Kachi	...	...	...	...	...	...	...	...	...	...	...	...	...	...	...	...	...	...	...	...	...	...	...	...	...	...	...	8	8	...
		Kumbi	16	9	7	72	34	38	12	6	6	33	13	20	15	10	5	18	9	9	31	18	13	11	8	3	...	...	...	1,061	572	489
		Mali	...	...	...	17	11	6	6	3	3	28	20	8	2	2	...	...	...	...	...	...	...	3	...	3	...	...	...	136	87	49
		Munurwad	19	4	15	...	...	...	6	6	...	...	...	...	...	...	...	1	1	...	4	2	2	3	3	...	...	...	...	142	74	68
		Mutrasi	...	...	...	...	...	...	2	...	2	...	...	...	...	...	...	...	...	...	2	...	2	...	...	...	...	...	...	248	122	121
		Pichakuntla	...	...	...	...	...	...	...	...	...	...	...	...	...	...	...	...	...	...	1	1	...	...	...	...	...	...	...	4	3	1
		Satani	...	...	...	...	...	...	...	...	...	...	...	...	...	...	...	...	...	...	...	...	...	...	...	...	...	...	...	6	1	5
		Vanjari	...	...	...	...	...	...	...	...	...	...	...	...	...	...	...	...	...	...	...	...	...	...	...	...	...	...	...	8	1	2
		Total......	40	16	24	89	45	44	26	15	11	70	36	34	18	18	5	19	10	9	38	21	17	17	11	6	...	...	...	1,615	870	745
	2b	Ahir	...	...	...	...	...	...	...	...	...	1	1	...	...	...	...	...	...	...	...	...	...	...	...	...	...	...	...	9	6	3
		Koli	28	16	12	13	11	2	59	24	35	13	8	5	1	...	1	47	26	21	...	...	...	...	...	...	...	...	...	199	98	101
		Total......	28	16	12	13	11	2	59	24	35	14	9	5	1	...	1	47	26	21	...	...	...	...	...	...	...	...	...	208	104	104
	2c	Dher	87	38	49	76	41	35	80	49	31	113	72	41	6	1	5	26	13	13	28	16	12	27	13	14	...	...	...	1,098	610	488
		Mang	22	13	9	32	23	9	59	28	31	18	11	7	1	...	1	15	10	5	...	...	...	...	...	...	...	...	...	318	176	142
		Total......	109	51	58	108	64	44	139	77	62	131	83	48	7	1	6	41	23	18	28	16	12	27	13	14	...	...	...	1,416	786	630
	4	Gond	...	...	...	...	...	...	...	...	...	...	...	...	29	14	15	...	...	...	...	...	...	...	...	...	...	...	...	30	14	16
		Gond H	...	...	...	1	1	...	2	2	...	...	...	...	...	...	...	2	2	...	...	...	...	...	...	...	...	...	...	13	10	3
		Koya	...	...	...	...	...	...	...	...	...	...	...	...	...	...	...	...	...	...	...	...	...	...	...	...	...	...	...	11	6	5
		Total......	...	...	...	1	1	...	2	2	...	...	...	...	29	14	15	2	2	...	...	...	...	...	...	...	...	...	...	54	30	24

TABLE XIV A.

Blind by Caste, Tribe or Race.—*Continued.*

Class.	Group.	Castes.	City and suburbs including Secunderabad.			Atraf-i-Balda.			Mahabubnagar. (Nagar Karnul.)			Nalgonda.			Warangal. (Khamam.)			Elgandal.			Indur.			Medak.			Aurangabad.			Birh.		
			Total.	Males.	Females.	Total.	Males.	Females.	Total.	Males.	Females.	Total.	Males.	Females.	Total.	Males.	Females.	Total.	Males.	Females.	Total.	Males.	Females.	Total.	Males.	Females.	Total.	Males.	Females.	Total.	Males.	Females.
1	2	3	4	5	6	7	8	9	10	11	12	13	14	15	16	17	18	19	20	21	22	23	24	25	26	27	28	29	30	31	32	33
B. Professional.	5 ...	Brahmin	16	12	4	6	2	4	10	6	4	8	6	2	16	12	4	15	7	8	9	5	4	12	10	2	34	20	14	30	19	11
		Jangam	...	...	...	2	1	1	9	9	...	4	2	2	...	...	...	2	2	...	...	...	...	4	4	...	...	...	...	...	...	...
		Total......	16	12	4	8	3	5	19	15	4	12	8	4	16	12	4	17	9	8	9	5	4	16	14	2	34	20	14	30	19	11
	6 ...	Bairagi	...	...	...	...	...	...	...	...	...	...	...	...	...	...	...	...	...	...	...	...	...	...	...	...	4	2	2	...	...	...
		Gosain		...	...	...	...	...	...	...	...	...	...	...	...	...	...	...	...	...	...	...	...	...	...	...	2	1	1	9	8	1
		Jogi	...	...	...	...	...	...	...	...	...	...	...	...	...	...	...	...	...	...	...	...	...	...	...	...	...	...	...	...	...	...
		Total......	...	...	...	...	...	...	...	...	...	...	...	...	...	...	...	...	...	...	...	...	...	...	...	...	6	3	3	9	8	1
	7 ...	Gurao	...	...	...	...	...	...	...	...	...	...	...	...	...	...	...	...	...	...	1	1	...	...	...	...	3	1	2	1	1	...
		Total......	...	...	...	...	...	...	...	...	...	...	...	...	...	...	...	...	...	...	1	1	...	...	...	...	3	1	2	1	1	...
	8 ...	Bhat	...	...	...	...	...	...	2	1	1	...	...	...	...	...	...	...	...	...	...	...	...	...	...	...	...	...	...	...	...	...
		Total......	...	...	...	...	...	...	2	1	1	...	...	...	...	...	...	...	...	...	...	...	...		...	...	...	...	...	...	...	...
	11 ...	Gondhali	...	...	...	...	...	...	...	...	...	...	...	...	...	...	...	...	...	...	...	...	...	...	...	...	...	...	...	...	...	...
		Tammadi	...	...	...	1	1	...	...	...	...	1	...	1	4	3	1	...	...	...	...	...	...	...	...	...	...	...	...	...	...	...
		Total......	...	...	...	1	1	...	...	...	...	1	...	1	4	3	1	...	...	...	...	...	...	...	...	...	...	...	...	...	...	...
	12 ...	Kanchani	1	...	1	...	...	...	...	...	...	1	1	...	...	...	...	...	...	...	...	...	...	...	...	...	...	...	...	...	...	...
		Total......	1	...	1	...	...	...	...	...	...	1	1	...	...	...	...	...	...	...	...	...	...	...	...	...	...	...	...	...	...	...
C. Commercial.	14 ...	Balija	...	...	...	14	6	8	15	9	6	7	3	4	2	...	2	7	4	3	..	...	...	31	20	11	...	...	...	...	...	...
		Komti	1	...	1	32	19	.13	37	25	12	23	13	10	32	18	14	61	38	23	2	...	2	21	13	8	1	1	...	3	1	2
		Wani	14	10	4	...	...	...	9	6	3	...	...	...	...	...	...	...	...	...	14	6	8	...	...	...	21	8	13	11	4	7
		Total......	15	10	5	46	25	21	61	40	21	30	16	14	34	18	16	68	42	26	16	6	10	52	33	19	22	9	13	14	5	9

TABLE XIV A.

Blind by Caste, Tribe or Race.—*Continued.*

Class.	Group.	Castes.	Nander. Total.	Nander. Males.	Nander. Females.	Naldrug. Total.	Naldrug. Males.	Naldrug. Females.	Bidar. Total.	Bidar. Males.	Bidar. Females.	Parbhani. Total.	Parbhani. Males.	Parbhani. Females.	Sirpur Tandur. Total.	Sirpur Tandur. Males.	Sirpur Tandur. Females.	Gulbarga. Total.	Gulbarga. Males.	Gulbarga. Females.	Raichur. Total.	Raichur. Males.	Raichur. Females.	Lingasugur. Total.	Lingasugur. Males.	Lingasugur. Females.	Railways. Total.	Railways. Males.	Railways. Females.	Total. Total.	Total. Males.	Total. Females.
			34	35	36	37	38	39	40	41	42	43	44	45	46	47	48	49	50	51	52	53	54	55	56	57	58	59	60	61	62	63
B. Professional.	5 ...	Brahmin	8	6	2	16	12	4	30	16	14	21	12	9	2	2	...	10	8	2	4	3	1	8	5	3	...	...	...	255	163	92
		Jangam	18	8	10	6	5	1	44	22	22	4	3	1	...	...	...	11	4	7	...	...	...	...	...	...	...	...	...	104	60	44
		Total.....	26	14	12	22	17	5	74	38	36	25	15	10	2	2	...	21	12	9	4	3	1	8	5	3	...	...	...	359	228	136
	6 ...	Bairagi	...	...	...	...	...	...	...	...	...	...	...	...	...	...	...	...	...	...	...	...	...	...	...	...	...	...	...	4	2	2
		Gosain	11	7	4	5	4	1	6	5	1	8	6	2	...	...	...	...	...	...	...	...	...	...	...	...	...	...	...	41	31	10
		Jogi	1	...	1	1	...	1	...	...	...	...	...	...	...	...	...	...	...	...	...	...	...	...	...	...	...	...	...	2	...	2
		Total ...	12	7	5	6	4	2	6	5	1	8	6	2	...	...	...	...	...	...	...	...	...	...	...	...	...	...	...	47	33	14
	7 ...	Gurao	4	2	2	4	4	...	6	6	...	...	...	...	1	1	...	1	...	1	...	...	...	...	...	...	...	...	...	21	16	5
		Total......	4	2	2	4	4	...	6	6	...	...	...	...	1	1	...	1	...	1	...	...	...	...	...	...	...	...	...	21	16	5
	8 ...	Bhat	...	...	...	...	...	...	...	...	...	...	...	...	...	...	...	...	...	...	...	...	...	...	...	...	...	...	...	2	1	1
		Total......	...	...	...	...	...	...	...	...	...	...	...	...	...	...	...	...	...	...	...	...	...	...	...	...	...	...	...	2	1	1
	11 ...	Gondhali	...	...	...	...	...	...	2	...	2	...	...	...	...	...	...	...	...	...	...	...	...	...	...	...	...	...	...	2	...	2
		Tammadi	...	...	...	...	...	...	...	...	...	...	...	...	...	...	...	...	...	...	2	1	1	...	...	...	...	...	...	8	5	3
		Total.....	...	...	...	...	...	...	2	...	2	...	...	...	...	...	...	...	...	...	2	1	1	...	...	...	...	...	...	10	5	5
	12 ...	Kanchani	...	...	...	...	...	...	...	...	...	1	...	1	...	...	...	...	...	...	...	...	...	...	...	...	...	...	...	3	1	2
		Total......	...	...	...	...	...	...	...	...	...	1	...	1	...	...	...	...	...	...	...	...	...	...	...	...	...	...	...	3	1	2
C. Commercial.	14 ...	Balija	...	...	...	...	...	...	5	1	4	...	...	...	...	...	...	...	...	...	35	17	18	...	...	...	...	...	...	116	60	56
		Komti	14	12	2	...	...	...	19	11	8	8	...	8	2	2	...	6	4	2	3	3	...	1	1	...	...	...	...	266	161	105
		Wani	46	20	26	48	26	22	232	125	107	32	19	13	...	...	...	112	79	33	...	...	...	56	31	25	...	...	...	595	334	261
		Total......	60	32	28	48	26	22	256	137	119	40	19	21	2	2	...	118	83	35	38	20	18	57	32	25	...	...	...	977	555	422

TABLE XIV A.

Blind by Caste, Tribe or Race.—*Continued.*

Class.	Group.	Castes.	City and suburbs including Secunderabad.			Atraf-i-Balda.			Mahabubnagar. (Nagar Karnul).			Nalgonda.			Warangal. (Khamam.)			Elgandal.			Indur.			Medak.			Aurangabad.			Birh.		
			Total.	Males.	Females.	Total.	Males.	Females.	Total.	Males.	Females.	Total.	Males.	Females.	Total.	Males.	Females.	Total.	Males.	Females.	Total.	Males.	Females.	Total.	Males.	Females.	Total.	Males.	Females.	Total.	Males.	Females.
1	2	3	4	5	6	7	8	9	10	11	12	13	14	15	16	17	18	19	20	21	22	23	24	25	26	27	28	29	30	31	32	33
C. Commercial.	16 ...	Banjara	2	2	...	...	...	...	...	...	...	...	...	...	...	...	...	5	3	2	11	3	8	...	...	...	7	3	4	80	40	40
		Lad	...	...	...	...	...	...	...	...	...	...	...	...	...	...	...	...	...	...	...	...	...	...	...	...	...	...	...	...	...	...
		Lambani	2	...	2	1	1	...	3	2	1	5	2	3	14	10	4	...	...	...	2	2	...	...	...	...	...	...	...	2	...	2
		Total......	4	2	2	1	1	...	3	2	1	5	2	3	14	10	4	5	3	2	13	5	8	...	...	...	7	3	4	82	40	42
D. Artisan and Village Menial.	17 ...	Panchal	...	...	...	...	...	...	...	...	...	...	...	...	...	...	...	1	1	...	...	...	...	1	1	...	...	...	...	...	...	...
		Sonar	3	3	...	8	6	2	4	3	1	3	2	1	7	3	4	11	6	5	3	2	1	12	7	5	11	7	4	9	2	7
		Total......	8	3	...	8	6	2	4	3	1	3	2	1	7	3	4	12	7	5	3	2	1	13	8	5	11	7	4	9	2	7
	18 ...	Hajjam	2	2	...	7	5	2	9	5	4	10	6	4	6	4	2	3	2	1	...	...	...	8	5	3	12	8	4	7	6	1
		Total......	2	2	...	7	5	2	9	5	4	10	6	4	6	4	2	3	2	1	...	...	...	8	5	3	12	8	4	7	6	1
	19 ...	Lohar	...	...	...	...	...	...	3	3	...	2	1	1	7	1	6	5	4	1	...	...	...	...	...	...	10	7	3	16	10	6
		Total......	...	...	...	...	...	...	3	3	...	2	1	1	7	1	6	5	4	1	...	...	...	...	...	...	10	7	3	16	10	6
	20 ...	Gaondi	...	...	...	...	...	...	6	4	2	...	...	...	...	...	...	...	...	...	...	...	...	...	...	...	...	...	...	...	...	...
		Hanigaru	...	...	...	...	...	...	...	...	...	...	...	...	...	...	...	...	...	...	...	...	...	...	...	...	...	...	...	...	...	...
		Nakashgar	...	...	...	...	...	...	...	...	...	...	...	...	1	...	1	...	...	...	...	...	...	...	...	...	...	...	...	...	...	...
		Sutar (or Barhai)... ...	...	...	...	2	1	1	6	3	3	3	2	1	4	2	2	9	6	3	...	...	...	4	2	2	6	4	2	11	4	7
		Total......	...	...	...	2	1	1	12	7	5	3	2	1	5	2	3	9	6	3	...	...	...	4	2	2	6	4	2	11	4	7
	21 ...	Kasar	...	...	...	1	1	...	1	...	1	...	...	...	2	...	2	...	...	...	2	...	2	...	...	...	4	2	2	6	2	4
		Total......	...	...	...	1	1	...	1	...	1	...	...	...	2	...	2	...	...	...	2	...	2	...	...	...	4	2	2	6	2	4
	22 ...	Darzi	...	...	...	...	...	...	...	...	...	...	...	...	...	...	...	3	2	1	...	...	...	2	2	...	...	...	...	5	3	2
		Zingar	...	...	...	...	...	...	...	...	...	...	...	...	...	...	...	...	...	...	...	...	...	...	...	...	1	1	...	...	...	...
		Total......	...	...	...	...	...	...	...	...	...	...	...	...	...	...	...	3	2	1	...	...	...	2	2	...	1	1	...	5	3	2

TABLE XIV A.

Blind by Caste, Tribe or Race.—*Continued.*

Class.	Group.	Castes.	Nander. Total.	Nander. Males.	Nander. Females.	Naldrug. Total.	Naldrug. Males.	Naldrug. Females.	Bidar. Total.	Bidar. Males.	Bidar. Females.	Parbhani. Total.	Parbhani. Males.	Parbhani. Females.	Sirpur Tandur. Total.	Sirpur Tandur. Males.	Sirpur Tandur. Females.	Gulbarga. Total.	Gulbarga. Males.	Gulbarga. Females.	Raichur. Total.	Raichur. Males.	Raichur. Females.	Lingasugur. Total.	Lingasugur. Males.	Lingasugur. Females.	Railways. Total.	Railways. Males.	Railways. Females.	Total. Total.	Total. Males.	Total. Females.
			34	35	36	37	38	39	40	41	42	43	44	45	46	47	48	49	50	51	52	53	54	55	56	57	58	59	60	61	62	63
C. Commercial.	16 ...	Banjara	13	6	7	5	2	3	9	4	5	27	21	6	2	2	...	...	...	...	...	...	...	...	...	...	...	...	...	161	86	75
		Lad	...	...	...	...	...	...	...	...	...	5	...	5	...	...	...	3	...	3	...	...	...	...	...	...	...	...	...	8	...	8
		Lambani	4	1	3	1	...	1	3	2	1	9	3	6	1	1	...	3	1	2	1	1	...	2	1	1	...	...	...	53	27	26
		Total......	17	7	10	6	2	4	12	6	6	41	24	17	3	3	...	6	1	5	1	1	...	2	1	1	...	...	...	272	113	109
D. Artisan and Village Menial.	17 ..	Panchal	...	...	...	...	...	...	3	3	...	2	...	2	1	...	1	8	2	6	4	2	2	4	1	3	...	...	...	24	10	14
		Sonar	4	1	3	5	2	3	7	3	4	5	5	...	...	...	...	1	...	1	8	7	1	2	...	2	...	...	...	103	59	44
		Total......	4	1	3	5	2	3	10	6	4	7	5	2	1	...	1	9	2	7	12	9	3	6	1	5	...	...	...	127	69	58
	18 ...	Hajjam	7	7	...	11	7	4	11	5	6	15	7	8	8	4	4	6	4	2	2	1	1	1	1	...	...	...	...	125	79	46
		Total......	7	7	...	11	7	4	11	5	6	15	7	8	8	4	4	6	4	2	2	1	1	1	1	...	...	...	...	125	79	46
	19 ...	Lohar	8	1	2	4	3	1	2	1	1	2	2	...	7	4	3	2	1	1	13	4	9	32	17	15	...	...	...	108	59	49
		Total......	3	1	2	4	3	1	2	1	1	2	2	...	7	4	3	2	1	1	13	4	9	32	17	15	...	...	...	108	59	49
	20 ...	Gaondi	3	1	2	...	...	...	2	...	2	...	...	...	1	...	1	1	...	1	3	1	2	...	...	...	...	...	...	16	6	10
		Hanigaru	...	...	...	...	...	...	...	...	...	...	...	...	...	...	...	...	...	...	...	...	...	8	3	5	...	...	...	8	3	5
		Nakashgar	...	...	...	...	...	...	...	...	...	...	...	...	...	...	...	...	...	...	...	...	...	...	...	...	...	...	...	1	...	1
		Sutar (or Barhai)	12	6	6	5	5	...	16	9	7	13	6	7	...	...	...	10	4	6	...	...	...	4	2	2	...	...	...	105	56	49
		Total......	15	7	8	5	5	...	18	9	9	13	6	7	1	...	1	11	4	7	3	1	2	12	5	7	...	...	...	130	65	65
	21 ...	Kasar	1	...	1	3	2	1	...	...	...	9	3	6	2	...	2	...	...	...	...	...	...	...	...	...	...	...	...	31	10	21
		Total......	1	...	1	3	2	1	...	...	...	9	3	6	2	...	2	...	...	...	...	...	...	...	...	...	...	...	...	31	10	21
	22 ...	Darzi	2	1	1	...	...	...	3	3	...	2	1	1	...	...	...	4	2	2	...	...	...	2	2	...	...	...	...	23	16	7
		Zingar	...	...	...	...	...	...	...	...	...	1	...	1	...	...	...	1	1	...	...	...	...	...	...	...	...	...	...	3	2	1
		Total......	2	1	1	...	...	...	3	3	...	3	1	2	...	...	...	5	3	2	...	...	...	2	2	...	...	...	...	26	18	8

TABLE XIV A.

Blind by Caste, Tribe or Race.—*Continued.*

Class.	Group.	Castes.	City and suburbs including Secunderabad.			Atraf-i-Balda.			Mahabubnagar (Nagar Karnul.)			Nalgonda.			Warangal. (Khamam.)			Elgandal.			Indur.			Medak.			Aurangabad.			Birh.		
			Total.	Males.	Females.	Total.	Males.	Females.	Total.	Males.	Females.	Total.	Males.	Females.	Total.	Males.	Females.	Total.	Males.	Females.	Total.	Males.	Females.	Total.	Males.	Females.	Total.	Males.	Females.	Total.	Males.	Females.
1	2	3	4	5	6	7	8	9	10	11	12	13	14	15	16	17	18	19	20	21	22	23	24	25	26	27	28	29	30	31	32	33
D. Artisan and Village Menial.	22b	Attar	...	...	...	...	...	...	...	...	...	...	...	...	...	...	...	...	...	...	...	...	...	...	...	...	...	...	...	...	...	...
		Total......	...	...	...	...	...	...	...	...	...	...	...	...	...	...	...	...	...	...	...	...	...	...	...	...	...	...	...	...	...	...
	23	Julaha	...	...	...	14	6	8	5	3	2	17	10	7	27	17	10	50	30	20	18	7	11	21	13	8	9	1	8	5	2	3
		Khatri	...	...	...	...	...	...	...	...	...	...	...	...	...	...	...	...	...	...	...	...	...	...	...	...	...	...	...	...	...	...
		Patkari	...	...	...	...	...	...	...	...	...	...	...	...	...	...	...	...	...	...	...	...	...	2	1	1	...	...	...	...	...	...
		Rangari or Rangrez	1	...	1	...	...	...	...	...	...	...	...	...	...	...	...	...	...	...	...	...	...	1	...	1	...	...	...	2	1	1
		Total......	1	...	1	14	6	8	5	3	2	17	10	7	27	17	10	50	30	20	18	7	11	24	14	10	9	1	8	7	3	4
	24	Dhobi	7	4	3	14	4	10	18	9	9	31	18	13	16	10	6	17	11	6	14	8	6	12	9	3	8	5	3	3	2	1
		Total......	7	4	3	14	4	10	18	9	9	31	18	13	16	10	6	17	11	6	14	8	6	12	9	3	8	5	3	3	2	1
	25	Pinjari	...	...	...	...	...	...	...	...	...	1	1	...	...	...	...	1	1	...	...	...	...	1	...	1	...	...	...	...	...	...
		Total......	...	...	...	...	...	...	...	...	...	1	1	...	...	...	...	1	1	...	...	...	...	1	...	1	...	...	...	...	...	...
	26	Dhangar	6	2	4	54	29	25	109	47	62	106	45	61	60	29	31	41	22	19	26	20	6	40	19	21	48	20	28	53	28	25
		Total......	6	2	4	54	29	25	109	47	62	106	45	61	60	29	31	41	22	19	26	20	6	40	19	21	48	20	28	53	28	25
	27	Teli	1	1	...	6	1	5	...	...	...	...	...	...	...	...	...	5	3	2	...	...	...	...	...	...	20	11	9	9	6	3
		Total......	1	1	...	6	1	5	...	...	...	...	...	...	...	...	...	5	3	2	...	...	...	...	...	...	20	11	9	9	6	3
	28	Kumbhar	1	1	...	7	4	3	...	...	...	14	8	6	10	6	4	7	5	2	...	...	...	14	9	5	4	2	2	7	4	3
		Total......	1	1	...	7	4	3	...	...	...	14	8	6	10	6	4	7	5	2	...	...	...	14	9	5	4	2	2	7	4	3

TABLE XIV A.

Blind by Caste, Tribe or Race.—*Continued.*

Class.	Group.	Caste.	Nander. Total.	Nander. Males.	Nander. Females.	Naldrug. Total.	Naldrug. Males.	Naldrug. Females.	Bidar. Total.	Bidar. Males.	Bidar. Females.	Parbhani. Total.	Parbhani. Males.	Parbhani. Females.	Sirpur Tandur. Total.	Sirpur Tandur. Males.	Sirpur Tandur. Females.	Gulbarga. Total.	Gulbarga. Males.	Gulbarga. Females.	Raichur. Total.	Raichur. Males.	Raichur. Females.	Lingasugur. Total.	Lingasugur. Males.	Lingasugur. Females.	Railways. Total.	Railways. Males.	Railways. Females.	Total. Total.	Total. Males.	Total. Females.
			34	35	36	37	38	39	40	41	42	43	44	45	46	47	48	49	50	51	52	53	54	55	56	57	58	59	60	61	62	63
D. Artisan and Village Menial.	22b ...	Attar	...	...	...	...	...	...	...	...	...	2	2	...	...	...	...	...	...	...	...	...	...	...	...	...	...	...	...	2	2	...
		Total......	...	...	...	...	...	...	...	...	...	2	2	...	...	...	...	...	...	...	...	...	...	...	...	...	...	...	...	2	2	...
	23 ...	Julaha	10	6	4	4	2	2	38	24	14	3	3	...	1	1	...	5	2	3	...	...	...	5	2	3	...	...	...	232	129	103
		Khatri	1	...	1	...	...	...	...	...	...	5	1	4	...	...	...	...	...	...	...	...	...	...	...	...	...	...	...	6	1	5
		Patkari	...	...	...	...	...	...	...	...	...	...	...	...	...	...	...	...	...	...	...	...	...	...	...	...	...	...	...	2	1	1
		Rangari or Rangrez ...	3	1	2	1	1	...	...	...	...	2	1	1	1	1	...	4	3	1	...	...	...	...	...	...	...	...	...	15	8	7
		Total......	14	7	7	5	3	2	38	24	14	10	5	5	2	2	...	9	5	4	...	...	...	5	2	3	...	...	...	255	139	116
	24 ...	Dhobi	6	6	...	5	4	1	11	3	8	8	4	4	...	...	...	5	4	1	...	...	...	...	...	...	...	...	...	175	101	74
		Total......	6	6	...	5	4	1	11	3	8	8	4	4	...	...	...	5	4	1	...	...	...	...	...	...	...	...	...	175	101	74
	25 ...	Pinjari	...	...	...	...	...	...	...	...	...	...	...	...	...	...	...	...	...	...	...	...	...	...	...	...	...	...	...	3	2	1
		Total......	...	...	...	...	...	...	...	...	...	...	...	...	...	...	...	...	...	...	...	...	...	...	...	...	...	...	...	3	2	1
	26 ...	Dhangar	66	37	29	41	20	21	186	77	59	100	45	55	2	2	...	39	17	22	33	17	16	36	23	13	...	...	...	996	499	497
		Total......	66	37	29	41	20	21	136	77	59	100	45	55	2	2	...	39	17	22	33	17	16	36	23	13	...	...	...	996	499	497
	27 ...	Teli	5	3	2	9	4	5	5	3	2	16	10	6	...	...	...	5	3	2	1	1	...	...	...	...	...	...	...	82	46	36
		Total......	5	3	2	9	4	5	5	3	2	16	10	6	...	...	...	5	3	2	1	1	...	...	...	...	...	...	...	82	46	36
	28 ...	Kumhar	2	2	...	3	1	2	4	1	3	4	4	...	7	4	3	6	3	3	3	1	2	1	1	...	...	...	...	94	56	38
		Total......	2	2	...	3	1	2	4	1	3	4	4	...	7	4	3	6	3	3	3	1	2	1	1	...	...	...	...	94	56	38

TABLE XIV A.

Blind by Caste, Tribe or Race.—*Continued.*

Class.	Group.	Castes.	City and suburbs including Secunderabad. Total.	Males.	Females.	Atraf-i-Balda. Total.	Males.	Females.	Mahabubnagar. (Nagar Karnul.) Total.	Males.	Females.	Nalgonda. Total.	Males.	Females.	Warangal. (Khamam.) Total.	Males.	Females.	Elgandal. Total.	Males.	Females.	Indur. Total.	Males.	Females.	Medak. Total.	Males.	Females.	Aurangabad. Total.	Males.	Females.	Bir. Total.	Males.	Females.
1	2	3	4	5	6	7	8	9	10	11	12	13	14	15	16	17	18	19	20	21	22	23	24	25	26	27	28	29	30	31	32	33
D. Artisan and Village Menial.	35	Besta	...	...	...	...	...	...	12	6	6	3	2	1	5	4	1	13	5	8	...	...	...	1	1	...	...	...	...	...	...	...
		Bhoi	...	...	...	1	1	...	...	...	...	...	...	...	...	...	...	...	...	...	7	4	3	...	...	...	3	1	2	2	2	...
		Total	...	...	...	1	1	...	12	6	6	3	2	1	5	4	1	13	5	8	7	4	3	1	1	...	3	1	2	2	2	...
	36	Goundla	3	3	...	31	21	10	27	14	13	30	15	15	47	24	23	36	24	12	...	...	...	23	19	4	...	...	...	...	...	...
		Kalal	...	...	...	...	...	...	...	...	...	...	...	...	...	...	...	...	...	...	...	...	...	...	...	...	...	...	...	1	1	...
		Total	3	3	...	31	21	10	27	14	13	30	15	15	47	24	23	36	24	12	...	...	...	23	19	4	...	...	...	1	1	...
	37	Kasai	...	...	...	...	...	...	1	1	...	1	1	...	2	2	...	...	...	...	...	...	...	...	...	...	...	...	...	...	...	...
		Total	...	...	...	...	...	...	1	1	...	1	1	...	2	2	...	...	...	...	...	...	...	...	...	...	...	...	...	...	...	...
	38	Chamar	1	1	...	...	...	...	...	...	...	...	...	...	...	...	...	...	...	...	...	...	...	...	...	...	10	6	4	16	14	2
		Dhore	...	...	...	...	...	...	...	...	...	...	...	...	...	...	...	...	...	...	...	...	...	...	...	...	...	...	...	2	1	1
		Dakkala	...	...	...	...	...	...	...	...	...	...	...	...	...	...	...	51	29	22	...	...	...	...	...	...	...	...	...	...	...	...
		Total	1	1	...	...	...	...	...	...	...	...	...	...	...	...	...	51	29	22	...	...	...	...	...	...	10	6	4	18	15	3
	38a	Bedar	3	...	3	...	...	...	6	3	3	...	...	...	...	...	...	...	...	...	...	...	...	...	...	...	...	...	...	...	...	...
		Naik	...	...	...	...	...	...	...	...	...	...	...	...	...	...	...	3	...	3	...	...	...	...	...	...	...	...	...	...	...	...
		Total	3	...	3	...	...	...	6	3	3	...	...	...	...	...	...	3	...	3	...	...	...	...	...	...	...	...	...	...	...	...
E. Vagrant Minor Artisans & Performers.	40	Waddewar	2	...	2	...	...	...	4	4	...	8	6	2	7	4	3	1	...	1	...	...	...	1	1	...	1	...	1	...	...	...
		Total	2	...	2	...	...	...	4	4	...	8	6	2	7	4	3	1	...	1	...	...	...	1	1	...	1	...	1	...	...	...
	41	Beldar	...	...	...	...	...	...	...	...	...	...	...	...	...	...	...	...	...	...	...	...	...	...	...	...	2	1	1	...	...	...
		Total	...	...	...	...	...	...	...	...	...	...	...	...	...	...	...	...	...	...	...	...	...	...	...	...	2	1	1	...	...	...

TABLE XIV A.

Blind by Caste, Tribe or Race.—*Continued.*

Class.	Group.	Castes.	Nander. Total.	Nander. Males.	Nander. Females.	Naldrug. Total.	Naldrug. Males.	Naldrug. Females.	Bidar. Total.	Bidar. Males.	Bidar. Females.	Parbhani. Total.	Parbhani. Males.	Parbhani. Females.	Sirpur Tandur. Total.	Sirpur Tandur. Males.	Sirpur Tandur. Females.	Gulbarga. Total.	Gulbarga. Males.	Gulbarga. Females.	Raichur. Total.	Raichur. Males.	Raichur. Females.	Lingasugur. Total.	Lingasugur. Males.	Lingasugur. Females.	Railways. Total.	Railways. Males.	Railways. Females.	Total. Total.	Total. Males.	Total. Females.
			34	35	36	37	38	39	40	41	42	43	44	45	46	47	48	49	50	51	52	53	54	55	56	57	58	59	60	61	62	63
D. Artisan and Village Menial.	35	Besta	...	...	...	...	...	...	...	...	...	...	...	...	...	...	...	...	...	...	1	...	1	...	...	...	...	...	...	35	18	17
		Bhoi	6	2	4	1	...	1	1	...	1	1	1	...	11	5	6	1	1	...	...	...	...	...	...	...	...	...	...	34	17	17
		Total......	6	2	4	1	...	1	1	...	1	1	1	...	11	5	6	1	1	...	1	...	1	...	...	...	...	...	...	69	35	34
	36	Goundla	...	...	...	...	...	...	6	8	8	...	...	...	...	...	...	...	...	...	2	1	1	1	...	1	...	...	...	206	124	82
		Kalal	1	1	...	...	...	...	...	...	...	...	...	...	...	...	...	...	...	...	...	...	...	...	...	...	...	...	...	2	2	...
		Total......	1	1	—	...	...	...	6	8	3	...	...	...	...	...	...	...	...	...	2	1	1	1	...	1	...	...	...	208	126	82
	37	Kasai	...	...	...	...	...	...	...	...	...	...	...	...	...	...	...	...	...	...	...	...	...	...	...	...	...	...	...	4	4	...
		Total......	...	...	...	...	...	...	...	...	...	...	...	...	...	...	...	...	...	...	...	...	...	...	...	...	...	...	...	4	4	...
	38	Chamar	8	2	6	4	...	4	6	8	8	8	6	2	...	...	...	...	...	...	...	...	...	...	...	...	...	...	...	53	32	21
		Dhore	...	—	...	1	...	1	2	2	...	...	...	...	...	...	...	1	...	1	...	...	...	...	...	...	...	...	...	6	3	3
		Dakkala	...	—	...	...	...	...	...	...	...	...	...	...	...	...	...	...	...	...	...	...	...	...	...	...	...	...	...	51	29	22
		Total......	8	2	6	5	...	5	8	5	3	8	6	2	...	...	...	1	...	1	...	...	...	...	...	...	...	...	...	110	64	46
	38a	Bedar	...	...	...	2	1	1	...	...	...	2	1	1	1	1	...	2	1	1	20	9	11	21	10	11	...	...	...	57	26	31
		Naik	...	...	...	...	...	...	...	...	...	...	...	...	...	...	...	1	...	1	...	...	...	...	...	...	...	...	...	4	...	4
		Total......	...	...	...	2	1	1	...	...	...	2	1	1	1	1	...	3	1	2	20	9	11	21	10	11	...	...	...	61	26	35
E. Vagrant Minor, Artisans & Performers.	40	Waddowar...	3	1	2	...	...	...	4	3	1	5	2	3	...	...	...	6	4	2	...	...	...	4	1	3	...	...	...	46	26	20
		Total......	3	1	2	...	...	...	4	3	1	5	2	3	...	...	...	6	4	2	...	...	...	4	1	3	...	...	...	46	26	20
	41	Bedar	...	...	...	...	...	...	...	...	...	...	...	...	4	4	...	...	...	...	...	...	...	...	...	...	...	...	...	6	5	1
		Total......	...	...	...	...	...	...	...	...	...	...	...	...	4	4	...	...	...	...	...	...	...	...	...	...	...	...	...	6	5	1

TABLE XIV A.

Blind by Caste, Tribe or Race.—*Continued.*

Class.	Group.	Castes.	City and suburbs including Secunderabad. Total.	Males.	Females.	Atraf-i-Balda. Total.	Males.	Females.	Mahabubnagar. (Nagar Karnul.) Total.	Males.	Females.	Nalgonda. Total.	Males.	Females.	Warangal. (Khamam.) Total.	Males.	Females.	Elgandal. Total.	Males.	Females.	Indur. Total.	Males.	Females.	Medak. Total.	Males.	Females.	Aurangabad. Total.	Males.	Females.	Birh. Total.	Males.	Females.
1	2	3	4	5	6	7	8	9	10	11	12	13	14	15	16	17	18	19	20	21	22	23	24	25	26	27	28	29	30	31	32	33
R. Vagrant Minor Artisans & Performers.	43 ...	Burud	...	...	...	...	...	...	3	1	2	...	...	...	3	1	2	2	1	1	...	...	...	2	1	1	...	...	...	...	...	...
		Kaikadi	...	...	...	...	...	...	...	...	...	...	...	...	...	...	...	...	...	...	...	...	...	...	...	...	...	...	...	2	1	1
		Total......	...	...	...	...	...	...	3	1	2	...	...	...	3	1	2	2	1	1	...	...	...	2	1	1	...	...	...	2	1	1
	44 ...	Erkulwad	1	...	1	1	...	1	...	...	...	1	...	1	4	2	2	1	1	...	...	...	...	6	3	3	...	...	...	...	...	...
		Total......	1	...	1	1	...	1	...	...	...	1	...	1	4	2	2	1	1	...	...	...	...	6	3	3	...	...	...	...	...	...
	46 ...	Domari	...	...	...	...	...	...	...	...	...	...	...	...	...	...	...	1	...	1	...	...	...	...	...	...	...	...	...	...	...	...
		Total......	...	...	...	...	...	...	...	...	...	...	...	...	...	...	...	1	...	1	...	...	...	...	...	...	...	...	...	...	...	...
E. Races and Nationalities.	48 ...	Mugbal	...	...	...	...	...	...	...	...	...	...	...	...	...	...	...	...	...	...	...	...	...	...	...	...	1	1	...	1	1	...
		Other Mussulmans ...	4	3	1	3	1	2	15	6	9	19	10	9	48	24	24	20	14	6	11	...	11	22	9	13	70	47	23	32	22	10
		Pathan	7	6	1	...	...	...	2	1	1	1	1	...	...	...	...	...	...	...	...	...	...	...	...	...	12	8	4	1	...	1
		Sheikh	53	26	27	33	20	13	32	11	21	6	4	2	...	...	...	...	...	...	16	16	...	13	10	3	30	11	19	11	7	4
		Syed	16	11	5	...	...	...	3	2	1	1	1	...	...	...	...	...	...	...	...	...	...	2	1	1	2	2	...	...	...	...
		Total......	80	46	34	36	21	15	52	20	32	27	16	11	48	24	24	20	14	6	27	16	11	37	20	17	115	69	46	45	30	15
	49b ...	Dasri	...	...	...	1	...	1	3	...	3	...	...	...	...	...	...	1	1	...	...	...	...	2	2	...	...	...	...	...	...	...
		Jain	...	...	...	...	...	...	...	...	...	...	...	...	...	...	...	...	...	...	2	2	...	...	...	...	3	2	1	3	3	...
		Other Hindus	14	8	6	3	2	1	16	13	3	20	14	6	1	1	...	1	1	...	2	1	1	4	2	2	61	40	21	7	2	5
		Perika	...	...	...	...	...	...	3	2	1	12	11	1	5	2	3	5	4	1	...	...	...	...	...	...	...	...	...	...	...	...
		Sikh	1	1	...	...	...	...	...	...	...	...	...	...	...	...	...	2	2	...	...	...	...	...	...	...	...	...	...	...	...	...
		Telinga	5	5	...	18	10	8	66	32	34	27	11	16	47	23	24	34	23	11	2	2	...	17	6	11	2	1	1	...	...	...
		Total......	20	14	6	22	12	10	88	47	41	59	36	23	53	26	27	43	31	12	6	5	1	23	10	13	66	43	23	10	5	5
	52 ...	Christians (Native) ...	3	2	1	...	...	...	...	...	...	...	...	...	...	...	...	...	...	...	...	...	...	1	1	...	5	5	...	...	...	...
		Total......	3	2	1	...	...	...	...	...	...	...	...	...	...	...	...	...	...	...	...	...	...	1	1	...	5	5	...	...	...	...
		Grand Total ...	263	149	114	430	229	201	703	373	330	580	292	288	601	338	263	601	356	245	284	162	122	530	306	224	1,121	637	484	845	459	386

TABLE XIV A.

Blind by Caste, Tribe or Race.—*Continued.*

Class.	Group.	Caste.	Nander.			Naldrug.			Bidar.			Parbhani.			Sirpur Tandur.			Gulbarga.			Raichur.			Lingasugur.			Railways.			Total.		
			Total.	Males.	Females.	Total.	Males.	Females.	Total.	Males.	Females.	Total.	Males.	Females.	Total.	Males.	Females.	Total.	Males.	Females.	Total.	Males.	Females.	Total.	Males.	Females.	Total.	Males.	Females.	Total.	Males.	Females.
			34	35	36	37	38	39	40	41	42	43	44	45	46	47	48	49	50	51	52	53	54	55	56	57	58	59	60	61	62	63
E. Vagrant Minor Artisans & Performers.	43 ...	Burud	...	...	...	...	...	...	1	...	1	...	...	...	...	...	...	2	...	2	...	...	...	1	...	1	...	...	...	14	4	10
		Kaikadi	1	...	1	...	...	...	1	...	1	1	1	...	...	...	...	2	1	1	...	...	...	3	2	1	...	...	...	10	5	5
		Total......	1	...	1	...	...	...	2	...	2	1	1	...	...	...	...	4	1	3	...	...	...	4	2	2	...	...	...	24	9	15
	44 ...	Erkulwad	...	...	...	...	...	...	...	...	...	...	...	...	...	...	...	...	...	...	...	...	...	...	...	...	...	...	...	14	6	8
		Total......	...	...	...	...	...	...	...	...	...	...	...	...	...	...	...	...	...	...	...	...	...	...	...	...	...	...	...	14	6	8
	46 ...	Domari	...	...	...	...	...	...	...	...	...	...	...	...	2	...	2	7	...	7	...	...	...	...	...	...	...	...	...	10	...	10
		Total......	...	...	...	...	...	...	...	...	...	...	...	...	2	...	2	7	...	7	...	...	...	...	...	...	...	...	...	10	...	10
F. Races and Nationalities.	48 ...	Mughal	...	...	...	2	2	...	8	...	8	1	1	...	...	...	...	...	...	...	...	...	...	...	...	...	...	...	...	18	5	8
		Other Mussulmans ...	1	...	1	...	...	...	46	14	32	...	...	...	...	...	...	21	21	...	12	5	7	6	...	6	...	...	...	330	176	154
		Pathan	...	...	...	6	3	3	...	...	...	4	3	1	...	...	...	4	3	1	...	...	...	...	...	...	...	...	...	37	25	12
		Sheikh	39	20	19	21	11	10	79	60	19	47	27	20	8	5	3	12	6	6	4	2	2	14	14	...	1	1	...	419	251	168
		Syed	...	...	...	3	1	2	...	...	...	11	6	5	...	...	...	...	...	...	...	...	...	...	...	...	...	...	...	38	24	14
		Total......	40	20	20	32	17	15	133	74	59	63	37	26	8	5	3	37	30	7	16	7	9	20	14	6	1	1	...	837	481	356
	49b ...	Dasri	1	...	1	...	...	...	...	...	...	...	...	...	...	...	...	...	...	...	...	...	...	...	...	...	...	...	...	8	3	5
		Jain	7	6	1	3	3	...	3	...	3	10	5	5	...	...	...	...	...	...	...	...	...	...	...	...	...	...	...	31	21	10
		Other Hindus	16	12	4	23	13	10	12	12	...	16	8	8	6	1	5	11	2	9	3	2	1	9	2	7	1	1	...	226	137	89
		Perika	1	...	1	...	...	...	...	...	...	...	...	...	...	...	...	...	...	...	...	...	...	...	...	...	...	...	...	26	19	7
		Sikh	1	1	...	...	...	...	...	...	...	1	...	1	...	...	...	...	...	...	...	...	...	...	...	...	...	...	...	5	4	1
		Telinga	2	2	...	1	...	1	...	...	...	4	1	3	1	...	1	8	6	2	...	...	...	...	...	...	...	...	...	234	122	112
		Total......	28	21	7	27	16	11	15	12	3	31	14	17	7	1	6	19	8	11	3	2	1	9	2	7	1	1	...	530	306	224
	52 ...	Christians (Native) ...	...	...	...	...	...	...	...	...	...	...	...	...	...	...	...	...	...	...	...	...	...	...	...	...	...	...	...	9	8	1
		Total......	...	...	...	...	...	...	...	...	...	...	...	...	...	...	...	...	...	...	...	...	...	...	...	...	...	...	...	9	8	1
		Grand Total......	715	371	344	670	389	281	1,244	679	565	1,009	551	458	140	75	65	445	256	189	222	117	105	277	151	126	2	2	...	10,632	5,892	4,740

TABLE XV.

LEPERS BY AGE.

TABLE XV.

Lepers by Age.

District or State.	Total Lepers. Total.	Total Lepers. Males.	Total Lepers. Females.	0—4 Males.	0—4 Females.	5—9 Males.	5—9 Females.	10—14 Males.	10—14 Females.	15—19 Males.	15—19 Females.	20—24 Males.	20—24 Females.	25—29 Males.	25—29 Females.	30—34 Males.	30—34 Females.	35—39 Males.	35—39 Females.	40—44 Males.	40—44 Females.	45—49 Males.	45—49 Females.	50—54 Males.	50—54 Females.	55—59 Males.	55—59 Females.	60 and over. Males.	60 and over. Females.	Unspecified. Males.	Unspecified. Females.
1	2	3	4	5	6	7	8	9	10	11	12	13	14	15	16	17	18	19	20	21	22	23	24	25	26	27	28	29	30	31	32
Telingana. Hyderabad. City	29	20	9	1	...	...	...	...	2	...	...	3	...	3	...	3	...	2	1	3	1	3	...	1	2	...	...	1	3	...	...
Suburbs including Secunderabad	76	52	24	...	...	...	...	1	...	1	1	...	2	5	...	8	1	4	2	12	7	4	1	5	3	2	2	9	5	1	...
Total......	105	72	33	1	...	...	...	1	2	1	1	3	2	8	...	11	1	6	3	15	8	7	1	6	5	2	2	10	8	1	...
Atraf-i-Balda District	105	89	16	...	...	...	...	2	2	1	...	6	...	6	...	12	2	6	...	12	4	7	2	19	3	4	1	14	2	...	...
Mahabubnagar (Nagar Karnul) ...	106	74	32	1	...	...	1	...	2	3	3	5	1	9	4	6	7	3	1	14	1	14	3	7	3	2	1	8	5	2	...
Nalgonda	91	73	18	...	...	...	...	1	...	3	1	3	...	5	2	9	2	5	2	9	4	7	...	12	4	1	2	18	1	...	...
Warangal (Khamam)	157	105	52	...	1	1	2	1	3	4	9	10	4	6	...	17	6	4	7	22	7	9	4	17	2	...	3	14	4	...	...
Elgandal	200	150	50	3	2	1	2	6	6	13	5	12	7	13	6	19	7	10	2	16	6	9	...	14	1	4	2	30	3	...	1
Indur	171	123	48	...	...	2	1	4	3	6	4	20	4	13	5	14	5	12	6	17	5	7	4	14	7	2	2	12	2	...	...
Medak	223	183	40	...	...	2	2	2	...	8	1	10	4	8	3	24	6	14	2	44	8	17	2	21	7	7	1	26	4	...	...
Mahratwara. Aurangabad	306	227	79	1	...	1	5	5	6	6	10	17	9	19	9	27	6	23	9	45	9	27	2	28	2	5	4	22	8	1	...
Birh	236	183	53	2	...	3	2	6	2	13	5	9	3	11	10	21	3	17	5	31	8	15	6	25	4	9	...	21	5	...	...
Nander	92	70	22	1	...	...	...	1	...	1	1	3	1	5	2	13	1	6	...	10	7	11	1	8	4	3	1	8	4	...	...
Naldrug	330	265	65	...	...	1	1	5	7	14	9	20	1	33	8	29	9	35	6	40	8	24	5	34	5	14	1	16	4	...	1
Bidar	213	163	50	...	...	1	2	1	1	8	2	12	1	13	7	19	3	6	4	31	9	18	6	24	8	9	1	20	6	1	...
Parbhani	112	88	29	1	1	...	1	...	3	5	1	3	4	7	3	9	3	12	...	8	4	12	...	18	4	3	...	10	5	...	...
Sirpur Tandur	57	44	13	...	1	...	...	...	2	2	2	1	1	6	1	4	3	3	...	11	...	6	2	6	1	1	...	4	...	...	...
Karnatic or Kanada. Gulbarga	161	119	42	...	...	...	3	5	...	6	3	7	4	7	4	14	3	15	2	26	7	17	1	11	4	4	2	7	9	...	...
Raichur	119	91	28	...	...	1	...	2	2	2	2	5	2	13	3	17	7	11	1	12	1	7	5	13	1	...	...	8	4	...	...
Lingasugur	198	147	46	...	1	...	1	4	2	9	3	10	3	7	3	20	12	16	4	25	4	21	5	21	5	4	...	10	3	...	...
Total Districts......	2,872	2,189	683	9	6	13	23	45	41	104	61	153	49	181	70	274	85	198	51	373	92	228	48	287	65	72	21	248	69	4	2
Total Districts including Hyderabad ...	2,977	2,261	716	10	6	13	23	46	43	105	62	156	51	189	70	285	86	204	54	388	100	285	49	298	70	74	23	258	77	5	2
Railways......	...	...	...	...	...	...	...	...	...	...	...	...	...	...	...	...	...	...	...	...	...	...	...	...	...	...	...	...	...	...	...
Grand Total......	2,977	2,261	716	10	6	13	23	46	43	105	62	156	51	189	70	285	86	204	54	388	100	285	49	298	70	74	23	258	77	5	2

TABLE XV A.

LEPERS BY CASTE, TRIBE OR RACE.

TABLE XV A.

Lepers by Castes, Tribe or Race.

Class.	Group.	Castes.	City and suburbs including Secunderabad.			Atraf-i-Balda.			Mahabubnagar (Nagar Karnul.)			Nalgonda.			Warangal. (Khamam).			Elgandal.			Indur.			Medak.			Aurangabad.			Birh.		
			Total.	Males.	Females.	Total.	Males.	Females.	Total.	Males.	Females.	Total.	Males.	Females.	Total.	Males.	Females.	Total.	Males.	Females.	Total.	Males.	Females.	Total.	Males.	Females.	Total.	Males.	Females.	Total.	Males.	Females.
1	2	3	4	5	6	7	8	9	10	11	12	13	14	15	16	17	18	19	20	21	22	23	24	25	26	27	28	29	30	31	32	33
A. Agricultural.	1 ...	Elma	...	...	...	...	...	...	...	...	...	...	...	...	2	1	1	1	1	...	...	...	...	...	...	...	...	...	...	...	...	...
	...	Mahratta	2	1	1	1	1	...	...	...	...	...	...	...	...	...	...	4	3	1	11	8	3	2	1	1	29	25	4	57	44	13
	...	Rajput	...	...	...	...	...	...	3	1	2	...	...	...	1	1	...	...	...	...	2	1	1	...	...	...	3	1	2	3	2	1
		Total......	2	1	1	1	1	...	3	1	2	...	...	...	3	2	1	5	4	1	13	9	4	2	1	1	32	26	6	60	46	14
	2a ...	Andh	...	...	...	...	...	...	...	...	...	...	...	...	...	...	...	...	...	...	...	...	...	...	...	...	...	...	...	...	...	...
		Kunbi	3	2	1	3	3	...	7	5	2	9	7	2	6	6	...	23	16	7	15	12	3	16	12	4	106	78	28	48	38	10
		Mali	...	...	...	...	...	...	...	...	...	...	...	...	...	...	...	...	...	...	...	...	...	...	...	...	7	6	1	9	7	2
		Munurwad	1	1	...	3	2	1	...	...	...	...	...	...	2	...	2	9	8	1	8	...	8	3	1	2	...	...	...	...	...	...
		Mutrasi	...	...	...	12	10	2	6	6	...	6	6	...	14	6	8	7	6	1	...	...	...	33	28	5	...	...	...	...	...	...
		Pichakuntla	...	...	...	...	...	...	1	1	...	...	...	...	1	1	...	...	...	...	...	...	...	...	...	...	...	...	...	...	...	...
		Total......	4	3	1	18	15	3	14	12	2	15	13	2	23	13	10	39	30	9	23	12	11	52	41	11	113	84	29	57	45	12
	2b ...	Koli	...	...	...	1	1	...	...	...	...	...	...	...	...	...	...	...	...	...	8	6	2	...	...	...	4	2	2	3	2	1
		Gaoli	...	...	...	...	...	...	...	...	...	1	1	...	...	...	...	...	...	...	...	...	...	...	...	...	...	...	...	...	...	...
		Total......	...	...	...	1	1	...	...	...	...	1	1	...	...	...	...	...	...	...	8	6	2	...	...	...	4	2	2	3	2	1
	2c ...	Dher	23	15	8	14	12	2	13	10	3	17	12	5	11	6	5	48	26	17	42	33	9	47	40	7	34	30	4	26	22	4
		Mang	3	3	...	...	...	...	...	...	...	...	...	...	...	...	...	...	...	...	28	21	7	...	...	...	10	7	3	9	8	1
		Total......	26	18	8	14	12	2	13	10	3	17	12	5	11	6	5	48	26	17	70	54	16	47	40	7	44	37	7	35	30	5
	4 ...	Chenchwad	...	...	...	...	...	...	1	1	...	...	...	...	...	...	...	...	...	...	...	...	...	...	...	...	...	...	...	...	...	...
		Gond	...	...	...	...	...	...	...	...	...	...	...	...	...	...	...	...	...	...	3	3	...	...	...	...	...	...	...	...	...	...
		Gond H	...	...	...	...	...	...	...	...	...	...	...	...	...	...	...	...	...	...	...	...	...	...	...	...	6	4	2	...	...	...
		Koya	...	...	...	...	...	...	...	...	...	...	...	...	10	4	6	6	5	1	...	...	...	...	...	...	...	...	...	...	...	...
		Total......	...	...	...	...	...	...	1	1	...	...	...	...	10	4	6	6	5	1	3	3	...	...	...	...	6	4	2	...	...	...
B. Professional.	5 ...	Brahmin	3	2	1	...	...	...	...	...	...	1	1	...	3	1	2	6	6	...	1	1	...	3	1	2	6	4	2	1	1	...
		Jangam	...	...	...	1	1	...	2	1	1	...	...	...	1	1	...	1	1	...	...	...	...	5	4	1	...	...	...	3	3	...
		Total......	3	2	1	1	1	...	2	1	1	1	1	...	4	2	2	7	7	...	1	1	...	8	5	3	6	4	2	4	4	...

TABLE XV A.

Lepers by Castes, Tribe or Race.—*Continued.*

Class.	Group.	Castes.	Nander. Total.	Nander. Males.	Nander. Females.	Naldrug. Total.	Naldrug. Males.	Naldrug. Females.	Bidar. Total.	Bidar. Males.	Bidar. Females.	Parbhani. Total.	Parbhani. Males.	Parbhani. Females.	Sirpur Tandur. Total.	Sirpur Tandur. Males.	Sirpur Tandur. Females.	Gulbarga. Total.	Gulbarga. Males.	Gulbarga. Females.	Raichur. Total.	Raichur. Males.	Raichur. Females.	Lingasugur. Total.	Lingasugur. Males.	Lingasugur. Females.	Railways. Total.	Railways. Males.	Railways. Females.	Total. Total.	Total. Males.	Total. Females.
			34	35	36	37	38	39	40	41	42	43	44	45	46	47	48	49	50	51	52	53	54	55	56	57	58	59	60	61	62	63
A. Agricultural.	1	Elma	...	...	...	...	...	...	5	3	2	1	...	1	...	...	...	2	1	1	...	...	...	...	...	...	...	...	...	11	6	5
		Mahratta	16	12	4	114	94	20	27	23	4	45	37	8	5	3	2	4	3	1	1	1	...	1	1	...	...	...	...	319	257	62
		Rajput	1	...	1	1	1	...	...	...	...	4	2	2	...	...	...	...	...	...	1	1	...	3	1	2	...	...	...	22	11	11
		Total......	17	12	5	115	95	20	32	26	6	50	39	11	5	3	2	6	4	2	2	2	...	4	2	2	...	...	...	352	274	78
	2a	Andh	1	1	...	...	...	...	...	...	...	...	...	...	...	...	...	...	...	...	...	...	...	...	...	...	...	...	...	1	1	...
		Kunbi	2	2	...	34	29	5	9	6	3	11	4	7	9	9	...	7	4	3	5	4	1	10	7	3	...	...	...	323	244	79
		Mali	3	2	1	8	5	3	7	5	2	5	4	1	...	...	...	1	1	...	...	...	...	...	...	...	...	...	...	40	30	10
		Munurwad	2	...	2	...	...	...	1	1	...	...	...	...	3	...	3	...	...	...	1	1	...	...	...	...	...	...	...	33	14	19
		Mutrasi	...	...	...	...	...	...	2	2	...	...	...	...	...	...	...	...	...	...	...	...	...	...	...	...	...	...	...	80	64	16
		Pichakuntla	...	...	...	...	...	...	...	...	...	...	...	...	...	...	...	...	...	...	...	...	...	...	...	...	...	...	...	2	2	...
		Total......	8	5	3	42	34	8	19	14	5	16	8	8	12	9	3	8	5	3	6	5	1	10	7	3	...	...	...	479	355	124
	2b	Kali...	2	2	...	5	4	1	8	3	5	...	...	...	...	...	...	24	16	8	7	5	2	23	15	8	...	...	...	85	56	29
		Gaoli	...	...	...	...	...	...	...	...	...	...	...	...	...	...	...	...	...	...	...	...	...	...	...	...	...	...	...	1	1	...
		Total......	2	2	..	5	4	1	8	3	5	...	...	...	...	...	...	24	16	8	7	5	2	23	15	8	...	...	...	86	57	29
	2c	Dher	9	8	1	49	37	12	22	18	4	16	13	3	6	6	...	3	2	1	8	7	1	12	9	3	...	...	...	395	306	89
		Mang	11	10	1	27	20	7	22	15	7	3	1	2	3	1	2	7	5	2	...	...	...	...	...	...	...	...	...	123	91	32
		Total......	20	18	2	76	57	19	44	33	11	19	14	5	9	7	2	10	7	3	8	7	1	12	9	3	...	...	...	518	397	121
	4	Chenchwad	...	...	...	...	...	...	...	...	...	...	...	...	...	...	...	...	...	...	...	...	...	...	...	...	...	...	...	1	1	...
		Gond	...	...	...	...	...	...	...	...	...	...	...	...	20	17	3	...	...	...	...	...	...	...	...	...	...	...	...	23	20	3
		Gond II	...	...	...	...	...	...	...	...	...	...	...	...	...	...	...	...	...	...	...	...	...	...	...	...	...	...	...	6	4	2
		Koya	...	...	...	...	...	...	...	...	...	...	...	...	...	...	...	...	...	...	...	...	...	...	...	...	...	...	...	16	9	7
		Total......	...	...	...	...	...	...	...	...	...	...	...	...	20	17	3	...	...	...	...	...	...	...	...	...	...	...	...	46	34	12
B. Professional.	5	Brahmin	4	2	2	2	2	...	3	...	3	2	2	...	...	...	...	2	2	...	1	...	1	1	1	...	...	...	...	39	26	13
		Jangam	...	...	...	1	...	1	7	7	...	...	...	...	...	...	...	6	5	1	...	...	...	...	...	...	...	...	...	27	23	4
		Total......	4	2	2	3	2	1	10	7	3	2	2	...	...	...	...	8	7	1	1	...	1	1	1	...	...	...	...	66	49	17

TABLE XV A.

Lepers by Castes, Tribe or Race.—*Continued.*

Class.	Group.	Castes.	City and suburbs including Secunderabad, Total.	Males.	Females.	Atraf-i-Balda, Total.	Males.	Females.	Mahabubnagar (Nagar Karnul), Total.	Males.	Females.	Nalgonda, Total.	Males.	Females.	Warangal (Khamam), Total.	Males.	Females.	Elgandal, Total.	Males.	Females.	Indur, Total.	Males.	Females.	Medak, Total.	Males.	Females.	Aurangabad, Total.	Males.	Females.	Birh, Total.	Males.	Females.
1	2	3	4	5	6	7	8	9	10	11	12	13	14	15	16	17	18	19	20	21	22	23	24	25	26	27	28	29	30	31	32	33
B. Professional.	6	Bairagi	...	...	...	...	...	...	...	...	...	...	...	...	...	...	...	...	...	...	...	...	...	...	...	...	2	2	...	1	1	...
		Gosain	...	...	...	...	...	...	...	...	...	...	...	...	...	...	...	...	...	...	...	...	...	...	...	...	1	...	1	...	...	...
		Jogi	...	...	...	...	...	...	...	...	...	...	...	...	...	...	...	...	...	...	...	...	...	...	...	...	1	...	1	...	...	...
		Manbhao	...	...	...	...	...	...	...	...	...	...	...	...	...	...	...	...	...	...	...	...	...	...	...	...	...	...	...	1	1	...
		Total	...	...	...	...	...	...	...	...	...	...	...	...	...	...	...	...	...	...	...	...	...	...	...	...	4	2	2	2	2	...
	7	Gurao	...	...	...	...	...	...	...	...	...	...	...	...	...	...	...	...	...	...	...	...	...	...	...	...	...	...	...	...	...	...
		Total	...	...	...	...	...	...	...	...	...	...	...	...	...	...	...	...	...	...	...	...	...	...	...	...	...	...	...	...	...	...
	9	Kayesth	...	...	...	...	...	...	...	...	...	...	...	...	...	...	...	...	...	...	...	...	...	...	...	...	...	...	...	...	...	...
		Total	...	...	...	...	...	...	...	...	...	...	...	...	...	...	...	...	...	...	...	...	...	...	...	...	...	...	...	...	...	...
	11	Gondhali	...	...	...	...	...	...	...	...	...	...	...	...	...	...	...	...	...	...	...	...	...	...	...	...	...	...	...	1	...	1
		Total	...	...	...	...	...	...	...	...	...	...	...	...	...	...	...	...	...	...	...	...	...	...	...	...	...	...	...	1	...	1
	12	Kanchani	...	...	...	...	...	...	1	...	1	2	1	1	...	...	...	...	...	...	1	1	...	...	...	...	...	...	...	...	...	...
		Total	...	...	...	...	...	...	1	...	1	2	1	1	...	...	...	...	...	...	1	1	...	...	...	...	...	...	...	...	...	...
C. Commercial.	14	Balija	...	...	...	1	...	1	2	2	...	1	1	...	2	1	1	...	...	...	...	...	...	9	9	...	1	...	1	...	...	...
		Komti	1	1	...	6	5	1	10	8	2	8	5	3	3	3	...	...	...	...	2	1	1	8	5	3	...	...	...	...	...	...
		Wani	1	1	...	...	...	...	2	2	...	...	...	...	...	...	...	5	4	1	4	2	2	...	...	...	3	2	1	4	4	...
		Total	2	2	...	7	5	2	14	12	2	9	6	3	5	4	1	5	4	1	6	3	3	17	14	3	4	2	2	4	4	...
	16	Banjara	1	1	...	...	...	...	...	...	...	...	...	...	...	...	...	1	1	...	7	6	1	...	...	...	...	...	...	...	...	...
		Lad	...	...	...	...	...	...	...	...	...	...	...	...	...	...	...	...	...	...	...	...	...	...	...	...	...	...	...	...	...	...
		Lambani	...	...	...	...	...	...	...	...	...	2	2	...	4	4	...	...	...	...	...	...	...	...	...	...	...	...	...	...	...	...
		Total	1	1	...	...	...	...	...	...	...	2	2	...	4	4	...	1	1	...	7	6	1	...	...	...	...	...	...	...	...	...

TABLE XV A.

Lepers by Caste, Tribe or Race.—*Continued.*

Class.	Group.	Castes.	Nander. Total.	Nander. Males.	Nander. Females.	Naldrug. Total.	Naldrug. Males.	Naldrug. Females.	Bidar. Total.	Bidar. Males.	Bidar. Females.	Parbhani. Total.	Parbhani. Males.	Parbhani. Females.	Sirpur Tandur. Total.	Sirpur Tandur. Males.	Sirpur Tandur. Females.	Gulbarga. Total.	Gulbarga. Males.	Gulbarga. Females.	Raichur. Total.	Raichur. Males.	Raichur. Females.	Lingasugur. Total.	Lingasugur. Males.	Lingasugur. Females.	Railways. Total.	Railways. Males.	Railways. Females.	Total. Total.	Total. Males.	Total. Females.
			34	35	36	37	38	39	40	41	42	43	44	45	46	47	48	49	50	51	52	53	54	55	56	57	58	59	60	61	62	63
B. Professional.	6 ...	Bairagi	...	...	...	1	1	...	...	...	...	...	...	...	...	...	...	...	...	...	...	...	...	...	...	...	...	...	...	4	4	...
		Gosain	...	...	...	3	3	...	4	4	...	1	1	...	...	...	...	...	...	...	...	...	...	...	...	...	...	...	...	9	8	1
		Jogi...	...	...	...	...	...	...	...	...	...	...	...	...	...	...	...	...	...	...	...	...	...	...	...	...	...	...	...	1	...	1
		Manbhao	...	...	...	...	...	...	...	...	...	...	...	...	...	...	...	...	...	...	...	...	...	...	...	...	...	...	...	1	1	...
		Total......	...	...	...	4	4	...	4	4	...	1	1	...	...	...	...	...	...	...	...	...	...	...	...	...	...	...	...	15	13	2
	7 ...	Gurao	1	...	1	3	2	1	...	...	...	...	...	...	...	...	...	...	...	...	...	...	...	...	...	...	...	...	...	4	2	2
		Total......	1	...	1	3	2	1	...	...	...	...	...	...	...	...	...	...	...	...	...	...	...	...	...	...	...	...	...	4	2	2
	9 ...	Kayesth	...	...	...	...	...	...	...	...	...	...	...	...	...	...	...	...	...	...	1	1	...	...	...	...	...	...	...	1	1	...
		Total......	...	...	...	...	...	...	...	...	...	...	...	...	...	...	...	...	...	...	1	1	...	...	...	...	...	...	...	1	1	...
	11 ...	Gondhali	...	...	...	...	...	...	2	2	...	...	...	...	...	...	...	...	...	...	...	...	...	...	...	...	...	...	...	3	2	1
		Total......	...	...	...	...	...	...	2	2	...	...	...	...	...	...	...	...	...	...	...	...	...	...	...	...	...	...	...	3	2	1
	12 ...	Kanchani	...	...	...	1	...	1	...	...	...	...	...	...	...	...	...	...	...	...	...	...	...	...	...	...	...	...	...	5	2	3
		Total......	...	...	...	1	...	1	...	...	...	...	...	...	...	...	...	...	...	...	...	...	...	...	...	...	...	...	...	5	2	3
C. Commercial.	14 ...	Balija	...	...	...	...	...	...	2	2	...	...	...	...	...	...	...	...	...	...	18	13	5	...	...	...	...	...	...	36	28	8
		Komti	5	5	...	...	...	...	5	5	...	...	...	...	...	...	...	...	...	...	...	...	...	...	...	...	...	...	...	48	38	10
		Wani	7	6	1	13	10	3	37	29	8	2	1	1	1	1	...	45	35	10	...	...	...	28	21	7	...	...	...	152	118	34
		Total......	12	11	1	13	10	3	44	36	8	2	1	1	1	1	...	45	35	10	18	13	5	28	21	7	...	...	...	236	184	52
	16 ...	Banjara	...	...	...	...	...	...	...	...	...	...	...	...	...	...	...	...	...	...	...	...	...	...	...	...	...	...	...	9	8	1
		Lad	...	...	...	...	...	...	...	...	...	1	1	...	...	...	...	...	...	...	...	...	...	...	...	...	...	...	...	1	1	...
		Lambani	...	...	...	...	...	...	...	...	...	...	...	...	...	...	...	2	1	1	1	1	...	...	...	...	...	...	...	9	8	1
		Total......	...	...	...	...	...	...	...	...	...	1	1	...	...	...	...	2	1	1	1	1	...	...	...	...	...	...	...	19	17	2

TABLE XV A.

Lepers by Caste, Tribe or Race.—*Continued.*

Class.	Group.	Castes.	City and suburbs including Secunderabad.			Atraf-i-Balda.			Mahabubnagar (Nagar Karnul.)			Nalgonda.			Warangal. (Khamam.)			Elgandal.			Indur.			Medak.			Aurangabad.			Birh.		
			Total.	Males.	Females.	Total.	Males.	Females.	Total.	Males.	Females.	Total.	Males.	Females.	Total.	Males.	Females.	Total.	Males.	Females.	Total.	Males.	Females.	Total.	Males.	Females.	Total.	Males.	Females.	Total.	Males.	Females.
1	2	3	4	5	6	7	8	9	10	11	12	13	14	15	16	17	18	19	20	21	22	23	24	25	26	27	28	29	30	31	32	33
D. Artisan and Village Menial.	17 ...	Panchal	...	...	...	...	...	...	...	...	...	...	...	...	...	...	...	...	...	...	1	1	...	...	...	...	...	...	...	...	...	...
		Sonar	2	1	1	...	...	...	...	...	...	...	...	...	3	3	...	2	2	...	...	...	...	...	...	...	2	...	2	2	...	2
		Total......	2	1	1	...	...	...	...	...	...	...	...	...	3	3	...	2	2	...	1	1	...	...	...	...	2	...	2	2	...	2
	18 ...	Hajjam	...	...	...	3	3	...	1	1	...	3	3	...	4	4	...	4	4	...	2	2	...	4	4	...	6	5	1	2	1	1
		Total......	...	...	...	3	3	...	1	1	...	3	3	...	4	4	...	4	4	...	2	2	...	4	4	...	6	5	1	2	1	1
	19 ...	Lohar	...	...	...	...	...	...	1	1	...	3	3	...	3	1	2	2	2	...	...	...	...	...	...	...	2	2	...	3	2	1
		Total......	...	...	...	...	...	...	1	1	...	3	3	...	3	1	2	2	2	...	...	...	...	...	...	...	2	2	...	3	2	1
	20 ...	Gaondi	...	...	...	...	...	...	3	3	...	...	...	...	...	...	...	1	1	...	...	...	...	...	...	...	...	...	...	...	...	...
		Sutar or Barhai	1	1	...	...	...	...	...	...	...	...	...	...	2	2	...	3	3	...	1	1	...	1	1	...	...	...	...	6	4	2
		Total......	1	1	...	...	...	...	3	3	...	...	...	...	2	2	...	4	4	...	1	1	...	1	1	...	...	...	...	6	4	2
	21 ...	Kasar	...	...	...	...	...	...	...	...	...	...	...	...	...	...	...	...	...	...	...	...	...	...	...	...	...	...	...	2	1	1
		Total......	...	...	...	...	...	...	...	...	...	...	...	...	...	...	...	...	...	...	...	...	...	...	...	...	...	...	...	2	1	1
	22 ...	Darzi	...	...	...	...	...	...	...	...	...	1	1	...	...	...	...	...	...	...	...	...	...	...	...	...	...	...	...	2	...	2
		Zingar	...	...	...	...	...	...	...	...	...	...	...	...	...	...	...	...	...	...	...	...	...	...	...	...	...	...	...	...	...	...
		Total......	...	...	...	...	...	...	...	...	...	1	1	...	...	...	...	...	...	...	...	...	...	...	...	...	...	...	...	2	...	2
	23 ...	Khatri	4	1	3	...	...	...	...	...	...	...	...	...	...	...	...	...	...	...	...	...	...	...	...	...	...	...	...	...	...	...
		Rangari or Rangrez ...	...	...	...	...	...	...	...	...	...	...	...	...	...	...	...	...	...	...	...	...	...	...	...	...	...	...	...	3	2	1
		Sali or Julaha	...	...	...	2	1	1	1	1	...	4	4	...	7	5	2	17	13	4	...	...	...	6	6	...	2	2	...	...	...	...
		Total......	4	1	3	2	1	1	1	1	...	4	4	...	7	5	2	17	13	4	...	...	...	6	6	...	2	2	...	3	2	1
	24 ...	Dhobi	2	...	2	2	2	...	2	2	...	5	5	...	7	6	1	6	4	2	2	2	...	5	5	...	2	1	1	...	...	...
		Total......	2	...	2	2	2	...	2	2	...	5	5	...	7	6	1	6	4	2	2	2	...	5	5	...	2	1	1	...	...	...

TABLE XV A.

Lepors by Caste, Tribe or Race.—*Continued.*

Class.	Group.	Castes.	Nander.			Naldrug.			Bidar.			Parbhani.			Sirpur Tandur.			Gulbarga.			Raichur.			Lingasugur.			Railways.			Total.		
			Total.	Males.	Females.	Total.	Males.	Females.	Total.	Males.	Females.	Total.	Males.	Females.	Total.	Males.	Females.	Total.	Males.	Females.	Total.	Males.	Females.	Total.	Males.	Females.	Total.	Males.	Females.	Total.	Males.	Females.
		...	34	35	36	37	38	39	40	41	42	43	44	45	46	47	48	49	50	51	52	53	54	55	56	57	58	59	60	61	62	63
D. Artisan and Village Menial.	17	Panchal	...	...	...	1	1	...	1	...	1	...	...	...	1	1	...	2	1	1	8	8	...	13	12	1	...	...	...	22	19	3
		Sonar	3	3	...	2	2	...	1	...	1	...	...	...	...	...	...	...	...	...	...	...	...	...	...	...	...	...	...	17	11	6
		Total......	3	3	...	3	3	...	2	...	2	...	...	...	1	1	...	2	1	1	8	8	...	13	12	1	...	...	...	39	30	9
	18	Hajjam	3	2	1	2	2	...	2	2	...	...	...	...	...	...	...	2	2	...	...	...	...	...	...	...	...	...	...	38	35	3
		Total......	3	2	1	2	2	...	2	2	...	...	...	...	...	...	...	2	2	...	...	...	...	...	...	...	...	...	...	38	35	3
	19	Lohar	2	...	2	...	...	...	1	...	1	1	1	...	...	...	...	...	...	...	...	...	...	...	...	...	...	...	...	18	12	6
		Total......	2	...	2	...	...	...	1	...	1	1	1	...	...	...	...	...	...	...	...	...	...	...	...	...	...	...	...	18	12	6
	20	Gaondi	...	...	...	...	...	...	...	...	...	...	...	...	...	...	...	1	1	...	1	1	...	...	...	...	...	...	...	6	6	...
		Sutar or Barhai	1	1	...	6	6	...	1	...	1	...	...	...	...	...	...	...	...	...	...	...	...	...	...	...	...	...	...	22	19	3
		Total......	1	1	...	6	6	...	1	...	1	...	...	...	...	...	...	1	1	...	1	1	...	...	...	...	...	...	...	28	25	3
	21	Kasar	...	...	...	1	...	1	...	...	...	...	...	...	2	...	2	...	...	...	...	...	...	...	...	...	...	...	...	5	1	4
		Total......	...	...	...	1	...	1	...	...	...	...	...	...	2	...	2	...	...	...	...	...	...	...	...	...	...	...	...	5	1	4
	22	Darzi	...	...	...	2	2	...	...	...	...	...	...	...	...	...	...	3	2	1	...	...	...	...	...	...	...	...	...	8	5	3
		Zingar	...	...	...	1	1	...	...	...	...	...	...	...	...	...	...	...	...	...	1	1	...	...	...	...	...	...	...	2	2	...
		Total......	...	...	...	3	3	...	...	...	...	...	...	...	...	...	...	3	2	1	1	1	...	...	...	...	...	...	...	10	7	3
	23	Julaha	...	...	...	...	...	...	...	...	...	1	1	...	...	...	...	...	...	...	...	...	...	3	2	1	...	...	...	43	35	8
		Khatri	1	1	...	2	2	...	...	...	...	2	1	1	...	...	...	...	...	...	...	...	...	1	1	...	...	...	...	7	3	4
		Rangari or Rangrez ...	...	...	...	...	...	...	...	...	...	...	...	...	...	...	...	1	...	1	...	...	...	...	...	...	...	...	...	7	5	2
		Total......	1	1	...	2	2	...	...	...	...	3	2	1	...	...	...	1	...	1	...	...	...	4	3	1	...	...	...	57	43	14
	24	Dhobi	...	...	...	1	1	...	1	1	...	...	...	...	1	1	...	2	2	...	1	1	...	7	6	1	...	...	...	46	39	7
		Total......	...	...	...	1	1	...	1	1	...	...	...	...	1	1	...	2	2	...	1	1	...	7	6	1	...	...	...	46	39	7

TABLE XV A.

Lepers by Caste, Tribe or Race.—*Continued.*

Class.	Group.	Castes.	City and suburbs including Secunderabad. Total.	Males.	Females.	Atraf-i-Balda. Total.	Males.	Females.	Mahabubnagar. (Nagar Karnul.) Total.	Males.	Females.	Nalgonda. Total.	Males.	Females.	Warangal. (Khamam.) Total.	Males.	Females.	Elgandal. Total.	Males.	Females.	Indur. Total.	Males.	Females.	Medak. Total.	Males.	Females.	Aurangabad. Total.	Males.	Females.	Birh. Total.	Males.	Females.
1	2	3	4	5	6	7	8	9	10	11	12	13	14	15	16	17	18	19	20	21	22	23	24	25	26	27	28	29	30	31	32	33
D. Artisan and Village Menial.	26	Dhangar	1	1	...	10	8	2	10	8	2	9	6	3	5	3	2	7	4	3	5	5	...	16	13	3	8	6	2	15	13	2
		Total	1	1	...	10	8	2	10	8	2	9	6	3	5	3	2	7	4	3	5	5	...	16	13	3	8	6	2	15	13	2
	27	Teli	1	...	1	...	...	...	1	1	...	...	...	...	...	...	...	2	2	...	...	...	...	...	...	...	3	3	...	2	2	...
		Total	1	...	1	...	...	...	1	1	...	...	...	...	...	...	...	2	2	...	...	...	...	...	...	...	3	3	...	2	2	...
	28	Kumbhar	...	...	...	1	1	...	...	...	...	...	...	...	...	...	...	4	3	1	...	...	...	1	1	...	7	4	3	1	...	1
		Total	...	...	...	1	1	...	...	...	...	...	...	...	...	...	...	4	3	1	...	...	...	1	1	...	7	4	3	1	...	1
	35	Besta	...	...	...	...	...	...	4	1	3	...	...	...	1	1	...	3	2	1	...	...	...	...	...	...	...	...	...	...	...	...
		Bhoi	1	1	...	...	...	...	...	...	...	...	...	...	...	...	...	...	...	...	13	7	6	...	...	...	4	2	2	1	...	1
		Total	1	1	...	...	...	...	4	1	3	...	...	...	1	1	...	3	2	1	13	7	6	...	...	...	4	2	2	1	...	1
	36	Kalal	1	...	1	...	...	...	3	3	...	...	...	...	...	...	...	...	...	...	1	...	1	9	6	3	...	...	...	...	...	...
		Geundla	...	...	...	10	10	...	...	...	...	...	...	...	12	7	5	14	9	5	...	...	...	...	...	...	...	...	...	...	...	...
		Total	1	...	1	10	10	...	3	3	...	...	...	...	12	7	5	14	9	5	1	...	1	9	6	3	...	...	...	...	...	...
	37	Kasai	...	...	...	...	...	...	1	...	1	1	1	...	...	...	...	...	...	...	...	...	...	...	...	...	...	...	...	...	...	...
		Total	...	...	...	...	...	...	1	...	1	1	1	...	...	...	...	...	...	...	...	...	...	...	...	...	...	...	...	...	...	...
	38	Chamar	4	2	2	20	18	2	...	...	...	...	...	...	...	...	...	...	...	...	...	...	...	29	23	6	3	3	...	6	6	...
		Dhore	...	...	...	...	...	...	...	...	...	...	...	...	34	22	12	...	...	...	...	...	...	...	...	...	...	...	...	...	...	...
		Mochi	...	...	...	...	...	...	11	5	6	...	...	...	...	...	...	...	...	...	...	...	...	...	...	...	...	...	...	...	...	...
		Total	4	2	2	20	18	2	11	5	6	...	...	...	34	22	12	...	...	...	...	...	...	29	23	6	3	3	...	6	6	...
	38a	Bedar	...	...	...	...	...	...	...	...	...	...	...	...	...	...	...	...	...	...	...	...	...	...	...	...	...	...	...	...	...	...
		Naik	...	...	...	...	...	...	...	...	...	...	...	...	...	...	...	...	...	...	3	1	2	...	...	...	...	...	...	...	...	...
		Total	...	...	...	...	...	...	...	...	...	...	...	...	...	...	...	...	...	...	3	1	2	...	...	...	...	...	...	...	...	...

TABLE XV A.

Lepers by Caste, Tribe or Race.—*Continued.*

Class.	Group.	Castes.		Nander. Total.	Nander. Males.	Nander. Females.	Naldrug. Total.	Naldrug. Males.	Naldrug. Females.	Bidar. Total.	Bidar. Males.	Bidar. Females.	Parbhani. Total.	Parbhani. Males.	Parbhani. Females.	Sirpur Tandur. Total.	Sirpur Tandur. Males.	Sirpur Tandur. Females.	Gulbarga. Total.	Gulbarga. Males.	Gulbarga. Females.	Raichur. Total.	Raichur. Males.	Raichur. Females.	Lingsugur. Total.	Lingsugur. Males.	Lingsugur. Females.	Railways. Total.	Railways. Males.	Railways. Females.	Total. Total.	Total. Males.	Total. Females.
				34	35	36	37	38	39	40	41	42	43	44	45	46	47	48	49	50	51	52	53	54	55	56	57	58	59	60	61	62	63
D. Artisan and Village Menial.	26	Bhangar	...	6	5	1	12	9	3	10	7	3	2	2	...	3	3	...	14	9	5	3	3	...	1	...	1	...	...	...	137	105	32
			Total	6	5	1	12	9	3	10	7	3	2	2	...	3	3	...	14	9	5	3	3	...	1	...	1	...	...	...	137	105	32
	27	Teli	...	...	...	...	3	2	1	...	...	...	5	4	1	...	...	...	1	1	...	1	1	...	...	...	...	...	...	...	19	16	3
			Total	...	...	...	3	2	1	...	...	...	5	4	1	...	...	...	1	1	...	1	1	...	...	...	...	...	...	...	19	16	3
	28	Kumbar	...	1	1	...	4	4	...	...	...	...	...	...	...	...	...	...	...	...	...	14	11	3	16	10	6	...	...	...	69	55	14
			Total	1	1	...	4	4	...	...	...	...	...	...	...	...	...	...	...	...	...	14	11	3	16	10	6	...	...	...	69	55	14
	35	[illegible]	...	...	...	...	...	...	...	...	...	...	...	...	...	...	...	...	...	...	...	...	...	...	...	...	...	...	...	...	8	4	4
		Bhoi	...	2	2	...	...	...	...	...	...	...	...	...	...	...	...	...	...	...	...	...	...	...	...	...	...	...	...	...	21	12	9
			Total	2	2	...	...	...	...	...	...	...	...	...	...	...	...	...	...	...	...	...	...	...	...	...	...	...	...	...	29	16	13
	36	Kalal	...	...	...	...	1	1	...	1	1	...	...	...	...	...	...	...	2	1	1	3	2	1	4	2	2	...	...	...	35	26	9
		Goundla	...	...	...	...	...	...	...	...	...	...	...	...	...	...	...	...	...	...	...	...	...	...	...	...	...	...	...	...	26	16	10
			Total	...	...	...	1	1	...	1	1	...	...	...	...	...	...	...	2	1	1	3	2	1	4	2	2	...	...	...	61	42	19
	37	Kasai	...	...	...	...	...	...	...	...	...	...	...	...	...	...	...	...	...	...	...	...	...	...	...	...	...	...	...	...	2	1	1
			Total	...	...	...	...	...	...	...	...	...	...	...	...	...	...	...	...	...	...	...	...	...	...	...	...	...	...	...	2	1	1
	38	Chamar	...	...	...	...	1	1	...	1	...	1	1	1	...	...	...	...	2	1	1	...	...	...	...	...	...	...	...	...	67	55	12
		Dhore	...	...	...	...	...	...	...	5	5	...	...	...	...	...	...	...	...	...	...	...	...	...	...	...	...	...	...	...	39	27	12
		Mochi	...	...	...	...	1	1	...	...	...	...	...	...	...	...	...	...	...	...	...	...	...	...	...	...	...	...	...	...	12	6	6
			Total	...	...	...	2	2	...	6	5	1	1	1	...	...	...	...	2	1	1	...	...	...	...	...	...	...	...	...	118	88	30
	38a.	Bedar	...	...	...	...	1	1	...	...	...	...	...	...	...	...	...	...	2	2	...	26	19	7	10	7	3	...	...	...	39	29	10
		Naik	...	...	...	...	...	...	...	...	...	...	...	...	...	1	1	...	...	...	...	...	...	...	...	...	...	...	...	...	4	2	2
			Total	...	...	...	1	1	...	...	...	...	...	...	...	1	1	...	2	2	...	26	19	7	10	7	3	...	...	...	43	31	12

TABLE XV A.

Lepers by Caste, Tribe or Race.—*Continued.*

Class.	Group.	Castes.	City and suburbs including Secunderabad. Total.	Males.	Females.	Atraf-i-Balda. Total.	Males.	Females.	Mahabubnagar. (Nagar Karnul.) Total.	Males.	Females.	Nalgonda. Total.	Males.	Females.	Warangal. (Khamam.) Total.	Males.	Females.	Elgandal. Total.	Males.	Females.	Indur. Total.	Males.	Females.	Medak. Total.	Males.	Females.	Aurangabad. Total.	Males.	Females.	Birh. Total.	Males.	Females.
1	2	3	4	5	6	7	8	9	10	11	12	13	14	15	16	17	18	19	20	21	22	23	24	25	26	27	28	29	30	31	32	33
E. Vagrant Minor Artisans and Performers.	40 ...	Waddewar	...	...	...	...	...	...	...	...	...	1	1	...	...	...	...	6	5	1	1	...	1	1	1	...	1	1	...	...	...	...
		Total......	...	...	...	...	...	...	...	...	...	1	1	...	...	...	...	6	5	1	1	...	1	1	1	...	1	1	...	...	...	...
	41 ...	Baldar	...	...	...	...	...	...	...	...	...	...	...	...	...	...	...	...	...	...	...	...	...	...	...	...	3	...	3	...	...	...
		Total......	...	...	...	...	...	...	...	...	...	...	...	...	...	...	...	...	...	...	...	...	...	...	...	...	3	...	3	...	...	...
	43 ...	Barud	...	...	...	...	...	...	...	...	...	...	...	...	...	...	...	2	1	1	...	...	...	1	1	...	...	...	...	...	...	...
		Kaikadi	...	...	...	...	...	...	...	...	...	...	...	...	...	...	...	...	...	...	...	...	...	...	...	...	...	...	...	...	...	...
		Total......	...	...	...	...	...	...	...	...	...	...	...	...	...	...	...	2	1	1	...	...	...	1	1	...	...	...	...	...	...	...
	44 ...	Erkulwad	...	...	...	...	...	...	...	...	...	...	...	...	2	2	...	...	...	...	...	...	...	...	...	...	...	...	...	...	...	...
		Total......	...	...	...	...	...	...	...	...	...	...	...	...	2	2	...	...	...	...	...	...	...	...	...	...	...	...	...	...	...	...
F. Races and Nationalities.	48 ...	Mughal	1	1	...	...	...	...	...	...	...	...	...	...	...	...	...	...	...	...	...	...	...	...	...	...	...	...	...	...	...	...
		Pathan	4	3	1	...	...	...	1	...	1	...	...	...	...	...	...	...	...	...	...	...	...	...	...	...	...	...	...	5	3	2
		Syed	7	6	1	2	1	1	2	1	1	...	...	...	...	...	...	...	...	...	...	...	...	1	...	1	2	1	1	...	...	...
		Sheikh	26	21	5	9	6	3	5	5	...	2	2	...	...	...	...	...	...	...	8	8	...	9	8	1	13	12	1	4	2	2
		Other Mussalmans ...	8	1	2	...	...	...	...	...	...	1	1	...	5	5	...	7	5	2	...	...	...	9	8	1	16	9	7	13	11	2
		Total......	41	32	9	11	7	4	8	6	2	3	3	...	5	5	...	7	5	2	8	8	...	19	16	3	31	22	9	22	16	6
	49b ...	Jain	...	...	...	...	...	...	...	...	...	...	...	...	...	...	...	...	...	...	...	...	...	...	...	...	3	3	...	3	3	...
		Other Hindus	7	4	3	1	1	...	...	...	...	5	5	...	...	...	...	2	1	1	1	...	1	...	...	...	16	12	4	...	...	...
		Perika	...	...	...	1	1	...	...	...	...	1	1	...	1	1	...	...	...	...	...	...	...	...	...	...	...	...	...	...	...	...
		Telinga	1	1	...	2	2	...	12	5	7	8	4	4	11	8	3	12	12	...	1	1	...	5	5	...	...	...	...	...	...	...
		Total......	8	5	3	4	4	...	12	5	7	14	10	4	12	9	3	14	13	1	2	1	1	5	5	...	19	15	4	3	3	...
	52 ...	Christians (Native) ...	1	1	...	...	...	...	...	...	...	...	...	...	...	...	...	...	...	...	...	...	...	...	...	...	...	...	...	...	...	...
		Total......	1	1	...	...	...	...	...	...	...	...	...	...	...	...	...	...	...	...	...	...	...	...	...	...	...	...	...	...	...	...
		Grand Total......	105	72	33	105	89	16	106	74	32	91	73	18	157	105	52	200	150	50	171	123	48	228	188	40	306	227	79	236	183	53

TABLE XV A.

Lepers by Caste, Tribe or Race.—*Continued.*

Class.	Group.	Castes.	Nander. Total.	Nander. Males.	Nander. Females.	Naldrug. Total.	Naldrug. Males.	Naldrug. Females.	Bidar. Total.	Bidar. Males.	Bidar. Females.	Parbhani. Total.	Parbhani. Males.	Parbhani. Females.	Sirpur. Tandur. Total.	Sirpur. Tandur. Males.	Sirpur. Tandur. Females.	Gulbarga. Total.	Gulbarga. Males.	Gulbarga. Females.	Raichur. Total	Raichur. Males.	Raichur. Females.	Lingasugur. Total.	Lingasugur. Males.	Lingasugur. Females.	Railways. Total.	Railways. Males.	Railways. Females.	Total. Total.	Total. Males.	Total. Females.
			34	35	36	37	38	39	40	41	42	43	44	45	46	47	48	49	50	51	52	53	54	55	56	57	58	59	60	61	62	63
E. Vagrant Minor Artisans and Performers.	40 ...	Waddewar	...	...	...	...	...	...	8	2	1	...	...	...	...	...	...	...	...	...	8	8	...	10	8	2	...	...	...	26	21	5
		Total......	...	...	...	...	...	...	8	2	1	...	...	...	...	...	...	...	...	...	8	8	...	10	8	2	...	...	...	26	21	5
	41 ...	Beldar	...	...	...	...	...	...	...	...	...	...	...	...	...	...	...	...	...	...	...	...	...	...	...	...	...	...	...	3	...	3
		Total......	...	...	...	...	...	...	...	...	...	...	...	...	...	...	...	...	...	...	...	...	...	...	...	...	...	...	...	3	...	3
	43 ...	Burud	...	...	...	...	...	...	...	...	...	...	...	...	...	...	...	...	...	...	...	...	...	...	...	...	...	...	...	3	2	1
		Kaikadi	...	...	...	...	...	...	...	...	...	...	...	...	...	...	...	...	...	...	1	1	...	2	...	2	...	...	...	3	1	2
		Total......	...	...	...	...	...	...	...	...	...	...	...	...	...	...	...	...	...	...	1	1	...	2	...	2	...	...	...	6	3	3
	44 ...	Erkulwad	...	...	...	...	...	...	...	...	...	...	...	...	...	...	...	...	...	...	...	...	...	...	...	...	...	...	...	2	2	...
		Total......	...	...	...	...	...	...	...	...	...	...	...	...	...	...	...	...	...	...	...	...	...	...	...	...	...	...	...	2	2	...
F. Races and Nationalities.	48 ...	Mughal	...	...	...	...	...	...	...	...	...	...	...	...	...	...	...	...	...	...	...	...	...	...	...	...	...	...	...	1	1	...
		Pathan	...	...	...	2	2	...	...	...	...	1	1	...	...	...	...	...	...	...	...	...	...	...	...	...	...	...	...	13	9	4
		Syed	...	...	...	...	...	...	...	...	...	...	...	...	...	...	...	...	...	...	...	...	...	...	...	...	...	...	...	14	9	5
		Sheikh	6	3	3	20	15	5	4	4	...	...	...	...	...	...	...	18	12	1	1	1	...	...	...	...	...	...	...	120	99	21
		Other Mussulmans ...	...	...	...	...	...	...	18	15	3	7	5	2	...	...	...	8	5	3	15	10	5	28	19	4	...	...	...	125	94	31
		Total......	6	3	3	22	17	5	22	19	3	8	6	2	...	...	...	21	17	4	16	11	5	28	19	4	...	...	...	273	212	61
	49b ...	Jain	...	...	...	...	...	...	...	...	...	...	...	...	...	...	...	...	...	...	...	...	...	...	...	...	...	...	...	6	6	...
		Other Hindus	3	2	1	5	4	1	...	...	...	1	1	...	2	1	1	3	3	...	2	...	2	5	5	...	...	...	...	53	39	14
		Perika	...	...	...	...	...	...	...	...	...	...	...	...	...	...	...	...	...	...	...	...	...	...	...	...	...	...	...	3	3	...
		Telinga	...	...	...	...	...	...	1	1	...	...	...	...	...	...	...	2	2	...	...	...	...	...	...	...	...	...	...	55	41	14
		Total......	3	2	1	5	4	1	1	1	...	1	1	...	2	1	1	5	5	...	2	...	2	5	5	...	...	...	...	117	89	28
	52 ...	Christian (Native)... ...	...	...	...	...	...	...	...	...	...	...	...	...	...	...	...	...	...	...	...	...	...	...	...	...	...	...	...	1	1	...
		Total......	...	...	...	...	...	...	...	...	...	...	...	...	...	...	...	...	...	...	...	...	...	...	...	...	...	...	...	1	1	...
		Grand Total......	92	70	22	330	265	65	213	163	50	112	83	29	57	44	13	161	119	42	119	91	28	193	147	46	...	...	...	2,977	2,261	716

TABLE XVI.

CASTES AND SUB-DIVISIONS.

TABLE XVI.

Castes and Sub-divisions.

Class.	Group.	Castes.	Sub-division of Castes.	Religion.	Total. Total.	Total. Males.	Total. Females.	Hyderabad. Total.	Hyderabad. Males.	Hyderabad. Females.	Atraf-i-Balda. Total.	Atraf-i-Balda. Males.	Atraf-i-Balda. Females.	Mahabubnagar. Total.	Mahabubnagar. Males.	Mahabubnagar. Females.	Nalgonda. Total.	Nalgonda. Males.	Nalgonda. Females.
1	2	3	4	5	6	7	8	9	10	11	12	13	14	15	16	17	18	19	20
A	1 ...	Mahratta ...	Abidar	Hindu ...	9	2	7	9	2	7	...	...	...	...	...	...	...	...	...
		do ...	Adhve	do ...	640	640	...	...	...	...	...	...	...	...	...	...	...	...	...
		do ...	Agadhi	do ...	1	...	1	...	...	...	...	...	...	...	...	...	...	...	...
		do ...	Agli	do ...	34	18	16	...	...	...	...	...	...	...	...	...	...	...	...
		do ...	Ahair	do ...	17	8	9	...	...	...	...	...	...	...	...	...	...	...	...
		do ...	Ahle	do ...	17	16	1	...	...	...	...	...	...	...	...	...	...	...	...
		do ...	Alitikar	do ...	82	48	34	...	...	...	...	...	...	...	...	...	...	...	...
		do ...	Andhvan	do ...	88	50	38	...	...	...	...	...	...	...	...	...	...	...	...
		do ...	Angarvaha	do ...	4	1	3	4	1	3	...	...	...	...	...	...	...	...	...
		do ...	Anim	do ...	13	6	7	13	6	7	...	...	...	...	...	...	...	...	...
		do ...	Anvar...	do ...	6	6	...	...	...	...	...	...	...	...	...	...	...	...	...
		do ...	Are	do ...	22,765	11,886	10,879	...	...	...	1,604	830	774	1,161	604	557	1,339	671	668
		do ...	Arge	do ...	8	2	6	...	...	...	...	...	...	...	...	...	...	...	...
		do ...	Arya	do ...	9	5	4	4	3	1	...	...	...	...	...	...	...	...	...
		do ...	Asal	do ...	5	3	2	...	...	...	...	...	...	...	...	...	...	...	...
		do ...	Atri	do ...	25	8	17	...	...	...	...	...	...	...	...	...	...	...	...
		do ...	Anchekar	do ...	19	11	8	...	...	...	...	...	...	...	...	...	...	...	...
		do ...	Avali	do ...	2	2	...	...	...	...	...	...	...	...	...	...	...	...	...
		do ...	Babre	do ...	20	10	10	...	...	...	...	...	...	...	...	...	...	...	...
		do ...	Badgur	do ...	9	9	...	...	...	...	...	...	...	...	...	...	...	...	...
		do ...	Badvan	do ...	109	63	46	...	...	...	...	...	...	...	...	...	...	...	...
		do ...	Bagar...	do ...	7	5	2	...	...	...	...	...	...	...	...	...	...	...	...
		do ...	Bagle	do ...	4	1	3	...	...	...	...	...	...	...	...	...	...	...	...
		do ...	Bahare	do ...	5	1	4	...	...	...	...	...	...	...	...	...	...	...	...
		do ...	Bakre	do ...	6	4	2	...	...	...	...	...	...	...	...	...	...	...	...
		do ...	Bal	do ...	5	3	2	...	...	...	...	...	...	...	...	...	...	...	...
		do ...	Bale	do ...	36	16	20	...	...	...	...	...	...	...	...	...	...	...	...
		do ...	Balgoti	do ...	3	3	...	...	...	...	...	...	...	...	...	...	...	...	...
		do ...	Balkar...	do ...	100	49	51	...	...	...	...	...	...	...	...	...	...	...	...
		do ...	Balve	do ...	20	12	8	...	...	...	...	...	...	...	...	...	...	...	...
		do ...	Bande...	do ...	6	2	4	...	...	...	...	...	...	...	...	...	...	...	...
		do ...	Baoli	do ...	2	2	...	...	...	...	...	...	...	...	...	...	...	...	...
		do ...	Baoro	do ...	2	...	2	...	...	...	...	...	...	...	...	...	...	...	...
		do ...	Baphale	do ...	4	1	3	...	...	...	...	...	...	...	...	...	...	...	...
		do ...	Baramase	do ...	21,887	11,229	10,658	584	310	274	60	32	28	...	...	...	...	...	...
		do ...	Bardare	do ...	78	37	41	...	...	...	...	...	...	...	...	...	...	...	...
		do ...	Bargale	do ...	3	2	1	...	...	...	...	...	...	...	...	...	...	...	...
		do ...	Barkat	do ...	5	2	3	...	...	...	...	...	...	...	...	...	...	...	...
		do ...	Basar	do ...	33	16	17	...	...	...	...	...	...	...	...	...	...	...	...
		do ...	Basett	do ...	1	1	...	1	1	...	...	...	...	...	...	...	...	...	...
		do ...	Basgad	do ...	12	8	4	...	...	...	...	...	...	...	...	...	...	...	...
		do ...	Basve	do ...	46	22	24	...	...	...	...	...	...	...	...	...	...	...	...
		do ...	Baseri	do ...	24	11	13	24	11	13	...	...	...	...	...	...	...	...	...
		do ...	Bavagre	do ...	2	2	...	...	...	...	...	...	...	...	...	...	...	...	...

TABLE XVI.

Castes and Sub-divisions.—*Continued.*

Class.	Group.	Castes.	Sub-division of Castes.	Religion.	Warangal. Total.	Warangal. Males.	Warangal. Females.	Elgandal. Total.	Elgandal. Males.	Elgandal. Females.	Indur. Total.	Indur. Males.	Indur. Females.	Medak. Total.	Medak. Males.	Medak. Females.	Aurangabad. Total.	Aurangabad. Males.	Aurangabad. Females.
					21	22	23	24	25	26	27	28	29	30	31	32	33	34	35
A	1	Mahratta	Abidar	Hindu	...	...	...	...	...	...	...	...	...	...	...	...	...	...	...
		do	Adhvo	do	...	...	...	...	...	...	...	...	...	...	...	...	...	...	...
		do	Agadhi	do	...	...	...	...	...	...	...	...	...	...	...	...	...	...	...
		do	Agli	do	...	...	...	...	...	...	34	18	16	...	...	...	...	...	...
		do	Ahuir	do	...	...	...	...	...	...	...	...	...	...	...	...	...	...	...
		do	Able	do	...	...	...	...	...	...	...	...	...	...	...	...	17	8	9
		do	Alitikar	do	...	...	...	...	...	...	...	...	...	...	...	...	...	...	...
		do	Andhvan	do	...	...	...	...	...	...	...	...	...	...	...	...	82	48	34
		do	Angarvaha	do	...	...	...	...	...	...	...	...	...	...	...	...	54	29	25
		do	Anim	do	...	...	...	...	...	...	...	...	...	...	...	...	...	...	...
		do	Anvar	do	...	...	...	...	...	...	...	...	...	...	...	...	...	...	...
		do	Are	do	7,411	3,923	3,488	9,517	4,950	4,567	480	248	232	1,252	659	593	...	...	...
		do	Argo	do	...	...	...	...	...	...	...	...	...	...	...	...	...	...	...
		do	Arya	do	...	...	...	...	...	...	...	...	...	...	...	...	...	...	...
		do	Asal	do	...	...	...	...	...	...	...	...	...	...	...	...	5	2	3
		do	Atri	do	...	...	...	...	...	...	...	...	...	...	...	...	5	3	2
		do	Anchokar	do	...	...	...	...	...	...	...	...	...	...	...	...	25	8	17
		do	Avali	do	...	...	...	...	...	...	...	...	...	...	...	...	...	...	...
		do	Babre	do	...	...	...	...	...	...	...	...	...	...	...	...	...	...	...
		do	Badgur	do	...	...	...	...	...	...	...	...	...	...	...	...	...	...	...
		do	Badvan	do	...	...	...	...	...	...	...	...	...	...	...	...	...	...	...
		do	Bagar	do	...	...	...	...	...	...	...	...	...	...	...	...	...	...	...
		do	Baglo	do	...	...	...	...	...	...	...	...	...	...	...	...	...	...	...
		do	Bahare	do	...	...	...	...	...	...	...	...	...	...	...	...	...	...	...
		do	Bakre	do	...	...	...	...	...	...	...	...	...	...	...	...	...	...	...
		do	Bal	do	...	...	...	...	...	...	...	...	...	...	...	...	...	...	...
		do	Bale	do	...	...	...	...	...	...	...	...	...	...	...	...	...	...	...
		do	Balgoti	do	...	...	...	...	...	...	...	...	...	...	...	...	3	3	...
		do	Balkar	do	...	...	...	...	...	...	...	...	...	...	...	...	...	...	...
		do	Balve	do	...	...	...	...	...	...	...	...	...	...	...	...	...	...	...
		do	Bando	do	...	...	...	...	...	...	...	...	...	...	...	...	...	...	...
		do	Baoli	do	...	...	...	...	...	...	...	...	...	...	...	...	...	...	...
		do	Baore	do	...	...	...	...	...	...	...	...	...	...	...	...	...	...	...
		do	Baphale	do	...	...	...	...	...	...	...	...	...	...	...	...	...	...	...
		do	Baramase	do	128	59	69	3,042	1,596	1,446	7	4	3	...	...	...	240	130	110
		do	Bardare	do	...	...	...	...	...	...	...	...	...	...	...	...	...	...	...
		do	Bargale	do	...	...	...	...	...	...	...	...	...	...	...	...	...	...	...
		do	Barkat	do	...	...	...	...	...	...	...	...	...	...	...	...	...	...	...
		do	Basar	do	...	...	...	...	...	...	...	...	...	...	...	...	...	...	...
		do	Basett	do	...	...	...	...	...	...	...	...	...	...	...	...	...	...	...
		do	Basgad	do	...	...	...	...	...	...	...	...	...	...	...	...	...	...	...
		do	Basvo	do	...	...	...	...	...	...	...	...	...	...	...	...	...	...	...
		do	Bateri	do	...	...	...	...	...	...	...	...	...	...	...	...	...	...	...
		do	Bavagre	do	...	...	...	...	...	...	...	...	...	...	...	...	...	...	...

TABLE XVI.

Castes and Sub-divisions.—*Continued.*

Class.	Group.	Castes.	Sub-division of Castes.	Religion.	Birh. Total.	Birh. Males.	Birh. Females.	Nander. Total.	Nander. Males.	Nander. Females.	Naldrug. Total.	Naldrug. Males.	Naldrug. Females.	Bidar. Total.	Bidar. Males.	Bidar. Females.	Parbhani. Total.	Parbhani. Males.	Parbhani. Females.
					36	37	38	39	40	41	42	43	44	45	46	47	48	49	50
A	1 ...	Mahratta ...	Abidar	Hindu ...	...	...	...	...	...	...	...	...	...	...	...	...	...	...	...
		do ...	Adhve...	do ...	...	...	...	640	640	...	...	...	...	...	...	...	...	...	...
		do ...	Agadhi	do ...	...	...	...	...	...	...	1	...	1	...	...	...	...	...	...
		do ...	Agli	do ...	...	...	...	...	...	...	...	...	...	...	...	...	...	...	...
		do ...	Ahair	do ...	...	...	...	...	...	...	...	...	...	...	...	...	...	...	...
		do ...	Ahle	do ...	...	...	...	17	16	1	...	...	...	...	...	...	...	...	...
		do ...	Alitikar	do ...	...	...	...	...	...	...	...	...	...	...	...	...	...	...	...
		do ...	Andhvan	do ...	12	5	7	22	16	6	...	...	...	...	...	...	...	...	...
		do ...	Angarvaha	do ...	...	...	...	...	...	...	...	...	...	...	...	...	...	...	...
		do ...	Anim	do ...	...	...	...	...	...	...	...	...	...	...	...	...	...	...	...
		do ...	Anvar...	do ...	...	...	...	6	6	...	...	...	...	...	...	...	...	...	...
		do ...	Are	do ...	...	...	...	...	...	...	...	...	...	...	...	...	...	...	...
		do ...	Argo	do ...	...	...	...	...	...	...	8	2	6	...	...	...	...	...	...
		do ...	Arya	do ...	...	...	...	...	...	...	...	...	...	...	...	...	...	...	...
		do ...	Asal	do ...	...	...	...	...	...	...	...	...	...	...	...	...	...	...	...
		do ...	Asri	do ...	...	...	...	...	...	...	...	...	...	...	...	...	...	...	...
		do ...	Anchekar	do ...	...	...	...	...	...	...	19	11	8	...	...	...	...	...	...
		do ...	Avali	do ...	...	...	...	2	2	...	...	...	...	...	...	...	...	...	...
		do ...	Babre	do ...	...	...	...	...	...	...	20	10	10	...	...	...	...	...	...
		do ...	Badgur	do ...	...	...	...	...	...	...	...	...	...	...	...	...	...	...	...
		do ...	Badvan	do ...	...	...	...	109	63	46	...	...	...	...	...	...	...	...	...
		do ...	Bagar	do ...	...	...	...	7	5	2	...	...	...	...	...	...	...	...	...
		do ...	Bagle	do ...	...	...	...	...	...	...	4	1	3	...	...	...	...	...	...
		do ...	Bahare	do ...	...	...	...	...	...	...	5	1	4	...	...	...	...	...	...
		do ...	Bakre	do ...	...	...	...	...	...	...	6	4	2	...	...	...	...	...	...
		do ...	Bal	do ...	...	...	...	...	...	...	...	...	...	5	3	2	...	...	...
		do ...	Bale	do ...	...	...	...	...	...	...	36	16	20	...	...	...	...	...	...
		do ...	Balgoti	do ...	...	...	...	...	...	...	...	...	...	...	...	...	...	...	...
		do ...	Balkar...	do ...	...	...	...	100	49	51	...	...	...	...	...	...	...	...	...
		do ...	Balvo	do ...	3	...	3	...	...	...	10	6	4	...	...	...	...	...	...
		do ...	Bande...	do ...	...	...	...	...	...	...	6	2	4	...	...	...	...	...	...
		do ...	Baoli	do ...	...	...	...	2	2	...	...	...	...	...	...	...	...	...	...
		do ...	Baore	do ...	...	...	...	...	...	...	2	...	2	...	...	...	...	...	...
		do ...	Baphale	do ...	...	...	...	...	...	...	4	1	3	...	...	...	...	...	...
		do ...	Baramase	do ...	371	203	168	87	43	44	16,822	8,578	8,244	8	6	2	...	...	...
		do ...	Bardare	do ...	...	...	...	78	37	41	...	...	...	...	...	...	...	...	...
		do ...	Bargale	do ...	...	...	...	3	2	1	...	...	...	...	...	...	...	...	...
		do ...	Barkat...	do ...	...	...	...	...	...	...	5	2	3	...	...	...	...	...	...
		do ...	Basar...	do ...	...	...	...	...	...	...	...	...	...	33	16	17	...	...	...
		do ...	Basett	do ...	...	...	...	...	...	...	...	...	...	...	...	...	...	...	...
		do ...	Basgad	do ...	...	...	...	12	8	4	...	...	...	...	...	...	...	...	...
		do ...	Basve	do ...	...	...	...	...	...	...	46	22	24	...	...	...	...	...	...
		do ...	Bazeri	do ...	...	...	...	...	...	...	...	...	...	...	...	...	...	...	...
		do ...	Bavagre	do ...	...	...	...	...	...	...	2	2	...	...	...	...	...	...	...

TABLE XVI.

Castes and Sub-divisions.—*Continued*.

Class.	Group.	Castes.	Sub-division of Castes.	Religion.	Sirpur Tandur. Total.	Sirpur Tandur. Males.	Sirpur Tandur. Females.	Gulbarga. Total.	Gulbarga. Males.	Gulbarga. Females.	Raichur. Total.	Raichur. Males.	Raichur. Females.	Lingasugur. Total.	Lingasugur. Males.	Lingasugur. Females.	Railways. Total.	Railways. Males.	Railways. Females.
					51	52	53	54	55	56	57	58	59	60	61	62	63	64	65
A	1 ...	Mahratta ...	Abidar	Hindu ...	...	...	...	...	...	...	...	...	...	...	...	...	...	...	...
		do ...	Adhvo	do ...	...	...	...	...	...	...	...	...	...	...	...	...	...	...	...
		do ...	Agadhi	do ...	...	...	...	...	...	...	...	...	...	...	...	...	...	...	...
		do ...	Agli	do ...	...	...	...	...	...	...	...	...	...	...	...	...	...	...	...
		do ...	Ahair	do ...	...	...	...	...	...	...	...	...	...	...	...	...	...	...	...
		do ...	Ahle	do ...	...	...	...	...	...	...	...	...	...	...	...	...	...	...	...
		do ...	Alitikar	do ...	...	...	...	...	...	...	...	...	...	...	...	...	...	...	...
		do ...	Andhvan	do ...	...	...	...	...	...	...	...	...	...	...	...	...	...	...	...
		do ...	Angarvaha	do ...	...	...	...	...	...	...	...	...	...	...	...	...	...	...	...
		do ...	Anim	do ...	...	...	...	...	...	...	...	...	...	...	...	...	...	...	...
		do ...	Anvar	do ...	...	...	...	...	...	...	...	...	...	...	...	...	...	...	...
		do ...	Are	do ...	...	...	...	...	...	...	...	...	...	...	...	...	1	1	...
		do ...	Arge	do ...	...	...	...	...	...	...	...	...	...	...	...	...	...	...	...
		do ...	Arya	do ...	...	...	...	...	...	...	...	...	...	...	...	...	...	...	...
		do ...	Asal	do ...	...	...	...	...	...	...	...	...	...	...	...	...	...	...	...
		do ...	Atri	do ...	...	...	...	...	...	...	...	...	...	...	...	...	...	...	...
		do ...	Anchekar	do ...	...	...	...	...	...	...	...	...	...	...	...	...	...	...	...
		do ...	Avali...	do ...	...	...	...	...	...	...	...	...	...	...	...	...	...	...	...
		do ...	Babre	do ...	...	...	...	...	...	...	...	...	...	...	...	...	...	...	...
		do ...	Badgur	do ...	...	...	...	...	...	...	9	9	...	...	...	...	...	...	...
		do ...	Badvan	do ...	...	...	...	...	...	...	...	...	...	...	...	...	...	...	...
		do ...	Bagar	do ...	...	...	...	...	...	...	...	...	...	...	...	...	...	...	...
		do ...	Bagle	do ...	...	...	...	...	...	...	...	...	...	...	...	...	...	...	...
		do ...	Baharo	do ...	...	...	...	...	...	...	...	...	...	...	...	...	...	...	...
		do ...	Bakre	do ...	...	...	...	...	...	...	...	...	...	...	...	...	...	...	...
		do ...	Bal	do ...	...	...	...	...	...	...	...	...	...	...	...	...	...	...	...
		do ...	Bale	do ...	...	...	...	...	...	...	...	...	...	...	...	...	...	...	...
		do ...	Bolgoti	do ...	...	...	...	...	...	...	...	...	...	...	...	...	...	...	...
		do ...	Balkar	do ...	...	...	...	...	...	...	...	...	...	...	...	...	...	...	...
		do ...	Balvo	do ...	...	...	...	7	6	1	...	...	...	...	...	...	...	...	...
		do ...	Baude...	do ...	...	...	...	...	...	...	...	...	...	...	...	...	...	...	...
		do ...	Baoli	do ...	...	...	...	...	...	...	...	...	...	...	...	...	...	...	...
		do ...	Baore	do ...	...	...	...	...	...	...	...	...	...	...	...	...	...	...	...
		do ...	Baphalo	do ...	...	...	...	...	...	...	...	...	...	...	...	...	...	...	...
		do ...	Baramase	do ...	5	5	...	422	211	211	88	40	48	23	12	11	...	...	...
		do ...	Bardaro	do ...	...	...	...	...	...	...	...	...	...	...	...	...	...	...	...
		do ...	Bargalo	do ...	...	...	...	...	...	...	...	...	...	...	...	...	...	...	...
		do ...	Barkat	do ...	...	...	...	...	...	...	...	...	...	...	...	...	...	...	...
		do ...	Basar	do ...	...	...	...	...	...	...	...	...	...	...	...	...	...	...	...
		do ...	Basett	do ...	...	...	...	...	...	...	...	...	...	...	...	...	...	...	...
		do ...	Basgad	do ...	...	...	...	...	...	...	...	...	...	...	...	...	...	...	...
		do ...	Basve	do ...	...	...	...	...	...	...	...	...	...	...	...	...	...	...	...
		do ...	Bateri	do ...	...	...	...	...	...	...	...	...	...	...	...	...	...	...	...
		do ...	Bavagro	do ...	...	...	...	...	...	...	...	...	...	...	...	...	...	...	...

TABLE XVI.

Castes and Sub-divisions.—*Continued.*

Class.	Group.	Castes.	Sub-division of Castes.	Religion.	Total.			Hyderabad.			Atraf-i-Balda.			Mahabubnagar.			Nalgonda.		
					Total.	Males.	Females.	Total.	Males.	Females.	Total.	Males.	Females.	Total.	Males.	Females.	Total.	Males.	Females.
1	2	3	4	5	6	7	8	9	10	11	12	13	14	15	16	17	18	19	20
A	1 ...	Mahratta ...	Bavapura	Hindu ...	18	9	9	18	9	9	...	...	...	...	...	...	...	...	...
		do ...	Bekar	do ...	10	4	6	...	...	...	...	...	...	...	...	...	...	...	...
		do ...	Belladoulu	do ...	94	45	49	...	...	...	...	...	...	...	...	...	...	...	...
		do ...	Bhadao	do ...	4	2	2	...	...	...	...	...	...	...	...	...	...	...	...
		do ...	Bhairs...	do ...	1	1	...	...	...	...	...	...	...	...	...	...	...	...	...
		do ...	Bhale	do ...	68	...	68	...	...	...	...	...	...	...	...	...	...	...	...
		do ...	Bhalke...	do ...	5	2	3	...	...	...	...	...	...	...	...	...	...	...	...
		do ...	Bhaoke	do ...	24	16	8	...	...	...	...	...	...	...	...	...	...	...	...
		do ...	Bhaorak	do ...	2	1	1	2	1	1	...	...	...	...	...	...	...	...	...
		do ...	Bharave	do ...	14	6	8	...	...	...	...	...	...	...	...	...	...	...	...
		do ...	Bharvad	do ...	28	18	10	...	...	...	...	...	...	...	...	...	...	...	...
		do ...	Bhavale	do ...	193	106	87	...	...	...	...	...	...	...	...	...	...	...	...
		do ...	Bhavesi	do ...	17	8	9	17	8	9	...	...	...	...	...	...	...	...	...
		do ...	Bhavechar	do ...	5	2	3	5	2	3	...	...	...	...	...	...	...	...	...
		do ...	Bhosagar	do ...	7	4	3	7	4	3	...	...	...	...	...	...	...	...	...
		do ...	Bhosle...	do ...	1,256	610	646	...	...	...	...	...	...	...	...	...	...	...	...
		do ...	Bhubhal	do ...	28	16	12	...	...	...	...	...	...	...	...	...	...	...	...
		do ...	Bhugod	do ...	2	2	...	...	...	...	...	...	...	...	...	...	...	...	...
		do ...	Bhuke	do ...	56	30	26	...	...	...	...	...	...	...	...	...	...	...	...
		do ...	Bhupal	do ...	12	7	5	...	...	...	...	...	...	...	...	...	...	...	...
		do ...	Bhupevar	do ...	8	8	...	...	...	...	...	...	...	...	...	...	...	...	...
		do ...	Bhusmat	do ...	23	8	15	23	8	15	...	...	...	...	...	...	...	...	...
		do ...	Bhutale	do ...	6	1	5	...	...	...	...	...	...	...	...	...	...	...	...
		do ...	Biltani...	do ...	1	1	...	...	...	...	...	...	...	...	...	...	...	...	...
		do ...	Bimat	do ...	4	1	3	...	...	...	...	...	...	...	...	...	...	...	...
		do ...	Birhadi	do ...	1	1	...	...	...	...	...	...	...	...	...	...	...	...	...
		do ...	Bokt	do ...	1	1	...	...	...	...	...	...	...	...	...	...	...	...	...
		do ...	Budhle	do ...	13	10	3	...	...	...	...	...	...	...	...	...	...	...	...
		do ...	Chadukal	do ...	2	...	2	2	...	2	...	...	...	...	...	...	...	...	...
		do ...	Changle	do ...	12	7	5	...	...	...	...	...	...	...	...	...	...	...	...
		do ...	Changul	do ...	6	4	2	...	...	...	...	...	...	...	...	...	...	...	...
		do ...	Chanhal	do ...	6	...	6	...	...	...	...	...	...	...	...	...	...	...	...
		do ...	Chankal	do ...	18	11	7	...	...	...	...	...	...	...	...	...	...	...	...
		do ...	Chaodhari	do ...	6	1	5	...	...	...	...	...	...	...	...	...	...	...	...
		do ...	Chaple...	do ...	7	5	2	...	...	...	...	...	...	...	...	...	...	...	...
		do ...	Chapsinge	do ...	5	3	2	...	...	...	...	...	...	...	...	...	...	...	...
		do ...	Charvangi	do ...	25	...	25	...	...	...	...	...	...	...	...	...	...	...	...
		do ...	Chatai...	do ...	6	6	...	...	...	...	...	...	...	...	...	...	...	...	...
		do ...	Chaval	do ...	5	...	5	...	...	...	...	...	...	...	...	...	...	...	...
		do ...	Chavan	do ...	629	414	215	...	...	...	...	...	...	...	...	...	...	...	...
		do ...	Chhapro	do ...	4	3	1	...	...	...	...	...	...	...	...	...	...	...	...
		do ...	Chinchole	do ...	5	3	2	...	...	...	...	...	...	...	...	...	...	...	...
		do ...	Chitki...	do ...	50	50	...	...	...	...	...	...	...	...	...	...	...	...	...
		do ...	Chhoan	do ...	9	5	4	9	5	4	...	...	...	...	...	...	...	...	...

TABLE XVI.

Castes and Sub-divisions.—*Continued.*

Class.	Group.	Castes.	Sub-division of Castes.	Religion.	Warangal. Total.	Warangal. Males.	Warangal. Females.	Elgandal. Total.	Elgandal. Males.	Elgandal. Females.	Indur. Total.	Indur. Males.	Indur. Females.	Medak. Total.	Medak. Males.	Medak. Females.	Aurangabad. Total.	Aurangabad. Males.	Aurangabad. Females.
					21	22	23	24	25	26	27	28	29	30	31	32	33	34	35
A	1 ...	Mahratta ...	Bavapura	Hindu ...	...	...	...	...	...	...	...	...	...	...	...	...	...	...	...
		do ...	Bekar	do ...	...	...	...	...	...	...	...	...	...	...	...	...	...	...	...
		do ...	Belladoulu	do ...	...	...	...	...	...	...	...	...	...	...	...	...	...	...	...
		do ...	Bhadao	do ...	...	...	...	...	...	...	...	...	...	...	...	...	...	...	...
		do ...	Bhairs...	do ...	...	...	...	...	...	...	...	...	...	...	...	...	...	...	...
		do ...	Bhale	do ...	...	...	...	...	...	...	...	...	...	...	...	...	1	1	...
		do ...	Bhalke...	do ...	...	...	...	...	...	...	...	...	...	...	...	...	...	...	...
		do ...	Bhaoke	do ...	...	...	...	...	...	...	...	...	...	...	...	...	...	...	...
		do ...	Bhaorak	do ...	...	...	...	...	...	...	...	...	...	...	...	...	...	...	...
		do ...	Bharavo	do ...	...	...	...	...	...	...	...	...	...	...	...	...	...	...	...
		do ...	Bharvad	do ...	...	...	...	...	...	...	...	...	...	...	...	...	...	...	...
		do ...	Bhavale	do ...	...	...	...	...	...	...	...	...	...	...	...	...	...	...	...
		do ...	Bhavesi	do ...	...	...	...	...	...	...	...	...	...	...	...	...	...	...	...
		do ...	Bhavechar	do ...	...	...	...	...	...	...	...	...	...	...	...	...	...	...	...
		do ...	Bhosagar	do ...	...	...	...	...	...	...	...	...	...	...	...	...	...	...	...
		do ...	Bhosle...	do ...	...	...	...	...	...	...	...	...	...	...	...	...	...	...	...
		do ...	Bhubhal	do ...	...	...	...	...	...	...	...	...	...	...	...	...	26	13	13
		do ...	Bhugod	do ...	...	...	...	...	...	...	...	...	...	...	...	...	...	...	...
		do ...	Bhuke...	do ...	...	...	...	...	...	...	...	...	...	...	...	...	...	...	...
		do ...	Bhupal	do ...	...	...	...	...	...	...	...	...	...	...	...	...	...	...	...
		do ...	Bhupevar	do ...	...	...	...	...	...	...	...	...	...	...	...	...	...	...	...
		do ...	Bhusmat	do ...	...	...	...	...	...	...	...	...	...	...	...	...	...	...	...
		do ...	Bhutale	do ...	...	...	...	...	...	...	...	...	...	...	...	...	...	...	...
		do ...	Biltani...	do ...	...	...	...	...	...	...	...	...	...	...	...	...	...	...	...
		do ...	Bimat	do ...	...	...	...	...	...	...	...	...	...	...	...	...	...	...	...
		do ...	Birbadi	do ...	...	...	...	...	...	...	...	...	...	...	...	...	...	...	...
		do ...	Bokt	do ...	...	...	...	...	...	...	...	...	...	...	...	...	1	1	...
		do ...	Budhle	do ...	...	...	...	...	...	...	...	...	...	...	...	...	...	...	...
		do ...	Chadukal	do ...	...	...	...	...	...	...	...	...	...	...	...	...	13	10	3
		do ...	Changle	do ...	...	...	...	...	...	...	...	...	...	...	...	...	...	...	...
		do ...	Changul	do ...	...	...	...	...	...	...	...	...	...	...	...	...	...	...	...
		do ...	Chanhal	do ...	...	...	...	...	...	...	...	...	...	...	...	...	...	...	...
		do ...	Chankal	do ...	...	...	...	...	...	...	...	...	...	...	...	...	...	...	...
		do ...	Chaodhari	do ...	...	...	...	...	...	...	...	...	...	...	...	...	...	...	...
		do ...	Chaple...	do ...	...	...	...	...	...	...	...	...	...	...	...	...	...	...	...
		do ...	Chapsinge	do ...	...	...	...	...	...	...	...	...	...	...	...	...	...	...	...
		do ...	Charvangi	do ...	...	...	...	...	...	...	...	...	...	...	...	...	...	...	...
		do ...	Chatai...	do ...	...	...	...	...	...	...	...	...	...	...	...	...	...	...	...
		do ...	Chaval	do ...	...	...	...	...	...	...	...	...	...	...	...	...	...	...	...
		do ...	Chavan	do ...	...	...	...	...	...	...	...	...	...	...	...	...	...	...	...
		do ...	Chhapre	do ...	...	...	...	...	...	...	...	...	...	...	...	...	...	...	...
		do ...	Chinchole	do ...	...	...	...	...	...	...	...	...	...	...	...	...	...	...	...
		do ...	Chitki	do ...	...	...	...	...	...	...	...	...	...	...	...	...	...	...	...
		do ...	Chhoan	do ...	...	...	...	...	...	...	...	...	...	...	...	...	...	...	...

TABLE XVI.

Castes and Sub-divisions.—*Continued.*

Class.	Group	Castes.	Sub-division of Castes.	Religion.	Birh.			Nander.			Naldrug.			Bidar.			Parbhani.		
					Total.	Males.	Females.	Total.	Males.	Females.	Total.	Males.	Females.	Total.	Males.	Females.	Total.	Males.	Females.
					36	37	38	39	40	41	42	43	44	45	46	47	48	49	50
A	1 ...	Mahratta ...	Bavapura	Hindu ...	...	...	...	...	...	...	...	...	...	...	...	...	...	...	...
		do ...	Bekar	do ...	...	...	...	...	...	...	10	4	6	...	...	...	...	...	...
		do ...	Belladoulu	do ...	...	...	...	...	...	...	...	...	...	...	...	...	...	...	...
		do ...	Bhadao	do ...	...	...	...	...	...	...	4	2	2	...	...	...	...	...	...
		do ...	Bhairs	do ...	...	...	...	...	...	...	...	...	...	...	...	...	...	...	...
		do ...	Bhale	do ...	...	...	...	...	...	...	...	...	...	...	...	...	68	...	68
		do ...	Bhalke	do ...	...	...	...	...	...	...	...	...	...	5	2	3	...	...	...
		do ...	Bhaoke	do ...	...	...	...	...	...	...	16	8	8	8	8	...	...	...	...
		do ...	Bhaerak	do ...	...	...	...	...	...	...	...	...	...	...	...	...	...	...	...
		do ...	Bharave	do ...	...	...	...	14	6	8	...	...	...	...	...	...	...	...	...
		do ...	Bharvad	do ...	...	...	...	28	18	10	...	...	...	...	...	...	...	...	...
		do ...	Bhavale	do ...	...	...	...	7	7	...	184	97	87	...	...	...	2	2	...
		do ...	Bhavesi	do ...	...	...	...	...	...	...	...	...	...	...	...	...	...	...	...
		do ...	Bhavechar	do ...	...	...	...	...	...	...	...	...	...	...	...	...	...	...	...
		do ...	Bhosagar	do ...	...	...	...	...	...	...	...	...	...	...	...	...	...	...	...
		do ...	Bhosle...	do ...	...	...	...	128	66	62	194	88	106	876	428	448	...	...	...
		do ...	Bhubhal	do ...	...	...	...	28	16	12	...	...	...	...	...	...	...	...	...
		do ...	Bhugod	do ...	...	...	...	...	...	...	2	2	...	...	...	...	...	...	...
		do ...	Bhuke...	do ...	...	...	...	...	...	...	56	30	26	...	...	...	...	...	...
		do ...	Bhupal	do ...	...	...	...	...	...	...	...	...	...	12	7	5	...	...	...
		do ...	Bhupevar	do ...	...	...	...	...	...	...	...	...	...	8	8	...	...	...	...
		do ...	Bhusmat	do ...	...	...	...	...	...	...	...	...	...	...	...	...	...	...	...
		do ...	Bhutale	do ...	...	...	...	...	...	...	...	...	...	6	1	5	...	...	...
		do ...	Biltani	do ...	...	...	...	...	...	...	...	...	...	...	...	...	...	...	...
		do ...	Bimat	do ...	...	...	...	...	...	...	4	1	3	...	...	...	...	...	...
		do ...	Birhadi	do ...	...	...	...	...	...	...	...	...	...	...	...	...	...	...	...
		do ...	Bokt	do ...	...	...	...	1	1	...	...	...	...	...	...	...	...	...	...
		do ...	Budhle	do ...	...	...	...	...	...	...	...	...	...	...	...	...	...	...	...
		do ...	Chadukal	do ...	...	...	...	...	...	...	...	...	...	...	...	...	...	...	...
		do ...	Changle	do ...	...	...	...	12	7	5	...	...	...	...	...	...	...	...	...
		do ...	Changul	do ...	...	...	...	...	...	...	6	4	2	...	...	...	...	...	...
		do ...	Chanhal	do ...	...	...	...	...	...	...	6	...	6	...	...	...	...	...	...
		do ...	Chankal	do ...	...	...	...	...	...	...	...	...	...	...	...	...	...	...	...
		do ...	Chaodhari	do ...	...	...	...	...	...	...	6	1	5	...	...	...	...	...	...
		do ...	Chaple	do ...	...	...	...	...	...	...	...	...	...	7	5	2	...	...	...
		do ...	Chapsinge	do ...	5	8	2	...	...	...	...	...	...	...	...	...	...	...	...
		do ...	Charvangi	do ...	...	...	...	...	...	...	...	...	...	25	...	25	...	...	...
		do ...	Chatai...	do ...	6	6	...	...	...	...	...	...	...	...	...	...	...	...	...
		do ...	Chaval	do ...	...	...	...	...	...	...	...	...	...	...	...	...	...	...	...
		do ...	Chavan	do ...	...	...	...	629	414	215	...	...	...	...	...	...	...	...	...
		do ...	Chhapre	do ...	...	...	...	...	...	...	4	3	1	...	...	...	...	...	...
		do ...	Chinchole	do ...	...	...	...	...	...	...	5	3	2	...	...	...	...	...	...
		do ...	Chitki...	do ...	...	...	...	...	...	...	...	...	...	50	50	...	...	...	...
		do ...	Chhoan	do ...	...	...	...	...	...	...	...	...	...	...	...	...	...	...	...

TABLE XVI.

Castes and Sub-divisions.—*Continued.*

Class.	Group.	Castes.	Sub-division of Castes.	Religion.	Sirpur Tandur. Total.	Sirpur Tandur. Males.	Sirpur Tandur. Females.	Gulbarga. Total.	Gulbarga. Males.	Gulbarga. Females.	Raichur. Total.	Raichur. Males.	Raichur. Females.	Lingasugur. Total.	Lingasugur. Males.	Lingasugur. Females.	Railways. Total.	Railways. Males.	Railways. Females.
					51	52	53	54	55	56	57	58	59	60	61	62	63	64	65
A	1 ...	Mahratta ...	Bavapura	Hindu ...	...	...	...	...	...	...	...	...	...	...	...	...	...	...	...
		do ...	Bekar	do ...	...	...	...	...	...	...	...	...	...	...	...	...	...	...	...
		do ...	Belladonlu	do ...	...	...	...	...	...	...	...	...	...	...	...	...	...	...	...
		do ...	Bhadao	do ...	...	...	...	...	...	...	...	...	...	94	45	49	...	...	...
		do ...	Bhairs...	do ...	...	...	...	...	...	...	...	...	...	...	...	...	...	...	...
		do ...	Bhale	do ...	...	...	...	...	...	...	...	...	...	...	...	...	...	...	...
		do ...	Bhalke	do ...	...	...	...	...	...	...	...	...	...	...	...	...	...	...	...
		do ...	Bhaoke	do ...	...	...	...	...	...	...	...	...	...	...	...	...	...	...	...
		do ...	Bhaorak	do ...	...	...	...	...	...	...	...	...	...	...	...	...	...	...	...
		do ...	Bharave	do ...	...	...	...	...	...	...	...	...	...	...	...	...	...	...	...
		do ...	Bharvad	do ...	...	...	...	...	...	...	...	...	...	...	...	...	...	...	...
		do ...	Bhavale	do ...	...	...	...	...	...	...	...	...	...	...	...	...	...	...	...
		do ...	Bhavesi	do ...	...	...	...	...	...	...	...	...	...	...	...	...	...	...	...
		do ...	Bhavechar ...	do ...	...	...	...	...	...	...	...	...	...	...	...	...	...	...	...
		do ...	Bhosagar	do ...	...	...	...	...	...	...	...	...	...	...	...	...	...	...	...
		do ...	Bhosle	do ...	...	...	...	27	13	14	5	2	8	...	...	...	...	...	...
		do ...	Bhubhal	do ...	...	...	...	...	...	...	...	...	...	...	...	...	...	...	...
		do ...	Bhugod	do ...	...	...	...	...	...	...	...	...	...	...	...	...	...	...	...
		do ...	Bhuke...	do ...	...	...	...	...	...	...	...	...	...	...	...	...	...	...	...
		do ...	Bhupal	do ...	...	...	...	...	...	...	...	...	...	...	...	...	...	...	...
		do ...	Bhupevar	do ...	...	...	...	...	...	...	...	...	...	...	...	...	...	...	...
		do ...	Bhusmat	do ...	...	...	...	...	...	...	...	...	...	...	...	...	...	...	...
		do ...	Bhutali	do ...	...	...	...	...	...	...	...	...	...	...	...	...	...	...	...
		do ...	Biltani...	do ...	1	1	...	...	...	...	...	...	...	...	...	...	...	...	...
		do ...	Bimat	do ...	...	...	...	...	...	...	...	...	...	...	...	...	...	...	...
		do ...	Birhadi	do ...	...	...	...	...	...	...	...	...	...	...	...	...	...	...	...
		do ...	Bokt	do ...	...	...	...	...	...	...	...	...	...	...	...	...	...	...	...
		do ...	Budhle	do ...	...	...	...	...	...	...	...	...	...	...	...	...	...	...	...
		do ...	Chadukal	do ...	...	...	...	...	...	...	...	...	...	...	...	...	...	...	...
		do ...	Changle	do ...	...	...	...	...	...	...	...	...	...	...	...	...	...	...	...
		do ...	Changul	do ...	...	...	...	...	...	...	...	...	...	...	...	...	...	...	...
		do ...	Chauhal	do ...	...	...	...	...	...	...	...	...	...	...	...	...	...	...	...
		do ...	Chaokal	do ...	...	...	...	...	...	...	...	...	...	18	11	7	...	...	...
		do ...	Chaodhari	do ...	...	...	...	...	...	...	...	...	...	...	...	...	...	...	...
		do ...	Chaple	do ...	...	...	...	...	...	...	...	...	...	...	...	...	...	...	...
		do ...	Chapeinge	do ...	...	...	...	...	...	...	...	...	...	...	...	...	...	...	...
		do ...	Charvangi	do ...	...	...	...	...	...	...	...	...	...	...	...	...	...	...	...
		do ...	Chatai...	do ...	...	...	...	...	...	...	...	...	...	...	...	...	...	...	...
		do ...	Chaval	do ...	5	...	5	...	...	...	...	...	...	...	...	...	...	...	...
		do ...	Chavan	do ...	...	...	...	...	...	...	...	...	...	...	...	...	...	...	...
		do ...	Chhapre	do ...	...	...	...	...	...	...	...	...	...	...	...	...	...	...	...
		do ...	Chinchole	do ...	...	...	...	...	...	...	...	...	...	...	...	...	...	...	...
		do ...	Chitki	do ...	...	...	...	...	...	...	...	...	...	...	...	...	...	...	...
		do ...	Chhoan	do ...	...	...	...	...	...	...	...	...	...	...	...	...	...	...	...

TABLE XVI.

Castes and Sub-divisions.—*Continued.*

Class.	Group.	Castes.	Sub-division of Castes.	Religion.	Total. Total.	Total. Males.	Total. Females.	Hyderabad. Total.	Hyderabad. Males.	Hyderabad. Females.	Atraf-i-Balda. Total.	Atraf-i-Balda. Males.	Atraf-i-Balda. Females.	Mahabubnagar. Total.	Mahabubnagar. Males.	Mahabubnagar. Females.	Nalgonda. Total.	Nalgonda. Males.	Nalgonda. Females.
1	2	3	4	5	6	7	8	9	10	11	12	13	14	15	16	17	18	19	20
A	1 ...	Mahratta ...	Dadge...	Hindu ...	1	1	...	...	...	...	...	...	...	...	...	...	...	...	...
		do ...	Dagan	do ...	9	5	4	...	...	...	...	...	...	...	...	...	...	...	...
		do ...	Dagde...	do ...	10	6	4	...	...	...	...	...	...	...	...	...	...	...	...
		do ...	Dakar...	do ...	16	9	7	...	...	...	...	...	...	...	...	...	...	...	...
		do ...	Dakhne	do ...	8,287	4,238	4,049	...	...	...	...	...	...	...	...	...	...	...	...
		do ...	Dangve	do ...	5	3	2	...	...	...	...	...	...	...	...	...	...	...	...
		do ...	Daore	do ...	9	9	...	...	...	...	...	...	...	...	...	...	...	...	...
		do ...	Davagir	do ...	26	12	14	...	...	...	...	...	...	...	...	...	...	...	...
		do ...	Daske	do ...	41	21	20	...	...	...	...	...	...	...	...	...	...	...	...
		do ...	Daree	do ...	5	1	4	...	...	...	...	...	...	...	...	...	...	...	...
		do ...	Davalkar	do ...	6	2	4	...	...	...	...	...	...	...	...	...	...	...	...
		do ...	Dayal	do ...	34	18	16	...	...	...	...	...	...	...	...	...	...	...	...
		do ...	Dhahanker	do ...	9	5	4	...	...	...	...	...	...	...	...	...	...	...	...
		do ...	Dhandi	do ...	4	1	3	...	...	...	...	...	...	...	...	...	...	...	...
		do ...	Dhanuj	do ...	48	31	17	...	...	...	...	...	...	...	...	...	...	...	...
		do ...	Dhaole	do ...	18	9	9	...	...	...	...	...	...	...	...	...	...	...	...
		do ...	Dhaonare	do ...	10	3	7	...	...	...	...	...	...	...	...	...	...	...	...
		do ...	Dhape...	do ...	54	47	7	...	...	...	...	...	...	...	...	...	...	...	...
		do ...	Dharoti	do ...	15	7	8	...	...	...	...	...	...	...	...	...	...	...	...
		do ...	Dhasim	do ...	8	4	4	...	...	...	...	...	...	...	...	...	...	...	...
		do ...	Dhavan	do ...	114	43	71	...	...	...	...	...	...	...	...	...	...	...	...
		do ...	Dhomale	do ...	532	313	219	...	...	...	...	...	...	...	...	...	...	...	...
		do ...	Dokre	do ...	15	6	9	...	...	...	...	...	...	...	...	...	...	...	...
		do ...	Dongre	do ...	35	16	19	...	...	...	...	...	...	...	...	...	...	...	...
		do ...	Doshant	do ...	10	4	6	...	...	...	...	...	...	...	...	...	...	...	...
		do ...	Dubad...	do ...	86	73	13	...	...	...	...	...	...	...	...	...	...	...	...
		do ...	Gabad...	do ...	18	7	11	...	...	...	...	...	...	...	...	...	...	...	...
		do ...	Gade	do ...	2	...	2	...	...	...	...	...	...	...	...	...	...	...	...
		do ...	Gadiko	do ...	11	8	3	...	...	...	...	...	...	...	...	...	...	...	...
		do ...	Gadvine	do ...	5	5	...	...	...	...	...	...	...	...	...	...	...	...	...
		do ...	Gaike	do ...	18	7	11	...	...	...	...	...	...	...	...	...	...	...	...
		do ...	Galkaput	do ...	35	19	16	...	...	...	...	...	...	...	...	...	...	...	...
		do ...	Galve	do ...	3	1	2	...	...	...	...	...	...	...	...	...	...	...	...
		do ...	Gangotri	do ...	17	13	4	...	...	...	...	...	...	...	...	...	...	...	...
		do ...	Gania	do ...	12	6	6	...	...	...	...	...	...	...	...	...	...	...	...
		do ...	Gaone	do ...	8	4	4	...	...	...	...	...	...	...	...	...	...	...	...
		do ...	Gaosi	do ...	1	1	...	...	...	...	...	...	...	...	...	...	...	...	...
		do ...	Garad	do ...	19	11	8	...	...	...	...	...	...	...	...	...	...	...	...
		do ...	Garikad	do ...	9	5	4	9	5	4	...	...	...	...	...	...	...	...	...
		do ...	Gayakvad	do ...	931	494	437	...	...	...	...	...	...	...	...	...	...	...	...
		do ...	Ghadge	do ...	8	4	4	...	...	...	...	...	...	...	...	...	...	...	...
		do ...	Ghagar	do ...	4	4	...	...	...	...	...	...	...	...	...	...	...	...	...
		do ...	Ghataise	do ...	27	3	24	...	...	...	...	...	...	...	...	...	...	...	...
		do ...	Ghatse...	do ...	4	2	2	...	...	...	...	...	...	...	...	...	...	...	...

TABLE XVI.

Castes and Sub-divisions.—*Continued.*

Class.	Group.	Castes.	Sub-division of Castes.	Religion.	Warangal. Total.	Warangal. Males.	Warangal. Females.	Elgandal. Total	Elgandal. Males.	Elgandal. Females.	Indur. Total.	Indur. Males.	Indur. Females.	Medak. Total.	Medak. Males.	Medak. Females.	Aurangabad. Total.	Aurangabad. Males.	Aurangabad. Females.
					21	22	23	24	25	26	27	28	29	30	31	32	33	34	35
A	1	Mahratta	Dadge	Hindu	...	...	...	...	...	...	...	...	...	...	...	...	...	...	...
		do	Dagan	do	...	...	...	...	...	...	...	...	...	...	...	...	...	...	...
		do	Dagde	do	...	...	...	...	...	...	...	...	...	...	...	...	...	...	...
		do	Dakar	do	...	...	...	...	...	...	...	...	...	...	...	...	...	...	...
		do	Dakhne	do	...	...	...	...	...	...	...	...	...	...	...	...	...	...	...
		do	Dangve	do	...	...	...	...	...	...	...	...	...	...	...	...	...	...	...
		do	Daore	do	...	...	...	...	...	...	...	...	...	...	...	...	...	...	...
		do	Davagir	do	...	...	...	...	...	...	...	...	...	...	...	...	...	...	...
		do	Daske	do	...	...	...	...	...	...	...	...	...	...	...	...	...	...	...
		do	Daree	do	...	...	...	...	...	...	...	...	...	...	...	...	...	...	...
		do	Davalkar	do	...	...	...	...	...	...	...	...	...	...	...	...	...	...	...
		do	Dayal	do	...	...	...	...	...	...	...	...	...	...	...	...	...	...	...
		do	Dhahanker	do	...	...	...	...	...	...	...	...	...	...	...	...	...	...	...
		do	Dhandi	do	...	...	...	...	...	...	...	...	...	...	...	...	...	...	...
		do	Dhanuj	do	...	...	...	...	...	...	...	...	...	...	...	...	...	...	...
		do	Dhaole	do	...	...	...	...	...	...	...	...	...	...	...	...	...	...	...
		do	Dhaonare	do	...	...	...	...	...	...	...	...	...	...	...	...	...	...	...
		do	Dhape	do	...	...	...	...	...	...	...	...	...	...	...	...	...	...	...
		do	Dharoti	do	...	...	...	...	...	...	...	...	...	...	...	...	15	7	8
		do	Dhasim	do	...	...	...	...	...	...	...	...	...	...	...	...	...	...	...
		do	Dhavan	do	...	...	...	...	...	...	...	...	...	...	...	...	...	...	...
		do	Dhomale	do	...	...	...	...	...	...	...	...	...	...	...	...	...	...	...
		do	Dokre	do	...	...	...	...	...	...	...	...	...	...	...	...	...	...	...
		do	Dongre	do	...	...	...	...	...	...	...	...	...	...	...	...	...	...	...
		do	Doshant	do	...	...	...	...	...	...	...	...	...	...	...	...	...	...	...
		do	Dubad	do	...	...	...	...	...	...	...	...	...	...	...	...	...	...	...
		do	Gabad	do	...	...	...	...	...	...	...	...	...	...	...	...	...	...	...
		do	Gade	do	...	...	...	...	...	...	...	...	...	...	...	...	...	...	...
		do	Gadike	do	...	...	...	...	...	...	...	...	...	...	...	...	...	...	...
		do	Gadvine	do	...	...	...	...	...	...	...	...	...	...	...	...	5	5	...
		do	Gaike	do	...	...	...	—	...	...	...	...	...	...	...	...	...	...	...
		do	Galkaput	do	...	...	...	—	...	...	...	...	...	...	...	...	...	...	...
		do	Galve	do	...	...	...	...	...	...	...	...	...	...	...	...	...	...	...
		do	Gangotri	do	...	...	...	...	...	...	...	...	...	...	...	...	...	...	...
		do	Gania	do	...	...	...	...	...	...	...	...	...	...	...	...	...	...	...
		do	Gaone	do	...	...	...	...	...	...	...	...	...	...	...	...	...	...	...
		do	Gaosi	do	...	...	...	...	...	...	...	...	...	...	...	...	...	...	...
		do	Garad	do	...	...	...	...	...	...	...	...	...	...	...	...	...	...	...
		do	Garikad	do	...	...	...	...	...	...	...	...	...	...	...	...	...	...	...
		do	Gayakvad	do	...	...	...	...	...	...	36	20	16	...	...	...	21	10	11
		do	Ghadge	do	...	...	...	...	...	...	...	...	...	...	...	...	...	...	...
		do	Ghagar	do	...	...	...	...	...	...	...	...	...	...	...	...	...	...	...
		do	Ghatsise	do	...	...	...	...	...	...	...	...	...	...	...	...	...	...	...
		do	Ghatte	do	...	...	...	...	...	...	...	...	...	...	...	...	...	...	...

TABLE XVI.

Castes and Sub-divisions.—*Continued.*

Class.	Group.	Castes.	Sub-division of Castes.	Religion.	Birh. Total.	Birh. Males.	Birh. Females.	Nander. Total.	Nander. Males.	Nander. Females.	Naldrug. Total.	Naldrug. Males.	Naldrug. Females.	Bidar. Total.	Bidar. Males.	Bidar. Females.	Parbhani. Total.	Parbhani. Males.	Parbhani. Females.
					36	37	38	39	40	41	42	43	44	45	46	47	48	49	50
A	1 ...	Mahratta ...	Dadge	Hindu ...	...	...	...	...	...	...	1	1	...	...	...	...	...	...	...
		do ...	Dagan	do ...	...	...	...	9	5	4	...	...	...	...	...	...	...	...	...
		do ...	Dagde...	do ...	...	...	...	...	...	...	10	6	4	...	...	...	...	...	...
		do ...	Dakar...	do ...	...	...	...	...	...	...	16	9	7	...	...	...	...	...	...
		do ...	Dakhne	do ...	...	...	...	...	...	...	...	...	...	...	...	...	8,287	4,288	4,049
		do ...	Dangve	do ...	...	...	...	...	...	...	...	...	...	5	3	2	...	...	...
		do ...	Daore	do ...	...	...	...	...	...	...	9	9	...	...	...	...	...	...	...
		do ...	Davagir	do ...	...	...	...	...	...	...	...	...	...	26	12	14	...	...	...
		do ...	Daske	do ...	...	...	...	...	...	...	41	21	20	...	...	...	...	...	...
		do ...	Dare	de ...	...	...	...	...	...	...	5	1	4	...	...	...	...	...	...
		do ...	Davalkar	do ...	...	...	...	6	2	4	...	...	...	...	...	...	...	...	...
		do ...	Dayal	do ...	...	...	...	...	...	...	34	18	16	...	...	...	...	...	...
		do ...	Dhahanker	do ...	...	...	...	...	...	...	...	...	...	9	5	4	...	...	...
		do ...	Dhandi	do ...	...	...	...	...	...	...	4	1	3	...	...	...	...	...	...
		do ...	Dhanuj	do ...	...	...	...	...	...	...	...	...	...	...	...	...	48	31	17
		do ...	Dhaole	do ...	...	...	...	...	...	...	...	...	...	18	9	9	...	...	...
		do ...	Dhaonare	do ...	...	...	...	...	...	...	10	3	7	...	...	...	...	...	...
		do ...	Dhape...	do ...	...	...	...	...	...	...	...	...	...	44	42	2	...	...	...
		do ...	Dharoti	do ...	...	...	...	...	...	...	...	...	...	...	...	...	...	...	...
		do ...	Dhasim	do ...	...	...	...	...	...	...	8	4	4	...	...	...	...	...	...
		do ...	Dhavan	do ...	...	...	...	58	24	34	...	...	...	56	19	37	...	...	...
		do ...	Dhomale	do ...	...	...	...	...	...	...	34	15	19	498	298	200	...	...	...
		do ...	Dokre	do ...	...	...	...	...	...	...	15	6	9	...	...	...	...	...	...
		do ...	Dongre	de ...	...	...	...	...	...	...	7	4	3	...	...	...	...	...	...
		do ...	Doshant	do ...	...	...	...	...	...	...	10	4	6	...	...	...	...	...	...
		do ...	Dubad	do ...	...	...	...	86	73	13	...	...	...	...	...	...	...	...	...
		do ...	Gabad...	do ...	...	...	...	...	...	...	18	7	11	...	...	...	...	...	...
		do ...	Gade	do ...	...	...	...	...	...	...	2	...	2	...	...	...	...	...	...
		do ...	Gadike	do ...	...	...	...	...	...	...	...	...	...	...	...	...	...	...	...
		do ...	Gadvine	do ...	...	...	...	...	...	...	...	...	...	...	...	...	...	...	...
		do ...	Gaike...	do ...	...	...	...	18	7	11	...	...	...	...	...	...	...	...	...
		do ...	Galkaput	do ...	...	...	...	35	19	16	...	...	...	...	...	...	...	...	...
		do ...	Galve	do ...	...	...	...	...	...	...	3	1	2	...	...	...	...	...	...
		do ...	Gangotri	do ...	...	...	...	...	...	...	...	...	...	...	...	...	17	13	4
		do ...	Gania...	do ...	...	...	...	...	...	...	...	...	...	12	6	6	...	...	...
		do ...	Gaone...	do ...	...	...	...	...	...	...	8	4	4	...	...	...	...	...	...
		do ...	Gaosi	do ...	...	...	...	...	...	...	...	...	...	1	1	...	...	...	...
		do ...	Garad...	do ...	...	...	...	19	11	8	...	...	...	...	...	...	...	...	...
		do ...	Garikad	do ...	...	...	...	...	...	...	...	...	...	...	...	...	...	...	...
		do ...	Gayakvad	do ...	54	33	21	874	193	181	401	211	190	5	4	1	...	...	...
		do ...	Ghadge	do ...	...	...	...	6	8	3	2	1	1	...	...	...	...	...	...
		do ...	Ghagar	do ...	...	...	...	4	4	...	...	...	...	...	...	...	...	...	...
		do ...	Ghatsise	do ...	27	3	24	...	...	...	...	...	...	...	...	...	...	...	...
		do ...	Ghatte	do ...	...	...	...	...	...	...	4	2	2	...	...	...	...	...	...

TABLE XVI.

Castes and Sub-divisions.—*Continued.*

Class.	Group.	Castes.	Sub-division of Castes.	Religion.	Sirpur Tandur. Total.	Sirpur Tandur. Males.	Sirpur Tandur. Females.	Gulbarga. Total.	Gulbarga. Males.	Gulbarga. Females.	Raichur. Total.	Raichur. Males.	Raichur. Females.	Lingasugur. Total.	Lingasugur. Males.	Lingasugur. Females	Railways. Total.	Railways. Males.	Railways. Females.
					51	52	53	54	55	56	57	58	59	60	61	62	63	64	65
A	1	Mahratta	Dadge	Hindu	...	...	...	...	...	...	...	...	...	...	...	...	...	...	...
		do	Dagan	do	...	...	...	...	...	...	...	...	...	...	...	...	...	...	...
		do	Dagde	do	...	...	...	...	...	...	...	...	...	...	...	...	...	...	...
		do	Dakar	do	...	...	...	...	...	...	...	...	...	...	...	...	...	...	...
		do	Dakhne	do	...	...	...	...	...	...	...	...	...	...	...	...	...	...	...
		do	Dangvo	do	...	...	...	...	...	...	...	...	...	...	...	...	...	...	...
		do	Daore	do	...	...	...	...	...	...	...	...	...	...	...	...	...	...	...
		do	Davagir	do	...	...	...	...	...	...	...	...	...	...	...	...	...	...	...
		do	Daske	do	...	...	...	...	...	...	...	...	...	...	...	...	...	...	...
		do	Daro	do	...	...	...	...	...	...	...	...	...	...	...	...	...	...	...
		do	Davalkar	do	...	...	...	...	...	...	...	...	...	...	...	...	...	...	...
		do	Dayal	do	...	...	...	...	...	...	...	...	...	...	...	...	...	...	...
		do	Dhahaurkor	do	...	...	...	...	...	...	...	...	...	...	...	...	...	...	...
		do	Dhandi	do	...	...	...	...	...	...	...	...	...	...	...	...	...	...	...
		do	Dhanuj	do	...	...	...	...	...	...	...	...	...	...	...	...	...	...	...
		do	Dhaole	do	...	...	...	...	...	...	...	...	...	...	...	...	...	...	...
		do	Dhaonare	do	...	...	...	...	...	...	...	...	...	...	...	...	...	...	...
		do	Dhape	do	...	...	...	...	...	...	...	...	...	10	5	5	...	...	...
		do	Dharoti	do	...	...	...	...	...	...	...	...	...	...	...	...	...	...	...
		do	Dhasim	do	...	...	...	...	...	...	...	...	...	...	...	...	...	...	...
		do	Dhavan	do	...	...	...	...	...	...	...	...	...	...	...	...	...	...	...
		do	Dhomale	do	...	...	...	...	...	...	...	...	...	...	...	...	...	...	...
		do	Dokre	do	...	...	...	...	...	...	...	...	...	...	...	...	...	...	...
		do	Dongre	do	...	...	...	28	12	16	...	...	...	...	...	...	...	...	...
		do	Doshant	do	...	...	...	...	...	...	...	...	...	...	...	...	...	...	...
		do	Dubad	do	...	...	...	...	...	...	...	...	...	...	...	...	...	...	...
		do	Gabad	do	...	...	...	...	...	...	...	...	...	...	...	...	...	...	...
		do	Gade	do	...	...	...	...	...	...	...	...	...	...	...	...	...	...	...
		do	Gadike	do	11	8	8	...	...	...	...	...	...	...	...	...	...	...	...
		do	Gadvine	do	...	...	...	...	...	...	...	...	...	...	...	...	...	...	...
		do	Gaike	do	...	...	...	...	...	...	...	...	...	...	...	...	...	...	...
		do	Galkaput	do	...	...	...	...	...	...	...	...	...	...	...	...	...	...	...
		do	Galve	do	...	...	...	...	...	...	...	...	...	...	...	...	...	...	...
		do	Gangotri	do	...	...	...	...	...	...	...	...	...	...	...	...	...	...	...
		do	Gania	do	...	...	...	...	...	...	...	...	...	...	...	...	...	...	...
		do	Gaone	do	...	...	...	...	...	...	...	...	...	...	...	...	...	...	...
		do	Gaosi	do	...	...	...	...	...	...	...	...	...	...	...	...	...	...	...
		do	Garad	do	...	...	...	...	...	...	...	...	...	...	...	...	...	...	...
		do	Garikad	do	...	...	...	...	...	...	...	...	...	...	...	...	...	...	...
		do	Gayakvad	do	5	2	3	35	21	14	...	...	...	...	...	...	...	...	...
		do	Ghadge	do	...	...	...	...	...	...	...	...	...	...	...	...	...	...	...
		do	Ghagar	do	...	...	...	...	...	...	...	...	...	...	...	...	...	...	...
		do	Ghatsise	do	...	...	...	...	...	...	...	...	...	...	...	...	...	...	...
		do	Ghatte	do	...	...	...	...	...	...	...	...	...	...	...	...	...	...	...

TABLE XVI.
Castes and Sub-divisions.—*Continued.*

Class.	Group.	Castes.	Sub-division of Castes.	Religion.	Total. Total.	Total. Males.	Total. Females.	Hyderabad. Total.	Hyderabad. Males.	Hyderabad. Females.	Atraf-i-Balda. Total.	Atraf-i-Balda. Males.	Atraf-i-Balda. Females.	Mahabubnagar. Total.	Mahabubnagar. Males.	Mahabubnagar. Females.	Nalgonda. Total.	Nalgonda. Males.	Nalgonda. Females.
1	2	3	4	5	6	7	8	9	10	11	12	13	14	15	16	17	18	19	20
A	1 ...	Mahratta ...	Ghatvale	Hindu ...	84	84	...	...	...	...	...	...	...	...	...	...	...	...	...
		do ...	Ghoped	do ...	8	2	1	...	...	...	...	...	...	...	...	...	...	...	...
		do ...	Ghotak	do ...	81	15	16	...	...	...	...	...	...	...	...	...	...	...	...
		do ...	Giaramasi	do ...	18	4	9	18	4	9	...	...	...	...	...	...	...	...	...
		do ...	Giugne	do ...	51	22	29	...	...	...	...	...	...	...	...	...	...	...	...
		do ...	Gokule	do ...	6	2	4	...	...	...	...	...	...	...	...	...	...	...	...
		do ...	Gole	do ...	93	62	31	...	...	...	...	...	...	...	...	...	...	...	...
		do ...	Gotkar	do ...	42	32	10	...	...	...	...	...	...	...	...	...	...	...	...
		do ...	Goono	do ...	8	4	4	...	...	...	...	...	...	...	...	...	...	...	...
		do ...	Gorpade	do ...	87	40	47	...	...	...	...	...	...	...	...	...	...	...	...
		do ...	Gorud	do ...	15	8	7	...	...	...	...	...	...	...	...	...	...	...	...
		do ...	Got	do ...	12	7	5	...	...	...	...	...	...	...	...	...	...	...	...
		do ...	Goto	do ...	8	...	3	...	...	...	...	...	...	...	...	...	...	...	...
		do ...	Had	do ...	87	2	85	...	...	...	...	...	...	...	...	...	...	...	...
		do ...	Haladjole	do ...	244	116	128	...	...	...	...	...	...	...	...	...	...	...	...
		do ...	Halve	do ...	5	2	3	...	...	...	...	...	...	...	...	...	...	...	...
		do ...	Handelawaru	do ...	4	3	1	...	...	...	...	...	...	...	...	...	...	...	...
		do ...	Haro	do ...	81	...	81	...	...	...	...	...	...	...	...	...	...	...	...
		do ...	Hartake	do ...	6	1	5	...	...	...	...	...	...	...	...	...	...	...	...
		do ...	Hartal...	do ...	6	6	...	...	...	...	...	...	...	...	...	...	...	...	...
		do ...	Havanjat ...	do ...	4	2	2	...	...	...	...	...	...	...	...	...	...	...	...
		do ...	Hendri Marathi ...	do ...	167	82	85	...	...	...	...	...	...	...	...	...	...	...	...
		do ...	Hingnero	do ...	5	3	2	...	...	...	...	...	...	...	...	...	...	...	...
		do ...	Holkar...	do ...	47	25	22	...	...	...	...	...	...	...	...	...	...	...	...
		do ...	Icho	do ...	6	6	...	...	...	...	...	...	...	...	...	...	...	...	...
		do ...	Idge	do ...	2	2	...	...	...	...	...	...	...	...	...	...	...	...	...
		do ...	Ingle	do ...	558	294	264	...	...	...	...	...	...	...	...	...	...	...	...
		do ...	Isve	do ...	1	1	...	...	...	...	...	...	...	...	...	...	...	...	...
		do ...	Jabando	do ...	1	...	1	...	...	...	...	...	...	...	...	...	...	...	...
		do ...	Jabute...	do ...	8	2	1	...	...	...	...	...	...	...	...	...	...	...	...
		do ...	Jadalval	do ...	8	8	...	...	...	...	...	...	...	...	...	...	...	...	...
		do ...	Jadho	do ...	24,068	12,044	12,024	65	22	43	...	...	...	...	...	...	...	...	...
		do ...	Jagdal...	do ...	22	7	15	...	...	...	...	...	...	...	...	...	...	...	...
		do ...	Jagnab	do ...	1	1	...	1	1	...	...	...	...	...	...	...	...	...	...
		do ...	Jagtal	do ...	1	1	...	...	...	...	...	...	...	...	...	...	...	...	...
		do ...	Jagtap...	do ...	149	69	80	...	...	...	...	...	...	...	...	...	...	...	...
		do ...	Jagthale	do ...	79	43	36	...	...	...	...	...	...	...	...	...	...	...	...
		do ...	Jakate...	do ...	18	7	6	...	...	...	...	...	...	...	...	...	...	...	...
		do ...	Jakhle...	do ...	7	3	4	...	...	...	...	...	...	...	...	...	...	...	...
		do ...	Jamale	do ...	1	1	...	...	...	...	...	...	...	...	...	...	...	...	...
		do ...	Janesari	do ...	18	...	18	...	...	...	...	...	...	...	...	...	...	...	...
		do ...	Janvare	do ...	25	10	15	...	...	...	...	...	...	...	...	...	...	...	...
		do ...	Jaole	do ...	28	9	19	...	...	...	...	...	...	...	...	...	...	...	...

TABLE XVI.

Castes and Sub-divisions.—*Continued.*

Class.	Group.	Castes.	Sub-division of Castes.	Religion.	Warangal.			Elgandal.			Indur.			Medak.			Aurangabad.		
					Total.	Males.	Females.	Total.	Males.	Females.	Total.	Males.	Females.	Total.	Males.	Females.	Total.	Males.	Females.
					21	22	23	24	25	26	27	28	29	30	31	32	33	34	35
A	1 ...	Mahratta ...	Ghatvale	Hindu ...	...	...	...	...	...	...	...	...	...	...	...	...	84	84	...
		do ...	Ghoped	do ...	...	...	...	...	...	...	...	...	...	...	...	...	...	...	...
		do ...	Ghotak	do ...	...	...	...	...	...	...	...	...	...	...	...	...	...	...	...
		do ...	Giaramasi	do ...	...	...	...	...	...	...	...	...	...	...	...	...	...	...	...
		do ...	Gingne	do ...	...	...	...	...	...	...	...	...	...	...	...	...	...	...	...
		do ...	Gokule	do ...	...	...	...	...	...	...	...	...	...	...	...	...	...	...	...
		do ...	Gole	do ...	...	...	...	...	...	...	...	...	...	...	...	...	...	...	...
		do ...	Gotkar	do ...	...	...	...	...	...	...	...	...	...	...	...	...	...	...	...
		do ...	Goone	do ...	...	...	...	...	...	...	...	...	...	...	...	...	...	...	...
		do ...	Gorpade	do ...	...	...	...	...	...	...	...	...	...	...	...	...	...	...	...
		do ...	Gorud	do ...	...	...	...	...	...	...	...	...	...	...	...	...	...	...	...
		do ...	Got	do ...	...	...	...	...	...	...	...	...	...	...	...	...	...	...	...
		do ...	Gote	do ...	...	...	...	...	...	...	...	...	...	...	...	...	...	...	...
		do ...	Had	do ...	...	...	...	...	...	...	...	...	...	...	...	...	...	...	...
		do ...	Haladjole	do ...	...	...	...	...	...	...	...	...	...	...	...	...	244	116	128
		do ...	Halve	do ...	...	...	...	...	...	...	...	...	...	...	...	...	...	...	...
		do ...	Handelawaru	do ...	...	...	...	...	...	...	...	...	...	...	...	...	...	...	...
		do ...	Hare	do ...	...	...	...	...	...	...	...	...	...	...	...	...	81	...	31
		do ...	Hartako	do ...	...	...	...	...	...	...	...	...	...	...	...	...	...	...	...
		do ...	Hartal...	do ...	...	...	...	...	...	...	...	...	...	...	...	...	...	...	...
		do ...	Havanjat	do ...	...	...	...	...	...	...	...	...	...	...	...	...	...	...	...
		do ...	Hendri Marathi ...	do ...	...	...	...	...	...	...	...	...	...	...	...	...	...	...	...
		do ...	Hingnere	do ...	...	...	...	...	...	...	...	...	...	...	...	...	...	...	...
		do ...	Holkar...	do ...	...	...	...	...	...	...	...	...	...	...	...	...	...	...	...
		do ...	Icho	do ...	...	...	...	...	...	...	...	...	...	...	...	...	...	...	...
		do ...	Idgo	do ...	...	...	...	...	...	...	...	...	...	...	...	...	...	...	...
		do ...	Ingle	do ...	...	...	...	...	...	...	...	...	...	...	...	...	...	...	...
		do ...	Isve	do ...	...	...	...	...	...	...	1	1	...	...	...	...	...	...	...
		do ...	Jabande	do ...	...	...	...	...	...	...	...	...	...	...	...	...	...	...	...
		do ...	Jabute...	do ...	...	...	...	...	...	...	...	...	...	...	...	...	...	...	...
		do ...	Jadalval	do ...	...	...	...	...	...	...	...	...	...	...	...	...	...	...	...
		do ...	Jadho	do ...	...	...	...	...	...	...	698	885	863	...	...	...	128	65	63
		do ...	Jagdal...	do ...	...	...	...	...	...	...	...	...	...	...	...	...	...	...	...
		do ...	Jagnab	do ...	...	...	...	...	...	...	...	...	...	...	...	...	...	...	...
		do ...	Jagtal	do ...	...	...	...	...	...	...	...	...	...	...	...	...	...	...	...
		do ...	Jagtap...	do ...	...	...	...	...	...	...	...	...	...	...	...	...	...	...	...
		do ...	Jagthale	do ...	...	...	...	...	...	...	...	...	...	...	...	...	...	...	...
		do ...	Jakate...	do ...	...	...	...	...	...	...	...	...	...	...	...	...	...	...	...
		do ...	Jakhle...	do ...	...	...	...	...	...	...	...	...	...	...	...	...	...	...	...
		do ...	Jamale	do ...	...	...	...	...	...	...	...	...	...	...	...	...	...	...	...
		do ...	Janesari	do ...	...	...	...	...	...	...	...	...	...	...	...	...	...	...	...
		do ...	Janvaro	do ...	...	...	...	...	...	...	...	...	...	...	...	...	...	...	...
		do ...	Jaole	do ...	...	...	...	...	...	...	...	...	...	...	...	...	...	...	...

TABLE XVI.

Castes and Sub-divisions.—*Continued.*

Class.	Group.	Castes.	Sub-division of Castes.	Religion.	Birh. Total.	Birh. Males.	Birh. Females.	Nander. Total.	Nander. Males.	Nander. Females.	Naldrug. Total.	Naldrug. Males.	Naldrug. Females.	Bidar. Total.	Bidar. Males.	Bidar. Females.	Parbhani. Total.	Parbhani. Males.	Parbhani. Females.
					36	37	38	39	40	41	42	43	44	45	46	47	48	49	50
A	1 ...	Mahratta ...	Ghatvale	Hindu ...	...	...	...	...	...	...	...	...	...	...	...	...	...	...	...
		do ...	Ghoped	do ...	...	...	...	...	...	...	3	2	1	...	...	...	...	...	...
		do ...	Ghotak	do ...	...	...	...	...	...	...	...	...	...	31	15	16	...	...	...
		do ...	Giaramasl	do ...	...	...	...	...	...	...	...	...	...	...	...	...	...	...	...
		do ...	Gingno	do ...	5	2	3	...	...	...	46	20	26	...	...	...	...	...	...
		do ...	Gokule	do ...	...	...	...	...	...	...	...	...	...	6	2	4	...	...	...
		do ...	Gole	do ...	...	...	...	...	...	...	32	14	18	61	48	13	...	...	...
		do ...	Gotkar	do ...	...	...	...	42	32	10	...	...	...	...	...	...	...	...	...
		do ...	Goone	do ...	...	...	...	...	...	...	8	4	4	...	...	...	...	...	...
		do ...	Gorpade	do ...	...	...	...	...	...	...	...	...	...	...	...	...	...	...	...
		do ...	Gorud... ...	do ...	...	...	...	...	...	...	...	...	...	15	8	7	...	...	...
		do ...	Got	do ...	...	...	...	12	7	5	...	...	...	...	...	...	...	...	...
		do ...	Gote	do ...	...	...	...	...	...	...	3	...	3	...	...	...	...	...	...
		do ...	Had	do ...	...	...	...	37	2	35	...	...	...	...	...	...	...	...	...
		do ...	Haladjole	do ...	...	...	...	...	...	...	...	...	...	...	...	...	...	...	...
		do ...	Halve	do ...	...	...	...	...	...	...	5	2	3	...	...	...	...	...	...
		do ...	Handelawaru... ...	do ...	...	...	...	...	...	...	...	...	...	...	...	...	...	...	...
		do ...	Hare	do ...	...	...	...	...	...	...	...	...	...	...	...	...	...	...	...
		do ...	Hartake	do ...	...	...	...	...	...	...	6	1	5	...	...	...	...	...	...
		do ...	Hartal... ...	do ...	...	...	...	...	...	...	...	...	...	6	6	...	...	...	...
		do ...	Havanjat	do ...	...	...	...	...	...	...	4	2	2	...	...	...	...	...	...
		do ...	Hendri Marathi ...	do ...	...	...	...	...	...	...	...	...	...	...	...	...	...	...	...
		do ...	Hingnere	do ...	...	...	...	...	...	...	5	3	2	...	...	...	...	...	...
		do ...	Holkar	do ...	...	...	...	...	...	...	22	12	10	25	13	12	...	...	...
		do ...	Iche	do ...	6	6	...	...	...	...	...	...	...	...	...	...	...	...	...
		do ...	Idge	do ...	...	...	...	2	2	...	...	...	...	...	...	...	...	...	...
		do ...	Ingle	do ...	6	2	4	284	149	135	122	63	59	138	76	62	...	...	...
		do ...	Isve	do ...	...	...	...	...	...	...	...	...	...	...	...	...	...	...	...
		do ...	Jabando	do ...	...	...	...	...	...	...	1	...	1	...	...	...	...	...	...
		do ...	Jabute	do ...	...	...	...	...	...	...	3	2	1	...	...	...	...	...	...
		do ...	Jadalval	do ...	...	...	...	...	...	...	...	...	...	...	...	...	...	...	...
		do ...	Jadho	do ...	95	10	85	19,590	9,873	9,717	1,841	881	960	65	35	30	988	603	385
		do ...	Jagdal... ...	do ...	...	...	...	...	...	...	22	7	15	...	...	...	...	...	...
		do ...	Jagnab	do ...	...	...	...	...	...	...	...	...	...	...	...	...	...	...	...
		do ...	Jagtal... ...	do ...	...	...	...	...	...	...	...	...	...	...	...	...	...	...	...
		do ...	Jagtap... ...	do ...	29	15	14	...	...	...	119	53	66	...	...	...	1	1	...
		do ...	Jagthale	do ...	...	...	...	79	43	36	...	...	...	...	...	...	...	...	...
		do ...	Jakate... ...	do ...	...	...	...	...	...	...	13	7	6	...	...	...	...	...	...
		do ...	Jakhle... ...	do ...	...	...	...	7	3	4	...	...	...	...	...	...	...	...	...
		do ...	Jamale	do ...	...	...	...	1	1	...	...	...	...	...	...	...	...	...	...
		do ...	Janesari	do ...	...	...	...	...	...	...	...	...	...	...	...	...	...	...	...
		do ...	Janvare	do ...	...	...	...	...	...	...	25	10	15	...	...	...	...	...	...
		do ...	Jaole	do ...	...	...	...	4	4	...	15	5	10	...	...	...	...	...	...

TABLE XVI.

Castes and Sub-divisions.—*Continued.*

Class.	Group.	Castes.	Sub-division of Castes.	Religion.	Sirpur Tandur. Total.	Sirpur Tandur. Males.	Sirpur Tandur. Females.	Gulbarga. Total.	Gulbarga. Males.	Gulbarga. Females.	Raichur. Total.	Raichur. Males.	Raichur. Females.	Lingsugur. Total.	Lingsugur. Males.	Lingsugur. Females.	Railways. Total.	Railways. Males.	Railways. Females.
					51	52	53	54	55	56	57	58	59	60	61	62	63	64	65
A	1 ...	Mahratta ...	Ghatvale	Hindu ...	...	...	...	...	...	...	...	...	...	...	...	...	...	...	...
		do ...	Ghoped	do ...	...	...	...	...	...	...	...	...	...	...	...	...	...	...	...
		do ...	Ghotak	do ...	...	...	...	...	...	...	...	...	...	...	...	...	...	...	...
		do ...	Giaramasi	do ...	...	...	...	...	...	...	...	...	...	...	...	...	...	...	...
		do ...	Gingne	do ...	...	...	...	...	...	...	...	...	...	...	...	...	...	...	...
		do ...	Gokule	do ...	...	...	...	...	...	...	...	...	...	...	...	...	...	...	...
		do ...	Gale	do ...	...	...	...	...	...	...	...	...	...	...	...	...	...	...	...
		do ...	Gotkar	do ...	...	...	...	...	...	...	...	...	...	...	...	...	...	...	...
		do ...	Goone	do ...	...	...	...	...	...	...	...	...	...	...	...	...	...	...	...
		do ...	Gorpade	do ...	...	...	...	...	...	...	...	...	...	87	40	47	...	...	...
		do ...	Gorud...	do ...	...	...	...	...	...	...	...	...	...	...	...	...	...	...	...
		do ...	Got	do ...	...	...	...	...	...	...	...	...	...	...	...	...	...	...	...
		do ...	Geto	do ...	...	...	...	...	...	...	...	...	...	...	...	...	...	...	...
		do ...	Had	do ...	...	...	...	...	...	...	...	...	...	...	...	...	...	...	...
		do ...	Haladjolo	do ...	...	...	...	...	...	...	...	...	...	...	...	...	...	...	...
		do ...	Halve	do ...	...	...	...	...	...	...	...	...	...	...	...	...	...	...	...
		do ...	Handelawaru... ...	do ...	...	...	...	...	...	...	...	...	...	4	3	1	...	...	...
		do ...	Hare	do ...	...	...	...	...	...	...	...	...	...	...	...	...	...	...	...
		do ...	Hartake	do ...	...	...	...	...	...	...	...	...	...	...	...	...	...	...	...
		do ...	Hartal...	do ...	...	...	...	...	...	...	...	...	...	...	...	...	...	...	...
		do ...	Havanjat	do ...	...	...	...	...	...	...	...	...	...	...	...	...	...	...	...
		do ...	Hendri Marathi ...	do ...	167	82	85	...	...	...	...	...	...	...	...	...	...	...	...
		do ...	Hinguere	do ...	...	...	...	...	...	...	...	...	...	...	...	...	...	...	...
		do ...	Holkar	do ...	...	...	...	...	...	...	...	...	...	...	...	...	...	...	...
		do ...	Icho	do ...	...	...	...	...	...	...	...	...	...	...	...	...	...	...	...
		do ...	Idgo	do ...	...	...	...	...	...	...	...	...	...	...	...	...	...	...	...
		do ...	Ingle	do ...	...	...	...	8	4	4	...	...	...	...	...	...	...	...	...
		do ...	Isve	do ...	...	...	...	...	...	...	...	...	...	...	...	...	...	...	...
		do ...	Jabande	do ...	...	...	...	...	...	...	...	...	...	...	...	...	...	...	...
		do ...	Jabute	do ...	...	...	...	...	...	...	...	...	...	...	...	...	...	...	...
		do ...	Jadalval	do ...	3	3	...	...	...	...	...	...	...	...	...	...	...	...	...
		do ...	Jadho	do ...	25	18	7	493	159	334	41	22	19	39	21	18	...	...	...
		do ...	Jagdal	do ...	...	...	...	...	...	...	...	...	...	...	...	...	...	...	...
		do ...	Jagnab	do ...	...	...	...	...	...	...	...	...	...	...	...	...	...	...	...
		do ...	Jagtal...	do ...	...	...	...	...	...	...	...	...	...	1	1	...	...	...	...
		do ...	Jagtap	do ...	...	...	...	...	...	...	...	...	...	...	...	...	...	...	...
		do ...	Jagthale	do ...	...	...	...	...	...	...	...	...	...	...	...	...	...	...	...
		do ...	Jakate	do ...	...	...	...	...	...	...	...	...	...	...	...	...	...	...	...
		do ...	Jakhle	do ...	...	...	...	...	...	...	...	...	...	...	...	...	...	...	...
		do ...	Jamale	do ...	...	...	...	...	...	...	...	...	...	...	...	...	...	...	...
		do ...	Janesari	do ...	13	...	13	...	...	...	...	...	...	...	...	...	...	...	...
		do ...	Janvare	do ...	...	...	...	...	...	...	...	...	...	...	...	...	...	...	...
		do ...	Jaole	do ...	9	...	9	...	...	...	...	...	...	...	...	...	...	...	...

TABLE XVI.

Castes and Sub-divisions.—*Continued.*

Class.	Group.	Castes.	Sub-division of Castes.	Religion.	Total.			Hyderabad.			Atraf-i-Balda.			Mahabubnagar.			Nalgonda.		
					Total.	Males.	Females.	Total.	Males.	Females.	Total.	Males.	Females.	Total.	Males.	Females.	Total.	Males.	Females.
1	2	3	4	5	6	7	8	9	10	11	12	13	14	15	16	17	18	19	20
A	1 ...	Mahratta ...	Jaosagar	Hindu ...	81	12	19	...	...	...	...	...	...	...	...	...	...	...	...
		do ...	Japete	do ...	6	3	3	...	...	...	...	...	...	...	...	...	...	...	...
		do ...	Japhasan	do ...	1	1	...	...	...	...	...	...	...	...	...	...	...	...	...
		do ...	Jarbad	do ...	6	3	3	...	...	...	...	...	...	...	...	...	...	...	...
		do ...	Jate	do ...	8	6	2	...	...	...	...	...	...	...	...	...	...	...	...
		do ...	Jatpati	do ...	6	4	2	...	...	...	...	...	...	...	...	...	...	...	...
		do ...	Jasvan	do ...	30	22	8	30	22	8	...	...	...	...	...	...	...	...	...
		do ...	Jhamble	do ...	114	36	78	...	...	...	...	...	...	...	...	...	...	...	...
		do ...	Jhoned	do ...	7	4	3	...	...	...	...	...	...	...	...	...	...	...	...
		do ...	Jotvad	do ...	21	21	...	...	...	...	...	...	...	...	...	...	...	...	...
		do ...	Kadam	do ...	9,779	4,930	4,849	...	...	...	...	...	...	...	...	...	...	...	...
		do ...	Kadap... ...	do ...	58	26	32	...	...	...	...	...	...	...	...	...	...	...	...
		do ...	Kaddar	do ...	1	1	...	...	...	...	...	...	...	...	...	...	...	...	...
		do ...	Kadade	do ...	40	18	22	...	...	...	...	...	...	...	...	...	...	...	...
		do ...	Kadgar	do ...	39	21	18	...	...	...	...	...	...	...	...	...	...	...	...
		do ...	Kadikod	do ...	9	3	6	9	3	6	...	...	...	...	...	...	...	...	...
		do ...	Kadkan	do ...	2	...	2	...	...	...	...	...	...	...	...	...	...	...	...
		do ...	Kadsal	do ...	10	5	5	...	...	...	...	...	...	...	...	...	...	...	...
		do ...	Kaduri	do ...	8	4	4	...	...	...	...	...	...	...	...	...	...	...	...
		do ...	Kahankar	do ...	8	4	4	...	...	...	...	...	...	...	...	...	...	...	...
		do ...	Kaka	do ...	8	7	1	...	...	...	...	...	...	...	...	...	...	...	...
		do ...	Kakde... ...	do ...	15	9	6	...	...	...	...	...	...	...	...	...	...	...	...
		do ...	Kakse... ...	do ...	7	5	2	...	...	...	...	...	...	...	...	...	...	...	...
		do ...	Kalanki	do ...	19	8	11	...	...	...	...	...	...	...	...	...	...	...	...
		do ...	Kale	do ...	823	302	521	...	...	...	...	...	...	...	...	...	...	...	...
		do ...	Kalleyan	do ...	19	15	4	...	...	...	...	...	...	...	...	...	...	...	...
		do ...	Kamle... ...	do ...	115	30	85	...	...	...	...	...	...	...	...	...	...	...	...
		do ...	Kansaie	do ...	10	6	4	...	...	...	...	...	...	...	...	...	...	...	...
		do ...	Kanshia	do ...	10	5	5	...	...	...	...	...	...	...	...	...	...	...	...
		do ...	Kaolibar	do ...	28	...	28	...	...	...	...	...	...	...	...	...	...	...	...
		do ...	Kar	do ...	137	54	83	137	54	83	...	...	...	...	...	...	...	...	...
		do ...	Karanwar	do ...	2	1	1	...	...	...	...	...	...	...	...	...	...	...	...
		do ...	Karle	do ...	38	17	21	...	...	...	...	...	...	...	...	...	...	...	...
		do ...	Karnag	do ...	19	11	8	...	...	...	...	...	...	...	...	...	...	...	...
		do ...	Karod... ...	do ...	7	4	3	...	...	...	...	...	...	...	...	...	...	...	...
		do ...	Kasdi	do ...	26	12	14	...	...	...	...	...	...	...	...	...	...	...	...
		do ...	Katvat	do ...	9	6	3	...	...	...	...	...	...	...	...	...	...	...	...
		do ...	Kavi Mahratti ...	do ...	18	18	...	...	...	...	...	...	...	...	...	...	...	...	...
		do ...	Kedar... ...	do ...	17	8	9	...	...	...	...	...	...	...	...	...	...	...	...
		do ...	Keni	do ...	47	46	1	...	...	...	...	...	...	...	...	...	...	...	...
		do ...	Khalbhangi	do ...	9	4	5	...	...	...	...	...	...	...	...	...	...	...	...
		do ...	Khamunsar	do ...	4	1	3	...	...	...	...	...	...	...	...	...	...	...	...
		do ...	Khaolo	do ...	38	20	18	...	...	...	...	...	...	...	...	...	...	...	...

TABLE XVI.

Castes and Sub-divisions.—*Continued.*

Class.	Group.	Castes.	Sub-division of Castes.	Religion.	Warangal. Total.	Warangal. Males.	Warangal. Females.	Elgandal. Total.	Elgandal. Males.	Elgandal. Females.	Indur. Total.	Indur. Males.	Indur. Females.	Medak. Total.	Medak. Males.	Medak. Females.	Aurangabad. Total.	Aurangabad. Males.	Aurangabad. Females.
					21	22	23	24	25	26	27	28	29	30	31	32	33	34	35
A	1 ...	Mahratta ...	Jaosagar	Hindu ...	...	...	...	...	...	...	...	...	...	...	...	...	...	...	...
		do ...	Japete...	do ...	...	...	...	...	...	...	...	...	...	...	...	...	...	...	...
		do ...	Japhasan	do ...	...	...	...	...	...	...	...	...	...	...	...	...	...	...	...
		do ...	Jarbad	do ...	...	...	...	...	...	...	...	...	...	...	...	...	...	...	...
		do ...	Jato	do ...	...	...	...	...	...	...	...	...	...	...	...	...	...	...	...
		do ...	Jatpati	do ...	...	...	...	...	...	...	...	...	...	...	...	...	...	...	...
		do ...	Jasvan	do ...	...	...	...	...	...	...	...	...	...	...	...	...	...	...	...
		do ...	Jhamble	do ...	...	...	...	...	...	...	...	...	...	...	...	...	...	...	...
		do ...	Jhoned	do ...	...	...	...	...	...	...	...	...	...	...	...	...	...	...	...
		do ...	Jotvad	do ...	...	...	...	...	...	...	...	...	...	...	...	...	...	...	...
		do ...	Kadam	do ...	...	...	...	...	...	...	205	110	95	...	...	...	19	11	8
		do ...	Kadap	do ...	...	...	...	...	...	...	...	...	...	...	...	...	58	26	82
		do ...	Kaddar	do ...	...	...	...	...	...	...	...	...	...	...	...	...	...	...	...
		do ...	Kadade	do ...	...	...	...	...	...	...	...	...	...	...	...	...	40	18	22
		do ...	Kadgar	do ...	...	...	...	...	...	...	...	...	...	...	...	...	...	...	...
		do ...	Kadikod	do ...	...	...	...	...	...	...	...	...	...	...	...	...	...	...	...
		do ...	Kadkan	do ...	...	...	...	...	...	...	...	...	...	...	...	...	...	...	...
		do ...	Kadsal	do ...	...	...	...	...	...	...	...	...	...	...	...	...	...	...	...
		do ...	Kaduri	do ...	...	...	...	...	...	...	...	...	...	...	...	...	8	4	4
		do ...	Kahankar	do ...	...	...	...	...	...	...	...	...	...	...	...	...	...	...	...
		do ...	Kaka	do ...	...	...	...	...	...	...	...	...	...	...	...	...	...	...	...
		do ...	Kakdo...	do ...	...	...	...	...	...	...	...	...	...	...	...	...	...	...	...
		do ...	Kakse	do ...	...	...	...	...	...	...	...	...	...	...	...	...	...	...	...
		do ...	Kalanki	do ...	...	...	...	...	...	...	...	...	...	...	...	...	...	...	...
		do ...	Kale	do ...	...	...	...	...	...	...	...	...	...	...	...	...	...	...	...
		do ...	Kalleyan	do ...	...	...	...	...	...	...	...	...	...	...	...	...	...	...	...
		do ...	Kamle...	do ...	...	...	...	...	...	...	...	...	...	...	...	...	...	...	...
		do ...	Kansaie	do ...	...	...	...	...	...	...	...	...	...	...	...	...	...	...	...
		do ...	Kanshia	do ...	...	...	...	...	...	...	...	...	...	...	...	...	...	...	...
		do ...	Kaolibar	do ...	...	...	...	...	...	...	...	...	...	...	...	...	...	...	...
		do ...	Kar	do ...	...	...	...	...	...	...	...	...	...	...	...	...	...	...	...
		do ...	Karanwar	do ...	...	...	...	...	...	...	...	...	...	...	...	...	...	...	...
		do ...	Karlo	do ...	...	...	...	...	...	...	...	...	...	...	...	...	...	...	...
		do ...	Karnag	do ...	...	...	...	...	...	...	...	...	...	...	...	...	...	...	...
		do ...	Karod...	do ...	...	...	...	...	...	...	...	...	...	...	...	...	...	...	...
		do ...	Kasdi	do ...	...	...	...	...	...	...	...	...	...	...	...	...	...	...	...
		do ...	Katvat	do ...	...	...	...	...	...	...	...	...	...	...	...	...	...	...	...
		do ...	Kavi Mahratti ...	do ...	...	...	...	...	...	...	...	...	...	...	...	...	...	...	...
		do ...	Kedar...	do ...	...	...	...	...	...	...	1	1	...	...	...	...	...	...	...
		do ...	Keni	do ...	...	...	...	...	...	...	...	...	...	...	...	...	46	46	...
		do ...	Khalbhangi	do ...	...	...	...	...	...	...	...	...	...	...	...	...	9	4	5
		do ...	Khamunsar	do ...	...	...	...	...	...	...	...	...	...	...	...	...	...	...	...
		do ...	Khaole	do ...	...	...	...	...	...	...	...	...	...	...	...	...	...	...	...

TABLE XVI.
Castes and Sub-divisions.

TABLE XVI.

Castes and Sub-divisions—*Continued.*

Class.	Group.	Castes.	Sub-division of Castes.	Religion.	Bhir. Total.	Bhir. Males.	Bhir. Females.	Nander. Total.	Nander. Males.	Nander. Females.	Naldrug. Total.	Naldrug. Males.	Naldrug. Females.	Bidar. Total.	Bidar. Males.	Bidar. Females.	Parbhani. Total.	Parbhani. Males.	Parbhani. Females.
					36	37	38	39	40	41	42	43	44	45	46	47	48	49	50
A	1 ...	Mahratta ...	Jacsagar	Hindu ...	...	...	...	...	...	...	... 6	...	...	31	12	19	...	...	...
		do ...	Japete...	do ...	...	...	...	...	...	...	1	3	3	...	...	...	...	...	...
		do ...	Japhasan	do ...	...	...	...	...	...	...	...	1	...	...	...	...	...	...	...
		do ...	Jarbad	do ...	...	...	...	6	3	3	...	...	...	...	...	...	...	...	...
		do ...	Jate	do ...	...	...	...	...	...	...	8	6	2	...	...	...	...	...	...
		do ...	Jatpati... ...	do ...	...	...	...	6	4	2	...	...	...	...	...	...	...	...	...
		do ...	Jasvan	do ...	...	...	...	...	...	...	...	...	...	...	...	...	...	...	...
		do ...	Jhamble	do ...	...	...	...	75	7	68	20	16	4	19	13	6	...	...	...
		do ...	Jhoned	do ...	...	...	...	...	...	...	7	4	3	...	...	...	...	...	...
		do ...	Jotvad...	do ...	...	...	...	...	...	...	...	...	...	...	...	...	...	...	...
		do ...	Kadam	do ...	...	...	...	6,327	3,173	3,154	995	515	480	2,090	1,072	1,018	140	46	94
		do ...	Kadap...	do ...	...	...	...	...	...	...	...	...	...	...	...	...	...	...	...
		do ...	Kaddar	do ...	...	...	...	...	...	...	1	1	...	...	...	...	...	...	...
		do ...	Kadado	do ...	...	...	...	...	...	...	...	...	...	...	...	...	...	...	...
		do ...	Kadgar	do ...	...	...	...	...	...	...	89	21	18	...	...	...	...	...	...
		do ...	Kadikod	do ...	...	...	...	...	...	...	...	...	...	...	...	...	...	...	...
		do ...	Kadkan	do ...	...	...	...	2	...	2	...	...	...	...	...	...	...	...	...
		do ...	Kadsal	do ...	...	...	...	10	5	5	...	...	...	...	...	...	...	...	...
		do ...	Kaduri	do ...	...	...	...	...	...	...	...	...	...	...	...	...	...	...	...
		do ...	Kahankar	do ...	8	4	4	...	...	...	...	...	...	...	...	...	...	...	...
		do ...	Kaka	do ...	...	...	...	...	...	...	8	7	1	...	...	...	...	...	...
		do ...	Kakde	do ...	...	...	...	...	...	...	15	9	6	...	...	...	...	...	...
		do ...	Kakse	do ...	...	...	...	...	...	...	7	5	2	...	...	...	...	...	...
		do ...	Kalatki	do ...	...	...	...	...	...	...	...	...	...	...	...	...	...	...	...
		do ...	Kale	do ...	...	...	...	166	5	161	...	...	...	619	297	322	...	...	...
		do ...	Kalleyan	do ...	...	...	...	19	15	4	...	...	...	...	...	...	...	...	...
		do ...	Kamle	do ...	...	...	...	50	50	...	52	22	30	13	8	5	...	...	...
		do ...	Kansaie	do ...	...	...	...	...	...	...	...	...	...	10	6	4	...	...	...
		do ...	Kanihia	do ...	...	...	...	...	...	...	10	5	5	...	...	...	...	...	...
		do ...	Kaolibar	do ...	...	...	...	...	...	...	...	...	...	...	...	...	...	...	...
		do ...	Kar	do ...	...	...	...	...	...	...	...	...	...	...	...	...	...	...	...
		do ...	Karanwar	do ...	...	...	...	...	...	...	2	1	1	...	...	...	...	...	...
		do ...	Karle	do ...	...	...	...	...	...	...	...	...	...	...	...	...	38	17	21
		do ...	Karnag	do ...	...	...	...	19	11	8	...	...	...	...	...	...	...	...	...
		do ...	Kared	do ...	...	...	...	...	...	...	7	4	3	...	...	...	...	...	...
		do ...	Kasdi	do ...	...	...	...	2	...	2	...	...	...	...	...	...	...	...	...
		do ...	Katvat	do ...	...	...	...	...	...	...	9	6	3	...	...	...	...	...	...
		do ...	Kavi Mahratti ...	do ...	...	...	...	...	...	...	...	...	...	...	...	...	...	...	...
		do ...	Kedar	do ...	...	...	...	...	...	...	11	5	6	5	2	3	...	...	...
		do ...	Keni	do ...	...	...	...	...	...	...	1	...	1	...	...	...	...	...	...
		do ...	Khalbhangi	do ...	...	...	...	...	...	...	...	...	...	...	...	...	...	...	...
		do ...	Khamunsar	do ...	...	...	...	...	...	...	4	1	3	...	...	...	...	...	...
		do ...	Khaole	do ...	...	...	...	...	...	...	38	20	18	...	...	...	...	...	...

TABLE XVI.

Castes and Sub-divisions.—*Continued.*

Class.	Group.	Castes.	Sub-division of Castes.	Religion.	Sirpur Tandur. Total.	Sirpur Tandur. Males.	Sirpur Tandur. Females.	Gulbarga. Total.	Gulbarga. Males.	Gulbarga. Females.	Raichur. Total.	Raichur. Males.	Raichur. Females.	Lingsugur. Total.	Lingsugur. Males.	Lingsugur. Females.	Railways. Total.	Railways. Males.	Railways. Females.
					51	52	53	54	55	56	57	58	59	60	61	62	63	64	65
A	1 ...	Mahratta ...	Jasangar	Hindu ...	...	...	...	...	...	...	...	...	...	...	...	...	...	...	...
		do ...	Japete...	do ...	...	...	...	...	...	...	...	...	...	...	...	...	...	...	...
		do ...	Japhasan	do ...	...	...	...	...	...	...	...	...	...	...	...	...	...	...	...
		do ...	Jarbad	do ...	...	...	...	...	...	...	...	...	...	...	...	...	...	...	...
		do ...	Jate	do ...	...	...	...	...	...	...	...	...	...	...	...	...	...	...	...
		do ...	Jatpati	do ...	...	...	...	...	...	...	...	...	...	...	...	...	...	...	...
		do ...	Jasvan	do ...	...	...	...	...	...	...	...	...	...	...	...	...	...	...	...
		do ...	Jhamble	do ...	...	...	...	...	...	...	...	...	...	...	...	...	...	...	...
		do ...	Jhoned	do ...	...	...	...	...	...	...	...	...	...	...	...	...	...	...	...
		do ...	Jotvad	do ...	21	21	...	...	...	...	...	...	...	...	...	...	...	...	...
		do ...	Kadam	do ...	8	8	...	...	...	...	...	...	...	...	...	...	...	...	...
		do ...	Kadap...	do ...	...	...	...	...	...	...	...	...	...	...	...	...	...	...	...
		do ...	Kaddar	do ...	...	...	...	...	...	...	...	...	...	...	...	...	...	...	...
		do ...	Kadade	do ...	...	...	—	...	...	...	...	...	...	...	...	...	...	...	...
		do ...	Kadgar	do ...	...	...	...	...	...	...	...	...	...	...	...	...	...	...	...
		do ...	Kadikod	do ...	...	...	...	...	...	...	...	...	...	...	...	...	...	...	...
		do ...	Kadkan	do ...	...	...	...	...	...	...	...	...	...	...	...	...	...	...	...
		do ...	Kadsal	do ...	...	...	...	...	...	...	...	...	...	...	...	...	...	...	...
		do ...	Kaduri	do ...	...	...	...	...	...	...	...	...	...	...	...	...	...	...	...
		do ...	Kahankar	do ...	...	...	...	...	...	...	...	...	...	...	...	...	...	...	...
		do ...	Kaka...	do ...	...	...	...	...	...	...	...	...	...	...	...	...	...	...	...
		do ...	Kakde...	do ...	...	...	...	...	...	...	...	...	...	...	...	...	...	...	...
		do ...	Kakse...	do ...	...	...	...	...	...	...	...	...	...	...	...	...	...	...	...
		do ...	Kalanki	do ...	...	...	...	...	...	...	...	...	...	19	8	11	...	...	...
		do ...	Kale	do ...	38	...	38	...	...	...	...	...	...	...	...	...	...	...	...
		do ...	Kalleyan	do ...	...	...	...	...	...	...	...	...	...	...	...	...	...	...	...
		do ...	Kamle...	do ...	...	...	...	...	...	...	...	...	...	...	...	...	...	...	...
		do ...	Kansaie	do ...	...	...	...	...	...	...	...	...	...	...	...	...	...	...	...
		do ...	Kanshia	do ...	...	...	...	...	...	...	...	...	...	...	...	...	...	...	...
		do ...	Kaolibar	do ...	...	...	...	...	...	...	...	...	...	28	...	28	...	...	...
		do ...	Kar	do ...	...	...	...	...	...	...	...	...	...	...	...	...	...	...	...
		do ...	Karanwar	do ...	...	...	...	...	...	...	...	...	...	...	...	...	...	...	...
		do ...	Karle	do ...	...	...	...	...	...	...	...	...	...	...	...	...	...	...	...
		do ...	Karnag	do ...	...	...	...	...	...	...	...	...	...	...	...	...	...	...	...
		do ...	Karod	do ...	...	...	...	...	...	...	...	...	...	...	...	...	...	...	...
		do ...	Kasdi	do ...	24	12	12	...	...	...	...	...	...	...	...	...	...	...	...
		do ...	Katvat	do ...	...	...	...	...	...	...	...	...	...	...	...	...	...	...	...
		do ...	Kavi Mahratti ...	do ...	18	18	...	...	...	...	...	...	...	...	...	...	...	...	...
		do ...	Kedar	do ...	...	...	...	...	...	...	...	...	...	...	...	...	...	...	...
		do ...	Keni	do ...	...	...	...	...	...	...	...	...	...	...	...	...	...	...	...
		do ...	Khalbhangi	do ...	...	...	...	...	...	...	...	...	...	...	...	...	...	...	...
		do ...	Khamunsar	do ...	...	...	...	...	...	...	...	...	...	...	...	...	...	...	...
		do ...	Khaole	do	...	...	...	...	...	...	...	...	...	...	...	...	...	...	...

TABLE XVI.

Castes and Sub-divisions.—*Continued.*

Class.	Group.	Castes.	Sub-division of Castes.	Religion.	Total.			Hyderabad.			Atraf-i-Balda.			Mahabubnagar.			Nalgonda.		
					Total.	Males.	Females.	Total.	Males.	Females.	Total.	Males.	Females.	Total.	Males.	Females.	Total.	Males.	Females.
1	2	3	4	5	6	7	8	9	10	11	12	13	14	15	16	17	18	19	20
A	1 ...	Mahratta ...	Kharale	Hindu ...	144	75	69	...	...	...	...	...	...	...	...	...	...	...	...
		do ...	Kharde	do ...	5	3	2	...	...	...	...	...	...	...	...	...	...	...	...
		do ...	Khare...	do ...	217	123	94	...	...	...	...	...	...	...	...	...	...	...	...
		do ...	Kharkhod	do ...	6	3	3	...	...	...	...	...	...	...	...	...	...	...	...
		do ...	Khatvan	do ...	19	...	19	...	...	...	...	...	...	...	...	...	...	...	...
		do ...	Khedkar	do ...	149	82	67	...	...	...	...	...	...	...	...	...	...	...	...
		do ...	Khodke	do ...	16	12	4	...	...	...	...	...	...	...	...	...	...	...	...
		do ...	Khoshi	do ...	5	...	5	...	...	...	...	...	...	...	...	...	...	...	...
		do ...	Khutevat	do ...	96	56	40	...	...	...	...	...	...	...	...	...	...	...	...
		do ...	Kokar	do ...	10	1	9	...	...	...	...	...	...	...	...	...	...	...	...
		do ...	Koaher	do ...	6	6	...	...	...	...	...	...	...	...	...	...	...	...	...
		do ...	Kor	do ...	25	10	15	...	...	...	...	...	...	...	...	...	...	...	...
		do ...	Korsale	do ...	879	429	450	...	...	...	...	...	...	...	...	...	...	...	...
		do ...	Kote	do ...	8	8	...	...	...	...	...	...	...	...	...	...	...	...	...
		do ...	Kotle	do ...	16	16	...	...	...	...	...	...	...	...	...	...	...	...	...
		do ...	Lad	do ...	84	4	80	84	4	30	...	...	...	...	...	...	...	...	...
		do ...	Lagaya	do ...	4	4	...	4	4	...	...	...	...	...	...	...	...	...	...
		do ...	Lalsi	do ...	12	7	5	...	...	...	...	...	...	...	...	...	...	...	...
		do ...	Lamara	do ...	4	2	2	...	...	...	...	...	...	...	...	...	...	...	...
		do ...	Lasupne	do ...	12	...	12	...	...	...	...	...	...	...	...	...	...	...	...
		do ...	Lugde...	do ...	8	2	1	...	...	...	...	...	...	...	...	...	...	...	...
		do ...	Mabhal	do ...	8	1	2	...	...	...	...	...	...	...	...	...	...	...	...
		do ...	Madan	do ...	5	1	4	...	...	...	...	...	...	...	...	...	...	...	...
		do ...	Magtol	do ...	1	1	...	...	...	...	...	...	...	...	...	...	...	...	...
		do ...	Mahave	do ...	785	409	376	...	...	...	...	...	...	...	...	...	...	...	...
		do ...	Mainavat	do ...	99	...	99	...	...	...	...	...	...	...	...	...	...	...	...
		do ...	Maine	do ...	2,018	879	1,139	...	...	...	...	...	...	...	...	...	...	...	...
		do ...	Maki	do ...	3	2	1	3	2	1	...	...	...	...	...	...	...	...	...
		do ...	Malve...	do ...	16	9	7	...	...	...	...	...	...	...	...	...	...	...	...
		do ...	Mandria	do ...	4	2	2	4	2	2	...	...	...	...	...	...	...	...	...
		do ...	Mane	do ...	550	819	231	...	...	...	...	...	...	...	...	...	...	...	...
		do ...	Manjre	do ...	7	...	7	...	...	...	...	...	...	...	...	...	...	...	...
		do ...	Maoge...	do ...	4	4	...	...	...	...	...	...	...	...	...	...	...	...	...
		do ...	Marul	do ...	8	6	2	...	...	...	...	...	...	...	...	...	...	...	...
		do ...	Masik	do ...	30	15	15	...	...	...	...	...	...	...	...	...	...	...	...
		do ...	Maske	do ...	18	8	10	...	...	...	...	...	...	...	...	...	...	...	...
		do ...	Mate	do ...	10	4	6	...	...	...	...	...	...	...	...	...	...	...	...
		do ...	Mathsar	do ...	14	8	6	14	8	6	...	...	...	...	...	...	...	...	...
		do ...	Medhavant	do ...	22	11	11	...	...	...	...	...	...	...	...	...	...	...	...
		do ...	Meher	do ...	21	7	14	...	...	...	...	...	...	...	...	...	...	...	...
		do ...	Mogal...	do ...	8	4	4	...	...	...	...	...	...	...	...	...	...	...	...
		do ...	Mogan	do ...	9	5	4	9	5	4	...	...	...	...	...	...	...	...	...
		do ...	More	do ...	3,232	1,682	1,550	1	1	...	...	...	...	...	...	...	...	...	...
		do ...	Mundkar	do ...	1	1	...	...	...	...	...	...	...	...	...	...	...	...	...

TABLE XVI.

Castes and Sub-divisions.—*Continued.*

Class.	Group.	Castes.	Sub-division of Castes.	Religion.	Warangal. Total.	Warangal. Males.	Warangal. Females.	Elgandal. Total.	Elgandal. Males.	Elgandal. Females.	Indur. Total.	Indur. Males.	Indur. Females.	Medak. Total.	Medak. Males.	Medak. Females.	Aurangabad. Total.	Aurangabad. Males.	Aurangabad. Females.
					21	22	23	24	25	26	27	28	29	30	31	32	33	34	35
A	1 ...	Mahratta ...	Kharale	Hindu ...	...	...	...	...	...	...	...	...	...	...	...	...	...	...	...
		do ...	Kharde	do ...	...	...	...	...	...	...	...	...	...	...	...	...	...	...	...
		do ...	Khare	do ...	...	...	...	...	...	...	...	...	...	...	...	...	...	...	...
		do ...	Kharkhod	do ...	...	...	...	...	...	...	...	...	...	...	...	...	...	...	...
		do ...	Khatvan	do ...	...	...	...	...	...	...	...	...	...	...	...	...	...	...	...
		do ...	Khedkar	do ...	...	...	...	...	...	...	...	...	...	...	...	...	...	...	...
		do ...	Khodke	do ...	...	...	...	...	...	...	...	...	...	...	...	...	...	...	...
		do ...	Khoshi	do ...	...	...	...	...	...	...	...	...	...	...	...	...	...	...	...
		do ...	Khutevat	do ...	...	...	...	...	...	...	...	...	...	...	...	...	...	...	...
		do ...	Kokar...	do ...	...	...	...	...	...	...	...	...	...	...	...	...	...	...	...
		do ...	Konher	do ...	...	...	...	...	...	...	...	...	...	...	...	...	...	...	...
		do ...	Kor	do ...	...	...	...	...	...	...	...	...	...	...	...	...	6	6	...
		do ...	Korsale	do ...	...	...	...	...	...	...	...	...	...	...	...	...	...	...	...
		do ...	Kote	do ...	...	...	...	...	...	...	...	...	...	...	...	...	...	...	...
		do ...	Kotle	do ...	...	...	...	...	...	...	...	...	...	...	...	...	...	...	...
		do ...	Lad	do ...	...	...	...	...	...	...	...	...	...	...	...	...	...	...	...
		do ...	Lagaya	do ...	...	...	...	...	...	...	...	...	...	...	...	...	...	...	...
		do ...	Lalsi	do ...	...	...	...	...	...	...	...	...	...	...	...	...	...	...	...
		do ...	Lamara	do ...	...	...	...	...	...	...	...	...	...	...	...	...	...	...	...
		do ...	Lasupne	do ...	...	...	...	...	...	...	...	...	...	...	...	...	...	...	...
		do ...	Lugde...	do ...	...	...	...	...	...	...	...	...	...	...	...	...	...	...	...
		do ...	Mabhal	do ...	...	...	...	...	...	...	...	...	...	...	...	...	...	...	...
		do ...	Madan	do ...	...	...	...	...	...	...	...	...	...	...	...	...	...	...	...
		do ...	Magtol	do ...	...	...	...	...	...	...	...	...	...	...	...	...	...	...	...
		do ...	Mahave ...	do ...	...	...	...	...	...	...	...	...	...	...	...	...	...	...	...
		do ...	Mainavat ...	do ...	...	...	...	...	...	...	...	...	...	...	...	...	...	...	...
		do ...	Maine...	do ...	...	...	...	...	...	...	...	...	...	...	...	...	...	...	...
		do ...	Maki	do ...	...	...	...	...	...	...	...	...	...	...	...	...	...	...	...
		do ...	Malve...	do ...	...	...	...	...	...	...	...	...	...	...	...	...	...	...	...
		do ...	Mandria	do ...	...	...	...	...	...	...	...	...	...	...	...	...	...	...	...
		do ...	Mane	do ...	...	...	...	...	...	...	76	37	39	...	...	...	...	...	...
		do ...	Manjre	do ...	...	...	...	...	...	...	...	...	...	...	...	...	...	...	...
		do ...	Maoge	do ...	...	...	...	...	...	...	...	...	...	...	...	...	4	4	...
		do ...	Marul...	do ...	...	...	...	...	...	...	...	...	...	...	...	...	...	...	...
		do ...	Masik	do ...	...	...	...	...	...	...	...	...	...	...	...	...	...	...	...
		do ...	Maske...	do ...	...	...	...	...	...	...	...	...	...	...	...	...	...	...	...
		do ...	Mate	do ...	...	...	...	...	...	...	...	...	...	...	...	...	...	...	...
		do ...	Mathsar	do ...	...	...	...	...	...	...	...	...	...	...	...	...	...	...	...
		do ...	Medhavant	do ...	...	...	...	...	...	...	...	...	...	...	...	...	...	...	...
		do ...	Meher...	do ...	...	...	...	...	...	...	...	...	...	...	...	...	...	...	...
		do ...	Mogal...	do ...	...	...	...	...	...	...	...	...	...	...	...	...	...	...	...
		do ...	Mogan	do ...	...	...	...	...	...	...	...	...	...	...	...	...	...	...	...
		do ...	Moro	do ...	...	...	...	...	...	...	...	...	...	...	...	...	...	...	...
		do ...	Mundkar	do ...	...	...	...	...	...	...	...	...	...	...	...	...	...	...	...

TABLE XVI.

Castes and Sub-divisions.

TABLE XVI.

Castes and Sub-divisions.—*Continued.*

Class.	Group.	Castes.	Sub-division of Castes.	Religion.	Birh. Total.	Birh. Males.	Birh. Females.	Nander. Total.	Nander. Males.	Nander. Females.	Naldrug. Total.	Naldrug. Males.	Naldrug. Females.	Bidar. Total.	Bidar. Males.	Bidar. Females.	Parbhani. Total.	Parbhani. Males.	Parbhani. Females.
					36	37	38	39	40	41	42	43	44	45	46	47	48	49	50
A	1 ...	Mahratta ...	Kharale	Hindu ...	...	...	...	33	19	14	111	56	55	...	...	...	...	...	...
		do ...	Kharde	do ...	...	...	...	...	...	...	5	3	2	...	...	...	...	...	...
		do ...	Khare...	do ...	...	...	...	...	...	...	...	...	...	...	...	...	...	...	...
		do ...	Kharkhod	do ...	...	...	...	...	...	...	6	3	3	...	...	...	...	...	...
		do ...	Khatvan	do ...	19	...	19	...	...	...	...	...	...	...	...	...	...	...	...
		do ...	Khedkar	do ...	...	...	...	136	70	66	...	...	...	13	12	1	...	...	...
		do ...	Khodke	do ...	...	...	...	7	7	...	9	5	4	...	...	...	...	...	...
		do ...	Khoshi	do ...	...	...	...	5	...	5	...	...	...	...	...	...	...	...	...
		do ...	Khutevat	do ...	...	...	...	96	56	40	...	...	...	...	...	...	...	...	...
		do ...	Kokar...	do ...	...	...	...	10	1	9	...	...	...	...	...	...	...	...	...
		do ...	Konher	do ...	...	...	...	...	...	...	...	...	...	...	...	...	...	...	...
		do ...	Kor	do ...	...	...	...	...	...	...	25	10	15	...	...	...	...	...	...
		do ...	Korsala	do ...	...	...	...	...	...	...	...	...	...	86	...	86	...	...	...
		do ...	Kote	do ...	...	...	...	...	...	...	3	3	...	...	...	...	...	...	...
		do ...	Kotle	do ...	...	...	...	...	...	...	...	...	...	16	16	...	...	...	...
		do ...	Lad	do ...	...	...	...	...	...	...	...	...	...	...	...	...	...	...	...
		do ...	Lagaya	do ...	...	...	...	...	...	...	...	...	...	...	...	...	...	...	...
		do ...	Lalsi	do ...	...	...	...	...	...	...	...	...	...	...	...	...	...	...	...
		do ...	Lamara	do ...	...	...	...	...	...	...	...	...	...	...	...	...	...	...	...
		do ...	Lasupne	do ...	...	...	...	12	...	12	...	...	...	...	...	...	...	...	...
		do ...	Lugde...	do ...	...	...	...	...	...	...	3	2	1	...	...	...	...	...	...
		do ...	Mabhal	do ...	...	...	...	...	...	...	...	...	...	3	1	2	...	...	...
		do ...	Madan	do ...	...	...	...	...	...	...	...	...	...	5	1	4	...	...	...
		do ...	Magtol	do ...	1	1	...	...	...	...	...	...	...	...	...	...	...	...	...
		do ...	Mahave	do ...	...	...	...	785	409	376	...	...	...	...	...	...	...	...	...
		do ...	Mainavat	do ...	99	...	99	...	...	...	...	...	...	...	...	...	...	...	...
		do ...	Maine...	do ...	...	...	...	...	...	...	24	15	9	1,974	854	1,120	...	...	...
		do ...	Maki	do ...	...	...	...	...	...	...	...	...	...	...	...	...	...	...	...
		do ...	Malve...	do ...	...	...	...	...	...	...	16	9	7	...	...	...	...	...	...
		do ...	Mandria	do ...	...	...	...	...	...	...	...	...	...	...	...	...	...	...	...
		do ...	Mane	do ...	...	...	...	75	65	10	399	217	182	...	...	...	...	...	...
		do ...	Manjre	do ...	...	...	...	7	...	7	...	...	...	...	...	...	...	...	...
		do ...	Mauge...	do ...	...	...	...	...	...	...	...	...	...	...	...	...	...	...	...
		do ...	Marul...	do ...	...	...	...	...	...	...	...	...	...	8	6	2	...	...	...
		do ...	Masik	do ...	...	...	...	10	7	3	15	8	7	...	...	...	...	...	...
		do ...	Maske	do ...	...	...	...	11	6	5	7	2	5	...	...	...	...	...	...
		do ...	Mate	do ...	...	...	...	...	...	...	6	3	3	4	1	3	...	...	...
		do ...	Mathsar	do ...	...	...	...	...	...	...	...	...	...	...	...	...	...	...	...
		do ...	Medhavant	do ...	...	...	...	...	...	...	22	11	11	...	...	...	...	...	...
		do ...	Meher...	do ...	...	...	...	...	...	...	8	2	6	28	6	22	...	...	...
		do ...	Mogal...	do ...	...	...	...	...	...	...	...	...	...	8	4	4	...	...	...
		do ...	Mogan	do ...	...	...	...	...	...	...	...	...	...	...	...	...	...	...	...
		do ...	More	do ...	...	...	...	920	457	463	888	188	200	1,905	1,028	877	...	...	...
		do ...	Mundkar	do ...	...	...	...	...	...	...	...	...	...	...	...	...	1	1	...

TABLE XVI.

Castes and Sub-divisions.—*Continued.*

Class.	Group.	Castes.	Subdivision of Castes.	Religion.	Sirpur Tandur. Total.	Sirpur Tandur. Males.	Sirpur Tandur. Females.	Gulbarga. Total.	Gulbarga. Males.	Gulbarga. Females.	Raichur. Total.	Raichur. Males.	Raichur. Females.	Lingsaugur. Total.	Lingsaugur. Males.	Lingsaugur. Females.	Railways. Total.	Railways. Males.	Railways. Females.
					51	52	53	54	55	56	57	58	59	60	61	62	63	64	65
A	1 ...	Mahratta ...	Kharale	Hindu ...	...	...	...	...	...	...	...	...	...	...	...	...	...	...	...
		do ...	Kharde	do ...	...	...	...	...	...	...	...	...	...	...	...	...	...	...	...
		do ...	Khare...	do ...	217	123	94	...	...	...	...	...	...	...	...	...	...	...	...
		do ...	Kharkhod	do ...	...	...	...	...	...	...	...	...	...	...	...	...	...	...	...
		do ...	Khatvan	do ...	...	...	...	...	...	...	...	...	...	...	...	...	...	...	...
		do ...	Khedkar	do ...	...	...	...	...	...	...	...	...	...	...	...	...	...	...	...
		do ...	Khodke	do ...	...	...	...	...	...	...	...	...	...	...	...	...	...	...	...
		do ...	Khoshi	do ...	...	...	...	...	...	...	...	...	...	...	...	...	...	...	...
		do ...	Khutevat	do ...	...	...	...	...	...	...	...	...	...	...	...	...	...	...	...
		do ...	Kukar	do ...	...	...	...	...	...	...	...	...	...	...	...	...	...	...	...
		do ...	Konher	do ...	...	...	...	...	...	...	...	...	...	...	...	...	...	...	...
		do ...	Kor	do ...	...	...	...	...	...	...	...	...	...	...	...	...	...	...	...
		do ...	Korsale	do ...	843	429	414	...	...	...	...	...	...	...	...	...	...	...	...
		do ...	Kote	do ...	...	...	...	...	...	...	...	...	...	...	...	...	...	...	...
		do ...	Kotlo	do ...	...	...	...	...	...	...	...	...	...	...	...	...	...	...	...
		do ...	Lad	do ...	...	...	...	...	...	...	...	...	...	...	...	...	...	...	...
		do ...	Lagaya	do ...	...	...	...	...	...	...	...	...	...	...	...	...	...	...	...
		do ...	Lalsi	do ...	...	...	...	...	...	...	12	7	5	...	...	...	...	...	...
		do ...	Lamara	do ...	...	...	...	...	...	...	4	2	2	...	...	...	...	...	...
		do ...	Lasupne	do ...	...	...	...	...	...	...	...	...	...	...	...	...	...	...	...
		do ...	Lugde...	do ...	...	...	...	...	...	...	...	...	...	...	...	...	...	...	...
		do ...	Mabhaj	do ...	...	...	...	...	...	...	...	...	...	...	...	...	...	...	...
		do ...	Madan	do ...	...	...	...	...	...	...	...	...	...	...	...	...	...	...	...
		do ...	Magtol	do ...	...	...	...	...	...	...	...	...	...	...	...	...	...	...	...
		do ...	Mahavo	do ...	...	...	...	...	...	...	...	...	...	...	...	...	...	...	...
		do ...	Mainavat	do ...	...	...	...	...	...	...	...	...	...	...	...	...	...	...	...
		do ...	Maine...	do ...	...	...	...	20	10	10	...	...	...	...	...	...	...	...	...
		do ...	Maki	do ...	...	...	...	...	...	...	...	...	...	...	...	...	...	...	...
		do ...	Malve...	do ...	...	...	...	...	...	...	...	...	...	...	...	...	...	...	...
		do ...	Mandria	do ...	...	...	...	...	...	...	...	...	...	...	...	...	...	...	...
		do ...	Mane	do ...	...	...	...	...	...	...	...	...	...	...	...	...	...	...	...
		do ...	Manjre	do ...	...	...	...	...	...	...	...	...	...	...	...	...	...	...	...
		do ...	Maoge...	do ...	...	...	...	...	...	...	...	...	...	...	...	...	...	...	...
		do ...	Marul...	do ...	...	...	...	...	...	...	...	...	...	...	...	...	...	...	...
		do ...	Masik	do ...	5	...	5	...	...	...	...	...	...	...	...	...	...	...	...
		do ...	Maske...	do ...	...	...	...	...	...	...	...	...	...	...	...	...	...	...	...
		do ...	Mate	do ...	...	...	...	...	...	...	...	...	...	...	...	...	...	...	...
		do ...	Mathsar	do ...	...	...	...	...	...	...	...	...	...	...	...	...	...	...	...
		do ...	Medhavant	do ...	...	...	...	...	...	...	...	...	...	...	...	...	...	...	...
		do ...	Meher...	do ...	...	...	...	...	...	...	...	...	...	...	...	...	...	...	...
		do ...	Mogal...	do ...	...	...	...	...	...	...	...	...	...	...	...	...	...	...	...
		do ...	Mogan	do ...	...	...	...	...	...	...	...	...	...	...	...	...	...	...	...
		do ...	More	do ...	...	...	...	18	8	10	...	...	...	...	...	...	...	...	...
		do ...	Mundkar	do ...	...	...	...	...	...	...	...	...	...	...	...	...	...	...	...

TABLE XVI.

Castes and Sub-divisions.—*Continued.*

Class.	Group.	Castes.	Sub-division of Castes.	Religion.	Total.			Hyderabad.			Atraf-i-Balda.			Mahabubnagar.			Nalgonda.		
					Total.	Males.	Females.	Total.	Males.	Females.	Total.	Males.	Females.	Total.	Males.	Females.	Total.	Males.	Females.
1	2	3	4	5	6	7	8	9	10	11	12	13	14	15	16	17	18	19	20
A	1 ...	Mahratta ...	Musle ...	Hindu ...	81	81	...	...	...	...	...	...	...	...	...	...	...	...	...
		do ...	Mutali	do ...	20	11	9	...	...	...	...	...	...	...	...	...	...	...	...
		do ...	Nadri ...	do ...	1	1	...	...	...	...	...	...	...	...	...	...	...	...	...
		do ...	Nagedhar	do ...	82	14	18	...	...	...	...	...	...	...	...	...	...	...	...
		do ...	Nagre ...	do ...	80	20	10	...	...	...	...	...	...	...	...	...	...	...	...
		do ...	Nagtidke	do ...	12	5	7	...	...	...	...	...	...	...	...	...	...	...	...
		do ...	Nague	do ...	8	3	5	...	...	...	...	...	...	...	...	...	...	...	...
		do ...	Naikbhoale	do ...	11	5	6	...	...	...	...	...	...	...	...	...	...	...	...
		do ...	Nalvade	do ...	88	14	24	...	...	...	...	...	...	...	...	...	...	...	...
		do ...	Namdeo	do ...	4	2	2	4	2	2	...	...	...	...	...	...	...	...	...
		do ...	Narbi ...	do ...	82	15	17	...	...	...	...	...	...	...	...	...	...	...	...
		do ...	Nari ...	do ...	18	9	9	...	...	...	...	...	...	...	...	...	...	...	...
		do ...	Nastabi	do ...	5	2	3	...	...	...	...	...	...	...	...	...	...	...	...
		do ...	Nimalvar	do ...	8	8	...	...	...	...	...	...	...	...	...	...	...	...	...
		do ...	Nirali ...	do ...	2,640	1,328	1,312	...	...	...	...	...	...	...	...	...	...	...	...
		do ...	Nirgud	do ...	1	1	...	...	...	...	...	...	...	...	...	...	...	...	...
		do ...	Nod ...	do ...	4	...	4	...	...	...	...	...	...	...	...	...	...	...	...
		do ...	Nundoba	do ...	3	2	1	3	2	1	...	...	...	...	...	...	...	...	...
		do ...	Upmane	do ...	8	...	3	...	...	...	...	...	...	...	...	...	...	...	...
		do ...	Padhand	do ...	2	2	...	...	...	...	...	...	...	...	...	...	...	...	...
		do ...	Padri ...	do ...	8	...	3	...	...	...	...	...	...	...	...	...	...	...	...
		do ...	Padval	do ...	20	13	7	...	...	...	...	...	...	...	...	...	...	...	...
		do ...	Pakhre	do ...	81	15	16	...	...	...	...	...	...	...	...	...	...	...	...
		do ...	Pakiram	do ...	6	4	2	...	...	...	...	...	...	...	...	...	...	...	...
		do ...	Palantia	do ...	3	...	3	...	...	...	...	...	...	...	...	...	...	...	...
		do ...	Palas ...	do ...	137	50	87	...	...	...	...	...	...	...	...	...	...	...	...
		do ...	Palayan	do ...	8	...	3	3	...	3	...	...	...	...	...	...	...	...	...
		do ...	Palre ...	do ...	1	1	...	...	...	...	...	...	...	...	...	...	...	...	...
		do ...	Pandovai	do ...	84	21	13	34	21	13	...	...	...	...	...	...	...	...	...
		do ...	Paore ...	do ...	11	3	8	...	...	...	...	...	...	...	...	...	...	...	...
		do ...	Paose ...	do ...	8	8	...	...	...	...	...	...	...	...	...	...	...	...	...
		do ...	Papjadho	do ...	4	...	4	...	...	...	...	...	...	...	...	...	...	...	...
		do ...	Parvas	do ...	5	5	...	...	...	...	...	...	...	...	...	...	...	...	...
		do ...	Pasale ...	do ...	44	...	44	...	...	...	...	...	...	...	...	...	...	...	...
		do ...	Pathar	do ...	127	114	13	...	...	...	...	...	...	...	...	...	...	...	...
		do ...	Pathore	do ...	8	4	4	...	...	...	...	...	...	...	...	...	...	...	...
		do ...	Pavar ...	do ...	8,714	1,987	1,727	6	2	4	...	...	...	...	...	...	...	...	...
		do ...	Pavasre	do ...	2	1	1	...	...	...	...	...	...	...	...	...	...	...	...
		do ...	Phaonar	do ...	45	28	22	...	...	...	...	...	...	...	...	...	...	...	...
		do ...	Pharate	do ...	10	3	7	...	...	...	...	...	...	...	...	...	...	...	...
		do ...	Pingle ...	do ...	112	24	88	...	...	...	...	...	...	...	...	...	...	...	...
		do ...	Pisall ...	do ...	16	8	8	...	...	...	...	...	...	...	...	...	...	...	...
		do ...	Pudan	do ...	21	9	12	...	...	...	...	...	...	...	...	...	...	...	...
		do ...	Pure ...	do ...	11	11	...	...	...	...	...	...	...	...	...	...	...	...	...

TABLE XVI.

Castes and Sub-divisions.—*Continued.*

Class.	Group.	Castes.	Sub-division of Castes.	Religion.	Warangal.			Elgandal.			Indur.			Medak.			Aurangabad.		
					Total.	Males.	Females.	Total.	Males.	Females.	Total.	Males.	Females.	Total.	Males.	Females.	Total.	Males.	Females.
					21	22	23	24	25	26	27	28	29	30	31	32	33	34	35
A	1 ...	Mahratta ...	Musle	Hindu ...	...	...	...	...	...	...	...	...	...	...	...	...	...	...	...
		do ...	Mutali... ...	do ...	...	...	...	...	...	...	...	...	...	...	...	...	...	...	...
		do ...	Nadri	do ...	...	...	...	...	...	...	...	...	...	...	...	...	1	1	...
		do ...	Nagedhar ...	do ...	...	...	...	...	...	...	32	14	18	...	...	...	...	...	...
		do ...	Nagre ...	do ...	...	...	...	...	...	...	...	...	...	...	...	...	...	...	...
		do ...	Nagtidke ...	do ...	...	...	...	...	...	...	...	...	...	...	...	...	...	...	...
		do ...	Nague... ...	do ...	...	...	...	...	...	...	...	...	...	...	...	...	...	...	...
		do ...	Naikbhosle ...	do ...	...	...	...	...	...	...	...	...	...	...	...	...	...	...	...
		do ...	Nalvade ...	do ...	...	...	...	...	...	...	...	...	...	...	...	...	...	...	...
		do ...	Namdeo ...	do ...	...	...	...	...	...	...	...	...	...	...	...	...	...	...	...
		do ...	Narbi	do ...	...	...	...	...	...	...	...	...	...	...	...	...	...	...	...
		do ...	Nari	do ...	...	...	...	...	...	...	...	...	...	...	...	...	10	4	6
		do ...	Nastabi ...	do ...	...	...	...	...	...	...	...	...	...	...	...	...	...	...	...
		do ...	Nimalvar ...	do ...	...	...	...	...	...	...	8	8	...	...	...	...	...	...	...
		do ...	Nirali	do ...	...	...	...	...	...	...	72	39	33	...	...	...	2	1	1
		do ...	Nirgud ...	do ...	...	...	...	...	...	...	...	...	...	...	...	...	...	...	...
		do ...	Nod	do ...	...	...	...	...	...	...	...	...	...	...	...	...	...	...	...
		do ...	Nundoba ...	do ...	...	...	...	...	...	...	...	...	...	...	...	...	...	...	...
		do ...	Opmane ...	do ...	...	...	...	...	...	...	...	...	...	...	...	...	...	...	...
		do ...	Padhand ...	do ...	...	...	...	...	...	...	...	...	...	...	...	...	...	...	...
		do ...	Padri	do ...	...	...	...	...	...	...	...	...	...	...	...	...	2	2	...
		do ...	Padval ...	do ...	...	...	...	...	...	...	...	...	...	...	...	...	3	...	3
		do ...	Pakhre ...	do ...	...	...	...	...	...	...	...	...	...	...	...	...	...	...	...
		do ...	Pakiram ...	do ...	...	...	...	...	...	...	...	...	...	...	...	...	...	...	...
		do ...	Palantia ...	do ...	...	...	...	...	...	...	...	...	...	...	...	...	...	...	...
		do ...	Palas	do ...	...	...	...	...	...	...	...	...	...	...	...	...	...	...	...
		do ...	Palayan ...	do ...	...	...	...	...	...	...	...	...	...	...	...	...	...	...	...
		do ...	Palre	do ...	...	...	...	...	...	...	...	...	...	...	...	...	...	...	...
		do ...	Pandovai ...	do ...	...	...	...	...	...	...	...	...	...	...	...	...	...	...	...
		do ...	Paore	do ...	...	...	...	...	...	...	...	...	...	...	...	...	...	...	...
		do ...	Paose	do ...	...	...	...	...	...	...	...	...	...	...	...	...	...	...	...
		do ...	Papjadho ...	do ...	...	...	...	...	...	...	...	...	...	...	...	...	...	...	...
		do ...	Parvas ...	do ...	...	...	...	...	...	...	...	...	...	...	...	...	...	...	...
		do ...	Pasale... ...	do ...	...	...	...	...	...	...	...	...	...	...	...	...	...	...	...
		do ...	Pathar ...	do ...	...	...	...	...	...	...	...	...	...	...	...	...	...	...	...
		do ...	Pathore ...	do ...	...	...	...	...	...	...	...	...	...	...	...	...	...	...	...
		do ...	Pavar... ...	do ...	...	...	...	...	...	...	181	113	68	...	...	...	12	9	3
		do ...	Pavasre ...	do ...	...	...	...	...	...	...	...	...	...	...	...	...	...	...	...
		do ...	Phsonar ...	do ...	...	...	...	...	...	...	...	...	...	...	...	...	...	...	...
		do ...	Pharate ...	do ...	...	...	...	...	...	...	...	...	...	...	...	...	...	...	...
		do ...	Pingle... ...	do ...	...	...	...	...	...	...	...	...	...	...	...	...	...	...	...
		do ...	Pisali	do ...	...	...	...	...	...	...	...	...	...	...	...	...	...	...	...
		do ...	Pudan ...	do ...	...	...	...	...	...	...	...	...	...	...	...	...	...	...	...
		do ...	Pure	do ...	...	...	...	...	...	...	...	...	...	...	...	...	...	...	...

TABLE XVI.

Castes and Sub-divisions.—*Continued.*

Class.	Group.	Castes.	Sub-division of Castes.	Religion.	Birh. Total.	Birh. Males.	Birh. Females.	Nander. Total.	Nander. Males.	Nander. Females.	Naldrug. Total.	Naldrug. Males.	Naldrug. Females.	Bidar. Total.	Bidar. Males.	Bidar. Females.	Parbhani. Total.	Parbhani. Males.	Parbhani. Females.
					36	37	38	39	40	41	42	43	44	45	46	47	48	49	50
A	1	Mehratta	Musle	Hindu	...	...	...	...	...	...	...	...	...	31	31	...	...	...	...
		do	Mutali	do	...	...	...	20	11	9	...	...	...	...	...	...	...	...	...
		do	Nadri	do	...	...	...	...	...	...	...	...	...	...	...	...	...	...	...
		do	Nagedhar	do	...	...	...	...	...	...	...	...	...	...	...	...	...	...	...
		do	Nagze	do	...	...	...	...	...	...	20	13	7	...	...	...	10	7	3
		do	Nagtidke	do	...	...	...	...	...	...	12	5	7	...	...	...	...	...	...
		do	Nagne	do	...	...	...	...	...	...	8	3	5	...	...	...	...	...	...
		do	Naikbhosle	do	...	...	...	...	...	...	...	...	...	11	5	6	...	...	...
		do	Nalvade	do	...	...	...	30	9	21	8	5	3	...	...	...	...	...	...
		do	Namdeo	do	...	...	...	...	...	...	...	...	...	...	...	...	...	...	...
		do	Narbi	do	...	...	...	...	...	...	32	15	17	...	...	...	...	...	...
		do	Nari	do	...	...	...	...	...	...	...	...	...	...	...	...	8	5	3
		do	Nastabi	do	...	...	...	...	...	...	5	2	3	...	...	...	...	...	...
		do	Nimalvar	do	...	...	...	...	...	...	...	...	...	...	...	...	...	...	...
		do	Nirali	do	211	107	104	2,076	1,047	1,029	49	28	21	...	...	...	185	84	101
		do	Nirgud	do	...	...	...	...	...	...	1	1	...	...	...	...	...	...	...
		do	Nod	do	...	...	...	...	...	...	4	...	4	...	...	...	...	...	...
		do	Nundoba	do	...	...	...	...	...	...	...	...	...	...	...	...	...	...	...
		do	Opmane	do	...	...	...	...	...	...	3	...	3	...	...	...	...	...	...
		do	Padhand	do	...	...	...	...	...	...	...	...	...	...	...	...	...	...	...
		do	Padri	do	...	...	...	...	...	...	...	...	...	...	...	...	...	...	...
		do	Padval	do	...	...	...	8	8	...	12	5	7	...	...	...	...	...	...
		do	Pakhre	do	...	...	...	...	...	...	31	15	16	...	...	...	...	...	...
		do	Pakiram	do	...	...	...	6	4	2	...	...	...	...	...	...	...	...	...
		do	Palantia	do	...	...	...	...	...	...	...	...	...	3	...	3	...	...	...
		do	Palas	do	...	...	...	187	50	87	...	...	...	...	...	...	...	...	...
		do	Palayan	do	...	...	...	...	...	...	...	...	...	...	...	...	...	...	...
		do	Palre	do	...	...	...	...	...	...	...	...	...	1	1	...	...	...	...
		do	Pandovai	do	...	...	...	...	...	...	...	...	...	...	...	...	...	...	...
		do	Paore	do	...	...	...	1	1	...	4	1	3	...	...	...	...	...	...
		do	Paose	do	...	...	...	3	3	...	...	...	...	...	...	...	...	...	...
		do	Papjadho	do	...	...	...	...	...	...	...	...	...	4	...	4	...	...	...
		do	Parvas	do	5	5	...	...	...	...	...	...	...	...	...	...	...	...	...
		do	Pasale	do	...	...	...	44	...	44	...	...	...	...	...	...	...	...	...
		do	Pathar	do	111	106	5	...	...	...	16	8	8	...	...	...	...	...	...
		do	Pathore	do	...	...	...	...	...	...	...	...	...	8	4	4	...	...	...
		do	Pavar	do	6	6	...	2,775	1,491	1,284	484	238	246	4	3	1	191	95	96
		do	Pavasre	do	...	...	...	...	...	...	2	1	1	...	...	...	...	...	...
		do	Phaonar	do	...	...	...	45	23	22	...	...	...	...	...	...	...	...	...
		do	Pharate	do	...	...	...	...	...	...	10	3	7	...	...	...	...	...	...
		do	Pingle	do	...	...	...	73	...	73	39	24	15	...	...	...	...	...	...
		do	Pisali	do	...	...	...	...	...	...	16	8	8	...	...	...	...	...	...
		do	Pudan	do	...	...	...	...	...	...	21	9	12	...	...	...	...	...	...
		do	Pure	do	...	...	...	...	...	...	...	...	...	11	11	...	...	...	...

TABLE XVI.

Castes and Sub-divisions.—*Continued.*

Class.	Group.	Castes.	Sub-division of Castes.	Religion.	Sirpur-Tandur. Total.	Sirpur-Tandur. Males.	Sirpur-Tandur. Females.	Gulbarga. Total.	Gulbarga. Males.	Gulbarga. Females.	Raichur. Total.	Raichur. Males.	Raichur. Females.	Lingasugur. Total.	Lingasugur. Males.	Lingasugur. Females.	Railways. Total.	Railways. Males.	Railways. Females.
					51	52	53	54	55	56	57	58	59	60	61	62	63	64	65
A	1 ...	Mahratta ...	Musle ...	Hindu ...	...	...	...	...	...	...	...	...	...	...	...	...	...	...	...
		do ...	Mutali ...	do ...	...	...	...	...	...	...	...	...	...	...	...	...	...	...	...
		do ...	Nadri ...	do ...	...	...	...	...	...	...	...	...	...	...	...	...	...	...	...
		do ...	Nagedhar ...	do ...	...	...	...	...	...	...	...	...	...	...	...	...	...	...	...
		do ...	Nagre ...	do ...	...	...	...	...	...	...	...	...	...	...	...	...	...	...	...
		do ...	Nagtidke ...	do ...	...	...	...	...	...	...	...	...	...	...	...	...	...	...	...
		do ...	Nague ...	do ...	...	...	...	...	...	...	...	...	...	...	...	...	...	...	...
		do ...	Naikbhosle ...	do ...	...	...	...	...	...	...	...	...	...	...	...	...	...	...	...
		do ...	Nalvade ...	do ...	...	...	...	...	...	...	...	...	...	...	...	...	...	...	...
		do ...	Namdeo ...	do ...	...	...	...	...	...	...	...	...	...	...	...	...	...	...	...
		do ...	Narbi ...	do ...	...	...	...	...	...	...	...	...	...	...	...	...	...	...	...
		do ...	Nari ...	do ...	...	...	...	...	...	...	...	...	...	...	...	...	...	...	...
		do ...	Nastabi ...	do ...	...	...	...	...	...	...	...	...	...	...	...	...	...	...	...
		do ...	Nimalvar ...	do ...	...	...	...	...	...	...	...	...	...	...	...	...	...	...	...
		do ...	Nirali ...	do ...	...	...	...	45	22	23	...	...	...	...	...	...	...	...	...
		do ...	Nirgud ...	do ...	...	...	...	...	...	...	...	...	...	...	...	...	...	...	...
		do ...	Nod ...	do ...	...	...	...	...	...	...	...	...	...	...	...	...	...	...	...
		do ...	Nundoba ...	do ...	...	...	...	...	...	...	...	...	...	...	...	...	...	...	...
		do ...	Opmano ...	do ...	...	...	...	...	...	...	...	...	...	...	...	...	...	...	...
		do ...	Padhand ...	do ...	...	...	...	...	...	...	...	...	...	...	...	...	...	...	...
		do ...	Padri ...	do ...	...	...	...	...	...	...	...	...	...	...	...	...	...	...	...
		do ...	Padval ...	do ...	...	...	...	...	...	...	...	...	...	...	...	...	...	...	...
		do ...	Pakhre ...	do ...	...	...	...	...	...	...	...	...	...	...	...	...	...	...	...
		do ...	Pakiram ...	do ...	...	...	...	...	...	...	...	...	...	...	...	...	...	...	...
		do ...	Palantia ...	do ...	...	...	...	...	...	...	...	...	...	...	...	...	...	...	...
		do ...	Palas ...	do ...	...	...	...	...	...	...	...	...	...	...	...	...	...	...	...
		do ...	Palayan ...	do ...	...	...	...	...	...	...	...	...	...	...	...	...	...	...	...
		do ...	Palre ...	do ...	...	...	...	...	...	...	...	...	...	...	...	...	...	...	...
		do ...	Pandovai ...	do ...	...	...	...	...	...	...	...	...	...	...	...	...	...	...	...
		do ...	Paore ...	do ...	6	1	5	...	...	...	...	...	...	...	...	...	...	...	...
		do ...	Paose ...	do ...	...	...	...	...	...	...	...	...	...	...	...	...	...	...	...
		do ...	Papjadho ...	do ...	...	...	...	...	...	...	...	...	...	...	...	...	...	...	...
		do ...	Parvas ...	do ...	...	...	...	...	...	...	...	...	...	...	...	...	...	...	...
		do ...	Pasale ...	do ...	...	...	...	...	...	...	...	...	...	...	...	...	...	...	...
		do ...	Pathar ...	do ...	...	...	...	...	...	...	...	...	...	...	...	...	...	...	...
		do ...	Pathore ...	do ...	...	...	...	...	...	...	...	...	...	...	...	...	...	...	...
		do ...	Pavar ...	do ...	...	...	...	55	30	25	...	...	...	...	...	...	...	...	...
		do ...	Pavasre ...	do ...	...	...	...	...	...	...	...	...	...	...	...	...	...	...	...
		do ...	Phaonar ...	do ...	...	...	...	...	...	...	...	...	...	...	...	...	...	...	...
		do ...	Pharate ...	do ...	...	...	...	...	...	...	...	...	...	...	...	...	...	...	...
		do ...	Pingle ...	do ...	...	...	...	...	...	...	...	...	...	...	...	...	...	...	...
		do ...	Pisali ...	do ...	...	...	...	...	...	...	...	...	...	...	...	...	...	...	...
		do ...	Pudan ...	do ...	...	...	...	...	...	...	...	...	...	...	...	...	...	...	...
		do ...	Pure ...	do ...	...	...	...	...	...	...	...	...	...	...	...	...	...	...	...

TABLE XVI.

Castes and Sub-divisions.—*Continued.*

Class.	Group.	Castes.	Sub-division of Castes.	Religion.	Total. Total.	Total. Males.	Total. Females.	Hyderabad. Total.	Hyderabad. Males.	Hyderabad. Females.	Atraf-i-Balda. Total.	Atraf-i-Balda. Males.	Atraf-i-Balda. Females.	Mahabubnagar. Total.	Mahabubnagar. Males.	Mahabubnagar. Females.	Nalgonda. Total.	Nalgonda. Males.	Nalgonda. Females.
1	2	3	4	5	6	7	8	9	10	11	12	13	14	15	16	17	18	19	20
A	1 ...	Mahratta ...	Puvad...	Hindu ...	4	3	1	...	...	...	...	...	...	...	...	...	...	...	...
		do ...	Raghe...	do ...	4	2	2	...	...	...	...	...	...	...	...	...	...	...	...
		do ...	Rainand	do ...	5	2	3	...	...	...	...	...	...	...	...	...	...	...	...
		do ...	Rajade	do ...	241	120	121	...	...	...	...	...	...	...	...	...	...	...	...
		do ...	Rajut	do ...	29	20	9	29	20	9	...	...	...	...	...	...	...	...	...
		do ...	Ramathar	do ...	6	3	3	...	...	...	...	...	...	...	...	...	...	...	...
		do ...	Ramne	do ...	14	8	6	...	...	...	...	...	...	...	...	...	...	...	...
		do ...	Ramraj	do ...	7	4	3	7	4	3	...	...	...	...	...	...	...	...	...
		do ...	Rankham	do ...	17	10	7	...	...	...	...	...	...	...	...	...	...	...	...
		do ...	Raokad	do ...	17	6	11	...	...	...	...	...	...	...	...	...	...	...	...
		do ...	Rasan	do ...	2	1	1	...	...	...	...	...	...	...	...	...	...	...	...
		do ...	Ravat	do ...	84	27	7	84	27	7	...	...	...	...	...	...	...	...	...
		do ...	Sajpan	do ...	40	22	18	...	...	...	...	...	...	...	...	...	...	...	...
		do ...	Sakul	do ...	37	24	13	...	...	...	...	...	...	...	...	...	...	...	...
		do ...	Salunke	do ...	1,676	823	853	...	...	...	...	...	...	...	...	...	...	...	...
		do ...	Sanam...	do ...	20	15	5	...	...	...	...	...	...	...	...	...	...	...	...
		do ...	Sangjate	do ...	10	10	...	...	...	...	...	...	...	...	...	...	...	...	...
		do ...	Saole	do ...	50	27	23	...	...	...	...	...	...	...	...	...	...	...	...
		do ...	Sarangi	do ...	2	1	1	...	...	...	...	...	...	...	...	...	...	...	...
		do ...	Saraswat	do ...	7	4	3	7	4	3	...	...	...	...	...	...	...	...	...
		do ...	Sare	do ...	85	47	38	...	...	...	...	...	...	...	...	...	...	...	...
		do ...	Sarga	do ...	32	13	19	...	...	...	...	...	...	...	...	...	...	...	...
		do ...	Sarosi	do ...	9	9	...	3	3	...	...	...	...	...	...	...	...	...	...
		do ...	Satvan	do ...	33	15	18	...	...	...	...	...	...	...	...	...	...	...	...
		do ...	Savi	do ...	34	21	13	34	21	13	...	...	...	...	...	...	...	...	...
		do ...	Savase	do ...	43	26	17	...	...	...	...	...	...	...	...	...	...	...	...
		do ...	Savat	do ...	484	253	231	...	...	...	...	...	...	...	...	...	...	...	...
		do ...	Sekpao	do ...	9	5	4	...	...	...	...	...	...	...	...	...	...	...	...
		do ...	Seone	do ...	6	3	3	...	...	...	...	...	...	...	...	...	...	...	...
		do ...	Shahadesi	do ...	185	37	148	...	...	...	...	...	...	...	...	...	...	...	...
		do ...	Shilke	do ...	73	37	26	...	...	...	...	...	...	...	...	...	...	...	...
		do ...	Shalu	do ...	6,612	3,746	2,866	...	...	...	...	...	...	...	...	...	...	...	...
		do ...	Sidalke	do ...	1	1	...	...	...	...	...	...	...	...	...	...	...	...	...
		do ...	Silil	do ...	27	1	26	...	...	...	...	...	...	...	...	...	...	...	...
		do ...	Sinde	do ...	14,139	7,473	6,666	...	...	...	...	...	...	...	...	...	...	...	...
		do ...	Sirpevar	do ...	192	97	95	...	...	...	...	...	...	...	...	...	...	...	...
		do ...	Sirsait	do ...	70	...	70	...	...	...	...	...	...	...	...	...	...	...	...
		do ...	Sirsale...	do ...	144	3	141	...	...	...	...	...	...	...	...	...	...	...	...
		do ...	Sivije	do ...	46	20	26	...	...	...	...	...	...	...	...	...	...	...	...
		do ...	Somavamshi	do ...	149	47	102	81	46	35	...	...	...	...	...	...	...	...	...
		do ...	Songre...	do ...	4	4	...	...	...	...	...	...	...	...	...	...	...	...	...
		do ...	Sonsal	do ...	17	11	6	...	...	...	...	...	...	...	...	...	...	...	...
		do ...	Sri	do ...	98	90	8	98	90	8	...	...	...	...	...	...	...	...	...
		do ...	Sudhri...	do ...	40	40	...	...	...	...	...	...	...	...	...	...	...	...	...
		do ...	Sukarvale	do ...	1	1	...	...	...	...	...	...	...	...	...	...	...	...	...

TABLE XVI.

Castes and Sub-divisions.—*Continued.*

Class.	Group.	Castes.	Sub-division of Castes.	Religion.	Warangal. Total.	Warangal. Males.	Warangal. Females.	Elgandal. Total.	Elgandal. Males.	Elgandal. Females.	Indur. Total.	Indur. Males.	Indur. Females.	Medak. Total.	Medak. Males.	Medak. Females.	Aurangabad. Total.	Aurangabad. Males.	Aurangabad. Females.
					21	22	23	24	25	26	27	28	29	30	31	32	33	34	35
A	1 ...	Mahratta ...	Puvad...	Hindu ...	...	...	...	...	...	...	...	...	...	...	...	...	...	...	...
		do ...	Raghe...	do ...	...	...	...	...	...	...	...	...	...	...	...	...	...	...	...
		do ...	Rainand	do ...	...	...	...	...	...	...	...	...	...	...	...	...	...	...	...
		do ...	Rajade	do ...	...	...	...	...	...	...	...	...	...	...	...	...	...	...	...
		do ...	Rajut	do ...	...	...	...	...	...	...	...	...	...	...	...	...	...	...	...
		do ...	Ramathar	do ...	...	...	...	...	...	...	...	...	...	...	...	...	...	...	...
		do ...	Ramne	do ...	...	...	...	...	...	...	...	...	...	...	...	...	6	3	3
		do ...	Ramraj	do ...	...	...	...	...	...	...	...	...	...	...	...	...	...	...	...
		do ...	Rankham	do ...	...	...	...	...	...	...	...	...	...	...	...	...	...	...	...
		do ...	Raoked	do ...	...	...	...	...	...	...	...	...	...	...	...	...	...	...	...
		do ...	Rasan	do ...	...	...	...	...	...	...	...	...	...	...	...	...	...	...	...
		do ...	Ravat	do ...	...	...	...	...	...	...	...	...	...	...	...	...	...	...	...
		do ...	Sajpan	do ...	...	...	...	...	...	...	...	...	...	...	...	...	...	...	...
		do ...	Sakul	do ...	...	...	...	...	...	...	...	...	...	...	...	...	40	22	18
		do ...	Salunke	do ...	...	...	...	...	...	...	...	...	...	...	...	...	...	...	...
		do ...	Sanam...	do ...	...	...	...	...	...	...	51	26	25	...	...	...	...	...	...
		do ...	Sangjate	do ...	...	...	...	...	...	...	...	...	...	...	...	...	...	...	...
		do ...	Saole	do ...	...	...	...	...	...	...	...	...	...	...	...	...	...	...	...
		do ...	Sarangi	do ...	...	...	...	...	...	...	...	...	...	...	...	...	1	1	...
		do ...	Saraswat	do ...	...	...	...	...	...	...	...	...	...	...	...	...	...	...	...
		do ...	Sare	do ...	...	...	...	...	...	...	...	...	...	...	...	...	...	...	...
		do ...	Sarga	do ...	...	...	...	...	...	...	...	...	...	...	...	...	...	...	...
		do ...	Sarosi	do ...	...	...	...	...	...	...	...	...	...	...	...	...	...	...	...
		do ...	Satvan	do ...	...	...	...	...	...	...	...	...	...	...	...	...	...	...	...
		do ...	Savi	do ...	...	...	...	...	...	...	...	...	...	...	...	...	...	...	...
		do ...	Savase...	do ...	...	...	...	...	...	...	...	...	...	...	...	...	...	...	...
		do ...	Savat	do ...	...	...	...	...	...	...	...	...	...	...	...	...	...	...	...
		do ...	Sekpao...	do ...	...	...	...	...	...	...	28	12	16	...	...	...	...	...	...
		do ...	Seone	do ...	...	...	...	...	...	...	...	...	...	...	...	...	...	...	...
		do ...	Shahadesi	do ...	...	...	...	...	...	...	...	...	...	...	...	...	...	...	...
		do ...	Shilke	do ...	...	...	...	...	...	...	...	...	...	...	...	...	185	87	148
		do ...	Shalu	do ...	...	...	...	...	...	...	...	...	...	...	...	...	...	...	...
		do ...	Sidalke	do ...	...	...	...	...	...	...	222	98	124	...	...	...	...	...	...
		do ...	Silil	do ...	...	...	...	...	...	...	...	...	...	...	...	...	...	...	...
		do ...	Sinde	do ...	...	...	...	...	...	...	...	...	...	...	...	...	...	...	...
		do ...	Sirpevar	do ...	...	...	...	...	...	...	227	114	118	48	24	24	44	19	25
		do ...	Sirsait	do ...	...	...	...	...	...	...	...	...	...	...	...	...	...	...	...
		do ...	Sirsale...	do ...	...	...	...	...	...	...	...	...	...	...	...	...	...	...	...
		do ...	Sivije...	do ...	...	...	...	...	...	...	...	...	...	...	...	...	...	...	...
		do ...	Somavamshi	do ...	...	...	...	...	...	...	...	...	...	...	...	...	...	...	...
		do ...	Songre...	do ...	...	...	...	...	...	...	...	...	...	...	...	...	...	...	...
		do ...	Sonsal	do ...	...	...	...	...	...	...	...	...	...	...	...	...	...	...	...
		do ...	Sri	do ...	...	...	...	...	...	...	...	...	...	...	...	...	...	...	...
		do ...	Sudhri...	do ...	...	...	...	...	...	...	...	...	...	...	...	...	...	...	...
		do ...	Sukarvale	do ...	...	...	...	...	...	...	...	...	...	...	...	...	...	...	...

TABLE XVI.

Castes and Sub-divisions.—*Continued.*

Class.	Group.	Castes.	Sub-division of Castes.	Religion.	Birh. Total.	Birh. Males.	Birh. Females.	Nander. Total.	Nander. Males.	Nander. Females.	Naldrug. Total.	Naldrug. Males.	Naldrug. Females.	Bidar. Total.	Bidar. Males.	Bidar. Females.	Parbhani. Total.	Parbhani. Males.	Parbhani. Females.
					36	37	38	39	40	41	42	43	44	45	46	47	48	49	50
A	1 ...	Mahratta ...	Puvad...	Hindu ...	...	...	...	...	...	...	...	...	...	4	3	1	...	...	...
		do ...	Raghe	do ...	...	...	...	...	...	...	4	2	2	...	...	...	...	...	...
		do ...	Rainand	do ...	5	2	3	...	...	...	...	...	...	...	...	...	...	...	...
		do ...	Rajade	do ...	...	...	...	...	...	...	241	120	121	...	...	...	...	...	...
		do ...	Rajut	do ...	...	...	...	...	...	...	...	...	...	...	...	...	...	...	...
		do ...	Ramathar	do ...	...	...	...	...	...	...	...	...	...	...	...	...	...	...	...
		do ...	Ramne ...	do ...	...	...	...	...	...	...	14	8	6	...	...	...	...	...	...
		do ...	Ramraj	do ...	...	...	...	...	...	...	...	...	...	...	...	...	...	...	...
		do ...	Rankham	do ...	...	...	...	...	...	...	17	10	7	...	...	...	...	...	...
		do ...	Raokad	do ...	...	...	...	17	6	11	...	...	...	...	...	...	...	...	...
		do ...	Rasan	do ...	...	...	...	...	...	...	...	...	...	2	1	1	...	...	...
		do ...	Ravat	do ...	...	...	...	...	...	...	...	...	...	...	...	...	...	...	...
		do ...	Sajpan...	do ...	...	...	...	...	...	...	...	...	...	...	...	...	...	...	...
		do ...	Sakul	do ...	...	...	...	...	...	...	37	24	13	...	...	...	...	...	...
		do ...	Salunke	do ...	...	...	...	882	196	186	170	75	95	1,066	526	540	...	...	...
		do ...	Sanam...	do ...	...	...	...	...	...	...	20	15	5	...	...	...	...	...	...
		do ...	Sangjte	do ...	...	...	...	...	...	...	10	10	...	...	...	...	...	...	...
		do ...	Saole	do ...	...	...	...	...	...	...	49	26	23	...	...	...	...	...	...
		do ...	Sarangi	do ...	...	...	...	2	1	1	...	...	...	...	...	...	...	...	...
		do ...	Saraswat	do ...	...	...	...	...	...	...	...	...	...	...	...	...	...	...	...
		do ...	Saro	do ...	...	...	...	...	...	...	85	47	38	...	...	...	...	...	...
		do ...	Sarga	do ...	...	...	...	...	...	...	32	13	19	...	...	...	...	...	...
		do ...	Sarosi	do ...	...	...	...	...	...	...	...	...	...	...	...	...	...	...	...
		do ...	Satvan...	do ...	...	...	...	...	...	...	33	15	18	...	...	...	...	...	...
		do ...	Savi	do ...	...	...	...	...	...	...	...	...	...	...	...	...	...	...	...
		do ...	Savase...	do ...	...	...	...	...	...	...	43	26	17	...	...	...	...	...	...
		do ...	Savat	do ...	...	...	...	9	4	5	127	63	64	316	170	146	...	...	...
		do ...	Sokpao...	do ...	...	...	...	9	5	4	...	...	...	...	...	...	...	...	...
		do ...	Scone	do ...	...	...	...	...	...	...	6	3	3	...	...	...	...	...	...
		do ...	Shahadesi	do ...	...	...	...	...	...	...	...	...	...	...	...	...	...	...	...
		do ...	Shailke	do ...	...	...	...	...	...	...	7	4	3	66	33	33	...	...	...
		do ...	Shalu	do ...	10	5	5	5,129	2,894	2,235	11	10	1	12	4	8	1,228	785	493
		do ...	Sidalke	do ...	...	...	...	...	...	...	1	1	...	...	...	...	...	...	...
		do ...	Silil	do ...	...	...	...	...	...	...	...	...	...	27	1	26	...	...	...
		do ...	Sinde	do ...	5	5	...	7,999	4,301	3,698	816	422	394	4,776	2,428	2,348	8	8	...
		do ...	Sirpevar	do ...	...	...	...	192	97	95	...	...	...	...	...	...	...	...	...
		do ...	Sirsait	do ...	...	...	...	...	...	...	...	...	...	70	...	70	...	...	...
		do ...	Sirsale	do ...	...	...	...	...	...	...	...	...	...	144	3	141	...	...	...
		do ...	Sivije	do ...	...	...	...	...	...	...	...	...	...	...	...	...	...	...	...
		do ...	Somavamshi	do ...	...	...	...	...	...	...	...	...	...	...	...	...	...	...	...
		do ...	Songre...	do ...	...	...	...	...	...	...	...	...	...	...	...	...	4	4	...
		do ...	Sonsal	do ...	...	...	...	17	11	6	...	...	...	...	...	...	...	...	...
		do ...	Sri	do ...	...	...	...	...	...	...	...	...	...	...	...	...	...	...	...
		do ...	Sudhri...	do ...	...	...	...	40	40	...	...	...	...	...	...	...	...	...	...
		do ...	Sukarvale	do ...	...	...	...	...	...	...	...	...	...	...	...	...	...	...	...

TABLE XVI.

Castes and Sub-divisions—*Continued*.

Class.	Group.	Castes.	Sub-division of Castes.	Religion.	Sirpur Tandur. Total.	Sirpur Tandur. Males.	Sirpur Tandur. Females.	Gulbarga. Total.	Gulbarga. Males.	Gulbarga. Females.	Raichur. Total.	Raichur. Males.	Raichur. Females.	Lingasugur. Total.	Lingasugur. Males.	Lingasugur. Females.	Railways. Total.	Railways. Males.	Railways. Females.
					51	52	53	54	55	56	57	58	59	60	61	62	63	64	65
A	1	Mahratta	Puvad	Hindu	...	...	...	...	...	...	...	...	...	...	...	...	...	...	...
		do	Raghe	do	...	...	...	...	...	...	...	...	...	...	...	...	...	...	...
		do	Ramand	do	...	...	...	...	...	...	...	...	...	...	...	...	...	...	...
		do	Rajade	do	...	...	...	...	...	...	...	...	...	...	...	...	...	...	...
		do	Rajut	do	...	...	...	...	...	...	...	...	...	...	...	...	...	...	...
		do	Ramathar	do	...	...	...	...	...	...	...	...	...	...	...	...	...	...	...
		do	Ramne	do	...	...	...	...	...	...	...	...	...	...	...	...	...	...	...
		do	Ramraj	do	...	...	...	...	...	...	...	...	...	...	...	...	...	...	...
		do	Ramkham	do	...	...	...	...	...	...	...	...	...	...	...	...	...	...	...
		do	Raokad	do	...	...	...	...	...	...	...	...	...	...	...	...	...	...	...
		do	Rasan	do	...	...	...	...	...	...	...	...	...	...	...	...	...	...	...
		do	Ravat	do	...	...	...	...	...	...	...	...	...	...	...	...	...	...	...
		do	Sajpan	do	...	...	...	...	...	...	...	...	...	...	...	...	...	...	...
		do	Sakul	do	...	...	...	...	...	...	...	...	...	...	...	...	...	...	...
		do	Salunke	do	...	...	...	...	...	...	...	...	...	...	...	...	...	...	...
		do	Sanam	do	...	...	...	...	...	...	...	...	...	7	...	7	...	...	...
		do	Sangjato	do	...	...	...	...	...	...	...	...	...	...	...	...	...	...	...
		do	Saole	do	...	...	...	...	...	...	...	...	...	...	...	...	...	...	...
		do	Sarangi	do	...	...	...	...	...	...	...	...	...	...	...	...	...	...	...
		do	Saraswat	do	...	...	...	...	...	...	...	...	...	...	...	...	...	...	...
		do	Sare	do	...	...	...	...	...	...	...	...	...	...	...	...	...	...	...
		do	Sarga	do	...	...	...	...	...	...	...	...	...	...	...	...	...	...	...
		do	Sarosi	do	6	6	...	...	...	...	...	...	...	...	...	...	...	...	...
		do	Satvan	do	...	...	...	...	...	...	...	...	...	...	...	...	...	...	...
		do	Savi	do	...	...	...	...	...	...	...	...	...	...	...	...	...	...	...
		do	Savase	do	...	...	...	...	...	...	...	...	...	...	...	...	...	...	...
		do	Savat	do	...	...	...	...	...	...	...	...	...	...	...	...	...	...	...
		do	Sokpas	do	...	...	...	...	...	...	4	4	...	...	...	...	...	...	...
		do	Seone	do	...	...	...	...	...	...	...	...	...	...	...	...	...	...	...
		do	Shahadesi	do	...	...	...	...	...	...	...	...	...	...	...	...	...	...	...
		do	Shailke	do	...	...	...	...	...	...	...	...	...	...	...	...	...	...	...
		do	Shalu	do	...	...	...	...	...	...	...	...	...	...	...	...	...	...	...
		do	Sidalke	do	...	...	...	...	...	...	...	...	...	...	...	...	...	...	...
		do	Silil	do	...	...	...	...	...	...	...	...	...	...	...	...	...	...	...
		do	Sinde	do	...	...	...	...	...	...	...	...	...	...	...	...	...	...	...
		do	Sirpovar	do	2	...	2	112	60	52	13	8	5	89	84	5	...	...	...
		do	Sirsait	do	...	...	...	...	...	...	...	...	...	...	...	...	...	...	...
		do	Sirsale	do	...	...	...	...	...	...	...	...	...	...	...	...	...	...	...
		do	Sivije	do	...	...	...	...	...	...	...	...	...	...	...	...	...	...	...
		do	Somavamshi	do	...	...	...	...	...	...	...	...	...	46	20	26	...	...	...
		do	Songre	do	...	...	...	...	...	...	4	1	8	64	...	64	...	...	...
		do	Sonsal	do	...	...	...	...	...	...	...	...	...	...	...	...	...	...	...
		do	Shri	do	...	...	...	...	...	...	...	...	...	...	...	...	...	...	...
		do	Sudhri	do	...	...	...	...	...	...	...	...	...	...	...	...	...	...	...
		do	Sukarvale	do	...	...	...	...	...	...	...	...	...	1	1	...	...	...	...

TABLE XVI.

Castes and Sub-divisions.—*Continued.*

Class.	Group.	Castes.	Sub-division of Castes.	Religion.	Total.			Hyderabad.			Atraf-i-Balda.			Mahabubnagar.			Nalgonda.		
					Total.	Males.	Females.	Total.	Males.	Females.	Total.	Males.	Females.	Total.	Males.	Females.	Total.	Males.	Females.
1	2	3	4	5	6	7	8	9	10	11	12	13	14	15	16	17	18	19	20
A	1 ...	Mahratta ...	Suratyari	Hindu ...	7	3	4	...	...	...	...	...	...	...	...	...	...	...	...
		do ...	Suria	do ...	4	2	2	4	2	2	...	...	...	...	...	...	...	...	...
		do ...	Suriked	do ...	8	4	4	...	...	...	...	...	...	...	...	...	...	...	...
		do ...	Suror	do ...	12	12	...	...	...	...	...	...	...	...	...	...	...	...	...
		do ...	Survani	do ...	40	37	3	...	...	...	...	...	...	...	...	...	...	...	...
		do ...	Surve	do ...	5	2	3	...	...	...	...	...	...	...	...	...	...	...	...
		do ...	Tajavar	do ...	8	1	7	...	...	...	...	...	...	...	...	...	...	...	...
		do ...	Talkar	do ...	22	12	10	...	...	...	...	...	...	...	...	...	...	...	...
		do ...	Taluk	do ...	3	3	...	3	3	...	...	...	...	...	...	...	...	...	...
		do ...	Tapukar	do ...	38	38	...	...	...	...	...	...	...	...	...	...	...	...	...
		do ...	Tara	do ...	12	5	7	...	...	...	...	...	...	...	...	...	...	...	...
		do ...	Thanar	do ...	52	52	...	...	...	...	...	...	...	...	...	...	...	...	...
		do ...	Thorat	do ...	5	3	2	...	...	...	...	...	...	...	...	...	...	...	...
		do ...	Vadne...	do ...	42	21	21	...	...	...	...	...	...	...	...	...	...	...	...
		do ...	Vaghmar	do ...	24	13	11	...	...	...	...	...	...	...	...	...	...	...	...
		do ...	Vaher	do ...	20	20	...	...	...	...	...	...	...	...	...	...	...	...	...
		do ...	Vakal	do ...	5	3	2	...	...	...	...	...	...	...	...	...	...	...	...
		do ...	Valo	do ...	10	8	2	...	...	...	...	...	...	...	...	...	...	...	...
		do ...	Valkhed	do ...	74	85	89	...	...	...	...	...	...	...	...	...	...	...	...
		do ...	Valvane	do ...	5	2	3	...	...	...	...	...	...	...	...	...	...	...	...
		do ...	Vardhan	do ...	20	20	...	...	...	...	...	...	...	...	...	...	...	...	...
		do ...	Varval	do ...	137	135	2	...	...	...	...	...	...	...	...	...	...	...	...
		do ...	Vasai	do ...	24	13	11	...	...	...	...	...	...	...	...	...	...	...	...
		do ...	Vasekari	do ...	11	6	5	...	...	...	...	...	...	...	...	...	...	...	...
		do ...	Vasudeo	do ...	1,674	783	891	...	...	...	...	...	...	...	...	...	...	...	...
		do ...	Vatake	do ...	2	1	1	...	...	...	...	...	...	...	...	...	...	...	...
		do ...	Vatyal	do ...	75	55	20	...	...	...	...	...	...	...	...	...	...	...	...
		do ...	Vavangi	do ...	11	...	11	...	...	...	...	...	...	...	...	...	...	...	...
		do ...	Vavre...	do ...	2	1	1	...	...	...	...	...	...	...	...	...	...	...	...
		do ...	Vichsi...	do ...	1,842	945	897	...	...	...	...	...	...	...	...	...	...	...	...
		do ...	Vighal	do ...	55	55	...	...	...	...	...	...	...	...	...	...	...	...	...
		do ...	Vikrama	do ...	6	2	4	...	...	...	...	...	...	...	...	...	...	...	...
		do ...	Vishva	do ...	3	1	2	...	...	...	...	...	...	...	...	...	...	...	...
		do ...	Vottam	do ...	5	4	1	...	...	...	...	...	...	...	...	...	...	...	...
		do ...	Yalechore	do ...	5	4	1	...	...	...	...	...	...	...	...	...	...	...	...
		do ...	Yadukal	do ...	1	1	...	1	1	...	...	...	...	...	...	...	...	...	...
		do ...	Yaoda...	do ...	12	9	3	...	...	...	12	9	3	...	...	...	...	...	...
		do ...	Yaole	do ...	1	1	...	...	...	...	...	...	...	...	...	...	...	...	...
		do ...	Yapugalewar	do ...	279	169	110	...	...	...	...	...	...	...	...	...	...	...	...
		do ...	Yasde	do ...	14	7	7	...	...	...	...	...	...	...	...	...	...	...	...
		do ...	Yedke	do ...	6	3	3	...	...	...	...	...	...	...	...	...	...	...	...
		do ...	Unspecified	do ...	827,262	421,232	406,030	6,880	3,408	2,972	957	506	451	1,197	608	589	251	129	122
			Total.....		989,857	494,719	474,638	7,786	4,164	3,622	2,633	1,377	1,256	2,358	1,212	1,146	1,590	800	790

TABLE XVI.

Castes and Sub-divisions.—*Continued.*

Class.	Group.	Castes.	Sub-division of Castes.	Religion.	Warangal.			Elgandal.			Indur.			Medak.			Aurangabad.		
					Total.	Males.	Females.	Total.	Males.	Females.	Total.	Males.	Females.	Total.	Males.	Females.	Total.	Males.	Females.
					21	22	23	24	25	26	27	28	29	30	31	32	33	34	35
A	1 ...	Mahratta ...	Suratyari	Hindu ...	...	...	...	...	...	...	...	...	...	...	...	...	...	...	...
		do ...	Suria	do ...	...	...	...	...	...	...	...	...	...	...	...	...	...	...	...
		do ...	Suriked	do ...	...	...	...	...	...	...	...	...	...	...	...	...	...	...	...
		do ...	Surnor... ...	do ...	...	...	...	...	...	...	...	...	...	...	...	...	...	...	...
		do ...	Survani	do ...	...	...	...	...	...	...	...	...	...	...	...	...	...	...	...
		do ...	Surve	do ...	...	...	...	...	...	...	...	...	...	...	...	...	...	...	...
		do ...	Tajavar	do ...	...	...	...	...	...	...	...	...	...	...	...	...	...	...	...
		do ...	Talkar	do ...	...	...	...	...	...	...	...	...	...	...	...	...	...	...	...
		do ...	Taluk... ...	do ...	...	...	...	...	...	...	...	...	...	...	...	...	...	...	...
		do ...	Tapukar	do ...	...	...	...	...	...	...	...	...	...	...	...	...	...	...	...
		do ...	Tara	do ...	...	...	...	...	...	...	...	...	...	...	...	...	...	...	...
		do ...	Thanar	do ...	...	...	...	...	...	...	...	...	...	...	...	...	...	...	...
		do ...	Thorat	do ...	...	...	...	...	...	...	...	...	...	...	...	...	...	...	...
		do ...	Vadne... ...	do ...	...	...	...	...	...	...	...	...	...	...	...	...	...	...	...
		do ...	Vaghmar	do ...	...	...	...	...	...	...	...	...	...	...	...	...	...	...	...
		do ...	Vaher... ...	do ...	...	...	...	...	...	...	...	...	...	...	...	...	...	...	...
		do ...	Vakal... ...	do ...	...	...	...	...	...	...	...	...	...	...	...	...	...	...	...
		do ...	Vale... ...	do ...	...	...	...	...	...	...	...	...	...	...	...	...	...	...	...
		do ...	Valkhod	do ...	...	...	...	...	...	...	...	...	...	...	...	...	...	...	...
		do ...	Valvane	do ...	...	...	...	...	...	...	...	...	...	...	...	...	...	...	...
		do ...	Vardhan	do ...	...	...	...	...	...	...	...	...	...	...	...	...	...	...	...
		do ...	Varval	do ...	...	...	...	...	...	...	...	...	...	...	...	...	...	...	...
		do ...	Vasai	do ...	...	...	...	...	...	...	...	...	...	...	...	...	...	...	...
		do ...	Vasekari	do ...	...	...	...	...	...	...	...	...	...	...	...	...	...	...	...
		do ...	Vasudeo	do ...	...	...	...	...	...	...	...	...	...	...	...	...	...	...	...
		do ...	Vatake	do ...	...	...	...	...	...	...	...	...	...	...	...	...	188	62	76
		do ...	Vatyal	do ...	...	...	...	...	...	...	...	...	...	...	...	...	...	...	...
		do ...	Vavangi	do ...	...	...	...	...	...	...	...	...	...	...	...	...	8	8	...
		do ...	Vavre... ...	do ...	...	...	...	...	...	...	...	...	...	...	...	...	11	...	11
		do ...	Vichsi... ...	do ...	...	...	...	...	...	...	...	...	...	...	...	...	...	...	...
		do ...	Vighal	do ...	...	...	...	...	...	...	...	...	...	...	...	...	1,842	945	897
		do ...	Vikrama	do ...	...	...	...	...	...	...	...	...	...	...	...	...	...	...	...
		do ...	Vishva	do ...	...	...	...	...	...	...	...	...	...	...	...	...	...	...	...
		do ...	Vottam	do ...	...	...	...	...	...	...	...	...	...	...	...	...	8	1	2
		do ...	Yalechore	do ...	...	...	...	...	...	...	...	...	...	...	...	...	...	...	...
		do ...	Yadukal	do ...	...	...	...	...	...	...	...	...	...	...	...	...	...	...	...
		do ...	Yaoda... ...	do ...	...	...	...	...	...	...	...	...	...	...	...	...	...	...	...
		do ...	Yaole	do ...	...	...	...	...	...	...	...	...	...	...	...	...	...	...	...
		do ...	Yapugalewar	do ...	...	...	...	...	...	...	...	...	...	...	...	...	...	...	...
		do ...	Yasde... ...	do ...	...	...	...	...	...	...	...	...	...	...	...	...	...	...	...
		do ...	Yedke... ...	do ...	...	...	...	...	...	...	...	...	...	...	...	...	...	...	...
		do ...	Unspecified	do ...	4,794	2,535	2,259	753	408	345	17,507	8,944	8,563	685	364	821	28,765	14,610	14,155
			Total......		12,333	6,517	5,816	13,312	6,954	6,358	19,866	10,142	9,724	1,985	1,047	938	32,213	16,337	15,876

TABLE XVI.

Castes and Sub-divisions.—*Continued.*

Class.	Group.	Castes.	Sub-division of Castes.	Religion.	Birh. Total.	Birh. Males.	Birh. Females.	Nander. Total	Nander. Males.	Nander. Females.	Naldrug. Total.	Naldrug. Males.	Naldrug. Females.	Bidar. Total.	Bidar. Males.	Bidar. Females.	Parbhani. Total.	Parbhani. Males.	Parbhani. Females.
					36	37	38	39	40	41	42	43	44	45	46	47	48	49	50
A	1 ...	Mahratta ...	Suratyari	Hindu ...	...	...	...	...	...	...	7	3	4	...	...	...	...	...	...
		do ...	Suria	do ...	...	...	...	...	...	...	...	...	...	...	...	...	...	...	...
		do ...	Suriked	do ...	...	...	...	...	...	...	...	...	...	...	...	...	...	...	...
		do ...	Surur	do ...	...	...	...	12	12	...	...	...	...	...	...	...	...	...	...
		do ...	Survani	do ...	...	...	...	...	...	...	...	...	...	...	...	...	...	...	...
		do ...	Surve...	do ...	...	...	...	...	...	...	5	2	3	...	...	...	...	...	...
		do ...	Tajavar	do ...	...	...	...	...	...	...	...	...	...	...	...	...	8	1	7
		do ...	Talkar	do ...	...	...	...	...	...	...	...	...	...	...	...	...	...	...	...
		do ...	Taluk...	do ...	...	...	...	...	...	...	...	...	...	...	...	...	...	...	...
		do ...	Tapukar	do ...	...	...	...	38	38	...	...	...	...	...	...	...	...	...	...
		do ...	Tara	do ...	...	...	...	...	...	...	12	5	7	...	...	...	...	...	...
		do ...	Thanar	do ...	...	...	...	52	52	...	...	...	...	...	...	...	...	...	...
		do ...	Thorat	do ...	...	...	...	...	...	...	5	3	2	...	...	...	...	...	...
		do ...	Vadue	do ...	...	...	...	22	9	13	20	12	8	...	...	...	...	...	...
		do ...	Vaghmar	do ...	...	...	...	9	4	5	15	9	6	...	...	...	...	...	...
		do ...	Vaher...	do ...	...	...	...	...	...	...	...	...	...	20	20	...	...	...	...
		do ...	Vakal...	do ...	...	...	...	...	...	...	...	...	...	5	3	2	...	...	...
		do ...	Vale	do ...	...	...	...	...	...	...	5	5	...	5	3	2	...	...	...
		do ...	Valkhed	do ...	...	...	...	74	85	89	...	...	...	...	...	...	...	...	...
		do ...	Valvane	do ...	...	...	...	...	...	...	5	2	3	...	...	...	...	...	...
		do ...	Vardhan	do ...	...	...	...	...	...	...	...	...	...	...	...	...	...	...	...
		do ...	Varval	do ...	...	...	...	...	...	...	187	185	2	...	...	...	...	...	...
		do ...	Vasai	do ...	...	...	...	...	...	...	...	...	...	...	...	...	...	...	...
		do ...	Vasekar	do ...	...	...	...	...	...	...	11	6	5	...	...	...	...	...	...
		do ...	Vasudeo	do ...	181	81	100	196	102	94	304	150	154	281	94	187	494	228	266
		do ...	Vataka	do ...	...	...	...	...	...	...	2	1	1	...	...	...	...	...	...
		do ...	Vatyal	do ...	...	...	...	67	47	20	...	...	...	...	...	...	...	...	...
		do ...	Vavangi	do ...	...	...	...	...	...	...	...	...	...	...	...	...	...	...	...
		do ...	Vavre...	do ...	...	...	...	...	...	...	2	1	1	...	...	...	...	...	...
		do ...	Viobai...	do ...	...	...	...	...	...	...	...	...	...	...	...	...	...	...	...
		do ...	Vighal	do ...	...	...	...	55	55	...	...	...	...	...	...	...	...	...	...
		do ...	Vikrama	do ...	...	...	...	...	...	...	...	...	...	...	...	...	...	...	...
		do ...	Vishva	do ...	...	...	...	...	...	...	...	...	...	...	...	...	...	...	...
		do ...	Vottam	do ...	...	...	...	...	...	...	...	...	...	...	...	...	...	...	...
		do ...	Yalgohore	do ...	...	...	...	...	...	...	5	4	1	...	...	...	...	...	...
		do ...	Yadukal	do ...	...	...	...	...	...	...	...	...	...	...	...	...	...	...	...
		do ...	Yaoda...	do ...	...	...	...	...	...	...	...	...	...	...	...	...	...	...	...
		do ...	Yaole	do ...	...	...	...	...	...	...	...	...	...	...	...	...	...	...	...
		do ...	Yapugalewar	do ...	...	...	...	279	169	110	...	...	...	...	...	...	...	...	...
		do ...	Yasde...	do ...	...	...	...	...	...	...	14	7	7	...	...	...	...	...	...
		do ...	Yedke...	do ...	...	...	...	...	...	...	6	3	3	...	...	...	...	...	...
		do ...	Unspecified	do ...	164,383	83,738	80,645	104,525	52,627	51,898	175,158	89,124	86,034	105,454	54,085	51,419	192,086	97,778	94,313
			Total......		165,663	84,348	81,315	155,787	79,608	76,184	200,926	102,255	98,671	121,112	61,854	59,258	203,812	103,892	99,920

TABLE XVI.

Castes and Sub-divisions.—*Continued.*

Class.	Group.	Castes.	Sub-division of Castes.	Religion.	Sirpur Tandur. Total.	Sirpur Tandur. Males.	Sirpur Tandur. Females.	Gulbarga. Total.	Gulbarga. Males.	Gulbarga. Females.	Raichur. Total.	Raichur. Males.	Raichur. Females.	Lingasugur. Total.	Lingasugur. Males.	Lingasugur. Females.	Railways. Total.	Railways. Males.	Railways. Females.
					51	52	53	54	55	56	57	58	59	60	61	62	63	64	65
A	1 ...	Mahratta ...	Suratvari	Hindu ...	...	...	...	...	...	...	...	...	...	...	...	...	...	...	...
		do ...	Suria	do ...	...	...	...	...	...	...	8	4	4	...	...	...	...	...	...
		do ...	Suriked	do ...	...	...	...	...	...	...	...	...	...	...	...	...	...	...	...
		do ...	Surur...	do ...	...	...	...	...	...	...	...	...	...	...	...	...	...	...	...
		do ...	Survani	do ...	...	...	...	...	...	...	...	...	...	40	37	3	...	...	...
		do ...	Surve	do ...	...	...	...	...	...	...	...	...	...	...	...	...	...	...	...
		do ...	Tajavar	do ...	...	...	...	...	...	...	...	...	...	...	...	...	...	...	...
		do ...	Talkar	do ...	...	...	...	22	12	10	...	...	...	...	...	...	...	...	...
		do ...	Taluk...	do ...	...	...	...	...	...	...	...	...	...	...	...	...	...	...	...
		do ...	Tapukar	do ...	...	...	...	...	...	...	...	...	...	...	...	...	...	...	...
		do ...	Tara	do ...	...	...	...	...	...	...	...	...	...	...	...	...	...	...	...
		do ...	Thanar	do ...	...	...	...	...	...	...	...	...	...	...	...	...	...	...	...
		do ...	Thorat	do ...	...	...	...	...	...	...	...	...	...	...	...	...	...	...	...
		do ...	Vadne...	do ...	...	...	...	...	...	...	...	...	...	...	...	...	...	...	...
		do ...	Vaghmar	do ...	...	...	...	...	...	...	...	...	...	...	...	...	...	...	...
		do ...	Vaher...	do ...	...	...	...	...	...	...	...	...	...	...	...	...	...	...	...
		do ...	Vakal...	do ...	...	...	...	...	...	...	...	...	...	...	...	...	...	...	...
		do ...	Vale	do ...	...	...	...	...	...	...	...	...	...	...	...	...	...	...	...
		do ...	Valkhed	do ...	...	...	...	...	...	...	...	...	...	...	...	...	...	...	...
		do ...	Valvane	do ...	...	...	...	...	...	...	...	...	...	...	...	...	...	...	...
		do ...	Vardhan	do ...	20	20	...	...	...	...	...	...	...	...	...	...	...	...	...
		do ...	Varval	do ...	...	...	...	...	...	...	...	...	...	...	...	...	...	...	...
		do ...	Vasai	do ...	24	13	11	...	...	...	...	...	...	...	...	...	...	...	...
		do ...	Vasekari	do ...	...	...	...	...	...	...	...	...	...	...	...	...	...	...	...
		do ...	Vasudeo	do ...	125	64	61	5	2	3	...	...	...	...	...	...	...	...	...
		do ...	Vatake	do ...	...	...	...	...	...	...	...	...	...	...	...	...	...	...	...
		do ...	Vatyal	do ...	...	...	...	...	...	...	...	...	...	...	...	...	...	...	...
		do ...	Vavangi	do ...	...	...	...	...	...	...	...	...	...	...	...	...	...	...	...
		do ...	Vavre...	do ...	...	...	...	...	...	...	...	...	...	...	...	...	...	...	...
		do ...	Vichsi...	do ...	...	...	...	...	...	...	...	...	...	...	...	...	...	...	...
		do ...	Vighal	do ...	...	...	...	...	...	...	...	...	...	...	...	...	...	...	...
		do ...	Vikrama	do ...	...	...	...	...	...	...	...	...	...	6	2	4	...	...	...
		do ...	Vishva	do ...	...	...	...	...	...	...	...	...	...	...	...	...	...	...	...
		do ...	Vottam	do ...	...	...	...	...	...	...	5	4	1	...	...	...	...	...	...
		do ...	Yalechore	do ...	...	...	...	...	...	...	...	...	...	...	...	...	...	...	...
		do ...	Yadukal	do ...	...	...	...	...	...	...	...	...	...	...	...	...	...	...	...
		do ...	Yaoda	do ...	...	...	...	...	...	...	...	...	...	...	...	...	...	...	...
		do ...	Yaole	do ...	1	1	...	...	...	...	...	...	...	...	...	...	...	...	...
		do ...	Yapugulewar	do ...	...	...	...	...	...	...	...	...	...	...	...	...	...	...	...
		do ...	Yasde	do ...	...	...	...	...	...	...	...	...	...	...	...	...	...	...	...
		do ...	Yedke...	do ...	...	...	...	...	...	...	...	...	...	...	...	...	...	...	...
		do ...	Unspecified	do ...	3,521	1,818	1,703	12,800	6,609	6,191	3,300	1,603	1,697	4,398	2,186	2,212	348	207	141
			Total......		5,118	2,648	2,470	14,097	7,179	6,918	3,493	1,706	1,787	4,974	2,476	2,498	349	208	141

TABLE XVI.

Castes and Sub-divisions.—*Continued.*

Class.	Group.	Castes.	Sub-division of Castes.	Religion.	Total. Total.	Total. Males.	Total. Females.	Hyderabad. Total.	Hyderabad. Males.	Hyderabad. Females.	Atraf-i-Balda. Total.	Atraf-i-Balda. Males.	Atraf-i-Balda. Females.	Mahabubnagar. Total.	Mahabubnagar. Males.	Mahabubnagar. Females.	Nalgonda. Total.	Nalgonda. Males.	Nalgonda. Females.
1	2	3	4	5	6	7	8	9	10	11	12	13	14	15	16	17	18	19	20
A	2a ...	Kunbi ...	Abadvad	Hindu ...	13	7	6	...	...	...	...	...	...	...	...	...	...	...	...
		do ...	Achchhao	do ...	39	39	...	...	...	...	...	...	...	...	...	...	...	...	...
		do ...	Adava...	do ...	1	...	1	...	...	...	...	...	...	...	...	...	...	...	...
		do ...	Adi	do ...	88	45	43	25	11	14	...	...	...	...	...	...	...	...	...
		do ...	Adkapu	do ...	87	44	43	...	...	...	...	...	...	...	...	...	9	2	7
		do ...	Adle	do ...	2	2	...	...	...	...	...	...	...	...	...	...	...	...	...
		do ...	Ahal	do ...	8	5	3	...	...	...	...	...	...	...	...	...	...	...	...
		do ...	Ahervad	do ...	25	11	14	5	3	2	...	...	...	...	...	...	...	...	...
		do ...	Ahnale	do ...	12	5	7	...	...	...	...	...	...	...	...	...	...	...	...
		do ...	Aide	do ...	142	142	...	...	...	...	...	...	...	...	...	...	...	...	...
		do ...	Akramase	do ...	4,307	2,055	2,252	25	21	4	...	...	...	...	...	...	...	...	...
		do ...	Alivad	do ...	2	1	1	...	...	...	...	...	...	...	...	...	...	...	...
		do ...	Anjulvad	do ...	78	77	1	...	...	...	...	...	...	...	...	...	...	...	...
		do ...	Ansitivar	do ...	25	15	10	...	...	...	...	...	...	...	...	...	...	...	...
		do ...	Aogi	do ...	30	16	14	...	...	...	...	...	...	...	...	...	...	...	...
		do ...	Apar	do ...	5	3	2	...	...	...	...	...	...	...	...	...	...	...	...
		do ...	Arayatha	do ...	16	3	13	...	...	...	...	...	...	...	...	...	...	...	...
		do ...	Are	do ...	1,476	759	717	...	...	...	...	...	...	...	...	...	45	31	14
		do ...	Aroto	do ...	7	1	6	...	...	...	...	...	...	...	...	...	...	...	...
		do ...	Asal	do ...	22	10	12	...	...	...	...	...	...	...	...	...	...	...	...
		do ...	At	do ...	1	1	...	...	...	...	...	...	...	...	...	...	...	...	...
		do ...	Athva...	do ...	139	...	139	...	...	...	...	...	...	...	...	...	...	...	...
		do ...	Autad	do ...	7	3	4	...	...	...	...	...	...	...	...	...	...	...	...
		do ...	Aval	do ...	9	...	9	...	...	...	...	...	...	...	...	...	...	...	...
		do ...	Awat	do ...	8	3	5	...	...	...	...	...	...	...	...	...	...	...	...
		do ...	Badeole	do ...	6	3	3	...	...	...	...	...	...	...	...	...	...	...	...
		do ...	Bagle	do ...	81	42	39	...	...	...	...	...	...	...	...	...	...	...	...
		do ...	Bairaval	do ...	22	14	8	...	...	...	...	...	...	...	...	...	...	...	...
		do ...	Balwantvad	do ...	18	9	9	...	...	...	...	...	...	...	...	...	...	...	...
		do ...	Banavad	do ...	92	47	45	...	...	...	...	...	...	...	...	...	...	...	...
		do ...	Barsevad	do ...	31	14	17	...	...	...	...	...	...	...	...	...	...	...	...
		do ...	Basiput	do ...	1	...	1	...	...	...	...	...	...	...	...	...	...	...	...
		do ...	Basmad	do ...	5	3	2	5	3	2	...	...	...	...	...	...	...	...	...
		do ...	Begvad	do ...	236	80	156	...	...	...	...	...	...	...	...	...	...	...	...
		do ...	Bhadge	do ...	54	24	30	...	...	...	...	...	...	...	...	...	...	...	...
		do ...	Bhairkapu	do ...	10	6	4	...	...	...	...	...	...	...	...	...	...	...	...
		do ...	Bhajgod	do ...	60	32	28	...	...	...	...	...	...	...	...	...	...	...	...
		do ...	Bhamat	do ...	403	205	198	...	...	...	...	...	...	...	...	...	...	...	...
		do ...	Bhanor	do ...	1	1	...	...	...	...	...	...	...	...	...	...	...	...	...
		do ...	Bharadi	do ...	510	252	258	...	...	...	...	...	...	...	...	...	...	...	...
		do ...	Bharol	do ...	16	8	12	...	...	...	...	...	...	...	...	...	...	...	...
		do ...	Bhatvad	do ...	94	52	42	...	...	...	...	...	...	...	...	...	...	...	...

TABLE XVI.

Castes and Sub-divisions.—*Continued.*

Class.	Group.	Castes.	Sub-division of Castes.	Religion.	Warangal. Total.	Warangal. Males.	Warangal. Females.	Elgandal. Total.	Elgandal. Males.	Elgandal. Females.	Indur. Total.	Indur. Males.	Indur. Females.	Medak. Total.	Medak. Males.	Medak. Females.	Aurangabad. Total.	Aurangabad. Males.	Aurangabad. Females.
					21	22	23	24	25	26	27	28	29	30	31	32	33	34	35
A	2a	Kunbi	Abadv d	Hindu	...	...	...	...	...	...	...	...	...	...	...	...	...	...	...
		do	Achchhao	do	...	...	...	...	...	...	...	...	...	...	...	...	...	...	...
		do	Adava	do	...	...	...	...	...	...	...	...	...	...	...	...	...	...	...
		do	Adi	do	...	...	...	58	34	24	...	...	...	...	...	...	...	...	...
		do	Adkapu	do	...	...	...	74	39	35	...	...	...	...	...	...	...	...	...
		do	Adle	do	...	...	...	...	...	...	...	...	...	...	...	...	2	2	...
		do	Ahal	do	...	...	...	...	...	...	...	...	...	...	...	...	...	...	...
		do	Ahervad	do	...	...	...	...	...	...	20	8	12	...	...	...	...	...	...
		do	Ahnale	do	...	...	...	...	...	...	12	5	7	...	...	...	...	...	...
		do	Aide	do	...	...	...	...	...	...	...	...	...	...	...	...	142	142	...
		do	Akramase	do	...	...	...	14	9	5	...	...	...	...	...	...	2,823	1,351	1,472
		do	Alivad	do	...	...	...	...	...	...	...	...	...	...	...	...	...	...	...
		do	Anjulvad	do	...	...	...	...	...	...	...	...	...	...	...	...	78	77	1
		do	Ansitivar	do	...	...	...	...	...	...	25	15	10	...	...	...	...	...	...
		do	Aogi	do	...	...	...	...	...	...	...	...	...	...	...	...	...	...	...
		do	Apar	do	...	...	...	...	...	...	...	...	...	...	...	...	5	3	2
		do	Arayatha	do	...	...	...	...	...	...	...	...	...	...	...	...	...	...	...
		do	Are	do	...	...	...	...	...	...	1	1	...	...	...	...	...	...	...
		do	Arote	do	...	...	...	...	...	...	...	...	...	...	...	...	...	...	...
		do	Asal	do	...	...	...	...	...	...	22	10	12	...	...	...	...	...	...
		do	At	do	...	...	...	...	...	...	...	...	...	...	...	...	...	...	...
		do	Athva	do	...	...	...	...	...	...	...	...	...	...	...	...	...	...	...
		do	Antad	do	...	...	...	...	...	...	...	...	...	...	...	...	7	3	4
		do	Aval	do	...	...	...	...	...	...	...	...	...	...	...	...	...	...	...
		do	Awat	do	...	...	...	...	...	...	...	...	...	...	...	...	8	3	5
		do	Badeole	do	...	...	...	...	...	...	...	...	...	...	...	...	...	...	...
		do	Bagle	do	...	...	...	...	...	...	...	...	...	...	...	...	...	...	...
		do	Bairaval	do	...	...	...	...	...	...	...	...	...	...	...	...	...	...	...
		do	Balwantvad	do	...	...	...	...	...	...	18	9	9	...	...	...	...	...	...
		do	Banavad	do	...	...	...	...	...	...	45	22	23	...	...	...	...	...	...
		do	Barsevad	do	...	...	...	...	...	...	31	14	17	...	...	...	...	...	...
		do	Basiput	do	...	...	...	...	...	...	...	...	...	...	...	...	...	...	...
		do	Basmad	do	...	...	...	...	...	...	...	...	...	...	...	...	...	...	...
		do	Begvad	do	...	...	...	...	...	...	11	6	5	...	...	...	...	...	...
		do	Bhadge	do	...	...	...	...	...	...	...	...	...	...	...	...	28	10	18
		do	Bhairkapu	do	...	...	...	...	...	...	10	6	4	...	...	...	...	...	...
		do	Bhajgod	do	...	...	...	...	...	...	...	...	...	...	...	...	...	...	...
		do	Bhamat	do	...	...	...	...	...	...	...	...	...	...	...	...	...	...	...
		do	Bhanor	do	...	...	...	...	...	...	1	1	...	...	...	...	...	...	...
		do	Bharadi	do	...	...	...	...	...	...	...	...	...	...	...	...	874	191	183
		do	Bharol	do	...	...	...	...	...	...	...	...	...	...	...	...	9	...	9
		do	Bhatvad	do	...	...	...	...	...	...	74	40	34	...	...	...	...	...	...

TABLE XVI.

Castes and Sub-divisions.—*Continued.*

Class.	Group.	Castes.	Sub-division of Castes.	Religion.	Birh. Total.	Birh. Males.	Birh. Females.	Nander. Total.	Nander. Males.	Nander. Females.	Naldrug. Total.	Naldrug. Males.	Naldrug. Females.	Bidar. Total.	Bidar. Males.	Bidar. Females.	Parbhani. Total.	Parbhani. Males.	Parbhani. Females.
					36	37	38	39	40	41	42	43	44	45	46	47	48	49	50
A	2a ...	Kunbi ...	Abadvad	Hindu ...	...	...	...	13	7	6	...	...	...	...	...	...	...	...	...
		do ...	Achchhao	do ...	39	39	...	...	...	...	...	...	...	...	...	...	...	...	...
		do ...	Adava...	do ...	1	...	1	...	...	...	...	...	...	...	...	...	...	...	...
		do ...	Adi	do ...	...	...	...	...	...	...	...	...	...	...	...	...	...	...	...
		do ...	Adkapu	do ...	...	...	...	4	3	1	...	...	...	...	...	...	...	...	...
		do ...	Adle	do ...	...	...	...	...	...	...	...	...	...	...	...	...	...	...	...
		do ...	Ahal	do ...	...	...	...	8	5	3	...	...	...	...	...	...	...	...	...
		do ...	Ahervad	do ...	...	...	...	...	...	...	...	...	...	...	...	...	...	...	...
		do ...	Ahnale	do ...	...	...	...	...	...	...	...	...	...	...	...	...	...	...	...
		do ...	Aide	do ...	...	...	...	...	...	...	...	...	...	...	...	...	...	...	...
		do ...	Akramase	do ...	132	67	65	...	...	...	793	401	392	9	4	5	150	13	137
		do ...	Alivad	do ...	...	...	...	...	...	...	...	...	...	...	...	...	...	...	...
		do ...	Anjulvad	do ...	...	...	...	...	...	...	...	...	...	...	...	...	...	...	...
		do ...	Ansitivar	do ...	...	...	...	...	...	...	...	...	...	...	...	...	...	...	...
		do ...	Aogi	do ...	...	...	...	...	...	...	...	...	...	...	...	...	...	...	...
		do ...	Apar	do ...	...	...	...	...	...	...	...	...	...	...	...	...	...	...	...
		do ...	Arayatha	do ...	...	...	...	...	...	...	...	...	...	...	...	...	...	...	...
		do ...	Are	do ...	...	...	...	...	...	...	...	...	...	...	...	...	...	...	...
		do ...	Arote	do ...	...	...	...	...	...	...	...	...	...	...	...	...	...	...	...
		do ...	Asal	do ...	...	...	...	...	...	...	...	...	...	...	...	...	...	...	...
		do ...	At	do ...	1	1	...	...	...	...	...	...	...	...	...	...	...	...	...
		do ...	Athva...	do ...	...	...	...	...	...	...	...	...	...	...	...	...	...	...	...
		do ...	Autad...	do ...	...	...	...	...	...	...	...	...	...	...	...	...	139	...	139
		do ...	Aval	do ...	...	...	...	9	...	9	...	...	...	...	...	...	...	...	...
		do ...	Awat	do ...	...	...	...	...	...	...	...	...	...	...	...	...	...	...	...
		do ...	Badeole	do ...	...	...	...	6	3	3	...	...	...	...	...	...	...	...	...
		do ...	Bagle	do ...	...	...	...	...	...	...	...	...	...	...	...	...	...	...	...
		do ...	Bairaval	do ...	...	...	...	...	...	...	...	...	...	...	...	...	...	...	...
		do ...	Balwantvad	do ...	...	...	...	...	...	...	...	...	...	...	...	...	22	14	8
		do ...	Banavad	do ...	...	...	...	...	...	...	...	...	...	...	...	...	...	...	...
		do ...	Barsevad	do ...	...	...	...	...	...	...	...	...	...	...	...	...	...	...	...
		do ...	Basiput	do ...	1	...	1	...	...	...	...	...	...	...	...	...	...	...	...
		do ...	Basmad	do ...	...	...	...	...	...	...	...	...	...	...	...	...	...	...	...
		do ...	Begvad	do ...	...	...	...	225	74	151	...	...	...	...	...	...	...	...	...
		do ...	Bhadge	do ...	...	...	...	26	14	12	...	...	...	...	...	...	...	...	...
		do ...	Bhairkapu	do ...	...	...	...	...	...	...	...	...	...	...	...	...	...	...	...
		do ...	Bhajgod	do ...	...	...	...	60	32	28	...	...	...	...	...	...	...	...	...
		do ...	Bhamat	do ...	...	...	...	...	...	...	...	...	...	3	2	1	206	98	108
		do ...	Bhanor	do ...	...	...	...	...	...	...	...	...	...	...	...	...	...	...	...
		do ...	Bharadi	do ...	33	15	18	...	...	...	...	...	...	8	4	4	...	...	...
		do ...	Bharol...	do ...	...	...	...	...	...	...	...	...	...	...	...	...	7	3	4
		do ...	Bhatvad	do ...	...	...	...	20	12	8	...	...	...	...	...	...	...	...	...

TABLE XVI.

Castes and Sub-divisions.—*Continued.*

Class.	Group.	Castes.	Sub-division of Castes.	Religion.	Sirpur Tandur. Total.	Sirpur Tandur. Males.	Sirpur Tandur. Females.	Gulbarga. Total.	Gulbarga. Males.	Gulbarga. Females.	Raichur. Total.	Raichur. Males.	Raichur. Females.	Lingasugur. Total.	Lingasugur. Males.	Lingasugur. Females.	Railways. Total.	Railways. Males.	Railways. Females.
					51	52	53	54	55	56	57	58	59	60	61	62	63	64	65
A	2a ...	Kunbi ...	Abadvad	Hindu ...	...	...	...	...	...	...	...	...	...	...	...	...	...	...	...
		do ...	Achchhao	do ...	...	...	...	...	...	...	...	...	...	...	...	...	...	...	...
		do ...	Adava...	do ...	...	...	...	...	...	...	...	...	...	...	...	...	...	...	...
		do ...	Adi	do ...	...	...	...	...	...	...	...	...	...	...	...	...	...	...	...
		do ...	Adkapu	do ...	...	...	...	...	...	...	...	...	...	...	...	...	...	...	...
		do ...	Adle	do ...	...	...	...	...	...	...	...	...	...	...	...	...	...	...	...
		do ...	Ahla	do ...	...	...	...	...	...	...	...	...	...	...	...	...	...	...	...
		do ...	Ahervad	do ...	...	...	...	...	...	...	...	...	...	...	...	...	...	...	...
		do ...	Ahnale	do ...	...	...	...	...	...	...	...	...	...	...	...	...	...	...	...
		do ...	Aide	do ...	...	...	...	...	...	...	...	...	...	...	...	...	...	...	...
		do ...	Akramase	do ...	361	189	172	...	...	...	...	...	...	...	...	...	...	...	...
		do ...	Alivad...	do ...	2	1	1	...	...	...	...	...	...	...	...	...	...	...	...
		do ...	Anjulvad	do ...	...	...	...	...	...	...	...	...	...	...	...	...	...	...	...
		do ...	Ansitivar	do ...	...	...	...	...	...	...	...	...	...	...	...	...	...	...	...
		do ...	Aogi	do ...	80	16	14	...	...	...	...	...	...	...	...	...	...	...	...
		do ...	Apar	do ...	...	...	...	...	...	...	...	...	...	...	...	...	...	...	...
		do ...	Arayatha	do ...	...	...	...	...	...	...	...	...	...	16	3	18	...	...	...
		do ...	Are	do ...	1,093	561	532	...	...	...	337	166	171	...	...	...	...	...	...
		do ...	Arote	do ...	7	1	6	...	...	...	...	...	...	...	...	...	...	...	...
		do ...	Asal	do ...	...	...	...	...	...	...	...	...	...	...	...	...	...	...	...
		do ...	At	do ...	...	...	...	...	...	...	...	...	...	...	...	...	...	...	...
		do ...	Athva	do ...	...	...	...	...	...	...	...	...	...	...	...	...	...	...	...
		do ...	Autad	do ...	...	...	...	...	...	...	...	...	...	...	...	...	...	...	...
		do ...	Aval	do ...	...	...	...	...	...	...	...	...	...	...	...	...	...	...	...
		do ...	Awat	do ...	...	...	...	...	...	...	...	...	...	...	...	...	...	...	...
		do ...	Badeole	do ...	...	...	...	...	...	...	...	...	...	...	...	...	...	...	...
		do ...	Bagle	do ...	...	...	...	15	10	5	...	...	...	66	32	34	...	...	...
		do ...	Bairaval	do ...	...	...	...	...	...	...	...	...	...	...	...	...	...	...	...
		do ...	Balwantvad	do ...	...	...	...	...	...	...	...	...	...	...	...	...	...	...	...
		do ...	Banavad	do ...	47	25	22	...	...	...	...	...	...	...	...	...	...	...	...
		do ...	Barsevad	do ...	...	...	...	...	...	...	...	...	...	...	...	...	...	...	...
		do ...	Basiput	do ...	...	...	...	...	...	...	...	...	...	...	...	...	...	...	...
		do ...	Basmad	do ...	...	...	...	...	...	...	...	...	...	...	...	...	...	...	...
		do ...	Begvad	do ...	...	...	...	...	...	...	...	...	...	...	...	...	...	...	...
		do ...	Bhadge	do ...	...	...	...	...	...	...	...	...	...	...	...	...	...	...	...
		do ...	Bhairkapu	do ...	...	...	...	...	...	...	...	...	...	...	...	...	...	...	...
		do ...	Bhajgod	do ...	...	...	...	...	...	...	...	...	...	...	...	...	...	...	...
		do ...	Bhamat	do ...	194	105	89	...	...	...	...	...	...	...	...	...	...	...	...
		do ...	Bhanor	do ...	...	...	...	...	...	...	...	...	...	...	...	...	...	...	...
		do ...	Bharadi	do ...	95	42	53	...	...	...	...	...	...	...	...	...	...	...	...
		do ...	Bharol	do ...	...	...	...	...	...	...	...	...	...	...	...	...	...	...	...
		do ...	Bhatvad	do ...	...	...	...	...	...	...	...	...	...	...	...	...	...	...	...

TABLE XVI.

Castes and Sub-divisions.—*Continued.*

Class.	Group.	Castes.	Sub-division of Castes.	Religion.	Total.			Hyderabad.			Atraf-i-Balda.			Mahabubnagar.			Nalgonda.		
					Total.	Males.	Females.	Total.	Males.	Females.	Total.	Males.	Females.	Total.	Males.	Females.	Total.	Males.	Females.
1	2	3	4	5	6	7	8	9	10	11	12	13	14	15	16	17	18	19	20
A	2a ...	Kunbi ...	Bhavane	Hindu ...	9	7	2	...	...	...	...	...	...	...	...	...	...	...	...
		do ...	Bhavesal	do ...	28	15	13	...	...	...	...	...	...	...	...	...	...	...	...
		do ...	Bhavle	do ...	9	5	4	...	...	...	...	...	...	...	...	...	...	...	...
		do ...	Bhaval	do ...	52	30	22	...	...	...	...	...	...	...	...	...	...	...	...
		do ...	Bhayadvad	do ...	37	17	20	...	...	...	...	...	...	...	...	...	...	...	...
		do ...	Bhimle	do ...	32	17	15	...	...	...	...	...	...	...	...	...	...	...	...
		do ...	Bhishia	do ...	3	2	1	...	...	...	...	...	...	...	...	...	...	...	...
		do ...	Bhitur...	do ...	13	13	...	...	...	...	...	...	...	...	...	...	...	...	...
		do ...	Bhopi	do ...	4	3	1	...	...	...	...	...	...	...	...	...	...	...	...
		do ...	Bhororvad	do ...	9,515	4,847	4,668	...	...	...	...	...	...	...	...	...	...	...	...
		do ...	Bhoroti	do ...	91	50	41	...	...	...	...	...	...	...	...	...	...	...	...
		do ...	Bhosar	do ...	86	39	47	...	...	...	...	...	...	...	...	...	...	...	...
		do ...	Bhoval	do ...	5	1	4	...	...	...	...	...	...	...	...	...	...	...	...
		do ...	Bhuno...	do ...	14	13	1	...	...	...	...	...	...	...	...	...	...	...	...
		do ...	Bhuti	do ...	15	7	8	...	...	...	...	...	...	...	...	...	...	...	...
		do ...	Bondhle	do ...	7	4	3	...	...	...	...	...	...	...	...	...	...	...	...
		do ...	Bukalvar	do ...	8	2	6	...	...	...	...	...	...	...	...	...	...	...	...
		do ...	Chakradavaru ...	do ...	60	32	28	...	...	...	...	...	...	...	...	...	...	...	...
		do ...	Chari	do ...	4	3	1	...	...	...	...	...	...	...	...	...	...	...	...
		do ...	Charkli	do ...	81	34	47	...	...	...	...	...	...	...	...	...	...	...	...
		do ...	Chatamata	do ...	194	99	95	...	...	...	...	...	...	...	...	...	...	...	...
		do ...	Chansari	do ...	97	54	43	...	...	...	...	...	...	...	...	...	...	...	...
		do ...	Chikde	do ...	13	8	5	...	...	...	...	...	...	...	...	...	...	...	...
		do ...	Chinakanti	do ...	50	34	16	...	...	...	...	...	...	...	...	...	...	...	...
		do ...	Chitapvad	do ...	14,186	7,229	6,957	...	...	...	2,576	1,292	1,284	1,563	787	776	560	276	284
		do ...	Chitkod	do ...	4	2	2	...	...	...	...	...	...	...	...	...	...	...	...
		do ...	Chitlavad	do ...	157	82	75	...	...	...	...	...	...	...	...	...	...	...	...
		do ...	Chitpal	do ...	491	267	224	...	...	...	...	...	...	...	...	...	...	...	...
		do ...	Chorvaonshi	do ...	6	3	3	...	...	...	...	...	...	...	...	...	...	...	...
		do ...	Chubal	do ...	9	5	4	...	...	...	...	...	...	...	...	...	...	...	...
		do ...	Dag	do ...	5	1	4	...	...	...	...	...	...	...	...	...	...	...	...
		do ...	Dagi	do ...	4	2	2	4	2	2	...	...	...	...	...	...	...	...	...
		do ...	Dakakar	do ...	3	1	2	3	1	2	...	...	...	...	...	...	...	...	...
		do ...	Dalve	do ...	5	3	2	...	...	...	...	...	...	...	...	...	...	...	...
		do ...	Dandinoru	do ...	92	46	46	...	...	...	...	...	...	...	...	...	...	...	...
		do ...	Dhamegar	do ...	18	12	6	...	...	...	...	...	...	...	...	...	...	...	...
		do ...	Dawan	do ...	6	5	1	6	5	1	...	...	...	...	...	...	...	...	...
		do ...	Dayavad	do ...	18	5	13	...	...	...	...	...	...	...	...	...	...	...	...
		do ...	Deore	do ...	8	6	2	...	...	...	...	...	...	...	...	...	...	...	...
		do ...	Doosal...	do ...	3	1	2	...	...	...	...	...	...	...	...	...	...	...	...
		do ...	Dovangi	do ...	9	5	4	...	...	...	...	...	...	...	...	...	...	...	...
		do ...	Devaraju	do ...	3	1	2	3	1	2	...	...	...	...	...	...	...	...	...

TABLE XVI.

Castes and Sub-divisions.—*Continued.*

Class.	Group.	Castes.	Sub-division of Castes.	Religion.	Warangal. Total.	Warangal. Males.	Warangal. Females.	Elgandal. Total.	Elgandal. Males.	Elgandal. Females.	Indur. Total.	Indur. Males.	Indur. Females.	Medak. Total.	Medak. Males.	Medak. Females.	Aurangabad. Total.	Aurangabad. Males.	Aurangabad. Females.
					21	22	23	24	25	26	27	28	29	30	31	32	33	34	35
A	2a ...	Kunbi ...	Bhavane	Hindu ...	...	...	...	...	...	...	...	...	...	...	...	...	9	7	2
		do ...	Bhavesal	do ...	...	...	...	...	...	...	28	15	18	...	...	...	...	...	...
		do ...	Bhavle	do ...	...	...	...	...	...	...	...	...	...	...	...	...	6	4	2
		do ...	Bhaval	do ...	...	...	...	...	...	...	52	30	22	...	...	...	...	...	...
		do ...	Bhayadvad	do ...	...	...	...	...	...	...	14	6	8	...	...	...	22	10	12
		do ...	Bhimle	do ...	...	...	...	...	...	...	...	...	...	...	...	...	...	...	...
		do ...	Bhishia	do ...	...	...	...	...	...	...	...	...	...	...	...	...	...	...	...
		do ...	Bhitur...	do ...	...	...	...	...	...	...	...	...	...	...	...	...	13	13	...
		do ...	Bhopi	do ...	...	...	...	...	...	...	...	...	...	...	...	...	4	3	1
		do ...	Bhororvad	do ...	...	...	...	...	...	...	8,097	4,142	3,955	...	...	...	...	...	...
		do ...	Bhoroti	do ...	...	...	...	...	...	...	91	50	41	...	...	...	...	...	...
		do ...	Bhosar	do ...	...	...	...	...	...	...	...	...	...	...	...	...	15	5	10
		do ...	Bhoval	do ...	...	...	...	...	...	...	5	1	4	...	...	...	...	...	...
		do ...	Bhuno...	do ...	...	...	...	...	...	...	...	...	...	...	...	...	...	...	...
		do ...	Bhuti	do ...	...	...	...	...	...	...	6	2	4	...	...	...	...	...	...
		do ...	Bondhle	do ...	...	...	...	...	...	...	...	...	...	...	...	...	7	4	3
		do ...	Bukalvar	do ...	...	...	...	...	...	...	8	2	6	...	...	...	...	...	...
		do ...	Chakradavaru ...	do ...	...	...	...	...	...	...	...	...	...	...	...	...	...	...	...
		do ...	Chari	do ...	...	...	...	...	...	...	...	...	...	...	...	...	...	...	...
		do ...	Charkli	do ...	...	...	...	...	...	...	...	...	...	...	...	...	...	...	...
		do ...	Chatamata	do ...	...	...	...	...	...	...	...	...	...	...	...	...	...	...	...
		do ...	Chansari	do ...	...	...	...	...	...	...	...	...	...	...	...	...	...	...	...
		do ...	Chikde	do ...	...	...	...	...	...	...	...	...	...	...	...	...	...	...	...
		do ...	Chinakanti	do ...	...	...	...	...	...	...	...	...	...	...	...	...	...	...	...
		do ...	Chitapvad	do ...	2,005	1,040	965	4,566	2,362	2,204	982	505	477	1,934	967	967	...	...	...
		do ...	Chitkod	do ...	...	...	...	...	...	...	...	...	...	...	...	...	...	...	...
		do ...	Chitlavad	do ...	...	...	...	...	...	...	157	82	75	...	...	...	...	...	...
		do ...	Chitpal	do ...	...	...	...	...	...	...	...	...	...	...	...	...	...	...	...
		do ...	Chorvaonshi	do ...	...	...	...	...	...	...	...	...	...	...	...	...	...	...	...
		do ...	Chubal	do ...	...	...	...	...	...	...	...	...	...	...	...	...	...	...	...
		do ...	Dag	do ...	...	...	...	...	...	...	...	...	...	...	...	...	9	5	4
		do ...	Dagi	do ...	...	...	...	...	...	...	...	...	...	...	...	...	...	...	...
		do ...	Dakakar	do ...	...	...	...	...	...	...	...	...	...	...	...	...	...	...	...
		do ...	Dalvo	do ...	...	...	...	...	...	...	...	...	...	...	...	...	...	...	...
		do ...	Dandimoru	do ...	...	...	...	...	...	...	...	...	...	...	...	...	...	...	...
		do ...	Dhamegar	do ...	...	...	...	...	...	...	...	...	...	...	...	...	...	...	...
		do ...	Dawan	do ...	...	...	...	...	...	...	...	...	...	...	...	...	...	...	...
		do ...	Dayavad	do ...	...	...	...	...	...	...	18	5	13	...	...	...	...	...	...
		do ...	Deore	do ...	...	...	...	...	...	...	...	...	...	...	...	...	...	...	...
		do ...	Deosal...	do ...	...	...	...	...	...	...	3	1	2	...	...	...	...	...	...
		do ...	Devangi	do ...	...	...	...	...	...	...	...	...	...	...	...	...	...	...	...
		do ...	Devaraju	do ...	...	...	...	...	...	...	...	...	...	...	...	...	...	...	...

TABLE XVI.

Castes and Sub-divisions.—*Continued.*

Class.	Group.	Castes.	Sub-division of Castes.	Religion.	Birh. Total.	Birh. Males.	Birh. Females.	Nander. Total.	Nander. Males.	Nander. Females.	Naldrug. Total.	Naldrug. Males.	Naldrug. Females.	Bidar. Total.	Bidar. Males.	Bidar. Females.	Parbhani. Total.	Parbhani. Males.	Parbhani. Females.
					36	37	38	39	40	41	42	43	44	45	46	47	48	49	50
A	2a ...	Kunbi ...	Bhavane	Hindu ...	...	...	...	...	...	...	...	...	...	...	...	...	...	...	...
		do ...	Bhavesal	do ...	...	...	...	...	...	...	...	...	...	...	...	...	...	...	...
		do ...	Bhavle	do ...	...	...	...	3	1	2	...	...	...	...	...	...	...	...	...
		do ...	Bhaval	do ...	...	...	...	...	...	...	...	...	...	...	...	...	...	...	...
		do ...	Bhayadvad	do ...	...	...	...	...	...	...	...	...	...	...	...	...	...	...	...
		do ...	Bhimle	do ...	...	...	...	...	...	...	...	...	...	82	17	15	...	...	...
		do ...	Bhishia	do ...	...	...	...	3	2	1	...	...	...	...	...	...	...	...	...
		do ...	Bhitur...	do ...	...	...	...	...	...	...	...	...	...	...	...	...	...	...	...
		do ...	Bhopi	do ...	...	...	...	...	...	...	...	...	...	...	...	...	...	...	...
		do ...	Bhororvad	do ...	...	...	...	1,418	705	713	...	...	...	...	...	...	...	...	...
		do ...	Bhoroti	do ...	...	...	...	...	...	...	...	...	...	...	...	...	...	...	...
		do ...	Bhosar	do ...	71	34	37	...	...	...	...	...	...	...	...	...	...	...	...
		do ...	Bhoval	do ...	...	...	...	...	...	...	...	...	...	...	...	...	...	...	...
		do ...	Bhuno...	do ...	...	...	...	...	...	...	...	...	...	...	...	...	...	...	...
		do ...	Bhuti	do ...	...	...	...	...	...	...	...	...	...	...	...	...	14	13	1
		do ...	Bondhle	do ...	...	...	...	...	...	...	...	...	...	9	5	4	...	...	...
		do ...	Bukalvar	do ...	...	...	...	...	...	...	...	...	...	...	...	...	...	...	...
		do ...	Chakradavaru ...	do ...	...	...	...	...	...	...	...	...	...	...	...	...	...	...	...
		do ...	Chari	do ...	...	...	...	...	...	...	...	...	...	...	...	...	...	...	...
		do ...	Charkli	do ...	...	...	...	...	...	...	...	...	...	...	...	...	...	...	...
		do ...	Chatamata	do ...	...	...	...	...	...	...	...	...	...	...	...	...	...	...	...
		do ...	Chansari	do ...	...	...	...	...	...	...	...	...	...	...	...	...	...	...	...
		do ...	Chikde	do ...	...	...	...	...	...	...	...	...	...	...	...	...	...	...	...
		do ...	Chinakanti	do ...	...	...	...	...	...	...	...	...	...	...	...	...	...	...	...
		do ...	Chilapvad	do ...	...	...	...	...	...	...	...	...	...	...	...	...	...	...	...
		do ...	Chitkod	do ...	...	...	...	4	2	2	...	...	...	...	...	...	...	...	...
		do ...	Chitlavad	do ...	...	...	...	...	...	...	...	...	...	...	...	...	...	...	...
		do ...	Chitpal	do ...	...	...	...	...	...	...	...	...	...	...	...	...	...	...	...
		do ...	Chorvaonshi	do ...	6	3	3	...	...	...	...	...	...	...	...	...	...	...	...
		do ...	Chubal	do ...	...	...	...	...	...	...	...	...	...	...	...	...	...	...	...
		do ...	Dag	do ...	...	...	...	5	1	4	...	...	...	...	...	...	...	...	...
		do ...	Dagi	do ...	...	...	...	...	...	...	...	...	...	...	...	...	...	...	...
		do ...	Dakakar	do ...	...	...	...	...	...	...	...	...	...	...	...	...	...	...	...
		do ...	Dalve	do ...	...	...	...	...	...	...	...	...	...	...	...	...	...	...	...
		do ...	Dandinoru	do ...	...	...	...	...	...	...	...	...	...	...	...	...	...	...	...
		do ...	Dhamegar	do ...	...	...	...	...	...	...	...	...	...	18	12	6	...	...	...
		do ...	Dawan	do ...	...	...	...	...	...	...	...	...	...	...	...	...	...	...	...
		do ...	Dayavad	do ...	...	...	...	...	...	...	...	...	...	...	...	...	...	...	...
		do ...	Deore	do ...	...	...	...	...	...	...	...	...	...	...	...	...	...	...	...
		do ...	Deosal...	do ...	...	...	...	...	...	...	...	...	...	...	...	...	...	...	...
		do ...	Devangi	do ...	...	...	...	...	...	...	...	...	...	...	...	...	...	...	...
		do ...	Devaraju	do ...	...	...	...	...	...	...	...	...	...	...	...	...	...	...	...

TABLE XVI.

Castes and Sub-divisions.—*Continued.*

Class.	Group.	Castes.	Sub-division of Castes.	Religion.	Sirpur Tandur. Total.	Sirpur Tandur. Males.	Sirpur Tandur. Females.	Gulbarga. Total.	Gulbarga. Males.	Gulbarga. Females.	Raichur. Total.	Raichur. Males.	Raichur. Females.	Lingasugur. Total.	Lingasugur. Males.	Lingasugur. Females.	Railways. Total.	Railways. Males.	Railways. Females.
					51	52	53	54	55	56	57	58	59	60	61	62	63	64	65
A	2a ...	Kunbi ...	Bhavane	Hindu ...	...	...	...	...	...	...	...	...	...	...	...	...	...	...	...
		do ...	Bhavesal ...	do ...	...	...	...	...	...	...	...	...	...	...	...	...	...	...	...
		do ...	Bhavle	do ...	...	...	...	...	...	...	...	...	...	...	...	...	...	...	...
		do ...	Bhaval	do ...	...	...	...	...	...	...	...	...	...	...	...	...	...	...	...
		do ...	Bhayadvad	do ...	1	1	...	...	...	...	...	...	...	...	...	...	...	...	...
		do ...	Bhimle	do ...	...	...	...	...	...	...	...	...	...	...	...	...	...	...	...
		do ...	Bhishia	do ...	...	...	...	...	...	...	...	...	...	...	...	...	...	...	...
		do ...	Bhitur...	do ...	...	...	...	...	...	...	...	...	...	...	...	...	...	...	...
		do ...	Bhopi	do ...	...	...	...	...	...	...	...	...	...	...	...	...	...	...	...
		do ...	Bhororvad	do ...	...	...	...	...	...	...	...	...	...	...	...	...	...	...	...
		do ...	Bhoroti	do ...	...	...	...	...	...	...	...	...	...	...	...	...	...	...	...
		do ...	Bhosar	do ...	...	...	...	...	...	...	...	...	...	...	...	...	...	...	...
		do ...	Bhoval	do ...	...	...	...	...	...	...	...	...	...	...	...	...	...	...	...
		do ...	Bhuno...	do ...	...	...	...	...	...	...	...	...	...	...	...	...	...	...	...
		do ...	Bhuti	do ...	...	...	...	...	...	...	...	...	...	...	...	...	...	...	...
		do ...	Bondhle	do ...	...	...	...	...	...	...	...	...	...	...	...	...	...	...	...
		do ...	Bukalvar	do ...	...	...	...	...	...	...	...	...	...	...	...	...	...	...	...
		do ...	Chakradavaru ...	do ...	...	...	...	...	...	...	...	...	...	60	82	28	...	...	...
		do ...	Chari	do ...	4	8	1	...	...	...	...	...	...	...	...	...	...	...	...
		do ...	Charkli	do ...	81	34	47	...	...	...	...	...	...	...	...	...	...	...	...
		do ...	Chatamata	do ...	...	...	...	...	...	...	...	...	...	194	99	95	...	...	...
		do ...	Chansari	do ...	97	54	43	...	...	...	...	...	...	...	...	...	...	...	...
		do ...	Chikde	do ...	...	...	...	13	8	5	...	...	...	...	...	...	...	...	...
		do ...	Chinakanti	do ...	...	...	...	...	...	...	...	...	...	50	84	16	...	...	...
		do ...	Chitapvad	do ...	...	...	...	...	...	...	...	...	...	...	...	...	...	...	...
		do ...	Chitkod	do ...	...	...	...	...	...	...	...	...	...	...	...	...	...	...	...
		do ...	Chitlavad	do ...	...	...	...	...	...	...	...	...	...	...	...	...	...	...	...
		do ...	Chitpal	do ...	...	...	...	491	267	224	...	...	...	...	...	...	...	...	...
		do ...	Chorvaonshi	do ...	...	...	...	...	...	...	...	...	...	...	...	...	...	...	...
		do ...	Chubal	do ...	...	...	...	...	...	...	...	...	...	...	...	...	...	...	...
		do ...	Dag	do ...	...	...	...	...	...	...	...	...	...	...	...	...	...	...	...
		do ...	Dagi	do ...	...	...	...	...	...	...	...	...	...	...	...	...	...	...	...
		do ...	Dakakar	do ...	...	...	...	...	...	...	...	...	...	...	...	...	...	...	...
		do ...	Dalve	do ...	...	...	...	5	8	2	...	...	...	...	...	...	...	...	...
		do ...	Dandinoru	do ...	...	...	...	...	...	...	...	...	...	92	46	46	...	...	...
		do ...	Dhamegar	do ...	...	...	...	...	...	...	...	...	...	...	...	...	...	...	...
		do ...	Dawan	do ...	...	...	...	...	...	...	...	...	...	...	...	...	...	...	...
		do ...	Dayavad	do ...	...	...	...	...	...	...	...	...	...	...	...	...	...	...	...
		do ...	Deore	do ...	8	6	2	...	...	...	...	...	...	...	...	...	...	...	...
		do ...	Deosal...	do ...	...	...	...	...	...	...	...	...	...	...	...	...	...	...	...
		do ...	Devangi	do ...	...	...	...	9	5	4	...	...	...	...	...	...	...	...	...
		do ...	Devaraju	do	...	...	...	...	...	...	...	...	...	...	...	...	...	...	...

TABLE XVI.

Castes and Sub-divisions.—*Continued.*

Class.	Group.	Castes.	Sub-division of Castes.	Religion.	Total. Total.	Total. Males.	Total. Females.	Hyderabad. Total.	Hyderabad. Males.	Hyderabad. Females.	Atraf-i-Balda. Total.	Atraf-i-Balda. Males.	Atraf-i-Balda. Females.	Mahabubnagar. Total.	Mahabubnagar. Males.	Mahabubnagar. Females.	Nalgonda. Total.	Nalgonda. Males.	Nalgonda. Females.
1	2	3	4	5	6	7	8	9	10	11	12	13	14	15	16	17	18	19	20
A	2a ...	Kunbi ...	Devatgeru	Hindu ...	3	3	...	...	...	...	...	...	...	...	...	...	...	...	...
		do ...	Dhad	do ...	9	...	9	...	...	...	...	...	...	...	...	...	...	...	...
		do ...	Dhadalvad	do ...	4	2	2	...	...	...	...	...	...	...	...	...	...	...	...
		do ...	Dhadang	do ...	30	18	12	...	...	...	...	...	...	...	...	...	...	...	...
		do ...	Danoji	do ...	6,272	3,309	2,963	...	...	...	...	...	...	...	...	...	...	...	...
		do ...	Dhanor	do ...	4	3	1	...	...	...	...	...	...	...	...	...	...	...	...
		do ...	Dhapesi	do ...	145	40	105	...	...	...	...	...	...	...	...	...	...	...	...
		do ...	Dhatta	do ...	22	12	10	22	12	10	...	...	...	...	...	...	...	...	...
		do ...	Dhavai	do ...	2	2	...	...	...	...	...	...	...	...	...	...	...	...	...
		do ...	Dhulpavad	do ...	9	3	6	...	...	...	...	...	...	...	...	...	...	...	...
		do ...	Dhulwandar	do ...	134	65	69	...	...	...	...	...	...	...	...	...	...	...	...
		do ...	Dhumal	do ...	10	7	3	...	...	...	...	...	...	...	...	...	...	...	...
		do ...	Dilarvad	do ...	213	98	115	...	...	...	...	...	...	...	...	...	...	...	...
		do ...	Dimarvad	do ...	1,955	994	961	...	...	...	...	...	...	...	...	...	...	...	...
		do ...	Dinkar	do ...	64	39	25	...	...	...	...	...	...	...	...	...	...	...	...
		do ...	Dinkeli	do ...	547	236	311	...	...	...	...	...	...	...	...	...	...	...	...
		do ...	Divarle	do ...	4	2	2	...	...	...	...	...	...	...	...	...	...	...	...
		do ...	Dugal	do ...	33	4	29	...	...	...	...	...	...	...	...	...	...	...	...
		do ...	Gadanol	do ...	98	41	57	98	41	57	...	...	...	...	...	...	...	...	...
		do ...	Gantelavaru	do ...	95	44	51	...	...	...	...	...	...	...	...	...	...	...	...
		do ...	Gaoja	do ...	67	41	26	...	...	...	...	...	...	...	...	...	...	...	...
		do ...	Garasi	do ...	6	2	4	6	2	4	...	...	...	...	...	...	...	...	...
		do ...	Gatatri	do ...	6	4	2	6	4	2	...	...	...	...	...	...	...	...	...
		do ...	Gayavad	do ...	7	2	5	...	...	...	...	...	...	...	...	...	...	...	...
		do ...	Ghadge	do ...	20	8	12	...	...	...	...	...	...	...	...	...	...	...	...
		do ...	Gharpat	do ...	18	10	8	...	...	...	...	...	...	...	...	...	...	...	...
		do ...	Ghotole	do ...	131	64	67	...	...	...	...	...	...	...	...	...	...	...	...
		do ...	Ghatlavad	do ...	76	76	...	...	...	...	...	...	...	...	...	...	...	...	...
		do ...	Ghogri	do ...	8	3	5	...	...	...	...	...	...	...	...	...	...	...	...
		do ...	Ghosavad	do ...	12	12	...	...	...	...	...	...	...	...	...	...	...	...	...
		do ...	Gilvani	do ...	530	230	300	...	...	...	...	...	...	...	...	...	...	...	...
		do ...	Girali	do ...	7	7	...	7	7	...	...	...	...	...	...	...	...	...	...
		do ...	Girne	do ...	4	2	2	...	...	...	...	...	...	...	...	...	...	...	...
		do ...	Godadi	do ...	67,531	34,470	33,061	490	268	222	18,763	9,441	9,322	4,609	2,304	2,305	14,167	7,242	6,925
		do ...	Golas	do ...	11	1	10	...	...	...	...	...	...	...	...	...	...	...	...
		do ...	Godekari	do ...	9	...	9	...	...	...	...	...	...	...	...	...	...	...	...
		do ...	Godloi...	do ...	40	15	25	40	15	25	...	...	...	...	...	...	...	...	...
		do ...	Gogbhale	do ...	300	135	165	...	...	...	300	135	165	...	...	...	...	...	...
		do ...	Golkapu	do ...	19	8	11	...	...	...	...	...	...	...	...	...	...	...	...
		do ...	Golkor	do ...	35	22	13	...	...	...	...	...	...	...	...	...	...	...	...
		do ...	Golait	do ...	9	...	9	...	...	...	...	...	...	...	...	...	...	...	...
		do ...	Gotar	do ...	3,613	1,826	1,787	...	...	...	...	...	...	...	...	...	...	...	...

TABLE XVI.

Castes and Sub-divisions.—*Continued*.

Class.	Group.	Castes.	Sub-division of Castes.	Religion.	Warangal.			Elgandal.			Indur.			Medak.			Aurangabad.		
					Total.	Males.	Females.	Total.	Males.	Females.	Total.	Males.	Females.	Total.	Males.	Females.	Total.	Males.	Females.
					21	22	23	24	25	26	27	28	29	30	31	32	33	34	35
A	2a ...	Kunbi ...	Devatgeru	Hindu ...	...	...	...	...	...	...	...	...	...	...	...	...	...	...	...
		do ...	Dhad	do ...	...	...	...	...	...	...	...	...	...	...	...	...	9	...	9
		do ...	Dhadalvad	do ...	...	...	...	...	...	...	4	2	2	...	...	...	...	...	...
		do ...	Dhadang	do ...	...	...	...	...	...	...	...	...	...	...	...	...	80	18	12
		do ...	Danoji	do ...	...	...	...	...	...	...	...	...	...	...	...	...	...	...	...
		do ...	Dhanor	do ...	...	...	...	...	...	...	...	...	...	...	...	...	4	3	1
		do ...	Dhapesi	do ...	...	...	...	...	...	...	...	...	...	...	...	...	145	40	105
		do ...	Dhatta	do ...	...	...	...	...	...	...	...	...	...	...	...	...	...	...	...
		do ...	Dhavai	do ...	...	...	...	...	...	...	...	...	...	...	...	...	2	2	...
		do ...	Dhulpavad	do ...	...	...	...	...	...	...	...	...	...	...	...	...	...	...	...
		do ...	Dhulwandar	do ...	...	...	...	...	...	...	...	...	...	...	...	...	...	...	...
		do ...	Dhumal	do ...	...	...	...	...	...	...	...	...	...	...	...	...	10	7	8
		do ...	Dilarvad	do ...	...	...	...	...	...	...	213	98	115	...	...	...	...	...	...
		do ...	Dimarvad	do ...	...	...	...	...	...	...	1,955	994	961	...	...	...	...	...	...
		do ...	Dinkar	do ...	...	...	...	...	...	...	16	7	9	...	...	...	...	...	...
		do ...	Dinkeli	do ...	...	...	...	...	...	...	547	236	811	...	...	...	...	...	...
		do ...	Divarle	do ...	...	...	...	...	...	...	4	2	2	...	...	...	...	...	...
		do ...	Dugal...	do ...	...	...	...	...	...	...	9	4	5	...	...	...	...	...	...
		do ...	Gadanol	do ...	...	...	...	...	...	...	...	...	...	...	...	...	...	...	...
		do ...	Gantelavaru	do ...	...	...	...	...	...	...	...	...	...	...	...	...	...	...	...
		do ...	Gaoja...	do ...	...	...	...	...	...	...	...	...	...	...	...	...	...	...	...
		do ...	Garasi...	do ...	...	...	...	...	...	...	...	...	...	...	...	...	...	...	...
		do ...	Gatatri	do ...	...	...	...	...	...	...	...	...	...	...	...	...	...	...	...
		do ...	Gayavad	do ...	...	...	...	...	...	...	7	2	5	...	...	...	...	...	...
		do ...	Ghadge	do ...	...	...	...	...	...	...	...	...	...	...	...	...	...	...	...
		do ...	Gharpat	do ...	...	...	...	...	...	...	...	...	...	...	...	...	...	...	...
		do ...	Ghotole	do ...	...	...	...	...	...	...	...	...	...	...	...	...	131	64	67
		do ...	Ghatlavad	do ...	...	...	...	...	...	...	...	...	...	...	...	...	...	...	...
		do ...	Ghogri	do ...	...	...	...	...	...	...	...	...	...	...	...	...	8	3	5
		do ...	Ghosavad	do ...	...	...	...	...	...	...	...	...	...	...	...	...	...	...	...
		do ...	Gilvani	do ...	...	...	...	...	...	...	...	...	...	...	...	...	530	230	300
		do ...	Girali	do ...	...	...	...	...	...	...	...	...	...	...	...	...	...	...	...
		do ...	Girne	do ...	...	...	...	...	...	...	...	...	...	...	...	...	...	...	...
		do ...	Godadi	do ...	435	226	209	20,343	10,542	9,801	5,082	2,567	2,515	3,048	1,545	1,503	...	...	...
		do ...	Golas	do ...	...	...	...	...	...	...	...	...	...	...	...	...	10	...	10
		do ...	Godekari	do ...	...	...	...	...	...	...	...	...	...	...	...	...	9	...	9
		do ...	Godloi	do ...	...	...	...	...	...	...	...	...	...	...	...	...	...	...	...
		do ...	Gogbanle	do ...	...	...	...	...	...	...	...	...	...	...	...	...	...	...	...
		do ...	Golkapu	do ...	...	...	...	...	...	...	...	...	...	...	...	...	...	...	...
		do ...	Golkor	do ...	...	...	...	...	...	...	...	...	...	...	...	...	...	...	...
		do ...	Golait...	do ...	...	...	...	...	...	...	...	...	...	...	...	...	...	...	...
		do ...	Gotar	do ...	...	...	...	...	...	...	...	...	...	...	...	...	...	...	...

TABLE XVI.

Castes and Sub-divisions.—*Continued.*

Class.	Group.	Castes.	Sub-division of Castes.	Religion.	Birb. Total.	Birb. Males.	Birb. Females.	Nander. Total.	Nander. Males.	Nander. Females.	Naldrug. Total.	Naldrug. Males.	Naldrug. Females.	Bidar. Total.	Bidar. Males.	Bidar. Females.	Parbhani. Total.	Parbhani. Males.	Parbhani. Females.
					36	37	38	39	40	41	42	43	44	45	46	47	48	49	50
A	2a ...	Kunbi ...	Devatgeru ...	Hindu ...	...	...	...	...	...	...	...	...	...	...	...	...	...	...	...
		do ...	Dhad ...	do ...	...	...	...	...	...	...	...	...	...	...	...	...	...	...	...
		do ...	Dhadalvad ...	do ...	...	...	...	...	...	...	...	...	...	...	...	...	...	...	...
		do ...	Dhadang ...	do ...	...	...	...	...	...	...	...	...	...	...	...	...	...	...	...
		do ...	Danoji ...	do ...	...	...	...	...	...	...	...	...	...	...	...	...	...	...	...
		do ...	Dhanor ...	do ...	...	...	...	...	...	...	...	...	...	...	...	...	...	...	...
		do ...	Dhapesi ...	do ...	...	...	...	...	...	...	...	...	...	...	...	...	...	...	...
		do ...	Dhatta ...	do ...	...	...	...	...	...	...	...	...	...	...	...	...	...	...	...
		do ...	Dhavai ...	do ...	...	...	...	...	...	...	...	...	...	...	...	...	...	...	...
		do ...	Dhulpavad ...	do ...	...	...	...	...	...	...	...	...	...	...	...	...	...	...	...
		do ...	Dhulwandar ...	do ...	...	...	...	...	...	...	...	...	...	...	...	...	...	...	...
		do ...	Dhumal ...	do ...	...	...	...	...	...	...	...	...	...	...	...	...	...	...	...
		do ...	Dilarvad ...	do ...	...	...	...	...	...	...	...	...	...	...	...	...	...	...	...
		do ...	Dimarvad ...	do ...	...	...	...	...	...	...	...	...	...	...	...	...	...	...	...
		do ...	Dinkar ...	do ...	18	18	...	...	...	...	...	...	...	...	...	...	...	...	...
		do ...	Dinkeli ...	do ...	...	...	...	...	...	...	...	...	...	...	...	...	...	...	...
		do ...	Divarle ...	do ...	...	...	...	...	...	...	...	...	...	...	...	...	...	...	...
		do ...	Dugal ...	do ...	...	...	...	...	...	...	...	...	...	24	...	24	...	...	...
		do ...	Gadanol ...	do ...	...	...	...	...	...	...	...	...	...	...	...	...	...	...	...
		do ...	Gantelavaru ...	do ...	...	...	...	...	...	...	...	...	...	...	...	...	...	...	...
		do ...	Gaoja ...	do ...	...	...	...	...	...	...	...	...	...	...	...	...	...	...	...
		do ...	Garasi ...	do ...	...	...	...	...	...	...	...	...	...	...	...	...	...	...	...
		do ...	Gatatri ...	do ...	...	...	...	...	...	...	...	...	...	...	...	...	...	...	...
		do ...	Gayavad ...	do ...	...	...	...	...	...	...	...	...	...	...	...	...	...	...	...
		do ...	Ghadge ...	do ...	...	...	...	...	...	...	...	...	...	...	...	...	20	8	12
		do ...	Gharpat ...	do ...	...	...	...	18	10	8	...	...	...	...	...	...	...	...	...
		do ...	Ghotole ...	do ...	...	...	...	...	...	...	...	...	...	...	...	...	...	...	...
		do ...	Ghatlavad ...	do ...	76	76	...	...	...	...	...	...	...	...	...	...	...	...	...
		do ...	Ghogri ...	do ...	...	...	...	...	...	...	...	...	...	...	...	...	...	...	...
		do ...	Ghosavad ...	do ...	12	12	...	...	...	...	...	...	...	...	...	...	...	...	...
		do ...	Gilvani ...	do ...	...	...	...	...	...	...	...	...	...	...	...	...	...	...	...
		do ...	Girali ...	do ...	...	...	...	...	...	...	...	...	...	...	...	...	...	...	...
		do ...	Girne ...	do ...	4	2	2	...	...	...	...	...	...	...	...	...	...	...	...
		do ...	Godadi ...	do ...	...	...	...	21	12	9	...	...	...	147	84	63	...	...	...
		do ...	Golas ...	do ...	...	...	...	...	...	...	...	...	...	...	...	...	...	...	...
		do ...	Godekari ...	do ...	...	...	...	...	...	...	...	...	...	...	...	...	...	...	...
		do ...	Godloi ...	do ...	...	...	...	...	...	...	...	...	...	...	...	...	...	...	...
		do ...	Gogbanlo ...	do ...	...	...	...	...	...	...	...	...	...	...	...	...	...	...	...
		do ...	Golkapu ...	do ...	...	...	...	...	...	...	...	...	...	...	...	...	...	...	...
		do ...	Golkor ...	do ...	...	...	...	...	...	...	...	...	...	...	...	...	...	...	...
		do ...	Golait ...	do ...	...	...	...	...	...	...	...	...	...	...	...	...	...	...	...
		do ...	Gotar ...	do ...	...	...	...	...	...	...	...	...	...	...	...	...	...	...	...

TABLE XVI.

Castes and Sub-divisions.—*Continued.*

Class.	Group.	Castes.	Sub-division of Castes.	Religion.	Sirpur Tandur.			Gulbarga.			Raichur.			Lingasugur.			Railways.		
					Total.	Males.	Females.	Total.	Males.	Females.	Total.	Males.	Females.	Total.	Males.	Females.	Total.	Males.	Females.
					51	52	53	54	55	56	57	58	59	60	61	62	63	64	65
A	2a ...	Kunbi ...	Devatgeru	Hindu ...	...	...	...	...	...	...	...	...	...	8	8	...	...	...	...
		do ...	Dhad	do ...	...	...	...	...	...	...	...	...	...	...	...	...	...	...	...
		do ...	Dhadalvad	do ...	...	...	...	...	...	...	...	...	...	...	...	...	...	...	...
		do ...	Dhadang	do ...	...	...	...	...	...	...	...	...	...	...	...	...	...	...	...
		do ...	Danoji...	do ...	6,272	8,309	2,963	...	...	...	...	...	...	...	...	...	...	...	...
		do ...	Dhanor	do ...	...	...	...	...	...	...	...	...	...	...	...	...	...	...	...
		do ...	Dhapesi	do ...	...	...	...	...	...	...	...	...	...	...	...	...	...	...	...
		do ...	Dhatta...	do ...	...	...	...	...	...	...	...	...	...	...	...	...	...	...	...
		do ...	Dhavai	do ...	...	...	...	...	...	...	...	...	...	...	...	...	...	...	...
		do ...	Dhulpavad	do ...	...	...	...	...	...	...	9	8	6	...	...	...	...	...	...
		do ...	Dhulwandar	do ...	...	...	...	...	...	...	...	...	...	134	65	69	...	...	...
		do ...	Dhumal	do ...	...	...	...	...	...	...	...	...	...	...	...	...	...	...	...
		do ...	Dilarvad	do ...	...	...	...	...	...	...	...	...	...	...	...	...	...	...	...
		do ...	Dimarvad	do ...	...	...	...	...	...	...	...	...	...	...	...	...	...	...	...
		do ...	Dinkar	do ...	80	14	16	...	...	...	...	...	...	...	...	...	...	...	...
		do ...	Dinkeli	do ...	...	...	...	...	...	...	...	...	...	...	...	...	...	...	...
		do ...	Divarle	do ...	...	...	...	...	...	...	...	...	...	...	...	...	...	...	...
		do ...	Dugal	do ...	...	...	...	...	...	...	...	...	...	...	...	...	...	...	...
		do ...	Gadanol	do ...	...	...	...	...	...	...	...	...	...	...	...	...	...	...	...
		do ...	Gantelavaru	do ...	...	...	...	...	...	...	...	...	...	95	44	51	...	...	...
		do ...	Gaoja	do ...	67	41	26	...	...	...	...	...	...	...	...	...	...	...	...
		do ...	Garasi...	do ...	...	...	...	...	...	...	...	...	...	...	...	...	...	...	...
		do ...	Gatatri	do ...	...	...	...	...	...	...	...	...	...	...	...	...	...	...	...
		do ...	Gayavad	do ...	...	...	...	...	...	...	...	...	...	...	...	...	...	...	...
		do ...	Ghadge	do ...	...	...	...	...	...	...	...	...	...	...	...	...	...	...	...
		do ...	Gharpat	do ...	...	...	...	...	...	...	...	...	...	...	...	...	...	...	...
		do ...	Ghotole	do ...	...	...	...	...	...	...	...	...	...	...	...	...	...	...	...
		do ...	Ghatlavad	do ...	...	...	...	...	...	...	...	...	...	...	...	...	...	...	...
		do ...	Ghogri	do ...	...	...	...	...	...	...	...	...	...	...	...	...	...	...	...
		do ...	Ghosavad	do ...	...	...	...	...	...	...	...	...	...	...	...	...	...	...	...
		do ...	Gilvani	do ...	...	...	...	...	...	...	...	...	...	...	...	...	...	...	...
		do ...	Girali	do ...	...	...	...	...	...	...	...	...	...	...	...	...	...	...	...
		do ...	Girne	do ...	...	...	...	...	...	...	...	...	...	...	...	...	...	...	...
		do ...	Godadi	do ...	196	102	94	...	...	...	230	137	93	...	...	...	...	...	...
		do ...	Golas	do ...	...	...	...	1	1	...	...	...	...	...	...	...	...	...	...
		do ...	Godekari	do ...	...	...	...	...	...	...	...	...	...	...	...	...	...	...	...
		do ...	Godloi...	do ...	...	...	...	...	...	...	...	...	...	...	...	...	...	...	...
		do ...	Gogbanle	do ...	...	...	...	...	...	...	...	...	...	...	...	...	...	...	...
		do ...	Golkapu	do ...	19	8	11	...	...	...	...	...	...	...	...	...	...	...	...
		do ...	Golkor	do ...	35	22	13	...	...	...	...	...	...	...	...	...	...	...	...
		do ...	Golait...	do ...	9	...	9	...	...	...	...	...	...	...	...	...	...	...	...
		do ...	Gotar	do ...	...	...	...	3,613	1,826	1,787	...	...	...	...	...	...	...	...	...

TABLE XVI.

Castes and Sub-divisions.—*Continued.*

Class.	Group.	Castes.	Sub-division of Castes.	Religion.	Total. Total.	Total. Males.	Total. Females.	Hyderabad. Total.	Hyderabad. Males.	Hyderabad. Females.	Atraf-i-Balda. Total.	Atraf-i-Balda. Males.	Atraf-i-Balda. Females.	Mahabubnagar. Total.	Mahabubnagar. Males.	Mahabubnagar. Females.	Nalgonda. Total.	Nalgonda. Males.	Nalgonda. Females.
1	2	3	4	5	6	7	8	9	10	11	12	13	14	15	16	17	18	19	20
A	2a ...	Kunbi ...	Gone Kapu	Hindu ...	28,492	14,179	14,313	...	...	...	2,767	1,406	1,361	1,520	762	758	1,418	717	701
		do ...	Gonpat	do ...	19	12	7	...	...	...	...	...	...	...	...	...	...	...	...
		do ...	Goralvad	do ...	9,258	4,781	4,477	...	...	...	...	...	...	...	...	...	...	...	...
		do ...	Gorati	do ...	26	10	16	26	10	16	...	...	...	...	...	...	...	...	...
		do ...	Gorevad	do ...	204	114	90	...	...	...	...	...	...	...	...	...	...	...	...
		do ...	Govar	do ...	3	1	2	...	...	...	...	...	...	...	...	...	...	...	...
		do ...	Gosani...	do ...	36	14	22	...	...	...	...	...	...	...	...	...	...	...	...
		do ...	Guride	do ...	458	230	228	...	...	...	...	...	...	...	...	...	...	...	...
		do ...	Gurka	do ...	20	18	2	...	...	...	...	...	...	...	...	...	...	...	...
		do ...	Guvadvad	do ...	11	7	4	...	...	...	...	...	...	...	...	...	...	...	...
		do ...	Hachal	do ...	7	4	3	...	...	...	...	...	...	...	...	...	...	...	...
		do ...	Hadguralkar	do ...	33	18	15	...	...	...	...	...	...	...	...	...	...	...	...
		do ...	Haindri	do ...	194	124	70	...	...	...	...	...	...	...	...	...	...	...	...
		do ...	Haral	do ...	52	15	37	...	...	...	...	...	...	...	...	...	...	...	...
		do ...	Hardi	do ...	69	39	30	...	...	...	...	...	...	...	...	...	...	...	...
		do ...	Hatkakne	do ...	25	12	13	...	...	...	...	...	...	...	...	...	...	...	...
		do ...	Hazari	do ...	2	2	...	...	...	...	...	...	...	...	...	...	...	...	...
		do ...	Hingle...	do ...	17	11	6	...	...	...	...	...	...	...	...	...	...	...	...
		do ...	Hitte	do ...	31	5	26	...	...	...	...	...	...	...	...	...	...	...	...
		do ...	Hugane	do ...	22	13	9	...	...	...	...	...	...	...	...	...	...	...	...
		do ...	Idle	do ...	2	...	2	...	...	...	...	...	...	...	...	...	...	...	...
		do ...	Idve	do ...	106	55	51	...	...	...	...	...	...	...	...	...	...	...	...
		do ...	Ingle	do ...	38	22	16	...	...	...	...	...	...	...	...	...	...	...	...
		do ...	Irpael...	do ...	4	1	3	...	...	...	...	...	...	...	...	...	...	...	...
		do ...	Ityal	do ...	24	14	10	...	...	...	...	...	...	...	...	...	...	...	...
		do ...	Jalai	do ...	12	4	8	...	...	...	...	...	...	...	...	...	...	...	...
		do ...	Jadval...	do ...	3	1	2	...	...	...	...	...	...	...	...	...	...	...	...
		do ...	Jagadmal	do ...	65	28	37	...	...	...	...	...	...	...	...	...	...	...	...
		do ...	Javar	do ...	75	36	39	...	...	...	...	...	...	...	...	...	...	...	...
		do ...	Jagdund	do ...	4	3	1	...	...	...	...	...	...	...	...	...	...	...	...
		do ...	Kabeli	do ...	30	15	15	...	...	...	...	...	...	...	...	...	...	...	...
		do ...	Kabhar	do ...	169	88	81	...	...	...	...	...	...	...	...	...	...	...	...
		do ...	Kadai	do ...	3	1	2	3	1	2	...	...	...	...	...	...	...	...	...
		do ...	Kadkar	do ...	271	149	122	...	...	...	...	...	...	...	...	...	...	...	...
		do ...	Kadle	do ...	2	...	2	...	...	...	...	...	...	...	...	...	...	...	...
		do ...	Kadse	do ...	24	22	2	...	...	...	...	...	...	...	...	...	...	...	...
		do ...	Kadu	do ...	38	17	21	...	...	...	...	...	...	...	...	...	...	...	...
		do ...	Kakde...	do ...	23	3	20	...	...	...	...	...	...	...	...	...	...	...	...
		do ...	Kakne...	do ...	41	24	17	...	...	...	...	...	...	...	...	...	...	...	...
		do ...	Kakvat	do ...	2	...	2	...	...	...	...	...	...	...	...	...	...	...	...
		do ...	Kalyane	do ...	20	10	10	...	...	...	...	...	...	...	...	...	...	...	...
		do ...	Kamar...	do ...	6	3	3	...	...	...	...	...	...	...	...	...	...	...	...

TABLE XVI.

Castes and Sub-divisions.—*Continued.*

Class.	Group.	Castes	Sub-division of Castes.	Religion.	Warangal.			Elgandal.			Indur.			Modak.			Aurangabad.		
					Total.	Males.	Females.	Total.	Males.	Females.	Total.	Males.	Females.	Total.	Males.	Females.	Total.	Males.	Females.
					21	22	23	24	25	26	27	28	29	30	31	32	33	34	35
A	2a ...	Kunbi	Gonc Kapu	Hindu	4,520	2,198	2,322	15,393	7,785	7,608	2,134	1,024	1,110	897	200	197	...	...	...
		do	Goupat	do	...	...	...	...	...	...	...	...	...	...	...	...	...	...	...
		do	Goralvad	do	...	...	...	...	...	...	5,056	2,609	2,447	...	...	...	...	...	...
		do	Gorati...	do	...	...	...	...	...	...	...	...	...	...	...	...	...	...	...
		do	Gorevad	do	...	...	...	...	...	...	200	112	88	...	...	...	4	2	2
		do	Govar...	do	...	...	...	...	...	...	8	1	2	...	...	...	...	...	...
		do	Gosani	do	...	...	...	...	...	...	...	...	...	...	...	...	...	...	...
		do	Guride	do	...	...	...	101	51	50	...	...	...	...	...	...	...	...	...
		do	Gurka...	do	...	...	...	20	18	2	...	...	...	...	...	...	...	...	...
		do	Guvadvad	do	...	...	...	...	...	...	11	7	4	...	...	...	...	...	...
		do	Hachal	do	...	...	...	...	...	...	...	...	...	...	...	...	...	...	...
		do	Hadguralkar	do	...	...	...	...	...	...	...	...	...	...	...	...	...	...	...
		do	Haindri	do	...	...	...	...	...	...	...	...	...	...	...	...	...	...	...
		do	Haral...	do	...	...	...	...	...	...	...	...	...	...	...	...	...	...	...
		do	Hardi...	do	...	...	...	...	...	...	...	...	...	...	...	...	46	29	17
		do	Hatkakne	do	...	...	...	...	...	...	25	12	18	...	...	...	...	...	...
		do	Hazari	do	...	...	...	...	...	...	...	...	...	...	...	...	2	2	...
		do	Hingle	do	...	...	...	...	...	...	...	...	...	...	...	...	17	11	6
		do	Hitto...	do	...	...	...	...	...	...	...	...	...	...	...	...	81	5	26
		do	Hugane	do	...	...	...	...	...	...	...	...	...	...	...	...	...	...	...
		do	Idle	do	...	...	...	...	...	...	...	...	...	...	...	...	...	...	...
		do	Idve	do	...	...	...	...	...	...	...	...	...	...	...	...	...	...	...
		do	Ingle	do	...	...	...	...	...	...	...	...	...	...	...	...	...	...	...
		do	Irpael	do	...	...	...	...	...	...	...	...	...	...	...	...	4	1	8
		do	Ityal	do	...	...	...	...	...	...	...	...	...	...	...	...	24	14	10
		do	Jalai	do	...	...	...	...	...	...	...	...	...	...	...	...	...	...	...
		do	Jadval	do	...	...	...	...	...	...	...	...	...	...	...	...	...	...	...
		do	Jagadmal	do	...	...	...	...	...	...	65	28	37	...	...	...	...	...	...
		do	Javar...	do	...	...	...	...	...	...	...	...	...	...	...	...	...	...	...
		do	Jagdund	do	...	...	...	...	...	...	4	3	1	...	...	...	...	...	...
		do	Kabeli...	do	...	...	...	...	...	...	...	...	...	...	...	...	...	...	...
		do	Kabbar	do	...	...	...	...	...	...	...	...	...	...	...	...	169	88	81
		do	Kadai...	do	...	...	...	...	...	...	...	...	...	...	...	...	...	...	...
		do	Kadkar	do	...	...	...	...	...	...	...	...	...	...	...	...	271	149	122
		do	Kadlo...	do	...	...	...	...	...	...	...	...	...	...	...	...	2	...	2
		do	Kadse...	do	...	...	...	...	...	...	...	...	...	...	...	...	20	20	...
		do	Kadu...	do	...	...	...	...	...	...	...	...	...	...	...	...	30	13	17
		do	Kakdo...	do	...	...	...	...	...	...	...	...	...	...	...	...	23	3	20
		do	Kakne	do	...	...	...	...	...	...	...	...	...	...	...	...	...	...	...
		do	Kakvat	do	...	...	...	...	...	...	...	...	...	...	...	...	...	...	...
		do	Kalyane	do	...	...	...	...	...	...	20	10	10	...	...	...	...	...	...
		do	Kamar	do	...	...	...	...	...	...	...	...	...	...	...	...	...	...	...

TABLE XVI.
Castes and Sub-divisions.

TABLE XVI.

Castes and Sub-divisions.—*Continued.*

Class.	Group.	Castes.	Sub-division of Castes.	Religion.	Birh. Total.	Birh. Males.	Birh. Females.	Nander. Total.	Nander. Males.	Nander. Females.	Naldrug. Total.	Naldrug. Males.	Naldrug. Females.	Bidar. Total.	Bidar. Males.	Bidar. Females.	Parbhani. Total.	Parbhani. Males.	Parbhani. Females.
					36	37	38	39	40	41	42	43	44	45	46	47	48	49	50
A	2a ...	Kunbi ...	Gone Kapu	Hindu ...	...	...	...	54	27	27	...	...	...	...	...	...	...	...	...
A	2a ...	do ...	Gonpat	do ...	...	...	...	...	...	...	5	3	2	14	9	5	...	...	...
A	2a ...	do ...	Goralvad	do ...	...	...	...	...	...	...	...	...	...	...	...	...	...	...	...
A	2a ...	do ...	Gorati... ...	do ...	...	...	...	...	...	...	...	...	...	...	...	...	...	...	...
A	2a ...	do ...	Gorevad	do ...	...	...	...	...	...	...	...	...	...	...	...	...	...	...	...
A	2a ...	do ...	Govar... ...	do ...	...	...	...	...	...	...	...	...	...	...	...	...	...	...	...
A	2a ...	do ...	Gosani	do ...	...	...	...	...	...	...	...	...	...	...	...	...	...	...	...
A	2a ...	do ...	Guride	do ...	...	...	...	...	...	...	...	...	...	357	179	178	...	...	...
A	2a ...	do ...	Gurka	do ...	...	...	...	...	...	...	...	...	...	...	...	...	...	...	...
A	2a ...	do ...	Guvadvad	do ...	...	...	...	...	...	...	...	...	...	...	...	...	...	...	...
A	2a ...	do ...	Hachal	do ...	...	...	...	...	...	...	...	...	...	7	4	3	...	...	...
A	2a ...	do ...	Hadguralkar	do ...	...	...	...	...	...	...	...	...	...	...	...	...	...	...	...
A	2a ...	do ...	Haindri	do ...	...	...	...	...	...	...	...	...	...	...	...	...	...	...	...
A	2a ...	do ...	Haral... ...	do ...	32	15	17	...	...	...	...	...	...	...	...	...	20	...	20
A	2a ...	do ...	Hardi... ...	do ...	...	...	...	...	...	...	20	10	10	...	...	...	...	...	...
A	2a ...	do ...	Hatkakne	do ...	...	...	...	...	...	...	...	...	...	...	...	...	...	...	...
A	2a ...	do ...	Hazari	do ...	...	...	...	...	...	...	...	...	...	...	...	...	...	...	...
A	2a ...	do ...	Hingle	do ...	...	...	...	...	...	...	...	...	...	...	...	...	...	...	...
A	2a ...	do ...	Hitte	do ...	...	...	...	...	...	...	...	...	...	...	...	...	...	...	...
A	2a ...	do ...	Hugane	do ...	...	...	...	...	...	...	...	...	...	...	...	...	...	...	...
A	2a ...	do ...	Idle	do ...	...	...	...	...	...	...	...	...	...	...	...	...	...	...	...
A	2a ...	do ...	Idve	do ...	...	...	...	...	...	...	...	...	...	106	55	51	...	...	...
A	2a ...	do ...	Ingle	do ...	...	...	...	...	...	...	...	...	...	...	...	...	38	22	16
A	2a ...	do ...	Irpael	do ...	...	...	...	...	...	...	...	...	...	...	...	...	...	...	...
A	2a ...	do ...	Ityal	do ...	...	...	...	...	...	...	...	...	...	...	...	...	...	...	...
A	2a ...	do ...	Jalai	do ...	...	...	...	...	...	...	...	...	...	...	...	...	...	...	...
A	2a ...	do ...	Jadual	do ...	...	...	...	3	1	2	...	...	...	...	...	...	...	...	...
A	2a ...	do ...	Jagadmal	do ...	...	...	...	...	...	...	...	...	...	...	...	...	...	...	...
A	2a ...	do ...	Javar	do ...	...	...	...	...	...	...	...	...	...	...	...	...	...	...	...
A	2a ...	do ...	Jagdund	do ...	...	...	...	...	...	...	...	...	...	...	...	...	...	...	...
A	2a ...	do ...	Kabeli... ...	do ...	...	...	...	...	...	...	...	...	...	...	...	...	...	...	...
A	2a ...	do ...	Kabhar	do ...	...	...	...	...	...	...	...	...	...	...	...	...	...	...	...
A	2a ...	do ...	Kadai	do ...	...	...	...	...	...	...	...	...	...	...	...	...	...	...	...
A	2a ...	do ...	Kadkar	do ...	...	...	...	...	...	...	...	...	...	...	...	...	...	...	...
A	2a ...	do ...	Kadle	do ...	...	...	...	...	...	...	...	...	...	...	...	...	...	...	...
A	2a ...	do ...	Kadse	do ...	...	...	...	4	2	2	...	...	...	...	...	...	...	...	...
A	2a ...	do ...	Kadu	do ...	2	1	1	...	...	...	4	2	2	...	...	...	...	...	...
A	2a ...	do ...	Kakde... ...	do ...	...	...	...	...	...	...	...	...	...	...	...	...	...	...	...
A	2a ...	do ...	Kakne	do ...	...	...	...	...	...	...	...	...	...	...	...	...	...	...	...
A	2a ...	do ...	Kakat... ...	do ...	...	...	...	...	...	...	...	...	...	...	...	...	...	...	...
A	2a ...	do ...	Kalyane	do ...	...	...	...	...	...	...	...	...	...	...	...	...	...	...	...
A	2a ...	do ...	Kamar	do ...	6	3	3	...	...	...	...	...	...	...	...	...	...	...	...

TABLE XVI.

Castes and Sub-divisions.—*Continued.*

Class.	Group.	Castes.	Sub-division of Castes.	Religion.	Sirpur Tandur. Total.	Sirpur Tandur. Males.	Sirpur Tandur. Females.	Gulbarga. Total.	Gulbarga. Males.	Gulbarga. Females.	Raichur. Total.	Raichur. Males.	Raichur. Females.	Lingasugur. Total.	Lingasugur. Males.	Lingasugur. Females.	Railways. Total.	Railways. Males.	Railways. Females.
					51	52	53	54	55	56	57	58	59	60	61	62	63	64	65
A	2a ...	Kunbi ...	Gone Kapu	Hindu ...	246	38	208	20	10	10	23	12	11	...	...	...	...	...	...
		do ...	Gonpat	do ...	...	...	...	...	...	...	...	...	...	...	...	...	...	...	...
		do ...	Goralvad	do ...	4,177	2,160	2,017	25	12	13	...	...	...	...	...	...	...	...	...
		do ...	Gorati	do ...	...	...	...	...	...	...	...	...	...	...	...	...	...	...	...
		do ...	Gorevad	do ...	...	...	...	...	...	...	...	...	...	...	...	...	...	...	...
		do ...	Govar...	do ...	...	...	...	...	...	...	...	...	...	...	...	...	...	...	...
		do ...	Gosani	do ...	...	...	...	...	...	...	36	14	22	...	...	...	...	...	...
		do ...	Gurido	do ...	...	...	...	...	...	...	...	...	...	...	...	...	...	...	...
		do ...	Gurka...	do ...	...	...	...	...	...	...	...	...	...	...	...	...	...	...	...
		do ...	Guvadvad	do ...	...	...	...	...	...	...	...	...	...	...	...	...	...	...	...
		do ...	Hachal	do ...	...	...	...	...	...	...	...	...	...	...	...	...	...	...	...
		do ...	Hadguralkar	do ...	...	...	...	33	18	15	...	...	...	...	...	...	...	...	...
		do ...	Haindri	do ...	194	124	70	...	...	...	...	...	...	...	...	...	...	...	...
		do ...	Haral	do ...	...	...	...	...	...	...	...	...	...	...	...	...	...	...	...
		do ...	Hardi	do ...	...	...	...	3	...	3	...	...	...	...	...	...	...	...	...
		do ...	Hatkakne	do ...	...	...	...	...	...	...	...	...	...	...	...	...	...	...	...
		do ...	Hazari...	do ...	...	...	...	...	...	...	...	...	...	...	...	...	...	...	...
		do ...	Hingle	do ...	...	...	...	...	...	...	...	...	...	...	...	...	...	...	...
		do ...	Hitte	do ...	...	...	...	...	...	...	...	...	...	...	...	...	...	...	...
		do ...	Hugane	do ...	...	...	...	22	13	9	...	...	...	...	...	...	...	...	...
		do ...	Idle	do ...	...	...	...	2	...	2	...	...	...	...	...	...	...	...	...
		do ...	Idve	do ...	...	...	...	...	...	...	...	...	...	...	...	...	...	...	...
		do ...	Ingle	do ...	...	...	...	...	...	...	...	...	...	...	...	...	...	...	...
		do ...	Irpael	do ...	...	...	...	...	...	...	...	...	...	...	...	...	...	...	...
		do ...	Ityal	do ...	...	...	...	...	...	...	...	...	...	...	...	...	...	...	...
		do ...	Jalai	do ...	...	...	...	12	4	8	...	...	...	...	...	...	...	...	...
		do ...	Jadval	do ...	...	...	...	...	...	...	...	...	...	...	...	...	...	...	...
		do ...	Jagadmal	do ...	...	...	...	...	...	...	...	...	...	...	...	...	...	...	...
		do ...	Javar	do ...	...	...	...	75	36	39	...	...	...	...	...	...	...	...	...
		do ...	Jagdund	do ...	...	...	...	...	...	...	...	...	...	...	...	...	...	...	...
		do ...	Kabeli	do ...	...	...	...	30	15	15	...	...	...	...	...	...	...	...	...
		do ...	Kabhar	do ...	...	...	...	...	...	...	...	...	...	...	...	...	...	...	...
		do ...	Kadai	do ...	...	...	...	...	...	...	...	...	...	...	...	...	...	...	...
		do ...	Kadkar	do ...	...	...	...	...	...	...	...	...	...	...	...	...	...	...	...
		do ...	Kadle	do ...	...	...	...	...	...	...	...	...	...	...	...	...	...	...	...
		do ...	Kadse	do ...	...	...	...	...	...	...	...	...	...	...	...	...	...	...	...
		do ...	Kadu	do ...	...	...	...	2	1	1	...	...	...	...	...	...	...	...	...
		do ...	Kakde...	do ...	...	...	...	...	...	...	...	...	...	...	...	...	...	...	...
		do ...	Kakne...	do ...	41	24	17	...	...	...	...	...	...	...	...	...	...	...	...
		do ...	Kakvat	do ...	...	...	...	2	...	2	...	...	...	...	...	...	...	...	...
		do ...	Kalyane	do ...	...	...	...	...	...	...	...	...	...	...	...	...	...	...	...
		do ...	Kamar	do ...	...	...	...	...	...	...	...	...	...	...	...	...	...	...	...

TABLE XVI.

Castes and Sub-divisions.—*Continued.*

Class.	Group.	Castes.	Sub-division of Castes.	Religion.	Total. Total.	Total. Males.	Total. Females.	Hyderabad. Total.	Hyderabad. Males.	Hyderabad. Females.	Atraf-i-Balda. Total.	Atraf-i-Balda. Males.	Atraf-i-Balda. Females.	Mahabubnagar. Total.	Mahabubnagar. Males.	Mahabubnagar. Females.	Nalgonda. Total.	Nalgonda. Males.	Nalgonda. Females.
1	2	3	4	5	6	7	8	9	10	11	12	13	14	15	16	17	18	19	20
A	2a ...	Kunbi ...	Kame ...	Hindu ...	2	...	2	...	...	...	...	...	...	...	...	...	...	...	...
		do ...	Kanale ...	do ...	54	31	23	...	...	...	...	...	...	...	...	...	...	...	...
		do ...	Kanavad ...	do ...	34	2	32	...	...	...	...	...	...	...	...	...	...	...	...
		do ...	Kanchi ...	do ...	185	102	83	...	...	...	...	...	...	...	...	...	...	...	...
		do ...	Kauda... ...	do ...	5	2	3	...	...	...	...	...	...	...	...	...	...	...	...
		do ...	Kandvi ...	do ...	3	3	...	3	3	...	...	...	...	...	...	...	...	...	...
		do ...	Kanthibagi ...	do ...	114	63	51	...	...	...	...	...	...	...	...	...	...	...	...
		do ...	Kaple	do ...	23	6	17	...	...	...	...	...	...	...	...	...	...	...	...
		do ...	Karikal ...	do ...	373	237	136	...	...	...	...	...	...	...	...	...	...	...	...
		do ...	Karku... ...	do ...	6	2	4	...	...	...	...	...	...	...	...	...	...	...	...
		do ...	Katali... ...	do ...	1	1	...	1	1	...	...	...	...	...	...	...	...	...	...
		do ...	Katati ...	do ...	7	2	5	7	2	5	...	...	...	...	...	...	...	...	...
		do ...	Katilkute ...	do ...	2	1	1	...	...	...	...	...	...	...	...	...	...	...	...
		do ...	Kathwas ...	do ...	3	2	1	...	...	...	...	...	...	...	...	...	...	...	...
		do ...	Khadalvar ...	do ...	12	6	6	...	...	...	...	...	...	...	...	...	...	...	...
		do ...	Khade... ...	do ...	43	21	22	...	...	...	...	...	...	...	...	...	...	...	...
		do ...	Khalipo ...	do ...	94	...	94	...	...	...	...	...	...	...	...	...	...	...	...
		do ...	Khaludak ...	do ...	3	2	1	...	...	...	...	...	...	...	...	...	...	...	...
		do ...	Khandan ...	do ...	15	4	11	...	...	...	...	...	...	...	...	...	...	...	...
		do ...	Kharari ...	do ...	10	5	5	...	...	...	...	...	...	...	...	...	...	...	...
		do ...	Khand ...	do ...	4	4	...	...	...	...	...	...	...	...	...	...	...	...	...
		do ...	Khel	do ...	619	297	322	...	...	...	...	...	...	...	...	...	...	...	...
		do ...	Khumal ...	do ...	22	5	17	...	...	...	...	...	...	...	...	...	...	...	...
		do ...	Kirikola ...	do ...	4,509	2,153	2,356	...	...	...	...	...	...	...	...	...	...	...	...
		do ...	Kisalvar ...	do ...	2	2	...	...	...	...	...	...	...	...	...	...	...	...	...
		do ...	Kobsadvaru ...	do ...	6	5	1	...	...	...	...	...	...	...	...	...	...	...	...
		do ...	Kodael... ...	do ...	14	2	12	8	2	6	...	...	...	...	...	...	...	...	...
		do ...	Kodhle ...	do ...	16	16	...	...	...	...	...	...	...	...	...	...	...	...	...
		do ...	Kodide ...	do ...	107	51	56	...	...	...	...	...	...	...	...	...	107	51	56
		do ...	Kodikal ...	do ...	19	...	19	...	...	...	...	...	...	...	...	...	...	...	...
		do ...	Kodvakal ...	do ...	2,126	971	1,155	...	...	...	...	...	...	...	...	...	...	...	...
		do ...	Kolkadgi ...	do ...	4,290	2,150	2,140	...	...	...	...	...	...	...	...	...	...	...	...
		do ...	Kondalwaru ...	do ...	103	55	48	...	...	...	...	...	...	...	...	...	...	...	...
		do ...	Konri	do ...	38	16	22	...	...	...	...	...	...	...	...	...	...	...	...
		do ...	Kopaskaute ...	do ...	60	35	25	...	...	...	...	...	...	...	...	...	...	...	...
		do ...	Kotiad ...	do ...	4	1	3	...	...	...	...	...	...	...	...	...	...	...	...
		do ...	Korudvad ...	do ...	5	...	5	...	...	...	...	...	...	...	...	...	...	...	...
		do ...	Kulwe ...	do ...	91	48	43	...	...	...	...	...	...	...	...	...	...	...	...
		do ...	Kunepal ...	do ...	7	5	2	...	...	...	...	...	...	...	...	...	...	...	...
		do ...	Kunkar ...	do ...	7	2	5	...	...	...	...	...	...	...	...	...	...	...	...
		do ...	Kurausheti ...	do ...	94	45	49	...	...	...	...	...	...	...	...	...	...	...	...
		do ...	Kurni... ...	do ...	27	...	27	...	...	...	...	...	...	...	...	...	...	...	...

TABLE XVI.

Castes and Sub-divisions.—*Continued.*

Class.	Group.	Castes.	Sub-division of Castes.	Religion.	Warangal.			Elgandal.			Indur.			Medak.			Aurangabad.		
					Total.	Males.	Females.	Total.	Males.	Females.	Total.	Males.	Females.	Total.	Males.	Females.	Total.	Males.	Females.
					21	22	23	24	25	26	27	28	29	30	31	32	33	34	35
A	2a ...	Kunbi ...	Kame	Hindu ...	...	...	...	...	...	...	...	...	...	...	...	...	2	...	2
		do ...	Kanale...	do ...	...	...	...	...	...	...	...	...	...	...	...	...	...	...	...
		do ...	Kanavad	do ...	...	...	...	...	...	...	5	2	3	...	...	...	...	...	...
		do ...	Kauchi	do ...	...	...	...	...	...	...	...	...	...	185	102	83	...	...	...
		do ...	Kauda	do ...	...	...	...	...	...	...	...	...	...	...	...	...	...	...	...
		do ...	Kandvi	do ...	...	...	...	...	...	...	...	...	...	...	...	...	...	...	...
		do ...	Kauthibagi	do ...	...	...	...	...	...	...	...	...	...	...	...	...	...	...	...
		do ...	Kaple	do ...	...	...	...	...	...	...	...	...	...	...	...	...	...	...	...
		do ...	Karikal	do ...	...	...	...	...	...	...	...	...	...	...	...	...	...	...	...
		do ...	Karku...	do ...	...	...	...	...	...	...	...	...	...	...	...	...	6	2	4
		do ...	Katali	do ...	...	...	...	...	...	...	...	...	...	...	...	...	...	...	...
		do ...	Katati	do ...	...	...	...	...	...	...	...	...	...	...	...	...	...	...	...
		do ...	Katilkute	do ...	...	...	...	...	...	...	...	...	...	...	...	...	2	1	1
		do ...	Kathwas	do ...	...	...	...	...	...	...	...	...	...	...	...	...	3	2	1
		do ...	Khadalvar	do ...	...	...	...	...	...	...	...	...	...	...	...	...	12	6	6
		do ...	Khade...	do ...	...	...	...	...	...	...	...	...	...	...	...	...	...	...	...
		do ...	Khalipo	do ...	...	...	...	...	...	...	...	...	...	...	...	...	...	...	...
		do ...	Khaludak	do ...	...	...	...	...	...	...	...	...	...	...	...	...	...	...	...
		do ...	Khandan	do ...	...	...	...	...	...	...	...	...	...	...	...	...	...	...	...
		do ...	Kharari	do ...	...	...	...	...	...	...	...	...	...	...	...	...	10	5	5
		do ...	Khaud	do ...	...	...	...	...	...	...	...	...	...	...	...	...	...	...	...
		do ...	Khel	do ...	...	...	...	...	...	...	...	...	...	...	...	...	...	...	...
		do ...	Khumal	do ...	...	...	...	...	...	...	...	...	...	...	...	...	22	5	17
		do ...	Kirikola	do ...	...	...	...	...	...	...	...	...	...	...	...	...	...	...	...
		do ...	Kisalvar	do ...	...	...	...	...	...	...	...	...	...	...	...	...	...	...	...
		do ...	Kobsadvaru	do ...	...	...	...	...	...	...	...	...	...	...	...	...	...	...	...
		do ...	Kodael...	do ...	...	...	...	...	...	...	...	...	...	...	...	...	6	...	6
		do ...	Kodhle	do ...	...	...	...	...	...	...	...	...	...	...	...	...	...	...	...
		do ...	Kodide...	do ...	...	...	...	...	...	...	...	...	...	...	...	...	...	...	...
		do ...	Kodikal	do ...	...	...	...	...	...	...	...	...	...	...	...	...	...	...	...
		do ...	Kodvakal	do ...	...	...	...	...	...	...	65	28	37	...	...	...	...	...	...
		do ...	Kolkadgi	do ...	...	...	...	...	...	...	196	95	101	...	...	...	...	...	...
		do ...	Kondalwaru	do ...	...	...	...	...	...	...	...	...	...	...	...	...	...	...	...
		do ...	Konri	do ...	...	...	...	...	...	...	...	...	...	...	...	...	...	...	...
		do ...	Kopaskaute	do ...	...	...	...	...	...	...	...	...	...	...	...	...	...	...	...
		do ...	Kotlad...	do ...	...	...	...	...	...	...	...	...	...	...	...	...	...	...	...
		do ...	Korudvad	do ...	...	...	...	...	...	...	...	...	...	...	...	...	...	...	...
		do ...	Kulwe...	do ...	...	...	...	...	...	...	...	...	...	...	...	...	...	...	...
		do ...	Kunepal	do ...	...	...	...	...	...	...	...	...	...	...	...	...	...	...	...
		do ...	Kunkar	do ...	...	...	...	...	...	...	7	2	5	...	...	...	...	...	...
		do ...	Kurausheti	do ...	...	...	...	...	...	...	...	...	...	...	...	...	...	...	...
		do ...	Kurni...	do ...	...	...	...	...	...	...	...	...	...	...	...	...	27	...	27

TABLE XVI.

Castes and Sub-divisions.—*Continued.*

Class.	Group.	Castes.	Sub-division of Castes.	Religion.	Birh. Total.	Birh. Males.	Birh. Females.	Nander. Total.	Nander. Males.	Nander. Females.	Naldrug. Total.	Naldrug. Males.	Naldrug. Females.	Bidar. Total.	Bidar. Males.	Bidar. Females.	Parbhani. Total.	Parbhani. Males.	Parbhani. Females.
					36	37	38	39	40	41	42	43	44	45	46	47	48	49	50
A	2a ...	Kunbi ...	Kame	Hindu ...	...	...	...	...	...	...	...	...	...	...	...	...	...	...	...
		do ...	Kanale	do ...	54	31	23	...	...	...	...	...	...	...	...	...	...	...	...
		do ...	Kanavad	do ...	...	...	...	...	...	...	...	...	...	...	...	...	...	...	...
		do ...	Kauchi	do ...	...	...	...	...	...	...	...	...	...	...	...	...	...	...	...
		do ...	Kauda...	do ...	5	2	8	...	...	...	...	...	...	...	...	...	...	...	...
		do ...	Kandvi	do ...	...	...	...	...	...	...	...	...	...	...	...	...	...	...	...
		do ...	Kauthibagi	do ...	...	...	...	...	...	...	...	...	...	...	...	...	...	...	...
		do ...	Kaple	do ...	7	...	7	...	...	...	...	...	...	16	6	10	...	...	...
		do ...	Karikal	do ...	...	...	...	...	...	...	...	...	...	...	...	...	...	...	...
		do ...	Karku...	do ...	...	...	...	...	...	...	...	...	...	...	...	...	...	...	...
		do ...	Katali...	do ...	...	...	...	...	...	...	...	...	...	...	...	...	...	...	...
		do ...	Katati...	do ...	...	...	...	...	...	...	...	...	...	...	...	...	...	...	...
		do ...	Katilkute	do ...	...	...	...	...	...	...	...	...	...	...	...	...	...	...	...
		do ...	Kathwas	do ...	...	...	...	...	...	...	...	...	...	...	...	...	...	...	...
		do ...	Khadalvar	do ...	...	...	...	...	...	...	...	...	...	...	...	...	...	...	...
		do ...	Khade...	do ...	...	...	...	...	...	...	...	...	...	...	...	...	...	...	...
		do ...	Khalipo	do ...	...	...	...	...	...	...	...	...	...	...	...	...	94	...	94
		do ...	Khaludak	do ...	...	...	...	...	...	...	...	...	...	...	...	...	...	...	...
		do ...	Khandan	do ...	...	...	...	...	...	...	...	...	...	...	...	...	...	...	...
		do ...	Kharari	do ...	...	...	...	...	...	...	...	...	...	...	...	...	...	...	...
		do ...	Khaud...	do ...	...	...	...	...	...	...	...	...	...	...	...	...	...	...	...
		do ...	Khel	do ...	...	...	...	...	...	...	...	...	...	619	297	322	...	...	...
		do ...	Khumal	do ...	...	...	...	...	...	...	...	...	...	...	...	...	...	...	...
		do ...	Kirikola	do ...	...	...	...	...	...	...	...	...	...	...	...	...	...	...	...
		do ...	Kisalvar	do ...	...	...	...	...	...	...	...	...	...	...	...	...	...	...	...
		do ...	Kobsadvaru	do ...	...	...	...	...	...	...	...	...	...	...	...	...	...	...	...
		do ...	Kodsel	do ...	...	...	...	...	...	...	...	...	...	...	...	...	...	...	...
		do ...	Kodhle	do ...	...	...	...	...	...	...	...	...	...	16	16	...	...	...	...
		do ...	Kodide	do ...	...	...	...	...	...	...	...	...	...	...	...	...	...	...	...
		do ...	Kodikal	do ...	...	...	...	...	...	...	...	...	...	...	...	...	...	...	...
		do ...	Kodvakal	do ...	...	...	...	65	38	82	...	...	...	266	122	144	...	...	...
		do ...	Kolkadgi	do ...	2	2	...	3,894	1,955	1,939	18	11	7	...	...	...	5	4	1
		do ...	Kondalwaru	do ...	...	...	...	...	...	...	...	...	...	...	...	...	...	...	...
		do ...	Konri	do ...	...	...	...	38	16	22	...	...	...	...	...	...	...	...	...
		do ...	Kopaskaute	do ...	...	...	...	...	...	...	...	...	...	...	...	...	...	...	...
		do ...	Kotlad...	do ...	...	...	...	...	...	...	...	...	...	...	...	...	...	...	...
		do ...	Korudvad	do ...	...	...	...	...	...	...	...	...	...	...	...	...	...	...	...
		do ...	Kulwe	do ...	...	...	...	...	...	...	...	...	...	...	...	...	...	...	...
		do ...	Kunepal	do ...	...	...	...	7	5	2	...	...	...	...	...	...	...	...	...
		do ...	Kunkar	do ...	...	...	...	...	...	...	...	...	...	...	...	...	...	...	...
		do ...	Kurausheti	do ...	...	...	...	...	...	...	...	...	...	...	...	...	...	...	...
		do ...	Kurni	do ...	...	...	...	...	...	...	...	...	...	...	...	...	...	...	...

TABLE XVI.

Castes and Sub-divisions.—*Continued.*

Class.	Group.	Castes.	Sub-division of Castes.	Religion.	Sirpur Tandur. Total.	Sirpur Tandur. Males.	Sirpur Tandur. Females.	Gulbarga. Total.	Gulbarga. Males.	Gulbarga. Females.	Raichur. Total.	Raichur. Males.	Raichur. Females.	Lingasugur. Total.	Lingasugur. Males.	Lingasugur. Females.	Railways. Total.	Railways. Males.	Railways. Females.
					51	52	53	54	55	56	57	58	59	60	61	62	63	64	65
A	2a ...	Kunbi ...	Kame ...	Hindu ...	...	...	...	...	...	...	...	...	...	...	...	...	...	...	...
		do ...	Kanale	do ...	...	...	...	...	...	...	...	...	...	...	...	...	...	...	...
		do ...	Kanavad	do ...	...	...	...	29	...	29	...	...	...	...	...	...	...	...	...
		do ...	Kauchi	do ...	...	...	...	...	...	...	...	...	...	...	...	...	...	...	...
		do ...	Kauda ...	do ...	...	...	...	...	...	...	...	...	...	...	...	...	...	...	...
		do ...	Kandvi	do ...	...	...	...	...	...	...	...	...	...	...	...	...	...	...	...
		do ...	Kauthibagi	do ...	...	...	...	...	...	...	114	63	51	...	...	...	...	...	...
		do ...	Kaple ...	do ...	...	...	...	...	...	...	...	...	...	...	...	...	...	...	...
		do ...	Karikal	do ...	...	...	...	...	...	...	...	...	...	373	237	136	...	...	...
		do ...	Karku ...	do ...	...	...	...	...	...	...	...	...	...	...	...	...	...	...	...
		do ...	Katali ...	do ...	...	...	...	...	...	...	...	...	...	...	...	...	...	...	...
		do ...	Katuti ...	do ...	...	...	...	...	...	...	...	...	...	...	...	...	...	...	...
		do ...	Katilkute	do ...	...	...	...	...	...	...	...	...	...	...	...	...	...	...	...
		do ...	Kathwas	do ...	...	...	...	...	...	...	...	...	...	...	...	...	...	...	...
		do ...	Khadalvar	do ...	...	...	...	...	...	...	...	...	...	...	...	...	...	...	...
		do ...	Khade ...	do ...	43	21	22	...	...	...	...	...	...	...	...	...	...	...	...
		do ...	Khalipo	do ...	...	...	...	...	...	...	...	...	...	...	...	...	...	...	...
		do ...	Khaludak	do ...	...	...	...	3	2	1	...	...	...	...	...	...	...	...	...
		do ...	Khandan	do ...	15	4	11	...	...	...	...	...	...	...	...	...	...	...	...
		do ...	Kharari	do ...	...	...	...	...	...	...	...	...	...	...	...	...	...	...	...
		do ...	Khand	do ...	4	4	...	...	...	...	...	...	...	...	...	...	...	...	...
		do ...	Khel ...	do ...	...	...	...	...	...	...	...	...	...	...	...	...	...	...	...
		do ...	Khumal	do ...	...	...	...	...	...	...	...	...	...	...	...	...	...	...	...
		do ...	Kirikola	do ...	...	...	...	3,544	1,803	1,741	...	...	...	965	350	615	...	...	...
		do ...	Kisalvar	do ...	...	...	...	2	2	...	...	...	...	...	...	...	...	...	...
		do ...	Kobsadvaru	do ...	...	...	...	...	...	...	...	...	...	6	5	1	...	...	...
		do ...	Kodael	do ...	...	...	...	...	...	...	...	...	...	...	...	...	...	...	...
		do ...	Kodhle	do ...	...	...	...	...	...	...	...	...	...	...	...	...	...	...	...
		do ...	Kodide	do ...	...	...	...	...	...	...	...	...	...	...	...	...	...	...	...
		do ...	Kodikal	do ...	...	...	...	...	...	...	...	...	...	19	...	19	...	...	...
		do ...	Kodvakal	do ...	...	...	...	1,730	788	942	...	...	...	...	...	...	...	...	...
		do ...	Kolkadgi	do ...	...	...	...	175	83	92	...	...	...	...	...	...	...	...	...
		do ...	Kondalwaru	do ...	...	...	...	...	...	...	...	...	...	103	55	48	...	...	...
		do ...	Konri ...	do ...	...	...	...	...	...	...	...	...	...	...	...	...	...	...	...
		do ...	Kopaskante	do ...	...	...	...	...	...	...	...	...	...	60	35	25	...	...	...
		do ...	Kotlad ...	do ...	4	1	3	...	...	...	...	...	...	...	...	...	...	...	...
		do ...	Korudvad	do ...	5	...	5	...	...	...	...	...	...	...	...	...	...	...	...
		do ...	Kulwe	do ...	...	...	...	91	48	43	...	...	...	...	...	...	...	...	...
		do ...	Kunepal	do ...	...	...	...	...	...	...	...	...	...	...	...	...	...	...	...
		do ...	Kunkar	do ...	...	...	...	...	...	...	...	...	...	...	...	...	...	...	...
		do ...	Kurausheti	do ...	...	...	...	54	27	27	...	...	...	40	18	22	...	...	...
		do ...	Kurni ...	do ...	...	...	...	...	...	...	...	...	...	...	...	...	...	...	...

TABLE XVI.

Castes and Sub-divisions.—*Continued.*

Class.	Group.	Castes.	Sub-division of Castes.	Religion.	Total. Total.	Total. Males.	Total. Females.	Hyderabad. Total.	Hyderabad. Males.	Hyderabad. Females.	Atraf-i-Balda. Total.	Atraf-i-Balda. Males.	Atraf-i-Balda. Females.	Mahabubnagar. Total.	Mahabubnagar. Males.	Mahabubnagar. Females.	Nalgonda. Total.	Nalgonda. Males.	Nalgonda. Females.
1	2	3	4	5	6	7	8	9	10	11	12	13	14	15	16	17	18	19	20
A	2a ...	Kunbi ...	Kurniyavaru	Hindu ...	224	114	110	...	...	...	...	...	...	...	...	...	...	...	...
		do ...	Kushal	do ...	1	1	...	...	...	...	...	...	...	...	...	...	...	...	...
		do ...	Kutebal	do ...	84	18	16	...	...	...	...	...	...	...	...	...	...	...	...
		do ...	Kuveban	do ...	4	2	2	...	...	...	...	...	...	...	...	...	...	...	...
		do ...	Ladvan	do ...	115	51	64	...	...	...	...	...	...	...	...	...	...	...	...
		do ...	Lagad...	do ...	38	16	22	...	...	...	...	...	...	...	...	...	...	...	...
		do ...	Laghaun	do ...	88	46	42	...	...	...	...	...	...	...	...	...	...	...	...
		do ...	Lakhe...	do ...	4	1	3	...	...	...	...	...	...	...	...	...	...	...	...
		do ...	Lakmari	do ...	5,403	2,792	2,611	...	...	...	27	15	12	...	...	...	122	68	54
		do ...	Lalgoudu	do ...	8,455	1,738	1,717	...	...	...	...	...	...	...	...	...	...	...	...
		do ...	Loate	do ...	6	3	3	...	...	...	...	...	...	...	...	...	...	...	...
		do ...	Lokabadki	do ...	47	21	26	...	...	...	...	...	...	...	...	...	...	...	...
		do ...	Madak	do ...	13	7	6	...	...	...	...	...	...	...	...	...	...	...	...
		do ...	Made	do ...	2	...	2	...	...	...	...	...	...	...	...	...	...	...	...
		do ...	Madge...	do ...	2	1	1	...	...	...	...	...	...	...	...	...	...	...	...
		do ...	Madhukar	do ...	1	1	...	...	...	...	...	...	...	...	...	...	...	...	...
		do ...	Madke	do ...	6	4	2	...	...	...	...	...	...	...	...	...	...	...	...
		do ...	Magli	do ...	2	1	1	...	...	...	...	...	...	...	...	...	...	...	...
		do ...	Mahevad	do ...	3	...	3	...	...	...	...	...	...	...	...	...	...	...	...
		do ...	Mahud	do ...	8	5	3	...	...	...	...	...	...	...	...	...	...	...	...
		do ...	Maikot	do ...	548	267	281	...	...	...	...	...	...	...	...	...	...	...	...
		do ...	Mairal...	do ...	8	6	2	...	...	...	...	...	...	...	...	...	...	...	...
		do ...	Maitrani	do ...	12	12	...	...	...	...	...	...	...	...	...	...	...	...	...
		do ...	Makni...	do ...	8	...	8	...	...	...	...	...	...	...	...	...	...	...	...
		do ...	Malbegi	do ...	453	223	230	...	...	...	...	...	...	...	...	...	...	...	...
		do ...	Malhari	do ...	2	1	1	...	...	...	...	...	...	...	...	...	...	...	...
		do ...	Manale	do ...	54	31	23	...	...	...	...	...	...	...	...	...	...	...	...
		do ...	Mane	do ...	28	15	13	...	...	...	...	...	...	...	...	...	...	...	...
		do ...	Manedvad	do ...	2,643	1,371	1,272	...	...	...	...	...	...	...	...	...	...	...	...
		do ...	Maneve	do ...	38	22	16	...	...	...	...	...	...	...	...	...	...	...	...
		do ...	Manod	do ...	29	29	...	...	...	...	...	...	...	...	...	...	...	...	...
		do ...	Maole	do ...	5	4	1	...	...	...	...	...	...	...	...	...	...	...	...
		do ...	Masevad	do ...	276	150	126	...	...	...	...	...	...	...	...	...	...	...	...
		do ...	Mashau	do ...	4	2	2	...	...	...	...	...	...	...	...	...	...	...	...
		do ...	Matmatkai	do ...	6,204	3,048	3,156	...	...	...	...	...	...	...	...	...	...	...	...
		do ...	Milbadki	do ...	1,266	639	627	...	...	...	...	...	...	...	...	...	...	...	...
		do ...	Mochal	do ...	6	4	2	...	...	...	...	...	...	...	...	...	...	...	...
		do ...	Mond	do ...	9	3	6	...	...	...	...	...	...	...	...	...	...	...	...
		do ...	Mondbal	do ...	2	1	1	...	...	...	...	...	...	...	...	...	...	...	...
		do ...	Motadvad	do ...	789	399	390	...	...	...	...	...	...	...	...	...	...	...	...
		do ...	More	do ...	8	1	7	...	...	...	...	...	...	...	...	...	...	...	...
		do ...	Motati...	do ...	176,246	89,775	86,471	891	199	192	18,627	6,988	6,694	42,706	21,467	21,239	85,862	18,410	17,452

TABLE XVI.

Castes and Sub-divisions.—*Continued.*

Class.	Group.	Castes.	Sub-division of Castes.	Religion.	Warangal. Total.	Warangal. Males.	Warangal. Females.	Elgandal. Total.	Elgandal. Males.	Elgandal. Females.	Indur. Total.	Indur. Males.	Indur. Females.	Medak. Total.	Medak. Males.	Medak. Females.	Aurangabad. Total.	Aurangabad. Males.	Aurangabad. Females.
					21	22	23	24	25	26	27	28	29	30	31	32	33	34	35
A	2a ...	Kunbi ...	Kurniyavaru	Hindu ...	...	...	...	...	...	...	...	...	...	...	...	...	...	...	...
		do ...	Kushal	do ...	...	...	...	...	...	...	...	...	...	...	...	...	...	...	...
		do ...	Kutebal	do ...	...	...	...	...	...	...	4	2	2	...	...	...	...	...	...
		do ...	Kuveban	do ...	...	...	...	...	...	...	4	2	2	...	...	...	...	...	...
		do ...	Ladvan	do ...	...	...	...	...	...	...	...	...	...	...	...	...	...	...	...
		do ...	Lagad	do ...	...	...	...	...	...	...	...	...	...	...	...	...	...	...	...
		do ...	Laghaun	do ...	...	...	...	...	...	...	...	...	...	...	...	...	...	...	...
		do ...	Lakhe	do ...	...	...	...	...	...	...	...	...	...	...	...	...	4	1	3
		do ...	Lakmari	do ...	3,582	1,849	1,733	1,672	860	812	...	...	...	...	...	...	...	...	...
		do ...	Lalgoudu	do ...	...	...	...	...	...	...	...	...	...	...	...	...	...	...	...
		do ...	Loate	do ...	...	...	...	...	...	...	...	...	...	...	...	...	...	...	...
		do ...	Lokabadki	do ...	...	...	...	...	...	...	...	...	...	...	...	...	...	...	...
		do ...	Madak...	do ...	...	...	...	...	...	...	...	...	...	...	...	...	...	...	...
		do ...	Made	do ...	...	...	...	...	...	...	...	...	...	...	...	...	...	...	...
		do ...	Madge	do ...	...	...	...	...	...	...	...	...	...	...	...	...	...	...	...
		do ...	Madhukar	do ...	...	...	...	...	...	...	...	...	...	...	...	...	1	1	...
		do ...	Madko	do ...	...	...	...	...	...	...	...	...	...	...	...	...	...	...	...
		do ...	Magli	do ...	...	...	...	...	...	...	2	1	1	...	...	...	...	...	...
		do ...	Mahevad	do ...	...	...	...	...	...	...	8	...	8	...	...	...	...	...	...
		do ...	Mahud	do ...	...	...	...	...	...	...	...	...	...	...	...	...	...	...	...
		do ...	Maikot	do ...	...	...	...	...	...	...	...	...	...	...	...	...	...	...	...
		do ...	Mairal...	do ...	...	...	...	...	...	...	...	...	...	...	...	...	...	...	...
		do ...	Maitrani	do ...	...	...	...	...	...	...	...	...	...	...	...	...	12	12	...
		do ...	Makni	do ...	...	...	...	...	...	...	...	...	...	...	...	...	8	...	8
		do ...	Malbegi	do ...	...	...	...	...	...	...	...	...	...	...	...	...	...	...	...
		do ...	Malhari	do ...	...	...	...	...	...	...	...	...	...	...	...	...	...	...	...
		do ...	Manalo	do ...	...	...	...	...	...	...	...	...	...	...	...	...	...	...	...
		do ...	Mane	do ...	...	...	...	...	...	...	...	...	...	...	...	...	...	...	...
		do ...	Manedvad	do ...	...	...	...	...	...	...	2,643	1,371	1,272	...	...	...	...	...	...
		do ...	Maneve	do ...	...	...	...	...	...	...	...	...	...	...	...	...	...	...	...
		do ...	Manod...	do ...	...	...	...	...	...	...	...	...	...	...	...	...	...	...	...
		do ...	Maole	do ...	...	...	...	...	...	...	...	...	...	...	...	...	5	4	1
		do ...	Masevad	do ...	...	...	...	...	...	...	...	...	...	...	...	...	...	...	...
		do ...	Mashau	do ...	...	...	...	...	...	...	...	...	...	...	...	...	...	...	...
		do ...	Matmatkai	do ...	...	...	...	...	...	...	...	...	...	...	...	...	...	...	...
		do ...	Milbadki	do ...	...	...	...	...	...	...	...	...	...	...	...	...	...	...	...
		do ...	Mochal	do ...	...	...	...	...	...	...	...	...	...	...	...	...	...	...	...
		do ...	Mond	do ...	...	...	...	...	...	...	...	...	...	...	...	...	...	...	...
		do ...	Mondbal	do ...	...	...	...	...	...	...	...	...	...	...	...	...	...	...	...
		do ...	Motadvad	do ...	...	...	...	...	...	...	545	280	265	...	...	...	...	...	...
		do ...	More	do ...	...	...	...	...	...	...	...	...	...	...	...	...	8	1	7
		do ...	Motati...	do ...	18,006	9,317	8,689	39,433	20,212	19,221	7,740	3,902	3,838	9,026	4,572	4,454	...	...	...

TABLE XVI.
Castes and Sub-divisions.

TABLE XVI.

Castes and Sub-divisions.—*Continued.*

Class.	Group.	Castes.	Sub-division of Castes.	Religion.	Firb. Total.	Firb. Males.	Firb. Females.	Nandor. Total.	Nandor. Males.	Nandor. Females.	Naldrug. Total.	Naldrug. Males.	Naldrug. Females.	Bidar. Total.	Bidar. Males.	Bidar. Females.	Parbhani. Total.	Parbhani. Males.	Parbhani. Females.
					36	37	38	39	40	41	42	43	44	45	46	47	48	49	50
A	2a ...	Kunbi ...	Kurniyavaru	Hindu ...	...	...	...	...	...	...	...	...	...	...	...	...	...	...	...
		do ...	Kushal	do ...	...	...	...	...	...	...	...	...	...	...	...	...	...	...	...
		do ...	Kutcbal	do ...	...	...	...	15	8	7	...	...	...	5	2	8	...	...	...
		do ...	Kuveban	do ...	...	...	...	...	...	...	...	...	...	...	...	...	...	...	...
		do ...	Ladvan	do ...	...	...	...	...	...	...	...	...	...	...	...	...	18	8	10
		do ...	Lagad...	do ...	...	...	...	38	16	22	...	...	...	...	...	...	...	...	...
		do ...	Laghaun	do ...	...	...	...	...	...	...	...	...	...	...	...	...	...	...	...
		do ...	Lakhe...	do ...	...	...	...	...	...	...	...	...	...	...	...	...	...	...	...
		do ...	Lakmari	do ...	...	...	...	...	...	...	...	...	...	...	...	...	...	...	...
		do ...	Lalgoudu	do ...	...	...	...	...	...	...	...	...	...	...	...	...	...	...	...
		do ...	Loate	do ...	...	...	...	6	3	3	...	...	...	...	...	...	...	...	...
		do ...	Lokabadki	do ...	...	...	...	...	...	...	...	...	...	...	...	...	...	...	...
		do ...	Madak	do ...	...	...	...	...	...	...	...	...	...	13	7	6	...	...	...
		do ...	Made	do ...	...	...	...	...	...	...	...	...	...	...	...	...	2	...	2
		do ...	Madge	do ...	...	...	...	...	...	...	...	...	...	2	1	1	...	...	...
		do ...	Madhukar	do ...	...	...	...	...	...	...	...	...	...	...	...	...	...	...	...
		do ...	Madke...	do ...	6	4	2	...	...	...	...	...	...	...	...	...	...	...	...
		do ...	Magli	do ...	...	...	...	...	...	...	...	...	...	...	...	...	...	...	...
		do ...	Mahevad	do ...	...	...	...	...	...	...	...	...	...	...	...	...	...	...	...
		do ...	Mahud	do ...	...	...	...	...	...	...	...	...	...	...	...	...	...	...	...
		do ...	Maikot	do ...	...	...	...	...	...	...	...	...	...	...	...	...	...	...	...
		do ...	Mairal...	do ...	7	5	2	...	...	...	...	...	...	...	...	...	...	...	...
		do ...	Maitrani	do ...	...	...	...	...	...	...	...	...	...	...	...	...	...	...	...
		do ...	Makni...	do ...	...	...	...	...	...	...	...	...	...	...	...	...	...	...	...
		do ...	Malbegi	do ...	...	...	...	...	...	...	...	...	...	...	...	...	...	...	...
		do ...	Malhari	do ...	...	...	...	2	1	1	...	...	...	...	...	...	...	...	...
		do ...	Manale	do ...	54	31	23	...	...	...	...	...	...	...	...	...	...	...	...
		do ...	Mane	do ...	28	15	13	...	...	...	...	...	...	...	...	...	...	...	...
		do ...	Manedvad	do ...	...	...	...	...	...	...	...	...	...	...	...	...	...	...	...
		do ...	Maneve	do ...	...	...	...	...	...	...	...	...	...	...	...	...	...	...	...
		do ...	Manod	do ...	...	...	...	1	1	...	...	...	...	...	...	...	...	...	...
		do ...	Maole	do ...	...	...	...	...	...	...	...	...	...	...	...	...	...	...	...
		do ...	Masevad	do ...	127	70	57	...	...	...	...	...	...	...	...	...	...	...	...
		do ...	Mashau	do ...	...	...	...	4	2	2	...	...	...	...	...	...	...	...	...
		do ...	Matmatkai	do ...	...	...	...	...	...	...	...	...	...	...	...	...	...	...	...
		do ...	Milbadki	do ...	...	...	...	...	...	...	...	...	...	...	...	...	...	...	...
		do ...	Mochal	do ...	...	...	...	...	...	...	6	4	2	...	...	...	...	...	...
		do ...	Mond	do ...	...	...	...	...	...	...	...	...	...	...	...	...	...	...	...
		do ...	Mondbal	do ...	...	...	...	2	1	1	...	...	...	...	...	...	...	...	...
		do ...	Motadvad	do ...	...	...	...	1	...	1	...	...	...	...	...	...	130	60	70
		do ...	More	do ...	...	...	...	...	...	...	...	...	...	...	...	...	...	...	...
		do ...	Motati...	do ...	...	...	...	...	...	...	...	...	...	484	259	225	...	...	...

TABLE XVI.
Castes and Sub-divisions.—*Continued.*

Class.	Group.	Castes.	Sub-division of Castes.	Religion.	Sirpur Tandur. Total.	Sirpur Tandur. Males.	Sirpur Tandur. Females.	Gulbarga. Total.	Gulbarga. Males.	Gulbarga. Females.	Raichur. Total.	Raichur. Males.	Raichur. Females.	Lingasugur. Total.	Lingasugur. Males.	Lingasugur. Females.	Railways. Total.	Railways. Males.	Railways. Females.
					51	52	53	54	55	56	57	58	59	60	61	62	63	64	65
A	2a ...	Kunbi ...	Kutniyavaru	Hindu ...	...	...	...	...	...	...	...	...	...	224	114	110	...	...	...
		do ...	Kushal	do ...	1	1	...	...	...	...	...	...	...	...	...	...	...	...	...
		do ...	Kutebal	do ...	...	...	...	10	6	4	...	...	...	...	...	...	...	...	...
		do ...	Kuveban	do ...	...	...	...	...	...	...	...	...	...	...	...	...	...	...	...
		do ...	Ladvan	do ...	97	43	54	...	...	...	...	...	...	...	...	...	...	...	...
		do ...	Lagad	do ...	...	...	...	...	...	...	...	...	...	...	...	...	...	...	...
		do ...	Laghaun	do ...	88	46	42	...	...	...	...	...	...	...	...	...	...	...	...
		do ...	Lakhe...	do ...	...	...	...	...	...	...	...	...	...	...	...	...	...	...	...
		do ...	Lakmari	do ...	...	...	...	...	...	...	...	...	...	...	...	...	...	...	...
		do ...	Lalgondu	do ...	...	...	...	...	...	...	2,776	1,399	1,377	679	839	840	...	...	...
		do ...	Loate	do ...	...	...	...	...	...	...	...	...	...	...	...	...	...	...	...
		do ...	Lokabadki	do ...	...	...	...	...	...	...	...	...	...	47	21	26	...	...	...
		do ...	Madak	do ...	...	...	...	...	...	...	...	...	...	...	...	...	...	...	...
		do ...	Made	do ...	...	...	...	...	...	...	...	...	...	...	...	...	...	...	...
		do ...	Madge	do ...	...	...	...	...	...	...	...	...	...	...	...	...	...	...	...
		do ...	Madhukar	do ...	...	...	...	...	...	...	...	...	...	...	...	...	...	...	...
		do ...	Madke	do ...	...	...	...	...	...	...	...	...	...	...	...	...	...	...	...
		do ...	Magli...	do ...	...	...	...	...	...	...	...	...	...	...	...	...	...	...	...
		do ...	Mahevad	do ...	...	...	...	...	...	...	...	...	...	...	...	...	...	...	...
		do ...	Mahud	do ...	8	5	3	...	...	...	...	...	...	...	...	...	...	...	...
		do ...	Maikot	do ...	...	...	...	548	267	281	...	...	...	...	...	...	...	...	...
		do ...	Mairal	do ...	...	...	...	...	...	...	...	...	...	...	...	...	1	1	...
		do ...	Maitrani	do ...	...	...	...	...	...	...	...	...	...	...	...	...	...	...	...
		do ...	Makni	do ...	...	...	...	...	...	...	...	...	...	...	...	...	...	...	...
		do ...	Malbegi	do ...	...	...	...	...	...	...	38	18	20	420	210	210	...	...	...
		do ...	Malhari	do ...	...	...	...	...	...	...	...	...	...	...	...	...	...	...	...
		do ...	Manale	do ...	...	...	...	...	...	...	...	...	...	...	...	...	...	...	...
		do ...	Mane	do ...	...	...	...	...	...	...	...	...	...	...	...	...	...	...	...
		do ...	Manedvad	do ...	...	...	...	...	...	...	...	...	...	...	...	...	...	...	...
		do ...	Maneve	do ...	...	...	...	38	22	16	...	...	...	...	...	...	...	...	...
		do ...	Manod	do ...	...	...	...	28	28	...	...	...	...	...	...	...	...	...	...
		do ...	Maole	do ...	...	...	...	...	...	...	...	...	...	...	...	...	...	...	...
		do ...	Masevad	do ...	149	80	69	...	...	...	...	...	...	...	...	...	...	...	...
		do ...	Mashau	do ...	...	...	...	...	...	...	...	...	...	...	...	...	...	...	...
		do ...	Matmatkai	do ...	...	...	...	8	4	4	2,575	1,222	1,353	3,621	1,822	1,799	...	...	...
		do ...	Milbadki	do ...	...	...	...	...	...	...	4	2	2	1,262	637	625	...	...	...
		do ...	Mochal	do ...	...	...	...	...	...	...	...	...	...	...	...	...	...	...	...
		do ...	Mond	do ...	...	...	...	9	3	6	...	...	...	...	...	...	...	...	...
		do ...	Mondbal	do ...	...	...	...	...	...	...	...	...	...	...	...	...	...	...	...
		do ...	Motadvad	do ...	...	...	...	113	59	54	...	...	...	...	...	...	...	...	...
		do ...	More	do ...	...	...	...	...	...	...	...	...	...	...	...	...	...	...	...
		do ...	Motati	do ...	...	...	...	...	...	...	8,971	4,504	4,467	...	...	...	...	...	...

TABLE XVI.

Castes and Sub-divisions.—*Continued.*

Class.	Group.	Castes.	Sub-division of Castes.	Religion.	Total.			Hyderabad.			Atraf-i-Balda.			Mahabubnagar.			Nalgonda.		
					Total.	Males.	Females.	Total.	Males.	Females.	Total.	Males.	Females.	Total.	Males.	Females.	Total.	Males.	Females.
1	2	3	4	5	6	7	8	9	10	11	12	13	14	15	16	17	18	19	20
A	2a ...	Kunbi ...	Mothri	Hindu ...	188	69	69	...	...	...	...	...	...	...	...	...	...	...	...
		do ...	Mule	do ..	8	1	2	...	...	...	...	...	...	...	...	...	...	...	...
		do ...	Mukhadi	do ...	4	4	...	...	...	...	...	...	...	...	...	...	...	...	...
		do ...	Munati ...	do ...	6	4	2	...	...	...	...	...	...	...	...	...	...	...	...
		do ...	Munurvad	do ...	1,440	721	719	...	...	...	...	...	...	...	...	...	...	...	...
		do ...	Mushti	do ...	105	48	57	...	...	...	...	...	...	...	...	...	...	...	...
		do ...	Muttinipende... ...	do ...	34	17	17	...	...	...	...	...	...	...	...	...	...	...	...
		do ...	Nagdad	do ...	51	10	41	...	...	...	...	...	...	...	...	...	...	...	...
		do ...	Nagri	do ...	20	9	11	...	...	...	...	...	...	...	...	...	...	...	...
		do ...	Nakarle	do ...	79	45	34	...	...	...	...	...	...	...	...	...	...	...	...
		do ...	Nakod... ...	do ...	18	8	5	...	...	...	...	...	...	...	...	...	...	...	...
		do ...	Narda... ...	do ...	187	75	62	...	...	...	...	...	...	...	...	...	...	...	...
		do ...	Narwal	do ...	1,022	526	496	...	...	...	...	...	...	...	...	...	...	...	...
		do ...	Nati Kunbi	do ...	817	443	374	...	...	...	...	...	...	...	...	...	...	...	...
		do ...	Naur	do ...	74	85	89	...	...	...	...	...	...	...	...	...	...	...	...
		do ...	Neyapu	do ...	17	7	10	...	...	...	...	...	...	...	...	...	...	...	...
		do ...	Nidole... ...	do ...	4	1	8	...	...	...	...	...	...	...	...	...	...	...	...
		do ...	Nilevar	do ...	218	106	112	...	...	...	...	...	...	...	...	...	...	...	...
		do ...	Nilkantnoda	do ...	25	15	10	...	...	...	...	...	...	...	...	...	...	...	...
		do ...	Nirvate	do ...	15	18	2	...	...	...	...	...	...	...	...	...	...	...	...
		do ...	Odkari	do ...	4	2	2	...	...	...	...	...	...	...	...	...	...	...	...
		do ...	Pachhte	do ...	1	1	...	...	...	...	...	...	...	...	...	...	...	...	...
		do ...	Pâchikadvad	do ...	14	4	10	...	...	...	...	...	...	...	...	...	...	...	...
		do ...	Padad... ...	do ...	14	5	9	...	...	...	...	...	...	...	...	...	...	...	...
		do ...	Padamvad	do ...	29	19	10	...	...	...	...	...	...	...	...	...	...	...	...
		do ...	Padwalbagi	do ...	234	106	128	...	...	...	...	...	...	...	...	...	...	...	...
		do ...	Pairadu	do ...	8	8	5	...	...	...	...	...	...	...	...	...	...	...	...
		do ...	Paknati	do ...	71,239	36,192	35,047	295	258	37	3,367	1,690	1,677	14,580	7,252	7,328	3,923	1,929	1,994
		do ...	Palamunural ...	do ...	262	137	125	...	...	...	...	...	...	...	...	...	...	...	...
		do ...	Pangal	do ...	240	131	109	...	...	...	...	...	...	...	...	...	...	...	...
		do ...	Panmod	do ...	22	9	13	...	...	...	...	...	...	...	...	...	...	...	...
		do ...	Paralwal	do ...	4	3	1	...	...	...	...	...	...	...	...	...	...	...	...
		do ...	Pasodni	do ...	3	1	2	...	...	...	...	...	...	...	...	...	...	...	...
		do ...	Parkevar	do ...	599	284	315	...	...	...	...	...	...	...	...	...	...	...	...
		do ...	Parmavad	do ...	147	72	75	...	...	...	...	...	...	...	...	...	...	...	...
		do ...	Parvad	do ...	53	25	28	...	...	...	...	...	...	...	...	...	...	...	...
		do ...	Patal	do ...	8	5	3	...	...	...	...	...	...	...	...	...	...	...	...
		do ...	Patansetti	do ...	5	4	1	...	...	...	...	...	...	...	...	...	...	...	...
		do ...	Patkar	do ...	89	87	2	...	...	...	...	...	...	...	...	...	...	...	...
		do ...	Patti	do ...	18	10	8	...	...	...	...	...	...	...	...	...	18	10	8
		do ...	Patyar	do ...	5	3	2	5	3	2	...	...	...	...	...	...	...	...	...
		do ...	Pedakanti	do ...	736	378	358	...	...	...	...	...	...	...	...	...	445	225	220

TABLE XVI.

Castes and Sub-divisions.—*Continued.*

Class.	Group.	Castes.	Sub-division of Castes.	Religion.	Warangal. Total.	Warangal. Males.	Warangal. Females.	Elgandal. Total.	Elgandal. Males.	Elgandal. Females.	Indur. Total.	Indur. Males.	Indur. Females.	Medak. Total.	Medak. Males.	Medak. Females.	Aurangabad. Total.	Aurangabad. Males.	Aurangabad. Females.
					21	22	23	24	25	26	27	28	29	30	31	32	33	34	35
A	2a ...	Kunbi ...	Mothri	Hindu ...	...	...	...	...	...	...	...	...	...	...	...	...	...	...	...
		do ...	Mule	do ...	...	...	...	...	...	...	...	...	...	...	...	...	3	1	2
		do ...	Mukhadi	do ...	...	...	...	...	...	...	...	...	...	...	...	...	4	4	...
		do ...	Munati	do ...	...	...	...	...	...	...	...	...	...	...	...	...	...	...	...
		do ...	Munurvad	do ...	...	...	...	...	...	...	...	...	...	...	...	...	...	...	...
		do ...	Mushti	do ...	...	...	...	...	...	...	...	...	...	...	...	...	...	...	...
		do ...	Muttinipende	do ...	...	...	...	...	...	...	...	...	...	...	...	...	...	...	...
		do ...	Nagdad	do ...	...	...	...	...	...	...	...	...	...	...	...	...	...	...	...
		do ...	Nagri	do ...	...	...	...	...	...	...	...	...	...	...	...	...	...	...	...
		do ...	Nakarle	do ...	...	...	...	...	...	...	...	...	...	...	...	...	79	45	34
		do ...	Nakod...	do ...	...	...	...	...	...	...	...	...	...	...	...	...	13	8	5
		do ...	Narda...	do ...	...	...	...	...	...	...	...	...	...	...	...	...	...	...	...
		do ...	Narwal	do ...	...	...	...	...	...	...	...	...	...	...	...	...	...	...	...
		do ...	Nati Kunbi	do ...	...	...	...	...	...	...	817	443	374	...	...	...	...	...	...
		do ...	Naur	do ...	...	...	...	...	...	...	...	...	...	...	...	...	...	...	...
		do ...	Neyapu	do ...	17	7	10	...	...	...	...	...	...	...	...	...	...	...	...
		do ...	Nidole...	do ...	...	...	...	...	...	...	...	...	...	...	...	...	...	...	...
		do ...	Nilevar	do ...	...	...	...	...	...	...	214	105	109	...	...	...	4	1	3
		do ...	Nilkantnoda	do ...	...	...	...	...	...	...	...	...	...	...	...	...	...	...	...
		do ...	Nirvate	do ...	...	...	...	...	...	...	15	13	2	...	...	...	...	...	...
		do ...	Odkari	do ...	...	...	...	...	...	...	...	...	...	...	...	...	...	...	...
		do ...	Pachhte	do ...	...	...	...	...	...	...	...	...	...	...	...	...	4	2	2
		do ...	Pachikadvad	do ...	...	...	...	...	...	...	14	4	10	...	...	...	1	1	...
		do ...	Padad...	do ...	...	...	...	...	...	...	...	...	...	...	...	...	...	...	...
		do ...	Padamvad	do ...	...	...	...	...	...	...	8	8	...	...	...	...	...	...	...
		do ...	Padwalbagi	do ...	...	...	...	...	...	...	...	...	...	...	...	...	...	...	...
		do ...	Pairadu	do ...	...	...	...	...	...	...	...	...	...	...	...	...	...	...	...
		do ...	Paknati	do ...	988	482	506	7,525	3,812	3,713	3,200	1,639	1,561	5,769	2,904	2,865	...	...	...
		do ...	Palamunural	do ...	...	...	...	...	...	...	262	137	125	...	...	...	...	...	...
		do ...	Pangal	do ...	...	...	...	...	...	...	...	...	...	...	...	...	...	...	...
		do ...	Panmod	do ...	...	...	...	...	...	...	...	...	...	...	...	...	...	...	...
		do ...	Paralwal	do ...	...	...	...	...	...	...	...	...	...	...	...	...	...	...	...
		do ...	Pasodni	do ...	...	...	...	...	...	...	...	...	...	...	...	...	...	...	...
		do ...	Parkevar	do ...	...	...	...	...	...	...	...	...	...	...	...	...	...	...	...
		do ...	Parmavad	do ...	...	...	...	...	...	...	147	72	75	...	...	...	...	...	...
		do ...	Parvad	do ...	...	...	...	...	...	...	53	25	28	...	...	...	...	...	...
		do ...	Patal	do ...	...	...	...	...	...	...	...	...	...	...	...	...	8	5	3
		do ...	Patansetti	do ...	...	...	...	...	...	...	...	...	...	...	...	...	...	...	...
		do ...	Patkar	do ...	...	...	...	...	...	...	...	...	...	...	...	...	89	87	2
		do ...	Patti	do ...	...	...	...	...	...	...	...	...	...	...	...	...	...	...	...
		do ...	Patyar...	do ...	...	...	...	...	...	...	...	...	...	...	...	...	...	...	...
		do ...	Pedakanti	do ...	291	153	138	...	...	...	...	...	...	...	...	...	...	...	...

TABLE XVI.
Castes and Sub-divisions.

TABLE XVI.

Castes and Sub-divisions.—*Continued.*

Class.	Group.	Castes.	Sub-division of Castes.	Religion.	Birh, Total.	Birh, Males.	Birh, Females.	Nander. Total.	Nander. Males.	Nander. Females.	Naldrug. Total.	Naldrug. Males.	Naldrug. Females.	Bidar. Total.	Bidar. Males.	Bidar. Females.	Parbhani. Total.	Parbhani. Males.	Parbhani. Females.
					36	37	38	39	40	41	42	43	44	45	46	47	48	49	50
A	2a ...	Kunbi ...	Móthri	Hindu ...	...	...	...	...	...	...	...	...	...	138	69	69	...	...	...
		do ...	Mule	do ...	...	...	...	...	...	...	...	...	...	...	...	...	...	...	...
		do ...	Mukhadi ...	do ...	...	...	...	...	...	...	...	...	...	...	...	...	...	...	...
		do ...	Munati ...	do ...	...	...	...	...	...	...	...	...	...	...	...	...	...	...	...
		do ...	Munurvad ...	do ...	...	...	...	...	...	...	...	...	...	5	1	4	...	...	...
		do ...	Mushti ...	do ...	...	...	...	...	...	...	...	...	...	...	...	...	...	...	...
		do ...	Muttinipende ...	do ...	...	...	...	...	...	...	...	...	...	...	...	...	...	...	...
		do ...	Nagdad ...	do ...	...	...	...	51	10	41	...	...	...	...	...	...	...	...	...
		do ...	Nagri ...	do ...	...	...	...	...	...	...	...	...	...	...	...	...	...	...	...
		do ...	Nakarle ...	do ...	...	...	...	...	...	...	...	...	...	...	...	...	...	...	...
		do ...	Nakod... ...	do ...	...	...	...	...	...	...	...	...	...	...	...	...	...	...	...
		do ...	Narda... ...	do ...	...	...	...	...	...	...	...	...	...	...	...	...	...	...	...
		do ...	Narwal ...	do ...	...	...	...	...	...	...	...	...	...	...	...	...	...	...	...
		do ...	Nati Kunbi ...	do ...	...	...	...	...	...	...	...	...	...	...	...	...	...	...	...
		do ...	Naur... ...	do ...	...	...	...	...	...	...	...	...	...	...	...	...	...	...	...
		do ...	Neyapu ...	do ...	...	...	...	...	...	...	...	...	...	...	...	...	...	...	...
		do ...	Nidole... ...	do ...	...	...	...	...	...	...	...	...	...	...	...	...	...	...	...
		do ...	Nilevar ...	do ...	...	...	...	...	...	...	...	...	...	...	...	...	...	...	...
		do ...	Nilkantnoda ...	do ...	...	...	...	...	...	...	...	...	...	...	...	...	...	...	...
		do ...	Nirvate ...	do ...	...	...	...	...	...	...	...	...	...	...	...	...	...	...	...
		do ...	Odkari ...	do ...	...	...	...	...	...	...	...	...	...	...	...	...	...	...	...
		do ...	Pachhte ...	do ...	...	...	...	...	...	...	...	...	...	...	...	...	...	...	...
		do ...	Pachikadvad ...	do ...	...	...	...	...	...	...	...	...	...	...	...	...	...	...	...
		do ...	Padad... ...	do ...	...	...	...	14	5	9	...	...	...	...	...	...	...	...	...
		do ...	Padamvad ...	do ...	...	...	...	...	...	...	...	...	...	...	...	...	...	...	...
		do ...	Padwalbagi ...	do ...	...	...	...	...	...	...	...	...	...	...	...	...	...	...	...
		do ...	Pairadu ...	do ...	...	...	...	...	...	...	...	...	...	...	...	...	...	...	...
		do ...	Paknati ...	do ...	...	...	...	13	8	5	...	...	...	94	47	47	...	...	...
		do ...	Palamunural ...	do ...	...	...	...	...	...	...	...	...	...	...	...	...	...	...	...
		do ...	Pangal ...	do ...	...	...	...	19	10	9	...	...	...	...	...	...	221	121	100
		do ...	Panmod ...	do ...	...	...	...	22	9	13	...	...	...	...	...	...	...	...	...
		do ...	Paralwal ...	do ...	4	3	1	...	...	...	...	...	...	...	...	...	...	...	...
		do ...	Pasodni ...	do ...	3	1	2	...	...	...	...	...	...	...	...	...	...	...	...
		do ...	Parkevar ...	do ...	...	...	...	268	138	130	...	...	...	...	...	...	...	...	...
		do ...	Parmavad ...	do ...	...	...	...	...	...	...	...	...	...	...	...	...	...	...	...
		do ...	Parvad ...	do ...	...	...	...	...	...	...	...	...	...	...	...	...	...	...	...
		do ...	Patal	do ...	...	...	...	...	...	...	...	...	...	...	...	...	...	...	...
		do ...	Patansetti ...	do ...	...	...	...	...	...	...	...	...	...	...	...	...	...	...	...
		do ...	Patkar ...	do ...	...	...	...	...	...	...	...	...	...	...	...	...	...	...	...
		do ...	Patti	do ...	...	...	...	...	...	...	...	...	...	...	...	...	...	...	...
		do ...	Patyar ...	do ...	...	...	...	...	...	...	...	...	...	...	...	...	...	...	...
		do ...	Pedakanti ...	do ...	...	...	...	...	...	...	...	...	...	...	...	...	...	...	...

TABLE XVI.

Castes and Sub-divisions.—*Continued.*

Class.	Group.	Castes.	Sub-division of Castes.	Religion.	Sirpur Tandur. Total.	Sirpur Tandur. Males.	Sirpur Tandur. Females.	Gulbarga. Total.	Gulbarga. Males.	Gulbarga. Females.	Raichur. Total.	Raichur. Males.	Raichur. Females.	Lingasugur. Total.	Lingasugur. Males.	Lingasugur. Females.	Railways. Total.	Railways. Males.	Railways. Females.
					51	52	53	54	55	56	57	58	59	60	61	62	63	64	65
A	2a ...	Kunbi ...	Mothri	Hindu ...	...	...	...	...	...	...	...	...	...	...	...	...	...	...	...
		do ...	Mule	do ...	...	...	...	...	...	...	...	...	...	...	...	...	...	...	...
		do ...	Mukhadi	do ...	...	...	...	...	...	...	...	...	...	...	...	...	...	...	...
		do ...	Munati	do ...	...	...	...	...	...	...	6	4	2	...	...	...	...	...	...
		do ...	Munurvad	do ...	...	...	...	1,485	720	715	...	...	...	...	...	...	...	...	...
		do ...	Mushti	do ...	105	48	57	...	...	...	...	...	...	...	...	...	...	...	...
		do ...	Muttinipende	do ...	...	...	...	...	...	...	34	17	17	...	...	...	...	...	...
		do ...	Nagdad	do ...	...	...	...	...	...	...	...	...	...	...	...	...	...	...	...
		do ...	Nagri	do ...	...	...	...	20	9	11	...	...	...	...	...	...	...	...	...
		do ...	Nakarle	do ...	...	...	...	...	...	...	...	...	...	...	...	...	...	...	...
		do ...	Nakod...	do ...	...	...	...	...	...	...	...	...	...	...	...	...	...	...	...
		do ...	Narda...	do ...	...	...	...	137	75	62	...	...	...	...	...	...	...	...	...
		do ...	Narwal	do ...	...	...	...	...	...	...	...	...	...	1,022	526	496	...	...	...
		do ...	Nati Kunbi	do ...	...	...	...	...	...	...	...	...	...	...	...	...	...	...	...
		do ...	Naur...	do ...	...	...	...	74	85	39	...	...	...	...	...	...	...	...	...
		do ...	Neyapu	do ...	...	...	...	...	...	...	...	...	...	...	...	...	...	...	...
		do ...	Nidole...	do ...	...	...	...	...	...	...	...	...	...	...	...	...	...	...	...
		do ...	Nilevar	do ...	...	...	...	4	1	8	...	...	...	...	...	...	...	...	...
		do ...	Nilkantnoda	do ...	...	...	...	25	15	10	...	...	...	...	...	...	...	...	...
		do ...	Nirvate	do ...	...	...	...	...	...	...	...	...	...	...	...	...	...	...	...
		do ...	Odkari	do ...	...	...	...	...	...	...	...	...	...	...	...	...	...	...	...
		do ...	Pachhte	do ...	...	...	...	...	...	...	...	...	...	...	...	...	...	...	...
		do ...	Pachikadvad	do ...	...	...	...	...	...	...	...	...	...	...	...	...	...	...	...
		do ...	Padad...	do ...	...	...	...	...	...	...	...	...	...	...	...	...	...	...	...
		do ...	Padamvad	do ...	21	11	10	...	...	...	...	...	...	...	...	...	...	...	...
		do ...	Padwalbagi	do ...	...	...	...	...	...	...	8	8	5	226	103	123	...	...	...
		do ...	Pairadu	do ...	8	3	5	...	...	...	...	...	...	...	...	...	...	...	...
		do ...	Paknati	do ...	24	10	14	75	41	34	15,749	8,119	7,630	15,637	8,001	7,636	...	...	...
		do ...	Palamunural... ...	do ...	...	...	...	...	...	...	...	...	...	...	...	...	...	...	...
		do ...	Pangal	do ...	...	...	...	...	...	...	...	...	...	...	...	...	...	...	...
		do ...	Panmod	do ...	...	...	...	...	...	...	...	...	...	...	...	...	...	...	...
		do ...	Paralwal	do ...	...	...	...	...	...	...	...	...	...	...	...	...	...	...	...
		do ...	Pasodni	do ...	...	...	...	...	...	...	...	...	...	...	...	...	...	...	...
		do ...	Parkevar	do ...	331	146	185	...	...	...	...	...	...	...	...	...	...	...	...
		do ...	Parmavad	do ...	...	...	...	...	...	...	...	...	...	...	...	...	...	...	...
		do ...	Parvad	do ...	...	...	...	...	...	...	...	...	...	...	...	...	...	...	...
		do ...	Patal	do ...	...	...	...	...	...	...	...	...	...	...	...	...	...	...	...
		do ...	Patansetti	do ...	...	...	...	...	...	...	...	...	...	5	4	1	...	...	...
		do ...	Patkar	do ...	...	...	...	...	...	...	...	...	...	...	...	...	...	...	...
		do ...	Patti	do ...	...	...	...	...	...	...	...	...	...	...	...	...	...	...	...
		do ...	Patyar...	do ...	...	...	...	...	...	...	...	...	...	...	...	...	...	...	...
		do ...	Pedakanti	do ...	...	...	...	...	...	...	...	...	...	...	...	...	...	...	...

TABLE XVI.

Castes and Sub-divisions.—*Continued.*

Class.	Group.	Castes.	Sub-division of Castes.	Religion.	Total.			Hyderabad.			Atraf-i-Balda.			Mahabubnagar.			Nalgonda.		
					Total.	Males.	Females.	Total.	Males.	Females.	Total.	Males.	Females.	Total.	Males.	Females.	Total.	Males.	Females.
1	2	3	4	5	6	7	8	9	10	11	12	13	14	15	16	17	18	19	20
A	2a ...	Kunbi ...	Phadao	Hindu ...	8	2	6	...	...	...	...	...	...	...	...	...	...	...	...
		do ...	Phadsi	do ...	7	3	4	...	...	...	...	...	...	...	...	...	...	...	...
		do ...	Phaked	do ...	31	16	15	...	...	...	...	...	...	...	...	...	...	...	...
		do ...	Phakre	do ...	31	16	15	...	...	...	...	...	...	...	...	...	...	...	...
		do ...	Pikarad	do ...	9	7	2	...	...	...	...	...	...	...	...	...	...	...	...
		do ...	Pile	do ...	1	1	...	...	...	...	...	...	...	...	...	...	...	...	...
		do ...	Rahidvad	do ...	89	54	35	...	...	...	...	...	...	...	...	...	...	...	...
		do ...	Rajgona	do ...	17	14	3	...	...	...	...	...	...	...	...	...	...	...	...
		do ...	Ranal	do ...	19	19	...	...	...	...	...	...	...	...	...	...	...	...	...
		do ...	Rane	do ...	68	32	31	...	...	...	...	...	...	...	...	...	...	...	...
		do ...	Ranke	do ...	10	5	5	...	...	...	...	...	...	...	...	...	...	...	...
		do ...	Raol	do ...	136	73	63	...	...	...	...	...	...	...	...	...	...	...	...
		do ...	Raot	do ...	161	81	80	...	...	...	...	...	...	...	...	...	...	...	...
		do ...	Reddi	do ...	6,528	3,266	3,262	...	...	...	...	...	...	1	1	...	...	...	...
		do ...	Rogari	do ...	1	1	...	...	...	...	...	...	...	...	...	...	...	...	...
		do ...	Rohidas	do ...	3	3	...	...	...	...	...	...	...	...	...	...	...	...	...
		do ...	Salonke	do ...	179	81	98	...	...	...	...	...	...	...	...	...	...	...	...
		do ...	Saghban	do ...	10	4	6	...	...	...	...	...	...	...	...	...	...	...	...
		do ...	Saitvar	do ...	5	3	2	...	...	...	...	...	...	...	...	...	...	...	...
		do ...	Sakri	do ...	3	2	1	...	...	...	...	...	...	...	...	...	...	...	...
		do ...	Sanam	do ...	5	3	2	...	...	...	...	...	...	...	...	...	...	...	...
		do ...	Sanami	do ...	75	75	...	...	...	...	...	...	...	...	...	...	...	...	...
		do ...	Sangalvad	do ...	19	11	8	...	...	...	...	...	...	...	...	...	...	...	...
		do ...	Sangpal	do ...	59	28	31	...	...	...	...	...	...	...	...	...	...	...	...
		do ...	Sankar	do ...	25	5	20	...	...	...	...	...	...	...	...	...	...	...	...
		do ...	Sarke	do ...	3	2	1	...	...	...	...	...	...	...	...	...	...	...	...
		do ...	Sarsude	do ...	2	1	1	...	...	...	...	...	...	...	...	...	...	...	...
		do ...	Satar	do ...	58	22	36	...	...	...	...	...	...	...	...	...	...	...	...
		do ...	Satkut	do ...	43	17	26	...	...	...	...	...	...	...	...	...	...	...	...
		do ...	Savan	do ...	4	2	2	...	...	...	...	...	...	...	...	...	...	...	...
		do ...	Savli	do ...	10	4	6	...	...	...	...	...	...	...	...	...	...	...	...
		do ...	Serol	do ...	22	12	10	...	...	...	...	...	...	...	...	...	...	...	...
		do ...	Setsainavad ...	do ...	7	7	...	...	...	...	...	...	...	...	...	...	...	...	...
		do ...	Shetve... ...	do ...	67	37	30	...	...	...	...	...	...	...	...	...	...	...	...
		do ...	Sigarvad	do ...	6	4	2	...	...	...	...	...	...	...	...	...	...	...	...
		do ...	Silbadki	do ...	586	300	286	...	...	...	...	...	...	...	...	...	...	...	...
		do ...	Sirsat	do ...	7	2	5	...	...	...	...	...	...	...	...	...	...	...	...
		do ...	Sirmani	do ...	2	2	...	...	...	...	...	...	...	...	...	...	...	...	...
		do ...	Sirur	do ...	4	4	...	...	...	...	...	...	...	...	...	...	...	...	...
		do ...	Sodle	do ...	4	4	...	...	...	...	...	...	...	...	...	...	...	...	...
		do ...	Sogal	do ...	6	6	...	...	...	...	...	...	...	...	...	...	...	...	...
		do ...	Sokal	do ...	5	3	2	...	...	...	...	...	...	...	...	...	...	...	...

TABLE XVI.

Castes and Sub-divisions.—*Continued.*

Class.	Group.	Castes.	Sub-division of Castes.	Religion.	Warangal. Total.	Warangal. Males.	Warangal. Females.	Elgandal. Total.	Elgandal. Males.	Elgandal. Females.	Indur. Total.	Indur. Males.	Indur. Females.	Medak. Total.	Medak. Males.	Medak. Females.	Aurangabad. Total.	Aurangabad. Males.	Aurangabad. Females.
					21	22	23	24	25	26	27	28	29	30	31	32	33	34	35
A	2a ...	Kunbi ...	Phadao	Hindu ...	...	...	...	...	...	...	8	2	6	...	...	...	...	...	...
		do ...	Phadsi	do ...	...	...	...	...	...	...	...	...	...	...	...	...	...	...	...
		do ...	Phaked	do ...	...	...	...	...	...	...	...	...	...	...	...	...	...	...	...
		do ...	Phakre	do ...	...	...	...	...	...	...	...	...	...	...	...	...	...	...	...
		do ...	Pikarad	do ...	...	...	...	...	...	...	9	7	2	...	...	...	...	...	...
		do ...	Pile	do ...	...	...	...	...	...	...	...	...	...	...	...	...	...	...	...
		do ...	Rahidvad	do ...	...	...	...	...	...	...	89	54	35	...	...	...	...	...	...
		do ...	Rajgona	do ...	...	...	...	...	...	...	...	...	...	...	...	...	...	...	...
		do ...	Ranal...	do ...	...	...	...	...	...	...	...	...	...	...	...	...	19	19	...
		do ...	Rane	do ...	...	...	...	...	...	...	63	32	31	...	...	...	...	...	...
		do ...	Ranke	do ...	...	...	...	...	...	...	...	...	...	...	...	...	...	...	...
		do ...	Raol	do ...	...	...	...	...	...	...	...	...	...	...	...	...	18	11	7
		do ...	Raot	do ...	...	...	...	...	...	...	...	...	...	...	...	...	54	26	28
		do ...	Reddi	do ...	319	164	155	...	...	...	...	...	...	397	197	200	8	...	8
		do ...	Rogari	do ...	...	...	...	...	...	...	1	1	...	...	...	...	...	...	...
		do ...	Rohidas	do ...	...	...	...	...	...	...	...	...	...	...	...	...	8	8	...
		do ...	Salonke	do ...	...	...	...	...	...	...	...	...	...	...	...	...	172	80	92
		do ...	Saghban	do ...	...	...	...	...	...	...	10	4	6	...	...	...	...	...	...
		do ...	Saitvar	do ...	...	...	...	...	...	...	...	...	...	...	...	...	...	...	...
		do ...	Sakri	do ...	...	...	...	...	...	...	...	...	...	...	...	...	...	...	...
		do ...	Sanam	do ...	...	...	...	...	...	...	...	...	...	...	...	...	5	8	2
		do ...	Sanami	do ...	...	...	...	...	...	...	...	...	...	...	...	...	75	75	...
		do ...	Sangalvad	do ...	...	...	...	...	...	...	...	...	...	...	...	...	...	...	...
		do ...	Sangpal	do ...	...	...	...	...	...	...	59	28	31	...	...	...	...	...	...
		do ...	Sankar	do ...	...	...	...	...	...	...	...	...	...	...	...	...	11	...	11
		do ...	Sarke	do ...	...	...	...	...	...	...	...	...	...	...	...	...	...	...	...
		do ...	Sarsude	do ...	...	...	...	...	...	...	...	...	...	...	...	...	...	...	...
		do ...	Satar	do ...	...	...	...	...	...	...	...	...	...	...	...	...	...	...	...
		do ...	Satkut	do ...	...	...	...	...	...	...	...	...	...	...	...	...	48	17	26
		do ...	Savan	do ...	...	...	...	...	...	...	...	...	...	...	...	...	...	...	...
		do ...	Savli	do ...	...	...	...	...	...	...	...	...	...	...	...	...	...	...	...
		do ...	Serol	do ...	...	...	...	...	...	...	...	...	...	...	...	...	22	12	10
		do ...	Setsainavad	do ...	...	...	...	...	...	...	...	...	...	...	...	...	7	7	...
		do ...	Shetve	do ...	...	...	...	...	...	...	...	...	...	...	...	...	...	...	...
		do ...	Sigarvad	do ...	...	...	...	...	...	...	...	...	...	...	...	...	...	...	...
		do ...	Silbadki	do ...	...	...	...	...	...	...	...	...	...	...	...	...	...	...	...
		do ...	Sirsat	do ...	...	...	...	...	...	...	...	...	...	...	...	...	...	...	...
		do ...	Sirmani	do ...	...	...	...	...	...	...	...	...	...	...	...	...	...	...	...
		do ...	Sirur	do ...	...	...	...	...	...	...	...	...	...	...	...	...	...	...	...
		do ...	Sodle	do ...	...	...	...	...	...	...	...	...	...	...	...	...	4	4	...
		do ...	Sogal	do ...	...	...	...	...	...	...	...	...	...	...	...	...	...	...	...
		do ...	Sokal	do ...	...	...	...	...	...	...	...	...	...	...	...	...	...	...	...

TABLE XVI.

Castes and Sub-divisions.—*Continued.*

Class.	Group.	Castes.	Sub-division of Castes.	Religion.	Birh. Total.	Birh. Males.	Birh. Females.	Nander. Total.	Nander. Males.	Nander. Females.	Naldrug. Total.	Naldrug. Males.	Naldrug. Females.	Bidar. Total.	Bidar. Males.	Bidar. Females.	Parbhani. Total.	Parbhani. Males.	Parbhani. Females.
					36	37	38	39	40	41	42	43	44	45	46	47	48	49	50
A	2a ...	Kunbi ...	Phadao	Hindu ...	...	...	...	...	...	...	...	...	...	...	...	...	...	...	...
		do ...	Phadsi...	do ...	7	3	4	...	...	...	...	...	...	...	...	...	...	...	...
		do ...	Phaked	do ...	...	...	...	...	...	...	...	...	...	...	...	...	...	...	...
		do ...	Phakre	do ...	...	...	...	...	...	...	...	...	...	...	...	...	...	...	...
		do ...	Pikarad	do ...	...	...	...	...	...	...	...	...	...	...	...	...	...	...	...
		do ...	Pile	do ...	...	...	...	...	...	...	...	...	...	...	...	...	...	...	...
		do ...	Rahidvad	do ...	...	...	...	...	...	...	...	...	...	...	...	...	...	...	...
		do ...	Rajgona	do ...	...	...	...	...	...	...	...	...	...	...	...	...	...	...	...
		do ...	Ranal	do ...	...	...	...	...	...	...	...	...	...	...	...	...	...	...	...
		do ...	Rane	do ...	...	...	...	...	...	...	...	...	...	...	...	...	...	...	...
		do ...	Ranke...	do ...	...	...	...	...	...	...	...	...	...	10	5	5	...	...	...
		do ...	Raol	do ...	11	6	5	9	6	3	50	25	25	...	...	...	48	25	23
		do ...	Raot	do ...	6	5	1	...	...	...	...	...	...	2	1	1	14	7	7
		do ...	Reddi	do ...	...	...	...	...	...	...	...	...	...	...	...	...	...	...	...
		do ...	Rogari	do ...	...	...	...	...	...	...	...	...	...	...	...	...	...	...	...
		do ...	Rohidas	do ...	...	...	...	...	...	...	...	...	...	...	...	...	...	...	...
		do ...	Salonke	do ...	7	1	6	...	...	...	...	...	...	...	...	...	...	...	...
		do ...	Saghban	do ...	...	...	...	...	...	...	...	...	...	...	...	...	...	...	...
		do ...	Saitvar	do ...	...	...	...	5	3	2	...	...	...	...	...	...	...	...	...
		do ...	Sakri	do ...	...	...	...	...	...	...	3	2	1	...	...	...	...	...	...
		do ...	Sanam	do ...	...	...	...	...	...	...	...	...	...	...	...	...	...	...	...
		do ...	Sanami	do ...	...	...	...	...	...	...	...	...	...	...	...	...	...	...	...
		do ...	Sangalvad	do ...	...	...	...	...	...	...	...	...	...	...	...	...	...	...	...
		do ...	Sangpal	do ...	...	...	...	...	...	...	...	...	...	...	...	...	...	...	...
		do ...	Sankar	do ...	...	...	...	...	...	...	14	5	9	...	...	...	...	...	...
		do ...	Sarke	do ...	...	...	...	...	...	...	...	...	...	3	2	1	...	...	...
		do ...	Sarsude	do ...	2	1	1	...	...	...	...	...	...	...	...	...	...	...	...
		do ...	Satar	do ...	...	...	...	58	22	36	...	...	...	...	...	...	...	...	...
		do ...	Satkut...	do ...	...	...	...	...	...	...	...	...	...	...	...	...	...	...	...
		do ...	Savan	do ...	...	...	...	4	2	2	...	...	...	...	...	...	...	...	...
		do ...	Savli	do ...	...	...	...	10	4	6	...	...	...	...	...	...	...	...	...
		do ...	Sarol	do ...	...	...	...	...	...	...	...	...	...	...	...	...	...	...	...
		do ...	Setsainavad	do ...	...	...	...	...	...	...	...	...	...	...	...	...	...	...	...
		do ...	Shetve	do ...	...	...	...	...	...	...	...	...	...	67	37	30	...	...	...
		do ...	Sigarvad	do ...	...	...	...	6	4	2	...	...	...	...	...	...	...	...	...
		do ...	Silbadki	do ...	...	...	...	...	...	...	...	...	...	...	...	...	...	...	...
		do ...	Sirsat	do ...	...	...	...	...	...	...	...	...	...	7	2	5	...	...	...
		do ...	Sirmani	do ...	...	...	...	2	2	...	...	...	...	...	...	...	...	...	...
		do ...	Sirur	do ...	...	...	...	4	4	...	...	...	...	...	...	...	...	...	...
		do ...	Sodle	do ...	...	...	...	...	...	...	...	...	...	...	...	...	...	...	...
		do ...	Sogal	do ...	...	...	...	6	6	...	...	...	...	...	...	...	...	...	...
		do ...	Sokal	do ...	...	...	...	...	...	...	...	...	...	...	...	...	...	...	...

TABLE XVI.

Castes and Sub-divisions.—*Continued.*

Class.	Group.	Castes.	Sub-division of Castes.	Religion.	Sirpur Tandur. Total.	Sirpur Tandur. Males.	Sirpur Tandur. Females.	Gulbarga. Total.	Gulbarga. Males.	Gulbarga. Females.	Raichur. Total.	Raichur. Males.	Raichur. Females.	Lingasugur. Total.	Lingasugur. Males.	Lingasugur. Females.	Railways. Total.	Railways. Males.	Railways. Females.
					51	52	53	54	55	56	57	58	59	60	61	62	63	64	65
A	2a ...	Kunbi ...	Phadao	Hindu ...	...	...	...	...	...	...	...	...	...	...	...	...	...	...	...
		do ...	Phadsi	do ...	...	...	...	...	...	...	...	...	...	...	...	...	...	...	...
		do ...	Phakod	do ...	31	16	15	...	...	...	...	...	...	...	...	...	...	...	...
		do ...	Phakre	do ...	31	16	15	...	...	...	...	...	...	...	...	...	...	...	...
		do ...	Pikarad	do ...	...	...	...	...	...	...	...	...	...	...	...	...	...	...	...
		do ...	Pile	do ...	...	...	...	...	...	...	...	...	...	...	...	...	1	1	...
		do ...	Rahidvad	do ...	...	...	...	...	...	...	...	...	...	...	...	...	...	...	...
		do ...	Rajgona	do ...	17	14	3	...	...	...	...	...	...	...	...	...	...	...	...
		do ...	Ranal	do ...	...	...	...	...	...	...	...	...	...	...	...	...	...	...	...
		do ...	Rane	do ...	...	...	...	...	...	...	...	...	...	...	...	...	...	...	...
		do ...	Ranke	do ...	...	...	...	...	...	...	...	...	...	...	...	...	...	...	...
		do ...	Raol	do ...	...	...	...	...	...	...	...	...	...	...	...	...	...	...	...
		do ...	Raot	do ...	...	...	...	82	41	41	...	...	...	...	...	...	8	1	2
		do ...	Reddi	do ...	...	...	...	3,262	1,628	1,634	638	309	324	1,913	967	946	...	...	...
		do ...	Rogari	do ...	...	...	...	...	...	...	...	...	...	...	...	...	...	...	...
		do ...	Rohidas	do ...	...	...	...	...	...	...	...	...	...	...	...	...	...	...	...
		do ...	Salonke	do ...	...	...	...	...	...	...	...	...	...	...	...	...	...	...	...
		do ...	Saghban	do ...	...	...	...	...	...	...	...	...	...	...	...	...	...	...	...
		do ...	Saitvar	do ...	...	...	...	...	...	...	...	...	...	...	...	...	...	...	...
		do ...	Sakri	do ...	...	...	...	...	...	...	...	...	...	...	...	...	...	...	...
		do ...	Sanam	do ...	...	...	...	...	...	...	...	...	...	...	...	...	...	...	...
		do ...	Sanami	do ...	...	...	...	...	...	...	...	...	...	...	...	...	...	...	...
		do ...	Sangalvad	do ...	19	11	8	...	...	...	...	...	...	...	...	...	...	...	...
		do ...	Sangpal	do ...	...	...	...	...	...	...	...	...	...	...	...	...	...	...	...
		do ...	Sankar	do ...	...	...	...	...	...	...	...	...	...	...	...	...	...	...	...
		do ...	Sarke	do ...	...	...	...	...	...	...	...	...	...	...	...	...	...	...	...
		do ...	Sarsude	do ...	...	...	...	...	...	...	...	...	...	...	...	...	...	...	...
		do ...	Satar	do ...	...	...	...	...	...	...	...	...	...	...	...	...	...	...	...
		do ...	Satkut	do ...	...	...	...	...	...	...	...	...	...	...	...	...	...	...	...
		do ...	Savan	do ...	...	...	...	...	...	...	...	...	...	...	...	...	...	...	...
		do ...	Savli	do ...	...	...	...	...	...	...	...	...	...	...	...	...	...	...	...
		do ...	Serol	do ...	...	...	...	...	...	...	...	...	...	...	...	...	...	...	...
		do ...	Setsainavad	do ...	...	...	...	...	...	...	...	...	...	...	...	...	...	...	...
		do ...	Shetve	do ...	...	...	...	...	...	...	...	...	...	...	...	...	...	...	...
		do ...	Sigarvad	do ...	...	...	...	...	...	...	...	...	...	...	...	...	...	...	...
		do ...	Silbadki	do ...	...	...	...	...	...	...	586	300	286	...	...	...	...	...	...
		do ...	Sirsat	do ...	...	...	...	...	...	...	...	...	...	...	...	...	...	...	...
		do ...	Sirmani	do ...	...	...	...	...	...	...	...	...	...	...	...	...	...	...	...
		do ...	Sirur	do ...	...	...	...	...	...	...	...	...	...	...	...	...	...	...	...
		do ...	Sodlo	do ...	...	...	...	...	...	...	...	...	...	...	...	...	...	...	...
		do ...	Sogal	do ...	...	...	...	...	...	...	...	...	...	...	...	...	...	...	...
		do ...	Sokal	do ...	...	...	...	...	...	...	...	...	...	5	3	2	...	...	...

TABLE XVI.

Castes and Sub-divisions.

TABLE XVI.

Castes and Sub-divisions.—*Continued.*

Class.	Group.	Castes.	Sub-division of Castes.	Religion.	Total. Total.	Total. Males.	Total. Females.	Hyderabad. Total.	Hyderabad. Males.	Hyderabad. Females.	Atraf-i-Balda. Total.	Atraf-i-Balda. Males.	Atraf-i-Balda. Females.	Mahabubnagar. Total.	Mahabubnagar. Males.	Mahabubnagar. Females.	Nalgonda. Total.	Nalgonda. Males.	Nalgonda. Females.
1	2	3	4	5	6	7	8	9	10	11	12	13	14	15	16	17	18	19	20
A	2a ...	Kunbi ...	Sond ...	Hindu ...	5	5	...	...	...	...	...	...	...	...	...	...	...	...	...
		do ...	Surialad	do ...	43	23	20	...	...	...	...	...	...	...	...	...	...	...	...
		do ...	Sutni ...	do ...	127	49	78	...	...	...	...	...	...	...	...	...	...	...	...
		do ...	Suvase	do ...	1	...	1	...	...	...	...	...	...	...	...	...	...	...	...
		do ...	Tal ...	do ...	5	2	3	...	...	...	...	...	...	...	...	...	...	...	...
		do ...	Tarti ...	do ...	1	1	...	...	...	...	...	...	...	...	...	...	...	...	...
		do ...	Tatavad	do ...	11	4	7	...	...	...	...	...	...	...	...	...	...	...	...
		do ...	Thating	do ...	8	4	4	...	...	...	...	...	...	...	...	...	...	...	...
		do ...	Tidan	do ...	7	6	1	...	...	...	...	...	...	...	...	...	...	...	...
		do ...	Tidbuj	do ...	1,598	1,085	513	...	...	...	...	...	...	...	...	...	...	...	...
		do ...	Tilvar	do ...	32	32	...	...	...	...	...	...	...	...	...	...	...	...	...
		do ...	Tilvan	do ...	116,105	59,578	56,527	...	...	...	...	...	...	...	...	...	...	...	...
		do ...	Tikhali	do ...	124	124	...	...	...	...	...	...	...	...	...	...	...	...	...
		do ...	Tikun ...	do ...	3	2	1	...	...	...	...	...	...	...	...	...	...	...	...
		do ...	Tilane...	do ...	520	88	432	...	...	...	...	...	...	...	...	...	...	...	...
		do ...	Tirad ...	do ...	1,364	351	1,013	...	...	...	...	...	...	...	...	...	...	...	...
		do ...	Tirak ...	do ...	88	46	42	...	...	...	...	...	...	...	...	...	...	...	...
		do ...	Todwe	do ...	587	270	317	...	...	...	...	...	...	...	...	...	...	...	...
		do ...	Tolse ...	do ...	74	26	48	...	...	...	...	...	...	...	...	...	...	...	...
		do ...	Uranseti	do ...	13	6	7	...	...	...	...	...	...	...	...	...	...	...	...
		do ...	Vadkar	do ...	6	4	2	...	...	...	...	...	...	...	...	...	...	...	...
		do ...	Vadmavad	do ...	10	10	...	...	...	...	...	...	...	...	...	...	...	...	...
		do ...	Vadud	do ...	...	...	...	...	...	...	...	...	...	...	...	...	...	...	...
		do ...	Vaghe	do ...	477	153	324	...	...	...	...	...	...	...	...	...	...	...	...
		do ...	Vahilevar	do ...	49	26	23	...	...	...	...	...	...	...	...	...	...	...	...
		do ...	Vakkalgri	do ...	4	2	2	...	...	...	...	...	...	...	...	...	...	...	...
		do ...	Valhalkri	do ...	19	7	12	...	...	...	...	...	...	...	...	...	...	...	...
		do ...	Valvale	do ...	58	32	26	...	...	...	...	...	...	...	...	...	...	...	...
		do ...	Vange	do ...	5	4	1	...	...	...	...	...	...	...	...	...	...	...	...
		do ...	Vanjal	do ...	85	...	85	...	...	...	...	...	...	...	...	...	...	...	...
		do ...	Vansri	do ...	4	2	2	...	...	...	...	...	...	...	...	...	...	...	...
		do ...	Vari ...	do ...	85	85	...	...	...	...	...	...	...	...	...	...	...	...	...
		do ...	Vartad	do ...	2	2	...	...	...	...	...	...	...	...	...	...	...	...	...
		do ...	Vashadu	do ...	2	2	...	...	...	...	...	...	...	...	...	...	...	...	...
		do ...	Vatwan	do ...	69	69	...	...	...	...	...	...	...	...	...	...	...	...	...
		do ...	Yadao ...	do ...	193	95	98	...	...	...	...	...	...	...	...	...	...	...	...
		do ...	Yaravar	do ...	4	4	...	...	...	...	...	...	...	...	...	...	...	...	...
		do ...	Yarra Kunbi ...	do ...	14	14	...	...	...	...	...	...	...	...	...	...	...	...	...
		do ...	Yoradvar	do ...	4	2	2	...	...	...	...	...	...	...	...	...	...	...	...
		do ...	Unspecified ...	do ...	658,944	334,261	324,683	8,719	4,483	4,236	1,517	734	783	6,872	3,684	3,288	4,417	2,214	2,203
			Total......		1,233,930	626,539	607,391	10,203	5,358	4,845	42,944	21,646	21,298	71,851	36,207	35,644	61,093	31,175	29,918

TABLE XVI.

Castes and Sub-divisions.—*Continued.*

Class.	Group.	Castes.	Sub-division of Castes.	Religion.	Warangal. Total.	Warangal. Males.	Warangal. Females.	Elgandal. Total.	Elgandal. Males.	Elgandal. Females.	Indur. Total.	Indur. Males.	Indur. Females.	Medak. Total.	Medak. Males.	Medak. Females.	Aurangabad. Total.	Aurangabad. Males.	Aurangabad. Females.
					21	22	23	24	25	26	27	28	29	30	31	32	33	34	35
A	2a ...	Kunbi ...	Sond ...	Hindu ...	...	...	...	...	...	...	...	...	...	...	...	...	...	...	...
		do ...	Surialad ...	do ...	...	...	...	...	...	...	48	28	20	...	...	...	...	...	...
		do ...	Sutni ...	do ...	...	...	...	...	...	...	...	...	...	...	...	...	...	...	...
		do ...	Suvase ...	do ...	...	...	...	...	...	...	...	...	...	...	...	...	1	...	1
		do ...	Tal ...	do ...	...	...	...	...	...	...	...	...	...	...	...	...	5	2	8
		do ...	Tarti ...	do ...	...	...	...	...	...	...	...	...	...	...	...	...	...	...	...
		do ...	Tatavad ...	do ...	...	...	...	...	...	...	11	4	7	...	...	...	...	...	...
		do ...	Thating ...	do ...	...	...	...	...	...	...	...	...	...	...	...	...	...	...	...
		do ...	Tidan ...	do ...	...	...	...	...	...	...	...	...	...	...	...	...	7	6	1
		do ...	Tidbuj ...	do ...	...	...	...	...	...	...	...	...	...	...	...	...	...	...	...
		do ...	Tilvar ...	do ...	...	...	...	...	...	...	...	...	...	...	...	...	32	82	...
		do ...	Tilvan ...	do ...	...	...	...	...	...	...	...	...	...	...	...	...	116,084	59,567	56,517
		do ...	Tikhali ...	do ...	...	...	...	...	...	...	...	...	...	...	...	...	124	124	...
		do ...	Tikun ...	do ...	...	...	...	...	...	...	...	...	...	...	...	...	...	...	...
		do ...	Tilane ...	do ...	...	...	...	...	...	...	...	...	...	...	...	...	520	88	432
		do ...	Tirad ...	do ...	...	...	...	...	...	...	...	...	...	...	...	...	...	...	...
		do ...	Tirak ...	do ...	...	...	...	...	...	...	...	...	...	...	...	...	...	...	...
		do ...	Todwe ...	do ...	...	...	...	...	...	...	...	...	...	...	...	...	...	...	...
		do ...	Tolse ...	do ...	...	...	...	...	...	...	...	...	...	...	...	...	...	...	...
		do ...	Uranseti ...	do ...	...	...	...	...	...	...	...	...	...	...	...	...	...	...	...
		do ...	Vadkar ...	do ...	...	...	...	...	...	...	6	4	2	...	...	...	...	...	...
		do ...	Vadmavad ...	do ...	...	...	...	...	...	...	10	10	...	...	...	...	...	...	...
		do ...	Vadud ...	do ...	...	...	...	...	...	...	...	...	...	...	...	...	...	...	...
		do ...	Vaghe ...	do ...	...	...	...	...	...	...	...	...	...	...	...	...	114	16	98
		do ...	Vahilevar ...	do ...	...	...	...	...	...	...	...	...	...	...	...	...	...	...	...
		do ...	Vakkalgri ...	do ...	...	...	...	...	...	...	...	...	...	...	...	...	...	...	...
		do ...	Valbalki ...	do ...	...	...	...	...	...	...	...	...	...	...	...	...	...	...	...
		do ...	Valvale ...	do ...	...	...	...	...	...	...	...	...	...	...	...	...	...	...	...
		do ...	Vange ...	do ...	...	...	...	...	...	...	...	...	...	...	...	...	...	...	...
		do ...	Vanjal ...	do ...	...	...	...	...	...	...	...	...	...	...	...	...	...	...	...
		do ...	Vansri ...	do ...	...	...	...	...	...	...	...	...	...	...	...	...	...	...	...
		do ...	Vari ...	do ...	...	...	...	...	...	...	...	...	...	...	...	...	85	85	...
		do ...	Vartad ...	do ...	...	...	...	...	...	...	...	...	...	...	...	...	2	2	...
		do ...	Vashadu ...	do ...	...	...	...	...	...	...	...	...	...	...	...	...	...	...	...
		do ...	Vatwan ...	do ...	...	...	...	...	...	...	...	...	...	...	...	...	...	...	...
		do ...	Yadao ...	do ...	...	...	...	...	...	...	2	2	...	...	...	...	...	...	...
		do ...	Yaravar ...	do ...	...	...	...	...	...	...	4	4	...	...	...	...	...	...	...
		do ...	Yarra Kunbi ...	do ...	...	...	...	...	...	...	...	...	...	...	...	...	...	...	...
		do ...	Yeradvar ...	do ...	...	...	...	...	...	...	4	2	2	...	...	...	...	...	...
		do ...	Unspecified ...	do ...	35,216	17,974	17,242	44,100	22,809	21,291	65,382	82,915	32,467	4,740	2,407	2,333	169,518	85,482	84,036
			Total......		65,379	33,410	31,969	133,299	68,533	64,766	106,731	53,919	52,812	25,496	12,894	12,602	292,353	148,392	143,961

TABLE XVI.

Castes and Sub-divisions.—*Continued.*

Class.	Group.	Castes.	Sub-division of Castes.	Religion.	Birh. Total.	Birh. Males.	Birh. Females.	Nander. Total.	Nander. Males.	Nander. Females.	Naldrug. Total.	Naldrug. Males.	Naldrug. Females.	Bidar. Total.	Bidar. Males.	Bidar. Females.	Parbhani. Total.	Parbhani. Males.	Parbhani. Females.
					36	37	38	39	40	41	42	43	44	45	46	47	48	49	50
A	2a	Kunbi	Sond	Hindu	...	...	...	...	...	...	...	...	...	...	...	...	...	...	...
		do	Surialad	do	...	...	...	...	...	...	...	...	...	...	...	...	...	...	...
		do	Sutni	do	...	...	...	127	49	78	...	...	...	...	...	...	...	...	...
		do	Suvase	do	...	...	...	...	...	...	...	...	...	...	...	...	...	...	...
		do	Tal	do	...	...	...	...	...	...	...	...	...	...	...	...	...	...	...
		do	Tarti	do	...	...	...	...	...	...	...	...	...	1	1	...	...	...	...
		do	Tatavad	do	...	...	...	...	...	...	...	...	...	...	...	...	...	...	...
		do	Thating	do	...	...	...	...	...	...	...	...	...	...	...	...	...	...	...
		do	Tidan	do	...	...	...	...	...	...	...	...	...	...	...	...	8	4	4
		do	Tidbuj	do	...	...	...	...	...	...	...	...	...	...	...	...	...	...	...
		do	Tilvar	do	...	...	...	...	...	...	...	...	...	...	...	...	...	...	...
		do	Tilvan	do	21	11	10	...	...	...	...	...	...	...	...	...	...	...	...
		do	Tikhali	do	...	...	...	...	...	...	...	...	...	...	...	...	...	...	...
		do	Tikun	do	...	...	...	...	...	...	...	...	...	3	2	1	...	...	...
		do	Tilaue	do	...	...	...	...	...	...	...	...	...	...	...	...	...	...	...
		do	Tirad	do	...	...	...	...	...	...	...	...	...	...	...	...	...	...	...
		do	Tirak	do	...	...	...	...	...	...	...	...	...	...	...	...	...	...	...
		do	Todwe	do	...	...	...	...	...	...	...	...	...	...	...	...	...	...	...
		do	Tolse	do	...	...	...	...	...	...	...	...	...	74	26	48	...	...	...
		do	Uransoti	do	...	...	...	...	...	...	...	...	...	...	...	...	...	...	...
		do	Vadkar	do	...	...	...	...	...	...	...	...	...	...	...	...	...	...	...
		do	Vadmayad	do	...	...	...	...	...	...	...	...	...	...	...	...	...	...	...
		do	Vadud	do	...	...	...	...	...	...	...	...	...	...	...	...	...	...	...
		do	Vaghe	do	32	19	18	32	15	17	107	102	5	...	...	...	192	1	191
		do	Vahilevar	do	...	...	...	...	...	...	49	26	23	...	...	...	...	...	...
		do	Vakkalgri	do	...	...	...	...	...	...	...	...	...	...	...	...	...	...	...
		do	Valbalki	do	...	...	...	...	...	...	...	...	...	...	...	...	...	...	...
		do	Valvale	do	...	...	...	58	32	26	...	...	...	...	...	...	...	...	...
		do	Vango	do	...	...	...	3	2	1	...	...	...	...	...	...	2	2	...
		do	Vanjal	do	...	...	...	85	...	85	...	...	...	...	...	...	...	...	...
		do	Vansri	do	4	2	2	...	...	...	...	...	...	...	...	...	...	...	...
		do	Vari	do	...	...	...	...	...	...	...	...	...	...	...	...	...	...	...
		do	Vartad	do	...	...	...	...	...	...	...	...	...	...	...	...	...	...	...
		do	Vashadu	do	...	...	...	...	...	...	...	...	...	...	...	...	...	...	...
		do	Vatwan	do	69	69	...	...	...	...	...	...	...	...	...	...	...	...	...
		do	Yadao	do	...	...	...	137	64	73	...	...	...	...	...	...	...	...	...
		do	Yaravar	do	...	...	...	...	...	...	...	...	...	...	...	...	...	...	...
		do	Yarra Kunbi	do	...	...	...	...	...	...	...	...	...	...	...	...	...	...	...
		do	Yeradvar	do	...	...	...	...	...	...	...	...	...	...	...	...	...	...	...
		do	Unspecified	do	79,740	40,476	39,264	22,731	11,466	11,265	39,553	20,030	19,523	7,924	3,922	4,002	91,473	46,579	44,894
			Total		80,680	41,043	39,587	29,591	14,815	14,776	40,622	20,621	20,001	10,488	5,200	5,288	92,823	46,982	45,841

TABLE XVI.

Castes and Sub-divisions.—*Continued.*

Class.	Group.	Castes.	Sub-division of Castes.	Religion.	Sirpur Tandur. Total.	Sirpur Tandur. Males.	Sirpur Tandur. Females.	Gulbarga. Total.	Gulbarga. Males.	Gulbarga. Females.	Raichur. Total.	Raichur. Males.	Raichur. Females.	Lingasugur. Total.	Lingasugur. Males.	Lingasugur. Females.	Railways. Total.	Railways. Males.	Railways. Females.
					51	52	53	54	55	56	57	58	59	60	61	62	63	64	65
A	2a ...	Kunbi ...	Sond ...	Hindu ...	5	5	...	...	...	...	...	...	...	...	...	...	...	...	...
		do ...	Surialad	do ...	...	...	...	...	...	...	...	...	...	...	...	...	...	...	...
		do ...	Sutni ...	do ...	...	...	...	...	...	...	...	...	...	...	...	...	...	...	...
		do ...	Suvase	do ...	...	...	...	...	...	...	...	...	...	...	...	...	...	...	...
		do ...	Tal ...	do ...	...	...	...	...	...	...	...	...	...	...	...	...	...	...	...
		do ...	Tarti ...	do ...	...	...	...	...	...	...	...	...	...	...	...	...	...	...	...
		do ...	Tatavad	do ...	...	...	...	...	...	...	...	...	...	...	...	...	...	...	...
		do ...	Thating	do ...	...	...	...	...	...	...	...	...	...	...	...	...	...	...	...
		do ...	Tidan ...	do ...	...	...	...	...	...	...	...	...	...	...	...	...	...	...	...
		do ...	Tidbuj	do ...	1,598	1,085	518	...	...	...	...	...	...	...	...	...	...	...	...
		do ...	Tilvar	do ...	...	...	...	...	...	...	...	...	...	...	...	...	...	...	...
		do ...	Tilvan...	do ...	...	...	...	...	...	...	...	...	...	...	...	...	...	...	...
		do ...	Tikhali	do ...	...	...	...	...	...	...	...	...	...	...	...	...	...	...	...
		do ...	Tikun ...	do ...	...	...	...	...	...	...	...	...	...	...	...	...	...	...	...
		do ...	Tilane...	do ...	...	...	...	...	...	...	...	...	...	...	...	...	...	...	...
		do ...	Tirad ...	do ...	1,864	851	1,018	...	...	...	...	...	...	...	...	...	...	...	...
		do ...	Tirak ...	do ...	88	46	42	...	...	...	...	...	...	...	...	...	...	...	...
		do ...	Todwe	do ...	...	...	...	587	270	817	...	...	...	...	...	...	...	...	...
		do ...	Tolse ...	do ...	...	...	...	...	...	...	...	...	...	...	...	...	...	...	...
		do ...	Uranseti	do ...	...	...	...	13	6	7	...	...	...	...	...	...	...	...	...
		do ...	Vadkar	do ...	...	...	...	...	...	...	...	...	...	...	...	...	...	...	...
		do ...	Vadmavad	do ...	...	...	...	...	...	...	...	...	...	...	...	...	...	...	...
		do ...	Vadud	do ...	...	...	...	...	...	...	...	...	...	...	...	...	...	...	...
		do ...	Vaghe	do ...	...	...	...	...	...	...	...	...	...	...	...	...	...	...	...
		do ...	Vahilevar	do ...	...	...	...	...	...	...	...	...	...	...	...	...	...	...	...
		do ...	Vakkalgri	do ...	...	...	...	4	2	2	...	...	...	...	...	...	...	...	...
		do ...	Valbalki	do ...	...	...	...	...	...	...	...	...	...	19	7	12	...	...	...
		do ...	Valvale	do ...	...	...	...	...	...	...	...	...	...	...	...	...	...	...	...
		do ...	Vange	do ...	...	...	...	...	...	...	...	...	...	...	...	...	...	...	...
		do ...	Vanjal	do ...	...	...	...	...	...	...	...	...	...	...	...	...	...	...	...
		do ...	Vansri	do ...	...	...	...	...	...	...	...	...	...	...	...	...	...	...	...
		do ...	Vari ...	do ...	...	...	...	...	...	...	...	...	...	...	...	...	...	...	...
		do ...	Vartad	do ...	...	...	...	...	...	...	...	...	...	...	...	...	...	...	...
		do ...	Vashadu	do ...	2	2	...	...	...	...	...	...	...	...	...	...	...	...	...
		do ...	Vatwan	do ...	...	...	...	...	...	...	...	...	...	...	...	...	...	...	...
		do ...	Yadao...	do ...	42	22	20	...	...	...	...	...	...	...	...	...	12	7	5
		do ...	Yaravar	do ...	...	...	...	...	...	...	...	...	...	...	...	...	...	...	...
		do ...	Yarra Kunbi	do ...	14	14	...	...	...	...	...	...	...	...	...	...	...	...	...
		do ...	Yeradvar	do ...	...	...	...	...	...	...	...	...	...	...	...	...	...	...	...
		do ...	Unspecified ...	do ...	29,825	14,956	14,869	10,887	5,698	5,194	7,079	8,628	8,456	29,004	14,706	14,298	247	158	89
			Total......		47,245	28,841	23,404	27,360	13,907	13,453	39,203	19,910	19,293	56,360	28,518	27,842	264	168	96

TABLE XVI.

Castes and Sub-divisions.—*Continued.*

Class.	Group.	Castes.	Sub-division of Castes.	Religion.	Total. Total.	Total. Males.	Total. Females.	Hyderabad. Total.	Hyderabad. Males.	Hyderabad. Females.	Atraf-i-Balda. Total.	Atraf-i-Balda. Males.	Atraf-i-Balda. Females.	Mahabubnagar. Total.	Mahabubnagar. Males.	Mahabubnagar. Females.	Nalgonda. Total.	Nalgonda. Males.	Nalgonda. Females.
1	2	3	4	5	6	7	8	9	10	11	12	13	14	15	16	17	18	19	20
A	5 ...	Brahmins ...	Adharvanvedam ...	Hindu ...	24	7	17	...	...	...	...	...	...	15	5	10	9	2	7
		do ...	Adhvaitam	do ...	84	47	37	...	...	...	...	...	...	8	2	6	27	18	9
		do ...	Adhya	do ...	2	2	...	...	...	...	...	...	...	...	...	...	...	...	...
		do ...	Aidad	do ...	8	2	6	8	2	6	...	...	...	...	...	...	...	...	...
		do ...	Andrulu	do ...	2,322	1,183	1,139	...	...	...	...	...	...	36	18	28	601	314	287
		do ...	Ankyavate	do ...	7	4	3	...	...	...	...	...	...	...	...	...	...	...	...
		do ...	Anoli	do ...	1	1	...	1	1	...	...	...	...	...	...	...	...	...	...
		do ...	Apastambh	do ...	3,169	1,637	1,532	...	...	...	42	22	20	...	...	...	...	...	...
		do ...	Apayeti	do ...	8	3	5	...	...	...	...	...	...	...	...	...	...	...	...
		do ...	Araddhia	do ...	375	176	199	...	...	...	31	16	15	...	...	...	21	10	11
		do ...	Aravalukkulu ...	do ...	2	1	1	...	...	...	...	...	...	...	...	...	...	...	...
		do ...	Arva	do ...	3	1	2	...	...	...	...	...	...	...	...	...	3	1	2
		do ...	Arveilu	do ...	458	236	222	...	...	...	...	...	...	102	49	53	16	9	7
		do ...	Asletu... ...	do ...	78	42	36	...	...	...	...	...	...	...	...	...	...	...	...
		do ...	Asvalain	do ...	8,998	4,765	4,233	230	100	130	...	...	...	...	...	...	...	...	...
		do ...	Atrigotri	do ...	39	...	39	...	...	...	...	...	...	...	...	...	...	...	...
		do ...	Ayavar	do ...	5,939	2,903	3,036	995	498	497	2	2	...	31	17	14	163	92	71
		do ...	Baduri... ...	do ...	11	5	6	...	...	...	...	...	...	...	...	...	...	...	...
		do ...	Baharkath ...	do ...	4	2	2	4	2	2	...	...	...	...	...	...	...	...	...
		do ...	Bedpar	do ...	13	13	...	13	13	...	...	...	...	...	...	...	...	...	...
		do ...	Bejabargi	do ...	12	7	5	12	7	5	...	...	...	...	...	...	...	...	...
		do ...	Betka	do ...	1	1	...	...	...	...	...	...	...	...	...	...	...	...	...
		do ...	Beyas	do ...	6	4	2	6	4	2	...	...	...	...	...	...	...	...	...
		do ...	Bhagwat	do ...	707	417	290	1	1	...	...	...	...	20	10	10	1	1	...
		do ...	Bramha	do ...	43	21	22	43	21	22	...	...	...	...	...	...	...	...	...
		do ...	Bhargao	do ...	3	2	1	...	...	...	...	...	...	...	...	...	...	...	...
		do ...	Charakshaie ...	do ...	29	12	17	...	...	...	...	...	...	...	...	...	...	...	...
		do ...	Chirunchee ...	do ...	18	6	12	...	...	...	...	...	...	...	...	...	18	6	12
		do ...	Chitpavan	do ...	55	28	27	...	...	...	...	...	...	...	...	...	...	...	...
		do ...	Daim	do ...	1	...	1	...	...	...	...	...	...	...	...	...	...	...	...
		do ...	Dandni	do ...	3	2	1	...	...	...	...	...	...	...	...	...	...	...	...
		do ...	Dasnu	do ...	6	6	...	...	...	...	...	...	...	...	...	...	...	...	...
		do ...	Dava	do ...	107	56	51	32	15	17	...	...	...	...	...	...	21	14	7
		do ...	Davag	do ...	66	32	34	...	...	...	...	...	...	...	...	...	...	...	...
		do ...	Daya	do ...	6	5	1	6	5	1	...	...	...	...	...	...	...	...	...
		do ...	Deshust	do ...	20,271	10,552	9,719	...	...	...	...	...	...	...	...	...	...	...	...
		do ...	Dravid	do ...	5,902	3,054	2,848	...	...	...	59	34	25	658	307	351	96	48	48
		do ...	Duli	do ...	1	1	...	1	1	...	...	...	...	...	...	...	...	...	...
		do ...	Dundval	do ...	2	2	...	...	...	...	...	...	...	...	...	...	...	...	...
		do ...	Gaitri	do ...	3	1	2	...	...	...	...	...	...	...	...	...	...	...	...
		do ...	Gaivadi	do ...	1	1	...	...	...	...	...	...	...	...	...	...	...	...	...
		do ...	Gangotre	do ...	12	9	3	...	...	...	...	...	...	...	...	...	...	...	...

TABLE XVI.

Castes and Sub-divisions.—*Continued.*

Class.	Group.	Castes.	Sub-division of Castes.	Religion.	Warangal.			Elgandal.			Indur.			Medak.			Aurangabad.		
					Total.	Males.	Females.	Total.	Males.	Females.	Total.	Males.	Females.	Total.	Males.	Females.	Total.	Males.	Females.
					21	22	23	24	25	26	27	28	29	30	31	32	33	34	35
A	5 ...	Brahmins ...	Adharvanvedam ...	Hindu ...	...	...	...	...	...	...	...	...	...	...	...	...	...	...	...
		do ...	Adhvaitam	do ...	49	27	22	...	...	...	...	...	...	...	...	...	...	...	...
		do ...	Adhya	do ...	...	...	...	...	...	...	...	...	...	...	...	...	...	...	...
		do ...	Aidad	do ...	...	...	...	...	...	...	...	...	...	...	...	...	...	...	...
		do ...	Andrulu	do ...	1,560	790	770	96	53	48	...	...	...	5	8	2	...	...	...
		do ...	Ankyavate	do ...	7	4	3	...	...	...	...	...	...	...	...	...	...	...	...
		do ...	Anoli	do ...	...	...	...	...	...	...	...	...	...	...	...	...	...	...	...
		do ...	Apastambh	do ...	155	79	76	825	368	457	65	37	28	60	82	28	107	83	24
		do ...	Apayeti	do ...	...	...	...	...	...	...	8	8	5	...	...	...	...	...	...
		do ...	Araddhia	do ...	47	26	21	175	78	97	...	...	...	92	41	51	...	...	...
		do ...	Aravalukkulu... ...	do ...	...	...	...	2	1	1	...	...	...	...	...	...	...	...	...
		do ...	Arva	do ...	...	...	...	...	...	...	...	...	...	...	...	...	...	...	...
		do ...	Arveilu	do ...	69	36	83	10	5	5	...	...	...	8	8	...	...	...	...
		do ...	Asletu	do ...	...	...	...	78	42	36	...	...	...	...	...	...	...	...	...
		do ...	Asvalain	do ...	81	13	18	18	11	7	352	175	177	10	4	6	526	314	212
		do ...	Atrigotri	do ...	...	...	...	...	...	...	...	...	...	...	...	...	...	...	...
		do ...	Ayavar...	do ...	369	185	184	265	146	119	2,812	1,327	1,485	17	10	7	20	14	6
		do ...	Baduri...	do ...	...	...	...	...	...	...	11	5	6	...	...	...	...	...	...
		do ...	Baharkath	do ...	...	...	...	...	...	...	...	...	...	...	...	...	...	...	...
		do ...	Bedpar...	do ...	...	...	...	...	...	...	...	...	...	...	...	...	...	...	...
		do ...	Bejabargi	do ...	...	...	...	...	...	...	...	...	...	...	...	...	...	...	...
		do ...	Betka	do ...	...	...	...	...	...	...	...	...	...	...	...	...	...	...	...
		do ...	Beyas	do ...	...	...	...	...	...	...	...	...	...	...	...	...	...	...	...
		do ...	Bhagwat	do ...	2	1	1	...	...	...	89	53	36	5	4	1	54	30	24
		do ...	Bramha	do ...	...	...	...	...	...	...	...	...	...	...	...	...	...	...	...
		do ...	Bhargao	do ...	...	...	...	...	...	...	1	1	...	...	...	...	2	1	1
		do ...	Charakshaie	do ...	...	...	...	...	...	...	...	...	...	...	...	...	29	12	17
		do ...	Chirunchee	do ...	...	...	...	...	...	...	...	...	...	...	...	...	...	...	...
		do ...	Chitpavan	do ...	...	...	...	...	...	...	16	6	10	...	...	...	20	13	7
		do ...	Daim	do ...	...	...	...	...	...	...	...	...	...	...	...	...	...	...	...
		do ...	Dandni	do ...	...	...	...	...	...	...	...	...	...	...	...	...	...	...	...
		do ...	Dasnu	do ...	...	...	...	...	...	...	...	...	...	...	...	...	...	...	...
		do ...	Dava	do ...	8	4	4	46	23	23	...	...	...	...	...	...	...	...	...
		do ...	Davag	do ...	...	...	...	...	...	...	...	...	...	...	...	...	1	1	...
		do ...	Daya	do ...	...	...	...	...	...	...	...	...	...	...	...	...	...	...	...
		do ...	Deshust	do ...	...	...	...	...	...	...	122	67	55	23	17	6	863	452	411
		do ...	Dravid...	do ...	531	259	272	914	463	451	738	875	863	167	94	73	27	20	7
		do ...	Duli	do ...	...	...	...	...	...	...	...	...	...	...	...	...	...	...	...
		do ...	Dundval	do ...	...	...	...	...	...	...	...	...	...	...	...	...	...	...	...
		do ...	Gaitri	do ...	...	...	...	3	1	2	...	...	...	...	...	...	...	...	...
		do ...	Gaivadi	do ...	...	...	...	...	...	...	...	...	...	...	...	...	...	...	...
		do ...	Gangotre	do ...	...	...	...	...	...	...	...	...	...	...	...	...	...	...	...

TABLE XVI.

Castes and Sub-divisions.—*Continued.*

Class.	Group.	Castes.	Sub-division of Castes.	Religion.	Birh. Total.	Birh. Males.	Birh. Females.	Nander. Total.	Nander. Males.	Nander. Females.	Naldrug. Total.	Naldrug. Males.	Naldrug. Females.	Bidar. Total.	Bidar. Males.	Bidar. Females.	Parbhani. Total.	Parbhani. Males.	Parbhani. Females.
					36	37	38	39	40	41	42	43	44	45	46	47	48	49	50
A	5 ...	Brahmins ...	Adharvanvedam ...	Hindu ...	...	...	...	...	...	...	...	...	...	...	...	...	...	...	...
		do ...	Adhvaitam	do ...	...	...	...	...	...	...	...	...	...	...	...	...	...	...	...
		do ...	Adhya	do ...	...	...	...	...	...	...	...	...	...	...	...	...	...	...	...
		do ...	Aidad	do ...	...	...	...	...	...	...	...	...	...	...	...	...	...	...	...
		do ...	Andrulu	do ...	...	...	...	...	...	...	...	...	...	...	...	...	...	...	...
		do ...	Ankyavate	do ...	...	...	...	...	...	...	...	...	...	...	...	...	...	...	...
		do ...	Anoli	do ...	...	...	...	...	...	...	...	...	...	...	...	...	...	...	...
		do ...	Apastambh	do ...	479	271	208	320	164	156	13	9	4	467	233	234	20	14	6
		do ...	Apayeti	do ...	...	...	...	...	...	...	...	...	...	...	...	...	...	...	...
		do ...	Araddhia	do ...	...	...	...	...	...	...	...	...	...	...	...	...	...	...	...
		do ...	Aravalukkulu... ...	do ...	...	...	...	...	...	...	...	...	...	...	...	...	...	...	...
		do ...	Arva	do ...	...	...	...	...	...	...	...	...	...	...	...	...	...	...	...
		do ...	Arveilu	do ...	...	...	...	...	...	...	...	...	...	...	...	...	...	...	...
		do ...	Alsetu	do ...	...	...	...	...	...	...	...	...	...	...	...	...	...	...	...
		do ...	Asvalain	do ...	8,017	1,581	1,486	1,094	553	541	188	104	84	549	818	231	2,520	1,861	1,159
		do ...	Atrigotri	do ...	...	...	...	...	...	...	...	...	...	...	...	...	...	...	...
		do ...	Ayavar	do ...	...	...	...	801	138	163	88	16	22	79	89	40	115	80	85
		do ...	Baduri... ...	do ...	...	...	...	...	...	...	...	...	...	...	...	...	...	...	...
		do ...	Baharkath	do ...	...	...	...	...	...	...	...	...	...	...	...	...	...	...	...
		do ...	Bedpar... ...	do ...	...	...	...	...	...	...	...	...	...	...	...	...	...	...	...
		do ...	Bejabergi	do ...	...	...	...	...	...	...	...	...	...	...	...	...	...	...	...
		do ...	Betka	do ...	...	...	...	...	...	...	...	...	...	...	...	...	1	1	...
		do ...	Beyas	do ...	...	...	...	...	...	...	...	...	...	...	...	...	...	...	...
		do ...	Bhagwat	do ...	221	150	71	50	25	25	12	6	6	114	69	45	96	45	51
		do ...	Bramha	do ...	...	...	...	...	...	...	...	...	...	...	...	...	...	...	...
		do ...	Bhargao	do ...	...	...	...	...	...	...	...	...	...	...	...	...	...	...	...
		do ...	Charakshaie	do ...	...	...	...	...	...	...	...	...	...	...	...	...	...	...	...
		do ...	Chirunchee	do ...	...	...	...	...	...	...	...	...	...	...	...	...	...	...	...
		do ...	Chitpavan	do ...	2	2	...	...	...	...	5	8	2	...	...	...	9	4	5
		do ...	Daim	do ...	1	...	1	...	...	...	...	...	...	...	...	...	...	...	...
		do ...	Dandni	do ...	8	2	1	...	...	...	...	...	...	...	...	...	...	...	...
		do ...	Damu	do ...	6	6	...	...	...	...	...	...	...	...	...	...	...	...	...
		do ...	Dava	do ...	...	...	...	...	...	...	...	...	...	...	...	...	...	...	...
		do ...	Davag	do ...	...	...	...	...	...	...	...	...	...	65	81	84	...	...	...
		do ...	Daya	do ...	...	...	...	...	...	...	...	...	...	...	...	...	...	...	...
		do ...	Deshust	do ...	543	289	254	29	20	9	8,516	4,473	4,048	...	...	...	1	...	1
		do ...	Dravid... ...	do ...	...	...	...	28	1	27	10	5	5	268	149	119	223	106	117
		do ...	Duli	do ...	...	...	...	...	...	...	...	...	...	...	...	...	...	...	...
		do ...	Dundval	do ...	...	...	...	...	...	...	...	...	...	...	...	...	2	2	...
		do ...	Gaitri	do ...	...	...	...	...	...	...	...	...	...	...	...	...	...	...	...
		do ...	Gaivadi	do ...	...	...	...	...	...	...	...	...	...	...	...	...	1	1	...
		do ...	Gangotre	do ...	...	...	...	...	...	...	...	...	...	...	...	...	12	9	8

TABLE XVI.

Castes and Sub-divisions.—*Continued.*

Class.	Group.	Castes.	Sub-division of Castes.	Religion.	Sirpur Tandur. Total.	Sirpur Tandur. Males.	Sirpur Tandur. Females.	Gulbarga. Total.	Gulbarga. Males.	Gulbarga. Females.	Raichur. Total.	Raichur. Males.	Raichur. Females.	Lingasugur. Total.	Lingasugur. Males.	Lingasugur. Females.	Railways. Total.	Railways. Males.	Railways. Females.
					51	52	53	54	55	56	57	58	59	60	61	62	63	64	65
A	5 ...	Brahmins ...	Adharvanvedam ...	Hindu	...	...	...	...	...	...	...	...	...	...	...	...	...	...	...
		do ...	Adhvaitam	do ...	...	...	...	...	...	...	...	...	...	...	...	...	...	...	...
		do ...	Adhya...	do ...	...	...	...	...	...	...	...	...	...	2	2	...	...	...	...
		do ...	Aidad	do ...	...	...	...	...	...	...	...	...	...	...	...	...	...	...	...
		do ...	Andrulu	do ...	...	...	...	...	...	...	24	10	14	...	...	...	...	...	...
		do ...	Ankyavate	do ...	...	...	...	...	...	...	...	...	...	...	...	...	...	...	...
		do ...	Anoli	do ...	...	...	...	...	...	...	...	...	...	...	...	...	...	...	...
		do ...	Apastambh	do ...	378	187	191	238	138	100	...	...	...	...	...	...	...	...	...
		do ...	Apayeti	do ...	...	...	...	...	...	...	...	...	...	...	...	...	...	...	...
		do ...	Araddhia	do ...	...	...	...	...	...	...	9	5	4	...	...	...	...	...	...
		do ...	Aravalukkulu ...	do ...	...	...	...	...	...	...	...	...	...	...	...	...	...	...	...
		do ...	Arva	do ...	...	...	...	...	...	...	...	...	...	...	...	...	...	...	...
		do ...	Arveilu	do ...	...	...	...	...	...	...	258	134	124	...	...	...	...	...	...
		do ...	Asletu	do ...	...	...	...	...	...	...	...	...	...	...	...	...	...	...	...
		do ...	Asvalaiu	do ...	23	16	7	347	181	166	...	...	...	93	84	9	...	...	...
		do ...	Atrigotri	do ...	...	...	...	...	...	...	...	...	...	89	...	89	...	...	...
		do ...	Ayavar	do ...	534	253	281	76	38	38	5	2	3	112	44	68	5	2	8
		do ...	Baduri	do ...	...	...	...	...	...	...	...	...	...	...	...	...	...	...	...
		do ...	Baharkath	do ...	...	...	...	...	...	...	...	...	...	...	...	...	...	...	...
		do ...	Bedpar	do ...	...	...	...	...	...	...	...	...	...	...	...	...	...	...	...
		do ...	Bejabargi	do ...	...	...	...	...	...	...	...	...	...	...	...	...	...	...	...
		do ...	Betka	do ...	...	...	...	...	...	...	...	...	...	...	...	...	...	...	...
		do ...	Beyas	do ...	...	...	...	...	...	...	...	...	...	...	...	...	...	...	...
		do ...	Bhagwat	do ...	...	...	...	40	20	20	2	2	...	...	...	...	...	...	...
		do ...	Bramha	do ...	...	...	...	...	...	...	...	...	...	...	...	...	...	...	...
		do ...	Bhargao	do ...	...	...	...	...	...	...	...	...	...	...	...	...	...	...	...
		do ...	Charakshaie ...	do ...	...	...	...	...	...	...	...	...	...	...	...	...	...	...	...
		do ...	Chirunchee ...	do ...	...	...	...	...	...	...	...	...	...	...	...	...	...	...	...
		do ...	Chitpavan	do ...	2	...	2	1	...	1	...	...	...	...	...	...	...	...	...
		do ...	Daim	do ...	...	...	...	...	...	...	...	...	...	...	...	...	...	...	...
		do ...	Dandni	do ...	...	...	...	...	...	...	...	...	...	...	...	...	...	...	...
		do ...	Damu	do ...	...	...	...	...	...	...	...	...	...	...	...	...	...	...	...
		do ...	Dava	do ...	...	...	...	...	...	...	...	...	...	...	...	...	...	...	...
		do ...	Davag	do ...	...	...	...	...	...	...	...	...	...	...	...	...	...	...	...
		do ...	Daya	do ...	...	...	...	...	...	...	...	...	...	...	...	...	...	...	...
		do ...	Deshuet	do ...	7	2	5	1,634	884	750	1,370	710	660	7,163	3,638	3,525	...	...	...
		do ...	Dravid...	do ...	691	338	353	9	5	4	1,483	850	633	...	...	...	...	...	...
		do ...	Duli	do ...	...	...	...	...	...	...	...	...	...	...	...	...	...	...	...
		do ...	Dundval	do ...	...	...	...	...	...	...	...	...	...	...	...	...	...	...	...
		do ...	Gaitri	do ...	...	...	...	...	...	...	...	...	...	...	...	...	...	...	...
		do ...	Gaivadi	do ...	...	...	...	...	...	...	...	...	...	...	...	...	...	...	...
		do ...	Gangotre	do ...	...	...	...	...	...	...	...	...	...	...	...	...	...	...	...

TABLE XVI.

Castes and Sub-divisions.—*Continued.*

Class.	Group.	Castes.	Sub-division of Castes.	Religion.	Total.			Hyderabad.			Atraf-i-Balda.			Mahabubnagar.			Nalgonda.		
					Total.	Males.	Females.	Total.	Males.	Females.	Total.	Males.	Females.	Total.	Males.	Females.	Total.	Males.	Females.
1	2	3	4	5	6	7	8	9	10	11	12	13	14	15	16	17	18	19	20
A	5 ...	Brahmins ...	Garg ...	Hindu ...	1	1	...	...	...	...	...	...	...	...	...	...	...	...	...
		do ...	Good ...	do ...	1,529	945	584	398	242	156	24	14	10	22	13	9	14	8	6
		do ...	Gojargoad ...	do ...	65	27	38	...	...	...	...	...	...	...	...	...	...	...	...
		do ...	Gojrati ...	do ...	46	29	17	43	27	16	...	...	...	...	...	...	...	...	...
		do ...	Gokudi ...	do ...	11	5	6	11	5	6	...	...	...	...	...	...	...	...	...
		do ...	Goverdhan ...	do ...	28	14	14	...	...	...	...	...	...	...	...	...	...	...	...
		do ...	Gujarpand ...	do ...	1	1	...	...	...	...	...	...	...	...	...	...	...	...	...
		do ...	Gundikota ...	do ...	56	28	28	...	...	...	...	...	...	53	26	27	...	...	...
		do ...	Harak...	do ...	5	5	...	...	...	...	...	...	...	...	...	...	...	...	...
		do ...	Haridas ...	do ...	9	5	4	...	...	...	...	...	...	...	...	...	...	...	...
		do ...	Hiras...	do ...	17	8	9	...	...	...	...	...	...	...	...	...	...	...	...
		do ...	Hirpati ...	do ...	17	10	7	17	10	7	...	...	...	...	...	...	...	...	...
		do ...	Jamnath ...	do ...	1	1	...	1	1	...	...	...	...	...	...	...	...	...	...
		do ...	Jiyangaru ...	do ...	11	7	4	...	...	...	...	...	...	11	7	4	...	...	...
		do ...	Johi ...	do ...	7	6	1	7	6	1	...	...	...	...	...	...	...	...	...
		do ...	Joshi ...	do ...	108	63	45	66	38	28	...	...	...	...	...	...	...	...	...
		do ...	Kaili ...	do ...	1	1	...	1	1	...	...	...	...	...	...	...	...	...	...
		do ...	Kalikunj ...	do ...	2	1	1	2	1	1	...	...	...	...	...	...	...	...	...
		do ...	Kamkoti ...	do ...	4	4	...	4	4	...	...	...	...	...	...	...	...	...	...
		do ...	Kankobj ...	do ...	240	130	110	155	93	62	...	...	...	...	...	...	...	...	...
		do ...	Kanno...	do ...	2,404	1,357	1,047	...	...	...	...	...	...	...	...	...	...	...	...
		do ...	Karadi ...	do ...	92	45	47	...	...	...	...	...	...	...	...	...	...	...	...
		do ...	Kaseyap ...	do ...	7	2	5	...	...	...	...	...	...	...	...	...	...	...	...
		do ...	Kathri ...	do ...	2	1	1	2	1	1	...	...	...	...	...	...	...	...	...
		do ...	Katiyaiani ...	do ...	8	2	1	...	...	...	...	...	...	...	...	...	...	...	...
		do ...	Koknast ...	do ...	636	329	307	...	...	...	...	...	...	...	...	...	...	...	...
		do ...	Kondnia ...	do ...	4	2	2	...	...	...	...	...	...	...	...	...	...	...	...
		do ...	Krishnpukshi...	do ...	160	85	75	...	...	...	...	...	...	...	...	...	...	...	...
		do ...	Kunojia ...	do ...	6,889	4,057	2,832	3,679	2,292	1,387	272	178	94	158	90	68	33	14	19
		do ...	Kurvatiki ...	do ...	1,409	710	699	...	...	...	...	...	...	...	...	...	16	9	7
		do ...	Lavai...	do ...	2	1	1	2	1	1	...	...	...	...	...	...	...	...	...
		do ...	Lingdhari ...	do ...	5	4	1	1	1	...	...	...	...	...	...	...	4	3	1
		do ...	Machuri ...	do ...	22	20	2	22	20	2	...	...	...	...	...	...	...	...	...
		do ...	Madhianjun ...	do ...	870	445	425	...	...	...	...	...	...	...	...	...	...	...	...
		do ...	Madhinale ...	do ...	138	72	66	...	...	...	...	...	...	...	...	...	...	...	...
		do ...	Madhva ...	do ...	3,098	1,558	1,540	19	11	8	290	133	157	946	459	487	18	11	7
		do ...	Malvi ...	do ...	276	159	117	...	...	...	...	...	...	...	...	...	...	...	...
		do ...	Mahrashtra ...	do ...	8,327	4,506	3,821	668	426	242	...	...	...	18	11	7	4	3	1
		do ...	Mekhil ...	do ...	57	57	...	...	...	...	...	...	...	...	...	...	...	...	...
		do ...	Modanchakdu ...	do ...	3	1	2	...	...	...	...	...	...	...	...	...	...	...	...
		do ...	Morkinati ...	do ...	25	14	11	...	...	...	...	...	...	9	4	5	...	...	...
		do ...	Morti ...	do ...	10	6	4	...	...	...	...	...	...	...	...	...	...	...	...

TABLE XVI.

Castes and Sub-divisions.—*Continued.*

Class.	Group.	Castes.	Sub-division of Castes.	Religion.	Warangal.			Elgandal.			Indur.			Medak.			Aurangabad.		
					Total.	Males.	Females.	Total.	Males.	Females.	Total.	Males.	Females.	Total.	Males.	Females.	Total.	Males.	Females.
					21	22	23	24	25	26	27	28	29	30	31	32	33	34	35
A	5 ...	Brahmins ...	Garg	Hindu ...	...	...	...	...	...	...	...	...	...	...	...	...	...	...	...
		do ...	Good	do ...	8	8	...	175	101	74	79	47	82	7	5	2	240	143	97
		do ...	Gojargoad	do ...	...	...	...	...	...	...	...	...	...	...	...	...	65	27	38
		do ...	Gojrati...	do ...	...	...	...	...	...	...	...	...	...	...	...	...	...	...	...
		do ...	Gokudi...	do ...	...	...	...	...	...	...	...	...	...	...	...	...	...	...	...
		do ...	Goverdhan	do ...	...	...	...	...	...	...	...	...	...	...	...	...	25	12	13
		do ...	Gujarpand	do ...	...	...	...	...	...	...	...	...	...	...	...	...	...	...	...
		do ...	Gundikota	do ...	...	...	...	...	...	...	...	...	...	3	2	1	...	...	...
		do ...	Harak	do ...	...	...	...	...	...	...	...	...	...	...	...	...	...	...	...
		do ...	Haridas	do ...	...	...	...	...	...	...	...	...	...	...	...	...	...	...	...
		do ...	Hiras	do ...	...	...	...	...	...	...	...	...	...	...	...	...	...	...	...
		do ...	Hirpati	do ...	...	...	...	...	...	...	...	...	...	...	...	...	...	...	...
		do ...	Jamnath	do ...	...	...	...	...	...	...	...	...	...	...	...	...	...	...	...
		do ...	Jiyangaru	do ...	...	...	...	...	...	...	...	...	...	...	...	...	...	...	...
		do ...	Johi	do ...	...	...	...	...	...	...	...	...	...	...	...	...	...	...	...
		do ...	Joshi	do ...	...	...	...	...	...	...	3	1	2	...	...	...	26	11	15
		do ...	Kaili	do ...	...	...	...	...	...	...	...	...	...	...	...	...	...	...	...
		do ...	Kalikunj	do ...	...	...	...	...	...	...	...	...	...	...	...	...	...	...	...
		do ...	Kamkoti	do ...	...	...	...	...	...	...	...	...	...	...	...	...	...	...	...
		do ...	Kankobj	do ...	...	...	...	...	...	...	...	...	...	...	...	...	23	14	9
		do ...	Kanno	do ...	...	...	...	...	...	...	195	119	76	...	...	...	140	95	45
		do ...	Karadi...	do ...	...	...	...	...	...	...	48	23	25	...	...	...	...	...	...
		do ...	Kaseyap	do ...	...	...	...	...	...	...	...	...	...	...	...	...	...	...	...
		do ...	Kathri...	do ...	...	...	...	...	...	...	...	...	...	...	...	...	...	...	...
		do ...	Katiyaiani	do ...	...	...	...	...	...	...	...	...	...	...	...	...	...	...	...
		do ...	Koknast	do ...	...	...	...	...	...	...	11	5	6	...	...	...	328	166	162
		do ...	Kondnia	do ...	...	...	...	...	...	...	4	2	2	...	...	...	...	...	...
		do ...	Krishnpukshi... ...	do ...	...	...	...	...	...	...	...	...	...	...	...	...	8	7	1
		do ...	Kunojia	do ...	159	75	84	52	31	21	139	71	68	114	59	55	638	859	279
		do ...	Kurvatiki	do ...	75	41	84	1	1	...	...	...	...	...	...	...	21	11	10
		do ...	Lavai	do ...	...	...	...	...	...	...	...	...	...	...	...	...	...	...	...
		do ...	Lingdhari	do ...	...	...	...	...	...	...	...	...	...	...	...	...	...	...	...
		do ...	Machuri	do ...	...	...	...	...	...	...	...	...	...	...	...	...	...	...	...
		do ...	Madhianjun	do ...	...	...	...	...	...	...	105	58	52	...	...	...	...	...	...
		do ...	Madhinale	do ...	...	...	...	...	...	...	...	...	...	...	...	...	138	72	66
		do ...	Madhva	do ...	113	69	44	356	155	201	84	88	46	309	157	152	42	21	21
		do ...	Malvi	do ...	...	...	...	...	...	...	...	...	...	...	...	...	88	19	19
		do ...	Mahrashtra	do ...	62	47	15	...	...	...	...	...	...	6	6	...	4,717	2,540	2,177
		do ...	Mekhil...	do ...	...	...	...	...	...	...	...	...	...	...	...	...	...	...	...
		do ...	Modanchakdu... ...	do ...	3	1	2	...	...	...	...	...	...	...	...	...	...	...	...
		do ...	Morkinati	do ...	...	...	...	...	...	...	...	...	...	...	...	...	...	...	...
		do ...	Morli	do ...	...	...	...	...	...	...	...	...	...	...	...	...	...	...	...

TABLE XVI.
Castes and Sub-divisions.

TABLE XVI.

Castes and Sub-divisions.—*Continued.*

Class.	Group.	Castes.	Sub-division of Castes.	Religion.	Birh. Total.	Birh. Males.	Birh. Females.	Nander. Total.	Nander. Males.	Nander. Females.	Naldrug. Total.	Naldrug. Males.	Naldrug. Females.	Bidar. Total.	Bidar. Males.	Bidar. Females.	Parbhani. Total.	Parbhani. Males.	Parbhani. Females.
					36	37	38	39	40	41	42	43	44	45	46	47	48	49	50
A	5 ...	Brahmins ...	Garg ...	Hindu ...	1	1	...	...	...	...	...	...	...	...	...	...	...	...	...
		do ...	Good ...	do ...	26	25	1	8	4	4	37	25	12	...	...	...	402	250	152
		do ...	Gojargoad ...	do ...	...	...	...	...	...	...	...	...	...	...	...	...	...	...	...
		do ...	Gojrati ...	do ...	...	...	...	...	...	...	...	...	...	...	...	...	...	...	...
		do ...	Gokudi ...	do ...	...	...	...	...	...	...	...	...	...	...	...	...	...	...	...
		do ...	Goverdhan ...	do ...	3	2	1	...	...	...	...	...	...	...	...	...	...	...	...
		do ...	Gujarpand ...	do ...	1	1	...	...	...	...	...	...	...	...	...	...	...	...	...
		do ...	Gundikota ...	do ...	...	...	...	...	...	...	...	...	...	...	...	...	...	...	...
		do ...	Harak... ...	do ...	5	5	...	...	...	...	...	...	...	...	...	...	...	...	...
		do ...	Haridas ...	do ...	2	1	1	...	...	...	...	...	...	6	3	3	...	...	...
		do ...	Hiras ...	do ...	...	...	...	...	...	...	...	...	...	17	8	9	...	...	...
		do ...	Hirpati ...	do ...	...	...	...	...	...	...	...	...	...	...	...	...	...	...	...
		do ...	Jamnath ...	do ...	...	...	...	...	...	...	...	...	...	...	...	...	...	...	...
		do ...	Jiyangaru ...	do ...	...	...	...	...	...	...	...	...	...	...	...	...	...	...	...
		do ...	Johi ...	do ...	...	...	...	...	...	...	...	...	...	...	...	...	...	...	...
		do ...	Joshi ...	do ...	...	...	...	...	...	...	...	...	...	...	...	...	18	18	...
		do ...	Kaili ...	do ...	...	...	...	...	...	...	...	...	...	...	...	...	...	...	...
		do ...	Kalikunj ...	do ...	...	...	...	...	...	...	...	...	...	...	...	...	...	...	...
		do ...	Kamkoti ...	do ...	...	...	...	...	...	...	...	...	...	...	...	...	...	...	...
		do ...	Kankobj ...	do ...	...	...	...	22	5	17	40	18	22	...	...	...	...	...	...
		do ...	Kanno... ...	do ...	818	410	408	199	114	85	94	61	83	25	14	11	461	261	200
		do ...	Karadi ...	do ...	...	...	...	9	5	4	85	17	18	...	...	...	...	...	...
		do ...	Kasyap ...	do ...	7	2	5	...	...	...	...	...	...	...	...	...	...	...	...
		do ...	Kathri... ...	do ...	...	...	...	...	...	...	...	...	...	...	...	...	...	...	...
		do ...	Katiyaiani ...	do ...	...	...	...	...	...	...	...	...	...	...	...	...	...	...	...
		do ...	Koknast ...	do ...	19	10	9	...	...	...	99	50	49	23	7	16	14	4	10
		do ...	Kondnia ...	do ...	...	...	...	...	...	...	...	...	...	...	...	...	...	...	...
		do ...	Krishnpukshi...	do ...	...	...	...	40	22	18	...	...	...	17	11	6	...	...	...
		do ...	Kunojia ...	do ...	801	147	154	133	82	51	201	121	80	18	10	8	188	74	64
		do ...	Kurvatiki ...	do ...	...	...	...	...	...	...	14	9	5	...	...	...	...	...	...
		do ...	Lavai ...	do ...	...	...	...	...	...	...	...	...	...	...	...	...	...	...	...
		do ...	Lingdhari ...	do ...	...	...	...	...	...	...	...	...	...	...	...	...	...	...	...
		do ...	Machuri ...	do ...	...	...	...	...	...	...	...	...	...	...	...	...	...	...	...
		do ...	Madhianjun ...	do ...	139	78	61	76	36	40	2	1	1	11	2	9	378	211	167
		do ...	Madhinale ...	do ...	...	...	...	...	...	...	...	...	...	...	...	...	...	...	...
		do ...	Madhva ...	do ...	...	...	...	126	63	68	2	1	1	62	26	36	...	...	...
		do ...	Malvi ...	do ...	47	25	22	...	...	...	34	13	21	...	...	...	157	102	55
		do ...	Mahrashtra ...	do ...	...	...	...	8	5	8	2,778	1,431	1,347	...	...	...	...	...	...
		do ...	Mekhil ...	do ...	57	57	...	...	...	...	...	...	...	...	...	...	...	...	...
		do ...	Modanchakdu ...	do ...	...	...	...	...	...	...	...	...	...	...	...	...	...	...	...
		do ...	Mokinati ...	do ...	...	...	...	...	...	...	...	...	...	...	...	...	...	...	...
		do ...	Morti ...	do ...	...	...	...	...	...	...	...	...	...	...	...	...	...	...	...

TABLE XVI.

Castes and Sub-divisions.—*Continued.*

Class.	Group.	Castes.	Sub-division of Castes.	Religion.	Sirpur Tandur. Total.	Sirpur Tandur. Males.	Sirpur Tandur. Females.	Gulbarga. Total.	Gulbarga. Males.	Gulbarga. Females.	Raichur. Total.	Raichur. Males.	Raichur. Females.	Lingasugur. Total.	Lingasugur. Males.	Lingasugur. Females.	Railways. Total.	Railways. Males.	Railways. Females.
					51	52	53	54	55	56	57	58	59	60	61	62	63	64	65
A	5 ...	Brahmins ...	Garg	Hindu ...	...	...	...	...	...	...	...	...	...	...	...	...	...	...	...
		do ...	Good	do ...	9	4	5	2	2	...	41	80	11	87	24	18	...	...	...
		do ...	Gojargoad	do ...	...	...	...	...	...	...	...	...	...	...	...	...	...	...	...
		do ...	Gojrati...	do ...	...	...	...	3	2	1	...	...	...	...	...	...	...	...	...
		do ...	Gokudi	do ...	...	...	...	...	...	...	...	...	...	...	...	...	...	...	...
		do ...	Goverdhan	do ...	...	...	...	...	...	...	...	...	...	...	...	...	...	...	...
		do ...	Gujarpand	do ...	...	...	...	...	...	...	...	...	...	...	...	...	...	...	...
		do ...	Gundikota	do ...	...	...	...	...	...	...	...	...	...	...	...	...	...	...	...
		do ...	Harak...	do ...	...	...	...	...	...	...	...	...	...	...	...	...	...	...	...
		do ...	Haridas	do ...	...	...	...	1	1	...	...	...	...	...	...	...	...	...	...
		do ...	Hiras	do ...	...	...	...	...	...	...	...	...	...	...	...	...	...	...	...
		do ...	Hirpati	do ...	...	...	...	...	...	...	...	...	...	...	...	...	...	...	...
		do ...	Jamnath	do ...	...	...	...	...	...	...	...	...	...	...	...	...	...	...	...
		do ...	Jiayangaru	do ...	...	...	...	...	...	...	...	...	...	...	...	...	...	...	...
		do ...	Johi	do ...	...	...	...	...	...	...	...	...	...	...	...	...	...	...	...
		do ...	Joshi	do ...	...	...	...	...	...	...	...	...	...	...	...	...	...	...	...
		do ...	Kaili	do ...	...	...	...	...	...	...	...	...	...	...	...	...	...	...	...
		do ...	Kalikunj	do ...	...	...	...	...	...	...	...	...	...	...	...	...	...	...	...
		do ...	Kamkoti	do ...	...	...	...	...	...	...	...	...	...	...	...	...	...	...	...
		do ...	Kankobj	do ...	...	...	...	...	...	...	...	...	...	...	...	...	...	...	...
		do ...	Kanno...	do ...	55	82	28	79	44	85	69	23	46	269	184	85	...	...	...
		do ...	Karadi	do ...	...	...	...	...	...	...	...	...	...	...	...	...	...	...	...
		do ...	Kaseyap	do ...	...	...	...	...	...	...	...	...	...	...	...	...	...	...	...
		do ...	Kathri	do ...	...	...	...	...	...	...	...	...	...	...	...	...	...	...	...
		do ...	Katiyaiani	do ...	...	...	...	3	2	1	...	...	...	...	...	...	...	...	...
		do ...	Koknast	do ...	3	2	1	79	48	81	18	13	5	42	24	18	...	...	...
		do ...	Kondnia	do ...	...	...	...	...	...	...	...	...	...	...	...	...	...	...	...
		do ...	Krishnpukshi... ...	do ...	95	45	50	...	...	...	...	...	...	...	...	...	...	...	...
		do ...	Kunojia	do ...	103	47	56	271	162	109	92	53	89	888	192	196	...	...	...
		do ...	Kurvatiki	do ...	...	...	...	143	75	68	64	83	31	1,075	531	544	...	...	...
		do ...	Lavai	do ...	...	...	...	...	...	...	...	...	...	...	...	...	...	...	...
		do ...	Lingdhari	do ...	...	...	...	...	...	...	...	...	...	...	...	...	...	...	...
		do ...	Machuri	do ...	...	...	...	...	...	...	...	...	...	...	...	...	...	...	...
		do ...	Madhianjun	do ...	111	85	76	9	4	5	1	1	...	88	24	14	...	...	...
		do ...	Madhinale	do ...	...	...	...	...	...	...	...	...	...	...	...	...	...	...	...
		do ...	Madhva	do ...	13	6	7	295	161	134	181	66	65	292	181	111	...	...	...
		do ...	Malvi...	do ...	...	...	...	...	...	...	...	...	...	...	...	...	...	...	...
		do ...	Mahrashtra	do ...	...	...	...	40	24	16	2	2	...	24	11	18	...	...	...
		do ...	Mekhil	do ...	...	...	...	...	...	...	...	...	...	...	...	...	...	...	...
		do ...	Modanchakdu ...	do ...	...	...	...	...	...	...	...	...	...	...	...	...	...	...	...
		do ...	Morkinati	do ...	...	...	...	...	...	...	16	10	6	...	...	...	...	...	...
		do ...	Morti	do ...	...	...	...	...	...	...	...	...	...	10	6	4	...	...	...

TABLE XVI.

Castes and Sub-divisions.—*Continued.*

Class.	Group.	Castes.	Sub-division of Castes.	Religion.	Total.			Hyderabad.			Atraf-i-Balda.			Mahabubnagar.			Nalgonda.		
					Total.	Males.	Females.	Total.	Males.	Females.	Total.	Males.	Females.	Total.	Males.	Females.	Total.	Males.	Females.
1	2	3	4	5	6	7	8	9	10	11	12	13	14	15	16	17	18	19	20
A	5 ...	Brahmins ...	Nagar...	Hindu ...	4	1	3	...	...	...	...	...	...	...	...	...	...	...	...
		do ...	Nannas	do ...	17	8	9	...	...	...	...	...	...	...	...	...	...	...	...
		do ...	Neaglu	do ...	2,383	1,223	1,160	...	...	...	13	9	4	130	63	67	935	463	472
		do ...	Pakshi...	do ...	1	1	...	...	...	...	...	...	...	...	...	...	...	...	...
		do ...	Panasth	do ...	16	...	16	...	...	...	...	...	...	...	...	...	...	...	...
		do ...	Panchdraved	do ...	2,162	1,093	1,069	...	...	...	...	...	...	10	3	7	...	...	...
		do ...	Panchgod	do ...	425	292	133	...	...	...	...	...	...	...	...	...	...	...	...
		do ...	Pande	do ...	41	40	1	3	2	1	...	...	...	...	...	...	...	...	...
		do ...	Parshaki	do ...	4	2	2	4	2	2	...	...	...	...	...	...	...	...	...
		do ...	Pavari...	do ...	22	1	21	22	1	21	...	...	...	...	...	...	...	...	...
		do ...	Phatak	do ...	7	5	2	...	...	...	...	...	...	...	...	...	...	...	...
		do ...	Piuda	do ...	2	1	1	2	1	1	...	...	...	...	...	...	...	...	...
		do ...	Porashwar	do ...	8	6	2	...	...	...	...	...	...	...	...	...	...	...	...
		do ...	Prabhu	do ...	11	4	7	...	...	...	...	...	...	...	...	...	...	...	...
		do ...	Prathamshake ...	do ...	2,135	981	1,154	...	...	...	9	3	6	70	37	33	56	27	29
		do ...	Puncharashram ...	do ...	2	2	...	...	...	...	...	...	...	...	...	...	2	2	...
		do ...	Radhar	do ...	16	6	10	16	6	10	...	...	...	...	...	...	...	...	...
		do ...	Ramanandi	do ...	50	34	16	50	34	16	...	...	...	...	...	...	...	...	...
		do ...	Ramanj	do ...	8,054	1,441	1,613	60	34	26	400	172	228	1,236	581	655	286	120	166
		do ...	Rudra	do ...	1	1	...	...	...	...	...	...	...	...	...	...	...	...	...
		do ...	Rugvedi	do ...	19,313	9,887	9,426	...	...	...	2	1	1	75	38	37	2	1	1
		do ...	Rukhe...	do ...	5	...	5	...	...	...	...	...	...	...	...	...	...	...	...
		do ...	Sajgoad	do ...	1	...	1	...	...	...	...	...	...	...	...	...	...	...	...
		do ...	Sakar	do ...	1	1	...	...	...	...	...	...	...	...	...	...	...	...	...
		do ...	Salbar	do ...	1	...	1	...	...	...	...	...	...	...	...	...	...	...	...
		do ...	Samnedi	do ...	259	139	120	...	...	...	...	...	...	...	...	...	...	...	...
		do ...	Sandel...	do ...	1	1	...	1	1	...	...	...	...	...	...	...	...	...	...
		do ...	Sanewad	do ...	21	11	10	...	...	...	...	...	...	...	...	...	...	...	...
		do ...	Sanodu	do ...	9	3	6	9	3	6	...	...	...	...	...	...	...	...	...
		do ...	Sannudia	do ...	28	9	19	28	9	19	...	...	...	...	...	...	...	...	...
		do ...	Sanpuj	do ...	2	2	...	...	...	...	...	...	...	...	...	...	...	...	...
		do ...	Saraswut	do ...	89	63	26	28	21	7	...	...	...	...	...	...	...	...	...
		do ...	Shainto	do ...	7	5	2	...	...	...	...	...	...	...	...	...	...	...	...
		do ...	Shainve	do ...	71	37	34	...	...	...	...	...	...	...	...	...	...	...	...
		do ...	Shawa...	do ...	405	196	209	...	...	...	...	...	...	...	...	...	...	...	...
		do ...	Shikwan	do ...	26	17	9	...	...	...	...	...	...	...	...	...	...	...	...
		do ...	Shormati	do ...	242	158	84	242	158	84	...	...	...	...	...	...	...	...	...
		do ...	Shrimali	do ...	15	9	6	...	...	...	...	...	...	...	...	...	...	...	...
		do ...	Silvarta	do ...	37	37	...	...	...	...	...	...	...	...	...	...	...	...	...
		do ...	Smarth	do ...	14,860	7,576	7,284	18	10	8	699	358	341	1,235	612	623	1,242	642	600
		do ...	Sirajphur	do ...	2	2	...	...	...	...	...	...	...	...	...	...	...	...	...
		do ...	Sodar	do ...	12	5	7	12	5	7	...	...	...	...	...	...	...	...	...

TABLE XVI.

Castes and Sub-divisions.—*Continued.*

Class.	Group.	Castes.	Sub-division of Castes.	Religion.	Warangal. Total.	Warangal. Males.	Warangal. Females.	Elgandal. Total.	Elgandal. Males.	Elgandal. Females.	Indur. Total.	Indur. Males.	Indur. Females.	Medak. Total.	Medak. Males.	Medak. Females.	Aurangabad. Total.	Aurangabad. Males.	Aurangabad. Females.
					21	22	23	24	25	26	27	28	29	30	31	32	33	34	35
A	5 ...	Brahmins ...	Nagar ...	Hindu ...	...	...	...	...	...	...	...	...	...	...	...	...	...	...	...
		do ...	Nannas	do ...	...	...	...	...	...	...	...	...	...	...	...	...	17	8	9
		do ...	Neaglu...	do ...	1,242	660	582	56	23	33	...	...	...	7	5	2	...	...	...
		do ...	Pakshi ...	do ...	...	...	...	...	...	...	...	...	...	...	...	...	...	...	...
		do ...	Panasth	do ...	...	...	...	...	...	...	...	...	...	...	...	...	16	...	16
		do ...	Panchdraved ...	do ...	...	...	...	...	...	...	...	...	...	17	8	9	6	6	...
		do ...	Panchgod	do ...	...	...	...	...	...	...	1	1	...	...	...	...	76	63	18
		do ...	Pande ...	do ...	...	...	...	...	...	...	83	88	...	...	...	...	...	...	...
		do ...	Parshaki	do ...	...	...	...	...	...	...	...	...	...	...	...	...	...	...	...
		do ...	Pavari	do ...	...	...	...	...	...	...	...	...	...	...	...	...	...	...	...
		do ...	Phatak	do ...	...	...	...	...	...	...	...	...	...	...	...	...	7	5	2
		do ...	Pinda ...	do ...	...	...	...	...	...	...	...	...	...	...	...	...	...	...	...
		do ...	Porashwar	do ...	...	...	...	...	...	...	...	...	...	...	...	...	5	8	2
		do ...	Prabhu...	do ...	...	...	...	...	...	...	...	...	...	...	...	...	...	...	...
		do ...	Prathamshake	do ...	52	23	29	60	32	28	95	27	68	67	84	88	192	98	94
		do ...	Puncharashram	do ...	...	...	...	...	...	...	...	...	...	...	...	...	...	...	...
		do ...	Radhar	do ...	...	...	...	...	...	...	...	...	...	...	...	...	...	...	...
		do ...	Ramanandi	do ...	...	...	...	...	...	...	...	...	...	...	...	...	...	...	...
		do ...	Ramanj	do ...	466	225	241	86	48	38	212	118	94	227	98	129	...	...	...
		do ...	Rudra ...	do ...	...	...	...	...	...	...	...	...	...	...	...	...	...	...	...
		do ...	Rugvedi	do ...	49	29	20	65	27	38	730	355	875	29	12	17	3,689	1,817	1,872
		do ...	Rukhe ...	do ...	...	...	...	...	...	...	...	...	...	...	...	...	5	...	5
		do ...	Sajgoad	do ...	...	...	...	...	...	...	...	...	...	...	...	...	...	...	...
		do ...	Sakar ...	do ...	...	...	...	...	...	...	...	...	...	...	...	...	1	1	...
		do ...	Salbar	do ...	...	...	...	...	...	...	...	...	...	...	...	...	...	...	...
		do ...	Samnedi	do ...	...	...	...	...	...	...	...	...	...	...	...	...	242	129	118
		do ...	Sandel...	do ...	...	...	...	...	...	...	...	...	...	...	...	...	...	...	...
		do ...	Sanewad	do ...	...	...	...	...	...	...	...	...	...	...	...	...	...	...	...
		do ...	Sanodu	do ...	...	...	...	...	...	...	...	...	...	...	...	...	...	...	...
		do ...	Sannudia	do ...	...	...	...	...	...	...	...	...	...	...	...	...	...	...	...
		do ...	Sanpuj...	do ...	...	...	...	...	...	...	...	...	...	...	...	...	...	...	...
		do ...	Saraswut	do ...	...	...	...	...	...	...	...	...	...	...	...	...	...	...	...
		do ...	Shainte	do ...	...	...	...	...	...	...	...	...	...	...	...	...	7	5	2
		do ...	Shainve	do ...	...	...	...	...	...	...	...	...	...	...	...	...	55	28	27
		do ...	Shawa ...	do ...	36	18	18	118	62	56	151	68	83	...	...	...	...	...	...
		do ...	Shikwan	do ...	...	...	...	...	...	...	...	...	...	...	...	...	...	...	...
		do ...	Shormati	do ...	...	...	...	...	...	...	...	...	...	...	...	...	...	...	...
		do ...	Shrimali	do ...	...	...	...	...	...	...	...	...	...	...	...	...	15	9	6
		do ...	Silvarta	do ...	...	...	...	...	...	...	...	...	...	...	...	...	...	...	...
		do ...	Smarth	do ...	1,711	895	816	1,530	746	784	959	438	521	608	825	288	880	427	453
		do ...	Sirajphur	do ...	...	...	...	...	...	...	...	...	...	...	...	...	...	...	...
		do ...	Sodar ...	do ...	...	...	...	...	...	...	...	...	...	...	...	...	...	...	...

TABLE XVI.
Castes and Sub-divisions.

TABLE XVI.

Castes and Sub-divisions.—*Continued.*

Class.	Group.	Castes.	Sub-division of Castes.	Religion.	Birh. Total.	Birh. Males.	Birh. Females.	Nander. Total.	Nander. Males.	Nander. Females.	Naldrug. Total.	Naldrug. Males.	Naldrug. Females.	Bidar. Total.	Bidar. Males.	Bidar. Females.	Parbhani. Total.	Parbhani. Males.	Parbhani. Females.
					36	37	38	39	40	41	42	43	44	45	46	47	48	49	50
A	5 ...	Brahmins ...	Negar ...	Hindu ...	...	...	...	...	...	...	...	...	...	...	...	...	4	1	3
		do ...	Nannas ...	do ...	...	...	...	...	...	...	...	...	...	...	...	...	...	...	...
		do ...	Neaglu ...	do ...	...	...	...	...	...	...	...	...	...	...	...	...	...	...	...
		do ...	Pakshi ...	do ...	...	...	...	...	...	...	...	...	...	...	...	...	...	...	...
		do ...	Panasth ...	do ...	...	...	...	...	...	...	...	...	...	...	...	...	...	...	...
		do ...	Panchdraved ...	do ...	...	...	...	...	...	...	89	48	41	2,026	1,016	1,010	5	3	2
		do ...	Panchgod ...	do ...	17	10	7	5	4	1	25	18	7	222	131	91	79	65	14
		do ...	Pande ...	do ...	...	...	...	...	...	...	...	...	...	...	...	...	...	...	...
		do ...	Parshaki ...	do ...	...	...	...	...	...	...	...	...	...	...	...	...	...	...	...
		do ...	Pavari... ...	do ...	...	...	...	...	...	...	...	...	...	...	...	...	...	...	...
		do ...	Phatak ...	do ...	...	...	...	...	...	...	...	...	...	...	...	...	...	...	...
		do ...	Pinda ...	do ...	...	...	...	...	...	...	...	...	...	...	...	...	...	...	...
		do ...	Porashwar ...	do ...	...	...	...	...	...	...	...	...	...	...	...	...	...	...	...
		do ...	Prabhu ...	do ...	...	...	...	...	...	...	...	...	...	...	...	...	3	3	...
		do ...	Prathamshake ...	do ...	487	232	255	245	130	115	69	39	30	43	25	18	168	87	81
		do ...	Puncharashram ...	do ...	...	...	...	...	...	...	...	...	...	...	...	...	...	...	...
		do ...	Radhar ...	do ...	...	...	...	...	...	...	...	...	...	...	...	...	...	...	...
		do ...	Ramanandi ...	do ...	...	...	...	...	...	...	...	...	...	...	...	...	...	...	...
		do ...	Ramanj ...	do ...	7	5	2	13	8	5	2	1	1	...	...	...	...	...	...
		do ...	Rudra ...	do ...	1	1	...	...	...	...	...	...	...	...	...	...	...	...	...
		do ...	Rugvedi ...	do ...	3,705	1,942	1,763	1,704	859	845	727	394	333	1,752	931	821	4,580	2,324	2,256
		do ...	Rukhe ...	do ...	...	...	...	...	...	...	...	...	...	...	...	...	...	...	...
		do ...	Sajgoad ...	do ...	...	...	...	...	...	...	...	...	...	...	...	...	...	...	...
		do ...	Sakar ...	do ...	...	...	...	...	...	...	...	...	...	...	...	...	...	...	...
		do ...	Salbar ...	do ...	...	...	...	1	...	1	...	...	...	...	...	...	...	...	...
		do ...	Samnedi ...	do ...	2	2	...	...	...	...	...	...	...	...	...	...	...	...	...
		do ...	Sandel... ...	do ...	...	...	...	...	...	...	...	...	...	...	...	...	...	...	...
		do ...	Sanewad ...	do ...	...	...	...	...	...	...	21	11	10	...	...	...	...	...	...
		do ...	Sanodu ...	do ...	...	...	...	...	...	...	...	...	...	...	...	...	...	...	...
		do ...	Sannudia ...	do ...	...	...	...	...	...	...	...	...	...	...	...	...	...	...	...
		do ...	Sanpuj ...	do ...	...	...	...	...	...	...	2	2	...	...	...	...	...	...	...
		do ...	Saraswut ...	do ...	28	16	12	6	2	4	...	...	...	7	5	2	11	10	1
		do ...	Shainte ...	do ...	...	...	...	...	...	...	...	...	...	...	...	...	...	...	...
		do ...	Shainve ...	do ...	6	6	...	...	...	...	3	2	1	...	...	...	7	1	6
		do ...	Shawa ...	do ...	86	40	46	2	2	...	...	...	...	12	6	6	...	...	...
		do ...	Shikwan ...	do ...	...	...	...	...	...	...	...	...	...	...	...	...	26	17	9
		do ...	Shormati ...	do ...	...	...	...	...	...	...	...	...	...	...	...	...	...	...	...
		do ...	Shrimali ...	do ...	...	...	...	...	...	...	...	...	...	...	...	...	...	...	...
		do ...	Silvarta ...	do ...	37	37	...	...	...	...	...	...	...	...	...	...	...	...	...
		do ...	Smarth ...	do ...	1,443	751	692	621	331	290	275	141	184	966	525	441	1,167	545	622
		do ...	Sirajphur ...	do ...	...	...	...	...	...	...	...	...	...	...	...	...	...	...	...
		do ...	Sodar ...	do ...	...	...	...	...	...	...	...	...	...	...	...	...	...	...	...

TABLE XVI.

Castes and Sub-divisions.—*Continued.*

Class.	Group.	Castes.	Sub-division of Castes.	Religion.	Sirpur Tandur. Total.	Sirpur Tandur. Males.	Sirpur Tandur. Females.	Gulbarga. Total.	Gulbarga. Males.	Gulbarga. Females.	Raichur. Total.	Raichur. Males.	Raichur. Females.	Lingasugur. Total.	Lingasugur. Males.	Lingasugur. Females.	Railways. Total.	Railways. Males.	Railways. Females.
					51	52	53	54	55	56	57	58	59	60	61	62	63	64	65
A	5 ...	Brahmins ...	Nagar ...	Hindu	...	...	...	...	...	...	...	...	...	...	...	...	...	...	...
		do ...	Nannas	do	...	...	...	...	...	...	...	...	...	...	...	...	...	...	...
		do ...	Neaglu	do	...	...	...	...	...	...	...	...	...	...	...	...	...	...	...
		do ...	Pakhi ...	do	1	1	...	...	...	...	...	...	...	...	...	...	...	...	...
		do ...	Panasth	do	...	...	...	...	...	...	...	...	...	...	...	...	...	...	...
		do ...	Panchdraved ...	do	1	1	...	8	8	...	...	...	...	...	...	...	...	...	...
		do ...	Panchgod	do	...	...	...	...	...	...	...	...	...	...	...	...	...	...	...
		do ...	Pande ...	do	...	...	...	...	...	...	...	...	...	...	...	...	...	...	...
		do ...	Parshaki	do	...	...	...	...	...	...	...	...	...	...	...	...	...	...	...
		do ...	Pavari ...	do	...	...	...	...	...	...	...	...	...	...	...	...	...	...	...
		do ...	Phatak	do	...	...	...	...	...	...	...	...	...	...	...	...	...	...	...
		do ...	Pinda ...	do	...	...	...	...	...	...	...	...	...	...	...	...	...	...	...
		do ...	Porashwar	do	...	...	...	...	...	...	...	...	...	...	...	...	...	...	...
		do ...	Prabhu	do	...	...	...	11	4	7	...	...	...	...	...	...	...	...	...
		do ...	Prathamshake	do	4	...	4	156	66	90	59	81	28	808	90	213	...	...	...
		do ...	Puncharashram	do	...	...	...	...	...	...	...	...	...	...	...	...	...	...	...
		do ...	Radhar	do	...	...	...	...	...	...	...	...	...	...	...	...	...	...	...
		do ...	Ramanandi	do	...	...	...	...	...	...	...	...	...	...	...	...	...	...	...
		do ...	Ramanj	do	...	...	...	29	14	15	30	17	18	...	...	...	...	...	...
		do ...	Rudra ...	do	...	...	...	...	...	...	...	...	...	...	...	...	...	...	...
		do ...	Rugvodi	do	307	147	160	915	481	484	740	898	842	242	181	111	...	...	...
		do ...	Rukhe ...	do	...	...	...	...	...	...	...	...	...	...	...	...	...	...	...
		do ...	Sajgoad	do	1	...	1	...	...	...	...	...	...	...	...	...	...	...	...
		do ...	Sakar ...	do	...	...	...	...	...	...	...	...	...	...	...	...	...	...	...
		do ...	Salbar ...	do	...	...	...	...	...	...	...	...	...	...	...	...	...	...	...
		do ...	Samnedi	do	...	...	...	15	8	7	...	...	...	...	...	...	...	...	...
		do ...	Sandel...	do	...	...	...	...	...	...	...	...	...	...	...	...	...	...	...
		do ...	Sanewad	do	...	...	...	...	...	...	...	...	...	...	...	...	...	...	...
		do ...	Sanodu	do	...	...	...	...	...	...	...	...	...	...	...	...	...	...	...
		do ...	Sannudia	do	...	...	...	...	...	...	...	...	...	...	...	...	...	...	...
		do ...	Sanpuj...	do	...	...	...	...	...	...	...	...	...	...	...	...	...	...	...
		do ...	Saraswut	do	...	...	...	9	9	...	...	...	...	...	...	...	...	...	...
		do ...	Shainte	do	...	...	...	...	...	...	...	...	...	...	...	...	...	...	...
		do ...	Shainve	do	...	...	...	...	...	...	...	...	...	...	...	...	...	...	...
		do ...	Shawa	do	...	...	...	...	...	...	...	...	...	...	...	...	...	...	...
		do ...	Shikwan	do	...	...	...	...	...	...	...	...	...	...	...	...	...	...	...
		do ...	Shormati	do	...	...	...	...	...	...	...	...	...	...	...	...	...	...	...
		do ...	Shrimali	do	...	...	...	...	...	...	...	...	...	...	...	...	...	...	...
		do ...	Silvarta	do	...	...	...	...	...	...	...	...	...	...	...	...	...	...	...
		do ...	Smarth	do	20	11	9	499	248	251	252	176	76	735	895	840	...	...	...
		do ...	Sirajphur	do	2	2	...	...	...	...	...	...	...	...	...	...	...	...	...
		do ...	Sodar ...	do	...	...	...	...	...	...	...	...	...	...	...	...	...	...	...

TABLE XVI.

Castes and Sub-divisions.—*Continued.*

Class.	Group.	Castes.	Sub-division of Castes.	Religion.	Total.			Hyderabad.			Atraf-i-Balda.			Mahabubnagar.			Nalgonda.		
					Total.	Males.	Females.	Total.	Males.	Females.	Total.	Males.	Females.	Total.	Males.	Females.	Total.	Males.	Females.
1	2	3	4	5	6	7	8	9	10	11	12	13	14	15	16	17	18	19	20
A	5 ...	Brahmins ...	Sribastan	Hindu ...	10	5	5	10	5	5	...	...	...	...	...	...	...	...	...
		do ...	Sringodd	do ...	5	5	...	...	...	...	...	...	...	...	...	...	...	...	...
		do ...	Srivaishnao	do ...	2,079	1,057	1,022	45	28	17	...	...	...	299	142	157	...	...	...
		do ...	Srivardhan	do ...	2	2	...	...	...	...	...	...	...	...	...	...	...	...	...
		do ...	Srivartavin	do ...	3	2	1	...	...	...	...	...	...	...	...	...	...	...	...
		do ...	Srya	do ...	5	4	1	5	4	1	...	...	...	...	...	...	...	...	...
		do ...	Survurya	do ...	230	121	109	196	96	100	...	...	...	1	...	1	...	...	...
		do ...	Telangi	do ...	809	430	379	282	162	120	...	...	...	...	...	...	...	...	...
		do ...	Tergul...	do ...	768	442	326	...	...	...	...	...	...	...	...	...	...	...	...
		do ...	Tertuyashaki	do ...	25	11	14	...	...	...	...	...	...	...	...	...	...	...	...
		do ...	Fenhala	do ...	22	13	9	...	...	...	...	...	...	8	5	3	...	...	...
		do ...	Tevari	do ...	137	29	108	125	21	104	...	...	...	1	1	...	...	...	...
		do ...	Teradarti	do ...	83	21	12	83	21	12	...	...	...	...	...	...	...	...	...
		do ...	Vadagalu	do ...	19	8	11	...	...	...	19	8	11	...	...	...	...	...	...
		do ...	Vadahala	do ...	224	115	109	...	...	...	...	...	...	19	8	11	15	11	4
		do ...	Vaidikulu	do ...	1,572	780	792	...	...	...	124	64	60	144	69	75	...	...	...
		do ...	Vaikhanas	do ...	2	1	1	...	...	...	...	...	...	...	...	...	...	...	...
		do ...	Vaitrshakha	do ...	8	8	...	...	...	...	...	...	...	...	...	...	...	...	...
		do ...	Vapisni	do ...	1,838	951	887	...	...	...	...	...	...	...	...	...	...	...	...
		do ...	Varkar	do ...	27	13	14	22	11	11	...	...	...	...	...	...	...	...	...
		do ...	Vasist	do ...	20	20	...	...	...	...	...	...	...	...	...	...	...	...	...
		do ...	Vegunedu	do ...	24	10	14	...	...	...	...	...	...	...	...	...	...	...	...
		do ...	Vrishtam	do ...	1	...	1	1	...	1	...	...	...	...	...	...	...	...	...
		do ...	Vellabhachau... ...	do ...	15	8	7	6	3	3	9	5	4	...	...	...	...	...	...
		do ...	Velnadeo	do ...	109	59	50	...	...	...	...	...	...	11	7	4	16	10	6
		do ...	Veshniatara	do ...	29	12	17	29	12	17	...	...	...	...	...	...	...	...	...
		do ...	Veshnao	do ...	6,478	3,326	3,152	501	263	238	278	149	124	894	428	466	591	318	273
		do ...	Veshva	do ...	25	15	10	...	...	...	...	...	...	...	...	...	25	15	10
		do ...	Yadosrakolu	do ...	19	12	7	...	...	...	...	...	...	19	12	7	...	...	...
		do ...	Yajoshshakha ...	do ...	80	44	36	...	...	...	...	...	...	...	...	...	...	...	...
		do ...	Yegniyatarkolu ...	do ...	3	...	3	...	...	...	...	...	...	...	...	...	...	...	...
		do ...	Yegniyawalki ...	do ...	70	30	40	...	...	...	...	...	...	...	...	...	12	7	5
		do ...	Yejurvedi	do ...	18,992	9,852	9,140	...	...	...	81	42	39	93	56	37	119	49	70
		do ...	Yellandsu	do ...	24	14	10	...	...	...	...	...	...	...	...	...	...	...	...
		do ...	Yelnatte	do ...	1	...	1	1	...	1	...	...	...	...	...	...	...	...	...
		do ...	Unspecified	do ...	115,558	60,191	55,367	9,309	5,309	4,000	2,837	1,467	1,370	4,480	2,247	2,233	4,727	2,346	2,381
			Total......	......	270,432	140,884	129,548	17,510	10,072	7,438	5,186	2,677	2,509	10,812	5,322	5,490	9,093	4,574	4,519

TABLE XVI.

Castes and Sub-divisions.—*Continued.*

Class.	Group.	Castes.	Sub-division of Castes.	Religion.	Warangal.			Elgandal.			Indur.			Medak.			Aurangabad.		
					Total.	Males.	Females.	Total.	Males.	Females.	Total.	Males.	Females.	Total.	Males.	Females.	Total.	Males.	Females.
					21	22	23	24	25	26	27	28	29	30	31	32	33	34	35
A	5 ...	Brahmins ...	Sribastan	Hindu ...	...	...	...	...	...	...	...	...	...	...	...	...	...	...	...
		do ...	Sringodd	do ...	...	...	...	...	...	...	...	...	...	...	...	...	...	...	...
		do ...	Srivaishnao	do ...	541	274	267	656	339	317	94	47	47	346	184	162	...	...	...
		do ...	Srivardhan	do ...	...	...	...	...	...	...	...	...	...	...	...	...	...	...	...
		do ...	Srivartavin	do ...	...	...	...	...	...	...	...	...	...	...	...	...	3	2	1
		do ...	Srya	do ...	...	...	...	...	...	...	...	...	...	...	...	...	...	...	...
		do ...	Survurya	do ...	...	...	...	...	...	...	...	...	...	...	...	...	...	...	...
		do ...	Telangi	do ...	327	178	149	...	...	...	...	...	...	161	72	89	7	3	4
		do ...	Tergul	do ...	...	...	...	...	...	...	...	...	...	...	...	...	151	121	30
		do ...	Tertuyashaki	do ...	...	...	...	...	...	...	...	...	...	...	...	...	...	...	...
		do ...	Tenhala	do ...	14	8	6	...	...	...	...	...	...	...	...	...	...	...	...
		do ...	Tevari...	do ...	...	...	...	...	...	...	...	...	...	...	...	...	...	...	...
		do ...	Teradarti	do ...	...	...	...	...	...	...	...	...	...	...	...	...	...	...	...
		do ...	Vadagalu	do ...	...	...	...	...	...	...	...	...	...	...	...	...	...	...	...
		do ...	Vadahala	do ...	...	...	...	...	...	...	...	...	...	130	56	74	...	...	...
		do ...	Vaidikulu	do ...	1,217	605	612	54	27	27	...	...	...	33	15	18	...	...	...
		do ...	Vaikhanas	do ...	...	...	...	...	...	...	...	...	...	...	...	...	...	...	...
		do ...	Vaitrshakha	do ...	...	...	...	8	8	...	...	...	...	...	...	...	...	...	...
		do ...	Vapisni	do ...	...	...	...	...	...	...	...	...	...	...	...	...	46	14	32
		do ...	Varkar	do ...	...	...	...	...	...	...	...	...	...	...	...	...	...	...	...
		do ...	Vasist	do ...	...	...	...	...	...	...	...	...	...	...	...	...	...	...	...
		do ...	Vegunedu	do ...	24	10	14	...	...	...	...	...	...	...	...	...	...	...	...
		do ...	Vrishtam	do ...	...	...	...	...	...	...	...	...	...	...	...	...	...	...	...
		do ...	Vellabhachau... ...	do ...	...	...	...	...	...	...	...	...	...	...	...	...	...	...	...
		do ...	Velnadeo	do ...	82	42	40	...	...	...	...	...	...	...	...	...	...	...	...
		do ...	Veshniatara	do ...	...	...	...	...	...	...	...	...	...	...	...	...	...	...	...
		do ...	Veshnao	do ...	...	...	...	...	...	...	161	71	90	117	55	62	49	32	17
		do ...	Veshva...	do ...	...	...	...	...	...	...	...	...	...	...	...	...	...	...	...
		do ...	Yadostakolu	do ...	...	...	...	...	...	...	...	...	...	...	...	...	...	...	...
		do ...	Yajoshshakha... ...	do ...	18	10	8	14	7	7	...	...	...	48	27	21	...	...	...
		do ...	Yegniyatarkolu ...	do ...	...	...	...	3	...	3	...	...	...	...	...	...	...	...	...
		do ...	Yegniyawalki... ...	do ...	19	10	9	...	...	...	31	10	21	...	...	...	...	...	...
		do ...	Yejurvedi	do ...	94	53	41	9	6	3	587	303	284	23	10	13	5,181	2,668	2,513
		do ...	Yellandsu	do ...	...	...	...	...	...	...	...	...	...	...	...	...	...	...	...
		do ...	Yelnatte	do ...	...	...	...	...	...	...	...	...	...	...	...	...	...	...	...
		do ...	Unspecified	do ...	8,346	4,246	4,100	13,273	6,359	6,914	6,944	3,504	3,440	2,867	1,425	1,442	12,494	6,611	5,883
			Total......	......	17,486	8,951	8,535	18,948	9,163	9,785	14,885	7,388	7,497	5,501	2,763	2,738	31,242	16,487	14,755

TABLE XVI.

Castes and Sub-divisions.—*Continued.*

Class.	Group.	Castes.	Sub-division of Castes.	Religion.	Birh. Total.	Birh. Males.	Birh. Females.	Nander. Total.	Nander. Males.	Nander. Females.	Naldrug. Total.	Naldrug. Males.	Naldrug. Females.	Bidar. Total.	Bidar. Males.	Bidar. Females.	Parbhani. Total.	Parbhani. Males.	Parbhani. Females.
					36	37	38	39	40	41	42	43	44	45	46	47	48	49	50
A	5 ...	Brahmins ...	Sribastan	Hindu ...	...	...	...	...	...	...	...	...	...	...	...	...	...	...	...
		do ...	Sringodd	do ...	5	5	...	...	...	...	...	...	...	...	...	...	...	...	...
		do ...	Srivaishnao	do ...	...	...	...	11	5	6	...	...	...	2	1	1	...	...	...
		do ...	Srivardhan	do ...	...	...	...	...	...	...	2	2	...	...	...	...	...	...	...
		do ...	Srivartavin	do ...	...	...	...	...	...	...	...	...	...	...	...	...	...	...	...
		do ...	Srya	do ...	...	...	...	...	...	...	...	...	...	...	...	...	...	...	...
		do ...	Survurya	do ...	28	23	5	...	...	...	...	...	...	...	...	...	5	2	3
		do ...	Telangi	do ...	...	...	...	...	...	...	...	...	...	...	...	...	...	...	...
		do ...	Tergul...	do ...	362	187	175	8	1	2	237	124	118	5	1	4	6	4	2
		do ...	Tertuyashaki... ...	do ...	25	11	14	...	...	...	...	...	...	...	...	...	...	...	...
		do ...	Tenhala	do ...	...	...	...	...	...	...	...	...	...	...	...	...	...	...	...
		do ...	Tevari...	do ...	...	...	...	...	...	...	...	...	...	...	...	...	...	...	...
		do ...	Teradarti	do ...	...	...	...	...	...	...	...	...	...	...	...	...	...	...	...
		do ...	Vadagalu	do ...	...	...	...	...	...	...	...	...	...	...	...	...	...	...	...
		do ...	Vadahala	do ...	...	...	...	...	...	...	...	...	...	...	...	...	...	...	...
		do ...	Vaidikulu	do ...	...	...	...	...	...	...	...	...	...	...	...	...	...	...	...
		do ...	Vaikhanas	do ...	...	...	...	...	...	...	...	...	...	...	...	...	...	...	...
		do ...	Vaitrahakha	do ...	...	...	...	...	...	...	...	...	...	...	...	...	...	...	...
		do ...	Vapisni	do ...	1,413	732	681	100	56	44	4	1	3	155	80	75	120	68	52
		do ...	Varkar	do ...	...	...	...	...	...	...	...	...	...	...	...	...	...	...	...
		do ...	Vasist...	do ...	20	20	...	...	...	...	...	...	...	...	...	...	...	...	...
		do ...	Vegunedu	do ...	...	...	...	...	...	...	...	...	...	...	...	...	...	...	...
		do ...	Vrishtam	do ...	...	...	...	...	...	...	...	...	...	...	...	...	...	...	...
		do ...	Vellabhachau ...	do ...	...	...	...	...	...	...	...	...	...	...	...	...	...	...	...
		do ...	Velnadeo	do ...	...	...	...	...	...	...	...	...	...	...	...	...	...	...	...
		do ...	Veshniatara	do ...	...	...	...	...	...	...	...	...	...	...	...	...	...	...	...
		do ...	Veshnao	do ...	137	59	78	112	45	67	149	73	76	599	306	293	129	83	46
		do ...	Veshva	do ...	...	...	...	...	...	...	...	...	...	...	...	...	...	...	...
		do ...	Yadostakolu	do ...	...	...	...	...	...	...	...	...	...	...	...	...	...	...	...
		do ...	Yajoshshakha ...	do ...	...	...	...	...	...	...	...	...	...	...	...	...	...	...	...
		do ...	Yegniyatarkolu ...	do ...	...	...	...	...	...	...	...	...	...	...	...	...	...	...	...
		do ...	Yegniyawalki ...	do ...	...	...	...	...	...	...	...	...	...	8	3	5	...	...	...
		do ...	Yejurvedi	do ...	5,244	2,754	2,490	1,364	789	625	870	198	172	859	188	171	4,708	2,408	2,300
		do ...	Yellandsu	do ...	...	...	...	...	...	...	...	...	...	...	...	...	...	...	...
		do ...	Yelnatte	do ...	...	...	...	...	...	...	...	...	...	...	...	...	...	...	...
		do ...	Unspecified	do ...	5,960	3,111	2,849	4,803	2,551	2,252	5,549	2,940	2,609	10,111	5,205	4,906	7,095	3,983	3,112
			Total......	......	24,711	12,959	11,752	11,488	5,970	5,468	19,642	10,357	9,285	17,988	9,843	8,645	22,676	12,142	10,534

TABLE XVI.

Castes and Sub-divisions.—*Continued.*

Class.	Group.	Castes.	Sub-division of Castes.	Religion.	Sirpur Tandur. Total.	Sirpur Tandur. Males.	Sirpur Tandur. Females.	Gulbarga. Total.	Gulbarga. Males.	Gulbarga. Females.	Raichur. Total.	Raichur. Males.	Raichur. Females.	Lingasugur. Total.	Lingasugur. Males.	Lingasugur. Females.	Railways. Total.	Railways. Males.	Railways. Females.
					51	52	53	54	55	56	57	58	59	60	61	62	63	64	65
A	5 ...	Brahmins ...	Sribastan	Hindu ...	...	...	...	...	...	...	...	...	...	...	...	...	...	...	...
		do ...	Sringodd	do ...	...	...	...	...	...	...	...	...	...	...	...	...	...	...	...
		do ...	Srivaishnao	do ...	...	...	...	22	7	15	63	80	83	...	...	...	...	...	...
		do ...	Srivardhan	do ...	...	...	...	...	...	...	...	...	...	...	...	...	...	...	...
		do ...	Srivartavin	do ...	...	...	...	...	...	...	...	...	...	...	...	...	...	...	...
		do ...	Srya	do ...	...	...	...	...	...	...	...	...	...	...	...	...	...	...	...
		do ...	Survurya	do ...	...	...	...	...	...	...	...	...	...	...	...	...	...	...	...
		do ...	Telangi	do ...	...	...	...	...	...	...	32	15	17	...	...	...	...	...	...
		do ...	Tergul...	do ...	...	...	...	4	4	...	...	...	...	...	...	...	...	...	...
		do ...	Tertuyashaki	do ...	...	...	...	...	...	...	...	...	...	...	...	...	...	...	...
		do ...	Tenhala	do ...	...	...	...	...	...	...	...	...	...	...	...	...	...	...	...
		do ...	Tevari	do ...	...	...	...	11	7	4	...	...	...	...	...	...	...	...	...
		do ...	Teradarti	do ...	...	...	...	...	...	...	...	...	...	...	...	...	...	...	...
		do ...	Vadagalu	do ...	...	...	...	...	...	...	...	...	...	...	...	...	...	...	...
		do ...	Vadahala	do ...	...	...	...	...	...	...	52	82	20	8	8	...	...	...	...
		do ...	Vaidikulu	do ...	...	...	...	...	...	...	...	...	...	...	...	...	...	...	...
		do ...	Vaikhanas	do ...	...	...	...	...	...	...	2	1	1	...	...	...	...	...	...
		do ...	Vaitrshakha	do ...	...	...	...	...	...	...	...	...	...	...	...	...	...	...	...
		do ...	Vapisni	do ...	...	...	...	...	...	...	...	...	...	...	...	...	...	...	...
		do ...	Varkar	do ...	...	...	...	...	...	...	...	...	...	5	2	8	...	...	...
		do ...	Vasist	do ...	...	...	...	...	...	...	...	...	...	...	...	...	...	...	...
		do ...	Vegunedu	do ...	...	...	...	...	...	...	...	...	...	...	...	...	...	...	...
		do ...	Vrishtam	do ...	...	...	...	...	...	...	...	...	...	...	...	...	...	...	...
		do ...	Vellabhachau... ...	do ...	...	...	...	...	...	...	...	...	...	...	...	...	...	...	...
		do ...	Velnadeo	do ...	...	...	...	...	...	...	...	...	...	...	...	...	...	...	...
		do ...	Veshniatara	do ...	...	...	...	...	...	...	...	...	...	...	...	...	...	...	...
		do ...	Veshnao	do ...	2	2	...	...	...	...	1,433	739	694	1,329	701	628	2	2	...
		do ...	Veshva	do ...	...	...	...	...	...	...	...	...	...	...	...	...	...	...	...
		do ...	Yadostakolu	do ...	...	...	...	...	...	...	...	...	...	...	...	...	...	...	...
		do ...	Yajoshshakha... ...	do ...	...	...	...	...	...	...	...	...	...	...	...	...	...	...	...
		do ...	Yegniyatarkolu ...	do ...	...	...	...	...	...	...	...	...	...	...	...	...	...	...	...
		do ...	Yegniyawalki... ...	do ...	...	...	...	...	...	...	...	...	...	...	...	...	...	...	...
		do ...	Yejurvedi	do ...	169	93	76	296	133	163	207	98	109	88	54	84	...	...	...
		do ...	Yellandsu	do ...	...	...	...	...	...	...	24	14	10	...	...	...	...	...	...
		do ...	Yelnatte	do ...	...	...	...	...	...	...	...	...	...	...	...	...	...	...	...
		do ...	Unspecified	do ...	1,275	673	602	10,255	5,302	4,953	2,172	1,306	866	2,636	1,356	1,280	425	250	175
			Total......		3,806	1,897	1,909	15,500	8,082	7,418	8,651	4,801	3,850	14,930	7,682	7,248	432	254	178

TABLE XVI.

Castes and Sub-divisions.—*Continued.*

Class.	Group.	Castes.	Sub-division of Castes.	Religion.	Total. Total.	Total. Males.	Total. Females.	Hyderabad. Total.	Hyderabad. Males.	Hyderabad. Females.	Atraf-i-Balda. Total.	Atraf-i-Balda. Males.	Atraf-i-Balda. Females.	Mahabubnagar. Total.	Mahabubnagar. Males.	Mahabubnagar. Females.	Nalgonda. Total.	Nalgonda. Males.	Nalgonda. Females.
1	2	3	4	5	6	7	8	9	10	11	12	13	14	15	16	17	18	19	20
C	14 ...	Komti ...	Adgota	Hindu ...	2	...	2	2	...	2	...	...	...	...	...	...	...	...	...
		do ...	Adhor	do ...	28	19	9	...	...	...	...	...	...	...	...	...	...	...	...
		do ...	Adi	do ...	10	3	7	...	...	...	10	3	7	...	...	...	...	...	...
		do ...	Agar	do ...	165	68	97	158	64	94	7	4	3	...	...	...	...	...	...
		do ...	Aleshaie ...	do ...	2	1	1	...	...	...	...	...	...	...	...	...	...	...	...
		do ...	Apitdar ...	do ...	41	23	18	41	23	18	...	...	...	...	...	...	...	...	...
		do ...	Are	do ...	6	3	3	...	...	...	...	...	...	...	...	...	6	3	3
		do ...	Arva	do ...	1,602	802	800	...	...	...	12	4	8	...	...	...	1,176	594	582
		do ...	Atralkar ...	do ...	3	2	1	...	...	...	...	...	...	...	...	...	...	...	...
		do ...	Badavar ...	do ...	10	7	3	...	...	...	...	...	...	...	...	...	...	...	...
		do ...	Balevar ...	do ...	48	24	24	...	...	...	...	...	...	...	...	...	...	...	...
		do ...	Balvant ...	do ...	2	1	1	...	...	...	...	...	...	...	...	...	...	...	...
		do ...	Bandhuvad ...	do ...	9	8	1	...	...	...	...	...	...	...	...	...	...	...	...
		do ...	Banma... ...	do ...	76	...	76	...	...	...	...	...	...	...	...	...	...	...	...
		do ...	Balurvad ...	do ...	51	32	19	...	...	...	...	...	...	...	...	...	...	...	...
		do ...	Bejabargi ...	do ...	228	152	76	228	152	76	...	...	...	...	...	...	...	...	...
		do ...	Bekadvad ...	do ...	11	3	8	...	...	...	...	...	...	...	...	...	...	...	...
		do ...	Bekam... ...	do ...	1	...	1	...	...	...	...	...	...	...	...	...	...	...	...
		do ...	Bhanni Komti ...	do ...	6	3	3	6	3	3	...	...	...	...	...	...	...	...	...
		do ...	Bheri	do ...	1,144	597	547	...	...	...	...	...	...	...	...	...	...	...	...
		do ...	Butekar ...	do ...	11	2	9	...	...	...	...	...	...	...	...	...	...	...	...
		do ...	Chadarvad ...	do ...	85	22	13	...	...	...	...	...	...	...	...	...	...	...	...
		do ...	Chilkul ...	do ...	3	2	1	...	...	...	...	...	...	...	...	...	...	...	...
		do ...	Chitawbari ...	do ...	8	5	3	...	...	...	...	...	...	...	...	...	...	...	...
		do ...	Dadulvar ...	do ...	53	29	24	...	...	...	...	...	...	...	...	...	...	...	...
		do ...	Dagam ...	do ...	1	1	...	1	1	...	...	...	...	...	...	...	...	...	...
		do ...	Davasar ...	do ...	7	5	2	7	5	2	...	...	...	...	...	...	...	...	...
		do ...	Deochar ...	do ...	8	6	2	...	...	...	...	...	...	...	...	...	...	...	...
		do ...	Dikshavant ...	do ...	4	2	2	...	...	...	...	...	...	...	...	...	...	...	...
		do ...	Duvar... ...	do ...	12	3	9	...	...	...	...	...	...	...	...	...	...	...	...
		do ...	Ganevar ...	do ...	10	10	...	...	...	...	...	...	...	...	...	...	...	...	...
		do ...	Ganti	do ...	31	13	18	31	13	18	...	...	...	...	...	...	...	...	...
		do ...	Ghisadvad ...	do ...	24	11	13	...	...	...	...	...	...	...	...	...	...	...	...
		do ...	Goara	do ...	173	90	83	...	...	...	...	...	...	...	...	...	...	...	...
		do ...	Gojrati ...	do ...	5	4	1	5	4	1	...	...	...	...	...	...	...	...	...
		do ...	Gopevad ...	do ...	33	22	11	...	...	...	...	...	...	...	...	...	...	...	...
		do ...	Goshevad ...	do ...	5	2	3	5	2	3	...	...	...	...	...	...	...	...	...
		do ...	Goth	do ...	12	3	9	...	...	...	...	...	...	...	...	...	...	...	...
		do ...	Hari	do ...	16	11	5	...	...	...	...	...	...	...	...	...	...	...	...
		do ...	Jaisvar ...	do ...	23	12	11	23	12	11	...	...	...	...	...	...	...	...	...
		do ...	Janga	do ...	19	12	7	19	12	7	...	...	...	...	...	...	...	...	...
		do ...	Javari... ...	do ...	8	5	3	...	...	...	...	...	...	...	...	...	...	...	...
		do ...	Jodevar ...	do ...	9	7	2	...	...	...	...	...	...	...	...	...	...	...	...

TABLE XVI.

Castes and Sub-divisions.—*Continued.*

Class.	Group.	Castes.	Sub-division of Castes.	Religion.	Warangal.			Elgandal.			Indur.			Medak.			Aurangabad.		
					Total.	Males.	Females.	Total.	Males.	Females.	Total.	Males.	Females.	Total.	Males.	Females.	Total.	Males.	Females.
					21	22	23	24	25	26	27	28	29	30	31	32	33	34	35
C	14 ...	Komti ...	Adgota	Hindu ...	...	...	...	...	...	...	...	...	...	...	...	...	...	...	...
		do ...	Adbor	do ...	...	...	...	...	...	...	...	...	...	...	...	...	...	...	...
		do ...	Adi	do ...	...	...	...	...	...	...	...	...	...	...	...	...	...	...	...
		do ...	Agar	do ...	...	...	...	...	...	...	...	...	...	...	...	...	...	...	...
		do ...	Aleshaie	do ...	...	...	...	...	...	...	...	...	...	...	...	...	...	...	...
		do ...	Apitdar	do ...	...	...	...	...	...	...	...	...	...	...	...	...	...	...	...
		do ...	Are	do ...	...	...	...	...	...	...	...	...	...	...	...	...	...	...	...
		do ...	Arva	do ...	...	...	...	414	204	210	...	...	...	...	...	...	...	...	...
		do ...	Atralkar	do ...	...	...	...	...	...	...	...	...	...	...	...	...	...	...	...
		do ...	Badavar	do ...	...	...	...	...	...	...	...	...	...	...	...	...	...	...	...
		do ...	Balevar	do ...	...	...	...	...	...	...	...	...	...	...	...	...	...	...	...
		do ...	Balvant	do ...	...	...	...	...	...	...	...	...	...	...	...	...	...	...	...
		do ...	Bandhuvad	do ...	...	...	...	...	...	...	...	...	...	...	...	...	...	...	...
		do ...	Banma	do ...	...	...	...	...	...	...	...	...	...	...	...	...	...	...	...
		do ...	Balurvad	do ...	...	...	...	...	...	...	...	...	...	...	...	...	...	...	...
		do ...	Bejabargi	do ...	...	...	...	...	...	...	...	...	...	...	...	...	...	...	...
		do ...	Bekadvad	do ...	...	...	...	...	...	...	...	...	...	...	...	...	...	...	...
		do ...	Bekam...	do ...	...	...	...	...	...	...	...	...	...	...	...	...	...	...	...
		do ...	Bhanni Komti ...	do ...	...	...	...	...	...	...	...	...	...	...	...	...	1	...	1
		do ...	Bheri	do ...	86	42	44	185	105	80	...	...	...	8	1	2	846	442	404
		do ...	Butekar	do ...	...	...	...	...	...	...	...	...	...	...	...	...	...	...	...
		do ...	Chadarvad	do ...	...	...	...	...	...	...	...	...	...	...	...	...	...	...	...
		do ...	Chilkul	do ...	...	...	...	...	...	...	...	...	...	...	...	...	...	...	...
		do ...	Chitawbari	do ...	...	...	...	...	...	...	1	1	...	...	...	...	...	...	...
		do ...	Dadulvar	do ...	...	...	...	...	...	...	...	...	...	...	...	...	...	...	...
		do ...	Dagam	do ...	...	...	...	...	...	...	...	...	...	...	...	...	...	...	...
		do ...	Davasar	do ...	...	...	...	...	...	...	...	...	...	...	...	...	...	...	...
		do ...	Deochar	do ...	...	...	...	...	...	...	...	...	...	...	...	...	...	...	...
		do ...	Dikshavant	do ...	4	2	2	...	...	...	...	...	...	...	...	...	...	...	...
		do ...	Duvar	do ...	...	...	...	...	...	...	...	...	...	...	...	...	...	...	...
		do ...	Ganevar	do ...	...	...	...	...	...	...	...	...	...	...	...	...	...	...	...
		do ...	Ganti	do ...	...	...	...	...	...	...	...	...	...	...	...	...	...	...	...
		do ...	Ghisadvad	do ...	...	...	...	...	...	...	...	...	...	...	...	...	...	...	...
		do ...	Goara	do ...	173	90	83	...	...	...	...	...	...	...	...	...	...	...	...
		do ...	Gojrati	do ...	...	...	...	...	...	...	...	...	...	...	...	...	...	...	...
		do ...	Gopevad	do ...	...	...	...	...	...	...	2	1	1	...	...	...	...	...	...
		do ...	Goshevad	do ...	...	...	...	...	...	...	...	...	...	...	...	...	...	...	...
		do ...	Goth	do ...	...	...	...	...	...	...	...	...	...	...	...	...	...	...	...
		do ...	Hari	do ...	...	...	...	...	...	...	...	...	...	...	...	...	...	...	...
		do ...	Jaisvar	do ...	...	...	...	...	...	...	...	...	...	...	...	...	...	...	...
		do ...	Janga	do ...	...	...	...	...	...	...	...	...	...	...	...	...	...	...	...
		do ...	Javari	do ...	...	...	...	...	...	...	...	...	...	...	...	...	...	...	...
		do ...	Jodevar	do ...	...	...	...	...	...	...	...	...	...	...	...	...	...	...	...

TABLE XVI.

Castes and Sub-divisions.—*Continued.*

Class.	Group.	Castes.	Sub-division of Castes.	Religion.	Birh. Total.	Birh. Males.	Birh. Females.	Nander. Total.	Nander. Males.	Nander. Females.	Naldrug. Total.	Naldrug. Males.	Naldrug. Females.	Bidar. Total.	Bidar. Males.	Bidar. Females.	Parbhani. Total.	Parbhani. Males.	Parbhani. Females.
					36	37	38	39	40	41	42	43	44	45	46	47	48	49	50
C	14 ...	Komti ...	Adgota	Hindu ...	16	12	4	...	...	...	12	7	5	...	...	...	...	...	...
		do ...	Adhor	do ...	...	...	...	...	...	...	...	...	...	...	...	...	...	...	...
		do ...	Adi	do ...	...	...	...	...	...	...	...	...	...	...	...	...	...	...	...
		do ...	Agar	do ...	...	...	...	...	...	...	...	...	...	...	...	...	...	...	...
		do ...	Aleshaie	do ...	...	...	...	...	...	...	...	...	...	...	...	...	...	...	...
		do ...	Apitdar	do ...	...	...	...	...	...	...	...	...	...	...	...	...	2	1	1
		do ...	Are	do ...	...	...	...	...	...	...	...	...	...	...	...	...	...	...	...
		do ...	Arva	do ...	...	...	...	...	...	...	...	...	...	...	...	...	...	...	...
		do ...	Atralkar	do ...	...	...	...	3	2	1	...	...	...	...	...	...	...	...	...
		do ...	Badavar	do ...	...	...	...	10	7	3	...	...	...	...	...	...	...	...	...
		do ...	Balevar	do ...	...	...	...	48	24	24	...	...	...	...	...	...	...	...	...
		do ...	Balvant	do ...	...	...	...	2	1	1	...	...	...	...	...	...	...	...	...
		do ...	Bandhuvad	do ...	...	...	...	9	8	1	...	...	...	...	...	...	...	...	...
		do ...	Banma	do ...	...	...	...	76	...	76	...	...	...	...	...	...	...	...	...
		do ...	Balurvad	do ...	...	...	...	51	32	19	...	...	...	...	...	...	...	...	...
		do ...	Bejabargi	do ...	...	...	...	...	...	...	...	...	...	...	...	...	...	...	...
		do ...	Bekadvad	do ...	...	...	...	11	3	8	...	...	...	...	...	...	...	...	...
		do ...	Bekam...	do ...	...	...	...	...	...	...	...	...	...	...	...	...	...	...	...
		do ...	Bhanni Komti ...	do ...	...	...	...	...	...	...	...	...	...	...	...	...	...	...	...
		do ...	Bheri	do ...	...	...	...	...	...	...	11	2	9	...	...	...	...	...	...
		do ...	Butekar	do ...	...	...	...	...	...	...	...	...	...	...	...	...	...	...	...
		do ...	Chadarvad	do ...	...	...	...	35	22	13	...	...	...	...	...	...	...	...	...
		do ...	Chilkul	do ...	...	...	...	3	2	1	...	...	...	...	...	...	...	...	...
		do ...	Chitawbari	do ...	...	...	...	7	4	3	...	...	...	...	...	...	...	...	...
		do ...	Dadulvar	do ...	...	...	...	53	29	24	...	...	...	...	...	...	...	...	...
		do ...	Dagam	do ...	...	...	...	...	...	...	...	...	...	...	...	...	...	...	...
		do ...	Davasar	do ...	...	...	...	...	...	...	...	...	...	...	...	...	...	...	...
		do ...	Deochar	do ...	...	...	...	8	6	2	...	...	...	...	...	...	...	...	...
		do ...	Dikshavant	do ...	...	...	...	...	...	...	...	...	...	...	...	...	...	...	...
		do ...	Duvar	do ...	10	10	...	...	...	...	...	...	...	...	...	...	12	3	9
		do ...	Ganevar	do ...	...	...	...	...	...	...	...	...	...	...	...	...	...	...	...
		do ...	Ganti	do ...	...	...	...	...	...	...	...	...	...	...	...	...	...	...	...
		do ...	Ghisadvad	do ...	...	...	...	24	11	13	...	...	...	...	...	...	...	...	...
		do ...	Goara	do ...	...	...	...	...	...	...	...	...	...	...	...	...	...	...	...
		do ...	Gojrati...	do ...	...	...	...	...	...	...	...	...	...	...	...	...	...	...	...
		do ...	Gopevad	do ...	...	...	...	31	21	10	...	...	...	...	...	...	...	...	...
		do ...	Goshevad	do ...	...	...	...	...	...	...	...	...	...	...	...	...	...	...	...
		do ...	Goth	do ...	...	...	...	...	...	...	...	...	...	12	3	9	...	...	...
		do ...	Hari	do ...	...	...	...	...	...	...	...	...	...	16	11	5	...	...	...
		do ...	Jaisvar	do ...	...	...	...	...	...	...	...	...	...	...	...	...	...	...	...
		do ...	Janga	do ...	...	...	...	...	...	...	...	...	...	...	...	...	...	...	...
		do ...	Javari	do ...	...	...	...	...	...	...	...	...	...	...	...	...	...	...	...
		do ...	Jodevar...	do ...	...	...	...	9	7	2	...	...	...	...	...	...	...	...	...

TABLE XVI.

Castes and Sub-divisions.—*Continued.*

Class.	Group.	Castes.	Sub-division of Castes.	Religion.	Sirpur Tandur.			Gulbarga.			Raichur.			Lingasugur.			Railways.		
					Total.	Males.	Females.	Total.	Males.	Females.	Total.	Males.	Females.	Total.	Males.	Females.	Total.	Males.	Females.
					51	52	53	54	55	56	57	58	59	60	61	62	63	64	65
C	14 ...	Komti ...	Adgota	Hindu ...	...	...	...	...	...	...	...	...	...	...	...	...	...	...	...
		do ...	Adhor	do ...	...	...	...	...	...	...	...	...	...	...	...	...	...	...	...
		do ...	Adi	do ...	...	...	...	...	...	...	...	...	...	...	...	...	...	...	...
		do ...	Agar	do ...	...	...	...	...	...	...	...	...	...	...	...	...	...	...	...
		do ...	Aleshaie ...	do ...	...	...	...	...	...	...	...	...	...	...	...	...	...	...	...
		do ...	Apitdar ...	do ...	...	...	...	...	...	...	...	...	...	...	...	...	...	...	...
		do ...	Are	do ...	...	...	...	...	...	...	...	...	...	...	...	...	...	...	...
		do ...	Arva	do ...	...	...	...	...	...	...	...	...	...	...	...	...	...	...	...
		do ...	Atralkar ...	do ...	...	...	...	...	...	...	...	...	...	...	...	...	...	...	...
		do ...	Badavar ...	do ...	...	...	...	...	...	...	...	...	...	...	...	...	...	...	...
		do ...	Balevar ...	do ...	...	...	...	...	...	...	...	...	...	...	...	...	...	...	...
		do ...	Balvant ...	do ...	...	...	...	...	...	...	...	...	...	...	...	...	...	...	...
		do ...	Bandhuvad ...	do ...	...	...	...	...	...	...	...	...	...	...	...	...	...	...	...
		do ...	Banma ...	do ...	...	...	...	...	...	...	...	...	...	...	...	...	...	...	...
		do ...	Balurvad ...	do ...	...	...	...	...	...	...	...	...	...	...	...	...	...	...	...
		do ...	Bejabargi ...	do ...	...	...	...	...	...	...	...	...	...	...	...	...	...	...	...
		do ...	Bekadvad ...	do ...	...	...	...	...	...	...	...	...	...	...	...	...	...	...	...
		do ...	Bekam... ...	do ...	...	...	...	...	...	...	...	...	...	...	...	...	...	...	...
		do ...	Bhanni Komti	do ...	...	...	...	...	...	...	...	...	...	...	...	...	...	...	...
		do ...	Bheri	do ...	...	...	...	...	...	...	24	7	17	...	...	...	...	...	...
		do ...	Butekar ...	do ...	...	...	...	...	...	...	...	...	...	...	...	...	...	...	...
		do ...	Chadarvad ...	do ...	...	...	...	...	...	...	...	...	...	...	...	...	...	...	...
		do ...	Chilkul ...	do ...	...	...	...	...	...	...	...	...	...	...	...	...	...	...	...
		do ...	Chitawbari ...	do ...	...	...	...	...	...	...	...	...	...	...	...	...	...	...	...
		do ...	Dadulvar ...	do ...	...	...	...	...	...	...	...	...	...	...	...	...	...	...	...
		do ...	Dagam ...	do ...	...	...	...	...	...	...	...	...	...	...	...	...	...	...	...
		do ...	Davasar ...	do ...	...	...	...	...	...	...	...	...	...	...	...	...	...	...	...
		do ...	Deochar ...	do ...	...	...	...	...	...	...	...	...	...	...	...	...	...	...	...
		do ...	Dikshavant ...	do ...	...	...	...	...	...	...	...	...	...	...	...	...	...	...	...
		do ...	Duvar	do ...	...	...	...	...	...	...	...	...	...	...	...	...	...	...	...
		do ...	Ganevar ...	do ...	...	...	...	...	...	...	...	...	...	...	...	...	...	...	...
		do ...	Ganti	do ...	...	...	...	...	...	...	...	...	...	...	...	...	...	...	...
		do ...	Ghisadvad ...	do ...	...	...	...	...	...	...	...	...	...	...	...	...	...	...	...
		do ...	Goara	do ...	...	...	...	...	...	...	...	...	...	...	...	...	...	...	...
		do ...	Gojrati ...	do ...	...	...	...	...	...	...	...	...	...	...	...	...	...	...	...
		do ...	Gopevad ...	do ...	...	...	...	...	...	...	...	...	...	...	...	...	...	...	...
		do ...	Goshevad ...	do ...	...	...	...	...	...	...	...	...	...	...	...	...	...	...	...
		do ...	Goth	do ...	...	...	...	...	...	...	...	...	...	...	...	...	...	...	...
		do ...	Hari	do ...	...	...	...	...	...	...	...	...	...	...	...	...	...	...	...
		do ...	Jaisvar ...	do ...	...	...	...	...	...	...	...	...	...	...	...	...	...	...	...
		do ...	Janga	do ...	...	...	...	...	...	...	...	...	...	...	...	...	...	...	...
		do ...	Javari ...	do ...	...	...	...	...	...	...	8	5	8	...	...	...	...	...	...
		do ...	Jodevar ...	do ...	...	...	...	...	...	...	...	...	...	...	...	...	...	...	...

TABLE XVI.

Castes and Sub-divisions.—*Continued.*

Class.	Group.	Castes.	Sub-division of Castes.	Religion.	Total.			Hyderabad.			Atraf-i-Balda.			Mahabubnagar.			Nalgonda.		
					Total.	Males.	Females.	Total.	Males.	Females.	Total.	Males.	Females.	Total.	Males.	Females.	Total.	Males.	Females.
1	2	3	4	5	6	7	8	9	10	11	12	13	14	15	16	17	18	19	20
C	14 ...	Komti ...	Jovarpai	Hindu ...	36	23	13	...	...	...	...	...	...	...	...	...	...	...	...
		do ...	Jutipao	do ...	4	3	1	2	2	...	...	...	...	...	...	...	...	...	...
		do ...	Kachevar	do ...	42	19	23	...	...	...	...	...	...	...	...	...	...	...	...
		do ...	Kadavutar	do ...	128	67	61	...	...	...	...	...	...	...	...	...	...	...	...
		do ...	Kadhurti	do ...	8	4	4	...	...	...	...	...	...	...	...	...	...	...	...
		do ...	Kalakomti	do ...	59	33	26	...	...	...	...	...	...	...	...	...	...	...	...
		do ...	Kauvant	do ...	1	...	1	...	...	...	...	...	...	...	...	...	...	...	...
		do ...	Kardani	do ...	1	1	...	1	1	...	...	...	...	...	...	...	...	...	...
		do ...	Karlevar	do ...	84	45	39	...	...	...	...	...	...	...	...	...	...	...	...
		do ...	Karve	do ...	54	34	20	...	...	...	...	...	...	...	...	...	...	...	...
		do ...	Katepar	do ...	6	2	4	...	...	...	...	...	...	...	...	...	...	...	...
		do ...	Kochu	do ...	81	45	36	...	...	...	81	45	36	...	...	...	...	...	...
		do ...	Kokalvar	do ...	15	12	3	...	...	...	...	...	...	...	...	...	...	...	...
		do ...	Kokuti... ...	do ...	1	1	...	...	...	...	...	...	...	...	...	...	...	...	...
		do ...	Korgir	do ...	51	26	25	...	...	...	...	...	...	...	...	...	...	...	...
		do ...	Kotulvar	do ...	70	30	40	...	...	...	...	...	...	...	...	...	...	...	...
		do ...	Kuchi	do ...	105	56	49	...	...	...	...	...	...	105	56	49	...	...	...
		do ...	Lingayet	do ...	142	66	76	103	50	53	25	11	14	...	...	...	...	...	...
		do ...	Lovdnar	do ...	4	3	1	4	3	1	...	...	...	...	...	...	...	...	...
		do ...	Madana	do ...	4	3	1	...	...	...	...	...	...	...	...	...	...	...	...
		do ...	Mahasvas	do ...	8	3	5	...	...	...	...	...	...	...	...	...	...	...	...
		do ...	Maisri	do ...	318	153	165	318	153	165	...	...	...	...	...	...	...	...	...
		do ...	Mamadvar	do ...	22	9	13	...	...	...	...	...	...	...	...	...	...	...	...
		do ...	Margalvad	do ...	11	6	5	...	...	...	...	...	...	...	...	...	...	...	...
		do ...	Mirvar	do ...	3	...	3	...	...	...	...	...	...	...	...	...	...	...	...
		do ...	Modgujrati	do ...	8	5	3	8	5	3	...	...	...	...	...	...	...	...	...
		do ...	Mogunia	do ...	6	5	1	6	5	1	...	...	...	...	...	...	...	...	...
		do ...	Molhar	do ...	4	...	4	4	...	4	...	...	...	...	...	...	...	...	...
		do ...	Monevad	do ...	11	4	7	...	...	...	...	...	...	...	...	...	...	...	...
		do ...	Muratvan	do ...	8	4	4	...	...	...	...	...	...	...	...	...	...	...	...
		do ...	Neti	do ...	273	141	132	...	...	...	1	1	...	...	...	...	...	...	...
		do ...	Nakahat	do ...	1	...	1	1	...	1	...	...	...	...	...	...	...	...	...
		do ...	Padamvar	do ...	16	9	7	...	...	...	...	...	...	...	...	...	...	...	...
		do ...	Parakh	do ...	23	4	19	...	...	...	...	...	...	...	...	...	...	...	...
		do ...	Parasvar	do ...	41	22	19	...	...	...	...	...	...	...	...	...	...	...	...
		do ...	Paravar	do ...	5	3	2	...	...	...	...	...	...	...	...	...	...	...	...
		do ...	Patekar	do ...	25	11	14	...	...	...	...	...	...	...	...	...	...	...	...
		do ...	Pechari	do ...	12	5	7	...	...	...	...	...	...	...	...	...	...	...	...
		do ...	Peshtevar	do ...	14	6	8	...	...	...	...	...	...	...	...	...	...	...	...
		do ...	Pianevar	do ...	3	2	1	...	...	...	...	...	...	...	...	...	...	...	...
		do ...	Pichchu	do ...	10	6	4	...	...	...	10	6	4	...	...	...	...	...	...
		do ...	Pimadvad	do ...	5	4	1	...	...	...	...	...	...	...	...	...	...	...	...
		do ...	Pimparvar	do ...	9	4	5	...	...	...	...	...	...	...	...	...	...	...	...

TABLE XVI.

Castes and Sub-divisions.—*Continued.*

Class.	Group.	Castes.	Sub-division of Castes.	Religion.	Warangal. Total.	Warangal. Males.	Warangal. Females.	Elgandal. Total.	Elgandal. Males.	Elgandal. Females.	Indur. Total.	Indur. Males.	Indur. Females.	Medak. Total.	Medak. Males.	Medak. Females.	Aurangabad. Total.	Aurangabad. Males.	Aurangabad. Females.
					21	22	23	24	25	26	27	28	29	30	31	32	33	34	35
C	14 ...	Komti ...	Jovarpal	Hindu ...	...	...	...	...	...	...	...	...	...	...	...	...	...	...	...
		do ...	Jutipao	do ...	...	...	...	...	...	...	2	1	1	...	...	...	...	...	...
		do ...	Kachevar	do ...	...	...	...	...	...	...	...	...	...	...	...	...	...	...	...
		do ...	Kadavatar	do ...	...	...	...	...	...	...	...	...	...	...	...	...	...	...	...
		do ...	Kadhurti	do ...	...	...	...	...	...	...	...	...	...	...	...	...	...	...	...
		do ...	Kalakomti	do ...	...	...	...	...	...	...	...	...	...	...	...	...	...	...	...
		do ...	Kauvant	do ...	...	...	...	...	...	...	...	...	...	...	...	...	...	...	...
		do ...	Kardani	do ...	...	...	...	...	...	...	...	...	...	...	...	...	...	...	...
		do ...	Karlevar	do ...	...	...	...	...	...	...	...	...	...	...	...	...	...	...	...
		do ...	Karve	do ...	...	...	...	...	...	...	...	...	...	...	...	...	...	...	...
		do ...	Katepar	do ...	...	...	...	...	...	...	...	...	...	...	...	...	...	...	...
		do ...	Kochu	do ...	...	...	...	...	...	...	...	...	...	...	...	...	...	...	...
		do ...	Kokalvar	do ...	...	...	...	...	...	...	...	...	...	...	...	...	...	...	...
		do ...	Kokuti	do ...	...	...	...	...	...	...	...	...	...	...	...	...	...	...	...
		do ...	Korgir	do ...	...	...	...	...	...	...	...	...	...	...	...	...	...	...	...
		do ...	Kotulvar	do ...	...	...	...	...	...	...	...	...	...	...	...	...	...	...	...
		do ...	Kuchi	do ...	...	...	...	...	...	...	...	...	...	...	...	...	...	...	...
		do ...	Lingayet	do ...	...	...	...	...	...	...	...	...	...	...	...	...	...	...	...
		do ...	Lovdnar	do ...	...	...	...	...	...	...	...	...	...	...	...	...	...	...	...
		do ...	Madana	do ...	...	...	...	...	...	...	...	...	...	...	...	...	...	...	...
		do ...	Mahasvas	do ...	...	...	...	...	...	...	...	...	...	...	...	...	...	...	...
		do ...	Maisri	do ...	...	...	...	...	...	...	...	...	...	...	...	...	...	...	...
		do ...	Mamadvar	do ...	...	...	...	...	...	...	6	8	3	...	...	...	...	...	...
		do ...	Margalvad	do ...	...	...	...	...	...	...	...	...	...	...	...	...	...	...	...
		do ...	Mirvar	do ...	...	...	...	...	...	...	...	...	...	...	...	...	...	...	...
		do ...	Modgujrati	do ...	...	...	...	...	...	...	...	...	...	...	...	...	...	...	...
		do ...	Mogunia	do ...	...	...	...	...	...	...	...	...	...	...	...	...	...	...	...
		do ...	Molhar	do ...	...	...	...	...	...	...	...	...	...	...	...	...	...	...	...
		do ...	Monevad	do ...	...	...	...	...	...	...	...	...	...	...	...	...	...	...	...
		do ...	Muratvan	do ...	...	...	...	...	...	...	8	4	4	...	...	...	...	...	...
		do ...	Neti	do ...	241	124	117	...	...	...	...	...	...	23	12	11	...	...	...
		do ...	Nakahat	do ...	...	...	...	...	...	...	...	...	...	...	...	...	...	...	...
		do ...	Padamvar	do ...	...	...	...	...	...	...	16	9	7	...	...	...	...	...	...
		do ...	Parakh	do ...	...	...	...	...	...	...	...	...	...	...	...	...	23	4	19
		do ...	Parasvar	do ...	...	...	...	...	...	...	...	...	...	...	...	...	...	...	...
		do ...	Paravar	do ...	...	...	...	...	...	...	...	...	...	...	...	...	...	...	...
		do ...	Patekar	do ...	...	...	...	...	...	...	...	...	...	...	...	...	25	11	14
		do ...	Pechari	do ...	...	...	...	...	...	...	...	...	...	...	...	...	...	...	...
		do ...	Peshtevar	do ...	...	...	...	...	...	...	...	...	...	...	...	...	...	...	...
		do ...	Pianevar	do ...	...	...	...	...	...	...	...	...	...	...	...	...	...	...	...
		do ...	Pichchu	do ...	...	...	...	...	...	...	...	...	...	...	...	...	...	...	...
		do ...	Pimadvad	do ...	...	...	...	...	...	...	...	...	...	...	...	...	...	...	...
		do ...	Pimparvar	do ...	...	...	...	...	...	...	...	...	...	...	...	...	...	...	...

TABLE XVI.

Castes and Sub-divisions.—*Continued.*

Class.	Group.	Castes.	Sub-division of Castes.	Religion.	Birh. Total.	Birh. Males.	Birh. Females.	Nander. Total.	Nander. Males.	Nander. Females.	Naldrug. Total.	Naldrug. Males.	Naldrug. Females.	Bidar. Total.	Bidar. Males.	Bidar. Females.	Parbhani. Total.	Parbhani. Males.	Parbhani. Females.
					36	37	38	39	40	41	42	43	44	45	46	47	48	49	50
O	14 ...	Komti ...	Jovarpai	Hindu ...	...	...	...	86	23	13	...	...	...	...	...	...	...	...	...
		do ...	Jutipao	do ...	...	...	...	...	...	...	...	...	...	...	...	...	...	...	...
		do ...	Kachevar	do ...	...	...	...	42	19	23	...	...	...	...	...	...	...	...	...
		do ...	Kadavatar	do ...	...	...	...	128	67	61	...	...	...	...	...	...	...	...	...
		do ...	Kadhurti	do ...	...	...	...	8	4	4	...	...	...	...	...	...	...	...	...
		do ...	Kalakomti	do ...	...	...	...	59	33	26	...	...	...	...	...	...	...	...	...
		do ...	Kauvant	do ...	1	...	1	...	...	...	...	...	...	...	...	...	...	...	...
		do ...	Kardani	do ...	...	...	...	...	...	...	...	...	...	...	...	...	...	...	...
		do ...	Karlevar	do ...	...	...	...	...	...	...	...	...	...	84	45	39	...	...	...
		do ...	Karve	do ...	...	...	...	...	...	...	...	...	...	...	...	...	...	...	...
		do ...	Katepar	do ...	...	...	...	6	2	4	...	...	...	...	...	...	...	...	...
		do ...	Kochu	do ...	...	...	...	...	...	...	...	...	...	...	...	...	...	...	...
		do ...	Kokalvar	do ...	...	...	...	...	...	...	...	...	...	15	12	3	...	...	...
		do ...	Kokuti	do ...	...	...	...	...	...	...	...	...	...	1	1	...	...	...	...
		do ...	Korgir	do ...	...	...	...	51	26	25	...	...	...	...	...	...	...	...	...
		do ...	Kotulvar	do ...	...	...	...	65	27	38	...	...	...	...	...	...	...	...	...
		do ...	Kuchi	do ...	...	...	...	...	...	...	...	...	...	5	3	2	...	...	...
		do ...	Lingayet	do ...	...	...	...	...	...	...	...	...	...	...	...	...	...	...	...
		do ...	Lovdnar	do ...	...	...	...	...	...	...	...	...	...	...	...	...	...	...	...
		do ...	Madana	do ...	...	...	...	...	...	...	...	...	...	...	...	...	...	...	...
		do ...	Mahasvas	do ...	...	...	...	8	3	5	...	...	...	...	...	...	...	...	...
		do ...	Maisri	do ...	...	...	...	...	...	...	...	...	...	...	...	...	...	...	...
		do ...	Mamadvar	do ...	...	...	...	16	6	10	...	...	...	...	...	...	...	...	...
		do ...	Margalvad	do ...	...	...	...	11	6	5	...	...	...	...	...	...	...	...	...
		do ...	Mirvar...	do ...	...	...	...	8	...	3	...	...	...	...	...	...	...	...	...
		do ...	Modgujrati	do ...	...	...	...	...	...	...	...	...	...	...	...	...	...	...	...
		do ...	Mogunia	do ...	...	...	...	...	...	...	...	...	...	...	...	...	...	...	...
		do ...	Molhar...	do ...	...	...	...	...	...	...	...	...	...	...	...	...	...	...	...
		do ...	Monevad	do ...	...	...	...	11	4	7	...	...	...	...	...	...	...	...	...
		do ...	Muratvan	do ...	...	...	...	...	...	...	...	...	...	...	...	...	...	...	...
		do ...	Neti	do ...	...	...	...	...	...	...	...	...	...	...	...	...	...	...	...
		do ...	Nakahat	do ...	...	...	...	...	...	...	...	...	...	...	...	...	...	...	...
		do ...	Padamvar	do ...	...	...	...	...	...	...	...	...	...	...	...	...	...	...	...
		do ...	Parakh...	do ...	...	...	...	...	...	...	...	...	...	...	...	...	...	...	...
		do ...	Parasvar	do ...	...	...	...	41	22	19	...	...	...	...	...	...	...	...	...
		do ...	Paravar	do ...	...	...	...	5	3	2	...	...	...	...	...	...	...	...	...
		do ...	Patekar	do ...	...	...	...	...	...	...	...	...	...	...	...	...	...	...	...
		do ...	Pechari	do ...	...	...	...	12	5	7	...	...	...	...	...	...	...	...	...
		do ...	Peshtevar	do ...	...	...	...	14	6	8	...	...	...	...	...	...	...	...	...
		do ...	Pianevar	do ...	...	...	...	8	2	1	...	...	...	...	...	...	...	...	...
		do ...	Pichchu	do ...	...	...	...	...	...	...	...	...	...	...	...	...	...	...	...
		do ...	Pimadvad	do ...	...	...	...	5	4	1	...	...	...	...	...	...	...	...	...
		do ...	Pimparvar	do ...	...	...	...	9	4	5	...	...	...	...	...	...	...	...	...

TABLE XVI.

Castes and Sub-divisions.—*Continued.*

Class.	Group.	Castes.	Sub-division of Castes.	Religion.	Sirpur Tandur. Total.	Sirpur Tandur. Males.	Sirpur Tandur. Females.	Gulbarga. Total.	Gulbarga. Males.	Gulbarga. Females.	Raichur. Total.	Raichur. Males.	Raichur. Females.	Lingasugur. Total.	Lingasugur. Males.	Lingasugur. Females.	Railways. Total.	Railways. Males.	Railways. Females.
					51	52	53	54	55	56	57	58	59	60	61	62	63	64	65
C	14 ...	Komti ...	Jovarpai	Hindu ...	...	...	...	...	...	...	...	...	...	...	...	...	...	...	...
		do ...	Jutipao	do ...	...	...	...	...	...	...	...	...	...	...	...	...	...	...	...
		do ...	Kachevar	do ...	...	...	...	...	...	...	...	...	...	...	...	...	...	...	...
		do ...	Kadavatar	do ...	...	...	...	...	...	...	...	...	...	...	...	...	...	...	...
		do ...	Kadhurti	do ...	...	...	...	...	...	...	...	...	...	...	...	...	...	...	...
		do ...	Kalakomti	do ...	...	...	...	...	...	...	...	...	...	...	...	...	...	...	...
		do ...	Kauvant	do ...	...	...	...	...	...	...	...	...	...	...	...	...	...	...	...
		do ...	Kardani	do ...	...	...	...	...	...	...	...	...	...	...	...	...	...	...	...
		do ...	Karlevar	do ...	...	...	...	...	...	...	...	...	...	...	...	...	...	...	...
		do ...	Karve	do ...	...	...	...	...	...	...	...	...	...	...	...	...	...	...	...
		do ...	Katepar	do ...	...	...	...	54	34	20	...	...	...	...	...	...	...	...	...
		do ...	Kochu	do ...	...	...	...	...	...	...	...	...	...	...	...	...	...	...	...
		do ...	Kokalvar	do ...	...	...	...	...	...	...	...	...	...	...	...	...	...	...	...
		do ...	Kokuti	do ...	...	...	...	...	...	...	...	...	...	...	...	...	...	...	...
		do ...	Korgir...	do ...	...	...	...	...	...	...	...	...	...	...	...	...	...	...	...
		do ...	Kotulvar	do ...	...	...	...	...	...	...	...	...	...	...	...	...	...	...	...
		do ...	Kuchi	do ...	...	...	...	...	...	...	...	...	...	...	...	...	...	...	...
		do ...	Lingayet	do ...	...	...	...	...	...	...	...	...	...	...	...	...	...	...	...
		do ...	Lovdnar	do ...	...	...	...	14	5	9	...	...	...	...	...	...	...	...	...
		do ...	Madana	do ...	...	...	...	...	...	...	...	...	...	...	...	...	...	...	...
		do ...	Mahasvas	do ...	...	...	...	...	...	...	4	3	1	...	...	...	...	...	...
		do ...	Maisri	do ...	...	...	...	...	...	...	...	...	...	...	...	...	...	...	...
		do ...	Mamadvar	do ...	...	...	...	...	...	...	...	...	...	...	...	...	...	...	...
		do ...	Margalvad	do ...	...	...	...	...	...	...	...	...	...	...	...	...	...	...	...
		do ...	Mirvar	do ...	...	...	...	...	...	...	...	...	...	...	...	...	...	...	...
		do ...	Modgujrati	do ...	...	...	...	...	...	...	...	...	...	...	...	...	...	...	...
		do ...	Mogunia	do ...	...	...	...	...	...	...	...	...	...	...	...	...	...	...	...
		do ...	Molhar...	do ...	...	...	...	...	...	...	...	...	...	...	...	...	...	...	...
		do ...	Monevad	do ...	...	...	...	...	...	...	...	...	...	...	...	...	...	...	...
		do ...	Muratvan	do ...	...	...	...	...	...	...	...	...	...	...	...	...	...	...	...
		do ...	Neti	do ...	...	...	...	...	...	...	...	...	...	...	...	...	...	...	...
		do ...	Nakahat	do ...	...	...	...	...	...	...	8	4	4	...	...	...	...	...	...
		do ...	Padamvar	do ...	...	...	...	...	...	...	...	...	...	...	...	...	...	...	...
		do ...	Parakh	do ...	...	...	...	...	...	...	...	...	...	...	...	...	...	...	...
		do ...	Parasvar	do ...	...	...	...	...	...	...	...	...	...	...	...	...	...	...	...
		do ...	Paravar	do ...	...	...	...	...	...	...	...	...	...	...	...	...	...	...	...
		do ...	Patekar	do ...	...	...	...	...	...	...	...	...	...	...	...	...	...	...	...
		do ...	Pechari	do ...	...	...	...	...	...	...	...	...	...	...	...	...	...	...	...
		do ...	Peshtevar	do ...	...	...	...	...	...	...	...	...	...	...	...	...	...	...	...
		do ...	Pianevar	do ...	...	...	...	...	...	...	...	...	...	...	...	...	...	...	...
		do ...	Pichchu	do ...	...	...	...	...	...	...	...	...	...	...	...	...	...	...	...
		do ...	Pimadvad	do ...	...	...	...	...	...	...	...	...	...	...	...	...	...	...	...
		do ...	Pimparvar	do ...	...	...	...	...	...	...	...	...	...	...	...	...	...	...	...

TABLE XVI.

Castes and Sub-divisions.—*Continued.*

Class.	Group.	Castes.	Sub-division of Castes.	Religion.	Total. Total.	Total. Males.	Total. Females.	Hyderabad. Total.	Hyderabad. Males.	Hyderabad. Females.	Atraf-i-Balda. Total.	Atraf-i-Balda. Males.	Atraf-i-Balda. Females.	Mahabubnagar. Total.	Mahabubnagar. Males.	Mahabubnagar. Females.	Nalgonda. Total.	Nalgonda. Males.	Nalgonda. Females.
1	2	3	4	5	6	7	8	9	10	11	12	13	14	15	16	17	18	19	20
C	14 ...	Komti ...	Pitgol	Hindu ...	1	1	...	...	...	...	...	...	...	...	...	...	...	...	...
		do ...	Puja	do ...	76	45	31	...	...	...	76	45	31	...	...	...	...	...	...
		do ...	Rajupa...	do ...	2	1	1	...	...	...	...	...	...	...	...	...	...	...	...
		do ...	Raspak	do ...	8	3	5	...	...	...	...	...	...	...	...	...	...	...	...
		do ...	Rudrakanthi	do ...	8	5	3	...	...	...	...	...	...	...	...	...	...	...	...
		do ...	Saraji	do ...	4	4	...	4	4	...	...	...	...	...	...	...	...	...	...
		do ...	Saramvar	do ...	7	3	4	...	...	...	...	...	...	...	...	...	...	...	...
		do ...	Satgulvar	do ...	8	2	6	...	...	...	...	...	...	...	...	...	...	...	...
		do ...	Soevar...	do ...	1	1	...	...	...	...	...	...	...	...	...	...	...	...	...
		do ...	Sojue	do ...	60	23	37	...	...	...	...	...	...	...	...	...	...	...	...
		do ...	Somasvar	do ...	8	4	4	...	...	...	...	...	...	...	...	...	...	...	...
		do ...	Somashetti	do ...	19	11	8	...	...	...	...	...	...	...	...	...	...	...	...
		do ...	Telang...	do ...	30	13	17	27	12	15	...	...	...	...	...	...	...	...	...
		do ...	Tilevari	do ...	23	9	14	...	...	...	...	...	...	...	...	...	...	...	...
		do ...	Trivar	do ...	2	2	...	...	...	...	...	...	...	...	...	...	...	...	...
		do ...	Vadukal	do ...	9	4	5	...	...	...	...	...	...	...	...	...	...	...	...
		do ...	Vagan...	do ...	17	7	10	...	...	...	...	...	...	...	...	...	...	...	...
		do ...	Vaghots	do ...	23	...	23	...	...	...	...	...	...	...	...	...	...	...	...
		do ...	Vahevar	do ...	5	3	2	...	...	...	...	...	...	...	...	...	...	...	...
		do ...	Vahit	do ...	7	4	3	...	...	...	...	...	...	...	...	...	...	...	...
		do ...	Vaisarga	do ...	109	31	78	...	...	...	...	...	...	...	...	...	...	...	...
		do ...	Vaishatvar	do ...	2	1	1	...	...	...	...	...	...	...	...	...	...	...	...
		do ...	Vakevar	do ...	72	37	35	...	...	...	...	...	...	...	...	...	...	...	...
		do ...	Varamvar	do ...	17	14	3	...	...	...	...	...	...	...	...	...	...	...	...
		do ...	Varde	do ...	5	3	2	...	...	...	5	3	2	...	...	...	...	...	...
		do ...	Vasnaw	do ...	27	23	4	...	...	...	...	...	...	...	...	...	...	...	...
		do ...	Vatil	do ...	6	6	...	...	...	...	...	...	...	...	...	...	...	...	...
		do ...	Veshamma	do ...	22	11	11	22	11	11	...	...	...	...	...	...	...	...	...
		do ...	Virasevad	do ...	1	...	1	...	...	...	...	...	...	...	...	...	...	...	...
		do ...	Yaguvar	do ...	5	4	1	...	...	...	...	...	...	...	...	...	...	...	...
		do ...	Yallavar	do ...	16	8	8	...	...	...	...	...	...	...	...	...	...	...	...
		do ...	Yalgavia	do ...	12	10	2	12	10	2	...	...	...	...	...	...	...	...	...
		do ...	Yalni	do ...	2	1	1	...	...	...	...	...	...	...	...	...	...	...	...
		do ...	Yanna...	do ...	1,082	540	542	...	...	...	...	...	...	...	...	...	...	...	...
		do ...	Yapakvar	do ...	15	7	8	...	...	...	...	...	...	...	...	...	...	...	...
		do ...	Yastasri	do ...	25	12	13	...	...	...	...	...	...	...	...	...	...	...	...
		do ...	Yeginavar	do ...	124,059	63,053	61,006	...	...	...	10,679	5,346	5,333	16,982	8,621	8,361	15,178	7,728	7,455
		do ...	Yeralshakh	do ...	2	2	...	...	...	...	...	...	...	...	...	...	...	...	...
		do ...	Yesakvar	do ...	61	33	28	...	...	...	...	...	...	...	...	...	...	...	...
		do ...	Yesan	do ...	3	3	...	...	...	...	...	...	...	...	...	...	...	...	...
		do ...	Unspecified	do ...	81,317	41,261	40,056	8,909	4,828	4,081	2,253	1,151	1,102	2,819	1,466	1,353	6,824	8,505	8,319
			Total......		212,865	108,111	104,754	9,947	5,875	4,572	13,159	6,619	6,540	19,906	10,148	9,763	23,184	11,825	11,359

TABLE XVI.

Castes and Sub-divisions.—*Continued.*

Class.	Group.	Castes.	Sub-division of Castes.	Religion.	Warangal. Total.	Warangal. Males.	Warangal. Females.	Elgandal. Total.	Elgandal. Males.	Elgandal. Females.	Indur. Total.	Indur. Males.	Indur. Females.	Medak. Total.	Medak. Males.	Medak. Females.	Aurangabad. Total.	Aurangabad. Males.	Aurangabad. Females.
					21	22	23	24	25	26	27	28	29	30	31	32	33	34	35
C	14 ...	Komti ...	Pitgol ...	Hindu ...	...	...	...	...	...	...	...	...	...	...	...	...	...	...	...
		do ...	Puja ...	do ...	...	...	...	...	...	...	...	...	...	...	...	...	...	...	...
		do ...	Rajupa...	do ...	...	...	...	...	...	...	2	1	1	...	...	...	...	...	...
		do ...	Raspak...	do ...	...	...	...	...	...	...	8	8	5	...	...	...	...	...	...
		do ...	Rudrakanthi ...	do ...	...	...	...	...	...	...	...	...	...	...	...	...	...	...	...
		do ...	Saraji ...	do ...	...	...	...	...	...	...	...	...	...	...	...	...	...	...	...
		do ...	Saramvar ...	do ...	...	...	...	...	...	...	...	...	...	...	...	...	...	...	...
		do ...	Satgulvar ...	do ...	...	...	...	...	...	...	...	...	...	...	...	...	...	...	...
		do ...	Soevar...	do ...	...	...	...	...	...	...	...	...	...	...	...	...	...	...	...
		do ...	Sajue ...	do ...	...	...	...	...	...	...	60	28	37	...	...	...	...	...	...
		do ...	Somasvar ...	do ...	...	...	...	...	...	...	...	...	...	...	...	...	...	...	...
		do ...	Somshetti ...	do ...	...	...	...	...	...	...	...	...	...	...	...	...	...	...	...
		do ...	Telang...	do ...	...	...	...	...	...	...	...	...	...	...	...	...	...	...	...
		do ...	Tilevari ...	do ...	...	...	...	...	...	...	...	...	...	...	...	...	1	1	...
		do ...	Trivar ...	do ...	...	...	...	...	...	...	...	...	...	...	...	...	2	2	...
		do ...	Vadukal ...	do ...	...	...	...	...	...	...	...	...	...	...	...	...	...	...	...
		do ...	Vagan ...	do ...	...	...	...	...	...	...	17	7	10	...	...	...	...	...	...
		do ...	Vaghote ...	do ...	...	...	...	...	...	...	...	...	...	...	...	...	...	...	...
		do ...	Vahevar ...	do ...	...	...	...	...	...	...	...	...	...	...	...	...	...	...	...
		do ...	Vahit ...	do ...	...	...	...	...	...	...	...	...	...	...	...	...	...	...	...
		do ...	Vaisarga ...	do ...	...	...	...	...	...	...	...	...	...	...	...	...	...	...	...
		do ...	Vaishatvar ...	do ...	...	...	...	...	...	...	...	...	...	...	...	...	...	...	...
		do ...	Vakevar ...	do ...	...	...	...	...	...	...	...	...	...	...	...	...	...	...	...
		do ...	Varamvar ...	do ...	...	...	...	...	...	...	...	...	...	...	...	...	...	...	...
		do ...	Varde ...	do ...	...	...	...	...	...	...	...	...	...	...	...	...	...	...	...
		do ...	Vasmaw ...	do ...	...	...	...	...	...	...	...	...	...	...	...	...	...	...	...
		do ...	Vatil ...	do ...	...	...	...	...	...	...	...	...	...	...	...	...	...	...	...
		do ...	Veshamma ...	do ...	...	...	...	...	...	...	...	...	...	...	...	...	...	...	...
		do ...	Virasevad ...	do ...	...	...	...	...	...	...	...	...	...	...	...	...	...	...	...
		do ...	Yaguvar ...	do ...	...	...	...	...	...	...	...	...	...	...	...	...	...	...	...
		do ...	Yallavar ...	do ...	...	...	...	...	...	...	...	...	...	...	...	...	...	...	...
		do ...	Yalgavia ...	do ...	...	...	...	...	...	...	...	...	...	...	...	...	...	...	...
		do ...	Yalni ...	do ...	...	...	...	...	...	...	...	...	...	...	...	...	2	1	1
		do ...	Yanna...	do ...	...	...	...	...	...	...	...	...	...	...	...	...	...	...	...
		do ...	Yapakvar ...	do ...	...	...	...	...	...	...	...	...	...	...	...	...	...	...	...
		do ...	Yastasri ...	do ...	...	...	...	...	...	...	25	12	13	...	...	...	...	...	...
		do ...	Yeginavar ...	do ...	22,241	11,338	10,908	83,786	17,809	16,427	...	...	...	12,492	6,291	6,201	...	...	...
		do ...	Yeralshakh ...	do ...	...	...	...	...	...	...	...	...	...	...	...	...	...	...	...
		do ...	Yesakvar ...	do ...	...	...	...	...	...	...	...	...	...	...	...	...	...	...	...
		do ...	Yesan ...	do ...	...	...	...	...	...	...	...	...	...	...	...	...	...	...	...
		do ...	Unspecified ...	do ...	6,416	3,321	8,095	2,551	1,339	1,212	15,880	7,883	7,997	2,186	1,122	1,064	576	287	339
			Total......		29,161	14,912	14,249	86,886	18,957	17,929	16,027	7,948	8,079	14,704	7,426	7,278	1,476	698	778

TABLE XVI.

Castes and Sub-divisions.—*Continued.*

Class.	Group.	Castes.	Sub-division of Castes.	Religion.	Birh. Total.	Birh. Males.	Birh. Females.	Nander. Total.	Nander. Males.	Nander. Females.	Naldrug. Total.	Naldrug. Males.	Naldrug. Females.	Bidar. Total.	Bidar. Males.	Bidar. Females.	Parbhani. Total.	Parbhani. Males.	Parbhani. Females.
					36	37	38	39	40	41	42	43	44	45	46	47	48	49	50
C	14 ...	Komti ...	Pitgol ...	Hindu ...	...	...	...	...	...	...	1	1	...	...	...	...	...	...	...
		do ...	Puja ...	do ...	...	...	...	...	...	...	...	...	...	...	...	...	...	...	...
		do ...	Rajupa	do ...	...	...	...	...	...	...	...	...	...	...	...	...	...	...	...
		do ...	Raspak	do ...	...	...	...	...	...	...	...	...	...	...	...	...	...	...	...
		do ...	Rudrakanthi ...	do ...	...	...	...	...	...	...	...	...	...	...	...	...	8	5	3
		do ...	Saraji ...	do ...	...	...	...	...	...	...	...	...	...	...	...	...	...	...	...
		do ...	Saramvar	do ...	...	...	...	7	3	4	...	...	...	...	...	...	...	...	...
		do ...	Sa'gulvar	do ...	...	...	...	8	2	6	...	...	...	...	...	...	...	...	...
		do ...	Soevar...	do ...	...	...	...	1	1	...	...	...	...	...	...	...	...	...	...
		do ...	Sojue ...	do ...	...	...	...	...	...	...	...	...	...	...	...	...	...	...	...
		do ...	Somasvar	do ...	...	...	...	8	4	4	...	...	...	...	...	...	...	...	...
		do ...	Somashetti	do ...	...	...	...	...	...	...	...	...	...	...	...	...	...	...	...
		do ...	Telang	do ...	...	...	...	...	...	...	...	...	...	...	...	...	...	...	...
		do ...	Tilevari	do ...	...	...	...	22	8	14	...	...	...	...	...	...	...	...	...
		do ...	Trivar	do ...	...	...	...	...	...	...	...	...	...	...	...	...	...	...	...
		do ...	Vadukal	do ...	...	...	...	9	4	5	...	...	...	...	...	...	...	...	...
		do ...	Vagan ...	do ...	...	...	...	...	...	...	...	...	...	...	...	...	...	...	...
		do ...	Vaghote	do ...	28	...	28	...	...	...	...	...	...	...	...	...	...	...	...
		do ...	Vahevar	do ...	...	...	...	5	3	2	...	...	...	...	...	...	...	...	...
		do ...	Vahit ...	do ...	...	...	...	...	...	...	...	...	...	...	...	...	7	4	3
		do ...	Vaisarga	do ...	109	31	78	...	...	...	...	...	...	...	...	...	...	...	...
		do ...	Vaishatvar	do ...	...	...	...	...	...	...	...	...	...	2	1	1	...	...	...
		do ...	Vakevar	do ...	...	...	...	72	37	35	...	...	...	...	...	...	...	...	...
		do ...	Varamvar	do ...	...	...	...	17	14	3	...	...	...	...	...	...	...	...	...
		do ...	Varde...	do ...	...	...	...	...	...	...	...	...	...	...	...	...	...	...	...
		do ...	Vamaw	do ...	...	...	...	27	23	4	...	...	...	...	...	...	...	...	...
		do ...	Vatil...	do ...	...	...	...	...	...	...	...	...	...	...	...	...	...	...	...
		do ...	Veshamma	do ...	...	...	...	...	...	...	...	...	...	...	...	...	...	...	...
		do ...	Virasevad	do ...	...	...	...	1	...	1	...	...	...	...	...	...	...	...	...
		do ...	Yagnvar	do ...	...	...	...	5	4	1	...	...	...	...	...	...	...	...	...
		do ...	Yallavar	do ...	...	...	...	16	8	8	...	...	...	...	...	...	...	...	...
		do ...	Yallgavia	do ...	...	...	...	...	...	...	...	...	...	...	...	...	...	...	...
		do ...	Yalni ...	do ...	...	...	...	...	...	...	...	...	...	...	...	...	...	...	...
		do ...	Yanna ...	do ...	...	...	...	...	...	...	...	...	...	...	...	...	...	...	...
		do ...	Yapakwar	do ...	...	...	...	...	...	...	...	...	...	15	7	8	...	...	...
		do ...	Yastaeri	do ...	...	...	...	...	...	...	...	...	...	...	...	...	...	...	...
		do ...	Yeginavar	do ...	...	...	...	1,777	847	980	12	9	3	4,678	2,377	2,301	33	24	9
		do ...	Yeralshakh	do ...	...	...	...	...	...	...	...	...	...	2	2	...	...	...	...
		do ...	Yesakvar	do ...	...	...	...	61	33	28	...	...	...	...	...	...	...	...	...
		do ...	Yesan ...	do ...	...	...	...	...	...	...	...	...	...	3	3	...	...	...	...
		do ...	Unspecified ...	do ...	1,087	550	537	9,902	5,018	4,889	493	238	255	5,454	2,777	2,677	3,205	1,434	1,771
			Total......		1,246	603	643	12,851	6,449	6,402	529	257	272	10,287	5,242	5,045	3,267	1,471	1,796

TABLE XVI.

Castes and Sub-divisions.—*Continued.*

Class.	Group.	Castes.	Sub-division of Castes.	Religion.	Sirpur Tandur.			Gulbarga.			Raichur.			Lingasugur.			Railways.		
					Total.	Males.	Females.	Total.	Males.	Females.	Total.	Males.	Females.	Total.	Males.	Females.	Total.	Males.	Females.
					51	52	53	54	55	56	57	58	59	60	61	62	63	64	65
C	14 ...	Komti ...	Pitgol ...	Hindu ...	...	...	...	...	...	...	...	...	...	...	...	...	...	...	...
		do ...	Puja ...	do ...	...	...	...	...	...	...	...	...	...	...	...	...	...	...	...
		do ...	Ra.ui a	do ...	...	...	...	...	...	...	...	...	...	...	...	...	...	...	...
		do ...	Raspak	do ...	...	...	...	...	...	...	...	...	...	...	...	...	...	...	...
		do ...	Rudrakanthi ...	do ...	...	...	...	...	...	...	...	...	...	...	...	...	...	...	...
		do ...	Saraji ...	do ...	...	...	...	...	...	...	...	...	...	...	...	...	...	...	...
		do ...	Saramvar	do ...	...	...	...	...	...	...	...	...	...	...	...	...	...	...	...
		do ...	Sitgu var	do ...	...	...	...	...	...	...	...	...	...	...	...	...	...	...	...
		do ...	So var	do ...	...	...	...	...	...	...	...	...	...	...	...	...	...	...	...
		do ...	Sojne ...	do ...	...	...	...	...	...	...	...	...	...	...	...	...	...	...	...
		do ...	Somasvar	do ...	...	...	...	...	...	...	...	...	...	...	...	...	...	...	...
		do ...	Somasbetti	do ...	...	...	...	19	11	8	...	...	...	...	...	...	...	...	...
		do ...	Telang	do ...	...	...	...	3	1	2	...	...	...	...	...	...	...	...	...
		do ...	Televari	do ...	...	...	...	...	...	...	...	...	...	...	...	...	...	...	...
		do ...	Trivar	do ...	...	...	...	...	...	...	...	...	...	...	...	...	...	...	...
		do ...	Vadukal	do ...	...	...	...	...	...	...	...	...	...	...	...	...	...	...	...
		do ...	Vagan...	do ...	...	...	...	...	...	...	...	...	...	...	...	...	...	...	...
		do ...	Vaghote	do ...	...	...	...	...	...	...	...	...	...	...	...	...	...	...	...
		do ...	Vahevar	do ...	...	...	...	...	...	...	...	...	...	...	...	...	...	...	...
		do ...	Vahit ...	do ...	...	...	...	...	...	...	...	...	...	...	...	...	...	...	...
		do ...	Vaisarga	do ...	...	...	...	...	...	...	...	...	...	...	...	...	...	...	...
		do ...	Vaishatvar	do ...	...	...	...	...	...	...	...	...	...	...	...	...	...	...	...
		do ...	Vakevar	do ...	...	...	...	...	...	...	...	...	...	...	...	...	...	...	...
		do ...	Varamvar	do ...	...	...	...	...	...	...	...	...	...	...	...	...	...	...	...
		do ...	Vaide ...	do ...	...	...	...	...	...	...	...	...	...	...	...	...	...	...	...
		do ...	Va..aw	do ...	...	...	...	...	...	...	...	...	...	...	...	...	...	...	...
		do ...	Vatil ...	do ...	6	6	...	...	...	...	...	...	...	...	...	...	...	...	...
		do ...	Vesamma	do ...	...	...	...	...	...	...	...	...	...	...	...	...	...	...	...
		do ...	Virasevad	do ...	...	...	...	...	...	...	...	...	...	...	...	...	...	...	...
		do ...	Yaguvar	do ...	...	...	...	...	...	...	...	...	...	...	...	...	...	...	...
		do ...	Yallavar	do ...	...	...	...	...	...	...	...	...	...	...	...	...	...	...	...
		do ...	Yalgavia	do ...	...	...	...	...	...	...	...	...	...	...	...	...	...	...	...
		do ...	Yalni ...	do ...	...	...	...	...	...	...	...	...	...	...	...	...	...	...	...
		do ...	Yanna...	do ...	...	...	...	...	...	...	5	2	3	1,077	538	539	...	...	...
		do ...	Yapakvar	do ...	...	...	...	...	...	...	...	...	...	...	...	...	...	...	...
		do ...	Ya.tasri	do ...	...	...	...	...	...	...	...	...	...	...	...	...	...	...	...
		do ...	Yeginavar	do ...	2,012	960	1,052	1,765	933	832	2,466	1,274	1,192	8	6	2	...	...	...
		do ...	Yeralshakh	do ...	...	...	...	...	...	...	...	...	...	...	...	...	...	...	...
		do ...	Ye-akvar	do ...	...	...	...	...	...	...	...	...	...	...	...	...	...	...	...
		do ...	Yesau ...	do ...	...	...	...	...	...	...	...	...	...	...	...	...	...	...	...
		do ...	Unspecified ...	do ...	2,252	1,055	1,197	2,065	1,009	1,056	5,225	2,637	2,588	3,201	1,681	1,520	19	15	4
			Total.....		4,270	2,021	2,249	3,920	1,993	1,927	7,740	3,932	3,808	4,286	2,225	2,061	19	15	4

TABLE XVI.

Castes and Sub-divisions.—*Continued.*

Class.	Group.	Castes.	Sub-division of Castes.	Religion.	Total.			Hyderabad.			Atraf-i-Balda.			Mahabubnagar.			Nalgonda.		
					Total.	Males.	Females.	Total.	Males.	Females.	Total.	Males.	Females.	Total.	Males.	Females.	Total.	Males.	Females.
1	2	3	4	5	6	7	8	9	10	11	12	13	14	15	16	17	18	19	20
C	14 ...	Vani ...	Adi ...	Hindu ...	4,299	2,192	2,107	...	...	...	...	...	...	...	...	...	...	...	...
		do ...	Agarval ...	do ...	1,479	920	559	856	420	236	...	...	...	...	...	...	...	...	...
		do ...	Aghari ...	do ...	7	5	2	...	...	...	...	...	...	...	...	...	...	...	...
		do ...	Agea ...	do ...	7	4	3	7	4	3	...	...	...	...	...	...	...	...	...
		do ...	Andbalki ...	do ...	205	100	105	...	...	...	...	...	...	...	...	...	...	...	...
		do ...	Balkevar ...	do ...	7	3	4	...	...	...	...	...	...	...	...	...	...	...	...
		do ...	Bamlachinivar	do ...	7	3	4	...	...	...	...	...	...	...	...	...	...	...	...
		do ...	Baturale ...	do ...	3	3	...	...	...	...	...	...	...	...	...	...	...	...	...
		do ...	Bejabargi ...	do ...	10	7	3	10	7	3	...	...	...	...	...	...	...	...	...
		do ...	Bhadao ...	do ...	25	...	25	...	...	...	...	...	...	...	...	...	...	...	...
		do ...	Bhimashankari ...	do ...	109	30	79	...	...	...	...	...	...	...	...	...	...	...	...
		do ...	Bilenki ...	do ...	17	10	7	...	...	...	...	...	...	...	...	...	...	...	...
		do ...	Biruhmashetti ...	do ...	8	...	8	...	...	...	...	...	...	...	...	...	...	...	...
		do ...	Bondu ...	do ...	15	7	8	15	7	8	...	...	...	...	...	...	...	...	...
		do ...	Chad ...	do ...	56	36	20	...	...	...	...	...	...	...	...	...	...	...	...
		do ...	Chaikri ...	do ...	6	3	3	...	...	...	...	...	...	...	...	...	...	...	...
		do ...	Ghatur ...	do ...	30	17	13	30	17	13	...	...	...	...	...	...	...	...	...
		do ...	Cheti ...	do ...	10	10	...	10	10	...	...	...	...	...	...	...	...	...	...
		do ...	Chilvant ...	do ...	18,429	9,455	8,974	...	...	...	...	...	...	...	...	...	...	...	...
		do ...	Chilvar ...	do ...	22	13	9	...	...	...	...	...	...	...	...	...	...	...	...
		do ...	Desgans ...	do ...	27	12	15	...	...	...	...	...	...	...	...	...	...	...	...
		do ...	Dhaba ...	do ...	17	7	10	...	...	...	...	...	...	...	...	...	...	...	...
		do ...	Dhase ...	do ...	2	1	1	...	...	...	...	...	...	...	...	...	...	...	...
		do ...	Diksat ...	do ...	15	...	15	...	...	...	...	...	...	...	...	...	...	...	...
		do ...	Dikshbadki ...	do ...	2,245	1,040	1,205	...	...	...	...	...	...	...	...	...	...	...	...
		do ...	Dikshparetan ...	do ...	48	25	18	...	...	...	...	...	...	...	...	...	...	...	...
		do ...	Dikshvant ...	do ...	158,526	80,651	77,875	...	...	...	174	86	88	...	...	...	...	...	...
		do ...	Govardan ...	do ...	11	7	4	...	...	...	...	...	...	...	...	...	...	...	...
		do ...	Govhar ...	do ...	11	...	11	...	...	...	...	...	...	...	...	...	...	...	...
		do ...	Gujrati ...	do ...	3	1	2	3	1	2	...	...	...	...	...	...	...	...	...
		do ...	Gurastulu ...	do ...	704	362	342	...	...	...	63	34	29	511	254	257	15	7	8
		do ...	Gurval ...	do ...	2	...	2	...	...	...	...	...	...	...	...	...	...	...	...
		do ...	Gululbansi ...	do ...	3	3	...	3	3	...	...	...	...	...	...	...	...	...	...
		do ...	Hanjan ...	do ...	4	3	1	...	...	...	...	...	...	...	...	...	...	...	...
		do ...	Hatvan ...	do ...	3	...	3	...	...	...	...	...	...	...	...	...	...	...	...
		do ...	Huper ...	do ...	51	20	31	...	...	...	...	...	...	...	...	...	...	...	...
		do ...	Jangam ...	do ...	1,013	599	414	...	...	...	...	...	...	...	...	...	...	...	...
		do ...	Janu ...	do ...	4	...	4	...	...	...	...	...	...	...	...	...	...	...	...
		do ...	Jasval ...	do ...	48	24	24	...	...	...	...	...	...	...	...	...	...	...	...
		do ...	Jathvani ...	do ...	49	30	19	7	4	3	...	...	...	...	...	...	...	...	...

TABLE XVI.

Castes and Sub-divisions.—*Continued.*

Class.	Group.	Castes.	Sub-division of Castes.	Religion.	Warangal. Total.	Warangal. Males.	Warangal. Females.	Elgandal. Total.	Elgandal. Males.	Elgandal. Females.	Indur. Total.	Indur. Males.	Indur. Females.	Medak. Total.	Medak. Males.	Medak. Females.	Aurangabad. Total.	Aurangabad. Males.	Aurangabad. Females.
					21	22	23	24	25	26	27	28	29	30	31	32	33	34	35
C	14 ...	Vâni ...	Adi	Hindu ...	...	...	...	...	...	...	...	...	...	...	...	...	...	...	...
		do ...	Agarvál	do ...	5	2	3	...	...	...	7	5	2	...	...	...	70	40	30
		do ...	Akhati	do ...	...	...	...	...	...	...	...	...	...	...	...	...	7	5	2
		do ...	Agêa	do ...	...	...	...	...	...	...	...	...	...	...	...	...	...	...	...
		do ...	Andbâdki	do ...	...	...	...	...	...	...	...	...	...	...	...	...	...	...	...
		do ...	Balkevar	do ...	...	...	...	...	...	...	...	...	...	...	...	...	...	...	...
		do ...	Bamlachinivar	do ...	...	...	...	...	...	...	...	...	...	...	...	...	...	...	...
		do ...	Baturâte	do ...	...	...	...	...	...	...	...	...	...	...	...	...	...	...	...
		do ...	Bejabargi	do ...	...	...	...	...	...	...	...	...	...	...	...	...	...	...	...
		do ...	Bhadâo...	do ...	...	...	...	...	...	...	...	...	...	...	...	...	...	...	...
		do ...	Bhasamdhani	do ...	...	...	...	...	...	...	98	24	74	...	...	...	...	...	...
		do ...	Bilenal	do ...	...	...	...	...	...	...	...	...	...	...	...	...	17	10	7
		do ...	Birhamshetti ...	do ...	...	...	...	...	...	...	...	...	...	...	...	...	...	...	...
		do ...	Bondus	do ...	...	...	...	...	...	...	...	...	...	...	...	...	...	...	...
		do ...	Chad	do ...	...	...	...	...	...	...	...	...	...	...	...	...	...	...	...
		do ...	Chaikri... ...	do ...	...	...	...	...	...	...	...	...	...	...	...	...	...	...	...
		do ...	Châtur... ...	do ...	...	...	...	...	...	...	...	...	...	...	...	...	...	...	...
		do ...	Cheri	do ...	...	...	...	...	...	...	...	...	...	...	...	...	...	...	...
		do ...	Chilvant ...	do ...	...	...	...	...	...	...	168	102	66	...	...	...	...	...	...
		do ...	Chilvar... ...	do ...	...	...	...	...	...	...	...	...	...	...	...	...	...	...	...
		do ...	Deogana ...	do ...	...	...	...	...	...	...	...	...	...	...	...	...	27	12	15
		do ...	Dhabu	do ...	...	...	...	...	...	...	...	...	...	...	...	...	...	...	...
		do ...	Dhase	do ...	...	...	...	...	...	...	...	...	...	...	...	...	...	...	...
		do ...	Diksat	do ...	...	...	...	...	...	...	...	...	...	...	...	...	...	...	...
		do ...	Dikshbadki ...	do ...	...	...	...	...	...	...	...	...	...	...	...	...	...	...	...
		do ...	Dikshpaneban ...	do ...	...	...	...	...	...	...	...	...	...	...	...	...	...	...	...
		do ...	Dikshvant ...	do ...	...	...	...	...	...	...	4,785	2,368	2,367	37	21	16	927	451	476
		do ...	Govardan ...	do ...	...	...	...	...	...	...	...	...	...	...	...	...	11	7	4
		do ...	Govhar... ...	do ...	...	...	...	...	...	...	...	...	...	...	...	...	...	...	...
		do ...	Gujerati ...	do ...	...	...	...	...	...	...	...	...	...	...	...	...	...	...	...
		do ...	Gurastuln ...	do ...	...	...	...	17	11	6	...	...	...	98	56	42	...	...	...
		do ...	Gursal	do ...	...	...	...	...	...	...	2	...	2	...	...	...	...	...	...
		do ...	Gululbansi ...	do ...	...	...	...	...	...	...	...	...	...	...	...	...	...	...	...
		do ...	Hanjan... ...	do ...	...	...	...	...	...	...	...	...	...	...	...	...	...	...	...
		do ...	Hatvan ...	do ...	...	...	...	...	...	...	...	...	...	...	...	...	...	...	...
		do ...	Huper	do ...	...	...	...	...	...	...	...	...	...	...	...	...	...	...	...
		do ...	Jangam ...	do ...	...	...	...	...	...	...	...	...	...	...	...	...	61	37	24
		do ...	Janu	do ...	...	...	...	...	...	...	...	...	...	...	...	...	...	...	...
		do ...	Jasval	do ...	...	...	...	...	...	...	...	...	...	...	...	...	...	...	...
		do ...	Jathvani ...	do ...	...	...	...	...	...	...	...	...	...	...	...	...	...	...	...

TABLE XVI.
Castes and Sub-divisions.

TABLE XVI.

Castes and Sub-divisions.—*Continued.*

Class.	Group.	Castes.	Sub-division of Castes.	Religion.	Birh. Total.	Birh. Males.	Birh. Females.	Nander. Total.	Nander. Males.	Nander. Females.	Naldrug. Total.	Naldrug. Males.	Naldrug. Females.	Bidar. Total.	Bidar. Males.	Bidar. Females.	Parbhani. Total.	Parbhani. Males.	Parbhani. Females.
					36	37	38	39	40	41	42	43	44	45	46	47	48	49	50
C	14 ...	Vani ...	Adi	Hindu ...	...	...	...	...	...	...	133	71	62	...	...	...	...	...	...
		do ...	Agarval	do ...	48	24	24	59	32	27	79	44	35	7	5	2	514	329	185
		do ...	Aghati	do ...	...	...	...	...	...	...	...	...	...	...	...	...	...	...	...
		do ...	Agra	do ...	...	...	...	...	...	...	...	...	...	...	...	...	...	...	...
		do ...	Andhadki	do ...	...	...	...	...	...	...	...	...	...	...	...	...	...	...	...
		do ...	Balkivar	do ...	...	...	...	...	...	...	...	...	...	...	...	...	...	...	...
		do ...	Bambchinivar ...	do ...	...	...	...	7	3	4	...	...	...	...	...	...	...	...	...
		do ...	Baturate	do ...	3	3	...	...	...	...	...	...	...	...	...	...	...	...	...
		do ...	Bejahargi	do ...	...	...	...	...	...	...	...	...	...	...	...	...	...	...	...
		do ...	Bhadao...	do ...	...	...	...	25	...	25	...	...	...	...	...	...	...	...	...
		do ...	Bhasamdhani	do ...	...	...	...	...	...	...	...	...	...	11	6	5	...	...	...
		do ...	Bilnai	do ...	...	...	...	...	...	...	...	...	...	...	...	...	...	...	...
		do ...	Birhamshetti	do ...	...	...	...	...	...	...	...	...	...	8	...	8	...	...	...
		do ...	Bondus...	do ...	...	...	...	...	...	...	...	...	...	...	...	...	...	...	...
		do ...	Chad	do ...	...	...	...	56	36	20	...	...	...	...	...	...	...	...	...
		do ...	Chaikri...	do ...	...	...	...	6	3	3	...	...	...	...	...	...	...	...	...
		do ...	Chatur...	do ...	...	...	...	...	...	...	...	...	...	...	...	...	...	...	...
		do ...	Cheri	do ...	...	...	...	...	...	...	...	...	...	...	...	...	...	...	...
		do ...	Chilvant	do ...	891	484	407	1,645	795	850	1,242	622	620	8,856	4,669	4,187	1,678	812	866
		do ...	Chilvar	do ...	...	...	...	22	13	9	...	...	...	...	...	...	...	...	...
		do ...	Deogana	do ...	...	...	...	...	...	...	...	...	...	...	...	...	...	...	...
		do ...	Dhabu	do ...	...	...	...	17	7	10	...	...	...	...	...	...	...	...	...
		do ...	Dhase	do ...	2	1	1	...	...	...	...	...	...	...	...	...	...	...	...
		do ...	Dikaat	do ...	...	...	...	15	...	15	...	...	...	...	...	...	...	...	...
		do ...	Dikshbadki	do ...	...	...	...	...	...	...	24	24	...	6	3	3	...	...	...
		do ...	Dikshpaneban	do ...	...	...	...	...	...	...	...	...	...	...	...	...	...	...	...
		do ...	Dikshvant	do ...	3,950	2,048	1,902	21,387	10,857	10,530	13,649	7,104	6,545	93,162	47,037	46,125	6,681	3,379	3,302
		do ...	Govardan	do ...	...	...	...	...	...	...	...	...	...	...	...	...	...	...	...
		do ...	Govhar	do ...	11	...	11	...	...	...	...	...	...	...	...	...	...	...	...
		do ...	Gujrati...	do ...	...	...	...	...	...	...	...	...	...	...	...	...	...	...	...
		do ...	Gurastulu	do ...	...	...	...	...	...	...	...	...	...	...	...	...	...	...	...
		do ...	Gurval	do ...	...	...	...	...	...	...	...	...	...	...	...	...	...	...	...
		do ...	Gulalbansi	do ...	...	...	...	...	...	...	...	...	...	...	...	...	...	...	...
		do ...	Hanjan...	do ...	...	...	...	...	...	...	...	...	...	...	...	...	...	...	...
		do ...	Hatvau	do ...	3	...	3	...	...	...	...	...	...	...	...	...	...	...	...
		do ...	Huper	do ...	...	...	...	...	...	...	...	...	...	...	...	...	...	...	...
		do ..	Jangam	do ...	23	9	14	...	...	...	...	...	...	...	...	...	156	84	72
		do ...	Janu	do ...	...	...	...	4	...	4	...	...	...	...	...	...	...	...	...
		do ...	Jasval	do ...	...	...	...	...	...	...	...	...	...	...	...	...	48	24	24
		do ...	Jathvani	do ...	...	...	...	...	...	...	...	...	...	...	...	...	...	...	...

TABLE XVI.

Castes and Sub-divisions.—*Continued.*

Class.	Group.	Castes.	Sub-division of Castes.	Religion.	Sirpur Tandur.			Gulbarga.			Raichur.			Lingsugur.			Railways.		
					Total.	Males.	Females.	Total.	Males.	Females.	Total.	Males.	Females.	Total.	Males.	Females.	Total.	Males.	Females.
					51	52	53	54	55	56	57	58	59	60	61	62	63	64	65
C	14 ...	Vani ...	Adi	Hindu ...	...	...	...	4,166	2,121	2,045	...	...	...	...	...	...	...	...	...
		do ...	Agarval	do ...	32	17	15	1	1	...	1	1	...	...	...	...	...	...	...
		do ...	Aghati	do ...	...	...	...	...	...	...	...	...	...	...	...	...	...	...	...
		do ...	Ages	do ...	...	...	...	...	...	...	...	...	...	...	...	...	...	...	...
		do ...	Andbadli	do ...	...	...	...	205	100	105	...	...	...	...	...	...	...	...	...
		do ...	Balkevar	do ...	...	...	...	7	8	4	...	...	...	...	...	...	...	...	...
		do ...	Bamlachinivar... ...	do ...	...	...	...	...	...	...	...	...	...	...	...	...	...	...	...
		do ...	Baturate	do ...	...	...	...	...	...	...	...	...	...	...	...	...	...	...	...
		do ...	Bejabargi	do ...	...	...	...	...	...	...	...	...	...	...	...	...	...	...	...
		do ...	Bhadao...	do ...	...	...	...	...	...	...	...	...	...	...	...	...	...	...	...
		do ...	Bhasandhani	do ...	...	...	...	...	...	...	...	...	...	...	...	...	...	...	...
		do ...	Bilenai...	do ...	...	...	...	...	...	...	...	...	...	...	...	...	...	...	...
		do ...	Birhamshetti	do ...	...	...	...	...	...	...	...	...	...	...	...	...	...	...	...
		do ...	Bondus...	do ...	...	...	...	...	...	...	...	...	...	...	...	...	...	...	...
		do ...	Chad	do ...	...	...	...	...	...	...	...	...	...	...	...	...	...	...	...
		do ...	Chaikri...	do ...	...	...	...	...	...	...	...	...	...	...	...	...	...	...	...
		do ...	Chatur...	do ...	...	...	...	...	...	...	...	...	...	...	...	...	...	...	...
		do ...	Cheri	do ...	...	...	...	...	...	...	...	...	...	...	...	...	...	...	...
		do ...	Chilvant	do ...	38	21	17	3,911	1,950	1,961	...	...	...	...	...	...	...	...	...
		do ...	Chilvar	do ...	...	...	...	...	...	...	...	...	...	...	...	...	...	...	...
		do ...	Deogana	do ...	...	...	...	...	...	...	...	...	...	...	...	...	...	...	...
		do ...	Dhabu	do ...	...	...	...	...	...	...	...	...	...	...	...	...	...	...	...
		do ...	Dhase	do ...	...	...	...	...	...	...	...	...	...	...	...	...	...	...	...
		do ...	Diksat	do ...	...	...	...	...	...	...	...	...	...	...	...	...	...	...	...
		do ...	Dikshbadki	do ...	...	...	...	2,215	1,013	1,202	...	...	...	...	...	...	...	...	...
		do ...	Dikshpaneban	do ...	...	...	...	43	25	18	...	...	...	...	...	...	...	...	...
		do ...	Dikshvant	do ...	49	44	5	13,773	7,256	6,517	...	...	...	2	...	2	...	...	...
		do ...	Govardan	do ...	...	...	...	...	...	...	...	...	...	...	...	...	...	...	...
		do ...	Govhar	do ...	...	...	...	...	...	...	...	...	...	...	...	...	...	...	...
		do ...	Gujrati...	do ...	...	...	...	...	...	...	...	...	...	...	...	...	...	...	...
		do ...	Gurastulu	do ...	...	...	...	...	...	...	...	...	...	...	...	...	...	...	...
		do ...	Gursal	do ...	...	...	...	...	...	...	...	...	...	...	...	...	...	...	...
		do ...	Gululbansi	do ...	...	...	...	...	...	...	...	...	...	...	...	...	...	...	...
		do ...	Haujan...	do ...	...	...	...	...	...	...	...	...	...	4	8	1	...	...	...
		do ...	Hatvan...	do ...	...	...	...	...	...	...	...	...	...	...	...	...	...	...	...
		do ...	Huper	do ...	...	...	...	51	20	31	...	...	...	...	...	...	...	...	...
		do ...	Jengam	do ...	3	...	8	770	469	301	...	...	...	...	...	...	...	...	...
		do ...	Janu	do ...	...	...	...	...	...	...	...	...	...	...	...	...	...	...	...
		do ...	Jasval	do ...	...	...	...	...	...	...	...	...	...	...	...	...	...	...	...
		do ...	Jathvani	do ...	...	...	...	42	26	16	...	...	...	...	...	...	...	...	...

TABLE XVI.

Castes and Sub-divisions.—*Continued.*

Class.	Group.	Castes.	Sub-division of Castes.	Religion.	Total.			Hyderabad.			Atraf-i-Balda.			Mahabubnagar.			Nalgonda.		
					Total.	Males.	Females.	Total.	Males.	Females.	Total.	Males.	Females.	Total.	Males.	Females.	Total.	Males.	Females.
1	2	3	4	5	6	7	8	9	10	11	12	13	14	15	16	17	18	19	20
C	14 ...	Vani ...	Johari ...	Hindu ...	2	2	...	...	...	...	...	...	...	...	...	...	...	...	...
		do ...	Kadhar...	do ...	1	1	...	...	...	...	...	...	...	...	...	...	...	...	...
		do ...	Kakangar	do ...	5	2	3	...	...	...	...	...	...	...	...	...	...	...	...
		do ...	Kalji ...	do ...	5	3	2	...	...	...	...	...	...	...	...	...	...	...	...
		do ...	Kandi ...	do ...	162	88	74	...	...	...	...	...	...	...	...	...	...	...	...
		do ...	Kavlekar	do ...	29	19	10	...	...	...	...	...	...	...	...	...	...	...	...
		do ...	Kasid ...	do ...	60	31	29	...	...	...	...	...	...	...	...	...	...	...	...
		do ...	Khadalvar	do ...	55	42	13	...	...	...	...	...	...	...	...	...	...	...	...
		do ...	Khadkar	do ...	40	20	20	...	...	...	...	...	...	...	...	...	...	...	...
		do ...	Kulne ...	do ...	42	19	23	...	...	...	...	...	...	...	...	...	...	...	...
		do ...	Kumnvat	do ...	7	3	4	...	...	...	...	...	...	...	...	...	...	...	...
		do ...	Kuvar ...	do ...	7	5	2	...	...	...	...	...	...	...	...	...	...	...	...
		do ...	Lingait ...	do ...	41,701	21,221	20,480	7	5	2	...	...	...	...	...	...	...	...	...
		do ...	Maisri ...	do ...	4,089	2,379	1,710	419	267	152	1	1	...	...	...	...	...	...	...
		do ...	Majun ...	do ...	10	4	6	10	4	6	...	...	...	...	...	...	...	...	...
		do ...	Malesar	do ..	2	2	...	...	...	...	...	...	...	...	...	...	...	...	...
		do ...	Malsati	do ...	9	3	6	...	...	...	...	...	...	...	...	...	...	...	...
		do ...	Manad ...	do ...	87	87	...	...	...	...	...	...	...	...	...	...	...	...	...
		do ...	Mantri ...	do ...	6	2	4	...	...	...	2	1	1	...	...	...	...	...	...
		do ...	Mutijpati	do ...	5	2	3	...	...	...	...	...	...	...	...	...	...	...	...
		do ...	Natkar ...	do ...	1	1	...	...	...	...	...	...	...	...	...	...	...	...	...
		do ...	Oparak	do ...	12	5	7	...	...	...	...	...	...	...	...	...	...	...	...
		do ...	Osval ...	do ...	1,474	789	685	6	2	4	...	...	...	...	...	...	...	...	...
		do ...	Padsagar	do ...	5	2	3	...	...	...	...	...	...	...	...	...	...	...	...
		do ...	Panchambadki	do ...	2,752	1,244	1,508	...	...	...	...	...	...	...	...	...	...	...	...
		do ...	Panchamvar ...	do ...	17,848	9,390	8,458	...	...	...	...	...	...	...	...	...	...	...	...
		do ...	Pardesi...	do ...	39	23	16	...	...	...	...	...	...	...	...	...	...	...	...
		do ...	Parvar...	do ...	12	8	4	...	...	...	...	...	...	...	...	...	...	...	...
		do ...	Phalbad	do ...	207	114	93	...	...	...	...	...	...	...	...	...	...	...	...
		do ...	Pindari	do ...	37	17	20	37	17	20	...	...	...	...	...	...	...	...	...
		do ...	Purvant	do ...	59	29	30	...	...	...	...	...	...	...	...	...	...	...	...
		do ...	Rai ...	do ...	2	2	...	...	...	...	...	...	...	...	...	...	...	...	...
		do ...	Rasphal	do ...	12	6	6	...	...	...	...	...	...	...	...	...	...	...	...
		do ...	Rasvat ...	do ...	34,298	17,216	17,082	...	...	...	357	182	175	...	...	...	...	...	...
		do ...	Rudra ...	do ...	11	7	4	...	...	...	...	...	...	...	...	...	...	...	...
		do ...	Sajan ...	do ...	10	4	6	...	...	...	...	...	...	...	...	...	...	...	...
		do ...	Saraogi	do ...	2,251	1,201	1,050	20	12	8	...	...	...	...	...	...	...	...	...
		do ...	Saravan	do ...	8	1	2	3	1	2	...	...	...	...	...	...	...	...	...
		do ...	Sargoingnath ...	do ...	2	...	2	2	...	2	...	...	...	...	...	...	...	...	...
		do ...	Sarsetti...	do ...	9	3	6	...	...	...	...	...	...	...	...	...	...	...	...

TABLE XVI.

Castes and Sub-divisions.—*Continued.*

Class.	Group.	Castes.	Sub-division of Castes.	Religion.	Warangal. Total.	Warangal. Males.	Warangal. Females.	Elgandal. Total.	Elgandal. Males.	Elgandal. Females.	Indur. Total.	Indur. Males.	Indur. Females.	Medak. Total.	Medak. Males.	Medak. Females.	Aurangabad. Total.	Aurangabad. Males.	Aurangabad. Females.
					21	22	23	24	25	26	27	28	29	30	31	32	33	34	35
C	14 ...	Vani ...	Johari	Hindu ...	...	...	...	...	...	...	...	...	...	...	...	...	2	2	...
		do ...	Kadhar...	do ...	...	...	...	...	...	...	...	...	...	...	...	...	1	1	...
		do ...	Kakangar	do ...	...	...	...	...	...	...	5	2	8	...	...	...	...	...	...
		do ...	Kalji	do ...	...	...	...	...	...	...	...	...	...	...	...	...	...	...	...
		do ...	Kaudi	do ...	...	...	...	...	...	...	...	...	...	...	...	...	162	88	74
		do ...	Kavlekar	do ...	...	...	...	...	...	...	...	...	...	...	...	...	...	...	...
		do ...	Kasid	do ...	...	...	...	...	...	...	...	...	...	...	...	...	...	...	...
		do ...	Khadalvar	do ...	...	...	...	...	...	...	...	...	...	...	...	...	55	42	13
		do ...	Khadkar	do ...	...	...	...	...	...	...	...	...	...	...	...	...	40	20	20
		do ...	Kulne	do ...	...	...	...	...	...	...	...	...	...	...	...	...	42	19	23
		do ...	Kumuvat	do ...	...	...	...	...	...	...	...	...	...	...	...	...	...	...	...
		do ...	Kuvar	do ...	...	...	...	...	...	...	...	...	...	...	...	...	7	5	2
		do ...	Lingait	do ...	...	...	...	...	...	...	1,044	508	536	...	...	...	1,494	764	730
		do ...	Maisri	do ...	...	...	...	2	2	...	4	3	1	...	...	...	1,031	544	487
		do ...	Majun	do ...	...	...	...	...	...	...	...	...	...	...	...	...	...	...	...
		do ...	Malesar	do ...	...	...	...	...	...	...	...	...	...	...	...	...	...	...	...
		do ...	Malseti...	do ...	...	...	...	...	...	...	...	...	...	...	...	...	...	...	...
		do ...	Manad...	do ...	...	...	...	...	...	...	...	...	...	...	...	...	...	...	...
		do ...	Mantri	do ...	...	...	...	4	1	8	...	...	...	...	...	...	...	...	...
		do ...	Mutijpati	do ...	...	...	...	...	...	...	...	...	...	...	...	...	...	...	...
		do ...	Natkar	do ...	...	...	...	...	...	...	...	...	...	...	...	...	...	...	...
		do ...	Oparak...	do ...	...	...	...	...	...	...	...	...	...	...	...	...	12	5	7
		do ...	Osval	do ...	...	...	...	...	...	...	...	...	...	...	...	...	447	263	184
		do ...	Padsagar	do ...	...	...	...	...	...	...	...	...	...	...	...	...	...	...	...
		do ...	Panchambadki ...	do ...	...	...	...	...	...	...	...	...	...	...	...	...	...	...	...
		do ...	Panchamvar	do ...	...	...	...	...	...	...	...	...	...	...	...	...	38	18	20
		do ...	Pardesi...	do ...	...	...	...	...	...	...	...	...	...	...	...	...	39	23	16
		do ...	Parvar...	do ...	...	...	...	...	...	...	...	...	...	...	...	...	12	8	4
		do ...	Phalbad	do ...	...	...	...	...	...	...	...	...	...	...	...	...	...	...	...
		do ...	Pindari	do ...	...	...	...	...	...	...	...	...	...	...	...	...	...	...	...
		do ...	Purvant	do ...	...	...	...	...	...	...	59	29	30	...	...	...	...	...	...
		do ...	Rai	do ...	...	...	...	...	...	...	2	2	...	...	...	...	...	...	...
		do ...	Rasphal	do ...	...	...	...	...	...	...	...	...	...	...	...	...	...	...	...
		do ...	Rasvat...	do ...	...	...	...	...	...	...	3,789	1,886	1,903	28	14	14	...	...	...
		do ...	Rudra	do ...	...	...	...	...	...	...	...	...	...	...	...	...	...	...	...
		do ...	Sajan	do ...	...	...	...	...	...	...	...	...	...	...	...	...	...	...	...
		do ...	Saraogi	do ...	...	...	...	...	...	...	28	12	16	...	...	...	1,018	572	446
		do ...	Saravan	do ...	...	...	...	...	...	...	...	...	...	...	...	...	...	...	...
		do ...	Sargoingnath ...	do ...	...	...	...	...	...	...	...	...	...	...	...	...	...	...	...
		do ...	Sarsetti	do ...	...	...	...	...	...	...	9	8	6	...	...	...	...	...	...

TABLE XVI.

Castes and Sub-divisions.—*Continued.*

Class.	Group.	Castes.	Sub-division of Castes.	Religion.	Birh. Total.	Birh. Males.	Birh. Females.	Nander. Total.	Nander. Males.	Nander. Females.	Naldrug. Total.	Naldrug. Males.	Naldrug. Females.	Bidar. Total.	Bidar. Males.	Bidar. Females.	Parbhani. Total.	Parbhani. Males.	Parbhani. Females.
					36	37	38	39	40	41	42	43	44	45	46	47	48	49	50
C	14 ...	Vani ...	Johari	Hindu ...	...	...	...	...	...	...	...	...	...	...	...	...	...	...	...
		do ...	Kadhar	do ...	...	...	...	...	...	...	...	...	...	...	...	...	...	...	...
		do ...	Kakangar	do ...	...	...	...	...	...	...	...	...	...	...	...	...	...	...	...
		do ...	Kalji	do ...	...	...	...	5	3	2	...	...	...	...	...	...	...	...	...
		do ...	Kaudi	do ...	...	...	...	...	...	...	...	...	...	...	...	...	...	...	...
		do ...	Kavlekar	do ...	...	...	...	17	13	4	...	...	...	...	...	...	12	6	6
		do ...	Kasid	do ...	60	31	29	...	...	...	...	...	...	...	...	...	...	...	...
		do ...	Khadalvar	do ...	...	...	...	...	...	...	...	...	...	...	...	...	...	...	...
		do ...	Khadkar	do ...	...	...	...	...	...	...	...	...	...	...	...	...	...	...	...
		do ...	Kulne	do ...	...	...	...	...	...	...	...	...	...	...	...	...	...	...	...
		do ...	Kumuvat	do ...	7	3	4	...	...	...	...	...	...	...	...	...	...	...	...
		do ...	Kuvar	do ...	...	...	...	...	...	...	...	...	...	...	...	...	...	...	...
		do ...	Lingait...	do ...	2,173	1,162	1,011	...	...	...	8,696	1,884	6,812	5,240	2,722	2,518	3,644	1,912	1,732
		do ...	Maisri	do ...	335	197	138	269	181	88	1	1	...	491	281	210	1,506	888	618
		do ...	Majun	do ...	...	...	...	...	...	...	...	...	...	...	...	...	...	...	...
		do ...	Makesar	do ...	...	...	...	2	2	...	...	...	...	...	...	...	...	...	...
		do ...	Malseti...	do ...	...	...	...	...	...	...	...	...	...	9	3	6	...	...	...
		do ...	Manad	do ...	37	37	...	...	...	...	...	...	...	...	...	...	...	...	...
		do ...	Mantri	do ...	...	...	...	...	...	...	...	...	...	...	...	...	...	...	...
		do ...	Mutijpati	do ...	...	...	...	...	...	...	...	...	...	5	2	3	...	...	...
		do ...	Natkar...	do ...	1	1	...	...	...	...	...	...	...	...	...	...	...	...	...
		do ...	Oparak...	do ...	...	...	...	...	...	...	...	...	...	...	...	...	...	...	...
		do ...	Osval	do ...	101	53	48	33	22	11	206	122	84	5	2	3	477	196	281
		do ...	Padmagar	do ...	...	...	...	...	...	...	...	...	...	...	...	...	...	...	...
		do ...	Panchambadki ...	do ...	...	...	...	...	...	...	...	...	...	...	...	...	...	...	...
		do ...	Panchamvar	do ...	220	143	77	66	44	22	10,448	5,401	5,047	470	437	33	43	11	32
		do ...	Pardesi...	do ...	...	...	...	...	...	...	...	...	...	...	...	...	...	...	...
		do ...	Parvar...	do ...	...	...	...	...	...	...	...	...	...	...	...	...	...	...	...
		do ...	Phalbad	do ...	...	...	...	207	114	93	...	...	...	...	...	...	...	...	...
		do ...	Pindari...	do ...	...	...	...	...	...	...	...	...	...	...	...	...	...	...	...
		do ...	Purvant	do ...	...	...	...	...	...	...	...	...	...	...	...	...	...	...	...
		do ...	Rai	do ...	...	...	...	...	...	...	...	...	...	...	...	...	...	...	...
		do ...	Rasphal	do ...	12	6	6	...	...	...	...	...	...	...	...	...	...	...	...
		do ...	Rasvat...	do ...	745	865	880	13,138	6,640	6,498	4,754	2,367	2,387	6,916	3,324	3,592	4,571	2,438	2,133
		do ...	Rudra	do ...	11	7	4	...	...	...	...	...	...	...	...	...	...	...	...
		do ...	Sajan	do ...	...	...	...	...	...	...	...	...	...	...	...	...	...	...	...
		do ..	Saraogi	do ...	30	16	14	63	26	37	395	214	181	10	5	5	614	307	307
		do ..	Saravan	do ...	...	...	...	...	...	...	...	...	...	...	...	...	...	...	...
		do ...	Sargoingnath	do ...	...	...	...	...	...	...	...	...	...	...	...	...	...	...	...
		do ...	Sarsetti...	do ...	...	...	...	...	...	...	...	...	...	...	...	...	...	...	...

TABLE XVI.

Castes and Sub-divisions.—*Continued.*

Class.	Group.	Castes.	Sub-division of Castes.	Religion.	Sirpur Tandur.			Gulbarga.			Raichur.			Lingasugur.			Railways.		
					Total.	Males.	Females.	Total.	Males.	Females.	Total.	Males.	Females.	Total.	Males.	Females.	Total.	Males.	Females.
					51	52	53	54	55	56	57	58	59	60	61	62	63	64	65
C	14 ...	Vani ...	Johari	Hindu ...	...	...	...	...	...	...	...	...	...	...	...	...	...	...	...
		do ...	Kadhar...	do ...	...	...	...	...	...	...	...	...	...	...	...	...	...	...	...
		do ...	Kakangar	do ...	...	...	...	...	...	...	...	...	...	...	...	...	...	...	...
		do ...	Kalji	do ...	...	...	...	...	...	...	...	...	...	...	...	...	...	...	...
		do ...	Kaudi	do ...	...	...	...	...	...	...	...	...	...	...	...	...	...	...	...
		do ...	Kavlekar	do ...	...	...	...	...	...	...	...	...	...	...	...	...	...	...	...
		do ...	Kasid	do ...	...	...	...	...	...	...	...	...	...	...	...	...	...	...	...
		do ...	Khadalvar	do ...	...	...	...	...	...	...	...	...	...	...	...	...	...	...	...
		do ...	Khadkar	do ...	...	...	...	...	...	...	...	...	...	...	...	...	...	...	...
		do ...	Kulne	do ...	...	...	...	...	...	...	...	...	...	...	...	...	...	...	...
		do ...	Kumuvat	do ...	...	...	...	...	...	...	...	...	...	...	...	...	...	...	...
		do ...	Kuvar	do ...	...	...	...	...	...	...	...	...	...	...	...	...	...	...	...
		do ...	Lingait...	do ...	...	...	...	24,188	12,159	12,029	...	...	...	215	105	110	...	...	...
		do ...	Maisri	do ...	21	7	14	...	...	...	...	...	...	9	7	2	...	...	...
		do ...	Majun	do ...	...	...	...	...	...	...	...	...	...	...	...	...	...	...	...
		do ...	Malesar	do ...	...	...	...	...	...	...	...	...	...	...	...	...	...	...	...
		do ...	Malseti...	do ...	...	...	...	...	...	...	...	...	...	...	...	...	...	...	...
		do ...	Manad...	do ...	...	...	...	...	...	...	...	...	...	...	...	...	...	...	...
		do ...	Mantri...	do ...	...	...	...	...	...	...	...	...	...	...	...	...	...	...	...
		do ...	Mutijpati	do ...	...	...	...	...	...	...	...	...	...	...	...	...	...	...	...
		do ...	Natkar...	do ...	...	...	...	...	...	...	...	...	...	...	...	...	...	...	...
		do ...	Oparak...	do ...	...	...	...	...	...	...	...	...	...	...	...	...	...	...	...
		do ...	Osval	do ...	...	...	...	81	16	15	88	55	88	80	58	22	...	...	...
		do ...	Padsagar	do ...	...	...	...	5	2	3	...	...	...	...	...	...	...	...	...
		do ...	Panchambadki ...	do ...	...	...	...	2,752	1,244	1,508	...	...	...	...	...	...	...	...	...
		do ...	Panchamvar	do ...	...	...	...	6,568	3,341	3,227	...	...	...	...	...	...	...	...	...
		do ...	Pardesi...	do ...	...	...	...	...	...	...	...	...	...	...	...	...	...	...	...
		do ...	Parvar...	do ...	...	...	...	...	...	...	...	...	...	...	...	...	...	...	...
		do ...	Phalbad	do ...	...	...	...	...	...	...	...	...	...	...	...	...	...	...	...
		do ...	Pindari...	do ...	...	...	...	...	...	...	...	...	...	...	...	...	...	...	...
		do ...	Purvant	do ...	...	...	...	...	...	...	...	...	...	...	...	...	...	...	...
		do ...	Rai	do ...	...	...	...	...	...	...	...	...	...	...	...	...	...	...	...
		do ...	Rasphal	do ...	...	...	...	...	...	...	...	...	...	...	...	...	...	...	...
		do ...	Rasvat...	do ...	...	...	...	...	...	...	...	...	...	...	...	...	...	...	...
		do ...	Rudra	do ...	...	...	...	...	...	...	...	...	...	...	...	...	...	...	...
		do ...	Sajan	do ...	...	...	...	10	4	6	...	...	...	...	...	...	...	...	...
		do ...	Saraogi	do ...	...	...	...	71	86	85	...	...	...	...	...	...	2	1	1
		do ...	Saravan	do ...	...	...	...	...	...	...	...	...	...	...	...	...	...	...	...
		do ...	Sargoingnath	do ...	...	...	...	...	...	...	...	...	...	...	...	...	...	...	...
		do ...	Sarsetti...	do ...	...	...	...	...	...	...	...	...	...	...	...	...	...	...	...

TABLE XVI.

Castes and Sub-divisions.—*Continued.*

Class.	Group.	Castes.	Sub-division of Castes.	Religion.	Total. Total.	Total. Males.	Total. Females.	Hyderabad. Total.	Hyderabad. Males.	Hyderabad. Females.	Atraf-i-Balda. Total.	Atraf-i-Balda. Males.	Atraf-i-Balda. Females.	Mahabubnagar. Total.	Mahabubnagar. Males.	Mahabubnagar. Females.	Nalgonda. Total.	Nalgonda. Males.	Nalgonda. Females.
1	2	3	4	5	6	7	8	9	10	11	12	13	14	15	16	17	18	19	20
C	14 ...	Vani ...	Seoti	Hindu ...	17	10	7	...	...	...	...	...	...	...	...	...	...	...	...
		do ...	Setval	do ...	755	391	364	...	...	...	...	...	...	...	...	...	...	...	...
		do ...	Sheobalki	do ...	33	15	18	...	...	...	...	...	...	...	...	...	...	...	...
		do ...	Sheodas	do ...	3	1	2	...	...	...	...	...	...	...	...	...	...	...	...
		do ...	Sikmepancham ...	do ...	2	1	1	...	...	...	...	...	...	...	...	...	...	...	...
		do ...	Sikshivant	do ...	23	22	1	...	...	...	...	...	...	...	...	...	...	...	...
		do ...	Simeseti	do ...	75	39	36	...	...	...	...	...	...	...	...	...	...	...	...
		do ...	Sirul	do ...	4	...	4	...	...	...	...	...	...	...	...	...	...	...	...
		do ...	Somale	do .	9	9	...	9	9	...	...	...	...	...	...	...	...	...	...
		do ...	Vashe	do ...	133	49	84	...	...	...	...	...	...	...	...	...	...	...	...
		do ...	Vibhutidar	do ...	2	2	...	...	...	...	...	...	...	...	...	...	...	...	...
		do ...	Virpankh	do ...	41	22	19	...	...	...	...	...	...	...	...	...	...	...	...
		do ...	Virsheo...	do ...	52	45	7	...	...	...	...	...	...	...	...	...	...	...	...
		do ...	Zangriwar	do ...	58	58	...	...	...	...	...	...	...	...	...	...	...	...	...
		do ...	Unspecified	do ...	121,156	62,945	58,211	3,837	2,240	1,597	99	56	43	116	91	25	10	6	4
			Total......	......	415,208	213,154	202,054	5,091	3,030	2,061	696	360	336	627	345	282	25	13	12
F	48 ...	Sheikh ...	Abbasi	Musulman...	316	292	24	316	292	24	...	...	...	...	...	...	...	...	...
		do ...	Ansari	do ...	1,713	795	918	938	414	524	...	...	...	...	...	...	34	13	21
		do ...	Askari	do ...	1	...	1	...	...	...	...	...	...	...	...	...	...	...	...
		do ...	Faruki	do ...	5,463	2,787	2,676	2,232	1,165	1,067	...	...	...	349	171	178	...	...	...
		do ...	Kureshi	do ..	131,710	66,772	64,938	66,734	33,400	33,334	4,179	2,163	2,016	6	3	3	2,233	1,148	1,085
		do ...	Osmani...	do ...	418	229	189	264	140	124	...	...	...	...	...	...	...	...	...
		do ...	Sharif	do ...	198	105	93	20	20	...	17	7	10	54	24	30	60	32	28
		do ...	Siddiki	do ...	20,184	10,040	10,144	6,511	3,245	3,266	69	30	39	1,270	614	656	11	7	4
		do ...	Tarkash	do ...	8	6	2	...	...	...	...	...	...	...	...	...	...	...	...
		do ...	Unspecified	do ...	696,113	354,241	341,872	33,308	17,015	16,293	27,287	14,235	13,052	42,665	21,354	21,311	19,832	10,146	9,686
			Total......	......	856,124	435,267	420,857	110,323	55,691	54,632	31,552	16,435	15,117	44,344	22,166	22,178	22,170	11,346	10,824

TABLE XVI.

Castes and Sub-divisions.—*Continued.*

Class.	Group.	Castes.	Sub-division of Castes.	Religion.	Warangal. Total.	Warangal. Males.	Warangal. Females.	Elgandal. Total.	Elgandal. Males.	Elgandal. Females.	Indur. Total.	Indur. Males.	Indur. Females.	Medak. Total.	Medak. Males.	Medak. Females.	Aurangabad. Total.	Aurangabad. Males.	Aurangabad. Females.
					21	22	23	24	25	26	27	28	29	30	31	32	33	34	35
C	14 ...	Vani ...	Seoti	Hindu ..	...	...	...	...	...	...	...	...	...	...	...	...	...	...	...
		do ...	Setval	do ..	...	...	...	...	...	...	...	...	...	...	...	...	257	189	118
		do ...	Sheobalki	do ..	...	...	...	...	...	...	...	...	...	...	...	...	...	...	...
		do ...	Sheodas	do ...	...	...	...	...	...	...	...	...	...	...	...	...	...	...	...
		do ...	Sikmepancham ...	do ...	...	...	...	...	...	...	...	...	...	...	...	...	...	...	...
		do ...	Sikshivant	do ..	...	...	...	...	...	...	...	...	...	...	...	...	...	...	...
		do ...	Simeseti	do ..	...	...	...	...	...	...	...	...	...	...	...	...	...	...	...
		do ...	Sirul	do ..	...	...	...	...	...	...	...	...	...	...	...	...	...	...	...
		do ...	Somale...	do ..	...	...	...	...	...	...	...	...	...	...	...	...	...	...	...
		do ...	Vashe	do ..	...	...	...	...	...	...	133	49	84	...	...	...	...	...	...
		do ...	Vibhutidar	do ..	...	...	...	...	...	...	...	...	...	...	...	...	...	...	...
		do ...	Virpankh	do ..	...	...	...	...	...	...	41	22	19	...	...	...	...	...	...
		do ...	Virsheo	do ...	...	...	...	...	...	...	...	...	...	...	...	...	...	...	...
		do ...	Zangriwar	do ..	...	...	...	...	...	...	53	53	...	...	...	...	...	...	...
		do ...	Unspecified	do ..	102	64	38	236	139	97	8,913	4,585	4,328	74	47	27	10,372	5,663	4,709
			Total......	......	107	66	41	259	153	106	19,090	9,653	9,437	237	138	99	16,144	8,733	7,411
	48 ...	Sheikh ...	Abbasi...	Mussulman	...	...	...	...	...	...	...	...	...	...	...	...	...	...	...
		do ...	Ansari...	do ..	...	...	...	...	...	...	73	87	36	...	...	...	65	35	30
		do ...	Askari...	do ..	...	...	...	...	...	...	...	...	...	...	...	...	...	...	...
		do ...	Faruki...	do ..	...	...	...	8	4	4	399	208	191	91	36	55	230	122	108
		do ...	Kureshi	do ..	1,598	817	781	5,659	2,924	2,735	6,714	3,270	3,444	6,776	3,412	8,864	8,474	4,484	8,990
		do ...	Osmani	do ..	...	...	...	...	...	...	57	81	26	67	48	24	...	...	...
		do ...	Sharif	do .	41	19	22	...	...	...	...	...	...	6	3	3	...	...	...
		do ..	Siddiki	do ..	16	12	4	119	50	69	539	292	247	428	217	211	1,039	486	553
		do ..	Tarkash	do ..	...	...	...	...	...	...	...	...	...	...	...	...	...	...	...
		do ..	Unspecified	do ..	31,306	16,191	15,115	26,608	13,681	12,927	82,425	16,018	16,407	22,509	11,284	11,225	54,540	27,447	27,098
			Total......	......	82,961	17,039	15,922	82,894	16,659	15,785	40,207	19,856	20,351	29,877	14,995	14,882	64,348	32,574	81,774

TABLE XVI.

Castes and Sub-divisions.—*Continued.*

Class.	Group.	Castes.	Sub-division of Castes.	Religion.	Birh. Total.	Birh. Males.	Birh. Females.	Nander. Total.	Nander. Males.	Nander. Females.	Naldrug. Total.	Naldrug. Males.	Naldrug. Females.	Bidar. Total.	Bidar. Males.	Bidar. Females.	Parbhani. Total.	Parbhani. Males.	Parbhani. Females.
					36	37	38	39	40	41	42	43	44	45	46	47	48	49	50
C	14 ...	Vani ...	Seoti	Hindu ...	...	...	...	...	...	...	...	...	...	17	10	7	...	...	...
		do ...	Setval	do ...	101	52	49	116	55	61	106	52	54	...	...	...	175	93	82
		do ...	Sheobalki	do ...	...	...	...	...	...	...	...	...	...	...	...	...	...	...	...
		do ...	Sheodas	do ...	...	...	...	...	...	...	8	1	2	...	...	...	...	...	...
		do ...	Sikmepancham ...	do ...	...	...	...	...	...	...	...	...	...	2	1	1	...	...	...
		do ...	Sikshivant	do ...	...	...	...	...	...	...	...	...	...	23	22	1	...	...	...
		do ...	Sineseti	do ...	...	...	...	75	39	36	...	...	...	...	...	...	...	...	...
		do ...	Sirul	do ...	...	...	...	4	...	4	...	...	...	...	...	...	...	...	...
		do ...	Somale...	do ...	...	...	...	...	...	...	...	...	...	...	...	...	...	...	...
		do ...	Vashe	do ...	...	...	...	...	...	...	...	...	...	...	...	...	...	...	...
		do ...	Vibhutidar	do ...	...	...	...	...	...	...	2	2	...	...	...	...	...	...	...
		do ...	Virpankh	do ...	...	...	...	...	...	...	...	...	...	...	...	...	...	...	...
		do ...	Virsheo	do ...	...	...	...	...	...	...	...	...	...	...	...	...	...	...	...
		do ...	Zangriwar	do ...	...	...	...	...	...	...	...	...	...	...	...	...	...	...	...
		do ...	Unspecified	do ...	9,054	4,825	4,229	12,045	6,276	5,769	15,978	8,388	7,590	25,971	13,114	12,857	8,400	4,714	3,686
			Total......	......	17,818	9,467	8,351	49,283	25,161	24,122	50,711	26,292	24,419	141,209	71,643	69,566	28,519	15,193	13,326
F	48 ...	Sheikh ...	Abbasi	Musulman...	...	...	...	...	...	...	...	...	...	...	...	...	...	...	...
		do ...	Ansari	do ...	10	6	4	69	29	40	222	109	113	212	104	108	56	25	31
		do ...	Askari	do ...	...	...	...	...	...	...	...	...	...	...	...	...	...	...	...
		do ...	Faruki	do ...	619	302	317	129	46	83	...	...	...	98	43	55	1,105	574	531
		do ...	Kureshi	do ...	1,629	910	719	2,812	1,509	1,303	2,308	1,227	1,081	7,589	3,812	3,777	4,040	1,989	2,051
		do ...	Osmani...	do ...	...	...	...	...	...	...	...	...	...	...	...	...	...	...	...
		do ...	Sharif	do ...	...	...	...	...	...	...	...	...	...	...	...	...	...	...	...
		do ...	Siddiki	do ...	623	350	273	512	188	324	854	450	404	1,995	1,032	963	3,551	1,803	1,748
		do ...	Tarkash	do ...	...	...	...	...	...	...	...	...	...	...	...	...	...	...	...
		do ...	Unspecified	do ...	34,666	17,725	16,941	40,452	20,717	19,785	40,739	20,729	20,010	85,760	43,642	42,118	39,502	20,187	19,365
			Total......	......	37,547	19,293	18,254	43,974	22,489	21,485	44,128	22,515	21,608	95,654	48,688	47,021	48,254	24,528	23,726

TABLE XVI.

Castes and Sub-divisions.—*Continued.*

Class.	Group.	Castes.	Sub-division of Castes.	Religion.	Sirpur Tandur. Total.	Sirpur Tandur. Males.	Sirpur Tandur. Females.	Gulbarga. Total.	Gulbarga. Males.	Gulbarga. Females.	Raichur. Total.	Raichur. Males.	Raichur. Females.	Lingasugur. Total.	Lingasugur. Males.	Lingasugur. Females.	Railways. Total.	Railways. Males.	Railways. Females.
					51	52	53	54	55	56	57	58	59	60	61	62	63	64	65
C	14 ...	Vani ...	Seoti ...	Hindu ...	...	...	...	...	...	...	...	...	...	...	...	...	...	...	...
		do ...	Setval ...	do ...	...	...	...	...	...	...	...	...	...	...	...	...	...	...	...
		do ...	Sheobalki ...	do ...	...	...	...	83	15	18	...	...	...	...	...	...	...	...	...
		do ...	Seodas ...	do ...	...	...	...	...	...	...	...	...	...	...	...	...	...	...	...
		do ...	Sikmepancham ...	do ...	...	...	...	...	...	...	...	...	...	...	...	...	...	...	...
		do ...	Sikshivant ...	do ...	...	...	...	...	...	...	...	...	...	...	...	...	...	...	...
		do ...	Simeseti ...	do ...	...	...	...	...	...	...	...	...	...	...	...	...	...	...	...
		do ...	Sirul ...	do ...	...	...	...	...	...	...	...	...	...	...	...	...	...	...	...
		do ...	Somale ...	do ...	...	...	...	...	...	...	...	...	...	...	...	...	...	...	...
		do ...	Vasbe ...	do ...	...	...	...	...	...	...	...	...	...	...	...	...	...	...	...
		do ...	Vibhutidar ...	do ...	...	...	...	...	...	...	...	...	...	...	...	...	...	...	...
		do ...	Virpankh ...	do ...	...	...	...	...	...	...	...	...	...	...	...	...	...	...	...
		do ...	Virsheo ...	do ...	...	...	...	52	45	7	...	...	...	...	...	...	...	...	...
		do ...	Zangriwar ...	do ...	...	...	...	...	...	...	...	...	...	...	...	...	...	...	...
		do ...	Unspecified ...	do ...	548	274	274	11,284	5,460	5,824	22	14	8	13,993	6,914	7,079	107	80	27
			Total......	......	691	363	328	70,178	35,306	34,872	111	70	41	14,303	7,087	7,216	109	81	28
T	48 ...	Sheikh ...	Abbasi ...	Mussulman...	...	...	...	...	...	...	...	...	...	...	...	...	...	...	...
		do ...	Ansari ...	do ...	5	8	2	12	7	5	8	1	2	14	12	2	...	...	...
		do ...	Askari ...	do ...	1	...	1	...	...	...	...	...	...	...	...	...	...	...	...
		do ...	Faruki ...	do ...	1	1	...	164	99	65	38	16	22	...	...	...	...	...	...
		do ...	Kureshi ...	do ...	797	407	390	1,658	850	808	7,730	4,011	3,719	773	435	338	1	1	...
		do ...	Osmani ...	do ...	3	2	1	22	10	12	5	3	2	...	...	...	...	...	...
		do ...	Sharif ...	do ...	...	...	...	...	...	...	...	...	...	...	...	...	...	...	...
		do ...	Siddiki ...	do ...	203	85	118	117	72	45	1,708	806	902	619	801	818	...	...	...
		do ...	Tarkash ...	do ...	...	...	...	...	...	...	...	...	...	8	6	2	...	...	...
		do ...	Unspecified ...	do ...	6,210	3,115	3,095	78,406	39,953	38,453	32,981	16,918	16,063	46,279	23,511	22,768	688	423	215
			Total......	......	7,220	3,613	3,607	80,379	40,991	39,388	42,465	21,755	20,710	47,693	24,265	23,428	639	424	215

TABLE XVI.

Castes and Sub-divisions.—*Continued.*

Class.	Group.	Castes.	Sub-division of Castes.	Religion.	Total. Total.	Total. Males.	Total. Females.	Hyderabad. Total.	Hyderabad. Males.	Hyderabad. Females.	Atraf-i-Balda. Total.	Atraf-i-Balda. Males.	Atraf-i-Balda. Females.	Mahabubnagar. Total.	Mahabubnagar. Males.	Mahabubnagar. Females.	Nalgonda. Total.	Nalgonda. Males.	Nalgonda. Females.
1	2	3	4	5	6	7	8	9	10	11	12	13	14	15	16	17	18	19	20
F	48 ...	Syed ...	Alvi	Musulman...	750	471	279	529	346	183	...	...	...	10	4	6	...	...	...
		do ...	Bakari	do ...	59	34	25	59	34	25	...	...	...	...	...	...	...	...	...
		do ...	Hasni	do ...	20,158	10,297	9,861	20,016	10,231	9,785	...	...	...	...	...	...	...	...	...
		do ...	Hasan-ul-Husaini ...	do ...	2	2	...	2	2	...	...	...	...	...	...	...	...	...	...
		do ...	Husaini	do ...	5,640	2,929	2,711	...	...	...	246	133	118	955	443	512	170	81	89
		do ...	Jafari	do ...	545	253	292	534	247	287	...	...	...	...	...	...	11	6	5
		do ...	Mahdvi	do ...	13	6	10	16	6	10	...	...	...	...	...	...	...	...	...
		do ...	Musavi...	do ...	225	100	125	225	100	125	...	...	...	...	...	...	...	...	...
		do ...	Nakvi	do ...	63	55	8	63	55	8	...	...	...	...	...	...	...	...	...
		do ...	Razvi	do ...	1,755	723	1,072	1,522	610	912	14	9	5	31	13	18	...	...	...
		do ...	Zaidi	do ...	249	114	135	249	114	135	...	...	...	...	...	...	...	...	...
		do ...	Unspecified	do ...	83,785	42,640	41,145	7,721	4,042	3,679	5,974	2,961	3,013	3,956	2,027	1,929	2,808	1,423	1,385
			Total......	......	113,287	57,624	55,663	20,936	15,787	15,149	6,234	3,103	3,131	4,952	2,487	2,465	2,989	1,510	1,479
F	48 ...	Arab ...	Ajfi	Musulman...	5	5	...	...	...	...	...	...	...	...	...	...	...	...	...
		do ...	Badvi	do ...	42	13	29	...	...	...	...	...	...	...	...	...	...	...	...
		do ...	Balirsar	do ...	1	1	...	...	...	...	...	...	...	...	...	...	...	...	...
		do ...	Basri	do ...	26	26	...	...	...	...	...	...	...	...	...	...	...	...	...
		do ...	Darvan	do ...	4	2	2	...	...	...	...	...	...	...	...	...	...	...	...
		do ...	Habib	do ...	6	5	1	6	5	1	...	...	...	...	...	...	...	...	...
		do ...	Hazramut	do ...	1	1	...	...	...	...	...	...	...	...	...	...	...	...	...
		do ...	Kalabtar	do ...	1	...	1	...	...	...	...	...	...	...	...	...	...	...	...
		do ...	Kohavi...	do ...	1	1	...	...	...	...	...	...	...	...	...	...	...	...	...
		do ...	Movallad	do ...	3	3	...	...	...	...	...	...	...	...	...	...	...	...	...
		do ...	Nadi	do ...	8	3	5	...	...	...	...	...	...	...	...	...	...	...	...
		do ...	Rafai	do ...	22	12	10	...	...	...	...	...	...	...	...	...	...	...	...
		do ...	Saori	do ...	7	3	4	...	...	...	...	...	...	...	...	...	...	...	...
		do ...	Sharif	do ...	1	1	...	...	...	...	...	...	...	...	...	...	...	...	...
		do ...	Unspecified	do ...	1,612	935	677	19	16	3	92	67	25	199	100	99	6	6	...
			Total......	......	1,740	1,011	729	25	21	4	92	67	25	199	100	99	6	6	...
			Grand Total......	......	4,072,943	2,077,309	1,995,634	191,821	99,498	92,323	102,496	52,284	50,212	155,049	77,982	77,067	120,150	61,249	58,901

Note.—The total of this Table does not tally with the Provincial Total; because only the sub-castes of nine important main castes were abstracted districtwar. The distribution of the population among the main castes will be seen from Supplementary Table C.

TABLE XVI.

Castes and Sub-divisions.—*Continued.*

Class.	Group.	Castes.	Sub-division of Castes.	Religion.	Warangal.			Elgandal.			Indur.			Medak.			Aurangabad.		
					Total.	Males.	Females.	Total.	Males.	Females.	Total.	Males.	Females.	Total.	Males.	Females.	Total.	Males.	Females.
					21	22	23	24	25	26	27	28	29	30	31	32	33	34	35
F	48 ...	Syed ...	Alvi	Mussulman...	...	...	...	28	14	14	10	5	5	4	3	1	...	...	...
		do ...	Bakari	do ...	...	...	...	...	...	...	...	...	...	...	...	...	...	...	...
		do ...	Hasani...	do ...	...	...	...	...	...	...	...	...	...	...	...	...	...	...	...
		do ...	Hasan-ul-Hussini ...	do ...	...	...	...	...	...	...	...	...	...	...	...	...	...	...	...
		do ...	Husaini	do ...	158	88	70	467	248	219	282	146	136	467	257	210	510	276	234
		do ...	Jafari	do ...	...	...	...	...	...	...	...	...	...	...	...	...	...	...	...
		do ...	Mahdvi	do ...	...	...	...	...	...	...	...	...	...	...	...	...	...	...	...
		do ...	Musavi	do ...	...	...	...	...	...	...	...	...	...	...	...	...	...	...	...
		do ...	Nakvi	do ...	...	...	...	...	...	...	...	...	...	...	...	...	...	...	...
		do ...	Razvi	do ...	...	...	...	...	...	...	...	...	...	11	4	7	16	12	4
		do ...	Zaidi	do ...	...	...	...	...	...	...	...	...	...	...	...	...	...	...	...
		do ...	Unspecified	do ...	4,184	2,234	1,950	5,129	2,538	2,591	3,314	1,649	1,665	3,993	1,967	2,026	5,325	2,679	2,646
			Total......	......	4,342	2,322	2,020	5,624	2,800	2,824	3,606	1,800	1,806	4,475	2,231	2,244	5,851	2,967	2,884
F	48 ...	Arab ...	Ajfi	Mussulman...	...	...	...	...	...	...	...	...	...	...	...	...	...	...	...
		do ...	Badvi	do ...	...	...	...	...	...	...	...	...	...	...	...	...	24	1	23
		do ...	Balirsar	do ...	...	...	...	...	...	...	...	...	...	...	...	...	1	1	...
		do ...	Basri	do ...	...	...	...	...	...	...	...	...	...	...	...	...	26	26	...
		do ...	Durvan	do ...	...	...	...	...	...	...	...	...	...	...	...	...	4	2	2
		do ...	Habib	do ...	...	...	...	...	...	...	...	...	...	...	...	...	...	...	...
		do ...	Hazramut	do ...	...	...	...	...	...	...	...	...	...	...	...	...	...	...	...
		do ...	Kalabtar	do ...	...	...	...	...	...	...	...	...	...	...	...	...	...	...	...
		do ...	Kohavi...	do ...	...	...	...	...	...	...	...	...	...	...	...	...	...	...	...
		do ...	Movallad	do ...	...	...	...	...	...	...	3	3	...	...	...	...	...	...	...
		do ...	Nadi	do ...	...	...	...	...	...	...	...	...	...	...	...	...	8	3	5
		do ...	Rafai	do ...	...	...	...	...	...	...	1	1	...	...	...	...	...	...	...
		do ...	Saori	do ...	...	...	...	...	...	...	...	...	...	...	...	...	...	...	...
		do ...	Sharif	do ...	...	...	...	...	...	...	...	...	...	...	...	...	...	...	...
		do ...	Unspecified	do ...	26	13	13	41	30	11	77	39	38	241	136	105	210	109	101
			Total......	......	26	13	13	41	30	11	81	43	38	241	136	105	273	142	131
			Grand Total......	......	161,795	83,230	78,565	240,763	123,249	117,514	220,493	110,749	109,744	82,516	41,630	40,886	448,900	226,880	217,570

TABLE XVI.

Castes and Sub-divisions.—*Continued.*

Class.	Group.	Castes.	Sub-division of Castes.	Religion.	Birh. Total.	Birh. Males.	Birh. Females.	Nander. Total.	Nander. Males.	Nander. Females.	Naldrug. Total.	Naldrug. Males.	Naldrug. Females.	Bidar. Total.	Bidar. Males.	Bidar. Females.	Parbhani. Total.	Parbhani. Males.	Parbhani. Females.
					36	37	38	39	40	41	42	43	44	45	46	47	48	49	50
F	48 ...	Syed ...	Alvi	Mussulman...	...	...	...	...	...	...	11	4	7	...	...	...	2	2	...
		do ...	Bakari	do ...	...	...	...	...	...	...	...	...	...	...	...	...	...	...	...
		do ...	Hasani...	do ...	12	1	11	12	6	6	3	2	1	...	...	...	5	2	3
		do ...	Hasan-ul-Husaini ...	do ...	...	...	...	...	...	...	...	...	...	...	...	...	...	...	...
		do ...	Husaini	do ...	274	151	123	198	77	121	219	123	96	1	1	...	592	299	293
		do ...	Jafari	do ...	...	...	...	...	...	...	...	...	...	...	...	...	...	...	...
		do ...	Mahdvi	do ...	...	...	...	...	...	...	...	...	...	...	...	...	...	...	...
		do ...	Musavi	do ...	...	...	...	...	...	...	...	...	...	...	...	...	...	...	...
		do ...	Nakvi	do ...	...	...	...	...	...	...	...	...	...	...	...	...	...	...	...
		do ...	Razvi	do ...	...	...	...	...	...	...	75	32	43	40	2	38	21	12	9
		do ...	Zaidi	do ...	...	...	...	...	...	...	...	...	...	...	...	...	...	...	...
		do ...	Unspecified	do ...	2,944	1,506	1,438	3,233	1,685	1,548	4,390	2,256	2,134	7,117	3,591	3,526	3,151	1,618	1,533
			Total......	......	3,230	1,658	1,572	3,443	1,768	1,675	4,698	2,417	2,281	7,158	3,594	3,564	3,771	1,933	1,838
F	48 ...	Arab ...	Ajfi	Mussulman...	...	...	...	5	5	...	...	...	...	...	...	...	...	...	...
		do ...	Badvi	do ...	18	12	6	...	...	...	...	...	...	...	...	...	...	...	...
		do ...	Balirsar	do ...	...	...	...	...	...	...	...	...	...	...	...	...	...	...	...
		do ...	Basri	do ...	...	...	...	...	...	...	...	...	...	...	...	...	...	...	...
		do ...	Darvan	do ...	...	...	...	...	...	...	...	...	...	...	...	...	...	...	...
		do ...	Habib	do ...	...	...	...	...	...	...	...	...	...	...	...	...	...	...	...
		do ...	Hazramut	do ...	...	...	...	...	...	...	...	...	...	1	1	...	...	...	...
		do ...	Kalabsar	do ...	...	...	...	...	...	...	1	...	1	...	...	...	...	...	...
		do ...	Kohavi	do ...	...	...	...	...	...	...	...	...	...	...	...	...	...	...	...
		do ...	Movallad	do ...	...	...	...	...	...	...	...	...	...	...	...	...	...	...	...
		do ...	Nadi	do ...	...	...	...	...	...	...	...	...	...	...	...	...	...	...	...
		do ...	Rafai	do ...	...	...	...	2	1	1	...	...	...	...	...	...	...	...	...
		do ...	Saori	do ...	...	...	...	...	...	...	...	...	...	...	...	...	7	3	4
		do ...	Sharif	do ...	...	...	...	...	...	...	...	...	...	...	...	...	1	1	...
		do ...	Unspecified	do ...	58	30	28	52	30	22	128	95	33	156	81	75	106	68	38
			Total......	......	76	42	34	59	36	23	129	95	34	157	82	75	114	72	42
			Grand Total......	......	330,921	169,413	161,508	306,371	156,291	150,080	361,380	184,809	176,571	404,048	205,591	198,457	403,236	206,213	197,023

TABLE XVI.

Castes and Sub-divisions.—*Continued.*

Class.	Group.	Castes.	Sub-division of Castes.	Religion.	Sirpur Tandur. Total.	Sirpur Tandur. Males.	Sirpur Tandur. Females.	Gulbarga. Total.	Gulbarga. Males.	Gulbarga. Females.	Raichur. Total.	Raichur. Males.	Raichur. Females.	Lingasugur. Total.	Lingasugur. Males.	Lingasugur. Females.	Railways. Total.	Railways. Males.	Railways. Females.
					51	52	53	54	55	56	57	58	59	60	61	62	63	64	65
F	48 ...	Syed ...	Alvi ...	Musulman...	...	...	...	55	39	16	...	...	...	101	54	47	...	...	...
		do ...	Bakari ...	do ...	...	...	...	...	...	...	...	...	...	...	...	...	...	...	...
		do ...	Hasani...	do ...	...	...	...	55	25	30	55	30	25	...	...	...	...	...	...
		do ...	Hasan-ul-Husaini ...	do ...	...	...	...	...	...	...	...	...	...	...	...	...	...	...	...
		do ...	Husaini ...	do ...	65	41	24	176	106	70	749	393	356	111	66	45	...	...	...
		do ...	Jafari ...	do ...	...	...	...	...	...	...	...	...	...	...	...	...	...	...	...
		do ...	Mahdvi ...	do ...	...	...	...	...	...	...	...	...	...	...	...	...	...	...	...
		do ...	Musavi...	do ...	...	...	...	...	...	...	...	...	...	...	...	...	...	...	...
		do ...	Nakvi ...	do ...	...	...	...	...	...	...	...	...	...	...	...	...	...	...	...
		do ...	Razvi ...	do ...	30	12	18	24	11	13	2	2	...	9	4	5	...	...	...
		do ...	Zaidi ...	do ...	...	...	...	...	...	...	...	...	...	...	...	...	...	...	...
		do ...	Unspecified ...	do ...	761	341	420	6,206	3,149	3,057	5,256	2,668	2,588	8,114	4,163	3,951	209	143	66
			Total......	......	856	394	462	6,516	3,330	3,186	6,062	3,098	2,969	8,335	4,287	4,048	209	143	66
F	48 ...	Arab ...	Ajfi ...	Musulman...	...	...	...	...	...	...	...	...	...	...	...	...	...	...	...
		do ...	Badvi ...	do ...	...	...	...	...	...	...	...	...	...	...	...	...	...	...	...
		do ...	Balirsar ...	do ...	...	...	...	...	...	...	...	...	...	...	...	...	...	...	...
		do ...	Basri ...	do ...	...	...	...	...	...	...	...	...	...	...	...	...	...	...	...
		do ...	Darvan ...	do ...	...	...	...	...	...	...	...	...	...	...	...	...	...	...	...
		do ...	Habib ...	do ...	...	...	...	...	...	...	...	...	...	...	...	...	...	...	...
		do ...	Hazramut ...	do ...	...	...	...	...	...	...	...	...	...	...	...	...	...	...	...
		do ...	Kalabtar ...	do ...	...	...	...	...	...	...	...	...	...	...	...	...	...	...	...
		do ...	Kohavi...	do ...	1	1	...	...	...	...	...	...	...	...	...	...	...	...	...
		do ...	Movallad ...	do ...	...	...	...	...	...	...	...	...	...	...	...	...	...	...	...
		do ...	Nadi ...	do ...	...	...	...	...	...	...	...	...	...	...	...	...	...	...	...
		do ...	Rafai ...	do ...	19	10	9	...	...	...	...	...	...	...	...	...	...	...	...
		do ...	Saori ...	do ...	...	...	...	...	...	...	...	...	...	...	...	...	...	...	...
		do ...	Sharif ...	do ...	...	...	...	...	...	...	...	...	...	...	...	...	...	...	...
		do ...	Unspecified ...	do ...	7	5	2	127	74	53	...	...	...	65	34	31	2	2	...
			Total......	......	27	16	11	127	74	53	...	...	...	65	34	31	2	2	...
			Grand Total......	......	69,238	34,798	34,440	218,077	110,862	107,215	107,725	55,267	52,458	150,946	76,574	74,372	2,023	1,295	728

TABLE XVII A.

OCCUPATIONS BY AGE.

Class.	Order.	Sub-order and Group.	Serial No.	Occupations.	PROVINCIAL TOTAL. Total. Total.	Total. 0—4	Total. 5—14	Total. 15 and over.	Total. Unspecified.	Males. Total.	Males. 0—4	Males. 5—14	Males. 15 and over.	Males. Unspecified.	Females. Total.	Females. 0—4	Females. 5—14	Females. 15 and over.	Females. Unspecified.
1	2	3	4	5	6	7	8	9	10	11	12	13	14	15	16	17	18	19	20
Class A.	I. Administration.	1. Service of the Imperial and Provincial Governments.	1	The Viceroy, Governors, Lieutenant-Governors, and Chief Commissioners and their families	1,500	18	105	257	1,120	24	2	8	14	...	1,476	16	97	243	1,120
			2	Officers	1,585	155	295	1,123	12	827	80	150	597	...	758	75	145	526	12
			3	Officers, Superintendents, and Clerical Establishments, Police, Excise Inspectors, Sub-Registrars, &c.	16,090	1,912	3,367	10,713	98	8,106	875	1,694	5,586	1	7,984	1,037	1,678	5,177	97
			4	Messengers, Constables, Bailiffs, Warders, Menials, &c.	190,169	22,403	37,112	130,194	460	105,921	11,150	19,917	74,768	86	84,248	11,253	17,195	55,426	374
				Total Sub-order 1......	209,344	24,488	40,879	142,287	1,690	114,878	12,107	21,769	80,915	87	94,466	12,381	19,110	61,372	1,603
		2. Services of Local & Municipal Bodies.	5	Inspecting and Supervising Officials ...	6	...	1	5	...	3	...	...	3	...	3	...	1	2	...
			6	Clerical Establishments...	46	3	17	26	...	34	2	12	20	...	12	1	5	6	...
			7	Menials	3,141	363	550	2,228	...	1,531	182	279	1,070	...	1,610	181	271	1,158	...
				Total Sub-order 2......	3,193	366	568	2,259	...	1,568	184	291	1,093	...	1,625	182	277	1,166	...
		3. Village Service.	8	Headmen, when not Agriculturists ...	83,458	10,684	18,654	54,031	89	45,151	5,425	9,948	29,764	14	38,307	5,259	8,706	24,267	75
			9	Accountants	54,744	6,394	11,158	37,147	45	27,884	3,190	5,721	18,957	16	26,860	3,204	5,437	18,190	29
			11	Watchmen and other Menials	190,871	31,079	42,677	116,467	148	114,118	16,809	25,418	71,840	51	76,253	14,270	17,259	44,627	97
				Total Sub-order 3......	328,573	48,157	72,489	207,645	282	187,153	25,424	41,087	120,561	81	141,420	22,733	31,402	87,084	201
				Total Order I......	541,110	73,011	113,936	352,191	1,972	303,599	37,715	63,147	202,569	168	237,511	35,296	50,789	149,622	1,804
	II. Defence.	4. Army.	12	Officers	1,029	133	217	679	...	591	60	113	418	...	438	73	104	261	...
			13	Non-Commissioned Officers and Privates	40,816	4,610	7,824	28,301	81	24,305	2,304	3,975	18,025	1	16,511	2,306	3,849	10,276	80
			14	Followers	20,500	2,429	3,864	14,204	3	12,535	1,220	2,060	9,253	2	7,965	1,209	1,804	4,951	1
			15	Administrative Establishments ...	954	106	183	665	...	495	57	89	349	...	459	49	94	316	...
				Total Sub-order 4......	63,299	7,278	12,088	43,849	84	37,926	3,641	6,237	28,045	3	25,373	3,637	5,851	15,804	81
		5. Navy & Marine.	16	Officers	...	...	...	...	...	...	...	...	...	...	...	...	...	...	...
			17	Engineers, Warrant Officers and Seamen	...	...	...	...	...	...	...	...	...	...	...	...	...	...	...
			18	Administrative Staff	...	...	...	...	...	...	...	...	...	...	...	...	...	...	...
				Total Sub-order 5......	...	...	...	...	...	...	...	...	...	...	...	...	...	...	...
				Total Order II......	63,299	7,278	12,088	43,849	84	37,926	3,641	6,237	28,045	3	25,373	3,637	5,851	15,804	81

TABLE XVII A.

Occupations by Age.—*Continued.*

Class.	Order.	Sub-Order and Group.	Serial No.	Occupations.	TOWN. Total. Total.	Total. 0—4	Total. 5—14	Total. 15 and over.	Total. Unspecified.	Males. Total.	Males. 0—4	Males. 5—14	Males. 15 and over.	Males. Unspecified.	Females. Total.	Females. 0—4	Females. 5—14	Females. 15 and over.	Females. Unspecified.
					21	22	23	24	25	26	27	28	29	30	31	32	33	34	35
Class A.	I. Administration.	1. Service of the Imperial and Provincial Governments.	1	The Viceroy, Governors, Lieutenant-Governors, and Chief Commissioners and their families	1,500	18	105	257	1,120	24	2	8	14	...	1,476	16	97	243	1,120
			2	Officers	1,196	118	223	846	9	604	61	117	426	...	592	57	106	420	9
			3	Officers, Superintendents and Clerical Establishments, Police, Excise Inspectors, Sub-Registrars, &c.	3,710	420	815	2,475	...	2,046	220	480	1,346	...	1,664	200	385	1,129	...
			4	Messengers, Constables, Bailiffs, Warders, Menials, &c.	95,358	10,387	17,769	67,035	217	50,688	5,083	9,200	36,423	32	44,670	5,304	8,569	30,612	185
				Total Sub-order 1	101,764	10,893	18,912	70,613	1,846	53,362	5,316	9,805	38,209	32	48,402	5,577	9,107	32,404	1,314
		2. Services of Local & Municipal Bodies.	5	Inspecting and Supervising Officials ...	6	...	1	5	...	3	...	...	3	...	3	...	1	2	...
			6	Clerical Establishments	18	1	5	12	...	15	1	4	10	...	3	...	1	2	...
			7	Menials	3,019	346	521	2,152	...	1,478	175	267	1,036	...	1,541	171	254	1,116	...
				Total Sub-order 2	3,043	347	527	2,169	...	1,496	176	271	1,049	...	1,547	171	256	1,120	...
		3. Village Service.	8	Headmen, when not Agriculturists ...	1,421	148	287	985	1	749	75	155	519	...	672	73	132	466	1
			9	Accountants	2,715	311	574	1,830	...	1,359	176	281	902	...	1,356	135	293	928	...
			11	Watchmen and other Menials ...	5,042	702	1,152	3,188	...	2,684	359	631	1,694	...	2,358	343	521	1,494	...
				Total Sub-order 3......	9,178	1,161	2,013	6,003	1	4,792	610	1,067	3,115	...	4,386	551	946	2,888	1
				Total Order I	118,985	12,401	21,452	78,785	1,347	59,650	6,102	11,143	42,378	32	54,335	6,299	10,309	36,412	1,315
	II. Defence.	4. Army.	12	Officers	883	127	197	559	...	468	55	96	317	...	415	72	101	242	...
			13	Non-Commissioned Officers and Privates	34,724	3,887	6,582	24,202	53	21,228	2,000	3,374	15,854	...	13,496	1,887	3,208	8,348	53
			14	Followers	19,102	2,262	3,646	13,191	3	11,504	1,101	1,918	8,483	2	7,598	1,161	1,728	4,708	1
			15	Administrative Establishments ...	954	106	183	665	...	495	57	89	349	...	459	49	94	316	...
				Total Sub-order 4......	55,663	6,382	10,608	38,617	56	33,695	3,213	5,477	25,003	2	21,968	3,169	5,131	13,614	54
		5. Navy & Marine.	16	Officers	...	...	...	...	...	...	...	...	...	...	...	...	...	...	...
			17	Engineers, Warrant Officers and Seamen	...	...	...	...	...	...	...	...	...	...	...	...	...	...	...
			18	Administrative Staff	...	...	...	...	...	...	...	...	...	...	...	...	...	...	...
				Total Sub-order 5	...	...	...	...	...	...	...	...	...	...	...	...	...	...	...
				Total Order II	55,663	6,382	10,608	38,617	56	33,695	3,213	5,477	25,003	2	21,968	3,169	5,131	13,614	54

TABLE XVII A.

Occupations by Age.—*Continued.*

Class.	Order.	Sub-order and Group.	Serial No.	Occupations.	COUNTRY. Total. Total.	Total. 0—4	Total. 5—14	Total. 15 and over.	Total. Unspecified.	Males. Total.	Males. 0—4	Males. 5—14	Males. 15 and over.	Males. Unspecified.	Females. Total.	Females. 0—4	Females. 5—14	Females. 15 and over.	Females. Unspecified.
					36	37	38	39	40	41	42	43	44	45	46	47	48	49	50
Class A.	I. Administration.	1. Service of the Imperial and Provincial Governments.	1	The Viceroy, Governors, Lieutenant-Governors, and Chief Commissioners and their families	...	...	...	...	...	...	...	...	...	...	...	...	...	...	...
			2	Officers	389	87	72	277	8	228	19	38	171	...	166	18	39	106	8
			3	Officers, Superintendents, and Clerical Establishments, Police, Excise Inspectors, Sub-Registrars, &c.	12,380	1,492	2,552	8,238	98	6,060	655	1,214	4,190	1	6,820	837	1,338	4,048	97
			4	Messengers, Constables, Bailiffs, Warders, Menials, &c.	94,811	12,066	19,343	63,159	243	55,233	6,117	10,717	38,345	54	39,578	5,949	8,626	24,814	189
				Total Sub-order 1......	107,580	13,595	21,967	71,674	844	61,516	6,791	11,964	42,706	55	46,064	6,804	10,003	28,968	289
		2. Service of Local & Municipal Bodies.	5	Inspecting and Supervising Officials ...	...	...	...	...	...	...	...	...	...	...	...	...	...	...	...
			6	Clerical Establishments	28	2	12	14	...	19	1	8	10	...	9	1	4	4	...
			7	Menials	122	17	29	76	...	53	7	12	34	...	69	10	17	42	...
				Total Sub-order 2......	150	19	41	90	...	72	8	20	44	...	78	11	21	46	...
		3. Village Service.	8	Headmen, when not Agriculturists ...	82,037	10,536	18,367	53,046	88	44,402	5,350	9,793	29,245	14	37,635	5,186	8,574	23,801	74
			9	Accountants	52,029	6,083	10,584	35,317	45	26,525	3,014	5,440	18,055	16	25,504	3,069	5,144	17,262	29
			11	Watchmen and other Menials... ...	185,329	30,377	41,525	113,279	148	111,434	16,450	24,787	70,146	51	73,895	13,927	16,738	43,183	97
				Total Sub-order 3......	319,395	46,996	70,476	201,642	281	182,361	24,814	40,020	117,446	81	137,034	22,182	30,456	84,196	200
				Total Order I......	427,125	60,610	92,484	273,406	625	243,949	31,613	52,004	160,196	136	183,176	28,997	40,480	113,210	489
	II. Defence.	4. Army.	12	Officers	146	6	20	120	...	123	5	17	101	...	23	1	3	19	...
			13	Non-Commissioned Officers and Privates	6,092	723	1,242	4,099	28	3,077	304	601	2,171	1	3,015	419	641	1,928	27
			14	Followers	1,398	167	218	1,013	...	1,031	119	142	770	...	367	48	76	243	...
			15	Administrative Establishments ...	...	...	...	...	...	...	...	...	...	...	...	...	...	...	...
				Total Sub-order 4......	7,636	896	1,480	5,232	28	4,231	428	760	3,042	1	3,405	468	720	2,190	27
		5. Navy & Marine.	16	Officers	...	...	...	...	...	...	...	...	...	...	...	...	...	...	...
			17	Engineers, Warrant Officers and Sea men	...	...	...	...	...	...	...	...	...	...	...	...	...	...	...
			18	Administrative Staff	...	...	...	...	...	...	...	...	...	...	...	...	...	...	...
				Total Sub-order 3......	...	...	...	...	...	...	...	...	...	...	...	...	...	...	...
				Total Order II......	7,636	896	1,480	5,232	28	4,231	428	760	3,042	1	3,405	468	720	2,190	27

TABLE XVII A.

Occupations by Age.—*Continued.*

Class.	Order.	Sub-order and Group.	Serial No.	Occupations.	PROVINCIAL TOTAL. Total. Total.	Total. 0—4	Total. 5—14	Total. 15 and over.	Total. Unspecified.	Males. Total.	Males. 0—4	Males. 5—14	Males. 15 and over.	Males. Unspecified.	Females. Total.	Females. 0—4	Females. 5—14	Females. 15 and over.	Females. Unspecified.
1	2	3	4	5	6	7	8	9	10	11	12	13	14	15	16	17	18	19	20
Class A.—*concld.*	III. Foreign and Feudatory State Service.	6. Administrative Service.	19	Chiefs, Consuls and Officers ...	671	68	162	441	...	851	25	91	235	...	320	43	71	206	...
			20	Clerical Establishments	1,522	164	276	1,082	...	850	72	156	622	...	672	92	120	460	...
			21	Menials, &c.	2,315	244	429	1,639	3	1,763	159	287	1,314	3	552	85	142	325	...
				Total Sub-order 6......	4,508	476	867	3,162	3	2,964	256	534	2,171	3	1,544	220	333	991	...
		7. Army and Marine.	22	Officers	1	...	...	1	...	1	...	...	1	...	...	...	...	...	...
			23	Privates and Seamen, &c.	...	...	...	...	...	...	...	...	...	...	...	...	...	...	...
				Total Sub-order 7......	1	...	...	1	...	1	...	...	1	...	...	...	...	...	...
				Total Order III......	4,509	476	867	3,168	3	2,965	256	534	2,172	3	1,544	220	333	991	...
Class B.	IV. Live-Stock.	8. Stock breeding and dealing. (a) Horses & horned cattle.	24	Horse breeders and dealers	610	87	148	375	...	439	56	117	266	...	171	31	31	109	...
			25	Cattle breeders and dealers, and Commissariat Farm Establishment ...	23,049	2,894	8,204	11,946	5	16,482	1,639	6,475	8,366	2	6,567	1,255	1,729	8,580	3
			26	Herdsmen	87,627	9,641	40,242	37,701	43	61,901	4,871	33,350	23,661	19	25,726	4,770	6,892	14,040	24
			27	Buffalo breeders and dealers	242	34	71	137	...	171	18	49	104	...	71	16	22	33	...
		(b)—Other draught, &c., animals.	28	Elephant catchers and breeders ...	...	...	...	...	...	...	...	...	...	...	...	...	...	...	...
			29	Camel breeders and dealers	3	...	1	2	...	2	...	1	1	...	1	...	...	1	...
			30	Ass and mule breeders and dealers...	40	5	10	25	...	21	...	3	18	...	19	5	7	7	...
		(c) Small stock.	31	Sheep and goat breeders and dealers.	170,820	27,891	47,477	95,878	74	108,802	14,677	295,69	59,515	41	67,018	13,214	17,908	35,863	33
			32	Pig breeders and dealers	180	24	48	108	...	161	24	46	91	...	19	...	2	17	...
				Total Sub-order 8......	282,571	40,576	96,201	145,672	122	182,979	21,285	69,610	92,022	62	99,592	19,291	26,591	58,650	60
		9. Subsidiary Services to stock. (a) Training and doctoring live-stock.	33	Veterinary Surgeons and Assistants...	22	2	6	14	...	15	1	4	10	...	7	1	2	4	...
			34	Farriers and gelders	1,049	143	218	688	...	558	82	107	869	...	491	61	111	819	...
			35	Horse and elephant breakers and trainers, &c.	264	88	71	150	5	152	22	44	86	...	112	16	27	64	5
		(b) Vermin destroying.	36	Rat, monkey, jackal crocodile, &c., catchers	...	...	...	...	...	...	...	...	...	...	...	...	...	...	...
				Total Sub-order 9......	1,335	183	295	852	5	725	105	155	465	...	610	78	140	387	5
				Total Order IV......	283,906	40,759	96,496	146,524	127	183,704	21,390	69,765	92,487	62	100,202	19,869	26,731	54,087	65
	V. Agriculture.	10. Interest in land.	37	Land occupants not cultivating ...	100,993	18,946	22,368	64,379	800	51,376	6,899	11,837	32,615	25	49,617	7,047	10,531	31,764	275
			38	Land occupants cultivating	4,976	800	1,245	2,933	...	3,257	522	807	1,928	...	1,721	278	488	1,005	...
			39	Lessees of villages, &c.	46	6	3	37	...	25	4	3	18	...	21	2	...	19	...
			40	Tenants not cultivating	6,188	886	1,479	3,809	14	3,519	491	863	2,164	1	2,669	395	616	1,645	13
			41	Tenants and sharers cultivating ...	4,501,683	715,518	1,057,793	2,725,907	2,465	2,844,949	849,821	560,501	1,433,664	963	2,156,734	865,697	497,292	1,292,243	1,502
				Total Sub-order 10......	4,613,888	731,156	1,082,888	2,797,065	2,779	2,403,126	857,737	574,011	1,470,389	989	2,210,762	378,419	508,877	1,326,676	1,790

TABLE XVII A.

Occupations by Age.—*Continued.*

Class.	Order.	Sub-order and Group.	Serial No.	Occupations.	TOWN. Total. Total.	Total. 0—4	Total. 5—14	Total. 15 and over.	Total. Unspecified.	Males. Total.	Males. 0—4	Males. 5—14	Males. 15 and over.	Males. Unspecified.	Females. Total.	Females. 0—4	Females. 5—14	Females. 15 and over.	Females. Unspecified.
					21	22	23	24	25	26	27	28	29	30	31	32	33	34	35
Class A.—*concld.*	III. Foreign and Feudatory State Service.	6. Administrative Service.	19	Chiefs, Consuls and Officers	671	68	162	441	...	351	25	91	235	...	320	48	71	206	...
			20	Clerical Establishments	1,481	161	272	1,048	...	818	71	154	593	...	663	90	118	455	...
			21	Menials, &c.	1,677	168	286	1,223	...	1,128	83	144	901	...	549	85	142	322	...
				Total Sub-order 6......	3,829	397	720	2,712	...	2,297	179	389	1,729	...	1,532	218	331	983	...
		7. Army and Marine.	22	Officers	1	...	...	1	...	1	...	...	1	...	...	...	...	...	...
			23	Privates and Seamen, &c.	...	...	...	...	...	...	...	...	...	...	...	...	...	...	...
				Total Sub-order 7......	1	...	...	1	...	1	...	...	1	...	...	...	...	...	...
				Total Order III......	3,830	397	720	2,713	...	2,298	179	389	1,730	...	1,532	218	331	983	...
Class B.	IV. Live-Stock.	8. Stock breeding & dealing. (a) Horses & horned cattle.	24	Horse breeders and dealers	229	30	42	157	...	132	17	23	92	...	97	13	19	65	...
			25	Cattle breeders and dealers, and Commissariat Farm Establishment ...	513	69	128	316	...	352	42	93	217	...	161	27	85	99	...
			26	Herdsmen	2,121	232	747	1,142	...	1,298	125	584	589	...	823	107	163	553	...
			27	Buffalo breeders and dealers... ...	1	...	...	1	...	...	...	...	...	...	1	...	...	1	...
		(b) Other draught, &c., animals.	28	Elephant catchers and breeders ...	...	...	...	...	...	...	...	...	...	...	...	...	...	...	...
			29	Camel breeders and dealers	3	...	1	2	...	2	...	1	1	...	1	...	...	1	...
			30	Ass and mule breeders and dealers...	3	...	1	2	...	3	...	1	2	...	...	...	...	...	...
		(c) Small stock.	31	Sheep and goat breeders and dealers.	3,156	463	772	1,919	2	1,720	237	443	1,039	1	1,436	226	329	880	1
			32	Pig breeders and dealers	12	1	4	7	...	7	1	2	4	...	5	...	2	3	...
				Total Sub-order 8......	6,038	795	1,695	3,546	2	3,514	422	1,147	1,944	1	2,524	373	548	1,602	1
		9. Subsidiary Services to stock. (a) Training and doctoring live-stock.	33	Veterinary Surgeons and Assistants...	20	2	6	12	...	13	1	4	8	...	7	1	2	4	...
			34	Farriers and gelders	607	83	129	395	...	314	45	68	201	...	293	38	61	194	...
			35	Horse and elephant breakers and trainers, &c.	85	9	26	50	...	48	8	16	24	...	37	1	10	26	...
		(b) Vermin destroying.	36	Rat, monkey, jackal, crocodile, &c., catchers	...	...	...	...	...	...	...	...	...	...	...	...	...	...	...
				Total Sub-order 9......	712	94	161	457	...	375	54	88	233	...	337	40	73	224	...
				Total Order IV......	6,750	889	1,856	4,003	2	3,889	476	1,235	2,177	1	2.861	413	621	1,826	1
	V. Agriculture.	10. Interest in land.	37	Land occupants not cultivating ...	13,906	1,318	2,492	10,086	10	6,279	658	1,218	4,401	2	7,627	660	1,274	5,685	8
			38	Land occupants cultivating	927	172	251	503	...	430	85	116	229	...	497	88	135	274	...
			39	Lessees of villages, &c.	25	2	1	22	...	8	1	1	6	...	17	1	...	16	...
			40	Tenants not cultivating	152	15	34	103	...	71	7	19	45	...	81	8	15	58	...
			41	Tenants and sharers cultivating ...	117,236	16,795	25,676	74,646	119	61,692	8,259	13,889	39,507	37	55,544	8,536	11,787	35,139	82
				Total Sub-order 10......	132,246	18,303	28,454	85,360	129	68,480	9,010	15,248	44,188	39	63,766	9,293	13,211	41,172	90

TABLE XVII A.

Occupations by Age.—*Continued.*

Class.	Order.	Sub-order and Group.	Serial No.	Occupations.	COUNTRY. Total. Total.	Total. 0—4	Total. 5—14	Total. 15 and over.	Total. Unspecified.	Males. Total.	Males. 0—4	Males. 5—14	Males. 15 and over.	Males. Unspecified.	Females. Total.	Females. 0—4	Females. 5—14	Females. 15 and over.	Females. Unspecified.
					36	37	38	39	40	41	42	43	44	45	46	47	48	49	50
Class A.—*concld.*	III. Foreign and Feudatory State Service.	6. Administrative service.	19	Chiefs, Consuls and Officers... ...	...	...	...	...	...	...	...	...	...	...	...	...	...	...	...
			20	Clerical Establishments	41	8	4	34	...	32	1	2	29	...	9	2	2	5	...
			21	Menials, &c.	638	76	143	416	3	635	76	143	413	3	3	...	...	3	...
				Total Sub-order 6......	679	79	147	450	3	667	77	145	442	3	12	2	2	8	...
		7. Army and Marine.	22	Officers	...	...	...	...	...	...	...	...	...	...	...	...	...	...	...
			23	Privates and Seamen, &c.	...	...	...	...	...	...	...	...	...	...	...	...	...	...	...
				Total Sub-order 7......	...	...	...	...	...	...	...	...	...	...	...	...	...	...	...
				Total Order III......	679	79	147	450	3	667	77	145	442	3	12	2	2	8	...
Class B.	IV. Live-Stock.	8. Stock breeding & dealing. (a) Horses & horned cattle.	24	Horse breeders and dealers	881	57	106	218	...	807	39	94	174	...	74	18	12	44	...
			25	Cattle breeders and dealers, and Commissariat Farm Establishment ...	22,536	2,825	8,076	11,630	5	16,130	1,597	6,382	8,149	2	6,406	1,228	1,694	3,481	3
			26	Herdsmen	85,506	9,409	39,495	36,559	43	60,603	4,746	32,766	23,072	19	24,903	4,663	6,729	13,487	24
			27	Buffalo breeders and dealers ...	241	34	71	136	...	171	18	49	104	...	70	16	22	32	...
		(b)—Other draught, &c., animals.	28	Elephant catchers and breeders ...	...	...	...	...	...	...	...	...	...	...	...	...	...	...	...
			29	Camel breeders and dealers	...	...	...	...	...	...	...	...	...	...	...	...	...	...	...
			30	Ass and mule breeders and dealers...	37	5	9	23	...	18	...	2	16	...	19	5	7	7	...
		(c) Small stock.	31	Sheep and goat breeders and dealers.	167,664	27,428	46,705	93,459	72	102,082	14,440	29,126	58,476	40	65,582	12,988	17,579	34,983	32
			32	Pig breeders and dealers	168	23	44	101	...	154	23	44	87	...	14	...	...	14	...
				Total Sub-order 8......	276,533	39,781	94,506	142,126	120	179,465	20,863	68,463	90,078	61	97,068	18,918	26,043	52,048	59
		9. Subsidiary Services to stock. (a) Training and doctoring live-stock.	33	Veterinary Surgeons and Assistants...	2	...	...	2	...	2	...	...	2	...	...	...	...	...	...
			34	Farriers and gelders	442	60	89	293	...	244	37	89	168	...	198	23	50	125	...
			35	Horse and elephant breakers and trainers, &c.	179	29	45	100	5	104	14	28	62	...	75	15	17	38	5
		(b) Vermin destroying.	36	Rat, monkey, jackal, crocodile, &c., catchers	...	...	...	...	...	...	...	...	...	...	...	...	...	...	...
				Total Sub-order 9......	623	89	134	395	5	350	51	67	232	...	273	38	67	163	5
				Total Order IV......	277,156	39,870	94,640	142,521	125	179,815	20,914	68,530	90,310	61	97,341	18,956	26,110	52,211	64
	V. Agriculture.	10. Interest in land.	37	Land occupants not cultivating ...	87,087	12,628	19,876	54,293	290	45,097	6,241	10,619	28,214	23	41,990	6,387	9,257	26,079	267
			38	Land occupants cultivating	4,051	627	994	2,430	...	2,827	437	691	1,699	...	1,224	190	303	731	...
			39	Lessees of villages, &c....	21	4	2	15	...	17	3	2	12	...	4	1	...	3	...
			40	Tenants not cultivating	6,036	871	1,445	3,706	14	3,448	484	844	2,119	1	2,588	387	601	1,587	13
			41	Tenants and sharers cultivating ...	4,384,447	698,723	1,032,117	2,651,261	2,346	2,283,257	341,562	546,612	1,394,157	926	2,101,190	357,161	485,505	1,257,104	1,420
				Total Sub-order 10......	4,481,642	712,853	1,054,434	2,711,705	2,650	2,334,646	348,727	558,768	1,426,201	950	2,146,996	364,126	495,666	1,285,504	1,700

TABLE XVII A.

Occupations by Age.—*Continued.*

Class.	Order.	Sub-order and Group.	Serial No.	Occupations.	PROVINCIAL TOTAL. Total. Total.	Total. 0—4	Total. 5—14	Total. 15 and over.	Total. Unspecified.	Males. Total.	Males. 0—4	Males. 5—14	Males. 15 and over.	Males. Unspecified.	Females. Total.	Females. 0—4	Females. 5—14	Females. 15 and over.	Females. Unspecified.
1	2	3	4	5	6	7	8	9	10	11	12	13	14	15	16	17	18	19	20
Class B.—*concld.*	V. Agriculture—*concld.*	11. Agricultural labourers.	42	Farm servants	124,534	18,514	27,802	78,158	60	79,624	10,139	17,220	52,242	28	44,910	8,375	10,582	25,916	37
			43	Field labourers and crop watchers ...	432,925	62,445	92,051	278,228	201	172,345	27,133	43,138	102,018	56	260,580	35,312	48,913	176,210	145
				Total Sub-order 11......	557,459	80,959	119,853	356,386	261	251,969	37,272	60,358	154,260	79	305,490	43,687	59,495	202,126	182
		12. Growers of special products and trees.	44	Tea, coffee and cinchona planters, Managers and Assistants ...	...	...	...	...	...	...	...	...	...	...	...	...	...	...	...
			45	Cocoanut growers	...	...	...	...	...	...	...	...	...	...	...	...	...	...	...
			46	Beetel-vine and areca-nut growers ...	348	44	72	232	...	167	14	81	122	...	181	30	41	110	...
			47	Waternut growers	1	...	...	1	...	...	...	...	...	...	1	...	...	1	...
			48	Cardamom and pepper growers ...	...	...	...	...	...	...	...	...	...	...	...	...	...	...	...
			49	Indigo planters, Managers, &c. ...	...	...	...	...	...	...	...	...	...	...	...	...	...	...	...
			50	Fruit growers	386	49	90	247	...	344	42	84	218	...	42	7	6	29	...
			51	Market gardeners, (vegetable growers)	3,707	511	735	2,459	2	1,621	204	322	1,094	1	2,086	807	413	1,865	1
			52	Gardeners, seedsmen, &c.	2,046	258	380	1,407	1	1,258	143	222	887	1	798	115	158	520	...
			53	Manure preparers and sellers, (sometimes also scavengers)	22	3	8	11	...	12	1	4	7	...	10	2	4	4	...
			54	Forest Officers	23	4	7	12	...	17	4	5	8	...	6	...	2	4	...
			55	Forest rangers, Guards, Peons ...	429	49	101	276	3	296	23	74	199	...	133	26	27	77	3
				Total Sub-order 12......	6,962	918	1,398	4,645	6	3,710	481	742	2,585	2	3,252	487	651	2,110	4
		13. Agricultural training and supervision.	56	Directors of Agriculture and their Assistants	7	1	2	4	...	4	1	2	1	...	3	...	...	3	...
			57	Model Farm Managers, &c.	...	...	...	...	...	...	...	...	...	...	...	...	...	...	...
			58	Agents and Managers of landed estates, (not planters)	18	2	5	6	...	5	...	2	3	...	8	2	3	3	...
				Total Sub-order 13......	20	3	7	10	...	9	1	4	4	...	11	2	3	6	...
				Total order V......	5,178,829	813,036	1,204,141	3,158,106	3,046	2,658,814	395,441	635,115	1,627,188	1,070	2,519,515	417,595	569,026	1,580,918	1,976
Class C.	VI. Personal and household services.	14. Personal and domestic services.	59	Barbers	85,741	13,041	19,932	52,717	51	45,985	6,437	10,747	28,775	26	39,756	6,604	9,185	23,942	25
			60	Ear pickers	...	...	...	...	...	...	...	...	...	...	...	...	...	...	...
			61	Tattooers	26	4	2	20	...	18	4	2	12	...	8	...	...	8	...
			62	Caste-mark appliers	...	...	...	...	...	...	...	...	...	...	...	...	...	...	...
			63	Washermen, (sometimes also dyers) ...	157,901	25,233	39,190	93,399	79	78,903	12,202	20,336	46,345	20	78,998	13,031	18,854	47,054	59
			64	Water carriers	7,441	993	1,587	4,859	2	3,829	493	817	2,518	1	3,612	500	770	2,341	1
			65	Cooks	5,765	672	1,198	3,897	8	3,087	348	600	2,139	...	2,678	324	593	1,758	3
			66	Indoor servants...	372,235	46,393	75,098	249,769	975	204,803	22,466	41,571	140,673	93	167,432	23,927	33,527	109,096	882
			67	Grooms, coachmen and dog boys, &c. ...	16,325	1,966	3,077	11,276	6	9,672	912	1,599	7,159	2	6,653	1,054	1,478	4,117	4
			68	Door-keepers, &c.	2,519	385	551	1,581	2	1,585	196	347	1,041	1	934	189	204	590	1
				Total Sub-order 14......	647,958	88,687	140,680	417,568	1,118	347,882	43,058	76,019	228,662	148	300,071	45,579	64,611	188,906	975

TABLE XVII A.

Occupations by Age.—*Continued.*

Class.	Order.	Sub-order and Group.	Serial No.	Occupations.	TOWN. Total. Total.	Total. 0—4	Total. 5—14	Total. 15 and over.	Total. Unspecified.	Males. Total.	Males. 0—4	Males. 5—14	Males. 15 and over.	Males. Unspecified.	Females. Total.	Females. 0—4	Females. 5—14	Females. 15 and over.	Females. Unspecified.
					21	22	23	24	25	26	27	28	29	30	31	32	33	34	35
Class B.—*concld.*	V. Agriculture.—*concld.*	11. Agricultural labourers.	42	Farm servants	11,511	1,605	2,390	7,515	1	7,725	1,020	1,694	5,010	1	8,786	585	696	2,505	...
			43	Field labourers and crop watchers ...	11,552	1,752	2,430	7,370	...	5,808	868	1,860	3,580	...	5,744	884	1,070	3,790	...
				Total Sub-order 11......	23,063	3,357	4,820	14,885	1	13,533	1,888	3 054	8,590	1	9,530	1,469	1,766	6,295	...
		12. Growers of special products and trees.	44	Tea, coffee and cinchona planters, Managers and Assistants ...	...	...	...	...	...	...	...	...	...	...	...	...	...	...	...
			45	Cocoanut growers	...	...	...	...	...	...	...	...	...	...	...	...	...	...	...
			46	Betel-vine and areca-nut growers ...	9	1	1	7	...	9	1	1	7	...	...	...	...	...	...
			47	Waternut growers	...	...	...	...	...	...	...	...	...	...	...	...	...	...	...
			48	Cardamom and pepper growers ...	...	...	...	...	...	...	...	...	...	...	...	...	...	...	...
			49	Indigo planters, Managers, &c. ...	...	...	...	...	...	...	...	...	...	...	...	...	...	...	...
			50	Fruit growers	119	13	24	82	...	79	6	18	55	...	40	7	6	27	...
			51	Market gardeners, (vegetable growers)	1,214	129	222	863	...	641	60	109	472	...	573	69	113	891	...
			52	Gardeners, Seedsmen, &c.	1,254	141	222	891	...	639	64	105	470	...	615	77	117	421	...
			53	Manure preparers and sellers, (sometimes also scavengers)	...	...	...	...	...	...	...	...	...	...	...	...	...	...	...
			54	Forest Officers	...	...	...	...	...	...	...	...	...	...	...	...	...	...	...
			55	Forest rangers, Guards, Peons ...	134	21	28	82	8	84	9	20	55	...	50	12	8	27	8
				Total Sub-order 12......	2,730	805	497	1,925	8	1,452	140	253	1,059	...	1,278	165	244	866	8
		13. Agricultural training and supervision.	56	Directors of Agriculture and their Assistants	7	1	2	4	...	4	1	2	1	...	3	...	...	3	...
			57	Model Farm Managers, &c.	...	...	...	...	...	...	...	...	...	...	...	...	...	...	...
			58	Agents and Managers of landed estates (not planters)	13	2	5	6	...	5	...	2	3	...	8	2	3	3	...
				Total Sub-order 13......	20	3	7	10	...	9	1	4	4	...	11	2	3	6	...
				Total Order V......	158,059	21,968	33,778	102,180	133	83,474	11,039	18,554	53,841	40	74,585	10,929	15,224	48,389	93
Class. C.	VI. Personal and household services.	14. Personal and domestic services.	59	Barbers	9,328	1,168	2,081	6,077	2	4,890	586	1,133	3,171	...	4,438	582	948	2,906	2
			60	Ear pickers	...	...	...	...	...	...	...	...	...	...	...	...	...	...	...
			61	Tattooers	...	...	...	...	...	...	...	...	...	...	...	...	...	...	...
			62	Caste-mark appliers	...	...	...	...	...	...	...	...	...	...	...	...	...	...	...
			63	Washermen, (sometimes also dyers)...	12,277	1,703	2,869	7,696	9	6,284	852	1,548	3,882	2	5,993	851	1,321	3,814	7
			64	Water carriers	3,651	426	769	2,456	...	1,763	198	381	1,184	...	1,888	228	388	1,272	...
			65	Cooks	4,184	470	904	2,808	2	2,161	244	441	1,476	...	2,023	226	463	1,382	2
			66	Indoor servants	118,508	11,579	19,676	86,908	845	64,341	5,865	10,823	47,636	17	54,167	5,714	8,853	39,272	828
			67	Grooms, coachmen and dog boys, &c.	12,228	1,326	2,232	8,668	2	7,579	674	1,216	5,688	1	4,649	652	1,016	2,980	1
			68	Door-keepers, &c.	39	4	10	25	...	37	4	9	24	...	2	...	1	1	...
				Total Sub-order 14......	160,215	16,676	28,541	114,638	360	87,055	8,423	15,551	63,061	20	73,160	8,258	12,990	51,577	840

TABLE XVII A.

Occupations by Age.—*Continued.*

Class.	Order.	Sub-order and Group.	Serial No.	Occupations.	COUNTRY. Total. Total.	Total. 0—4	Total. 5—14	Total. 15 and over.	Total. Unspecified.	Males. Total.	Males. 0—4	Males. 5—14	Males. 15 and over.	Males. Unspecified.	Females. Total.	Females. 0—4	Females. 5—14	Females. 15 and over.	Females. Unspecified.
					36	37	38	39	40	41	42	43	44	45	46	47	48	49	50
Class B.—*contd.*	V. Agriculture.—*contd.*	11. Agricultural labourers.	42	Farm servants	113,023	16,909	25,412	70,648	59	71,899	9,119	15,526	47,232	22	41,124	7,790	9,886	23,411	87
			43	Field labourers and crop watchers ...	421,373	60,693	89,621	270,858	201	16,657	26,265	41,778	98,438	56	254,836	34,428	47,843	172,420	145
				Total Sub-order 11......	534,396	77,602	115,038	341,501	260	238,486	35,384	57,304	145,670	78	295,960	42,218	57,729	195,831	182
		12. Growers of special products and trees.	44	Tea, coffee and cinchona planters, Managers and Assistants	...	...	...	...	...	...	...	...	...	...	...	...	...	...	...
			45	Cocoanut growers	...	...	...	...	...	...	...	...	...	...	...	...	...	...	...
			46	Betel-vine and areca-nut growers ...	389	48	71	225	...	158	18	30	115	...	181	30	41	110	...
			47	Waternut growers	1	...	...	1	...	...	...	...	...	...	1	...	...	1	...
			48	Cardamom and pepper growers ...	...	...	...	...	...	...	...	...	...	...	...	...	...	...	...
			49	Indigo planters, Managers, &c. ...	...	...	...	...	...	...	...	...	...	...	...	...	...	...	...
			50	Fruit growers	267	36	66	165	...	265	36	66	163	...	2	...	...	2	...
			51	Market gardeners, (vegetable growers).	2,493	382	513	1,596	2	980	144	213	622	1	1,513	238	300	974	1
			52	Gardeners, seedsmen, &c.	792	117	158	516	1	614	79	117	417	1	178	38	41	99	...
			53	Manure preparers and sellers, (sometimes also scavengers)	22	3	8	11	...	12	1	4	7	...	10	2	4	4	...
			54	Forest Officers...	23	4	7	12	...	17	4	5	8	...	6	...	1	4	...
			55	Forest rangers, Guards, Peons ...	295	28	73	194	...	212	14	54	144	...	83	14	19	50	...
				Total Sub-order 12......	4,232	618	896	2,720	3	2,258	291	489	1,476	2	1,974	322	407	1,244	1
		13. Agricultural training and supervision.	56	Directors of Agriculture and their Assistants	...	...	...	...	...	...	...	...	...	...	...	...	...	...	...
			57	Model Farm Managers, &c, ...	...	...	...	...	...	...	...	...	...	...	...	...	...	...	...
			58	Agents and Managers of landed estates, (not planters)...	...	...	...	...	...	...	...	...	...	...	...	...	...	...	...
				Total Sub-order 13......	...	...	...	...	...	...	...	...	...	...	...	...	...	...	...
				Total Order V......	5,020,270	791,068	1,170,368	3,055,926	2,913	2,575,340	384,402	616,561	1,573,347	1,030	2,444,930	406,666	558,802	1,482,579	1,888
Class C.	VI. Personal and household services.	14. Personal and domestic services.	59	Barbers...	76,413	11,873	17,851	46,640	49	41,095	5,851	9,614	25,604	26	35,318	6,022	8,237	21,036	23
			60	Ear pickers	...	...	...	...	...	...	...	...	...	...	...	...	...	...	...
			61	Tattooers	26	4	2	20	...	18	4	2	12	...	8	...	...	8	...
			62	Caste-mark appliers	...	...	...	...	...	...	...	...	...	...	...	...	...	...	...
			63	Washermen, (sometimes also dyers)...	145,624	23,530	36,321	85,703	70	72,619	11,350	18,788	42,468	18	73,005	12,180	17,583	43,240	52
			64	Water carriers...	3,790	567	818	2,403	2	2,066	295	436	1,334	1	1,724	272	382	1,069	1
			65	Cooks	1,581	202	289	1,089	1	926	104	159	663	...	655	98	130	426	1
			66	Indoor servants	253,727	34,814	55,422	162,861	630	140,462	16,601	30,748	93,087	76	113,265	18,213	24,674	69,824	554
			67	Grooms, coachmen and dog boys, &c.	4,097	640	845	2,608	4	2,093	238	383	1,471	1	2,004	402	462	1,137	3
			68	Door-keepers, &c.	2,480	331	541	1,606	2	1,548	192	338	1,017	1	932	139	208	589	3
				Total Sub-order 14......	487,788	71,961	112,089	302,980	758	260,827	34,635	60,468	165,601	123	226,911	37,326	51,621	137,329	635

TABLE XVII A.

Occupations by Age.—*Continued.*

Class.	Order.	Sub-order and Group.	Serial No.	Occupations.	PROVINCIAL TOTAL. Total. Total.	Total. 0—4	Total. 5—14	Total. 15 and over.	Total. Unspecified.	Males. Total.	Males. 0—4	Males. 5—14	Males. 15 and over.	Males. Unspecified.	Females. Total.	Females. 0—4	Females. 5—14	Females. 15 and over.	Females. Unspecified.
1	2	3	4	5	6	7	8	9	10	11	12	13	14	15	16	17	18	19	20
Class. C.—*concld.*	VI. Personal and household services.—*concld.*	15. Non-domestic Establishment.	69	Hotel, Lodging and Boarding house, Bar and Refreshment-room-keepers ...	360	49	76	235	...	188	29	43	116	...	172	20	88	119	...
			70	Rest-house, Serai, Bath house, &c., Owners and Managers	18	1	2	10	...	10	...	1	9	...	3	1	1	1	...
			71	Club-Secretaries, Managers, Stewards, &c.	...	...	...	...	...	...	...	...	...	...	...	...	...	...	...
				Total Sub-order 15	373	50	78	245	...	198	29	44	125	...	175	21	34	120	...
		16. Sanitation.	72	Sanitary Officers of Government ...	...	...	...	...	...	...	...	...	...	...	...	...	...	...	...
			73	Sanitary Inspectors, &c., Local and Municipal	249	46	49	154	...	168	28	36	104	...	81	18	13	50	...
			74	Sweepers and scavengers	3,046	407	684	1,953	2	1,338	162	316	860	...	1,708	245	368	1,093	2
			75	Dust and sweeping contractors ...	8	...	...	8	...	...	...	...	...	...	8	...	...	8	...
				Total Sub-order 16	3,303	453	733	2,115	2	1,506	190	352	964	...	1,797	263	381	1,151	2
				Total Order VI	65,629	89,140	141,441	419,928	1,120	349,586	43,277	76,415	229,751	143	302,043	45,863	65,026	190,177	977
Class D.—Preparation and supply of material substances.	VII. Food and drink.	17. Animal food.	76	Cow and buffalo-keepers, and milk and butter sellers	16,871	2,235	8,907	10,721	8	7,576	1,003	1,867	4,703	3	9,295	1,232	2,040	6,018	5
			77	Ghee preparers and sellers	1,436	196	319	921	...	376	51	97	228	...	1,060	145	222	693	...
			78	Cheese-makers and sellers	...	...	...	...	...	...	...	...	...	...	...	...	...	...	...
			79	Butchers...	21,704	3,099	5,153	13,413	89	11,091	1,430	2,740	6,918	3	10,613	1,669	2,413	6,495	86
			80	Fowl and egg dealers	405	75	90	240	...	186	32	48	106	—	219	43	42	134	...
			81	Fishermen and fish-curers, (many are also boatmen and palki bearers) ...	38,535	7,010	10,259	21,243	23	19,709	3,317	5,611	10,775	6	18,826	3,693	4,648	10,468	17
			82	Fish dealers	12,872	2,272	3,010	7,084	6	7,053	1,130	1,811	4,111	1	5,319	1,142	1,199	2,978	5
				Total Sub-order 17	91,323	14,887	22,738	53,622	76	45,991	6,963	12,174	26,841	13	45,332	7,924	10,564	26,781	63
		18. Vegetable food.	83	Grain dealers	90,486	11,131	20,061	59,233	61	46,973	5,434	10,598	30,934	7	43,513	5,697	9,463	28,299	54
			84	Grain parchers	3,824	465	799	2,535	25	1,428	180	371	876	1	2,396	285	428	1,659	24
			85	Pulse and flour preparers and sellers ...	1,984	194	380	1,408	2	473	74	143	256	...	1,511	120	237	1,152	2
			86	Flour mill service and management ...	...	...	...	...	...	...	...	...	...	...	...	...	...	...	...
			87	Bakers	1,179	105	221	853	...	665	57	127	481	...	514	48	94	872	...
			88	Bran sellers	11	1	2	8	...	6	1	2	8	...	5	—	—	5	—
			89	Vegetable sellers	25,781	3,982	6,074	15,716	9	12,780	1,928	3,275	7,572	5	13,001	2,054	2,799	8,144	4
			90	Fruit sellers	24,996	4,429	6,356	14,203	8	12,505	2,139	3,409	6,952	5	12,491	2,290	2,947	7,251	3
			91	Cocoanut dealers	156	28	36	92	...	71	15	13	43	...	85	13	23	49	...

TABLE XVII A.

Occupations by Age.—*Continued.*

Class.	Order.	Sub-order and Group.	Serial No.	Occupations.	TOWN. Total. Total.	Total. 0—4	Total. 5—14	Total. 15 and over.	Total. Unspecified.	Males. Total.	Males. 0—4	Males. 5—14	Males. 15 and over.	Males. Unspecified.	Females. Total.	Females. 0—4	Females. 5—14	Females. 15 and over.	Females. Unspecified.
					21	22	23	24	25	26	27	28	29	30	31	32	33	34	35
Class C.—*concld.*	VI. Personal and household services.—*concld.*	15. Non-domestic Establishment.	69	Hotel, Lodging and Boarding house, Bar and Refreshment-room-keepers ...	251	36	61	154	...	132	20	34	78	...	119	16	27	76	...
			70	Rest-house, Serai, Bath house, &c, owners and Managers	7	1	2	4	...	4	...	1	3	...	3	1	1	1	...
			71	Club-Secretaries, Managers, Stewards, &c.	...	...	...	...	...	...	...	...	...	...	...	...	...	...	...
				Total Sub-order 15	258	37	63	158	...	136	20	35	81	...	122	17	28	77	...
		16. Sanitation.	72	Sanitary Officers of Government ...	...	...	...	...	...	...	...	...	...	...	...	...	...	...	...
			73	Sanitary Inspectors, &c., Local and Municipal	129	25	24	80	...	88	18	17	53	...	41	7	7	27	...
			74	Sweepers and scavengers	2,391	301	534	1,556	...	1,153	131	276	746	...	1,238	170	258	810	...
			75	Dust and sweeping contractors ...	5	...	...	5	...	...	...	...	...	...	5	...	...	5	...
				Total Sub-order 16	2,525	326	558	1,641	...	1,241	149	293	799	...	1,284	177	265	842	...
				Total Order VI	162,998	17,039	29,162	116,437	360	88,432	8,592	15,879	63,941	20	74,566	8,447	13,288	52,496	340
Class D.—Preparation and supply of material substances.	VII. Food and drink.	17. Animal food.	76	Cow and buffalo-keepers, and milk and butter sellers...	7,663	1,010	1,709	4,987	7	430	517	955	2,555	3	3,688	493	754	2,382	4
			77	Ghee preparers and sellers	86	4	17	65	...	43	2	9	32	...	43	2	8	33	...
			78	Cheese-makers and sellers	...	...	...	...	...	...	...	...	...	...	...	...	...	...	...
			79	Butchers	9,867	1,268	2,292	6,302	5	5,261	655	1,261	3,344	1	4,606	613	1,031	2,958	4
			80	Fowl and egg dealers	191	26	39	126	...	97	13	23	61	...	94	13	16	65	...
			81	Fishermen and fish curers, (many are also boatmen and palki bearers) ...	4,411	721	1,182	2,508	...	2,528	288	701	1,439	...	1,883	333	481	1,069	...
			82	Fish dealers	1,546	236	360	950	...	608	72	154	382	...	938	164	206	568	...
				Total Sub-order 17	23,764	3,265	5,599	14,888	12	12,567	1,647	3,108	7,813	4	11,197	1,618	2,496	7,075	8
		18. Vegetable food.	83	Grain dealers	15,751	1,588	2,982	11,169	12	8,460	821	1,605	6,034	...	7,291	767	1,377	5,135	12
			84	Grain parchers	1,202	143	246	813	...	525	72	129	324	...	677	71	117	489	...
			85	Pulse and flour preparers and sellers ...	633	64	184	435	...	261	34	82	145	...	372	30	52	290	...
			86	Flour mill service and management ...	...	...	...	...	...	...	...	...	...	...	...	...	...	...	...
			87	Bakers	1,157	104	212	841	...	656	57	121	478	...	501	47	91	368	...
			88	Bran sellers	11	1	2	8	...	6	1	2	3	...	5	...	...	5	...
			89	Vegetable sellers...	5,447	720	1,229	3,496	2	2,343	330	610	1,402	1	3,104	390	619	2,094	1
			90	Fruit sellers	3,012	422	667	1,928	...	1,369	196	338	835	...	1,643	226	329	1,088	...
			91	Cocoanut dealers	69	12	17	40	...	35	10	9	16	...	34	2	8	24	...

TABLE XVII A.

Occupations by Age.—*Continued.*

Class.	Order.	Sub-order and Group.	Serial No.	Occupations.	COUNTRY. Total. Total.	Total. 0—4	Total. 5—14	Total. 15 and over.	Total. Unspecified.	Males. Total.	Males. 0—4	Males. 5—14	Males. 15 and over.	Males. Unspecified.	Females. Total.	Females. 0—4	Females. 5—14	Females. 15 and over.	Females. Unspecified.
					36	37	38	39	40	41	42	43	44	45	46	47	48	49	50
Class C.—*concld.*	VI. Personal and household services.—*concld.*	15. Non-domestic establishment.	69	Hotel, Lodging and Boarding house, Bar and Refreshment-room-keepers ...	109	13	15	81	...	56	9	9	38	...	53	4	6	43	...
			70	Rest-house, Serai, Bath house, &c., Owners and Managers	6	...	...	6	...	6	...	...	6	...	...	...	...	...	...
			71	Club-Secretaries, Managers, Stewards, &c.	...	...	...	...	...	...	...	...	...	...	...	...	...	...	...
				Total Sub-order 15	115	13	15	87	...	62	9	9	44	...	53	4	6	43	...
		16. Sanitation.	72	Sanitary Officers of Government ...	...	...	...	...	...	...	...	...	...	...	...	...	...	...	...
			73	Sanitary Inspectors, &c., Local and Municipal	120	21	25	74	...	80	10	19	51	...	40	11	6	23	...
			74	Sweepers and scavengers	655	106	150	397	2	185	31	40	114	...	470	75	110	283	2
			75	Dust and sweeping contractors... ...	3	...	...	3	...	...	...	...	...	...	3	...	...	3	...
				Total Sub-order 16	778	127	175	474	2	265	41	59	165	...	513	86	116	309	2
				Total Order VI......	488,681	72,101	112,279	303,491	760	261,154	34,685	60,536	165,810	123	227,477	37,416	51,743	137,681	637
Class D.—Preparation and supply of material substances.	VII. Food and drink.	17. Animal food.	76	Cow and buffalo-keepers and milk and butter sellers	9,208	1,225	2,198	5,784	1	8,546	486	912	2,148	...	5,662	739	1,286	3,636	1
			77	Ghee preparers and sellers	1,350	192	302	856	...	333	49	88	196	...	1,017	143	214	660	...
			78	Cheese-makers and sellers	...	...	...	...	...	...	...	...	...	...	...	...	...	...	...
			79	Butchers	11,837	1,831	2,861	7,111	34	5,830	775	1,479	3,574	2	6,007	1,056	1,382	3,537	32
			80	Fowl and egg dealers	214	49	51	114	...	89	19	25	45	...	125	30	26	69	...
			81	Fishermen and fish curers, (many are also boatmen and palki bearers) ...	34,124	6,289	9,077	18,735	23	17,181	2,929	4,910	9,336	6	16,943	3,360	4,167	9,399	17
			82	Fish dealers	10,826	2,036	2,650	6,134	6	6,445	1,058	1,657	3,729	1	4,381	978	993	2,405	5
				Total Sub-order 17	67,559	11,622	17,139	38,734	64	33,424	5,316	9,071	19,028	9	34,135	6,306	8,068	19,706	55
		18. Vegetable food.	83	Grain dealers	74,735	9,543	17,079	48,064	49	88,513	4,613	8,993	24,900	7	86,222	4,930	8,086	23,164	42
			84	Grain parchers	2,622	322	553	1,722	25	903	108	242	552	1	1,719	214	311	1,170	24
			85	Pulse and flour preparers and sellers ...	1,351	130	246	973	2	212	40	61	111	...	1,139	90	185	862	2
			86	Flour mill service and management ...	...	...	...	...	...	...	...	...	...	...	...	...	...	...	...
			87	Bakers	22	1	9	12	...	9	...	6	3	...	13	1	3	9	...
			88	Bran sellers	...	...	...	...	...	...	...	...	...	...	...	...	...	...	...
			89	Vegetable sellers	20,334	3,262	4,845	12,220	7	10,437	1,598	2,665	6,170	4	9,897	1,664	2,180	6,050	3
			90	Fruit sellers	21,984	4,007	5,689	12,280	8	11,136	1,943	3,071	6,117	5	10,848	2,064	2,618	6,163	3
			91	Cocoanut dealers	84	16	19	52	...	36	5	4	27	...	51	11	15	25	...

TABLE XVII A.

Occupations by Age.—*Continued.*

Class.	Order.	Sub-order and Group.	Serial No.	Occupations.	PROVINCIAL TOTAL. Total. Total.	Total. 0—4	Total. 5—14	Total. 15 and over.	Total. Unspecified.	Males. Total.	Males. 0—4	Males. 5—14	Males. 15 and over.	Males. Unspecified.	Females. Total.	Females. 0—4	Females. 5—14	Females. 15 and over.	Females. Unspecified.
1	2	3	4	5	6	7	8	9	10	11	12	13	14	15	16	17	18	19	20
Class D.—Preparation and supply of material substances—*contd.*	VII. Food and drink.—*concld.*	18. Vegetable food.—*contd.*	92	Confectioners and sweetmeat makers, and sellers, and cooks, who are also sometimes fishermen and water carriers	5,122	607	1,058	3,462	...	2,603	291	533	1,779	...	2,519	316	520	1,683	...
			93	Sweetmeat pedlars	181	17	25	139	...	117	10	19	88	...	64	7	6	51	...
				Total Sub order 18......	153,720	20,959	85,007	97,649	105	77,621	10,129	18,490	48,984	18	76,099	10,830	16,517	48,665	87
		19. Drink Condiments and Narcotics.	94	Ice manufacturers and sellers	300	36	53	209	2	181	25	31	125	...	119	11	22	84	2
			95	Sodawater, Lemonade, &c., manufacturers and sellers	24	2	5	17	...	8	...	1	7	...	16	2	4	10	...
			96	Sharbat preparers and sellers	20	2	8	10	...	14	2	7	5	...	6	...	1	5	...
			97	Country spirits distillers and sellers ...	62,636	9,860	15,222	37,560	24	30,220	4,562	7,581	18,`67	10	32,446	5,298	7,641	19,493	14
			98	Toddy-drawers and sellers	209,229	32,755	53,104	123,292	78	111,361	16,013	28,797	66,510	41	97,868	16,742	24,807	56,782	37
			99	Foreign wine and spirit dealers ...	472	44	76	282	70	209	23	36	150	...	263	21	40	182	70
			100	Brewers	...	...	...	...	...	...	...	...	...	...	...	...	...	...	...
			101	Tea sellers and tasters, (not planters) ...	104	9	21	74	...	75	8	12	55	...	29	1	9	19	...
			102	Coffee preparers and sellers, (not planters)	18	3	1	9	...	4	...	1	3	...	9	3	...	6	...
			103	Sugar manufacturers and sellers ...	106	14	18	74	...	90	13	14	63	...	16	1	4	11	...
			104	Molasses (jaggery, gur, &c.,) makers and sellers	689	97	123	469	...	243	30	38	175	...	446	67	85	294	...
			105	Salt preparers and sellers	13,509	1,950	3,221	8,328	10	7,874	1,071	1,931	4,868	4	5,635	879	1,290	3,460	6
			106	Assafœtida, turmeric, &c., sellers ...	7,527	879	1,710	4,936	2	3,577	411	830	2,336	...	3,950	468	880	2,600	2
			107	Vinegar manufacturers and sellers ...	13	...	4	9	...	8	...	2	6	...	5	...	2	3	...
			108	Pickle makers and sellers	33	3	8	22	...	12	1	2	9	...	21	2	6	13	...
			109	Grocers and general condiment dealers..	100,393	12,588	21,492	66,250	63	56,648	6,632	12,287	37,701	28	43,745	5,956	9,205	28,549	35
			110	Cardamom preparers and dealers ...	...	...	...	...	...	...	...	...	...	...	...	...	...	...	...
			111	Betel leaf and areca-nut sellers ...	18,927	1,874	3,015	9,020	18	7,170	923	1,610	4,631	6	6,757	951	1,405	4,389	12
			112	Tobacco and snuff manufacturers and sellers	2,814	311	617	1,882	4	1,347	148	319	880	...	1,467	163	298	1,002	4
			113	Prepared hukka pedlars	9	7	1	1	...	2	1	1	...	...	7	6	...	1	...
			114	Opium, &c., manufacturers and sellers..	608	57	145	402	4	321	28	70	223	...	287	29	75	179	4
			115	Bhang, ganja, &c., preparers and sellers.	172	18	31	123	...	68	9	8	51	...	104	9	23	72	...
				Total Sub-order 19......	412,628	60,509	98,875	252,969	275	219,432	29,900	53,578	135,865	89	193,196	30,609	45,297	117,104	186
				Total Order VII......	657,671	96,355	156,620	404,240	456	343,044	46,992	84,242	211,690	120	314,627	49,363	72,378	192,550	336

TABLE XVII A.

Occupations by Age.—*Continued.*

Class D.—Preparation and supply of material substances—*contd.* VII. Food and drink.—*contd.*

Serial No.	Occupations.	TOWN. Total. Total.	Total. 0—4	Total. 5—14	Total. 15 and over.	Total. Unspecified.	Males. Total.	Males. 0—4	Males. 5—14	Males. 15 and over.	Males. Unspecified.	Females. Total.	Females. 0—4	Females. 5—14	Females. 15 and over.	Females. Unspecified.
		21	22	23	24	25	26	27	28	29	30	31	32	33	34	35
	18. Vegetable food.—*contd.*															
92	Confectioners and sweetmeat makers, and sellers, and cooks, who are also sometimes fishermen and water carriers	1,851	194	847	1,810	...	1,029	94	183	752	...	822	100	164	558	...
93	Sweetmeat pedlars	181	17	25	189	...	117	10	19	88	...	64	7	6	51	...
	Total Sub-order 18......	29,314	8,265	5,861	20,174	14	14,801	1,625	3,098	10,077	1	14,513	1,640	2,768	10,097	13
	19. Drink Condiments and Narcotics.															
94	Ice manufacturers and sellers	112	10	25	75	2	54	4	8	42	...	58	6	17	33	2
95	Sodawater, Lemonade, &c., manufacturers and sellers	24	2	5	17	...	8	...	1	7	...	16	2	4	10	...
96	Sharbat preparers and sellers	5	1	1	3	...	3	1	1	1	...	2	...	...	2	...
97	Country spirits distillers and sellers ...	3,964	485	867	2,610	2	2,033	233	459	1,339	2	1,931	252	408	1,271	...
98	Toddy-drawers and sellers	7,888	943	1,734	5,210	1	3,881	459	846	2,476	...	4,057	484	888	2,784	1
99	Foreign wine and spirit dealers ...	443	88	70	265	70	209	23	86	150	...	284	15	84	115	70
100	Brewers...	...	...	...	...	...	...	...	...	...	...	...	...	...	...	...
101	Tea sellers and tasters, (not planters)...	104	9	21	74	...	75	8	12	55	...	29	1	9	19	...
102	Coffee preparers and sellers, (not planters)	13	8	1	9	...	4	...	1	3	...	9	3	...	6	...
103	Sugar manufacturers and sellers ...	21	4	7	10	...	15	4	6	5	...	6	...	1	5	...
104	Molasses (jaggery, gur, &c.,) makers and sellers	259	27	51	181	...	116	13	20	83	...	143	14	31	98	...
105	Salt preparers and sellers	658	76	160	422	...	331	39	76	216	...	327	37	84	206	...
106	Assafœtida, turmeric, &c., sellers ...	248	31	58	159	...	165	25	45	95	...	83	6	13	64	...
107	Vinegar manufacturers and sellers ...	10	...	4	6	...	6	...	2	4	...	4	...	2	2	...
108	Pickle makers and sellers	5	...	1	4	...	1	...	...	1	...	4	...	1	3	...
109	Grocers and general condiment dealers..	14,880	1,757	2,916	10,197	10	6,984	800	1,862	4,769	3	7,946	957	1,554	5,428	7
110	Cardamom preparers and dealers ...	...	...	...	...	...	...	...	...	...	...	...	...	...	...	...
111	Betel leaf and areca-nut sellers ...	3,358	415	683	2,260	...	1,642	202	338	1,102	...	1,716	213	345	1,158	...
112	Tobacco and snuff manufacturers and sellers	1,062	102	208	752	...	459	89	106	314	...	603	63	102	438	...
113	Prepared hukka pedlars	9	7	1	1	...	2	1	1	...	...	7	6	...	1	...
114	Opium, &c., manufacturers and sellers.	198	18	42	138	...	131	12	25	94	...	67	6	17	44	...
115	Bhang, ganja, &c., preparers and sellers.	107	10	21	76	...	45	7	6	82	...	62	3	15	44	...
	Total Sub-order 19......	33,368	3,938	6,876	22,469	85	16,064	1,870	3,401	10,788	5	17,304	2,068	3,475	11,681	80
	Total Order VII......	86,446	10,468	18,336	57,581	111	43,432	5,142	9,602	28,678	10	43,014	5,326	8,734	28,858	101

TABLE XVII A.

Occupations by Age.—*Continued.*

Class.	Order.	Sub-order and Group.	Serial No.	Occupations.	COUNTRY. Total. Total.	Total. 0—4	Total. 5—14	Total. 15 and over.	Total. Unspecified.	Males. Total.	Males. 0—4	Males. 5—14	Males. 15 and over.	Males. Unspecified.	Females. Total.	Females. 0—4	Females. 5—14	Females. 15 and over.	Females. Unspecified.
					36	37	38	39	40	41	42	43	44	45	46	47	48	49	50
Class D.—Preparation and supply of material substances.—*contd.*	VII. Food and drink.—*contd.*	18. Vegetable food.—*contd.*	92	Confectioners and sweetmeat makers, and sellers, and cooks, who are also sometimes fishermen and water carriers	3,271	413	706	2,152	...	1,574	197	350	1,027	...	1,697	216	356	1,125	...
			93	Sweetmeat pedlars	...	...	...	...	...	...	...	...	...	...	...	...	...	...	...
				Total Sub-order 18......	124,406	17,694	29,146	77,475	91	62,820	8,504	15,392	38,907	17	61,586	9,190	13,754	38,568	74
		19. Drink Condiments and Narcotics.	94	Ice manufacturers and sellers	188	26	28	134	...	127	21	23	83	...	61	5	5	51	...
			95	Sodawater, Lemonade, &c., manufacturers and sellers	...	...	...	...	...	...	...	...	...	...	...	...	...	...	...
			96	Sharbat preparers and sellers	15	1	7	7	...	11	1	6	4	...	4	...	1	3	...
			97	Country spirits distillers and sellers ...	58,702	9,375	14,355	34,950	22	28,187	4,329	7,122	16,728	8	30,515	5,046	7,233	18,222	14
			98	Toddy-drawers and sellers	201,341	31,812	51,370	118,082	77	107,530	15,554	27,901	64,034	41	93,811	16,258	23,469	54,048	36
			99	Foreign wine and spirit dealers ...	29	6	6	17	...	...	...	...	...	...	29	6	6	17	...
			100	Brewers...	...	...	...	...	...	...	...	...	...	...	...	...	...	...	...
			101	Tea sellers and tasters, (not planters)...	...	...	...	...	...	...	...	...	...	...	...	...	...	...	...
			102	Coffee preparers and sellers, (not planters)	...	...	...	...	...	...	...	...	...	...	...	...	...	...	...
			103	Sugar manufacturers and sellers ...	85	10	11	64	...	75	9	8	58	...	10	1	3	6	...
			104	Molasses (jaggery, gur, &c.,) makers and sellers	430	70	72	288	...	127	17	18	92	...	303	53	54	196	...
			105	Salt preparers and sellers	12,851	1,874	3,061	7,906	10	7,543	1,032	1,855	4,652	4	5,308	842	1,206	3,254	6
			106	Assafœtida, turmeric, &c., sellers ...	7,279	848	1,652	4,777	2	3,412	386	785	2,241	...	3,867	462	867	2,536	2
			107	Vinegar manufacturers and sellers ...	3	...	...	3	...	2	...	...	2	...	1	...	...	1	...
			108	Pickle makers and sellers	28	3	7	18	...	11	1	2	8	...	17	2	5	10	...
			109	Grocers and general condiment dealers..	85,513	10,881	18,576	56,053	53	49,714	5,832	10,925	32,932	25	35,799	4,999	7,651	23,121	28
			110	Cardamom preparers and dealers ...	...	...	...	...	...	...	...	...	...	...	...	...	...	...	...
			111	Betel leaf and areca-nut sellers ...	10,569	1,459	2,332	6,760	18	5,528	721	1,272	3,529	6	5,041	738	1,060	3,231	12
			112	Tobacco and snuff manufacturers and sellers	1,752	209	409	1,130	4	888	109	213	566	...	864	100	196	564	4
			113	Prepared hukka pedlars	...	...	...	...	...	...	...	...	...	...	...	...	...	...	...
			114	Opium, &c., manufacturers and sellers..	410	39	103	264	4	190	16	45	129	...	220	23	58	135	4
			115	Bhang, ganja, &c., preparers and sellers.	65	8	10	47	...	23	2	2	19	...	42	6	8	28	...
				Total Sub-order 19......	379,260	56,571	91,999	230,500	190	203,368	28,030	50,177	125,077	84	175,892	28,541	41,822	105,423	106
				Total Order VII......	571,225	85,887	138,284	346,709	345	299,612	41,850	74,640	183,012	110	271,613	44,037	63,644	163,697	235

TABLE XVII A.

Occupations by Age.—*Continued.*

Class.	Order.	Sub-order and Group.	Serial No.	Occupations.	PROVINCIAL TOTAL. Total. Total.	Total. 0—4	Total. 5—14	Total. 15 and over.	Total. Unspecified.	Males. Total.	Males. 0—4	Males. 5—14	Males. 15 and over.	Males. Unspecified.	Females. Total.	Females. 0—4	Females. 5—14	Females. 15 and over.	Females. Unspecified.
1	2	3	4	5	6	7	8	9	10	11	12	13	14	15	16	17	18	19	20
Class D.—Preparation and supply of material substances.—*contd.*	VIII. Light, firing and forage.	20. Lighting.	116	Oil pressers and sellers	53,885	7,100	11,698	34,568	24	27,079	8,368	6,068	17,637	11	26,306	3,732	5,635	16,926	13
			117	Oil and salt sellers	159	24	36	99	...	42	10	9	23	...	117	14	27	76	...
			118	Oil cake dealers	643	79	134	430	...	429	52	80	297	...	214	27	54	133	...
			119	Candle makers and sellers	11	2	4	5	...	11	2	4	5	...	...	...	...	...	...
			120	Torch makers and sellers	100	17	24	59	...	54	12	17	25	...	46	5	7	84	...
			121	Kerosine oil dealers	45	8	11	26	...	82	6	9	17	...	18	2	2	9	...
			122	Matches makers and sellers	24	...	7	17	...	9	...	4	5	...	15	...	3	12	...
			123	Lamp and lantern makers and sellers ...	109	11	22	76	...	61	7	14	40	...	48	4	8	36	...
			124	Gas workers, Gas Company Managers, &c.	...	...	...	...	...	...	...	...	...	...	...	...	...	...	...
				Total Sub-order 20......	54,476	7,241	11,936	35,275	24	27,717	3,457	6,200	18,049	11	26,759	3,784	5,786	17,226	13
		21. Fuel and forage.	125	Firewood and grass gatherers and sellers	35,952	5,382	7,757	22,792	21	15,631	2,521	3,787	9,869	4	20,321	2,861	4,020	13,423	17
			126	Firewood contractors and dealers ...	255	39	52	164	...	99	18	26	55	...	156	21	26	109	...
			127	Coal miners, &c....	...	...	...	...	...	...	...	...	...	...	...	...	...	...	...
			128	Coal dealers, brokers, Coal Company Managers, &c...	21	8	3	10	...	8	1	...	7	...	13	7	3	3	...
			129	Charcoal burners and dealers	488	77	116	295	...	274	89	63	172	...	214	38	53	123	...
			130	Cowdung-fuel preparers and sellers (are often also scavengers)	544	70	127	347	...	104	19	33	52	...	440	51	94	295	...
			131	Hay, &c., contractors and dealers ...	953	112	223	618	...	244	42	71	181	...	709	70	152	487	...
				Total Sub-order 21	38,213	5,688	8,278	24,226	21	16,360	2,640	3,980	9,786	4	21,853	3,048	4,348	14,440	17
				Total Order VIII	92,689	12,929	20,214	59,501	45	44,077	6,097	10,130	27,835	15	48,612	6,832	10,084	31,666	30
	IX. Buildings.	22. Building materials.	132	Brick and tile burners and sellers ...	967	115	215	637	...	512	44	122	346	...	455	71	93	291	...
			133	Lime, chunam and shell burners and sellers	1,922	307	449	1,165	1	1,120	168	256	695	1	802	139	193	470	...
			134	Stone quarry owners, contractors, marble dealers, &c.	1,727	313	372	1,042	...	1,188	208	274	706	...	539	105	98	336	...
			135	Thatch dealers and thatchers	189	20	53	116	...	93	10	21	62	...	96	10	82	54	...
				Total Sub-order 22	4,805	755	1,089	2,960	1	2,913	430	678	1,809	1	1,892	325	416	1,151	...

TABLE XVII A.

Occupations by Age.—*Continued.*

Class.	Order.	Sub-order and Group.	Serial No.	Occupations.	TOWN. Total. Total.	Total. 0—4	Total. 5—14	Total. 15 and over.	Total. Unspecified.	Males. Total.	Males. 0—4	Males. 5—14	Males. 15 and over.	Males. Unspecified.	Females. Total.	Females. 0—4	Females. 5—14	Females. 15 and over.	Females. Unspecified.
					21	22	23	24	25	26	27	28	29	30	31	32	33	34	35
Class D.—Preparation and supply of material substances.—*contd.*	VIII. Light, firing and forage.	20. Lighting.	116	Oil pressers and sellers...	7,067	869	1,562	4,632	4	3,565	445	802	2,316	2	3,502	424	760	2,316	2
			117	Oil and salt sellers	74	12	13	49	...	34	7	7	20	...	40	5	6	29	...
			118	Oil cake dealers...	33	6	6	21	...	17	4	1	12	...	16	2	5	9	...
			119	Candle makers and sellers	11	2	4	5	...	11	2	4	5	...	...	...	...	...	...
			120	Torch makers and sellers	60	7	14	39	...	31	3	9	19	...	29	4	5	20	...
			121	Kerosine oil dealers	18	3	2	13	...	6	1	...	5	...	12	2	2	8	...
			122	Matches makers and sellers	24	...	7	17	...	9	...	4	5	...	15	...	3	12	...
			123	Lamp and lantern makers and sellers ...	109	11	22	76	...	61	7	14	40	...	48	4	8	36	...
			124	Gas workers, Gas Company Managers, &c.	...	...	...	...	...	...	...	...	...	...	...	...	...	...	...
				Total Sub-order 20	7,396	910	1,630	4,852	4	3,734	469	841	2,422	2	3,662	441	789	2,430	2
		21. Fuel and forage.	125	Firewood and grass gatherers and sellers	7,901	1,018	1,664	5,209	10	3,110	457	779	1,871	3	4,791	561	885	3,338	7
			126	Firewood contractors and dealers ...	192	34	37	121	...	72	15	16	41	...	120	19	21	80	...
			127	Coal-miners, &c.	...	...	...	...	...	...	...	...	...	...	...	...	...	...	...
			128	Coal dealers, brokers, Coal Company Managers, &c.	...	...	...	...	...	...	...	...	...	...	...	...	...	...	...
			129	Charcoal burners and dealers	166	19	39	108	...	84	13	19	52	...	82	6	20	56	...
			130	Cowdung-fuel preparers and sellers (are often also scavengers)	224	32	49	143	...	30	11	10	9	...	194	21	39	134	...
			131	Hay, &c., contractors and dealers ...	664	65	150	449	...	118	27	39	52	...	546	38	111	397	...
				Total Sub-order 21	9,147	1,168	1,939	6,030	10	3,414	523	863	2,025	3	5,733	645	1,076	4,005	7
				Total Order VIII	16,543	2,078	3,569	10,882	14	7,148	992	1,704	4,447	5	9,395	1,086	1,865	6,435	9
	IX. Buildings.	22. Building materials.	132	Brick and tile burners and sellers ...	802	96	181	525	...	440	38	107	295	...	362	58	74	230	...
			133	Lime, chunam and shell burners and sellers	459	63	122	274	...	207	25	63	119	...	252	38	59	155	...
			134	Stone quarry owners, contractors, marble dealers, &c.	85	15	23	47	...	55	10	15	30	...	30	5	8	17	...
			135	Thatch dealers and thatchers	92	10	22	60	...	58	6	15	37	...	34	4	7	23	...
				Total Sub-order 22	1,438	184	348	906	...	760	79	200	481	...	678	105	148	425	...

TABLE XVII A.

Occupations by Age.—*Continued.*

Class.	Order.	Sub-order and Group.	Serial No.	Occupations.	COUNTRY. Total. Total.	Total. 0—4	Total. 5—14	Total. 15 and over.	Total. Unspecified.	Males. Total.	Males. 0—4	Males. 5—14	Males. 15 and over.	Males. Unspecified.	Females. Total.	Females. 0—4	Females. 5—14	Females. 15 and over.	Females. Unspecified.
					36	37	38	39	40	41	42	43	44	45	46	47	48	49	50
Class D.—Preparation and supply of material substances.—*contd.*	VIII. Light, firing and forage.	20. Lighting.	116	Oil pressers and sellers	46,318	6,231	10,136	29,931	20	23,514	2,923	5,261	15,321	9	22,804	3,308	4,875	14,610	11
			117	Oil and salt sellers	85	12	23	50	...	8	8	2	3	...	77	9	21	47	...
			118	Oil cake dealers...	610	73	128	409	...	412	48	79	285	...	198	25	49	124	...
			119	Candle makers and sellers	...	...	...	...	...	...	...	...	...	...	...	...	...	...	...
			120	Torch makers and sellers	40	10	10	20	...	23	9	8	6	...	17	1	2	14	...
			121	Kerosine oil dealers	27	5	9	13	...	26	5	9	12	...	1	...	...	1	...
			122	Matches makers and sellers	...	...	...	...	...	...	...	...	...	...	...	...	...	...	...
			123	Lamp and lantern makers and sellers ...	...	...	...	...	...	...	...	...	...	...	...	...	...	...	...
			124	Gas workers, Gas Company Managers, &c.	...	...	...	...	...	...	...	...	...	...	...	...	...	...	...
				Total Sub-order 20	47,080	6,331	10,306	30,423	20	23,983	2,988	5,359	15,627	9	23,097	3,343	4,947	14,796	11
		21. Fuel and forage.	125	Firewood and grass gatherers and sellers	28,051	4,364	6,093	17,583	11	12,521	2,064	2,958	7,498	1	15,530	2,300	3,135	10,085	10
			126	Firewood contractors and dealers ...	63	5	15	43	...	27	3	10	14	...	36	2	5	29	...
			127	Coal miners, &c....	...	...	...	...	...	...	...	...	...	...	...	...	...	...	...
			128	Coal dealers, brokers, Coal Company Managers, &c....	21	8	3	10	...	8	1	...	7	...	13	7	3	3	...
			129	Charcoal burners and dealers	322	58	77	187	...	190	26	44	120	...	132	32	33	67	...
			130	Cowdung-fuel preparers and sellers (are often also scavengers)	320	38	78	204	...	74	8	23	43	...	246	30	55	161	...
			131	Hay, &c., contractors and dealers ...	289	47	73	169	...	126	15	32	79	...	163	32	41	90	...
				Total Sub-order 21	29,066	4,520	6,339	18,196	11	12,946	2,117	3,067	7,761	1	16,120	2,403	3,272	10,435	10
				Total Order VIII	76,146	10,851	16,645	48,619	31	36,929	5,105	8,426	23,388	10	39,217	5,746	8,219	25,231	21
	IX. Buildings.	22. Building materials.	132	Brick and tile burners and sellers ...	165	19	34	112	...	72	6	15	51	...	93	13	19	61	...
			133	Lime, chunam and shell burners and sellers	1,463	244	327	891	1	913	143	193	576	1	550	101	134	315	...
			134	Stone quarry owners, contractors, marble dealers, &c.	1,642	298	349	995	...	1,133	198	259	676	...	509	100	90	319	...
			135	Thatch dealers and thatchers... ...	97	10	31	56	...	35	4	6	25	...	62	6	25	31	...
				Total Sub-order 22......	3,367	571	741	2,054	1	2,153	351	473	1,328	1	1,214	220	268	726	...

TABLE XVII A.

Occupations by Age.—*Continued.*

Class.	Order.	Sub-order and Group.	Serial No.	Occupations.	PROVINCIAL TOTAL. Total. Total.	Total. 0—4	Total. 5—14	Total. 15 and over.	Total. Unspecified.	Males. Total.	Males. 0—4	Males. 5—14	Males. 15 and over.	Males. Unspecified.	Females. Total.	Females. 0—4	Females. 5—14	Females. 15 and over.	Females. Unspecified.
1	2	3	4	5	6	7	8	9	10	11	12	13	14	15	16	17	18	19	20
Class D.—Preparation and supply of material substances.—*contd.*	IX. Buildings—*concld.*	23. Artificers in building.	136	Building contractors	151	19	31	97	4	44	7	8	29	...	107	12	28	68	4
			137	Stone and marble workers	4,794	942	1,122	2,725	5	2,592	489	671	1,429	3	2,202	453	451	1,296	2
			138	Masons	34,512	5,486	8,046	20,952	28	18,721	2,783	4,326	11,599	13	15,791	2,703	3,720	9,353	15
			139	Builders and Joiners	4,174	752	1,101	2,321	...	3,172	558	839	1,780	...	1,002	199	262	541	...
			140	Plasterers and house painters	70	5	11	54	...	25	...	5	20	...	45	5	6	34	...
			141	Mud wall and roof builders	12,285	2,084	2,982	7,214	5	6,662	1,032	1,628	4,002	5	5,623	1,052	1,359	3,212	...
			142	Plumbers and tile turners	60	11	10	39	...	50	9	8	33	...	10	2	2	6	...
			143	Tilers and tile turners	8	1	3	4	...	5	...	2	3	...	3	1	1	1	...
				Total Sub-order 23	56,054	9,300	13,306	33,406	42	31,271	4,873	7,482	18,895	21	24,783	4,427	5,824	14,511	21
				Total order IX	60,859	10,055	14,395	36,366	43	34,184	5,303	8,155	20,704	22	26,675	4,752	6,240	15,662	21
	X. Vehicles and Vessels.	24. Railway Plant.	144	Railway Mechanics (Fitters, painters, boiler makers, rivetters, &c.)... ...	481	66	100	315	...	268	33	54	181	...	213	33	46	134	...
			145	Railway permanent-way Foremen, plate-layers, Inspectors, &c.	589	80	75	434	...	404	44	43	317	...	185	36	32	117	...
				Total Sub-order 24	1,070	146	175	749	...	672	77	97	498	...	398	69	78	251	...
		25. Carts, carriages, &c.	146	Cart makers, carriage makers and sellers	2,460	333	553	1,568	6	1,440	171	317	952	...	1,020	162	236	616	6
			147	Palki, Dandi, Rickshaw, &c., makers and sellers	19	4	5	10	...	8	2	3	3	...	11	2	2	7	...
				Total Sub-order 25	2,479	337	558	1,578	6	1,448	173	320	955	...	1,031	164	238	623	6
		26. Ships and Boats.	148	Ship wrights, boat-builders, &c. ...	...	...	...	...	...	...	...	...	...	...	...	...	...	...	...
			149	Boat and ship painters, tarrers, &c. ...	...	...	...	...	...	...	...	...	...	...	...	...	...	...	...
			150	Sail-makers	...	...	...	...	...	...	...	...	...	...	...	...	...	...	...
			151	Wicker-boat makers, canoe diggers, &c.	...	...	...	...	...	...	...	...	...	...	...	...	...	...	...
			152	Ship chandlers and marine store dealers.	...	...	...	...	...	...	...	...	...	...	...	...	...	...	...
				Total Sub-order 26	...	...	...	...	...	...	...	...	...	...	...	...	...	...	...
				Total Order X	3,549	483	733	2,327	6	2,120	250	417	1,453	...	1,429	233	316	874	6
	XI. Supplementary requirements.	27. Paper, &c.	153	Paper makers and sellers, and palm leaf binders	1,779	289	448	1,042	...	941	124	262	555	...	838	165	186	487	...
			154	Stationers	153	15	30	108	...	126	14	23	89	...	27	1	7	19	...
			155	Waste paper and rag dealers	...	...	...	...	...	...	...	...	...	...	...	...	...	...	...
			156	Waxed-cloth preparers and sellers ...	...	...	...	...	...	...	...	...	...	...	...	...	...	...	...
				Total Sub-order 27......	1,932	304	478	1,150	...	1,067	138	285	644	...	865	166	193	506	...

TABLE XVII A.

Occupations by Age.—*Continued.*

Class.	Order.	Sub-order and Group.	Serial No.	Occupations.	TOWN. Total. Total.	Total. 0—4	Total. 5—14	Total. 15 and over.	Total. Unspecified.	Males. Total.	Males. 0—4	Males. 5—14	Males. 15 and over.	Males. Unspecified.	Females. Total.	Females. 0—4	Females. 5—14	Females. 15 and over.	Females. Unspecified.
					21	22	23	24	25	26	27	28	29	30	31	32	33	34	35
Class D.—Preparation and supply of material substances.—*contd.*	IX. Buildings.—*concld.*	23. Artificers in building.	136	Building contractors	24	2	2	16	4	3	...	...	3	...	21	2	2	13	4
			137	Stone and marble workers	735	129	137	469	...	391	61	76	254	...	344	68	61	215	...
			138	Masons	7,011	957	1,461	4,588	5	3,611	470	736	2,402	3	3,400	487	725	2,186	2
			139	Builders and Joiners	31	1	9	21	...	16	...	7	9	...	15	1	2	12	...
			140	Plasterers and house painters	44	3	6	35	...	18	...	3	15	...	26	3	3	20	...
			141	Mud wall and roof builders	719	100	144	474	1	297	42	55	199	1	422	58	89	275	...
			142	Plumbers and tile turners	11	1	3	7	...	4	...	1	3	...	7	1	2	4	...
			143	Tilers and tile turners	...	...	...	...	...	...	...	...	...	...	...	...	...	...	...
				Total Sub-order 23	8,575	1,193	1,762	5,610	10	4,340	573	878	2,885	4	4,235	620	884	2,725	6
				Total Order IX	10,013	1,377	2,110	6,516	10	5,100	652	1,078	3,366	4	4,913	725	1,032	3,150	6
	X. Vehicles and Vessels.	24. Railway Plant.	144	Railway Mechanics (Fitters, painters, boiler makers, rivetters, &c.)	385	44	86	255	...	208	19	45	144	...	177	25	41	111	...
			145	Railway permanent-way Foremen, plate-layers, Inspectors, &c.	30	3	3	24	...	21	2	2	17	...	9	1	1	7	...
				Total Sub-order 24	415	47	89	279	...	229	21	47	161	...	186	26	42	118	...
		25. Carts, carriages, &c.	146	Cart makers, carriage makers and sellers	158	18	33	107	...	97	10	24	63	...	61	8	9	44	...
			147	Palki, Dandi, Rickshaw, &c., makers and sellers	15	4	3	8	...	6	2	1	3	...	9	2	2	5	...
				Total Sub-order 25	173	22	36	115	...	103	12	25	66	...	70	10	11	49	...
		26. Ships and Boats.	148	Ship wrights, boat-builders, &c.... ...	...	...	...	...	...	...	...	...	...	...	...	...	...	...	...
			149	Boat and ship painters, tarrers, &c. ...	...	...	...	...	...	...	...	...	...	...	...	...	...	...	...
			150	Sail-makers	...	...	...	...	...	...	...	...	...	...	...	...	...	...	...
			151	Wicker-boat makers, canoe diggers, &c...	...	...	...	...	...	...	...	...	...	...	...	...	...	...	...
			152	Ship chandlers and marine store dealers.	...	...	...	...	...	...	...	...	...	...	...	...	...	...	...
				Total Sub-order 26	...	...	...	...	...	...	...	...	...	...	...	...	...	...	...
				Total Order X	588	69	125	394	...	332	33	72	227	...	256	36	53	167	...
	XI. Supplementary requirements.	27. Paper, &c.	153	Paper makers and sellers, and palm leaf binders...	739	98	218	423	...	474	59	145	270	...	265	39	73	153	...
			154	Stationers	30	1	7	22	...	19	...	5	14	...	11	1	2	8	...
			155	Waste paper and rag dealers ...	...	...	...	...	...	...	...	...	...	...	...	...	...	...	...
			156	Waxed-cloth preparers and sellers ...	...	...	...	...	...	...	...	...	...	...	...	...	...	...	...
				Total Sub-order 27	769	99	225	445	...	493	59	150	284	...	276	40	75	161	...

TABLE XVII A.

Occupations by Age.—*Continued.*

Class.	Order	Sub-order and Group.	Serial No.	Occupations.	COUNTRY. Total. Total.	Total. 0—4	Total. 5—14	Total. 15 and over.	Total. Unspecified.	Males. Total.	Males. 0—4	Males. 5—14	Males. 15 and over.	Males. Unspecified.	Females. Total.	Females. 0—4	Females. 5—14	Females. 15 and over.	Females. Unspecified.
					36	37	38	39	40	41	42	43	44	45	46	47	48	49	50
Class D.—Preparation and supp'y of material substances.—*concld.*	IX. Buildings.—*concld.*	23. Artificers in building.	136	Building contractors	127	17	29	81	...	41	7	8	26	...	86	10	21	55	...
			137	Stone and marble workers	4,059	813	985	2,256	5	2,201	428	595	1,175	3	1,858	885	890	1,081	2
			138	Masons	27,501	4,529	6,585	16,364	23	15,110	2,313	8,590	9,197	10	12,391	2,216	2,995	7,167	13
			139	Builders and Joiners	4,143	751	1,092	2,300	...	3,156	553	832	1,771	...	987	198	260	529	...
			140	Plasterers and house painters	26	2	5	19	...	7	...	2	5	...	19	2	8	14	...
			141	Mud wall and roof builders	11,566	1,984	2,838	6,740	4	6,365	990	1,568	3,803	4	5,201	994	1,270	2,937	...
			142	Plumbers and tile turners	49	10	7	32	...	46	9	7	30	...	3	1	...	2	...
			143	Tilers and tile turners	8	1	3	4	...	5	...	2	3	...	3	1	1	1	...
				Total Sub-order 23	47,479	8,107	11,544	27,796	32	26,931	4,300	6,604	16,010	17	20,548	3,807	4,940	11,786	15
				Total Order IX	50,846	8,678	12,285	29,850	38	29,084	4,651	7,077	17,338	18	21,762	4,027	5,208	12,512	15
	X. Vehicles and Vessels.	24. Railway Plant.	144	Railway Mechanics (Fitters, painters, boiler makers, rivetters, &c.)	96	22	14	60	...	60	14	9	37	...	36	8	5	23	...
			145	Railway permanent-way Foremen, plate-layers, Inspectors, &c.	559	77	72	410	...	383	42	41	300	...	176	35	31	110	...
				Total Sub-order 24	655	99	86	470	...	443	56	50	337	...	212	43	36	133	...
		25. Carts, carriages, &c.	146	Cart makers, carriage makers and sellers	2,302	315	520	1,461	6	1,343	161	293	889	...	959	154	227	572	6
			147	Palki, Dandi, Rickshaw, &c., makers and sellers	4	...	2	2	...	2	...	2	...	...	2	...	...	2	...
				Total Sub-order 25	2,306	315	522	1,463	6	1,345	161	295	889	...	961	154	227	574	6
		26. Ships and Boats.	148	Ship wrights, boat-builders, &c. ...	...	...	...	...	...	...	...	...	...	...	...	...	...	...	...
			149	Boat and ship painters, tarrers, &c. ...	...	...	...	...	...	...	...	...	...	...	...	...	...	...	...
			150	Sail-makers	...	...	...	...	...	...	...	...	...	...	...	...	...	...	...
			151	Wicker-boat makers, canoe diggers, &c.	...	...	...	...	...	...	...	...	...	...	...	...	...	...	...
			152	Ship chandlers and marine store dealers.	...	...	...	...	...	...	...	...	...	...	...	...	...	...	...
				Total Sub-order 26	...	...	...	...	...	...	...	...	...	...	...	...	...	...	...
				Total Order X	2,961	414	608	1,933	6	1,788	217	345	1,226	...	1,173	197	263	707	6
	XI. Supplementary requirements.	27. Paper, &c.	153	Paper makers and sellers, and palm leaf binders	1,040	191	230	619	...	467	65	117	285	...	573	126	113	334	...
			154	Stationers	123	14	23	86	...	107	14	18	75	...	16	...	5	11	...
			155	Waste paper and rag dealers	...	...	...	...	...	...	...	...	...	...	...	...	...	...	...
			156	Waxed-cloth preparers and sellers ...	...	...	...	...	...	...	...	...	...	...	...	...	...	...	...
				Total Sub-order 27	1,168	205	258	705	...	574	79	185	360	...	589	126	118	345	...

TABLE XVII A.

Occupations by Age.—*Continued.*

Class.	Order.	Sub-order and Group.	Serial No.	Occupations.	PROVINCIAL TOTAL. Total. Total.	Total. 0—4	Total. 5—14	Total. 15 and over.	Total. Unspecified.	Males. Total.	Males. 0—4	Males. 5—14	Males. 15 and over.	Males. Unspecified.	Females. Total.	Females. 0—4	Females. 5—14	Females. 15 and over.	Females. Unspecified.
1	2	3	4	5	6	7	8	9	10	11	12	13	14	15	16	17	18	19	20
Class D.—Preparation and supply of material substances.—*contd.*	XI. Supplementary requirements.—*contd.*	28. Books & Prints, &c.	157	Press proprietors, Lithographers and Printers	507	53	116	338	...	294	30	63	201	...	218	23	58	137	...
			158	Book-binders	170	23	40	107	...	108	15	23	70	...	62	8	17	37	...
			159	Book-sellers and publishers	314	26	40	248	...	120	12	17	91	...	194	14	23	157	...
			160	Newspaper proprietors and Managers	59	5	15	39	...	27	2	6	19	...	32	3	9	20	...
			161	News Agents, Book Agents and News-paper sellers, &c.	5	1	1	3	...	3	1	1	1	...	2	...	...	2	...
			162	Print and picture dealers	28	3	3	22	...	7	1	1	5	...	21	2	2	17	...
				Total Sub-order 28	1,083	111	215	757	...	559	61	111	387	...	524	50	104	370	...
		29. Watches, clocks, and scientific instruments.	163	Watch and clock makers and sellers	233	22	46	165	...	131	13	21	97	...	102	9	25	68	...
			164	Opticians	...	...	...	...	...	...	...	...	...	...	...	...	...	...	...
			165	Surgical instrument makers and sellers	...	...	...	...	...	...	...	...	...	...	...	...	...	...	...
			166	Photographic apparatus dealers	...	...	...	...	...	...	...	...	...	...	...	...	...	...	...
			167	Other scientific instrument makers, menders and sellers	...	...	...	...	...	...	...	...	...	...	...	...	...	...	...
			168	Scale makers and sellers	...	...	...	...	...	...	...	...	...	...	...	...	...	...	...
				Total Sub-order 29	233	22	46	165	...	131	13	21	97	...	102	9	25	68	...
		30. Carving, engraving, &c.	169	Wood and ebony carvers	13	2	6	5	...	9	1	5	3	...	4	1	1	2	...
			170	Ivory carvers	...	...	...	...	...	...	...	...	...	...	...	...	...	...	...
			171	Cotton stamp makers and sellers	...	...	...	...	...	...	...	...	...	...	...	...	...	...	...
			172	Turners and lacquerers	28	5	6	17	...	12	2	3	7	...	16	3	3	10	...
			173	Die sinkers and seal, &c., engravers	33	2	12	19	...	18	1	10	7	...	15	1	2	12	...
			174	Type-founders	...	...	...	...	...	...	...	...	...	...	...	...	...	...	...
			175	Mica, flint and Talc workers and sellers	22	1	2	19	...	1	...	...	1	...	21	1	2	18	...
			176	Mosaic and Alabaster workers and sellers	...	...	...	...	...	...	...	...	...	...	...	...	...	...	...
				Total Sub-order 30	96	10	26	60	...	40	4	18	18	...	56	6	8	42	...
		Toys, curiosities, &c.	177	Toy, kite and cage makers and sellers, Bird stuffers	155	20	37	98	...	125	19	28	78	...	30	1	9	20	...
			178	Hukka stem makers and sellers	143	17	28	98	...	85	11	17	57	...	58	6	11	41	...
			179	Papier-maché workers and sellers	377	53	72	252	...	...	...	...	...	...	377	53	72	252	...
			180	Card-makers and sellers	...	...	...	...	...	...	...	...	...	...	...	...	...	...	...
			181	Tábut and Tázia makers and sellers	26	5	2	19	...	26	5	2	19	...	...	...	...	...	...
			182	Curiosity dealers	23	1	6	16	...	14	...	2	12	...	9	1	4	4	...
				Total Sub-order 31	724	96	145	483	...	250	35	49	166	...	474	61	96	317	...

TABLE XVII A.

Occupations by Age.—*Continued.*

Class D.—Preparation and supply of material substances.—*contd.*

XI. Supplementary requirements.—*contd.*

Sub-order and Group.	Serial No.	Occupations.	TOWN. Total. Total.	TOWN. Total. 0—4	TOWN. Total. 5—14	TOWN. Total. 15 and over.	TOWN. Total. Unspecified.	TOWN. Males. Total.	TOWN. Males. 0—4	TOWN. Males. 5—14	TOWN. Males. 15 and over.	TOWN. Males. Unspecified.	TOWN. Females. Total.	TOWN. Females. 0—4	TOWN. Females. 5—14	TOWN. Females. 15 and over.	TOWN. Females. Unspecified.
			21	22	23	24	25	26	27	28	29	30	31	32	33	34	35
28. Books & Prints, &c.	157	Press proprietors, Lithographers and Printers	426	42	98	286	...	232	21	48	163	...	194	21	50	123	...
	158	Book-binders	152	20	37	95	...	90	12	20	58	...	62	8	17	87	...
	159	Book-sellers and publishers	165	14	25	126	...	93	6	14	73	...	72	8	11	53	...
	160	Newspaper proprietors and Managers	59	5	15	89	...	27	2	6	19	...	82	8	9	20	...
	161	News Agents, Book Agents and Newspaper sellers, &c.	5	1	1	8	...	3	1	1	1	...	2	...	...	2	...
	162	Print and picture dealers	...	...	...	...	...	...	...	...	...	...	...	...	...	...	...
		Total Sub-order 28	807	82	176	549	...	445	42	89	314	...	362	40	87	285	...
29. Watches, clocks, and scientific instruments.	163	Watch and clock makers and sellers	222	22	44	156	...	123	13	20	90	...	99	9	24	66	...
	164	Opticians...	...	...	...	...	...	...	...	...	...	...	...	...	...	...	...
	165	Surgical instrument makers and sellers	...	...	...	...	...	...	...	...	...	...	...	...	...	...	...
	166	Photographic apparatus dealers...	...	...	...	...	...	...	...	...	...	...	...	...	...	...	...
	167	Other scientific instrument makers, menders and sellers	...	...	...	...	...	...	...	...	...	...	...	...	...	...	...
	168	Scale makers and sellers	...	...	...	...	...	...	...	...	...	...	...	...	...	...	...
		Total Sub-order 29	222	22	44	156	...	123	13	20	90	...	99	9	24	66	...
30. Carving, engraving, &c.	169	Wood and ebony carvers	13	2	6	5	...	9	1	5	3	...	4	1	1	2	...
	170	Ivory carvers	...	...	...	...	...	...	...	...	...	...	...	...	...	...	...
	171	Cotton stamp makers and sellers	...	...	...	...	...	...	...	...	...	...	...	...	...	...	...
	172	Turners and lacquerers...	2	...	1	1	...	2	...	1	1	...	...	...	...	...	...
	173	Die sinkers and seal, &c., engravers	33	2	12	19	...	18	1	10	7	...	15	1	2	12	...
	174	Type-founders	...	...	...	...	...	...	...	...	...	...	...	...	...	...	...
	175	Mica, flint and Talc workers and sellers.	...	...	...	...	...	...	...	...	...	...	...	...	...	...	...
	176	Mosaic and Alabaster workers and sellers	...	...	...	...	...	...	...	...	...	...	...	...	...	...	...
		Total Sub-order 30	48	4	19	25	...	29	2	16	11	...	19	2	8	14	...
Toys, curiosities, &c.	177	Toy, kite and cage makers and sellers, Bird stuffers	40	1	12	27	...	80	1	10	19	...	10	...	2	8	...
	178	Hukka stem makers and sellers	136	15	27	94	...	78	9	16	58	...	58	6	11	41	...
	179	Papier-maché workers and sellers	...	...	...	...	...	...	...	...	...	...	...	...	...	...	...
	180	Card-makers and sellers	...	...	...	...	...	...	...	...	...	...	...	...	...	...	...
	181	Tábut and Tázia makers and sellers	...	...	...	...	...	...	...	...	...	...	...	...	...	...	...
	182	Curiosity dealers...	23	1	6	16	...	14	...	2	12	...	9	1	4	4	...
		Total Sub-order 31	199	17	45	137	...	122	10	28	84	...	77	7	17	58	...

TABLE XVII A.

Occupations by Age.—*Continued.*

Class D.—Preparation and supply of material substances.—*contd.*

XI. Supplementary requirements.—*contd.*

Sub-order and Group.	Serial No.	Occupations.	COUNTRY. Total. Total.	Total. 0—4	Total. 5—14	Total. 15 and over.	Total. Unspecified.	Males. Total.	Males. 0—4	Males. 5—14	Males. 15 and over.	Males. Unspecified.	Females. Total.	Females. 0—4	Females. 5—14	Females. 15 and over.	Females. Unspecified.
			36	37	38	39	40	41	42	43	44	45	46	47	48	49	50
28. Books & Prints, &c.	157	Press proprietors, Lithographers and Printers...	81	11	18	52	...	62	9	15	88	...	19	2	8	14	...
	158	Book-binders	18	8	8	12	...	18	8	8	12	...	...	...	...	...	...
	159	Book-sellers and publishers	149	12	15	122	...	27	6	3	18	...	122	6	12	104	...
	160	Newspapers proprietors and Managers...	...	...	...	...	...	...	...	...	...	...	...	...	...	...	...
	161	News Agents, Book Agents and News-paper sellers, &c.	...	...	...	...	...	...	...	...	...	...	...	...	...	...	...
	162	Print and picture dealers	28	8	8	22	...	7	1	1	5	...	21	2	2	17	...
		Total Sub-order 28	276	29	89	208	...	114	19	22	73	...	162	10	17	185	...
29. Watches, clocks, and scientific instruments.	163	Watch and clock makers and sellers	11	...	2	9	...	8	...	1	7	...	8	...	1	2	...
	164	Opticians...	...	...	...	...	...	...	...	...	...	...	...	...	...	...	...
	165	Surgical instrument makers and sellers ...	...	...	...	...	...	...	...	...	...	...	...	...	...	...	...
	166	Photographic apparatus dealers...	...	...	...	...	...	...	...	...	...	...	...	...	...	...	...
	167	Other scientific instrument makers, menders and sellers	...	...	...	...	...	...	...	...	...	...	...	...	...	...	...
	168	Scale makers and sellers	...	...	...	...	...	...	...	...	...	...	...	...	...	...	...
		Total Sub-order 29	11	...	2	9	...	8	...	1	7	...	8	...	1	2	...
30. Carving, engraving, &c.	169	Wool and ebony carvers	...	...	...	...	...	...	...	...	...	...	...	...	...	...	...
	170	Ivory carvers	...	...	...	...	...	...	...	...	...	...	...	...	...	...	...
	171	Cotton stamp makers and sellers	...	...	...	...	...	...	...	...	...	...	...	...	...	...	...
	172	Turners and lacquerers...	26	5	5	16	...	10	2	2	6	...	16	3	3	10	...
	173	Die sinkers and seal, &c., engravers	...	...	...	...	...	...	...	...	...	...	...	...	...	...	...
	174	Type-founders	...	...	...	...	...	...	...	...	...	...	...	...	...	...	...
	175	Mica, flint and Talc workers and sellers.	22	1	2	19	...	1	...	...	1	...	21	1	2	18	...
	176	Mosaic and Alabaster workers and sellers ...	...	...	...	...	...	...	...	...	...	...	...	...	...	...	...
		Total Sub-order 30	48	6	7	35	...	11	2	2	7	...	37	4	5	28	...
Toys, curiosities, &c.	177	Toy, kite and cage makers and sellers, Bird stuffers	115	19	25	71	...	95	18	18	59	...	20	1	7	12	...
	178	Hukka stem makers and sellers	7	2	1	4	...	7	2	1	4	...	...	...	...	...	...
	179	Papier maché workers and sellers	877	53	72	252	...	...	...	...	...	...	877	58	72	252	...
	180	Card-makers and sellers...	...	...	...	...	...	...	...	...	...	...	...	...	...	...	...
	181	Tábut and Tázia makers and sellers	26	5	2	19	...	26	5	2	19	...	...	...	...	...	...
	182	Curiosity dealers	...	...	...	...	...	...	...	...	...	...	...	...	...	...	...
		Total Sub-order 31	525	79	100	846	...	128	25	21	82	...	897	54	79	264	...

TABLE XVII A.

Occupations by Age.—*Continued.*

Class.	Order.	Sub-order and Group.	Serial No.	Occupations.	PROVINCIAL TOTAL. Total. Total.	Total. 0—4	Total. 5—14	Total. 15 and over.	Total. Unspecified.	Males. Total.	Males. 0—4	Males. 5—14	Males. 15 and over.	Males. Unspecified.	Females. Total.	Females. 0—4	Females. 5—14	Females. 15 and over.	Females. Unspecified.
1	2	3	4	5	6	7	8	9	10	11	12	13	14	15	16	17	18	19	20
Class D.—Preparation and supply of material substances.—*contd.*	XI. Supplementary requirements.—*contd.*	32. Music and musical instruments.	183	Music and musical instrument dealers.	40	5	8	82	...	6	2	...	4	...	84	8	3	28	...
			184	Conch dealers, drum and horn makers, &c.	181	19	21	90	1	77	12	11	54	...	54	7	10	86	1
				Total Sub-order 32......	171	24	24	122	1	83	14	11	58	...	88	10	18	64	1
		33. Necklaces, bracelets, beads, sacred threads, &c.	185	Bangle makers and sellers in lac ...	218	36	44	138	...	106	19	22	65	...	107	17	22	68	...
			186	Bangle makers and sellers in stone ...	...	...	...	...	...	...	...	...	...	...	...	...	...	...	...
			187	Bangle makers and sellers in wood and bone	28	4	9	15	...	26	4	9	13	...	2	...	...	2	...
			188	Bangle makers and sellers in clay ...	...	...	...	...	...	...	...	...	...	...	...	...	...	...	...
			189	Bangle makers and sellers in glass ...	14,817	1,966	3,275	9,570	6	7,023	878	1,542	4,601	2	7,794	1,088	1,733	4,969	4
			190	Bangle fitters	2,036	273	467	1,296	...	1,235	157	300	778	...	801	116	167	518	...
			191	Imitation and pewter jewelry makers and sellers	5	1	...	4	...	5	1	...	4	...	...	...	...	...	...
			192	Bead makers and sellers	1,375	251	370	754	...	685	126	192	367	...	690	125	178	387	...
			193	Rosary and necklace makers and sellers.	45	5	13	27	...	44	5	12	27	...	1	...	1	...	...
			194	Flower garland makers and sellers ...	3,676	447	779	2,450	...	1,951	237	430	1,284	...	1,725	210	849	1,166	...
			195	Artificial flower and caste-mark spangle makers and sellers	36	1	6	29	...	20	1	8	16	...	16	...	8	13	...
			196	Sacred thread makers and sellers ...	15	1	4	10	...	13	1	4	8	...	2	...	...	2	...
				Total Sub-order 33	22,246	2,985	4,967	14,288	6	11,108	1,429	2,514	7,168	2	11,138	1,556	2,458	7,125	4
		34. Furniture.	197	Upholsterers	...	...	...	...	...	...	...	...	...	...	...	...	...	...	...
			198	Furniture makers	22	...	7	15	...	9	...	1	8	...	13	...	6	7	...
			199	Frame makers	240	23	61	156	...	144	14	41	89	...	96	9	20	67	...
			200	Looking-glass makers and sellers ...	15	1	2	12	...	4	...	...	4	...	11	1	2	8	...
				Total Sub-order 34......	277	24	70	183	...	157	14	42	101	...	120	10	28	82	...
		35. Harness.	201	Saddlery and harness makers and sellers...	1,929	286	426	1,215	2	954	135	287	582	...	975	151	189	633	2
			202	Saddle cloth makers, embroiderers and sellers	430	48	72	810	...	226	26	87	163	...	204	22	85	147	...
			203	Whip, goad, &c., makers	116	24	22	70	...	...	...	...	...	...	116	24	22	70	...
				Total Sub-order 35	2,475	358	520	1,595	2	1,180	161	274	745	...	1,295	197	246	850	2

TABLE XVII A.

Occupations by Age.—*Continued.*

Class.	Order.	Sub-order and Group.	Serial No.	Occupations.	TOWN. Total. Total.	Total. 0—4	Total. 5—14	Total. 15 and over.	Total. Unspecified.	Males. Total.	Males. 0—4	Males. 5—14	Males. 15 and over.	Males. Unspecified.	Females. Total.	Females. 0—4	Females. 5—14	Females. 15 and over.	Females. Unspecified.
					21	22	23	24	25	26	27	28	29	30	31	32	33	34	35
Class D.—Preparation and supply of material substances.—*contd.*	XI. Supplementary requirements.—*contd.*	32. Music and musical instruments.	183	Music and musical instrument dealers...	10	...	2	8	...	3	...	...	3	...	7	...	2	5	...
			184	Conch dealers, drum and horn makers, &c.	104	15	18	71	...	54	8	9	87	...	50	7	9	84	...
				Total Sub-order 32......	114	15	20	79	...	57	8	9	40	...	57	7	11	39	...
		33. Necklaces, bracelets, beads, sacred threads, &c.	185	Bangle makers and sellers in lac ...	2	...	...	2	...	...	...	...	...	...	2	...	...	2	...
			186	Bangle makers and sellers in stone ...	...	...	...	...	...	...	...	...	...	...	...	...	...	...	...
			187	Bangle makers and sellers in wood and bone.	...	...	...	...	...	...	...	...	...	...	...	...	...	...	...
			188	Bangle makers and sellers in clay ...	...	...	...	...	...	...	...	...	...	...	...	...	...	...	...
			189	Bangle makers and sellers in glass ...	2,281	263	476	1,540	2	981	112	195	624	...	1,350	151	281	916	2
			190	Bangle fitters	291	45	59	187	...	182	29	34	119	...	109	16	25	68	...
			191	Imitation and pewter jewelry makers and sellers	...	...	...	...	...	...	...	...	...	...	...	...	...	...	...
			192	Bead makers and sellers...	244	42	57	145	...	119	24	23	72	...	125	18	34	73	...
			193	Rosary and necklace makers and sellers.	...	...	...	...	...	...	...	...	...	...	...	...	...	...	...
			194	Flower garland makers and sellers ...	1,769	174	337	1,258	...	876	85	176	615	...	893	89	161	643	...
			195	Artificial flower and caste-mark spangle makers and sellers	35	1	6	28	...	20	1	3	16	...	15	...	3	12	...
			196	Sacred thread makers and sellers ...	3	...	1	2	...	1	...	1	...	...	2	...	...	2	...
				Total Sub-order 33......	4,625	525	936	3,162	2	2,129	251	432	1,446	...	2,496	274	504	1,716	2
		34. Furniture.	197	Upholsterers	...	...	...	...	...	...	...	...	...	...	...	...	...	...	...
			198	Furniture makers	13	...	3	10	...	9	...	1	8	...	4	...	2	2	...
			199	Frame makers	186	16	52	118	...	118	11	36	71	...	68	5	16	47	...
			200	Looking-glass makers and sellers ...	2	...	...	2	...	1	...	...	1	...	1	...	...	1	...
				Total Sub-order 34......	201	16	55	130	...	128	11	37	80	...	73	5	18	50	...
		35. Harness.	201	Saddlery and harness makers and sellers	597	88	135	374	...	313	47	82	184	...	284	41	53	190	...
			202	Saddle cloth makers, embroiderers and sellers	275	33	41	201	...	144	16	23	105	...	131	17	18	96	...
			203	Whip, goad, &c., makers	...	...	...	...	...	...	...	...	...	...	...	...	...	...	...
				Total Sub-order 35......	872	121	176	575	...	457	63	105	289	...	415	58	71	286	...

TABLE XVII A.

Occupations by Age.—*Continued.*

Class.	Order.	Sub-order and Group.	Serial No.	Occupations.	COUNTRY. Total. Total.	Total. 0—4	Total. 5—14	Total. 15 and over.	Total. Unspecified.	Males. Total.	Males. 0—4	Males. 5—14	Males. 15 and over.	Males. Unspecified.	Females. Total.	Females. 0—4	Females. 5—14	Females. 15 and over.	Females. Unspecified.
					36	37	38	39	40	41	42	43	44	45	46	47	48	49	50
Class D.—Preparation and supply of material substances.—*contd.*	XI. Supplementary requirements.—*contd.*	32. Music and musical instruments.	183	Music and musical instrument dealers ...	30	5	1	24	...	3	2	...	1	...	27	2	1	23	...
			184	Conch dealers, drum and horn makers, &c.	27	4	3	19	1	23	4	2	17	...	4	...	1	2	1
				Total Sub-order 32	57	9	4	43	1	26	6	2	18	...	31	2	2	25	1
		33. Necklaces, bracelets, beads, sacred threads, &c.	185	Bangle makers and sellers in lac ...	211	86	44	131	...	106	19	22	65	...	105	17	22	66	...
			186	Bangle makers and sellers in stone ...	...	...	...	...	...	...	...	...	...	...	...	...	...	...	...
			187	Bangle makers and sellers in wood and bone	28	4	9	15	...	26	4	9	18	...	2	...	...	2	...
			188	Bangle makers and sellers in clay ...	...	...	...	...	...	...	...	...	...	...	...	...	...	...	...
			189	Bangle makers and sellers in glass ...	12,536	1,703	2,799	8,030	4	6,092	766	1,347	3,977	2	6,444	987	1,452	4,058	2
			190	Bangle fitters	1,745	228	408	1,109	...	1,053	128	266	659	...	692	100	142	450	...
			191	Imitation and pewter jewelry makers and sellers	5	1	...	4	...	5	1	...	4	...	...	...	...	...	...
			192	Bead makers and sellers	1,131	209	313	609	...	566	102	169	295	...	565	107	144	314	...
			193	Rosary and necklace makers and sellers	45	5	13	27	...	44	5	12	27	...	1	...	1	...	...
			194	Flower garland makers and sellers ...	1,907	273	442	1,192	...	1,075	152	254	669	...	832	121	188	523	...
			195	Artificial flower and caste-mark spangle makers and sellers	1	...	...	1	...	...	...	...	...	...	1	...	...	1	...
			196	Sacred thread makers and sellers ...	12	1	3	8	...	12	1	3	8	...	...	...	...	...	...
				Total Sub-order 33	17,621	2,460	4,031	11,126	4	8,979	1,178	2,082	5,717	2	8,642	1,282	1,949	5,409	2
		34. Furniture.	197	Upholsterers	...	...	...	...	...	...	...	...	...	...	...	...	...	...	...
			198	Furniture makers	9	...	4	5	...	...	...	...	...	...	9	...	4	5	...
			199	Frame makers	54	7	9	38	...	26	3	5	18	...	28	4	4	20	...
			200	Looking-glass makers and sellers ...	18	1	2	10	...	3	...	...	8	...	10	1	2	7	...
				Total Sub-order 34	76	8	15	53	...	29	3	5	21	...	47	5	10	32	...
		35. Harness.	201	Saddlery and harness makers and sellers	1,332	198	291	841	2	641	88	155	398	...	691	110	136	443	2
			202	Saddle cloth makers, embroiderers and sellers	155	15	81	109	...	82	10	14	58	...	73	5	17	51	...
			203	Whip, goad, &c., makers	116	24	22	70	...	...	...	...	...	...	116	24	22	70	...
				Total Sub-order 35	1,603	237	344	1,020	2	723	98	169	456	...	880	139	175	564	2

TABLE XVII A.

Occupations by Age.—*Continued.*

Class.	Order.	Sub-order and Group.	Serial No.	Occupations.	PROVINCIAL TOTAL. Total. Total.	Total. 0—4	Total. 5—14	Total. 15 and over.	Total. Unspecified.	Males. Total.	Males. 0—4	Males. 5—14	Males. 15—and over.	Males. Unspecified.	Females. Total.	Females. 0—4	Females. 5—14	Females. 15 and over.	Females. Unspecified.
1	2	3	4	5	6	7	8	9	10	11	12	13	14	15	16	17	18	19	20
Class D.—Preparation and supply of material substances.—*contd.*	XI. Supplementary requirements —*contd.*	36. Tools and machinery.	204	Knife and tool makers and sellers ...	73	15	12	46	...	27	6	5	16	...	46	9	7	30	...
			205	Knife and tool grinders	1,122	150	284	685	3	604	79	156	369	...	518	71	128	816	3
			206	Looms and Loom-comb makers and sellers	154	22	40	92	...	131	21	31	79	...	23	1	9	13	...
			207	Mechanic, (not railway)	307	35	63	209	...	177	21	37	119	...	130	14	26	90	...
			208	Machinery dealers, &c....	...	...	...	...	...	...	...	...	...	...	...	...	...	...	...
				Total Sub-order 36	1,653	222	399	1,032	3	939	127	229	583	...	717	95	170	449	3
		37. Arms and Ammunition.	209	Gun makers, menders and sellers ...	65	6	12	44	3	43	4	7	32	...	22	2	5	12	...
			210	Ammunition and cap dealers	8	...	1	7	...	5	...	...	5	...	3	...	1	2	...
			211	Gun-powder makers and sellers ...	227	29	51	147	...	114	10	29	75	...	113	19	22	72	...
			212	Firework makers and sellers	645	103	164	378	...	500	89	125	286	...	145	14	39	92	...
			213	Sword and scabbard makers and sellers.	395	38	91	266	...	159	5	34	120	...	236	33	57	146	...
			214	Spear-head, shield, &c., makers and sellers	23	4	6	13	...	12	2	2	8	...	11	2	4	5	...
			215	Bow and arrow makers and sellers ...	...	...	...	...	...	...	...	...	...	...	...	...	...	...	...
			216	Cudgel (láthi) makers and sellers ...	4	2	...	2	...	1	...	...	1	...	3	2	...	1	...
				Total Sub-order 37	1,337	182	325	857	3	834	110	197	527	...	533	72	128	330	3
				Total Order XI	32,260	4,338	7,215	20,692	15	16,348	2,106	8,751	10,489	2	15,912	2,232	3,464	10,203	13
	XII. Textile fabrics and dress.	38. Wool and Fur.	217	Carpet weavers and sellers	1,212	183	340	688	1	673	104	178	390	1	539	79	162	298	...
			218	Shawl weavers and sellers	151	12	32	107	...	92	4	27	61	...	59	8	5	46	...
			219	Felt and pashm workers and sellers ...	114	13	24	77	...	62	7	12	43	...	52	6	12	34	...
			220	Blanket weavers and sellers (often also shepherds)...	92,338	15,715	22,022	54,545	56	49,895	7,877	11,964	30,027	27	42,443	7,838	10,058	24,518	29
			221	Woollen cloth manufacturers and dealers	74,380	12,418	20,898	41,038	26	40,030	5,968	11,463	22,588	11	34,350	6,450	9,435	18,450	15
			222	Woollen yarn spinners and sellers ...	4,593	474	856	3,262	1	478	98	144	236	...	4,115	376	712	3,026	1
			223	Wool carders	208	11	24	173	...	11	4	1	6	...	197	7	23	167	...
			224	Wool dyers	...	...	...	...	...	...	...	...	...	...	...	...	...	...	...
			225	Fur dealers	267	70	57	140	...	6	2	2	2	...	261	68	55	138	...
				Total Sub-order 38	173,263	28,896	44,253	100,030	84	91,247	14,064	23,791	53,353	39	82,016	14,832	20,462	46,677	45
		39. Silk.	226	Silkworm rearers and cocoon gatherers	...	...	...	...	...	...	...	...	...	...	...	...	...	...	...
			227	Silk carders and spinners	8,555	393	698	2,463	1	1,400	200	362	838	...	2,155	193	336	1,625	1
			228	Silk weavers and dealers	2,525	309	593	1,617	6	722	92	174	456	...	1,803	217	419	1,161	6
			229	Silk printers and dyers...	39	8	3	28	...	19	3	2	14	...	20	4	1	14	...
			230	Braid and ribbon makers and sellers ...	1,835	218	411	1,205	1	780	99	162	518	1	1,055	119	249	687	...
				Total Sub-order 39	7,954	928	1,705	5,313	8	2,921	394	700	1,826	1	5,033	534	1,005	3,487	7

TABLE XVII A.

Occupations by Age.—*Continued.*

Class.	Order.	Sub-order and Group.	Serial No.	Occupations.	TOWN. Total. Total.	Total. 0—4	Total. 5—14	Total. 15 and over.	Total. Unspecified.	Males. Total.	Males. 0—4	Males. 5—14	Males. 15 and over.	Males. Unspecified.	Females. Total.	Females. 0—4	Females. 5—14	Females. 15 and over.	Females. Unspecified.
					21	22	23	24	25	26	27	28	29	30	31	32	33	34	35
Class D.—Preparation and supply of material substances.—*concld.*	XI. Supplementary requirements.—*concld.*	36. Tools and machinery.	204	Knife and tool makers and sellers ...	8	1	1	6	...	2	...	...	2	...	6	1	1	4	...
			205	Knife and tool grinders	553	56	144	353	...	332	35	83	214	...	221	21	61	139	...
			206	Looms and Loom-comb makers and sellers	91	14	23	54	...	87	14	22	51	...	4	...	1	3	...
			207	Mechanic, (not railway)	203	24	36	143	...	73	10	10	53	...	130	14	26	90	...
			208	Machinery dealers, &c.	...	...	...	...	...	...	...	...	...	...	...	...	...	...	...
				Total Sub-order 36	855	95	204	556	...	494	59	115	320	...	361	36	89	236	...
		37. Arms and Ammunition.	209	Gun makers, menders and sellers ...	43	3	8	29	3	28	2	5	21	...	15	1	8	8	3
			210	Ammunition and cap dealers	4	...	...	4	...	3	...	...	3	...	1	...	...	1	...
			211	Gun-powder makers and sellers ...	57	8	11	38	...	20	2	1	17	...	37	6	10	21	...
			212	Firework makers and sellers	181	28	34	119	...	137	25	22	90	...	44	8	12	29	...
			213	Sword and scabbard makers and sellers	242	13	53	176	...	180	4	29	97	...	112	9	24	79	...
			214	Spear-head, shield, &c., makers and sellers	19	2	5	12	...	8	...	1	7	...	11	2	4	5	...
			215	Bow and arrow makers and sellers ...	...	...	...	...	...	...	...	...	...	...	...	...	...	...	...
			216	Cudgel (láthi) makers and sellers ...	4	2	...	2	...	1	...	...	1	...	3	2	...	1	...
				Total Sub-order 37	550	56	111	380	3	327	33	58	236	...	223	23	53	144	3
				Total Order XI	9,262	1,052	2,011	6,194	5	4,804	551	1,059	3,194	...	4,458	501	952	3,000	5
	XII. Textile fabrics and dress.	38. Wool and Fur.	217	Carpet weavers and sellers	587	86	171	330	...	262	41	70	151	...	325	45	101	179	...
			218	Shawl weavers and sellers	146	12	32	102	...	90	4	27	59	...	56	8	5	43	...
			219	Felt and pashm workers and sellers ...	3	...	...	3	...	3	...	...	3	...	...	...	...	...	...
			220	Blanket weavers and sellers (often also shepherds)...	2,987	474	713	1,797	3	1,518	227	885	906	...	1,469	247	328	891	3
			221	Woollen cloth manufacturers and dealers	3,224	499	899	1,826	...	1,115	164	801	650	...	2,109	335	598	1,176	...
			222	Woollen yarn spinners and sellers ...	132	7	28	97	...	10	1	1	8	...	122	6	27	89	...
			223	Wool carders	...	...	...	...	...	...	...	...	...	...	...	...	...	...	...
			224	Wool dyers	...	...	...	...	...	...	...	...	...	...	...	...	...	...	...
			225	Fur dealers	...	...	...	...	...	...	...	...	...	...	...	...	...	...	...
				Total Sub-order 38......	7,079	1,078	1,843	4,155	8	2,998	437	784	1,777	...	4,081	641	1,059	2,378	8
		39. Silk.	226	Silkworm rearers and cocoon gatherers	...	...	...	...	...	...	...	...	...	...	...	...	...	...	...
			327	Silk carders and spinners	1,667	174	283	1,210	...	491	79	114	298	...	1,176	95	169	912	...
			228	Silk weavers and dealers	1,045	126	250	669	...	123	16	29	78	...	922	110	221	591	...
			229	Silk printers and dyers	11	2	1	8	...	7	1	1	5	...	4	1	...	3	...
			230	Braid and ribbon makers and sellers ...	741	87	179	475	...	308	33	69	206	...	433	54	110	269	...
				Total Sub-order 39	3,464	889	713	2,362	...	929	129	213	587	...	2,585	260	500	1,775	...

TABLE XVII A.

Occupations by Age.—*Continued.*

Class.	Order.	Sub-order and Group.	Serial No.	Occupations.	COUNTRY. Total. Total.	Total. 0—4	Total. 5—14	Total. 15 and over.	Total. Unspecified.	Males. Total.	Males. 0—4	Males. 5—14	Males. 15 and over.	Males. Unspecified.	Females. Total.	Females. 0—4	Females. 5—14	Females. 15 and over.	Females. Unspecified.
					36	37	38	39	40	41	42	43	44	45	46	47	48	49	50
Class D.—Preparation and supply of material substances.—*contd.*	XI. Supplementary requirements.—*concld.*	36. Tools and machinery.	204	Knife and tool makers and sellers ...	65	14	11	40	...	25	6	5	14	...	40	8	6	26	...
			205	Knife and tool grinders	569	94	140	332	3	272	44	73	155	...	297	50	67	177	3
			206	Looms and Loom-comb makers and sellers	68	8	17	38	...	44	7	9	28	...	19	1	8	10	...
			207	Mechanic, (not railway)	104	11	27	66	...	104	11	27	66	...	...	...	...	...	...
			208	Machinery dealers, &c	...	...	...	...	...	...	...	...	...	...	...	...	...	...	...
				Total Sub-order 36......	801	127	195	476	3	445	68	114	263	...	356	59	81	213	3
		37. Arms and Ammunition.	209	Gun makers, menders and sellers ...	22	3	4	15	...	15	2	2	11	...	7	1	2	4	...
			210	Ammunition and cap dealers	4	...	1	3	...	2	...	...	2	...	2	...	1	1	...
			211	Gun-powder makers and sellers ...	170	21	40	109	...	94	8	28	58	...	76	13	12	51	...
			212	Firework makers and sellers	464	75	130	259	...	863	64	103	196	...	101	11	27	63	...
			213	Sword and scabbard makers and sellers.	153	25	38	90	...	29	1	5	23	...	124	24	33	67	...
			214	Spear-head, shield, &c., makers and sellers	4	2	1	1	...	4	2	1	1	...	...	...	...	...	...
			215	Bow and arrow makers and sellers ...	...	...	...	...	...	...	...	...	...	...	...	...	...	...	...
			216	Cudgel (láthi) makers and sellers ...	...	...	...	...	...	...	...	...	...	...	...	...	...	...	...
				Total Sub-order 37......	817	126	214	477	...	507	77	139	291	...	810	49	75	186	...
				Total Order XI	22,998	3,286	5,204	14,498	10	11,544	1,555	2,692	7,295	2	11,454	1,731	2,512	7,203	8
	XII. Textile fabrics and dress.	38. Wool and Fur.	217	Carpet weavers and sellers	625	97	169	358	1	411	63	108	239	1	214	34	61	119	...
			218	Shawl weavers and sellers	5	...	...	5	...	2	...	...	2	...	3	...	...	3	...
			219	Felt and pashm workers and sellers ...	111	13	24	74	...	59	7	12	40	...	52	6	12	34	...
			220	Blanket weavers and sellers (often also shepherds)...	89,351	15,241	21,309	52,748	53	48,377	7,650	11,579	29,121	27	40,974	7,591	9,730	23,627	26
			221	Woollen cloth manufacturers and dealers	71,156	11,919	19,999	39,212	26	38,915	5,804	11,162	21,938	11	32,241	6,115	8,837	17,274	15
			222	Woollen yarn spinners and sellers ...	4,461	467	828	3,165	1	468	97	143	228	...	3,993	370	685	2,937	1
			223	Wool carders	208	11	24	173	...	11	4	1	6	...	197	7	23	167	...
			224	Wool dyers	...	...	...	...	...	...	...	...	...	...	...	...	...	...	...
			225	Fur dealers	267	70	57	140	...	6	2	2	2	...	261	68	55	138	...
				Total Sub-order 38......	166,184	27,818	42,410	95,875	81	88,249	18,627	23,007	51,576	39	77,935	14,191	19,403	44,299	42
		39. Silk.	226	Silk worm rearers and cocoon gatherers.	...	...	...	...	...	...	...	...	...	...	...	...	...	...	...
			227	Silk carders and spinners	1,888	219	415	1,253	1	909	121	248	540	...	979	98	167	713	1
			228	Silk weavers and dealers	1,480	183	843	948	6	599	76	145	378	...	881	107	198	570	6
			229	Silk printers and dyers...	28	6	2	20	...	12	2	1	9	...	16	4	1	11	...
			230	Braid and ribbon makers and sellers ...	1,094	131	232	730	1	472	66	98	812	1	622	65	139	418	...
				Total Sub-order 39	4,490	539	992	2,951	8	1,992	265	487	1,239	1	2,498	274	505	1,712	7

TABLE XVII A.

Occupations by Age.—*Continued.*

Class.	Order.	Sub-order and Group.	Serial No.	Occupations.	PROVINCIAL TOTAL.														
					TOTAL.					MALES.					FEMALES.				
					Total.	0—4	5—14	15 and over.	Unspecified.	Total.	0—4	5—14	15 and over.	Unspecified.	Total.	0—4	5—14	15 and over.	Unspecified.
1	2	3	4	5	6	7	8	9	10	11	12	13	14	15	16	17	18	19	20
Class D.—Preparation and supply of material substances.—*contd.*	XII. Textile fabrics and dress.—*contd.*	40. Cotton.	231	Cotton cleaners, pressers and ginners...	33,422	4,571	7,081	21,753	17	13,135	2,047	3,106	7,976	6	20,287	2,524	3,975	13,777	11
			232	Cotton carpet and rug makers and sellers	156	25	34	96	1	89	15	18	56	...	67	10	16	40	1
			233	Cotton spinners, sizers and yarn beaters	54,752	6,311	11,168	37,230	43	12,833	2,206	3,936	6,688	3	41,919	4,105	7,232	30,542	40
			234	Cotton weavers, Mill-owners and Managers	295,441	45,849	69,631	179,734	227	158,327	22,692	37,410	98,155	70	137,114	23,157	32,221	81,579	157
			235	Cotton factory hands (undefined) ...	1,813	233	381	1,198	1	954	113	224	617	...	859	120	157	581	1
			236	Calenderers, fullers and printers ...	45	5	10	30	...	21	4	6	11	...	24	1	4	19	...
			237	Cotton dyers	17,084	2,329	3,965	10,763	27	8,988	1,135	2,116	5,728	9	8,096	1,194	1,849	5,035	18
			238	Tape makers and sellers	253	47	58	148	...	101	15	22	64	...	152	32	36	84	...
			239	Tent manufacturers and sellers ...	11	1	5	5	...	11	1	5	5	...	...	...	...	...	...
				Total Sub-order 40	402,977	59,371	92,333	250,957	316	194,459	28,228	46,843	119,300	88	208,518	31,143	45,490	131,657	228
		41. Jute, flax, coir, &c.	240	Flax spinners, weavers and sellers ...	144	25	26	93	...	109	22	16	71	...	35	3	10	22	...
			241	Hemp rope makers and sellers ...	1,888	244	297	847	...	675	125	154	396	...	713	119	143	451	...
			242	Jute manufacturers, Managers and Agents	29	2	3	24	...	27	2	3	22	...	2	...	...	2	...
			243	Sacking, tarpaulin and gunny makers and sellers	4,205	701	983	2,519	2	2,432	869	572	1,491	...	1,773	332	411	1,028	2
			244	Net makers and sellers...	48	8	12	28	...	31	7	9	15	...	17	1	3	13	...
			245	Fancy work dealers	21	5	5	11	...	21	5	5	11	...	...	...	...	...	...
			246	Coir preparers, manufacturers and sellers	947	160	213	574	...	378	61	93	224	...	569	99	120	350	...
				Total Sub-order 41	6,782	1,145	1,539	4,096	2	3,673	591	852	2,230	...	3,109	554	687	1,866	2
		42. Dress.	247	Tailors and darners	47,458	6,472	11,065	29,896	25	22,755	3,126	5,624	14,000	5	24,703	3,346	5,441	15,896	20
			248	Milliners and dressmakers	85	7	15	63	...	39	3	7	29	...	46	4	8	34	...
			249	Outfitters, and cloths and quilt dealers..	2,536	365	611	1,560	...	1,278	175	294	809	...	1,258	190	317	751	...
			250	Hosiers and haberdashers	4,300	616	1,018	2,659	7	1,998	267	517	1,213	1	2,302	349	501	1,446	6
			251	Hat, cap and turban makers and sellers	80	9	10	61	...	47	4	6	37	...	33	5	4	24	...
			252	Turban binders	209	36	40	133	...	93	14	22	57	...	116	22	18	76	...
			253	Umbrella makers and sellers	6	1	1	4	...	4	1	...	3	...	2	...	1	1	...
			254	Embroiderers and lace and muslin makers	203	23	41	139	...	31	4	8	19	...	172	19	33	120	...
			255	Button makers and sellers	19	3	4	12	...	8	...	3	5	...	11	3	1	7	...
			256	False plait makers and sellers ...	734	97	170	497	...	381	38	96	247	...	383	59	74	250	...
			257	Piece-goods dealers	77,702	10,540	17,669	49,382	111	41,096	5,237	9,328	26,517	14	36,606	5,303	8,341	22,865	97
				Total Sub-order 42	183,332	18,169	30,644	84,406	143	67,730	8,869	15,905	42,936	20	65,632	9,300	14,739	41,470	123
				Total Order XII......	724,838	108,509	170,474	444,802	553	360,030	52,146	88,091	219,645	148	364,808	56,363	82,388	225,157	405

TABLE XVII A.

Occupations by Age.—*Continued.*

Class.	Order.	Sub-order and Group.	Serial No.	Occupations.	TOWN. Total. Total.	Total. 0—4	Total. 5—14	Total. 15 and over.	Total. Unspecified.	Males. Total.	Males. 0—4	Males. 5—14	Males. 15 and over.	Males. Unspecified.	Females. Total.	Females. 0—4	Females. 5—14	Females. 15 and over.	Females. Unspecified.
					21	22	23	24	25	26	27	28	29	30	31	32	33	34	35
Class D.—Preparation and supply of material substances.—*cont'd.*	XII. Textile fabrics and dress.—*concld.*	40. Cotton.	231	Cotton cleaners, pressers and ginners ...	2,757	336	579	1,839	3	1,512	189	325	997	1	1,245	147	254	842	2
			232	Cotton carpet and rug makers and sellers...	32	2	12	18	...	16	2	4	10	...	16	...	8	8	...
			233	Cotton spinners, sizers and yarn beaters	2,516	256	513	1,745	2	654	107	198	849	...	1,862	149	815	1,896	2
			234	Cotton weavers, Mill-owners and Managers	50,646	7,083	10,884	32,623	56	26,651	3,507	5,739	17,388	17	23,995	3,576	5,145	15,235	39
			235	Cotton factory hand (undefined) ...	1,238	154	273	810	1	638	70	157	411	...	600	84	116	399	1
			236	Calenderers, fullers and printers ...	2	...	...	2	...	1	...	...	1	...	1	...	...	1	...
			237	Cotton dyers	6,493	845	1,466	4,162	20	3,221	399	722	2,092	8	3,272	446	744	2,070	12
			238	Tape makers and sellers	2	1	...	1	...	2	1	...	1	...	...	...	...	...	...
			239	Tent manufacturers and sellers ...	...	...	...	...	...	...	...	...	...	...	...	...	...	...	...
				Total Sub-order 40	63,686	8,677	13,727	41,200	82	32,695	4,275	7,145	21,249	26	30,991	4,402	6,582	19,951	56
		41. Jute, flax, coir, &c.	240	Flax spinners, weavers and sellers ...	22	5	3	14	...	22	5	3	14	...	...	...	...	...	...
			241	Hemp rope makers and sellers... ...	152	11	38	103	...	57	4	13	40	...	95	7	25	68	...
			242	Jute manufacturers, Managers and Agents	...	...	...	...	...	...	...	...	...	...	...	...	...	...	...
			243	Sacking, tarpaulin and gunny makers and sellers	69	7	17	45	...	33	4	11	18	...	36	3	6	27	...
			244	Net makers and sellers	7	2	1	4	...	7	2	1	4	...	...	...	...	...	...
			245	Fancy work dealers	...	...	...	...	...	...	...	...	...	...	...	...	...	...	...
			246	Coir preparers, manufacturers and sellers	...	...	...	...	...	...	...	...	...	...	...	...	...	...	...
				Total Sub-order 41	250	25	59	166	...	119	15	28	76	...	131	10	31	90	...
		42. Dress.	247	Tailors and darners	11,221	1,428	2,582	7,207	4	5,760	718	1,348	3,693	1	5,461	710	1,234	3,514	3
			248	Milliners and dressmakers	85	7	15	63	...	39	3	7	29	...	46	4	8	34	...
			249	Outfitters, and cloths and quilt dealers...	44	8	12	24	...	16	2	6	8	...	28	6	6	16	...
			250	Hosiers and haberdashers	1,215	139	265	811	...	562	64	157	341	...	653	75	108	470	...
			251	Hat, cap and turban makers and sellers...	68	8	10	50	...	38	4	6	28	...	30	4	4	22	...
			252	Turban binders	100	16	20	64	...	28	3	6	19	...	72	13	14	45	...
			253	Umbrella makers and sellers	...	...	...	...	...	...	...	...	...	...	...	...	...	...	...
			254	Embroiderers and lace and muslin makers	103	10	24	69	...	30	4	8	18	...	73	6	16	51	...
			255	Button makers and sellers	4	1	...	3	...	1	...	...	1	...	3	1	...	2	...
			256	False plait makers and sellers	241	31	48	162	...	112	12	24	76	...	129	19	24	86	...
			257	Piece-goods dealers	22,291	2,723	4,795	14,757	16	11,450	1,276	2,469	7,704	1	10,841	1,447	2,326	7,058	15
				Total Sub-order 42	35,372	4,371	7,771	23,210	20	18,036	2,086	4,081	11,917	2	17,336	2,285	3,740	11,298	18
				Total Order XII......	109,851	14,540	24,113	71,093	105	54,777	6,942	12,201	35,606	28	55,074	7,598	11,912	35,487	77

TABLE XVII A.

Occupations by Age.—*Continued.*

Class.	Order.	Sub-order and Group.	Serial No.	Occupations.	COUNTRY. Total. Total.	Total. 0—4	Total. 5—14	Total. 15 and over.	Total. Unspecified.	Males. Total.	Males. 0—4	Males. 5—14	Males. 15 and over.	Males. Unspecified.	Females. Total.	Females. 0—4	Females. 5—14	Females. 15 and over.	Females. Unspecified.
					36	37	38	39	40	41	42	43	44	45	46	47	48	49	50
Class D.—Preparation and supply of material substances.—*contd.*	XII. Textile fabrics and dress.—*contd.*	40. Cotton.	231	Cotton cleaners, pressers and ginners ...	30,665	4,235	6,502	19,914	14	11,623	1,858	2,781	6,979	5	19,042	2,377	3,721	12,935	9
			232	Cotton carpet and rug makers and sellers	124	23	22	78	1	73	18	14	46	...	51	10	8	32	1
			233	Cotton spinners, sizers and yarn beaters.	52,236	6,055	10,655	35,485	41	12,179	2,099	3,738	6,339	3	40,057	3,956	6,917	29,146	38
			234	Cotton weavers, Mill-owners and Managers	244,795	38,766	58,747	147,111	171	131,676	19,185	31,671	80,767	58	113,119	19,581	27,076	66,344	118
			235	Cotton factory hands (undefined) ...	575	79	108	388	...	316	43	67	206	...	259	36	41	182	...
			236	Calenderers, fullers and printers ...	43	5	10	28	...	20	4	6	10	...	23	1	4	18	...
			237	Cotton dyers	10,591	1,484	2,499	6,601	7	5,767	736	1,394	3,636	1	4,824	748	1,105	2,965	6
			238	Tape makers and sellers	251	46	58	147	...	99	14	22	63	...	152	32	36	84	...
			239	Tent manufacturers and sellers ...	11	1	5	5	...	11	1	5	5	...	...	...	...	...	...
				Total Sub-order 40	339,291	50,694	78,606	209,757	234	161,764	23,953	39,698	98,051	62	177,527	26,741	38,908	111,706	172
		41. Jute, flax, coir, &c.	240	Flax spinners, weavers and sellers ...	122	20	28	79	...	87	17	18	57	...	35	3	10	22	...
			241	Hemp rope makers and sellers	1,236	233	259	744	...	618	121	141	356	...	618	112	118	388	...
			242	Jute manufacturers, Managers and Agents	29	2	3	24	...	27	2	3	22	...	2	...	...	2	...
			243	Sacking, tarpaulin and gunny makers and sellers	4,136	694	966	2,474	2	2,399	365	561	1,473	...	1,737	329	405	1,001	2
			244	Net makers and sellers	41	6	11	24	...	24	5	8	11	...	17	1	3	13	...
			245	Fancy work dealers	21	5	5	11	...	21	5	5	11	...	...	...	...	...	...
			246	Coir prepareres, manufacturers and sellers	947	160	213	574	...	378	61	93	224	...	569	99	120	350	...
				Total Sub-order 41	6,532	1,120	1,480	3,930	2	3,554	576	824	2,154	...	2,978	544	656	1,776	2
		42. Dress.	247	Tailors and darners	36,287	5,044	8,483	22,689	21	16,995	2,408	4,276	10,307	4	19,242	2,686	4,207	12,382	17
			248	Milliners and dressmakers	...	...	...	...	...	...	...	...	...	...	...	...	...	...	...
			249	Outfitters, and cloths and quilt dealers...	2,492	857	599	1,536	...	1,262	173	288	801	...	1,230	184	311	735	...
			250	Hosiers and haberdashers	3,085	477	753	1,848	7	1,436	203	360	872	1	1,649	274	393	976	6
			251	Hat, cap and turban makers and sellers..	12	1	...	11	...	9	...	...	9	...	3	1	...	2	...
			252	Turban binders	109	20	20	69	...	65	11	16	38	...	44	9	4	31	...
			253	Umbrella makers and sellers	6	1	1	4	...	4	1	...	3	...	2	...	1	1	...
			254	Embroiderers and lace and muslin makers...	100	13	17	70	...	1	...	...	1	...	99	13	17	69	...
			255	Button makers and sellers	15	2	4	9	...	7	...	3	4	...	8	2	1	5	...
			256	False plait makers and sellers	523	66	122	335	...	269	26	72	171	...	254	40	50	164	...
			257	Piece-goods dealers	55,411	7,817	12,874	34,625	95	29,646	3,961	6,859	18,813	13	25,765	3,856	6,015	15,812	82
				Total Sub-order 42	97,990	13,798	22,873	61,196	123	49,694	6,788	11,874	31,019	18	48,296	7,015	10,999	30,177	105
				Total Order XII......	614,487	93,969	146,861	373,709	448	305,253	45,204	75,890	184,039	120	309,234	48,765	70,471	189,670	328

TABLE XVII A.

Occupations by Age.—*Continued.*

Class.	Order.	Sub-order and Group.	Serial No.	Occupations.	PROVINCIAL TOTAL. Total. Total.	Total. 0—4	Total. 5—14	Total. 15 and over.	Total. Unspecified.	Males. Total.	Males. 0—4	Males. 5—14	Males. 15 and over.	Males. Unspecified.	Females. Total.	Females. 0—4	Females. 5—14	Females. 15 and over.	Females. Unspecified.
1	2	3	4	5	6	7	8	9	10	11	12	13	14	15	16	17	18	19	20
Class D.—Preparation and supply of material substances.—contd.	XIII. Metals and precious stones.	43. Gold, silver and precious stones.	258	Gold and silver dealers...	1,033	93	226	714	...	736	65	169	502	...	297	28	57	212	...
			259	Gold and silver assayers	106	16	65	25	...	20	1	7	12	...	86	15	58	13	...
			260	Gold and silver workers	90,046	12,118	21,213	56,674	41	46,887	5,917	11,214	29,741	15	43,159	6,201	9,999	26,933	26
			261	Gold beaters	64	9	8	47	...	29	3	4	22	...	35	6	4	25	...
			262	Goldsmiths and dust washers	406	64	111	231	...	180	23	47	110	...	226	41	64	121	...
			263	Gold miners, managers and agents	51	5	5	41	...	39	2	2	35	...	12	3	3	6	...
			264	Enamellers	9	2	1	6	...	5	1	1	3	...	4	1	...	3	...
			265	Electro-platers	122	20	22	80	...	73	12	11	50	...	49	8	11	30	...
			266	Gold and silver wire drawers and braid makers...	1,275	127	229	919	...	678	67	116	495	...	597	60	113	424	...
			267	Plate and platedware dealers	3	...	...	3	...	1	...	...	1	...	2	...	...	2	...
			268	Diamond polishers and dealers	13	1	1	11	...	5	1	...	4	...	8	...	1	7	...
			269	Diamond diggers, washers, &c...	5	...	2	3	...	2	...	...	2	...	3	...	2	1	...
			270	Ruby workers	6	...	1	5	...	6	...	1	5	...	...	...	...	...	...
			271	Ruby and emerald, &c., dealers	1	...	...	1	...	1	...	...	1	...	...	...	...	...	...
			272	Pearl divers	2	...	1	1	...	...	...	...	...	...	2	...	1	1	...
			273	Pearl and other precious (stone unspecified) dealers	602	58	114	430	...	378	33	65	280	...	224	25	49	150	...
			274	Coral dealers	1	...	...	1	...	1	...	...	1	...	...	...	...	...	...
			275	Cornelian and agate cutters and sellers..	...	...	...	...	...	...	...	...	...	...	...	...	...	...	...
				Total Sub-order 43	93,745	12,513	21,999	59,192	41	49,041	6,125	11,637	31,264	15	44,704	6,388	10,362	27,928	26
		44. Brass, copper and bell metal.	276	Brass workers and sellers	7	...	1	6	...	4	...	1	3	...	3	...	...	3	...
			277	Brass pot makers and sellers	6,372	879	1,412	4,077	4	3,649	459	812	2,377	1	2,723	420	600	1,700	3
			278	Brass image casters and sellers...	8	2	...	6	...	3	1	...	2	...	5	1	...	4	...
			279	Copper workers and sellers	5,052	725	1,148	3,169	10	2,650	361	625	1,663	1	2,402	364	523	1,506	9
			280	Brass and copper wire drawers and sellers ...	3	...	1	2	...	...	...	...	...	...	3	...	1	2	...
			281	Bell metal workers and sellers ...	305	37	54	214	...	148	14	36	98	...	157	23	18	116	...
			282	General workers in brass, copper, and bell metal	7,989	1,082	1,967	4,931	9	4,327	545	1,021	2,758	8	3,662	537	946	2,178	6
			283	Brass and copper dealers	291	32	70	186	3	154	9	46	96	3	137	23	24	90	...
				Total Sub-order 44	20,027	2,757	4,653	12,591	26	10,935	1,389	2,541	6,997	8	9,092	1,368	2,112	5,594	18
		45. Tin, zinc, mercury and lead.	284	Tin workers and sellers	1,899	274	410	1,215	...	1,185	160	254	721	...	764	114	156	494	...
			285	Tinfoil makers and sellers	6	...	...	6	...	1	...	...	1	...	5	...	...	5	...
			286	Zinc workers and sellers	2	...	...	2	...	2	...	...	2	...	...	...	...	...	...
			287	Lead and quick-silver makers and sellers ...	4	...	1	3	...	2	...	...	2	...	2	...	1	1	...
			288	General workers in tin, lead and zinc ...	197	20	40	137	...	103	9	28	71	...	94	11	17	66	...
				Total Sub-order 45	2,108	294	451	1,363	...	1,243	169	277	797	...	865	125	174	566	...

TABLE XVII A.

Occupations by Age.—*Continued.*

Class.	Order.	Sub-order and Group.	Serial No.	Occupations.	TOWN. Total. Total.					Males.					Females.				
					Total.	0—4	5—14	15 and over.	Unspecified.	Total.	0—4	5—14	15 and over.	Unspecified.	Total.	0—4	5—14	15 and over.	Unspecified.
					21	22	23	24	25	26	27	28	29	30	31	32	33	34	35
Class D.—Preparation and supply of material substances.—contd.	XIII. Metals and precious stones.	43. Gold, silver and precious stones.	258	Gold and silver dealers...	476	26	80	370	...	271	11	42	218	...	205	15	88	152	...
			259	Gold and silver assayers	37	6	9	22	...	20	1	7	12	...	17	5	2	10	...
			260	Gold and silver workers	12,722	1,420	2,770	8,530	2	6,730	696	1,438	4,596	...	5,992	724	1,332	8,934	2
			261	Gold beaters	46	5	6	34	...	20	1	4	15	...	25	4	2	19	...
			262	Golsmiths and dust washers	101	14	22	65	...	55	7	13	35	...	46	7	9	30	...
			263	Gold miners, managers and agents	8	2	2	4	...	5	1	1	3	...	3	1	1	1	...
			264	Enamellers	4	1	...	3	...	2	1	...	1	...	2	...	...	2	...
			265	Electro-platers	120	20	22	78	...	71	12	11	48	...	49	8	11	30	...
			266	Gold and silver wire drawers and braid makers	1,241	125	224	892	...	644	65	111	468	...	597	60	113	424	...
			267	Plate and platedware dealers	3	...	...	3	...	1	...	...	1	...	2	...	...	2	...
			268	Diamond polishers and dealers...	13	1	1	11	...	5	1	...	4	...	8	...	1	7	...
			269	Diamond diggers, washers, &c.	5	...	2	3	...	2	...	...	2	...	3	...	2	1	...
			270	Ruby workers	...	...	...	...	...	...	...	...	...	...	...	...	...	...	...
			271	Ruby and emerald, &c., dealers	...	...	...	...	...	...	...	...	...	...	...	...	...	...	...
			272	Pearl divers	...	...	...	...	...	...	...	...	...	...	...	...	...	...	...
			273	Pearl and other precious (stone unspecified) dealers	342	33	75	234	...	206	18	40	148	...	136	15	85	86	...
			274	Coral dealers	...	...	...	...	...	...	...	...	...	...	...	...	...	...	...
			275	Cornelian and agate cutters and sellers	...	...	...	...	...	...	...	...	...	...	...	...	...	...	...
				Total Sub-order 43......	15,117	1,653	3,213	10,249	2	8,032	814	1,667	5,551	...	7,085	839	1,546	4,698	2
		44. Brass, copper and bell metal.	276	Brass workers and sellers	4	...	1	3	...	4	...	1	3	...	...	...	...	...	...
			277	Brass pot makers and sellers	943	134	193	616	...	619	90	131	398	...	324	44	62	218	...
			278	Brass image casters and sellers...	8	2	...	6	...	3	1	...	2	...	5	1	...	4	...
			279	Copper workers and sellers	670	98	152	420	...	300	42	67	191	...	370	56	85	229	...
			280	Brass and copper wire drawers and sellers	...	...	...	...	...	...	...	...	...	...	...	...	...	...	...
			281	Bell metal workers and sellers...	119	9	16	94	...	48	3	12	33	...	71	6	4	61	...
			282	General workers in brass, copper and bell metal	1,086	126	221	739	...	565	69	112	384	...	521	57	109	355	...
			283	Brass and copper dealers	204	23	49	132	...	94	6	29	59	...	110	17	20	73	...
				Total Sub-order 44......	3,034	392	632	2,010	...	1,633	211	352	1,070	...	1,401	181	280	940	...
		45. Tin, zinc, mercury and lead.	284	Tin workers and sellers...	793	101	163	529	...	428	52	82	294	...	365	49	81	235	...
			285	Tinfoil makers and sellers	...	...	...	...	...	...	...	...	...	...	...	...	...	...	...
			286	Zinc workers and sellers	1	...	...	1	...	1	...	...	1	...	...	...	...	...	...
			287	Lead and quick-silver makers and sellers	4	...	1	3	...	2	...	...	2	...	2	...	1	1	...
			288	General workers in tin, lead and zinc	48	5	8	35	...	31	2	6	23	...	17	3	2	12	...
				Total Sub-order 45......	846	106	172	568	...	462	54	88	320	...	384	52	84	248	...

TABLE XVII A.

Occupations by Age.—*Continued.*

Class.	Order.	Sub-order and Group.	Serial No.	Occupations.	COUNTRY. Total. Total.	Total. 0—4	Total. 5—14	Total. 15 and over.	Total. Unspecified.	Males. Total.	Males. 0—4	Males. 5—14	Males. 15 and over.	Males. Unspecified.	Females. Total.	Females. 0—4	Females. 5—14	Females. 15 and over.	Females. Unspecified.
					36	37	38	39	40	41	42	43	44	45	46	47	48	49	50
Class D.—Preparation and supply of material substances.—*contd.*	XIII. Metal and precious stones.	43. Gold, silver and precious stones.	258	Gold and silver dealers	557	67	146	344	...	465	54	127	284	...	92	13	19	60	...
			259	Gold and silver assayers	69	10	56	3	...	...	...	...	...	...	69	10	56	3	...
			260	Gold and silver workers	77,324	10,698	18,443	48,144	39	40,157	5,221	9,776	25,145	15	37,167	5,477	8,667	22,999	24
			261	Gold beaters	19	4	2	13	...	9	2	...	7	...	10	2	2	6	...
			262	Goldsmiths and dust washers	805	50	89	166	...	125	16	34	75	...	180	34	55	91	...
			263	Gold miners, managers and agents ...	43	3	3	37	...	34	1	1	32	...	9	2	2	5	...
			264	Enamellers	5	1	1	3	...	3	...	1	2	...	2	1	...	1	...
			265	Electro-platers	2	...	...	2	...	2	...	...	2	...	...	...	...	...	...
			266	Gold and silver wire drawers and braid makers	84	2	5	27	...	34	2	5	27	...	...	...	...	...	...
			267	Plate and platedware dealers... ...	...	...	...	...	...	...	...	...	...	...	...	...	...	...	...
			268	Diamond polishers and dealers... ...	...	...	...	...	...	...	...	...	...	...	...	...	...	...	...
			269	Diamond diggers, washers, &c.... ...	...	...	...	...	...	...	...	...	...	...	...	...	...	...	...
			270	Ruby workers	6	...	1	5	...	6	...	1	5	...	...	...	...	...	...
			271	Ruby and emerald, &c., dealers ...	1	...	...	1	...	1	...	...	1	...	...	...	...	...	...
			272	Pearl divers	2	...	1	1	...	...	...	...	...	...	2	...	1	1	...
			273	Pearl and other precious (stone unspecified) dealers	260	25	39	196	...	172	15	25	132	...	88	10	14	64	...
			274	Coral dealers	1	...	...	1	...	1	...	...	1	...	...	...	...	...	...
			275	Cornelian and agate cutters and sellers	...	...	...	...	...	...	...	...	...	...	...	...	...	...	...
				Total Sub-order 43	78,628	10,860	18,786	48,943	39	41,009	5,311	9,970	25,713	15	37,619	5,549	8,816	28,230	24
		44. Brass, copper and bell metal.	276	Brass workers and sellers	8	...	...	3	...	...	...	...	...	...	8	...	...	3	...
			277	Brass pot makers and sellers	5,429	745	1,219	3,461	4	3,030	369	681	1,979	1	2,399	376	538	1,482	3
			278	Brass image casters and sellers ...	...	...	...	...	...	...	...	...	...	...	...	...	...	...	...
			279	Copper workers and sellers	4,382	627	996	2,749	10	2,350	319	558	1,472	1	2,032	308	438	1,277	9
			280	Brass and copper wire drawers and sellers	3	...	1	2	...	...	...	...	...	...	3	...	1	2	...
			281	Bell metal workers and sellers... ...	186	28	38	120	...	100	11	24	65	...	86	17	14	55	...
			282	General workers in brass, copper, and bell metal	6,903	956	1,746	4,192	9	3,762	476	909	2,374	3	3,141	480	837	1,818	6
			283	Brass and copper dealers	87	9	21	54	3	60	3	17	37	3	27	6	4	17	...
				Total Sub-order 44	16,993	2,365	4,021	10,581	26	9,302	1,178	2,189	5,927	8	7,691	1,187	1,832	4,654	18
		45. Tin, zinc, mercury and lead.	284	Tin workers and sellers...	1,106	173	247	686	...	707	108	172	427	...	399	65	75	259	...
			285	Tinfoil makers and sellers	6	...	...	6	...	1	...	...	1	...	5	...	...	5	...
			286	Zinc workers and sellers	1	...	...	1	...	1	...	...	1	...	...	...	...	...	...
			287	Lead and quick-silver maker and sellers	...	...	...	...	...	...	...	...	...	...	...	...	...	...	...
			288	General workers in tin, lead and zinc...	149	15	32	102	...	72	7	17	48	...	77	8	15	54	...
				Total Sub-order 45	1,262	188	279	795	...	781	115	189	477	...	481	73	90	318	...

TABLE XVII A.

Occupations by Age.—*Continued.*

Class.	Order.	Sub-order and Group.	Serial No.	Occupations.	PROVINCIAL TOTAL. Total. Total.	Total. 0—4	Total. 5—14	Total. 15 and over.	Total. Unspecified.	Males. Total.	Males. 0—4	Males. 5—14	Males. 15 and over.	Males. Unspecified.	Females. Total.	Females. 0—4	Females. 5—14	Females. 15 and over.	Females. Unspecified.
1	2	3	4	5	6	7	8	9	10	11	12	13	14	15	16	17	18	19	20
Class D.—Preparation and supply of material substances.—*contd.*	XIII. Metals and precious stones.—*concld.*	46. Iron and steel.	289	Iron and steel founders, smelters and sellers ...	832	156	231	445	...	434	76	130	228	...	398	80	101	217	...
			290	Blacksmiths ...	54,851	7,929	12,858	34,032	32	29,290	8,937	6,852	18,490	11	25,561	8,992	6,006	15,542	21
			291	Iron and hardware dealers ...	626	94	124	408	...	139	22	31	86	...	487	72	93	322	...
			292	Nail makers and sellers...	...	...	...	...	...	...	...	...	...	...	...	...	...	...	...
			293	Lock makers, menders and sellers ...	16	8	8	10	...	10	8	2	5	...	6	...	1	5	...
			294	Weight makers and stampers ...	...	...	...	...	...	...	...	...	...	...	...	...	...	...	...
				Total Sub-order 46......	56,325	8,182	13,216	34,895	32	29,873	4,038	7,015	18,809	11	26,452	4,144	6,201	16,086	21
				Total Order XIII	172,205	23,746	40,319	108,041	99	91,092	11,721	21,470	57,867	34	81,113	12,025	18,849	50,174	65
	XIV. Glass, pottery and stone-ware.	47. Glass and Chinaware.	295	Glass-blowers, window-glass makers, &c.	32	7	8	22	...	2	...	1	1	...	30	7	2	21	...
			296	Bottle dealers ...	47	7	16	24	...	18	2	7	9	...	29	5	9	15	...
			297	Glass and Chinaware dealers ...	103	14	13	76	...	41	4	5	32	...	62	10	8	44	...
				Total Sub-order 47	182	28	32	122	...	61	6	13	42	...	121	22	19	80	...
		48. Earthen and stoneware.	298	Potters and pot and pipe bowl makers and sellers. (Some are also brick and tile makers) ...	91,488	14,569	22,030	54,850	39	47,772	7,098	11,616	29,039	19	43,716	7,471	10,414	25,811	20
			299	Grindstone and millstone makers and sellers ...	2,144	830	528	1,285	1	1,126	171	287	667	1	1,018	159	241	618	...
			300	Pestle and mortar makers and sellers ...	51	12	15	24	...	35	7	9	19	...	16	5	6	5	...
			301	Quartz and soapstone powder preparers and sellers ...	116	19	29	68	...	45	9	16	20	...	71	10	13	48	...
				Total Sub-order 48	93,799	14,930	22,602	56,227	40	48,978	7,285	11,928	29,745	20	44,821	7,645	10,674	26,482	20
				Total Order XIV	93,981	14,958	22,684	56,349	40	49,039	7,291	11,941	29,787	20	44,942	7,667	10,693	26,562	20
	XV. Wood, cane & leaves, &c.	49. Timber and wood.	302	Timber and bamboo agents and dealers..	691	103	163	425	...	390	57	91	242	...	301	46	72	183	...
			303	Wood cutters and sawyers ...	651	95	184	422	...	447	64	89	294	...	204	31	45	128	...
			304	Carpenters ...	110,013	15,894	25,591	68,465	63	59,038	7,875	13,988	37,146	29	50,975	8,019	11,603	31,319	34
			305	Coopers and box makers ...	53	4	16	33	...	7	...	3	4	...	46	4	13	29	...
				Total Sub-order 49	111,408	16,096	25,904	69,345	63	59,882	7,996	14,171	37,686	29	51,526	8,100	11,733	31,659	34
		50. Canework matting and leaves, &c.	306	Bamboo and rattan splitters, makers and sellers ...	10,609	1,663	2,581	6,407	8	5,467	822	1,362	3,278	5	5,142	841	1,169	3,129	3
			307	Basket weavers and winnowing pan makers and sellers ...	28,983	4,672	6,748	15,546	17	13,989	2,314	3,629	8,041	5	12,994	2,358	3,119	7,505	12
			308	Mat makers and sellers ...	7,598	1,872	1,876	4,347	8	3,739	630	1,001	2,107	1	3,859	742	875	2,240	2
			309	Screen (chik) makers and sellers ...	1	...	...	1	...	...	...	...	...	...	1	...	...	1	...

TABLE XVII A.

Occupations by Age.—*Continued.*

Class.	Order.	Sub-order and Group.	Serial No.	Occupations.	TOWN. Total. Total.	Total. 0—4	Total. 5—14	Total. 15 and over.	Total. Unspecified.	Males. Total.	Males. 0—4	Males. 5—14	Males. 15 and over.	Males. Unspecified.	Females. Total.	Females. 0—4	Females. 5—14	Females. 15 and over.	Females. Unspecified.
					21	22	23	24	25	26	27	28	29	30	31	32	33	34	35
Class D.—Preparation and supply of material substances.—*contd.*	XIII. Metals and precious stones.—*concld.*	46. Iron and steel.	289	Iron and steel founders, smelters and sellers ...	86	1	6	29	...	22	...	5	17	...	14	1	1	12	...
			290	Blacksmiths ...	4,794	622	1,007	3,165	...	2,512	808	527	1,677	...	2,282	814	480	1,488	...
			291	Iron and hardware dealers ...	64	8	10	46	...	89	5	7	27	...	25	8	3	19	...
			292	Nail makers and sellers... ...	...	...	...	...	...	...	...	...	...	...	...	...	...	...	...
			293	Lock makers, menders and sellers ...	7	...	1	6	...	8	...	...	8	...	4	...	1	3	...
			294	Weight makers and stampers ...	...	...	...	...	...	...	...	...	...	...	...	...	...	...	...
				Total Sub-order 46	4,901	631	1,024	3,246	...	2,576	313	539	1,724	...	2,325	318	485	1,522	...
				Total Order XIII	23,898	2,782	5,041	16,073	2	12,703	1,392	2,646	8,665	...	11,195	1,390	2,395	7,408	2
	XIV. Glass, pottery and stone-ware.	47. Glass and Chinaware.	295	Glass-blowers, window-glass makers, &c.	10	...	2	8	...	...	...	...	...	...	10	...	2	8	...
			296	Bottle dealers ...	47	7	16	24	...	18	2	7	9	...	29	5	9	15	...
			297	Glass and Chinaware dealers ...	89	10	10	69	...	40	4	5	31	...	49	6	5	38	...
				Total Sub-order 47	146	17	28	101	...	58	6	12	40	...	88	11	16	61	...
		48. Earthen and stoneware.	298	Potters and pot and pipe, bowl makers and sellers. (Some are also brick and tile makers) ...	5,887	846	1,296	8,744	1	2,789	397	654	1,738	...	3,098	449	642	2,006	1
			299	Grindstone and millstone makers and sellers ...	335	40	76	219	...	177	25	87	115	...	158	15	89	104	...
			300	Pestle and mortar makers and sellers ...	5	2	1	2	...	4	2	...	2	...	1	...	1	...	...
			301	Quartz and soapstone powder preparers and sellers ...	...	...	...	...	...	...	...	...	...	...	...	...	...	...	...
				Total Sub-order 48	6,227	888	1,378	8,965	1	2,970	424	691	1,855	...	3,257	464	682	2,110	1
				Total Order XIV	6,873	905	1,401	4,066	1	3,028	430	703	1,895	...	3,345	475	698	2,171	1
	XV. Wood, cane & leaves, &c.	49. Timber and wood.	302	Timber and bamboo agents and dealers.	102	17	22	63	...	52	9	9	34	...	50	8	13	29	...
			303	Wood cutters and sawyers ...	310	32	61	217	...	186	21	34	131	...	124	11	27	86	...
			304	Carpenters ...	8,425	1,094	1,786	5,541	4	4,386	529	902	2,954	1	4,039	565	884	2,587	3
			305	Coopers and box makers ...	14	1	4	9	...	2	...	...	2	...	12	1	4	7	...
				Total Sub-order 49	8,851	1,144	1,873	5,830	4	4,626	559	945	3,121	1	4,225	585	928	2,709	3
		50. Canework matting and leaves, &c.	306	Bamboo and rattan splitters, makers and sellers ...	1,664	247	348	1,069	...	768	111	177	480	...	896	136	171	589	...
			307	Basket weavers and winnowing pan makers and sellers ...	1,885	805	457	1,122	1	1,040	164	248	628	...	845	141	209	494	1
			308	Mat makers and sellers... ...	325	63	82	180	...	202	25	55	122	...	123	38	27	58	...
			309	Screen (chik) makers and sellers ...	1	...	...	1	...	...	...	...	...	...	1	...	...	1	...

TABLE XVII A.

Occupations by Age.—*Continued.*

Class.	Order.	Sub-order and Group.	Serial No.	Occupations.	COUNTRY. Total. Total.	Total. 0—4	Total. 5—14	Total. 15 and over.	Total. Unspecified.	Males. Total.	Males. 0—4	Males. 5—14	Males. 15 and over.	Males. Unspecified.	Females. Total.	Females. 0—4	Females. 5—14	Females. 15 and over.	Females. Unspecified.
					36	37	38	39	40	41	42	43	44	45	46	47	48	49	50
Class D.—Preparation and supply of material substances.—*contd.*	XIII. Metals and precious stones.—*concld.*	46. Iron and steel.	289	Iron and steel founders, melters and sellers ...	796	155	225	416	...	412	76	125	211	...	384	79	100	205	...
			290	Blacksmiths	50,057	7,307	11,851	30,867	32	26,778	3,629	6,325	16,813	11	23,279	3,678	5,526	14,054	2
			291	Iron and hardware dealers	562	86	114	362	...	100	17	24	59	...	462	69	90	303	...
			292	Nail makers and sellers	...	...	...	...	...	...	...	...	...	...	...	...	...	...	...
			293	Lock makers, menders and sellers	9	3	2	4	...	7	3	2	2	...	2	...	...	2	...
			294	Weight makers and stampers ...	...	...	...	...	...	...	...	...	...	...	...	...	...	...	...
				Total Sub-order 46......	51,424	7,551	12,192	31,649	32	27,297	3,725	6,476	17,085	11	24,127	3,826	5,716	14,564	21
				Total Order XIII......	148,307	20,964	35,278	91,968	97	78,389	10,329	18,824	49,202	34	69,918	10,635	16,454	42,766	63
	XIV. Glass, pottery and stoneware.	47. Glass and Chinaware.	295	Glass-blowers, window-glass makers, &c.	22	7	1	14	...	2	...	1	1	...	20	7	...	13	...
			296	Bottle dealers	...	...	...	...	...	...	...	...	...	...	...	...	...	...	...
			297	Glass and Chinaware dealers ...	14	4	3	7	...	1	...	...	1	...	13	4	3	6	...
				Total Sub-order 47......	36	11	4	21	...	3	...	1	2	...	33	11	3	19	...
		48. Earthern and stoneware.	298	Potters and pot and pipe, bowl makers and sellers. (Some are also brick and tile makers) ...	85,601	13,723	20,734	51,106	38	44,983	6,701	10,962	27,301	19	40,618	7,022	9,772	23,805	19
			299	Grindstone and millstone makers and sellers ...	1,809	290	452	1,066	1	949	146	250	552	1	860	144	202	514	...
			300	Pestle and mortar makers and sellers ...	46	10	14	22	...	31	5	9	17	...	15	5	5	5	...
			301	Quartz and soapstone powder preparers and sellers ...	116	19	29	68	...	45	9	16	20	...	71	10	13	48	...
				Total Sub-order 48......	87,572	14,042	21,229	52,262	39	46,008	6,861	11,237	27,890	20	41,564	7,181	9,992	24,372	19
				Total Order XIV......	87,608	14,053	21,233	52,283	39	46,011	6,861	11,238	27,892	20	41,597	7,192	9,995	24,391	19
	XV. Wood, cane & leaves, &c.	49. Timber and wood.	302	Timber and bamboo agents and dealers	589	86	141	362	...	338	48	82	208	...	251	38	59	154	...
			303	Wood cutters and sawyers ...	341	63	73	205	...	261	43	55	163	...	80	20	18	42	...
			304	Carpenters ...	101,588	14,800	28,805	62,924	59	54,652	7,346	18,086	34,192	28	46,936	7,454	10,719	28,732	31
			305	Coopers and box makers ...	39	3	12	24	...	5	...	3	2	...	34	3	9	22	...
				Total Sub-order 49......	102,557	14,952	24,031	63,515	59	55,256	7,437	13,226	34,565	28	47,301	7,515	10,805	28,950	31
		50. Canework matting and leaves, &c.	306	Bamboo and rattan splitters, makers and sellers ...	8,945	1,416	2,183	5,338	8	4,699	711	1,185	2,798	5	4,246	705	998	2,540	3
			307	Basket weavers and winnowing pan makers and sellers ...	25,098	4,367	6,291	14,424	16	12,949	2,150	3,381	7,413	5	12,149	2,217	2,910	7,011	11
			308	Mat makers and sellers...	7,273	1,309	1,794	4,167	3	3,537	605	946	1,985	1	3,736	704	848	2,182	2
			309	Screen (chik) makers and sellers ...	...	...	...	...	...	...	...	...	...	...	...	...	...	...	...

TABLE XVII A.

Occupations by Age.—*Continued.*

Class.	Order.	Sub-order and Group.	Serial No.	Occupations.	PROVINCIAL TOTAL. Total. Total.	Total. 0—4	Total. 5—14	Total. 15 and over.	Total. Unspecified.	Males. Total.	Males. 0—4	Males. 5—14	Males. 15 and over.	Males. Unspecified.	Females. Total.	Females. 0—4	Females. 5—14	Females. 15 and over.	Females. Unspecified.
1	2	3	4	5	6	7	8	9	10	11	12	13	14	15	16	17	18	19	20
Class D.—Preparation and supply of material substances.—*contd.*	XV. Wood, cane and leaves, &c.—*concld.*	50. Cane-work matting and leaves, &c.—*concld.*	310	Leaf plate makers and sellers, (Are also often temple servants)...	5,128	664	1,154	3,297	18	2,701	835	664	1,702	...	2,427	829	490	1,595	18
			311	Tooth-stick sellers	11	...	4	7	...	11	...	4	7	...	...	...	...	...	...
			312	Leaf-fan makers and sellers	5	2	1	2	...	1	...	...	1	...	4	2	1	1	...
			313	Brush and comb makers and sellers	389	42	80	267	...	148	19	29	100	...	241	23	51	167	...
			314	Broom makers and sellers	745	114	141	487	3	161	80	88	98	...	584	84	108	389	3
			315	Pith and bark collectors, workers and sellers	668	98	110	460	...	408	61	74	273	...	260	37	86	187	...
				Total Sub-order 50	52,187	8,627	12,645	30,821	44	26,625	4,211	6,796	15,607	11	25,512	4,416	5,849	15,214	33
				Total Order XV	163,545	24,723	38,549	100,166	107	86,507	12,297	20,967	53,293	40	77,038	12,516	17,582	46,873	67
	XVI. Drugs, gums, dyes, &c.	51. Gums, wax and similar forest produce.	316	India-rubber collectors and sellers	...	...	...	...	...	...	...	...	...	...	...	...	...	...	...
			317	Camphor and gum collectors and sellers	4	1	...	3	...	2	...	...	2	...	2	1	...	1	...
			318	Gallnut (myrobolan) collectors and sellers	11	8	...	3	...	6	2	...	4	...	5	1	...	4	...
			319	Catechu preparers and sellers	...	...	...	...	...	...	...	...	...	...	...	...	...	...	...
			320	Lac collectors and sellers	...	...	...	...	...	...	...	...	...	...	...	...	...	...	...
			321	Sealing-wax makers and sellers	8	1	2	5	...	8	1	2	5	...	...	...	...	...	...
			322	Tar preparers and sellers	...	...	...	...	...	...	...	...	...	...	...	...	...	...	...
			323	Wax, honey and general minor forest produce collectors and sellers	6,881	1,203	1,715	3,962	1	3,898	645	1,056	2,197	...	2,983	558	659	1,765	1
				Total Sub-order 51	6,904	1,208	1,717	3,978	1	3,914	648	1,058	2,208	...	2,990	560	659	1,770	1
		52. Drugs, dyes, pigments, &c.	324	Chemists and druggists	583	82	126	375	...	302	89	60	203	...	281	48	66	172	...
			325	Borax workers and sellers	...	...	...	...	...	...	...	...	...	...	...	...	...	...	...
			326	Saltpetre workers and sellers	98	11	23	64	...	79	10	18	51	...	19	1	5	13	...
			327	Alum, soda, &c., workers and sellers	...	...	...	...	...	...	...	...	...	...	...	...	...	...	...
			328	Soap makers and sellers	195	33	40	122	...	82	7	19	56	...	113	26	21	66	...
			329	Sulphur workers and sellers	13	...	5	8	...	11	...	4	7	...	2	...	1	1	...
			330	Indigo workers and dealers (not planters)	273	31	59	183	...	130	9	26	95	...	143	22	33	88	...
			331	Madder and logwood workers and dealers	326	42	77	207	...	206	25	43	138	...	120	17	34	69	...
			332	Ink makers and sellers	176	19	29	128	...	97	9	19	69	...	79	10	10	59	...
			333	Antimony preparers and sellers	98	19	19	60	...	48	12	12	24	...	50	7	7	36	...
			334	Henna " "	22	3	4	15	...	22	3	4	15	...	...	...	...	...	...
			335	Carmine " "	81	12	19	50	...	46	8	10	28	...	35	4	9	22	...
			336	Kanku (red powder) preparers and sellers	3,289	451	848	1,975	15	1,640	205	436	996	3	1,649	246	412	979	12
			337	Perfume preparers and sellers	7,659	1,074	1,764	4,812	9	3,844	504	937	2,398	5	3,815	570	827	2,414	4
				Total Sub-order 52	12,813	1,777	3,013	7,999	24	6,507	831	1,588	4,080	8	6,306	946	1,425	3,919	16
				Total Order XVI	19,717	2,985	4,730	11,977	25	10,421	1,479	2,646	6,288	8	9,296	1,506	2,084	5,689	17

TABLE XVII A.

Occupations by Age.—*Continued.*

Class.	Order.	Sub-order and Group.	Serial No.	Occupations.	TOWN. Total. Total.	Total. 0—4	Total. 5—14	Total. 15 and over.	Total. Unspecified.	Males. Total.	Males. 0—4	Males. 5—14	Males. 15 and over.	Males. Unspecified.	Females. Total.	Females. 0—4	Females. 5—14	Females. 15 and over.	Females. Unspecified.
					21	22	23	24	25	26	27	28	29	30	31	32	33	34	35
Class D.—Preparation and supply of material substances.—*contd.*	XV. Wood, cane and leaves, &c.—*concld.*	50. Cane-work matting and leaves, &c.—*concld.*	310	Leaf plate makers and sellers, (Are also often temple servants)	834	82	85	217	...	169	19	51	99	...	165	13	84	118	...
			311	Tooth-stick sellers	8	...	8	5	...	8	...	3	5	...	...	...	...	...	...
			312	Leaf-fan makers and sellers	3	2	1	...	...	...	...	...	...	...	3	2	1	...	...
			313	Brush and comb makers and sellers ...	151	19	80	102	...	59	8	16	35	...	92	11	14	67	...
			314	Broom makers and sellers	189	22	81	86	...	55	10	13	82	...	84	12	18	54	...
			315	Pith and bark collectors, workers and sellers	2	...	...	2	...	...	...	...	...	...	2	...	...	2	...
				Total Sub-order 50......	4,512	690	1,037	2,784	1	2,301	387	563	1,401	...	2,211	358	474	1,383	1
				Total Order XV......	13,368	1,834	2,910	8,614	5	6,927	896	1,508	4,522	1	6,436	938	1,402	4,092	4
	XVI. Drugs, gums, dyes, &c.	51. Gums, wax and similar forest produce.	316	India-rubber collectors and sellers ...	...	...	...	...	...	...	...	...	...	...	...	...	...	...	...
			317	Camphor and gum collectors and sellers.	4	1	...	8	...	2	...	...	2	...	2	1	...	1	...
			318	Gallnut (myrobolan) collectors and sellers	...	...	...	...	...	...	...	...	...	...	...	...	...	...	...
			319	Catechu preparers and sellers	...	...	...	...	...	...	...	...	...	...	...	...	...	...	...
			320	Lac collectors and sellers	...	...	...	...	...	...	...	...	...	...	...	...	...	...	...
			321	Sealing-wax makers and sellers ...	...	...	...	...	...	...	...	...	...	...	...	...	...	...	...
			322	Tar preparers and sellers	...	...	...	...	...	...	...	...	...	...	...	...	...	...	...
			323	Wax, honey and general minor forest produce collectors and sellers	15	2	2	11	...	8	...	...	8	...	12	2	2	8	...
				Total Sub-order 51......	19	3	2	14	...	5	...	...	5	...	14	3	2	9	...
		52. Drugs, dyes, pigments, &c.	324	Chemists and druggists...	218	24	88	156	...	108	15	15	78	...	110	9	82	78	...
			325	Borax workers and sellers	...	...	...	...	...	...	...	...	...	...	...	...	...	...	...
			326	Saltpetre workers and sellers	7	...	1	6	...	7	...	1	6	...	...	...	...	...	...
			327	Alum, soda, &c., workers and sellers ...	...	...	...	...	...	...	...	...	...	...	...	...	...	...	...
			328	Soap makers and sellers	...	...	...	...	...	...	...	...	...	...	...	...	...	...	...
			329	Sulphur workers and sellers	3	...	2	1	...	1	...	1	...	...	2	...	1	1	...
			330	Indigo workers and dealers (not planters).	76	4	17	55	...	54	1	10	43	...	22	3	7	12	...
			331	Madder and logwood workers and dealers	84	12	20	52	...	81	12	20	49	...	3	...	...	3	...
			332	Ink makers and sellers	109	14	18	77	...	59	7	13	39	...	50	7	5	38	...
			333	Antimony preparers and sellers ...	23	1	2	20	...	2	...	...	2	...	21	1	2	18	...
			334	Henna " "	...	...	...	...	...	...	...	...	...	...	...	...	...	...	...
			335	Carmine " "	21	4	3	14	...	14	4	1	9	...	7	...	2	5	...
			336	Kanku (red powder) preparers and sellers	482	49	105	276	2	259	28	61	170	...	173	21	44	106	2
			337	Perfume preparers and sellers	1,217	118	293	806	...	670	61	166	448	...	547	57	127	363	...
				Total Sub-order 52......	2,190	226	499	1,463	2	1,255	128	288	839	...	935	98	211	624	2
				Total Order XVI......	2,209	229	501	1,477	2	1,260	128	288	844	...	949	101	213	633	2

TABLE XVII A.

Occupations by Age.—*Continued.*

Class D.—Preparation and supply of material substances.—*contd.*

Order	Sub-order and Group	Serial No.	Occupations	COUNTRY. Total. Total. (36)	Total. 0—4 (37)	Total. 5—14 (38)	Total. 15 and over. (39)	Total. Unspecified. (40)	Males. Total. (41)	Males. 0—4 (42)	Males. 5—14 (43)	Males. 15 and over. (44)	Males. Unspecified. (45)	Females. Total. (46)	Females. 0—4 (47)	Females. 5—14 (48)	Females. 15 and over. (49)	Females. Unspecified. (50)
XV. Wood, cane and leaves, &c.—*concld.*	50. Canework matting and leaves, &c.—*concld.*	310	Leaf plate makers and sellers. (Are also often temple servants)	4,794	682	1,069	3,080	13	2,582	316	613	1,603	...	2,262	316	456	1,477	18
		311	Tooth-stick sellers	3	...	1	2	...	3	...	1	2	...	...	...	...	...	...
		312	Leaf-fan makers and sellers	2	...	...	2	...	1	...	...	1	...	1	...	...	1	...
		313	Brush and comb makers and sellers ...	238	23	50	165	...	89	11	13	65	...	149	12	87	100	...
		314	Broom makers and sellers	606	92	110	401	8	106	20	20	66	...	500	72	90	335	8
		315	Pith and bark collectors, workers and sellers	666	98	110	458	...	408	61	74	273	...	258	87	86	185	...
			Total Sub-order 50......	47,625	7,937	11,608	28,037	43	24,324	3,874	6,233	14,206	11	23,301	4,063	5,375	13,831	32
			Total Order XV	150,182	22,889	35,639	91,552	102	79,580	11,311	19,459	48,771	39	70,602	11,578	16,180	42,781	63
XVI. Drugs, gums, dyes, &c.	51. Gums, wax and similar forest produce.	316	India-rubber collectors and sellers ...	...	...	...	...	...	...	...	...	...	...	...	...	...	...	...
		317	Camphor and gum collectors and sellers	...	...	...	...	...	...	...	...	...	...	...	...	...	...	...
		318	Gallnut (myrobolan) collectors and sellers	11	8	...	8	...	6	2	...	4	...	5	1	...	4	...
		319	Catechu preparers and sellers	...	...	...	...	...	...	...	...	...	...	...	...	...	...	...
		320	Lac collectors and sellers	...	...	...	...	...	...	...	...	...	...	...	...	...	...	...
		321	Sealing-wax makers and sellers ...	8	1	2	5	...	8	1	2	5	...	...	...	...	...	...
		322	Tar preparers and sellers	...	...	...	...	...	...	...	...	...	...	...	...	...	...	...
		323	Wax, honey and general minor forest produce collectors and sellers	6,866	1,201	1,713	3,951	1	3,895	645	1,056	2,194	...	2,971	556	657	1,757	1
			Total Sub-order 51	6,885	1,205	1,715	3,964	1	3,909	648	1,058	2,203	...	2,976	557	657	1,761	1
	52. Drugs, dyes, pigments, &c.	324	Chemists and druggists	365	58	88	219	...	194	24	45	125	...	171	34	43	94	...
		325	Borax workers and sellers	...	...	...	...	...	...	...	...	...	...	...	...	...	...	...
		326	Saltpetre workers and sellers	91	11	22	58	...	72	10	17	45	...	19	1	5	13	...
		327	Alum, soda, &c., workers and sellers ...	...	...	...	...	...	...	...	...	...	...	...	...	...	...	...
		328	Soap makers and sellers	195	33	40	122	...	82	7	19	56	...	113	26	21	66	...
		329	Sulphur workers and sellers	10	...	3	7	...	10	...	3	7	...	...	...	...	...	...
		330	Indigo workers and dealers (not planters)	197	27	42	128	...	76	8	16	52	...	121	19	26	76	...
		331	Madder and logwood workers and dealers	242	30	57	155	...	125	13	23	89	...	117	17	84	66	...
		332	Ink makers and sellers	67	5	11	51	...	38	2	6	30	...	29	3	5	21	...
		333	Antimony preparers and sellers... ...	75	18	17	40	...	46	12	12	22	...	29	6	5	18	...
		334	Henna " "	22	3	4	15	...	22	3	4	15	...	...	...	...	...	...
		335	Carmine " "	60	8	16	36	...	32	4	9	19	...	28	4	7	17	...
		336	Kanku (red powder) preparers and sellers.	2,857	402	743	1,699	13	1,381	177	375	826	3	1,476	225	368	873	10
		337	Perfume preparers and sellers	6,442	956	1,471	4,006	9	3,174	443	771	1,955	5	3,268	513	700	2,051	4
			Total Sub-order 52	10,623	1,551	2,514	6,536	22	5,252	703	1,300	3,241	8	5,371	848	1,214	3,295	14
			Total Order XVI	17,508	2,756	4,229	10,500	23	9,161	1,351	2,358	5,444	8	8,347	1,405	1,871	5,056	15

TABLE XVII A.

Occupations by Age.—*Continued.*

Class.	Order.	Sub-order and Group.	Serial No.	Occupations.	PROVINCIAL TOTAL. Total. Total.	Total. 0—4	Total. 5—14	Total. 15 and over.	Total. Unspecified.	Males. Total.	Males. 0—4	Males. 5—14	Males. 15 and over.	Males. Unspecified.	Females. Total.	Females. 0—4	Females. 5—14	Females. 15 and over.	Females. Unspecified.
1	2	3	4	5	6	7	8	9	10	11	12	13	14	15	16	17	18	19	20
Class D.—Preparation, &c.—*concld.*	XVII. Leather, horn, bones and grease.	53. Leather, &c	338	Tanners, curriers and hide sellers (many also shoe-makers)	8,094	1,578	1,922	4,588	6	3,490	569	786	2,133	2	4,604	1,009	1,136	2,455	4
			339	Shoes, sandals, boot-makers and sellers...	92,409	15,754	21,845	54,757	53	54,164	8,633	13,091	32,407	33	38,245	7,121	8,754	22,350	20
			340	Leather dyers	3,224	518	757	1,947	2	1,496	242	353	900	1	1,728	276	404	1,047	1
			341	Water bag, well-bag, bucket and ghee-pot makers and sellers...	45,289	9,087	10,617	25,558	27	27,123	4,702	6,149	16,258	14	18,166	4,385	4,468	9,300	13
			342	Hide, horns and bone dealers	8,601	1,585	2,014	4,993	9	5,058	895	1,227	2,934	2	3,543	690	787	2,059	7
			343	Catgut preparers and sellers	52	7	13	32	...	43	7	11	25	...	9	...	2	7	...
			344	Glue makers and sellers	5	1	1	3	...	5	1	1	3	...	...	...	...	...	...
			345	Grease preparers and sellers	...	...	...	...	...	...	...	...	...	...	...	...	...	...	...
				Total Sub-order 53......	157,674	28,530	37,169	91,878	97	91,379	15,049	21,618	54,660	52	66,295	13,481	15,551	37,218	45
				Total Order XVII......	157,674	28,530	37,169	91,878	97	91,379	15,049	21,618	54,660	52	66,295	13,481	15,551	37,218	45
Class E.—Commerce, transport, storage.	XVIII. Commerce.	54. Dealers in money and securities.	346	Bankers and Bank managers	1,042	75	165	802	...	637	46	98	493	...	405	29	67	309	...
			347	Money-lenders and Pawnbrokers ...	20,358	2,658	4,431	13,204	65	9,293	1,102	2,040	6,150	1	11,065	1,556	2,391	7,054	64
			348	Bill-discounters	462	73	114	275	...	377	61	95	221	...	85	12	19	54	...
			349	Insurance Agents and under-writers ...	3	...	...	3	...	2	...	...	2	...	1	...	...	1	...
			350	Money changers and testers	10,973	1,265	2,382	7,324	2	5,828	643	1,283	3,900	2	5,145	622	1,099	3,424	...
			351	Bank clerks, cashiers, bill collectors, accountants, &c.	57	5	12	40	...	22	1	5	16	...	35	4	7	24	...
				Total Sub-order 54......	32,895	4,076	7,104	21,648	67	16,159	1,853	3,521	10,782	3	16,736	2,223	3,583	10,866	64
		55. General merchants.	352	General merchants	46,838	5,775	10,841	30,201	21	21,171	3,476	5,092	13,598	5	25,667	2,299	5,749	16,603	16
			353	Merchants' managers, accountants, clerks, assistants, &c.	511	49	108	354	...	272	25	49	198	...	239	24	59	156	...
				Total Sub-order 55......	47,349	5,824	10,949	30,555	21	21,443	2,501	5,141	13,796	5	25,906	3,323	5,808	16,759	16
		56. Dealing unspecified.	354	Shop-keepers' clerks, salesmen, &c. ...	522	55	95	372	...	285	28	49	208	...	237	27	46	164	...
			355	Shop-keepers and money-lenders' servants	9,893	1,275	1,940	6,670	8	5,908	654	1,149	4,101	4	3,985	621	791	2,569	4
			356	Shop-keepers otherwise unspecified ...	76,986	9,671	16,134	51,131	50	37,179	4,383	7,783	25,002	11	39,807	5,288	8,351	26,129	39
			357	Pedlars, Hawkers, &c.	260	29	57	174	...	139	10	31	98	...	121	19	26	76	...
				Total Sub-order 56......	87,661	11,030	18,226	58,347	58	43,511	5,075	9,012	29,409	15	44,150	5,955	9,214	28,938	43

TABLE XVII A.

Occupations by Age.—*Continued.*

Class.	Order.	Sub-order and Group.	Serial No.	Occupations.	TOWN. Total. Total.	Total. 0—4	Total. 5—14	Total. 15 and over.	Total. Unspecified.	Males. Total.	Males. 0—4	Males. 5—14	Males. 15 and over.	Males. Unspecified.	Females. Total.	Females. 0—4	Females. 5—14	Females. 15 and over.	Females. Unspecified.
					21	22	23	24	25	26	27	28	29	30	31	32	33	34	35
Class D.—Preparation, &c.—concld.	XVII. Leather, horn, bones, and grease.	53. Leather, &c.	338	Tanners, curriers and hide sellers (many also shoe-makers)	1,044	185	288	571	...	466	70	140	256	...	578	115	148	315	...
			339	Shoes, sandals, boot-makers and sellers	8,805	1,212	1,938	5,652	3	4,636	614	1,010	3,010	2	4,169	598	928	2,642	1
			340	Leather dyers	993	147	233	612	1	607	96	133	377	1	386	51	100	235	...
			341	Water bag, well-bag, bucket and ghee-pot makers and sellers	1,573	440	325	808	...	914	299	192	423	...	659	141	133	385	...
			342	Hide, horns and bone dealers	1,522	221	317	982	2	788	112	170	506	...	734	109	147	476	2
			343	Catgut preparers and sellers	52	7	13	32	...	43	7	11	25	...	9	...	2	7	...
			344	Glue makers and sellers	...	...	...	...	...	...	...	...	...	...	...	...	...	...	...
			345	Grease preparers and sellers	...	...	...	...	...	...	...	...	...	...	...	...	...	...	...
				Total Sub-order 53	13,989	2,212	3,114	8,657	6	7,454	1,198	1,656	4,597	3	6,535	1,014	1,458	4,060	3
				Total Order XVII......	13,989	2,212	3,114	8,657	6	7,454	1,198	1,656	4,597	3	6,535	1,014	1,458	4,060	3
Class E.—Commerce, transport, storage.	XVIII. Commerce.	54. Dealers in money and securities.	346	Bankers and Bank managers	796	49	109	638	...	508	34	70	404	...	288	15	39	234	...
			347	Money-lenders and Pawnbrokers ...	3,059	343	645	2,065	6	1,374	132	291	951	...	1,685	211	354	1,114	6
			348	Bill-discounters	181	20	50	111	...	139	14	33	92	...	42	6	17	19	...
			349	Insurance Agents and under-writers ...	3	...	...	3	...	2	...	...	2	...	1	...	...	1	...
			350	Money changers and testers	5,346	534	1,144	3,668	...	2,469	238	555	1,676	...	2,877	296	589	1,992	...
			351	Bank clerks, cashiers, bill collectors, accountants, &c.	57	5	12	40	...	22	1	5	16	...	35	4	7	24	...
				Total Sub-order 54......	9,442	951	1,960	6,525	6	4,514	419	954	3,141	...	4,928	532	1,006	3,384	6
		55. General merchants.	352	General merchants	4,850	551	1,041	3,258	...	2,338	254	519	1,565	...	2,512	297	522	1,693	...
			353	Merchants managers, accountants, clerks, assistants, &c.	510	49	108	353	...	271	25	49	197	...	239	24	59	156	...
				Total Sub-order 55......	5,360	600	1,149	3,611	...	2,609	279	568	1,762	...	2,751	321	581	1,849	...
		56. Dealing unspecified.	354	Shop-keepers' clerks, salesmen, &c. ...	469	49	85	335	...	256	25	46	185	...	213	24	39	150	...
			355	Shop-keepers and money lenders' servants.	1,689	178	306	1,205	...	945	101	159	685	...	744	77	147	520	...
			356	Shop-keepers otherwise unspecified ...	19,569	2,109	3,771	13,671	18	10,359	1,101	2,024	7,233	1	9,210	1,008	1,747	6,438	17
			357	Pedlars, Hawkers, &c.	259	29	57	173	...	138	10	31	97	...	121	19	26	76	...
				Total Sub-order 56......	21,986	2,365	4,219	15,384	18	11,698	1,237	2,260	8,200	1	10,288	1,128	1,959	7,184	17

TABLE XVII A.

Occupations by Age.—*Continued.*

Class.	Order.	Sub-order and Group.	Serial No.	Occupations.	COUNTRY. Total. Total.	Total. 0—4	Total. 5—14	Total. 15 and over.	Total. Unspecified.	Males. Total.	Males. 0—4	Males. 5—14	Males. 15 and over.	Males. Unspecified.	Females. Total.	Females. 0—4	Females. 5—14	Females. 15 and over.	Females. Unspecified.
					36	37	38	39	40	41	42	43	44	45	46	47	48	49	50
Class D.—Preparation, &c.—concld.	XVII. Leather, horn, bones, and grease.	53. Leather, &c.	338	Tanners, curriers and hide sellers (many also shoe-makers)	7,050	1,393	1,634	4,017	6	3,024	499	646	1,877	2	4,026	894	988	2,140	4
			339	Shoes, sandals, boot-makers and sellers	83,604	14,542	19,907	49,105	50	49,528	8,019	12,081	29,397	31	34,076	6,528	7,826	19,708	19
			340	Leather dyers	2,231	371	524	1,335	1	889	146	220	523	...	1,342	225	804	812	1
			341	Water bag, well-bag, bucket and ghee-pot makers and sellers...	43,716	8,647	10,292	24,750	27	26,209	4,408	5,957	15,835	14	17,507	4,244	4,335	8,915	13
			342	Hide, horns and bone dealers	7,079	1,364	1,697	4,011	7	4,270	783	1,057	2,428	2	2,809	581	640	1,588	5
			343	Catgut preparers and sellers	...	...	...	...	...	...	...	...	...	...	...	...	...	...	...
			344	Glue makers and sellers	5	1	1	3	...	5	1	1	3	...	...	...	...	...	...
			345	Grease preparers and sellers	...	...	...	...	...	...	...	...	...	...	...	...	...	...	...
				Total Sub-order 53......	143,685	26,318	34,055	83,221	91	83,925	13,851	19,962	50,063	49	59,760	12,467	14,093	33,158	42
				Total Order XVII......	143,685	26,318	34,055	83,221	91	83,925	13,851	19,962	50,063	49	59,760	12,467	14,093	33,158	42
Class E.—Commerce, transport, storage.	XVIII. Commerce.	54. Dealers in money and securities.	346	Bankers and Bank managers...	246	26	56	164	...	129	12	28	89	...	117	14	28	75	...
			347	Money-lenders and Pawnbrokers	17,299	2,315	3,786	11,139	59	7,919	970	1,749	5,199	1	9,380	1,345	2,037	5,940	58
			348	Bill-discounters	281	53	64	164	...	238	47	62	129	...	43	6	2	35	...
			349	Insurance Agents and under-writers	...	...	...	...	...	...	...	...	...	...	...	...	...	...	...
			350	Money changers and testers	5,627	731	1,238	3,656	2	3,359	405	728	2,224	2	2,268	326	510	1,432	...
			351	Bank clerks, cashiers, bill collectors, accountants, &c.	...	...	...	...	...	...	...	...	...	...	...	...	...	...	...
				Total Sub-order 54......	23,453	3,125	5,144	15,123	61	11,645	1,434	2,567	7,641	3	11,808	1,691	2,577	7,482	58
		55. General merchants.	352	General merchants	41,988	5,224	9,800	26,943	21	18,833	2,222	4,573	12,033	5	23,155	3,002	5,227	14,910	16
			353	Merchants' managers, accountants, clerks, assistants, &c....	1	...	...	1	...	1	...	...	1	...	...	...	...	...	...
				Total Sub-order 55......	41,989	5,224	9,800	26,944	21	18,834	2,222	4,578	12,034	5	23,155	3,002	5,227	14,910	16
		56. Dealing unspecified.	354	Shop-keepers' clerks, salesmen, &c.	53	6	10	37	...	29	3	8	28	...	24	3	7	14	...
			355	Shop-keepers and money-lenders' servants	8,204	1,097	1,634	5,465	8	4,963	553	990	3,416	4	3,241	544	644	2,049	4
			356	Shop-keepers otherwise unspecified	57,417	7,562	12,362	37,460	32	26,820	3,282	5,759	17,769	10	30,597	4,280	6,604	19,691	22
			357	Pedlars, Hawkers, &c.	1	...	...	1	...	1	...	...	1	...	...	...	...	...	...
				Total Sub-order 56......	65,675	8,665	14,007	42,963	40	31,813	3,838	6,752	21,209	14	33,862	4,827	7,255	21,754	26

TABLE XVII A.

Occupations by Age.—*Continued.*

Class.	Order.	Sub-order and Group.	Serial No.	Occupations.	PROVINCIAL TOTAL. Total. Total.	Total. 0—4	Total. 5—14	Total. 15 and over.	Total. Unspecified.	Males. Total.	Males. 0—4	Males. 5—14	Males. 15 and over.	Males. Unspecified.	Females. Total.	Females. 0—4	Females. 5—14	Females. 15 and over.	Females. Unspecified.
1	2	3	4	5	6	7	8	9	10	11	12	13	14	15	16	17	18	19	20
Class E.—Commerce, transport, storage.—*contd.*	XVIII. Commerce.—*concld.*	57. Middlemen, &c. (a—Brokers, &c.)	358	Brokers' Agents, Dubash...	1,076	117	197	762	...	501	47	82	372	...	575	70	115	390	...
			359	Auctioneers, Auditors, Actuaries, Notaries public, Appraisers and House agents	20	2	7	11	...	9	...	8	6	...	11	2	4	5	...
		(b) Contractors and farmers.	360	Farmers of tolls, ferries...	58	11	10	37	...	51	10	9	32	...	7	1	1	5	...
			361	Farmers of liquor, opium, &c. ...	3,484	496	796	2,191	1	1,146	158	243	745	...	2,338	338	553	1,446	1
			362	Lessees and superintendents of market stalls, &c.	175	19	34	122	...	84	5	13	66	...	91	14	21	56	...
			363	Contractors—otherwise unspecified	3,333	419	790	2,122	2	1,808	194	406	1,208	...	1,525	225	384	914	2
			364	Contractors for labour, Emigration agents, &c.	178	27	28	123	...	58	2	4	52	...	120	25	24	71	...
				Total Sub-order 57......	8,324	1,091	1,862	5,368	3	3,657	416	760	2,481	...	4,667	675	1,102	2,887	3
				Total Order XVIII......	176,229	22,021	38,141	115,918	149	84,770	9,845	18,434	56,468	23	91,459	12,176	19,707	59,450	126
	XIX. Transport and storage.	58. Railways. (a) Administration.	365	Agents, directors, managers and their assistants	17	2	3	12	...	7	...	...	7	...	10	2	3	5	...
			366	Traffic Managers, Superintendents and Assistants	6	...	2	4	...	6	...	2	4	...	...	...	...	...	...
			367	Locomotive Superintendents & Assistants.	38	...	9	29	...	21	...	4	17	...	17	...	5	12	...
			368	Auditors, Accountants, &c.	23	1	...	22	...	11	1	...	10	...	12	...	...	12	...
			369	Engineers (when not returned under general heading)...	151	16	20	115	...	85	7	7	71	...	66	9	13	44	...
		(b) Working staff.	370	Clerical Staff in Railway establishment...	595	76	107	412	...	355	40	58	257	...	240	36	49	155	...
			371	Station Masters and Assistants, Inspectors, Overseers, &c. ...	619	108	136	375	...	319	59	59	201	...	300	49	77	174	...
			372	Guards, drivers, firemen, &c. ...	400	53	89	258	...	222	21	47	154	...	178	32	42	104	...
			373	Pointsmen, shunters, porters, signallers, &c.	5,022	691	853	3,478	...	2,946	357	432	2,157	...	2,076	334	421	1,321	...
				Total Sub-order 58......	6,871	947	1,219	4,705	...	3,972	485	609	2,878	...	2,899	462	610	1,827	...
		59. Roads. (a) Cart, carriage and tramway owners and drivers.	374	Tramway, mail carriage, &c., companies contractors, &c...	...	...	...	...	...	...	...	...	...	...	...	...	...	...	...
			375	Cart owners & drivers, carting agents, &c.	27,901	3,617	5,721	18,546	17	17,764	1,959	3,453	12,343	9	10,137	1,658	2,268	6,203	8
			376	Livery stable keepers, &c.	1,108	155	196	757	...	582	59	104	419	...	526	96	92	338	...
			377	Drivers, stable boys, &c. (not private servants)	1,958	247	370	1,340	1	1,487	157	252	1,077	1	471	90	118	263	...
		(b) Carriers by pack animals.	378	Palki, &c., owners, bearers, &c.	4,851	661	928	3,259	3	3,053	349	545	2,157	2	1,798	312	382	1,102	1
			379	Pack bullock owners, drivers, &c.	24,024	3,524	5,681	14,795	20	13,558	1,741	3,158	8,653	6	10,466	1,783	2,528	6,146	14
			380	Pack camel, elephant, mule, &c., owners and drivers	1,555	211	366	978	...	796	95	192	509	...	759	116	174	469	...
				Total Sub-order 59......	61,397	8,415	13,262	39,679	41	37,240	4,360	7,704	25,158	18	24,157	4,055	5,558	14,521	23

TABLE XVII A.

Occupations by Age.—*Continued.*

Class.	Order.	Sub-order and Group.	Serial No.	Occupations.	TOWN. Total. Total.	Total. 0—4	Total. 5—14	Total. 15 and over.	Total. Unspecified.	Males. Total.	Males. 0—4	Males. 5—14	Males. 15 and over.	Males. Unspecified.	Females. Total.	Females. 0—4	Females. 5—14	Females. 15 and over.	Females. Unspecified.
					21	22	23	24	25	26	27	28	29	30	31	32	33	34	35
Class E.—Commerce, transport, storage.—*contd.*	XVIII. Commerce.—*concld.*	57. Middlemen, &c. (a)—Brokers, &c.	358	Brokers' Agents, Dubash	659	58	108	493	...	327	24	44	259	...	332	34	64	234	...
			359	Auctioneers, Auditors, Actuaries, Notaries public, Appraisers and House agents	19	2	7	10	...	9	...	3	6	...	10	2	4	4	...
		(b) Contractors and farmers.	360	Farmers of tolls, ferries	7	1	...	6	...	2	...	...	2	...	5	1	...	4	...
			361	Farmers of liquor, opium, &c.... ...	148	11	23	114	...	98	7	16	75	...	50	4	7	39	...
			362	Lessees and superintendents of market stalls, &c.	65	12	15	38	...	21	2	7	12	...	44	10	8	26	...
			363	Contractors—otherwise unspecified ...	1,389	161	337	890	1	709	79	166	464	...	680	82	171	426	1
			364	Contractors for labour, Emigration agents, &c.	3	1	...	2	...	2	1	...	1	...	1	...	...	1	...
				Total Sub-order 57......	2,290	246	490	1,553	1	1,168	113	236	819	...	1,122	133	254	734	1
				Total Order XVIII......	39,078	4,162	7,818	27,073	25	19,989	2,048	4,018	13,922	1	19,089	2,114	3,800	13,151	24
	XIX. Transport and storage.	58. Railways. (a) Administration.	365	Agents, directors, managers and their assistants	12	...	3	9	...	5	...	...	5	...	7	...	3	4	...
			366	Traffic Managers, Superintendents and Assistants	5	...	2	3	...	5	...	2	3	...	...	...	...	...	...
			367	Locomotive Superintendents & Assistants.	31	...	7	24	...	17	...	3	14	...	14	...	4	10	...
			368	Auditors, Accountants, &c.	9	1	...	8	...	6	1	...	5	...	3	...	...	3	...
			369	Engineers (when not returned under general heading)	71	12	14	45	...	29	6	4	19	...	42	6	10	26	...
		(b) Working staff.	370	Clerical Staff in Railway establishment...	476	68	85	323	...	274	35	43	196	...	202	33	42	127	...
			371	Station Masters and Assistants, Inspectors, Overseers, &c.	70	14	18	38	...	41	10	11	20	...	29	4	7	18	...
			372	Guards, drivers, firemen, &c.	222	30	62	130	...	103	10	31	62	...	119	20	31	68	...
			373	Pointsmen, shunters, porters, signallers, &c.	1,435	210	284	941	...	742	114	133	495	...	693	96	151	446	...
				Total Sub-order 58......	2,331	835	475	1,521	...	1,222	176	227	819	...	1,109	159	248	702	...
		59. Roads. (a) Cart, carriage and tramway owners and drivers.	374	Tramway, mail carriage, &c., companies contractors, &c.	...	...	...	...	...	...	...	...	...	...	...	...	...	...	...
			375	Cart owners & drivers, carting agents, &c.	5,002	595	946	3,461	...	2,792	277	489	2,026	...	2,210	318	457	1,435	...
			376	Livery stable keepers, &c.	537	83	99	355	...	274	33	54	187	...	263	50	45	168	...
			377	Drivers, stable boys, &c., (not private servants).	46	3	17	26	...	18	1	3	14	...	28	2	14	12	...
		(b) Carriers by pack animals.	378	Palki, &c., owners, bearers, &c... ...	2,230	207	304	1,719	...	1,609	125	177	1,307	...	621	82	127	412	...
			379	Pack bullock owners, drivers, &c. ...	1,928	228	377	1,318	5	965	86	191	688	...	963	142	186	630	5
			380	Pack camel, elephant, mule, &c., owners and drivers	964	116	243	605	...	542	61	148	333	...	422	55	95	272	...
				Total Sub-order 59......	10,707	1,232	1,986	7,484	5	6,200	583	1,062	4,555	...	4,507	649	924	2,929	5

TABLE XVII A.

Occupations by Age.—*Continued.*

Class.	Order.	Sub-order and Group.	Serial No.	Occupations.	COUNTRY. Total. Total.	Total. 0—4	Total. 5—14	Total. 15 and over.	Total. Unspecified.	Males. Total.	Males. 0—4	Males. 5—14	Males. 15 and over.	Males. Unspecified.	Females. Total.	Females. 0—4	Females. 5—14	Females. 15 and over.	Females. Unspecified.
					36	37	38	39	40	41	42	43	44	45	46	47	48	49	50
Class D.—Commerce, transport, storage.—*contd.*	XVIII. Commerce.—*concld.*	57. Middlemen, &c. (a)—Brokers, &c.	358	Brokers' Agents, Dubash	417	59	89	269	...	174	23	38	118	...	243	36	51	156	...
			359	Auctioneers, Auditors, Actuaries, Notaries public, Appraisers, and House agents...	1	...	...	1	...	...	...	...	...	...	1	...	...	1	...
		(b) Contractors and farmers.	360	Farmers of tolls, ferries	51	10	10	31	...	49	10	9	30	...	2	...	1	1	...
			361	Farmers of liquor, opium, &c.	3,336	485	773	2,077	1	1,048	151	227	670	...	2,288	334	546	1,407	1
			362	Lessees and superintendents of market stalls, &c.	110	7	19	84	...	63	3	6	54	..	47	4	13	30	...
			363	Contractors—otherwise unspecified ...	1,944	258	453	1,232	1	1,099	115	240	744	...	845	148	218	488	1
			364	Contractors for labour, Emigration agents, &c.	175	26	28	121	...	56	1	4	51	...	119	25	24	70	...
				Total Sub-order 57......	6,034	845	1,372	3,815	2	2,489	803	524	1,662	...	3,545	542	848	2,153	2
				Total Order XVIII......	137,151	17,859	30,323	88,845	124	64,781	7,797	14,416	42,546	22	72,370	10,062	15,907	46,299	102
	XIX. Transport and storage.	58. Railways. (a) Administration.	365	Agents, directors, managers and their assistants	5	2	...	3	...	2	...	...	2	...	3	2	...	1	...
			366	Traffic Managers, Superintendents, and Assistants	1	...	...	1	...	1	...	...	1	...	...	...	...	...	...
			367	Locomotive Superintendents & Assistants.	7	...	2	5	...	4	...	1	3	...	3	...	1	2	...
			368	Auditors, Accountants, &c.	14	...	...	14	...	5	...	...	5	...	9	...	...	9	...
			369	Engineers (when not returned under general heading)	80	4	6	70	...	56	1	3	52	...	24	3	3	18	...
			370	Clerical Staff in Railway establishment..	119	8	22	89	...	81	5	15	61	...	38	3	7	28	...
		(b) Working staff.	371	Station Masters and Assistants, Inspectors, Overseers, &c.	549	94	118	337	...	278	49	48	181	...	271	45	70	156	...
			372	Guards, drivers, firemen, &c.	178	23	27	128	...	119	11	16	92	...	59	12	11	36	...
			373	Pointsmen, shunters, porters, signallers, &c.	3,587	481	569	2,537	...	2,204	243	299	1,662	...	1,383	238	270	875	...
				Total Sub-order 58......	4,540	612	744	3,184	...	2,750	309	382	2,059	...	1,790	803	362	1,125	...
		59. Road. (a) Cart, carriage and tramway owners and drivers.	374	Tramway, mail carriage, &c., companies contractors, &c.	...	...	...	...	...	...	...	...	...	...	...	...	...	...	...
			375	Cart owners & drivers, carting agents, &c.	22,899	3,022	4,775	15,085	17	14,972	1,682	2,964	10,317	9	7,927	1,340	1,811	4,768	8
			376	Livery stable keepers, &c.	571	72	97	402	...	308	26	50	232	...	263	46	47	170	...
			377	Drivers, stable boys, &c., (not private servants)	1,912	244	353	1,314	1	1,469	156	249	1,063	1	443	88	104	251	...
		(b) Carriers by pack animals.	378	Palki, &c., owners, bearers, &c... ...	2,621	454	624	1,540	3	1,444	224	368	850	2	1,177	230	256	690	1
			379	Pack bullock owners, drivers, &c. ...	22,096	2,296	5,304	13,481	15	12,593	1,655	2,967	7,965	6	9,503	1,641	2,337	5,516	9
			380	Pack camel, elephant, mule, &c., owners and drivers	591	95	123	373	...	254	34	44	176	...	337	61	79	197	...
				Total Sub-order 59......	50,690	7,183	11,276	32,195	36	31,040	3,777	6,642	20,603	18	19,650	3,406	4,634	11,592	18

TABLE XVII A.

Occupations by Age.—*Continued.*

Class.	Order.	Sub-order and Group.	Serial No.	Occupations.	PROVINCIAL TOTAL. Total. Total.	Total. 0—4	Total. 5—14	Total. 15 and over.	Total. Unspecified.	Males. Total.	Males. 0—4	Males. 5—14	Males. 15 and over.	Males. Unspecified.	Females. Total.	Females. 0—4	Females. 5—14	Females. 15 and over.	Females. Unspecified.
1	2	3	4	5	6	7	8	9	10	11	12	13	14	15	16	17	18	19	20
Class E.—Commerce, transport, storage.—*concld.*	XIX.—Transport and storage.	60. Water. (a) Owners, &c. of vessels.	381	Ship owners, Companies, Agents ...	...	...	...	...	...	...	...	...	...	...	...	...	...	...	...
			382	Shipping clerks, supercargoes, and stevedores	...	...	...	...	...	...	...	...	...	...	...	...	...	...	...
			383	Boat and barge owners, &c, ...	...	...	...	...	...	...	...	...	...	...	...	...	...	...	...
		(b) Working staff of vessels.	384	Ships' Officers, Engineers, mariners and firemen...	13	...	...	13	...	12	...	...	12	...	1	...	...	1	...
			385	Boat and barge men	707	104	153	450	...	415	55	89	271	...	292	49	64	179	...
			386	Pilots	...	...	...	...	...	...	...	...	...	...	...	...	...	...	...
			387	Lock-keepers, &c., and canal service ...	5,179	852	1,175	3,127	25	3,021	442	654	1,924	1	2,158	410	521	1,208	24
			388	Dock and harbour service	...	...	...	...	...	...	...	...	...	...	...	...	...	...	...
			389	Divers (not for pearls)	15	1	4	10	...	9	1	2	6	...	6	...	2	4	...
				Total Sub-order 60......	5,914	957	1,332	3,600	25	3,457	498	745	2,213	1	2,457	459	587	1,887	24
		61. Messages. (a) Post, &c.	390	Postal Directors, Postmasters and clerks.	474	66	85	323	...	231	28	34	169	...	243	38	51	154	...
			391	Postal messengers, runners, &c, ...	2,314	299	448	1,559	8	1,410	139	249	1,014	8	904	160	199	545	...
			392	Messengers (unspecified)	1,302	189	240	873	...	664	79	119	466	...	638	110	121	407	...
		(b) Telegraph, & Telephone.	393	Telegraph officers (Government, Railway and others), and clerical, and accounts establishment	122	14	24	84	...	70	6	11	53	...	52	8	13	31	...
			394	Signallers and messengers	32	1	7	24	...	16	...	...	16	...	16	1	7	8	...
			395	Telephone Company's service	5	2	1	2	...	3	1	1	1	...	2	1	...	1	...
				Total Sub-order 61......	4,249	571	805	2,865	8	2,394	253	414	1,719	8	1,855	318	391	1,146	...
		62. Storage and weighing.	396	Warehouse owners, keepers, &c, ...	16	3	1	12	...	14	3	1	10	...	2	...	...	2	...
			397	Warehouse service	22	4	6	12	...	19	3	6	10	...	3	1	...	2	...
			398	Porters (general)	3,254	481	670	2,103	...	1,677	251	348	1,078	...	1,577	230	322	1,025	...
			399	Weighmen and measurers	897	95	180	622	...	482	48	100	334	...	415	47	80	288	...
			400	Watchmen (not village)	170	18	33	119	...	112	8	15	89	...	58	10	18	30	...
				Total Sub-order 62......	4,359	601	890	2,868	...	2,304	313	470	1,521	...	2,055	288	420	1,347	...
				Total Order XIX......	82,790	11,491	17,508	53,717	74	49,367	5,909	9,942	33,489	27	33,423	5,582	7,566	20,228	47

TABLE XVII A.

Occupations by Age.—*Continued.*

Class.	Order.	Sub-order and Group.	Serial No.	Occupations.	TOWN. Total. Total.	Total. 0—4	Total. 5—14	Total. 15 and over.	Total. Unspecified.	Males. Total.	Males. 0—4	Males. 5—14	Males. 15 and over.	Males. Unspecified.	Females. Total.	Females. 0—4	Females. 5—14	Females. 15 and over.	Females. Unspecified.
					21	22	23	24	25	26	27	28	29	30	31	32	33	34	35
Class E.—Commerce, transport, storage.—*concld.*	XIX.—Transport and storage.	60. Water. (a) Owners, &c. of vessels.	381	Ship owners, Companies Agents ...	...	...	...	...	...	...	...	...	...	...	...	...	...	...	...
			382	Shipping clerks, supercargoes, and stevedores	...	...	...	...	...	...	...	...	...	...	...	...	...	...	...
			383	Boat and barge owners, &c.	...	...	...	...	...	...	...	...	...	...	...	...	...	...	...
		(b) Working staff of vessels.	384	Ships' Officers, Engineers, mariners, and firemen...	2	...	...	2	...	1	...	...	1	...	1	...	...	1	...
			385	Boat and barge men	39	6	10	23	...	23	4	7	12	...	16	2	3	11	...
			386	Pilots	...	...	...	...	...	...	...	...	...	...	...	...	...	...	...
			387	Lock-keepers, &c., and canal service ...	106	15	27	64	...	48	8	9	31	...	58	7	18	33	
			388	Dock and harbour service	...	...	...	...	...	...	...	...	...	...	...	...	...	...	
			389	Divers (not for pearls)	14	1	4	9	...	8	1	2	4	...	6	...	2	4	
				Total Sub-order 60......	161	22	41	98	...	80	18	18	49	...	81	9	23	49	...
		61. Messages. (a) Post, &c.	390	Postal Directors, Postmasters and clerks.	240	82	87	171	...	136	19	17	100	...	104	18	20	71	...
			391	Postal messengers, runners, &c. ...	930	106	191	633	...	532	47	95	390	...	398	59	96	243	...
			392	Messengers (unspecified)	1,177	181	211	785	...	587	75	101	411	...	590	106	110	374	...
		(b) Telegraph, & Telephone.	393	Telegraph officers (Government, Railway and others), and clerical, and accounts establishment	58	6	14	38	...	32	2	6	24	...	26	4	8	14	...
			394	Signallers and messengers	21	...	4	17	...	13	...	...	13	...	8	...	4	4	...
			395	Telephone Company's service	5	2	1	2	...	3	1	1	1	...	2	1	...	1	...
				Total Sub-order 61......	2,431	327	458	1,646	...	1,303	144	220	939	...	1,128	183	238	707	...
		62. Storage and weighing.	396	Warehouse owners, keepers, &c. ...	3	...	...	3	...	1	...	...	1	...	2	...	...	2	...
			397	Warehouse service	20	4	6	10	...	17	3	6	8	...	3	1	...	2	...
			398	Porters (general)	2,171	287	418	1,466	...	1,034	134	208	692	...	1,137	153	210	774	...
			399	Weighmen and measurers	183	22	48	113	...	83	10	20	53	...	100	12	28	60	...
			400	Watchmen (not village)	125	16	26	83	...	80	6	11	63	...	45	10	15	20	...
				Total Sub-order 62......	2,502	329	498	1,675	...	1,215	153	245	817	...	1,287	176	253	858	...
				Total Order XIX......	18,132	2,245	3,458	12,424	5	10,020	1,069	1,772	7,179	...	8,112	1,176	1,686	5,245	5

TABLE XVII A.

Occupations by Age.—*Continued.*

Class.	Order.	Sub-order and Group.	Serial No.	Occupations.	COUNTRY. Total. Total.	Total. 0—4	Total. 5—14	Total. 15 and over.	Total. Unspecified.	Males. Total.	Males. 0—4	Males. 5—14	Males. 15 and over.	Males. Unspecified.	Females. Total.	Females. 0—4	Females. 5—14	Females. 15 and over.	Females. Unspecified.
					36	37	38	39	40	41	42	43	44	45	46	47	48	49	50
Class E.—Commerce, transport, storage—*concld.*	XIX.—Transport and storage.	60. Water. (a) Owners, &c. of vessels.	381	Ship owners, Companies Agents	...	...	...	...	...	...	...	...	...	...	...	...	...	...	...
			382	Shipping clerks, supercargoes, and stevedores	...	...	...	...	...	...	...	...	...	...	...	...	...	...	...
			383	Boat and barge owners, &c.	...	...	...	...	...	...	...	...	...	...	...	...	...	...	...
		(b) Working staff of vessels.	384	Ships' Officers, Engineers, mariners, and firemen	11	...	...	11	...	11	...	...	11	...	...	...	...	...	...
			385	Boat and barge men	668	98	143	427	...	392	51	82	259	...	276	47	61	168	...
			386	Pilots	...	...	...	...	...	...	...	...	...	...	...	...	...	...	...
			387	Lock-keepers, &c., and canal service	5,073	837	1,148	3,063	25	2,973	434	645	1,893	1	2,100	403	503	1,170	24
			388	Dock and harbour service	...	...	...	...	...	...	...	...	...	...	...	...	...	...	...
			389	Divers (not for pearls)...	1	...	...	1	...	1	...	...	1	...	...	...	...	...	...
				Total Sub-order 60......	5,753	935	1,291	3,502	25	3,377	485	727	2,164	1	2,376	450	564	1,338	24
		61. Messages. (a) Post, &c.	390	Postal Directors, Postmasters and clerks	234	34	48	152	...	95	9	17	69	...	139	25	31	83	...
			391	Postal messengers, runners, &c.	1,384	193	257	926	8	878	92	154	624	8	506	101	103	302	...
			392	Messengers (unspecified)	125	8	29	88	...	77	4	18	55	...	48	4	11	33	...
		(b) Telegraph, & Telephone.	393	Telegraph officers (Government, Railway and others), and clerical, and accounts establishment	64	8	10	46	...	38	4	5	29	...	26	4	5	17	...
			394	Signallers and messengers	11	1	3	7	...	3	...	...	3	...	8	1	3	4	...
			395	Telephone Company's service	...	...	...	...	...	...	...	...	...	...	...	...	...	...	...
				Total Sub-order 61......	1,818	244	347	1,219	8	1,091	109	194	780	8	727	135	153	439	...
		62. Storage and weighing.	396	Warehouse owners, keepers, &c.	13	3	1	9	...	13	3	1	9	...	...	...	...	...	...
			397	Warehouse service	2	...	...	2	...	2	...	...	2	...	...	...	...	...	...
			398	Porters (general)	1,083	194	252	637	...	643	117	140	386	...	440	77	112	251	...
			399	Weighmen and measurers	714	73	132	509	...	399	38	80	281	...	315	35	52	228	...
			400	Watchmen (not village)	45	2	7	36	...	32	2	4	26	...	13	...	3	10	...
				Total Sub-order 62......	1,857	272	392	1,193	...	1,089	160	225	704	...	768	112	167	489	...
				Total Order XIX......	64,658	9,246	14,050	41,293	69	39,347	4,840	8,170	26,310	27	25,311	4,406	5,880	14,983	42

TABLE XVII A.

Occupations by Age.—*Continued.*

Class.	Order.	Sub-order and Group.	Serial No.	Occupations.	PROVINCIAL TOTAL. Total. Total.	Total. 0—4	Total. 5—14	Total. 15 and over.	Total. Unspecified.	Males. Total.	Males. 0—4	Males. 5—14	Males. 15 and over.	Males. Unspecified.	Females. Total.	Females. 0—4	Females. 5—14	Females. 15 and over.	Females. Unspecified.
1	2	3	4	5	6	7	8	9	10	11	12	13	14	15	16	17	18	19	20
Class F.—Professions.	XX. Learned and artistic professions.	63. Religion. (a) Priests, Ministers, &c.	401	Priests, ministers, preachers, missionaries, &c.	8,455	927	1,765	5,735	28	3,826	364	834	2,626	2	4,629	563	931	3,109	26
			402	Catechists, readers, Zanána mission service, &c.	1,743	178	325	1,237	3	988	95	195	697	1	755	83	130	540	2
			403	Exorcists, hail-averters, amulettiers, &c.	1,457	214	340	902	1	790	116	188	486	...	667	98	152	416	1
		(b) Subsidiary religious services.	404	Religious mendicants, inmates of monasteries, convents, &c.	34,203	4,377	7,128	22,656	42	18,680	2,246	4,004	12,419	11	15,523	2,131	3,124	10,237	31
			405	Church, Temple, Masjid, Pagoda, ghat, burial or burning-ground service, pilgrim conductors, and Undertakers...	18,720	2,511	4,040	12,130	39	9,707	1,223	2,174	6,308	2	9,013	1,288	1,866	5,822	37
				Total Sub-order 63......	64,578	8,207	13,598	42,660	113	33,991	4,044	7,395	22,536	16	30,587	4,163	6,203	20,124	97
		64. Education.	406	Administrative and inspecting officials ...	52	3	18	31	...	20	1	7	12	...	32	2	11	19	...
			407	Principals, professors, and teachers in colleges, &c., schools, &c.	11,684	1,410	2,342	7,806	126	6,598	722	1,272	4,599	5	5,086	688	1,070	3,207	121
			408	Clerks, &c., on establishments of Educational Institution	132	15	27	90	...	76	7	13	56	...	56	8	14	34	...
				Total Sub-order 64......	11,868	1,428	2,387	7,927	126	6,694	730	1,292	4,667	5	5,174	698	1,095	3,260	121
		65. Literature.	409	Authors, Editors, Journalists, ballad-makers	11	1	1	6	3	6	...	...	6	...	5	1	1	...	3
			410	Reporters, Short-hand writers, Book copyists...	21	2	3	16	...	11	1	...	10	...	10	1	3	6	...
			411	Private Secretaries and Clerks	2,611	295	549	1,763	4	1,751	181	361	1,209	...	860	114	188	554	4
			412	Public Scribes and Copyists	196	26	37	133	...	100	7	14	79	...	96	19	23	54	...
			413	Service in Libraries and Literary Institutions	1	...	...	1	...	1	...	...	1	...	...	...	...	...	...
				Total Sub-order 65......	2,840	324	590	1,919	7	1,869	189	375	1,305	...	971	135	215	614	7
		66. Law.	414	Barristers, Advocates and Pleaders ...	3,653	407	650	2,584	12	1,995	213	339	1,443	...	1,658	194	311	1,141	12
			415	Solicitors and Attorneys...	46	4	9	33	...	22	3	1	18	...	24	1	8	15	...
			416	Law-agents, Mukhtiárs, &c.	9	2	1	6	...	4	...	1	3	...	5	2	...	3	...
			417	Articled clerks and other lawyers' clerks.	12	...	5	7	...	5	...	1	4	...	7	...	4	3	...
			418	Stamp-Vendors	168	32	34	102	...	41	8	8	25	...	127	24	26	77	...
			419	Petition-writers	426	39	77	310	...	233	28	36	169	...	193	11	41	141	...
				Total Sub-order 66......	4,314	484	776	3,042	12	2,300	252	386	1,662	...	2,014	232	390	1,380	12

TABLE XVII A.

Occupations by Age.—*Continued.*

Class.	Order.	Sub-order and Group.	Serial No.	Occupations.	TOWN. Total. Total.					Males.					Females.				
					Total.	0—4	5—14	15 and over.	Unspecified.	Total.	0—4	5—14	15 and over.	Unspecified.	Total.	0—4	5—14	15 and over.	Unspecified.
					21	22	23	24	25	26	27	28	29	30	31	32	33	34	35
Class F.—Professions.	XX. Learned and artistic professions.	63. Religion. (a) Priests, Ministers, &c.	401	Priests, ministers, preachers, missionaries, &c.	1,365	149	292	924	...	746	64	166	516	...	619	85	126	408	...
			402	Catechists, readers, Zanána mission service, &c.	581	54	124	403	...	328	39	75	214	...	253	15	49	189	...
			403	Exorcists, hail-averters, amulettiers, &c.	416	28	82	805	1	193	18	32	143	...	223	10	50	162	1
		(b) Subsidiary religious services.	404	Religious mendicants, inmates of monasteries, convents, &c.	4,204	420	799	2,978	7	2,352	210	436	1,704	2	1,852	210	368	1,274	5
			405	Church, Temple, Masjid, Pagoda, ghat, burial or burning-ground service, pilgrim conductors, and Undertakers	3,697	412	729	2,550	6	2,126	232	414	1,479	1	1,571	180	315	1,071	5
				Total Sub-order 63......	10,263	1,063	2,026	7,160	14	5,745	563	1,123	4,056	8	4,518	500	903	3,104	11
		64. Education.	406	Administrative and inspecting officials...	47	8	16	28	...	20	1	7	12	...	27	2	9	16	...
			407	Principals, professors, and teachers in colleges, &c., schools, &c.	3,576	385	737	2,341	113	1,755	189	367	1,197	2	1,821	196	370	1,144	111
			408	Clerks, &c., on establishments of Educational Institution	34	...	3	31	...	20	...	1	19	...	14	...	2	12	...
				Total Sub-order 64......	3,657	388	756	2,400	113	1,795	190	375	1,228	2	1,862	198	381	1,172	111
		65. Literature.	409	Authors, Editors, Journalists, ballad-makers...	9	1	1	4	3	4	...	...	4	...	5	1	1	...	3
			410	Reporters, Short-hand writers, Book copyists...	17	2	3	12	...	7	1	...	6	...	10	1	3	6	...
			411	Private Secretaries and Clerks ...	1,523	169	319	1,035	...	835	82	170	583	...	688	87	149	452	...
			412	Public Scribes and Copyists	125	14	24	87	...	67	3	10	54	...	58	11	14	33	...
			413	Service in Libraries and Literary Institutions	1	...	...	1	...	1	...	...	1	...	...	...	...	...	...
				Total Sub-order 65......	1,675	186	347	1,139	3	914	86	180	648	...	761	100	167	491	3
		66. Law.	414	Barristers, Advocates and Pleaders	2,866	309	493	2,058	6	1,517	153	236	1,128	...	1,349	156	257	930	6
			415	Solicitors and Attorneys...	46	4	9	33	...	22	3	1	18	...	24	1	8	15	...
			416	Law-agents, mukhtiárs, &c.	8	2	1	5	...	3	...	1	2	...	5	2	...	3	...
			417	Articled clerks and other lawyers' clerks.	12	...	5	7	...	5	...	1	4	...	7	...	4	3	...
			418	Stamp-Vendors ...	52	10	12	30	...	31	8	7	16	...	21	2	5	14	...
			419	Petition-writers ...	278	19	44	215	...	140	10	19	111	...	138	9	25	104	...
				Total Sub-order 66......	3,262	344	564	2,348	6	1,718	174	265	1,279	...	1,544	170	299	1,069	6

TABLE XVII A.

Occupations by Age.—*Continued.*

Class.	Order.	Sub-order and Group.	Serial No.	Occupations.	COUNTRY. Total. Total.	Total. 0—4	Total. 5—14	Total. 15 and over.	Total. Unspecified.	Males. Total.	Males. 0—4	Males. 5—14	Males. 15 and over.	Males. Unspecified.	Females. Total.	Females. 0—4	Females. 5—14	Females. 15 and over.	Females. Unspecified.
					36	37	38	39	40	41	42	43	44	45	46	47	48	49	50
Class F.—Professions.	XX. Learned and artistic professions.	63. Religion. (a) Priests, Ministers, &c.	401	Priests, ministers, preachers, missionaries, &c.	7,090	778	1,473	4,811	28	3,080	300	668	2,110	2	4,010	478	805	2,701	26
			402	Catechists, readers, Zanána mission service, &c.	1,162	124	201	834	3	660	56	120	483	1	502	68	81	351	2
		(b) Subsidiary religious services.	403	Exorcists, hail-averters, amulettiers, &c...	1,041	186	258	597	...	597	98	156	843	...	444	88	102	254	...
			404	Religious mendicants, inmates of monasteries, convents, &c.	29,999	3,957	6,329	19,678	35	16,328	2,086	3,568	10,715	9	13,671	1,921	2,761	8,963	26
			405	Church, Temple, Masjid, Pagoda, ghat, burial or burning-ground service, pilgrim conductors, and Undertakers...	15,023	2,099	3,311	9,580	33	7,581	991	1,760	4,829	1	7,442	1,108	1,551	4,751	32
				Total Sub-order 63......	54,315	7,144	11,572	35,500	99	28,246	3,481	6,272	18,480	13	26,069	3,663	5,300	17,020	86
		64. Education.	406	Administrative and inspecting officials...	5	...	2	3	...	...	...	...	...	...	5	...	2	3	...
			407	Principals, professors and teachers in colleges, &c., schools, &c.	8,108	1,025	1,605	5,465	13	4,843	533	905	3,402	3	3,265	492	700	2,063	10
			408	Clerks, &c., on establishments of Educational Institution	98	15	24	59	...	56	7	12	37	...	42	8	12	22	...
				Total Sub-order 64......	8,211	1,040	1,631	5,527	13	4,899	540	917	3,439	3	3,312	500	714	2,088	10
		65. Literature.	409	Authors, Editors, Journalists, ballad-makers	2	...	...	2	...	2	...	...	2	...	...	...	...	...	...
			410	Reporters, Short-hand writers, Book copyists	4	...	...	4	...	4	...	...	4	...	...	...	...	...	...
			411	Private Secretaries and Clerks... ...	1,088	126	230	728	4	916	99	191	626	...	172	27	39	102	4
			412	Public Scribes and Copyists	71	12	13	46	...	33	4	4	25	...	38	8	9	21	...
			413	Service in Libraries and Literary Institutions	...	...	...	...	...	...	...	...	...	...	...	...	...	...	...
				Total Sub-order 65......	1,165	138	243	780	4	955	103	195	657	...	210	35	48	123	4
		66. Law.	414	Barristers, Advocates and Pleaders ...	787	98	157	526	6	478	60	103	315	...	309	38	54	211	6
			415	Solicitors and Attorneys	...	...	...	...	...	...	...	...	...	...	...	...	...	...	...
			416	Law-agents, mukhtiárs, &c.	1	...	...	1	...	1	...	...	1	...	...	...	...	...	...
			417	Articled clerks and other lawyers' clerks.	...	...	...	...	...	...	...	...	...	...	...	...	...	...	...
			418	Stamp-Vendors...	116	22	22	72	...	10	...	1	9	...	106	22	21	63	...
			419	Petition-writers	148	20	33	95	...	93	18	17	58	...	55	2	16	37	...
				Total Sub-order 66......	1,052	140	212	694	6	582	78	121	383	...	470	62	91	311	6

TABLE XVII A.

Occupations by Age.—*Continued.*

Class.	Order.	Sub-order and Group.	Serial No.	Occupations.	PROVINCIAL TOTAL. Total. Total.	Total. 0—4	Total. 5—14	Total. 15 and over.	Total. Unspecified.	Males. Total.	Males. 0—4	Males. 5—14	Males. 15 and over.	Males. Unspecified.	Females. Total.	Females. 0—4	Females. 5—14	Females. 15 and over.	Females. Unspecified.
1	2	3	4	5	6	7	8	9	10	11	12	13	14	15	16	17	18	19	20
Class F.—Professions,—*contd.*	XX.—Learned and artistic professions,—*contd.*	67. Medicine. (a) Practitioners.	420	Administrative and Inspecting Staff (when not returned under general head) ...	37	8	12	17	...	14	3	3	8	...	23	5	9	9	...
			421	Practitioners by diploma ...	489	65	98	326	...	243	37	42	164	...	246	28	56	162	...
			422	Practitioners without diploma (Baid, Hakim, Kobiraj, &c.)...	12,442	1,627	2,773	8,030	12	6,697	857	1,477	4,361	2	5,745	770	1,296	3,669	10
			423	Dentists ...	...	...	...	...	...	...	...	...	...	...	...	...	...	...	...
			424	Oculists ...	2	...	...	2	...	1	...	...	1	...	1	...	...	1	...
			425	Vaccinators ...	197	24	43	130	...	139	18	35	86	...	58	6	8	44	...
		(b) Subsidiary medical service.	426	Midwifery ...	1,155	83	326	745	1	336	35	196	104	1	819	48	130	641	...
			427	Hospital and Asylum, Matrons, Assistants and Apothecaries...	350	55	91	204	...	174	28	46	100	...	176	27	45	104	...
			428	Compounders, Nurses and hospital, Asylum and dispensary service ...	223	32	69	122	...	127	20	41	66	...	96	12	28	56	...
				Total Sub-order 67......	14,895	1,894	3,412	9,576	13	7,731	998	1,840	4,890	3	7,164	896	1,572	4,686	10
		68. Engineering and surveying. (a)—(b) Subsidiary staff. Engineers, Architects and Surveyors.	429	Administrative and Inspecting Staff ...	5	...	...	5	...	1	...	...	1	...	4	...	...	4	...
			430	Civil Engineers and Architects...	102	16	12	73	...	57	8	5	44	...	45	8	8	29	...
			431	Topographical, Archæological and Revenue Surveyors ...	66	9	23	35	...	50	8	16	26	...	16	1	6	9	...
			432	Draughtsmen and Operators in Survey Offices, Overseers, &c....	707	70	152	485	...	372	33	73	266	...	335	37	79	219	...
			433	Clerks, &c., in offices of the above ...	812	89	168	555	...	451	40	93	318	...	361	49	75	237	...
				Total Sub-order 68......	1,692	184	355	1,153	...	931	89	187	655	...	761	95	168	498	...
		69. Other sciences. (a) Astronomy, &c.	434	Astronomers and Meteorologists, and establishments ...	1	...	...	1	...	1	...	...	1	...	...	...	...	...	...
			435	Botanists, Naturalists and officers of Scientific Institutions ...	...	...	...	...	...	...	...	...	...	...	...	...	...	...	...
			436	Metallurgists ...	1	...	...	1	...	1	...	...	1	...	...	...	...	...	...
		(b) Minor sciences.	437	Astrologers, Genealogists and Horoscope-casters ...	7,853	906	1,562	5,373	12	3,825	427	761	2,637	...	4,028	479	801	2,736	12
			438	Almanac-makers and sellers ...	4	...	...	4	...	2	...	...	2	...	2	...	...	2	...
			439	Diviners (selectors of well and house sites, &c.) ...	2	...	...	2	...	2	...	...	2	...	...	...	...	...	...
				Total Sub-order 69......	7,861	906	1,562	5,381	12	3,831	427	761	2,643	...	4,030	479	801	2,738	12

TABLE XVII A.

Occupations by Age.—*Continued.*

Class.	Order.	Sub-order and Group.	Serial No.	Occupations.	TOWN. Total. Total.	Total. 0—4	Total. 5—14	Total. 15 and over.	Total. Unspecified.	Males. Total.	Males. 0—4	Males. 5—14	Males. 15 and over.	Males. Unspecified.	Females. Total.	Females. 0—4	Females. 5—14	Females. 15 and over.	Females. Unspecified.
					21	22	23	24	25	26	27	28	29	30	31	32	33	34	35
Class F.—Professions.—*contd.*	XX. Learned and artistic professions.—*contd.*	67. Medicine. (a) Practitioners.	420	Administrative and Inspecting Staff (when not returned under general head) ...	32	7	9	16	...	14	3	3	8	...	18	4	6	8	...
			421	Practitioners by diploma...	388	56	79	253	...	186	30	35	121	...	202	26	44	132	...
			222	Practitioners without diploma (Baid, Hakim, Kobiraj, &c.)...	3,483	347	743	2,393	...	1,731	169	380	1,182	...	1,752	178	363	1,211	...
			423	Dentists ...	...	...	...	...	...	...	...	...	...	...	...	...	...	...	...
			424	Oculists ...	...	...	...	...	...	...	...	...	...	...	...	...	...	...	...
			425	Vaccinators	121	14	27	80	...	72	9	20	43	...	49	5	7	37	...
			426	Midwifery	577	44	97	436	...	78	18	26	34	...	499	26	71	402	...
		(b) Subsidiary medical service.	427	Hospital and Asylum, Matrons, Assistants and Apothecaries...	276	48	77	156	...	139	25	40	74	...	137	23	82	82	...
			428	Compounders, Nurses and hospital, Asylum and dispensary service	148	18	39	91	...	72	6	19	47	...	76	12	20	44	...
				Total Sub-order 67......	5,025	534	1,066	3,425	...	2,292	260	523	1,509	...	2,733	274	543	1,916	...
		68. Engineering and surveying. (a)—	429	Administrative and Inspecting Staff ...	5	...	...	5	...	1	...	...	1	...	4	...	...	4	...
			430	Civil Engineers and Architects ...	85	13	12	60	...	50	6	5	89	...	35	7	7	21	...
			431	Topographical, Archæological and Revenue Surveyors	23	4	8	11	...	7	3	2	2	...	16	1	6	9	...
		(b) Subsidiary staff.	432	Draughtsmen and Operators in Survey Offices, overseers, &c. ...	388	38	84	266	...	191	18	38	135	...	197	20	46	131	...
			433	Clerks, &c., in offices of the above	636	66	144	426	...	358	31	84	243	...	278	35	60	183	...
				Total Sub-order 68......	1,137	121	248	768	...	607	58	129	420	...	530	63	119	348	...
		69. Other sciences. (a) Astronomy, &c.	434	Astronomers and Meteorologists and establishments ...	1	...	...	1	...	1	...	...	1	...	...	...	...	...	...
			435	Botanists, Naturalists and officers of Scientific Institutions ...	...	...	...	...	...	...	...	...	...	...	...	...	...	...	...
		(b) Minor sciences.	436	Metallurgists ...	1	...	...	1	...	1	...	...	1	...	...	...	...	...	...
			437	Astrologers, Genealogists and Horoscope-casters ...	654	60	94	500	...	254	20	33	201	...	400	40	61	299	...
			438	Almanac-makers and sellers ...	4	...	...	4	...	2	...	...	2	...	2	...	...	2	...
			439	Diviners (selectors of well and house sites, &c.) ...	...	...	...	...	...	...	...	...	...	...	...	...	...	...	...
				Total Sub-order 69......	660	60	94	506	...	258	20	33	205	...	402	40	61	301	...

TABLE XVII A.

Occupations by Age.—*Continued.*

Class.	Order.	Sub-order and Group.	Serial No.	Occupations.	COUNTRY. Total. Total.	Total. 0—4	Total. 5—14	Total. 15 and over.	Total. Unspecified.	Males. Total.	Males. 0—4	Males. 5—14	Males. 15 and over.	Males. Unspecified.	Females. Total.	Females. 0—4	Females. 5—14	Females. 15 and over.	Females. Unspecified.
					36	37	38	39	40	41	42	43	44	45	46	47	48	49	50
Class F.—Professions.—*contd.*	XX. Learned and artistic professions.—*contd.*	67. Medicine. (a) Practitioners.	420	Administrative and Inspecting Staff (when not returned under general head) ...	5	1	3	1	...	...	...	...	...	...	5	1	3	1	...
			421	Practitioners by diploma	101	9	19	73	...	57	7	7	43	...	44	2	12	80	...
			422	Practitioners without diploma (Baid, Hakim, Kobiraj, &c.)...	8,959	1,280	2,030	5,637	12	4,966	688	1,097	3,179	2	3,993	592	933	2,458	10
			423	Dentists ...	...	...	...	...	...	...	...	...	...	...	...	...	...	...	...
			424	Oculists ...	2	...	...	2	...	1	...	...	1	...	1	...	...	1	...
			425	Vaccinators	76	10	16	50	...	67	9	15	43	...	9	1	1	7	...
		(b) Subsidiary medical service.	426	Midwifery	578	29	229	309	1	258	17	170	70	1	320	22	59	239	...
			427	Hospital and Asylum, Matrons, Assistants and Apothecaries	74	7	19	48	...	35	3	6	26	...	39	4	13	22	...
			428	Compounders, Nurses and hospital, Asylum and dispensary service	75	14	30	31	...	55	14	22	19	...	20	...	8	12	...
				Total Sub-order 67......	9,870	1,360	2,340	6,151	13	5,439	738	1,317	3,381	3	4,431	622	1,029	2,770	10
		68. Engineering and surveying. (a)—	429	Administrative and Inspecting Staff ...	...	...	...	...	...	...	...	...	...	...	...	...	...	...	...
		Engineers, Architects and Surveyors.	430	Civil Engineers and Architects	17	3	1	13	...	7	2	...	5	...	10	1	1	8	...
			431	Topographical, Archæological and Revenue Surveyors	43	5	14	24	...	43	5	14	24	...	...	...	...	...	...
		(b) Subsidiary staff.	432	Draughtsmen and Operators in Survey Offices, overseers, &c....	319	32	68	219	...	181	15	35	131	...	138	17	33	88	...
			433	Clerks, &c., in offices of the above	176	23	24	129	...	93	9	9	75	...	83	14	15	54	...
				Total Sub-order 68......	555	63	107	385	...	324	31	58	235	...	231	32	49	150	...
		69. Other sciences. (a) Astronomy, &c.	434	Astronomers and Meteorologists and establishments...	...	...	...	...	...	...	...	...	...	...	...	...	...	...	...
			435	Botanists, Naturalists and officers of Scientific Institution ...	...	...	...	...	...	...	...	...	...	...	...	...	...	...	...
			436	Metallurgists	...	...	...	...	...	...	...	...	...	...	...	...	...	...	...
		(b) Minor sciences.	437	Astrologers, Genealogists and Horoscope-casters ...	7,199	846	1,468	4,873	12	3,571	407	728	2,436	...	3,628	439	740	2,437	12
			438	Almanac-makers and sellers ...	...	...	...	...	...	...	...	...	...	...	...	...	...	...	...
			439	Diviners (selectors of well and house sites, &c.	2	...	...	2	...	2	...	...	2	...	...	...	...	...	...
				Total Sub-order 69......	7,201	846	1,468	4,875	12	3,573	407	728	2,438	...	3,628	439	740	2,437	12

TABLE XVII A.

Occupations by Age.—*Continued.*

Class.	Order.	Sub-order and Group.	Serial No.	Occupations.	PROVINCIAL TOTAL. Total. Total.	Total. 0—4	Total. 5—14	Total. 15 and over.	Total. Unspecified.	Males. Total.	Males. 0—4	Males. 5—14	Males. 15 and over.	Males. Unspecified.	Females. Total.	Females. 0—4	Females. 5—14	Females. 15 and over.	Females. Unspecified.
1	2	3	4	5	6	7	8	9	10	11	12	13	14	15	16	17	18	19	20
Class F.—Professions.—*contd.*	XX. Learned and artistic professions.—*contd.*	70. Pictorial art and sculpture.	440	Painters, Superintendents of Schools of Art, &c.	1,289	144	270	874	1	753	70	155	527	1	536	74	115	847	...
			441	Sculptors	25	3	2	20	...	11	...	1	10	...	14	3	1	10	...
			442	Photographers	44	5	9	30	...	25	2	7	16	...	19	8	2	14	...
				Total Sub-order 70......	1,358	152	281	924	1	789	72	163	553	1	569	80	118	371	...
		71. Music, acting, dancing.	443	Music Composers and Teachers... ...	447	59	121	267	...	427	57	114	256	...	20	2	7	11	...
			444	Bandmasters and players (not military)	14,917	2,063	3,197	9,652	5	8,140	1,083	1,728	5,326	8	6,777	980	1,469	4,326	2
			445	Piano-Tuners	158	14	37	107	...	1	...	...	1	...	157	14	37	106	...
			446	Actors, Singers and Dancers, and their accompanists	11,977	1,429	2,608	7,929	11	4,720	612	1,136	2,971	1	7,257	817	1,472	4,958	10
				Total Sub-order 71......	27,499	3,565	5,963	17,955	16	13,288	1,752	2,978	8,554	4	14,211	1,813	2,985	9,401	12
				Total Order XX......	136,905	17,144	28,924	90,537	300	71,424	8,553	15,377	47,465	29	65,481	8,591	13,547	43,072	271
	XXI.—Sport and amusement.	72. Sport.	447	Race-course service, Book-makers, Jockeys, &c.	2	...	...	2	...	...	...	...	...	...	2	...	...	2	...
			448	Shikaries, Falconers, Birdcatchers ...	2,162	344	593	1,225	...	1,122	180	316	626	...	1,040	164	277	599	...
			449	Huntsmen, whippers in	75	11	19	45	...	38	5	11	22	...	37	6	8	23	...
				Total Sub-order 72......	2,239	355	612	1,272	...	1,160	185	327	648	...	1,079	170	285	624	...
		73. Exhibition and games. (a) Catching, training & exhibiting animals.	450	Exhibitors of trained animals (Bulls, bears, snakes, monkeys, &c.)... ...	290	52	70	168	...	132	23	34	75	...	158	29	36	93	...
			451	Circus owners, managers, &c.... ...	172	32	40	100	...	143	23	36	84	...	29	9	4	16	...
			452	Cock and pigeon fanciers	...	...	...	...	...	...	...	...	...	...	...	...	...	...	...
		(b) Conjuring, Fortune-telling & other exhibitions.	453	Buffoons	440	62	99	279	...	147	17	30	100	...	293	45	69	179	...
			454	Story and ballad reciters	103	14	25	64	...	66	6	17	43	...	37	8	8	21	...
			455	Exhibitors of puppets	465	75	127	263	...	260	42	71	147	...	205	33	56	116	...
			456	Conjurors and fortune-tellers	3,178	518	747	1,911	2	1,385	221	341	823	...	1,793	297	406	1,088	2
		(c) Acrobatics & athletics.	457	Tumblers, Acrobats, Wrestlers, Professional cricketers, &c.	4,332	686	1,003	2,627	16	2,424	377	570	1,477	...	1,908	309	433	1,150	16
		(d) Service of places of entertainments.		Swing and merry-go-round keepers ...	...	...	...	...	...	...	...	...	...	...	...	...	...	...	...
			458 459	Tennis and Racquet Court, Gymkhana, and boat club service	18	2	2	14	...	13	2	2	9	...	5	...	...	5	...
			460	Billiard room and theatre ownership, managership and service	402	60	71	271	...	211	26	86	149	...	191	84	85	122	...
				Total Sub-order 73......	9,400	1,501	2,184	5,697	18	4,781	737	1,137	2,907	...	4,619	764	1,047	2,790	18
				Total Order XXI......	11,639	1,856	2,796	6,969	18	5,941	922	1,464	3,555	...	5,698	934	1,332	3,414	18

TABLE XVII A.

Occupations by Age.—*Continued.*

Class.	Order.	Sub-order and Group.	Serial No.	Occupations.	TOWN. Total. Total.	Total. 0—4	Total. 5—14	Total. 15 and over.	Total. Unspecified.	Males. Total.	Males. 0—4	Males. 5—14	Males. 15 and over.	Males. Unspecified.	Females. Total.	Females. 0—4	Females. 5—14	Females. 15 and over.	Females. Unspecified.
					21	22	23	24	25	26	27	28	29	30	31	32	33	34	35
Class F.—Professions.—*contd.*	XX.—Learned and artistic professions.—*contd.*	70. Pictorial art and sculpture.	440	Painters, Superintendents of Schools of Art, &c.	590	60	118	412	...	275	21	53	201	...	315	39	65	211	...
			441	Sculptors...	25	3	2	20	...	11	...	1	10	...	14	3	1	10	...
			442	Photographers ...	44	5	9	30	...	25	2	7	16	...	19	3	2	14	...
				Total Sub-order 70......	659	68	129	462	...	311	23	61	227	...	348	45	68	235	...
		71. Music, acting, dancing.	443	Music Composers and Teachers...	18	2	6	10	...	6	...	3	3	...	12	2	3	7	...
			444	Bandmasters and players (not military).	2,825	861	622	1,841	1	1,619	213	344	1,061	1	1,206	148	278	780	...
			445	Piano-Tuners ...	158	14	37	107	...	1	...	...	1	...	157	14	37	106	...
			446	Actors, Singers and Dancers, and their accompanists ...	4,011	368	705	2,936	2	801	104	166	531	...	3,210	264	539	2,405	2
				Total Sub-order 71......	7,012	745	1,370	4,894	3	2,427	317	513	1,596	1	4,585	428	857	3,298	2
				Total Order XX......	33,350	3,509	6,600	23,102	139	16,067	1,691	3,202	11,168	6	17,283	1,818	3,398	11,934	133
	XXI.—Sport and amusement.	72. Sport.	447	Race-course service, Book makers, Jockeys, &c.	...	...	...	...	...	...	...	...	...	...	...	...	...	...	...
			448	Shikaries, Falconers, Birdcatchers	201	18	39	144	...	106	10	20	76	...	95	8	19	68	...
			449	Huntsmen, whippers in...	...	...	...	...	...	...	...	...	...	...	...	...	...	...	...
				Total Sub-order 72......	201	18	39	144	...	106	10	20	76	...	95	8	19	68	...
		73. Exhibition and dames. (a) Catching, training & exhibiting animals.	450	Exhibitors of trained animals (Bulls, bears, snakes, monkeys, &c.) ...	43	4	6	33	...	25	...	5	20	...	18	4	1	13	...
			451	Circus owners, managers, &c. ...	24	1	4	19	...	21	1	4	16	...	3	...	...	3	...
			452	Cock and pigeon fanciers	...	...	...	...	...	...	...	...	...	...	...	...	...	...	...
		(b) Conjuring, Fortune-telling & other exhibitions.	453	Buffoons...	90	9	13	68	...	60	5	5	50	...	30	4	8	18	...
			454	Story and ballad reciters	10	1	3	6	...	1	...	...	1	...	9	1	3	5	...
			455	Exhibitors of puppets ...	45	5	17	23	...	28	4	9	15	...	17	1	8	8	...
			456	Conjurors and fortune-tellers ...	60	6	17	37	...	34	1	12	21	...	26	5	5	16	...
		(c) Acrobatics & athletics.	457	Tumblers, Acrobats, Wrestlers, Professional cricketers, &c. ...	578	79	133	366	...	211	37	44	130	...	367	42	89	236	...
		(d) Service of places of entertainment.	458	Swing and merry-go-round keepers ...	...	...	...	...	...	...	...	...	...	...	...	...	...	...	...
			459	Tennis and Racquet Court, Gymkhana, and boat club service ...	18	2	2	14	...	13	2	2	9	...	5	...	...	5	...
			460	Billiard room and theatre ownership, managership and service ...	12	1	...	11	...	11	1	...	10	...	1	...	...	1	...
				Total Sub-order 73......	880	108	195	577	...	404	51	81	272	...	476	57	114	305	...
				Total Order XXI......	1,081	126	234	721	...	510	61	101	348	...	571	65	133	373	...

TABLE XVII A.

Occupations by Age.—*Continued.*

Class.	Order.	Sub-order and Group.	Serial No.	Occupations.	COUNTRY. Total. Total.	Total. 0—4	Total. 5—14	Total. 15 and over.	Total. Unspecified.	Males. Total.	Males. 0—4	Males. 5—14	Males. 15 and over.	Males. Unspecified.	Females. Total.	Females. 0—4	Females. 5—14	Females. 15 and over.	Females. Unspecified.
					36	37	38	39	40	41	42	43	44	45	46	47	48	49	50
Class F.—Professions.—*contd.*	XX.—Learned and artistic professions.—*contd.*	70. Pictorial art and sculpture.	440	Painters, Superintendents of Schools of Art, &c.	699	84	152	462	1	478	49	102	326	1	221	35	50	136	...
			441	Sculptors...	...	...	...	...	...	...	...	...	...	...	...	...	...	...	...
			442	Photographers	...	...	...	...	...	...	...	...	...	...	...	...	...	...	...
				Total Sub-order 70......	699	84	152	462	1	478	49	102	326	1	221	35	50	136	...
		71. Music, acting, dancing.	443	Music Composers and Teachers ...	429	57	115	257	...	421	57	111	253	...	8	...	4	4	...
			444	Bandmasters and players (not military)	12,092	1,702	2,575	7,811	4	6,521	870	1,384	4,265	2	5,571	832	1,191	3,546	2
			445	Piano-Tuners	...	...	...	...	...	...	...	...	...	...	...	...	...	...	...
			446	Actors, Singers and Dancers, and their accompanists	7,966	1,061	1,908	4,993	9	3,919	508	970	2,440	1	4,047	553	983	2,553	8
				Total Sub-order 71......	20,487	2,820	4,593	13,061	13	10,861	1,435	2,465	6,958	3	9,626	1,385	2,128	6,103	10
				Total Order XX......	108,555	13,635	22,324	67,435	161	55,357	6,862	12,175	36,297	23	48,198	6,773	10,149	31,138	138
	XXI.—Sport and amusement.	72. Sport.	447	Race-course service, Book-makers, Jockeys, &c.	2	...	...	2	...	...	...	...	...	...	2	...	...	2	...
			448	Shikaries, Falconers, Birdcatchers ...	1,961	826	554	1,081	...	1,016	170	296	550	...	945	156	258	531	...
			449	Huntsmen, whippers in...	75	11	19	45	...	38	5	11	22	...	37	6	8	23	...
				Total Sub-order 72......	2,088	837	573	1,128	...	1,054	175	307	572	...	984	162	266	556	...
		73. Exhibition and games. (a) Catching, training & exhibiting animals.	450	Exhibitors of trained animals (Bulls, bears, snakes, monkeys, &c.) ...	247	48	64	185	...	107	23	29	55	...	140	25	35	80	...
			451	Circus owners, managers, &c. ...	148	31	36	81	...	122	22	32	68	...	26	9	4	13	...
			452	Cock and pigeon fanciers	...	...	...	...	...	...	...	...	...	...	...	...	...	...	...
		(b) Conjuring, Fortune-telling & other exhibitions.	453	Buffoons...	350	53	86	211	...	87	12	25	50	...	263	41	61	161	...
			454	Story and ballad reciters	93	13	22	58	...	65	6	17	42	...	28	7	5	16	...
			455	Exhibitors of puppets	420	70	110	240	...	232	38	62	132	...	188	32	48	108	...
			456	Conjurors and fortune-tellers	3,118	512	730	1,874	2	1,351	220	329	802	...	1,767	292	401	1,072	2
		(c) Acrobatics & athletics.	457	Tumblers, Acrobats, Wrestlers, Professional cricketers, &c.	3,754	607	870	2,261	16	2,213	340	526	1,347	...	1,541	267	344	914	16
		(d) Service of places of entertainment.	458	Swing and merry-go-round keepers ...	...	...	...	...	...	...	...	...	...	...	...	...	...	...	...
			459	Tennis and Racquet Court, Gymkhana and boat club service	...	...	...	...	...	...	...	...	...	...	...	...	...	...	...
			460	Billiard room and theatre ownership, managership and service	390	59	71	260	...	200	25	36	139	...	190	34	35	121	...
				Total Sub-order 73......	8,520	1,393	1,989	5,120	18	4,377	686	1,056	2,635	...	4,143	707	933	2,485	18
				Total Order XXI......	10,558	1,730	2,562	6,248	18	5,431	861	1,363	3,207	...	5,127	869	1,199	3,041	18

TABLE XVII A.

Occupations by Age.—*Continued.*

Class.	Order.	Sub-order and Group.	Serial No.	Occupations.	PROVINCIAL TOTAL. Total. Total.	Total. 0—4	Total. 5—14	Total. 15 and over.	Total. Unspecified.	Males. Total.	Males. 0—4	Males. 5—14	Males. 15 and over.	Males. Unspecified.	Females. Total.	Females. 0—4	Females. 5—14	Females. 15 and over.	Females. Unspecified.
1	2	3	4	5	6	7	8	9	10	11	12	13	14	15	16	17	18	19	20
Class G.—Indefinite and Independent.	XXII. Complex occupations.			(Village, &c., combined function to be specified provincially)	......	...	...	...	...	...	...	...	...	...	...	...	...	...	...
				Total Order XXII......	......	...	...	...	...	...	...	...	...	...	...	...	...	...	...
	XXIII. Indefinite.	74. Unskilled labour. (a) Special branches.	461	Well sinkers	1,465	254	371	836	4	741	113	183	442	3	724	141	188	394	1
			462	Tank diggers and excavators	3,089	573	764	1,752	...	1,001	154	229	618	...	2,088	419	535	1,134	...
			463	Road, Canal and Railway labourers ...	949	122	179	648	...	527	64	93	370	...	422	58	86	278	...
			464	Quarrymen (stone splitters, &c.) ...	23,609	4,087	5,834	13,680	8	12,181	1,940	3,084	7,154	3	11,428	2,147	2,750	6,526	5
			465	Miners (unspecified)	326	33	47	246	...	...	...	...	...	...	326	33	47	246	...
			466	Rice-pounders and huskers	9,251	1,048	1,955	6,248	...	2,825	446	885	1,494	...	6,426	602	1,070	4,754	...
		(b) General.	467	General labour	1,425,638	212,600	316,303	895,928	807	589,525	93,452	150,007	345,786	280	836,113	119,148	166,296	550,142	527
				Total Sub-order 74......	1,464,327	218,717	325,453	919,338	819	606,800	96,169	154,481	355,864	286	857,527	122,548	170,972	563,474	533
		75. Undefined, &c.	468	Undefined and disreputable means of livelihood	441,280	74,203	102,421	263,578	1,078	225,038	34,513	53,466	136,835	224	216,242	39,690	48,955	126,743	854
				Total Sub-order 75......	441,280	74,203	102,421	263,578	1,078	225,038	34,513	53,466	136,835	224	216,242	39,690	48,955	126,743	854
				Total Order XXIII......	1,905,607	292,920	427,874	1,182,916	1,897	831,838	130,682	207,947	492,699	510	1,073,769	162,238	219,927	690,217	1,387
	XXIV. Independent of work.	76. Property & alms. (a) Property & allowances.	469	House-rent, shares, and other property not being land	3,884	491	832	2,557	4	1,349	151	275	923	...	2,535	340	557	1,634	4
			470	Allowances from patrons or relatives ...	3,768	389	777	2,596	6	691	130	197	364	...	3,077	259	580	2,232	6
		(b) Charity and endowment.	471	Educational or other endowments, scholarship, &c.	197	19	79	99	...	59	4	22	33	...	138	15	57	66	...
			472	Mendicancy (not being affiliated to a religious order)	288,295	38,765	61,290	187,999	241	150,296	18,650	32,682	98,876	88	137,999	20,115	28,608	89,123	153
				Total Sub-order 76......	296,144	39,664	62,978	193,251	251	152,395	18,935	33,176	100,196	88	143,749	20,729	29,802	93,055	163
		77. Supported at the public charge. (a) Pension.	473	Pension, Civil Services	15,665	1,423	3,183	11,031	28	6,682	690	1,507	4,483	2	8,983	733	1,676	6,548	26
			474	Pension, Military Services	10,848	1,007	2,892	6,949	...	5,447	544	1,368	3,535	...	4,901	463	1,024	3,414	...
		(b) Prisoners.	475	Inmates of Asylums, &c.	......	...	...	...	...	...	...	...	...	...	...	...	...	...	...
			476	Prisoners, under trial	6	1	2	3	...	2	...	...	2	...	4	1	2	1	...
			477	Prisoners, for debt	294	44	57	193	...	294	44	57	193	...	...	...	...	...	...
			478	Prisoners, convicted or in Reformatories, &c.	143	2	...	141	...	134	1	...	133	...	9	1	...	8	...
				Total Sub-order 77......	26,456	2,477	5,684	18,317	28	12,559	1,279	2,932	8,346	2	13,897	1,198	2,702	9,971	26
				Total Order XXIV......	322,600	42,141	68,612	211,568	279	164,954	20,214	36,108	108,542	90	157,646	21,927	32,504	103,026	189
				Grand Total......	11,537,040	1,728,884	2,665,876	7,121,725	10,555	5,873,129	828,486	1,418,913	3,618,141	2,589	5,663,911	900,398	1,251,963	3,503,584	7,966

TABLE XVII A.

Occupations by Age.—*Continued.*

Class.	Order.	Sub-order and Group.	Serial No.	Occupations.	TOWN. Total. Total.	Total. 0—4	Total. 5—14	Total. 15 and over.	Total. Unspecified.	Males. Total.	Males. 0—4	Males. 5—14	Males. 15 and over.	Males. Unspecified.	Females. Total.	Females. 0—4	Females. 5—14	Females. 15 and over.	Females. Unspecified.
					21	22	23	24	25	26	27	28	29	30	31	32	33	34	35
Class G.—Indefinite and Independent.	XXII. Complex occupations.			(Village, &c., combined function to be specified provincially)	...	...	...	...	...	...	...	...	...	...	...	...	...	...	...
				Total Order XXII......	...	...	...	...	...	...	...	...	...	...	...	...	...	...	...
	XXIII. Indefinite.	74. Unskilled labour. (a) Special branches.	461	Well sinkers	...	...	...	...	...	...	...	...	...	...	...	...	...	...	...
			462	Tank diggers and excavators	87	8	17	62	...	49	3	7	39	...	38	5	10	23	...
			463	Road, Canal and Railway labourers ...	335	30	87	218	...	174	19	41	114	...	161	11	46	104	...
			464	Quarrymen (stone splitters, &c.) ...	1,775	277	427	1,070	1	883	150	231	501	1	892	127	196	569	...
			465	Miners (unspecified)	...	...	...	...	...	...	...	...	...	...	...	...	...	...	...
			466	Rice-pounders and huskers	513	43	90	380	...	149	25	45	79	...	364	18	45	301	...
		(b) General.	467	General labour	108,277	13,364	21,218	73,607	88	45,967	5,974	10,232	29,738	23	62,310	7,390	10,986	43,869	65
				Total Sub-order 74......	110,987	13,722	21,839	75,337	89	47,222	6,171	10,556	30,471	24	63,765	7,551	11,283	44,860	65
		75. Undefined, &c.	468	Undefined and disreputable means of livelihood	24,373	3,019	5,191	16,057	106	9,655	1,261	2,338	6,028	28	14,718	1,758	2,853	10,029	78
				Total Sub-order 75......	24,373	3,019	5,191	16,057	106	9,655	1,261	2,338	6,028	28	14,718	1,758	2,853	10,029	78
				Total Order XXIII......	135,360	16,741	27,030	91,394	195	56,877	7,432	12,894	36,[illegible]	52	78,483	9,309	14,136	54,895	143
	XXIV. Independent of work.	76. Property & alms. (a) Property & allowances.	469	House-rent, shares, and other property not being land...	1,555	154	318	1,083	...	634	66	123	445	...	921	88	195	638	...
			470	Allowances from patrons or relatives ...	554	34	103	414	3	130	19	85	76	...	424	15	68	338	3
		(b) Charity and endowment.	471	Educational or other endowments, scholarship, &c.	189	19	74	96	...	53	4	19	80	...	136	15	55	66	...
			472	Mendicancy (not being affiliated to a religious order)	38,517	3,931	7,320	27,247	19	19,742	1,855	3,766	14,117	4	18,775	2,076	3,554	13,130	15
				Total Sub-order 76......	40,815	4,138	7,815	28,840	22	20,559	1,944	3,943	14,668	4	20,256	2,194	3,872	14,177	18
		77. Supported at the public charge. (a) Pension.	473	Pension, Civil Services	12,572	1,054	2,433	9,058	27	5,541	547	1,208	3,784	2	7,031	507	1,225	5,274	25
			474	Pension, Military Services	9,225	881	2,098	6,246	...	4,773	485	1,192	3,096	...	4,452	396	906	3,150	...
		(b) Prisoners.	475	Inmates of Asylums, &c.	...	...	...	...	...	...	...	...	...	...	...	...	...	...	...
			476	Prisoners, under trial	6	1	2	3	...	2	...	...	2	...	4	1	2	1	...
			477	Prisoners, for debt	1	...	...	1	...	1	...	...	1	...	...	...	...	...	...
			478	Prisoners, convicted or in Reformatories, &c.	99	...	...	99	...	93	...	...	93	...	6	...	...	6	...
				Total Sub-order 77......	21,903	1,936	4,533	15,407	27	10,410	1,032	2,400	6,976	2	11,493	904	2,133	8,431	25
				Total Order XXIV......	62,718	6,074	12,348	44,247	49	30,969	2,976	6,343	21,644	6	31,749	3,098	6,005	27,603	43
				Grand Total......	1,083,539	129,479	218,295	733,193	2,572	552,835	63,234	113,524	375,866	211	530,704	66,245	104,771	357,327	2,361

TABLE XVII A.

Occupations by Age.—*Continued.*

Class.	Order.	Sub-order and Group.	Serial No.	Occupations.	COUNTRY.														
					TOTAL.					MALES.					FEMALES.				
					Total.	0—4	5—14	15 and over.	Unspecified.	Total.	0—4	5—14	15 and over.	Unspecified.	Total.	0—4	5—14	15 and over.	Unspecified.
					36	37	38	39	40	41	42	43	44	45	46	47	48	49	50
Class G.—Indefinite and Independent.	XXII. Complex occupations.			(Village, &c., combined function to be specified provincially)...	...	...	...	...	...	...	...	...	...	...	...	...	...	...	...
				Total Order XXII......	...	...	...	...	...	...	...	...	...	...	...	...	...	...	...
	XXIII. Indefinite.	74. Unskilled labour. (a) Special branches.	461	Well sinkers	1,465	254	871	836	4	741	113	183	442	8	724	141	188	894	1
			462	Tank diggers and excavators	8,002	565	747	1,690	...	952	151	222	579	...	2,050	414	525	1,111	...
			463	Road, Canal and Railway labourers ...	614	92	92	430	...	853	45	52	256	...	261	47	40	174	...
			464	Quarrymen (stone splitters, &c.) ...	21,834	8,810	5,407	12,610	7	11,298	1,790	2,853	6,653	2	10,536	2,020	2,554	5,957	5
			465	Miners (unspecified)	326	33	47	246	...	...	...	...	...	...	326	33	47	246	...
			466	Rice-pounders and huskers	8,738	1,005	1,865	5,868	...	2,676	421	840	1,415	...	6,062	584	1,025	4,453	...
		(b) General.	467	General labour	1,317,361	199,236	295,085	822,821	719	543,558	87,478	139,775	316,048	257	773,803	111,758	155,310	506,273	462
				Total Sub-order 74......	1,353,340	204,995	303,614	844,001	780	559,578	89,998	143,925	325,393	262	793,762	114,997	159,689	518,608	468
		75. Undefined, &c.	468	Undefined and disreputable means of livelihood	416,907	71,184	97,230	247,521	972	215,388	88,252	51,128	180,807	196	201,524	87,932	46,102	116,714	776
				Total Sub-order 75......	416,907	71,184	97,230	247,521	972	215,383	33,252	51,128	130,807	196	201,524	87,932	46,102	116,714	776
				Total Order XXIII......	1,770,247	276,179	400,844	1,091,522	1,702	774,961	128,250	195,053	456,200	458	995,286	152,929	205,791	685,822	1,244
	XXIV. Independent of work.	76. Property & alms. (a) Property & allowances.	469	House-rent, shares, and other property not being land...	2,329	837	514	1,474	4	715	85	152	478	...	1,614	252	362	996	4
			470	Allowances from patrons or relatives	3,214	855	674	2,182	3	561	111	162	288	...	2,653	244	512	1,894	3
		(b) Charity and endowment.	471	Educational or other endowments, scholarship, &c. ...	8	...	5	3	...	6	...	3	3	...	2	...	2	...	...
			472	Mendicancy (not being affiliated to a religious order)	249,778	84,834	58,970	160,752	222	130,554	16,795	28,916	84,759	84	1,198,224	18,039	25,054	75,998	138
				Total Sub-order 76......	255,329	85,526	55,163	164,411	229	131,836	16,991	29,288	85,528	84	123,498	18,535	25,930	78,883	145
		77. Supported at the public charge. (a) Pension.	473	Pension, Civil Services	3,093	369	750	1,973	1	1,141	143	299	699	...	1,952	226	451	1,274	1
			474	Pension, Military Services	1,123	126	294	708	...	674	59	176	489	...	449	67	118	264	...
		(b) Prisoners.	475	Inmates of Asylums, &c.	...	...	...	...	...	...	...	...	...	...	...	...	...	...	...
			476	Prisoners, under trial	...	...	...	...	...	...	...	...	...	...	...	...	...	...	...
			477	Prisoners, for debt	293	44	57	192	...	293	44	57	192	...	...	...	...	...	...
			478	Prisoners, convicted or in Reformatories, &c.	44	2	...	42	...	41	1	...	40	...	3	1	...	2	...
				Total Sub-order 77......	4,553	541	1,101	2,910	1	2,149	247	532	1,870	...	2,404	294	569	1,540	1
				Total Order XXIV......	259,882	86,067	56,264	167,821	280	133,985	17,238	29,765	86,898	84	125,897	18,829	26,499	80,423	146
				Grand Total......	10,453,501	1,609,405	2,447,581	6,388,532	7,983	5,320,294	775,252	1,800,889	3,242,275	2,878	5,133,20	834,153	1,147,192	3,146,257	5,605

TABLE XVII A.

Occupations by Age.

Abstract showing totals of each Class.

Class.	Total. Total.	Total. 0—4	Total. 5—14	Total. 15 and over.	Total. Unspecified.	Males. Total.	Males. 0—4	Males. 5—14	Males. 15 and over.	Males. Unspecified.	Females. Total.	Females. 0—4	Females. 5—14	Females. 15 and over.	Females. Unspecified.
1	2	3	4	5	6	7	8	9	10	11	12	13	14	15	16
PROVINCIAL TOTAL.															
A	608,918	80,765	126,891	399,208	2,059	344,490	41,612	69,918	232,786	174	264,428	39,153	56,973	166,417	1,885
B	5,462,235	853,795	1,300,637	3,304,630	3,178	2,842,518	416,831	704,880	1,719,675	1,182	2,619,717	486,964	595,757	1,584,955	2,041
C	651,629	89,140	141,441	419,928	1,120	349,586	43,277	76,415	229,751	143	302,043	45,863	65,026	190,177	977
D	2,178,488	327,611	513,052	1,336,339	1,486	1,128,241	160,641	273,428	693,711	461	1,050,247	166,970	239,624	642,628	1,025
E	259,019	33,512	55,649	169,635	223	134,137	15,754	28,376	89,957	50	124,882	17,758	27,273	79,678	173
F	148,544	19,000	31,720	97,506	318	77,365	9,475	16,841	51,020	29	71,179	9,525	14,879	46,486	289
G	2,228,207	335,061	496,486	1,394,484	2,176	996,792	150,896	244,055	601,241	600	1,231,415	184,165	252,431	793,243	1,576
Grand Total	11,537,040	1,738,884	2,665,876	7,121,725	10,555	5,873,129	838,486	1,413,913	3,618,141	2,589	5,663,911	900,398	125,1963	3,503,584	7,966
TOWN.															
A	173,478	19,180	32,780	120,115	1,403	95,643	9,494	17,009	69,106	84	77,835	9,686	15,771	51,009	1,369
B	164,809	22,857	35,634	106,183	135	87,363	11,515	19,789	56,018	41	77,446	11,342	15,845	50,165	94
C	162,998	17,039	29,162	116,437	360	88,432	8,592	15,879	63,941	20	74,566	8,447	13,283	52,496	340
D	292,535	37,546	63,231	191,497	261	146,965	18,356	32,517	96,041	51	145,570	19,190	30,714	95,456	210
E	57,210	6,407	11,276	39,497	30	30,009	3,117	5,790	21,101	1	27,201	3,290	5,486	18,396	29
F	34,431	3,635	6,834	23,823	139	16,577	1,752	3,308	11,516	6	17,854	1,883	3,531	12,307	133
G	198,078	22,815	39,378	135,641	244	87,846	10,408	19,237	58,143	58	110,232	12,407	20,141	77,498	186
Grand Total	1,083,539	1,289,479	218,295	733,193	2,572	552,835	63,234	113,524	375,866	211	530,704	66,245	104,771	357,327	2,361
COUNTRY.															
A	435,440	61,585	94,111	279,088	656	248,847	32,118	52,909	163,680	140	186,593	29,467	41,202	115,408	516
B	5,297,426	830,938	1,265,003	3,198,447	3,038	2,755,155	405,316	685,091	1,663,657	1,091	2,542,271	425,622	579,912	1,534,790	1,947
C	488,631	72,101	112,279	303,491	760	261,154	34,685	60,536	165,810	123	227,477	37,716	51,743	137,681	637
D	1,885,953	290,065	449,821	1,144,842	1,225	981,276	142,285	240,911	597,670	410	904,677	147,480	208,910	547,172	815
E	201,809	27,105	44,373	130,138	193	104,128	12,637	22,586	68,856	49	97,681	14,468	21,787	61,282	144
F	114,113	15,365	24,886	73,683	179	60,788	7,723	13,538	39,504	23	53,325	7,642	11,348	34,179	156
G	2,030,129	312,246	457,108	1,258,843	1,932	908,946	140,488	224,818	543,098	542	1,121,183	171,758	232,290	715,745	1,390
Grand Total	10,453,501	1,609,405	2,447,581	6,388,532	7,988	5,320,294	775,252	1,300,389	3,242,275	2,378	5,133,207	834,153	1,147,192	3,146,257	5,605

TABLE XVII B.

OCCUPATIONS BY DISTRICTS.

TABLE XVII B.

Occupations by Districts.

Class.	Order.	Sub-order and Group.	Serial No.	Occupations.	Grand Total. Total.	Grand Total. Males.	Grand Total. Females.	Hyderabad. Total.	Hyderabad. Males.	Hyderabad. Females.	Atraf-i-Balda. Total.	Atraf-i-Balda. Males.	Atraf-i-Balda. Females.	Mahabubnagar. Total.	Mahabubnagar. Males.	Mahabubnagar. Females.	Nalgonda. Total.	Nalgonda. Males.	Nalgonda. Females.
1	2	3	4	5	6	7	8	9	10	11	12	13	14	15	16	17	18	19	20
Class A	I. Administration.	1. Service of the Imperial and Provincial Governments.	1	The Viceroy, Governors, Lieutenant-Governors, and Chief Commissioners and their families	1,500	24	1,476	1,500	24	1,476	...	...	...	...	...	...	...	...	...
			2	Officers	1,585	827	758	690	293	397	16	14	2	71	33	38	47	23	24
			3	Office Superintendents, and Clerical establishments, Police and Excise Inspectors, Sub-Registrars, &c.... ...	16,090	8,106	7,984	1,867	953	914	314	171	143	663	343	320	616	407	209
			4	Messengers, constables, bailiffs, warders, menials, &c.	190,169	105,921	84,248	51,249	28,275	22,974	3,339	2,233	1,106	4,970	2,815	2,155	4,256	2,587	1,669
				Total Sub-order 1......	209,344	114,878	94,466	55,306	29,545	25,761	3,669	2,418	1,251	5,704	3,191	2,513	4,919	3,017	1,902
		2. Service of Local & Municipal Bodies.	5	Inspecting and supervising officials ...	6	3	3	6	3	3	...	...	...	...	...	...	...	...	...
			6	Clerical establishments...	46	34	12	11	9	2	...	...	...	20	18	2	...	...	...
			7	Menials	3,141	1,531	1,610	2,711	1,334	1,377	7	3	4	16	3	13	...	...	...
				Total Sub-order 2......	3,193	1,568	1,625	2,728	1,346	1,382	7	3	4	36	21	15	...	...	...
		3. Village Service.	8	Headmen, when not agriculturists ...	83,458	45,151	38,307	106	63	43	2,578	1,452	1,126	3,598	2,006	1,592	3,528	1,839	1,689
			9	Accountants	54,744	27,884	26,860	131	67	64	1,877	797	1,080	3,105	1,587	1,518	3,145	1,500	1,645
			11	Watchmen and other menials	190,371	114,118	76,253	333	169	164	6,047	4,090	1,957	11,335	7,490	3,845	4,834	2,460	2,374
				Total Sub-order 3......	328,573	187,153	141,420	570	299	271	10,502	6,339	4,163	18,038	11,083	6,955	11,507	5,799	5,708
				Total Order I......	51,110	303,599	237,511	58,604	31,190	27,414	14,178	8,760	5,418	23,778	14,295	9,483	16,426	8,816	7,610
	II. Defence.	4. Army.	12	Officers	1,029	591	438	698	382	316	17	7	10	...	...	...	11	10	1
			13	Non-Commissioned Officers and Privates	40,816	24,305	16,511	20,140	12,451	7,689	1,197	652	545	2,006	912	1,094	287	141	146
			14	Followers	20.500	12,535	7,965	18,682	11,252	7,430	...	...	...	...	...	...	...	...	...
			15	Administrative establishments ...	954	495	459	954	495	459	...	...	...	...	...	...	...	...	...
				Total Sub-order 4......	63,299	37,926	25,373	40,474	24,580	15,894	1,214	659	555	2,006	912	1,094	298	151	147
		5. Navy and Marine.	16	Officers	...	...	...	...	...	...	...	...	...	...	...	...	...	...	...
			17	Engineers, Warrant Officers, and seamen	...	...	...	...	...	...	...	...	...	...	...	...	...	...	...
			18	Administrative Staff	...	...	...	...	...	...	...	...	...	...	...	...	...	...	...
				Total Sub-order 5......	...	...	...	...	...	...	...	...	...	...	...	...	...	...	...
				Total Order II......	63,299	8,426	25,373	40,474	24,580	15,894	1,214	659	555	2,006	912	1,094	298	151	147

TABLE XVII B.

Occupations by Districts.—*Continued.*

Class.	Order.	Sub-order and Group.	Serial No.	Occupations.	Warangal. Total.	Warangal. Males.	Warangal. Females.	Elgandal. Total.	Elgandal. Males.	Elgandal. Females.	Indur. Total.	Indur. Males.	Indur. Females.	Medak. Total.	Medak. Males.	Medak. Females.	Aurangabad. Total.	Aurangabad. Males.	Aurangabad. Females.
					21	22	23	24	25	26	27	28	29	30	31	32	33	34	35
Class A.	I. Administration.	1. Service of the Imperial and Provincial Governments.	1	The Viceroy, Governors, Lieutenant-Governors, and Chief Commissioners and their families	...	...	...	...	...	...	...	...	...	...	...	...	...	...	...
			2	Officers	232	181	51	76	42	34	22	8	14	44	28	16	24	17	7
			3	Office Superintendents, and Clerical establishments, Police and Excise Inspectors, Sub-Registrars, &c.	757	561	196	699	400	299	5,162	778	4,384	297	138	159	172	58	114
			4	Messengers, constables, bailiffs, warders, menials, &c.	7,420	3,935	3,485	6,676	4,059	2,617	10,782	7,617	3,165	2,758	1,679	1,079	14,803	8,010	6,793
				Total Sub-order 1......	8,409	4,677	3,732	7,451	4,501	2,950	15,966	8,403	7,563	3,099	1,845	1,254	14,999	8,085	6,914
		2. Service of Local & Municipal Bodies.	5	Inspecting and supervising officials ...	...	...	...	...	...	...	...	...	...	...	...	...	...	...	...
			6	Clerical establishments	...	...	...	...	...	...	...	...	...	...	...	...	...	...	...
			7	Menials	...	...	...	...	...	...	4	...	4	10	10	...	23	23	...
				Total Sub-order 2......	...	...	...	...	...	...	4	...	4	10	10	...	23	23	...
		3. Village Service.	8	Headmen, when not agriculturists ...	3,686	2,097	1,589	6,560	3,278	2,282	4,684	2,464	2,220	3,110	1,583	1,527	5,230	2,572	2,658
			9	Accountants	3,933	2,059	1,874	3,050	1,463	1,587	2,540	1,369	1,171	1,480	760	720	6,189	3,478	2,711
			11	Watchmen and other menials... ...	6,753	3,935	2,818	9,917	5,984	3,933	12,004	7,894	4,110	8,453	4,305	4,148	30,167	25,275	4,892
				Total Sub-order 3......	14,372	8,091	6,281	19,527	10,725	8,802	19,228	11,727	7,501	13,043	6,648	6,395	41,586	31,325	10,261
				Total Order I......	22,781	12,768	10,013	26,978	15,226	11,752	35,198	20,130	15,068	16,152	8,503	7,649	56,608	39,433	17,175
	II. Defence.	4. Army.	12	Officers	3	...	3	4	1	3	...	...	...	95	93	2	67	40	27
			13	Non-Commissioned Officers and Privates	429	248	181	1,042	478	564	310	168	142	920	595	325	4,972	3,093	1,879
			14	Followers	...	...	...	...	...	...	...	...	...	...	...	...	...	...	...
			15	Administrative establishments... ...	...	...	...	...	...	...	...	...	...	...	...	...	...	...	...
				Total Sub-order 4......	432	248	184	1,046	479	567	310	168	142	1,015	688	327	5,039	3,133	1,906
		5. Navy and Marine.	16	Officers	...	...	...	...	...	...	...	...	...	...	...	...	...	...	...
			17	Engineers, Warrant Officers, and seamen	...	...	...	...	...	...	...	...	...	...	...	...	...	...	...
			18	Administrative Staff	...	...	...	...	...	...	...	...	...	...	...	...	...	...	...
				Total Sub-order 5......	...	...	...	...	...	...	...	...	...	...	...	...	...	...	...
				Total Order II......	432	248	184	1,046	479	567	310	168	142	1,015	688	327	5,039	3,133	1,906

TABLE XVII B.

Occupations by Districts.—*Continued.*

Class. / Order. / Sub-order and Group.	Serial No.	Occupations.	Birh. Total.	Birh. Males.	Birh. Females.	Nander. Total.	Nander. Males.	Nander. Females.	Naldrug. Total.	Naldrug. Males.	Naldrug. Females.	Bidar. Total.	Bidar. Males.	Bidar. Females.	Parbhani. Total.	Parbhani. Males.	Parbhani. Females.
			36	37	38	39	40	41	42	43	44	45	46	47	48	49	50
Class A.—*contd.* I. Administration. 1. Service of the Imperial and Provincial Governments.	1	The Viceroy, Governors Lieutenant-Governors, and Chief Commissioners and their families	...	...	...	...	...	...	...	...	...	...	...	...	...	...	...
	2	Officers	47	76	81	18	6	12	64	11	53	34	16	18	79	66	13
	3	Office Superintendents, and Clerical establishments, Police and Excise Inspectors, Sub-Registrars, &c.	198	114	84	2,882	2,473	409	130	68	62	1,413	1,282	131	75	35	40
	4	Messengers, constables, bailiffs, warders, menials, &c.	7,783	4,271	3,512	8,375	4,058	4,322	7,971	4,545	3,426	14,681	7,880	6,801	10,337	5,620	4,717
		Total Sub-order 1......	8,028	4,401	3,627	11,275	6,532	4,743	8,165	4,624	3,541	16,078	9,128	6,950	10,491	5,721	4,770
2. Service of Local & Municipal Bodies.	5	Inspecting and supervising officials ...	...	...	...	...	...	...	...	...	...	...	...	...	...	...	...
	6	Clerical establishments...	...	...	...	...	...	...	...	...	...	2	2	...	7	...	7
	7	Menials	6	1	5	107	61	46	8	...	8	84	6	28	...	...	...
		Total Sub-order 2......	6	1	5	107	61	46	8	...	8	86	8	28	7	...	7
3. Village Service.	8	Headmen, when not agriculturists ...	5,527	3,078	2,449	5,782	3,287	2,495	5,084	2,824	2,260	10,292	5,480	4,812	6,318	3,561	2,757
	9	Accountants	4,390	2,365	2,025	2,789	1,317	1,472	3,558	1,784	1,774	5,735	2,683	3,052	3,291	1,840	1,451
	11	Watchmen and other menials... ...	13,510	5,474	8,036	7,622	4,280	3,342	15,612	8,919	6,693	19,069	8,562	10,507	13,037	7,760	5,277
		Total Sub-order 3......	23,427	10,917	12,510	16,193	8,884	7,309	24,254	13,527	10,727	35,096	16,725	18,371	22,646	13,161	9,485
		Total Order I......	31,461	15,319	16,142	27,575	15,477	12,098	32,422	18,151	14,271	51,210	25,861	25,349	33,144	18,882	14,262
II. Defence. 4. Army.	12	Officers	13	7	6	...	...	...	...	...	...	...	...	...	18	...	18
	13	Non-Commissioned Officers and Privates	2,448	1,417	1,031	98	28	70	382	238	144	338	100	238	3,250	1,935	1,315
	14	Followers	...	...	...	...	...	...	...	...	...	...	...	...	...	...	...
	15	Administrative establishments ...	...	...	...	...	...	...	...	...	...	...	...	...	...	...	...
		Total Sub-order 4......	2,461	1,424	1,037	98	28	70	382	238	144	338	100	233	3,268	1,935	1,333
5. Navy and Marine.	16	Officers	...	...	...	...	...	...	...	...	...	...	...	...	...	...	...
	17	Engineers, Warrant Officers, and seamen	...	...	...	...	...	...	...	...	...	...	...	...	...	...	...
	18	Administrative Staff	...	...	...	...	...	...	...	...	...	...	...	...	...	...	...
		Total Sub-order 5......	...	...	...	...	...	...	...	...	...	...	...	...	...	...	...
		Total Order II......	2,461	1,424	1,037	98	28	70	382	238	144	338	100	238	3,268	1,935	1,333

TABLE XVII B.

Occupations by Districts.—*Continued.*

Class.	Order.	Sub-order and Group.	Serial No.	Occupations.	Sirpur Tandur. Total.	Sirpur Tandur. Males.	Sirpur Tandur. Females.	Gulbarga. Total.	Gulbarga. Males.	Gulbarga. Females.	Raichur. Total.	Raichur. Males.	Raichur. Females.	Lingasugur. Total.	Lingasugur. Males.	Lingasugur. Females.	Railways. Total.	Railways. Males.	Railways. Females.
					51	52	53	54	55	56	57	58	59	60	61	62	63	64	65
Class A.—*contd.*	I. Administration.	1. Service of the Imperial and Provincial Governments.	1	The Viceroy, Governors, Lieutenant-Governors, and Chief Commissioners and their families	...	...	...	...	...	...	...	...	...	...	...	...	...	...	...
			2	Officers	6	6	...	14	5	9	89	54	85	9	7	2	3	1	2
			3	Office Superintendents, and Clerical establishments, Police and Excise Inspectors, Sub-Registrars, &c.	2	2	...	493	134	359	262	154	108	68	27	41	20	8	12
			4	Messengers, constables, bailiffs, warders, menials, &c.	4,313	2,319	1,994	14,112	7,547	6,565	7,171	3,628	3,543	9,006	4,748	4,258	217	150	67
				Total Sub-order 1......	4,821	2,327	1 994	14,619	7,686	6,933	7,522	3,836	3,686	9,083	4,782	4,301	240	159	81
		2. Service of Local & Municipal Bodies.	5	Inspecting and supervising officials ...	...	...	...	...	...	...	...	...	...	...	...	...	...	...	...
			6	Clerical establishments	...	...	...	...	...	...	6	5	1	...	...	...	...	...	...
			7	Menials	...	...	...	11	...	11	152	66	86	57	24	33	...	...	...
				Total Sub-order 2......	...	...	...	11	...	11	158	71	87	57	24	33	...	...	...
		3. Village Service.	8	Headmen, when not agriculturists ...	1,238	736	502	6,409	3,491	2,918	3,899	2,095	1,804	5,829	3,245	2,584	...	...	...
			9	Accountants	865	174	191	4,144	2,052	2,092	2,172	1,139	1,033	2,847	1,448	1,399	3	2	1
			11	Watchmen and other menials... ...	609	309	300	7,649	4,218	3,431	12,390	7,070	5,320	11,030	5,924	5,106	...	...	...
				Total Sub-order 3......	2,212	1,219	993	18,202	9,761	8,441	18,461	10,304	8,157	19,706	10,617	9,089	3	2	1
				Total Order I......	6,533	3,546	2,987	32,832	17,447	15,385	26,141	14,211	11,930	28,846	15,423	13,423	243	161	82
	II. Defence.	4. Army.	12	Officers...	...	...	...	...	...	...	81	39	42	19	10	9	3	2	1
			13	Non-Commissioned Officers and Privates	106	97	9	797	434	363	2,085	1,304	781	...	...	...	14	14	...
			14	Followers	...	...	...	...	...	...	422	249	173	1,396	1,034	362	...	...	...
			15	Administrative establishments ...	...	...	...	...	...	...	...	...	...	...	...	...	...	...	...
				Total Sub-order 4......	106	97	9	797	434	363	2,588	1,592	996	1,415	1,044	371	17	16	1
		5. Navy and Marine.	16	Offices	...	...	...	...	...	...	...	...	...	...	...	...	...	...	...
			17	Engineers, Warrant Officers, and seamen	...	...	...	...	...	...	...	...	...	...	...	...	...	...	...
			18	Administrative Staff	...	...	...	...	...	...	...	...	...	...	...	...	...	...	...
				Total Sub-order 5......	...	...	...	...	...	...	...	...	...	...	...	...	...	...	...
				Total Order II......	106	97	9	797	434	363	2,588	1,592	996	1,415	1,044	371	17	16	1

TABLE XVII B.

Occupations by Districts.—*Continued.*

Class.	Order.	Sub-order and Group.	Serial No.	Occupations.	Grand Total. Total.	Grand Total. Males.	Grand Total. Females.	Hyderabad. Total.	Hyderabad. Males.	Hyderabad. Females.	Atraf-i-Balda. Total.	Atraf-i-Balda. Males.	Atraf-i-Balda. Females.	Mahabubnagar. Total.	Mahabubnagar. Males.	Mahabubnagar. Females.	Nalgonda. Total.	Nalgonda. Males.	Nalgonda. Females.
1	2	3	4	5	6	7	8	9	10	11	12	13	14	15	16	17	18	19	20
Class A.—*concld.*	III. Foreign and Feudatory State Service.	6. Administrative Service.	19	Chiefs, Consuls, and Officers ...	671	851	820	644	840	304	...	...	...	...	...	...	...	...	...
			20	Clerical Establishments	1,522	850	672	1,356	751	605	...	...	...	...	...	...	...	...	...
			21	Menials, &c.	2,815	1,763	552	1,560	1,062	497	...	...	...	...	...	...	...	...	...
				Total Sub-order 6......	4,508	2,964	1,544	3,560	2,154	1,406	...	...	...	...	...	...	...	...	...
		7. Army and Marine.	22	Officers	1	1	...	1	1	...	...	...	...	...	...	...	...	...	...
			23	Privates and seamen, &c.	...	...	...	...	...	...	...	...	...	...	...	...	...	...	...
				Total Sub-order 7......	1	1	...	1	1	...	...	...	...	...	...	...	...	...	...
				Total Order III......	4,509	2,965	1,544	3,561	2,155	1,406	...	...	...	...	...	...	...	...	...
Class B.	IV. Live Stock.	8. Stock breeding and dealing. (a) Horses & horned cattle.	24	Horse breeders and dealers	610	489	171	174	96	78	81	80	1	89	45	44	58	41	18
			25	Cattle breeders and dealers and Commissariat Farm establishment ...	28,049	16,482	6,567	18	12	6	824	476	348	9,151	7,351	1,800	1,785	1,222	563
			26	Herdsmen	87,627	61,901	25,726	165	91	74	2,477	2,120	357	1,994	1,798	196	13,773	8,494	5,279
		(b)—Other draught, &c., animals.	27	Buffalo breeders and dealers	242	171	71	...	...	...	10	9	1	...	...	...	114	78	36
			28	Elephant catchers and breeders ...	...	...	...	...	...	...	...	...	...	...	...	...	...	...	...
			29	Camel breeders and dealers	8	2	1	...	...	...	...	...	...	...	...	...	...	...	...
			30	Ass and mule breeders and dealers...	40	21	19	...	...	...	2	2	...	4	4	...	2	...	2
		(c) Small stock.	31	Sheep and goat breeders and dealers.	170,820	103,802	67,018	270	142	127	11,089	6,589	4,500	24,274	14,708	9,571	26,182	18,308	7,879
			32	Pig breeders and dealers	180	161	19	1	1	...	10	9	1	9	9	...	...	...	...
				Total Sub-order 8......	282,571	182,979	99,592	628	848	285	14,393	9,185	5,208	35,521	23,910	11,611	41,909	28,138	13,771
		9. Subsidiary Services to stock. (a) Training and doctoring live-stock.	33	Veterinary Surgeons and Assistants...	22	15	7	18	11	7	...	...	...	1	1	...	...	...	...
			34	Farriers and gelders	1,049	558	491	338	172	165	44	43	1	87	36	51	...	...	...
			35	Horse and elephant breakers and trainers, &c.	264	152	112	51	36	15	[illegible]	8	8	45	25	20	28	28	...
		(b) Vermin destroying.	36	Rat, monkey, jackal, crocodile, &c., catchers	...	...	...	...	...	...	...	...	...	...	...	...	...	...	...
				Total Sub-order 9......	1,335	725	610	407	220	187	50	46	4	133	62	71	28	28	...
				Total Order IV......	283,906	183,704	100,202	1,035	563	472	14,443	9,231	5,212	35,654	23,972	11,682	41,937	28,166	13,771
	V. Agriculture.	10. Interest in land.	37	Land occupants, not cultivating ...	100,993	51,376	49,617	4,904	1,764	3,140	4,870	2,360	2,510	10,788	5,594	5,194	6,987	3,398	3,589
			38	Land occupants, cultivating	4,978	3,257	1,721	36	22	14	593	534	59	2,467	1,585	882	168	146	22
			39	Lessees of villages, &c.	46	25	21	25	8	17	15	11	4	...	...	...	...	...	...
			40	Tenants, not cultivating	6,188	3,519	2,669	...	...	...	...	...	...	457	120	337	...	...	...
			41	Tenants and sharers, cultivating ...	4,501,683	2,344,949	2,156,784	2,838	1,631	1,207	100,569	53,101	47,468	188,648	106,577	82,071	226,858	120,586	105,772
				Total Sub-order 10......	4,613,888	2,403,126	2,210,762	7,803	3,425	4,378	106,047	56,006	50,041	202,860	113,876	88,484	233,518	124,130	109,382

TABLE XVII B.

Occupations by Districts.—*Continued.*

Class.	Order.	Sub-order and Group.	Serial No.	Occupations.	Warangal. Total.	Warangal. Males.	Warangal. Females.	Elgandal. Total.	Elgandal. Males.	Elgandal. Females.	Indur. Total.	Indur. Males.	Indur. Females.	Medak. Total.	Medak. Males.	Medak. Females.	Aurangabad. Total.	Aurangabad. Males.	Aurangabad. Females.
					21	22	23	24	25	26	27	28	29	30	31	32	33	34	35
Class A.—*concld.*	III. Foreign and Feudatory State Service.	6. Administrative Service.	19	Chiefs, Consuls, and Officers...	...	...	...	...	...	...	...	...	...	...	...	...	3	...	3
			20	Clerical Establishments	...	...	...	...	...	...	...	...	...	...	...	...	86	45	41
			21	Menials, &c.	...	...	...	...	...	...	3	1	2	...	...	...	674	643	31
				Total Sub-order 6......	...	...	...	...	...	...	3	1	2	...	...	...	763	688	75
		7. Army and Marine.	22	Officers ...	...	...	...	...	...	...	...	...	...	...	...	...	...	...	...
			23	Privates and seamen, &c.	...	...	...	...	...	...	...	...	...	...	...	...	...	...	...
				Total Sub-order 7......	...	...	...	...	...	...	...	...	...	...	...	...	...	...	...
				Total Order III......	...	...	...	...	...	...	3	1	2	...	...	...	763	688	75
Class B.	IV. Live Stock.	8. Stock breeding & dealing. (a) Horses & horned cattle.	24	Horse breeders and dealers ...	85	80	5	...	...	...	6	6	...	...	...	...	16	15	1
			25	Cattle breeders and dealers and Commissariat Farm establishment	1,047	455	592	5,725	4,206	1,519	919	520	399	988	741	247	408	190	218
			26	Herdsmen	8,474	6,389	2,085	4,782	3,569	1,213	4,910	8,575	1,335	1,780	1,613	167	3,027	1,807	1,220
			27	Buffalo breeders and dealers...	113	83	80	5	1	4	...	...	...	...	...	...	...	...	...
		(b)—Other (c) Small draught, stock, &c., animals.	28	Elephant catchers and breeders	...	...	...	...	...	...	...	...	...	...	...	...	...	...	...
			29	Camel breeders and dealers ...	...	...	...	...	...	...	...	...	...	...	...	...	...	...	...
			30	Ass and mule breeders and dealers...	3	3	...	26	9	17	...	...	...	...	...	...	...	...	...
			31	Sheep and goat breeders and dealers.	83,714	19,327	14,387	40,691	24,171	16,520	7,906	4,758	8,153	8,099	5,061	8,038	2,594	1,483	1,111
			32	Pig breeders and dealers	114	114	...	7	7	...	1	1	...	27	14	13	...	...	...
				Total Sub-order 8......	48,500	26,401	17,099	51,236	31,963	19,273	13,742	8,855	4,887	10,894	7,429	8,465	6,040	8,495	2,545
		9. Subsidiary Services to stock. (a) Training and doctoring live-stock.	33	Veterinary Surgeons and Assistants...	...	...	...	...	...	...	2	2	...	...	...	...	...	...	...
			34	Farriers and gelders ...	17	17	...	7	5	2	...	...	...	60	56	4	45	27	18
			35	Horse and elephant breakers and trainers, &c. ...	12	2	10	1	1	...	...	...	...	26	12	14	20	9	11
		(b) Vermin destroying.	36	Rat, monkey, jackal, crocodile, &c., catchers	...	...	...	...	...	...	...	...	...	...	...	...	...	...	...
				Total Sub-order 9......	29	19	10	8	6	2	2	2	...	86	68	18	65	86	29
				Total Order IV......	43,529	26,420	17,109	51,244	31,969	19,275	13,744	8,857	4,887	10,980	7,497	8,483	6,105	8,531	2,574
	V. Agriculture.	10. Interest in land.	37	Land occupants, not cultivating	10,251	5,671	4,580	4,724	2,263	2,461	7,703	8,595	4,108	7,729	8,852	8,877	5,634	2,628	3,006
			38	Land occupants, cultivating ...	119	99	20	1,064	539	525	...	...	...	520	321	199	...	...	...
			39	Lessees of villages, &c.	6	6	...	...	...	...	...	...	...	...	...	...	...	...	...
			40	Tenants, not cultivating	685	643	42	184	...	184	...	...	...	...	...	...	9	9	...
			41	Tenants and sharers, cultivating	832,777	171,814	160,963	333,243	180,994	152,249	225,874	117,706	108,168	103,259	54,558	48,701	371,829	190,637	181,192
				Total Sub-order 10......	843,838	178,233	165,605	339,215	183,796	155,419	238,577	121,301	112,276	111,508	58,731	52,777	377,472	198,274	184,198

TABLE XVII B.
Occupations by Districts.

TABLE XVII B.

Occupations by Districts.—*Continued.*

Class.	Order.	Sub-order and Group.	Serial No.	Occupations.	Birh. Total.	Birh. Males.	Birh. Females.	Nander. Total.	Nander. Males.	Nander. Females.	Naldrug. Total.	Naldrug. Males.	Naldrug. Females.	Bidar. Total.	Bidar. Males.	Bidar. Females.	Parbhani. Total.	Parbhani. Males.	Parbhani. Females.
					36	37	38	39	40	41	42	43	44	45	46	47	48	49	50
Class A.—*concld.*	III. Foreign and Feudatory State Service.	6. Administrative service.	19	Chiefs, Consuls and Officers... ...	...	...	...	...	...	...	...	...	...	...	...	...	24	11	13
			20	Clerical Establishments	12	9	3	6	6	...	...	...	...	...	...	...	32	18	14
			21	Menials, &c, ...	13	13	...	...	...	...	...	...	...	...	...	...	18	9	9
				Total Sub-order 6......	25	22	3	6	6	...	...	...	...	...	...	...	74	38	36
		7. Army and Marine.	22	Officers	...	...	...	...	...	...	...	...	...	...	...	...	...	...	...
			23	Privates and seamen, &c, ...	...	...	...	...	...	...	...	...	...	...	...	...	...	...	...
				Total Sub-order 7......	...	...	...	...	...	...	...	...	...	...	...	...	...	...	...
				Total Order III......	25	22	3	6	6	...	...	...	...	...	...	...	74	38	36
Class B.	IV. Live Stock.	8. Stock breeding & dealing. (a) Horses & horned cattle.	24	Horse breeders and dealers	42	25	17	9	9	...	3	2	1	10	10	...	127	127	...
			25	Cattle breeders and dealers and Commissariat Farm establishment ...	77	28	49	180	100	80	269	124	145	595	318	277	100	72	28
			26	Herdsmen	2,993	2,018	975	7,121	5,504	1,617	5,447	4,503	944	11,159	7,904	3,255	4,047	2,940	1,107
			27	Buffalo breeders and dealers ...	...	...	...	...	...	...	...	...	...	...	...	...	...	...	...
		(b)—Other draught, &c., animals.	28	Elephant catchers and breeders ...	...	...	...	...	...	...	...	...	...	...	...	...	...	...	...
			29	Camel breeders and dealers	3	2	1	...	...	...	...	...	...	...	...	...	...	...	...
			30	Ass and mule breeders and dealers...	...	...	...	...	...	...	3	3	...	...	...	...	...	...	...
		(c) Small stock.	31	Sheep and goat breeders and dealers.	1,759	1,275	484	234	190	44	186	186	...	815	389	426	2,789	1,298	1,441
			32	Pig breeders and dealers	...	...	...	...	...	...	11	6	5	...	...	...	...	...	...
				Total Sub-order 8......	4,874	3,348	1,526	7,544	5,803	1,741	5,919	4,824	1,095	12,579	8,621	3,958	7,013	4,437	2,576
		9. Subsidiary Services to stock. (a) Training and doctoring live-stock.	33	Veterinary Surgeons and Assistants...	...	...	...	...	...	...	...	...	...	1	1	...	...	...	...
			34	Farriers and gelders	47	28	19	13	4	9	7	4	3	100	80	70	17	4	13
			35	Horse and elephant breakers and trainers, &c.	...	...	...	1	1	...	40	19	21	16	2	14	16	13	3
		(b) Vermin destroying.	36	Rat, monkey, jackal, crocodile, &c., catchers	...	...	...	...	...	...	...	...	...	...	...	...	...	...	...
				Total Sub-order 9......	47	28	19	14	5	9	47	23	24	117	33	84	33	17	16
				Total Order IV......	4,921	3,376	1,545	7,558	5,808	1,750	5,966	4,847	1,119	12,696	8,654	4,042	7,046	4,454	2,592
	V. Agriculture.	10. Interest in land.	37	Land occupants, not cultivating ...	4,599	2,559	2,040	5,261	2,432	2,829	3,319	2,298	1,021	6,071	2,925	3,146	1,997	1,015	982
			38	Land occupants, cultivating	...	...	...	...	...	...	11	11	...	...	...	...	...	...	...
			39	Lessees of villages, &c....	...	...	...	...	...	...	...	...	...	...	...	...	...	...	...
			40	Tenants, not cultivating	...	...	...	...	...	...	...	...	...	23	23	...	4,330	2,724	2,106
			41	Tenants and sharers, cultivating ...	296,722	153,109	143,613	293,757	152,628	141,129	292,086	148,480	143,606	349,302	179,865	169,437	377,883	192,813	184,570
				Total Sub-order 10......	301,321	155,668	145,653	299,018	155,060	143,958	295,416	150,789	144,627	355,896	182,813	172,583	384,210	196,552	187,658

TABLE XVII B.

Occupations by Districts.—*Continued.*

Class.	Order.	Sub-order and Group.	Serial No.	Occupations.	Sirpur Tandur. Total.	Sirpur Tandur. Males.	Sirpur Tandur. Females.	Gulbarga. Total.	Gulbarga. Males.	Gulbarga. Females.	Raichur. Total.	Raichur. Males.	Raichur. Females.	Lingasugur. Total.	Lingasugur. Males.	Lingasugur. Females.	Railways. Total.	Railways. Males.	Railways. Females.
					51	52	53	54	55	56	57	58	59	60	61	62	63	64	65
Class A.—concld.	III. Foreign and Feudatory State Service.	6. Administrative Service.	19	Chiefs, Consuls and Officers	...	...	...	...	...	...	...	...	...	...	...	...	...	...	...
			20	Clerical Establishments	...	...	...	...	...	...	...	...	...	...	...	...	...	...	...
			21	Menials, &c.	...	...	...	47	34	13	1	1	...	...	...	...	29	20	9
				Total Sub-order 6......	...	...	...	47	34	13	1	1	...	...	...	...	29	20	9
		7. Army and Marine.	22	Officers	...	...	...	...	...	...	...	...	...	...	...	...	...	...	...
			23	Privates and seamen, &c.	...	...	...	...	...	...	...	...	...	...	...	...	...	...	...
				Total Sub-order 7......	...	...	...	...	...	...	...	...	...	...	...	...	...	...	...
				Total Order III......	...	...	...	47	34	13	1	1	...	...	...	...	29	20	9
Class B.	IV. Live Stock.	8. Stock breeding & dealing. (a) Horses & horned cattle.	24	Horse breeders and dealers	...	...	...	...	...	...	...	...	...	...	...	...	...	...	...
			25	Cattle breeders and dealers, and Commissariat Farm establishment ...	...	...	...	11	...	11	4	3	1	...	...	...	...	...	...
			26	Herdsmen	83	41	42	116	104	12	457	363	94	312	159	153	...	...	...
			27	Buffalo breeders and dealers	5,148	3,035	2,113	5,747	3,610	2,137	2,860	1,957	903	1,721	972	749	2	2	...
		(b)—Other draught, &c., animals.	28	Elephant catchers and breeders... ...	...	...	...	...	...	...	...	...	...	...	...	...	...	...	...
			29	Camel breeders and dealers	...	...	...	...	...	...	...	...	...	...	...	...	...	...	...
			30	Ass and mule breeders and dealers ...	...	...	...	...	...	...	...	...	...	...	...	...	...	...	...
		(c) Small stock.	31	Sheep and goat breeders and dealers ...	131	83	48	1,355	870	485	6,421	3,640	2,781	2,405	1,387	1,018	...	...	...
			32	Pig breeders and dealers	...	...	...	...	...	...	...	...	...	...	...	...	6	1	5
				Total Sub-order 8......	5,362	3,159	2,203	7,229	4,584	2,645	9,742	5,963	3,779	4,438	2,518	1,920	8	3	5
		9. Subsidiary Services to stock. (a) Training and doctoring live-stock.	33	Veterinary Surgeons and Assistants ...	...	...	...	...	...	...	...	...	...	...	...	...	...	...	...
			34	Farriers and gelders	...	...	...	...	...	...	...	...	...	...	...	...	...	...	...
			35	Horse and elephant breakers and trainers, &c.	...	...	...	69	36	33	46	25	21	151	69	82	1	1	...
		(b) Vermin destroying.	36	Rat, monkey, jackal, crocodile, &c., catchers	...	...	...	...	...	...	1	...	1	...	...	...	1	1	...
				Total Sub-order 9......	...	...	...	69	36	33	47	25	22	151	69	82	2	2	...
				Total Order IV......	5,362	3,159	2,203	7,298	4,620	2,678	9,789	5,988	3,801	4,589	2,587	2,002	10	5	5
	V. Agriculture.	10. Interest in land.	37	Land occupants, not cultivating ...	1,886	1,603	283	2,942	1,544	1,398	...	...	...	...	...	...	...	...	...
			38	Land occupants, cultivating	...	...	...	...	...	...	6,543	3,479	3,064	4,778	2,389	2,389	7	7	...
			39	Lessees of villages, &c.	...	...	...	...	...	...	...	...	...	...	...	...	...	...	...
			40	Tenants, not cultivating	...	...	...	...	...	...	...	...	...	...	...	...	...	...	...
			41	Tenants and sharers, cultivating ...	111,515	57,554	53,961	272,548	142,242	130,306	243,312	126,789	116,523	379,639	193,843	185,796	24	22	2
				Total Sub-order 10......	1,13,401	59,157	54,244	275,490	143,786	131,704	249,855	130,268	119,587	384,417	196,232	188,185	31	29	2

TABLE XVII B.

Occupations by Districts.—*Continued.*

Class.	Order.	Sub-order and Group.	Serial No.	Occupations.	Grand Total. Total.	Grand Total. Males.	Grand Total. Females.	Hyderabad. Total.	Hyderabad. Males.	Hyderabad. Females.	Atraf-i-Balda. Total.	Atraf-i-Balda. Males.	Atraf-i-Balda. Females.	Mahabubnagar. Total.	Mahabubnagar. Males.	Mahabubnagar. Females.	Nalgonda. Total.	Nalgonda. Males.	Nalgonda. Females.
1	2	3	4	5	6	7	8	9	10	11	12	13	14	15	16	17	18	19	20
Class B.—*concld.*	V. Agriculture.—*concld.*	11. Agri-cultural labourers.	42	Farm-servants	124,534	79,624	44,910	102	54	48	4,095	2,464	1,631	12,402	9,414	2,988	7,954	5,188	2,766
			43	Field labourers and crop-watchers ...	432,925	172,345	260,580	145	685	77	13,432	3,538	9,894	62,764	16,440	46,324	17,730	2,510	15,220
				Total Sub-order 11......	557,459	251,969	305,490	247	122	125	17,527	6,002	11,525	75,166	25,854	49,312	25,684	7,698	17,986
		12. Growers of special products and trees.	44	Tea, coffee and cinchona Planters, managers and assistants ...	...	...	...	...	...	...	...	...	...	...	...	...	...	...	...
			45	Cocoanut growers	...	...	...	...	...	...	...	...	...	...	...	...	...	...	...
			46	Betel-vine and areca-nut growers ...	348	167	181	...	...	...	67	67	...	...	...	...	...	...	...
			47	Waternut growers	1	...	1	...	...	...	...	...	...	...	...	...	...	...	...
			48	Cardamom and pepper growers ...	...	...	...	...	...	...	...	...	...	...	...	...	...	...	...
			49	Indigo planters, managers, &c. ...	...	...	...	...	...	...	...	...	...	...	...	...	...	...	...
			50	Fruit growers	386	344	42	94	54	40	...	...	...	...	...	...	...	...	...
			51	Market gardeners (vegetable growers)	8,707	1,621	2,086	975	508	467	...	...	...	...	...	...	...	...	...
			52	Gardener, seedsmen, &c.	2,046	1,253	793	1,228	620	608	457	420	37	99	70	29	87	47	40
			53	Manure preparers and sellers (*sometimes also scavengers*)	22	12	10	...	...	...	...	...	...	...	...	...	...	...	...
			54	Forest Officers	23	17	6	...	...	...	...	...	...	...	...	...	...	...	...
			55	Forest Rangers, guards, peons ...	429	296	133	69	37	32	38	14	24	61	30	31	16	10	6
				Total Sub-order 12......	6,932	3,710	3,252	2,366	1,219	1,147	562	501	61	160	100	60	103	57	46
		13. Agricultural training and supervision.	56	Directors of Agriculture and their Assistants	7	4	3	7	4	3	...	...	...	...	...	...	...	...	...
			57	Model-Farm Managers, &c.	...	...	...	...	...	...	...	...	...	...	...	...	...	...	...
			58	Agents and Managers of landed estates (not planters)	13	5	8	13	5	8	...	...	...	...	...	...	...	...	...
				Total Sub-order 13......	20	9	11	20	9	11	...	...	...	...	...	...	...	...	...
				Total Order V......	5,178,329	2,658,814	2,519,515	10,436	4,775	5,661	124,136	62,509	61,627	277,686	139,830	137,856	259,300	131,885	127,415
Class C.	VI. Personal and household services.	14. Personal and domestic services.	59	Barbers	85,741	45,985	39,756	3,756	1,983	1,773	3,143	1,785	1,358	4,053	2,407	1,646	3,128	1,835	1,293
			60	Ear-pickers	...	...	...	...	...	...	...	...	...	...	...	...	...	...	...
			61	Tattooers	26	18	8	...	...	...	8	...	8	...	...	...	...	...	...
			62	Caste-mark appliers	...	...	...	...	...	...	...	...	...	...	...	...	...	...	...
			63	Washermen (*sometimes also dyers*) ...	157,901	78,903	78,998	5,151	2,626	2,525	8,446	4,254	4,192	13,065	6,449	6,616	15,256	7,741	7,515
			64	Water carriers	7,441	3,829	3,612	2,113	1,074	1,039	26	17	9	83	39	44	44	2	42
			65	Cooks	5,765	3,087	2,678	3,528	1,844	1,684	182	90	92	111	37	74	129	42	87
			66	Indoor servants...	372,235	204,803	167,432	77,231	42,187	35,044	14,721	7,950	6,771	29,895	10,288	19,607	14,453	8,398	6,055
			67	Grooms, coachmen and dog-boys, &c. ...	16,325	9,672	6,653	9,667	6,131	3,536	750	400	350	980	491	489	270	187	83
			68	Doorkeepers, &c.	2,519	1,585	934	3	1	2	...	...	...	...	...	...	...	...	...
				Total Sub-order 14......	647,953	347,882	300,071	101,449	55,846	45,603	27,276	14,496	12,780	48,187	19,711	28,476	33,280	18,205	15,075

TABLE XVII B.

Occupations by Districts.—*Continued.*

Class.	Order.	Sub-order and Group.	Serial No.	Occupations.	Warangal. Total.	Warangal. Males.	Warangal. Females.	Elgandal. Total.	Elgandal. Males.	Elgandal. Females.	Indur. Total.	Indur. Males.	Indur. Females.	Medak. Total.	Medak. Males.	Medak. Females.	Aurangabad. Total.	Aurangabad. Males.	Aurangabad. Females.
					21	22	23	24	25	26	27	28	29	30	31	32	33	34	35
Class B.—*concld.*	V. Agriculture.—*concld.*	11. Agricultural labourers.	42	Farm-servants	8,671	5,840	2,831	20,718	13,489	7,229	6,551	4,118	2,433	3,578	2,129	1,449	6,053	4,717	1,336
			43	Field labourers and crop-watchers ...	23,066	8,708	14,358	20,859	13,123	7,736	17,214	6,019	11,195	9,978	4,027	5,951	33,713	15,645	18,068
				Total Sub-order 11......	31,737	14,548	17,189	41,577	26,612	14,965	23,765	10,137	13,628	13,556	6,156	7,400	39,766	20,362	19,404
		12. Growers of special products and trees.	44	Tea, coffee and cinchona Planters, managers and assistants	...	...	...	...	...	...	...	...	...	...	...	...	...	...	...
			45	Cocoanut growers	...	...	...	...	...	...	...	...	...	...	...	...	...	...	...
			46	Betel-vine and areca-nut growers ...	...	...	...	...	...	...	120	1	119	52	52	...	105	43	62
			47	Waternut growers	...	...	...	...	...	...	...	...	...	...	...	...	...	...	...
			48	Cardamom and pepper growers ...	...	...	...	...	...	...	...	...	...	...	...	...	...	...	...
			49	Indigo planters, managers, &c. ...	...	...	...	...	...	...	...	...	...	...	...	...	...	...	...
			50	Fruit growers	68	59	9	...	...	...	...	...	...	...	...	...	289	289	...
			51	Market gardeners, (vegetable growers).	...	...	...	...	...	...	35	...	35	54	29	25	385	5	380
			52	Gardeners, seedsmen, &c.	...	...	...	112	69	43	...	...	...	31	10	21	6	6	...
			53	Manure preparers and sellers, (*sometimes also scavengers*)	...	...	...	...	...	...	...	...	...	...	...	...	...	...	...
			54	Forest Officers	...	...	...	...	...	...	...	...	...	...	...	...	23	17	6
			55	Forest Rangers, guards, peons ...	40	33	7	85	61	24	87	87	...	7	6	1	2	2	...
				Total Sub-order 12......	108	92	16	197	130	67	242	88	154	144	97	47	810	362	448
		13. Agricultural training and supervision.	56	Directors of Agriculture and their Assistants	...	...	...	...	...	...	...	...	...	...	...	...	...	...	...
			57	Model-Farm Managers, &c.	...	...	...	...	...	...	...	...	...	...	...	...	...	...	...
			58	Agents and Managers of landed estates (not planters)	...	...	...	...	...	...	...	...	...	...	...	...	...	...	...
				Total Sub-order 13......	...	...	...	...	...	...	...	...	...	...	...	...	...	...	...
				Total Order V......	375,683	192,873	182,810	380,989	210,538	170,451	257,584	131,526	126,058	125,208	64,984	60,224	418,048	213,998	204,050
Class C.	VI. Personal and household services.	14. Personal and domestic services.	59	Barbers	4,778	2,760	2,018	8,168	4,396	3,772	5,518	2,927	2,591	2,361	1,405	956	7,309	3,783	3,526
			60	Ear-pickers	...	...	...	...	...	...	...	...	...	...	...	...	...	...	...
			61	Tattooers	...	...	...	...	...	...	...	...	...	...	...	...	...	...	...
			62	Caste-mark appliers	...	...	...	...	...	...	...	...	...	...	...	...	...	...	...
			63	Washermen (*sometimes also dyers*) ...	21,264	10,693	10,571	29,078	15,192	13,886	14,477	6,954	7,523	7,173	3,465	3,708	3,410	1,650	1,760
			64	Water-carriers	66	49	17	23	4	19	125	57	68	36	17	19	985	554	431
			65	Cooks	113	96	17	75	28	47	76	26	50	34	18	16	160	38	122
			66	Indoor servants...	12,547	7,196	5,351	28,550	16,898	11,652	20,913	10,892	10,021	7,710	4,659	3,051	28,569	18,597	9,972
			67	Grooms, coachmen and dog-boys, &c....	374	202	172	288	206	82	177	146	31	374	256	118	868	202	666
			68	Doorkeepers, &c.	...	...	...	...	...	...	...	...	...	1	1	...	...	...	...
				Total Sub-order 14......	39,142	20,996	18,146	66,182	36,724	29,458	41,286	21,002	20,284	17,689	9,821	7,868	36,301	19,824	16,477

TABLE XVII B.

Occupations by Districts.—*Continued.*

Class.	Order.	Sub-order and Group.	Serial No.	Occupations.	Birh. Total.	Birh. Males.	Birh. Females.	Nander. Total.	Nander. Males.	Nander. Females.	Naldrug. Total.	Naldrug. Males.	Naldrug. Females.	Bidar. Total.	Bidar. Males.	Bidar. Females.	Parbhani. Total.	Parbhani. Males.	Parbhani. Females.
					36	37	38	39	40	41	42	43	44	45	46	47	48	49	50
Class B.—*concld.*	V. Agriculture.—*concld.*	11. Agricultural labourers.	42	Farm-servants	2,964	1,512	1,452	3,290	1,741	1,549	12,374	9,240	3,134	19,200	9,979	9,221	6,973	4,099	2,874
			43	Field labourers and crop-watchers ...	12,548	6,585	5,963	17,736	8,295	9,441	42,377	19,581	22,796	32,595	12,058	20,537	36,495	16,373	20,122
				Total Sub-order 11......	15,512	8,097	7,415	21,026	10,036	10,990	54,751	28,821	25,930	51,795	22,037	29,758	43,468	20,472	22,996
		12. Growers of special products and trees.	44	Tea, coffee and cinchona Planters, managers and assistants	...	...	...	...	...	...	...	...	...	...	...	...	...	...	...
			45	Cocoanut growers	...	...	...	...	...	...	...	...	...	...	...	...	...	...	...
			46	Betel-vine and areca-nut growers ...	4	4	...	...	...	...	1	...	1	...	...	...	...	...	...
			47	Waternut growers	...	...	...	...	...	...	...	...	...	...	...	...	...	...	...
			48	Cardamom and pepper growers ...	...	...	...	...	...	...	...	...	...	...	...	...	...	...	...
			49	Indigo planters, managers, &c. ...	...	...	...	...	...	...	...	...	...	...	...	...	...	...	...
			50	Fruit growers	76	73	3	227	137	90	166	92	74	220	220	...	740	278	462
			51	Market gardeners (vegetable growers)	...	...	...	...	...	...	...	...	...	...	...	...	...	...	...
			52	Gardeners, seedsmen, &c.	...	...	...	...	...	...	...	...	...	...	...	...	...	...	...
			53	Manure preparers and sellers (*sometimes also scavengers*)	...	...	...	7	...	7	6	3	3	...	...	...	...	...	...
			54	Forest Officers	...	...	...	...	...	...	...	...	...	...	...	...	...	...	...
			55	Forest Rangers, guards, peons ...	...	...	...	...	...	...	...	...	...	...	...	...	...	...	...
				Total Sub-order 12......	80	77	3	234	137	97	173	95	78	220	220	...	740	278	462
		13. Agricultural training and supervision.	56	Directors of Agriculture and their Assistants	...	...	...	...	...	...	...	...	...	...	...	...	...	...	...
			57	Model-Farm Managers, &c.	...	...	...	...	...	...	...	...	...	...	...	...	...	...	...
			58	Agents and Managers of landed estates (not planters)	...	...	...	...	...	...	...	...	...	...	...	...	...	...	...
				Total Sub-order 13......	...	...	...	...	...	...	...	...	...	...	...	...	...	...	...
				Total Order V......	316,913	163,842	153,071	320,278	165,233	155,045	350,340	179,705	170,635	407,411	205,070	202,341	428,418	217,302	211,116
Class. C.	VI. Personal and household services.	14. Personal and domestic services.	59	Barbers	5,652	2,852	2,800	5,394	2,750	2,644	4,910	2,600	2,310	7,116	3,622	3,494	7,345	3,831	3,514
			60	Ear-pickers	...	...	...	...	...	...	...	...	...	...	...	...	...	...	...
			61	Tattooers	18	18	...	...	...	...	...	...	...	...	...	...	...	...	...
			62	Caste-mark appliers	...	...	...	...	...	...	...	...	...	...	...	...	...	...	...
			63	Washermen (*sometimes also dyers*) ...	2,691	1,321	1,370	6,200	2,908	3,292	2,807	1,392	1,415	7,032	3,433	3,599	2,290	1,198	1,092
			64	Water-carriers	1,119	623	496	130	28	102	1,013	492	521	345	127	218	802	487	315
			65	Cooks	133	65	68	122	63	59	64	38	26	128	82	46	316	287	29
			66	Indoor servants	15,788	8,928	6,860	20,309	11,831	8,478	13,109	8,495	4,614	35,649	20,976	14,673	19,942	10,886	9,056
			67	Grooms, coachmen and dog-boys, &c.	355	232	123	130	80	50	257	146	111	320	147	173	695	410	285
			68	Doorkeepers, &c.	2,264	1,516	748	78	66	12	...	...	...	172	...	172	...	...	...
				Total Sub-order 14......	28,020	15,555	12,465	32,363	17,726	14,637	22,160	13,163	8,997	50,762	28,187	22,575	31,390	17,099	14,291

TABLE XVII B.

Occupations by Districts.—*Continued.*

Class.	Order.	Sub-order and Group.	Serial No.	Occupations.	Sirpur Tandur. Total.	Sirpur Tandur. Males.	Sirpur Tandur. Females.	Gulbarga. Total.	Gulbarga. Males.	Gulbarga. Females.	Raichur. Total.	Raichur. Males.	Raichur. Females.	Lingsugur. Total.	Lingsugur. Males.	Lingsugur. Females.	Railways. Total.	Railways. Males.	Railways. Females.
					51	52	53	54	55	56	57	58	59	60	61	62	63	64	65
Class B.—*concld.*	V. Agriculture.—*concld.*	11. Agricultural labourers.	42	Farm-servants	6,021	2,807	3,214	3,329	2,603	726	...	...	...	259	230	29	...	...	...
			43	Field labourers and crop-watchers ...	3,191	1,095	2,096	20,151	8,235	11,916	50,115	21,495	28,620	18,802	8,543	10,259	14	7	7
				Total Sub-order 11......	9,212	3,902	5,310	23,480	10,838	12,642	50,115	21,495	28,620	19,061	8,773	10,288	14	7	7
		12. Growers of special products and trees.	44	Tea, coffee and cinchona Planters, managers and assistants	...	...	...	...	...	...	...	...	...	...	...	...	...	...	...
			45	Cocoanut growers	...	...	...	...	...	...	...	...	...	...	...	...	...	...	...
			46	Betel-vine and areca-nut growers ...	...	...	...	...	...	...	...	...	...	...	...	...	...	...	...
			47	Waternut growers	...	...	...	...	...	...	...	...	...	...	...	...	...	...	...
			48	Cardamom and pepper growers ...	...	...	...	...	...	...	...	...	...	...	...	...	...	...	...
			49	Indigo planters, managers, &c. ...	...	...	...	...	...	...	...	...	...	...	...	...	...	...	...
			50	Fruit growers	...	...	...	...	...	...	...	...	...	...	...	...	...	...	...
			51	Market gardeners (vegetable growers).	...	...	...	...	...	...	...	...	...	...	...	...	3	1	2
			52	Gardeners, seedsmen, &c.	44	7	37	235	...	235	170	65	105	312	148	164	...	...	...
			53	Manure preparers and sellers (*sometimes also scavengers*)	...	...	...	...	...	...	16	6	10	2	2	...	8	8	5
			54	Forest Officers...	...	...	...	9	9	...	...	...	...	...	...	...	...	...	...
			55	Forest Rangers, guards, peons ...	...	...	...	...	...	...	16	12	4	8	4	4	...	...	...
				Total Sub-order 12......	44	7	37	244	9	235	202	83	119	322	154	168	11	4	7
		13. Agricultural training and supervision.	56	Directors of Agriculture and their Assistants	...	...	...	...	...	...	...	...	...	...	...	...	...	...	...
			57	Model-Farm Managers, &c.	...	...	...	...	...	...	...	...	...	...	...	...	...	...	...
			58	Agents and Managers of landed estates (not planters)	...	...	...	...	...	...	...	...	...	...	...	...	...	...	...
				Total Sub-order 13......	...	...	...	...	...	...	...	...	...	...	...	...	...	...	...
				Total Order V......	122,657	63,066	59,591	299,214	154,633	144,581	300,172	151,846	148,326	403,800	205,159	198,641	56	40	16
Class C.	VI. Personal and household services.	14. Personal and domestic services.	59	Barbers...	1,895	996	899	4,684	2,498	2,136	2,506	1,424	1,082	4,073	2,129	1,944	2	2	...
			60	Ear-pickers	...	...	...	...	...	...	...	...	...	...	...	...	...	...	...
			61	Tattooers	...	...	...	...	...	...	...	...	...	...	...	...	...	...	...
			62	Caste-mark appliers	...	...	...	...	...	...	...	...	...	...	...	...	...	...	...
			63	Washermen (*sometimes also dyers*) ...	3,436	1,725	1,711	4,154	2,120	2,034	6,960	3,378	3,582	5,009	2,402	2,607	2	2	...
			64	Water carriers...	14	4	10	244	119	125	105	50	55	93	57	36	75	29	46
			65	Cooks	23	13	10	126	71	55	154	74	80	185	73	62	156	102	54
			66	Indoor servants	6,854	4,136	2,718	15,355	8,759	6,596	7,951	4,257	3,694	7,618	4,421	3,197	71	49	22
			67	Grooms, coachmen and dog-boys, &c.	9	8	...	243	120	123	317	152	165	177	115	62	80	46	34
			68	Doorkeepers, &c.	1	1	...	...	...	...	...	...	...	...	...	...	...	...	...
				Total Sub-order 14......	12,226	6,878	5,348	24,756	13,687	11,069	17,993	9,335	8,658	17,105	9,197	7,908	386	230	156

TABLE XVII B.

Occupations by Districts.—*Continued.*

Class.	Order.	Sub-order and Group.	Serial No.	Occupations.	Grand Total. Total.	Grand Total. Males.	Grand Total. Females.	Hyderabad. Total.	Hyderabad. Males.	Hyderabad. Females.	Atraf-i-Balda. Total.	Atraf-i-Balda. Males.	Atraf-i-Balda. Females.	Mahabubnagar. Total.	Mahabubnagar. Males.	Mahabubnagar. Females.	Nalgonda. Total.	Nalgonda. Males.	Nalgonda. Females.
1	2	3	4	5	6	7	8	9	10	11	12	13	14	15	16	17	18	19	20
Class C.—*concld.*	VI. Personal and household services.	15. Non-domestic establishment.	69	Hotel, Lodging and Boarding house, Bar and Refreshment-room-keepers ...	360	188	172	230	127	103	...	...	...	1	...	1	14	1	13
			70	Rest-house, serai, Bathhouse, &c., owners and managers	13	10	3	7	4	3	...	...	...	...	...	...	...	...	...
			71	Club-Secretaries, managers, Stewards, &c	...	...	...	...	...	...	...	...	...	...	...	...	...	...	...
				Total Sub-order 15......	373	198	175	237	131	106	...	...	...	1	...	1	14	1	13
		16. Sanitation.	72	Sanitary Officers of Government ...	...	...	...	...	...	...	...	...	...	...	...	...	...	...	...
			73	Sanitary Inspectors, &c., Local and Municipal	249	168	81	23	15	8	...	...	...	...	...	...	...	...	...
			74	Sweepers and scavengers	3,046	1,338	1,708	1,506	741	765	18	13	5	86	43	43	5	1	4
			75	Dust and sweepings contractors ...	8	...	8	...	...	...	3	...	3	...	...	...	...	...	...
				Total Sub-order 16......	3,303	1,506	1,797	1,529	756	773	21	13	8	86	43	43	5	1	4
				Total Order VI......	651,629	349,586	302,043	103,215	56,733	46,482	27,297	14,509	12,788	48,274	19,754	28,520	33,299	18,207	15,092
Class II.—Preparation and supply of material substances.	VII. Food and drink.	17. Animal food.	76	Cow and buffalo-keepers and milk and butter sellers...	16,871	7,576	9,295	3,679	1,728	1,951	585	281	304	286	77	209	138	29	109
			77	Ghee preparers and sellers	1,436	376	1,060	23	14	9	42	18	24	90	54	36	12	8	4
			78	Cheese makers and sellers	...	...	...	...	...	...	...	...	...	...	...	...	...	...	...
			79	Butchers	21,704	11,091	10,613	4,444	2,397	2,047	1,394	740	654	1,643	917	726	674	392	282
			80	Fowl and egg dealers	405	186	219	182	91	91	36	29	7	66	21	45	12	5	7
			81	Fishermen and fish-curers (*many are also boatmen and palki bearers*) ...	38,535	19,709	18,826	1,146	564	582	283	94	189	8	8	...	450	432	18
			82	Fish dealers	12,872	7,053	5,819	418	228	190	1,068	663	405	1,927	1,082	845	1,647	654	993
				Total Sub-order 17......	91,823	45,991	45,832	9,887	5,017	4,870	3,358	1,775	1,583	4,020	2,159	1,861	2,938	1,520	1,418
		18. Vegetable food.	83	Grain dealers	90,486	46,973	43,513	6,604	3,686	2,918	5,201	2,261	2,940	11,170	5,789	5,381	5,788	3,405	2,383
			84	Grain parchers	3,824	1,428	2,396	268	126	142	279	127	152	293	165	128	105	12	93
			85	Pulse and flour preparers and sellers ...	1,984	473	1,511	143	49	94	44	10	34	38	11	27	5	...	5
			86	Flour-mill service and management ...	...	...	...	...	...	...	...	...	...	...	...	...	...	...	...
			87	Bakers	1,179	665	514	1,111	628	483	...	...	...	5	3	2	...	...	...
			88	Bran sellers	11	6	5	11	6	5	...	...	...	...	...	...	...	...	...
			89	Vegetable sellers	25,781	12,780	13,001	1,581	596	985	552	184	368	4,436	2,227	2,209	664	317	347
			90	Fruit sellers	24,996	12,505	12,491	1,227	538	689	237	108	129	148	...	148	902	464	438
			91	Cocoanut dealers	156	71	85	8	3	5	...	...	...	...	...	...	...	...	...

TABLE XVII B.

Occupations by Districts.—*Continued.*

Class.	Order.	Sub-order and Group.	Serial No.	Occupations.	Warangal. Total.	Warangal. Males.	Warangal. Females.	Elgandal. Total.	Elgandal. Males.	Elgandal. Females.	Indur. Total.	Indur. Males.	Indur. Females.	Medak. Total.	Medak. Males.	Medak. Females.	Aurangabad. Total.	Aurangabad. Males.	Aurangabad. Females.
					21	22	23	24	25	26	27	28	29	30	31	32	33	34	35
Class C.—*concld.*	VI. Personal and household services.—*concld.*	15. Non-domestic establishment.	69	Hotel, Lodging and Boarding house, Bar and Refreshment-room-keepers ...	42	26	16	...	...	...	...	...	...	16	...	16	18	18	...
			70	Rest-house, serai, Bathhouse, &c., owners and managers	...	...	...	...	...	...	...	...	...	...	...	...	6	6	...
			71	Club-Secretaries, managers, Stewards, &c.	...	...	...	...	...	...	...	...	...	...	...	...	...	...	...
				Total Sub-order 15	42	26	16	...	...	...	...	...	...	16	...	16	19	19	...
		16. Sanitation.	72	Sanitary Officers of Government ...	...	...	...	...	...	...	...	...	...	...	...	...	...	...	...
			73	Sanitary Inspectors, &c., Local and Municipal	58	52	6	...	...	...	...	...	...	74	49	84	...	...	...
			74	Sweepers and scavengers	3	...	3	141	1	140	139	26	113	47	3	44	509	246	268
			75	Dust and sweepings contractors ...	...	...	...	...	...	...	...	...	...	...	...	...	5	...	5
				Total Sub-order 16	61	52	9	141	1	140	139	26	113	121	48	78	514	246	268
				Total Order VI	89,245	21,074	18,171	66,323	86,725	29,598	41,425	21,028	20,897	17,826	9,864	7,962	86,834	20,089	16,745
Class D.—Preparation and supply of material substances.	VII. Food and drink.	17. Animal food.	76	Cow and buffalo-keepers and milk and butter sellers	540	156	884	2,216	535	1,681	156	100	56	871	615	256	2,191	1,149	1,042
			77	Ghee preparers and sellers	128	50	78	1,022	164	858	15	10	5	6	4	2	13	6	7
			78	Cheese makers and sellers	...	...	...	...	...	...	...	...	...	...	...	...	...	...	...
			79	Butchers...	601	251	350	582	268	819	517	870	147	994	558	441	1,796	882	914
			80	Fowl and egg dealers	20	20	...	25	...	25	...	...	...	16	14	2	9	6	3
			81	Fishermen and fish-curers (*many are also boatmen and palki bearers*) ...	1,263	884	879	15,817	7,992	7,825	9,896	5,099	4,797	112	107	5	588	7	581
			82	Fish dealers	755	422	838	...	...	...	8,820	2,059	1,761	1,458	824	634	573	578	...
				Total Sub-order 17	8,307	1,283	2,024	19,162	8,954	10,208	14,404	7,638	6,766	8,457	2,117	1,340	5,170	2,623	2,547
		18. Vegetable food.	83	Grain dealers	8,488	1,550	1,938	15,584	8,411	7,178	6,894	8,645	2,749	4,558	2,608	1,950	1,550	921	629
			84	Grain parchers	517	26	491	124	48	81	255	78	182	256	102	154	115	57	58
			85	Pulse and flour preparers and sellers ...	19	14	5	46	18	28	175	5	170	123	1	122	494	128	366
			86	Flour-mill service and management ...	...	...	...	...	...	...	...	...	...	...	...	...	...	...	...
			87	Bakers	7	4	3	6	4	2	...	...	...	17	6	11	...	...	...
			88	Bran sellers	...	...	...	...	...	...	...	...	...	...	...	...	...	...	...
			89	Vegetable sellers	8,412	1,386	2,026	5,085	2,811	2,274	617	402	215	343	272	71	1,286	680	606
			90	Fruit sellers	8,317	1,662	1,655	16,785	8,457	8,278	96	...	96	135	69	66	219	135	84
			91	Cocoanut dealers	...	...	...	...	...	...	...	...	...	...	...	...	...	...	...

TABLE XVII B.

Occupations by Districts.—*Continued.*

Class.	Order.	Sub-order and Group.	Serial No.	Occupations.	Birh. Total.	Birh. Males.	Birh. Females.	Nander. Total.	Nander. Males.	Nander. Females.	Naldrug. Total.	Naldrug. Males.	Naldrug. Females.	Bidar. Total.	Bidar. Males.	Bidar. Females.	Parbhani. Total.	Parbhani. Males.	Parbhani. Females.
					36	37	38	39	40	41	42	43	44	45	46	47	48	49	50
Class C.—*concld.*	VI. Personal and household services.—*concld.*	15. Non-domestic establishment.	69	Hotel, Lodging and Boarding house, Bar and Refreshment-room-keepers ...	16	16	...	...	...	...	...	...	...	...	...	...	...	...	...
			70	Rest-house, serai, Bathhouse &c., owners and managers	...	...	...	...	...	...	...	...	...	...	...	...	...	...	...
			71	Club-Secretaries, managers, Stewards,&c.	...	...	...	...	...	...	...	...	...	...	...	...	...	...	...
				Total Sub-order 15	16	16	...	...	...	...	...	...	...	...	...	...	...	...	...
		16. Sanitation.	72	Sanitary Officers of Government ...	...	...	...	...	...	...	...	...	...	...	...	...	...	...	...
			73	Sanitary Inspectors, &c., Local and Municipal	94	61	33	...	...	...	...	...	...	...	...	...	...	...	...
			74	Sweepers and scavengers	46	40	6	15	2	13	21	8	13	20	12	8	193	84	109
			75	Dust and sweepings contractors ...	...	...	...	...	...	...	...	...	...	...	...	...	...	...	...
				Total Sub-order 16	140	101	39	15	2	13	21	8	13	20	12	8	193	84	109
				Total Order VI......	28,176	15,672	12,504	32,378	17,728	14,650	22,181	13,171	9,010	50,782	28,399	22,383	31,583	17,183	14,400
Class D.—Preparation and supply of material substances.	VII. Food and drink.	17. Animal food.	76	Cow and buffalo-keepers and milk and butter sellers	871	464	407	675	299	376	451	235	216	1,408	619	789	1,114	597	517
			77	Ghee preparers and sellers	...	...	...	...	...	...	6	...	6	67	86	31	12	12	...
			78	Cheese makers and sellers	...	...	...	...	...	...	...	...	...	...	...	...	...	...	...
			79	Butchers	732	388	344	857	437	420	386	189	197	2,178	1,061	1,117	1,614	792	822
			80	Fowl and egg dealers	...	...	...	...	...	...	...	...	...	20	...	20	...	...	...
			81	Fishermen and fish-curers (*many are also boatmen and palki bearers*) ...	1,055	587	468	2,214	1,298	916	414	210	204	134	89	45	460	112	348
			82	Fish dealers	...	...	...	...	...	...	...	...	...	260	160	100	...	...	...
				Total Sub-order 17	2,658	1,439	1,219	3,746	2,034	1,712	1,257	634	623	4,067	1,965	2,102	3,200	1,518	1,687
		18. Vegetable food.	83	Grain dealers	1,304	742	562	2,666	917	1,749	1,147	647	500	10,946	4,776	6,170	1,715	886	829
			84	Grain parchers	241	121	120	81	41	40	119	52	67	274	99	175	504	245	259
			85	Pulse and flour preparers and sellers ...	26	...	26	220	57	163	75	16	59	182	44	138	273	87	186
			86	Flour-mill service and management ...	...	...	...	...	...	...	...	...	...	...	...	...	...	...	...
			87	Bakers	...	...	...	...	...	...	...	...	...	...	...	...	...	...	...
			88	Bran sellers	...	...	...	...	...	...	...	...	...	...	...	...	...	...	...
			89	Vegetable sellers	1,567	619	948	989	500	489	911	464	447	2,244	1,081	1,163	63	63	...
			90	Fruit sellers	74	4	70	...	...	...	104	5	99	14	14	...	1,615	988	627
			91	Cocoanut dealers	...	...	...	...	...	...	...	...	...	...	...	...	...	...	...

TABLE XVII B.

Occupations by Districts.—*Continued.*

Class.	Order.	Sub-order and Group.	Serial No.	Occupations.	Sirpur Tandur. Total.	Sirpur Tandur. Males.	Sirpur Tandur. Females.	Gulbarga. Total.	Gulbarga. Males.	Gulbarga. Females.	Raichur. Total.	Raichur. Males.	Raichur. Females.	Lingasugur. Total.	Lingasugur. Males.	Lingasugur. Females.	Railways. Total.	Railways. Males.	Railways. Females.
					51	52	53	54	55	56	57	58	59	60	61	62	63	64	65
Class C.—*concld.*	VI. Personal and household services.—*concld.*	15. Non-domestic establishment.	69	Hotel, Lodging and Boarding house, Bar and Refreshment-room-keepers ...	...	...	...	18	5	18	10	...	10	...	...	...	...	...	...
			70	Rest-house, serai, Bathhouse, &c., owners and managers	...	...	...	...	...	...	...	...	...	...	...	...	...	...	...
			71	Club-Secretaries, managers, Stewards, &c.	...	...	...	...	...	...	...	...	...	...	...	...	...	...	...
				Total Sub-order 15	...	...	...	18	5	13	10	...	10	...	...	...	...	...	...
		16. Sanitation.	72	Sanitary Officers of Government ...	...	...	...	...	...	...	...	...	...	...	...	...	...	...	...
			73	Sanitary Inspectors, &c., Local and Municipal	...	...	...	...	...	...	...	...	...	...	...	...	...	...	...
			74	Sweepers and scavengers	13	1	12	28	4	19	201	78	128	2	1	1	58	34	24
			75	Dust and sweepings contractors ...	...	...	...	...	...	...	...	...	...	...	...	...	...	...	...
				Total Sub-order 16	13	1	12	28	4	19	201	78	128	2	1	1	58	34	24
				Total Order VI	12,239	6,879	5,360	24,797	13,696	11,101	18,204	9,413	8,791	17,107	9,198	7,909	444	264	180
Class D.—Preparation and supply of material substances.	VII. Food and drink.	17. Animal food.	76	Cow and buffalo-keepers and milk and butter sellers	294	63	231	733	320	413	858	159	199	851	196	155	4	4	...
			77	Ghee preparers and sellers	...	...	...	...	...	...	...	...	...	...	...	...	...	...	...
			78	Cheese makers and sellers	...	...	...	...	...	...	...	...	...	...	...	...	...	...	...
			79	Butchers	106	42	64	968	248	720	1,431	788	643	785	379	406	7	7	...
			80	Fowl and egg dealers	...	...	...	...	...	...	19	...	19	...	...	...	...	...	...
			81	Fishermen and fish-curers (*many are also boatmen and palki bearers*) ...	4,014	2,110	1,904	166	56	110	970	559	411	45	1	44	...	...	...
			82	Fish dealers	...	...	...	202	202	...	222	164	58	27	27	...	...	...	...
				Total Sub-order 17	4,414	2,215	2,199	2,064	821	1,248	3,000	1,670	1,380	1,208	603	605	11	11	...
		18. Vegetable food.	83	Grain dealers	1,538	700	838	5,581	3,327	2,254	3,398	1,770	1,628	1,847	927	920	7	5	2
			84	Grain parchers	19	5	14	5	...	5	869	134	285	...	...	...	...	...	...
			85	Pulse and flour preparers and sellers ...	...	...	...	105	22	83	16	11	5	...	...	...	...	...	...
			86	Flour-mill service and management ...	...	...	...	...	...	...	...	...	...	...	...	...	...	...	...
			87	Bakers	...	...	...	...	...	...	33	20	13	...	...	...	...	...	...
			88	Bran sellers	...	...	...	...	...	...	...	...	...	...	...	...	...	...	...
			89	Vegetable sellers...	83	39	44	1,060	674	386	586	255	331	402	210	192	...	...	...
			90	Fruit sellers	8	...	8	...	...	...	137	39	98	23	18	5	5	4	1
			91	Cocoanut dealers	...	...	...	...	...	...	...	...	...	148	68	80	...	...	...

TABLE XVII B.

Occupations by Districts.—*Continued.*

Class.	Order.	Sub-order and Group.	Serial No.	Occupations.	Grand Total.			Hyderabad.			Atraf-i-Balda.			Mahabubnagar.			Nalgonda.		
					Total.	Males.	Females.	Total.	Males.	Females.	Total.	Males.	Females.	Total.	Males.	Females.	Total.	Males.	Females.
1	2	3	4	5	6	7	8	9	10	11	12	13	14	15	16	17	18	19	20
Class D.—Preparation and supply of material substances.—*contd.*	VII. Food and drink.—*concld.*	18. Vegetable food.—*concld.*	92	Confectioners and sweetmeat makers and sellers, and cooks who are also sometimes fishermen and water-carriers	5,122	2,603	2,519	658	896	262	543	210	333	360	134	226	49	14	35
			93	Sweetmeat pedlars	181	117	64	181	117	64	...	...	...	...	...	...	...	...	...
				Total Sub-order 18......	153,720	77,621	76,099	11,742	6,145	5,597	6,856	2,900	3,956	16,450	8,329	8,121	7,513	4,212	3,301
		19. Drink condiments and narcotics.	94	Ice manufacturers and sellers	300	181	119	112	54	58	1	...	1	...	...	...	...	...	...
			95	Sodawater, Lemonade, &c., manufacturers and sellers	24	8	16	21	7	14	...	...	...	...	...	...	...	...	...
			96	Sharbat preparers and sellers	20	14	6	5	3	2	...	...	...	...	...	...	...	...	...
			97	Country spirits distillers, and sellers ...	62,666	30,220	32,446	1,369	701	668	4,681	2,063	2,618	3,883	2,354	1,529	27,426	11,506	15,920
			98	Toddydrawers, and sellers	209,229	111,361	97,868	3,418	1,635	1,783	25,101	13,419	11,682	21,324	11,581	9,743	18,997	11,889	7,108
			99	Foreign wine and spirit dealers ...	472	209	263	443	209	234	...	...	...	...	...	...	...	...	...
			100	Brewers	...	...	...	...	...	...	...	...	...	...	...	...	...	...	...
			101	Tea sellers and tasters, (not planters) ...	104	75	29	104	75	29	...	...	...	...	...	...	...	...	...
			102	Coffee preparers and sellers, (not planters)	13	4	9	13	4	9	...	...	...	...	...	...	...	...	...
			103	Sugar manufacturers and sellers ...	106	90	16	...	...	...	...	...	...	...	...	...	6	2	4
			104	Molasses (Jaggery, Gur, &c.), makers and sellers	689	243	446	49	23	26	...	...	...	3	3	...	7	4	3
			105	Salt preparers and sellers	13,509	7,874	5,635	39	21	18	49	9	40	482	291	191	243	176	67
			106	Assafœtida, turmeric, &c., sellers ...	7,527	3,577	3,950	21	14	7	2,356	1,065	1,291	21	20	1	4,365	2,108	2,257
			107	Vinegar manufacturers and sellers ...	13	8	5	10	6	4	...	...	...	...	...	...	...	...	...
			108	Pickle makers and sellers	33	12	21	5	1	4	...	...	...	1	...	1	...	...	...
			109	Grocers and general condiment dealers..	100,393	56,648	43,745	867	516	351	1,406	692	714	8,222	4,605	3,617	5,413	3,065	2,348
			110	Cardamom preparers and dealers ...	...	...	...	...	...	...	...	...	...	...	...	...	...	...	...
			111	Betel leaf and areca-nut sellers ...	13,927	7,170	6,757	1,380	667	713	412	162	250	646	335	311	277	79	198
			112	Tobacco and snuff manufacturers and sellers	2,814	1,347	1,467	542	267	275	151	117	34	121	77	44	17	3	14
			113	Prepared hukka pedlars	9	2	7	9	2	7	...	...	...	...	...	...	...	...	...
			114	Opium, &c., manufacturers and sellers..	608	321	287	100	59	41	2	...	2	1	1	...	8	8	...
			115	Bhang, ganja, &c., preparers and sellers.	172	68	104	31	12	19	15	8	7	...	...	...	...	...	...
				Total Sub-order 19......	412,628	219,432	193,196	8,538	4,276	4,262	34,174	17,535	16,639	34,704	19,267	15,437	56,759	28,840	27,919
				Total Order VII......	657,671	343,044	314,627	30,167	15,438	14,729	44,388	22,210	22,178	55,174	29,755	25,419	67,205	34,572	32,633

TABLE XVII B.

Occupations by Districts.—*Continued.*

Class.	Order.	Sub-order and Group.	Serial No.	Occupations.	Warangal. Total.	Warangal. Males.	Warangal. Females.	Elgandal. Total.	Elgandal. Males.	Elgandal. Females.	Indur. Total.	Indur. Males.	Indur. Females.	Medak. Total.	Medak. Males.	Medak. Females.	Aurangabad. Total.	Aurangabad. Males.	Aurangabad. Females.
					21	22	23	24	25	26	27	28	29	30	31	32	33	34	35
Class D.—Preparation and supply of material substances.—*contd.*	VII. Food and drink.—*concld.*	18. Vegetable food.—*concld.*	92	Confectioners and sweetmeat makers and sellers, and cooks who are also sometimes fishermen and water-carriers	163	100	63	174	141	83	94	47	47	75	31	44	1,076	530	546
			93	Sweetmeat pedlars	...	...	...	...	...	...	...	...	...	...	...	...	...	...	...
				Total Sub-order 18......	10,923	4,742	6,181	37,754	19,885	17,869	7,631	4,172	3,459	5,507	3,089	2,418	4,740	2,451	2,289
		19. Drink condiments and narcotics.	94	Ice manufacturers and sellers	...	...	...	...	...	...	98	49	49	...	...	...	1	...	1
			95	Sodawater, Lemonade, &c., manufacturers and sellers...	...	...	...	...	...	...	...	...	...	...	...	...	2	...	2
			96	Sharbat preparers and sellers	...	...	...	...	...	...	15	11	4	...	...	...	...	...	...
			97	Country spirits distillers, and sellers ...	1,137	772	365	1,379	790	589	3,945	2,344	1,601	2,062	919	1,143	2,438	1,216	1,222
			98	Toddydrawers, and sellers	40,387	20,457	19,930	55,194	28,507	26,687	8,583	4,433	4,150	14,297	7,532	6,765	482	336	146
			99	Foreign wine and spirit dealers... ...	...	...	...	...	...	...	...	...	...	29	...	29	...	...	...
			100	Brewers	...	...	...	...	...	...	...	...	...	...	...	...	...	...	...
			101	Tea sellers and tasters (not planters) ...	...	...	...	...	...	...	...	...	...	...	...	...	...	...	...
			102	Coffee preparers and sellers (not planters)	...	...	...	...	...	...	...	...	...	...	...	...	...	...	...
			103	Sugar manufacturers and sellers ...	...	...	...	...	...	...	...	...	...	6	...	6	...	...	...
			104	Molasses (Jaggery, Gur, &c.), makers and sellers	4	4	...	51	8	43	18	15	3	...	...	...	26	26	...
			105	Salt preparers and sellers	3,925	2,856	1,069	4,202	2,163	2,039	73	...	73	102	...	102	54	30	24
			106	Assafœtida, turmeric, &c., sellers ...	152	152	...	17	3	14	2	2	...	521	195	326	...	...	...
			107	Vinegar manufacturers and sellers ...	...	...	...	...	...	...	...	...	...	...	...	...	3	2	1
			108	Pickle makers and sellers	...	...	...	...	...	...	...	...	...	...	...	...	...	...	...
			109	Grocers and general condiment dealers.	1,292	878	414	1,477	1,014	463	9,742	6,509	3,233	2,444	1,627	817	10,478	5,757	4,721
			110	Cardamom preparers and dealers ...	...	...	...	...	...	...	...	...	...	...	...	...	...	...	...
			111	Betel leaf and areca-nut sellers ...	121	70	51	116	55	61	883	243	140	259	122	137	1,835	941	894
			112	Tobacco and snuff manufacturers and sellers	103	82	21	120	40	80	213	51	162	71	42	29	503	179	324
			113	Prepared hukka pedlars	...	...	...	...	...	...	...	...	...	...	...	...	...	...	...
			114	Opium, &c., manufacturers and sellers.	13	8	5	6	1	5	12	8	4	7	3	4	129	62	67
			115	Bhang, ganja, &c., preparers and sellers.	...	...	...	...	...	...	6	6	...	7	3	4	8	...	8
				Total Sub-order 19......	47,134	25,279	21,855	62,562	32,581	29,981	23,090	13,671	9,419	19,805	10,443	9,362	15,959	8,549	7,410
				Total Order VII......	61,364	31,304	30,060	119,478	61,420	58,058	45,125	25,481	19,644	28,769	15,649	13,120	25,869	13,623	12,246

TABLE XVII B.

Occupations by Districts.—*Continued.*

Class.	Order.	Sub-order and Group.	Serial No.	Occupations.	Birh. Total.	Birh. Males.	Birh. Females.	Nander. Total.	Nander. Males.	Nander. Females.	Naldrug. Total.	Naldrug. Males.	Naldrug. Females.	Bidar. Total.	Bidar. Males.	Bidar. Females.	Parbhani. Total.	Parbhani. Males.	Parbhani. Females.
					36	37	38	39	40	41	42	43	44	45	46	47	48	49	50
Class D.—Preparation and supply of material substances,—*contd.*	VII. Food and drink.—*concld.*	18. Vegetable food.—*concld.*	92	Confectioners and sweetmeat makers and sellers, and cooks who are also sometimes fishermen and water-carriers	269	101	168	189	97	92	224	140	84	227	115	112	431	220	211
			93	Sweetmeat pedlars	...	...	...	...	...	...	...	...	...	...	...	...	...	...	...
				Total Sub-order 18......	3,481	1,587	1,894	4,095	1,612	2,483	2,580	1,824	1,256	13,887	6,129	7,758	4,601	2,489	2,112
		19. Drink condiments and narcotics.	94	Ice manufacturers and sellers	...	...	...	...	...	...	72	72	...	...	...	...	...	...	...
			95	Sodawater, Lemonade, &c., manufacturers and sellers	...	...	...	...	...	...	...	...	...	...	...	...	1	1	...
			96	Sharbat preparers and sellers	...	...	...	...	...	...	...	...	...	...	...	...	...	...	...
			97	Country spirits distillers, and sellers ...	924	534	390	2,212	993	1,219	990	471	519	3,326	2,094	1,232	1,821	856	965
			98	Taddydrawers, and sellers	212	158	54	1,565	960	605	283	129	154	4,078	2,283	1,795	963	462	501
			99	Foreign wine and spirit dealers ...	...	...	...	...	...	...	...	...	...	...	...	...	...	...	...
			100	Brewers...	...	...	...	...	...	...	...	...	...	...	...	...	...	...	...
			101	Tea sellers and tasters (not planters) ...	...	...	...	...	...	...	...	...	...	...	...	...	...	...	...
			102	Coffee preparers and sellers (not planters)	...	...	...	...	...	...	...	...	...	...	...	...	...	...	...
			103	Sugar manufacturers and sellers ...	...	...	...	...	...	...	...	...	...	46	40	6	48	48	...
			104	Molasses (Jaggery, Gur, &c.,) makers and sellers	1	1	...	...	...	...	279	44	285	42	8	34	...	...	...
			105	Salt preparers and sellers	7	7	...	5	...	5	87	80	7	9	...	9	24	12	12
			106	Assafœtida, turmeric, &c., sellers ...	...	...	...	...	...	...	85	2	82	...	...	...	...	...	...
			107	Vinegar manufacturers and sellers ...	...	...	...	...	...	...	...	...	...	...	...	...	...	...	...
			108	Pickle makers and sellers	...	...	...	...	...	...	...	...	...	...	...	...	...	...	...
			109	Grocers and general condiment dealers..	6,855	4,099	2,756	7,881	4,329	3,552	6,408	3,423	2,985	10,092	5,604	4,488	10,111	5,201	4,910
			110	Cardamom preparers and dealers ...	...	...	...	...	...	...	...	...	...	...	...	...	...	...	...
			111	Betel leaf and areca-nut sellers ...	1,428	772	656	724	426	298	2,247	1,153	1,094	1,183	617	571	1,418	765	653
			112	Tobacco and snuff manufacturers and sellers	18	5	13	38	12	26	19	1	18	281	202	79	190	82	108
			113	Prepared hukka pedlars	...	...	...	...	...	...	...	...	...	...	...	...	...	...	...
			114	Opium, &c., manufacturers and sellers..	85	47	38	49	12	37	65	16	49	23	16	7	40	32	8
			115	Bhang, ganja, &c., preparers and sellers.	...	...	...	21	4	17	6	1	5	31	12	19	...	...	...
				Total Sub-order 19......	9,530	5,623	3,907	12,495	6,736	5,759	10,441	5,343	5,098	19,116	10,876	8,240	14,616	7,459	7,157
				Total Order VII......	15,669	8,649	7,020	20,336	10,382	9,954	14,278	7,301	6,977	87,070	18,970	18,100	22,417	11,461	10,956

TABLE XVII B.

Occupations by Districts.—*Continued.*

Class.	Order.	Sub-order and Group.	Serial No.	Occupations.	Sirpur Tandur. Total.	Sirpur Tandur. Males.	Sirpur Tandur. Females.	Gulbarga. Total.	Gulbarga. Males.	Gulbarga. Females.	Raichur. Total.	Raichur. Males.	Raichur. Females.	Lingasugur. Total.	Lingasugur. Males.	Lingasugur. Females.	Railways. Total.	Railways. Males.	Railways. Females.
					51	52	53	54	55	56	57	58	59	60	61	62	63	64	65
Class D.—Preparation and supply of material substances.—*concld.*	VII. Food and drink.—*concld.*	18. Vegetable food.—*concld.*	92	Confectioners and sweetmeat makers and sellers, and cooks who are also sometimes fishermen and water-carriers	11	5	6	184	113	71	158	86	72	234	121	113	8	2	1
			93	Sweetmeat pedlars	...	...	...	...	...	...	...	...	...	...	...	...	...	...	...
				Total Sub-order 18......	1,659	749	910	6,935	4,136	2,799	4,697	2,315	2,382	2,654	1,344	1,310	15	11	4
		19. Drink, condiments and narcotics.	94	Ice manufacturers and sellers	...	...	...	16	6	10	...	...	...	...	...	...	...	...	...
			95	Sodawater, Lemonade, &c., manufacturers and sellers	...	...	...	...	...	...	...	...	...	...	...	...	...	...	...
			96	Sharbat preparers and sellers	...	...	...	...	...	...	...	...	...	...	...	...	...	...	...
			97	Country spirits distillers, and sellers ...	1,057	591	466	2,518	1,306	1,212	785	446	339	711	262	449	2	2	...
			98	Toddydrawers, and sellers	1,039	451	588	6,441	3,270	3,171	4,334	2,421	1,913	2,531	1,438	1,093	...	...	...
			99	Foreign wine and spirit dealers ...	...	...	...	...	...	...	...	...	...	...	...	...	...	...	...
			100	Brewers...	...	...	...	...	...	...	...	...	...	...	...	...	...	...	...
			101	Tea sellers and tasters (not planters) ...	...	...	...	...	...	...	...	...	...	...	...	...	...	...	...
			102	Coffee preparers and sellers (not planters)	...	...	...	...	...	...	...	...	...	...	...	...	...	...	...
			103	Sugar manufacturers and sellers ...	...	...	...	...	...	...	...	...	...	...	...	...	...	...	...
			104	Molasses (Jaggery, Gur, &c.,) makers and sellors	...	...	...	...	...	...	84	21	13	175	86	89	...	...	...
			105	Salt preparers and sellers	...	...	...	7	...	7	2,369	1,336	1,033	1,882	943	989	...	...	...
			106	Assafœtida, turmeric, &c., sellers ...	...	...	...	...	...	...	19	7	12	18	8	10	...	...	...
			107	Vinegar manufacturers and sellers ...	...	...	...	...	...	...	...	...	...	...	...	...	...	...	...
			108	Pickle makers and sellers	8	...	8	...	...	...	19	11	8	...	...	...	...	...	...
			109	Grocers and general condiment dealers..	1,827	639	1,188	7,593	4,587	3,006	3,172	1,649	1,523	5,097	2,443	2,654	16	11	5
			110	Cardamom preparers and dealers ...	...	...	...	...	...	...	...	...	...	...	...	...	...	...	...
			111	Betel leaf and areca-nut sellers ...	209	97	112	541	302	239	460	243	217	281	119	162	2	2	...
			112	Tobacco and snuff manufacturers and sellers	81	12	19	82	50	32	117	73	44	197	52	145	...	...	...
			113	Prepared hukka pedlars	...	...	...	...	...	...	...	...	...	...	...	...	...	...	...
			114	Opium, &c., manufacturers and sellers.	7	7	...	...	...	...	2	1	1	59	40	19	...	...	...
			115	Bhang, ganja, &c., preparers and sellers.	...	...	...	...	...	...	47	22	25	...	...	...	...	...	...
				Total Sub-order 19......	4,178	1,797	2,381	17,198	9,521	7,677	11,358	6,230	5,128	10,951	5,391	5,560	20	15	5
				Total Order VII......	10,251	4,761	5,490	26,197	14,478	11,719	19,055	10,215	8,840	14,818	7,338	7,475	46	37	9

TABLE XVII B.

Occupations by Districts.—*Continued.*

Class.	Order.	Sub-order and Group.	Serial No.	Occupations.	Grand Total. Total.	Grand Total. Males.	Grand Total. Females.	Hyderabad. Total.	Hyderabad. Males.	Hyderabad. Females.	Atraf-i-Balda. Total.	Atraf-i-Balda. Males.	Atraf-i-Balda. Females.	Mahabubnagar. Total.	Mahabubnagar. Males.	Mahabubnagar. Females.	Nalgonda. Total.	Nalgonda. Males.	Nalgonda. Females.
1	2	3	4	5	6	7	8	9	10	11	12	13	14	15	16	17	18	19	20
Class D.—Preparation and supply of material substances.—*contd.*	VIII. Light, firing and forage.	20. Lighting.	116	Oil-pressers and sellers	53,885	27,079	26,306	472	240	282	1,288	568	670	2,083	1,053	980	989	470	519
			117	Oil and salt sellers	159	42	117	74	34	40	4	...	4	...	...	...	...	...	...
			118	Oilcake dealers...	643	429	214	...	...	...	...	...	...	178	133	45	898	250	148
			119	Candle makers and sellers	11	11	...	11	11	...	...	...	...	...	...	...	...	...	...
			120	Torch makers and sellers	100	54	46	60	31	29	...	...	...	...	...	...	...	...	...
			121	Kerosine oil dealers	45	32	13	18	6	12	...	...	...	...	...	...	...	...	...
			122	Matches makers and sellers	24	9	15	24	9	15	...	...	...	...	...	...	...	...	...
			123	Lamp and lantern makers and sellers...	109	61	48	100	56	44	...	...	...	...	...	...	...	...	...
			124	Gas workers, Gas Company Managers, &c.	...	...	...	...	...	...	...	...	...	...	...	...	...	...	...
				Total Sub-order 20......	54,476	27,717	26,759	759	387	372	1,237	563	674	2,231	1,186	1,025	1,387	720	667
		21. Fuel and forage.	125	Firewood and grass gatherers and sellers	35,952	15,631	20,321	2,832	1,078	1,754	3,475	1,584	1,891	6,838	3,150	3,688	1,374	573	801
			126	Firewood contractors and dealers ...	255	99	156	88	43	45	10	10	...	...	...	...	...	...	...
			127	Coal miners, &c....	...	...	...	...	...	...	...	...	...	...	...	...	...	...	...
			128	Coal dealers, brokers, Coal Company Managers, &c....	21	8	13	...	...	...	...	...	...	...	...	...	...	...	...
			129	Charcoal burners and dealers	488	274	214	63	34	29	23	20	3	7	3	4	45	25	20
			130	Cowdung-fuel preparers and sellers (*are often also scavengers*)	544	104	440	70	14	56	64	35	29	7	...	7	65	...	65
			131	Hay, &c., contractors and dealers ...	953	244	709	659	114	545	85	81	4	...	...	...	...	...	...
				Total Sub-order 21......	38,218	16,360	21,853	3,712	1,283	2,429	3,657	1,730	1,927	6,852	3,153	3,699	1,484	598	886
				Total Order VIII......	92,689	44,077	48,612	4,471	1,670	2,801	4,894	2,293	2,601	9,063	4,339	4,724	2,871	1,318	1,553
	IX. Building.	22. Building materials.	132	Brick and tile burners and sellers ...	967	512	455	702	368	334	56	29	27	16	15	1	3	1	2
			133	Lime, chunám and shell burners and sellers	1,922	1,120	802	193	90	103	261	144	117	498	382	116	67	43	24
			134	Stone-quarry owners, contractors, marble dealers, &c.	1,727	1,188	589	40	22	18	...	...	...	290	231	59	...	...	...
			135	Thatch dealers and thatchers	189	93	96	47	26	21	2	2	...	...	...	...	...	...	...
				Total Sub-order 22......	4,805	2,913	1,892	982	506	476	319	175	144	804	628	176	70	44	26

TABLE XVII B.

Occupations by Districts.—*Continued.*

Class.	Order.	Sub-order and Group.	Serial No.	Occupations.	Warangal. Total.	Warangal. Males.	Warangal. Females.	Elgandal. Total.	Elgandal. Males.	Elgandal. Females.	Indur. Total.	Indur. Males.	Indur. Females.	Medak. Total.	Medak. Males.	Medak. Females.	Aurangabad. Total.	Aurangabad. Males.	Aurangabad. Females.
					21	22	23	24	25	26	27	28	29	30	31	32	33	34	35
Class D.—Preparation and supply of material substances.—*contd.*	VIII Light, firing and forage.	20. Lighting.	116	Oil-pressers and sellers	1,855	856	999	4,961	2,518	2,443	3,018	1,535	1,483	984	472	462	7,424	3,820	3,604
			117	Oil and salt sellers	81	8	73	...	...	...	...	...	...	...	...	...	...	...	...
			118	Oilcake dealers	35	30	5	...	...	...	...	...	...	...	...	...	...	...	...
			119	Candle makers and sellers	...	...	...	...	...	...	...	...	...	...	...	...	...	...	...
			120	Torch makers and sellers	...	...	...	...	...	...	...	...	...	...	...	...	...	...	...
			121	Kerosine oil dealers	...	...	...	...	...	...	40	23	17	...	...	...	...	...	...
			122	Matches makers and sellers	...	...	...	...	...	...	...	...	...	...	...	...	1	...	1
			123	Lamp and lantern makers and sellers ...	...	...	...	...	...	...	...	...	...	...	...	...	...	...	...
			124	Gas workers, Gas Company Managers, &c.	...	...	...	...	...	...	...	...	...	...	...	...	...	...	...
				Total Sub-order 20......	1,971	894	1,077	4,961	2,518	2,443	3,058	1,558	1,500	984	472	462	7,425	3,820	3,605
		21. Fuel and forage.	125	Firewood and grass gatherers and sellers	1,486	675	811	1,278	463	815	3,342	1,709	1,633	463	266	197	2,207	713	1,494
			126	Firewood contractors and dealers ...	...	...	...	...	...	...	...	...	...	...	...	...	157	46	111
			127	Coal miners, &c...	...	...	...	...	...	...	...	...	...	...	...	...	...	...	...
			128	Coal dealers, brokers, Coal Company Managers, &c...	21	8	13	...	...	...	...	...	...	...	...	...	...	...	...
			129	Charcoal burners and dealers	...	...	...	111	83	28	89	50	39	...	...	...	70	31	39
			130	Cowdung-fuel preparers and sellers (*are often also scavengers*)	8	...	8	7	...	7	14	10	4	153	...	153	60	27	33
			131	Hay, &c., contractors and dealers ...	...	...	...	...	...	...	...	...	...	...	...	...	4	4	...
				Total Sub-order 21	1,515	683	832	1,396	546	850	3,445	1,769	1,676	616	266	350	2,498	821	1,677
				Total Order VIII	3,486	1,577	1,909	6,357	3,064	3,293	6,503	3,327	3,176	1,550	738	812	9,923	4,641	5,282
	IX. Buildings.	22. Building materials.	132	Brick and tile burners and sellers ...	19	16	3	3	...	3	9	9	...	...	...	...	...	...	...
			133	Lime, chunám and shell burners and sellers	41	24	17	24	13	11	17	8	9	...	...	...	127	60	67
			134	Stone-quarry owners, contractors, marble dealers, &c.	42	42	...	...	...	...	...	...	...	10	10	...	66	18	48
			135	Thatch dealers and thatchers	...	...	...	...	...	...	...	...	...	11	11	...	17	12	5
				Total Sub-order 22	102	82	20	27	13	14	26	17	9	21	21	...	210	90	120

TABLE XVII B.

Occupations by Districts.—*Continued.*

Class.	Order.	Sub-order and Group.	Serial No.	Occupations.	Birh. Total.	Birh. Males.	Birh. Females.	Nander. Total.	Nander. Males.	Nander. Females.	Naldrug. Total.	Naldrug. Males.	Naldrug. Females.	Bidar. Total.	Bidar. Males.	Bidar. Females.	Parbhani. Total.	Parbhani. Males.	Parbhani. Females.
					36	37	38	39	40	41	42	43	44	45	46	47	48	49	50
Class D.—Preparation and supply of material substances.—*contd.*	VIII. Light, firing and forage.	20. Lighting.	116	Oil-pressers and sellers...	4,917	2,493	2,424	3,251	1,612	1,639	5,450	2,732	2,718	4,650	2,406	2,244	5,845	2,950	2,895
			117	Oil and salt sellers	...	...	...	...	...	...	...	...	...	...	...	...	...	...	...
			118	Oilcake dealers	...	...	...	...	...	...	...	...	...	...	...	...	...	...	...
			119	Candle makers and sellers	...	...	...	...	...	...	...	...	...	...	...	...	...	...	...
			120	Torch makers and sellers	...	...	...	...	...	...	...	...	...	...	...	...	...	...	...
			121	Kerosine oil dealers	26	26	...	...	...	...	...	...	...	...	...	...	...	...	...
			122	Matches makers and sellers	...	...	...	...	...	...	...	...	...	...	...	...	...	...	...
			123	Lamp and lantern makers and sellers...	9	5	4	...	...	...	...	...	...	...	...	...	...	...	...
			124	Gas workers, Gas Company Managers, &c.	...	...	...	...	...	...	...	...	...	...	...	...	...	...	...
				Total Sub-order 20	4,952	2,524	2,428	3,251	1,612	1,639	5,450	2,732	2,718	4,650	2,406	2,244	5,845	2,950	2,895
		21. Fuel and forage.	125	Firewood and grass gatherers and sellers	1,168	546	622	1,648	705	943	688	408	280	1,272	610	662	2,414	1,166	1,248
			126	Firewood contractors and dealers ...	...	...	...	...	...	...	...	...	...	...	...	...	...	...	...
			127	Coal miners, &c.	...	...	...	...	...	...	...	...	...	...	...	...	...	...	...
			128	Coal dealers, brokers, Coal Company Managers, &c.	...	...	...	...	...	...	...	...	...	...	...	...	...	...	...
			129	Charcoal burners and dealers	14	2	12	...	...	...	...	...	...	45	10	35	9	7	2
			130	Cowdung-fuel preparers and sellers (*are often also scavengers*)	...	...	...	...	...	...	42	3	39	35	15	20	12	...	12
			131	Hay, &c., contractors and dealers ...	...	...	...	...	...	...	42	42	...	...	...	...	1	...	1
				Total Sub-order 21	1,182	548	634	1,648	705	943	772	453	319	1,352	635	717	2,436	1,173	1,263
				Total Order VIII	6,134	3,072	3,062	4,899	2,317	2,582	6,222	3,185	3,037	6,002	3,041	2,961	8,281	4,123	4,158
	IX. Buildings.	22. Building materials.	132	Brick and tile burners and sellers ...	5	2	3	...	...	...	...	...	...	...	...	...	2	...	2
			133	Lime, chunám and shell burners and sellers	119	20	99	28	28	...	46	24	22	316	239	77	86	4	82
			134	Stone-quarry owners, contractors, marble dealers, &c.	...	...	...	...	...	...	...	...	...	...	...	...	...	...	...
			135	Thatch dealers and thatchers	106	40	66	...	...	...	3	...	3	...	...	...	3	2	1
				Total Sub-order 22	230	62	168	28	28	...	49	24	25	316	239	77	91	6	85

TABLE XVII B.

Occupations by Districts.—*Continued.*

Class.	Order.	Sub-order and Group.	Serial No.	Occupations.	Sirpur Tandur. Total.	Sirpur Tandur. Males.	Sirpur Tandur. Females.	Gulbarga. Total.	Gulbarga. Males.	Gulbarga. Females.	Raichur. Total.	Raichur. Males.	Raichur. Females.	Lingasugur. Total.	Lingasugur. Males.	Lingasugur. Females.	Railways. Total.	Railways. Males.	Railways. Females.
					51	52	53	54	55	56	57	58	59	60	61	62	63	64	65
Class D.—Preparation and supply of material substances.—*contd.*	VIII. Light, firing and forage.	20. Lighting.	116	Oil-pressers and sellers	1,146	591	555	2,971	1,648	1,323	956	497	459	1,280	623	657	...	...	...
			117	Oil and salt sellers	...	...	...	...	...	...	...	...	...	...	...	...	...	...	...
			118	Oilcake dealers...	...	...	...	...	...	...	...	...	...	...	...	...	...	...	...
			119	Candle makers and sellers	...	...	...	...	...	...	32	16	16	...	...	...	...	...	...
			120	Torch makers and sellers	...	...	...	...	...	...	...	...	...	...	...	...	...	...	...
			121	Kerosine oil dealers	...	...	...	...	...	...	...	...	...	...	...	...	...	...	...
			122	Matches makers and sellers	...	...	...	...	...	...	...	...	...	...	...	...	...	...	...
			123	Lamp and lantern makers and sellers ...	...	...	...	...	...	...	...	...	...	...	...	...	...	...	...
			124	Gas workers, Gas Company Managers, &c.	...	...	...	...	...	...	...	...	...	...	...	...	...	...	...
				Total Sub-order 20	1,146	591	555	2,971	1,648	1,323	988	513	475	1,280	623	657	...	...	...
		21. Fuel and forage.	125	Firewood and grass gatherers and sellers	301	115	186	1,531	602	929	2,808	845	1,963	823	422	401	4	1	3
			126	Firewood contractors and dealers ...	...	...	...	...	...	...	...	...	...	...	...	...	...	...	...
			127	Coal miners, &c....	...	...	...	...	...	...	...	...	...	...	...	...	...	...	...
			128	Coal dealers, brokers, Coal Company Managers, &c....	...	...	...	...	...	...	...	...	...	...	...	...	...	...	...
			129	Charcoal burners and dealers	...	...	...	...	...	...	6	3	3	6	6	...	...	...	...
			130	Cowdung-fuel preparers and sellers, (*are often also scavengers*)	...	...	...	7	...	7	...	...	...	...	...	...	...	...	...
			131	Hay, &c., contractors and dealers ...	...	...	...	...	...	...	162	3	159	...	...	...	...	...	...
				Total Sub-order 21	301	115	186	1,538	602	936	2,976	851	2,125	829	428	401	4	1	3
				Total Order VIII	1,447	706	741	4,509	2,250	2,259	3,964	1,364	2,600	2,109	1,051	1,058	4	1	3
	IX. Buildings.	22. Building materials.	132	Brick and tile burners and sellers ...	...	...	...	...	...	...	16	5	11	...	...	...	9	7	2
			133	Lime, chunám and shell burners and sellers	...	...	...	69	33	86	19	12	7	72	38	34	...	...	...
			134	Stone-quarry owners, contractors, marble dealers, &c.	...	...	...	156	154	2	413	214	199	776	515	261	...	...	...
			135	Thatch dealers and thatchers... ...	...	...	...	...	...	...	...	...	...	...	...	...	...	...	...
				Total Sub-order 22......	...	...	...	225	187	88	448	281	217	848	553	295	9	7	2

TABLE XVII B.

Occupations by Districts.—*Continued.*

Class.	Order.	Sub-order and Group.	Serial No.	Occupations.	Grand Total. Total.	Grand Total. Males.	Grand Total. Females.	Hyderabad. Total.	Hyderabad. Males.	Hyderabad. Females.	Atraf-i-Balda. Total.	Atraf-i-Balda. Males.	Atraf-i-Balda. Females.	Mahabubnagar. Total.	Mahabubnagar. Males.	Mahabubnagar. Females.	Nalgonda. Total.	Nalgonda. Males.	Nalgonda. Females.
1	2	3	4	5	6	7	8	9	10	11	12	13	14	15	16	17	18	19	20
Class D.—Preparation and supply of material substances.—*contd.*	IX. Buildings—*concld.*	23. Artificers in building.	136	Building contractors	151	44	107	...	...	...	...	...	...	...	...	...	...	...	...
			137	Stone and marble workers	4,794	2,592	2,202	581	273	258	31	19	12	646	383	263	...	...	...
			138	Masons	84,512	18,721	15,791	8,085	1,641	1,444	2,094	1,232	862	4,371	2,428	1,943	992	468	524
			139	Builders and Joiners	4,174	3,172	1,002	8	...	8	61	61	...	...	...	...	8,394	2,632	762
			140	Plasterers and house painters	70	25	45	9	8	6	...	...	...	...	...	...	1	1	...
			141	Mud wall and roof builders	12,285	6,662	5,623	77	42	35	192	132	60	...	...	...	8,161	1,065	2,096
			142	Plumbers and glaziers	60	50	10	11	4	7	...	...	...	...	...	...	...	...	...
			143	Tilers and tile-turners	8	5	3	...	...	...	...	...	...	6	8	8	...	...	...
				Total Sub-order 23	56,054	31,271	24,783	3,716	1,963	1,753	2,378	1,444	934	5,023	2,814	2,209	7,548	4,166	3,382
				Total Order IX	60,859	34,184	26,675	4,698	2,469	2,229	2,697	1,619	1,078	5,827	3,442	2,385	7,618	4,210	3,408
	X. Vehicles and vessels.	24. Railway plant.	144	Railway mechanics (Fitters, painters, boiler makers, rivetters, &c.)... ...	481	268	213	373	199	174	...	...	...	...	...	...	...	...	...
			145	Railway permanent-way Foremen, plate-layers, Inspectors, &c.	589	404	185	21	15	6	...	...	...	...	...	...	...	...	...
				Total Sub-order 24	1,070	672	398	394	214	180	...	...	...	...	...	...	...	...	...
		25. Carts, carriages, &c.	146	Cart makers, carriage makers and sellers	2,460	1,440	1,020	103	60	43	453	292	161	747	356	391	456	359	97
			147	Palki, Dandi, Rickshaw, &c., makers and sellers	19	8	11	13	6	7	2	2	...	...	...	...	2	...	2
				Total Sub-order 25	2,479	1,448	1,031	116	66	50	455	294	161	747	356	391	458	359	99
		26. Ships and boats.	148	Shipwrights, boat-builders, &c. ...	...	...	...	...	...	...	...	...	...	...	...	...	...	...	...
			149	Boat and ship painters, tarrers, &c. ...	...	...	...	...	...	...	...	...	...	...	...	...	...	...	...
			150	Sail makers	...	...	...	...	...	...	...	...	...	...	...	...	...	...	...
			151	Wicker-boat-makers, canoe diggers, &c. .	...	...	...	...	...	...	...	...	...	...	...	...	...	...	...
			152	Ship chandlers and marine store dealers.	...	...	...	...	...	...	...	...	...	...	...	...	...	...	...
				Total Sub-order 26	...	...	...	...	...	...	...	...	...	...	...	...	...	...	...
				Total Order X	8,549	2,120	1,429	510	280	230	455	294	161	747	356	391	458	359	99
	XI. Supplementary requirements.	27. Paper, &c.	153	Paper makers and sellers, and palmleaf binders	1,779	941	838	94	45	49	39	27	32	201	93	108	26	14	12
			154	Stationers	153	126	27	9	6	3	...	...	...	1	1	...	...	...	...
			155	Waste paper and rag dealers	...	...	...	...	...	...	...	...	...	...	...	...	...	...	...
			156	Waxed-cloth preparers and sellers ...	...	...	...	...	...	...	...	...	...	...	...	...	...	...	...
				Total Sub-order 27	1,932	1,067	865	103	51	52	59	27	32	202	94	108	26	14	12

TABLE XVII B.

Occupations by Districts.—*Continued.*

Class.	Order.	Sub-order and Group.	Serial No.	Occupations.	Warangal. Total.	Warangal. Males.	Warangal. Females.	Elgandal. Total.	Elgandal. Males.	Elgandal. Females.	Indur. Total.	Indur. Males.	Indur. Females.	Medak. Total.	Medak. Males.	Medak. Females.	Aurangabad. Total.	Aurangabad. Males.	Aurangabad. Females.
					21	22	23	24	25	26	27	28	29	30	31	32	33	34	35
Class D.—Preparation and supply of material substances.—*contd.*	IX. Buildings.—*concld.*	23. Artificers in building.	136	Building contractors	...	...	...	91	...	91	43	29	14	...	...	...	...	...	...
			137	Stone and marble workers	823	156	167	259	165	94	3	3	...	139	79	60	...	...	...
			138	Masons	2,458	1,211	1,247	1,962	1,139	823	629	378	251	690	476	214	1,625	865	760
			139	Builders and Joiners	556	857	199	115	99	16	8	...	8	6	...	6	11	5	6
			140	Plasterers and house painters	...	...	...	...	...	...	...	...	...	...	...	...	...	...	...
			141	Mud wall and roof builders	1,962	1,505	457	1,756	978	778	360	191	169	240	76	164	1,793	1,112	681
			142	Plumbers and glaziers	...	...	...	...	...	...	...	...	...	...	...	...	...	...	...
			143	Tilers and tile-turners	2	2	...	...	...	...	...	...	...	...	...	...	...	...	...
				Total Sub-order 23	5,301	3,231	2,070	4,183	2,381	1,802	1,038	601	437	1,075	631	444	3,429	1,982	1,447
				Total Order IX	5,408	3,318	2,090	4,210	2,394	1,816	1,064	618	446	1,096	652	444	3,689	2,072	1,567
	X. Vehicles and vessels.	24. Railway plant.	144	Railway mechanics (Fitters, painters, boiler makers, rivetters, &c.)	...	...	...	12	11	1	...	...	...	...	...	...	...	...	.
			145	Railway permanent-way Foremen, plate-layers, Inspectors, &c.	...	...	...	...	...	...	...	...	...	...	...	...	...	...	...
				Total Sub-order 24	...	...	...	12	11	1	...	...	...	...	...	...	...	...	...
		25. Carts, carriages, &c.	146	Cart makers, carriage makers and sellers	177	118	59	27	16	11	8	...	8	102	21	81	133	14	119
			147	Palki, Dandi, Rickshaw, &c., makers and sellers	...	...	...	2	...	2	...	...	...	...	...	...	...	...	...
				Total Sub-order 25	177	118	59	29	16	13	8	...	8	102	21	81	133	14	119
		26. Ships and boats.	148	Shipwrights, boat-builders, &c. ...	...	...	...	...	...	...	...	...	...	...	...	...	...	...	...
			149	Boat and ship painters, tarrers, &c. ...	...	...	...	...	...	...	...	...	...	...	...	...	...	...	...
			150	Sail makers	...	...	...	...	...	...	...	...	...	...	...	...	...	...	...
			151	Wicker-boat-makers, canoe diggers, &c.	...	...	...	...	...	...	...	...	...	...	...	...	...	...	...
			152	Ship chandlers and marine store dealers.	...	...	...	...	...	...	...	...	...	...	...	...	...	...	...
				Total Sub-order 26	...	...	...	...	...	...	...	...	...	...	...	...	...	...	...
				Total Order X	177	118	59	41	27	14	8	...	8	102	21	81	133	14	119
	XI. Supplementary requirements.	27. Paper, &c.	153	Paper makers and sellers, and palmleaf binders	...	...	...	547	483	64	101	60	41	170	2	168	422	144	278
			154	Stationers	...	...	...	3	...	3	...	...	...	...	...	...	33	33	...
			155	Waste paper and rag dealers	...	...	...	...	...	...	...	...	...	...	...	...	...	...	...
			156	Waxed-cloth preparers and sellers ...	...	...	...	...	...	...	...	...	...	...	...	...	...	...	...
				Total Sub-order 27	...	...	...	550	483	67	101	60	41	170	2	168	455	177	278

TABLE XVII B.
Occupations by Districts.

TABLE XVII B.

Occupations by Districts.—*Continued.*

Class.	Order	Sub-order and Group.	Serial No.	Occupations.	Birh. Total.	Birh. Males.	Birh. Females.	Nander. Total.	Nander. Males.	Nander. Females.	Naldrug. Total.	Naldrug. Males.	Naldrug. Females.	Bidar. Total.	Bidar. Males.	Bidar. Females.	Parbhani. Total.	Parbhani. Males.	Parbhani. Females.
					36	37	38	39	40	41	42	43	44	45	46	47	48	49	50
Class D.—Preparation and supply of material substances.—*contd.*	IX. Buildings.—*concld.*	23. Artificers in building.	136	Building contractors	...	...	...	...	...	...	...	...	...	...	...	...	9	9	...
			137	Stone and marble workers	...	...	...	...	...	...	35	35	...	...	...	...	5	5	...
			138	Masons	1,191	570	621	2,436	1,391	1,045	1,459	767	692	3,544	1,925	1,619	3,202	1,808	1,899
			139	Builders and Joiners	...	...	...	...	...	...	18	18	...	...	...	...	...	...	...
			140	Plasterers and house painters	...	...	...	...	...	...	...	...	...	...	...	...	...	...	...
			141	Mud wall and roof builders	112	95	17	55	23	32	62	56	6	818	408	410	292	81	211
			142	Plumbers and glaziers	...	...	...	...	...	...	...	...	...	...	...	...	...	...	...
			143	Tilers and tile-turners	...	...	...	...	...	...	...	...	...	...	...	...	...	...	...
				Total Sub-order 23	1,303	665	638	2,491	1,414	1,077	1,574	876	698	4,362	2,333	2,029	3,508	1,898	1,610
				Total Order IX	1,533	727	806	2,519	1,442	1,077	1,623	900	723	4,678	2,572	2,106	3,599	1,904	1,695
	X. Vehicles and vessels.	24. Railway plant.	144	Railway mechanics (Fitters, painters, boiler makers, rivetters, &c.)	...	...	...	...	...	...	...	...	...	...	...	...	...	...	...
			145	Railway permanent-way Foremen, plate-layers, Inspectors, &c.	...	...	...	...	...	...	...	...	...	...	...	...	...	...	...
				Total Sub-order 24	...	...	...	...	...	...	...	...	...	...	...	...	...	...	...
		25. Carts, carriages, &c.	146	Cart makers, carriage makers and sellers	78	78	...	79	76	3	36	10	26	8	8	...	...	...	...
			147	Palki, Dandi, Rickshaw, &c., makers and sellers	...	...	...	...	...	...	...	...	...	...	...	...	...	...	...
				Total Sub-order 25	78	78	...	79	76	3	36	10	26	8	8	...	...	...	...
		26. Ships and boats.	148	Shipwrights, boat-builders, &c.	...	...	...	...	...	...	...	...	...	...	...	...	...	...	...
			149	Boat and ship painters, tarrers, &c.	...	...	...	...	...	...	...	...	...	...	...	...	...	...	...
			150	Sail makers	...	...	...	...	...	...	...	...	...	...	...	...	...	...	...
			151	Wicker-boat-makers, canoe diggers, &c.	...	...	...	...	...	...	...	...	...	...	...	...	...	...	...
			152	Ship chandlers and marine store dealers	...	...	...	...	...	...	...	...	...	...	...	...	...	...	...
				Total Sub-order 26	...	...	...	...	...	...	...	...	...	...	...	...	...	...	...
				Total Order X	78	78	...	79	76	3	36	10	26	8	8	...	...	...	...
	XI. Supplementary requirements.	27. Paper, &c.	153	Paper makers and sellers, and palmleaf binders	...	...	...	13	10	3	35	21	14	22	15	7	33	...	33
			154	Stationers	24	7	17	...	...	...	...	...	...	4	...	4	79	79	...
			155	Waste paper and rag dealers	...	...	...	...	...	...	...	...	...	...	...	...	...	...	...
			156	Waxed-cloth preparers and sellers	...	...	...	...	...	...	...	...	...	...	...	...	...	...	...
				Total Sub-order 27	24	7	17	13	10	3	35	21	14	26	15	11	112	79	33

TABLE XVII B.

Occupations by Districts.—*Continued.*

Class.	Order.	Sub-order and Group.	Serial No.	Occupations.	Sirpur Tandur. Total.	Sirpur Tandur. Males.	Sirpur Tandur. Females.	Gulbarga. Total.	Gulbarga. Males.	Gulbarga. Females.	Raichur. Total.	Raichur. Males.	Raichur. Females.	Lingasugur. Total.	Lingasugur. Males.	Lingasugur. Females.	Railways. Total.	Railways. Males.	Railways. Females.
					51	52	53	54	55	56	57	58	59	60	61	62	63	64	65
Class D.—Preparation and supply of material substances.—*contd.*	IX. Buildings.—*concld.*	23. Artificers in building.	136	Building contractors	...	...	...	...	...	...	8	6	2	...	...	...	...	...	...
			137	Stone and marble Workers	...	...	...	...	...	...	2,027	1,068	959	795	406	889	...	...	...
			138	Masons	166	82	134	2,106	1,182	924	560	321	239	1,916	871	1,045	26	21	5
			139	Builders and Joiners	...	...	...	...	...	7	...	7	...	...	...	...	...	...	...
			140	Plasterers and house painters	...	...	...	...	...	...	5	...	5	55	21	34	...	...	...
			141	Mud wall and roof builders	191	155	86	484	395	89	413	240	178	817	108	209	...	...	...
			142	Plumbers and glaziers	...	...	...	87	37	...	...	...	...	...	...	...	12	9	8
			143	Tilers and tile-turners	...	...	...	...	...	...	...	...	...	...	...	...	...	...	...
				Total Sub-order 23	357	187	170	2,634	1,614	1,020	3,013	1,635	1,378	3,083	1,406	1,677	38	30	8
				Total Order IX......	357	187	170	2,859	1,801	1,058	3,461	1,866	1,595	3,931	1,959	1,972	47	37	10
	X. Vehicles and vessels.	24. Railway plant.	144	Railway mechanics (Fitters, painters, boiler makers, rivetters, &c.)	...	...	...	...	...	...	11	8	3	...	...	...	85	50	35
			145	Railway permanent-way Foremen, plate-layers, Inspectors, &c.	...	...	...	...	...	...	9	6	3	...	...	...	559	383	176
				Total Sub-order 24......	...	...	...	...	...	...	20	14	6	...	...	...	644	433	211
		25. Carts, carriages, &c.	146	Cart makers, carriage makers and sellers	...	...	...	...	...	...	53	32	21	...	...	...	...	...	...
			147	Palki, Dandi, Rickshaw, &c., makers and sellers	...	...	...	...	...	...	...	...	...	...	...	...	...	...	...
				Total Sub-order 25......	...	...	...	...	...	...	53	32	21	...	...	...	...	...	...
		26. Ships and boats.	148	Shipwrights, boat builders, &c. ...	...	...	...	...	...	...	...	...	...	...	...	...	...	...	...
			149	Boat and ship painters, tarrers, &c. ...	...	...	...	...	...	...	...	...	...	...	...	...	...	...	...
			150	Sail makers	...	...	...	...	...	...	...	...	...	...	...	...	...	...	...
			151	Wicker-boat-makers, canoe diggers, &c.	...	...	...	...	...	...	...	...	...	...	...	...	...	...	...
			152	Ship chandlers and marine store dealers.	...	...	...	...	...	...	...	...	...	...	...	...	...	...	...
				Total Sub-order 26......	...	...	...	...	...	...	...	...	...	...	...	...	...	...	...
				Total Order X......	...	...	...	...	...	...	73	46	27	...	...	...	644	433	211
	XI. Supplementary requirements.	27. Paper, &c.	153	Paper makers and sellers, and palmleaf binders...	6	...	6	35	21	14	15	6	9	...	...	...	...	...	...
			154	Stationers	...	...	...	...	...	...	...	...	...	...	...	...	...	...	...
			155	Waste paper and rag dealers	...	...	...	...	...	...	...	...	...	...	...	...	...	...	...
			156	Waxed-cloth preparers and sellers ...	...	...	...	...	...	...	...	...	...	...	...	...	...	...	...
				Total Sub-order 27......	6	...	6	35	21	14	15	6	9	...	...	...	...	...	...

TABLE XVII B.
Occupations by Districts.

TABLE XVII B.

Occupations by Districts.—*Continued.*

Class.	Order	Sub-orders and Group.	Serial No.	Occupations.	Grand Total. Total.	Grand Total. Males.	Grand Total. Females.	Hyderabad. Total.	Hyderabad. Males.	Hyderabad. Females.	Atraf-i-Balda. Total.	Atraf-i-Balda. Males.	Atraf-i-Balda. Females.	Mahabubnagar. Total.	Mahabubnagar. Males.	Mahabubnagar. Females.	Nalgonda. Total.	Nalgonda. Males.	Nalgonda. Females.
1	2	3	4	5	6	7	8	9	10	11	12	13	14	15	16	17	18	19	20
Class D.—Preparation and supply of material substances,—*contd.*	XI. Supplementary requirements.—*contd.*	28. Books & Prints, &c.	157	Press proprietors, Lithographers and Printers	507	294	213	385	202	183	22	15	7	7	5	2	...	...	...
			158	Book-binders	170	108	62	127	66	61	15	15	...	...	...	...	...	...	...
			159	Book-sellers and publishers	314	120	194	152	83	69	...	...	...	6	3	3	...	...	...
			160	Newspaper proprietors and managers ...	59	27	32	59	27	32	...	...	...	...	...	...	...	...	...
			161	News Agents, Book Agents and Newspaper sellers, &c.	5	3	2	5	3	2	...	...	...	...	...	...	...	...	...
			162	Print and picture dealers	28	7	21	...	...	...	2	...	2	...	...	...	1	...	1
				Total Sub-order 28	1,083	559	524	728	381	347	39	30	9	13	8	5	1	...	1
		29. Watches, clocks, and scientific instruments.	163	Watch and-clock makers and sellers ...	233	131	102	202	113	89	...	...	...	7	4	3	...	...	...
			164	Opticians...	...	...	...	...	...	...	...	...	...	...	...	...	...	...	...
			165	Surgical Instrument makers and sellers	...	...	...	...	...	...	...	...	...	...	...	...	...	...	...
			166	Photographic apparatus dealers	...	...	...	...	...	...	...	...	...	...	...	...	...	...	...
			167	Other scientific instrument makers, menders and sellers	...	...	...	...	...	...	...	...	...	...	...	...	...	...	...
			168	Scale makers and sellers	...	...	...	...	...	...	...	...	...	...	...	...	...	...	...
				Total Sub-order 29	233	131	102	202	113	89	...	...	...	7	4	3	...	...	...
		30. Carving, engraving, &c.	169	Wood and ebony carvers	13	9	4	13	9	4	...	...	...	...	...	...	...	...	...
			170	Ivory carvers	...	...	...	...	...	...	...	...	...	...	...	...	...	...	...
			171	Cotton-stamp makers and sellers ...	...	...	...	...	...	...	...	...	...	...	...	...	...	...	...
			172	Turners and lacquerers...	28	12	16	2	2	...	...	...	...	...	...	...	...	...	...
			173	Die-sinkers and seal, &c., engravers ...	33	18	15	33	18	15	...	...	...	...	...	...	...	...	...
			174	Type-founders	...	...	...	...	...	...	...	...	...	...	...	...	...	...	...
			175	Mica, flint and Talc workers and sellers.	22	1	21	...	...	...	21	...	21	...	...	...	...	...	...
			176	Mosaic and Alabaster workers and sellers	...	...	...	...	...	...	...	...	...	...	...	...	...	...	...
				Total Sub-order 30	96	40	56	48	29	19	21	...	21	...	...	...	...	...	...
		Toys, curiosities, &c.	177	Toy, kite, and cage makers and sellers. Bird stuffers	155	125	30	27	23	4	1	1	...	56	55	1	41	26	15
			178	Hukka-stem makers and sellers ...	143	85	58	134	78	56	...	...	...	...	...	...	...	...	...
			179	Papier-maché workers and sellers ...	377	...	377	...	...	...	...	...	...	...	...	...	...	...	...
			180	Card-makers and sellers	...	...	...	...	...	...	...	...	...	...	...	...	...	...	...
			181	Tábut and Tázia makers and sellers ...	26	26	...	...	...	...	...	...	...	...	...	...	...	...	...
			182	Curiosity dealers	23	14	9	23	14	9	...	...	...	...	...	...	...	...	...
				Total Sub-order 31	724	250	474	184	115	69	1	1	...	56	55	1	41	26	15

TABLE XVII B.

Occupations by Districts.—*Continued.*

Class.	Order.	Sub-order and Group.	Serial No.	Occupations.	Warangal. Total.	Warangal. Males.	Warangal. Females.	Elgandal. Total.	Elgandal. Males.	Elgandal. Females.	Indur. Total.	Indur. Males.	Indur. Females.	Medak. Total.	Medak. Males.	Medak. Females.	Aurangabad. Total.	Aurangabad. Males.	Aurangabad. Females.
					21	22	23	24	25	26	27	28	29	30	31	32	33	34	35
Class D.—Preparation and supply of material substances.—*contd.*	XI. Supplementary requirements.—*contd.*	28. Books & Prints, &c.	157	Press proprietors, Lithographers and Printers	40	37	3	...	...	...	3	3	...	9	9	...	2	1	1
			158	Book-binders	...	...	...	...	...	...	...	...	...	...	...	...	3	3	...
			159	Book-sellers and publishers	2	2	...	2	2	...	101	...	101	...	...	...	2	...	2
			160	Newspaper proprietors and managers ...	...	...	...	...	...	...	...	...	...	...	...	...	...	...	...
			161	News Agents, Book Agents and News-paper sellers, &c.	...	...	...	...	...	...	...	...	...	...	...	...	...	...	...
			162	Print and picture dealers	...	...	...	...	...	...	6	...	6	...	...	...	...	...	...
				Total Sub-order 28	42	39	3	2	2	...	110	3	107	9	9	...	7	4	3
		29. Watches, clocks, and scientific instruments.	163	Watch and clock makers and sellers ...	...	...	...	1	1	...	...	...	...	3	3	...	6	5	1
			164	Opticians...	...	...	...	...	...	...	...	...	...	...	...	...	...	...	...
			165	Surgical Instrument makers and sellers	...	...	...	...	...	...	...	...	...	...	...	...	...	...	...
			166	Photographic apparatus dealers... ...	...	...	...	...	...	...	...	...	...	...	...	...	...	...	...
			167	Other scientific instrument makers, menders and sellers	...	...	...	...	...	...	...	...	...	...	...	...	...	...	...
			168	Scale makers and sellers	...	...	...	...	...	...	...	...	...	...	...	...	...	...	...
				Total Sub-order 29	...	...	...	1	1	...	...	...	...	3	3	...	6	5	1
		30. Carving, engraving, &c.	169	Wood and ebony carvers	...	...	...	...	...	...	...	...	...	...	...	...	...	...	...
			170	Ivory carvers	...	...	...	...	...	...	...	...	...	...	...	...	...	...	...
			171	Cotton-stamp makers and sellers ...	...	...	...	...	...	...	...	...	...	...	...	...	...	...	...
			172	Turners and lacquerers...	...	...	...	...	...	...	...	...	...	15	...	15	...	...	...
			173	Die-sinkers and seal, &c., engravers ...	...	...	...	...	...	...	...	...	...	...	...	...	...	...	...
			174	Type-founders	...	...	...	...	...	...	...	...	...	...	...	...	...	...	...
			175	Mica, flint and Talc workers and sellers.	...	...	...	...	...	...	...	...	...	...	...	...	...	...	...
			176	Mosaic and Alabaster workers and sellers	...	...	...	...	...	...	...	...	...	...	...	...	...	...	...
				Total Sub-order 30	...	...	...	...	...	...	...	...	...	15	...	15	...	...	...
		Toys, curiosities, &c.	177	Toy, kite, and cage makers and sellers. Bird stuffers	2	1	1	10	7	3	...	...	...	...	...	...	7	7	...
			178	Hukka-stem makers and sellers ...	...	...	...	...	...	...	...	...	...	...	...	...	...	...	...
			179	Papier-maché workers and sellers ...	...	...	...	...	...	...	377	...	377	...	...	...	...	...	...
			180	Card-makers and sellers	...	...	...	...	...	...	...	...	...	...	...	...	...	...	...
			181	Tábut and Tázia makers and sellers ...	...	...	...	...	...	...	...	...	...	...	...	...	...	...	...
			182	Curiosity dealers...	...	...	...	...	...	...	...	...	...	...	...	...	...	...	...
				Total Sub-order 31	2	1	1	10	7	3	377	...	377	...	...	...	7	7	...

TABLE XVII B.
Occupations by Districts.

TABLE XVII B.

Occupations by Districts.—*Continued.*

Class.	Order.	Sub-order and Group.	Serial No.	Occupations.	Birh. Total.	Birh. Males.	Birh. Females.	Nander. Total.	Nander. Males.	Nander. Females.	Naldrug. Total.	Naldrug. Males.	Naldrug. Females.	Bidar. Total.	Bidar. Males.	Bidar. Females.	Parbhani. Total.	Parbhani. Males.	Parbhani. Females.
					36	37	38	39	40	41	42	43	44	45	46	47	48	49	50
Class D.—Preparation and supply of material substances.—*contd.*	XI. Supplementary requirements.—*contd.*	28. Books & Prints, &c.	157	Press proprietors, Lithographers and Printers...	3	1	2	...	...	...	...	...	...	...	...	...	...	...	...
			158	Book-binders	...	...	...	2	1	1	...	...	...	3	3	...	...	...	...
			159	Book-sellers and publishers	22	9	13	...	...	...	5	5	...	3	3	...	7	7	...
			160	Newspaper proprietors and managers...	...	...	...	...	...	...	...	...	...	...	...	...	...	...	...
			161	News Agents, Book Agents and Newspaper sellers, &c.	...	...	...	...	...	...	...	...	...	...	...	...	...	...	...
			162	Print and picture dealers	...	...	...	...	...	...	...	...	...	...	...	...	...	...	...
				Total Sub-order 28	25	10	15	2	1	1	5	5	...	6	6	...	7	7	...
		29. Watches, clocks, and scientific instruments.	163	Watch and clock makers and sellers	...	...	...	...	...	...	...	...	...	...	...	...	...	...	...
			164	Opticians...	...	...	...	...	...	...	...	...	...	...	...	...	...	...	...
			165	Surgical instrument makers and sellers	...	...	...	...	...	...	...	...	...	...	...	...	...	...	...
			166	Photographic apparatus dealers...	...	...	...	...	...	...	...	...	...	...	...	...	...	...	...
			167	Other scientific instrument makers, menders and sellers	...	...	...	...	...	...	...	...	...	...	...	...	...	...	...
			168	Scale makers and sellers	...	...	...	...	...	...	...	...	...	...	...	...	...	...	...
				Total Sub-order 29	...	...	...	...	...	...	...	...	...	...	...	...	...	...	...
		30. Carving, engraving, &c.	169	Wood and ebony carvers	...	...	...	...	...	...	...	...	...	...	...	...	...	...	...
			170	Ivory carvers	...	...	...	...	...	...	...	...	...	...	...	...	...	...	...
			171	Cotton-stamp makers and sellers	...	...	...	...	...	...	...	...	...	...	...	...	...	...	...
			172	Turners and lacquerers...	...	...	...	...	...	...	...	...	...	...	...	...	4	3	1
			173	Die sinkers and seal, &c., engravers	...	...	...	...	...	...	...	...	...	...	...	...	...	...	...
			174	Type-founders	...	...	...	...	...	...	...	...	...	...	...	...	...	...	...
			175	Mica, flint and Talc workers and sellers	...	...	...	...	...	...	...	...	...	...	...	...	...	...	...
			176	Mosaic and Alabaster workers and sellers ...	...	...	...	...	...	...	...	...	...	...	...	...	...	...	...
				Total Sub-order 30	...	...	...	...	...	...	...	...	...	...	...	...	4	3	1
		Toys, curiosities, &c.	177	Toy, kite, and cage makers and sellers. Bird stuffers	...	...	...	...	...	...	...	...	...	5	5	...	...	...	...
			178	Hukka-stem makers and sellers	...	...	...	5	5	...	...	...	...	4	2	2	...	...	...
			179	Papier-maché workers and sellers	...	...	...	...	...	...	...	...	...	...	...	...	...	...	...
			180	Card-makers and sellers...	...	...	...	...	...	...	...	...	...	...	...	...	...	...	...
			181	Tábut and Tázia makers and sellers	...	...	...	...	...	...	...	...	...	26	26	...	...	...	...
			182	Curiosity dealers	...	...	...	...	...	...	...	...	...	...	...	...	...	...	...
				Total Sub-order 31	...	...	...	5	5	...	...	...	...	35	33	2	...	...	...

TABLE XVII B.

Occupations by Districts.—*Continued.*

Class.	Order.	Sub-order and Group.	Serial No.	Occupations.	Sirpur Tandur. Total.	Sirpur Tandur. Males.	Sirpur Tandur. Females.	Gulbarga. Total.	Gulbarga. Males.	Gulbarga. Females.	Raichur. Total.	Raichur. Males.	Raichur. Females.	Lingasugur. Total.	Lingasugur. Males.	Lingasugur. Females.	Railways. Total.	Railways. Males.	Railways. Females.
					51	52	53	54	55	56	57	58	59	60	61	62	63	64	65
Class D.—Preparation and supply of material substances.—*contd.*	XI. Supplementary requirements.—*contd.*	28. Books & Prints, &c.	157	Press proprietors, Lithographers and Printers	...	...	...	4	...	4	23	16	7	9	5	4	...	...	...
			158	Book-binders	...	...	...	...	...	...	20	20	...	...	...	...	...	...	...
			159	Book-sellers and publishers	...	...	...	4	4	...	5	...	5	8	2	1	...	...	...
			160	Newspaper proprietors and managers...	...	...	...	...	...	...	...	...	...	...	...	...	...	...	...
			161	News Agents, Book Agents and News-paper sellers, &c.	...	...	...	...	...	...	...	...	...	...	...	...	...	...	...
			162	Print and picture dealers	...	...	...	...	...	...	...	...	...	19	7	12	...	...	...
				Total Sub-order 28......	...	...	...	8	4	4	48	36	12	31	14	17	...	...	...
		29. Watches, clocks, and scientific instruments.	163	Watch and clock makers and sellers ...	...	...	...	...	...	...	...	...	...	14	5	9	...	...	...
			164	Opticians	...	...	...	...	...	...	...	...	...	...	...	...	...	...	...
			165	Surgical Instrument makers and sellers	...	...	...	...	...	...	...	...	...	...	...	...	...	...	...
			166	Photographic apparatus dealers ...	...	...	...	...	...	...	...	...	...	...	...	...	...	...	...
			167	Other scientific instrument makers, menders and sellers	...	...	...	...	...	...	...	...	...	...	...	...	...	...	...
			168	Scale makers and sellers	...	...	...	...	...	...	...	...	...	...	...	...	...	...	...
				Total Sub-order 29	...	...	...	...	...	...	...	...	...	14	5	9	...	...	...
		30. Carving, engraving, &c.	169	Wood and ebony carvers	...	...	...	...	...	...	...	...	...	...	...	...	...	...	...
			170	Ivory carvers	...	...	...	...	...	...	...	...	...	...	...	...	...	...	...
			171	Cotton-stamp makers and sellers ...	...	...	...	...	...	...	...	...	...	...	...	...	...	...	...
			172	Turners and lacquerers...	...	...	...	7	7	...	...	...	...	...	...	...	...	...	...
			173	Die-sinkers and seal, &c., engravers...	...	...	...	...	...	...	...	...	...	...	...	...	...	...	...
			174	Type-founders	...	...	...	...	...	...	...	...	...	...	...	...	...	...	...
			175	Mica, flint and Talc workers and sellers.	...	...	...	...	...	...	1	1	...	...	...	...	...	...	...
			176	Mosaic and Alabaster workers and sellers	...	...	...	...	...	...	...	...	...	...	...	...	...	...	...
				Total Sub-order 30	...	...	...	7	7	...	1	1	...	...	...	...	...	...	...
		Toys, curiosities, &c.	177	Toy, kite, and cage makers and sellers, Bird stuffers	...	...	...	...	...	...	...	...	...	6	...	6	...	...	...
			178	Hukka-stem makers and sellers ...	...	...	...	...	...	...	...	...	...	...	...	...	...	...	...
			179	Papier-maché workers and sellers ...	...	...	...	...	...	...	...	...	...	...	...	...	...	...	...
			180	Card-makers and sellers	...	...	...	...	...	...	...	...	...	...	...	...	...	...	...
			181	Tábut and Tázia makers and sellers ...	...	...	...	...	...	...	...	...	...	...	...	...	...	...	...
			182	Curiosity dealers	...	...	...	...	...	...	...	...	...	...	...	...	...	...	...
				Total Sub-order 31	...	...	...	...	...	...	...	...	...	6	...	6	...	...	...

TABLE XVII B.
Occupations by Districts.

TABLE XVII B.

Occupations by Districts.—*Continued.*

Class.	Order.	Sub-order and Group.	Serial No.	Occupations.	Grand Total. Total.	Grand Total. Males.	Grand Total. Females.	Hyderabad. Total.	Hyderabad. Males.	Hyderabad. Females.	Atraf-i-Balda. Total.	Atraf-i-Balda. Males.	Atraf-i-Balda. Females.	Mahabubnagar. Total.	Mahabubnagar. Males.	Mahabubnagar. Females.	Nalgonda. Total.	Nalgonda. Males.	Nalgonda. Females.
1	2	3	4	5	6	7	8	9	10	11	12	13	14	15	16	17	18	19	20
Class D.—Preparation and supply of material substances.—*contd.*	XI. Supplementary requirements.—*contd.*	32. Music and musical instruments.	183	Music and musical instrument dealers ...	40	6	34	...	...	...	...	...	...	...	...	...	...	...	...
			184	Conch-dealers, drum and horn makers, &c.	131	77	54	104	54	50	...	...	...	...	...	...	...	...	...
				Total Sub-order 32	171	83	88	104	54	50	...	...	...	...	...	...	...	...	...
		33. Necklaces, Bracelets, beads, sacred threads, &c.	185	Bangle makers and sellers in lac ...	213	106	107	2	...	2	73	...	73	...	...	...	104	72	32
			186	Bangle makers and sellers in stone ...	...	...	...	...	...	...	...	...	...	...	...	...	...	...	...
			187	Bangle makers and sellers in wood and bone	28	26	2	...	...	...	...	...	...	7	5	2	8	8	...
			188	Bangle makers and sellers in clay ...	...	...	...	...	...	...	...	...	...	...	...	...	...	...	...
			189	Bangle makers and sellers in glass ...	14,817	7,023	7,794	722	847	375	453	218	235	1,954	1,092	862	657	314	343
			190	Bangle fitters	2,036	1,235	801	94	58	36	...	...	...	...	...	...	...	...	...
			191	Imitation and pewter jewelry makers and sellers	5	5	...	...	...	...	...	...	...	...	...	...	...	...	...
			192	Bead makers and sellers	1,875	685	690	8	...	8	140	69	71	136	77	59	551	247	304
			193	Rosary and necklace makers and sellers	45	44	1	...	...	...	9	9	...	34	34	...	...	...	...
			194	Flower garland makers and sellers ...	8,676	1,951	1,725	1,141	575	566	87	9	28	55	7	48	5	3	2
			195	Artificial flower and caste-mark spangle makers and sellers	86	20	16	85	20	15	...	...	...	...	...	...	...	...	...
			196	Sacred-thread makers and sellers ...	15	13	2	8	1	2	...	...	...	...	...	...	...	...	...
				Total Sub-order 33	22,246	11,108	11,138	2,005	1,001	1,004	712	305	407	2,186	1,215	971	1,320	639	681
		34. Furniture.	197	Upholsterers	...	...	...	...	...	...	...	...	...	...	...	...	...	...	...
			198	Furniture makers	22	9	13	13	9	4	...	...	...	...	...	...	...	...	...
			199	Frame-makers	240	144	96	...	...	...	...	...	...	...	...	...	...	...	...
			200	Looking-glass makers and sellers ...	15	4	11	2	1	1	8	8	...	...	...	...	...	...	...
				Total Sub-order 34	277	157	120	15	10	5	8	8	...	...	...	...	...	...	...
		35. Harness.	201	Saddlery and Harness makers and sellers	1,929	954	975	111	57	54	...	...	...	...	...	...	...	...	...
			202	Saddle cloth makers, embroiderers and sellers	480	226	204	246	132	114	17	12	5	82	46	36	...	...	...
			203	Whip, goad, &c., makers	116	...	116	...	...	...	...	...	...	...	...	...	...	...	...
				Total Sub-order 35	2,475	1,180	1,295	857	189	168	17	12	5	82	46	36	...	...	...

TABLE XVII B.

Occupations by Districts.—*Continued.*

Class D.—Preparation and supply of material substances.—*contd.*

Order XI. Supplementary requirements.—*contd.*

Sub-order and Group.	Serial No.	Occupations.	Warangal. Total.	Warangal. Males.	Warangal. Females.	Elgandal. Total.	Elgandal. Males.	Elgandal. Females.	Indur. Total.	Indur. Males.	Indur. Females.	Medak. Total.	Medak. Males.	Medak. Females.	Aurangabad. Total.	Aurangabad. Males.	Aurangabad. Females.
			21	22	23	24	25	26	27	28	29	30	31	32	33	34	35
32. Music and musical instruments.	183	Music and musical instrument dealers	...	...	...	...	...	...	...	...	...	...	...	...	40	6	84
	184	Conch-dealers, drum and horn makers, &c.	...	...	...	...	...	...	...	...	...	...	...	...	4	4	...
		Total Sub-order 32	...	...	...	...	...	...	...	...	...	...	...	...	44	10	84
33. Necklaces, Bracelets, beads, sacred threads, &c.	185	Bangle makers and sellers in lac	...	...	...	...	...	...	...	...	...	84	84	...	...	...	...
	186	Bangle makers and sellers in stone	...	...	...	...	...	...	...	...	...	...	...	...	...	...	...
	187	Bangle makers and sellers in wood and bone	13	13	...	...	...	...	...	...	...	...	...	...	...	...	...
	188	Bangle makers and sellers in clay	...	...	...	...	...	...	...	...	...	...	...	...	...	...	...
	189	Bangle makers and sellers in glass	658	841	817	958	474	484	297	...	297	408	229	179	1,841	787	604
	190	Bangle fitters	...	...	...	...	...	...	924	661	268	...	...	...	...	...	...
	191	Imitation and pewter jewelry makers and sellers	...	...	...	...	...	...	...	...	...	...	...	...	...	...	...
	192	Bead makers and sellers	192	94	98	7	...	7	...	...	...	85	80	5	...	...	...
	193	Rosary and necklace makers and sellers	...	...	...	2	1	1	...	...	...	...	...	...	...	...	...
	194	Flower garland makers and sellers	84	22	62	53	40	13	...	...	...	1	...	1	298	144	154
	195	Artificial flower and caste-mark spangle makers and sellers	...	...	...	...	...	...	...	...	...	...	...	...	...	...	...
	196	Sacred-thread makers and sellers	...	...	...	...	...	...	...	...	...	...	...	...	...	...	...
		Total Sub-order 33	947	470	477	1,020	515	505	1,221	661	560	478	293	185	1,639	881	758
34. Furniture.	197	Upholsterers	...	...	...	...	...	...	...	...	...	...	...	...	...	...	...
	198	Furniture makers	...	...	...	...	...	...	...	...	...	...	...	...	9	...	9
	199	Frame-makers	...	...	...	...	...	...	72	45	27	...	...	...	17	8	9
	200	Looking-glass makers and sellers	...	...	...	...	...	...	...	...	...	...	...	...	...	...	...
		Total Sub-order 34	...	...	...	...	...	...	72	45	27	...	...	...	26	8	18
35. Harness.	201	Saddlery and Harness makers and sellers	...	...	...	...	...	...	142	61	81	...	...	...	109	57	52
	202	Saddle cloth makers, embroiderers and sellers	86	17	19	34	4	30	...	...	...	15	15	...	...	...	...
	203	Whip, goad, &c., makers	...	...	...	...	...	...	...	...	...	...	...	...	...	...	...
		Total Sub-order 35	86	17	19	34	4	80	142	61	81	15	15	...	109	57	52

TABLE XVII B.

Occupations by Districts.—*Continued.*

Class.	Order.	Sub-order and Group.	Serial No.	Occupations.	Birh. Total.	Birh. Males.	Birh. Females.	Nander. Total.	Nander. Males.	Nander. Females.	Naldrug. Total.	Naldrug. Males.	Naldrug. Females.	Bidar. Total.	Bidar. Males.	Bidar. Females.	Parbhani. Total.	Parbhani. Males.	Parbhani. Females.
					36	37	38	39	40	41	42	43	44	45	46	47	48	49	50
Class D.—Preparation and supply of material substances.—*contd.*	XI. Supplementary requirements.—*contd.*	32. Music and musical instruments.	183	Music and musical instrument dealers.	...	...	...	...	...	...	...	...	...	...	...	...	...	...	...
			184	Conch-dealers, drum and horn makers, &c.	5	5	...	...	...	...	2	2	...	8	5	3	6	6	...
				Total Sub-order 32......	5	5	...	...	...	...	2	2	...	8	5	3	6	6	...
		33. Necklaces, Bracelets, beads, sacred threads, &c.	185	Bangle makers and sellers in lac ...	...	...	...	...	...	...	...	...	...	...	...	...	...	...	...
			186	Bangle makers and sellers in stone ...	...	...	...	...	...	...	...	...	...	...	...	...	...	...	...
			187	Bangle makers and sellers in wood and bone	...	...	...	...	...	...	...	...	...	...	...	...	...	...	...
			188	Bangle makers and sellers in clay ...	...	...	...	...	...	...	...	...	...	...	...	...	...	...	...
			189	Bangle makers and sellers in glass ...	1,169	517	652	976	853	628	...	...	...	...	...	...	832	808	524
			190	Bangle fitters	...	...	...	...	...	...	1,018	516	502	1,482	532	900	...	...	...
			191	Imitation and pewter jewelry makers and sellers	...	...	...	...	...	...	...	...	...	...	...	...	5	5	...
			192	Bead makers and sellers	...	...	...	...	...	...	...	...	...	...	...	...	...	...	...
			193	Rosary and necklace makers and sellers.	...	...	...	...	...	...	...	...	...	...	...	...	...	...	...
			194	Flower garland makers and sellers ...	124	110	14	303	155	148	74	...	74	726	423	303	157	106	51
			195	Artificial flower and caste-mark spangle makers and sellers	...	...	...	...	...	...	1	...	1	...	...	...	...	...	...
			196	Sacred-thread makers and sellers ...	6	6	...	...	...	...	1	1	...	...	...	...	...	...	...
				Total Sub-order 33	1,299	683	666	1,279	508	771	1,094	517	577	2,158	955	1,203	994	419	575
		34. Furniture.	197	Upholsterers	...	...	...	...	...	...	...	...	...	...	...	...	...	...	...
			198	Furniture makers	...	...	...	...	...	...	...	...	...	...	...	...	...	...	...
			199	Frame-makers	11	6	5	...	...	...	22	18	9	40	27	13	21	16	5
			200	Looking-glass makers and sellers ...	...	...	...	...	...	...	...	...	...	10	...	10	...	...	...
				Total Sub-order 34......	11	6	5	...	...	...	22	18	9	50	27	23	21	16	5
		35. Harness.	201	Saddlery and Harness makers and sellers...	83	48	85	112	52	60	102	55	47	606	286	870	254	149	105
			202	Saddle cloth makers, embroiderers and sellers...	...	...	...	...	...	...	...	...	...	...	...	...	...	...	...
			203	Whip, goad, &c., makers	...	...	...	...	...	...	116	...	116	...	...	...	...	...	...
				Total Sub-order 35	88	48	85	112	52	60	218	55	163	606	286	870	254	149	105

TABLE XVII B.

Occupations by Districts.—*Continued.*

Class.	Order.	Sub-order and Group.	Serial No.	Occupations.	Sirpur Tandur. Total.	Sirpur Tandur. Males.	Sirpur Tandur. Females.	Gulbarga. Total.	Gulbarga. Males.	Gulbarga. Females.	Raichur. Total.	Raichur. Males.	Raichur. Females.	Lingsugur. Total.	Lingsugur. Males.	Lingsugur. Females.	Railways. Total.	Railways. Males.	Railways. Females.
					51	52	53	54	55	56	57	58	59	60	61	62	63	64	65
Class D.—Preparation and supply of material substances.—*contd.*	XI. Supplementary requirements.—*contd.*	32. Music and musical instruments.	183	Music and musical instrument dealers...	...	...	...	...	...	...	...	...	...	...	...	...	...	...	...
			184	Conch-dealers, drum and horn makers, &c.	...	...	...	...	...	...	...	...	...	2	1	1	...	...	...
				Total Sub-order 32	...	...	...	...	...	...	...	...	...	2	1	1	...	...	...
		33. Necklaces, Bracelets, beads, sacred threads, &c.	185	Bangle makers and sellers in lac ...	...	...	...	...	...	...	...	...	...	...	...	...	...	...	...
			186	Bangle makers and sellers in stone ...	...	...	...	...	...	...	...	...	...	...	...	...	...	...	...
			187	Bangle makers and sellers in wood and bone	...	...	...	...	...	...	5	5	...	...	...	...	...	...	...
			188	Bangle makers and sellers in clay ...	...	...	...	...	...	...	...	...	...	...	...	...	...	...	...
			189	Bangle makers and sellers in glass ...	229	95	134	779	557	222	1,032	510	522	920	399	521	...	...	...
			190	Bangle fitters	...	...	...	...	...	...	...	...	...	...	...	...	...	...	...
			191	Imitation and pewter jewelry makers and sellers	...	...	...	...	...	...	...	...	...	...	...	...	...	...	...
			192	Bead makers and sellers	...	...	...	...	...	...	182	122	60	124	46	78	...	...	...
			193	Rosary and necklace makers and sellers	...	...	...	...	...	...	...	...	...	...	...	...	...	...	...
			194	Flower garland makers and sellers ...	32	29	3	370	188	182	66	49	17	147	88	59	8	8	...
			195	Artificial flower and caste-mark spangle makers and sellers	...	...	...	...	...	...	...	...	...	...	...	...	...	...	...
			196	Sacred-thread makers and sellers ...	5	5	...	...	...	...	...	...	...	...	...	...	...	...	...
				Total Sub-order 33	266	129	137	1,149	745	404	1,285	686	599	1,191	533	658	8	8	...
		34. Furniture.	197	Upholsterers	...	...	...	...	...	...	...	...	...	...	...	...	...	...	...
			198	Furniture makers	...	...	...	...	...	...	...	...	...	...	...	...	...	...	...
			199	Frame-makers	...	...	...	57	29	28	...	...	...	...	...	...	...	...	...
			200	Looking-glass makers and sellers ...	...	...	...	...	...	...	...	...	...	...	...	...	...	...	...
				Total Sub-order 34	...	...	...	57	29	28	...	...	...	...	...	...	...	...	...
		35. Harness.	201	Saddlery and Harness makers and sellers	45	20	25	347	208	189	12	7	5	6	4	2	...	...	...
			202	Saddle cloth makers, embroiderers and sellers	...	...	...	...	...	...	...	...	...	...	...	...	...	...	...
			203	Whip, goad, &c., makers	...	...	...	...	...	...	...	...	...	...	...	...	...	...	...
				Total Sub-order 35	45	20	25	347	208	139	12	7	5	6	4	2	...	...	...

TABLE XVII B.

Occupations by Districts.—*Continued.*

Class.	Order.	Sub-order and Group.	Serial No.	Occupations.	Grand Total. Total.	Grand Total. Males.	Grand Total. Females.	Hyderabad. Total.	Hyderabad. Males.	Hyderabad. Females.	Atraf-i-Balda. Total.	Atraf-i-Balda. Males.	Atraf-i-Balda. Females.	Mahabubnagar. Total.	Mahabubnagar. Males.	Mahabubnagar. Females.	Nalgonda. Total.	Nalgonda. Males.	Nalgonda. Females.
1	2	3	4	5	6	7	8	9	10	11	12	13	14	15	16	17	18	19	20
Class D.—Preparation and supply of material substances.—*contd.*	XI. Supplementary requirements.—*concld.*	36. Tools and machinery.	204	Knife and tool makers and sellers ...	73	27	46	...	...	...	...	...	...	2	1	1	2	1	1
			205	Knife and tool grinders	1,122	604	518	92	58	34	...	...	...	...	...	...	6	8	8
			206	Looms and Loom-comb makers and sellers	154	131	23	...	...	...	...	...	...	...	...	...	...	...	...
			207	Mechanic, (not railway)	307	177	130	203	73	130	104	104	...	...	...	...	...	...	...
			208	Machinery dealers, &c	...	...	...	...	...	...	...	...	...	...	...	...	...	...	...
				Total Sub-order 36......	1,656	939	717	295	131	164	104	104	...	2	1	1	8	4	4
		37. Arms and Ammunition.	209	Gun makers, menders, and sellers ...	65	43	22	24	14	10	...	...	...	6	6	...	5	8	2
			210	Ammunition and Cap dealers	8	5	3	4	3	1	...	...	...	...	...	...	...	...	...
			211	Gun-powder makers and sellers ...	227	114	113	28	14	14	8	4	4	22	15	7	6	4	2
			212	Fire-work makers, and sellers	645	500	145	65	29	36	19	9	10	21	11	10	...	...	...
			213	Sword and scabbard makers and sellers.	395	159	236	192	99	93	...	...	...	28	12	16	...	...	...
			214	Spear-head, shield, &c., makers and sellers	23	12	11	...	...	...	...	...	...	...	...	...	...	...	...
			215	Bow and arrow makers and sellers ...	...	...	...	...	...	...	...	...	...	...	...	...	...	...	...
			216	Cudgel (láthi) makers and sellers ...	4	1	3	4	1	3	...	...	...	...	...	...	...	...	...
				Total Sub-order 37......	1,367	834	533	317	160	157	27	13	14	77	44	33	11	7	4
				Total Order XI	32,260	16,348	15,912	4,358	2,234	2,124	983	495	488	2,625	1,467	1,158	1,407	690	717
	XII. Textile Fabrics and dress.	38. Wool and Fur.	217	Carpet weavers and sellers	1,212	673	539	4	2	2	...	...	...	...	...	...	...	...	...
			218	Shawl weavers and sellers	151	92	59	146	90	56	2	2	...	...	...	...	...	...	...
			219	Felt and pashm workers and sellers ...	114	62	52	3	3	...	...	...	...	...	...	...	...	...	...
			220	Blanket weavers and sellers (*often also shepherds*)	92,338	49,895	42,443	38	19	19	2,623	1,571	1,052	11,437	6,423	5,014	1,588	910	678
			221	Woollen cloth manufacturers and dealers	74,380	40,030	34,350	...	...	...	...	...	...	...	...	...	...	...	...
			222	Woollen yarn spinners and sellers ...	4,593	478	4,115	...	...	...	161	8	153	1,062	70	992	179	48	131
			223	Wool carders	208	11	197	...	...	...	...	...	...	208	11	197	...	...	...
			224	Wool dyers	...	...	...	...	...	...	...	...	...	...	...	...	...	...	...
			225	Fur dealers	267	6	261	...	...	...	...	...	...	267	6	261	...	...	...
				Total Sub-order 38......	178,268	91,247	82,016	191	114	77	2,786	1,581	1,205	12,974	6,510	6,464	1,767	958	809
		39. Silk.	226	Silk-worm rearers and cocoon gatherers.	...	...	...	...	...	...	...	...	...	...	...	...	...	...	...
			227	Silk carders and spinners	3,555	1,400	2,155	82	34	48	52	...	52	661	150	511	8	3	...
			228	Silk weavers and dealers	2,525	722	1,803	92	47	45	15	...	15	70	82	88	87	5	32
			229	Silk printers and dyers...	39	19	20	...	...	...	...	...	...	...	...	...	...	...	...
			230	Braid and ribbon makers and sellers ...	1,835	780	1,055	297	149	147	...	...	...	49	25	24	...	...	...
				Total Sub-order 39	7,954	2,921	5,033	470	230	240	67	...	67	780	207	573	40	8	32

TABLE XVII B.

Occupations by Districts.—*Continued.*

Class.	Order.	Sub-order and Group.	Serial No.	Occupations.	Warangal. Total.	Warangal. Males.	Warangal. Females.	Elgandal. Total.	Elgandal. Males.	Elgandal. Females.	Indur. Total.	Indur. Males.	Indur. Females.	Medak. Total.	Medak. Males.	Medak. Females.	Aurangabad. Total.	Aurangabad. Males.	Aurangabad. Females.
					21	22	23	24	25	26	27	28	29	30	31	32	33	34	35
Class D.—Preparation and supply of material substances.—*contd.*	XI. Supplementary requirements.—*concld.*	36. Tools and machinery.	204	Knife and tool makers and sellers	...	...	...	...	...	...	17	...	17	12	...	12	...	...	...
			205	Knife and tool grinders	...	...	...	...	...	...	55	30	25	...	...	...	96	54	42
			206	Looms and Loom-comb makers and sellers	...	...	...	81	15	16	...	...	...	...	...	...	...	...	...
			207	Mechanic, (not railway)	...	...	...	...	...	...	...	...	...	...	...	...	...	...	...
			208	Machinery dealers, &c.	...	...	...	...	...	...	...	...	...	...	...	...	...	...	...
				Total Sub-order 36	...	...	...	31	15	16	72	80	42	12	...	12	96	54	42
		37. Arms and Ammunition.	209	Gun makers, menders, and sellers	2	2	...	...	...	...	...	...	...	1	...	1	12	8	4
			210	Ammunition and Cap dealers	...	...	...	...	...	...	...	...	...	...	...	...	...	...	...
			211	Gun-powder makers and sellers	1	...	1	8	...	8	6	...	6	19	10	9	...	...	...
			212	Fire-work makers, and sellers	2	...	2	...	...	...	...	...	...	...	...	...	22	18	4
			213	Sword and scabbard makers and sellers	6	4	2	131	85	96	24	16	8	4	...	4	...	...	...
			214	Spear-head, shield, &c., makers and sellers	...	...	...	...	...	...	...	...	...	...	...	...	19	8	11
			215	Bow and arrow makers and sellers	...	...	...	...	...	...	...	...	...	...	...	...	...	...	...
			216	Cudgel (láthi) makers and sellers	...	...	...	...	...	...	...	...	...	...	...	...	...	...	...
				Total Sub-order 37	11	6	5	139	85	104	30	16	14	24	10	14	53	84	19
				Total Order XI	1,038	533	505	1,787	1,062	725	2,125	876	1,249	726	832	394	2,443	1,288	1,205
	XII. Textile Fabrics and dress.	38. Wool and Fur.	217	Carpet weavers and sellers	1,139	644	495	29	17	12	...	...	...	18	...	18	...	...	...
			218	Shawl weavers and sellers	...	...	...	3	...	8	...	...	...	...	...	...	...	...	...
			219	Felt and pashm workers and sellers	...	...	...	...	...	...	...	...	...	...	...	...	...	...	...
			220	Blanket weavers and sellers (*often also shepherds*)	3,466	2,064	1,402	8,708	4,888	8,820	7,148	8,368	8,780	2,600	1,585	1,015	7,708	4,480	8,278
			221	Woollen cloth manufacturers and dealers	3,078	1,628	1,450	71,181	38,402	32,779	...	...	...	14	...	14	...	...	...
			222	Woollen yarn spinners and sellers	471	86	385	1,418	91	1,327	...	...	...	506	81	425	...	...	...
			223	Wool carders	...	...	...	...	...	...	...	...	...	...	...	...	...	...	...
			224	Wool dyers	...	...	...	...	...	...	...	...	...	...	...	...	...	...	...
			225	Fur dealers	...	...	...	...	...	...	...	...	...	...	...	...	...	...	...
				Total Sub-order 38	8,154	4,422	3,732	81,339	43,398	37,941	7,148	3,368	8,780	3,138	1,666	1,472	7,708	4,430	8,278
		39. Silk.	226	Silk-worm rearers and cocoon gatherers	...	...	...	...	...	...	...	...	...	...	...	...	...	...	...
			327	Silk carders and spinners	...	...	...	...	...	...	615	582	33	...	...	...	280	197	83
			228	Silk weavers and dealers	337	102	235	418	111	307	617	2	615	226	62	164	108	8	105
			229	Silk printers and dyers	3	8	...	22	2	20	...	...	...	...	...	...	14	14	...
			230	Braid and ribbon makers and sellers	32	...	32	...	...	...	230	85	195	...	...	...	360	122	238
				Total Sub-order 39	372	105	267	440	113	327	1,462	619	843	226	62	164	762	336	426

TABLE XVII B.

Occupations by Districts.—*Continued.*

Class.	Order.	Sub-order and Group.	Serial No.	Occupations.	Birh. Total.	Birh. Males.	Birh. Females.	Nander. Total.	Nander. Males.	Nander. Females.	Naldrug. Total.	Naldrug. Males.	Naldrug. Females.	Bidar. Total.	Bidar. Males.	Bidar. Females.	Parbhani. Total.	Parbhani. Males.	Parbhani. Females.
					36	37	38	39	40	41	42	43	44	45	46	47	48	49	50
Class D.—Preparation and supply of material substances.—*contd.*	XI. Supplementary requirements.—*contd.*	36. Tools and machinery.	204	Knife and tool makers and sellers ...	4	...	4	...	...	...	21	11	10	12	12	...	8	2	1
			205	Knife and tool grinders	77	44	33	224	89	135	53	40	13	182	72	60	138	66	72
			206	Looms and Loom-comb makers and sellers	7	7	...	...	...	...	4	4	...	...	...	...	...	...	...
			207	Mechanic, (not railway)	...	...	...	...	...	...	...	...	...	...	...	...	...	...	...
			208	Machinery dealers, &c.,...	...	...	...	...	...	...	...	...	...	...	...	...	...	...	...
				Total Sub-order 36	88	51	37	224	89	135	78	55	23	144	84	60	141	68	73
		37. Arms and Ammunition.	209	Gun makers, menders, and sellers ...	...	...	...	...	...	...	5	5	...	...	...	...	8	3	5
			210	Ammunition and Cap dealers... ...	...	...	...	...	...	...	...	...	...	...	...	...	...	...	...
			211	Gun-powder makers and sellers ...	...	...	...	28	8	20	...	...	...	5	3	2	1	1	...
			212	Fire-work makers, and sellers ...	...	...	...	1	1	...	5	...	5	148	85	63	383	331	2
			213	Sword and scabbard makers and sellers.	...	...	...	...	...	...	...	...	...	17	1	16	...	...	...
			214	Spear-head, shield, &c., makers and sellers	...	...	...	...	...	...	...	...	...	4	4	...	...	...	...
			215	Bow and arrow makers and sellers ...	...	...	...	...	...	...	...	...	...	...	...	...	...	...	...
			216	Cudgel (láthi) makers and sellers ...	...	...	...	...	...	...	...	...	...	...	...	...	...	...	...
				Total Sub-order 37	...	...	...	29	9	20	10	5	5	174	93	81	342	335	7
				Total Order XI	1,535	760	775	1,664	674	990	1,464	673	791	3,207	1,454	1,753	1,881	1,082	799
	XII. Textile Fabrics and dress.	38. Wool and Fur.	217	Carpet weavers and sellers	...	...	...	...	...	...	10	10	...	...	...	...	...	...	...
			218	Shawl weavers and sellers	...	...	...	...	...	...	...	...	...	...	...	...	...	...	...
			219	Felt and pashm workers and sellers ...	...	...	...	...	...	...	...	...	...	59	59	...	...	...	...
			220	Blanket weavers and sellers (*often also shepherds*)	5,719	2,903	2,816	3,170	1,713	1,457	6,758	3,573	3,185	9,631	5,189	4,442	5,336	2,645	2,691
			221	Woollen cloth manufacturers and dealers	...	...	...	...	...	...	...	...	...	107	...	107	...	...	...
			222	Woollen yarn spinners and sellers ...	138	14	124	...	...	...	9	...	9	6	6	...	12	2	10
			223	Wool carders	...	...	...	...	...	...	...	...	...	...	...	...	...	...	...
			224	Wool dyers	...	...	...	...	...	...	...	...	...	...	...	...	...	...	...
			225	Fur dealers	...	...	...	...	...	...	...	...	...	...	...	...	...	...	...
				Total Sub-order 38	5,857	2,917	2,940	3,170	1,713	1,457	6,777	3,583	3,194	9,803	5,254	4,549	5,348	2,647	2,701
		39. Silk.	226	Silkworm rearers and cocoon gatherers	...	...	...	...	...	...	...	...	...	...	...	...	...	...	...
			227	Silk carders and spinners	130	42	88	...	...	...	65	20	45	128	[illegible]	110	83	83	...
			228	Silk weavers and dealers	15	15	...	18	17	1	...	...	...	105	105	...	212	...	211
			229	Silk printers and dyers...	...	...	...	...	...	...	...	...	...	...	...	...	...	...	...
			230	Braid and ribbon makers and sellers ...	210	152	58	152	83	69	65	41	24	318	143	175	103	20	83
				Total Sub-order 39	355	209	146	170	100	70	130	61	69	551	266	285	397	103	294

TABLE XVII B.

Occupations by Districts.—*Continued.*

Class.	Order.	Sub-order and Group.	Serial No.	Occupations.	Sirpur Tandur. Total.	Sirpur Tandur. Males.	Sirpur Tandur. Females.	Gulbarga. Total.	Gulbarga. Males.	Gulbarga. Females.	Raichur. Total.	Raichur. Males.	Raichur. Females.	Lingasugur. Total.	Lingasugur. Males.	Lingasugur. Females.	Railways. Total.	Railways. Males.	Railways. Females.
					51	52	53	54	55	56	57	58	59	60	61	62	63	64	65
Class D.—Preparation and supply of material substances.—*contd.*	XI. Supplementary requirements.—*contd.*	36. Tools and machinery.	204	Knife and tool makers and sellers ...	...	...	...	...	...	...	...	...	...	...	...	...	...	...	...
			205	Knife and tool grinders													...	...	...
			206	Looms and Loom-comb makers and sellers	71	57	14	91	42	49	28	18	10	59	31	28	...	...	...
			207	Mechanic, (not railway)	...	...	...	...	...	...	95	91	4	17	14	3	...	...	...
			208	Machinery dealers, &c, ...	...	...	...	...	...	...	...	...	...	...	...	...	...	...	...
				Total Sub-order 36......	71	57	14	91	42	49	123	109	14	76	45	31	...	...	...
		37. Arms and Ammunition.	209	Gun makers, menders, and sellers ...	...	...	...	...	...	...	...	...	...	...	...	...	...	...	...
			210	Ammunition and Cap dealers	...	...	...	2	2	...	...	...	...	...	...	...	...	...	...
			211	Gun-powder makers and sellers ...	...	...	...	...	...	...	...	...	...	...	...	...	...	...	...
			212	Fire-work makers, and sellers	...	...	...	70	51	19	18	...	18	7	4	3	4	2	2
			213	Sword and scabbard makers and sellers	...	...	...	5	...	5	...	...	...	...	...	...	...	...	...
			214	Spear-head, shield, &c., makers and sellers	...	...	...	...	...	...	...	...	...	16	7	9	...	...	...
			215	Bow and arrow makers and sellers ...	...	...	...	...	...	...	...	...	...	...	...	...	...	...	...
			216	Cudgel (láthi) makers and sellers ...	...	...	...	...	...	...	...	...	...	...	...	...	...	...	...
				Total Sub-order 37......	...	...	...	77	53	24	18	...	18	23	11	12	4	2	2
				Total Order XI......	888	206	182	1,771	1,109	662	1,502	845	657	1,349	613	736	7	5	2
	XII. Textile Fabrics and dress.	38. Wool and Fur.	217	Carpet weavers and sellers	...	...	...	12	...	12	...	...	...	...	...	...	...	...	...
			218	Shawl weavers and sellers	...	...	...	52	...	52	...	...	...	...	...	...	...	...	...
			219	Felt and pashm workers and sellers ...	...	...	...	...	...	...	...	...	...	...	...	...	...	...	...
			220	Blanket weavers and sellers (*often also shepherds*)	813	413	400	9,585	5,033	4,552	4,307	2,449	1,858	1,703	719	984	...	...	...
			221	Woollen cloth manufacturers and dealers	...	...	...	...	...	...	...	...	...	...	...	...	...	...	...
			222	Woollen yarn spinners and sellers ...	1	...	1	59	21	38	571	51	520	...	...	...	...	...	...
			223	Wool carders	...	...	...	...	...	...	...	...	...	...	...	...	...	...	...
			224	Wool dyers	...	...	...	...	...	...	...	...	...	...	...	...	...	...	...
			225	Fur dealers	...	...	...	...	...	...	...	...	...	...	...	...	...	...	...
				Total Sub-order 38......	814	413	401	9,708	5,054	4,654	4,878	2,500	2,378	1,703	719	984	...	...	...
		39. Silk.	226	Silk-worm rearers and cocoon gatherers.	...	...	...	...	...	...	...	...	...	...	...	...	...	...	...
			227	Silk carders and spinners	...	...	...	303	104	199	1,106	146	960	47	21	26	...	...	...
			228	Silk weavers and dealers	...	...	...	155	151	4	14	14	...	87	56	31	...	...	...
			229	Silk printers and dyers	...	...	...	...	...	...	...	...	...	...	...	...	...	...	...
			230	Braid and ribbon makers and sellers ...	...	...	...	20	10	10	...	...	...	...	...	...	...	...	...
				Total Sub-order 39......	...	...	...	478	265	213	1,120	160	960	134	77	57	...	...	...

TABLE XVII B.

Occupations by Districts.—*Continued.*

Class.	Order.	Sub-order and Group.	Serial No.	Occupations.	Grand Total. Total.	Grand Total. Males.	Grand Total. Females.	Hyderabad. Total.	Hyderabad. Males.	Hyderabad. Females.	Atraf-i-Balda. Total.	Atraf-i-Balda. Males.	Atraf-i-Balda. Females.	Mahabubnagar. Total.	Mahabubnagar. Males.	Mahabubnagar. Females.	Nalgonda. Total.	Nalgonda. Males.	Nalgonda. Females.
1	2	3	4	5	6	7	8	9	10	11	12	13	14	15	16	17	18	19	20
Class D.—Preparation and supply of material substances.—*contd.*	XII. Textile Fabrics and dress.—*concld.*	40. Cotton.	231	Cotton cleaners, pressers and ginners...	33,422	13,135	20,287	108	64	44	6	...	6	2,199	769	1,430	12	11	1
			232	Cotton carpet and rug makers and sellers	156	89	67	8	3	5	...	...	...	...	...	...	...	...	...
			233	Cotton spinners, sizers and yarn beaters	54,752	12,833	41,919	7	1	6	1,022	287	785	1,427	183	1,244	3,276	1,337	1,939
			234	Cotton weavers, Mill-owners and managers	295,441	158,327	137,114	1,139	620	519	11,244	6,226	5,018	24,641	13,413	11,228	28,365	15,821	12,544
			235	Cotton Factory hands (undefined) ...	1,813	954	859	497	264	233	9	9	...	67	25	42	...	...	...
			236	Calenderers, fullers and printers ...	45	21	24	2	1	1	...	...	...	43	20	23	...	...	...
			237	Cotton dyers	17,084	8,988	8,096	1,155	602	553	97	38	59	538	266	272	118	76	42
			238	Tape makers and sellers	258	101	152	...	...	...	...	...	...	21	8	13	33	14	19
			239	Tent manufacturers and sellers ...	11	11	...	...	...	...	...	...	...	...	...	...	...	...	...
				Total Sub-order 40	402,977	194,459	208,518	2,916	1,555	1,361	12,378	6,560	5,818	28,936	14,684	14,252	31,804	17,259	14,545
		41. Jute, flax, coir, &c.	240	Flax-spinners, weavers, and sellers ...	144	109	35	...	...	...	98	73	25	18	13	5	1	1	...
			241	Hemp rope makers and sellers ...	1,888	675	713	48	23	25	21	5	16	58	35	23	21	16	5
			242	Jute manufacturers, managers and agents	29	27	2	...	...	...	...	...	...	...	...	...	26	26	...
			243	Sacking, tarpaulin and gunny makers and sellers	4,205	2,432	1,773	10	8	2	263	144	119	166	119	47	29	26	3
			244	Net makers and sellers...	48	31	17	...	...	...	6	...	6	15	12	3	...	...	...
			245	Fancy work dealers	21	21	...	...	...	...	...	...	...	...	...	...	...	...	...
			246	Coir preparers, manufacturers and sellers	947	378	569	...	...	...	...	...	...	...	...	...	...	...	...
				Total Sub-order 41	6,782	3,673	3,109	58	31	27	388	222	166	257	179	78	77	69	8
		42. Dress.	247	Tailors and darners	47,458	22,755	24,703	5,719	3,007	2,712	1,668	585	1,083	2,777	912	1,865	3,822	1,890	1,932
			248	Milliners and dress-makers	85	39	46	85	39	46	...	...	...	...	...	...	...	...	...
			249	Outfitters, and clothes and quilt dealers..	2,536	1,278	1,258	2	1	1	...	...	...	7	1	6	...	...	...
			250	Hosiers and Haberdashers	4,300	1,998	2,302	273	153	120	436	179	257	85	48	37	4	1	3
			251	Hat, cap and turban makers and sellers	80	47	33	53	23	30	8	5	3	...	...	...	...	...	...
			252	Turban binders	209	93	116	63	20	43	...	...	...	...	...	...	...	...	...
			253	Umbrella makers and sellers	6	4	2	...	...	...	...	...	...	...	...	...	...	...	...
			254	Embroiderers and lace and muslin makers	208	31	172	18	7	11	...	...	...	1	...	1	...	...	...
			255	Button makers and sellers	19	8	11	4	1	3	...	...	...	...	...	...	...	...	...
			256	False-plait makers and sellers ...	764	381	383	...	...	...	1	...	1	148	73	75	15	14	1
			257	Piece-goods dealers	77,702	41,096	36,606	4,293	2,347	1,946	1,916	873	1,043	4,252	2,768	1,484	1,691	976	715
				Total Sub-order 42	133,862	67,730	65,632	10,510	5,598	4,912	4,029	1,643	2,386	7,270	3,802	3,468	5,082	2,381	2,651
				Total Order XII......	724,838	360,030	364,808	14,145	7,528	6,617	19,648	10,006	9,642	50,217	25,382	24,835	38,720	20,675	18,045

TABLE XVII B.

Occupations by Districts.—*Continued.*

Class.	Order.	Sub-order and Group.	Serial No.	Occupations.	Warangal. Total.	Warangal. Males.	Warangal. Females.	Elgandal. Total.	Elgandal. Males.	Elgandal. Females.	Indur. Total.	Indur. Males.	Indur. Females.	Medak. Total.	Medak. Males.	Medak. Females.	Aurangabad. Total.	Aurangabad. Males.	Aurangabad. Females.
					21	22	23	24	25	26	27	28	29	30	31	32	33	34	35
Class D.—Preparation and supply of material substances.—*contd.*	XII. Textile Fabrics and dress.—*contd.*	40. Cotton.	231	Cotton cleaners, pressers and ginners ...	1,000	12	988	225	12	213	8,252	1,484	6,768	545	196	349	1,862	601	1,261
			232	Cotton carpet and rug makers and sellers ...	32	26	6	13	7	6	...	...	...	...	...	...	...	...	...
			233	Cotton spinners, sizers and yarn beaters.	3,690	1,577	2,113	18,354	4,643	13,711	1,717	595	1,122	1,645	319	1,326	344	59	285
			234	Cotton weavers, Mill-owners and managers ...	40,466	22,761	17,705	184	40	144	29,097	15,080	14,017	17,833	9,628	8,205	8,757	4,512	4,245
			235	Cotton Factory hands (undefined) ...	...	...	...	10	10	...	...	...	...	10	5	5	94	30	64
			236	Calenderers, Fullers and printers ...	...	...	...	...	...	...	...	...	...	...	...	...	...	...	...
			237	Cotton dyers ...	282	129	153	1,568	806	762	1,583	806	777	533	313	220	1,041	522	519
			238	Tape makers and sellers ...	104	6	98	2	2	...	...	...	...	...	...	...	...	...	...
			239	Tent manufacturers and sellers ...	...	...	...	...	...	...	...	...	...	11	11	...	...	...	...
				Total Sub-order 40	45,574	24,511	21,063	20,356	5,520	14,836	40,649	17,965	22,684	20,577	10,472	10,105	12,098	5,724	6,374
		41. Jute, flax, coir, &c.	240	Flax-spinners, weavers, and sellers ...	...	...	...	...	...	...	...	...	...	...	...	...	5	...	5
			241	Hemp rope makers and sellers ...	253	94	159	239	170	69	82	36	46	32	23	9	66	39	27
			242	Jute manufacturers, managers and agents ...	...	...	...	...	...	...	...	...	...	...	...	...	...	...	...
			243	Sacking, tarpaulin and gunny makers and sellers ...	205	160	45	300	184	116	230	128	102	17	13	4	299	169	130
			244	Net makers and sellers ...	...	...	...	5	...	5	3	3	...	6	6	...	...	...	...
			245	Fancy work dealers ...	...	...	...	...	...	...	...	...	...	...	...	...	...	...	...
			246	Coir preparers, manufacturers and sellers	...	...	...	...	...	...	1	1	...	...	...	...	...	...	...
				Total Sub-order 41	458	254	204	544	354	190	316	168	148	55	42	13	370	208	162
		42. Dress.	247	Tailors and darners ...	4,365	2,022	2,343	6,100	2,809	3,291	4,312	2,107	2,205	2,156	1,253	903	2,136	1,104	1,032
			248	Milliners and dress-makers ...	...	...	...	...	...	...	...	...	...	...	...	...	...	...	...
			249	Outfitters, and clothes and quilt dealers...	...	...	...	...	...	...	...	...	...	...	...	...	9	...	9
			250	Hosiers and Haberdashers ...	56	33	23	474	222	252	580	216	364	154	90	64	346	185	161
			251	Hat, cap and turban makers and sellers...	...	...	...	...	...	...	...	...	...	17	17	...	...	...	...
			252	Turban binders ...	...	...	...	...	...	...	30	30	...	...	...	...	44	12	32
			253	Umbrella makers and sellers ...	...	...	...	...	...	...	...	...	...	6	4	2	...	...	...
			254	Embroiderers and lace and muslin makers...	...	...	...	5	...	5	50	...	50	...	...	...	75	...	75
			255	Button makers and sellers ...	...	...	...	...	...	...	...	...	...	...	...	...	...	...	...
			256	False-plait makers and sellers ...	2	2	...	12	12	...	...	...	...	86	80	6	...	...	...
			257	Piece-goods dealers ...	4,042	1,548	2,494	9,647	6,208	3,439	6,788	4,299	2,489	1,865	678	1,187	3,997	2,098	1,899
				Total Sub-order 42	8,465	3,605	4,860	16,238	9,251	6,987	11,760	6,652	5,108	4,234	2,072	2,162	6,607	3,399	3,208
				Total Order XII......	63,023	32,897	30,126	118,917	58,636	60,281	61,335	28,772	32,563	28,230	14,814	13,916	27,545	14,097	13,448

TABLE XVII B.

Occupations by Districts.—*Continued.*

Class.	Order.	Sub-order and Group.	Serial No.	Occupations.	Birh. Total.	Birh. Males.	Birh. Females.	Nander. Total.	Nander. Males.	Nander. Females.	Naldrug. Total.	Naldrug. Males.	Naldrug. Females.	Bidar. Total.	Bidar. Males.	Bidar. Females.	Parbhani. Total.	Parbhani. Males.	Parbhani. Females.
					36	37	38	39	40	41	42	43	44	45	46	47	48	49	50
Class D.—Preparation and supply of material substances.—*contd.*	XII. Textile Fabrics and dress.—*contd.*	40. Cotton.	231	Cotton cleaners, pressers and ginners ...	2,174	1,801	373	2,530	1,121	1,409	311	96	215	3,223	1,440	1,783	3,387	1,940	1,447
			232	Cotton carpet and rug makers and sellers...	13	...	13	...	...	...	...	...	...	...	...	...	2	...	2
			233	Cotton spinners, sizers and yarn beaters	344	127	217	7,714	1,234	6,480	321	120	201	2,703	466	2,237	1,858	876	982
			234	Cotton weavers, Mill-owners and managers	8,935	4,637	4,298	14,899	8,627	6,272	4,185	2,196	1,989	14,041	6,907	7,134	14,702	7,117	7,585
			235	Cotton Factory hands (undefined) ...	...	...	...	...	...	...	...	...	...	...	...	...	4	4	...
			236	Calenderers, fullers and printers ...	...	...	...	...	...	...	...	...	...	...	...	...	...	...	...
			237	Cotton dyers	852	466	386	2,034	1,092	942	799	390	409	1,445	871	574	2,048	1,108	940
			238	Tape makers and sellers	9	9	...	...	...	...	57	57	...	...	...	...	8	...	8
			239	Tent manufacturers and sellers ...	...	...	...	...	...	...	...	...	...	...	...	...	...	...	...
				Total Sub-order 40	12,327	7,040	5,287	27,177	12,074	15,103	5,673	2,859	2,814	21,412	9,684	11,728	21,504	10,540	10,964
		41. Jute, flax, coir, &c.	240	Flax-spinners, weavers, and sellers ...	...	...	...	...	...	...	...	...	...	...	...	...	22	22	...
			241	Hemp rope makers and sellers... ...	5	1	4	...	...	...	61	19	42	89	87	2	14	12	2
			242	Jute manufacturers, managers and agents	...	...	...	...	...	...	...	...	...	...	...	...	...	...	...
			243	Sacking, tarpaulin and gunny makers and sellers	56	8	48	108	34	74	556	296	260	1,506	845	661	309	206	103
			244	Net makers and sellers	...	...	...	...	...	...	...	...	...	...	...	...	3	...	3
			245	Fancy work dealers	...	...	...	...	...	...	...	...	...	...	...	...	...	...	...
			246	Coir preparers, manufacturers and sellers	...	...	...	923	370	553	7	7	...	16	...	16	...	...	...
				Total Sub-order 41	61	9	52	1,031	404	627	624	322	302	1,611	932	679	348	240	108
		42. Dress.	247	Tailors and darners	1,278	708	570	2,244	1,141	1,108	935	488	447	2,718	1,495	1,223	1,491	790	701
			248	Milliners and dress-makers	...	...	...	...	...	...	...	...	...	...	...	...	...	...	...
			249	Outfitters, and clothes and quilt dealers...	...	...	...	...	...	...	...	...	...	...	...	...	...	...	...
			250	Hosiers and Haberdashers	325	117	208	293	132	161	236	102	134	558	242	316	53	35	18
			251	Hat, cap and turban makers and sellers...	...	...	...	...	...	...	...	...	...	2	2	...	...	...	...
			252	Turban binders	5	...	5	12	11	1	...	...	...	40	18	22	...	...	...
			253	Umbrella makers and sellers	...	...	...	...	...	...	...	...	...	...	...	...	...	...	...
			254	Embroiderers and lace and muslin makers	...	...	...	...	...	...	...	...	...	...	...	...	53	23	30
			255	Button makers and sellers	...	...	...	...	...	...	...	...	...	...	...	...	...	...	...
			256	False-plait makers and sellers	...	...	...	...	...	...	...	...	...	49	16	33	...	...	...
			257	Piece-goods dealers	2,435	1,216	1,219	6,234	2,689	3,545	3,644	2,088	1,556	7,274	3,966	3,308	6,344	3,420	2,924
				Total Sub-order 42	4,043	2,041	2,002	8,783	3,973	4,810	4,815	2,678	2,137	10,641	5,739	4,902	7,941	4,268	3,673
				Total Order XII......	22,643	12,216	10,427	40,331	18,264	22,067	18,019	9,503	8,516	44,018	21,875	22,143	35,538	17,798	17,740

TABLE XVII B.

Occupations by Districts.—*Continued.*

Class D.—Preparation and supply of material substances.—*contd.*

XII. Textile Fabrics and dress.—*concld.*

Sub-order and Group.	Serial No.	Occupations.	Sirpur Tandur. Total.	Sirpur Tandur. Males.	Sirpur Tandur. Females.	Gulbarga. Total.	Gulbarga. Males.	Gulbarga. Females.	Raichur. Total.	Raichur. Males.	Raichur. Females.	Lingsugur. Total.	Lingsugur. Males.	Lingsugur. Females.	Railways. Total.	Railways. Males.	Railways. Females.
			51	52	53	54	55	56	57	58	59	60	61	62	63	64	65
40. Cotton.	231	Cotton cleaners, pressers and ginners ...	879	446	433	2,049	1,013	1,036	2,830	1,194	1,636	1,830	985	895	...	...	...
	232	Cotton carpet and rug makers and sellers ...	...	...	...	...	...	...	88	53	85	—	...	...	...	...	...
	233	Cotton spinners, sizers and yarn beaters	1,085	302	783	1,629	849	1,280	8,831	682	8,199	4,285	226	4,059	—	—	—
	234	Cotton weavers, Mill-owners and managers ...	13,772	7,874	5,898	27,894	14,646	13,248	20,103	10,170	9,935	15,171	8,042	7,129			
	235	Cotton Factory hands (undefined) ...	...	...	...	1,099	596	503	23	11	12	...	...	...	13	10	8
	236	Calenderers, fullers and printers ...	...	...	...	...	...	...	...	...	...	...	...	...	...	...	...
	237	Cotton dyers ...	264	108	156	2,502	742	760	512	325	187	718	333	385	...	...	...
	238	Tape makers and sellers ...	...	...	...	5	4	1	14	1	13	...	...	...	...	...	...
	239	Tent manufacturers and sellers ...	...	...	...	...	...	...	...	...	...	...	...	...	...	...	...
		Total Sub-order 40......	16,000	8,730	7,270	34,178	17,350	16,828	27,401	12,386	15,015	22,004	9,536	12,468	13	10	8
41. Jute, flax, coir, &c.	240	Flax-spinners, weavers, and sellers ...	...	...	...	...	...	...	...	...	...	...	...	...	...	...	...
	241	Hemp rope makers and sellers ...	...	...	...	1	1	...	199	24	175	199	90	109	...	...	...
	242	Jute manufacturers, managers and agents ...	...	...	...	...	...	...	8	1	2	...	...	...	...	...	...
	243	Sacking, tarpaulin and gunny makers and sellers ...	30	13	17	95	65	30	19	10	9	7	4	8	...	...	...
	244	Net makers and sellers ...	...	...	...	10	10	...	...	...	...	...	...	...	...	...	...
	245	Fancy work dealers ...	21	21	...	...	...	...	...	...	...	...	...	...	...	...	...
	246	Coir preparers, manufacturers and sellers	...	...	...	...	...	...	...	...	...	...	...	...	...	...	...
		Total Sub-order 41......	51	34	17	106	76	30	221	35	186	206	94	112	...	...	...
42. Dress.	247	Tailors and darners ...	972	484	488	2,448	1,128	1,320	1,310	654	656	1,483	664	819	24	14	10
	248	Milliners and dress-makers ...	...	...	...	...	...	...	...	...	...	...	...	...	...	...	...
	249	Outfitters, and clothes and quilt dealers...	...	...	...	...	...	...	252	125	127	2,266	1,151	1,115	...	...	...
	250	Hosiers and Haberdashers ...	88	9	29	889	234	155	...	...	...	...	...	...	...	...	...
	251	Hat, cap and turban makers and sellers.	...	...	...	...	...	...	...	...	...	...	...	...	...	...	...
	252	Turban binders ...	...	...	...	8	1	7	6	...	6	1	1	...	...	...	...
	253	Umbrella makers and sellers ...	...	...	...	...	...	...	...	...	...	...	...	...	...	...	...
	254	Embroiderers and lace and muslin makers...	1	1	...	...	...	...	...	...	...	...	...	...	...	...	...
	255	Button makers and sellers ...	...	...	...	...	...	...	15	7	8	...	...	...	...	...	...
	256	False-plait makers and sellers ...	...	...	...	...	...	...	501	233	268	...	...	...	...	...	...
	257	Piece-goods dealers ...	2,926	707	2,219	5,776	2,799	2,977	1,709	895	814	2,864	1,516	1,348	5	5	...
		Total Sub-order 42......	3,937	1,201	2,736	8,621	4,162	4,459	8,793	1,914	1,879	6,614	3,332	3,282	29	19	10
		Total Order XII......	20,802	10,378	10,424	53,091	26,907	26,184	37,413	16,995	20,418	30,661	13,758	16,903	42	29	13

TABLE XVII B.

Occupations by Districts.—*Continued.*

Class D.—Preparation and supply of material substances.—*contd.*

XIII. Metals and precious stones.

Sub-order and Group	Serial No.	Occupations	Grand Total: Total	Grand Total: Males	Grand Total: Females	Hyderabad: Total	Hyderabad: Males	Hyderabad: Females	Atraf-i-Balda: Total	Atraf-i-Balda: Males	Atraf-i-Balda: Females	Mahabubnagar: Total	Mahabubnagar: Males	Mahabubnagar: Females	Nalgonda: Total	Nalgonda: Males	Nalgonda: Females
3	4	5	6	7	8	9	10	11	12	13	14	15	16	17	18	19	20
43. Gold, silver and precious stones.	258	Gold and silver dealers...	1,083	736	297	431	249	182	6	6	...	28	12	16	8	8	...
	259	Gold and silver assayers	106	20	86	37	20	17	...	...	...	...	...	...	...	...	...
	260	Gold and silver workers	90,046	46,887	43,159	4,576	2,441	2,135	3,081	1,576	1,505	4,683	2,435	2,248	5,715	2,994	2,721
	261	Gold beaters	64	29	35	45	20	25	...	...	...	...	...	...	...	...	...
	262	Goldsmiths' dust washers	408	180	226	8	4	4	1	...	1	87	14	28	14	10	4
	263	Gold miners, managers, agents	51	89	12	...	...	...	...	...	...	...	...	...	...	...	...
	264	Enamellers	9	5	4	4	2	2	...	...	...	...	...	...	5	3	2
	265	Electro-platers	122	73	49	89	40	49	...	...	...	...	...	...	...	...	...
	266	Gold and silver wire drawers, and braid makers...	1,275	678	597	360	179	181	...	...	...	...	...	...	...	...	...
	267	Plate and plated ware dealers	3	1	2	3	1	2	...	...	...	...	...	...	...	...	...
	268	Diamond-polishers and dealers	18	5	8	13	5	8	...	...	...	...	...	...	...	...	...
	269	Diamond diggers, washers, &c...	5	2	3	5	2	3	...	...	...	...	...	...	...	...	...
	270	Ruby workers	6	6	...	...	...	...	...	...	...	...	...	...	...	...	...
	271	Ruby and emerald, &c., dealers	1	1	...	...	...	...	...	...	...	...	...	...	...	...	...
	272	Pearl divers	2	...	2	...	...	...	...	...	...	...	...	...	...	...	...
	273	Pearl and other precious (stone unspecified) dealers	602	378	224	285	155	130	6	2	4	45	38	7	21	21	...
	274	Coral dealers	1	1	...	...	...	...	1	1	...	...	...	...	...	...	...
	275	Cornelian and Agate cutters and sellers..	...	...	...	...	...	...	...	...	...	...	...	...	...	...	...
		Total Sub-order 43	93,745	49,041	44,704	5,856	3,118	2,738	3,095	1,585	1,510	4,793	2,499	2,294	5,765	3,038	2,727
44. Brass, copper and bell metal.	276	Brass workers and sellers	7	4	3	4	4	...	...	...	...	...	...	...	...	...	...
	277	Brass pot makers and sellers	6,372	3,649	2,723	58	28	30	124	10	114	166	123	43	69	10	59
	278	Brass Image casters and sellers...	8	3	5	8	3	5	...	...	...	...	...	...	...	...	...
	279	Copper workers and sellers	5,052	2,650	2,402	9	4	5	...	...	...	...	...	...	...	...	...
	280	Brass and copper wire drawers and sellers ...	8	...	3	...	...	...	...	...	...	...	...	...	...	...	...
	281	Bell metal workers and sellers ...	805	148	157	89	26	63	...	...	...	...	...	...	...	...	...
	282	General workers in brass, copper and bell-metal	7,989	4,327	3,662	363	203	160	1,110	605	505	561	325	236	1,060	548	512
	283	Brass and copper dealers	291	154	137	192	90	102	...	...	...	...	...	...	...	...	...
		Total Sub-order 44	20,027	10,935	9,092	718	353	365	1,234	615	619	727	448	279	1,129	558	571
45. Tin, zinc, mercury and lead.	284	Tin workers and sellers	1,899	1,135	764	422	228	194	6	6	...	...	...	...	...	...	...
	285	Tinfoil makers and sellers	6	1	5	...	...	...	...	...	...	...	...	...	...	...	...
	286	Zinc workers and sellers	2	2	...	1	1	...	...	...	...	...	...	...	...	...	...
	287	Lead and quick silver workers and sellers ...	4	2	2	4	2	2	...	...	...	...	...	...	...	...	...
	288	General workers in tin, lead and zinc ...	197	103	94	5	3	2	10	6	4	14	9	5	25	12	13
		Total Sub-order 45	2,108	1,243	865	482	284	198	16	12	4	14	9	5	25	12	13

TABLE XVII B.

Occupations by Districts.—*Continued.*

Class.	Order.	Sub-order and Group.	Serial No.	Occupations.	Warangal. Total.	Warangal. Males.	Warangal. Females.	Elgandal. Total.	Elgandal. Males.	Elgandal. Females.	Indur. Total.	Indur. Males.	Indur. Females.	Medak. Total.	Medak. Males.	Medak. Females.	Aurangabad. Total.	Aurangabad. Males.	Aurangabad. Females.
					21	22	23	24	25	26	27	28	29	30	31	32	33	34	35
Class D.—Preparation and supply of material substances.—*contd.*	XIII. Metals and precious stones.	43. Gold, silver and precious stones.	258	Gold and silver dealers	...	...	...	63	56	7	278	274	4	103	89	14	7	...	7
			259	Gold and silver assayers	...	...	...	...	...	...	67	...	67	...	...	...	...	...	...
			260	Gold and silver workers...	7,751	4,085	3,666	13,140	6,727	6,413	4,790	2,343	2,447	2,568	1,325	1,243	7,135	3,693	3,442
			261	Gold beaters	...	...	...	...	...	...	...	...	...	...	...	...	19	9	10
			262	Goldsmiths' dust washers	17	8	9	10	...	10	10	10	...	21	9	12	36	15	21
			263	Gold miners, managers, agents ...	...	...	...	...	...	...	...	...	...	...	...	...	...	...	...
			264	Enamellers	...	...	...	...	...	...	...	...	...	...	...	...	...	...	...
			265	Electro-platers	...	...	...	...	...	...	...	...	...	...	...	...	5	5	...
			266	Gold and silver wire drawers, and braid makers...	...	...	...	...	...	...	24	24	...	...	...	...	726	405	321
			267	Plate and plated ware dealers	...	...	...	...	...	...	...	...	...	...	...	...	...	...	...
			268	Diamond-polishers and dealers... ...	...	...	...	...	...	...	...	...	...	...	...	...	...	...	...
			269	Diamond diggers, washers, &c.... ...	...	...	...	...	...	...	...	...	...	...	...	...	...	...	...
			270	Ruby workers	...	...	...	...	...	...	...	...	...	...	...	...	...	...	...
			271	Ruby and emerald, &c., dealers ...	...	...	...	...	...	...	...	...	...	...	...	...	...	...	...
			272	Pearl divers	...	...	...	...	...	...	...	...	...	2	...	2	...	...	...
			273	Pearl and other precious (stone unspecified) dealers	2	2	...	18	3	15	4	4	...	84	34	50	7	7	...
			274	Coral dealers	...	...	...	...	...	...	...	...	...	...	...	...	...	...	...
			275	Cornelian and Agate cutters and sellers.	...	...	...	...	...	...	...	...	...	...	...	...	...	...	...
				Total Sub-order 43	7,770	4,095	3,675	13,231	6,786	6,445	5,173	2,655	2,518	2,778	1,457	1,321	7,985	4,134	3,801
		44. Brass, copper and bell metal.	276	Brass workers and sellers	3	...	3	...	...	...	...	...	...	...	...	...	...	...	...
			277	Brass pot makers and sellers	1	1	...	...	...	...	1,191	596	595	28	1	27	1,246	988	258
			278	Brass Image casters and sellers ...	...	...	...	...	...	...	...	...	...	...	...	...	...	...	...
			279	Copper workers and sellers	...	...	...	...	...	...	335	...	335	...	...	...	1,028	390	638
			280	Brass and copper wire drawers and sellers	...	...	...	...	...	...	...	...	...	...	...	...	3	...	3
			281	Bell metal workers and sellers	10	7	3	...	...	...	27	27	...	...	...	...	14	6	8
			282	General workers in brass, copper and bell-metal	1,185	589	596	2,389	1,296	1,093	106	73	33	443	272	171	24	24	...
			283	Brass and copper dealers	41	41	...	...	...	...	...	...	...	...	...	...	...	...	...
				Total Sub-order 44	1,240	638	602	2,389	1,296	1,093	1,659	696	963	471	273	198	2,315	1,408	907
		45. Tin zinc, mercury and lead.	284	Tin workers and sellers...	...	...	...	...	...	...	179	64	115	...	...	...	331	93	238
			285	Tinfoil makers and sellers	...	...	...	...	...	...	...	...	...	...	...	...	...	...	...
			286	Zinc workers and sellers	...	...	...	...	...	...	...	...	...	...	...	...	...	...	...
			287	Lead and quick silver workers and sellers	...	...	...	...	...	...	...	...	...	...	...	...	...	...	...
			288	General workers in tin, lead and zinc...	12	7	5	12	8	4	...	...	...	118	57	61	...	...	...
				Total Sub-order 45	12	7	5	12	8	4	179	64	115	118	57	61	331	93	238

TABLE XVII B.

Occupations by Districts.—*Continued.*

Class.	Order.	Sub-order and Group.	Serial No.	Occupations.	Birh. Total.	Birh. Males.	Birh. Females.	Nander. Total.	Nander. Males.	Nander. Females.	Naldrug. Total.	Naldrug. Males.	Naldrug. Females.	Bidar. Total.	Bidar. Males.	Bidar. Females.	Parbhani. Total.	Parbhani. Males.	Parbhani. Females.
					36	37	38	39	40	41	42	43	44	45	46	47	48	49	50
Class D.—Preparation and supply of material substances.—*contd.*	XIII. Metals and precious stones.	43. Gold, silver and precious stones.	258	Gold and silver dealers...	4	...	4	...	...	...	27	...	27	1	1	...	...	...	...
			259	Gold and silver assayers	2	...	2	...	...	...	...	...	...	...	...	...	...	...	...
			260	Gold and silver workers	5,339	2,738	2,601	4,338	2,231	2,107	3,806	2,065	1,741	5,494	2,885	2,609	5,705	3,045	2,660
			261	Gold beaters	...	...	...	...	...	...	...	...	...	...	...	...	...	...	...
			262	Goldsmiths' dust washers	15	...	15	...	...	...	39	17	22	94	37	57	6	...	6
			263	Gold miners, managers, agents ...	...	...	...	...	...	...	...	...	...	...	...	...	...	...	...
			264	Enamellers	...	...	...	...	...	...	...	...	...	...	...	...	...	...	...
			265	Electro-platers	28	28	...	...	...	...	...	...	...	...	...	...	...	...	...
			266	Gold and silver wire drawers, and braid makers	72	26	46	...	...	...	8	8	...	...	...	...	...	...	...
			267	Plate and plated ware dealers	...	...	...	...	...	...	...	...	...	...	...	...	...	...	...
			268	Diamond-polishers and dealers... ...	...	...	...	...	...	...	...	...	...	...	...	...	...	...	...
			269	Diamond diggers, washers, &c. ...	...	...	...	...	...	...	...	...	...	...	...	...	...	...	...
			270	Ruby workers	...	...	...	...	...	...	...	...	...	...	...	...	...	...	...
			271	Ruby and emerald, &c., dealers ...	...	...	...	...	...	...	...	...	...	...	...	...	...	...	...
			272	Pearl divers	...	...	...	...	...	...	...	...	...	...	...	...	...	...	...
			273	Pearl and other precious (stone unspecified) dealers	28	28	...	...	...	...	3	3	...	25	23	2	44	28	16
			274	Coral dealers	...	...	...	...	...	...	...	...	...	...	...	...	...	...	...
			275	Cornelian and Agate cutters and sellers.	...	...	...	...	...	...	...	...	...	...	...	...	...	...	...
				Total Sub-order 43......	5,488	2,820	2,668	4,338	2,231	2,107	3,878	2,088	1,790	5,614	2,946	2,668	5,755	3,073	2,682
		44. Brass, copper and bell metal.	276	Brass workers and sellers	...	...	...	...	...	...	...	...	...	...	...	...	...	...	...
			277	Brass pot makers and sellers	6	6	...	483	303	180	177	115	62	718	286	482	1,814	1,014	800
			278	Brass Image casters and sellers ...	...	...	...	...	...	...	...	...	...	...	...	...	...	...	...
			279	Copper workers and sellers	2,017	1,240	777	85	65	20	270	184	86	874	810	64	256	98	158
			280	Brass and copper wire drawers and sellers	...	...	...	...	...	...	...	...	...	...	...	...	...	...	...
			281	Bell metal workers and sellers... ...	...	...	...	...	...	...	...	...	...	27	25	2	102	27	75
			282	General workers in brass, copper and bell-metal	49	7	42	122	59	63	63	21	42	132	76	56	...	...	...
			283	Brass and copper dealers	...	...	...	...	...	...	...	...	...	...	...	...	...	...	...
				Total Sub-order 44......	2,072	1,253	819	690	427	263	510	320	190	1,251	697	554	2,172	1,139	1,033
		45. Tin, zinc, mercury and lead.	284	Tin workers and sellers...	56	6	45	19	18	1	11	9	2	227	150	77	33	11	22
			285	Tinfoil makers and sellers	...	...	...	...	...	...	...	...	...	1	1	...	...	...	...
			286	Zinc workers and sellers	...	...	...	...	...	...	...	...	...	1	1	...	...	...	...
			287	Lead and quick silver workers and sellers	...	...	...	...	...	...	...	...	...	...	...	...	...	...	...
			288	General workers in tin, lead and zinc.	...	...	...	...	...	...	...	...	...	...	...	...	...	...	...
				Total Sub-order 45......	51	6	45	19	18	1	11	9	2	229	152	77	33	11	22

TABLE XVII B.

Occupations by Districts.—*Continued.*

Class.	Order.	Sub-order and Group.	Serial No.	Occupations.	Sirpur Tandur. Total.	Sirpur Tandur. Males.	Sirpur Tandur. Females.	Gulbarga. Total.	Gulbarga. Males.	Gulbarga. Females.	Raichur. Total.	Raichur. Males.	Raichur. Females.	Lingasugur. Total.	Lingasugur. Males.	Lingasugur. Females.	Railways. Total.	Railways. Males.	Railways. Females.
					51	52	53	54	55	56	57	58	59	60	61	62	63	64	65
Class D.—Preparation and supply of material substances.—*contd.*	XIII. Metal and precious stones.	43. Gold, silver and precious stones.	258	Gold and silver dealers ...	...	...	...	...	...	...	26	20	6	51	21	30	...	...	...
			259	Gold and silver assayers	...	...	...	...	...	...	...	...	...	...	...	...	...	...	...
			260	Gold and silver workers	2,009	1,062	947	3,719	2,005	1,714	2,425	1,304	1,121	3,771	1,982	1,839	1	1	...
			261	Gold beaters	...	...	...	...	...	...	...	...	...	...	...	...	...	...	...
			262	Goldsmiths' dust washers	1	1	...	8	8	...	15	7	8	79	45	34	...	...	...
			263	Gold miners, managers, agents	...	...	...	...	...	...	5	2	3	46	37	9	...	...	...
			264	Enamellers	...	...	...	...	...	...	...	...	...	...	...	...	...	...	...
			265	Electro-platers	...	...	...	...	...	...	...	...	...	...	...	...	...	...	...
			266	Gold and silver wire drawers, and braid makers	1	1	..	81	32	49	8	8	...	...	...	...	...	...	...
			267	Plate and plated ware dealers...	...	...		...	...	...	...	...	...	...	...	...	...	...	...
			268	Diamond-polishers and dealers...	...	...	...	...	...	...	...	...	...	...	...	...	...	...	...
			269	Diamond diggers, washers, &c....	...	...	...	...	...	...	...	...	...	...	...	...	...	...	...
			270	Ruby workers	...	...	...	6	6	...	...	...	...	...	...	...	...	...	...
			271	Ruby and emerald, &c., dealers	...	...	...	...	...	...	1	1	...	...	...	...	...	...	...
			272	Pearl divers	...	...	...	...	...	...	...	...	...	...	...	...	...	...	...
			273	Pearl and other precious (stone unspecified) dealers	1	1	...	19	19	...	5	5	...	...	...	...	8	8	...
			274	Coral dealers	...	...	...	...	...	...	...	...	...	...	...	...	...	...	...
			275	Cornelian and Agate cutters and sellers	...	...	...	...	...	...	...	...	...	...	...	...	...	...	...
				Total Sub-order 43	2,012	1,065	947	3,828	2,065	1,763	2,485	1,347	1,138	3,947	2,035	1,912	4	4	...
		44. Brass, copper and bell metal.	276	Brass workers and sellers	...	...	...	...	...	...	...	...	...	...	...	...	...	...	...
			277	Brass pot makers and sellers	69	49	20	227	124	103	...	...	...	...	...	...	...	...	...
			278	Brass Image casters and sellers	...	...	...	...	...	...	...	...	...	...	...	...	...	...	...
			279	Copper workers and sellers	85	85	...	582	267	315	...	...	...	...	...	...	11	7	4
			280	Brass and copper wire drawers and sellers ...	...	...	...	...	...	...	...	...	...	...	...	...	...	...	...
			281	Bell metal workers and sellers...	...	...	...	36	30	6	...	...	...	...	...	...	...	...	...
			282	General workers in brass, copper and bell-metal	39	15	24	14	...	14	122	92	30	207	122	85	...	...	...
			283	Brass and copper dealers	...	...	...	...	...	...	33	10	23	25	13	12	...	...	...
				Total Sub-order 44	193	149	44	859	421	438	155	102	53	232	135	97	11	7	4
		45. Tin, zinc, mercury and lead.	284	Tin workers and sellers...	...	...	...	446	427	39	121	102	19	33	21	12	...	...	...
			285	Tinfoil makers and sellers	...	...	...	5	...	5	...	...	...	...	...	...	...	...	...
			286	Zinc workers and sellers	...	...	...	...	...	...	...	...	...	...	...	...	...	...	...
			287	Lead and quick-silver workers and sellers ...	...	...	...	...	...	...	...	...	...	...	...	...	...	...	...
			288	General workers in tin, lead and zinc...	...	...	...	...	...	...	1	1	...	...	...	...	...	...	...
				Total Sub-order 45	...	...	...	471	427	44	122	103	19	33	21	12	...	...	...

TABLE XVII B.

Occupations by Districts.—*Continued.*

Class.	Order.	Sub-order and Group.	Serial No.	Occupations.	Grand Total. Total.	Grand Total. Males.	Grand Total. Females.	Hyderabad. Total.	Hyderabad. Males.	Hyderabad. Females.	Atraf-i-Balda. Total.	Atraf-i-Balda. Males.	Atraf-i-Balda. Females.	Mahabubnagar. Total.	Mahabubnagar. Males.	Mahabubnagar. Females.	Nalgonda. Total.	Nalgonda. Males.	Nalgonda. Females.
1	2	3	4	5	6	7	8	9	10	11	12	13	14	15	16	17	18	19	20
Class D.—Preparation and supply of material substances.—*contd.*	XIII. Metals and precious stones.—*concld.*	46. Iron and steel.	289	Iron and steel founders, smelters and sellers ...	882	434	398	35	21	14	4	4	...	177	104	73	...	...	...
			290	Blacksmiths ...	54,851	29,290	25,561	1,909	1,048	861	2,159	981	1,178	3,554	1,882	1,672	2,981	1,618	1,318
			291	Iron and hardware dealers ...	626	139	487	29	12	17	2	...	2	...	...	...	8	...	8
			292	Nail makers and sellers...	...	...	...	...	...	...	...	...	...	...	...	...	...	...	...
			293	Lock makers, menders, and sellers ..	16	10	6	7	8	4	...	...	...	...	...	...	...	...	...
			294	Weight makers and stampers ...	...	...	...	...	...	...	...	...	...	...	...	...	...	...	...
				Total Sub-order 46	56,325	29,873	26,452	1,980	1,084	896	2,165	985	1,180	3,731	1,986	1,745	2,989	1,618	1,321
				Total Order XIII	172,205	91,092	81,113	8,986	4,789	4,197	6,510	3,197	3,313	9,265	4,942	4,328	9,858	5,226	4,632
	XIV. Glass, pottery and stone-ware.	47. Glass and Chinaware.	295	Glass-blowers, window glass makers, &c.	32	2	30	...	...	...	...	...	...	...	...	...	...	...	...
			296	Bottle dealers ...	47	18	29	47	18	29	...	...	...	...	...	...	...	...	...
			297	Glass and Chinaware dealers ...	103	41	62	46	20	26	...	...	...	1	1	...	...	...	...
				Total Sub-order 47	182	61	121	93	38	55	...	...	...	1	1	...	...	...	...
		48. Earthen and stoneware.	298	Potters and pot and pipe-bowl makers and sellers. (*Some are brick and tile makers also*) ...	91,488	47,772	43,716	1,290	656	634	4,749	2,467	2,282	4,618	2,631	1,987	5,890	3,277	2,613
			299	Grindstone and millstone makers, menders, and sellers ...	2,144	1,126	1,018	149	71	78	30	24	6	124	59	65	22	12	10
			300	Pestle and mortar makers and sellers ...	51	85	16	5	4	1	...	...	...	...	...	...	15	...	15
			301	Quartz and soapstone powder preparers and sellers ...	116	45	71	...	...	...	...	...	...	111	44	67	...	...	...
				Total Sub-order 48	93,799	48,978	44,821	1,444	731	713	4,779	2,491	2,288	4,853	2,734	2,119	5,927	3,289	2,638
				Total Order XIV	93,981	49,039	44,942	1,537	769	768	4,779	2,491	2,288	4,854	2,735	2,119	5,927	3,289	2,638
	XV. Wood, cane & leaves, &c.	49. Timber and wood.	302	Timber and bamboo agents, and dealers.	691	390	301	55	36	19	245	169	76	72	45	27	...	...	...
			303	Wood cutters and sawyers ...	651	447	204	255	149	106	172	152	20	1	1	...	...	...	...
			304	Carpenters ...	110,018	59,038	50,975	8,376	1,738	1,638	8,578	1,912	1,666	6,159	3,586	2,623	4,509	2,355	2,154
			305	Coopers and box makers ...	53	7	46	14	2	12	2	...	2	...	...	...	18	...	18
				Total Sub-order 49	111,408	59,882	51,526	3,700	1,925	1,775	8,997	2,233	1,764	6,232	3,582	2,650	4,527	2,355	2,172
		50. Canework, matting and leaves, &c.	306	Bamboo and rattan splitters, workers, and sellers ...	10,609	5,467	5,142	481	222	259	...	...	...	...	...	...	...	...	...
			307	Basket weavers and winnowing pan makers and sellers ...	26,983	13,989	12,994	263	180	133	1,466	768	708	3,031	1,756	1,275	2,742	1,386	1,856
			308	Mat makers and sellers...	7,598	3,739	3,859	95	39	56	445	151	294	2,062	1,232	830	279	133	146
			309	Screen (chik) makers and sellers ...	1	...	1	1	...	1	...	...	...	...	...	...	...	...	...

TABLE XVII B.

Occupations by Districts.—*Continued.*

Class.	Order.	Sub-order and Group.	Serial No.	Occupations.	Warangal. Total.	Warangal. Males.	Warangal. Females.	Elgandal. Total.	Elgandal. Males.	Elgandal. Females.	Indur. Total.	Indur. Males.	Indur. Females.	Medak. Total.	Medak. Males.	Medak. Females.	Aurangabad. Total.	Aurangabad. Males.	Aurangabad. Females.
					21	22	23	24	25	26	27	28	29	30	31	32	33	34	35
Class D.—Preparation and supply of material substances.—*contd.*	XIII. Metals and precious stones.—*concld.*	46. Iron and steel.	289	Iron and steel founders, smelters and sellers ...	253	108	145	348	193	155	...	...	...	11	...	11	...	...	...
			290	Blacksmiths	3,770	2,190	1,580	7,427	3,860	3,567	8,324	1,837	1,487	1,650	948	702	4,017	2,150	1,867
			291	Iron and hardware dealers	...	...	...	...	...	...	85	...	85	...	...	...	85	85	...
			292	Nail makers and sellers...	...	...	...	...	...	...	...	...	...	...	...	...	...	...	...
			293	Lock makers, menders, and sellers	...	...	...	...	...	...	...	...	...	...	...	...	...	...	...
			294	Weight makers and stampers ...	...	...	...	...	...	...	...	...	...	...	...	...	...	...	...
				Total Sub-order 46......	4,023	2,298	1,725	7,775	4,053	3,722	3,359	1,837	1,522	1,661	948	713	4,052	2,185	1,867
				Total Order XIII	13,045	7,038	6,007	23,407	12,143	11,264	10,370	5,252	5,118	5,028	2,735	2,293	14,633	7,820	6,813
	XIV. Glass, pottery and stoneware.	47. Glass and Chinaware.	295	Glass-blowers, window glass makers, &c.	...	...	...	...	...	...	1	...	1	...	...	...	...	...	...
			296	Bottle dealers	...	...	...	...	...	...	...	...	...	...	...	...	...	...	...
			297	Glass and Chinaware dealers ...	...	...	...	...	...	...	...	...	...	...	...	...	56	20	36
				Total Sub-order 47	...	...	...	...	...	...	1	...	1	...	...	...	56	20	36
		48. Earthen and stoneware.	298	Potters and pot and pipe-bowl makers and sellers. (*Some are brick and tile makers also*) ...	9,055	4,666	4,389	11,516	6,136	5,380	5,520	2,861	2,659	3,326	1,726	1,600	5,983	2,825	3,158
			299	Grindstone and millstone makers, menders, and sellers	32	23	9	77	48	29	97	53	44	33	14	19	316	174	142
			300	Pestle and mortar makers and sellers ...	...	...	...	...	...	...	...	...	...	...	...	...	...	...	...
			301	Quartz and soapstone powder preparers and sellers	...	...	...	...	...	...	...	...	...	5	1	4	...	...	...
				Total Sub-order 48	9,087	4,689	4,398	11,593	6,184	5,409	5,617	2,914	2,703	3,364	1,741	1,623	6,299	2,999	3,300
				Total Order XIV	9,087	4,689	4,398	11,593	6,184	5,409	5,618	2,914	2,704	3,364	1,741	1,623	6,355	3,019	3,336
	XV. Wood, cane & leaves, &c.	49. Timber and wood.	302	Timber and bamboo agents, and dealers.	49	43	6	59	48	11	9	9	...	23	7	16	...	...	...
			303	Wood cutters and sawyers	8	7	1	2	2	...	2	2	...	...	...	...	31	15	16
			304	Carpenters	7,539	3,972	3,567	10,899	6,145	4,754	6,158	3,169	2,989	2,930	1,613	1,317	8,220	4,484	3,736
			305	Coopers and box makers	9	4	5	...	...	...	...	...	...	10	1	9	...	...	...
				Total Sub-order 49	7,605	4,026	3,579	10,960	6,195	4,765	6,169	3,180	2,989	2,963	1,621	1,342	8,251	4,499	3,752
		50. Canework, matting and leaves, &c.	306	Bamboo and rattan splitters, workers, and sellers ...	...	...	...	...	...	...	1,714	835	879	7	4	3	1,119	643	476
			307	Basket weavers and winnowing pan makers and sellers	4,751	2,587	2,164	4,734	2,599	2,135	654	283	371	1,437	620	817	421	102	319
			308	Mat makers and sellers ...	893	497	396	1,627	635	992	...	...	...	644	290	354	62	52	10
			309	Screen (chik) makers and sellers	...	...	...	...	...	...	...	...	...	...	...	...	...	...	...

TABLE XVII B.

Occupations by Districts.—*Continued.*

Class.	Order.	Sub-order and Group.	Serial No.	Occupations.	Birh. Total.	Birh. Males.	Birh. Females.	Nander. Total.	Nander. Males.	Nander. Females.	Naldrug. Total.	Naldrug. Males.	Naldrug. Females.	Bidar. Total.	Bidar. Males.	Bidar. Females.	Parbhani. Total.	Parbhani. Males.	Parbhani. Females.
					36	37	38	39	40	41	42	43	44	45	46	47	48	49	50
Class D.—Preparation and supply of material substances.—*contd.*	XIII. Metals and precious stones.—*concld.*	46. Iron and steel.	289	Iron and steel founders, smelters and sellers ...	...	...	...	...	...	...	...	...	...	...	...	...	...	...	...
			290	Blacksmiths	3,376	1,727	1,649	2,631	1,260	1,371	2,443	1,434	1,009	4,162	2,157	2,005	2,603	1,427	1,176
			291	Iron and hardware dealers	18	18	...	...	...	...	387	...	387	63	39	24	28	14	14
			292	Nail makers and sellers	...	...	...	...	...	...	...	...	...	...	...	...	...	...	...
			293	Lock makers, menders, and sellers	...	...	...	...	...	...	9	7	2	...	...	...	...	...	...
			294	Weight makers and stampers ...	...	...	...	...	...	...	...	...	...	...	...	...	...	...	...
				Total Sub-order 46......	3,394	1,745	1,649	2,631	1,260	1,371	2,839	1,441	1,398	4,225	2,196	2,029	2,631	1,441	1,190
				Total Order XIII......	11,005	5,824	5,181	7,678	3,936	3,742	7,238	3,858	3,380	11,319	5,991	5,328	10,591	5,664	4,927
	XIV. Glass, pottery and stone-ware.—*concld.*	47. Glass and Chinaware.	295	Glass-blowers, window glass makers, &c.	...	...	...	5	2	3	...	...	...	...	...	...	26	...	26
			296	Bottle dealers	...	...	...	...	...	...	...	...	...	...	...	...	...	...	...
			297	Glass and Chinaware dealers ...	...	...	...	...	...	...	...	...	...	...	...	...	...	...	...
				Total Sub-order 47......	...	...	...	5	2	3	...	...	...	...	...	...	26	...	26
		48. Earthen and stoneware.	298	Potters and pot and pipe-bowl makers and sellers. (*Some are brick and tile makers also*) ...	4,775	2,513	2,262	5,834	2,800	3,034	4,593	2,435	2,158	6,753	3,387	3,366	5,859	3,061	2,798
			299	Grindstone and millstone makers, menders, and sellers...	255	157	98	...	...	...	434	192	242	193	154	39	102	38	64
			300	Pestle and mortar makers, and sellers ...	...	...	...	81	81	...	...	...	...	...	...	...	...	...	...
			301	Quartz and soapstone powder preparers and sellers ...	...	...	...	...	...	...	...	...	...	...	...	...	...	...	...
				Total Sub-order 48......	5,030	2,670	2,360	5,865	2,831	3,034	5,027	2,627	2,400	6,946	3,541	3,405	5,961	3,099	2,862
				Total Order XIV......	5,030	2,670	2,360	5,870	2,833	3,037	5,027	2,627	2,400	6,946	3,541	3,405	5,987	3,099	2,888
	XV. Wood, cane & leaves, &c.	49. Timber and wood.	302	Timber and bamboo agents, and dealers	...	...	...	...	...	...	27	5	22	...	...	...	108	...	108
			303	Wood cutters and sawyers ...	29	22	7	5	5	...	21	17	4	7	7	...	21	13	8
			304	Carpenters ...	7,007	3,647	3,360	8,036	4,241	3,795	6,724	3,590	3,134	9,743	5,049	4,694	9,050	4,759	4,291
			305	Coopers and box makers ...	...	...	...	...	...	...	...	...	...	...	...	...	...	...	...
				Total Sub-order 49......	7,036	3,669	3,367	8,041	4,246	3,795	6,772	3,612	3,160	9,750	5,056	4,694	9,179	4,772	4,407
		50. Canework, matting and leaves, &c.	306	Bamboo and rattan splitters, workers, and sellers ...	1,067	697	370	1,296	584	712	388	232	156	1,431	560	871	1,666	878	798
			307	Basket weavers and winnowing pan makers and sellers ...	409	136	273	301	231	70	965	430	535	903	558	345	267	105	162
			308	Mat makers and sellers...	56	6	50	...	...	...	...	...	...	56	25	31	...	...	...
			309	Screen (chik) makers and sellers ...	...	...	...	...	...	...	...	...	...	...	...	...	...	...	...

TABLE XVII B.

Occupations by Districts.—*Continued.*

Class.	Order.	Sub-order and Group.	Serial No.	Occupations.	Sirpur Tandur. Total.	Sirpur Tandur. Males.	Sirpur Tandur. Females.	Gulbarga. Total.	Gulbarga. Males.	Gulbarga. Females.	Raichur. Total.	Raichur. Males.	Raichur. Females.	Lingasugur. Total.	Lingasugur. Males.	Lingasugur. Females.	Railways. Total.	Railways. Males.	Railways. Females.
					51	52	53	54	55	56	57	58	59	60	61	62	63	64	65
Class D.—Preparation and supply of material substances.—*contd.*	XIII. Metals and precious stones.—*concld.*	46. Iron and steel.	289	Iron and steel founders, smelters and sellers ...	...	...	...	...	...	...	4	4	...	...	...	...	...	...	...
			290	Blacksmiths	1,792	972	820	2,942	1,620	1,322	1,757	895	862	2,892	1,276	1,116	12	8	4
			291	Iron and hardware dealers	...	...	...	18	18	...	3	3	...	...	...	...	...	...	...
			292	Nail makers and sellers...	...	...	...	...	...	...	...	...	...	...	...	...	...	...	...
			293	Lock makers, menders, and sellers	...	...	...	...	...	...	...	...	...	...	...	...	...	...	...
			294	Weight makers and stampers ...	...	...	...	...	...	...	...	...	...	...	...	...	...	...	...
				Total Sub-order 46......	1,792	972	820	2,960	1,638	1,322	1,764	902	862	2,892	1,276	1,116	12	8	4
				Total Order XIII	3,997	2,186	1,811	8,118	4,551	3,567	4,526	2,454	2,072	6,604	8,467	3,137	27	19	8
	XIV. Glass, pottery and stone-ware.	47. Glass and Chinaware.	295	Glass-blowers, window glass makers, &c.	...	...	...	...	...	...	...	...	...	...	...	...	...	...	...
			296	Bottle dealers ...	...	...	...	...	...	...	...	...	...	...	...	...	...	...	...
			297	Glass and Chinaware dealers ...	...	...	...	...	...	...	...	...	...	...	...	...	...	...	...
				Total Sub-order 47......	...	...	...	...	...	...	...	...	...	...	...	...	...	...	...
		48. Earthen and stoneware.	298	Potters and pot and pipe-bowl makers and sellers. (*Some are brick and tile makers also*) ...	1,306	620	686	4,298	2,410	1,888	8,227	1,783	1,444	2,896	1,518	1,378	...	...	...
			299	Grindstone and millstone makers, menders, and sellers	16	1	15	74	9	65	112	57	55	78	40	38	...	...	...
			300	Pestle and mortar makers and sellers ...	...	...	...	...	...	...	...	...	...	...	...	...	...	...	...
			301	Quartz and soapstone powder preparers and sellers ...	...	...	...	...	...	...	...	...	...	...	...	...	...	...	...
				Total Sub-order 48......	1,322	621	701	4,372	2,419	1,953	3,339	1,840	1,499	2,974	1,558	1,416	...	...	...
				Total Order XIV	1,322	621	701	4,372	2,419	1,953	3,339	1,840	1,499	2,974	1,558	1,416	...	...	...
	XV. Wood, cane & leaves, &c.	49. Timber and wood.	302	Timber and bamboo agents and dealers	1	1	...	...	...	...	86	20	16	...	...	...	7	7	...
			303	Wood cutters and sawyers ...	7	7	...	8	5	3	4	2	2	78	41	87	...	...	...
			304	Carpenters ...	2,670	1,417	1,253	5,749	3,298	2,451	2,974	1,597	1,877	4,667	2,491	2,176	25	25	...
			305	Coopers and box makers ...	...	...	...	...	...	...	...	...	...	...	...	...	...	...	...
				Total Sub-order 49......	2,678	1,425	1,253	5,757	3,303	2,454	3,014	1,619	1,395	4,745	2,532	2,218	32	32	...
		50. Canework, matting and leaves, &c.	306	Bamboo and rattan splitters, makers and sellers ...	606	366	240	884	451	388	...	...	...	...	...	...	...	...	...
			307	Basket weavers and winnowing pan makers and sellers ...	49	9	40	712	388	324	1,888	739	649	2,490	1,167	1,323	...	...	...
			308	Mat makers and sellers...	28	...	28	268	165	108	329	154	175	759	360	399	...	...	...
			309	Screen (chik) makers and sellers ...	...	...	...	...	...	...	...	...	...	...	...	...	...	...	...

TABLE XVII B.

Occupations by Districts.—*Continued.*

Class.	Order.	Sub-order and Group.	Serial No.	Occupations.	Grand Total. Total.	Grand Total. Males.	Grand Total. Females.	Hyderabad. Total.	Hyderabad. Males.	Hyderabad. Females.	Atraf-i-Balda. Total.	Atraf-i-Balda. Males.	Atraf-i-Balda. Females.	Mahabubnagar. Total.	Mahabubnagar. Males.	Mahabubnagar. Females.	Nalgonda. Total.	Nalgonda. Males.	Nalgonda. Females.
1	2	3	4	5	6	7	8	9	10	11	12	13	14	15	16	17	18	19	20
Class D.—Preparation and supply of material substances.—*contd.*	XV. Wood, cane and leaves, &c.—*concld.*	50. Canework, matting and leaves, &c.—*concld.*	310	Leaf-plate makers and sellers. (*Are also often temple servants*)	5,128	2,701	2,427	49	17	32	146	77	69	828	174	154	41	24	17
			311	Tooth-stick sellers	11	11	...	1	1	...	...	...	...	...	...	...	...	...	...
			312	Leaf-fan makers and sellers	5	1	4	3	...	3	...	...	...	...	...	...	...	...	...
			313	Brush and comb makers and sellers ...	389	148	241	45	12	33	1	1	...	16	...	16	8	8	...
			314	Broom makers and sellers	745	161	584	63	21	42	...	...	...	8	...	8	...	...	...
			315	Pith and bark collectors, workers, and sellers	668	408	260	...	...	...	52	35	17	111	51	60	102	96	6
				Total Sub-order 50	52,137	26,625	25,512	1,001	442	559	2,110	1,027	1,083	5,551	3,218	2,338	3,167	1,642	1,525
				Total Order XV	163,545	86,507	77,038	4,701	2,367	2,334	6,107	3,260	2,847	11,783	6,795	4,988	7,694	3,997	3,697
	XVI. Drugs, gums, dyes, &c.	51. Gums, wax and similar forest produce.	316	India-rubber collectors and sellers ...	...	...	...	...	...	...	...	...	...	...	...	...	...	...	...
			317	Camphor and gum collectors and sellers.	4	2	2	4	2	2	...	...	...	...	...	...	...	...	...
			318	Gallnut (myrobolan) collectors and sellers	11	6	5	...	...	...	...	...	...	...	...	...	...	...	...
			319	Catechu preparers and sellers	...	...	...	...	...	...	...	...	...	...	...	...	...	...	...
			320	Lac collectors and sellers	...	...	...	...	...	...	...	...	...	...	...	...	...	...	...
			321	Sealing-wax makers and sellers ...	8	8	...	...	...	...	...	...	...	...	...	...	...	...	...
			322	Tar preparers and sellers	...	...	...	...	...	...	...	...	...	...	...	...	...	...	...
			323	Wax, honey and general minor forest produce, collectors and sellers... ...	6,881	3,898	2,983	5	3	2	144	80	64	2,972	1,445	1,527	192	36	156
				Total Sub-order 51	6,904	3,914	2,990	9	5	4	144	80	64	2,972	1,445	1,527	192	36	156
		52. Drugs, dyes, pigments, &c.	324	Chemists and druggists...	583	302	281	195	93	102	8	8	...	10	8	2	59	11	48
			325	Borax workers and sellers	...	...	...	...	...	...	...	...	...	...	...	...	...	...	...
			326	Saltpetre workers and sellers	98	79	19	7	7	...	...	...	...	...	...	...	4	4	...
			327	Alum, soda, &c., workers and sellers ...	...	...	...	...	...	...	...	...	...	...	...	...	...	...	...
			328	Soap makers and sellers	195	82	113	...	...	...	4	4	...	27	2	25	153	73	80
			329	Sulphur workers and sellers	13	11	2	3	1	2	...	...	...	...	...	...	...	...	...
			330	Indigo workers and dealers (not planters)	278	130	148	...	...	...	12	2	10	27	12	15	10	...	10
			331	Madder and Logwood workers and dealers...	326	206	120	...	...	...	6	1	5	18	6	12	15	10	5
			332	Ink-makers and sellers	176	97	79	56	30	26	6	4	2	24	16	8	...	...	...
			333	Antimony preparers and sellers ...	98	48	50	19	2	17	49	24	25	23	22	1	3	...	3
			334	Henna " "	22	22	...	...	...	...	...	...	...	...	...	...	22	22	...
			335	Carmine " "	81	46	35	10	7	3	...	...	...	...	...	...	...	...	...
			336	Kanku (red powder) preparers and sellers	3,289	1,640	1,649	19	13	6	105	56	49	480	246	234	106	55	51
			337	Perfume preparers and sellers	7,659	3,844	3,815	283	193	90	127	100	27	116	57	59	43	22	21
				Total Sub-order 52	12,813	6,507	6,306	592	346	246	317	199	118	725	369	356	415	197	218
				Total Order XVI	19,717	10,421	9,296	601	351	250	461	279	182	3,697	1,814	1,883	607	233	374

TABLE XVII B.

Occupations by Districts.—*Continued.*

Class.	Order.	Sub-order and Group.	Serial No.	Occupations.	Warangal. Total.	Warangal. Males.	Warangal. Females.	Elgandal. Total.	Elgandal. Males.	Elgandal. Females.	Indur. Total.	Indur. Males.	Indur. Females.	Medak. Total.	Medak. Males.	Medak. Females.	Aurangabad. Total.	Aurangabad. Males.	Aurangabad. Females.
					21	22	23	24	25	26	27	28	29	30	31	32	33	34	35
Class D.—Preparation and supply of material substances—*contd.*	XV. Wood, cane and leaves, &c.—*concld.*	50. Canework, matting and leaves, &c.—*concld.*	310	Leaf-plate makers and sellers. (*Are also often temple servants*)	43	19	24	110	89	21	369	245	124	151	62	89	591	324	267
			311	Tooth-stick sellers	...	...	...	...	...	...	...	...	...	...	...	...	...	...	...
			312	Leaf-fan makers and sellers	...	...	...	1	...	1	...	...	...	...	...	...	...	...	...
			313	Brush and comb makers and sellers ...	21	9	12	...	...	...	117	72	45	45	...	45	22	1	21
			314	Broom makers and sellers	4	4	...	10	...	10	20	5	15	...	...	...	134	41	93
			315	Pith and bark collectors, workers, and sellers	806	169	137	5	3	2	...	...	...	...	...	...	...	...	...
				Total Sub-order 50	6,018	3,285	2,733	6,487	3,326	3,161	2,874	1,440	1,434	2,284	976	1,308	2,349	1,163	1,186
				Total Order XV	13,623	7,311	6,312	17,447	9,521	7,926	9,043	4,620	4,423	5,247	2,597	2,650	10,600	5,662	4,938
	XVI. Drugs, gums, dyes, &c.	51. Gums, wax and similar forest produce.	316	India-rubber collectors and sellers ...	...	...	...	...	...	...	...	...	...	...	...	...	...	...	...
			317	Camphor and gum collectors and sellers.	...	...	...	...	...	...	...	...	...	...	...	...	...	...	...
			318	Gallnut (myrobolan) collectors and sellers	...	...	...	11	6	5	...	...	...	...	...	...	...	...	...
			319	Catechu preparers and sellers	...	...	...	...	...	...	...	...	...	...	...	...	...	...	...
			320	Lac collectors and sellers	...	...	...	...	...	...	...	...	...	...	...	...	...	...	...
			321	Sealing-wax makers and sellers ...	...	...	...	...	...	...	...	...	...	...	...	...	...	...	...
			322	Tar preparers and sellers	...	...	...	...	...	...	...	...	...	...	...	...	8	8	...
			323	Wax, honey and general minor forest produce, collectors and sellers... ...	3,028	2,230	798	504	96	408	2	2	...	27	...	27	2	2	...
				Total Sub-order 51	3,028	2,230	798	515	102	413	2	2	...	27	...	27	10	10	...
		52. Drugs, dyes, pigments, &c.	324	Chemists and druggists	54	35	19	68	35	28	...	...	...	...	...	...	45	37	8
			325	Borax workers and sellers	...	...	...	...	...	...	...	...	...	...	...	...	...	...	...
			326	Saltpetre workers and sellers	...	...	...	...	...	...	...	...	...	...	...	...	14	8	6
			327	Alum, soda, &c., workers and sellers ...	...	...	...	...	...	...	...	...	...	...	...	...	...	...	...
			328	Soap makers and sellers...	...	...	...	...	...	...	...	...	...	...	...	...	6	...	6
			329	Sulphur workers and sellers	...	...	...	...	...	...	...	...	...	...	...	...	...	...	...
			330	Indigo workers and dealers (not planters).	...	...	...	...	...	...	...	...	...	...	...	...	...	...	...
			331	Madder and Logwood workers and dealers	90	56	34	49	42	7	...	...	...	92	55	37	8	8	...
			332	Ink-makers and sellers	6	1	5	16	6	10	5	1	4	1	1	...	...	...	...
			333	Antimony preparers and sellers ...	...	...	...	...	...	...	...	...	...	...	...	...	16	15	1
			334	Henna " "	...	...	...	...	...	...	...	...	...	...	...	...	4	...	4
			335	Carmine " "	...	...	...	...	...	...	10	5	5	...	...	...	...	...	...
			336	Kanku (red powder) preparers and sellers	503	277	226	943	448	495	189	80	109	220	100	120	81	...	81
			337	Perfume preparers and sellers	74	48	26	81	68	13	716	375	341	242	141	101	550	278	272
				Total Sub-order 52......	727	417	310	1,152	599	553	920	461	459	555	297	258	724	346	378
				Total Order XVI......	3,750	2,647	1,103	1,667	701	966	922	463	459	582	297	285	784	356	378

TABLE XVII B.

Occupations by Districts.—*Continued.*

Class.	Order.	Sub-order and Group.	Serial No.	Occupations.	Birh. Total.	Birh. Males.	Birh. Females.	Nander. Total.	Nander. Males.	Nander. Females.	Naldrug. Total.	Naldrug. Males.	Naldrug. Females.	Bidar. Total.	Bidar. Males.	Bidar. Females.	Parbhani. Total.	Parbhani. Males.	Parbhani. Females.
					36	37	38	39	40	41	42	43	44	45	46	47	48	49	50
Class D.—Preparation and supply of material substances.—*contd.*	XV. Wood, cane and leaves, &c.—*concld.*	50. Canework, matting and leaves, &c.—*concld.*	310	Leaf-plate makers and sellers. (*Are also often temple servants*)	585	288	297	154	95	59	589	304	285	1,088	547	541	498	239	259
			311	Tooth-stick sellers	...	...	...	...	...	...	...	...	...	10	10	...	...	...	...
			312	Leaf-fan makers and sellers	...	...	...	...	...	...	...	...	...	...	...	...	...	...	...
			313	Brush and comb makers and sellers ...	1	1	...	26	13	13	...	...	...	13	...	13	60	26	34
			314	Broom makers and sellers	184	43	141	...	...	...	29	19	10	210	2	208	54	...	54
			315	Pith and bark collectors, workers, and sellers	...	...	...	...	...	...	...	...	...	...	...	...	...	...	...
				Total Sub-order 50......	2,302	1,171	1,131	1,777	923	854	1,971	985	986	3,711	1,702	2,009	2,545	1,243	1,302
				Total Order XV......	9,338	4,840	4,498	9,818	5,169	4,649	8,743	4,597	4,146	13,461	6,758	6,703	11,724	6,015	5,709
	XVI. Drugs, gums, dyes, &c.	51. Gums, wax and similar forest produce.	316	India-rubber collectors and sellers ...	...	...	...	...	...	...	...	...	...	...	...	...	...	...	...
			317	Camphor and gum collectors and sellers.	...	...	...	...	...	...	...	...	...	...	...	...	...	...	...
			318	Gallnut (myrobolan) collectors and sellers	...	...	...	...	...	...	...	...	...	...	...	...	...	...	...
			319	Catechu preparers and sellers	...	...	...	...	...	...	...	...	...	...	...	...	...	...	...
			320	Lac collectors and sellers ...	...	...	...	...	...	...	...	...	...	...	...	...	...	...	...
			321	Sealing-wax makers and sellers ...	...	...	...	...	...	...	...	...	...	...	...	...	...	...	...
			322	Tar preparers and sellers	...	...	...	...	...	...	...	...	...	...	...	...	...	...	...
			323	Wax, honey and general minor forest produce, collectors and sellers... ...	...	...	...	1	...	1	...	...	...	2	1	1	...	...	...
				Total Sub-order 51......	...	...	...	1	...	1	...	...	...	2	1	1	...	...	...
		52. Drugs, dyes, pigments, &c.	324	Chemists and druggists...	...	...	...	2	2	...	110	54	56	...	...	...	...	...	...
			325	Borax workers and sellers	...	...	...	...	...	...	...	...	...	...	...	...	...	...	...
			326	Saltpetre workers and sellers	...	...	...	...	...	...	...	...	...	...	...	...	5	...	5
			327	Alum, soda, &c., workers and sellers ...	...	...	...	...	...	...	...	...	...	...	...	...	...	...	...
			328	Soap makers and sellers	...	...	...	...	...	...	...	...	...	...	...	...	...	...	...
			329	Sulphur workers and sellers	...	...	...	...	...	...	...	...	...	10	10	...	...	...	...
			330	Indigo workers and dealers (not planters.)	49	31	18	...	...	...	...	...	...	10	5	5	22	13	9
			331	Madder and Logwood workers and dealers	...	...	...	...	...	...	...	...	...	...	...	...	74	58	16
			332	Ink-makers and sellers	10	3	7	11	2	9	2	1	1	9	8	1	1	1	...
			333	Antimony preparers and sellers ...	...	...	...	...	...	...	...	...	...	...	...	...	...	...	...
			334	Henna " "	...	...	...	...	...	...	...	...	...	...	...	...	...	...	...
			335	Carmine " "	...	...	...	...	...	...	...	...	...	...	...	...	14	11	3
			336	Kanku (red powder) preparers and sellers	75	3	72	...	...	...	78	78	...	208	122	86	8	8	...
			337	Perfume preparers and sellers	632	378	254	778	341	437	539	262	277	1,361	737	624	576	306	270
				Total Sub-order 52......	766	415	351	791	345	446	724	390	334	1,598	882	716	700	397	303
				Total Order XVI......	766	415	351	792	345	447	724	390	334	1,600	883	717	700	397	303

TABLE XVII B.

Occupations by Districts.—*Continued.*

Class.	Order.	Sub-order and Group.	Serial No.	Occupations.	Sirpur Tandur. Total.	Sirpur Tandur. Males.	Sirpur Tandur. Females.	Gulbarga. Total.	Gulbarga. Males.	Gulbarga. Females.	Raichur. Total.	Raichur. Males.	Raichur. Females.	Lingasugur. Total.	Lingasugur. Males.	Lingasugur. Females.	Railways. Total.	Railways. Males.	Railways. Females.
					51	52	53	54	55	56	57	58	59	60	61	62	63	64	65
Class D.—Preparation and supply of material substances.—*contd.*	XV. Wood, cane and leaves, &c.—*concld.*	50. Canework, matting and leaves, &c.—*concld.*	310	Leaf-plate makers and sellers, (*Are also often temple servants*)	80	52	28	178	105	73	82	17	65	46	28	28	...	...	...
			311	Tooth-stick sellers	...	...	...	...	...	...	...	...	...	...	...	...	...	...	...
			312	Leaf-fan makers and sellers	...	...	...	...	...	...	...	...	...	...	...	...	1	1	...
			313	Brush and comb makers and sellers ...	...	...	...	19	10	9	...	...	...	...	...	...	...	...	...
			314	Broom makers and sellers	26	26	...	8	...	8	...	...	...	...	...	...	...	...	...
			315	Pith and bark collectors, workers, and sellers	...	...	...	...	...	...	72	38	34	20	16	4	...	...	...
				Total Sub-order 50......	784	453	331	2,019	1,119	900	1,871	948	923	8,315	1,566	1,749	1	1	...
				Total Order XV	3,462	1,878	1,584	7,776	4,422	3,354	4,885	2,567	2,318	8,060	4,098	3,962	83	83	...
	XVI. Drugs, gums, dyes, &c.	51. Gums, wax and similar forest produce.	316	India-rubber collectors and sellers ...	...	...	...	...	...	...	...	...	...	...	...	...	...	...	...
			317	Camphor and gum collectors and sellers	...	...	...	...	...	...	...	...	...	...	...	...	...	...	...
			318	Gallnut (myrobolan) collectors and sellers	...	...	...	...	...	...	...	...	...	...	...	...	...	...	...
			319	Catechu preparers and sellers	...	...	...	...	...	...	...	...	...	...	...	...	...	...	...
			320	Lac collectors and sellers	...	...	...	...	...	...	...	...	...	...	...	...	...	...	...
			321	Sealing-wax makers and sellers ...	...	...	...	...	...	...	...	...	...	...	...	...	...	...	...
			322	Tar preparers and sellers	...	...	...	...	...	...	...	...	...	...	...	...	...	...	...
			323	Wax, honey and general minor forest produce, collectors and sellers	...	...	...	...	...	...	7	3	4	...	...	...	...	...	...
				Total Sub-order 51	...	...	...	...	...	...	7	3	4	...	...	...	...	...	...
		52. Drugs, dyes, pigments, &c.	324	Chemists and druggists	...	...	...	...	...	...	37	19	18	...	...	...	...	...	...
			325	Borax workers and sellers	...	...	...	...	...	...	...	...	...	...	...	...	...	...	...
			326	Saltpetre workers and sellers	...	...	...	...	...	...	2	1	1	66	59	7	...	...	...
			327	Alum, soda, &c., workers and sellers ...	...	...	...	...	...	...	...	...	...	...	...	...	...	...	...
			328	Soap makers and sellers	...	...	...	...	...	...	5	3	2	...	...	...	...	...	...
			329	Sulphur workers and sellers	...	...	...	...	...	...	...	...	...	...	...	...	...	...	...
			330	Indigo workers and dealers (not planters)	...	...	...	43	4	39	...	...	...	...	...	...	...	...	...
			331	Madder and Logwood workers and dealers	...	...	...	...	...	...	74	33	41	...	...	...	...	...	...
			332	Ink-makers and sellers	5	5	...	1	1	...	2	...	2	5	2	3	...	...	...
			333	Antimony preparers and sellers... ...	...	...	...	...	...	...	...	...	...	...	...	...	...	...	...
			334	Henna " "	...	...	...	...	...	...	...	...	...	...	...	...	...	...	...
			335	Carmine " "	...	...	...	...	...	...	...	...	...	47	23	24	...	...	...
			336	Kanku (red powder) preparers and sellers.	...	...	...	65	39	26	208	118	90	6	2	4	...	...	...
			337	Perfume preparers and sellers	219	112	107	1,086	318	768	59	21	38	177	87	90	...	...	...
				Total Sub-order 52	224	117	107	1,195	362	833	387	195	192	301	173	128	...	...	...
				Total Order XVI	224	117	107	1,195	362	833	394	198	196	301	173	128	...	...	...

TABLE XVII B.
Occupations by Districts.

TABLE XVII B.

Occupations by Districts.—*Continued.*

Class.	Order.	Sub-order and Group.	Serial No.	Occupations.	Grant Total. Total.	Grant Total. Males.	Grant Total. Females.	Hyderabad. Total.	Hyderabad. Males.	Hyderabad. Females.	Atraf-i-Balda. Total.	Atraf-i-Balda. Males.	Atraf-i-Balda. Females.	Mahabubnagar. Total.	Mahabubnagar. Males.	Mahabubnagar. Females.	Nalgonda. Total.	Nalgonda. Males.	Nalgonda. Females.
1	2	3	4	5	6	7	8	9	10	11	12	13	14	15	16	17	18	19	20
Class D.—Preparation, &c.—*concld.*	XVII. Leather, horn, bones, and grease.	53. Leather, &c.	338	Tanners, curriers, and hide sellers (*many also shoe-makers*)	8,094	3,490	4,604	448	166	282	3,768	2,142	1,626	47	7	40	89	86	3
			339	Shoe, sandals, boot-makers and sellers.	92,409	54,164	38,245	2,866	1,642	1,224	2,619	1,578	1,041	3,582	2,306	1,276	3,100	1,483	1,617
			340	Leather dyers	3,224	1,496	1,728	58	30	28	...	...	...	...	...	...	...	...	...
			341	Water bag, well-bag, bucket and ghee-pot makers and sellers...	45,289	27,123	18,166	10	3	7	5,003	3,124	1,879	153	134	19	14,783	9,561	5,222
			342	Hide, horns, and bone dealers	8,601	5,058	3,543	416	250	166	236	128	108	647	426	221	292	244	48
			343	Catgut preparers and sellers	52	43	9	10	5	5	...	...	...	...	...	...	...	...	...
			344	Glue makers and sellers	5	5	...	...	...	...	...	...	...	...	...	...	...	...	...
			345	Grease preparers and sellers	...	...	...	...	...	...	...	...	...	...	...	...	...	...	...
				Total Sub-order 53......	157,674	91,379	66,295	3,808	2,096	1,712	11,626	6,972	4,654	4,429	2,873	1,556	18,264	11,374	6,890
				Total Order XVII......	157,674	91,379	66,295	3,808	2,096	1,712	11,626	6,972	4,654	4,429	2,873	1,556	18,264	11,374	6,890
Class E.—Commerce, transport, storage.	XVIII. Commerce.	54. Dealers in money and securities.	346	Bankers and Bank managers... ...	1,042	637	405	748	486	262	15	15	...	278	136	142	...	...	...
			347	Money lenders and Pawnbrokers ...	20,358	9,293	11,065	560	301	259	385	258	127	233	100	133	117	78	39
			348	Bill-discounters, &c.	462	377	85	22	16	6	...	...	...	...	...	...	...	...	...
			349	Insurance Agents and under-writers ...	3	2	1	3	2	1	...	...	...	...	...	...	...	...	...
			350	Money changers and testers	10,978	5,828	5,145	2,691	1,035	1,656	234	86	148	204	116	88	3	1	2
			351	Bank clerks, cashiers, bill-collectors, accountants, &c.	57	22	35	57	22	35	...	...	...	...	...	...	...	...	...
				Total Sub-order 54......	32,895	16,159	16,736	4,081	1,862	2,219	634	359	275	715	352	363	120	79	41
		55. General Merchants.	352	General merchants	46,838	21,171	25,667	2,694	1,413	1,281	6,912	3,186	3,726	89	3	86	6,900	3,324	3,576
			353	Merchants' managers, accountants, clerks, assistants, &c....	511	272	239	510	271	239	...	...	...	...	...	...	...	...	...
				Total Sub-order 55......	47,349	21,443	25,906	3,204	1,684	1,520	6,912	3,186	3,726	89	3	86	6,900	3,324	3,576
		56. Dealing unspecified.	354	Shopkeepers' clerks, salesmen, &c. ...	522	285	237	352	189	163	...	...	...	...	...	...	...	...	...
			355	Shopkeepers and Money lenders' servants	9,893	5,908	3,985	783	417	366	45	45	...	27	26	1	60	60	...
			356	Shopkeepers, otherwise unspecified ...	76,986	37,179	39,807	10,126	5,278	4,848	1,233	1,229	4	5,211	2,604	2,607	...	...	...
			357	Pedlars, Hawkers, &c.	260	139	121	259	138	121	...	...	...	...	...	...	...	...	...
				Total Sub-order 56......	87,661	43,511	44,150	11,520	6,022	5,498	1,278	1,274	4	5,238	2,630	2,608	60	60	...

TABLE XVII B.

Occupations by Districts.—*Continued.*

Class.	Order.	Sub-order and Group.	Serial No.	Occupations.	Warangal. Total.	Warangal. Males.	Warangal. Females.	Elgandal. Total.	Elgandal. Males.	Elgandal. Females.	Indur. Total.	Indur. Males.	Indur. Females.	Medak. Total.	Medak. Males.	Medak. Females.	Aurangabad. Total.	Aurangabad. Males.	Aurangabad. Females.
					21	22	23	24	25	26	27	28	29	30	31	32	33	34	35
Class D.—Preparation, &c.—*concld.*	XVII. Leather, horn, bones, and grease.	53. Leather, &c.	338	Tanners, curriers, and hide sellers (*many also shoe-makers*)	...	...	...	2,269	276	1,993	8	8	...	...	...	...	459	278	181
			339	Shoe, sandals, boot-makers and sellers ...	5,248	4,171	1,077	9,471	8,198	1,273	5,097	8,116	1,981	780	599	181	11,609	5,866	5,743
			340	Leather dyers	...	...	...	12	...	12	...	...	...	...	...	...	502	162	340
			341	Water bag, well-bag, bucket and ghee-pot makers and sellers...	2	2	...	73	42	31	585	561	24	2,062	1,036	1,026	74	74	...
			342	Hide, horns, and bone dealers	818	532	286	855	532	823	99	28	71	573	331	242	582	306	276
			343	Catgut preparers and sellers	...	...	...	...	...	...	...	...	...	...	...	...	42	38	4
			344	Glue makers and sellers	...	...	...	...	...	...	...	...	...	5	5	...	...	...	...
			345	Grease preparers and sellers	...	...	...	...	...	...	...	...	...	...	...	...	...	...	...
				Total Sub-order 53......	6,068	4,705	1,368	12,680	9,048	3,632	5,789	8,718	2,076	8,420	1,971	1,449	13,268	6,724	6,544
				Total Order XVII......	6,068	4,705	1,363	12,680	9,048	3,632	5,789	8,713	2,076	8,420	1,971	1,449	13,268	6,724	6,544
Class E.—Commerce, transport, storage.	XVIII. Commerce.	54. Dealers in money and securities.	346	Bankers and Bank managers	...	...	...	...	...	...	1	...	1	...	...	...	...	...	...
			347	Money lenders and Pawnbrokers ...	174	58	116	255	105	150	800	365	485	69	43	26	4,929	2,368	2,561
			348	Bill-discounters, &c.	...	...	...	...	...	...	382	317	65	...	...	...	11	11	...
			349	Insurance Agents and under-writers ...	...	...	...	...	...	...	...	...	...	...	...	...	...	...	...
			350	Money changers and testers	80	43	37	74	55	19	671	841	330	86	28	58	985	662	323
			351	Bank clerks, cashiers, bill-collectors, accountants, &c.	...	...	...	...	...	...	...	...	...	...	...	...	...	...	...
				Total Sub-order 54......	254	101	153	329	160	169	1,854	1,023	831	155	71	84	5,925	3,041	2,884
		55. General Merchants.	352	General merchants	7,804	2,763	5,041	15,189	7,076	8,068	8	8	...	6,959	3,157	3,802	25	24	1
			353	Merchants' managers, accountants, clerks, assistants, &c.	...	...	...	...	...	...	...	...	...	...	...	...	...	...	...
				Total Sub-order 55......	7,804	2,763	5,041	15,189	7,076	8,063	8	8	...	6,959	3,157	3,802	25	24	1
		56. Dealing unspecified.	354	Shopkeepers' clerks, salesmen, &c. ...	...	...	...	...	...	...	...	...	...	4	...	4	28	28	...
			355	Shopkeepers and Money lenders' servants	66	64	2	...	...	...	206	83	128	2	2	...	98	51	42
			356	Shopkeepers, otherwise unspecified ...	812	232	80	...	...	...	4,247	58	4,189	577	227	350	8,630	4,314	4,316
			357	Pedlars, Hawkers, &c.	...	...	...	...	...	...	...	...	...	...	...	...	...	...	...
				Total Sub-order 56......	378	296	82	...	...	...	4,453	141	4,312	583	229	354	8,751	4,393	4,358

TABLE XVII B.

Occupations by Districts.—*Continued.*

Class	Order.	Sub-order and Group.	Serial No.	Occupations.	Birh. Total.	Birh. Males.	Birh. Females.	Nander. Total.	Nander. Males.	Nander. Females.	Naldrug. Total.	Naldrug. Males.	Naldrug. Females.	Bidar. Total.	Bidar. Males.	Bidar. Females.	Parbhani. Total.	Parbhani. Males.	Parbhani. Females.
					36	37	38	39	40	41	42	43	44	45	46	47	48	49	50
Class D.—Preparation, &c.—*concld.*	XVII. Leathers, horn, bones, and grease.	53. Leather, &c.	338	Tanners, curriers, and hide sellers (*many also shoe-makers*)	...	...	...	25	20	5	198	119	79	110	65	45	440	236	204
			339	Shoe, sandals, boot-makers and sellers	10,249	5,189	5,060	4,521	2,452	2,069	8,846	4,753	4,093	7,650	4,013	3,637	7,635	3,984	3,651
			340	Leather dyers	366	230	136	71	25	46	573	350	223	717	273	444	89	...	89
			341	Water bag, well-bag, bucket and ghee-pot makers and sellers	...	...	...	76	47	29	75	14	61	219	154	65	2	2	...
			342	Hide, horns, and bone dealers	521	263	258	32	32	...	301	241	60	512	267	245	303	190	113
			343	Catgut preparers and sellers	...	...	...	...	...	...	...	...	...	...	...	...	...	...	...
			344	Glue makers and sellers	...	...	...	...	...	...	...	...	...	...	...	...	...	...	...
			345	Grease preparers and sellers	...	...	...	...	...	...	...	...	...	...	...	...	...	...	...
				Total Sub-order 53	11,136	5,682	5,454	4,725	2,576	2,149	9,993	5,477	4,516	9,208	4,772	4,436	8,469	4,412	4,057
				Total Order XVII......	11,136	5,682	5,454	4,725	2,576	2,149	9,993	5,477	4,516	9,208	4,772	4,436	8,469	4,412	4,057
Class E.—Commerce, transport, storage.	XVIII. Commerce.	54. Dealers in money and securities.	346	Bankers and Bank managers	...	...	...	...	...	...	...	...	...	...	...	...	...	...	...
			347	Money lenders and Pawnbrokers ...	2,625	1,165	1,460	739	372	367	2,354	1,115	1,239	2,047	1,053	994	2,305	953	1,352
			348	Bill-discounters, &c.	1	1	...	...	...	...	...	...	...	...	...	...	...	...	...
			349	Insurance Agents and under-writers ...	...	...	...	...	...	...	...	...	...	...	...	...	...	...	...
			350	Money changers and testers	816	527	289	523	222	301	689	402	286	1,190	674	516	1,323	703	620
			351	Bank clerks, cashiers, bill-collectors, accountants, &c.	...	...	...	...	...	...	...	...	...	...	...	...	...	...	...
				Total Sub-order 54......	3,442	1,693	1,749	1,262	594	668	3,043	1,518	1,525	3,237	1,727	1,510	3,628	1,656	1,972
		55. General Merchants.	352	General merchants	...	...	...	...	...	...	...	...	...	...	...	...	232	119	113
			353	Merchants' managers, accountants, clerks, assistants, &c.	...	...	...	...	...	...	...	...	...	...	...	...	...	...	...
				Total Sub-order 55......	...	...	...	...	...	...	...	...	...	...	...	...	232	119	113
		56. Dealing unspecified.	354	Shopkeepers' clerks, salesmen, &c. ...	...	...	...	...	...	...	3	1	2	...	...	...	12	4	8
			355	Shopkeepers and Money lenders' servants	5,738	3,571	2,167	240	116	124	35	11	24	164	164	...	672	373	299
			356	Shopkeepers, otherwise unspecified ...	3,794	991	2,803	6,483	3,170	3,313	4,867	2,363	2,504	7,378	4,755	2,623	4,963	2,415	2,548
			357	Pedlars, Hawkers, &c.	...	...	...	...	...	...	...	...	...	...	...	...	...	...	...
				Total Sub-order 56......	9,532	4,562	4,970	6,723	3,286	3,437	4,905	2,375	2,530	7,542	4,919	2,623	5,647	2,792	2,855

TABLE XVII B.

Occupations by Districts.—*Continued.*

Class.	Order.	Sub-order and Group.	Serial No.	Occupations.	Sirpur Tandur. Total.	Sirpur Tandur. Males.	Sirpur Tandur. Females.	Gulbarga. Total.	Gulbarga. Males.	Gulbarga. Females.	Raichur. Total.	Raichur. Males.	Raichur. Females.	Lingasugur. Total.	Lingasugur. Males.	Lingasugur. Females.	Railways. Total.	Railways. Males.	Railways. Females.
					51	52	53	54	55	56	57	58	59	60	61	62	63	64	65
Class D.—Preparation, &c.—*concld.*	XVII. Leather, horns, bones, and grease.	58. Leather, &c.	338	Tanners, curriers, and hide sellers (*many also shoe-makers*)	...	...	...	203	73	130	30	14	16	...	...	...	...	...	...
			339	Shoe, sandals, boot-makers and sellers...	2,860	1,410	1,450	3,794	2,113	1,681	1,019	513	506	1,462	777	685	1	1	...
			340	Leather dyers	501	225	276	332	200	132	1	1	...	2	...	2	...	...	...
			341	Water bag, well-bag, bucket and ghee-pot makers and sellers...	...	...	...	86	54	82	12,298	7,345	4,953	9,788	4,970	4,818	...	...	...
			342	Hide, horns, and bone dealers	306	241	65	122	17	105	1,560	800	760	426	230	196	...	...	...
			343	Catgut preparers and sellers	...	...	...	...	...	...	...	...	...	...	...	...	...	...	...
			344	Glue makers and sellers	...	...	...	...	...	...	...	...	...	...	...	...	...	...	...
			345	Grease preparers and sellers	...	...	...	...	...	...	...	...	...	...	...	...	...	...	...
				Total Sub-order 58......	3,667	1,876	1,791	4,537	2,457	2,080	14,908	8,673	6,235	11,678	5,977	5,701	1	1	...
				Total Order XVII......	3,667	1,876	1,791	4,537	2,457	2,080	14,908	8,673	6,235	11,678	5,977	5,701	1	1	...
Class E.—Commerce, transport, storage.	XVIII. Commerce.	54. Dealers in money and securities.	346	Bankers and Bank managers...	...	...	...	...	...	...	...	...	...	...	...	...	...	...	...
			347	Money lenders and Pawnbrokers	253	147	106	1,715	527	1,188	227	123	104	563	157	406	8	5	3
			348	Bill discounters, &c.	...	...	...	...	...	...	46	32	14	...	...	...	...	...	...
			349	Insurance Agents and under-writers	...	...	...	...	...	...	...	...	...	...	...	...	...	...	...
			350	Money changers and testers	97	19	78	871	673	198	196	128	68	238	110	128	2	2	...
			351	Bank clerks, cashiers, bill-collectors, accountants, &c.	...	...	...	...	...	...	...	...	...	...	...	...	...	...	...
				Total Sub-order 54......	350	166	184	2,586	1,200	1,386	469	283	186	801	267	534	10	7	3
		55. General Merchants.	352	General merchants	...	...	...	...	...	...	6	5	1	...	...	...	125	98	27
			353	Merchants' managers, accountants, clerks, assistants, &c.	...	...	...	...	...	...	...	...	...	...	...	...	1	1	...
				Total Sub-order 55......	...	...	...	...	...	...	6	5	1	...	...	...	126	99	27
		56. Dealing unspecified.	354	Shopkeepers' clerks, salesmen, &c.	...	...	...	...	...	...	118	60	58	5	3	2	...	...	...
			355	Shopkeepers and Money lenders' servants	4	...	4	1,757	924	833	...	...	...	...	...	...	1	1	...
			356	Shopkeepers, otherwise unspecified	1,628	1,023	605	8,354	3,372	4,982	3,776	1,938	1,838	5,403	3,207	2,196	4	3	1
			357	Pedlars, Hawkers, &c.	...	...	...	...	...	...	...	...	...	...	...	...	1	1	...
				Total Sub-order 56......	1,632	1,023	609	10,111	4,296	5,815	3,894	1,998	1,896	5,408	3,210	2,198	6	5	1

TABLE XVII B.

Occupations by Districts.—*Continued.*

Class.	Order.	Sub-order and Group.		Serial No.	Occupations.	Grand Total. Total.	Grand Total. Males.	Grand Total. Females.	Hyderabad. Total.	Hyderabad. Males.	Hyderabad. Females.	Atraf-i-Balda. Total.	Atraf-i-Balda. Males.	Atraf-i-Balda. Females.	Mahabubnagar. Total.	Mahabubnagar. Males.	Mahabubnagar. Females.	Nalgonda. Total.	Nalgonda. Males.	Nalgonda. Females.
1	2	3		4	5	6	7	8	9	10	11	12	13	14	15	16	17	18	19	20
Class E.—Commerce, transport, storage.—*concld.*	XVIII. Commerce.—*concld.*	57. Middlemen, &c.	(a)—Brokers, &c.	358	Brokers' Agents, Dubash	1,076	501	575	164	92	72	...	...	...	4	1	3	...	...	...
				359	Auctioneers, Auditors, Actuaries, Notaries public, Appraisers, and House-Agents, &c.	20	9	11	19	9	10	...	...	...	...	...	...	...	...	...
			(b) Contractors and farmers.	360	Farmers of Tolls, ferries	58	51	7	7	2	5	...	...	...	...	...	...	4	4	...
				361	Farmers of liquor, opium, &c.	3,484	1,146	2,338	11	4	7	100	15	85	234	172	62	100	40	60
				362	Lessees and Superintendents of markets, stalls, &c.	175	84	91	25	6	19	2	1	1	74	50	24	4	2	2
				363	Contractors—otherwise unspecified ...	3,333	1,808	1,525	824	414	410	297	194	103	165	94	71	151	125	26
				364	Contractors for labour, Emigration Agents, &c.	178	58	120	3	2	1	...	...	...	...	...	...	...	...	...
					Total Sub-order 57......	8,324	3,657	4,667	1,053	529	524	399	210	189	477	317	160	259	171	88
					Total Order XVIII......	176,229	84,770	91,459	19,858	10,097	9,761	9,223	5,029	4,194	6,469	3,302	3,167	7,389	3,684	3,705
	XIX. Transport and storage.	58. Railways.	(a) Administration.	365	Agents, directors, managers and their assistants	17	7	10	12	5	7	...	...	...	...	...	...	...	...	...
				366	Traffic Managers, Superintendents and Assistants	6	6	...	2	2	...	...	...	...	...	...	...	...	...	...
				367	Locomotive Superintendents, & Assistants	38	21	17	27	16	11	...	...	...	...	...	...	...	...	...
				368	Auditors, Accountants, &c.	23	11	12	4	3	1	...	...	...	...	...	...	...	...	...
				369	Engineers (when not returned under general heading)	151	85	66	69	28	41	...	...	...	...	...	...	...	...	...
			(b) Working staff.	370	Clerical Staff in Railway establishment.	595	355	240	409	226	183	...	...	...	...	...	...	...	...	...
				371	Station Masters and Assistants, Inspectors, Overseers, &c.	619	319	300	32	21	11	...	...	...	...	...	...	...	...	...
				372	Guards, drivers, firemen, &c.	400	222	178	153	77	76	2	2	...	...	...	...	...	...	...
				373	Pointsmen, shunters, porters, signallers, &c.	5,022	2,946	2,076	885	482	403	97	63	34	6	3	3	99	26	73
					Total Sub-order 58......	6,871	3,972	2,899	1,598	860	738	99	65	34	6	3	3	99	26	73
		59. Roads.	(a) Cart, carriage and tramway owners and drivers.	374	Tramway, mail carriage, &c., companies, contractors, &c.	...	...	...	...	...	...	...	...	...	...	...	...	...	...	...
				375	Cart owners & drivers, carting Agents, &c.	27,901	17,764	10,137	2,420	1,354	1,066	3,048	2,009	1,039	3,297	2,053	1,244	1,735	924	811
				376	Livery stable-keepers, &c.	1,108	582	526	140	69	71	11	...	11	9	3	6	...	...	...
				377	Drivers, stable-boys, &c., (*not private servants*)	1,958	1,487	471	41	14	27	1,413	1,197	216	106	39	67	208	136	72
			(b) Carriers by pack animals.	378	Palki, &c., owners, bearers, &c.	4,851	3,053	1,798	1,857	1,332	525	95	65	30	125	92	33	82	66	16
				379	Pack bullock owners, drivers, &c. ...	24,024	13,558	10,466	52	30	22	734	424	310	2,107	1,233	874	487	461	26
				380	Pack camel, elephant, mule, &c., owners and drivers	1,555	796	759	838	452	386	70	56	14	2	2	...	14	14	...
					Total Sub-order 59......	61,397	37,240	24,157	5,348	3,251	2,097	5,371	3,751	1,620	5,646	3,422	2,224	2,526	1,601	925

TABLE XVII B.

Occupations by Districts.—*Continued.*

Class.	Order.	Sub-order and Group.	Serial No.	Occupations.	Warangal. Total.	Warangal. Males.	Warangal. Females.	Elgandal. Total.	Elgandal. Males.	Elgandal. Females.	Indur. Total.	Indur. Males.	Indur. Females.	Medak. Total.	Medak. Males.	Medak. Females.	Aurangabad. Total.	Aurangabad. Males.	Aurangabad. Females.
					21	22	23	24	25	26	27	28	29	30	31	32	33	34	35
Class E.—Commerce, transport, storage.—*contd.*	XVIII. Commerce.—*concld.*	57. Middlemen, &c. (a)—Brokers, &c.	358	Brokers' Agents, Dubash	...	...	...	...	...	...	11	11	...	...	...	...	208	126	77
			359	Auctioneers, Auditors, Actuaries, Notaries public, Appraisers, and House-Agents, &c.	...	...	...	...	...	...	1	...	1	...	...	...	...	...	...
		(b) Contractors and farmers.	360	Farmers of Tolls, ferries	4	4	...	...	...	...	...	...	...	43	41	2	...	...	...
			361	Farmers of liquor, opium, &c.	65	58	7	10	7	3	11	11	...	19	11	8	4	4	...
			362	Lessees and Superintendents of markets, stalls, &c.	...	...	...	6	3	3	...	...	...	16	16	...	...	...	...
			363	Contractors—otherwise unspecified ...	358	273	85	206	156	50	506	141	365	50	37	13	198	103	95
			364	Contractors for labour, Emigration Agents, &c.	1	1	...	...	...	...	...	...	...	...	...	...	...	...	...
				Total Sub-order 57......	428	336	92	222	166	56	529	163	366	128	105	23	405	233	172
				Total Order XVIII......	8,864	3,496	5,368	15,690	7,402	8,288	6,839	1,330	5,509	7,825	3,562	4,263	15,106	7,691	7,415
	XIX. Transport and storage.	58. Railways. (a) Administration.	365	Agents, directors, managers and their assistants	...	...	...	...	...	...	...	...	...	...	...	...	5	2	3
			366	Traffic Managers, Superintendents, and Assistants	...	...	...	...	...	...	...	...	...	...	...	...	...	...	...
			367	Locomotive Superintendents, & Assistants.	...	...	...	...	...	...	...	...	...	...	...	...	...	...	...
			368	Auditors, Accountants, &c.	...	...	...	...	...	...	...	...	...	...	...	...	...	...	...
			369	Engineers (when not returned under general heading)	...	...	...	...	...	...	...	...	...	...	...	...	...	...	...
			370	Clerical Staff in Railway establishment..	...	...	...	...	...	...	...	...	...	...	...	...	...	...	...
		(b) Working staff.	371	Station Masters and Assistants, Inspectors, Overseers, &c.	...	...	...	...	...	...	...	...	...	...	...	...	...	...	...
			372	Guards, drivers, firemen, &c.	...	...	...	...	...	...	...	...	...	...	...	...	14	5	9
			373	Pointsmen, shunters, porters, signallers, &c.	210	148	62	4	4	...	...	...	...	21	19	2	15	15	—
				Total Sub-order 58......	210	148	62	4	4	...	...	...	...	21	19	2	34	22	12
		59. Road. (a) Cart, carriage and tramway owners and drivers.	374	Tramway, mail carriage, &c., companies, contractors, &c.	...	...	...	...	...	...	...	...	...	...	...	...	...	...	...
			375	Cart owners & drivers, carting Agents, &c.	1,928	1,268	660	103	88	20	3,220	2,754	466	1,727	1,178	549	3,654	1,785	1,869
			376	Livery stable-keepers, &c.	80	...	80	5	5	...	...	...	...	61	43	18	...	...	...
			377	Drivers, stable-boys, &c., (*not private servants*)	52	17	85	...	...	...	...	...	...	127	78	49	11	6	5
			378	Palki, &c., owners, bearers, &c... ...	79	57	22	177	67	110	1,147	638	509	102	49	53	84	49	35
		(b) Carriers by pack animals.	379	Pack bullock owners, drivers, &c. ...	170	85	85	2,229	1,168	1,061	4,173	1,766	2,407	2,445	1,204	1,241	559	352	207
			380	Pack camel, elephant, mule, &c., owners and drivers	...	...	...	...	...	...	82	28	4	2	...	2	90	23	67
				Total Sub-order 59......	2,259	1,427	832	2,514	1,328	1,191	8,572	5,186	3,386	4,464	2,552	1,912	4,398	2,215	2,183

TABLE XVII B.

Occupations by Districts.—*Continued.*

Class.	Order.	Sub-order and Group.	Serial No.	Occupations.	Birh. Total.	Birh. Males.	Birh. Females.	Nander. Total.	Nander. Males.	Nander. Females.	Naldrug. Total.	Naldrug. Males.	Naldrug. Females.	Bidar. Total.	Bidar. Males.	Bidar. Females.	Parbhani. Total.	Parbhani. Males.	Parbhani. Females.
					36	37	38	39	40	41	42	43	44	45	46	47	48	49	50
Class E.—Commerce, transport, storage.—*contd.*	XVIII. Commerce.—*concld.*	57. Middlemen, &c. (a)—Brokers, &c.	358	Brokers' Agents, Dubash	...	...	...	1	...	1	92	51	41	41	29	12	221	104	117
			359	Auctioneers, Auditors, Actuaries, Notaries public, Appraisers and House-Agents, &c.	...	...	...	...	...	...	...	...	...	...	...	...	...	...	...
		(b) Contractors and farmers.	360	Farmers of Tolls, ferries	...	...	...	...	...	...	...	...	...	...	...	...	...	...	...
			361	Farmers of liquor, opium, &c.... ...	29	29	...	...	...	...	69	69	...	1,638	49	1,589	26	...	26
			362	Lessees and Superintendents of markets, stalls, &c.	...	...	...	...	...	...	1	...	1	21	5	16	...	...	...
			363	Contractors—otherwise unspecified ...	47	11	36	47	27	20	29	24	5	19	14	5	222	72	150
			364	Contractors for labour, Emigration Agents, &c.	...	...	...	...	...	...	...	...	...	87	...	87	...	...	...
				Total Sub-order 57......	76	40	36	48	27	21	191	144	47	1,806	97	1,709	469	176	298
				Total Order XVIII......	13,050	6,295	6,755	8,033	3,907	4,126	8,139	4,037	4,102	12,585	6,743	5,842	9,976	4,748	5,233
	XIX. Transport and storage.	58. Railways. (a) Administration.	365	Agents, directors, managers and their assistants	...	...	...	...	...	...	...	...	...	...	...	...	...	...	...
			366	Traffic Managers, Superintendents and Assistants	...	...	...	...	...	...	...	...	...	...	...	...	...	...	...
			367	Locomotive Superintendents, & Assistants.	...	...	...	...	...	...	...	...	...	...	...	...	...	...	...
			368	Auditors, Accountants, &c.	...	...	...	...	...	...	...	...	...	...	...	...	...	...	...
			369	Engineers (when not returned under general heading)	...	...	...	...	...	...	...	...	...	...	...	...	...	...	...
			370	Clerical Staff in Railway establishment..	...	...	...	...	...	...	...	...	...	...	...	...	...	...	...
		(b) Working staff.	371	Station Masters and Assistants, Inspectors, Overseers, &c.	...	...	...	...	...	...	...	...	...	...	...	...	27	27	...
			372	Guards, drivers, firemen, &c.	...	...	...	...	...	...	...	...	...	...	...	...	18	...	18
			373	Pointsmen, shunters, porters, signallers, &c.	15	13	2	...	...	...	...	...	...	4	1	3	...	...	...
				Total Sub-order 58......	15	13	2	...	...	...	...	...	...	4	1	3	45	27	18
		59. Roads. (a) Cart, carriage and tramway owners and drivers.	374	Tramway, mail carriage, &c., companies, contractors, &c.	...	...	...	...	...	...	...	...	...	...	...	...	...	...	...
			375	Cart owners & drivers, carting Agents, &c.	862	801	61	1,070	734	336	1,496	1,155	341	1,329	766	563	1,710	883	827
			376	Livery stable-keepers, &c.	...	...	...	...	...	...	...	...	...	...	...	...	...	...	...
			377	Drivers, stable-boys, &c., (*not private servants*).	...	...	...	...	...	...	...	...	...	...	...	...	...	...	...
		(b) Carriers by pack animals.	378	Palki, &c., owners, bearers, &c... ...	...	...	...	...	...	...	80	41	39	232	86	146	422	858	64
			379	Pack bullock owners, drivers, &c. ...	1,539	912	627	1,212	674	538	571	280	341	2,334	1,654	680	2,982	1,886	1,046
			380	Pack camel, elephant, mule, &c., owners and drivers	43	36	7	83	15	68	...	...	...	25	17	8	142	4	138
				Total Sub-order 59......	1,944	1,249	695	2,365	1,423	942	2,147	1,426	721	3,920	2,523	1,397	5,206	3,131	2,075

TABLE XVII B.

Occupations by Districts.—*Continued.*

Class.	Order.	Sub-order and Group.	Serial No.	Occupations.	Sirpur Tandur. Total.	Males.	Females.	Gulbarga. Total.	Males.	Females.	Raichur. Total.	Males.	Females.	Lingasugur. Total.	Males.	Females.	Railways. Total.	Males.	Females.
					51	52	53	54	55	56	57	58	59	60	61	62	63	64	65
Class E.—Commerce, transport, storage.—*contd.*	XVIII. Commerce.—*concld.*	57. Middlemen, &c. (a)—Brokers, &c.	358	Brokers' Agents, Dubash...	...	...	...	166	...	166	132	63	69	40	23	17	1	1	...
			359	Auctioneers, Auditors, Actuaries, Notaries public, Appraisers and House-Agents, &c.	...	...	...	...	...	...	...	...	...	...	...	...	...	...	...
		(b) Contractors and farmers.	360	Farmers of Tolls, ferries...	...	...	...	...	...	...	...	...	...	...	...	...	...	...	...
			361	Farmers of liquor, opium, &c. ...	32	1	31	83	51	32	994	585	409	59	40	19	...	...	...
			362	Lessees and Superintendents of markets, stalls, &c.	...	...	...	26	1	25	...	...	...	...	...	...	...	...	...
			363	Contractors—otherwise unspecified ...	26	4	22	2	2	...	87	43	44	71	46	25	28	28	...
			364	Contractors for labour, Emigration Agents, &c. ...	...	...	...	...	...	...	...	...	...	...	...	...	87	55	32
				Total Sub-order 57......	58	5	53	277	54	223	1,213	691	522	170	109	61	116	84	32
				Total Order XVIII......	2,040	1,194	846	12,974	5,550	7,424	5,582	2,977	2,605	6,379	2,586	2,793	258	195	63
	XIX. Transport and storage.	58. Railways. (a) Administration.	365	Agents, directors, managers and their assistants ...	...	...	...	...	...	...	...	...	...	...	...	...	...	...	...
			366	Traffic Managers, Superintendents and Assistants ...	...	...	...	...	...	...	3	3	...	...	...	...	1	1	...
			367	Locomotive Superintendents, & Assistants.	...	...	...	1	1	...	4	1	3	...	...	...	6	8	8
			368	Auditors, Accountants, &c. ...	...	...	...	...	...	...	5	3	2	...	...	...	14	5	9
			369	Engineers (when not returned under general heading) ...	...	...	...	...	...	...	2	1	1	...	...	...	80	56	24
			370	Clerical Staff in Railway establishment...	...	...	...	...	...	...	40	21	19	...	...	...	119	81	38
		(b) Working staff.	371	Station Masters and Assistants, Inspectors, Overseers, &c. ...	...	...	...	...	...	...	38	20	18	...	...	...	549	278	271
			372	Guards, drivers, firemen, &c. ...	...	...	...	...	...	...	36	20	16	...	...	...	176	117	59
			373	Pointsmen, shunters, porters, signallers, &c. ...	...	...	...	396	167	229	746	397	349	11	5	6	2,514	1,604	910
				Total Sub-order 58......	...	...	...	397	168	229	874	466	408	11	5	6	3,459	2,145	1,314
		59. Roads. (a) Cart, carriage and tramway owners and drivers.	374	Tramway, mail carriage, &c., companies, contractors, &c...	...	...	...	...	...	...	...	...	...	...	...	...	...	...	...
			375	Cart owners & drivers, carting Agents, &c.	76	38	38	452	257	195	262	220	42	12	2	10	...	...	...
			376	Livery stable-keepers, &c.	...	...	...	10	...	10	520	286	234	322	176	146	...	...	...
			377	Drivers, stable-boys, &c., (*not private servants*) ...	...	...	...	...	...	...	...	...	...	...	...	...	...	...	...
		(b) Carriers by pack animals.	378	Palki, &c., owners, bearers, &c. ...	147	28	119	75	32	43	106	73	33	41	20	21	...	...	...
			379	Pack bullock owners, drivers, &c. ...	33	5	28	1,947	1,099	848	414	810	104	86	65	21	...	...	...
			380	Pack camel, elephant, mule, &c., owners and drivers ...	...	...	...	35	16	19	175	129	46	4	4	...	...	...	...
				Total Sub-order 59......	256	71	185	2,519	1,404	1,115	1,477	1,018	459	465	267	198	...	...	...

TABLE XVII B.

Occupations by Districts.—*Continued.*

Class.	Order.	Sub-order and Group.	Serial No.	Occupations.	Grand Total. Total.	Grand Total. Males.	Grand Total. Females.	Hyderabad. Total.	Hyderabad. Males.	Hyderabad. Females.	Atraf-i-Balda. Total.	Atraf-i-Balda. Males.	Atraf-i-Balda. Females.	Mahabubnagar. Total.	Mahabubnagar. Males.	Mahabubnagar. Females.	Nalgonda. Total.	Nalgonda. Males.	Nalgonda. Females.
1	2	3	4	5	6	7	8	9	10	11	12	13	14	15	16	17	18	19	20
Class E.—Commerce, transport, storage,—*concld.*	XIX.—Transport and storage.	60. Water. (a) Owners, &c. of vessels.	381	Ship owners, Companies, Agents ...	...	...	...	...	...	...	...	...	...	...	...	...	...	...	...
			382	Shipping clerks, supercargoes, and stevedores	...	...	...	...	...	...	...	...	...	...	...	...	...	...	...
			383	Boat and barge owners, &c.	...	...	...	...	...	...	...	...	...	...	...	...	...	...	...
		(b) Working staff of vessels.	384	Ships' Officers, Engineers, mariners, and firemen	13	12	1	2	1	1	...	...	...	...	...	...	...	...	...
			385	Boat and barge men	707	415	292	11	5	6	8	...	8	...	...	...	6	5	1
			386	Pilots	...	...	...	...	...	...	...	...	...	...	...	...	...	...	...
			387	Lock-keepers, &c., and canal service ...	5,179	3,021	2,158	4	2	2	474	305	169	616	357	259	133	75	58
			388	Dock and harbour service	...	...	...	...	...	...	...	...	...	...	...	...	...	...	...
			389	Divers (not for pearls)...	15	9	6	10	4	6	...	...	...	...	...	...	...	...	...
				Total Sub-order 60......	5,914	3,457	2,457	27	12	15	482	305	177	616	357	259	139	80	59
		61. Messages. (a) Post, &c.	390	Postal Directors, Postmasters and clerks,	474	231	243	148	71	77	8	8	...	13	11	2	95	47	48
			391	Postal messengers, runners, &c. ...	2,814	1,410	904	504	287	217	67	38	29	160	99	61	90	75	15
			392	Messengers (unspecified)	1,802	664	638	1,128	560	568	...	...	...	...	...	...	...	...	...
		(b) Telegraph & Telephone.	393	Telegraph officers (Government, Railway and others), and clerical, and accounts establishment	122	70	52	53	28	25	1	1	...	...	...	...	...	...	...
			394	Signallers and messengers	32	16	16	19	11	8	...	...	...	...	...	...	...	...	...
			395	Telephone Company s service	5	3	2	...	...	...	...	...	...	...	...	...	...	...	...
				Total Sub-order 61......	4,249	2,394	1,855	1,852	957	895	76	47	29	173	110	63	185	122	63
		62. Storage and weighing.	396	Warehouse owners, keepers, &c. ...	16	14	2	3	1	2	...	...	...	...	...	...	...	...	...
			397	Warehouse service	22	19	3	20	17	3	...	...	...	...	...	...	...	...	...
			398	Porters (general)	3,254	1,677	1,577	1,470	660	810	13	...	13	717	493	224	...	...	...
			399	Weighmen and measurers	897	482	415	122	64	58	129	78	51	26	15	11	7	2	5
			400	Watchmen (not village)	170	112	58	102	66	36	...	...	...	...	...	...	...	...	...
				Total Sub-order 62......	4,359	2,304	2,055	1,717	808	909	142	78	64	743	508	235	7	2	5
				Total Order XIX......	82,790	49,367	33,423	10,537	5,888	4,649	6,170	4,246	1,924	7,184	4,400	2,784	2,956	1,831	1,125

TABLE XVII B.

Occupations by Districts.—*Continued.*

Class.	Order.	Sub-order and Group.	Serial No	Occupations.	Warangal. Total.	Warangal. Males.	Warangal. Females.	Elgandal. Total.	Elgandal. Males.	Elgandal. Females.	Indur. Total.	Indur. Males.	Indur. Females.	Medak. Total.	Medak. Males.	Medak. Females.	Aurangabad. Total.	Aurangabad. Males.	Aurangabad. Females.
					21	22	23	24	25	26	27	28	29	30	31	32	33	34	35
Class E.—Commerce, transport, storage.—*contd.*	XIX.—Transport and storage.	60. Water. (a) Owners, &c. of vessels.	381	Ship owners, Companies, Agents ...	...	...	...	...	...	...	...	...	...	...	...	...	...	...	...
			382	Shipping clerks, supercargoes, and stevedores	...	...	...	...	...	...	...	...	...	...	...	...	...	...	...
			383	Boat and barge owners, &c.	...	...	...	...	...	...	...	...	...	...	...	...	...	...	...
		(b) Working staff of vessels.	384	Ships' Officers, Engineers, mariners, and firemen...	...	...	...	...	...	...	...	...	...	5	5	...	...	...	...
			385	Boat and barge men	40	21	19	56	37	19	149	109	40	9	9	...	50	82	18
			386	Pilots	...	...	...	...	...	...	...	...	...	...	...	...	...	...	...
			387	Lock-keepers, &c., and canal service ...	897	531	366	1,701	934	767	...	...	...	1,229	754	475	...	...	...
			388	Dock and harbour service	...	...	...	...	...	...	...	...	...	...	...	...	...	...	...
			389	Divers (not for pearls)	...	...	...	...	...	...	...	...	...	...	...	...	...	...	...
				Total Sub-order 60......	937	552	385	1,757	971	786	149	109	40	1,243	768	475	50	82	18
		61. Messages. (a) Post, &c.	390	Postal Directors, Postmasters and clerks.	16	15	1	21	14	7	...	...	...	4	4	...	3	8	...
			391	Postal messengers, runners, &c. ...	215	110	105	158	90	68	242	202	40	45	27	18	166	86	80
			392	Messengers (unspecified)	...	...	...	...	...	...	...	...	...	...	...	...	...	...	...
		(b) Telegraph & Telephone.	393	Telegraph officers (Government, Railway and others), and clerical, and accounts establishment	4	2	2	...	...	...	1	...	1	...	...	...	...	...	...
			394	Signallers and messengers	...	...	...	...	...	...	...	...	...	...	...	...	...	...	...
			395	Telephone Company's service	...	...	...	...	...	...	...	...	...	...	...	...	5	3	2
				Total Sub-order 61......	235	127	108	179	104	75	243	202	41	49	31	18	174	92	82
		62. Storage and weighing.	396	Warehouse owners, keepers, &c. ...	...	...	...	...	...	...	...	...	...	...	...	...	...	...	...
			397	Warehouse service	...	...	...	...	...	...	...	...	...	...	...	...	...	...	...
			398	Porters (general)	11	9	2	8	8	...	9	9	...	68	...	68	586	818	268
			399	Weighmen and measurers	22	18	4	30	12	18	114	60	54	50	31	19	20	3	17
			400	Watchmen (not village)	...	...	...	...	...	...	...	...	...	...	...	...	...	...	...
				Total Sub-order 62......	33	27	6	38	20	18	123	69	54	118	31	87	606	321	285
				Total Order XIX......	8,674	2,281	1,393	4,492	2,422	2,070	9,087	5,566	3,521	5,895	3,401	2,494	5,262	2,682	2,580

TABLE XVII B.

Occupations by Districts.—*Continued.*

Class.	Order.	Sub-order and Group.	Serial No.	Occupations.	Birh. Total.	Birh. Males.	Birh. Females.	Nander. Total.	Nander. Males.	Nander. Females.	Naldrug. Total.	Naldrug. Males.	Naldrug. Females.	Bidar. Total.	Bidar. Males.	Bidar. Females.	Parbhani. Total.	Parbhani. Males.	Parbhani. Females.
					36	37	38	39	40	41	42	43	44	45	46	47	48	49	50
Class E.—Commerce, transport, storage.—*concld.*	XIX.—Transport and storage.	60. Water. (a) Owners, &c., of vessels.	381	Ship owners, Companies, Agents ...	...	...	...	...	...	...	...	...	...	...	...	...	...	...	...
			382	Shipping clerks, supercargoes, and stevedores ...	...	...	...	...	...	...	...	...	...	...	...	...	...	...	...
			383	Boat and barge owners, &c. ...	...	...	...	...	...	...	...	...	...	...	...	...	...	...	...
		(b) Working staff of vessels.	384	Ships' Officers, Engineers, mariners and firemen...	...	...	...	...	...	...	...	...	...	...	...	...	...	...	...
			385	Boat and barge men ...	22	13	9	7	7	...	...	...	...	57	23	34	24	23	1
			386	Pilots ...	...	...	...	...	...	...	...	...	...	...	...	...	...	...	...
			387	Lock-keepers, &c., and canal service ...	...	...	...	...	...	...	...	...	...	...	...	...	...	...	...
			388	Dock and harbour service ...	...	...	...	...	...	...	...	...	...	...	...	...	...	...	...
			389	Divers (not for pearls) ...	...	...	...	5	5	...	...	...	...	...	...	...	...	...	...
				Total Sub-order 60......	22	13	9	12	12	...	...	...	...	57	23	34	24	23	1
		61. Messages. (a) Post, &c.	390	Postal Directors, Postmasters and clerks.	8	8	...	...	...	...	...	...	...	...	...	...	146	45	101
			391	Postal messengers, runners, &c. ...	123	57	66	43	29	14	80	67	13	106	53	53	1	1	...
			392	Messengers (unspecified) ...	...	...	...	...	...	...	...	...	...	...	...	...	...	...	...
		(b) Telegraph & Telephone.	393	Telegraph Officers (Government, Railway and others), and clerical, and accounts establishment ...	...	...	...	...	...	...	...	...	...	...	...	...	1	1	...
			394	Signallers and messengers ...	...	...	...	...	...	...	...	...	...	...	...	...	...	...	...
			395	Telephone Company's service ...	...	...	...	...	...	...	...	...	...	...	...	...	...	...	...
				Total Sub-order 61......	126	60	66	43	29	14	80	67	13	106	53	53	148	47	101
		62. Storage and weighing.	396	Warehouse owners, keepers, &c. ...	...	...	...	13	13	...	...	...	...	...	...	...	...	...	...
			397	Warehouse service ...	...	...	...	...	...	...	...	...	...	2	2	...	...	...	...
			398	Porters (general) ...	69	24	45	3	...	3	17	...	17	...	...	...	...	...	...
			399	Weighmen and measurers ...	32	32	...	...	...	...	9	...	9	134	73	61	10	6	4
			400	Watchmen (not village) ...	...	...	...	...	...	...	...	...	...	...	...	...	...	...	...
				Total Sub-order 62......	101	56	45	16	13	3	26	...	26	136	75	61	10	6	4
				Total Order XIX......	2,208	1,391	817	2,436	1,477	959	2,253	1,493	760	4,223	2,675	1,548	5,433	3,234	2,199

TABLE XVII B.

Occupations by Districts.—*Continued.*

Class.	Order.	Sub-order and Group.	Serial No.	Occupations.	Sirpur Tandur. Total.	Sirpur Tandur. Males.	Sirpur Tandur. Females.	Gulbarga. Total.	Gulbarga. Males.	Gulbarga. Females.	Raichur. Total.	Raichur. Males.	Raichur. Females.	Lingasugur. Total.	Lingasugur. Males.	Lingasugur. Females.	Railways. Total.	Railways. Males.	Railways. Females.
					51	52	53	54	55	56	57	58	59	60	61	62	63	64	65
Class E.—Commerce, transport, storage.—*concld.*	XIX. Transport and storage.	60. Water. (a) Owners, &c. of vessels.	381	Ship owners Companies, Agents ...	...	...	...	...	...	...	...	...	...	...	...	...	...	...	...
			382	Shipping clerks, supercargoes, and stevedores	...	...	...	...	...	...	...	...	...	...	...	...	...	...	...
			383	Boat and barge owners, &c.	...	...	...	...	...	...	...	...	...	...	...	...	...	...	...
		(b) Working staff of vessels.	384	Ships' Officers, Engineers, mariners and firemen...	...	...	...	...	...	...	...	...	...	...	...	...	6	6	...
			385	Boat and barge men	...	...	...	109	20	89	153	105	48	6	6	...	...	...	...
			386	Pilots	...	...	...	...	...	...	...	...	...	...	...	...	...	...	...
			387	Lock-keepers, &c., and canal service ...	...	...	...	...	...	...	23	12	11	102	51	51	...	...	...
			388	Dock and harbour service	...	...	...	...	...	...	...	...	...	...	...	...	...	...	...
			389	Divers (not for pearls)	...	...	...	...	...	...	...	...	...	...	...	...	...	...	...
				Total Sub-order 60......	...	...	...	109	20	89	176	117	59	108	57	51	6	6	...
		61. Messages. (a) Post, &c.	390	Postal Directors, Postmasters and clerks	...	...	...	...	...	...	5	3	2	...	...	...	12	7	5
			391	Postal messengers, runners, &c. ...	9	6	3	22	4	18	206	138	68	70	86	84	7	5	2
			392	Messengers (unspecified)	...	...	...	...	...	...	12	8	4	115	55	60	47	41	6
		(b) Telegraph & Telephone.	393	Telegraph officers (Government, Railways, and others), and clerical and accounts establishment	...	...	...	...	...	...	30	17	13	4	3	1	28	18	10
			394	Signallers and messengers	...	...	...	...	...	...	2	2	...	...	...	...	11	8	8
			395	Telephone Company's service	...	...	...	...	...	...	...	...	...	...	...	...	...	...	...
				Total Sub-order 61......	9	6	3	22	4	18	255	168	87	189	94	95	105	74	31
		62. Storage and weighing.	396	Warehouse owners, keepers, &c. ...	...	...	...	...	...	...	...	...	...	...	...	...	...	...	...
			397	Warehouse service	...	...	...	...	...	...	...	...	...	...	...	...	...	...	...
			398	Porters (general)	26	...	26	237	142	95	...	...	...	...	...	...	20	14	6
			399	Weighmen and measurers	1	1	...	162	79	83	2	2	...	27	6	21	...	...	...
			400	Watchman (not village)	...	...	...	...	...	...	23	14	9	...	...	...	45	82	18
				Total Sub-order 62......	27	1	26	399	221	178	25	16	9	27	6	21	65	46	19
				Total Order XIX......	292	78	214	3,446	1,817	1,629	2,807	1,785	1,022	800	429	371	3,635	2,271	1,364

TABLE XVII B.

Occupations by Districts.—*Continued.*

Class.	Order.	Sub-order and Group.	Serial No.	Occupations.	Grand Total. Total.	Grand Total. Males.	Grand Total. Females.	Hyderabad. Total.	Hyderabad. Males.	Hyderabad. Females.	Atraf-i-Balda. Total.	Atraf-i-Balda. Males.	Atraf-i-Balda. Females.	Mahabubnagar. Total.	Mahabubnagar. Males.	Mahabubnagar. Females.	Nalgonda. Total.	Nalgonda. Males.	Nalgonda. Females.
1	2	3	4	5	6	7	8	9	10	11	12	13	14	15	16	17	18	19	20
Class F.—Professions.	XX. Learned and artistic professions.	63. Religion. (a) Priests, Ministers, &c.	401	Priests, ministers, preachers, missionaries, &c.	8,455	8,826	4,629	535	280	255	41	15	26	65	29	36	17	11	6
			402	Catechists, readers, Zanána mission service, &c.	1,743	988	755	354	200	154	40	30	10	718	872	846	83	12	21
			403	Exorcists, hail-averters, amulettiers, &c.	1,457	790	667	392	173	219	201	72	129	81	48	33	160	74	86
		(b) Subsidiary religious services.	404	Religious mendicants, inmates of monasteries, convents, &c.	84,208	18,680	15,523	626	376	250	898	511	387	1,487	817	670	3,358	1,549	1,809
			405	Church, Temple, Masjid, Pagoda, ghat, burial or burning-ground service, pilgrim conductors, and Undertakers ...	18,720	9,707	9,013	1,274	718	556	801	456	345	1,458	805	653	796	483	313
				Total Sub-order 63......	64,578	3,3991	80,587	3,181	1,747	1,434	1,981	1,084	897	3,809	2,071	1,738	4,364	2,129	2,235
		64. Education.	406	Administrative and inspecting officials...	52	20	32	38	13	25	...	...	...	5	...	5	...	...	...
			407	Principals, professors, and teachers in colleges, &c., schools, &c.	11,684	6,598	5,086	1,975	948	1,027	571	349	222	867	518	349	600	361	239
			408	Clerks, &c., on establishments of Educational Institution	132	76	56	31	17	14	26	1	25	8	8	...	46	31	15
				Total Sub-order 64......	11,868	6,694	5,174	2,044	978	1,066	597	350	247	880	526	354	646	392	254
		65. Literature.	409	Authors, Editors, Journalists, balladmakers...	11	6	5	9	4	5	...	...	...	...	...	...	...	...	...
			410	Reporters, Short-hand writers, Book copyists...	21	11	10	17	7	10	...	...	...	...	...	...	...	...	...
			411	Private Secretaries and Clerks	2,611	1,751	860	1,134	611	523	6	...	6	41	27	14	22	7	15
			412	Public Scribes and Copyists ...	196	100	96	84	40	44	1	1	...	84	18	16	...	...	...
			413	Service in Libraries and Literary Institutions	1	1	...	1	1	...	...	...	...	...	...	...	...	...	...
				Total Sub-order 65......	2,840	1,869	971	1,245	663	582	7	1	6	75	45	80	22	7	15
		66. Law.	414	Barristers, Advocates and Pleaders ...	8,653	1,995	1,658	1,588	842	746	20	5	15	97	42	55	41	25	16
			415	Solicitors and Attorneys...	46	22	24	46	22	24	...	...	...	...	...	...	...	...	...
			416	Law-agents, mukhtiárs, &c.	9	4	5	8	3	5	...	...	...	...	...	...	...	...	...
			417	Articled clerks and other lawyers' clerks.	12	5	7	12	5	7	...	...	...	...	...	...	...	...	...
			418	Stamp-Vendors	168	41	127	18	7	11	...	...	...	8	8	...	...	...	...
			419	Petition-writers	426	233	193	51	35	16	...	...	...	...	...	...	...	...	...
				Total Sub-order 66......	4,814	2,300	2,014	1,723	914	809	20	5	15	100	45	55	41	25	16

TABLE XVII B.

Occupations by Districts.—*Continued.*

Class.	Order.	Sub-order and Group.	Serial No.	Occupations.	Warangal. Total.	Warangal. Males.	Warangal. Females.	Elgandal. Total.	Elgandal. Males.	Elgandal. Females.	Indur. Total.	Indur. Males.	Indur. Females.	Medak. Total.	Medak. Males.	Medak. Females.	Aurangabad. Total.	Aurangabad. Males.	Aurangabad. Females.
					21	22	23	24	25	26	27	28	29	30	31	32	33	34	35
Class F.—Professions.	XX. Learned and artistic professions.	63. Religion. (a) Priests, Ministers, &c.	401	Priests, ministers, preachers, missionaries, &c.	2,331	1,091	1,240	2,851	1,441	1,410	238	121	117	881	85	796	845	155	190
			402	Catechists, readers, Zanána mission service, &c.	13	3	10	4	4	...	...	...	...	57	48	9	...	...	...
		(b) Subsidiary religious services.	403	Exorcists, hail-averters, amulettiers, &c...	97	50	47	437	317	120	...	...	...	43	29	14	22	22	...
			404	Religious mendicants, inmates of monasteries, convents, &c.	976	481	495	1,504	785	719	3,081	1,654	1,427	988	510	478	1,621	597	1,024
			405	Church, Temple, Masjid, Pagoda, ghat, burial or burning-ground service, pilgrim conductors, and Undertakers...	1,181	623	558	1,135	567	568	186	162	24	726	411	315	1,773	909	864
				Total Sub-order 63......	4,598	2,248	2,350	5,931	3,114	2,817	3,505	1,937	1,568	2,645	1,033	1,612	3,761	1,683	2,078
		64. Education.	406	Administrative and inspecting officials...	...	...	...	...	...	...	...	...	...	...	...	...	9	7	2
			407	Principals, professors and teachers in colleges, &c., schools, &c.	887	544	343	1,046	548	498	362	240	122	479	293	186	763	426	337
			408	Clerks, &c., on establishments of Educational Institution	8	8	...	...	...	...	...	...	...	10	10	...	2	...	2
				Total Sub-order 64......	895	552	343	1,046	548	498	362	240	122	489	303	186	774	433	341
		65. Literature.	409	Authors, Editors, Journalists, ballad-makers	2	2	...	...	...	...	...	...	...	...	...	...	...	...	...
			410	Reporters, Short-hand writers, Book copyists	...	...	...	...	...	...	...	...	...	...	...	...	4	4	...
			411	Private Secretaries and Clerks... ...	83	43	40	8	4	4	1	1	...	25	9	16	468	467	1
			412	Public Scribes and Copyists	...	...	...	8	...	8	1	1	...	2	2	...	...	...	...
			413	Service in Libraries and Literary Institutions	...	...	...	...	...	...	...	...	...	...	...	...	...	...	...
				Total Sub-order 65......	85	45	40	16	4	12	2	2	...	27	11	16	472	471	1
		66. Law.	414	Barristers, Advocates and Pleaders ...	113	80	33	86	39	47	77	41	36	50	28	22	821	803	118
			415	Solicitors and Attorneys	...	...	...	...	...	...	...	...	...	...	...	...	...	...	...
			416	Law-agents, mukhtiárs, &c.	...	...	...	1	1	...	...	...	...	...	...	...	...	...	...
			417	Articled clerks and other lawyers' clerks.	...	...	...	...	...	...	...	...	...	...	...	...	...	...	...
			418	Stamp-Vendors...	2	2	...	...	...	...	...	...	...	64	...	64	2	1	1
			419	Petition-writers	4	4	...	4	4	...	18	12	6	...	...	...	109	55	54
				Total Sub-order 66......	119	86	33	91	44	47	95	53	42	114	28	86	432	259	173

TABLE XVII B.

Occupations by Districts.—*Continued.*

Class.	Order.	Sub-order and Group.	Serial No.	Occupations.	Birh. Total.	Birh. Males.	Birh. Females.	Nander. Total.	Nander. Males.	Nander. Females.	Naldrug. Total.	Naldrug. Males.	Naldrug. Females.	Bidar. Total.	Bidar. Males.	Bidar. Females.	Parbhani. Total.	Parbhani. Males.	Parbhani. Females.
					36	37	38	39	40	41	42	43	44	45	46	47	48	49	50
Class F.—Professions.	XX. Learned and artistic professions.	63. Religion. (a) Priests, Ministers, &c.	401	Priests, ministers, preachers, missionaries, &c.	103	63	40	102	63	89	145	80	65	129	58	71	229	100	129
			402	Catechists, readers, Zanâna mission service, &c.	51	50	1	4	4	...	...	...	...	...	...	...	5	5	...
			403	Exorcists, hail-averters, amulettiers, &c.	...	...	...	8	3	5	1	1	...	7	1	6	...	...	...
		(b) Subsidiary religious services.	404	Religious mendicants, inmates of monasteries, convents, &c.	2,565	1,490	1,075	2,670	1,869	1,801	2,222	1,058	1,164	2,513	1,663	850	8,699	1,845	1,854
			405	Church, Temple, Masjid, Pagoda, ghat, burial or burning-ground service, pilgrim conductors, and Undertakers...	1,567	781	786	740	272	468	1,850	657	693	2,011	974	1,087	790	892	898
				Total Sub-order 63......	4,286	2,384	1,902	3,524	1,711	1,813	3,718	1,796	1,922	4,660	2,696	1,964	4,723	2,342	2,381
		64. Education.	406	Administrative and inspecting officials.	...	...	...	...	...	...	...	...	...	...	...	...	...	...	...
			407	Principals, professors, and teachers in colleges, &c., schools, &c.	367	224	143	242	159	83	445	214	231	751	362	389	576	369	207
			408	Clerks, &c., on establishments of Educational Institution	1	1	...	...	...	...	...	...	...	...	...	...	...	...	...
				Total Sub-order 64......	368	225	143	242	159	83	445	214	231	751	362	389	576	369	207
		65. Literature.	409	Authors, Editors, Journalists, ballad-makers...	...	...	...	...	...	...	...	...	...	...	...	...	...	...	...
			410	Reporters, Short-hand writers, Book copyists...	...	...	...	...	...	...	...	...	...	...	...	...	...	...	...
			411	Private Secretaries and Clerks... ...	7	2	5	73	73	...	...	...	...	...	...	...	44	40	4
			412	Public Scribes and Copyists	...	...	...	...	...	...	...	...	...	...	...	...	...	...	...
			413	Service in Libraries and Literary Institutions	...	...	...	...	...	...	...	...	...	...	...	...	...	...	...
				Total Sub-order 65......	7	2	5	73	73	...	...	...	...	...	...	...	44	40	4
		66. Law.	414	Barristers, Advocates and Pleaders ...	190	94	96	135	70	65	137	79	58	170	89	81	249	148	106
			415	Solicitors and Attorneys	...	...	...	...	...	...	...	...	...	...	...	...	...	...	...
			416	Law-agents, mukhtiârs, &c.	...	...	...	...	...	...	...	...	...	...	...	...	...	...	...
			417	Articled clerks and other lawyers' clerks.	...	...	...	...	...	...	...	...	...	...	...	...	...	...	...
			418	Stamp-Vendors	11	11	...	4	2	2	5	2	3	...	...	...	2	2	...
			419	Petition-writers	58	40	18	17	16	1	27	7	20	67	40	27	36	5	31
				Total Sub-order 66......	259	145	114	156	88	68	169	88	81	287	129	108	287	150	187

TABLE XVII B.

Occupations by Districts.—*Continued.*

Class.	Order.	Sub-order and Group.	Serial No.	Occupations.	Sirpur Tandur. Total.	Sirpur Tandur. Males.	Sirpur Tandur. Females.	Gulbarga. Total.	Gulbarga. Males.	Gulbarga. Females.	Raichur. Total.	Raichur. Males.	Raichur. Females.	Lingasugur. Total.	Lingasugur. Males.	Lingasugur. Females.	Railways. Total.	Railways. Males.	Railways. Females.
					51	52	53	54	55	56	57	58	59	60	61	62	63	64	65
Class F.—Professions.	XX. Learned and artistic professions.	63. Religion. (a) Priests, Ministers, &c.	401	Priests, ministers, preachers, missionaries, &c.	56	24	32	119	84	35	129	74	55	156	76	80	33	26	
			402	Catechists, readers, Zanána mission service, &c.	...	...	...	...	...	...	85	60	25	379	200	179	...	...	...
		(b) Subsidiary religious services.	403	Exorcists, hail-averters, amulettiers, &c.	...	...	...	8	...	8	...	...	...	...	...	...	...	...	...
			404	Religious mendicants, inmates of monasteries, convents, &c.	1,420	1,332	88	4,181	2,383	1,798	365	246	119	29	14	15	...	...	...
			405	Church, Temple, Masjid, Pagoda, ghat, burial or burning-ground service, pilgrim conductors, and Undertakers...	83	36	47	874	443	481	1,265	675	590	710	843	867	...	...	...
				Total Sub-order 63......	1,559	1,392	167	5,182	2,910	2,272	1,844	1,055	789	1,274	633	641	33	26	7
		64. Education.	406	Administrative and inspecting officials ...	...	...	...	...	...	...	...	...	...	...	...	...	...	...	...
			407	Principals, professors, and teachers in colleges, &c., schools, &c.	30	23	7	516	353	163	688	370	318	511	290	221	8	7	1
			408	Clerks, &c., on establishments of Educational Institution	...	...	...	...	...	...	...	...	...	...	...	...	...	...	...
				Total Sub-order 64......	30	23	7	516	353	163	688	370	318	511	290	221	8	7	1
		65. Literature.	409	Authors, Editors, Journalists, ballad-makers	...	...	...	...	...	...	...	...	...	...	...	...	...	...	...
			410	Reporters, Short-hand writers, Book copyists...	...	...	...	...	...	...	...	...	...	...	...	...	...	...	...
			411	Private Secretaries and Clerks	...	...	...	28	26	2	272	222	50	361	190	171	38	29	9
			412	Public Scribes and Copyists	...	...	...	...	...	...	57	35	22	9	3	6	...	...	...
			413	Service in Libraries and Literary Institutions	...	...	...	...	...	...	...	...	...	...	...	...	...	...	...
				Total Sub-order 65......	...	...	...	28	26	2	329	257	72	370	193	177	38	29	9
		66. Law.	414	Barristers, Advocates and Pleaders ...	8	...	8	81	45	36	146	79	67	139	82	57	10	9	1
			415	Solicitors and Attorneys...	...	...	...	...	...	...	...	...	...	...	...	...	...	...	...
			416	Law-agents, Mukhtiárs, &c.	...	...	...	...	...	...	...	...	...	...	...	...	...	...	...
			417	Articled clerks and other lawyers' clerks.	...	...	...	...	...	...	...	...	...	...	...	...	...	...	...
			418	Stamp-Vendors	...	...	...	42	...	42	...	...	...	11	7	4	4	4	...
			419	Petition-writers	1	1	...	34	14	20	...	...	...	...	...	...	...	...	...
				Total Sub-order 66......	4	1	3	157	59	98	146	79	67	150	89	61	14	13	1

TABLE XVII B.

Occupations by Districts.—*Continued.*

Class.	Order.	Sub-order and Group.	Serial No.	Occupations.	Grand Total. Total.	Grand Total. Males.	Grand Total. Females.	Hyderabad. Total.	Hyderabad. Males.	Hyderabad. Females.	Atraf-i-Balda. Total.	Atraf-i-Balda. Males.	Atraf-i-Balda. Females.	Mahabubnagar. Total.	Mahabubnagar. Males.	Mahabubnagar. Females.	Nalgonda. Total.	Nalgonda. Males.	Nalgonda. Females.
1	2	3	4	5	6	7	8	9	10	11	12	13	14	15	16	17	18	19	20
Class F.—Professions.—*contd.*	XX.—Learned and artistic professions.—*contd.*	67. Medicine. (a) Practitioners.	420	Administrative and Inspecting Staff (when not returned under general head)	87	14	23	...	...	...	...	...	...	...	...	...	5	...	5
			421	Practitioners by diploma	489	243	246	817	150	167	2	2	...	27	18	9	7	...	7
			422	Practitioners without diploma (Baid, Hakim, Kobiraj, &c.)...	12,442	6,697	5,745	2,046	1,033	1,013	707	371	336	986	514	472	952	544	408
			423	Dentists	...	...	...	...	...	...	...	...	...	...	...	...	...	...	...
			424	Oculists	2	1	1	...	...	...	...	...	...	...	...	...	...	...	...
			425	Vaccinators	197	139	58	89	56	33	...	...	...	1	1	...	...	...	...
			426	Midwifery	1,155	336	819	439	66	373	46	2	44	8	1	7	107	9	98
		(b) Subsidiary medical service.	427	Hospital and Asylum, Matrons, Assistants and Apothecaries...	850	174	176	240	122	118	...	...	...	...	...	...	...	...	...
			428	Compounders, Nurses and hospital, Asylum and dispensary service ...	223	127	96	74	40	84	44	38	6	13	8	5	36	...	36
				Total Sub-order 67......	14,895	7,731	7,164	3,205	1,467	1,738	799	413	386	1,035	542	493	1,107	553	554
		68. Engineering and surveying. (a)—	429	Administrative and Inspecting Staff ...	5	1	4	4	1	3	...	...	...	...	...	...	...	...	...
			430	Civil Engineers and Architects... ...	102	57	45	76	46	30	...	...	...	5	2	3	1	...	1
			431	Topographical, Archæological and Revenue Surveyors	66	50	16	...	...	...	...	...	...	2	2	...	14	5	9
		(b) Subordinary staff, Engineers, Architects and Surveyors.	432	Draughtsmen and Operators in Survey Offices, overseers, &c.	707	372	335	234	113	121	...	...	...	12	12	...	86	81	5
			433	Clerks, &c., in offices of the above ...	812	451	361	356	209	147	2	2	...	82	42	40	59	56	3
				Total Sub-order 68......	1,692	931	761	670	369	301	2	2	...	101	58	43	110	92	18
		69. Other sciences. (a) Astronomy, &c.	434	Astronomers and Meteorologists, and establishments	1	1	...	1	1	...	...	...	...	...	...	...	...	...	...
			435	Botanists, Naturalists and officers of Scientific Institutions	...	...	...	...	...	...	...	...	...	...	...	...	...	...	...
			436	Metallurgists	1	1	...	...	...	...	...	...	...	...	...	...	...	...	...
		(b) Minor sciences.	437	Astrologers, Genealogists and Horoscope-casters	7,853	3,825	4,028	157	86	71	261	149	112	9	5	4	15	7	8
			438	Almanac-makers and sellers	4	2	2	4	2	2	...	...	...	...	...	...	...	...	...
			439	Diviners (selectors of well and house sites, &c.)	2	2	...	...	...	...	...	...	...	...	...	...	...	...	...
				Total Sub-order 69......	7,861	3,831	4,030	162	89	73	261	149	112	9	5	4	15	7	8

TABLE XVII B.

Occupations by Districts.—*Continued.*

Class.	Order.	Sub-order and Group.	Serial No.	Occupations.	Warangal. Total.	Warangal. Males.	Warangal. Females.	Elgandal. Total.	Elgandal. Males.	Elgandal. Females.	Indur. Total.	Indur. Males.	Indur. Females.	Medak. Total.	Medak. Males.	Medak. Females.	Aurangabad. Total.	Aurangabad. Males.	Aurangabad. Females.
					21	22	23	24	25	26	27	28	29	30	31	32	33	34	35
Class F.—Professions.—*contd.*	XX. Learned and artistic professions.—*contd.*	67. Medicine. (a) Practitioners.	420	Administrative and Inspecting Staff (when not returned under general head) ...	...	...	...	...	...	...	...	...	...	...	...	...	...	...	...
			421	Practitioners by diploma...	6	6	...	...	...	...	6	...	6	...	...	...	22	8	14
			422	Practitioners without diploma (Baid, Hakim, Kobiraj, &c.) ...	1,797	1,005	792	879	504	375	765	880	885	842	171	171	1,222	642	580
			423	Dentists ...	...	...	...	...	...	...	...	...	...	...	...	...	...	...	...
			424	Oculists ...	...	...	...	...	...	...	...	...	...	...	...	...	...	...	...
			425	Vaccinators ...	10	8	2	2	1	1	...	...	...	...	...	...	...	...	...
			426	Midwifery ...	70	8	62	13	4	9	...	...	...	...	...	...	2	2	...
		(b) Subsidiary medical service.	427	Hospital and Asylum, Matrons, Assistants and Apothecaries...	1	1	...	12	...	12	5	...	5	8	...	8	122	10	112
			428	Compounders, Nurses and hospital, Asylum and dispensary service ...	12	6	6	28	24	4	...	...	...	1	1	...	...	...	...
				Total Sub-order 67......	1,896	1,034	862	934	533	401	776	880	896	846	172	174	1,368	662	706
		68. Engineering and surveying. (a)—Engineers, Architects and Surveyors.	429	Administrative and Inspecting Staff ...	...	...	...	...	...	...	...	...	...	...	...	...	...	...	...
			430	Civil Engineers and Architects ...	8	4	4	8	2	6	...	...	...	...	...	...	...	...	...
			431	Topographical, Archæological and Revenue Surveyors ...	85	85	...	15	8	7	...	...	...	...	...	...	1	...	1
		(b) Subsidiary staff.	432	Draughtsmen and Operators in Survey Offices, overseers, &c. ...	19	12	7	82	12	20	130	52	78	22	22	...	66	84	82
			433	Clerks, &c., in offices of the above ...	117	72	45	...	...	...	50	16	84	9	4	5	12	6	6
				Total Sub-order 68......	179	123	56	55	22	33	180	68	112	31	26	5	79	40	39
		69. Other sciences. (a) Astronomy, &c.	434	Astronomers and Meteorologists and establishments ...	...	...	...	...	...	...	...	...	...	...	...	...	...	...	...
			435	Botanists, Naturalists and officers of Scientific Institutions ...	...	...	...	...	...	...	...	...	...	...	...	...	...	...	...
		(b) Minor sciences.	436	Metallurgists ...	...	...	...	...	...	...	...	...	...	...	...	...	...	...	...
			437	Astrologers, Genealogists and Horoscope-casters ...	5	3	2	7	1	6	1,043	550	493	259	153	106	1,406	769	637
			438	Almanac-makers and sellers ...	...	...	...	...	...	...	...	...	...	...	...	...	...	...	...
			439	Diviners (selectors of well and house sites, &c.) ...	...	...	...	...	...	...	...	...	...	...	...	...	...	...	...
				Total Sub-order 69......	5	3	2	7	1	6	1,043	550	493	259	153	106	1,406	769	637

TABLE XVII B.
Occupations by Districts.

TABLE XVII B.

Occupations by Districts.—*Continued.*

Class.	Order.	Sub-order and Group.	Serial No.	Occupations.	Birh. Total.	Birh. Males.	Birh. Females.	Nander. Total.	Nander. Males.	Nander. Females.	Naldrug. Total.	Naldrug. Males.	Naldrug. Females.	Bidar. Total.	Bidar. Males.	Bidar. Females.	Parbhani. Total.	Parbhani. Males.	Parbhani. Females.
					36	37	38	39	40	41	42	43	44	45	46	47	48	49	50
Class F.—Professions.—*contd.*	XX.—Learned and artistic professions.—*contd.*	67. Medicine. (a) Practitioners.	420	Administrative and Inspecting Staff (when not returned under general head)	32	14	18	...	...	...	...	...	...	...	...	...	...	...	...
			421	Practitioners by diploma	10	3	7	...	...	...	...	...	...	...	...	...	17	17	...
			422	Practitioners without diploma (Baid, Hakim, Kobiraj, &c.)	433	214	219	204	111	93	188	106	77	448	284	164	339	181	158
			423	Dentists	...	...	...	...	...	...	...	...	...	...	...	...	...	...	...
			424	Oculists	...	...	...	...	...	...	...	...	...	...	...	...	...	...	...
			425	Vaccinators	12	8	4	...	...	...	62	57	5	5	3	2	8	...	8
			426	Midwifery	1	...	1	6	...	6	2	2	...	237	214	23	15	...	15
		(b) Subsidiary medical service.	427	Hospital and Asylum, Matrons, Assistants and Apothecaries	33	11	22	...	...	...	...	...	...	...	...	...	...	...	...
			428	Compounders, Nurses and Hospital, Asylum and dispensary service ...	...	...	...	...	...	...	...	...	...	...	...	...	...	...	...
				Total Sub-order 67......	521	250	271	210	111	99	247	165	82	690	501	189	374	198	176
		68. Engineering and surveying. (a) Engineers, Architects and Surveyors.	429	Administrative and Inspecting Staff ...	...	...	...	...	...	...	...	...	...	...	...	...	...	...	...
			430	Civil Engineers and Architects... ...	...	...	...	...	...	...	...	...	...	...	...	...	...	...	...
			431	Topographical, Archæological and Revenue Surveyors ...	...	...	...	...	...	...	...	...	...	...	...	...	...	...	...
		(b) Subsidiary staff.	432	Draughtsmen and Operators in Survey Offices, overseers, &c.	...	...	...	...	...	...	...	...	...	8	...	8	1	...	1
			433	Clerks, &c., in offices of the above ...	13	4	9	14	9	5	12	...	12	13	2	11	11	4	7
				Total Sub-order 68......	13	4	9	14	9	5	12	...	12	16	2	14	12	4	8
		69. Other sciences. (a) Astronomy, &c.	434	Astronomers and Meteorologists, and establishments	...	...	...	...	...	...	...	...	...	...	...	...	...	...	...
			435	Botanists, Naturalists and officers of scientific Institutions	...	...	...	...	...	...	...	...	...	...	...	...	...	...	...
			436	Metallurgists	...	...	...	...	...	...	...	...	...	...	...	...	...	...	...
		(b) Minor sciences.	437	Astrologers, Genealogists and Horoscope-casters	1,018	424	594	1,090	515	575	24	11	13	1,349	601	748	4	2	2
			438	Almanac-makers and sellers	...	...	...	...	...	...	...	...	...	...	...	...	...	...	...
			439	Diviners (selectors of well and house sites, &c.)	...	...	...	2	2	...	...	...	...	...	...	...	...	...	...
				Total Sub-order 69......	1,018	424	594	1,092	517	575	24	11	13	1,349	601	748	4	2	2

TABLE XVII B.

Occupations by Districts.—*Continued.*

Class.	Order.	Sub-order and Group.	Serial No.	Occupations.	Sirpur Tandur. Total.	Sirpur Tandur. Males.	Sirpur Tandur. Females.	Gulbarga. Total.	Gulbarga. Males.	Gulbarga. Females.	Raichur. Total.	Raichur. Males.	Raichur. Females.	Lingasugur. Total.	Lingasugur. Males.	Lingasugur. Females.	Railways. Total.	Railways. Males.	Railways. Females.
					51	52	53	54	55	56	57	58	59	60	61	62	63	64	65
Class F.—Professions.—*contd.*	XX. Learned and artistic professions.—*contd.*	67. Medicine. (a) Practitioners.	420	Administrative and Inspecting Staff (when not returned under general head) ...	...	...	...	...	...	...	...	...	...	...	...	...	...	...	...
			421	Practitioners by diploma	4	4	...	22	8	19	28	14	8	21	12	9	6	6	...
			422	Practitioners without diploma (Baid, Hakim, Kobiraj, &c.)...	...	...	...	620	848	277	826	196	180	189	96	93	4	2	2
			423	Dentists ...	...	...	...	...	...	...	...	...	...	...	...	...	...	...	...
			424	Oculists ...	...	...	...	...	...	...	...	...	...	...	...	...	...	...	...
			425	Vaccinators	...	...	...	...	...	...	...	...	...	...	...	...	...	...	...
			426	Midwifery	...	...	...	4	...	4	21	4	17	41	18	28	16	2	14
		(b) Subsidiary medical service.	427	Hospital and Asylum, Matrons, Assistants and Apothecaries	78	88	85	...	...	...	8	2	1	...	...	...	...	...	...
			428	Compounders, Nurses and hospital, Asylum and dispensary service ...	5	4	1	...	...	...	8	5	8	...	...	...	2	1	1
				Total Sub-order 67......	82	46	36	646	846	300	880	221	159	251	126	125	28	11	17
		68. Engineering and surveying. (a)—Engineers, Architects and Surveyors.	429	Administrative and Inspecting Staff ...	...	...	...	...	...	...	...	...	...	...	...	...	...	...	...
			430	Civil Engineers and Architects	...	...	...	...	...	...	...	...	...	...	...	...	4	8	1
			431	Topographical, Archæological and Revenue Surveyors ...	...	...	...	...	...	...	...	...	...	...	...	...	...	...	...
		(b) Subdiary staff.	432	Draughtsmen and Operators in Survey Offices, overseers, &c....	57	20	87	9	9	...	45	81	14	25	15	10	16	9	7
			433	Clerks, &c., in offices of the above ...	8	4	4	17	6	11	87	15	22	...	...	...	...	...	...
				Total Sub-order 68......	65	24	41	26	15	11	82	46	36	25	15	10	20	12	8
		69. Other sciences. (a) Astronomy, &c.	434	Astronomers and Meteorologists and establishments...	...	...	...	...	...	...	...	...	...	...	...	...	...	...	...
			435	Botanists, Naturalists and officers of Scientific Institution ...	...	...	...	...	...	...	...	...	...	...	...	...	...	...	...
			436	Metallurgists ...	...	...	...	...	...	...	...	...	...	...	...	...	...	...	...
		(b) Minor sciences.	437	Astrologers, Genealogists and Horoscope-casters ...	121	47	74	554	215	839	186	78	63	896	215	181	...	...	...
			438	Almanac-makers and sellers ...	...	...	...	...	...	...	...	...	...	...	...	...	...	...	...
			439	Diviners (selectors of well and house sites, &c.	...	...	...	...	...	...	...	...	...	...	...	...	...	...	...
				Total Sub-order 69......	121	47	74	554	215	839	136	78	63	896	215	181	...	...	...

TABLE XVII B.

Occupations by Districts.

TABLE XVII B.

Occupations by Districts.—*Continued.*

Class.	Order.	Sub-order and Group.	Serial No.	Occupations.	Grand Total. Total.	Grand Total. Males.	Grand Total. Females.	Hyderabad. Total.	Hyderabad. Males.	Hyderabad. Females.	Atraf-i-Balda. Total.	Atraf-i-Balda. Males.	Atraf-i-Balda. Females.	Mahabubnagar. Total.	Mahabubnagar. Males.	Mahabubnagar. Females.	Nalgonda. Total.	Nalgonda. Males.	Nalgonda. Females.
1	2	3	4	5	6	7	8	9	10	11	12	13	14	15	16	17	18	19	20
Class F.—Professions.—*contd.*	XX.—Learned and artistic professions.—*contd.*	70. Pictorial art and sculpture.	440	Painters, Superintendents of Schools of Art, &c.	1,289	753	536	899	202	197	14	12	2	43	29	14	57	28	29
			441	Sculptors...	25	11	14	25	11	14	...	...	...	...	...	...	...	...	...
			442	Photographers	44	25	19	44	25	19	...	...	...	...	...	...	...	...	...
				Total Sub-order 70......	1,858	789	569	468	238	230	14	12	2	43	29	14	57	28	29
		71. Music, acting, dancing.	443	Music Composers and Teachers ...	447	427	20	7	8	4	...	...	...	...	...	...	...	...	...
			444	Bandmasters and players (not military).	14,917	8,140	6,777	757	421	336	889	446	393	952	585	417	590	362	228
			445	Piano-Tuners	158	1	157	158	1	157	...	...	...	...	...	...	...	...	...
			446	Actors, Singers and Dancers, and their accompanists.	11,977	4,720	7,257	2,672	377	2,295	775	363	412	821	435	386	775	269	506
				Total Sub-order 71......	27,499	13,288	14,211	3,594	802	2,792	1,614	809	805	1,773	970	803	1,365	631	734
				Total Order XX......	186,905	71,424	65,481	16,292	7,267	9,025	5,295	2,825	2,470	7,825	4,291	3,534	7,727	3,864	3,863
	XXI.—Sport and amusement.	72. Sport.	447	Race-course service, Book-makers, Jockeys, &c.	2	...	2	...	...	...	...	...	...	...	...	...	...	...	...
			448	Shikaries, Falconers, Birdcatchers ...	2,162	1,122	1,040	125	66	59	424	230	194	541	226	315	65	36	29
			449	Huntsmen, whippers in...	75	38	37	...	...	...	1	...	1	...	...	...	...	...	...
				Total Sub-order 72	2,289	1,160	1,079	125	66	59	425	230	195	541	226	315	65	36	29
		73. Exhibition and games. (a) Conjuring, Catching, training & exhibiting animals.	450	Exhibitors of trained animals (Bulls, bears, snakes, monkeys, &c).	290	132	158	88	20	18	46	7	39	41	25	16	31	15	16
			451	Circus owners, managers, &c.	172	143	29	8	5	3	...	...	...	...	...	...	...	...	...
			452	Cock and pigeon fanciers	...	...	...	...	...	...	...	...	...	...	...	...	...	...	...
		(b) Fortune-telling & other exhibitions.	453	Buffoons	440	147	293	63	33	30	6	4	2	22	22	...	1	1	...
			454	Story and ballad reciters	108	66	37	9	...	9	25	15	10	5	5	...	11	1	10
			455	Exhibitors of puppets	465	260	205	4	1	3	...	...	...	89	38	51	88	54	34
			456	Conjurors and fortune-tellers	3,178	1,385	1,793	21	14	7	388	80	308	658	282	376	40	20	20
		(c) Acrobatics & athletics.	457	Tumblers, Acrobats, Wrestlers, Professional cricketers, &c	4,332	2,424	1,908	290	13	277	42	17	25	105	42	63	80	31	49
		(d) Service of places of entertainment.	458	Swing and merry-go-round keepers ...	...	...	...	...	...	...	...	...	...	...	...	...	...	...	...
			459	Tennis and Racquet Court, Gymkhana, and boat club service	18	13	5	18	13	5	...	...	...	...	...	...	...	...	...
			460	Billiard room and theatre ownership, managership and service	402	211	191	...	...	...	...	...	...	...	...	...	...	...	...
				Total Sub-order 73......	9,400	4,781	4,619	451	99	352	507	123	384	920	414	506	251	122	129
				Total Order XXI......	11,689	5,941	5,698	576	165	411	982	853	579	1,461	640	821	316	158	158

TABLE XVII B.

Occupations by Districts.—*Continued.*

Class.	Order.	Sub-order and Group.	Serial No.	Occupations.	Warangal. Total.	Warangal. Males.	Warangal. Females.	Elgandal. Total.	Elgandal. Males.	Elgandal. Females.	Indur. Total.	Indur. Males.	Indur. Females.	Medak. Total.	Medak. Males.	Medak. Females.	Aurangabad. Total.	Aurangabad. Males.	Aurangabad. Females.
					21	22	23	24	25	26	27	28	29	30	31	32	33	34	35
Class F.—Professions.—*contd.*	XX.—Learned and artistic professions.—*contd.*	70. Pictorial art and sculpture.	440	Painters, Superintendents of Schools of Art, &c.	281	110	171	41	82	9	...	...	...	216	216	...	...	...	...
			441	Sculptors...	...	...	...	...	...	...	...	...	...	...	...	...	...	...	...
			442	Photographers	...	...	...	...	...	...	...	...	...	...	...	...	...	...	...
				Total Sub-order 70......	281	110	171	41	82	9	...	...	...	216	216	...	...	...	...
		71. Music, acting, dancing.	443	Music Composers and Teachers... ...	...	...	...	24	10	14	...	...	...	...	...	...	...	...	...
			444	Bandmasters and players (not military).	692	472	220	1,846	875	971	387	185	202	715	422	293	875	456	419
			445	Piano-Tuners	...	...	...	...	...	...	...	...	...	...	...	...	...	...	...
			446	Actors, Singers and Dancers, and their accompanists	929	521	408	1,109	530	579	1,795	724	1,071	736	261	475	466	894	272
				Total Sub-order 71......	1,621	993	628	2,979	1,415	1,564	2,182	909	1,273	1,451	683	768	1,341	650	691
				Total Order XX......	9,679	5,194	4,485	11,100	5,713	5,387	8,145	4,139	4,006	5,578	2,625	2,953	9,633	4,967	4,666
	XXI.—Sport and amusement.	72. Sport.	447	Race-course service, Book makers, Jockeys, &c.	...	...	...	...	...	...	...	...	...	2	...	2	...	...	...
			448	Shikaries, Falconers, Birdcatchers ...	11	8	3	21	6	15	20	4	16	89	47	42	186	184	52
			449	Huntsmen, whippers in...	48	21	27	22	15	8	...	...	...	3	2	1	...	...	...
				Total Sub-order 72......	59	29	30	44	21	23	20	4	16	94	49	45	186	134	52
		73. Exhibition and games. (a) Catching, training & exhibiting animals.	450	Exhibitors of trained animals (Bulls, bears, snakes, monkeys, &c.)	1	1	...	2	2	...	...	...	...	12	12	...	4	4	...
			451	Circus owners, managers, &c.	...	...	...	...	...	...	...	...	...	...	...	...	...	...	...
			452	Cock and pigeon fanciers	...	...	...	...	...	...	...	...	...	...	...	...	...	...	...
		(b) Conjuring, Fortune-telling & other exhibitions.	453	Buffoons...	...	...	...	11	2	9	...	...	...	12	...	12	9	2	7
			454	Story and ballad reciters	18	18	...	13	9	4	...	...	...	3	1	2	...	...	...
			455	Exhibitors of puppets	7	7	...	21	8	13	...	...	...	14	14	...	...	...	...
			456	Conjurors and fortune-tellers	87	48	39	17	17	...	47	...	47	263	182	81	208	22	181
		(c) Acrobatics & athletics.	457	Tumblers, Acrobats, Wrestlers, Professional cricketers, &c.	228	191	37	170	100	70	166	118	48	111	48	63	298	252	46
		(d) Service of places of entertainment.	458	Swing and merry-go-round keepers ...	...	...	...	...	...	...	...	...	...	...	...	...	...	...	...
			459	Tennis and Racquet Court, Gymkhana, and boat club service	...	...	...	...	...	...	...	...	...	...	...	...	...	...	...
			460	Billiard room and theatre ownership, managership and service	...	...	...	...	...	...	...	...	...	...	...	...	...	...	...
				Total Sub-order 73......	341	265	76	234	138	96	213	118	95	415	257	158	514	280	284
				Total Order XXI......	400	294	106	278	159	119	233	122	111	509	306	203	700	414	286

TABLE XVII B.

Occupations by Districts.—*Continued.*

Class.	Order.	Sub-order and Group.	Serial No.	Occupations.	Birh. Total.	Birh. Males.	Birh. Females.	Nander. Total.	Nander. Males.	Nander. Females.	Naldrug. Total.	Naldrug. Males.	Naldrug. Females.	Bidar. Total.	Bidar. Males.	Bidar. Females.	Parbhani. Total.	Parbhani. Males.	Parbhani. Females.
					36	37	38	39	40	41	42	43	44	45	46	47	48	49	50
Class F.—Professions.—*contd.*	XX. Learned and artistic professions.—*contd.*	70. Pictorial art and sculpture.	440	Painters, Superintendents of Schools of Art, &c.	...	...	...	...	...	...	...	...	...	...	...	...	...	...	...
			441	Sculptors	...	...	...	...	...	...	...	...	...	...	...	...	...	...	...
			442	Photographers	...	...	...	...	...	...	...	...	...	...	...	...	...	...	...
				Total Sub-order 70......	...	...	...	...	...	...	...	...	...	...	...	...	...	...	...
		71. Music, acting, dancing.	443	Music Composers and Teachers...	...	...	...	...	...	...	...	...	...	...	...	...	412	412	...
			444	Bandmasters and players (not military)	406	230	176	806	542	264	456	257	199	1,526	727	799	1,029	562	467
			445	Piano-Tuners	...	...	...	...	...	...	...	...	...	...	...	...	...	...	...
			446	Actors, Singers and Dancers, and their accompanists	163	97	66	131	97	34	218	99	119	366	211	155	356	193	168
				Total Sub-order 71......	569	327	242	937	639	298	674	356	318	1,892	938	954	1,797	1,167	630
				Total Order XX......	7,041	3,761	3,280	6,248	3,307	2,941	5,289	2,630	2,659	9,595	5,229	4,366	7,817	4,272	3,545
	XXI.—Sport and amusement.	72. Sport.	447	Race-course service, Book-makers, Jockeys, &c.	...	...	...	...	...	...	...	...	...	...	...	...	...	...	...
			448	Shikaries, Falconers, Birdcatchers	95	40	55	100	48	52	54	30	24	85	65	20	161	71	90
			449	Huntsmen, whippers in	...	...	...	...	...	...	...	...	...	...	...	...	...	...	...
				Total Sub-order 72......	95	40	55	100	48	52	54	30	24	85	65	20	161	71	90
		73. Exhibition and games. (a) Catching, training & exhibiting animals.	450	Exhibitors of trained animals (Bulls, bears, snakes, monkeys, &c.)...	...	...	...	...	...	...	...	...	...	...	...	...	...	...	...
			451	Circus owners, managers, &c.	...	...	...	63	42	21	...	...	...	63	63	...	...	...	...
			452	Cock and pigeon fanciers	...	...	...	...	...	...	...	...	...	...	...	...	...	...	...
		(b) Conjuring, Fortune-telling and other exhibitions.	453	Buffoons	31	24	7	2	2	...	...	...	...	88	19	69	100	4	96
			454	Story and ballad reciters	...	...	...	...	...	...	...	...	...	...	...	...	...	...	...
			455	Exhibitors of puppets	...	...	...	...	...	...	...	...	...	...	...	...	...	...	...
			456	Conjurors and fortune-tellers	343	173	170	...	...	...	500	174	326	...	...	...	51	13	38
		(c) Acrobatics & athletics.	457	Tumblers, Acrobats, Wrestlers, Professional cricketers, &c.	198	76	122	510	289	221	429	275	154	350	136	214	530	371	159
				Swing and merry-go-round keepers	...	...	...	...	...	...	...	...	...	...	...	...	...	...	...
		(d) Service of places of entertainment.	458 459	Tennis and Racquet Court, Gymkhana, and boat club service	...	...	...	...	...	...	...	...	...	...	...	...	...	...	...
			460	Billiard room and theatre ownership, managership and service	...	...	...	...	...	...	...	...	...	...	...	...	...	...	...
				Total Sub-order 73......	572	273	299	575	333	242	929	449	480	501	218	283	681	388	293
				Total Order XXI......	667	313	354	675	381	294	983	479	504	586	283	303	842	459	383

TABLE XVII B.

Occupations by Districts.—*Continued.*

Class.	Order.	Sub-order and Group.	Serial No.	Occupations.	Sirpur Tandur. Total.	Sirpur Tandur. Males.	Sirpur Tandur. Females.	Gulbarga. Total.	Gulbarga. Males.	Gulbarga. Females.	Raichur. Total.	Raichur. Males.	Raichur. Females.	Lingasugur. Total.	Lingasugur. Males.	Lingasugur. Females.	Railways. Total.	Railways. Males.	Railways. Females.
					51	52	53	54	55	56	57	58	59	60	61	62	63	64	65
Class F.—Professions.—*contd.*	XX.—Learned and artistic professions.—*contd.*	70. Pictorial art and sculpture.	440	Painters, Superintendents of Schools of Art, &c. ...	...	...	...	...	...	...	131	65	66	107	59	48	...	...	...
			441	Sculptors...	...	...	...	...	...	...	...	...	...	...	...	...	...	...	...
			442	Photographers ...	...	...	...	...	...	...	...	...	...	...	...	...	...	...	...
				Total Sub-order 70......	...	...	...	...	...	...	131	65	66	107	59	48	...	...	...
		71. Music, acting, dancing.	443	Music Composers and Teachers ...	...	...	...	...	...	...	3	1	2	1	1	...	...	...	...
			444	Bandmasters and players (not military)	122	70	52	970	525	445	709	445	264	1,240	608	632	...	...	...
			445	Piano-Tuners ...	...	...	...	...	...	...	...	...	...	...	...	...	...	...	...
			446	Actors, Singers and Dancers, and their accompanists ...	75	16	59	322	197	125	122	81	41	143	55	88	8	...	8
				Total Sub-order 71......	197	86	111	1,292	722	570	834	527	807	1,384	664	720	8	...	3
				Total Order XX......	2,058	1,619	439	8,401	4,646	3,755	4,570	2,693	1,877	4,468	2,284	2,184	144	98	46
	XXI.—Sport and amusement.	72. Sport.	447	Race-course service, Book-makers, Jockeys, &c. ...	...	...	...	...	...	...	...	...	...	...	...	...	...	...	...
			448	Shikaries, Falconers, Birdcatchers ...	44	29	15	43	34	9	33	16	17	65	32	33	...	...	...
			449	Huntsmen, whippers in... ...	...	...	...	...	...	...	...	...	...	...	...	...	...	...	...
				Total Sub-order 72......	44	29	15	43	34	9	33	16	17	65	32	33	...	...	...
		73. Exhibition and games. (a) Conjuring, Catching, training & exhibiting animals.	450	Exhibitors of trained animals (Bulls, bears, snakes, monkeys, &c.) ...	...	...	...	...	...	...	11	6	5	104	40	64	...	...	...
			451	Circus owners, managers, &c. ...	20	15	5	...	...	...	18	18	...	...	...	...	...	...	...
			452	Cock and pigeon fanciers ...	...	...	...	...	...	...	...	...	...	...	...	...	...	...	...
		(b) Fortune-telling & other exhibitions.	453	Buffoons... ...	...	...	...	67	26	41	...	...	...	28	7	20	...	...	...
			454	Story and ballad reciters ...	...	...	...	...	...	...	19	17	2	...	...	...	...	...	...
			455	Exhibitors of puppets ...	...	...	...	6	4	2	123	69	54	113	65	48	...	...	...
			456	Conjurors and fortune-tellers ...	162	130	32	109	76	33	51	36	15	238	118	120	...	...	...
		(c) Acrobatics & athletics.	457	Tumblers, Acrobats, Wrestlers, Professional cricketers, &c. ...	9	...	9	170	86	84	357	213	144	289	166	123	...	...	...
		(d) Service of places of entertainment.	458	Swing and merry-go-round keepers ...	...	...	...	...	...	...	...	...	...	...	...	...	...	...	...
			459	Tennis and Racquet Court, Gymkhana and boat club service ...	...	...	...	...	...	...	...	...	...	...	...	...	...	...	...
			460	Billiard room and theatre ownership, managership and service ...	...	...	...	...	...	...	105	70	35	297	141	156	...	...	...
				Total Sub-order 73......	191	145	46	352	192	160	684	429	255	1,069	538	581	...	...	...
				Total Order XXI......	235	174	61	395	226	169	717	445	272	1,134	570	564	...	...	...

TABLE XVII B.

Occupations by Districts.—*Continued.*

Class.	Order.	Sub-order and Group.	Serial No.	Occupations.	Grand Total. Total.	Grand Total. Males.	Grand Total. Females.	Hyderabad. Total.	Hyderabad. Males.	Hyderabad. Females.	Atraf-i-Balda. Total.	Atraf-i-Balda. Males.	Atraf-i-Balda. Females.	Mahabubnagar. Total.	Mahabubnagar. Males.	Mahabubnagar. Females.	Nalgonda. Total.	Nalgonda. Males.	Nalgonda. Females.
1	2	3	4	5	6	7	8	9	10	11	12	13	14	15	16	17	18	19	20
Class G.—Indefinite and Independent.	XXII. Complex occupations.			(Village, &c., combined function to be specified provincially)	...	...	...	...	...	...	...	...	...	...	...	...	...	...	...
				Total Order XXII......	...	...	...	...	...	...	...	...	...	...	...	...	...	...	...
	XXIII. Indefinite.	74. Unskilled labour. (a) Special branches.	461	Well sinkers	1,465	741	724	...	...	...	290	177	113	348	175	173	765	383	382
			462	Tank diggers and excavators	3,089	1,001	2,088	...	...	...	2	2	...	139	109	30	439	2	437
			463	Road, Canal and Railway labourers ...	949	527	422	233	115	118	21	17	4	57	9	48	14	9	5
			464	Quarrymen (stone splitters, &c.) ...	23,609	12,181	11,428	246	134	112	1,572	905	667	1,784	913	871	1,048	539	509
			465	Miners (unspecified)	326	...	326	...	...	...	...	...	...	...	...	...	...	...	...
			466	Rice-pounders and huskers	9,251	2,825	6,426	145	62	83	520	111	409	1,506	257	1,249	3,018	1,682	1,336
		(b) General.	467	General labour	1,425,638	589,525	836,113	35,627	15,685	19,992	48,263	17,531	30,732	51,813	17,943	33,870	57,860	19,211	38,649
				Total Sub-order 74......	1,464,327	606,800	857,527	36,251	15,946	20,305	50,668	18,743	31,925	55,647	19,406	36,241	63,144	21,826	41,318
		75. Undefined, &c.	468	Undefined and disreputable means of livelihood	441,280	225,038	216,242	5,168	2,089	3,079	24,738	13,700	11,038	40,452	21,611	18,841	21,970	10,423	11,547
				Total Sub-order 75......	441,280	225,038	216,242	5,168	2,089	3,079	24,738	13,700	11,038	40,452	21,611	18,841	21,970	10,423	11,547
				Total Order XXIII......	1,905,607	831,838	1,073,769	41,419	18,035	23,384	75,406	32,443	42,963	96,099	41,017	55,082	85,114	32,249	52,865
	XXIV. Independent of work.	76. Property & alms. (a) Property & allowances.	469	House-rent, shares, and other property not being land...	3,884	1,349	2,535	975	410	565	89	17	72	105	69	36	23	7	16
			470	Allowances from patrons or relatives ...	3,768	691	3,077	435	123	312	3	...	3	20	7	13	2	...	2
		(b) Charity and endowment.	471	Educational or other endowments, scholarship, &c.	197	59	138	189	53	136	...	...	...	...	...	...	...	...	...
			472	Mendicancy (not being affiliated to a religious order)	288,295	150,296	137,999	9,782	5,428	4,354	8,402	4,326	4,076	10,143	5,071	5,072	9,047	4,832	4,215
				Total Sub-order 76......	296,144	152,395	143,749	11,381	6,014	5,367	8,494	4,343	4,151	10,268	5,147	5,121	9,072	4,839	4,233
		77. Supported at the public charge. (a) Pension.	473	Pension, Civil Services	15,665	6,682	8,983	11,487	4,984	6,503	357	144	213	264	141	123	204	80	124
			474	Pension, Military Services	10,348	5,447	4,901	8,082	3,793	4,289	91	91	...	...	...	...	...	...	...
		(b) Prisoners.	475	Inmates of Asylums, &c.	...	...	...	...	...	...	...	...	...	...	...	...	...	...	...
			476	Prisoners, under trial	6	2	4	1	1	...	...	...	...	...	...	...	...	...	...
			477	Prisoners, for debt	294	294	...	1	1	...	...	...	...	...	...	...	...	...	...
			478	Prisoners, convicted or in Reformatories, &c	148	134	9	98	92	6	...	...	...	...	...	...	...	...	...
				Total Sub-order 77......	26,456	12,559	13,897	19,669	8,871	10,798	448	235	213	264	141	123	204	80	124
				Total Order XXIV......	322,600	164,954	157,646	31,050	14,885	16,165	8,942	4,578	4,364	10,582	5,288	5,244	9,276	4,919	4,857
				Grand Total......	11587040	5,878,129	5,663,911	415,089	216,324	198,715	389,784	198,258	191,526	674,649	341,601	333,048	624,617	319,823	304,794

TABLE XVII B.

Occupations by Districts.—*Continued.*

Class.	Order.	Sub-order and Group.	Serial No.	Occupations.	Warangal. Total.	Warangal. Males.	Warangal. Females.	Elgandal. Total.	Elgandal. Males.	Elgandal. Females.	Indur. Total.	Indur. Males.	Indur. Females.	Medak. Total.	Medak. Males.	Medak. Females.	Aurangabad. Total.	Aurangabad. Males.	Aurangabad. Females.
					21	22	23	24	25	26	27	28	29	30	31	32	33	34	35
Class G.—Indefinite and Independent.	XXII. Complex occupations.			(Village, &c., combined function to be specified provincially)	...	...	...	...	...	...	...	...	...	...	...	...	...	...	...
				Total Order XXII......	...	...	...	...	...	...	...	...	...	...	...	...	...	...	...
	XXIII. Indefinite.	74. Unskilled labour. (a) Special branches.	461	Well sinkers	...	...	...	6	6	...	...	...	...	24	...	24	...	...	...
			462	Tank diggers and excavators	2,207	805	1,402	243	60	183	...	...	...	20	14	6	39	9	30
			463	Road, Canal and Railway labourers ...	8	...	8	...	...	...	...	...	...	6	4	2	83	81	2
			464	Quarrymen (stone splitters, &c.) ...	36	3	33	325	136	189	1,443	779	664	791	485	306	1,600	775	825
			465	Miners (unspecified)	326	...	326	...	...	...	...	...	...	...	...	...	...	...	...
			466	Rice-pounders and huskers	466	45	421	433	130	303	1,211	189	1,022	1,452	183	1,269	...	...	...
		(b) General.	467	General labour	86,673	34,488	52,185	132,758	45,790	86,968	88,089	36,027	52,062	67,553	26,958	40,595	96,293	32,905	63,388
				Total Sub-order 74......	89,716	35,341	54,375	133,765	46,122	87,643	90,743	36,995	58,748	69,846	27,644	42,202	97,965	33,720	64,245
		75. Undefined, &c.	468	Undefined and disreputable means of livelihood	63,386	34,023	29,363	61,561	31,064	30,497	11,906	5,464	6,442	18,013	9,816	8,197	33,806	16,812	16,994
				Total Sub-order 75......	63,386	34,023	29,363	61,561	31,064	30,497	11,906	5,464	6,442	18,013	9,816	8,197	33,806	1,6312	16,994
				Total Order XXIII......	153,102	69,364	83,738	195,326	77,186	118,140	102,649	42,459	60,190	87,859	37,460	50,399	131,271	50,032	81,239
	XXIV. Independent of work.	76. Property & alms. (a) Property & allowances.	469	House-rent, shares, and other property not being land...	71	17	54	185	87	98	356	4	352	69	...	69	192	124	68
			470	Allowances from patrons or relatives ...	230	12	218	1	...	1	186	116	70	33	26	7	905	49	856
		(b) Charity and endowment.	471	Educational or other endowments, scholarship, &c.	...	...	...	...	...	...	...	...	...	...	...	...	...	...	...
			472	Mendicancy (not being affiliated to a religious order)	15,115	8,265	6,849	23,184	11,668	11,516	15,605	7,618	7,987	6,867	3,375	3,492	25,562	13,998	11,564
				Total Sub-order 76......	15,415	8,294	7,121	23,320	11,705	11,615	16,147	7,738	8,409	6,969	3,401	3,568	26,659	14,171	12,488
		77. Supported at the public charge. (a) Pension.	473	Pension, Civil Services	261	197	64	231	121	110	332	137	195	477	242	235	987	105	882
			474	Pension, Military Services	...	...	...	...	...	...	...	...	...	...	...	...	818	818	...
		(b) Prisoners.	475	Inmates of Asylums, &c.	...	...	...	...	...	...	...	...	...	...	...	...	...	...	...
			476	Prisoners, under trial	...	...	...	...	...	...	...	...	...	...	...	...	...	...	...
			477	Prisoners, for debt	...	...	...	...	...	...	...	...	...	293	293	...	...	...	...
			478	Prisoners, convicted or in Reformatories, &c.	...	...	...	...	...	...	...	...	...	35	35	...	...	...	...
				Total Sub-order 77......	261	197	64	231	121	110	332	137	195	805	570	235	1,805	923	882
				Total Order XXIV......	15,676	8,491	7,185	23,551	11,826	11,725	16,479	7,875	8,604	7,774	3,971	3,803	28,464	15,094	13,370
				Grand Total......	853,129	438,635	414,494	1,094,601	563,845	530,756	639,598	319,237	320,361	364,735	183,908	180,827	828,975	421,018	407,957

TABLE XVII B.

Occupations by Districts.—*Continued.*

Class.	Order.	Sub-order and Group.	Serial No.	Occupations.	Birh. Total.	Birh. Males.	Birh. Females.	Nander. Total.	Nander. Males.	Nander. Females.	Naldrug. Total.	Naldrug. Males.	Naldrug. Females.	Bidar. Total.	Bidar. Males.	Bidar. Females.	Parbhani. Total.	Parbhani. Males.	Parbhani. Females.
					36	37	38	39	40	41	42	43	44	45	46	47	48	49	50
Class G.—Indefinite and Independent.	XXII. Complex occupations.			(Village, &c., combined function to be specified provincially)...	...	...	...	...	...	...	...	...	...	...	...	...	...	...	...
				Total Order XXII......	...	...	...	...	...	...	...	...	...	...	...	...	...	...	...
	XXIII. Indefinite.	74. Unskilled labour. (a) Special branches.	461	Well sinkers ...	...	...	...	...	...	...	...	...	...	...	...	...	...	...	...
			462	Tank diggers and excavators ...	...	...	...	...	...	...	...	...	...	...	...	...	...	...	...
			463	Road, Canal and Railway labourers ...	15	7	8	...	...	...	4	3	1	17	8	14	60	21	39
			464	Quarrymen (stone splitters, &c.) ...	1,889	979	910	1,988	976	1,012	2,111	1,131	980	2,557	1,570	987	2,265	954	1,311
			465	Miners (unspecified) ...	...	...	...	...	...	...	...	...	...	...	...	...	...	...	...
			466	Rice-pounders and huskers ...	...	...	...	...	...	...	...	...	...	...	...	...	15	15	...
		(b) General.	467	General labour ...	99,763	46,102	53,661	86,852	36,921	49,931	101,740	45,801	55,939	146,499	66,531	79,968	112,143	53,662	58,481
				Total Sub-order 74......	101,667	47,088	54,579	88,840	37,897	50,943	103,855	46,935	56,920	149,073	68,104	80,969	114,483	54,652	59,831
		75. Undefined, &c.	468	Undefined and disreputable means of livelihood ...	28,671	14,285	14,386	21,230	11,099	10,131	22,000	9,610	12,390	31,919	18,871	13,048	27,116	12,887	14,229
				Total Sub-order 75......	28,671	14,285	14,386	21,230	11,099	10,131	22,000	9,610	12,390	31,919	18,871	13,048	27,116	12,887	14,229
				Total Order XXIII......	130,338	61,373	68,965	110,070	48,996	61,074	125,855	56,545	69,310	180,992	86,975	94,017	141,599	67,539	74,060
	XXIV. Independent of work.	76. Property & alms. (a) Property & allowances.	469	House-rent, shares, and other property not being land...	220	83	137	14	...	14	50	5	45	178	131	47	73	44	29
			470	Allowances from patrons or relatives	90	1	89	513	95	418	...	...	...	722	104	618	116	42	74
		(b) Charity and endowment.	471	Educational or other endowments, scholarship, &c. ...	...	...	...	...	...	...	...	...	...	...	...	...	...	...	...
			472	Mendicancy (not being affiliated to a religious order) ...	19,836	10,490	9,346	17,905	9,674	8,231	22,020	11,920	10,100	32,901	16,883	16,018	25,738	13,842	11,896
				Total Sub-order 76......	20,146	10,574	9,572	18,432	9,769	8,663	22,070	11,925	10,145	33,801	17,118	16,683	25,927	13,928	11,999
		77. Supported at the public charge. (a)—Pension.	473	Pension, Civil Services ...	401	224	177	16	...	16	18	3	15	197	91	106	86	54	32
			474	Pension, Military Services ...	42	10	32	15	5	10	7	2	5	56	25	31	935	521	414
		(b) Prisoners.	475	Inmates of Asylums, &c. ...	...	...	...	...	...	...	...	...	...	...	...	...	...	...	...
			476	Prisoners, under trial ...	5	1	4	...	...	...	...	...	...	...	...	...	...	...	...
			477	Prisoners, for debt ...	...	...	...	...	...	...	...	...	...	...	...	...	...	...	...
			478	Prisoners, convicted or in Reformatories, &c.	...	...	...	...	...	...	...	...	...	...	...	...	...	...	...
				Total Sub-order 77......	448	235	213	31	5	26	25	5	20	253	116	137	1,021	575	446
				Total Order XXIV......	20,594	10,809	9,785	18,463	9,774	8,689	22,095	11,930	10,165	34,054	17,234	16,820	26,948	14,503	12,445
				Grand Total......	642,722	328,530	314,192	632,529	320,136	312,393	649,272	331,747	317,525	901,984	457,088	444,896	805,335	410,499	394,836

TABLE XVII B.

Occupations by Districts.—*Continued.*

Class.	Order.	Sub-order and Group.	Serial No.	Occupations.	Sirpur Tandur. Total.	Sirpur Tandur. Males.	Sirpur Tandur. Females.	Gulbarga. Total.	Gulbarga. Males.	Gulbarga. Females.	Raichur. Total.	Raichur. Males.	Raichur. Females.	Lingasugur. Total.	Lingasugur. Males.	Lingasugur. Females.	Railways. Total.	Railways. Males.	Railways. Females.
					51	52	53	54	55	56	57	58	59	60	61	62	63	64	65
Class G.—Indefinite and Independent.	XXII. Complex occupations.			(Village, &c., combined function to be specified provincially)	...	...	...	...	...	...	...	...	...	...	...	...	...	...	...
				Total Order XXII......	...	...	...	...	...	...	...	...	...	...	...	...	...	...	...
	XXIII. Indefinite.	74. Unskilled labour. (a) Special branches.	461	Well sinkers	...	...	...	...	...	...	82	...	82	...	...	...	...	...	...
			462	Tank diggers and excavators	...	...	...	...	...	...	...	...	...	...	...	...	...	...	...
			463	Road, Canal and Railway labourers ...	...	...	...	80	80	...	17	7	10	28	15	13	406	256	150
			464	Quarrymen (stone splitters, &c.) ...	84	80	54	3,868	1,870	1,998	...	...	...	...	...	...	2	2	...
			465	Miners (unspecified)	...	...	...	...	...	...	...	...	...	...	...	...	...	...	...
			466	Rice-pounders and huskers	...	...	...	...	...	...	861	114	247	124	37	87	...	...	...
		(b) General.	467	General labour	26,620	10,878	15,742	100,864	44,240	56,624	85,800	16,122	19,178	50,698	22,606	28,087	285	174	61
				Total Sub-order 74......	26,704	10,908	15,796	104,762	46,140	58,622	85,710	16,243	19,467	50,845	22,658	28,187	648	482	211
		75. Undefined, &c.	468	Undefined and disreputable means of livelihood	3,572	1,840	1,732	20,888	10,408	10,485	2,058	624	1,429	3,160	837	2,323	171	80	91
				Total Sub-order 75......	3,572	1,840	1,732	20,888	10,408	10,485	2,053	624	1,429	3,160	837	2,323	171	80	91
				Total Order XXIII......	30,276	12,748	17,528	125,650	56,543	69,107	87,768	16,867	20,896	54,005	23,495	30,510	814	512	302
	XXIV. Independent of work.	76. Property & alms. (a) Property & allowances.	469	House-rent, shares, and other property not being land	23	10	13	412	89	878	856	109	247	525	226	299	18	17	1
			470	Allowances from patrons or relatives ...	114	108	6	843	6	887	54	1	53	1	1	...	...	...	...
		(b) Charity and endowment.	471	Educational or other endowments, scholarship, &c.	...	...	...	...	...	...	...	...	...	...	...	...	8	6	2
			472	Mendicancy (not being affiliated to a religious order)	3,869	1,350	2,519	18,070	9,144	8,926	9,907	5,059	4,848	14,819	7,889	6,980	24	14	10
				Total Sub-order 76......	4,006	1,468	2,538	18,825	9,189	9,636	10,317	5,169	5,148	14,845	7,566	7,279	50	37	13
		77. Supported at the public charge. (a) Pension.	473	Pension, Civil Services	83	11	22	108	50	58	60	87	23	146	61	85	...	...	...
			474	Pension, Military Services	...	...	...	49	87	12	228	129	94	...	...	...	80	16	14
		(b) Prisoners.	475	Inmates of Asylums, &c.	...	...	...	...	...	...	...	...	...	...	...	...	...	...	...
			476	Prisoners, under trial	...	...	...	...	...	...	...	...	...	...	...	...	...	...	...
			477	Prisoners, for debt	...	...	...	...	...	...	...	...	...	...	...	...	...	...	...
			478	Prisoners, convicted or in Reformatories, &c.	...	...	...	...	...	...	1	1	...	...	...	...	9	6	3
				Total Sub-order 77......	83	11	22	157	87	70	284	167	117	146	61	85	89	22	17
				Total Order XXIV......	4,089	1,479	2,560	18,982	9,276	9,706	10,601	5,336	5,265	14,991	7,627	7,364	89	59	30
				Grand Total......	231,754	116,955	114,799	649,258	329,678	319,580	512,455	260,217	252,238	620,014	311,894	308,620	6,590	4,236	2,354

TABLE XVII B.

Occupations by Districts.

Abstract showing totals of each Class.

Class.	Grand Total.			Hyderabad.			Atraf-i-Balda.			Mahabubnagar.			Nalgonda.		
	Total.	Males.	Females.	Total.	Males.	Females.	Total.	Males.	Females.	Total.	Males.	Females.	Total.	Males.	Females.
1	2	3	4	5	6	7	8	9	10	11	12	13	14	15	16
A	608,918	844,490	264,428	102,639	57,925	44,714	15,892	9,419	5,973	25,784	15,207	10,577	16,724	8,967	7,757
B	5,462,285	2,842,518	2,619,717	11,471	5,388	6,133	138,579	71,740	66,839	313,340	163,802	149,538	301,237	160,051	141,186
C	651,629	349,586	302,043	103,215	56,733	46,482	27,297	14,509	12,788	48,274	19,754	28,520	33,299	18,207	15,092
D	2,178,488	1,128,241	1,050,247	77,982	89,991	87,991	102,548	53,116	49,432	157,681	83,900	73,781	160,629	85,943	74,686
E	259,019	134,137	124,882	30,395	15,985	14,410	15,398	9,275	6,118	13,653	7,702	5,951	10,295	5,465	4,830
F	148,544	77,365	71,179	16,868	7,432	9,436	6,227	3,178	3,049	9,286	4,931	4,355	8,043	4,012	4,021
G	2,228,207	996,792	1,231,415	72,469	82,920	89,549	84,348	37,021	47,327	106,631	46,305	60,326	94,390	37,168	57,222
Grand Total......	11,537,040	5,873,129	5,663,911	415,039	216,324	198,715	389,784	198,258	191,526	674,649	341,601	333,048	624,617	319,823	304,794

Class.	Warangal.			Elgandal.			Indur.			Medak.			Aurangabad.		
	Total.	Males.	Females.	Total.	Males.	Females.	Total.	Males.	Females.	Total.	Males.	Females.	Total.	Males.	Females.
	17	18	19	20	21	22	23	24	25	26	27	28	29	30	31
A	23,213	13,016	10,197	28,024	15,705	12,319	35,511	20,299	15,212	17,167	9,191	7,976	62,410	43,254	19,156
B	419,212	219,293	199,919	432,233	242,507	189,726	271,328	140,883	130,945	136,188	72,481	63,707	424,153	217,529	206,624
C	39,245	21,074	18,171	66,323	36,725	29,598	41,425	21,028	20,397	17,826	9,864	7,962	36,834	20,089	16,745
D	180,064	96,132	83,932	317,584	164,200	153,384	147,902	76,036	71,866	78,114	41,047	37,067	115,142	59,266	55,876
E	12,538	5,777	6,761	20,182	9,824	10,358	15,926	6,896	9,030	13,720	6,963	6,757	20,868	10,873	9,995
F	10,079	5,488	4,591	11,378	5,872	5,506	8,378	4,261	4,117	6,087	2,931	3,156	10,333	5,381	4,952
G	168,778	77,855	90,923	218,877	89,012	129,865	119,128	50,334	68,794	95,683	41,481	54,202	159,735	65,126	94,609
Grand Total......	853,129	438,635	414,494	1,094,601	563,845	530,756	639,598	319,287	320,361	364,735	183,908	180,827	828,975	421,018	407,957

TABLE XVII B.

OCCUPATIONS BY DISTRICTS.

Abstract showing totals of each Class.—*Continued.*

Class.	Birh. Total.	Birh. Males.	Birh. Females.	Nander. Total.	Nander. Males.	Nander. Females.	Naldrug. Total.	Naldrug. Males.	Naldrug. Females.	Bidar. Total.	Bidar. Males.	Bidar. Females.	Parbhani. Total.	Parbhani. Males.	Parbhani. Females.
	32	33	34	35	36	37	38	39	40	41	42	43	44	45	46
A	33,947	16,765	17,182	27,679	15,511	12,168	32,804	18,389	14,415	51,543	25,961	25,582	36,486	20,855	15,631
B	321,834	167,218	154,616	327,836	171,041	156,795	356,306	184,552	171,754	420,107	213,724	206,383	435,464	221,756	213,708
C	28,176	15,672	12,504	32,378	17,728	14,650	22,181	13,171	9,010	50,782	28,399	22,383	31,588	17,188	14,400
D	84,867	44,983	39,884	98,711	48,014	50,697	73,367	38,521	34,846	137,517	69,865	67,652	109,187	55,955	53,232
E	15,258	7,686	7,572	10,469	5,384	5,085	10,392	5,530	4,862	16,808	9,418	7,390	15,409	7,977	7,432
F	7,708	4,074	3,634	6,923	3,688	3,235	6,272	3,109	3,163	10,181	5,512	4,669	8,659	4,731	3,928
G	150,932	72,182	78,750	128,538	58,770	69,768	147,950	68,475	79,475	215,046	104,209	110,837	168,547	82,042	86,505
Grand Total......	642,722	328,580	314,192	632,529	320,136	312,393	649,272	331,747	317,525	901,984	457,088	444,896	805,335	410,499	394,836

Class.	Sirpur Tandur. Total.	Sirpur Tandur. Males.	Sirpur Tandur. Females.	Gulbarga. Total.	Gulbarga. Males.	Gulbarga. Females.	Raichur. Total.	Raichur. Males.	Raichur. Females.	Lingasugur. Total.	Lingasugur. Males.	Lingasugur. Females.	Railways. Total.	Railways. Males.	Railways. Females.
	47	48	49	50	51	52	53	54	55	56	57	58	59	60	61
A	6,639	3,643	2,996	33,676	17,915	15,761	28,730	15,804	12,926	30,261	16,467	13,794	289	197	92
B	128,019	66,225	61,794	306,512	159,253	147,259	309,961	157,834	152,127	408,389	207,746	200,643	66	45	21
C	12,239	6,879	5,360	24,797	13,696	11,101	18,204	9,413	8,791	17,107	9,198	7,909	444	264	180
D	45,917	22,916	23,001	114,425	60,756	53,669	93,520	47,063	46,457	82,480	39,992	42,488	851	595	256
E	2,332	1,272	1,060	16,420	7,867	9,058	8,389	4,762	3,627	7,179	4,015	3,164	3,893	2,466	1,427
F	2,293	1,793	500	8,796	4,872	3,924	5,287	3,138	2,149	5,602	2,854	2,748	144	98	46
G	34,315	14,227	20,088	144,632	65,819	78,813	48,364	22,203	26,161	68,996	31,122	37,874	903	571	332
Grand Total......	231,754	116,955	114,799	649,258	329,678	319,580	512,455	260,217	252,238	620,014	311,394	308,620	6,590	4,236	2,354

TABLE XVII C.

OCCUPATION COMBINED WITH AGRICULTURE.

(Both sexes.)

TABLE XVII C.

Occupation combined with Agriculture.—(*Both sexes.*)

Sub-order.	Occupations.	Total persons returned under each in Table XVII A including those combining it with Agriculture.	PERSONS RETURNED AS COMBINING THE OCCUPATION WITH AGRICULTURE: Total persons.	CONNECTION WITH THE LAND: (a) Owners or Occupants.	(b) Tenants.	(c) Farm servants or field labourers.
1	2	3	4	5	6	7
1. Service of the Imperial & Provincial Governments.	Total Sub-order......	49,856	66	4	62	......
	3. Office Superintendents, &c.	8,676	10	4	6	......
	4. Messengers, Constables, &c.	45,596	56	......	56	......
	Others	584	......	......	......	......
3. Village Service.	Total Sub-order......	327,800	154,432	3,444	145,065	5,923
	8. Headmen, when not agriculturists ...	83,152	76,559	135	76,424	......
	9. Accountants	54,610	50,796	29	50,767	......
	11. Watchmen and other menials ...	190,038	27,077	3,280	17,874	5,923
	Others...	......	......	......	......	......
4. Army.	Total Sub-order......	10,014	11	10	1	......
	12. Officers	230	10	10	......	......
	13. Non-Commissioned Officers and Privates	7,986	1	......	1	......
	Others	1,818	......	......	......	......
8. Stock breeding and dealing.	Total Sub-order......	281,935	1,409	22	1,386	1
	25. Cattle breeders, &c.	23,031	851	......	851	......
	26. Herdsmen	37,861	55	......	55	......
	31. Sheep and goat breeders and dealers ...	170,544	1,003	22	980	1
	Others	50,499	......	......	......	......
9. Subsidiary services to stock.	Total Sub-order......	532	12	......	12	......
	35. Horse and elephant breakers and trainers, &c.	119	12	......	12	......
	Others...	413	......	......	......	......
12. Growers of special products & trees.	Total Sub-order......	4,585	304	1	303	......
	46. Betel growers, &c.	229	2	......	2	......
	51. Market gardeners, &c.	2,128	289	......	289	......
	52. Gardeners, seedsmen, &c.	804	13	1	12	......
	Others...	1,424	......	......	......	......
14. Personal & domestic services.	Total Sub-order......	546,118	27,657	827	24,042	2,788
	59. Barbers...	81,988	12,066	72	11,593	401
	63. Washermen, &c.	152,748	14,980	158	12,435	2,387
	66. Indoor servants	123,445	611	597	14	......
	Others...	187,942	......	......	......	......
16. Sanitation.	Total Sub-order......	636	5	......	5	......
	74. Sweepers, &c.	503	5	......	5	......
	Others	133	......	......	......	......
17. Animal food.	Total Sub-order......	81,425	3,840	......	3,840	......
	79. Butchers	8,104	9	......	9	......
	81. Fishermen, &c....	18,941	3,831	......	3,831	......
	Others	54,380	......	......	......	......
18. Vegetable food.	Total Sub-order......	141,963	670	......	670	......
	83. Grain dealers	83,875	670	......	670	......
	Others...	58,088	......	......	......	......
19. Drink, condiments & Narcotics.	Total Sub-order......	404,070	7,920	......	7,404	516
	97. Country spirits sellers, &c.	42,064	1,709	......	1,709	......
	98. Toddydrawers and sellers	182,165	8,454	......	2,938	516
	105. Salt preparers and sellers	13,254	121	......	121	......
	106. Assafoetida, &c., sellers	7,469	1	......	1	......
	109. Grocers and general condiment dealers.	99,510	2,635	......	2,635	......
	Others	59,608	......	......	......	......

TABLE XVII C.

Occupation combined with Agriculture.—(*Both sexes.*)

Sub-order.	Occupations.	Total persons returned under each in Table XVII A including those combining it with Agriculture.	PERSONS RETURNED AS COMBINING THE OCCUPATION WITH AGRICULTURE. Total persons.	CONNECTION WITH THE LAND. (a) Owners or Occupants.	(b) Tenants.	(c) Farm servants or field labourers.
1	2	3	4	5	6	7
20. Lighting.	Total Sub-order......	53,717	2,394	......	2,394	......
	116. Oil-pressers and sellers	52,913	2,390	......	2,390	......
	118. Oil-cake dealers	643	4	......	4	......
	Others	161	......	......	......	......
21. Fuel & forage.	Total Sub-order......	19,325	6	......	6	......
	125. Firewood and grass gatherers & sellers	18,545	5	......	5	......
	131. Hay, &c., contractors and dealers ...	247	1	......	1	......
	Others	533	......	......	......	......
23. Artificers in building.	Total Sub-order......	31,604	250	6	240	4
	137. Stone and marble workers	4,220	4	......	4	......
	138. Masons	15,043	235	6	225	4
	141. Mud-wall and roof builders... ...	8,041	11	......	11	......
	Others	4,300	......	......	......	......
27. Paper, &c.	Total Sub-order......	1,022	6	......	6	......
	153. Paper makers, &c.	1,018	6	......	6	......
	Others	4	......	......	......	......
33. Necklaces, bracelets, beads, sacred threads, &c.	Total Sub-order......	20,238	80	......	80	......
	189. Bangle makers and sellers in glass ...	7,040	7	......	7	......
	192. Bead makers and sellers	1,367	11	......	11	......
	194. Flower garland makers and sellers ...	2,084	62	......	62	......
	Others	9,747	......	......	......	......
38. Wool & fur.	Total Sub-order......	173,072	473	......	298	175
	120. Blanket weavers and sellers, &c. ...	92,300	448	......	273	175
	121. Woollen cloth manufacturers & dealers	74,273	25	......	25	......
	Others	6,499	......	......	......	......
39. Silk.	Total Sub-order......	3,179	2	......	2	......
	228. Silk weavers and dealers	1,204	2	......	2	......
	Others	1,975	......	......	......	......
40. Cotton.	Total Sub-order......	400,048	1,951	......	1,951	......
	231. Cotton cleaners, &c.	33,314	46	......	46	......
	233. Cotton spinners, &c.	37,330	63	......	63	......
	234. Cotton weavers, &c.	194,289	644	......	644	......
	237. Cotton dyers...	11,563	1,198	......	1,198	......
	Others	123,552	......	......	......	......
41. Jute, flax, coir, &c.	Total Sub-order......	2,206	43	......	43	......
	241. Hemp rope makers and sellers ...	1,022	43	......	43	......
	Others	1,184	......	......	......	......
42. Dress.	Total Sub-order......	55,675	78	9	69	......
	247. Tailors ond darners	23,181	69	9	60	......
	250. Hosiers and Haberdashers	1,209	2	......	2	......
	257. Piece-goods dealers	27,986	7	......	7	......
	Others	3,299	......	......	......	......
43. Gold, silver & precious stones.	Total Sub-order......	43,864	3,431	......	3,431	......
	260. Gold and silver workers	43,134	2,431	......	3,431	......
	Others	730	......	......	......	......
44. Brass, copper & bell metal.	Total Sub-order......	7,577	25	......	25	......
	282. General workers in brass, copper and bell metal	7,077	25	......	25	......
	Others	500	......	......	......	......

TABLE XVII C.

Occupation combined with Agriculture.—(*Both sexes.*)

Sub-order.	Occupations.	Total persons returned under each in Table XVII A including those combining it with Agriculture.	PERSONS RETURNED AS COMBINING THE OCCUPATION WITH AGRICULTURE. Total persons.	Connection with the land. (a) Owners or Occupants.	(b) Tenants.	(c) Farm servants or field labourers.
1	2	3	4	5	6	7
46. Iron & steel.	Total Sub-order......	54,333	14,563	97	14,466	......
	290. Blacksmiths	52,930	14,563	97	14,466	......
	Others	1,403	......	......	......	......
48. Earthen and stone-ware.	Total Sub-order......	92,355	17,362	46	17,316	......
	298. Potters, &c.	90,198	17,362	46	17,316	......
	Others	2,157	......	......	......	......
49. Timber and wood.	Total Sub-order......	107,676	34,096	311	33,785	......
	304. Carpenters	106,612	34,096	311	33,785	......
	Others	1,064	......	......	......	......
50. Cane-work, matting & leaves, &c.	Total Sub-order......	30,803	5	......	5	......
	310. Leaf-plate makers and sellers, &c. ...	947	5	......	5	......
	Others	29,856	......	......	......	......
51. Gums, wax & similar forest produce.	Total Sub-order......	6,880	19	......	19	......
	323. Forest produce collectors, &c... ...	6,869	19	......	19	......
	Others	11	......	......	......	......
53. Leather, &c.	Total Sub-order......	153,865	32,273	1,944	23,226	7,103
	338. Tanners, &c.	1,443	730	......	405	325
	339. Shoe-makers, &c.	89,542	18,465	215	13,676	4,574
	341. Water-bag makers, &c.	17,948	13,078	1,729	9,145	2,204
	Others	44,932	......	......	......	......
54. Dealers in money and securities.	Total Sub-order......	28,804	5,037	......	5,037	......
	347. Money lenders, &c.	19,790	5,030	......	5,030	......
	350. Money changers and testers	1,115	7	......	7	......
	Others	7,899	......	......	......	......
55. General merchants.	Total Sub-order......	43,759	97	6	91	......
	352. General merchants	43,759	97	6	91	......
	Others	......	......	......	......	......
56. Dealing unspecified.	Total Sub-order......	76,135	10,750	......	10,750	......
	356. Shop-keepers unspecified	66,856	10,750	......	10,750	......
	Others	9,279	......	......	......	......
57. Middlemen, &c.	Total Sub-order......	3,296	8	......	8	......
	361. Farmers of liquor, opium, &c. ...	1,581	8	......	8	......
	Others	1,715	......	......	......	......
59. Roads.	Total Sub-order......	56,049	1,082	......	1,007	75
	375. Cart owners, &c.	12,112	14	......	14	......
	377. Livery stable-keepers, &c.	1,906	203	......	203	......
	378. Palki, &c., owners, bearers, &c. ...	807	13	......	13	......
	379. Pack bullock owners, drivers, &c. ...	23,972	852	......	777	75
	Others	17,252	......	......	......	......
60. Water.	Total Sub-order......	5,458	625	385	240	......
	387. Lock-keepers, &c., and canal service...	5,177	625	385	240	......
	Others	281	......	......	......	......
62. Storage and weighing.	Total Sub-order......	1,133	2	2	......	......
	399. Weighmen and measurers	293	2	2	......	......
	Others	840	......	......	......	......

TABLE XVII C.

Occupation combined with Agriculture.—(*Both sexes.*)

Sub-order.	Occupations.	Total persons returned under each in Table XVII A including those combining it with Agriculture.	PERSONS RETURNED AS COMBINING THE OCCUPATION WITH AGRICULTURE. Total persons.	CONNECTION WITH THE LAND. (a) Owners or Occupants.	(b) Tenants.	(c) Farm servants or field labourers.
1	2	3	4	5	6	7
63. Religion.	Total Sub-order......	61,884	3,215	403	2,812	......
	401. Priests, &c.	7,887	74	......	74	......
	402. Catechists, &c.	1,829	99	30	69	......
	403. Exorcists, &c.	1,019	14	7	7	......
	404. Religious mendicants, &c.	33,577	2,702	148	2,554	......
	405. Church, Temple conductors, &c. ...	8,072	326	218	108	......
	Others	9,480	......	......	......	......
64. Education.	Total Sub-order......	5,752	3	3	......	......
	407. Principals, &c...	5,649	3	3	......	......
	Others	103	......	......	......	......
65. Literature.	Total Sub-order......	931	1	......	1	......
	411. Private Secretaries and clerks ...	818	1	......	1	......
	Others	113	......	......	......	......
67. Medicine.	Total Sub-order......	6,748	28	7	21	......
	422. Practitioners without diploma ...	6,178	28	7	21	......
	Others	570	......	......	......	......
69. Other science.	Total Sub-order......	7,699	571	31	540	......
	437. Astrologers, &c.	7,697	571	31	540	......
	Others	2	......	......	......	......
70. Pictorial art and sculpture.	Total Sub-order......	890	212	212	......	......
	440. Painters, &c....	890	212	212	......	......
	Others	......	......	......	......	......
71. Music, acting, dancing.	Total Sub-order......	13,021	121	41	80	......
	444. Bandmasters and players	7,583	121	41	80	......
	Others	5,438	......	......	......	......
72. Sport.	Total Sub-order......	1,326	1	......	1	......
	448. Shikaris, &c....	1,249	1	......	1	......
	Others	77	......	......	......	......
74. Unskilled labour.	Total Sub-order......	549,841	2,845	2,794	51	......
	462. Tank diggers and excavators ...	8,050	1	......	1	......
	464. Quarrymen	5,556	30	......	30	......
	466. Rice-pounders and huskers	7,880	2,794	2,794	......	......
	467. General labour	530,918	20	......	20	......
	Others	1,942	......	......	......	......
75. Undefined, &c.	Total Sub-order......	235,833	3,192	1,394	1,798	......
	468. Undefined and disreputable means of livelihood...	235,833	3,192	1,394	1,798	......
	Others	......	......	......	......	......
76. Property and alms.	Total Sub-order......	98,700	410	78	332	......
	472. Mendicancy	96,983	410	78	332	......
	Others	1,717	......	......	......	......
77. Supported at the public charge.	Total Sub-order......	6,748	14	8	6	......
	473. Pension, Civil Services	4,178	14	8	6	......
	Others	2,570	......	......	......	......
	Total......	4,808,860	331,597	12,085	302,927	16,585

TABLE A.

CHRISTIANS BY SECTS AND RACE.—PART I.—SECTS.

TABLE A.

Christians by sects and race.—Part I.—Sects.

District or State.	Total Christians.			Roman Catholic.								Church of England.								Baptist.							
				Total.		Foreign.		Eurasian.		Native.		Total.		Foreign.		Eurasian.		Native.		Total.		Foreign.		Eurasian.		Native.	
	Total.	Males.	Females.	Males.	Females.	Males.	Females.	Males.	Females.	Males.	Females.	Males.	Females.	Males.	Females.	Males.	Females.	Males.	Females.	Males.	Females.	Males.	Females.	Males.	Females.	Males.	Females.
1	2	3	4	5	6	7	8	9	10	11	12	13	14	15	16	17	18	19	20	21	22	23	24	25	26	27	28
Tellingana. Hyderabad. City	44	27	17	20	14	3	1	11	3	6	10	2	...	1	...	...	...	1	...	...	...	...	...	...	...	...	...
Tellingana. Hyderabad. Suburbs including Secunderabad	13,785	8,129	5,656	4,222	3,741	857	275	875	862	2,990	3,104	3,192	1,336	2,500	617	422	458	270	261	38	28	6	...	2	7	30	21
Total......	13,829	8,156	5,673	4,242	3,755	860	276	886	865	2,996	3,114	3,194	1,336	2,501	617	422	458	271	261	38	28	6	...	2	7	30	21
Atraf-i-Balda District	450	216	234	201	209	2	2	1	...	198	207	1	1	1	1	...	...	...	...	...	...	...	...	...	...	...	...
Mahabubnagar (Nagar Karnul) ...	121	67	54	9	8	...	...	2	...	7	8	...	...	...	...	...	...	...	...	42	33	2	6	...	...	40	27
Nalgonda	135	73	62	7	3	...	...	...	...	7	3	...	...	...	...	...	...	...	...	...	...	...	...	...	...	...	...
Warangal (Khamam)	1,484	794	690	119	113	11	9	10	2	98	102	518	454	21	11	8	...	484	448	11	11	...	...	...	...	11	11
Elgandal	193	122	71	10	12	2	4	2	...	6	8	1	1	1	...	...	1	...	...	...	...	...	...	...	...	...	...
Indur...	40	22	18	15	11	2	...	5	6	8	5	...	...	...	...	...	...	...	...	...	...	...	...	...	...	...	...
Medak	106	53	53	13	11	3	1	1	...	9	10	10	5	5	2	3	2	2	1	...	...	...	...	...	...	...	...
Mahratwara. Aurangabad	1,929	960	969	232	211	...	1	5	4	227	206	263	246	40	20	3	2	220	224	67	62	...	...	1	...	66	62
Birh	148	86	62	64	45	3	1	2	...	59	44	10	4	5	3	...	...	5	1	4	4	1	...	...	1	3	3
Nander	2	2	...	...	...	...	...	...	...	...	...	2	...	2	...	...	...	...	...	...	...	...	...	...	...	...	...
Naldrug	214	107	107	76	74	...	...	...	...	76	74	...	...	...	...	...	...	...	...	...	1	...	...	...	...	...	1
Bidar	21	12	9	9	7	1	3	2	2	6	2	3	2	1	1	...	...	2	1	...	...	...	...	...	...	...	...
Parbhani	67	41	26	26	23	2	2	1	...	23	21	15	3	13	3	...	...	2	...	...	...	...	...	...	...	...	...
Sirpur Tandur	...	...	...	...	...	...	...	...	...	...	...	...	...	...	...	...	...	...	...	...	...	...	...	...	...	...	...
Karnatic or Kanada. Gulbarga	287	150	137	98	103	7	5	9	13	82	85	6	9	6	1	...	8	...	...	10	8	...	...	...	...	10	8
Raichur	335	177	158	92	83	14	6	20	19	58	58	58	56	18	19	33	33	7	4	...	...	...	...	...	...	...	...
Lingasugur	398	203	195	57	48	5	6	10	5	42	37	11	9	6	2	5	7	...	...	...	...	...	...	...	...	...	...
Total Districts......	5,930	3,085	2,845	1,028	961	52	40	70	51	906	870	893	790	119	63	52	53	722	674	184	119	3	6	1	1	180	112
Total Districts including Hyderabad...	19,759	11,241	8,518	5,270	4,716	912	316	456	416	3,902	3,984	4,087	2,126	2,620	680	474	511	993	935	172	147	9	6	3	8	160	133
Railways......	670	389	281	155	133	10	5	53	61	92	67	181	117	69	46	93	57	19	14	1	1	...	1	1	...	...	...
Grand Total......	20,429	11,630	8,799	5,425	4,849	922	321	509	477	3,994	4,051	4,268	2,243	2,689	726	567	568	1,012	949	173	148	9	7	4	8	160	133

TABLE A.

Christians by sects and race.—Part I.—Sects.—*Continued.*

District or State.	Methodist.								Wesleyan.								Presbyterian.								Church of Scotland.							
	Total.		Foreign.		Eurasian.		Native.		Total.		Foreign.		Eurasian.		Native.		Total.		Foreign.		Eurasian.		Native.		Total.		Foreign.		Eurasian.		Native.	
	Males.	Females.	Males.	Females.	Males.	Females.	Males.	Females.	Males.	Females.	Males.	Females.	Males.	Females.	Males.	Females.	Males.	Females.	Males.	Females.	Males.	Females.	Males.	Females.	Males.	Females.	Males.	Females.	Males.	Females.	Males.	Females.
	29	30	31	32	33	34	35	36	37	38	39	40	41	42	43	44	45	46	47	48	49	50	51	52	53	54	55	56	57	58	59	60
Telingana. Hyderabad. City	2	1	...	...	2	1	...	...	...	...	...	...	...	...	...	...	...	...	...	...	...	...	...	...	...	...	...	...	...	...	...	...
Suburbs including Secunderabad	97	97	28	31	25	39	44	27	217	176	158	44	29	29	30	103	147	72	124	50	10	13	13	9	2	2	1	...	1	2	...	...
Total......	99	98	28	31	27	40	44	27	217	176	158	44	29	29	30	103	147	72	124	50	10	13	13	9	2	2	1	...	1	2	...	...
Atraf-i-Balda District	...	...	...	...	...	...	...	...	...	...	...	...	...	...	...	...	...	...	...	...	...	...	...	...	...	...	...	...	...	...	...	...
Mahabubnagar (Nagar Karnul) ...	...	...	...	...	...	...	...	...	...	...	...	...	...	...	...	...	...	...	...	...	...	...	...	...	...	...	...	...	...	...	...	...
Nalgonda	...	...	...	...	...	...	...	...	...	...	...	...	...	...	...	...	...	...	...	...	...	...	...	...	...	...	...	...	...	...	...	...
Warangal (Khamam)	47	36	1	2	7	4	39	30	...	...	...	...	...	...	...	...	...	...	...	...	...	...	...	...	...	...	...	...	...	...	...	...
Elgandal	63	15	3	2	4	1	56	12	15	13	1	...	...	...	14	13	...	...	...	...	...	...	...	...	...	...	...	...	...	...	...	...
Indur	...	...	...	...	...	...	...	...	...	...	...	...	...	...	...	...	2	1	2	1	...	...	...	...	...	...	...	...	...	...	...	...
Medak	...	...	...	...	...	...	...	...	9	6	1	1	...	...	8	5	...	...	...	...	...	...	...	...	1	...	1	...	...	...	...	...
Mahratwara. Aurangabad	64	87	...	...	...	1	64	86	...	...	...	...	...	...	...	...	192	198	3	3	...	...	189	195	3	6	...	1	...	...	3	5
Birh...	...	...	...	...	...	...	...	...	...	...	...	...	...	...	...	...	2	4	2	4	...	...	...	...	...	...	...	...	...	...	...	...
Nander	...	...	...	...	...	...	...	...	...	...	...	...	...	...	...	...	...	...	...	...	...	...	...	...	...	...	...	...	...	...	...	...
Naldrug	27	28	...	...	...	...	27	28	...	...	...	...	...	...	...	...	...	...	...	...	...	...	...	...	...	...	...	...	...	...	...	...
Bidar	...	...	...	...	...	...	...	...	...	...	...	...	...	...	...	...	...	...	...	...	...	...	...	...	...	...	...	...	...	...	...	...
Parbhani	...	...	...	...	...	...	...	...	...	...	...	...	...	...	...	...	...	...	...	...	...	...	...	...	...	...	...	...	...	...	...	...
Sirpur Tandur	...	...	...	...	...	...	...	...	...	...	...	...	...	...	...	...	...	...	...	...	...	...	...	...	...	...	...	...	...	...	...	...
Karnatic or Kanada. Gulbarga...	29	12	...	...	...	...	29	12	...	...	...	...	...	...	...	...	...	...	...	...	...	...	...	...	...	...	...	...	...	...	...	...
Raichur	1	...	...	...	1	...	...	...	1	1	1	1	...	...	...	...	...	...	...	...	...	...	...	...	2	3	1	...	1	3	...	...
Lingasugur	5	6	2	3	...	...	3	3	...	...	...	...	...	...	...	...	3	1	...	...	3	...	...	1	...	...	...	...	...	...	...	...
Total Districts......	236	184	6	7	12	6	218	171	25	20	3	2	...	...	22	18	199	204	7	8	3	...	189	196	6	9	2	1	1	3	3	5
Total Districts including Hyderabad...	335	282	34	38	39	46	262	198	242	196	161	46	29	29	52	121	346	276	181	58	13	13	202	205	8	11	3	1	2	5	3	5
Railways......	14	16	2	3	11	13	1	...	12	3	4	2	1	...	7	1	8	5	1	2	7	3	...	...	3	...	2	...	1	...	...	...
Grand Total......	349	298	36	41	50	59	263	198	254	199	165	48	30	29	59	122	354	281	182	60	20	16	202	205	11	11	5	1	3	5	3	5

TABLE A.

Christians by sects and race.—Part I.—Sects.—*Continued.*

District or State.	Free Church of Scotland. Total. Males.	Females.	Foreign. Males.	Females.	Eurasian. Males.	Females.	Native. Males.	Females.	Unsectarian. Total. Males.	Females.	Foreign. Males.	Females.	Eurasian. Males.	Females.	Native. Males.	Females.
	61	62	63	64	65	66	67	68	69	70	71	72	73	74	75	76
Telingana. Hyderabad. City	1	...	...	...	...	...	1	...	...	...	...	...	...	...	...	...
Suburbs including Secunderabad	12	19	...	...	...	...	12	19	88	60	4	1	14	22	70	37
Total......	13	19	...	...	...	...	13	19	88	60	4	1	14	22	70	37
Atraf-i-Balda District...	...	...	...	...	...	...	...	...	...	...	...	...	...	...	...	...
Mahabubnagar (Nagar Karnul) ...	...	...	...	...	...	...	...	...	...	...	...	...	...	...	...	...
Nalgonda	...	...	...	...	...	...	...	...	...	...	...	...	...	...	...	...
Warangal (Khamam)	...	...	...	...	...	...	...	...	...	...	...	...	...	...	...	...
Elgandal	...	...	...	...	...	...	...	...	...	...	...	...	...	...	...	...
Indur	...	...	...	...	...	...	...	...	...	...	...	...	...	...	...	...
Medak	...	...	...	...	...	...	...	...	...	...	...	...	...	...	...	...
Mahratwara. Aurangabad	7	8	...	...	...	...	7	8	2	1	1	...	...	...	1	1
Birh	...	...	...	...	...	...	...	...	6	5	4	1	...	...	2	4
Nander	...	...	...	...	...	...	...	...	...	...	...	...	...	...	...	...
Naldrug	...	...	...	...	...	...	...	...	...	...	...	...	...	...	...	...
Bidar	...	...	...	...	...	...	...	...	...	...	...	...	...	...	...	...
Parbhani	...	...	...	...	...	...	...	...	...	...	...	...	...	...	...	...
Sirpur Tandur	...	...	...	...	...	...	...	...	...	...	...	...	...	...	...	...
Karnatic or Kanada. Gulbarga	...	...	...	...	...	...	...	...	...	...	...	...	...	...	...	...
Raichur	...	...	...	...	...	...	...	...	4	1	1	...	...	...	8	1
Lingasugur	...	...	...	...	...	...	...	...	...	...	...	...	...	...	...	...
Total Districts......	7	8	...	...	...	...	7	8	12	7	6	1	...	...	6	6
Total Districts including Hyderadad...	20	27	...	...	...	...	20	27	100	67	10	2	14	22	76	43
Railways......	...	...	...	...	...	...	...	...	11	5	2	1	1	1	8	8
Grand Total......	20	27	...	...	...	...	20	27	111	72	12	3	15	23	84	46

District or State.	Congregationalist. Total. Males.	Females.	Foreign. Males.	Females.	Eurasian. Males.	Females.	Native. Males.	Females.	Episcopalian. Total. Males.	Females.	Foreign. Males.	Females.	Eurasian. Males.	Females.	Native. Males.	Females.
	77	78	79	80	81	82	83	84	85	86	87	88	89	90	91	92
Telingana. Hyderabad. City	...	...	...	...	...	...	...	...	...	...	...	...	...	...	...	...
Suburbs including Secunderabad	4	...	4	...	...	...	...	...	11	1	8	1	4	...	4	...
Total......	4	...	4	...	...	...	...	...	11	1	8	1	4	...	4	...
Atraf-i-Balda District...	...	...	...	...	...	...	...	...	...	...	...	...	...	...	...	...
Mahabubnagar (Nagar Karnul) ...	...	...	...	...	...	...	...	...	...	...	...	...	...	...	...	...
Nalgonda	...	...	...	...	...	...	...	...	...	...	...	...	...	...	...	...
Warangal (Khamam)	...	...	...	...	...	...	...	...	...	...	...	...	...	...	...	...
Elgandal	...	...	...	...	...	...	...	...	...	...	...	...	...	...	...	...
Indur	...	...	...	...	...	...	...	...	...	...	...	...	...	...	...	...
Medak	...	...	...	...	...	...	...	...	...	...	...	...	...	...	...	...
Mahratwara. Aurangabad	...	...	...	...	...	...	...	...	...	...	...	...	...	...	...	...
Birh	...	...	...	...	...	...	...	...	...	...	...	...	...	...	...	...
Nander	...	...	...	...	...	...	...	...	...	...	...	...	...	...	...	...
Naldrug	...	...	...	...	...	...	...	...	...	...	...	...	...	...	...	...
Bidar	...	...	...	...	...	...	...	...	...	...	...	...	...	...	...	...
Parbhani	...	...	...	...	...	...	...	...	...	...	...	...	...	...	...	...
Sirpur Tandur	...	...	...	...	...	...	...	...	...	...	...	...	...	...	...	...
Karnatic or Kanada. Gulbarga	...	...	...	...	...	...	...	...	...	...	...	...	...	...	...	...
Raichur	...	...	...	...	...	...	...	...	...	...	...	...	...	...	...	...
Lingasugur	...	...	...	...	...	...	...	...	...	...	...	...	...	...	...	...
Total Districts......	...	...	...	...	...	...	...	...	...	...	...	...	...	...	...	...
Total Districts including Hyderadad...	4	...	4	...	...	...	...	...	11	1	8	1	4	...	4	...
Railways......	...	...	...	...	...	...	...	...	...	...	...	...	...	...	...	...
Grand Total......	4	...	4	...	...	...	...	...	11	1	8	1	4	...	4	...

TABLE A.

Christians by sects and race.—Part I.—Sects.—*Continued.*

District or State.	Protestant.								Greek Church.							
	Total.		Foreign.		Eurasian.		Native.		Total.		Foreign.		Eurasian.		Native.	
	Males.	Females.	Males.	Females.	Males.	Females.	Males.	Females.	Males.	Females.	Males.	Females.	Males.	Females.	Males.	Females.
	93	94	95	96	97	98	99	100	101	102	103	104	105	106	107	108
Telingana. Hyderabad. City	2	2	2	2	...	...	...	...	...	...	...	...	...	...	...	...
Suburbs including Secunderabad	94	119	18	12	18	13	63	94	1	2	...	...	1	2	...	...
Total	96	121	15	14	18	13	63	94	1	2	...	...	1	2	...	...
Atraf-i-Balda District	14	24	...	1	...	...	14	23	...	...	...	...	...	...	...	...
Mahabubnagar (Nagar Karnul)	16	13	7	5	1	...	8	8	...	...	...	...	...	...	...	...
Nalgonda	66	59	1	1	...	...	65	58	...	...	...	...	...	...	...	...
Warangal (Khamam)	71	47	7	...	4	5	60	42	...	...	...	...	...	...	...	...
Elgandal	33	30	2	3	14	8	17	19	...	...	...	...	...	...	...	...
Indur	5	6	3	4	2	...	...	2	...	...	...	...	...	...	...	...
Medak	20	31	...	...	...	...	20	31	...	...	...	...	...	...	...	...
Mahratwara. Aurangabad	130	150	8	5	17	14	110	131	...	...	...	...	...	...	...	...
Birh	...	...	...	...	...	...	...	...	...	...	...	...	...	...	...	...
Nander	...	...	...	...	...	...	...	...	...	...	...	...	...	...	...	...
Naldrug	4	4	...	...	...	...	4	4	...	...	...	...	...	...	...	...
Bidar	...	...	...	...	...	...	...	...	...	...	...	...	...	...	...	...
Parbhani	...	...	...	...	...	...	...	...	...	...	...	...	...	...	...	...
Sirpur Tandur	...	...	...	...	...	...	...	...	...	...	...	...	...	...	...	...
Karnatic or Kanada. Gulbarga	7	5	...	...	...	...	7	5	...	...	...	...	...	...	...	...
Raichur	2	3	...	...	2	...	...	3	...	...	...	...	...	...	...	...
Lingasugur	14	6	...	...	9	4	5	2	...	...	...	...	...	...	...	...
Total Districts	382	378	23	19	49	31	310	328	...	...	...	...	...	...	...	...
Total Districts including Hyderabad	478	499	38	33	67	44	373	422	1	2	...	...	1	2	...	...
Railways	4	1	...	...	...	...	4	1	...	...	...	...	...	...	...	...
Grand Total	482	500	38	33	67	44	377	423	1	2	...	...	1	2	...	...

District or State.	Lutheran.								Puritan.								Unspecified.							
	Total.		Foreign.		Eurasian.		Native.		Total.		Foreign.		Eurasian.		Native.		Total.		Foreign.		Eurasian.		Native.	
	Males.	Females.	Males.	Females.	Males.	Females.	Males.	Females.	Males.	Females.	Males.	Females.	Males.	Females.	Males.	Females.	Males.	Females.	Males.	Females.	Males.	Females.	Males.	Females.
	109	110	111	112	113	114	115	116	117	118	119	120	121	122	123	124	125	126	127	128	129	130	131	132
Telingana. Hyderabad. City	...	...	...	...	...	...	...	...	...	...	...	...	...	...	...	...	...	...	...	...	...	...	...	...
Suburbs including Secunderabad	3	2	3	2	...	...	...	...	1	1	...	...	...	...	1	1	...	...	...	...	...	...	...	...
Total	3	2	3	2	...	...	...	...	1	1	...	...	...	...	1	1	...	...	...	...	...	...	...	...
Atraf-i-Balda District	...	...	...	...	...	...	...	...	...	...	...	...	...	...	...	...	...	...	...	...	...	...	...	...
Mahabubnagar (Nagar Karnul)	...	...	...	...	...	...	...	...	...	...	...	...	...	...	...	...	...	...	...	...	...	...	...	...
Nalgonda	...	...	...	...	...	...	...	...	...	...	...	...	...	...	...	...	...	...	...	...	...	...	...	...
Warangal (Khamam)	...	...	...	...	...	...	...	...	...	...	...	...	...	...	...	...	...	...	...	...	...	...	...	...
Elgandal	...	...	...	...	...	...	...	...	...	...	...	...	...	...	...	...	33	29	...	...	...	...	33	29
Indur	...	...	...	...	...	...	...	...	...	...	...	...	...	...	...	...	...	...	...	...	...	...	...	...
Medak	...	...	...	...	...	...	...	...	...	...	...	...	...	...	...	...	...	...	...	...	...	...	...	...
Mahratwara. Aurangabad	...	...	...	...	...	...	...	...	...	...	...	...	...	...	...	...	...	...	...	...	...	...	...	...
Birh	...	...	...	...	...	...	...	...	...	...	...	...	...	...	...	...	...	...	...	...	...	...	...	...
Nander	...	...	...	...	...	...	...	...	...	...	...	...	...	...	...	...	...	...	...	...	...	...	...	...
Naldrug	...	...	...	...	...	...	...	...	...	...	...	...	...	...	...	...	...	...	...	...	...	...	...	...
Bidar	...	...	...	...	...	...	...	...	...	...	...	...	...	...	...	...	...	...	...	...	...	...	...	...
Parbhani	...	...	...	...	...	...	...	...	...	...	...	...	...	...	...	...	...	...	...	...	...	...	...	...
Sirpur Tandur	...	...	...	...	...	...	...	...	...	...	...	...	...	...	...	...	...	...	...	...	...	...	...	...
Karnatic or Kanada. Gulbarga	...	...	...	...	...	...	...	...	...	...	...	...	...	...	...	...	...	...	...	...	...	...	...	...
Raichur	...	...	...	...	...	...	...	...	...	...	...	...	...	...	...	...	...	...	...	...	...	...	...	...
Lingasugur	...	...	...	...	...	...	...	...	...	...	...	...	...	...	...	...	17	11	...	...	6	...	11	11
																	113	125	...	...	...	...	113	125
Total Districts	...	...	...	...	...	...	...	...	...	...	...	...	...	...	...	...	163	165	...	...	6	...	157	165
Total Districts including Hyderabad	3	2	3	2	...	...	...	...	1	1	...	...	...	...	1	1	163	165	...	...	6	...	157	165
Railways	...	...	...	...	...	...	...	...	...	...	...	...	...	...	...	...	...	...	...	...	...	...	...	...
Grand Total	3	2	3	2	...	...	...	...	1	1	...	...	...	...	1	1	163	165	...	...	6	...	157	165

TABLE A.

CHRISTIANS BY SECTS AND RACE.—PART II.—RACES.

TABLE A.

Christians by sects and race.—Part II.—Races.

District or State.	Total Christians. Total.	Total Christians. Males.	Total Christians. Females.	Distribution by Race. A. Foreign. Total. Total.	Total. Males.	Total. Females.	Roman Catholic. Males.	Roman Catholic. Females.	Church of England. Males.	Church of England. Females.	Baptist. Males.	Baptist. Females.	Methodist. Males.	Methodist. Females.	Wesleyan. Males.	Wesleyan. Females.	Presbyterian. Males.	Presbyterian. Females.	Church of Scotland. Males.	Church of Scotland. Females.	Unsectarian. Males.	Unsectarian. Females.	Congregationalist. Males.	Congregationalist. Females.	Episcopalian. Males.	Episcopalian. Females.	Protestant. Males.	Protestant. Females.	Lutheran. Males.	Lutheran. Females.	Unspecified. Males.	Unspecified. Females.
1	2	3	4	5	6	7	8	9	10	11	12	13	14	15	16	17	18	19	20	21	22	23	24	25	26	27	28	29	30	31	32	33
Tellngana. Hyderabad. City	44	27	17	9	6	3	3	1	1	...	...	...	...	...	...	...	...	...	...	...	...	...	...	...	...	...	2	2	...	...	...	...
Suburbs including Secunderabad	18,785	8,129	5,656	4,734	3,701	1,033	857	275	2,500	617	6	...	28	31	158	44	124	50	1	...	4	1	4	...	3	1	13	12	3	2	...	...
Total......	18,829	8,156	5,673	4,743	3,707	1,036	860	276	2,501	617	6	...	28	31	158	44	124	50	1	...	4	1	4	...	3	1	15	14	3	2	...	...
Atraf-i-Balda District	450	216	234	7	3	4	2	2	1	1	...	...	...	...	...	...	...	...	...	...	...	...	...	...	...	...	...	1	...	...	...	...
Mahabubnagar (Nagar Karnul) ...	121	67	54	20	9	11	...	...	...	...	2	6	...	...	...	...	...	...	...	...	...	...	...	...	...	...	7	5	...	...	...	...
Nalgonda	185	73	62	2	1	1	...	...	...	...	...	...	...	...	...	...	...	...	...	...	...	...	...	...	...	...	1	1	...	...	...	...
Warangal (Khamam)	1,484	794	690	62	40	22	11	9	21	11	...	...	1	2	...	...	...	...	...	...	...	...	...	...	...	...	7	...	...	...	...	...
Elgandal	193	122	71	18	9	9	2	4	1	...	...	...	3	2	1	...	...	...	...	...	...	...	...	...	...	...	2	3	...	...	...	...
Indur	40	22	18	12	7	5	2	...	...	...	...	...	...	...	...	...	2	1	...	...	...	...	...	...	...	...	3	4	...	...	...	...
Medak	106	53	53	14	10	4	3	1	5	2	...	...	...	...	1	1	...	...	1	...	...	...	...	...	...	...	...	...	...	...	...	...
Mahratwara. Aurangabad	1,929	960	969	77	47	30	...	1	40	20	...	...	...	...	...	...	3	3	...	1	1	...	...	...	...	...	3	5	...	...	...	...
Birh	148	86	62	24	15	9	3	1	5	3	1	...	...	...	...	...	2	4	...	...	4	1	...	...	...	...	...	...	...	...	...	...
Nander	2	2	...	2	2	...	...	...	2	...	...	...	...	...	...	...	...	...	...	...	...	...	...	...	...	...	...	...	...	...	...	...
Naldrug	214	107	107	...	...	...	...	...	...	...	...	...	...	...	...	...	...	...	...	...	...	...	...	...	...	...	...	...	...	...	...	...
Bidar	21	12	9	6	2	4	1	3	1	1	...	...	...	...	...	...	...	...	...	...	...	...	...	...	...	...	...	...	...	...	...	...
Parbhani	67	41	26	20	15	5	2	2	13	3	...	...	...	...	...	...	...	...	...	...	...	...	...	...	...	...	...	...	...	...	...	...
Sirpur Tandur	...	...	...	...	...	...	...	...	...	...	...	...	...	...	...	...	...	...	...	...	...	...	...	...	...	...	...	...	...	...	...	...
Karnatic or Kanada. Gulbarga	287	150	137	19	13	6	7	5	6	1	...	...	...	...	...	...	...	...	...	...	...	...	...	...	...	...	...	...	...	...	...	...
Raichur	335	177	158	61	35	26	14	6	18	19	...	...	...	...	1	1	...	...	1	...	1	...	...	...	...	...	...	...	...	...	...	...
Lingasugur	398	203	195	24	13	11	5	6	6	2	...	...	2	3	...	...	...	...	...	...	...	...	...	...	...	...	...	...	...	...	...	...
Total Districts......	5,930	3,085	2,845	368	221	147	52	40	119	68	3	6	6	7	3	2	7	8	2	1	6	1	...	...	...	...	23	19	...	...	...	...
Total Districts including Hyderabad	19,759	11,241	8,518	5,111	3,928	1,183	912	316	2,620	680	9	6	34	38	161	46	131	58	3	1	10	2	4	...	3	1	38	33	3	2	...	...
Railways......	670	389	281	150	90	60	10	5	69	46	...	1	2	3	4	2	1	2	2	...	2	1	...	...	...	...	...	...	...	...	...	...
Grand Total......	20,429	11,630	8,799	5,261	4,018	1,243	922	321	2,689	726	9	7	36	41	165	48	132	60	5	1	12	3	4	...	3	1	38	33	3	2	...	...

TABLE A.

Christians by sects and race.—Part II.—Races.

District or State.	Total Christians.			Distribution by Race. B. Eurasian. Total.			Roman Catholic.		Church of England.		Baptist.		Methodist.		Wesleyan.		Presbyterian.		Church of Scotland.		Unsectarian.		Episcopalian.		Protestant.		Greek Church.		Unspecified.	
	Total.	Males.	Females.	Total.	Males.	Females.	Males.	Females.	Males.	Females.	Males.	Females.	Males.	Females.	Males.	Females.	Males.	Females.	Males.	Females.	Males.	Females.	Males.	Females.	Males.	Females.	Males.	Females.	Males.	Females.
1	2	3	4	5	6	7	8	9	10	11	12	13	14	15	16	17	18	19	20	21	22	23	24	25	26	27	28	29	30	31
Telingana. Hyderabad. City	44	27	17	17	13	4	11	3	...	...	...	...	2	1	...	...	...	...	...	...	...	...	...	...	...	...	...	...	...	...
Suburbs including Secunderabad	13,785	8,129	5,656	1,848	901	947	875	362	422	458	2	7	25	39	29	29	10	18	1	2	14	22	4	...	18	23	1	2	...	...
Total	13,829	8,156	5,673	1,865	914	951	886	365	422	458	2	7	27	40	29	29	10	13	1	2	14	22	4	...	18	13	1	2	...	...
Atraf-i-Balda District	450	216	234	1	1	...	1	...	...	...	...	...	...	...	...	...	...	...	...	...	...	...	...	...	...	...	...	...	...	...
Mahabubnagar (Nagar Karnul)	121	67	54	3	3	...	2	...	...	...	...	...	...	...	...	...	...	...	...	...	...	...	...	...	1	...	...	...	...	...
Nalgonda	135	73	62	...	...	...	...	...	...	...	...	...	...	...	...	...	...	...	...	...	...	...	...	...	...	...	...	...	...	...
Warangal (Khamam)	1,484	794	690	40	29	11	10	2	8	...	...	...	7	4	...	...	...	...	...	...	...	...	...	...	4	5	...	...	...	...
Elgandal	193	122	71	30	20	10	2	...	...	1	...	...	4	1	...	...	...	...	...	...	...	...	...	...	14	8	...	...	...	...
Indur	40	22	18	13	7	6	5	6	...	...	...	...	...	...	...	...	...	...	...	...	...	...	...	...	2	...	...	...	...	...
Medak	106	53	53	6	4	2	1	...	3	2	...	...	...	...	...	...	...	...	...	...	...	...	...	...	...	...	...	...	...	...
Mahratwara. Aurangabad	1,929	960	969	47	26	21	5	4	3	2	1	...	...	1	...	...	...	...	...	...	...	...	...	...	17	14	...	...	...	...
Birh	148	86	62	3	2	1	2	...	...	...	...	1	...	...	...	...	...	...	...	...	...	...	...	...	...	...	...	...	...	...
Nander	2	2	...	...	...	...	...	...	...	...	...	...	...	...	...	...	...	...	...	...	...	...	...	...	...	...	...	...	...	...
Naldrug	214	107	107	...	...	...	...	...	...	...	...	...	...	...	...	...	...	...	...	...	...	...	...	...	...	...	...	...	...	...
Bidar	21	12	9	4	2	2	2	2	...	...	...	...	...	...	...	...	...	...	...	...	...	...	...	...	...	...	...	...	...	...
Parbhani	67	41	26	1	1	...	1	...	...	...	...	...	...	...	...	...	...	...	...	...	...	...	...	...	...	...	...	...	...	...
Sirpur Tandur	...	...	...	...	...	...	...	...	...	...	...	...	...	...	...	...	...	...	...	...	...	...	...	...	...	...	...	...	...	...
Karnatic or Kanada. Gulbarga	287	150	137	30	9	21	9	13	...	8	...	...	...	...	...	...	...	...	...	...	...	...	...	...	...	...	...	...	...	...
Raichur	335	177	158	118	63	55	20	19	33	33	...	...	1	...	...	...	...	...	1	3	...	...	...	...	2	...	...	...	6	...
Lingasugur	398	203	195	43	27	16	10	5	5	7	...	...	...	...	...	...	8	...	...	...	...	...	...	...	9	4	...	...	...	...
Total Districts	5,930	3,085	2,845	339	194	145	70	51	52	53	1	1	12	6	...	...	8	...	1	3	...	...	...	...	49	31	...	...	6	...
Total Districts including Hyderabad	19,759	11,241	8,518	2,204	1,108	1,096	456	416	474	511	3	8	39	46	29	29	18	13	2	5	14	22	4	...	67	44	1	2	6	...
Railways	670	389	281	303	168	135	53	61	93	57	1	...	11	13	1	...	7	3	1	...	1	1	...	...	...	...	...	...	...	...
Grand Total	20,429	11,630	8,799	2,507	1,276	1,231	509	477	567	568	4	8	50	59	30	29	20	16	3	5	15	23	4	...	67	44	1	2	6	...

TABLE A.

Christians by sects and race.—Part II.—Races.

District or State.	Total Christians.			Distribution by Race. C, Native. Total.			Roman Catholic.		Church of England.		Baptist.		Methodist.		Wesleyan.		Presbyterian.		Church of Scotland.		Unsectarian.		Episcopalian.		Protestant.		Free Church of Scotland.		Puritan.		Unspecified.	
	Total.	Males.	Females.	Total.	Males.	Females.	Males.	Females.	Males.	Females.	Males.	Females.	Males.	Females.	Males.	Females.	Males.	Females.	Males.	Females.	Males.	Females.	Males.	Females.	Males.	Females.	Males.	Females.	Males.	Females.	Males.	Females.
1	2	3	4	5	6	7	8	9	10	11	12	13	14	15	16	17	18	19	20	21	22	23	24	25	26	27	28	29	30	31	32	33
Telingana. Hyderabad.																																
City	44	27	17	18	8	10	6	10	1	...	...	...	...	...	...	...	...	...	...	...	...	...	...	...	...	...	1	...	...	...	...	...
Suburbs including Secunderabad	13,785	8,129	5,656	7,203	3,527	3,676	2,990	3,104	270	261	30	21	44	27	30	103	13	9	...	...	70	37	4	...	63	94	12	19	1	1	...	...
Total......	13,829	8,156	5,673	7,221	3,535	3,686	2,996	3,114	271	261	30	21	44	27	30	103	13	9	...	...	70	37	4	...	62	94	13	19	1	1	...	...
Atraf-i-Balda District	450	216	234	442	212	230	198	207	...	...	...	...	...	...	...	...	...	...	...	...	...	...	...	...	14	28	...	...	...	...	...	...
Mahabubnagar (Nargar Karnul)	121	67	54	98	55	43	7	8	...	...	40	27	...	...	...	...	...	...	...	...	...	...	...	...	8	8	...	...	...	...	...	...
Nalgonda	135	73	62	133	72	61	7	8	...	...	...	...	...	...	...	...	...	...	...	...	...	...	...	...	65	58	...	...	...	...	...	...
Warangal (Khamam)	1,484	794	690	1,382	725	657	98	102	484	443	11	11	89	80	...	...	...	...	...	...	...	...	...	...	60	42	...	...	...	...	33	29
Elgandal	193	122	71	145	93	52	6	8	...	...	...	...	56	12	14	18	...	...	...	...	...	...	...	...	17	19	...	...	...	...	...	...
Indur	40	22	18	15	8	7	8	5	...	...	...	...	...	...	...	...	...	...	...	...	...	...	...	...	...	2	...	...	...	...	...	...
Medak	106	53	53	86	39	47	9	10	2	1	...	...	...	...	8	5	...	...	...	...	...	...	...	...	20	31	...	...	...	...	...	...
Mahratwara.																																
Aurangabad	1,929	960	969	1,805	887	918	227	206	220	224	66	62	64	86	...	...	189	195	8	5	1	1	...	...	110	131	7	8	...	...	...	...
Birh	148	86	62	121	69	52	59	44	5	1	8	8	...	...	...	...	...	...	...	...	2	4	...	...	...	...	...	...	...	...	...	...
Nander	2	2	...	...	...	...	...	...	...	...	...	...	...	...	...	...	...	...	...	...	...	...	...	...	...	...	...	...	...	...	...	...
Naldrug	214	107	107	214	107	107	76	74	...	...	...	1	27	28	...	...	...	...	...	...	...	...	...	...	4	4	...	...	...	...	...	...
Bidar	21	12	9	11	8	3	6	2	2	1	...	...	...	...	...	...	...	...	...	...	...	...	...	...	...	...	...	...	...	...	...	...
Parbhani...	67	41	26	46	25	21	23	21	2	...	...	...	...	...	...	...	...	...	...	...	...	...	...	...	...	...	...	...	...	...	...	...
Sirpur Tandur	...	...	...	...	...	...	...	...	...	...	...	...	...	...	...	...	...	...	...	...	...	...	...	...	...	...	...	...	...	...	...	...
Karnatic or Kanada.																																
Gulbarga	287	150	137	238	128	110	82	85	...	...	10	8	29	12	...	...	...	...	...	...	...	...	...	...	7	5	...	...	...	...	...	...
Raichur	335	177	158	156	79	77	58	58	7	4	...	...	...	...	...	...	...	...	...	...	3	1	...	...	...	3	...	...	...	...	11	11
Lingasugur...	398	203	195	331	163	168	42	87	...	...	...	...	3	3	...	...	...	1	...	...	...	...	...	...	5	2	...	...	...	...	113	125
Total Districts......	5,930	3,085	2,845	5,223	2,670	2,553	906	870	722	674	180	112	218	171	22	18	189	196	3	5	6	6	...	...	310	328	7	8	...	...	157	165
Total Districts including Hyderabad...	19,759	11,241	8,518	12,444	6,205	6,239	3,902	3,984	993	985	160	133	262	198	52	121	202	205	8	5	76	43	4	...	373	422	20	27	1	1	157	165
Railways......	670	389	281	217	131	86	92	67	19	14	...	...	1	...	7	1	...	...	...	...	8	3	...	...	4	1	...	...	...	...	...	...
Grand Total......	20,429	11,630	8,799	12,661	6,336	6,325	3,994	4,051	1,012	949	160	133	263	198	59	122	202	205	8	5	84	46	4	...	377	423	20	27	1	1	157	165

TABLE B.

Race and Age of the European, Eurasian, Armenian, and American Population.

TABLE B.

Showing by Race and Age the European, Eurasian, Armenian, and American Population.

District or State.	Total. Total. Males.	Total. Total. Females.	Total. 0—14 Males.	Total. 0—14 Females.	Total. 15—34 Males.	Total. 15—34 Females.	Total. 35—49 Males.	Total. 35—49 Females.	Total. 50 and over. Males.	Total. 50 and over. Females.	Total. Unspecified. Males.	Total. Unspecified. Females.	European. Total. Males.	European. Total. Females.	European. 0—14 Males.	European. 0—14 Females.	European. 15—34 Males.	European. 15—34 Females.	European. 35—49 Males.	European. 35—49 Females.	European. 50 and over. Males.	European. 50 and over. Females.	European. Unspecified. Males.	European. Unspecified. Females.
1	2	3	4	5	6	7	8	9	10	11	12	13	14	15	16	17	18	19	20	21	22	23	24	25
Telingana, Hyderabad, City	20	8	2	2	12	4	4	1	2	1	...	...	7	4	1	1	4	3	...	...	2	...	...	...
Suburbs including Secunderabad	4,605	1,981	747	787	3,329	830	370	244	159	120	...	...	3,699	1,038	389	404	3,012	459	232	117	66	58	...	...
Total......	4,625	1,989	749	789	3,341	834	374	245	161	121	...	...	3,706	1,037	390	405	3,016	462	232	117	68	58	...	...
Atraf-i-Balda District	4	4	2	1	1	2	...	...	1	1	...	...	3	4	2	1	...	2	...	...	1	1	...	...
Mahabubnagar (Nagar Karnul) ...	12	11	4	7	4	2	3	2	1	...	...	...	9	11	4	7	1	2	3	2	1	...	...	...
Nalgonda	1	1	...	...	...	1	1	...	...	...	...	...	1	1	...	...	...	1	1	...	...	...	...	...
Warangal (Khamam)	69	33	15	15	35	15	15	2	4	1	...	...	40	22	8	9	18	10	11	2	3	1	...	...
Elgandal	29	19	11	6	10	11	7	2	1	...	...	...	9	9	2	3	5	5	2	1	...	...	...	...
Indur	14	11	6	4	2	5	2	2	3	...	1	...	7	5	2	2	...	2	1	1	3	...	1	...
Medak...	14	6	4	2	8	3	2	1	...	...	...	...	10	4	3	1	5	2	2	1	...	...	...	...
Mahratwara, Aurangabad	73	51	20	19	34	21	15	7	4	4	...	...	46	30	8	11	26	12	10	5	2	2	...	...
Birh	17	10	2	2	10	6	5	2	...	...	...	...	15	9	2	2	8	5	5	2	...	...	...	...
Nander	2	...	...	...	...	...	2	...	...	...	...	...	2	...	...	...	...	...	2	...	...	...	...	...
Naldrug	...	...	...	...	...	...	...	...	...	...	...	...	...	...	...	...	...	...	...	...	...	...	...	...
Bidar	4	6	1	3	2	2	1	...	...	1	...	...	2	4	...	2	1	2	1	...	...	...	...	...
Parbhani	16	5	3	1	9	4	4	...	...	...	...	...	15	5	2	1	9	4	4	...	...	...	...	...
Sirpur Tandur	...	...	...	...	...	...	...	...	...	...	...	...	...	...	...	...	...	...	...	...	...	...	...	...
Karnatic or Kanada, Gulbarga...	22	27	12	9	6	13	3	4	1	1	...	...	13	6	7	3	3	2	3	1	...	...	...	...
Raichur	98	81	37	37	37	31	19	11	5	2	...	...	35	26	11	9	12	10	10	6	2	1	...	...
Lingasugur	41	27	7	6	20	15	8	3	6	3	...	...	13	10	2	3	5	5	3	1	3	1	...	...
Total Districts......	416	292	124	112	178	131	87	36	26	13	1	...	220	146	53	54	93	64	58	22	15	6	1	...
Total Districts including Hyderabad...	5,041	2,281	873	901	3,519	965	461	281	187	134	1	...	3,926	1,183	443	459	3,109	526	290	139	83	59	1	...
Railways......	258	195	82	85	126	83	37	18	13	9	...	...	89	60	24	23	46	25	14	8	5	4	...	...
Grand Total......	5,299	2,476	955	986	3,645	1,048	498	299	200	143	1	...	4,015	1,243	467	482	3,155	551	304	147	88	63	1	...

TABLE B.

Showing by Race and Age the European, Eurasian, Armenian, and American Population.—*Continued.*

District or State.	Eurasian.												Armenian.												American.											
	Total.		0—14		15—34		35—49		50 and over.		Unspecified.		Total.		0—14		15—34		35—49		50 and over.		Unspecified.		Total.		0—14		15—34		35—49		50 and over.		Unspecified.	
	Males.	Females.	Males.	Females.	Males.	Females.	Males.	Females.	Males.	Females.	Males.	Females.	Males.	Females.	Males.	Females.	Males.	Females.	Males.	Females.	Males.	Females.	Males.	Females.	Males.	Females.	Males.	Females.	Males.	Females.	Males.	Females.	Males.	Females.	Males.	Females.
	26	27	28	29	30	31	32	33	34	35	36	37	38	39	40	41	42	43	44	45	46	47	48	49	50	51	52	53	54	55	56	57	58	59	60	61
Tellingana. Hyderabad. City	13	4	1	1	8	1	4	1	...	1	...	...	...	...	...	...	...	...	...	...	...	...	...	...	...	...	...	...	...	...	...	...	...	...	...	...
Suburbs including Secunderabad	901	947	358	383	315	371	135	126	93	67	...	...	5	1	...	...	2	...	3	1	...	...	...	...	...	...	...	...	...	...	...	...	...	...	...	...
Total......	914	951	359	384	323	372	139	127	93	68	...	...	5	1	...	...	2	...	3	1	...	...	...	...	...	...	...	...	...	...	...	...	...	...	...	...
Atraf-i-Balda District	1	...	...	...	1	...	...	...	...	...	...	...	...	...	...	...	...	...	...	...	...	...	...	...	...	...	...	...	...	...	...	...	...	...	...	...
Mahabubnagar (Nagar Karnul) ...	3	...	...	...	3	...	...	...	...	...	...	...	...	...	...	...	...	...	...	...	...	...	...	...	...	...	...	...	...	...	...	...	...	...	...	...
Nalgonda	...	...	...	...	...	...	...	...	...	...	...	...	...	...	...	...	...	...	...	...	...	...	...	...	...	...	...	...	...	...	...	...	...	...	...	...
Warangal (Khamam)	29	11	7	6	17	5	4	...	1	...	...	...	...	...	...	...	...	...	...	...	...	...	...	...	...	...	...	...	...	...	...	...	...	...	...	...
Elgandal	20	10	9	3	5	6	5	1	1	...	...	...	...	...	...	...	...	...	...	...	...	...	...	...	...	...	...	...	...	...	...	...	...	...	...	...
Indur	7	6	4	2	2	3	1	1	...	...	...	...	...	...	...	...	...	...	...	...	...	...	...	...	...	...	...	...	...	...	...	...	...	...	...	...
Medak...	4	2	1	1	3	1	...	...	...	...	...	...	...	...	...	...	...	...	...	...	...	...	...	...	...	...	...	...	...	...	...	...	...	...	...	...
Mahratwara. Aurangabad	26	21	12	8	8	9	4	2	2	2	...	...	1	...	...	...	...	...	1	...	...	...	...	...	...	...	...	...	...	...	...	...	...	...	...	...
Birh	2	1	...	...	2	1	...	...	...	...	...	...	...	...	...	...	...	...	...	...	...	...	...	...	...	...	...	...	...	...	...	...	...	...	...	...
Nander	...	...	...	...	...	...	...	...	...	...	...	...	...	...	...	...	...	...	...	...	...	...	...	...	...	...	...	...	...	...	...	...	...	...	...	...
Naldrug	...	...	...	...	...	...	...	...	...	...	...	...	...	...	...	...	...	...	...	...	...	...	...	...	...	...	...	...	...	...	...	...	...	...	...	...
Bidar	2	2	1	1	1	...	...	...	...	1	...	...	...	...	...	...	...	...	...	...	...	...	...	...	...	...	...	...	...	...	...	...	...	...	...	...
Parbhani	1	...	1	...	...	...	...	...	...	...	...	...	...	...	...	...	...	...	...	...	...	...	...	...	...	...	...	...	...	...	...	...	...	...	...	...
Sirpur Tandur	...	...	...	...	...	...	...	...	...	...	...	...	...	...	...	...	...	...	...	...	...	...	...	...	...	...	...	...	...	...	...	...	...	...	...	...
Karnatic or Kanada. Gulbarga	9	21	5	6	3	11	...	3	1	1	...	...	...	...	...	...	...	...	...	...	...	...	...	...	...	...	...	...	...	...	...	...	...	...	...	...
Raichur	63	55	26	28	25	21	9	5	3	1	...	...	...	...	...	...	...	...	...	...	...	...	...	...	...	...	...	...	...	...	...	...	...	...	...	...
Lingasugur	27	16	5	3	15	9	4	2	3	2	...	...	...	...	...	...	...	...	...	...	...	...	...	...	1	1	...	...	...	1	1	...	...	...	...	...
Total Districts......	194	145	71	58	85	66	27	14	11	7	...	...	1	...	...	...	...	...	1	...	...	...	...	...	1	1	...	...	...	1	1	...	...	...	...	...
Total Districts including Hyderabad.	1,108	1,096	430	442	408	438	166	141	104	75	...	...	6	1	...	...	2	...	4	1	...	...	...	...	1	1	...	...	...	1	1	...	...	...	...	...
Railways......	168	135	58	62	80	58	22	10	8	5	...	...	1	...	...	...	...	...	1	...	...	...	...	...	...	...	...	...	...	...	...	...	...	...	...	...
Grand Total......	1,276	1,231	488	504	488	496	188	151	112	80	...	...	7	1	...	...	2	...	5	1	...	...	...	...	1	1	...	...	...	1	1	...	...	...	...	...

TABLE C.

SHOWING BY CASTE, TRIBE, AND RACE, THE LITERATE POPULATION, DISTINGUISHING THOSE WHO KNOW ENGLISH FROM THOSE WHO DO NOT.

TABLE C.

Literate by Language known.—Provincial (Summary).

Class.	Group.	Caste.	Religion.	TOTAL STRENGTH.						HYDERABAD.						ATRAF-I-BALDA.					
				Males.			Females.			Males.			Females.			Males.			Females.		
				Total Males.	Literate.		Total Females.	Literate.		Total Males.	Literate.		Total Females.	Literate.		Total Males.	Literate.		Total Females.	Literate.	
					Total.	English.		Total.	English.		Total.	English.		Total.	English.		Total.	English.		Total.	English.
1	2	3	4	5	6	7	8	9	10	11	12	13	14	15	16	17	18	19	20	21	22
A. Agricultural.	1	Elma		47,801	3,088	18	46,293	39	...	97	20	7	84	1	...	173	26	...	187	...	...
		Kshatri		10,006	1,717	16	9,047	29	...	1,669	350	7	1,294	13	...	417	108	...	410	1	...
		Kshatri (Sikh)		22	4	...	8	...	...	8	1	...	2	...	...	...	...	...	...	...	...
		Lodi		1,968	125	2	1,851	1	...	1,343	95	1	1,237	...	...	152	4	...	126	...	...
		Mahratta (Hindu)		4,94,710	8,593	55	4,74,630	113	...	4,164	509	30	3,622	4	...	1,377	65	...	1,256	2	...
		Mahratta (Jain)		5	2	...	4	...	...	...	...	...	...	...	...	...	...	...	...	...	...
		Munnewar		10,719	28	1	10,230	6	...	91	8	1	74	6	...	68	5	...	67	...	...
		Parbhu		265	19	5	276	1	...	7	3	2	7	1	...	...	...	...	...	...	...
		Purbiah		1,526	219	4	1,311	3	..	101	19	...	81	...	...	220	60	2	164	2	...
		Rajpoot (Hindu)		25,279	2,942	70	23,192	38	...	4,106	974	55	3,494	18	...	501	76	...	459	2	...
		Rajpoot (Jain)		7	2	...	...	...	...	4	2	...	...	...	...	...	...	...	...	...	...
		Rajpoot (Sikh)		21	9	..	12	...	...	5	2	...	1	...	...	...	...	...	...	...	...
		Rathor		264	27	...	196	...	...	90	11	...	43	...	...	...	...	...	...	...	...
		Thakur		1,756	146	3	1,732	1	...	196	72	3	135	1	...	1	...	...	...	...	...
		Total Group 1......		5,94,319	16,921	174	5,68,782	231	...	11,881	1,996	106	10,074	44	...	2,909	344	2	2,669	7	...
	2 A	Andh		9,289	15	...	8,920	2	..	...	...	...	...	...	...	...	...	...	...	...	...
		Anjani		314	2	...	325	...	...	...	...	...	...	...	...	...	...	...	...	...	...
		Aryan		1,246	255	40	1,231	9	...	1,051	214	28	1,017	7	...	4	...	...	3	...	...
		Hegari		2,351	24	2	2,485	...	...	...	...	...	...	...	...	345	2	...	366	...	...
		Gujar (Hindu)		775	225	3	729	1	...	17	6	...	17	...	...	...	...	...	...	...	...
		Gujar (Jain)		270	163	...	243	2	...	...	...	...	...	...	...	...	...	...	...	...	...
		Jat (Hindu)...		188	34	...	107	...	...	54	14	...	9	...	...	...	...	...	...	...	...
		Jat (Sikh)		173	66	1	38	1	...	12	5	...	11	...	...	...	...	...	...	...	...
		Kachhi		233	9	1	810	...	...	196	6	1	173	...	...	...	...	...	...	...	...
		Kunbi		6,26,539	21,449	360	6,07,391	391	9	5,358	1,323	314	4,845	143	9	21,646	1,200	4	21,298	16	...

TABLE C.

Literate by Language known.—Provincial (Summary)—*continued.*

Class.	Group.	Caste.	Religion.	MAHBUBNAGAR. Males. Total Males.	MAHBUBNAGAR. Males. Literate. Total.	MAHBUBNAGAR. Males. Literate. English.	MAHBUBNAGAR. Females. Total Females.	MAHBUBNAGAR. Females. Literate. Total.	MAHBUBNAGAR. Females. Literate. English.	NALGONDA. Males. Total Males.	NALGONDA. Males. Literate. Total.	NALGONDA. Males. Literate. English.	NALGONDA. Females. Total Females.	NALGONDA. Females. Literate. Total.	NALGONDA. Females. Literate. English.	WARANGAL. Males. Total Males.	WARANGAL. Males. Literate. Total.	WARANGAL. Males. Literate. English.	WARANGAL. Females. Total Females	WARANGAL. Females. Literate. Total.	WARANGAL. Females. Literate. English.
				23	24	25	26	27	28	29	30	31	32	33	34	35	36	37	38	39	40
A. Agricultural—*contd.*	1	Elma		1,942	251	...	1,888	10	...	2,222	211	...	2,155	4	...	2,883	337	...	2,735	5	...
		Kshatri		426	88	..	459	...	...	71	21	...	66	...	...	287	64	1	275	5	...
		Kshatri (Sikh)		...	...	...	...	...	...	...	...	...	...	...	...	...	...	...	...	...	...
		Lodi		2	1	...	4	...	...	...	...	...	...	...	...	8	...	...	...	...	...
		Mahratta (Hindu)		1,212	60	...	1,146	6	...	800	20	...	790	...	...	6,517	106	1	5,816	3	...
		Mahratta (Jain)		...	...	...	...	...	...	...	...	...	...	...	...	...	...	...	...	...	...
		Munnewar		18	3	...	26	...	...	...	...	...	...	...	...	759	5	...	672	...	...
		Parbhu		...	...	...	...	...	...	...	...	...	...	...	...	...	...	...	...	...	...
		Purbiah		52	11	2	46	...	...	5	2	...	2	...	...	5	2	...	4	...	...
		Rajpoot (Hindu)		722	135	1	731	1	...	225	35	...	216	3	...	696	105	...	703	...	...
		Rajpoot (Jain)		...	...	...	...	...	...	...	...	...	...	...	...	...	...	...	...	...	...
		Rajpoot (Sikh)		...	...	...	...	...	...	...	...	...	...	...	...	...	...	...	...	...	...
		Rathor		...	...	...	...	...	...	...	...	...	...	...	...	...	...	...	...	...	..
		Thakur		14	...	...	11	...	...	...	...	...	...	...	...	...	...	...	...	...	...
		Total Group 1......		4,388	549	3	4,311	17	...	3,323	289	...	3,229	7	...	11,155	619	2	10,205	13	...
	2 A	Andh			...	...	...	...	...	...	...	...	...	...	...	...	...	...	...	...	...
		Anjani		...	...	...	...	...	...	...	...	...	...	...	...	...	...	..	...	...	...
		Aryan		16	14	2	15	1	...	...	...	...	1	...	...	35	11	5	49	...	...
		Begar		89	...	..	96	...	...	...	...	...	...	...	...	33	...	...	33	...	...
		Gujar (Hindu)		...	...	...	...	...	...	...	...	...	...	...	...	...	...	...	...	...	...
		Gujar (Jain)		...	...	...	...	...	...	...	...	...	...	...	...	...	...	...	...	...	...
		Jat (Hindu)		1	...	...	...	...	...	...	...	...	...	...	...	...	...	...	...	...	..
		Jat (Sikh)		...	...	...	...	...	...	...	...	...	...	...	...	...	...	...	...	...	...
		Kachhi		...	...	...	...	...	...	...	...	...	...	...	...	...	...	...	...	...	...
		Kunbi		36,207	2,718	[illegible]	35 644	54	...	31,175	1,358	7	29,918	11	...	33,410	1,295	3	31 969	19	...

TABLE C.

Literate by Language known.—Provincial (Summary)—*continued.*

Class.	Group.	Caste.	Religion.	ELGANDAL.						INDUR.						MEDAK.					
				MALES.			FEMALES.			MALES.			FEMALES.			MALES.			FEMALES.		
				Total Males.	Literate.		Total Females.	Literate.		Total Males.	Literate.		Total Females.	Literate.		Total Males.	Literate.		Total Females.	Literate.	
					Total.	English.		Total.	English.		Total.	English.		Total.	English.		Total.	English.		Total.	English.
				41	42	43	44	45	46	47	48	49	50	51	52	53	54	55	56	57	58
A. Agricultural—(*contd*).	1	Elma		95,95	1,665	7	9,171	16	...	1,936	76	...	1,946	...	...	559	91	1	539	...	...
		Kshatri		111	15	...	97	...	...	794	71	...	775	...	...	530	161	...	498	2	...
		Kshatri (Sikh)		...	...	...	...	...	...	13	3	...	5	...	...	...	...	...	...	...	...
		Lodi		...	...	...	...	...	...	213	...	...	232	...	...	14	...	...	35	...	...
		Mahratta (Hindu)		6,954	95	...	6,358	3	...	10,142	334	...	9 724	3	...	1,047	73	...	938	...	...
		Mahratta (Jain)		...	...	...	..	...	...	...	...	...	...	...	...	...	...	...	...	...	...
		Munnewar		9,613	6	...	9,242	...	...	159	1	...	137	...	...	...	...	...	...	...	...
		Parbhu		217	...	...	205	...	...	..	...	...	...	...	...	...	...	...	...	...	...
		Purbiah		5	1	...	5	...	...	28	9	...	30	...	...	89	14	...	90	...	...
		Rajpoot (Hindu)		796	111	2	752	...	...	551	60	...	552	...	...	311	42	...	296	1	...
		Rajpoot (Jain)		...	...	...	...	...	...	...	...	...	...	...	...	...	...	...	...	...	...
		Rajpoot (Sikh)		...	...	...	...	...	...	...	...	...	...	...	...	...	...	...	...	...	...
		Rathor		3	...	...	2	...	...	1	...	...	1	...	...	4	1	...	...	...	...
		Thakur		...	...	...	...	...	...	1	...	...	...	...	...	...	...	...	...	...	...
		Total Group 1		27,294	1,893	9	25,832	19	...	13,838	554	...	13,402	3	...	2,554	382	1	2,396	3	...
	2 A	Andh...		...	...	...	...	...	...	425	...	...	465	...	...	...	...	...	...	...	...
		Anjani		...	...	...	...	...	...	...	...	...	...	...	...	...	...	...	...	...	...
		Aryan		15	6	2	10	...	...	...	...	...	9	...	...	12	3	...	9	...	...
		Begari		...	...	...	...	..	...	3	1	...	8	1	...	95	2	...	95	...	...
		Gujar (Hindu)		...	...	...	...	...	...	1	...	...	...	...	...	...	...	...	...	...	...
		Gujar (Jain)		...	...	...	...	...	...	...	...	...	...	...	...	...	...	...	...	...	...
		Jat (Hindu)		...	...	...	...	...	...	...	...	...	...	...	...	...	...	...	...	...	...
		Jat (Sikh)		...	...	...	...	...	...	...	...	...	...	...	...	...	...	...	...	...	...
		Kachhi		...	...	...	...	...	...	...	...	...	...	...	...	...	...	...	...	...	...
		Kunbi		68,533	2,572	6	64,766	47	...	53,919	1,670	...	52,812	29	...	12,894	1,707	5	12,602	16	...

TABLE C.

Literate by Language known.—Provincial (Summary)—*continued.*

Class	Group.	Caste.	Religion.	AURANGABAD. Males. Total Males.	AURANGABAD. Males. Literate. Total.	AURANGABAD. Males. Literate. English.	AURANGABAD. Females. Total Females.	AURANGABAD. Females. Literate. Total.	AURANGABAD. Females. Literate. English.	BIRH. Males. Total Males.	BIRH. Males. Literate. Total.	BIRH. Males. Literate. English.	BIRH. Females. Total Females.	BIRH. Females. Literate. Total.	BIRH. Females. Literate. English.	NANDER. Males. Total Males.	NANDER. Males. Literate. Total.	NANDER. Males. Literate. English.	NANDER. Females. Total Females.	NANDER. Females. Literate. Total.	NANDER. Females. Literate. English.
				59	60	61	62	63	64	65	66	67	68	69	70	71	72	73	74	75	76
A. Agricultural—(*contd.*)		Elma		...	...	..	...	...	...	1,370	17	...	1,293	...	...	710	8	...	695	...	...
		Kshatri		816	2:6	3	566	4	...	59	...	...	43	..	...	475	13	...	472	...	...
		Kshatri (Sikh)		...	...	..	...	...	...	...	...	...	...	..	...	1	...	...	1	...	...
		Lodi		159	13	1	150	...	...	4	...	...	3	...	...	...	...	...	4	...	...
		Mahratta (Hindu)		16,332	392	3	15,872	3	...	84,348	1,145	...	81,315	24	...	79 603	1,328	2	76,134	35	...
		Mahratta (Jain)		5	2	...	4	...	...	...	...	...	...	...	...	..	...	...	...	...	...
		Munnewar		...	...	...	...	...	...	...	...	...	...	...	...	...	...	...	...	...	...
		Parbhu		2	2	...	...	...	...	...	...	...	...	..	...	...	...	...	...	...	...
		Purbiah		764	64	...	68[illegible]	1	...	18	5	...	12	...	...	21	4	...	17	...	...
		Rajpoot (Hindu)		5,404	370	6	4,84[illegible]	2	...	1,115	104	...	1,011	3	...	1,571	147	...	1,533	2	...
		Rajpoot (Jain)		...	...	...	...	...	...	...	...	...	...	...	...	...	...	...	...	...	...
		Rajpoot (Sikh)		...	...	...	...	...	...	...	...	...	...	...	...	...	...	...	...	...	...
		Rather		32	7	...	31	...	...	17	...	...	18	...	...	3	2	...	6	...	...
		Thakur		494	21	...	481	...	...	190	10	...	163	...	...	167	14	...	197	...	...
		Total Group 1.....		21,008	1,077	13	22,630	10	...	87,121	1,281	...	83,858	27	...	82,551	1,516	2	79,059	37	...
	2-A.	Andh...		36	...	...	44	...	...	...	...	...	...	...	...	2,717	7	...	2,588	2	...
		Anjani		...	...	...	...	...	...	...	...	...	...	...	...	3	...	...	3	...	...
		Aryan		13	1	...	15	...	...	4	1	...	2	..	...	..	...	...	...	...	...
		Begari		...	...	...	...	..	...	...	...	...	...	...	...	1	...	...	4	...	...
		Gujar (Hindu)		416	208	3	405	1	...	266	2	...	250	...	...	1	1	...	...	...	...
		Gujar (Jain)...		...	..	...	...	...	...	62	35	...	51	1	...	...	...	...	...	...	..
		Jat (Hindu)		22	14	...	1	...	...	101	4	...	97	...	...	...	...	...	...	...	...
		Jat (Sikh)		...	...	...	...	...	...	...	...	...	...	...	...	...	...	...	...	...	...
		Kachhi		29	...	...	25	...	...	...	...	...	...	...	...	3	...	...	...	...	...
		Kunbi		148,392	1,312	3	1,43,961	20	...	41,043	328	...	39,587	2	...	14,815	126	...	14,776	5	...

TABLE C.

Literate by Language known—Provincial (Summary)—*continued.*

Class.	Group.	Caste.	Religion.	NALDRUG. Males. Total Males.	NALDRUG. Males. Literate. Total.	NALDRUG. Males. Literate. English.	NALDRUG. Females. Total Females.	NALDRUG. Females. Literate. Total.	NALDRUG. Females. Literate. English.	BIDAR. Males. Total Males.	BIDAR. Males. Literate. Total.	BIDAR. Males. Literate. English.	BIDAR. Females. Total Females.	BIDAR. Females. Literate. Total.	BIDAR. Females. Literate. English.	PARBHANI. Males. Total Males.	PARBHANI. Males. Literate. Total.	PARBHANI. Males. Literate. English.	PARBHANI. Females. Total Females.	PARBHANI. Females. Literate. Total.	PARBHANI. Females. Literate. English.
				77	78	79	80	81	82	83	84	85	86	87	88	89	90	91	92	93	94
A. Agricultural.—(*contd.*)		Elma ...		2,038	22	...	1,863	...	...	19,599	292	...	19,298	...	...	405	...	...	410	...	...
		Kshatri		64	20	...	53	...	...	605	9	...	544	...	...	258	16	...	225	...	...
		Kshatri (Sikh)		...	...	...	...	...	...	...	...	...	...	...	...	...	...	..	...	...	...
		Lodi ...		31	1	...	24	...	...	...	...	...	...	...	...	24	8	...	18	1	...
		Mahratta (Hindu)		102,251	1,965	...	98,667	9	...	61,854	1,118	...	59,258	12	...	103,892	899	...	99,920	5	...
		Mahratta (Jain)		...	..	...	...	...	...	...	...	...	...	...	...	..	...	...	...	...	...
		Munnewar		...	...	...	...	...	...	10	...	...	8	...	...	...	...	...	...	...	...
		Parbhu		3	1	...	2	...	...	2	1	...	3	...	...	4	3	...	6	...	...
		Purbiah		25	1	...	42	...	...	34	10	...	7	...	...	154	15	..	120	...	...
		Rajpoot (Hindu)		1,497	118	...	1,329	...	...	1,494	130	...	1,464	1	...	1,548	236	1	1,272	3	...
		Rajpoot (Jain)		...	...	...	...	...	...	...	...	...	...	...	...	3	...	...	...	...	...
		Rajpoot (Sikh)		...	...	...	...	...	...	...	...	...	...	...	...	16	7	...	11	...	...
		Rathor		...	...	...	...	...	...	19	...	...	10	...	...	25	6	...	15	..	...
		Thakur		234	7	...	216	...	...	118	9	...	165	...	...	316	11	...	337	...	...
		Total Group 1 ...		106,143	2,135	...	102,196	9	...	83,735	1,651	...	80,757	13	...	106,645	1,201	1	102,334	9	...
	2-A.	Andh ..		...	...	...	...	...	...	...	...	...	...	...	...	5,892	8	...	5,614	...	...
		Anjani		...	...	...	..	...	...	...	...	...	...	...	...	7	...	...	8	...	...
		Aryan		8	...	...	8	...	...	...	...	...	...	...	...	1	...	...	2	...	...
		Begari		...	...	...	...	...	...	...	...	...	...	...	...	12	1	...	4	...	...
		Gujar (Hindu)		...	...	...	...	...	...	13	4	...	10	...	...	6	...	...	...	...	...
		Gujar (Jain) ...		204	125	...	188	1	...	...	...	...	...	...	...	...	...	...	...	...	...
		Jat (Hindu) ...		...	...	...	...	...	...	...	...	...	...	...	...	6	2	...	...	...	...
		Jat (Sikh) ...		...	...	..	...	...	...	...	...	...	...	...	...	161	61	1	27	1	...
		Kachhi		...	...	...	...	...	...	...	...	...	...	...	...	...	...	...	...	...	...
		Kunbi		20,621	215	...	20,001	...	...	5,200	147	...	5,283	4	...	46,982	395	1	45,841	...	...

TABLE C.

Literate by Language known.—Provincial (Summary)—*continued.*

Class.	Group.	Caste.	Religion.	SIRPUR TANDUR.						GULBARGA.						RAICHUR					
				Males.			Females.			Males.			Females.			Males.			Females.		
				Total Males.	Literate. Total.	Literate. English.	Total Females.	Literate. Total.	Literate. English.	Total Males	Literate. Total.	Literate. English.	Total Females.	Literate. Total.	Literate. English.	Total Males.	Literate. Total.	Literate. English.	Total Females.	Literate. Total.	Literate. English.
				85	86	87	88	89	90	91	92	93	94	95	96	97	98	99	100	101	102
A. Agricultural—(contd.)	1	Elma...		4'3	17	...	473	...	...	2,230	43	1	2,083	...	...	1,47[illegible]	5	...	1,403	...	...
		Kshatri		...	...	...	...	...	...	1,412	192	2	1,412	1	...	958	272	3	759	3	...
		Kshatri (Sikh)		...	...	...	...	...	...	...	...	...	...	...	...	...	...	...	...	...	...
		Lodi ...		8	...	...	14	...	...	2	...	...	...	...	...	8	3	...	4	...	...
		Mahratta (Hindu)		2,648	25	...	2,470	...	...	7,179	192	10	6,918	1	...	1,706	126	1	1,787	2	...
		Mahratta (Jain)		...	...	...	...	...	...	...	...	...	...	...	...	...	...	...	...	...	...
		Munnewar		...	...	...	...	...	...	...	...	...	...	...	...	1	...	...	4	...	...
		Parbhu		...	...	...	...	...	...	22	5	1	44	...	...	6	2	1	6	...	...
		Purbiah		1	1	...	1	...	...	2	1	...	5	...	...	...	...	...	...	...	...
		Rajpoot (Hindu)		242	25	...	2:4	...	...	2,163	124	1	2,016	...	...	886	111	...	885	1	...
		Rajpoot (Jain)		...	...	...	...	...	...	...	...	...	...	...	...	...	...	...	...	...	...
		Rajpoot (Sikh)		...	...	...	...	...	...	...	...	...	...	...	...	...	...	...	...	...	...
		Rathor		...	...	...	...	...	...	68	...	...	67	...	...	2	...	...	3	...	...
		Thakur		7	...	...	7	...	...	7	1	...	8	...	...	11	1	...	12	...	...
		Total Group 1......		3,399	68	...	3,189	...	...	13,085	558	15	12,553	2	...	5,053	520	5	4,863	6	...
	2 A	Andh ..		219	...	...	209	...	...	...	...	...	...	...	...	...	...	...	...	...	...
		Anjani		304	2	...	314	...	...	...	...	...	...	...	...	...	...	...	...	...	...
		Aryan		...	...	...	...	...	...	18	3	2	17	...	...	52	...	...	59	...	...
		Begari		...	...	...	..	...	...	10	...	...	15	...	...	749	2	...	759	...	...
		Gujar (Hindu)		2	...	...	1	...	...	...	...	...	...	...	...	23	4	...	19	...	...
		Gujar (Jain)...		...	...	...	...	...	...	4	3	...	4	...	...	...	...	...	...	...	...
		Jat (Hindu)...		...	...	...	...	...	...	...	...	...	...	...	...	...	...	...	...	...	...
		Jat (Sikh)		...	...	..	...	...	...	...	...	...	...	...	...	...	...	...	...	...	...
		Kachhi		...	...	...	...	...	...	...	...	...	...	...	...	5	3	...	2	...	...
		Kunbi		23,841	173	1	23,404	...	...	13,907	412	1	13,453	2	...	19,910	2,409	4	19,293	19	...

TABLE C.

Literate by Language known.—Provincial (Summary)—*continued.*

Class.	Group.	Caste.	Religion.	LINGASUGUR.						RAILWAYS.					
				MALES.			FEMALES.			MALES.			FEMALES.		
				Total Males.	Literate. Total.	Literate. English.	Total Females.	Literate. Total.	Literate. English.	Total Males.	Literate. Total.	Literate. English.	Total Females.	Literate. Total.	Literate. English.
				103	104	105	106	107	108	109	110	111	112	113	114
A. Agricultural—(*contd.*)	1	Elma ..	...	68	4	...	66	...	...	6	2	2	4	3	...
		Kshatri	...	1,054	30	...	1,099	...	...	...	...	...	...	...	...
		Kshatri (Sikh)	...	...	...	...	...	...	...	...	...	...	...	...	...
		Lodi ...	...	...	...	...	...	...	...	...	...	...	...	...	...
		Mahratta (Hindu)	...	2,476	111	...	2,498	1	...	208	30	8	141	...	...
		Mahratta (Jain)	...	...	...	...	...	...	...	...	...	...	...	...	...
		Munnewar	...	...	...	...	...	...	...	...	...	...	...	...	...
		Parbhu	...	1	1	...	...	...	...	1	1	1	3	...	...
		Purbiah	...	2	...	...	2	...	...	...	...	...	...	...	...
		Rajpoot (Hindu)	...	1,396	95	1	1,384	1	...	55	14	3	28	...	...
		Rajpoot (Jain)	...	...	...	...	...	...	...	...	...	...	...	...	...
		Rajpoot (Sikh)	...	...	...	...	...	...	...	...	...	...	...	...	...
		Rathor	...	...	...	...	...	...	...	...	...	...	...	...	...
		Thakur	...	...	...	...	...	...	...	...	...	...	...	...	...
		Total Group 1 ...		4,997	241	1	5,049	2	...	270	47	14	176	3	...
	2 A	Andh ...	...	...	...	...	...	...	...	...	...	...	...	...	...
		Anjani	...	...	...	...	...	...	...	...	...	...	...	...	...
		Aryan	...	15	...	...	15	...	...	2	2	1	...	...	...
		Begari	...	1,014	16	2	1,105	...	...	...	...	...	...	...	...
		Gujar (Hindu)	...	30	...	...	27	...	...	...	...	...	...	...	...
		Gujar (Jain)...	...	...	...	...	...	...	...	...	...	...	...	...	...
		Jat (Hindu) ...	...	...	...	...	...	...	...	4	...	...	...	...	...
		Jat (Sikh)	...	...	...	...	...	...	...	...	...	...	...	...	...
		Kachhi	...	...	...	...	...	...	...	...	...	...	...	...	...
		Kunbi	...	28,518	2,060	1	27,842	1	...	168	29	7	96	3	...

TABLE C.

Literate by Language known—Provincial (Summary)—*continued.*

Class.	Group.	Caste.	Religion	TOTAL STRENGTH.						HYDERABAD.						ATRAF-I-BALDA.					
				Males.			Females.			Males.			Females.			Males.			Females.		
				Total Males.	Literate.		Total Females.	Literate.		Total Males.	Literate.		Total Females.	Literate.		Total Males.	Literate.		Total Females.	Literate.	
					Total.	English.		Total.	English.		Total.	English.		Total.	English.		Total.	English.		Total.	English.
1	2	3	4	5	6	7	8	9	10	11	12	13	14	15	16	17	18	19	20	21	22
A. Agricultural—(contd.)	2-A.	Mali ...		50,290	371	13	49,693	9	...	368	56	10	371	4	...	...	...	...	...	...	...
		Morai...		9	4	1	5	...	...	...	...	...	...	...	...	...	...	...	...	...	...
		Munnurwar ...		60,772	1,929	14	61,211	182	1	3,482	462	11	3,707	31	1	3,424	247	...	3,868	25	...
		Mushti		4,763	53	...	4,554	1	...	...	...	...	...	...	...	...	...	...	...	...	...
		Mutrasi		93,365	936	29	89,195	55	...	3,716	465	17	3,612	13	...	10,446	96	2	10,108	15	...
		Naidu...		297	134	67	258	7	2	259	115	56	227	7	2	...	...	...	...	...	...
		Pichakuntla ...		2,631	21	...	2,462	..	...	...	...	...	...	...	...	557	2	...	539	...	...
		Reddi		27,263	1,737	30	26,976	32	2	126	41	5	107	...	...	125	21	1	120	...	...
		Satani		6,105	2,290	12	5,907	45	...	31	17	7	40	3	...	314	159	...	366	4	...
		Tirmali		405	2	...	426	...	...	...	...	...	...	...	...	...	...	...	...	...	...
		Vanjari		3,430	258	...	3,380	2	...	69	26	...	43	...	...	543	8	...	587	2	...
		Total Group 2-A		890,716	29,977	573	865,736	739	14	14,749	2,750	449	14,179	208	12	37,404	1,809	7	37,195	62	...
	2-B.	Ahir		832	144	4	603	1	..	203	47	3	142	...	...	...	...	...	...	...	...
		Gaoli		7,932	145	9	6,637	2	...	1,274	78	9	1,210	1	...	353	8	...	312	...	...
		Koli		135,297	766	6	134,911	43	...	1,667	93	3	1,623	3	...	586	6	...	578	...	...
		Total Group 2-B		143,131	1,055	19	142,151	46	...	3,144	218	15	2,975	4	...	939	14	...	890	...	...
	2-C.	Dher		635,199	1,961	117	624,260	63	1	19,141	697	94	19,490	16	1	26,332	32	...	25,189	4	...
		Mang		156,134	424	6	156,988	8	...	1,762	107	6	1,906	1	...	293	3	...	284	...	...
		Total Group 2-C		791,333	2,385	123	781,248	71	1	20,903	804	100	21,396	17	1	26,625	35	...	25,473	4	...
	4	Bhil	Bhil	235	...	...	235	...	...	...	...	...	...	...	...	...	...	...	...	...	...
		Do. (Hindu)	Hindu	5,179	9	2	5,366	...	...	9	3	2	5	...	...	...	...	...	...	...	...
		Do. (Mussulman)	Mussalman	37	...	...	45	...	...	...	...	...	...	...	...	...	...	...	...	...	...
		Chentchulawad	Hindu	5,441	5	...	5,200	...	...	...	...	...	...	...	...	36	2	...	45	...	...
		Gond	Gond	14,637	11	...	14,023	1	..	...	...	...	...	...	...	...	...	...	...	...	...
		Gond	Hindu	4,737	34	...	4,598	...	...	...	...	...	...	...	...	...	...	...	...	...	...
		Koya	Hindu	30,724	67	...	30,687	2	...	...	...	...	...	...	...	7	...	...	9	...	...

TABLE C.

Literate by Language known—Provincial (Summary)—*continued.*

Class.	Group.	Caste.	Religion.	MAHBUBNAGAR.						NALGONDA.						WARANGAL.					
				Males.			Females.			Males.			Females.			Males.			Females.		
				Total Males.	Literate.		Total Females.	Literate.		Total Males.	Litorate.		Total Females.	Literate.		Total Males.	Literate.		Total Females.	Literate.	
					Total.	English.		Total.	English.		Total	English.		Total.	English.		Total.	English.		Total.	English.
				23	24	25	26	27	28	29	30	31	32	33	34	35	36	37	38	39	40
A. Agricultural—(*contd.*)	2-A.	Mali ...		...	...	...	...	...	...	...	...	...	...	...	...	...	...	...	...	...	...
		Morai		...	...	...	...	...	...	...	...	...	...	...	...	...	...	...	...	...	...
		Munnurwar		5,089	198	...	5,108	20	...	1,413	40	...	1,403	2	...	3,453	92	...	3,401	7	...
		Mushti		4,565	40	...	4,362	1	...	...	...	...	...	...	...	15	...	...	18	...	...
		Mutrasi		18,515	65	...	17,740	7	...	16,019	106	8	15,570	...	...	19,472	64	...	17,917	12	...
		Naidu...		3	2	...	1	...	...	3	2	...	2	...	...	2	2	...	6	...	...
		Pichakuntla		920	1	...	845	...	...	355	8	...	310	...	...	294	6	...	215	...	...
		Reddi ...		75	18	5	69	11	2	5,692	441	12	5,653	4	...	8,786	570	4	8,868	9	...
		Satani		434	198	...	395	4	...	575	241	...	527	6	...	1,300	498	3	1,137	9	...
		Tirmali		...	...	...	..	...	...	...	...	...	...	...	...	...	...	...	...	...	...
		Vanjari		64	2	...	21	...	...	361	38	...	456	...	...	465	8	...	429	...	...
		Total Group 2 A		65,987	3,256	10	64,296	107	2	55,593	2,234	28	53,840	24	...	67,265	2,476	15	64,142	56	..
	2-B.	Ahir ...		...	...	...	...	...	...	...	...	...	...	...	...	...	...	...	...	...	...
		Gaoli...		95	1	...	77	...	...	2	...	...	1	...	...	6	...	...	2	...	...
		Koli ...		...	...	...	...	...	...	...	...	...	...	...	...	582	2	...	450	...	...
		Total Group 2-B		95	1	...	77	...	...	2	...	...	1	...	...	588	2	...	452	...	...
	2-C.	Dher ...		43,973	31	2	41,661	5	...	46,514	72	...	43,914	1	...	53,786	83	1	50,076	8	...
		Mang ..		...	...	...	...	...	...	...	...	...	...	...	...	82	...	...	68	...	...
		Total Group 2-C		43,973	31	2	41,661	5	...	46,514	72	...	43,914	1	...	53,868	83	1	50,144	8	...
	4	Bhil ...	Bhil ...	...	...	...	...	...	...	...	...	...	...	...	...	...	...	...	...	...	...
		Do. (Hindu)	Hindu ..	...	...	...	...	...	...	...	...	...	...	...	...	...	...	...	...	...	...
		Do. (Mussulman)...	Mussulman	...	...	...	...	...	...	...	...	...	...	...	...	...	...	...	...	...	...
		Chentchulawad	Hindu ...	1,278	...	...	1,249	...	...	270	...	...	223	...	...	104	2	...	101	...	...
		Gond...	Gond ...	...	...	...	...	...	...	...	...	...	...	...	...	...	...	...	...	...	...
		Gond...	Hindu ..	...	...	...	...	...	...	...	...	...	...	...	...	...	...	...	...	...	...
		Koya...	Hindu ...	2	1	...	2	1	...	22	...	...	21	...	...	28,263	45	...	27,560	1	...

TABLE C.

Literate by Language known—Provincial (Summary)—*continued.*

Class.	Group.	Caste.	Religion.	ELGANDAL.						INDUR.						MEDAK.					
				Males.			Females.			Males.			Females.			Males.			Females.		
				Total Males.	Literate. Total.	Literate. English.	Total Females.	Literate. Total.	Literate. English.	Total Males.	Literate. Total.	Literate. English.	Total Females.	Literate. Total.	Literate. English.	Total Maels.	Literate. Total	Literate. English.	Total Females.	Literate. Total.	Literate. English.
				41	42	43	44	45	46	47	48	49	50	51	52	53	54	55	56	57	58
A. Agricultural—(*contd.*)	2-A.	Mali		...	...	...	...	...	...	362	1	...	335	1	...	...	...	...	...	...	...
		Morai		...	...	...	...	...	...	...	...	...	...	...	...	...	...	...	...	...	...
		Munnurwar		11,182	173	...	10,762	21	...	11,906	229	...	11,912	11	...	4,331	242	...	4,462	18	...
		Mushti		...	...	...	...	...	...	...	...	...	...	...	...	183	12	...	174	...	...
		Mutrasi		10,148	28	...	9,608	4	...	452	1	...	445	...	...	13,409	98	1	13,031	4	...
		Naidu		...	...	...	...	...	...	...	...	...	...	...	...	...	...	...	...	...	...
		Pichakuntla		90	...	...	74	..	...	29	3	...	24	...	...	230	1	...	229	...	...
		Reddi		44	12	...	51	...	...	373	4	..	352	...	...	9	1	...	6	...	...
		Satani		2,139	724	1	2,151	7	...	202	91	...	228	1	...	624	277	...	659	10	...
		Tirmali		...	...	...	...	...	...	...	...	...	...	...	...	...	...	...	...	...	...
		Vanjari		895	17	...	770	...	...	...	...	...	...	...	...	997	85	...	1,013	...	...
		Group Total 2 A		93,096	3,532	9	88,192	79	...	67,672	2,000	...	66,610	43	...	32,779	2,429	6	32,310	48	...
	2-B.	Ahir		...	...	...	...	...	...	...	...	...	...	...	...	...	...	...	...	...	...
		Gaoli		14	...	...	12	...	...	121	10	...	122	...	...	2	...	...	4	...	...
		Koli		595	...	...	501	...	...	18,521	75	...	19,100	8	...	278	...	...	286	...	...
		Total Group 2-B		609	...	...	513	...	...	18,642	85	...	19,222	8	...	280	...	...	290	...	...
	2-C.	Dher		60,725	37	...	56,849	1	...	31,114	79	...	32,097	3	...	21,194	42	...	20,981	2	...
		Mang		41	...	...	39	...	...	23,628	15	...	23,840	...	...	64	...	...	62	...	...
		Total Group 2 C		60,766	37	...	56,888	1	...	547,42	94	...	55,927	3	...	21 258	42	...	21,043	2	...
	4	Bhil	Bhil	...	...	...	...	...	...	...	...	...	...	...	...	...	...	...	...	...	...
		Do. (Hindu)	Hindu	...	...	...	...	...	...	30	...	...	27	...	...	...	...	...	...	...	...
		Do. (Mussulman)	Mussulman	...	...	...	...	...	...	...	...	...	...	...	...	...	...	...	...	...	...
		Chentchulawad	Hindu	3,632	1	...	3,484	...	...	8	...	...	7	...	...	34	...	...	30	...	...
		Gond	Gond	...	...	...	...	...	...	273	5	...	265	...	...	...	...	...	...	...	...
		Gond	Hindu	...	...	...	...	...	...	...	...	...	...	...	...	...	...	...	...	...	...
		Koya	Hindu	2,015	2	...	2,014	...	...	...	...	...	...	...	...	...	...	...	..	...	...

TABLE C.

Literate by Language known—Provincial (Summary)—*continued.*

Class.	Group.	Caste.	Religion.	AURANGABAD.						BIRH.						NANDER.					
				Males.			Females.			Males.			Females.			Males.			Females		
				Total Males.	Literate.		Total Females.	Literate.		Total Males.	Literate.		Total Females.	Literate.		Total Males.	Literate.		Total Females.	Literate.	
					Total.	English.		Total.	English.		Total.	English.		Total.	English.		Total.	English.		Total.	English.
				59	60	61	62	63	64	65	66	67	68	69	70	71	72	73	74	75	76
A. Agricultural—(*contd.*)	2-A.	Mali		14 553	99	...	14,542	...	...	8,819	52	...	8,699	...	...	1,493	7	...	1,416	...	...
		Morai		5	3	...	2	...	...	...	...	...	...	...	...	...	...	...	...	...	...
		Munnurwar		12	5	...	36	...	...	...	...	...	...	...	...	9,586	60	...	9,634	6	...
		Mushti		...	...	...	...	...	...	...	...	...	...	...	...	...	...	...	...	...	...
		Mutrasi		21	5	...	21	...	...	...	...	...	...	...	...	...	...	...	...	...	...
		Naidu		...	...	...	...	...	...	...	...	...	...	...	...	...	...	...	...	...	...
		Pichakuntla		...	...	...	...	...	...	...	...	...	...	...	...	...	...	...	...	...	...
		Reddi		1	1	...	2	...	...	..	...	...	...	...	...	7	...	...	7	...	...
		Satani		...	...	...	...	...	...	23	...	...	21	...	...	...	...	...	...	...	...
		Tirmali		89	...	...	72	...	...	165	1	...	199	...	...	...	...	...	...	...	...
		Vanjari		...	...	...	...	...	...	...	...	...	...	...	...	...	...	...	...	...	...
		Total Group 2-A		163,589	1,648	6	159,126	21	...	50,483	423	...	48.906	3	...	28,626	201	...	28,428	13	...
	2-B.	Ahir		338	39	...	271	...	...	7	...	...	7	...	...	...	...	...	...	...	...
		Gaoli		791	8	...	736	...	...	419	2	...	408	...	...	1,210	11	...	1,199	...	...
		Koli		4,120	16	...	4,056	...	...	2,053	10	...	1,945	2	...	10,101	28	...	10,248	6	...
		Total Group 2-B		5,252	63	..	5,063	...	...	2 479	12	...	2,360	2	...	11.311	39	...	11.447	6	...
	2-C.	Dher		41,195	162	...	42,807	7	...	29.241	33	...	28,882	...	...	30,534	38	...	31,471	1	...
		Mang		12,316	146	...	12,481	3	...	14,234	3	...	13 873	...	...	19,773	5	...	20.307	...	...
		Total Group 2-C		53,511	308	...	55,288	10	...	43,475	36	...	42,755	...	...	50,307	43	...	51,778	1	...
	4	Bhil	Bhil ...	...	...	...	...	...	...	...	...	...	...	...	...	...	...	...	...	...	...
		Do. (Hindu)	Hindu	4,517	6	...	4,725	...	...	355	..	...	341	...	...	3	...	...	...	...	...
		Do. (Mussulman)	Mussulman	37	...	...	45	...	...	...	...	...	...	...	...	...	...	...	...	...	...
		Chentchulawad	Hindu ...	...	...	...	...	...	...	...	...	...	...	..	...	12	...	...	8	...	...
		Gond	Gond ...	...	...	...	...	...	...	...	...	...	...	...	...	4	...	...	2	...	...
		Gond	Hindu ..	42	5	...	31	...	...	149	8	...	135	...	...	188	5	...	191	...	...
		Koya	Hindu ...	...	...	...	...	...	...	...	...	...	...	...	...	...	...	...	...	...	...

TABLE C.

Literature by Language known—Provincial (Summary).—*continued.*

Class.	Group.	Caste.	Religion.	NALDRUG.						BIDAR.						PARBHANI.					
				Males.			Females.			Males.			Females.			Males.			Females.		
				Total Males.	Literate.		Total Females.	Literate.		Total Males.	Literate.		Total Females.	Literate.		Total Males.	Literate.		Total Females.	Literate.	
					Total.	English.		Total.	English.		Total.	English.		Total.	English.		Total.	English.		Total.	English.
				77	78	79	80	81	82	83	84	85	86	87	88	80	90	91	92	93	94
A. Agricultural—(*contd*).	2-A.	Mali ...		7791	61	...	7,536	1	...	1,423	15	...	1 361	2	...	13 172	52	...	13,110	1	...
		Morai		...	...	...	...	...	...	...	...	...	...	...	...	4	1	1	2	...	...
		Munnurwar ...		7	6	...	3	...	..	1,261	25	...	1,323	...	...	31	3	...	21	...	...
		Mushti		...	...	...	...	...	..	...	...	...	...	..	...	...	...	...	...	...	...
		Mutrasi		...	...	...	...	...	...	48	...	...	48	...	...	5	1	1	4	...	...
		Naidu		...	...	...	...	...	...	...	...	...	...	...	...	...	...	...	...	...	...
		Pichakuntla ...		...	...	...	...	...	...	19	...	...	16	...	...	...	...	...	...	...	...
		Reddi		27	...	...	29	..	...	1,140	29	1	1,192	2	...	...	...	...	...	...	...
		Satani		...	...	...	..	...	...	6	6	...	4	...	...	...	...	...	...	...	...
		Tirmali		...	...	...	...	...	...	9	...	...	11	...	...	129	...	...	130	...	...
		Vanjari		...	...	...	...	...	...	...	...	...	...	...	...	...	...	...	...	...	...
		Total Group 2-A		28,658	407	...	27,765	2	...	9,119	226	1	9,248	8	...	66,408	524	4	64 764	2	...
	2-B.	Ahir ...		...	...	...	...	...	...	...	...	...	...	...	...	102	19	1	54	...	...
		Gaoli...		286	10	...	256	1	...	554	3	...	513	...	...	862	7	...	767	...	...
		Koli ...		5.569	46	...	5,474	...	...	23,631	70	...	23,699	...	...	3,234	42	...	3 245	2	...
		Total Group 2-B		5,855	56	...	5,730	1	...	24 185	73	...	24,212	...	...	4,198	68	1	4,665	2	...
	2-C.	Dher ...		34 820	47	...	34,362	...	...	41,720	16	...	41.795	2	...	48 392	170	...	48,997	1	...
		Mang...		16.665	5	...	16,670	...	...	34.357	4	...	34.402	...	...	14.144	116	...	14,628	3	...
		Total Group 2-C		51,485	52	...	51,032	...	...	76,077	20	...	76,197	2	..	62,536	286	...	63,625	4	...
	4	Bhil ...	Bhil ...	...	...	...	...	...	...	...	...	...	...	...	...	...	...	...	...	...	...
		Do. (Hindu)	Hindu ...	...	...	...	...	...	...	...	...	...	...	...	...	117	...	...	111	...	...
		Do. (Mussulman)...	Mussulman	...	...	...	...	...	...	...	...	...	...	...	...	...	...	...	...	...	...
		Chentchulawad	Hindu ...	...	...	...	...	...	...	26	...	...	24	...	...	...	...	...	...	...	...
		Gond	Gond ...	...	...	...	...	...	...	...	...	...	...	...	...	...	...	...	...	...	...
		Gond	Hindu ...	9	...	...	11	...	...	137	2	...	129	...	...	31	...	...	24	...	...
		Koya	Hindu ...	...	...	...	...	...	...	...	...	...	...	...	...	...	...	...	...	...	...

TABLE C.

Literate by Language known—Provincial (Summary)—*continued.*

Class.	Group.	Caste.	Religion.	SIRPUR TANDUR. Males. Total Males.	SIRPUR TANDUR. Males. Literate. Total.	SIRPUR TANDUR. Males. Literate. English.	SIRPUR TANDUR. Females. Total Females.	SIRPUR TANDUR. Females. Literate. Total.	SIRPUR TANDUR. Females. Literate. English.	GULBURGA. Males. Total Males.	GULBURGA. Males. Literate. Total.	GULBURGA. Males. Literate. English.	GULBURGA. Females. Total Females.	GULBURGA. Females. Literate. Total.	GULBURGA. Females. Literate. English.	RAICHUR. Males. Total Males.	RAICHUR. Males. Literate. Total.	RAICHUR. Males. Literate. English.	RAICHUR. Females. Total Females.	RAICHUR. Females. Literate. Total.	RAICHUR. Females. Literate. English.
				95	96	97	98	99	100	101	102	103	104	105	106	107	108	109	110	111	112
A. Agricultural—(*contd*).	2-A.	Mali ...		966	3	...	989	...	...	801	17	1	827	...	...	469	2	...	442	...	..
		Morai		...	...	...	...	...	...	...	...	...	...	...	...	...	...	...	...	...	...
		Munnurwar ...		1,387	6	...	1,354	...	...	1,245	24	...	1,309	4	...	2,842	109	...	2,783	27	...
		Mushti		...	...	...	...	...	...	...	...	...	...	...	...	...	...	...	...	...	...
		Mutrasi		...	...	...	...	...	...	975	4	...	988	...	...	86	...	...	86	...	...
		Naidu		...	...	...	...	...	...	8	1	1	5	...	...	5	...	...	6	...	...
		Pichakuntla...		...	...	...	...	...	...	2	...	...	2	...	...	125	...	...	104	...	...
		Reddi		...	...	...	...	...	...	2,864	148	1	2,897	...	...	2,187	99	...	2,006	4	...
		Satani		...	...	...	...	...	...	1	...	...	1	...	...	3`8	52	...	286	...	...
		Tirmali		13	1	...	14	...	...	...	...	...	...	...	...	...	...	...	...	...	...
		Vanjari		...	...	...	...	...	...	...	...	...	...	...	...	7	...	...	9	...	...
		Total Group 2-A		26 732	185	1	26,315	...	...	19,835	612	6	19,518	6	...	26,76?	2,68?	4	25,854	50	...
	2-B.	Ahir ...		4	1	...	3	...	...	1	...	...	...	...	...	48	21	...	12	1	...
		Gaoli...		642	...	...	624	...	...	299	6	...	272	...	...	3?	1	...	37	...	...
		Koli ...		1,315	6	...	1,278	...	...	36,484	98	1	35,891	5	...	12,222	128	...	11,870	1	...
		Total Group 2-B		1 961	7	...	1,905	...	...	3,6784	104	1	36,163	5	...	12,303	150	...	11,919	2	...
	2.C.	Dher ...		11,935	24	...	11,913	...	...	30,156	30	...	29,331	...	...	36,621	272	14	35,226	12	...
		Mang		2,510	...	...	2,482	...	...	16 028	14	...	15,817	1	...	...	...	...	...	...	...
		Total Group 2-C		14,445	24	...	14 395	...	...	46 184	44	...	45,148	1	...	36,621	272	14	35,226	12	...
	4	Bhil ...	Bhil ...	235	...	...	235	...	...	...	...	...	...	...	...	...	...	...	...	...	...
		Do. (Hindu)	Hindu ...	134	...	...	138	...	...	12	...	...	12	...	...	...	...	...	...	...	...
		Do. (Mussulman)	Mussulman	...	...	...	...	...	...	...	...	...	...	...	...	...	...	...	...	...	...
		Chentchulawad	Hindu ...	...	...	...	...	...	...	...	...	...	...	...	...	41	...	...	29	...	...
		Gond...	Gond ..	14,360	6	...	13,716	1	...	...	...	...	...	...	...	...	...	...	...	...	...
		Gond...	Hindu ...	4,160	14	...	4,060	...	...	19	...	...	17	...	...	...	...	...	...	...	...
		Koya...	Hindu ...	...	...	...	...	...	...	...	...	...	...	...	...	...	...	...	...	...	...

TABLE C.

Literate by Language known.—Provincial Summary—*continued.*

Class.	Group.	Caste.	Religion.	LINGASUGUR. Males. Total Males.	LINGASUGUR. Males. Literate. Total.	LINGASUGUR. Males. Literate. English.	LINGASUGUR. Females. Total Females.	LINGASUGUR. Females. Literate. Total.	LINGASUGUR. Females. Literate. English.	RAILWAY. Males. Total Males.	RAILWAY. Males. Literate. Total.	RAILWAY. Males. Literate. English.	RAILWAY. Females. Total Females.	RAILWAY. Females. Literate. Total.	RAILWAY. Females. Literate. English.
				113	114	115	116	117	118	119	120	121	122	123	124
A. Agricultural—*contd.*	2 A.	Mali		55	2	...	54	...	...	18	4	2	11	...	...
		Morai		...	...	...	...	...	...	...	...	...	...	...	...
		Munnurwar		113	7	3	132	...	...	8	1	...	2	...	...
		Mushti		...	...	...	...	...	...	...	...	...	...	...	...
		Mutrasi		...	...	...	...	...	...	43	3	...	17	...	...
		Naidu		...	...	...	...	...	...	17	12	10	11	...	...
		Pichakuntla		4	...	...	4	...	...	...	...	...	...	...	...
		Reddi		5,806	415	...	5,617	2	...	11	7	...	...	...	...
		Satani		93	26	1	86	1	...	5	1	...	4	...	...
		Tirmali		...	...	...	...	...	...	...	...	...	...	...	...
		Vanjari		31	...	...	22	...	...	..	...	...	...	...	...
		Total Group 2-A		35,682	2,526	7	34,907	4	...	276	59	20	141	3	...
	2-B.	Ahir		98	16	...	114	...	...	1	1	...	...	...	...
		Gaoli		65	...	...	83	...	...	1	...	...	2	...	...
		Koli		14,250	144	2	14,632	16	...	89	2	...	35	...	...
		Total Group 2-B		14,413	160	2	14,829	16	...	91	3	...	37	...	...
	2-C.	Dher		27,327	74	3	28,872	...	...	479	22	3	347	...	...
		Mang		...	...	...	...	...	...	237	6	...	129	...	...
		Total Group 2-C		27,327	74	3	28,872	...	...	716	28	3	476	...	...
	4	Bhil	Bhil ...	...	...	...	...	...	...	...	...	...	...	...	...
		Do. (Hindu)	Hindu ...	...	...	...	...	...	...	2	...	...	7	...	...
		Do. (Mussulman)	Mussulman	...	...	...	...	...	...	...	...	...	...	...	...
		Chentchulawad	Hindu ...	...	...	...	...	...	...	...	...	...	...	...	...
		Gond...	Gond ...	...	...	...	...	...	...	...	...	...	...	...	...
		Gond...	Hindu ...	...	...	...	...	...	...	2	...	...	...	...	...
		Koya...	Hindu ...	415	19	...	472	...	...	...	...	...	...	...	...

TABLE C.

Literate by Language known.—Provincial (Summary)—*continued.*

Class.	Group.	Caste.	Religion.	TOTAL STRENGTH.						HYDERABAD.						ATRAF-I-BALDA.					
				Males.			Females.			Males.			Females.			Males.			Females.		
				Total Males.	Literate.		Total Females.	Literate.		Total Males.	Literate.		Total Females.	Literate.		Total Males.	Literate.		Total Females.	Literate.	
					Total.	English.		Total.	English.		Total.	English.		Total.	English.		Total.	English.		Total.	English.
1	2	3	4	5	6	7	8	9	10	11	12	13	14	15	16	17	18	19	20	21	22
A. Agricultural—(*concld.*)		Oterwani		2	...	...	2	...	...	...	...	...	...	...	...	...	...	...	...	...	...
		Total Group 4.....		60,992	126	2	59,556	3	...	9	3	2	5	...	...	43	2	...	54	...	...
		Total Class A		2,490,521	50,464	891	2,417,473	1,090	15	50,686	5,771	672	48,629	273	13	67,920	2,204	9	66,281	73	...
	5	Brahmin		140,884	80,171	589	129,548	821	5	10,072	4,211	263	7,438	118	2	2,677	1 694	3	2,509	27	...
		Jangam		52,694	9,122	17	52,688	93	...	406	84	3	361	5	...	1,355	476	...	1,358	6	...
		Total Group 5		193,569	89,293	606	182,236	914	5	10,478	4,295	266	7,799	123	2	4,032	2,170	3	3,867	33	...
(B). Professional.	6	Aghore		5	...	...	6	...	...	...	...	...	...	...	...	...	...	...	...	...	...
		Arti		1	...	...	2	...	...	...	...	...	...	...	...	...	...	...	...	...	...
		Bairagi		2 875	181	1	2,207	3	...	178	36	1	95	1	...	125	7	...	67	...	...
		Degamber Hindu		58	1	...	46	...	...	...	...	...	...	...	...	...	...	...	...	...	...
		Devara		1	...	...	1	...	...	...	...	...	...	...	...	...	...	...	...	...	...
		Gadaria		3	...	...	1	...	...	...	...	...	...	...	...	...	...	...	...	...	...
		Gondarwandlu		4	...	...	6	...	...	...	...	...	...	...	...	...	...	...	...	...	...
		Gosain		14,971	1,100	3	12,171	6	...	493	161	3	236	...	...	106	15	...	7[illegible]	...	...
		Gosiga		734	10	...	666	1	...	...	...	...	...	...	...	...	...	...	...	...	...
		Gotralvarn		4	...	...	3	...	...	...	...	...	...	...	...	...	...	...	...	...	...
		Gayansagar		3	...	...	5	...	...	...	...	...	...	...	...	...	...	...	...	...	...
		Jogi		2,917	78	...	2,922	...	...	86	6	...	76	...	...	...	...	...	...	...	...
		Kulpand		6	...	...	4	...	...	...	...	...	...	...	...	...	...	...	...	...	...

TABLE C.

Literate by Language known.—Provincial (Summary).—*continued.*

Class.	Group.	Caste.	Religion.	MAHBUBNAGAR. Males. Total Males.	MAHBUBNAGAR. Males. Literate. Total.	MAHBUBNAGAR. Males. Literate. English.	MAHBUBNAGAR. Females. Total Females.	MAHBUBNAGAR. Females. Literate. Total.	MAHBUBNAGAR. Females. Literate. English.	NALGONDA. Males. Total Males.	NALGONDA. Males. Literate. Total.	NALGONDA. Males. Literate. English.	NALGONDA. Females. Total Females.	NALGONDA. Females. Literate. Total.	NALGONDA. Females. Literate. English.	WARANGAL. Males. Total Males.	WARANGAL. Males. Literate. Total.	WARANGAL. Males. Literate. English.	WARANGAL. Females. Total Females.	WARANGAL. Females. Literate. Total.	WARANGAL. Females. Literate. English.
				23	24	25	26	27	28	29	30	31	32	33	34	35	36	37	38	39	40
A. Agricultural—(concld.)		Oterwani		...	...	...	...	...	...	...	...	...	...	...	...	...	...	...	...	...	...
		Total Group 4		1,280	1	...	1,251	1	...	292	...	...	244	...	...	28,367	47	...	27,670	1	...
		Total Class A		115,723	3,838	15	111,596	130	2	105,724	2,595	28	101,228	32	...	161,243	3,227	18	152,513	78	...
	5	Brahmin		5,322	3,624	10	5,490	92	...	4,574	3,100	7	4,519	55	...	8,951	5,843	45	8,535	87	...
		Jangam		2,585	844	...	2,618	13	...	562	139	...	541	1	...	1,145	331	2	1,055	5	...
		Total Group 5		7,907	4,468	10	8,108	105	...	5,136	3,230	7	5,06	56	...	10,096	6,174	47	9,590	92	...
(B). Professional.	6	Aghore		...	...	...	...	...	...	...	...	...	...	...	...	...	...	...	...	...	...
		Arti		1	...	...	2	...	...	...	...	...	...	...	...	...	...	...	...	...	...
		Baigari		40	3	...	11	...	...	56	2	...	64	...	...	546	4	...	479	...	...
		Degamber Hindu		...	...	...	...	...	...	...	...	...	...	...	...	...	...	...	...	...	...
		Devara		...	...	...	...	...	...	...	...	...	...	...	...	...	...	...	...	...	...
		Gadaria		...	...	...	...	...	...	...	...	...	...	...	...	...	...	...	...	...	...
		Gondarwandlu		...	...	...	...	...	...	...	...	...	...	...	...	4	...	...	6	...	...
		Gosain		42	11	...	19	...	...	3	1	...	1	...	...	...	...	...	...	...	...
		Gosiga		...	...	...	...	...	...	...	...	...	...	...	...	...	...	...	...	...	...
		Gotralvaru		...	...	...	...	...	...	...	...	...	...	...	...	...	...	...	...	...	...
		Gayansagar		...	...	...	...	...	...	...	...	...	...	...	...	4	...	...	3	...	...
		Jogi		...	...	...	...	...	...	...	...	...	...	...	...	27	1	...	22	...	...
		Kulpand		...	...	...	...	...	...	...	...	...	...	...	...	...	...	...	...	...	...

TABLE C.

Literate by Language known.—Provincial (Summary).

TABLE C.

Literate by Language known.—Provincial (Summary)—*continued*.

Class.	Group.	Caste.	Religion.	ELGANDAL.						INDUR.						MEDAK.					
				Males.			Females.			Males.			Females.			Males.			Females.		
				Total Males.	Literate.		Total Females.	Literate.		Total Males.	Literate.		Total Females.	Literate.		Total Males.	Literate.		Total Females.	Literate.	
					Total.	English.		Total.	English.		Total.	English.		Total.	English.		Total.	English.		Total.	English.
				41	42	43	44	45	46	47	48	49	50	51	52	53	54	55	56	57	58
A. Agricultural—(*concld.*)		Oterwani		...	...	...	...	...	...	...	...	...	...	...	...	...	...	...	...	...	...
		Total Group 4		5,647	3	...	5,498	...	...	311	5	...	299	...	...	34	...	...	30	...	...
		Total Class A		187,412	5,465	18	176,923	99	...	155,205	2,738	...	155,470	57	...	56,905	2,853	7	56,669	53	...
	5	Brahmin		9,163	5,336	8	9,785	88	...	7,368	3,993	3	7,497	32	...	2,763	1,796	13	2,738	23	...
		Jangam		1,755	508	...	1,878	10	...	1,734	344	...	1,810	3	...	1,482	449	...	1,548	3	...
		Total Group 5		10,918	5,844	8	11,663	98	...	9,122	4,337	3	9,307	35	...	4,245	2,245	13	4,286	26	...
(B). Professional.	6	Aghore		...	...	...	...	...	...	...	...	...	...	...	...	...	...	...	...	...	...
		Arti		...	...	...	...	...	...	...	...	...	...	...	...	...	...	...	...	...	...
		Baigari		197	3	...	227	...	...	50	6	...	64	...	...	15	1	...	5	...	...
		Degomber Hindu		...	...	...	...	...	...	...	...	...	...	...	...	...	...	...	...	...	...
		Devara		1	...	...	1	...	...	...	...	...	...	...	...	...	...	...	...	...	...
		Gadaria		...	...	...	...	...	...	...	...	...	...	...	...	...	...	...	...	...	...
		Gondarwandlu		...	3	...	...	...	...	...	...	...	...	...	...	...	...	...	...	...	...
		Gosain		24	10	...	47	...	...	229	14	...	242	...	...	39	1	...	21	...	...
		Gosiga		734	...	...	666	1	...	...	...	...	...	...	...	...	...	...	...	...	...
		Gotralvaru		...	...	...	...	...	...	...	...	...	...	...	...	...	...	...	...	...	...
		Gayansagar...		...	...	...	...	...	...	...	...	...	...	...	...	...	...	...	...	...	...
		Jogi		...	...	...	...	...	...	1	...	...	5	...	...	...	...	...	...	...	...
		Kulpand		...	...	...	...	...	...	...	...	...	...	...	...	...	...	...	...	...	...

TABLE C.

Literate by Language known.—Provincial (Summary)—*continued.*

Class.	Group.	Caste.	Religion.	AURUNGABAD. Males. Total Males.	AURUNGABAD. Males. Literate. Total.	AURUNGABAD. Males. Literate. English.	AURUNGABAD. Females. Total Females.	AURUNGABAD. Females. Literate. Total.	AURUNGABAD. Females. Literate. English.	BIRH. Males. Total Males.	BIRH. Males. Literate. Total.	BIRH. Males. Literate. English.	BIRH. Females. Total Females.	BIRH. Females. Literate. Total.	BIRH. Females. Literate. English.	NANDER. Males. Total Males.	NANDER. Males. Literate. Total.	NANDER. Males. Literate. English.	NANDER. Females. Total Females.	NANDER. Females. Literate. Total.	NANDER. Females. Literate. English.
				59	60	61	62	63	64	65	66	67	68	69	70	71	72	73	74	75	76
A. Agricultural—(*concld.*)		Oterwani		...	...	...	...	...	...	...	...	...	...	...	...	...	...	...	...	...	...
		Total Group 4		4,596	11	...	4,801	...	...	504	8	...	476	...	...	207	5	...	201	...	...
		Total Class A		250,956	3,107	19	246,908	41	...	184,062	1,760	...	178,355	32	...	173,002	1,804	2	170,913	57	...
	5	Brahmin		16,487	8,787	40	14,755	57	...	12,959	7,012	5	11,752	31	...	5,970	3,527	3	5,463	16	...
		Jangam		185	19	...	184	...	...	536	106	...	459	1	...	3,096	344	...	2,955	3	...
		Total Group 5		16,672	8,806	40	14,939	57	...	13,495	7,118	5	12,211	32	...	9,066	3,871	3	8,418	19	...
(B). Professional.	6	Aghore		1	...	...	...	...	...	...	...	...	...	...	...	...	...	...	...	...	...
		Arti		...	...	...	...	...	...	...	...	...	...	...	...	...	...	...	...	...	...
		Bairagi		873	62	...	618	...	...	154	14	...	94	2	...	127	3	...	110	...	...
		Degamber Hindu		...	...	...	...	...	...	...	...	...	...	...	...	...	...	...	...	...	..
		Devara		...	...	...	...	...	...	...	...	...	...	...	...	...	...	...	...	...	...
		Gadaria		...	...	...	...	...	...	...	...	...	...	...	...	...	...	...	...	...	...
		Gondarwandlu		...	...	...	...	...	...	..	...	...	...	...	...	...	...	...	...	...	...
		Gosain		2,376	115	...	2,106	1	...	2,000	98	...	1,696	1	...	1,551	100	...	1,312		...
		Gosiga		...	...	...	...	..	...	...	...	...	...	...	...	...	...	...	...	...	...
		Gotralvaru		...	...	...	...	...	...	...	...	...	...	...	...	...	...	...	...	..	...
		Gayansagar		...	...	...	...	...	...	...	...	...	...	...	...	...	...	...	...	...	...
		Jogi		338	4	...	309	...	...	326	20	...	301	...	...	109	2	...	109	...	...
		Kulpand		...	...	...	...	...	...	...	...	...	...	...	...	...	...	...	...	...	...

TABLE C.

Literate by Language known.—Provincial (Summary).—*continued.*

Class.	Group.	Caste.	Religion.	NALDRUG.						BIDAR.						PARBAHNI.					
				MALES.			FEMALES.			MALES.			FEMALES.			MALES.			FEMALES.		
				Total Males.	Literate. Total.	Literate. English.	Total Females.	Literate. Total.	Literate. English.	Total Males.	Literate. Total.	Literate. English.	Total Females.	Literate. Total.	Literate. English.	Total Males.	Literate. Total.	Literate. English.	Total Females	Literate. Total.	Literate. English.
				77	78	79	80	81	82	83	84	85	86	87	88	89	90	91	92	93	94
(A). Agricultural—(*concld.*)		Oterwani		...	...	...	...	...	...	...	...	...	...	...	...	...	...	...	...	...	...
		Total Group 4		9	...	...	11	...	...	163	2	...	153	...	...	148	...	...	135	...	...
		Total Class A.		192,150	2,650	...	186,734	12	...	193,279	1,972	1	190,567	23	...	239,935	2,079	6	234,924	17	...
	5	Brahmin		10,357	6,004	4	9,285	31	...	9,343	5,506	3	8,615	27	...	12,142	6,774	3	10,534	42	...
		Jangam		1,911	240	...	1,713	1	...	11,285	1,114	...	11,021	3	...	1,228	184	...	1,128	1	...
		Total Group 5......		12,268	6,244	4	10,998	32	...	20,628	6,620	3	19,666	30	...	13,370	6,958	3	11,662	43	...
(B). Professional.	6	Aghore		...	...	...	...	...	...	2	...	...	1	...	...	...	...	...	...	...	...
		Arti...		...	...	...	...	...	...	...	...	...	...	...	...	...	...	...	...	...	...
		Bairagi		103	9	...	64	...	...	80	8	...	78	...	...	287	20	...	203	...	...
		Degamber Hindu		...	...	...	...	...	...	...	...	...	...	...	...	...	...	...	...	...	...
		Devara		...	...	...	...	...	...	...	...	...	...	...	...	...	...	...	...	...	...
		Gadaria		...	...	...	...	...	...	...	...	...	...	...	...	...	...	...	...	...	...
		Gondarwandlu		...	...	...	...	...	...	...	...	...	...	...	...	...	...	...	...	...	...
		Gosain		2,233	188	...	1,833	1	...	1,757	183	...	1,290	1	...	3,468	164	...	2,876	1	...
		Gosiga		...	...	...	...	...	...	...	...	...	...	...	...	...	...	...	...	...	...
		Gotralvaru		...	...	...	...	...	...	...	...	...	...	...	...	...	...	...	...	...	...
		Gayansagar...		...	...	...	...	...	...	...	...	...	...	...	...	...	...	...	...	...	...
		Jogi		426	13	...	404	...	...	285	8	...	321	...	...	836	17	...	860	...	...
		Kulpand		...	...	...	...	...	...	...	...	...	...	...	...	6	...	...	4	...	...

TABLE C.

Literate by Language known.—Provincial (Summary)—*continued.*

Class.	Group.	Caste.	Religion.	SIRPUR TANDUR. Males. Total Males.	Males. Literate. Total.	Males. Literate. English.	Females. Total Females.	Females. Literate. Total.	Females. Literate. English.	GULBARGA. Males. Total Males.	Males. Literate. Total.	Males. Literate. English.	Females. Total Females.	Females. Literate. Total.	Females. Literate. English.	RAICHUR. Males. Total Males.	Males. Literate. Total.	Males. Literate. English.	Females. Total Females.	Females. Literate. Total.	Females. Literate. English.
				95	93	97	98	99	100	101	102	103	101	105	106	107	108	109	110	111	112
(A). Agricultural—(*concld.*)		Oterwani		...	...	...	...	...	...	...	...	...	...	...	...	...	...	...	...	...	...
		Total Group 4.....		18,839	20	...	18,189	1	...	31	...	...	29	...	...	41	...	...	29	...	...
		Total Class A......		65,426	304	1	63,993	1	...	115,919	1,318	22	113,411	14	...	80,781	3,622	23	77,891	70	...
	5	Brahmin		1,897	1,007	3	1,909	3	...	8,082	4,826	80	7,418	26	...	4,801	2,877	18	3,850	34	...
		Jangam		324	40	...	366	...	...	7,292	936	8	7,29[illegible]	2	...	4,603	1,164	...	4,829	8	...
		Total Group 5 ...		2,221	1,047	3	2,275	3	...	15,374	5,762	88	14,708	28	...	9,404	4,041	18	8,679	42	...
(B). Professional.	6	Aghore		2	...	...	5	...	...	...	...	...	...	...	...	...	...	...	...	...	...
		Arti		...	...	...	...	...	...	...	...	...	...	...	...	...	...	...	...	...	...
		Bairagi		6	...	...	8	...	...	29	2	...	20	...	...	4	...	...	...	...	...
		Degamber Hindu		...	...	...	...	...	...	...	...	...	...	...	...	...	...	...	...	...	...
		Devara		...	...	...	...	...	...	...	...	...	...	...	...	...	...	...	...	...	...
		Gadaria		...	...	...	...	...	...	...	...	...	...	...	...	3	...	...	1	...	...
		Gondarwandlu		...	...	...	...	...	...	...	...	...	...	...	...	...	...	...	...	...	...
		Gosain		375	...	...	209	...	...	129	13	...	101	...	...	30	9	...	15	...	...
		Gosiga		...	20	...	...	...	...	...	...	...	...	...	...	...	...	...	...	...	...
		Gotralvaru		...	...	...	...	...	...	...	...	...	...	...	...	...	...	...	...	...	...
		Gayansagar		...	...	...	...	...	...	...	...	...	...	...	...	...	...	...	...	...	...
		Jogi		33	...	...	32	...	...	244	2	...	260	...	...	25	...	...	16	...	...
		Kulpand		...	...	...	...	...	...	...	...	...	...	...	...	...	...	...	...	...	...

TABLE C.

Literate by Language known.—Provincial (Summary)—*continued.*

Class.	Group.	Caste.	Religion.	LINGASUGUR. Males. Total Males.	LINGASUGUR. Males. Literate. Total.	LINGASUGUR. Males. Literate. English.	LINGASUGUR. Females. Total Females.	LINGASUGUR. Females. Literate. Total.	LINGASUGUR. Females. Literate. English.	RAILWAYS. Males. Total Males.	RAILWAYS. Males. Literate. Total.	RAILWAYS. Males. Literate. English.	RAILWAYS. Females. Total Females.	RAILWAYS. Females. Literate. Total.	RAILWAYS. Females. Literate. English.
				113	114	115	116	117	118	119	120	121	123	123	124
(A). Agricultural—(*concld.*)		Oterwani		2	...	...	2	...	...	...	...	...	...	...	...
		Total Group 4		417	19	...	471	...	...	4	...	...	7	...	...
		Total Class A.		82,836	3,020	13	84,131	22	...	1,357	137	37	837	6	...
	5	Brahmin		7,682	4,072	16	7,248	20	...	254	182	62	178	11	3
		Jangam		11,195	1,797	2	11,570	28	...	5	3	2	4	...	...
		Total Group 5		18,877	5,869	18	18,818	48	...	259	185	64	182	12	3
(B). Professional.	6	Aghore		...	...	...	...	...	...	...	...	...	...	...	...
		Arti		...	...	...	...	...	...	...	...	...	...	...	...
		Bairagi		1	...	...	...	...	...	3	...	...	...	...	...
		Degamber Hindu		58	1	...	46	...	...	...	...	...	...	...	...
		Devara		...	...	...	...	...	...	...	...	...	...	...	...
		Gadaria		...	...	...	...	...	...	...	...	...	...	...	...
		Gondarwandlu		...	...	...	...	...	...	...	...	...	...	...	...
		Gosain		114	3	...	94	...	...	2	1	...	...	...	...
		Gosiga		...	...	...	...	...	...	...	...	...	...	...	...
		Gotralavaru		...	...	...	...	...	...	...	...	...	...	...	...
		Gayansagar...		3	...	...	5	...	...	...	...	...	...	...	...
		Jogi		181	5	...	207	...	...	...	...	...	...	...	...
		Kulpand		...	...	...	...	...	...	...	...	...	...	...	...

TABLE C.

Literate by Language known—Provincial (Summary).

Class.	Group.	Caste.	Religion.	TOTAL STRENGTH. Males. Total Males.	Males. Literate. Total.	Males. Literate. English.	Females. Total Females.	Females. Literate. Total.	Females. Literate. English.	HYDERABAD. Males. Total Males.	Males. Literate. Total.	Males. Literate. English.	Females. Total Females.	Females. Literate. Total.	Females. Literate. English.	ATRAF-I-BALDA. Males. Total Males.	Males. Literate. Total.	Males. Literate. English.	Females. Total Females.	Females. Literate. Total.	Females. Literate. English.
1	2	3	4	5	6	7	8	9	10	11	12	13	14	15	16	17	18	19	20	21	22
B. Professional—(contd.)		Manbhao (Hindu)		1,233	246	...	1,086	14	...	...	...	...	...	...	...	...	...	...	...	...	...
		„ (Jain)		1	..	...	2	...	...	...	...	...	...	...	...	...	...	...	...	...	...
		Nanakshahi		37	4	...	22	...	...	...	...	...	...	...	...	...	...	...	...	...	...
		Odhmat		1	...	...	...	...	...	...	...	...	...	...	...	...	...	...	...	...	...
		Panasa		23	10	...	29	...	...	...	...	...	...	...	...	...	...	...	...	...	...
		Rinja		8	...	...	7	...	...	...	...	...	...	...	...	...	...	...	...	...	...
		Tonier		6	..	...	6	...	...	...	...	...	...	...	...	...	...	...	...	...	...
		Total Group 6		22,888	1,630	4	19,192	24	...	757	203	4	407	1	...	231	22	...	140	...	...
	7	Gurao (Hindu)		8,896	357	2	8,724	2	...	...	...	...	...	...	...	...	...	...	...	...	...
		„ (Jain)		11	...	...	6	...	...	...	...	...	...	...	...	...	...	...	...	...	...
		Guruvaria		16	...	...	26	...	...	16	...	...	26	...	...	...	...	...	...	...	...
		Kulugapiyar...		7	...	...	9	...	...	...	...	...	...	...	...	...	...	...	...	...	...
		Total Group 7		8 930	357	2	8,765	2	...	16	...	...	26	...	...	...	...	..	...	...	...
	8	Bhat (Hindu)		4,118	1,232	2	3,753	21	...	83	24	2	55	1	...	406	62	...	428	1	...
		„ (Jain)...		5	5	...	...	...	...	...	...	...	...	...	...	...	...	...	...	...	...
		Total Group 8		4,123	1,237	2	3,753	21	...	83	24	2	55	1	...	406	62	...	428	1	...
	9	Brahmanjai		29	...	...	9	...	...	...	...	...	...	...	...	...	...	...	...	...	...
		Golak		90	14	...	118	...	...	...	...	...	3	...	...	...	...	...	...	...	...
		Kayasth		1,697	743	37	1,536	22	...	1,196	596	25	1,081	16	...	13	6	...	13	1	...
		Mudliar		333	132	63	301	10	...	245	111	51	225	8	...	1	...	...	...	...	...
		Patiki		112	61	...	121	...	...	...	...	...	...	...	...	...	...	...	...	...	...
		Vidur		3,814	579	2	3,906	5	...	5	1	...	1	...	...	13	7	...	17	...	...
		Total Group 9		6,105	1,529	102	5,991	37	...	1,446	708	76	1,310	24	...	27	13	...	30	1	...

TABLE C.

Literate by Language known—Provincial (Summary)—*continued.*

Class.	Group.	Caste.	Religion.	MAHBUBNAGAR. Males. Total Males.	Males. Literate. Total.	Males. Literate. English.	Females. Total Females.	Females. Literate. Total.	Females. Literate. English.	NALGONDA. Males. Total Males.	Males. Literate. Total.	Males. Literate. English.	Females. Total Females.	Females. Literate. Total.	Females. Literate. English.	WARANGAL. Males. Total Males.	Males. Literate. Total.	Males. Literate. English.	Females. Total Females.	Females. Literate. Total.	Females. Literate. English.
				23	24	25	26	27	28	29	30	31	32	33	34	35	36	37	38	39	40
(B). Professional—(*contd.*)		Manbhao (Hindu)		...	...	...	...	...	...	...	...	...	...	...	...	...	...	...	...	...	...
		" (Jain)		...	...	...	...	...	...	...	...	...	...	...	...	...	...	...	...	...	...
		Nanakshahi		3	1	...	1	...	...	...	...	...	...	...	...	...	...	...	...	...	...
		Odhmat		...	...	...	...	...	...	...	...	...	...	...	...	...	...	...	...	...	...
		Panasa		...	...	...	...	...	...	6	1	...	5	...	...	8	8	...	10	...	...
		Rinja		...	...	...	...	...	...	...	...	...	...	...	...	...	...	...	...	...	...
		Tonier		...	...	...	...	...	...	...	...	...	...	...	...	...	...	...	...	...	...
		Total Group 6		86	15	...	33	...	...	65	5	...	7	...	...	589	13	...	520	...	...
	7	Gurao (Hindu)		...	...	...	...	...	...	...	...	...	...	...	...	...	...	...	...	...	...
		" (Jain)		...	...	...	...	...	...	...	...	...	...	...	...	...	...	...	...	...	...
		Guruvaria		...	...	...	...	...	...	...	...	...	...	...	...	...	...	...	...	...	...
		Kulugapiyar		...	...	...	...	...	...	...	...	...	...	...	...	...	...	...	...	...	...
		Total Group 7		...	...	...	...	...	...	...	...	...	...	...	...	...	...	...	...	...	...
	8	Bhat (Hindu)		190	72	...	236	6	...	635	209	...	464	2	...	859	268	...	865	3	...
		" (Jain)		...	...	...	...	...	...	...	...	...	...	...	...	...	...	...	...	...	...
		Total Group 8		190	72	...	236	6	...	635	209	...	464	2	...	859	268	...	865	3	...
	9	Brahmanjai		...	...	...	...	...	...	...	...	...	...	...	...	...	...	...	...	...	...
		Golak		...	...	...	...	...	...	...	...	...	...	...	...	...	...	...	...	...	...
		Kayasth		8	1	...	15	...	...	1	1	...	...	...	...	19	7	...	4	...	...
		Mudliar		...	...	...	...	...	...	1	1	...	...	...	...	9	4	2	6	...	...
		Patiki		...	...	...	...	...	...	...	...	...	...	...	...	...	...	...	...	...	...
		Vidur		6	2	...	9	...	...	5	...	...	2	...	...	5	...	...	7	...	...
		Total Group 9		14	3	...	24	...	...	7	2	...	2	...	...	33	11	2	17	...	...

TABLE C.

Literate by Langunge known—Provincial (Summary)—*continued.*

Class.	Group.	Caste.	Religion.	ELGANDAL. Males. Total Males.	ELGANDAL. Males. Literate. Total.	ELGANDAL. Males. Literate. English.	ELGANDAL. Females. Total Females.	ELGANDAL. Females. Literate. Total.	ELGANDAL. Females. Literate. English.	INDUR. Males. Total Males.	INDUR. Males. Literate. Total.	INDUR. Males. Literate. English.	INDUR. Females. Total Females.	INDUR. Females. Literate. Total.	INDUR. Females. Literate. English.	MEDAK. Males. Total Males.	MEDAK. Males. Literate. Total.	MEDAK. Males. Literate. English.	MEDAK. Females. Total Females.	MEDAK. Females. Literate. Total.	MEDAK. Females. Literate. English.
				41	42	43	44	45	46	47	48	49	50	51	52	53	54	55	56	57	58
(B). Professional—(*contd.*)		Manbhao (Hindu)		...	...	...	...	...	...	8	...	...	8	...	...	...	...	...	...	...	...
		„ (Jain)		...	...	...	...	...	...	...	...	...	...	...	...	...	...	...	...	...	...
		Nanakshaki		...	...	...	...	...	...	...	...	...	3	...	...	...	...	...	...	...	...
		Odhmat		...	...	...	...	...	...	...	...	...	...	...	...	...	...	...	...	...	...
		Panasa		9	1	...	14	...	...	...	...	...	...	...	...	...	...	...	...	...	...
		Rinja		8	...	...	7	...	...	...	...	...	...	...	...	...	...	...	...	...	...
		Tonier		6	...	...	6	...	...	...	...	...	...	...	...	...	...	...	...	...	...
		Total Group 6		979	17	...	968	1	...	288	20	...	322	...	...	54	2	...	26	...	...
	7	Gurao (Hindu)		...	...	...	...	...	...	361	37	...	363	...	...	...	...	...	...	...	...
		„ (Jain)		...	...	...	...	...	...	...	...	...	...	...	...	...	...	...	...	...	...
		Guruvaria		...	...	...	...	...	...	...	...	...	...	...	...	...	...	...	...	...	...
		Kulugapiyar...		...	...	...	...	...	...	...	...	...	...	...	...	...	...	...	...	...	...
		Total Group 7		...	...	...	...	...	...	361	37	...	363	...	...	...	...	...	...	...	...
	8	Bhat (Hindu)		680	253	...	651	4	...	162	37	...	140	1	...	145	66	...	143	2	...
		„ (Jain)		...	...	...	...	...	...	...	...	...	...	...	...	...	...	...	...	...	...
		Total Group 8		680	253	...	651	4	...	162	37	...	140	1	...	145	66	...	143	2	...
	9	Brahmanjai		...	...	...	...	...	...	...	...	...	...	...	...	...	...	...	...	...	...
		Golak		...	...	...	...	...	...	...	...	...	...	...	...	...	...	...	...	...	...
		Kayasth		6	5	...	1	...	...	56	2	...	43	...	...	8	6	...	6	...	...
		Mudliar		10	7	2	7	2	...	...	...	...	...	...	...	...	...	...	...	...	...
		Patiki		...	...	...	...	...	...	...	...	...	...	...	...	...	...	...	...	...	...
		Vidur		31	8	..	34	...	...	288	34	...	272	...	...	4	...	...	2	...	...
		Total Group 9		47	20	2	42	2	...	344	36	...	315	...	...	12	6	...	8	...	...

TABLE C.

Literate by Language known—Provincial (Summary)—*continued.*

Class.	Group.	Caste.	Religion.	AURANGABAD.						BIRH.						NANDER.					
				Males.			Females.			Males.			Females.			Males.			Females		
				Total Males.	Literate. Total.	Literate. English.	Total Females.	Literate. Total.	Literate. English.	Total Males.	Literate. Total.	Literate. English.	Total Females.	Literate. Total.	Literate. English.	Total Males.	Literate. Total.	Literate. English.	Total Females.	Literate. Total.	Literate. English.
				59	60	61	62	63	64	65	66	67	68	69	70	71	72	73	74	75	76
(B.) Professional—(contd.)		Manbhao (Hindu)		438	71	...	406	...	...	244	60	...	193	5	...	216	52	...	191	4	...
		„ (Jain)		1	...	...	2	...	...	...	...	...	...	...	...	...	...	...	...	...	...
		Nanakshahi		8	...	...	11	...	...	...	...	...	...	...	...	...	...	...	1	...	...
		Odhmat		...	...	...	...	...	...	...	...	...	...	...	...	...	...	...	...	...	...
		Panasa		...	...	...	...	...	...	...	...	...	...	...	...	...	...	...	...	...	...
		Rinja		...	...	...	...	...	...	...	...	...	...	...	...	...	...	...	...	...	...
		Tonier		...	...	...	...	...	...	...	...	...	...	...	...	...	...	...	...	...	...
		Total Group 6		4,035	252	...	3,452	1	...	2,724	192	...	2,284	8	...	2,003	157	...	1,723	5	...
	7	Gurao (Hindu)		778	29	2	739	...	...	783	20	...	743	1	...	605	19	...	579	...	...
		„ (Jain)		...	...	...	...	...	...	...	...	...	...	...	...	...	...	...	...	...	...
		Guruvaria		...	...	...	...	...	...	...	...	...	...	...	...	...	...	...	...	...	...
		Kulugapiyar		...	...	...	...	...	...	...	...	...	...	...	...	...	...	...	...	...	...
		Total Group 7		778	29	2	739	...	...	783	20	...	743	1	...	605	19	...	579	...	...
	8	Bhat (Hindu)		346	59	...	331	...	...	58	20	...	45	...	...	16	...	...	14	...	...
		„ (Jain)		5	5	...	...	...	...	...	...	...	...	...	...	...	...	...	...	...	...
		Total Group 8		351	64	...	331	...	...	58	20	...	45	...	...	16	...	...	14	...	...
	9	Brahmanjai		2	...	...	2	...	...	2	...	...	2	...	...	10	...	...	1	...	...
		Golak		31	9	...	38	...	...	17	4	...	12	...	...	7	...	...	12	...	...
		Kayasth		119	36	9	118	1	...	41	14	...	47	...	...	13	5	...	11	2	...
		Mudliar		...	...	...	...	...	...	...	...	...	...	...	...	...	...	...	...	...	...
		Patiki		...	...	...	...	...	...	...	...	...	...	...	...	...	...	...	...	...	...
		Vidur		320	75	...	327	1	...	300	45	...	264	...	...	640	109	...	715	1	...
		Total Group 9		472	120	9	485	2	...	360	63	...	325	...	...	670	114	...	739	3	...

TABLE C.

Literate by Language known—Provincial (Summary)—*continued.*

Class.	Group.	Caste.	Religion.	NALDRUG.						BIDAR.						PARBHANI.					
				MALES.			FEMALES.			MALES.			FEMALES.			MALES.			FEMALES.		
				Total Males.	Literate.		Total Females.	Literate.		Total Males.	Literate.		Total Females.	Literate.		Total Males.	Literate.		Total Females.	Literate.	
					Total.	English.		Total.	English.		Total.	English.		Total.	English.		Total	English.		Total.	English.
				77	78	79	80	81	82	83	84	85	86	87	88	89	90	91	92	93	94
(B). Professional—(*contd.*)		Manbhao (Hindu)		53	9	...	53	...	...	14	...	...	7	...	...	244	53	...	213	5	...
		" (Jain)		...	...	...	...	...	...	...	...	...	...	...	...	...	...	...	...	...	...
		Nanakshahi...		4	1	...	...	...	...	6	...	...	...	...	...	7	2	...	4	...	...
		Odhmat		...	...	...	...	...	...	...	...	...	...	...	...	...	...	...	...	...	...
		Panasa		...	...	...	...	...	...	...	...	...	...	...	...	...	...	...	...	...	...
		Rinja		...	...	...	...	...	...	...	...	...	...	...	...	...	...	...	...	...	...
		Tonier		...	...	...	...	...	...	...	...	...	...	...	...	...	...	...	...	...	...
		Total Group 6		2,320	220	...	2,354	1	...	2,144	199	...	1,697	1	...	4 848	256	...	4,160	6	...
	7	Gurao (Hindu)		2,334	95	...	2,340	...	...	1,880	74	...	1,853	...	...	1,039	29	...	994	...	...
		" (Jain)...		...	...	...	...	...	...	...	...	...	...	...	...	11	...	...	6	...	...
		Guruvaria		...	...	...	...	...	...	...	...	...	...	...	...	...	...	...	...	...	...
		Kulugapiyar...		...	...	...	...	...	...	...	...	...	...	...	...	...	...	...	...	...	...
		Total Group 7		2,334	95	...	2,340	...	...	1,880	74	...	1,853	...	...	1,050	29	...	1,000	...	...
	8	Bhat (Hindu)		...	...	...	...	...	...	48	8	...	36	...	...	132	14	...	137	...	...
		" (Jain)		...	...	...	...	...	...	...	...	...	...	...	...	...	...	...	...	...	...
		Total Group 8		...	...	...	...	...	...	48	8	...	36	...	...	132	14	...	137	...	...
	9	Brahmanjai		...	...	...	...	...	...	...	...	...	...	...	...	15	...	...	4	...	...
		Golak		4	...	...	5	...	...	20	...	...	32	...	...	11	1	...	16	...	...
		Kayasth		14	6	...	5	1	...	36	13	...	50	...	...	52	6	1	45	...	...
		Mudliar		...	...	...	...	...	...	...	...	...	...	...	...	...	...	...	...	...	...
		Patiki		4	...	...	3	...	...	108	61	...	118	...	...	...	...	...	...	...	...
		Vidur		220	45	...	220	...	...	785	82	...	700	2	...	606	138	1	581	1	...
		Total Group 9		242	51	...	233	1	...	949	156	...	960	2	...	684	145	2	646	1	...

TABLE C.

Literate by Language known—Provincial (Summary)—*continued.*

Class.	Group.	Caste.	Religion.	SIRPUR TANDUR.						GULBURGA.						RAICHUR.					
				MALES.			FEMALES.			MALES.			FEMALES.			MALES.			FEMALES.		
				Total Males.	Literate.		Total Females.	Literate.		Total Males.	Literate.		Total Females.	Literate.		Total Males.	Literate.		Total Females.	Literate.	
					Total.	English.		Total.	English.		Total.	English.		Total.	English.		Total.	English.		Total.	English.
				95	96	97	98	99	100	101	102	103	104	105	106	107	108	109	110	111	113
B. Professional—(*contd.*)		Manbhao (Hindu)		12	1	...	14	...	...	1	...	...	1	...	...	...	...	...	...	...	...
		,, Jain		...	...	...	...	...	...	...	...	...	...	...	...	...	...	...	...	...	...
		Nanakshahi		8	...	...	1	...	...	1	...	...	1	...	...	...	...	...	...	...	...
		Odhmat		...	...	...	...	...	...	...	...	...	...	...	...	...	...	...	...	...	...
		Panasa		...	...	...	...	...	...	...	...	...	...	...	...	...	...	...	...	...	...
		Rinja		...	...	...	...	...	...	...	...	...	...	...	...	...	...	...	...	...	...
		Tonier		...	...	...	...	...	...	...	...	...	...	...	...	...	...	...	...	...	...
		Total Group 6...... ..		436	21	...	269	...	...	404	17	...	383	...	...	62	9	...	32	...	...
	7	Gurao (Hindu)		113	13	...	116	...	...	1,002	41	...	997	1	...	...	...	...	...	...	...
		,, (Jain)		...	...	...	...	...	...	...	...	...	...	...	...	...	...	...	...	...	...
		Guruvaria		...	...	...	...	...	...	...	...	...	...	...	...	...	...	...	...	...	...
		Kulugapiyar		...	...	...	...	...	...	...	...	...	...	...	...	...	...	...	...	...	...
		Total Group 7.........		113	13	...	116	...	...	1,002	41	...	997	1	...	...	...	...	...	...	...
	8	Bhat (Hindu)		108	14	...	102	...	...	18	...	...	17	...	...	211	126	...	69	1	...
		,, Jain		...	...	...	...	...	...	...	...	...	...	...	...	...	...	...	...	...	...
		Total Group 8.........		108	14	...	102	...	...	18	...	...	17	...	...	211	126	...	69	1	...
	9	Brahmanjai		...	...	...	...	...	...	...	...	...	...	...	...	...	...	...	...	...	...
		Golak		...	...	...	...	...	...	...	...	...	...	...	...	...	...	...	...	...	...
		Kayash		6	4	...	...	...	...	31	16	2	29	...	...	35	15	...	25	1	...
		Mudliar		...	...	...	...	...	...	...	...	...	...	...	...	64	8	7	61	...	...
		Patiki...		...	...	...	...	...	...	...	...	...	...	...	...	...	...	...	...	...	...
		Vidur...		219	25	...	253	...	...	303	8	1	334	...	...	1	...	...	1	...	...
		Total Group 9.........		225	29	...	253	...	...	334	24	3	363	...	...	100	23	7	87	1	...

TABLE C.

Literate by Language known.—Provincial (Summary)—*continued.*

Class.	Group.	Caste.	Religion.	LINGASUGUR.						RAILWAYS.					
				Males.			Females.			Males.			Females.		
				Total Males.	Literate. Total.	Literate. English.	Total Females.	Literate. Total.	Literate. English.	Total Males.	Literate. Total.	Literate. English.	Total Females.	Literate. Total.	Literate. English.
				113	114	115	116	117	118	119	120	121	122	123	124
B. Professional—(contd.)		Manbhao (Hindu)		...	...	...	...	...	...	...	...	...	...	...	...
		" Jain		...	...	...	...	...	...	...	...	...	...	...	...
		Nanakshahi		...	...	...	...	...	...	...	...	...	...	...	...
		Odhmat		1	...	...	...	...	...	...	...	...	...	...	...
		Panasa		...	...	...	...	...	...	...	...	...	...	...	...
		Rinja		...	...	...	...	...	...	...	...	...	...	...	...
		Tonier		...	...	...	...	...	...	...	...	...	...	...	...
		Total Group 6		358	9	...	352	...	...	5	1	...	...	...	...
	7	Gurao (Hindu)		...	...	...	...	...	...	1	...	...	...	...	...
		" (Jain)		...	...	...	...	...	...	...	...	...	...	...	...
		Guruvaria		...	...	...	...	...	...	...	...	...	...	...	...
		Kulugapiyar		7	...	...	9	...	...	...	...	...	...	...	...
		Total Group 7		7	...	...	9	...	...	1	...	...	...	...	...
	8	Bhat (Hindu)		21	...	...	20	...	...	...	...	...	...	...	...
		" Jain		...	...	...	...	...	...	...	...	...	...	...	...
		Total Group 8		21	...	...	20	...	...	...	...	...	...	...	...
	9	Brahmanjai		...	...	...	...	...	...	...	...	...	...	...	...
		Golak		...	...	...	...	...	...	...	...	...	...	...	...
		Kayash		40	2	...	40	...	...	3	2	...	3	...	...
		Mudliar		...	...	...	...	...	...	3	1	1	2	...	...
		Patiki		...	...	...	...	...	...	...	...	...	...	...	...
		Vidur		93	...	...	107	...	...	...	...	...	...	...	...
		Total Group 9		133	2	...	147	...	...	6	3	1	5	...	...

TABLE C.

Literate by Language known—Provincial (Summary)—*continued.*

Class.	Group.	Caste.	Religion.	TOTAL STRENGTH.						HYDERABAD.						ATRAF-I-BALDA.					
				MALES.			FEMALES.			MALES.			FEMALES.			MALES.			FEMALES.		
				Total Males.	Literate. Total.	Literate. English.	Total Females.	Literate. Total.	Literate. English.	Total Males.	Literate. Total.	Literate. English.	Total Females.	Literate. Total.	Literate. English.	Total Males.	Literate. Total.	Literate. English.	Total Females.	Literate. Total.	Literate. English.
1	2	3	4	5	6	7	8	9	10	11	12	13	14	15	16	17	18	19	20	21	22
B. Professional—(*concld.*)	10	Joshi...		966	37	...	955	9	...	80	15	...	81	...	...	...	...	...	...	...	...
		Vaidya		5	...	...	3	...	...	...	...	...	...	...	...	...	...	...	...	...	...
		Total Group 10		971	37	...	958	9	...	80	15	...	81	...	...	...	...	...	...	...	...
	11	Aradhya		14	4	...	12	...	...	...	...	...	...	...	...	...	...	...	...	...	...
		Chinai		3	...	...	3	...	...	...	...	...	...	...	...	...	...	...	...	...	...
		Dom (Mussulman)		3	...	...	6	...	...	...	...	...	...	...	...	...	...	...	...	...	...
		Gondhle		2,428	71	...	2,507	...	...	20	3	...	21	...	...	...	...	...	...	...	...
		Halgar		3	1	...	...	...	...	...	...	...	...	...	...	...	...	...	...	...	...
		Kinara		9	...	...	11	...	...	...	...	...	...	...	...	...	...	...	...	...	...
		Pulari		860	19	...	815	1	...	...	...	...	...	...	...	...	...	...	...	...	...
		Sonnayi		321	19	...	292	...	...	...	...	...	...	...	...	5	...	...	2	...	...
		Singadi		157	1	...	131	...	...	...	...	...	...	...	...	...	...	...	...	...	...
		Tammadi		5,934	874	...	5,972	5	...	11	1	...	4	...	...	275	53	...	319	...	...
		Total Group 11		9,732	989	...	9,749	6	...	31	4	...	25	...	...	280	53	...	321	...	...
	12	Kanchani or Bogam (Jain) ..		3	...	...	2	...	...	...	...	...	...	...	...	...	...	...	...	...	...
		Do. (Hindu)		1,908	364	...	3,193	483	...	39	10	...	155	29	...	136	25	...	258	41	...
		Do. Mussulman		94	1	...	132	...	...	...	...	...	...	...	...	...	...	...	...	...	...
		Total Group 12		2,005	365	...	3,327	482	...	39	10	...	155	29	...	136	25	...	258	41	...
	13	Bahurupi (Hindu)		124	1	...	160	...	...	...	...	...	...	...	...	...	...	...	...	...	...
		Do. (Mussulman)		1	...	...	3	...	...	...	...	...	...	...	...	...	...	...	...	...	...
		Bhagavatulu		38	13	...	35	3	...	12	5	...	4	...	...	...	...	...	...	...	...
		Bhand		152	...	...	131	...	...	...	...	...	1	...	...	...	...	...	...	...	...
		Bommalavaru		17	...	...	22	...	...	...	...	...	...	...	...	17	...	...	22	...	...
		Total Group 13		332	14	...	351	3	...	12	5	...	5	...	...	17	...	...	22	...	...
		Total Class B.		2,41,654	95,451	716	2,34,322	1,499	5	12,942	5,264	348	9,863	178	2	5,129	2,345	3	5,066	76	...

TABLE C.

Literate by Language known—Provincial (Summary)—*continued.*

Class.	Group.	Caste.	Religion.	MAHBUBNAGAR. Males. Total Males.	MAHBUBNAGAR. Males. Literate. Total.	MAHBUBNAGAR. Males. Literate. English.	MAHBUBNAGAR. Females. Total Females.	MAHBUBNAGAR. Females. Literate. Total.	MAHBUBNAGAR. Females. Literate. English.	NALGONDA. Males. Total Males.	NALGONDA. Males. Literate. Total.	NALGONDA. Males. Literate. English.	NALGONDA. Females. Total Females.	NALGONDA. Females. Literate. Total.	NALGONDA. Females. Literate. English.	WARANGAL. Males. Total Males.	WARANGAL. Males. Literate. Total.	WARANGAL. Males. Literate. English.	WARANGAL. Females. Total Females.	WARANGAL. Females. Literate. Total.	WARANGAL. Females. Literate. English.
				23	24	25	26	27	28	29	30	31	32	33	34	35	36	37	38	39	40
B. Professional—(concld.)	10	Joshi ...		...	...	...	...	...	...	...	...	...	...	...	...	...	...	...	...	...	...
		Vaidya		...	...	...	...	...	...	...	...	...	...	...	...	...	...	...	...	...	...
		Total Group 10		...	...	...	...	...	...	...	...	...	...	...	...	...	...	...	...	...	...
	11	Aradhya		...	...	...	...	...	...	...	...	...	...	...	...	...	...	...	...	...	...
		Chinai		...	...	...	...	...	...	...	...	...	...	...	...	...	...	...	...	...	...
		Dom (Mussulman)		...	...	...	...	...	...	...	...	...	...	...	...	...	...	...	...	...	...
		Gondhle		...	...	...	...	...	...	1	1	...	...	...	...	...	...	...	...	...	...
		Halgar		...	...	...	...	...	...	...	...	...	...	...	...	...	...	...	...	...	...
		Kinara		...	...	...	...	...	...	9	...	...	11	...	...	...	...	...	...	...	...
		Pulari		...	...	...	...	...	...	...	...	...	...	...	...	...	...	...	...	...	...
		Sonnayi		6	...	...	2	...	...	19	2	...	12	...	...	15	...	...	19	...	...
		Singadi		5	...	...	7	...	...	...	...	...	...	...	...	6	...	...	6	...	...
		Tammadi		510	93	...	531	1	...	265	82	...	265	...	...	432	132	...	438	...	...
		Total Group 11		521	93	...	540	1	...	294	85	...	288	...	...	453	132	...	463	...	...
	12	Kanchani or Bogam (Jain)		...	...	...	...	...	...	...	...	...	...	...	...	...	...	...	...	...	...
		Do. (Hindu)		371	63	...	637	119	...	270	72	...	377	68	...	314	76	...	435	92	...
		Do. Mussulman		...	...	...	...	...	...	...	...	...	...	...	...	...	...	...	...	...	...
		Total Group 12		371	63	...	637	119	...	270	72	...	377	68	...	314	76	...	435	92	...
	13	Bahurupi (Hindu)		10	1	...	12	...	...	...	...	...	...	...	...	...	...	...	...	...	...
		Do. (Mussulman)		...	...	...	...	...	...	...	...	...	...	...	...	...	...	...	...	...	...
		Bhagavatulu		...	...	...	...	...	...	2	1	...	1	...	...	5	2	...	8	3	...
		Bhand		...	...	...	...	...	...	...	...	...	...	...	...	...	...	...	...	...	...
		Bommalavaru		...	...	...	...	...	...	...	...	...	...	...	...	...	...	...	...	...	...
		Total Group 13		10	1	...	12	...	...	2	1	...	1	...	...	5	2	...	8	3	...
		Total Class B		9,099	4,715	10	9,590	231	...	6,409	3,613	7	6,262	126	...	12,349	6,676	49	11,898	190	...

TABLE C.

Literate by Language known—Provincial (Summary).

TABLE C.

Literate by Language known—Provincial (Summary)—*continued.*

Class.	Group.	Caste.	Religion.	ELGANDAL. Males. Total Males.	ELGANDAL. Males. Literate. Total.	ELGANDAL. Males. Literate. English.	ELGANDAL. Females. Total Females.	ELGANDAL. Females. Literate. Total.	ELGANDAL. Females. Literate. English.	INDUR. Males. Total Males.	INDUR. Males. Literate. Total.	INDUR. Males. Literate. English.	INDUR. Females. Total Females.	INDUR. Females. Literate. Total.	INDUR. Females. Literate. English.	MEDAK. Males. Total Males.	MEDAK. Males. Literate. Total.	MEDAK. Males. Literate. English.	MEDAK. Females. Total Females.	MEDAK. Females. Literate. Total.	MEDAK. Females. Literate. English.
				41	42	43	44	45	46	47	48	49	50	51	52	53	54	55	56	57	58
B. Professional—(*concld.*)	10	Joshi		...	...	...	...	...	...	...	...	...	1	...	...	...	...	...	...	...	...
		Vaidya		...	...	...	...	...	...	...	...	...	...	...	...	...	...	...	...	...	...
		Total Group 10		...	...	...	...	...	...	...	...	...	1	...	...	...	...	...	...	...	...
	11	Aradhya		...	...	...	...	...	...	6	4	...	7	...	...	...	...	...	...	...	...
		Chinai		...	...	...	...	...	...	...	...	...	...	...	...	...	...	...	...	...	...
		Dom (Mussulman)		...	...	...	...	...	...	...	...	...	...	...	...	...	...	...	...	...	...
		Gondhle		...	...	...	...	...	...	30	...	...	66	...	...	...	...	...	...	...	...
		Halgar		...	...	...	...	...	...	...	...	...	...	...	...	...	...	...	...	...	...
		Kinara		...	...	...	...	...	...	...	...	...	...	...	...	...	...	...	...	...	...
		Pulari		...	...	...	...	...	...	2	...	...	...	...	...	...	...	...	...	...	...
		Sonnayi		219	17	...	204	...	...	3	...	...	...	...	...	4	...	...	3	...	...
		Singadi		4	...	...	4	...	...	13	...	...	10	...	...	...	...	...	...	...	...
		Tammadi		548	123	...	579	4	...	9	...	...	9	...	...	382	76	...	408	...	...
		Total Group 11		771	140	...	787	4	...	63	4	...	92	...	...	386	76	...	411	...	...
	12	Kanchani or Bogam (Jain)		...	...	...	...	...	...	...	...	...	...	...	...	...	...	...	...	...	...
		Do. (Hindu)		299	52	...	513	94	...	46	6	...	88	1	...	64	7	...	162	7	...
		Do. (Mussulman)		...	...	...	...	...	...	...	...	...	...	...	...	...	...	...	...	...	...
		Total Group 12		299	52	...	513	94	...	46	6	...	88	1	...	64	7	...	162	7	...
	13	Bahurupi (Hindu)		50	...	...	63	...	...	...	...	...	...	...	...	7	...	...	8	...	...
		Do. (Mussulman)		...	...	...	...	...	...	...	...	...	...	...	...	...	...	...	...	...	...
		Bhagavatulu		11	...	...	16	...	...	...	...	...	...	...	...	...	...	...	...	...	...
		Bhand		...	...	...	...	...	...	...	...	...	...	...	...	...	...	...	...	...	...
		Bommalavaru		...	...	...	...	...	...	...	...	...	...	...	...	...	...	...	...	...	...
		Total Group 13		61	...	...	79	...	...	...	...	...	...	...	...	7	...	...	8	...	...
		Total Class B		13,755	6,326	10	1,4703	203	...	10,386	4,477	3	10,628	37	...	4,913	2,402	13	5,044	35	...

TABLE C.

Literate by Language known—Provincial (Summary)—*continued.*

Class.	Group.	Caste.	Religion.	AURUNGABAD. Males. Total Males.	AURUNGABAD. Males. Literate. Total.	AURUNGABAD. Males. Literate. English.	AURUNGABAD. Females. Total Females.	AURUNGABAD. Females. Literate. Total.	AURUNGABAD. Females. Literate. English.	BIRH. Males. Total Males.	BIRH. Males. Literate. Total.	BIRH. Males. Literate. English.	BIRH. Females. Total Females.	BIRH. Females. Literate. Total.	BIRH. Females. Literate. English.	NANDER. Males. Total Males.	NANDER. Males. Literate. Total.	NANDER. Males. Literate. English.	NANDER. Females. Total Females.	NANDER. Females. Literate. Total.	NANDER. Females. Literate. English.
				59	60	61	62	63	64	65	66	67	68	69	70	71	72	73	74	75	76
B. Professional—(*concld*).	10	Joshi ...		321	16	...	326	9	...	187	2	...	192	...	...	16	2	...	8	...	...
		Vaidya		...	...	...	...	...	...	5	...	...	3	...	...	...	...	...	...	...	...
		Total Group 10		321	16	...	326	9	...	192	2	...	195	...	...	16	2	...	8	...	...
	11	Aradhya		...	...	...	...	...	...	..	...	...	...	...	...	...	...	...	...	...	...
		Chinai		3	...	...	3	...	...	...	...	...	...	...	...	...	...	...	...	...	...
		Dom (Mussulman)		...	...	...	...	...	...	...	...	...	...	...	...	...	...	...	...	...	...
		Gondhle		321	15	...	318	...	...	371	7	...	404	...	...	110	...	...	98	...	...
		Halgar		...	...	...	...	...	...	...	...	...	...	...	...	...	...	...	...	...	...
		Kinara		...	...	...	...	...	...	...	...	...	...	...	...	...	...	...	...	...	...
		Pulari		...	...	...	...	...	...	21	1	...	15	...	...	136	...	...	125	...	...
		Sonnayi		...	...	...	...	...	...	...	...	...	...	...	...	...	...	...	...	...	...
		Singadi		...	...	...	...	...	...	...	...	...	...	...	...	7	...	...	1	...	...
		Tammadi		79	...	...	81	...	...	7	...	...	...	...	...	...	...	...	...	...	...
		Total Group 11......		403	15	...	402	...	...	399	8	...	419	...	...	253	...	...	224	...	...
	12	Kanchani or Bogam (Jain)		...	...	...	...	...	...	...	...	...	...	...	...	...	...	...	...	...	...
		Do. (Hindu)		13	5	...	9	1	...	...	...	...	...	...	...	4	...	...	14	...	...
		Do. (Mussulman)		8	...	...	18	...	...	41	1	...	52	...	...	...	...	...	...	...	...
		Total Group 12......		21	5	...	27	1	...	41	1	...	52	...	...	4	...	...	14	...	..
	13	Bahurupi (Hindu) ...		...	...	...	...	...	...	43	...	...	59	...	...	...	...	...	...	...	...
		Do. (Musulman)		...	...	...	...	...	...	...	...	...	...	...	...	...	...	...	...	...	...
		Bhagavatulu...		2	2	...	...	...	...	...	...	...	...	...	...	...	...	...	...	...	...
		Bhand		...	...	...	...	...	...	...	...	...	...	...	...	...	...	...	...	...	...
		Bommalavaru		...	...	...	...	...	...	...	...	...	...	...	...	...	...	...	...	...	...
		Total Group 13......		2	2	...	...	...	...	43	...	...	59	...	...	...	...	...	...	...	...
		Total Class B......		23,055	9,309	51	20,701	70	...	18,095	7,424	5	16,333	41	...	12,633	4,163	3	11,719	27	...

TABLE C.

Literate by Language known—Provincial (Summary)—*continued.*

Class.	Group.	Caste.	Religion.	NALDRUG. Males. Total Males.	NALDRUG. Males. Literate. Total.	NALDRUG. Males. Literate. English.	NALDRUG. Females. Total Females.	NALDRUG. Females. Literate. Total.	NALDRUG. Females. Literate. English.	BIDAR. Males. Total Males.	BIDAR. Males. Literate. Total.	BIDAR. Males. Literate. English.	BIDAR. Females. Total Females.	BIDAR. Females. Literate. Total.	BIDAR. Females. Literate. English.	PARBHANI. Males. Total Males.	PARBHANI. Males. Literate. Total.	PARBHANI. Males. Literate. English.	PARBHANI. Females. Total Females.	PARBHANI. Females. Literate. Total.	PARBHANI. Females. Literate. English.
				77	78	79	80	81	82	83	84	85	86	87	88	89	90	91	92	93	94
B. Professional—(concld).	10	Joshi ...		83	...	...	80	...	...	99	1	...	98	...	...	114	1	...	121	...	...
		Vaidya ...		...	...	...	...	...	...	...	...	...	...	...	...	...	...	...	...	...	...
		Total Group 10		83	...	...	80	...	...	99	1	...	98	...	...	114	1	...	121	...	...
	11	Aradhya ...		...	...	...	...	...	...	...	...	...	...	...	...	7	...	...	4	...	...
		Chinai ...		...	...	...	...	...	...	...	...	...	...	...	...	...	...	...	...	...	...
		Dom (Mussulman) ...		...	...	...	...	...	...	...	...	...	...	...	...	...	...	...	...	...	...
		Gondhle ...		449	10	...	484	...	...	519	22	...	474	...	...	329	8	...	343	...	...
		Halgar ...		...	...	...	...	...	...	3	1	...	...	...	...	...	...	...	...	...	...
		Kinara ...		...	...	...	...	...	...	...	...	...	...	...	...	...	...	...	...	...	...
		Pulari ...		4	...	...	3	...	...	376	14	...	356	...	...	56	3	...	60	...	...
		Sonnayi ...		...	...	...	...	...	...	1	...	...	...	...	...	34	...	...	28	...	...
		Singadi ...		...	...	...	...	...	...	46	1	...	42	...	...	...	...	...	...	...	...
		Tammadi ...		...	...	...	...	...	...	176	4	...	157	...	...	...	...	...	...	...	...
		Total Group 11		453	10	...	487	...	...	1,121	42	...	1,029	...	...	426	11	...	435	...	...
	12	Kanchani or Bogam (Jain) ...		...	...	...	...	...	...	...	...	...	...	...	...	3	...	...	2	...	...
		Do. (Hindu) ...		1	...	...	6	...	...	29	9	...	54	...	...	23	...	...	23	...	...
		Do. (Mussulman) ...		6	...	...	9	...	...	1	...	...	11	...	...	38	...	...	42	...	...
		Total Group 12		7	...	...	15	...	...	30	9	...	65	...	...	64	...	...	67	...	...
	13	Bahurupi (Hindu) ...		10	...	...	14	...	...	...	...	...	...	...	...	...	...	...	1	...	...
		Do. (Mussulman) ...		...	...	...	...	...	...	1	...	...	3	...	...	...	...	...	...	...	...
		Bhagavatulu... ...		...	...	...	...	...	...	...	...	...	...	...	...	...	...	...	...	...	...
		Bhand ...		...	...	...	...	...	...	...	...	...	...	...	...	...	...	...	...	...	...
		Bommalavaru ...		...	...	...	...	...	...	...	...	...	...	...	...	...	...	...	...	...	...
		Total Group 13		10	...	...	14	...	...	1	...	...	3	...	...	...	...	...	1	...	...
		Total Class B		18,217	6,620	4	16,521	34	...	26,900	7,109	3	25,407	33	...	20,688	7,414	5	18,229	50	...

TABLE C.

Literate by Language known.—Provincial (Summary)—*continued.*

Class.	Group.	Caste.	Religion.	SIRPUR TANDUR. Males. Total Males.	SIRPUR TANDUR. Males. Literate. Total.	SIRPUR TANDUR. Males. Literate. English.	SIRPUR TANDUR. Females. Total Females.	SIRPUR TANDUR. Females. Literate. Total.	SIRPUR TANDUR. Females. Literate. English.	GULBURGA. Males. Total Males.	GULBURGA. Males. Literate. Total.	GULBURGA. Males. Literate. English.	GULBURGA. Females. Total Females.	GULBURGA. Females. Literate. Total.	GULBURGA. Females. Literate. English.	RAICHUR. Males. Total Males.	RAICHUR. Males. Literate. Total.	RAICHUR. Males. Literate. English.	RAICHUR. Females. Total Females.	RAICHUR. Females. Literate. Total.	RAICHUR. Females. Literate. English.
				95	96	97	98	99	100	101	102	103	104	105	106	107	108	109	110	111	112
B. Professional—(*concld*).	10	Joshi		...	...	...	...	...	...	66	...	...	48	...	...	...	...	...	...	...	...
		Vaidya		...	...	...	...	...	...	...	...	...	...	...	...	...	...	...	...	...	...
		Total Group 10		...	...	...	...	...	...	66	...	...	48	...	...	...	...	...	...	...	...
	11	Aradhya		...	...	...	...	...	...	1	...	...	1	...	...	...	...	...	...	...	...
		Chinai		...	...	...	...	...	...	...	...	...	...	...	...	...	...	...	...	...	...
		Dom (Mussulman)		...	...	...	...	...	...	3	...	...	6	...	...	...	...	...	...	...	...
		Gondhle		...	...	...	...	...	...	262	4	...	294	...	...	9	1	...	2	...	...
		Halgar		...	...	...	...	...	...	...	...	...	...	...	...	...	...	...	...	...	...
		Kinara		...	...	...	...	...	...	...	...	...	...	...	...	...	...	...	...	...	...
		Pulari		...	...	...	...	...	...	265	1	...	256	1	...	...	...	...	...	...	...
		Sonnayi		...	...	...	...	...	...	7	...	...	3	...	...	8	...	...	19	...	...
		Singadi		...	...	...	...	...	...	...	...	...	...	...	...	...	...	...	...	...	...
		Tammadi		24	8	...	28	...	...	73	2	...	88	...	...	973	110	...	970	...	...
		Total Group 11		24	8	...	28	...	...	611	7	...	648	1	...	990	111	...	991	...	...
	12	Kanchani or Bogam (Jain) ...		...	...	...	...	...	...	...	...	...	...	...	...	...	...	...	...	...	...
		Do. (Hindu)		62	9	...	100	6	...	29	...	...	73	7	...	120	21	...	155	13	...
		Do. (Mussulman)		...	...	...	...	...	...	...	...	...	...	...	...	...	...	...	...	...	...
		Total Group 12		62	9	...	100	6	...	29	...	...	73	7	...	120	21	...	155	13	...
	13	Bahurupi (Hindu)		...	...	...	...	...	...	4	...	...	2	...	...	...	...	...	1	...	...
		Do. (Mussulman)		...	...	...	...	...	...	...	...	...	...	...	...	...	...	...	...	...	...
		Bhagavatulu		2	2	...	2	...	...	...	...	...	...	...	...	...	...	...	...	...	...
		Bhand		...	...	...	...	...	...	...	...	...	...	...	...	152	...	...	130	...	...
		Bommalavaru		...	...	...	...	...	...	...	...	...	...	...	...	...	...	...	...	...	...
		Total Group 13		2	2	...	2	...	...	4	...	...	2	...	...	152	...	...	131	...	...
		Total Class B.		3,191	1,143	3	3,145	9	...	17,842	5,851	91	17,239	37	...	11,039	4,331	25	10,144	57	...

TABLE C.

Literate by Language known.—(Provincial Summary)—*continued.*

Class.	Group.	Caste.	Religion.	LINGSUGUR. Males. Total Males.	LINGSUGUR. Males. Literate. Total.	LINGSUGUR. Males. Literate. English.	LINGSUGUR. Females. Total Females.	LINGSUGUR. Females. Literate. Total.	LINGSUGUR. Females. Literate. English.	RAILWAYS. Males. Total Males.	RAILWAYS. Males. Literate. Total.	RAILWAYS. Males. Literate. English.	RAILWAYS. Females. Total Females.	RAILWAYS. Females. Literate. Total.	RAILWAYS. Females. Literate. English.
				113	114	115	116	117	118	119	120	121	122	123	124
B. Professional—(*concluded*).	10	Joshi...	Hindu	...	...	...	...	...	...	...	...	...	...	...	...
		Vaidya	"	...	...	...	...	...	...	...	...	...	...	...	...
		Total Group 10	......	...	...	...	...	...	...	...	...	...	...	...	...
	11	Aradhya	Hindu	...	...	...	...	...	...	...	...	...	...	...	...
		Chinai	"	...	...	...	...	...	...	...	...	...	...	...	...
		Dom	Mussulman	...	...	...	...	...	...	...	...	...	...	...	...
		Goudhle	Hindu	7	...	...	3	...	...	...	...	...	...	...	...
		Halgar	"	...	...	...	...	...	...	...	...	...	...	...	...
		Kinara	"	...	...	...	...	...	...	...	...	...	...	...	...
		Pulari	"	...	...	...	...	...	...	...	...	...	...	...	...
		Sonnayi	"	...	...	...	...	...	...	...	...	...	...	...	...
		Singadi	"	76	...	...	61	...	...	...	...	...	...	...	...
		Tammadi	"	2,170	190	...	2,095	...	...	...	...	...	...	...	...
		Total Group 11	......	2,253	190	...	2,159	...	...	...	...	...	...	...	...
	12	Kanchani or Bogam	Jain	...	...	...	...	...	...	...	...	...	...	...	...
		Do.	Hindu	88	9	...	134	5	...	...	...	...	...	...	...
		Do.	Mussulman	...	...	...	...	...	...	...	...	...	...	...	...
		Total Group 12	......	88	9	...	134	5	...	...	...	...	...	...	...
	13	Bahurupi	Hindu	...	...	...	...	...	...	...	...	...	...	...	...
		Do.	Mussulman	...	...	...	...	...	...	...	...	...	...	...	...
		Bhagavatulu...	Hindu	4	1	...	4	...	...	...	...	...	...	...	...
		Bhand	"	...	...	...	...	...	...	...	...	...	...	...	...
		Bommalavaru	"	...	...	...	...	...	...	...	...	...	...	...	...
		Total Group 13	......	4	1	...	4	...	...	...	...	...	...	...	...
		Total Class B.	......	21,741	6,080	18	21,643	53	...	271	189	65	187	12	3

TABLE C.

Literate by Language known.—(Provincial Summary)—*continued.*

Class.	Group.	Caste.	Religion.	TOTAL STRENGTH. Males. Total Males.	Males. Literate. Total.	Males. Literate. English.	Females. Total Females.	Females. Literate. Total.	Females. Literate. English.	HYDERABAD. Males. Total Males.	Males. Literate. Total.	Males. Literate. English.	Females. Total Females.	Females. Literate. Total.	Females. Literate. English.	ATRAF-I-BALDA. Males. Total Males.	Males. Literate. Total.	Males. Literate. English.	Females. Total Females.	Females. Literate. Total.	Females. Literate. English.
1	2	3	4	5	6	7	8	9	10	11	12	13	14	15	16	17	18	19	20	21	22
C. Commercial.	14	Aoti ...	Hindu ...	18	10	...	17	...	...	...	...	...	...	...	...	...	...	...	...	...	...
		Balija	"	41.548	9,048	125	41,386	191	1	1,739	738	110	1,687	6[illegible]	1	3,935	933	5	3,743	13	...
		Bhattia	"	105	19	...	88	...	...	...	...	...	...	...	...	...	...	...	...	...	...
		Bora ...	Mussulman	123	30	2	105	1	...	100	33	2	84	1	...	...	...	...	...	...	...
		Chanewar	Hindu ...	4,199	48	...	4,092	...	...	...	...	...	...	...	...	...	...	...	...	...	...
		Eginawar	"	26	9	...	26	...	...	...	...	...	...	...	...	...	...	...	...	...	...
		Guzerati	"	302	84	3	237	1	...	123	43	2	99	...	...	9	1	...	2	...	...
		Ghâsi...	"	15	...	...	6	...	...	...	...	...	...	...	...	...	...	...	...	...	...
		Do. ...	Jain	13	10	...	13	...	...	...	...	...	...	...	...	...	...	...	...	...	...
		Jayarkhani	Hindu ...	202	...	...	214	...	...	...	...	...	...	...	...	...	...	...	...	...	...
		Josaputri	"	8	3	...	4	...	...	...	...	...	...	...	...	...	...	...	...	...	...
		Kapur	"	7	1	...	5	1	...	...	...	...	...	...	...	...	...	...	...	...	...
		Kasad	"	393	109	...	358	...	...	...	...	...	...	...	...	...	...	...	...	...	...
		Komati	Hindu ...	108,111	51,428	148	104,754	440	...	5.375	2,862	74	4,572	36	...	6,619	3,600	6	6,540	26	...
		Kutchi	"	2	...	...	2	...	...	...	...	...	...	...	...	...	...	...	...	...	...
		Lingayet	"	49,055	4,447	22	48,477	22	...	264	43	...	226	...	...	738	179	...	718	...	...
		Memon	Mussulman	42	37	...	3	...	...	42	37	...	3	...	...	...	...	...	...	...	...
		Saiti ...	Hindu ...	744	81	1	811	...	...	129	32	1	135	...	...	6	2	...	6	...	...
		Wani	"	207,820	24,734	68	197,733	140	...	3,030	1,603	59	2,061	30	...	360	72	...	336	1	...
		Do. ...	Jain	5 511	2,665	6	4,437	20	...	92	68	3	49	1	...	...	...	...	...	...	...
		Yelgar or Elgar	Hindu ...	2	...	...	2	...	...	...	...	...	...	...	...	...	...	...	...	...	...
		Total Group 14.....	......	418,246	92,769	375	402,770	816	1	10,894	5,459	251	8,916	133	1	11,667	4.787	11	11,345	40	...
	15	Pusala	......	980	29	...	943	...	...	...	...	...	...	...	...	46	2	..	33	...	...
		Total Group 15	......	980	29	...	943	...	..	...	...	...	...	...	...	46	2	...	33	...	...

TABLE C.

Literate by Language known.—(Provincial Summary)—*continued.*

Class.	Group.	Caste.	Religion.	MAHBUBNAGAR. Males. Total Males.	Males. Literate. Total.	Males. Literate. English.	Females. Total Females.	Females. Literate. Total.	Females. Literate. English.	NALGONDA. Males. Total Males.	Males. Literate. Total.	Males. Literate. English.	Females. Total Females.	Females. Literate. Total.	Females. Literate. English.	WARANGAL. Males. Total Males.	Males. Literate. Total.	Males. Literate. English.	Females. Total Females.	Females. Literate. Total.	Females. Literate. English.
				23	24	25	26	27	28	29	30	31	32	33	34	35	36	37	38	39	40
C. Commercial—(*contd.*)	14	Aoti ...	Hindu	...	...	...	...	...	...	...	...	...	...	...	...	...	...	...	...	...	...
		Balija	"	6,599	2,185	2	6,884	43	...	1,982	205	...	1,927	3	...	1,134	136	...	1,113	3	...
		Bhattia	"	...	...	...	...	...	...	...	...	...	...	...	...	...	...	...	...	...	...
		Bora ...	Mussulman	...	...	...	...	...	...	...	...	...	...	...	...	...	...	...	...	...	...
		Chanewar	Hindu	...	...	...	...	...	...	...	...	...	...	...	...	...	...	...	...	...	...
		Eginawar	"	...	...	...	...	...	...	...	...	...	...	...	...	...	...	...	...	...	...
		Guzerati	"	...	...	...	...	...	...	4	...	...	4	...	...	1	1	...	1	...	...
		Ghási...	"	...	...	...	...	...	...	...	...	...	...	...	...	...	...	...	...	...	...
		Do.	Jain	...	...	...	...	...	...	...	...	...	...	...	...	...	...	...	...	...	...
		Jayarkhani	Hindu	...	...	...	...	...	...	...	...	...	...	...	...	...	...	...	...	...	...
		Josaputri	"	...	...	...	...	...	...	...	...	...	...	...	...	...	...	...	...	...	...
		Kapur	"	...	...	...	...	...	...	...	...	...	...	...	...	...	...	...	...	...	...
		Kasad	"	...	...	...	...	...	...	...	...	...	...	...	...	...	...	...	...	...	...
		Komati	Hindu	10,143	5,488	1	9,763	59	...	11,825	5,458	13	11,359	45	...	14,912	7,291	15	14,249	72	...
		Kutchi	"	...	...	...	...	...	...	...	...	...	...	...	...	...	...	...	...	...	...
		Lingayet	"	334	99	...	378	...	...	...	...	...	...	...	...	86	13	...	91	...	...
		Memon	Mussulman	...	...	...	...	...	...	...	...	...	...	...	...	...	...	...	...	...	...
		Saiti ...	Hindu	33	2	...	30	...	...	48	...	...	55	...	...	9	...	...	9	...	...
		Wani ...	"	345	141	...	282	1	...	13	6	...	12	...	...	66	41	...	41	2	...
		Do. ...	Jain	...	...	...	...	...	...	...	...	...	...	...	...	...	...	...	...	...	...
		Yelgar or Elgar	Hindu	...	...	...	...	...	...	...	...	...	...	...	...	...	...	...	...	...	...
		Total Group 14	......	17,454	7,915	3	17,337	103	...	13,872	5,669	13	13,357	48	...	16,208	7,482	15	15,504	77	...
	15	Pusala ...	......	...	...	...	...	...	...	507	17	...	471	...	...	129	8	...	143	...	...
		Total Group 15	......	...	...	...	...	...	...	507	17	...	471	...	...	129	8	...	143	...	...

TABLE C.

Literate by Language known.—(Provincial Summary)—*continued.*

Class.	Group.	Caste.	Religion.	ELGANDAL. Males. Total Males.	ELGANDAL. Males. Literate. Total.	ELGANDAL. Males. Literate. English.	ELGANDAL. Females. Total Females.	ELGANDAL. Females. Literate. Total.	ELGANDAL. Females. Literate. English.	INDUR. Males. Total Males.	INDUR. Males. Literate. Total.	INDUR. Males. Literate. English.	INDUR. Females. Total Females.	INDUR. Females. Literate. Total.	INDUR. Females. Literate. English.	MEDAK. Males. Total Males.	MEDAK. Males. Literate. Total.	MEDAK. Males. Literate. English.	MEDAK. Females. Total Females.	MEDAK. Females. Literate. Total.	MEDAK. Females. Literate. English.
				41	42	43	44	45	46	47	48	49	50	51	52	53	54	55	56	57	58
C. Commerci[illegible]—(contd.)	14	Aoti ...	Hindu ...	...	...	...	...	...	...	...	...	...	...	...	...	...	...	...	...	...	...
		Balija	„	2,461	243	...	2,393	9	...	...	...	...	...	...	...	4,822	1,121	1	4,787	10	...
		Bhattia	„	...	...	...	...	...	...	...	...	...	...	...	...	...	...	...	...	...	...
		Bora ...	Mussulman	...	...	...	...	...	...	...	...	...	...	...	...	...	...	...	...	...	...
		Chanewar	Hindu ...	...	...	...	...	...	...	386	9	...	416	...	...	...	...	...	...	...	...
		Eginawar	„	...	...	...	...	...	...	1	1	...	...	...	...	...	...	...	...	...	...
		Guzerati	„	...	...	...	...	...	...	1	...	...	...	...	...	13	...	...	12	...	...
		Ghâsi...	„	...	...	...	...	...	...	...	...	...	...	...	...	...	...	...	...	...	...
		Do.	Jain	...	...	...	...	...	...	...	...	...	...	...	...	...	...	...	...	...	...
		Jayarkhani	Hindu ...	...	...	...	...	...	...	...	...	...	...	...	...	...	...	...	...	...	...
		Josaputri	„	...	...	...	...	...	...	8	3	...	4	...	...	...	...	...	...	...	...
		Kapur	„	...	...	...	...	...	...	...	...	...	...	...	...	...	...	...	...	...	...
		Kasad	„	...	...	...	...	...	...	19	7	...	21	...	...	...	...	...	...	...	...
		Komati	Hindu ...	18,957	8,891	5	17,929	99	...	7,948	4,008	8	8,079	26	...	7,426	4,360	8	7,278	30	...
		Kutchi	„	...	...	...	...	...	...	...	...	...	...	...	...	...	...	...	...	...	...
		Lingayet	„	37	15	...	32	...	...	252	12	...	239	1	...	250	45	...	225	...	...
		Memon	Mussulman	...	...	...	...	...	...	...	...	...	...	...	...	...	...	...	...	...	...
		Saiti ...	Hindu ..	83	2	...	98	...	...	...	...	...	...	...	...	...	...	...	...	...	...
		Wani...	„	153	104	...	106	...	...	9,622	1,162	1	9,411	11	...	138	51	...	99	...	...
		Do. ...	Jain ..	...	...	...	...	...	...	31	19	...	26	...	...	...	...	...	...	...	...
		Yelgar or Elgar	Hindu ...	...	...	...	...	...	...	...	...	...	...	...	...	...	...	...	...	...	...
		Total Group 14	......	21,691	9,255	5	20,558	108	...	18,268	5,221	9	18,196	38	...	12,649	5,577	9	12,401	40	...
	15	Pusala	Hindu ...	292	2	...	294	...	...	...	...	...	...	...	...	6	...	...	2	...	...
		Total Group 15......	......	292	2	...	294	...	...	...	...	...	...	...	...	6	...	...	2	...	...

TABLE C.

Literate by Language known.—(Provincial Summary)—*continued.*

Class.	Group.	Caste.	Religion.	AURUNGABAD. Males. Total Males.	Males. Literate. Total.	Males. Literate. English.	Females. Total Females.	Females. Literate. Total.	Females. Literate. English.
				59	60	61	62	63	64
C. Commercial—(contd.)	14	Aoti	Hindu	15	10	...	13	...	...
		Balija	"	13	4	4	14	3	...
		Bhattia	"	44	18	...	4	...	...
		Bora	Mussulman	13	3	...	11	...	...
		Chanewar	Hindu	...	...	...	...	...	...
		Eginawar	"	...	...	...	...	...	...
		Guzerati	"	40	12	...	45	1	...
		Ghási	"	...	...	...	...	...	...
		Do.	Jain	12	9	...	13	...	...
		Jayarkhani	Hindu	187	...	...	201	...	...
		Josaputri	"	...	...	...	...	...	...
		Kapur	"	5	1	...	5	1	...
		Kasad	"	...	...	...	...	...	...
		Komati	Hindu	698	41	...	778	...	...
		Kutchi	"	...	...	...	...	...	...
		Lingayet	"	577	76	...	542	...	...
		Memon	Mussulman	...	...	...	...	...	...
		Saiti	Hindu	...	...	...	...	...	...
		Wani	"	6,342	2,168	...	5,535	12	...
		Do.	Jain	2,391	1,220	1	1,876	7	...
		Yelgar or Elgar	Hindu	...	...	...	...	...	...
		Total Group 14	......	10,337	3,562	5	9,037	24	...
	15	Pusala	Hindu	...	...	...	...	...	...
		Total Group 15	......	...	...	...	...	...	...

Caste.	Religion.	BIRH. Males. Total Males.	Males. Literate. Total.	Males. Literate. English.	Females. Total Females.	Females. Literate. Total.	Females. Literate. English.	NANDER. Males. Total Males.	Males. Literate. Total.	Males. Literate. English.	Females. Total Females.	Females. Literate. Total.	Females. Literate. English.
		65	66	67	68	69	70	71	72	73	74	75	76
Aoti	Hindu	...	...	...	...	...	...	...	...	...	...	...	...
Balija	"	...	...	...	...	...	...	...	...	...	...	...	...
Bhattia	"	...	...	...	...	...	...	...	...	...	...	...	...
Bora	Mussulman	9	...	...	8	...	...	...	...	...	...	...	...
Chanewar	Hindu	...	...	...	...	...	...	2,327	29	...	2,235	...	...
Eginawar	"	...	...	...	...	...	...	...	...	...	...	...	...
Guzerati	"	5	4	...	...	...	...	1	...	...	...	...	...
Ghási	"	...	...	...	...	...	...	15	...	...	6	...	...
Do.	Jain	...	...	...	...	...	...	...	...	...	...	...	...
Jayarkhani	Hindu	...	...	...	...	...	...	1	...	...	2	...	...
Josaputri	"	...	...	...	...	...	...	...	...	...	...	...	...
Kapur	"	...	...	...	...	...	...	...	...	...	...	...	...
Kasad	"	118	41	...	116	...	...	11	2	...	17	...	...
Komati	Hindu	603	162	...	643	...	...	6,449	2,694	...	6,402	9	...
Kutchi	"	2	...	...	2	...	...	...	...	...	...	...	...
Lingayet	"	667	75	...	611	1	...	257	20	...	269	...	...
Memon	Mussulman	...	...	...	...	...	...	...	...	...	...	...	...
Saiti	Hindu	...	...	...	...	...	...	...	...	...	...	...	...
Wani	"	8,330	2,246	...	7,383	11	...	25,023	1,444	...	23,990	10	...
Do.	Jain	1,137	584	...	968	4	...	138	65	...	132	...	...
Yelgar or Elgar	Hindu	...	...	...	...	...	...	...	...	...	...	...	...
Total Group 14	......	10,871	3,112	...	9,731	16	...	34,222	4,254	...	33,053	19	...
Pusala	Hindu	...	...	...	...	...	...	...	...	...	...	...	...
Total Group 15	......	...	...	...	...	...	...	...	...	...	...	...	...

TABLE C.

Literate by Language known.—(Provincial Summary)—*continued.*

Class.	Group.	Caste.	Religion.	NALDRUG. Males. Total Males.	NALDRUG. Males. Literate. Total.	NALDRUG. Males. Literate. English.	NALDRUG. Females. Total Females.	NALDRUG. Females. Literate. Total.	NALDRUG. Females. Literate. English.	BIDAR. Males. Total Males.	BIDAR. Males. Literate. Total.	BIDAR. Males. Literate. English.	BIDAR. Females. Total Females.	BIDAR. Females. Literate. Total.	BIDAR. Females. Literate. English.	PARBHANI. Males. Total Males.	PARBHANI. Males. Literate. Total.	PARBHANI. Males. Literate. English.	PARBHANI. Females. Total Females	PARBHANI. Females. Literate. Total.	PARBHANI. Females. Literate. English.
				77	78	79	80	81	82	83	84	85	86	87	88	89	90	91	92	93	94
C. Commercial—*continued.*	14	Aoti ...	Hindu ...	...	...	...	...	...	...	3	...	...	4	...	...	...	...	...	...	...	...
		Balija ..	"	...	...	...	...	...	...	95	11	...	86	...	...	...	...	...	...	...	...
		Bhattia ...	"	54	1	...	76	...	...	...	...	...	...	...	...	...	...	...	...	...	...
		Bora ...	Mussulman	...	...	...	...	...	...	...	...	...	...	...	...	...	...	...	...	...	...
		Chanewar ...	Hindu ...	5	...	...	7	...	...	1	...	...	5	...	...	1,476	8	...	1,427	...	...
		Eginawar ...	"	...	...	...	...	...	...	...	...	...	...	...	...	...	...	...	...	...	...
		Guzerati ...	"	19	4	...	18	...	...	30	3	...	19	...	...	28	1	...	28	...	...
		Ghasi...	"	...	...	...	...	...	...	...	...	...	...	...	...	...	...	...	...	...	...
		Do ...	Jain ...	1	1	...	...	...	...	...	...	...	...	...	...	...	...	...	...	...	...
		Jayarkhani ...	Hindu ...	...	...	...	...	...	...	...	...	...	...	...	...	...	...	...	...	...	...
		Josapurtri ...	"	...	...	...	...	...	...	...	...	...	...	...	...	...	...	...	...	...	...
		Kapur ...	"	...	...	...	...	...	...	...	...	...	...	...	...	1	...	...	...	...	...
		Kasad ...	"	1	...	...	1	...	...	...	...	...	...	...	...	244	59	...	203	...	...
		Komati ...	Hindu ...	257	54	...	272	...	...	5,242	2,150	...	5,045	8	...	1,471	644	...	1,796	2	...
		Kutchi ...	"	...	...	...	...	...	...	...	...	...	...	...	...	...	...	...	...	...	...
		Lingayet ...	"	273	42	...	226	...	...	6,639	473	...	6,423	2	...	158	13	...	111	...	...
		Memon ...	Mussulman	...	...	...	...	...	...	...	...	...	...	...	...	...	...	...	...	...	...
		Saiti ...	Hindu ...	...	...	...	...	...	...	23	...	...	22	...	...	...	...	...	...	...	...
		Wani ...	"	25,740	3,352	...	23,960	17	...	71,643	5,175	...	69,566	19	...	14,331	2,758	...	12,585	11	...
		Do. ..	Jain ...	552	232	...	459	2	...	85	32	...	67	...	...	862	289	...	741	6	...
		Yelgar or E'gar ...	Hindu ...	...	...	...	...	...	...	2	...	...	2	...	...	...	...	...	...	...	...
		Total Group 4		26,902	3,636	...	25,019	19	...	83,763	7 844	...	81,239	29	...	18,571	3,772	...	16,891	19	...
	15	Pusala ...	Hindu ...	...	...	...	...	...	...	...	...	...	...	...	...	...	...	...	...	...	...
		Total Group 5......		...	...	...	...	...	...	...	...	...	...	...	...	...	...	...	...	...	...

TABLE C.

Literate by Language known.—(Provincial Summary)—*continued.*

Class.	Group.	Caste.	Religion.	SIRPUR TANDUR.						GALBURGA.						RAICHUR.					
				Males.			Females.			Males.			Females.			Males.			Females.		
				Total Males.	Literate. Total.	Literate. English.	Total Females.	Literate. Total.	Literate. English.	Total Males.	Literate. Total.	Literate. English.	Total Females.	Literate. Total.	Literate. English.	Total Males.	Literate. Total.	Literate. English.	Total Females.	Literate. Total.	Literate. English.
				95	96	97	98	99	100	101	102	103	104	105	106	107	108	109	110	111	112
C. Commercial—(*continued.*)	14	Aoti	Hindu ...	...	...	...	...	...	...	...	...	...	...	...	...	...	...	...	...	...	...
		Balija	" ...	...	...	...	...	...	...	...	...	...	...	...	...	8,415	1,200	1	8,735	15	...
		Bhatta	" ...	...	...	...	...	...	...	7	...	...	8	...	...	...	...	...	...	...	...
		Bora	Mussulman	...	...	...	...	...	...	...	...	...	...	...	...	1	...	...	2	...	...
		Chanewar	Hindu ...	...	...	...	...	...	...	4	2	...	2	...	...	...	...	...	...	...	...
		Eginawar	" ...	25	8	...	26	...	...	...	...	...	...	...	...	...	...	.	...	...	...
		Guzerati	" ...	3	...	...	5	...	...	9	9	...	...	...	...	...	...	...	...	...	...
		Ghasi	" ...	...	...	...	...	...	...	...	...	...	...	...	...	...	...	...	...	...	...
		Do.	Jain ...	...	...	...	...	...	...	...	...	...	...	...	...	...	...	...	...	...	...
		Jayarkhani	Hindu ...	14	...	...	11	...	...	...	...	...	...	...	...	...	...	...	...	...	...
		Josaputri	" ..	...	...	...	...	...	...	...	...	...	...	...	...	...	...	...	...	...	...
		Kapur	" ...	1	...	...	...	...	...	...	...	...	...	...	...	...	...	...	...	...	...
		Kasad	" ...	...	...	...	...	...	...	...	...	...	...	...	...	...	...	...	...	...	...
		Komati	Hindu ..	2,021	697	4	2,249	3	...	1,993	912	6	1,927	6	...	3,932	1,463	7	3,808	15	...
		Kutchi	" ...	...	...	...	...	...	...	...	...	...	...	...	...	...	...	...	...	...	...
		Lingayet	" ...	41	...	...	40	...	...	29,650	2,000	22	29,308	7	...	4,082	685	...	4,101	3	...
		Memon	Mussulman	...	...	...	...	...	...	...	...	...	...	...	...	...	...	...	...	...	...
		Saiti	Hindu ..	...	...	...	...	...	...	33	...	...	32	...	...	380	43	...	424	...	...
		Wani	" ...	363	32	...	328	...	...	35,241	3,372	5	34,820	11	...	14	4	...	8	...	...
		Do.	Jain ..	...	...	...	...	...	...	65	29	...	52	...	...	56	50	...	33	...	...
		Yelgar or Elgar	Hindu ...	...	...	...	...	...	...	...	...	...	...	...	...	...	...	...	...	...	...
		Total Group 14	......	2,468	737	4	2,659	3	...	67 002	6,324	33	66,149	24	...	16,880	3,445	8	17,111	33	...
	15	Pusala	Hindu ...	...	...	...	...	...	...	...	...	...	...	...	...	...	...	...	...	...	...
		Total Group 15	......	...	...	...	...	...	...	...	...	...	...	...	...	...	...	...	...	...	...

TABLE C.

Literate by Language known.—(Provincial Summary)—*continued.*

Class.	Group.	Caste.	Religion.	LINGASUGUR. Males. Total Males.	Males. Literate. Total.	Males. Literate. English.	Females. Total Females.	Females. Literate. Total.	Females. Literate. English.	RAILWAY. Males. Total Males.	Males. Literate. Total.	Males. Literate. English.	Females. Total Females.	Females. Literate. Total.	Females. Literate. English.
				113	114	115	116	117	118	119	120	121	122	123	124
C. Commercial—*continued.*	14	Aoti ...	Hindu ...	...	...	...	...	...	...	...	...	...	...	...	...
		Balija ..	" ...	10,344	2,269	...	10,012	27	...	9	3	2	5	...	...
		Bhattia	" ...	...	...	...	...	...	...	...	...	...	...	...	...
		Bora ...	Mussulman	...	...	...	...	...	...	...	...	...	...	...	...
		Chanewar	Hindu ...	...	...	...	...	...	...	...	...	...	...	...	...
		Eginawar	" ...	...	...	...	...	...	...	...	...	...	...	...	...
		Gujzerati	" ...	6	2	1	4	...	...	10	4	...	...	...	...
		Ghasi ...	" ...	...	...	...	...	...	...	...	...	...	...	...	...
		Do.	Jain ...	...	...	...	...	...	...	...	...	...	...	...	...
		Jayarkhani	Hindu ...	...	...	...	...	...	...	...	...	...	...	...	...
		Josaputri	" ...	...	...	...	...	...	...	...	...	...	...	...	...
		Kapur	" ...	...	...	...	...	...	...	...	...	...	...	...	...
		Kasad	" ...	...	...	...	...	...	...	...	...	...	...	...	...
		Komati	Hindu ...	2,225	641	...	2,061	4	...	15	12	1	4	...	...
		Kutchi	" ...	...	...	...	...	...	...	...	...	...	...	...	...
		Lingayet	" ...	4,728	656	...	4,930	8	...	22	1	...	7	...	...
		Memon	Mussulman	...	...	...	...	...	...	...	...	...	...	...	...
		Saiti ...	Hindu ...	...	...	...	...	...	...	...	...	...	...	...	...
		Wani ...	" ...	6,989	971	1	7,183	4	...	77	32	2	27	...	...
		Do.	Jain ...	98	75	2	33	...	...	4	2	...	1	...	...
		Yelgar or Elgar	Hindu ...	...	...	...	...	...	...	...	...	...	...	...	...
		Total Group 14	......	24,390	4,614	4	24,223	43	...	137	54	5	44	...	...
	15	Pusala ...	Hindu ...	...	...	...	...	...	...	...	...	...	...	...	...
		Total Group 15	......	...	...	...	...	...	...	...	...	...	...	...	...

TABLE C.

Literate by Language known—(Provincial Summary)—*continued.*

Class.	Group.	Caste.	Religion.	TOTAL STRENGTH.						HYDERABAD.						ATRAF-I-BALDA.					
				Males.			Females.			Males.			Females.			Males.			Females.		
				Total Males.	Literate.		Total Females.	Literate.		Total Males.	Literate.		Total Females.	Literate.		Total Males.	Literate.		Total Females.	Literate.	
					Total.	English.		Total.	English.		Total.	English.		Total.	English.		Total.	English.		Total.	English.
1	2	3	4	5	6	7	8	9	10	11	12	13	14	15	16	17	18	19	20	21	22
C. Commercial—(*concluded*).	16	Banjara	Hindu ...	69,010	656	...	64,024	8	...	102	12	...	75	...	...	...	...	...	...	...	...
		Hammal	" ...	108	5	...	70	...	...	94	5	...	62	...	...	...	...	...	...	...	...
		Lad	" ...	2,685	301	...	2,530	1	...	13	...	...	6	...	...	...	...	...	...	...	...
		"	Jain ...	196	59	...	171	...	...	...	...	...	...	...	...	...	...	...	...	...	...
		Lamani	Hindu ...	89,051	124	...	72,348	4	...	28	4	...	17	...	...	1,255	4	...	833	...	...
		Total Group 16......	......	1,61,039	1,145	...	1,39,143	13	...	237	21	...	160	...	...	1,255	4	...	833	...	...
		Total Class C	......	5,80,258	93,942	375	5,42,856	829	1	11,131	5,480	251	9,076	133	1	12,958	4,793	11	12,211	40	...
D. Artisan and Village Menial.	17	Panchala	Hindu ...	8,385	683	...	8,193	3	...	10	...	...	1	...	...	249	14	...	217	...	...
		"	Jain ...	41	6	...	37	...	...	...	...	...	...	...	...	...	...	...	...	...	...
		Sonar or Ausala	Hindu ...	52,392	10,477	25	50,754	97	...	2,575	493	8	2,459	13	...	2,062	549	...	2,012	1	...
		"	Jain ...	56	9	...	34	...	...	...	...	...	...	...	...	...	...	...	...	...	...
		"	Mussulman	...	...	..	1	...	...	...	...	...	...	...	...	...	...	...	...	...	...
		Total Group 17......	......	60,874	11,175	25	59,019	100	...	2,585	493	8	2,460	13	...	2,311	563	...	2,229	1	...
	18	Hajjam or Mangala	Hindu ...	60,455	752	9	58,320	12	...	2,334	175	4	2,054	9	...	2,709	36	..	2,494	1	...
		" ..	Jain ...	20	4	...	8	...	...	...	...	...	...	...	...	...	...	...	...	...	...
		Total Group 18	......	60,475	756	9	58,328	12	..	2,334	175	4	2,054	9	...	2,709	36	...	2,494	1	...
	19	Ghisadi	Hindu ...	770	...	...	792	...	...	...	...	...	...	...	...	...	...	...	...	...	...
		Kirajgar	" ...	110	2	...	103	...	...	...	...	...	...	...	...	...	...	...	...	...	...
		Lohar	" ...	30,708	1,117	2	29,196	16	...	368	48	...	327	3	...	1,309	72	...	1,253	1	...
		Nalband	" ...	6	1	...	5	...	...	...	...	...	...	...	...	...	...	...	...	...	...
		Total Group 19	......	31,594	1,120	2	30,096	16	...	368	48	...	327	3	...	1,309	72	...	1,253	1	...
	20	Gaondi or Gaond	Hindu ...	14,477	299	4	14,330	3	1	491	88	4	469	2	1	617	22	...	609	...	...
		Hanigevaru	" ...	22	...	...	14	...	...	...	...	...	...	...	...	...	...	...	...	...	...
		Nakashgar	" ...	431	32	1	444	...	...	53	5	1	62	...	...	1	...	...	1	...	...
		"	Jain ...	3	..	...	1	...	...	...	...	...	...	...	...	...	...	...	...	...	...
		Sutar...	Hindu ...	52,833	1,870	2	50,614	27	...	1,015	65	...	932	5	...	1,919	128	...	1,875	2	...

TABLE C.

Literate by Language known—(Provincial Summary)—*continued.*

Class.	Group.	Caste.	Religion.	MAHBUBNAGAR. Males. Total Males.	Males. Literate. Total.	Males. Literate. English.	Females. Total Females.	Females. Literate. Total.	Females. Literate. English.	NALGONDA. Males. Total Males.	Males. Literate. Total.	Males. Literate. English.	Females. Total Females.	Females. Literate. Total.	Females. Literate. English.	WARANGAL. Males. Total Males.	Males. Literate. Total.	Males. Literate. English.	Females. Total Females.	Females. Literate. Total.	Females. Literate. English.
				23	24	25	26	27	28	29	30	31	32	33	34	35	36	37	38	39	40
C. Commercial—(*concluded*).	16	Banjara	Hindu	...	...	...	...	...	...	75	...	...	59	...	...	...	...	...	...	...	...
		Hammal	,,	...	...	...	...	...	...	...	...	...	...	...	...	...	...	...	...	...	...
		Lad	,,	...	...	...	...	...	...	...	...	...	...	...	...	...	...	...	...	...	...
		,,	Jain	...	...	...	...	...	...	...	...	...	...	...	...	...	...	...	...	...	...
		Lamani	Hindu	5,549	23	...	3,911	...	...	15,539	3	...	11,757	...	...	16,870	35	...	13,658	3	...
		Total Group 16	......	5,549	23	...	3,911	...	...	15,614	3	...	11,816	...	...	16,870	35	...	13,658	3	...
		Total Class C	......	23,003	7,938	3	21,248	103	...	29,993	5,689	13	25,644	48	...	33,207	7,525	15	29,305	80	...
D. Artisan and Village Menial.	17	Panchal	Hindu	...	...	...	...	...	...	153	22	...	173	...	...	51	9	...	40	...	...
		,,	Jain	...	...	...	...	...	...	...	...	...	...	...	...	...	...	...	...	...	...
		Sonar or Ausala	Hindu	2,939	895	...	2,940	8	...	3,485	1,063	4	3,319	6	...	5,065	1,383	4	4,906	24	...
		,,	Jain	...	...	...	...	...	...	...	...	...	...	...	...	...	...	...	...	...	...
		,,	Mussalman	...	...	...	...	...	...	...	...	...	...	...	...	...	...	...	...	...	...
		Total Group 17	......	2,939	895	...	2,940	8	...	3,638	1,085	4	3,492	6	...	5,116	1,392	4	4,946	24	...
	18	Hajjam or Mangala	Hindu	3,926	47	...	3,770	...	...	3,444	36	...	3,367	1	...	4,294	56	2	4,049	...	...
		,,	Jain	...	...	...	...	...	...	...	...	...	...	...	...	...	...	...	...	...	...
		Total Group 18	......	3,926	47	...	3,770	...	...	3,444	36	...	3,367	1	...	4,294	56	2	4,049	...	...
	19	Ghisadi	Hindu	...	...	...	...	...	...	...	...	...	...	...	...	...	...	...	...	...	...
		Kirajgar	,,	...	...	...	...	...	...	...	...	...	...	...	...	...	...	...	...	...	...
		Lohar	,,	2,083	137	...	2,010	7	...	2,599	125	...	2,461	...	...	4,324	176	1	4,042	...	...
		Nalband	,,	...	...	...	...	...	...	...	...	...	...	...	...	...	...	...	...	...	...
		Total Group 19	......	2,083	137	...	2,010	7	...	2,599	125	...	2,461	...	...	4,324	176	1	4,042	...	...
	20	Gaondi or Gaond	Hindu	4,356	40	...	4,243	...	...	343	3	...	304	...	...	1,097	10	...	1,126	...	...
		Hanigevaru	,,	...	...	...	...	...	...	...	...	...	...	...	...	...	...	...	...	...	...
		Nakashgar	,,	40	...	...	27	...	...	37	3	...	44	...	...	91	15	...	85	...	...
		,,	Jain	...	...	...	...	...	...	...	...	...	...	...	...	...	...	...	...	...	...
		Sutar	Hindu	3,299	214	...	3,089	4	...	2,851	164	1	2,795	...	...	3,794	210	1	3,740	4	...

TABLE C.

Literate by Language known—(Provincial Summary)—*continued.*

Class.	Group.	Caste.	Religion.	ELGANDAL. Males. Total Males.	ELGANDAL. Males. Literate. Total.	ELGANDAL. Males. Literate. English.	ELGANDAL. Females. Total Females.	ELGANDAL. Females. Literate. Total.	ELGANDAL. Females. Literate. English.	INDUR. Males. Total Males.	INDUR. Males. Literate. Total.	INDUR. Males. Literate. English.	INDUR. Females. Total Females.	INDUR. Females. Literate. Total.	INDUR. Females. Literate. English.	MEDAK. Males. Total Males.	MEDAK. Males. Literate. Total.	MEDAK. Males. Literate. English.	MEDAK. Females. Total Females.	MEDAK. Females. Literate. Total.	MEDAK. Females. Literate. English.
				41	42	43	44	45	46	47	48	49	50	51	52	53	54	55	56	57	58
C. Commercial—*concluded.*	16	Banjara	Hindu	96	...	...	99	...	...	2,612	120	...	2,896	...	...	380	33	...	325	...	...
		Hammal	,,	...	...	...	...	...	...	...	...	...	...	...	...	...	...	...	...	...	...
		Lad	,,	...	...	...	...	...	...	...	...	...	...	...	...	7	1	..	8	...	...
		,,	Jain	...	...	...	...	...	...	...	...	...	...	...	...	...	...	...	...	...	...
		Lamani	Hindu	5,432	4	...	4,437	...	...	6,404	5	...	5,398	...	...	2,059	1	...	1,395	...	...
		Total Group 16	......	5,528	4	...	4,536	...	...	9,016	125	...	8,294	...	...	2,446	35	...	1,728	..	...
		Total Class C	......	27,511	9,261	5	25,388	108	...	27,284	5,346	9	26,490	38	...	15,101	5,612	9	14,131	40	...
D. Artisan and Village Menial.	17	Panchal	Hindu	323	29	...	330	...	...	447	35	...	462	...	...	22	1	...	15	...	...
		,,	Jain	...	...	...	...	...	...	...	...	...	...	...	...	...	...	...	...	...	...
		Sonar or Ausala	Hindu	7,471	2,149	1	7,089	13	...	3,173	582	...	3,243	5	...	1,790	539	2	1,774	2	...
		,, ,,	Jain	...	...	...	...	...	...	...	...	...	...	...	...	...	...	...	...	...	...
		,, ,,	Mussulman	...	...	...	...	...	...	...	...	...	...	...	...	...	...	...	...	...	...
		Total Group 17	......	7,794	2,178	1	7,419	13	...	3,620	617	...	3,705	5	...	1,812	540	2	1,789	2	...
	18	Hajjam or Mangala	Hindu	5,876	15	...	5,570	1	...	3,478	62	...	3,688	...	...	2,592	23	...	2,501	...	...
		,, ,,	Jain	...	...	...	...	...	...	...	...	...	...	...	...	...	...	...	...	...	...
		Total Group 18	......	5,876	15	...	5,570	1	...	3,478	62	...	3,688	...	...	2,592	23	...	2,501	...	...
	19	Ghisadi	Hindu	...	...	...	...	...	...	...	...	...	...	...	...	...	...	...	...	...	...
		Kirajgar	,,	...	...	...	...	...	...	...	...	...	...	...	...	...	...	...	...	...	...
		Lohar	,,	4,791	136	...	4,402	...	...	1,581	52	...	1,548	1	...	1,156	79	...	1,143	...	...
		Nalband	,,	...	..	...	...	...	...	...	...	...	...	...	...	...	...	...	...	...	...
		Total Group 19	......	4,791	136	...	4,402	...	...	1,581	52	...	1,548	1	...	1, 56	79	...	1,143	...	...
	20	Gaondi or Gaond	Hindu	640	6	...	622	...	...	549	28	...	568	...	...	433	23	...	395	...	...
		Hanigevaru	,,	...	...	...	...	...	...	...	...	...	...	...	...	...	...	...	...	...	...
		Nakashgar	,,	30	8	...	37	...	...	61	1	...	66	...	...	...	...	...	...	...	...
		,,	Jain	...	...	...	...	...	...	...	...	...	...	...	...	...	...	...	...	...	...
		Sutar	Hindu	6,110	221	...	5,742	5	...	3,017	123	...	3,065	1	...	1,848	73	...	1,859	...	...

TABLE C.

Literate by Language known—(Provincial Summary)—*continued.*

Class.	Group.	Caste.	Religion.	AURUNGABAD. Males. Total Males.	Males. Literate. Total.	Males. Literate. English.	Females. Total Females.	Females. Literate. Total.	Females. Literate. English.	BIRH. Males. Total Males.	Males. Literate. Total.	Males. Literate. English.	Females. Total Females.	Females. Literate. Total.	Females. Literate. English.	NANDER. Males. Total Males.	Males. Literate. Total.	Males. Literate. English.	Females. Total Females.	Females. Literate. Total.	Females. Literate. English.
				59	60	61	62	63	64	65	66	67	68	69	70	71	72	73	74	75	76
C. Commercial—(*concluded*).	16	Banjara	Hindu	9,196	46	...	8,536	1	...	28,303	152	...	26,589	4	...	5,191	38	...	4,580	1	...
		Hammal	"	...	...	...	...	...	...	...	...	...	...	...	...	...	...	...	...	...	...
		Lad	"	463	98	...	366	...	...	370	59	...	346	...	...	...	...	...	...	...	...
		"	Jain	162	49	...	142	...	...	24	4	...	20	...	...	...	...	...	...	...	...
		Lamani	Hindu	2,774	2	...	2,407	...	...	1,809	2	...	1,598	...	...	4,205	7	...	3,845	1	...
		Total Group 16......	......	12,595	195	...	11,451	1	...	30,506	217	...	28,553	4	...	9,396	45	...	8,428	2	...
		Total Class C......	......	22,932	3,757	5	20,488	25	...	41,377	3,329	...	38,284	20	...	43,618	4,299	...	41,181	21	...
D. Artisan and Village Menial.	17	Panchal	Hindu	54	...	...	43	...	...	33	2	...	29	...	...	307	14	...	257	...	...
		"	Jain	...	...	...	...	...	...	...	...	...	...	...	...	5	...	...	8	...	...
		Sonar or Ausala	Hindu	4,303	375	1	4,086	5	...	3,464	374	...	3,162	4	...	2,333	249	...	2,382	1	...
		"	Jain	24	7	...	10	...	...	8	2	...	3	...	...	...	...	...	...	...	...
		"	Mussulman	...	...	...	...	...	...	...	...	...	...	...	...	...	...	...	...	...	...
		Total Group 17......	......	4,331	382	1	4,139	5	...	3,505	378	...	3,194	4	...	2,645	262	...	2,647	1	...
	18	Hajjam or Mangala	Hindu	4,164	29	...	4,073	...	...	3,247	14	...	3,153	...	...	3,29	9	...	3,178	...	...
		"	Jain	1	...	...	...	...	...	19	4	...	8	...	...	...	...	...	...	...	...
		Total Group 18......	......	4,165	29	...	4,073	...	...	3,266	18	...	3,161	...	...	3,293	9	...	3,178	...	...
	19	Ghisadi	Hindu	108	...	...	122	...	...	144	...	...	180	...	...	118	...	...	117	...	...
		Kirajgar	"	7	...	...	8	...	...	...	...	...	...	...	...	6	...	...	4	...	...
		Lohar	"	1,971	40	...	1,901	1	...	1,516	12	...	1,449	...	...	989	13	...	1,011	...	...
		Nalband	"	...	...	...	...	...	...	...	...	...	...	...	...	...	...	...	...	...	...
		Total Group 19......	......	2,086	40	...	2,031	1	...	1,660	12	...	1,629	...	...	1,113	12	...	1,132	...	...
	20	Gaondi or Gaond	Hindu	202	6	...	185	...	...	33	1	...	37	...	...	1,130	6	...	1,109	...	...
		Hanigevaru	"	...	...	...	...	...	...	...	...	...	...	...	...	...	...	...	...	...	...
		Nakashgar	"	45	...	...	50	...	...	...	...	...	...	...	...	...	...	...	...	...	...
		"	Jain	...	...	...	...	...	...	3	...	...	1	...	...	...	...	...	...	...	...
		Sutar	Hindu	3,439	70	...	3,325	1	...	3,387	56	...	3,186	1	...	3,738	60	...	3,605	2	...

TABLE C.

Literate by Language known—(Provincial Summary)—*continued.*

Class.	Group.	Caste.	Religion.	NALDRUG.						BIDAR.						PARBHANI.					
				MALES.			FEMALES.			MALES.			FEMALES.			MALES.			FEMALES.		
				Total Males.	Literate. Total.	Literate. English.	Total Females.	Literate. Total.	Literate. English.	Total Males.	Literate. Total.	Literate. English.	Total Females.	Literate. Total.	Literate. English.	Total Males.	Literate. Total.	Literate. English.	Total Females.	Literate. Total.	Literate. English.
				77	78	79	80	81	82	83	84	85	86	87	88	89	90	91	92	93	94
C. Commercial—(concluded).	16	Banjara	Hindu ...	3,419	79	...	3,153	1	...	6,624	77	...	5,863	...	...	12,033	91	...	10,964	1	...
		Hammal	" ...	...	...	...	...	...	...	13	...	...	8	...	...	...	...	...	...	...	...
		Lad	" ...	150	21	...	129	...	...	1,247	57	...	1,267	1	...	164	49	...	152	...	...
		"	Jain ..	2	2	...	1	...	...	8	4	...	8	...	...	...	...	...	...	...	...
		Lamani	Hindu ...	661	...	...	594	..	...	2,835	6	...	2,375	...	...	7,024	2	...	6,194	...	...
		Total Group 16......	......	4,232	102	...	3,877	1	...	10,727	144	...	9,521	1	...	19,221	142	...	17,310	1	...
		Total Class C.	......	31,134	3,788	...	28,896	20	...	94 490	7,988	...	90,760	30	...	37,792	3,914	...	34,201	20	...
	17	Panchal	Hindu ...	43	...	...	36	...	...	1,348	56	...	1,276	...	...	63	2	...	57	...	...
		"	Jain ...	10	...	...	9	...	...	11	3	...	3	...	...	15	3	...	17	...	...
		Sonar or Ausa'a	Hindu ...	2,423	338	...	2,279	...	...	2,737	250	...	2,667	...	...	3,372	324	1	3,274	...	...
		"	Jain ..	7	...	...	5	...	...	...	...	...	...	...	...	17	...	...	16	...	...
		"	Mussulman	...	...	...	...	...	...	...	...	...	1	...	...	...	...	...	...	...	...
		Total Group 17......	......	2,483	338	...	2,329	...	...	4,096	309	...	3,947	...	...	3 467	329	1	3,364	...	...
D. Artisan and Village Menial.	18	Hajjam or Manga'a	Hindu ...	3,452	17	...	3,235	...	...	4,088	22	...	3,988	...	...	3,937	28	...	3,955	...	...
		"	Jain ..	...	...	...	...	...	...	...	...	...	...	...	...	...	...	...	...	...	...
		Total Group 18......	......	3,452	17	...	3,235	...	...	4,058	22	...	3 988	...	...	3,937	28	...	3,955	...	...
	19	Ghisadi	Hindu ...	102	...	...	86	...	...	54	...	...	54	...	...	205	...	...	216	...	...
		Kirajgar	" ...	17	...	...	9	...	...	11	...	...	12	...	...	69	2	...	70	...	...
		Lohar	" ...	1,378	20	...	1,272	...	...	1,452	25	...	1,396	...	...	1,193	6	1	1,230	...	...
		Nalband	" ...	...	...	...	...	...	...	...	...	...	...	...	...	5	1	...	4	...	...
		Total Group 19......	......	1,497	20	..	1,367	...	...	1,517	25	...	1,462	...	...	1,472	9	1	1,520	...	...
	20	Gaondi or Gaond	Hindu ...	1,060	32	...	1,028	1	...	2,576	21	...	2,649	...	...	405	11	...	394	...	...
		Hanigevaru	" ...	...	...	...	...	...	...	...	...	...	..	...	...	...	...	...	...	...	...
		Nakashgar	" ...	...	...	...	...	...	...	16	...	...	13	...	...	4	...	...	6	...	...
		"	Jain ...	...	...	...	...	...	...	...	...	...	...	...	...	...	...	...	...	...	...
		Sutar	Hindu ...	2,572	57	...	3,276	..	..	3,535	46	..	3,286	...	...	3,938	46	...	3,557	...	...

TABLE C.

Literate by Language known—(Provincial Summary)—*continued.*

Class.	Group.	Caste.	Religion.	SIRPUR TANDUR. Males. Total Males.	Males. Literate. Total.	Males. Literate. English.	Females. Total Females.	Females. Literate. Total.	Females. Literate. English.	GULBARGA. Males. Total Males.	Males. Literate. Total.	Males. Literate. English.	Females. Total Females.	Females. Literate. Total.	Females. Literate. English.	RAICHUR. Males. Total Males.	Males. Literate. Total.	Males. Literate. English.	Females. Total Females.	Females. Literate. Total.	Females. Literate. English.
				95	96	97	98	99	100	101	102	103	104	105	106	107	108	109	110	111	112
C. Commercial—(*concld.*).	16	Banjara	Hindu	852	2	..	798	...	...	..	...	...	...	...	...	...	...	...	1	...	...
		Hammal	,,	...	...	...	...	...	...	...	...	...	...	...	...	...	...	...	...	...	...
		Lad	,,	...	...	...	...	...	...	212	11	...	216	...	...	...	...	...	...	...	...
		,,	Jain	...	...	...	...	...	...	...	...	...	...	...	...	...	...	...	...	...	...
		Lamani	Hindu	1,656	...	...	1,557	...	...	7,962	15	...	6,612	...	...	2,899	5	...	2,366	...	...
		Total Group 16	......	2,508	2	...	2,359	...	...	8,175	26	...	6,828	...	...	2,899	5	...	2,367	...	...
		Total Class C.	......	4,976	739	4	5,009	3	...	75,177	6,350	32	72,977	24	...	19,779	3,450	8	19,478	32	...
D. Artisan and Village Menial.	17	Panchal	Hindu	1,093	91	...	1,102	1	...	1,139	41	...	1,137	...	...	562	124	...	604	...	
		,,	Jain	...	...	...	...	...	...	...	...	...	...	...	...	...	...	...	...	...	...
		Sonar or Ausala	Hindu	710	70	...	712	...	...	1,584	228	2	1,613	1	...	1,384	328	...	1,331	6	...
		,,	Jain	...	...	...	...	...	...	...	...	...	...	...	...	...	...	...	...	...	...
		,,	Mussulman	...	...	...	...	...	...	...	...	...	...	...	...	...	...	...	...	...	...
		Total Group 17	......	1,803	161	...	1,814	1	...	2,723	269	2	2,750	1	...	1,946	452	...	1,935	6	..
	18	Hajjam or Mangala	Hindu	814	6	...	754	...	...	2,567	45	2	2,502	...	...	2,859	67	..	2,675	...	...
		,,	Jain	..	...	...	...	...	...	...	...	..	...	...	...	...	...	...	...	...	...
		Total Group 18	.....	814	6	...	754	...	...	2,567	45	2	2,502	...	...	2,859	67	...	2,675	...	...
	19	Ghisadi	Hindu	...	...	...	...	...	...	39	...	...	17	...	...	...	...	...	...	...	...
		Kirajgar	,,	...	...	...	...	...	...	...	...	...	...	...	...	...	...	...	...	...	...
		Lohar	,,	603	7	...	542	...	...	802	21	...	745	...	...	1,306	100	...	1,192	3	...
		Nalband	,,	...	...	...	...	...	...	1	...	...	1	...	...	...	...	...	...	...	...
		Total Group 19	......	603	7	..	542	...	...	812	21	...	763	...	...	1,306	100	...	1,192	3	...
	20	Gaondi or Gaond	Hindu	116	...	...	121	...	..	482	2	...	452	...	...	12	...	...	16	...	...
		Hanigevaru	,,	...	...	...	...	...	...	...	...	...	...	...	...	...	...	...	...	...	...
		Nakashgar	,,	23	...	...	38	...	...	26	...	...	15	...	...	...	...	...	..	...	...
		,,	Jain	...	...	...	...	...	...	...	...	..	...	...	..	...	...	...	...	...	...
		Sutar	Hindu	659	8		691	...	...	2,712	11[illegible]	..	2,684	...	.	1,778	93	..	1,768	2	...

TABLE C.

Literate by Language known—Provincial (Summary)—*continued.*

Class.	Group.	Caste.	Religion.	LINGASUGUR. Males. Total Males.	LINGASUGUR. Males. Literate. Total.	LINGASUGUR. Males. Literate. English.	LINGASUGUR. Females. Total Females.	LINGASUGUR. Females. Literate. Total.	LINGASUGUR. Females. Literate. English.	RAILWAYS. Males. Total Males.	RAILWAYS. Males. Literate. Total.	RAILWAYS. Males. Literate. English.	RAILWAYS. Females. Total Females.	RAILWAYS. Females. Literate. Total.	RAILWAYS. Females. Literate. English.
				113	114	115	116	117	118	119	120	121	122	123	124
C. Commercial—(*concluded*).	16	Banjara	Hindu	39	6	...	36	...	...	88	...	...	50	...	...
		Hammal	,,	1	...	...	...	...	...	...	...	...	...	...	...
		Lad	,,	39	5	...	40	...	...	...	...	...	...	...	...
		,,	Jain	...	...	...	...	...	...	...	...	...	...	...	...
		Lamani	Hindu	4,089	6	...	3,396	...	...	...	...	...	...	...	...
		Total Group 16	......	4,168	17	...	3,472	...	...	88	...	...	50	...	...
		Total Class C.	......	28,558	4,631	4	27,695	43	...	225	54	5	94	...	...
D. Artisan and Village Menial.	17	Panchal	Hindu	2,487	243	...	2,414	2	...	1	...	...	...	...	...
		,,	Jain	...	...	...	...	...	...	...	...	...	...	...	...
		Sonar or Ausala	Hindu	1,508	286	...	1,505	8	...	4	2	1	1	...	...
		,, ,,	Jain	...	...	...	...	...	...	...	...	...	...	...	...
		,, ,,	Mussalman	...	...	...	...	...	...	...	...	...	...	...	...
		Total Group 17	......	3,995	529	...	3,919	10	...	5	2	1	1	...	...
	18	Hajjam or Mangala	Hindu	3,367	64	...	3,309	...	...	14	1	...	4	...	...
		,, ,,	Jain	...	...	...	...	...	...	...	...	...	...	...	...
		Total Group 18	......	3,367	64	...	3,309	...	...	14	1	...	4	...	...
	19	Ghisadi	Hindu	...	...	...	...	...	...	...	...	...	...	...	...
		Kirajgar	,,	...	...	...	...	...	...	...	...	...	...	...	...
		Lohar	,,	1,286	45	...	1,272	...	...	1	...	...	...	...	...
		Nalband	,,	...	...	...	...	...	...	...	...	...	...	...	...
		Total Group 19	......	1,286	45	...	1,272	...	...	1	...	...	...	...	...
	20	Gaondi or Gaond	Hindu	...	...	...	...	...	...	3	...	...	...	...	...
		Hanigevaru	,,	22	...	...	14	...	...	...	...	...	...	...	...
		Nakashgar	,,	3	...	...	...	...	...	1	...	...	...	...	...
		,,	Jain	...	...	...	...	...	...	...	...	...	...	...	...
		Sutar	Hindu	2,180	105	...	2,049	...	...	1	...	...	...	...	...

TABLE C.

Literate by Language known—(Provincial Summary)—*continued.*

Class.	Group.	Caste.	Religion.	TOTAL STRENGTH. Males. Total Males.	Males. Literate. Total.	Males. Literate. English.	Females. Total Females.	Females. Literate. Total.	Females. Literate. English.	HYDERABAD. Males. Total Males.	Males. Literate. Total.	Males. Literate. English.	Females. Total Females.	Females. Literate. Total.	Females. Literate. English.	ATRAF-I-BALDA. Males. Total Males.	Males. Literate. Total.	Males. Literate. English.	Females. Total Females.	Females. Literate. Total.	Females. Literate. English.
1	2	3	4	5	6	7	8	9	10	11	12	13	14	15	16	17	18	19	20	21	22
D. Artisan and village Menial—(*contd.*).	20	Sutar...	Jain ...	2	...	...	...	...	...	...	...	...	...	...	...	...	...	...	...	...	...
		Total Group 20		67,739	2,201	7	65,403	30	1	1,559	159	5	1,463	7	1	2,537	150	...	2,485	2	...
	21	Kasar ...	Hindu ...	9,174	1,585	2	8,666	19	...	108	18	...	91	...	...	259	37	...	256	...	...
		Do. ...	Jain ...	842	169	...	820	...	...	...	...	...	...	...	...	...	...	...	...	...	...
		Tambatgar ...	Hindu ...	368	23	...	346	...	...	7	1	...	4	...	...	...	...	...	...	...	...
		Total Group 21		10,384	1,777	2	9,832	19	...	115	19	...	95	...	...	259	37	...	256	...	...
	22	Darzi ...	Hindu ...	18,841	1,717	18	17,937	22	1	1,842	288	14	1,485	6	1	524	85	1	490	1	...
		Do. ...	Jain ...	918	236	...	786	2	...	...	...	...	...	...	...	...	...	...	...	...	...
		Zingar ...	Hindu ...	2,377	106	...	2,330	...	...	2	...	...	2	...	...	31	...	...	37	...	...
		Total Group 22		22,136	2,059	18	21,053	24	1	1,844	288	14	1,487	6	1	555	85	1	527	1	...
	22a	Badbooj ...	Hindu ...	289	44	...	202	...	...	263	35	...	179	...	...	2	1	...	2	...	...
		Halwai ...	"	453	30	...	406	1	...	28	7	...	20	...	...	...	...	...	...	...	...
		Total Group 22a		742	74	...	608	1	...	291	42	...	199	...	...	2	1	...	2	...	...
	22b	Attar ...	Hindu ...	418	139	...	384	...	...	...	...	...	...	...	...	...	...	...	...	...	...
		Do. ...	Jain ...	2	...	...	2	...	...	...	...	...	...	...	...	...	...	...	...	...	...
		Do. ...	Mussulman	17	...	...	12	...	...	...	...	...	...	...	...	...	...	...	...	...	...
		Bagavan ...	Hindu ..	7	...	...	11	...	...	...	...	...	...	...	...	...	...	...	...	...	...
		Do. ...	Mussulman	53	...	...	40	...	...	...	...	...	...	...	...	...	...	...	...	...	...
		Bhatiari ...	"	3	...	...	5	...	...	...	...	...	...	...	...	...	...	...	...	...	...
		Bukavaru ...	Hindu ...	159	15	...	123	...	...	...	...	...	...	...	...	...	...	...	...	...	...
		Kachigundi ...	"	128	4	...	123	...	...	8	3	...	13	...	...	36	...	...	28	...	...
		Tamboli ...	"	199	20	...	202	...	...	7	1	...	5	...	...	...	...	...	...	...	...
		Do. ...	Jain ..	3	2	...	4	...	...	...	...	...	...	...	...	...	...	...	...	...	...
		Do. ...	Mussulman	15	1	...	12	...	...	1	...	...	...	...	...	...	...	...	...	...	...
		Total Group 22b		1,004	181	...	918	...	...	16	4	...	18	...	...	36	...	...	28	...	...

TABLE C.

Literate by language known—(Provincial Summary)—*continued.*

Class.	Group.	Caste.	Religion.	MAHBUBNAGAR. Males. Total Males.	MAHBUBNAGAR. Males. Literate. Total.	MAHBUBNAGAR. Males. Literate. English	MAHBUBNAGAR. Females. Total Females.	MAHBUBNAGAR. Females. Literate. Total.	MAHBUBNAGAR. Females. Literate. English.	NALGONDA. Males. Total Males.	NALGONDA. Males. Literate. Total.	NALGONDA. Males. Literate. English.	NALGONDA. Females. Total Females.	NALGONDA. Females. Literate. Total.	NALGONDA. Females. Literate. English.	WARANGAL. Males. Total Males.	WARANGAL. Males. Literate. Total.	WARANGAL. Males. Literate. English.	WARANGAL. Females. Total Females.	WARANGAL. Females. Literate. Total.	WARANGAL. Females. Literate. English.
				23	24	25	26	27	28	29	30	31	32	33	34	35	36	37	38	39	40
D. Artisan and Village-Menial—(*contd.*).	20	Sutar	Jain	...	...	...	...	...	...	...	...	...	...	...	...	...	...	...	...	...	...
		Total Group 20		7,695	274	...	7,359	4	...	3,231	170	1	3,143	...	...	4,982	235	1	4,951	4	...
	21	Kasar	Hindu	262	45	...	316	9	...	527	129	...	563	1	...	611	195	...	577	...	...
		Do.	Jain	...	...	...	...	...	...	...	...	...	...	...	...	...	...	...	...	...	...
		Tambatgar	Hindu	...	...	...	...	...	...	...	...	...	...	...	...	...	...	...	...	...	...
		Total Group 21		262	45	...	316	9	...	527	129	...	563	1	...	611	195	...	577	...	...
	22	Darzi	Hindu	674	113	...	636	...	...	1,352	108	...	1,261	2	...	1,933	138	...	1,746	2	...
		Do.	Jain	...	...	...	...	...	...	...	...	...	...	...	...	...	...	...	...	...	...
		Zingar	Hindu	62	10	...	65	...	...	12	...	...	7	...	...	44	2	...	49	2	...
		Total Group 22		736	123	...	701	...	...	1,364	108	...	1,268	2	...	1,977	140	...	1,795	...	...
	22-*a*	Badbooj	Hindu	...	...	...	...	...	...	...	...	...	...	...	...	1	1	...	1	...	...
		Halwai	„	...	...	...	...	...	...	...	...	...	...	...	...	...	...	...	...	...	...
		Total Group 22*a*		...	...	...	...	...	...	...	...	...	...	...	...	1	1	...	1	...	...
	22-*b*	Attar	Hindu	...	...	...	...	...	...	...	...	...	...	...	...	...	...	...	...	...	...
		Do.	Jain	...	...	...	...	...	...	...	...	...	...	...	...	...	...	...	...	...	...
		Do.	Mussulman	...	...	...	...	...	...	...	...	...	...	...	...	...	...	...	...	...	...
		Bagavan	Hindu	...	...	...	...	...	...	...	...	...	...	...	...	...	...	...	...	...	...
		Do.	Mussulman	...	...	...	...	...	...	...	...	...	...	...	...	...	...	...	...	...	...
		Bhatiari	„	...	...	...	...	...	...	...	...	...	...	...	...	...	...	...	...	...	...
		Bukavaru	Hindu	4	...	...	3	...	...	3	2	...	5	...	...	130	13	...	92	...	...
		Kachigundi	„	24	1	...	17	...	...	22	...	...	26	...	...	7	...	...	6	...	...
		Tamboli	„	4	...	...	1	...	...	...	...	...	...	...	...	...	...	...	...	...	...
		Do.	Jain	...	...	...	...	...	...	...	...	...	...	...	...	...	...	...	...	...	...
		Do.	Mussulman	...	...	...	...	...	...	...	...	...	...	...	...	...	...	...	...	...	...
		Total Group 22*b*		32	1	...	21	...	...	25	2	...	21	...	...	137	13	...	98	...	...

TABLE C.

Literate by language known—(Provincial Summary)—*continued.*

Class.	Group.	Caste.	Religion.	ELGANDAL. Males. Total Males.	ELGANDAL. Males. Literate. Total.	ELGANDAL. Males. Literate. English.	ELGANDAL. Females. Total Females.	ELGANDAL. Females. Literate. Total.	ELGANDAL. Females. Literate. English.	INDUR. Males. Total Males.	INDUR. Males. Literate. Total.	INDUR. Males. Literate. English.	INDUR. Females. Total Females.	INDUR. Females. Literate. Total.	INDUR. Females. Literate. English.	MEDAK. Males. Total Males.	MEDAK. Males. Literate. Total.	MEDAK. Males. Literate. English.	MEDAK. Females. Total Female.	MEDAK. Females. Literate. Total.	MEDAK. Females. Literate. English.
				41	42	43	44	45	46	47	48	49	50	51	52	53	54	55	56	57	58
D. Artisan and Village Menial—(*contd.*).	20	Sutar...	Jain	...	...	...	...	...	...	...	...	...	...	...	...	...	...	...	...	...	...
		Total Group 20		6,780	235	...	6,401	5	...	3,627	152	...	3,699	1	...	2,281	96	...	2,254	...	...
	21	Kasar	Hindu	1,279	343	...	1,106	3	...	478	66	...	384	1	...	115	30	1	116	...	...
		Do.	Jain	...	...	...	...	...	...	...	...	...	...	...	...	...	...	...	...	...	...
		Tambatgar	Hindu	...	...	...	...	...	...	...	...	...	...	...	...	...	...	...	...	...	...
		Total Group 21		1,279	343	...	1,106	3	..	478	66	...	384	1	...	115	30	1	116	...	...
	22	Darzi...	Hindu	3,320	72	...	3,190	4	...	1,853	93	...	2,014	...	...	698	75	...	688	...	...
		Do. ...	Jain	...	...	...	...	...	...	...	...	...	...	...	...	...	...	...	...	...	...
		Zingar	Hindu	362	9	...	343	...	...	166	3	...	156	...	...	35	3	...	42	...	...
		Total Group 22		3,682	81	...	3,533	4	...	2,019	96	...	2,170	...	...	733	78	...	730	...	...
	22a	Badbooj	Hindu	...	...	...	...	...	...	...	...	...	...	...	...	...	...	...	...	...	...
		Halwai	"	..	...	...	...	...	..	3	...	...	2	...	...	...	...	...	...	...	...
		Total Group 22a		...	...	...	..	...	...	3	...	...	2	...	...	...	...	...	...	...	...
	22b	Attar	Hindu	...	...	...	...	...	...	14	4	...	25	...	...	...	...	...	...	...	...
		Do.	Jain	...	...	...	...	...	...	...	...	...	1	...	...	...	...	...	...	...	...
		Do.	Mussulman	...	...	...	...	...	...	...	...	...	...	...	...	...	...	...	...	...	...
		Bagavan	Hindu	...	...	...	...	...	...	...	...	...	...	...	...	...	...	...	...	...	...
		Do.	Mussulman	...	...	...	...	...	...	...	...	...	...	...	...	...	...	...	...	...	...
		Bhatiari	"	...	...	...	...	...	...	...	...	...	...	...	...	...	...	...	...	...	...
		Bukkavaru	Hindu	...	...	...	...	...	...	...	...	...	...	...	...	...	...	...	...	...	...
		Kachigundi	"	14	...	...	20	...	...	...	...	...	...	...	...	...	...	...	13	...	...
		Támboli	"	...	...	...	...	...	...	21	...	...	32	...	...	17	...	...	...	...	...
		Do.	Jain	...	...	...	...	...	...	...	...	...	...	...	...	...	...	...	...	...	...
		Do.	Mussulman	..	...	...	...	...	...	...	...	...	...	...	...	...	...	...	...	...	...
		Total Group 22b		14	...	...	20	...	...	35	4	...	58	...	...	17	...	...	13	...	...

TABLE C.

Literate by Language known—(Provincial Summary)—*continued.*

Class.	Group.	Caste.	Religion.	AURANGABAD. Males. Total Males.	AURANGABAD. Males. Literate. Total.	AURANGABAD. Males. Literate. English.	AURANGABAD. Females. Total Females.	AURANGABAD. Females. Literate. Total.	AURANGABAD. Females. Literate. English.	BIRH. Males. Total Males.	BIRH. Males. Literate. Total.	BIRH. Males. Literate. English.	BIRH. Females. Total Females.	BIRH. Females. Literate. Total.	BIRH. Females. Literate. English.	NANDER. Males. Total Males.	NANDER. Males. Literate. Total.	NANDER. Males. Literate. English.	NANDER. Females. Total Females.	NANDER. Females. Literate. Total.	NANDER. Females. Literate. English.
				59	60	61	62	63	64	65	66	67	68	69	70	71	72	73	74	75	76
D. Artisan and Village Menial—(*contd.*).	20	Sutar	Jain ...	2	...	...	...	...	...	...	...	...	...	...	...	...	...	...	...	...	...
		Total Group 20		3,688	76	...	3,560	1	...	3,423	57	...	3,224	1	...	4,868	66	...	4,714	2	...
	21	Kasar	Hindu ...	1,381	251	...	1,324	2	...	1,075	163	...	1,022	...	...	348	30	...	350	...	...
		Do.	Jain ...	6	16	...	67	...	...	82	9	...	98	...	...	1	...	...	2	...	...
		Tambatgar	Hindu ...	46	3	.	49	...	...	88	5	...	86	...	...	19	7	...	11	...	...
		Total Group 21		1,488	270	...	1,440	2	...	1245	177	...	1,206	...	...	368	37	...	363	...	...
	22	Darzi	Hindu ...	789	109	1	753	1	...	495	66	...	444	...	...	955	62	...	951	...	...
		Do.	Jain ...	540	129	...	452	...	...	22	7	...	17	...	...	11	5	...	7	...	...
		Zingar	Hindu ...	103	5	...	95	...	...	60	1	...	46	...	...	78	8	...	81	...	...
		Total Group 22		1,432	243	1	1,300	1	...	577	74	...	507	...	...	1,044	75	...	1,039	...	...
	22a	Badbooj	Hindu ...	10	3	...	6	...	...	...	...	...	...	...	...	1	...	...	...	...	...
		Halwai	" ...	162	12	...	138	...	...	4	2	...	11	...	...	12	...	...	10	...	...
		Total Group 22 a		172	15	...	144	...	...	4	2	...	11	...	...	13	...	...	10	...	...
	22b	Attar	Hindu ...	228	120	...	217	...	...	23	5	...	12	...	...	5	...	...	10	...	...
		Do.	Jain ...	...	...	...	...	...	...	...	...	...	...	...	...	...	...	...	...	...	...
		Do.	Mussulman	...	...	...	...	...	...	2	...	...	2	...	...	...	...	...	...	...	...
		Bagavan	Hindu ...	...	...	...	...	...	...	...	...	...	...	...	...	...	...	...	...	...	...
		Do.	Mussulman	...	...	...	...	...	...	32	...	...	21	...	...	...	...	...	...	...	...
		Bhatiari	,, ...	...	...	...	...	...	...	...	...	...	...	...	...	...	...	...	...	...	...
		Bukkavaru	Hindu ...	...	...	...	...	...	...	...	...	...	...	...	...	...	...	...	...	...	...
		Kachigundi	" ...	...	...	...	...	...	...	...	...	...	...	...	...	...	...	...	...	...	...
		Tamboli	" ...	15	6	...	17	...	...	1	...	...	5	...	...	6	1	...	5	...	...
		Do.	Jain ...	3	2	...	4	...	...	...	...	...	...	...	...	...	...	...	...	...	...
		Do.	Mussulman	...	...	...	...	...	...	12	1	...	11	...	...	2	...	...	...	...	...
		Total Group 22b		246	128	...	238	...	...	70	6	...	51	...	...	13	1	...	15	...	...

TABLE C.

Literate by Language known—(Provincial Summary)—*continued.*

Class.	Group.	Caste.	Religion.	NALDRUG.						BIDAR.						PARBHANI.					
				MALES.			FEMALES.			MALES.			FEMALES.			MALES.			FEMALES.		
				Total Males.	Literate.		Total Females.	Literate.		Total Males.	Literate.		Total Females.	Literate.		Total Males.	Literate.		Total Females.	Literate.	
					Total.	English.		Total.	English.		Total.	English.		Total.	English.		Total.	English.		Total.	English.
				77	78	79	80	81	82	83	84	85	86	87	88	89	90	91	92	93	94
D. Artisan and Village Menial—(*contd.*)	20	Sutar	Jain	...	...	...	...	...	...	...	...	...	...	...	...	...	...	...	...	...	...
		Total Group 20		4,632	89	...	4,304	1	...	6,057	67	...	6,048	...	...	4,347	57	...	3,957	...	...
	21	Kasar	Hindu	579	115	...	501	1	...	384	33	...	335	1	...	810	64	...	797	...	..
		Do.	Jain	310	71	...	253	...	...	56	13	...	66	...	...	309	47	...	322	...	...
		Tambatgar	Hindu	77	3	...	75	...	...	27	...	...	28	...	...	36	...	...	35	...	...
		Total Group 21		966	189	...	829	1	...	467	46	...	429	1	...	1,155	111	...	1,154	...	...
	22	Darzi	Hindu	785	129	...	717	...	...	787	59	...	699	1	...	279	28	1	251	...	...
		Do.	Jain	6	...	...	9	...	...	...	...	...	...	...	...	339	95	...	301	2	...
		Zingar	Hindu	116	9	...	119	...	...	216	14	...	228	...	...	193	2	...	203	...	...
		Total Group 22		907	138	...	845	...	...	1,003	73	...	927	1	...	811	125	1	755	2	...
	22*a*	Badbooj	Hindu	...	...	...	...	...	...	...	...	...	...	...	...	9	3	...	12	...	...
		Halwai	„	...	...	...	...	...	...	31	8	...	34	1	...	19	...	...	10	...	...
		Total Group 22*a*		...	...	...	...	...	...	31	8	...	34	1	...	28	3	...	22	...	...
	22*b*	Attar	Hindu	...	...	...	...	...	...	62	...	...	50	...	...	54	3	...	42	...	...
		Do.	Jain	...	...	...	...	...	...	...	...	...	...	...	...	2	...	...	2	...	...
		Do.	Mussulman	2	...	...	1	...	...	...	...	...	...	...	...	13	...	...	8	...	...
		Bagavan	Hindu	...	...	...	...	...	...	...	...	...	2	...	...	...	..	...	...	...	...
		Do.	Mussulman	...	...	...	...	...	...	3	...	...	...	...	...	18	...	...	19	...	...
		Bhatiari	„	...	...	...	...	...	...	...	...	...	...	...	...	3	...	...	5	...	...
		Bukavaru	Hindu	...	...	...	...	...	...	...	...	...	...	...	...	...	...	...	...	...	...
		Kachigundi	„	...	...	...	...	...	...	...	...	...	...	...	...	...	...	...	...	...	...
		Tamboli	„	5	...	...	4	...	...	6	...	...	5	...	...	102	10	...	101	...	...
		Do.	Jain	...	...	...	...	...	...	...	...	...	...	...	...	...	...	...	...	...	...
		Do.	Mussulman	...	...	...	1	...	...	...	...	...	...	...	...	...	...	...	...	...	...
		Total Group 22*b*		7	...	...	6	...	...	71	...	...	57	...	...	192	13	...	177	...	...

TABLE C.

Literate by Language known—(Provincial Summary)—*continued.*

Class.	Group.	Caste.	Religion.	SIRPUR TANDUR.						GULBARGA.						RAICHUR.					
				Males.			Females.			Males.			Females.			Males.			Females.		
				Total Males.	Literate. Total.	Literate. English.	Total Females.	Literate. Total.	Literate. English.	Total Males.	Literate. Total.	Literate. English.	Total Females.	Literate. Total.	Literate. English.	Total Males.	Literate. Total.	Literate. English.	Total Females.	Literate. Total.	Literate. English.
				95	96	97	98	99	100	101	102	103	104	105	106	107	108	109	110	111	112
D. Artisan and Village Menial—(*contd.*)	20	Sutar	Jain	...	...	...	...	...	...	...	...	...	...	...	...	...	...	...	...	...	...
		Total Group 20		798	8	...	843	...	...	3,222	112	...	3,151	...	...	1,801	93	...	1,784	2	...
	21	Kasar	Hindu	524	10	...	503	...	...	224	12	1	212	1	...	123	25	...	111	...	...
		Do.	Jain	...	...	...	...	...	...	...	...	...	...	...	...	...	...	...	...	...	...
		Tambatgar	Hindu	...	...	...	...	...	...	57	3	...	55	...	...	3	1	...	1	...	...
		Total Group 21		524	10	...	503	...	...	281	15	1	267	1	...	126	26	...	112	...	...
	22	Darzi	Hindu	471	8	...	512	...	...	735	62	1	782	2	...	507	94	...	518	3	...
		Do.	Jain	...	...	...	...	...	...	...	...	...	...	...	...	...	...	...	...	...	...
		Zingar	Hindu	40	1	...	51	...	...	624	30	...	601	...	...	184	9	...	161	...	...
		Total Group 22		511	9	...	563	...	...	1,359	92	1	1,383	2	...	691	103	...	679	3	...
	22*a*	Badbooj	Hindu	...	...	...	...	...	...	...	...	...	...	...	...	3	1	...	2	...	...
		Halwai	"	104	1	...	88	...	...	25	...	...	33	...	...	4	...	...	3	...	...
		Total Group 22*a*		104	1	...	88	...	...	25	...	...	33	...	...	7	1	...	5	...	...
	22*b*	Attar	Hindu	15	5	...	13	...	...	2	...	...	3	...	...	...	...	...	...	...	...
		Do.	Jain	...	...	...	...	...	...	...	...	...	...	...	...	...	...	...	...	...	...
		Do.	Mussulman	...	...	...	...	...	...	...	...	...	...	...	...	...	...	...	...	...	...
		Bagavan	Hindu	...	...	...	...	...	...	7	...	...	9	...	...	...	...	...	...	...	...
		Do.	Mussulman	...	...	...	...	...	...	...	...	...	...	...	...	...	...	...	...	...	...
		Bhatiari	"	...	...	...	...	...	...	...	...	...	...	...	...	...	...	...	...	...	...
		Bukavaru	Hindu	...	...	...	...	...	...	...	...	...	...	...	...	11	...	...	4	...	...
		Kachigundi	"	...	...	...	...	...	...	...	...	...	...	...	...	...	...	...	...	...	...
		Tamboli	"	8	...	...	6	...	...	...	...	...	...	...	...	24	2	...	21	...	...
		Do.	Jain	...	...	...	...	...	...	...	...	...	...	...	...	...	...	...	...	...	...
		Do.	Mussulman	...	...	...	...	...	...	...	...	...	...	...	...	...	...	...	...	...	...
		Total Class 22*b*		23	5	...	19	...	...	9	...	...	12	...	...	35	2	...	25	...	...

TABLE C.

Literate by Language known—(Provincial Summary)—*continued.*

Class.	Group.	Caste.	Religion.	LINGASUGUR.						RAILWAYS.					
				MALES.			FEMALES.			MALES.			FEMALES.		
				Total Males.	Literate.		Total Females.	Literate.		Total Males.	Literate.		Total Females.	Literate.	
					Total.	English.		Total.	English.		Total.	English.		Total.	English.
				113	114	115	116	117	118	119	120	121	122	123	124
D. Artisan and Village Menial—(*contd.*)	20	Sutar...	Jain	...	...	...	...	...	...	...	...	...	...	...	...
		Total Group 20		2,205	105	...	2,063	...	...	5	...	...	...	...	...
	21	Kasar	Hindu	84	19	...	100	...	...	3	...	...	2	...	...
		Do.	Jain	23	13	...	12	...	...	...	...	...	...	...	...
		Tambatgar	Hindu	8	...	...	2	...	...	...	...	...	...	...	...
		Total Group 21		115	32	...	114	...	...	3	...	...	2	...	...
	22	Darzi...	Hindu	837	128	...	797	...	...	5	...	...	3	...	...
		Do. ...	Jain	...	...	...	...	...	...	...	...	...	...	...	...
		Zingar	Hindu	49	...	...	44	...	...	...	...	...	...	...	...
		Total Group 22		886	128	...	841	...	...	5	...	...	3	...	...
	22a	Badbooj	Hindu	...	...	...	...	...	...	...	...	...	...	...	...
		Halwai	,,	59	...	...	56	...	...	2	...	...	1	...	...
		Total Group 22a		59	...	...	56	...	...	2	...	...	1	...	...
	22b	Attar...	Hindu	14	1	...	12	...	...	1	1	...	...	...	...
		Do. ...	Jain	...	...	...	...	...	...	...	...	...	...	...	...
		Do. ...	Mussulman	...	...	...	...	...	...	...	...	...	...	...	...
		Bagavan	Hindu	...	...	...	...	...	...	...	...	...	...	...	...
		Do.	Mussulman	...	...	...	...	...	...	...	...	...	...	...	...
		Bhatiari	,,	...	...	...	...	...	...	...	...	...	...	...	...
		Bukavaru	Hindu	11	...	...	19	...	...	...	...	...	...	...	...
		Kachigundi	,,	...	...	...	...	...	...	...	...	...	...	...	...
		Tamboli	,,	...	...	...	...	...	...	...	...	...	...	...	...
		Do.	Jain	...	...	...	...	...	...	...	...	...	...	...	...
		Do.	Mussulman	...	...	...	...	...	...	...	...	...	...	...	...
		Total Group 22b		25	1	...	31	...	...	1	1	...	...	...	...

TABLE C.

Literate by Language known—(Provincial Summary)—*continued.*

Class.	Group.	Caste.	Religion.	TOTAL STRENGTH. Males. Total Males.	Males. Literate. Total.	Males. Literate. English.	Females. Total Females.	Females. Literate. Total.	Females. Literate. English.	HYDERABAD. Males. Total Males.	Males. Literate. Total.	Males. Literate. English.	Females. Total Females.	Females. Literate. Total.	Females. Literate. English.	ATRAF-I-BALDA. Males. Total Males.	Males. Literate. Total.	Males. Literate. English.	Females. Total Females.	Females. Literate. Total.	Females. Literate. English.
1	2	3	4	5	6	7	8	9	10	11	12	13	14	15	16	17	18	19	20	21	22
D. Artisan and Village Menial—(*contd.*)	23	Hatkar	Hindu ...	3.843	557	...	3,706	12	...	...	...	...	...	...	...	11	5	...	8	...	...
		Julaha or Salai	" ...	162.111	5,019	25	153,954	42	...	1,509	146	14	1,364	2	...	5,506	313	...	5,148	2	...
		Khatri	" ...	4,769	647	3	4,332	3	...	1,002	304	2	860	1	...	27	12	...	21	...	...
		Do.	Jain ...	1	1	...	...	...	...	...	...	...	...	...	...	...	...	...	...	...	...
		Do.	Sikh ...	15	1	...	4	...	...	15	1	...	4	...	...	...	...	...	...	...	...
		Kommu	Hindu ...	31	3	...	12	...	...	...	...	...	...	...	...	...	...	...	...	...	...
		Momin	Mussulman	96	24	1	118	2	...	40	23	1	51	2	...	...	...	...	...	...	...
		Nilgar	Hindu ...	612	37	...	577	...	...	2	...	...	...	...	...	54	3	...	53	...	...
		Pardhan	" ...	2,079	...	...	2,148	...	...	...	...	...	...	...	...	...	...	...	...	...	...
		Patkari	" ...	420	30	2	396	1	...	1	1	...	1	...	...	4	...	...	7	...	...
		Patwegar	" ...	320	43	...	266	...	...	8	...	...	11	...	...	6	2	...	8	...	...
		Do.	Mussulman	10	3	...	4	...	...	...	...	...	...	...	...	...	...	...	...	...	...
		Do.	Jain ...	85	10	...	77	...	...	...	...	...	...	...	...	...	...	...	...	...	...
		Rangrez	Hindu ...	8,278	1,346	3	7,794	14	...	339	90	2	311	9	...	93	23	...	69	1	...
		Do.	Jain ...	5	...	...	5	...	...	...	...	...	...	...	...	...	...	...	...	...	...
		Total Group 23		182.675	7,721	34	173 391	74	...	2,916	565	19	2,602	14	...	5,7[illegible]1	358	...	5,314	3	...
	24	Chakala	Hindu ...	98,253	284	5	95,743	14	...	1,336	48	5	1,174	2	...	5,185	...	...	5,049	...	...
		Do.	Mussulman	1	...	...	...	...	...	...	...	...	...	...	...	...	4	...	...	...	...
		Total Group 24		98,254	284	5	95,743	14	...	1,336	48	5	1,174	2	...	5,185	4	...	5,049	...	...
	25	Pinjari	Hindu ...	289	3	...	274	...	...	...	...	...	...	...	...	...	...	...	...	...	...
		Do.	Mussulman	2,811	37	1	2,700	...	...	3	...	...	5	...	...	128	4	...	120	...	...
		Total Group 25		3,100	40	1	2,974	...	...	3	...	...	5	...	...	128	4	...	120	...	...
	26	Dhangar	Hindu ...	37,8212	2,259	23	365,106	89	...	4,587	373	20	4,802	13	...	13,089	94	2	12,609	3	...
		Gandaria	" ...	21	10	...	5	...	...	...	...	...	...	...	...	...	...	...	...	...	...
		Agiala	" ...	4	2	...	7	...	...	...	...	...	...	...	...	...	...	...	...	...	...
		Aiyawar	" ...	101	...	...	115	...	...	...	...	...	...	...	...	...	...	...	...	...	...

TABLE C.

Literate by Language known—(Provincial Summary)—*continued.*

Class.	Group.	Caste.	Religion.	MAHBUBNAGAR. Males. Total Males.	Males. Literate. Total.	Males. Literate. English.	Females. Total Females.	Females. Literate. Total.	Females. Literate. English.	NALGONDA. Males. Total Males.	Males. Literate. Total.	Males. Literate. English.	Females. Total Females.	Females. Literate. Total.	Females. Literate. English.	WARANGAL. Males. Total Males.	Males. Literate. Total.	Males. Literate. English.	Females. Total Females.	Females. Literate. Total.	Females. Literate. English.
				23	24	25	26	27	28	29	30	31	32	33	34	35	36	37	38	39	40
D. Artisan and Village Menial—(contd).	23	Hatkar	Hindu	443	81	...	462	...	...	...	...	...	...	...	...	...	...	...	...	...	...
		Julaha or Salai	"	7,655	478	...	7,372	7	...	10,540	285	4	9,859	...	...	19,653	420	...	18,298	4	...
		Khatri	"	678	103	...	621	1	...	1	...	...	...	...	...	8	...	...	3	...	...
		Do.	Jain	...	...	...	...	...	...	...	...	...	...	...	...	...	...	...	...	...	...
		Do.	Sikh	...		...	...	...	...	...	...	...	...	...	...	...	...	...	...	...	...
		Kommu	Hindu	...	...	...	...	...	...	...	...	...	...	...	...	...	...	...	...	...	...
		Momin	Mussulman	...	...	...	...	...	...	1	...	...	...	...	...	...	...	...	...	...	...
		Nilgar	Hindu	134	13	...	125	...	...	...	...	...	...	...	...	...	...	...	...	...	...
		Pardhan	"	...	...	...	...	...	...	...	...	...	...	...	...	...	...	...	...	...	...
		Patkari	"	32	1	...	17	1	...	72	7	...	63	...	...	...	...	...	...	...	...
		Patwegar	"	...	...	...	...	...	...	...	...	...	...	...	...	151	27	...	147	...	...
		Do.	Mussulman	...	...	...	...	...	...	...	...	...	...	...	...	...	...	...	...	...	...
		Do.	Jain	...	...	...	...	...	...	...	...	...	...	...	...	...	...	...	...	...	...
		Rangrez	Hindu	172	23	...	193	...	...	29	7	...	16	...	...	144	33	...	151	...	...
		Do.	Jain	...	...	...	...	...	...	...	...	...	...	...	...	...	...	...	...	...	...
		Total Group 23		9,124	699	...	8,790	9	...	10,643	299	4	9,938	...	...	19,956	480	...	18,599	4	...
	24	Chakala	Hindu	8,999	27	...	9,000	1	...	11,117	29	...	10,597	7	...	13,422	19	...	12,830	...	...
		Do.	Mussulman	...	...	...	...	...	...	...	...	...	...	...	...	...	...	...	...	...	...
		Total Group 24		8,999	27	...	9,000	1	...	11,117	29	...	10,597	7	...	13,422	19	...	12,830	...	...
	25	Pinjari	Hindu	...	...	...	...	...	...	...	...	...	...	...	...	...	...	...	...	...	...
		Do.	Mussulman	290	5	...	308	...	...	506	10	...	483	...	...	592	4	1	561	...	...
		Total Group 25		290	5	...	308	...	...	506	10	...	483	...	...	592	4	1	561	...	...
	26	Dhangar	Hindu	28,554	125	...	28,045	8	...	40,635	103	...	38,934	11	...	35,708	170	...	34,493	21	...
		Gandaria	"	...	...	...	...	...	...	...	...	...	...	...	...	...	...	...	...	...	...
		Agiala	"	...	...	...	...	...	...	...	...	...	...	...	...	...	...	...	...	...	...
		Aiyawar	"	4	2	...	7	...	...	...	...	...	...	...	...	...	...	...	...	...	...

TABLE C.

Literate by Language known—(Provincial Summary)—*continued.*

Class.	Group.	Caste.	Religion.	ELGANDAL.						INDUR.						MEDAK.					
				Males.			Females.			Males.			Females.			Males.			Females.		
				Total Males.	Literate.		Total Females.	Literate.		Total Males.	Literate.		Total Females.	Literate.		Total Males.	Literate.		Total Females.	Literate.	
					Total.	English.		Total.	English.		Total.	English.		Total.	English.		Total.	English.		Total.	English.
				41	42	43	44	45	46	47	48	49	50	51	52	53	54	55	56	57	58
D. Artisan and village Menial—(contd).	23	Hatkar	Hindu ...	...	...	...	...	...	...	...	...	...	...	...	...	45	2	...	65	...	...
		Julaha or Salai	" ...	49,775	602	4	46,520	8	...	18,538	461	...	18,546	1	...	8,769	347	...	8,638	1	...
		Khatri	" ...	15	...	...	12	...	...	103	8	...	106	...	...	183	33	...	177	...	...
		Do.	Jain ...	...	...	...	...	...	...	...	...	...	...	...	...	...	...	...	...	...	...
		Do.	Sikh ...	...	...	...	...	...	...	...	...	...	...	...	...	...	...	...	...	...	...
		Kommu	Hindu ...	...	...	...	...	...	...	...	...	...	...	...	...	...	...	...	...	...	...
		Momin	Mussulman	...	...	...	...	...	...	37	...	...	49	...	...	...	...	...	...	...	...
		Nilgar	Hindu ...	41	...	...	37	...	...	...	...	...	...	...	...	369	21	...	352	...	...
		Pardhan	" ...	...	...	..	...	...	...	...	...	...	...	...	...	...	...	... 2	...	...	...
		Patkari	" ...	125	7	...	119	...	...	...	...	...	...	...	...	186	14		189	...	...
		Patwegar	" ...	9	1	...	10	...	...	14	5	...	15	...	...	...	...	...	...	...	...
		Do.	Mussulman	...	...	...	...	...	...	...	...	...	...	...	...	...	...	...	...	...	...
		Do.	Jain ...	...	...	...	...	...	...	...	...	...	...	...	...	...	...	...	...	...	...
		Rangrez	Hindu ...	261	16	...	227	...	...	555	85	...	570	...	...	277	76	...	313	2	...
		Do.	Jain ...	...	...	...	...	...	...	...	...	...	...	...	...	...	...	...	...	...	...
		Total Group 23		50,226	626	4	46,925	8	...	19,247	559	...	19,286	1	...	9,829	493	2	9,734	3	...
	24	Chakala	Hindu ...	16,619	17	...	15,363	1	...	8,311	14	...	8,517	...	...	4,782	6	...	4,652	...	...
		Do.	Mussulman	...	...	...	...	...	...	...	...	...	...	...	...	...	...	...	...	...	...
		Total Group 24		16,619	17	...	15,363	1	...	8,311	14	...	8,517	...	...	4,782	6	...	4,652	...	...
	25	Pinjari	Hindu ...	62	...	...	56	...	...	213	3	...	2[illegible]9	...	...	...	...	...	...	...	...
		Do.	Mussulman	601	5	...	557	...	...	171	3	...	16[illegible]	...	...	256	1	...	267	...	...
		Total Group 25		663	5	...	613	...	...	384	6	...	369	...	...	256	1	...	267	...	...
	26	Dhangar	Hindu ...	40,066	126	1	37,335	8	...	14,605	58	...	14,180	2	...	9,363	88	...	9,262	7	...
		Gandaria	" ...	...	...	...	...	...	...	...	...	...	...	...	...	...	...	...	...	...	...
		Agiala	" ...	...	...	...	...	...	...	...	...	...	...	...	...	...	...	...	...	...	...
		Aiyawar	" ...	...	...	...	...	...	...	...	...	...	...	...	...	...	...	...	...	...	...

TABLE C.

Literate by Language known—(Provincial Summary)—*continued.*

Class.	Group.	Caste.	Religion.	AURUNGABAD.						BIRH.						NANDER.					
				Males.			Females.			Males.			Females.			Males.			Females.		
				Total Males.	Literate. Total.	Literate. English.	Total Females.	Literate. Total.	Literate. English.	Total Males.	Literate. Total.	Literate. English.	Total Females.	Literate. Total.	Literate. English.	Total Males.	Literate. Total.	Literate. English.	Total Females.	Literate. Total.	Literate. English.
				59	60	61	62	63	64	65	66	67	68	69	70	71	72	73	74	75	76
D. Artisan and Village Menial—(contd.)	23	Hatkar	Hindu	...	...	...	...	...	...	...	...	...	...	...	...	...	...	...	...	...	...
		Ju'aha or Salai	„	2,766	197	1	2,587	...	...	3,522	215	...	3,320	1	...	4,325	95	...	4,287	4	...
		Khatri	„	31	22	...	10	1	...	264	39	...	248	...	...	33	...	...	35	...	...
		Do.	Jain	1	1	...	...	...	...	..	...	...	...	...	...	...	...	...	...	...	...
		Do.	Sikh	...	...	...	...	...	...	...	...	...	...	...	...	...	...	...	...	...	...
		Kommu	Hindu	1	...	...	...	...	...	7	...	...	7	...	...	...	...	...	...	...	...
		Momin	Mussulman	2	...	...	...	...	...	11	...	...	10	...	...	...	...	...	...	...	...
		Nilgar	Hindu	...	...	...	...	...	...	...	...	...	...	...	...	12	...	...	10	...	...
		Pardhan	„	...	...	...	...	...	...	...	...	...	...	...	...	...	...	...	...	...	...
		Patkari	„	...	...	...	...	...	...	...	...	...	...	...	...	...	...	...	...	...	...
		Patwegar	„	83	8	...	62	...	...	7	...	...	3	...	...	...	...	...	...	...	...
		Do.	Mussulman	...	...	...	...	...	...	..	...	...	...	...	...	...	...	...	...	...	...
		Do.	Jain	84	10	...	76	...	...	1	...	...	1	...	...	...	...	...	...	...	...
		Rangrez	Hindu	776	117	1	738	...	...	757	145	...	750	2	...	856	147	...	859	...	...
		Do.	Jain	3	...	...	2	...	...	...	...	...	...	...	...	...	...	...	...	...	...
		Total Group 23		3,747	355	2	3,475	1	...	4,569	399	...	4,330	3	...	5,226	242	...	5,191	4	...
	24	Chakala	Hindu	2,096	17	...	2,145	...	...	1,725	7	...	1,813	...	...	3,929	13	...	3,947	...	...
		Do.	Mussulman	...	...	...	...	...	...	...	...	...	...	...	...	...	...	...	...	...	..
		Total Group 24		2,096	17	...	2,145	...	...	1,725	7	..	1,813	...	...	3,929	13	...	3,947	...	...
	25	Pinjari	Hindu	...	...	...	...	...	...	1	...	...	...	...	...	8	...	...	5	...	...
		Do.	Mussulman	...	...	...	...	...	...	...	...	...	...	...	...	31	...	...	30	...	...
		Total Group 25		...	...	...	...	...	...	1	...	...	...	...	...	39	...	...	35	...	...
	26	Dhangar	Hindu	19,745	72	...	19,569	1	...	21,484	65	...	21,059	2	...	19,614	127	...	18,960	...	...
		Gandaria	„	12	6	...	1	...	...	...	...	...	...	...	...	...	...	...	...	...	...
		Agia'a	„	...	...	...	...	...	...	...	...	...	...	...	...	...	...	...	...	...	...
		Aiyawar	„	...	...	...	...	...	...	...	...	...	...	...	...	...	...	...	...	...	...

Literate by Language known—(Provincial Summary).

TABLE C.

Literate by Language known—(Provincial Summary)—*continued.*

Class.	Group.	Caste.	Religion.	NALDRUG.						BIDAR.						PARBHANI.					
				MALES.			FEMALES.			MALES.			FEMALES.			MALES.			FEMALES.		
				Total Males.	Literate.		Total Females.	Literate.		Total Males.	Literate.		Total Females.	Literate.		Total Males.	Literate.		Total Females.	Literate.	
					Total.	English.		Total.	English.		Total.	English.		Total.	English.		Total.	English.		Total.	English.
				77	78	79	80	81	82	83	84	85	86	87	88	89	90	91	92	93	94
D. Artisan and Village Menial—(*contd*).	23	Hatkar	Hindu	...	...	...	...	...	...	...	...	...	...	...	...	...	...	...	...	...	...
		Julaha or Salai	"	2,044	126	...	1,817	...	...	5,455	199	...	5,346	1	...	4,115	175	...	3,914	...	...
		Khatri	"	...	...	...	...	...	...	200	17	...	155	...	...	1,268	70	...	1,254	...	...
		Do.	Jain	...	...	...	...	...	...	...	...	...	...	...	...	...	...	...	...	...	...
		Do.	Sikh	...	...	...	...	...	...	...	...	...	...	...	...	...	...	...	...	...	...
		Kommu	Hindu	...	...	...	...	...	...	...	...	...	...	...	...	23	3	...	5	...	...
		Momin	Mussalman	...	...	...	...	...	...	...	...	...	...	...	...	2	1	...	5	...	...
		Nilgar	Hindu	...	...	...	...	...	...	...	...	...	...	...	...	...	...	...	...	...	...
		Pardhan	"	...	...	...	...	...	...	...	...	...	...	...	...	...	...	...	...	...	...
		P[illegible]i	"	...	...	...	...	...	...	...	...	...	...	...	...	...	...	...	...	...	...
		[illegible]gar	"	...	...	...	...	...	...	...	...	...	...	...	...	...	...	...	...	...	...
		Do.	Mussalman	...	...	...	...	...	...	...	...	...	...	...	...	...	...	...	...	...	...
		Do.	Jain	...	...	...	...	...	...	...	...	...	...	...	...	...	...	...	...	...	...
		Rangrez	Hindu	387	63	...	381	...	...	757	143	...	610	...	...	1,599	260	...	1,509	...	...
		Do.	Jain	2	...	...	3	...	...	...	...	...	...	...	...	...	...	...	...	...	...
		Total Group 23		2,433	189	...	2,201	...	...	6,412	359	...	6,111	1	...	7,007	509	...	6,687	...	...
	24	Chakala	Hindu	2,140	2	...	2,071	...	...	3,689	6	...	3,746	...	...	1,674	6	...	1,588	...	...
		Do.	Mussalman	1	...	...	...	...	...	...	...	...	...	...	...	...	...	...	...	...	...
		Total Group 24		2,141	2	...	2,071	...	...	3,689	6	...	3,746	...	...	1,674	6	...	1,588	...	...
	25	Pinjari	Hindu	...	...	...	...	...	...	...	...	...	...	...	...	...	...	...	...	...	...
		Do.	Mussalman	...	...	...	...	...	...	37	...	...	30	...	...	12	1	...	22	...	...
		Total Group 25		...	...	...	...	...	...	37	...	...	30	...	...	12	1	...	22	...	...
	26	Dhangar	Hindu	22,113	174	...	21,236	3	...	35,796	90	...	34,656	1	...	33,549	115	...	32,405	1	...
		Gandaria	"	...	...	...	...	...	...	...	...	...	...	...	...	9	4	...	4	...	...
		Agiala	"	...	...	...	...	...	...	...	...	...	...	...	...	...	...	...	...	...	...
		Aiyawar	"	...	...	...	...	...	...	...	...	...	...	...	...	...	...	...	...	...	...

TABLE C.

Literate by Language known.—(Provincial Summary)—*continued.*

Class.	Group.	Caste.	Religion.	SIRPUR TANDUR. Males. Total Males.	Males. Literate. Total.	Males. Literate. English.	Females. Total Females.	Females. Literate. Total.	Females. Literate. English.	GULBARGA. Males. Total Males.	Males. Literate. Total.	Males. Literate. English.	Females. Total Females.	Females. Literate. Total.	Females. Literate. English.	RAICHUR. Males. Total Males.	Males. Literate. Total.	Males. Literate. English.	Females. Total Females.	Females. Literate. Total.	Females. Literate. English.
				95	96	97	98	99	100	101	102	103	104	105	106	107	108	109	110	111	112
D. Artisan and Village Menial (*contd*).	23	Hatkar	Hindu	...	...	...	...	...	...	...	...	...	...	...	...	564	50	...	557	6	...
		Ju'aha or Salai	„	2,954	26	...	2,734	...	...	5,681	256	...	5,320	1	...	5,251	408	1	4,945	6	...
		Khatri	„	408	8	1	396	...	...	354	13	...	274	...	...	38	10	...	28	...	...
		Do.	Jain	...	...	...	...	...	...	...	...	...	...	...	...	...	...	...	...	...	...
		Do.	Sikh	...	...	...	...	...	...	...	...	...	...	...	...	...	...	...	...	...	...
		Kommu	Hindu	...	...	...	...	...	...	...	...	...	...	...	...	...	...	...	...	...	...
		Momin	Mussulman	...	...	...	...	...	...	2	...	...	2	...	...	...	...	...	...	...	...
		Nilgar	Hindu	...	...	...	...	...	...	...	...	...	...	...	...	...	...	...	...	...	...
		Pardhan	„	2,079	...	...	2,148	...	...	...	...	...	...	...	...	...	...	...	...	...	...
		Patkari	„	...	...	...	...	...	...	...	...	...	...	...	...	...	...	...	...	...	...
		Patwegar	„	...	...	...	...	...	...	...	...	...	...	...	...	...	...	...	...	...	...
		Do.	Mussulman	10	3	...	4	...	...	...	...	...	...	...	...	...	...	...	...	...	...
		Do.	Jain	...	...	...	...	...	...	...	...	...	...	...	...	...	...	...	...	...	...
		Rangrez	Hindu	169	6	...	160	...	...	843	85	...	684	...	...	33	7	...	37	...	...
		Do.	Jain	...	...	...	...	...	...	...	...	...	...	...	...	...	...	...	...	...	...
		Total Group 23		5,620	43	1	5,442	...	..	6,880	354	...	6,280	1	...	5,886	475	1	5,567	12	...
	24	Chakala	Hindu	1,779	3	..	1,769	...	...	2,791	5	...	2,764	...	...	5,196	32	...	5,196	...	...
		Do.	Mussulman	..	...	...	...	...	...	...	...	...	...	...	...	...	...	...	...	...	...
		Total Group 24		1,779	3	...	1,769	...	...	2,791	5	...	2,764	...	...	5,196	32	...	5,196	...	...
	25	Pinjari	Hindu	5	...	...	4	...	...	...	..	...	...	...	...	...	...	...	...	...	...
		Do.	Mussulman	10	2	...	7	...	...	43	...	..	38	...	...	36	2	...	36	...	...
		Total Group 25		15	2	...	11	...	...	43	...	...	38	...	...	36	2	...	36	...	...
	26	Dhangar	Hindu	3,097	6	...	3,035	...	...	25,332	318	...	24,020	2	...	8,081	137	...	7,909	6	...
		Gandaria	„	...	...	...	...	...	...	...	...	...	...	...	...	...	...	...	...	...	...
		Axiala	„	...	...	...	...	...	...	...	...	...	...	...	...	...	...	...	...	...	...
		Aiyawar	„	...	...	...	...	...	...	...	...	...	...	...	...	...	...	...	...	...	...

TABLE C.

Literate by Language known—(Provincial Summary)—*continued*.

Class.	Group.	Caste.	Religion.	LINGSUGUR. Males. Total Males.	LINGSUGUR. Males. Literate. Total.	LINGSUGUR. Males. Literate. English.	LINGSUGUR. Females. Total Females.	LINGSUGUR. Females. Literate. Total.	LINGSUGUR. Females. Literate. English.	RAILWAYS. Males. Total Males.	RAILWAYS. Males. Literate. Total.	RAILWAYS. Males. Literate. English.	RAILWAYS. Females. Total Females.	RAILWAYS. Females. Literate. Total.	RAILWAYS. Females. Literate. English.
				113	114	115	116	117	118	119	120	121	122	123	124
D. Artisan and Village Menial (*contd*).	23	Hatkar	Hindu	2,780	419	...	2,614	6	...	...	...	...	...	...	...
		Ju'aha or Salai	"	4,005	265	1	3,928	4	...	38	5	...	11	...	...
		Khatri	"	142	5	...	130	...	...	4	3	...	...	...	...
		Do.	Jain	...	...	...	...	...	...	...	...	...	...	...	...
		Do.	Sikh	...	...	...	...	...	...	...	...	...	...	...	...
		Kommu	Jain	...	...	...	...	...	...	...	...	...	...	...	...
		Momin	Mussulman	...	...	...	...	...	...	1	...	...	1	...	...
		Nilgar	Hindu	...	...	...	...	...	...	...	...	...	...	...	...
		Pardhan	"	...	...	...	...	...	...	...	...	...	...	...	...
		Patkari	"	...	...	...	...	...	...	...	...	...	...	...	...
		Patwegar	"	42	...	...	10	...	...	...	...	...	...	...	...
		Do.	Mussulman	...	...	...	...	...	...	...	...	...	...	...	...
		Do.	Jain	...	...	...	...	...	...	...	...	...	...	...	...
		Rangrez	Hindu	23[illegible]	20	...	216	...	...	1	...	...	...	...	...
		Do.	Jain	...	...	...	...	...	...	...	...	...	...	...	...
		Total Group 23		7,199	709	1	6,898	10	...	44	8	...	12	...	...
	24	Chakala	Hindu	3,437	27	...	3,506	3	...	26	2	...	16	...	...
		Do.	Mussulman	...	...	...	...	...	...	...	...	...	...	...	...
		Total Group 24		3437	27	...	3 506	3	...	26	2	...	16	...	...
	25	Pinjari	Hindu	...	...	...	...	...	...	...	...	...	...	...	...
		Do.	Mussulman	91	...	...	74	...	...	4	...	...	2	...	...
		Total Group 25		91	...	...	74	...	...	4	...	...	2	...	...
	26	Dhangar	Hindu	2,693	16	...	2,517	...		101	2	...	80	...	...
		Gandaria	"	...	...	...	...	...	...	...	...	...	...	...	...
		Agiala	"	...	...	...	...	...	...	...	...	...	...	...	...
		Aiyawar	"	101	...	...	115	...	...	...	...	...	...	...	...

TABLE C.

Literate by Language known—(Provincial Summary)—*continued.*

Class.	Group.	Caste.	Religion.	TOTAL STRENGTH.						HYDERABAD.						ATRAF-I-BALDA.					
				Males.			Females.			Males.			Females.			Males.			Females.		
				Total Males.	Literate. Total.	Literate. English.	Total Females.	Literate. Total.	Literate. English.	Total Males.	Literate. Total.	Literate. English.	Total Females.	Literate. Total.	Literate. English.	Total Males.	Literate. Total.	Literate. English.	Total Females.	Literate. Total.	Literate. English.
1	2	3	4	5	6	7	8	9	10	11	12	18	14	15	16	17	18	19	20	21	22
D. Artisan and Village Menial—(contd.).	26	Kurma	Hindu ...	1,22,826	715	2	1,18,609	21	...	45	67	1	488	1	...	8,002	48	1	7,794	4	...
		Total Group 26......		5,01,164	2,986	25	4,83,842	110	...	5,037	440	21	5,290	14	...	21,091	142	3	20,403	7	...
	27	Gandla	Hindu ...	43,716	3,540	3	41.978	51	...	296	32	...	220	...	...	1,167	345	...	1,082	3	...
		Do.	Mussulman	3	...	...	2	...	...	...	...	...	...	...	...	...	...	...	...	...	...
		Total Group 27		43,719	3,540	3	41,980	51	...	296	32	...	220	...	...	1,167	345	...	1,082	3	...
	28	Kummari	Hindu ...	54,709	521	...	52,306	6	...	680	35	...	680	...	...	2,711	13	...	2,613	1	...
		Total Group 28		54,709	521	3	52,306	6	...	680	35	...	680	...	...	2,711	13	...	2,613	1	...
	29	Kachari	Hindu ...	591	18	...	551	2	...	...	...	...	...	...	...	...	...	...	...	...	...
		Gajula	" ...	3.63	80	...	401	...	...	...	...	...	...	...	...	...	...	...	...	...	...
		Maniari	" ...	1,781	81	...	1,729	...	...	11	10	...	2	...	...	21	1	...	27	...	...
		Do.	Mussulman	3	...	...	5	...	...	...	...	...	...	...	...	...	...	...	...	...	...
		Total Group 29......		2,738	179	...	2,686	2	...	11	10	...	3	...	...	21	1	...	27	...	...
	30	Lonari	Hindu ...	183	3	...	220	...	...	...	...	...	...	...	...	9	1	...	6	...	...
		Uppara	" ...	11,625	82	..	1,17,86	...	...	...	...	...	...	...	...	...	...	...	...	...	...
		Total Group 30......		11,808	85	...	12,006	...	...	...	...	...	...	...	...	9	1	..	6	...	...
	32	Zarkari	Hindu ..	69	6	...	56	...	...	9	1	...	3	...	...	...	...	...	...	...	...
		Total Group 32......		69	6	...	56	...	...	9	1		3	...	...	...	...	...	...	...	...
	35	Besta	Hindu ...	42,499	96	...	42,051	1	...	...	...	...	...	...	...	932	8	...	889	1	...
		Bhoyi	" ...	24,639	303	3	25,043	5	...	4,265	195	2	2,837	5	...	...	...	...	...	...	...
		Kahar	" ...	519	12	...	457	...	...	180	8	...	93	...	...	...	...	...	...	...	...
		Do.	Sikh ...	2	...	...	...	...	...	...	...	...	...	...	...	...	...	...	...	...	...
		Malla or Mulli	Hindu ...	236	4	...	238	..	...	...	...	...	...	...	...	...	...	...	...	...	...
		Total Group 35......		67,945	415	3	67,789	6	...	4,445	203	2	2,930	5	...	932	8	...	889	1	...
	36	Bhandari	Hindu ..	644	12	...	666	..	...	4	2	...	2	...	...	20	2	...	16	...	...
		Gaondla	" ...	1,19,944	1 597	...	1,15,718	43	...	87	17	...	86	...	...	14,316	462	...	13,962	11	...
		Kalal...	" ...	24,757	1,191	4	24,408	7	...	1,511	245	2	1,421	2	...	...	...	...	...	...	...

TABLE C.

Literate by Language known—(Provincial Summary)—*continued.*

Class.	Group.	Caste.	Religion.	MAHBUBNAGAR. Males. Total Males.	Males. Literate. Total.	Males. Literate. English.	Females. Total Females.	Females. Literate. Total.	Females. Literate. English.	NALGONDA. Males. Total Males.	Males. Literate. Total.	Males. Literate. English.	Females. Total Females.	Females. Literate. Total.	Females. Literate. English.	WARANGAL. Males. Total Males.	Males. Literate. Total.	Males. Literate. English.	Females. Total Females.	Females. Literate. Total.	Females. Literate. English.
				23	24	25	26	27	28	29	30	31	32	33	34	35	36	37	38	39	40
D. Artisan and Village Menial—(*contd.*)	26	Kurma	Hindu	10,652	42	...	10,245	4	...	5,854	11	...	5,497	...	...	6,484	37	...	5,931	5	...
		Total Group 26		39,210	169	...	38,297	12	...	46,489	114	...	44,431	11	...	42,192	207	...	40,424	26	...
	27	Gandla	Hindu	963	274	...	924	4	...	905	76	...	888	...	...	986	150	...	958	...	...
		Do.	Mussalman	...	...	...	...	...	...	...	...	...	...	...	...	...	...	...	...	...	...
		Total Group 27		963	274	...	924	4	...	905	76	...	888	...	...	986	150	...	958	...	...
	28	Kummari	Hindu	3,906	42	...	3,773	1	...	5,315	54	...	5,115	2	...	5,702	31	...	5,531	...	...
		Total Group 28		3,906	42	...	3,773	1	...	5,315	54	...	5,115	2	...	5,702	31	...	5,531	...	...
	29	Kachari	Hindu	...	...	...	...	...	...	...	...	...	...	...	...	...	...	...	...	...	...
		Gajula	"	...	...	...	...	...	...	38	...	...	32	...	...	16	2	...	16	...	...
		Maniari	"	...	...	...	...	...	...	...	...	...	...	...	...	...	...	...	...	...	...
		Do.	Mussulman	...	...	...	...	...	...	...	...	...	...	...	...	...	...	...	...	...	...
		Total Group 29		...	...	...	...	...	...	38	...	...	32	...	...	16	2	...	16	...	...
	30	Lonari	Hindu	...	...	...	...	...	...	...	...	...	...	...	...	...	...	...	...	...	...
		Uppara	"	...	...	...	...	...	...	...	...	...	...	...	...	...	...	...	...	...	...
		Total Group 30		...	...	...	...	...	...	...	...	...	...	...	...	...	...	...	...	...	...
	32	Zarkari	Hindu	10	...	...	9	...	...	...	...	...	...	...	...	26	2	...	23	...	...
		Total Group 32		10	...	...	9	...	...	...	...	...	...	...	...	26	2	...	23	...	...
	35	Besta	Hindu	11,993	15	...	11,556	...	...	1,580	6	...	1,611	...	...	4,325	12	...	4,366	...	...
		Bhoyi	"	...	...	...	...	...	...	...	...	...	...	...	...	...	...	...	...	...	...
		Kahar	"	...	...	...	...	...	...	...	...	...	...	...	...	7	...	...	4	...	...
		Do.	Sikh	...	...	...	...	...	...	...	...	...	...	...	...	...	...	...	...	...	...
		Malla or Mulli	Hindu	...	...	...	...	...	...	...	...	...	...	...	...	...	...	...	...	...	...
		Total Group 35		11,993	15	...	11,556	...	...	1,580	6	...	1,611	...	...	4,332	12	...	4,370	...	...
	36	Bhandari	Hindu	...	...	...	...	...	...	...	...	...	...	...	...	...	...	...	...	...	...
		Gaondla	"	9,450	142	...	9,731	1	...	24,697	137	...	24,016	22	...	24,770	277	...	23,961	2	...
		Kalal	"	5,494	39	...	5,569	1	...	...	...	...	...	...	...	...	...	...	...	...	...

TABLE C.

Literate by Language known—(Provincial Summary)—*continued.*

Class.	Group.	Caste.	Religion.	ELGANDAL.						INDUR.						MEDAK.					
				MALES.			FEMALES.			MALES.			FEMALES.			MALES.			FEMALES.		
				Total Males.	Literate.		Total Females.	Literate.		Total Males.	Literate.		Total Females.	Literate.		Total Males.	Literate.		Total Females.	Literate.	
					Total.	English.		Total.	English.		Total.	English.		Total.	English.		Total.	English.		Total.	English.
				41	42	43	44	45	46	47	48	49	50	51	52	53	54	55	56	57	58
D. Artisan and Village Menial—(*contd*).	26	Kurma	Hindu ...	12,514	14	...	11,185	...	...	944	...	...	935	...	...	5,359	6	...	5,205	...	...
		Total Group 26......		52,580	140	1	48,520	8	...	15,549	58	...	15,115	2	...	14,722	94	...	14,467	7	...
	27	Gandla	Hindu ..	3,414	318	2	3,184	4	...	1,535	162	...	1,492	5	...	577	172	...	567	4	...
		Do.	Mussulman	...	...	...	...	...	...	...	...	...	...	...	...	...	...	...	...	...	...
		Total Group 27		3,414	318	2	3,184	4	...	1,535	162	...	1,492	5	...	577	172	...	567	4	...
	28	Kummari	Hindu ...	6,974	37	...	6,350	...	...	2,888	13	...	2,709	1	...	2,046	18	...	1,887	...	...
		Total Group 28		6,974	37	...	6,350	...	...	2,888	13	...	2,709	1	...	2,046	18	...	1,887	...	...
	29	Kachari	Hindu ...	...	...	...	...	...	...	...	...	...	...	...	...	...	...	...	...	...	...
		Gajula	,, ...	53	1	...	61	...	...	...	...	...	...	...	...	5	...	...	2	...	...
		Maniari	,, ...	...	...	...	...	...	...	1	...	...	9	...	...	...	...	...	...	...	...
		Do.	Mussulman	...	...	...	...	...	...	...	...	...	...	...	...	...	...	...	...	...	...
		Total Group 29		53	1	...	61	...	...	1	...	...	9	...	...	5	...	...	2	...	...
	30	Lonari	Hindu ...	...	...	...	...	...	...	...	...	...	...	...	...	...	...	...	...	...	...
		Uppara	,, ...	...	...	...	...	...	...	...	...	...	...	...	...	...	...	...	...	...	...
		Total Group 30......		...	...	...	...	...	...	...	...	...	...	...	...	...	...	...	...	...	...
	32	Zarkari	Hindu ...	...	...	...	...	...	...	...	...	...	...	...	...	9	...	...	10	...	...
		Total Group 32		...	...	...	...	...	...	...	...	...	...	...	...	9	...	...	10	...	...
	35	Besta	Hindu ..	10,255	22	...	10,315	...	...	10,905	42	...	...	...	...	952	13	...	1,001	...	...
		Bhoyi	,, ...	...	...	...	...	...	...	...	...	...	12,584	...	...	...	...	...	...	...	...
		Kahar	,, ...	...	...	...	...	...	...	...	...	...	...	...	...	...	...	...	...	...	...
		Do.	Sikh ..	...	...	...	...	...	...	5	...	...	...	...	...	...	...	...	...	...	...
		Malla or Mulli	Hindu ...	...	...	...	...	...	...	...	...	...	2	...	...	...	...	...	...	...	...
		Total Group 35		10,255	22	...	10,315	...	...	10,910	42	...	12,586	...	...	952	13	...	1,001	...	...
	36	Bhandari	Hindu ...	16	4	...	26	...	...	45	...	...	42	...	...	2	...	...	1	...	...
		Gaondla	,, ...	32,322	224	...	30,252	2	...	1,791	35	...	1,666	...	...	5,093	159	...	4,986	3	...
		Kalal	,, ...	...	...	...	...	...	...	4,507	396	...	4,327	2	...	3,379	138	...	3,254	1	...

TABLE C.

Literate by Language known—(Provincial Summary)—*continued.*

Class.	Group.	Caste.	Religion.	AURUNGABAD.						BIRH.						NANDER.					
				MALES.			FEMALES.			MALES.			FEMALES.			MALES.			FEMALES.		
				Total Males.	Literate.		Total Females.	Literate.		Total Males.	Literate.		Total Females.	Literate.		Total Males.	Literate.		Total Females.	Literate.	
					Total.	English.		Total.	English.		Total.	English.		Total.	English.		Total.	English.		Total.	English.
				59	60	61	62	63	64	65	66	67	68	69	70	71	72	73	74	75	76
D. Artisan and Village Menial—(*contd*).	26	Kurma	Hindu ..	12	6	...	6	...	...	...	...	...	...	...	...	...	...	...	...	...	...
		Total Group 26.....		19 769	84	...	19,576	1	...	21,484	65	...	21,059	2	...	19,614	127	...	18,966	...	...
	27	Gandla	Hindu ..	5,807	231	1	5,819	6	...	3,300	98	...	3,167	...	...	2,225	89	...	2,149	1	...
		Do	Mussalman	3	...	...	:	...	...	...	...	...	...	...	...	...	...	...	...	...	...
		Total Group 27.....		5,810	231	1	5,821	6	...	3,300	98	...	3,167	...	...	2,225	89	...	2,149	1	...
	28	Kummari	Hindu ..	3,062	42	...	3,119	...	...	2,698	12	...	2,692	...	...	2,709	6	...	2,650	...	...
		Total Group 28		3,062	42	...	3,119	...	...	2,698	12	...	2,692	...	...	2,709	6	...	2,650	...	...
	29	Kachari	Hindu ...	54	6	...	55	...	...	388	2	...	345	2	...	8	...	...	15	...	...
		Gajula	" ..	...	...	...	...	...	...	...	...	...	...	...	...	...	...	...	...	...	...
		Maniari	" ..	280	3	...	238	...	...	...	...	...	...	...	...	...	...	...	...	...	...
		Do.	Mussulman	...	...	...	...	...	...	...	...	...	...	...	...	...	...	...	...	...	...
		Total Group 29.....		334	9	...	293	...	...	383	2	...	345	2	...	8	...	...	15	..	...
	30	Lonari	Hindu ..	40	...	...	36	...	...	46	...	...	44	...	...	5	...	...	4	...	...
		Uppara	" ...	...	..	...	...	...	...	...	...	...	...	...	...	15	...	...	20	...	...
		Total Group 30		40	...	...	36	...	...	46	...	...	44	...	...	20	...	...	24	...	...
	32	Zarkari	Hindu ..	...	...	...	1	..	...	...	...	...	...	...	...	...	...	...	...	...	...
		Total Group 32.....		...	...	...	1	...	...	...	..	...	...	...	...	...	...	...	...	...	...
	35	Besta	Hindu ..	...	...	...	...	...	...	...	...	...	...	...	...	...	...	...	...	...	...
		Bhoyi	" ..	1,025	30	...	1,009	...	...	589	1	...	532	...	...	3,446	2	...	3,503	...	...
		Kahar	" ...	218	1	...	251	...	...	77	...	...	81	...	...	...	...	...	...	...	...
		Do.	Sikh ...	...	...	...	...	...	...	...	..	...	...	...	...	...	...	...	...	...	...
		Malla or Mulli	Hindu ...	179	1	...	177	...	...	34	1	...	42	...	...	...	...	...	...	...	...
		Total Group 35.....		1,412	32	...	1,437	...	...	700	2	...	655	...	...	3,446	2	...	3,503	...	...
	36	Bhandari	Hindu ..	...	..	...	...	...	...	7	...	...	8	...	...	127	...	...	138	...	...
		Gaond'a	" ...	1	..	..	3	...	...	...	...	...	...	...	...	...	...	...	...	...	...
		Kalal	" ...	907	79	1	871	...	...	234	32	...	218	...	...	1,176	74	...	1,202	...	...

TABLE C.

Literate by Language known.—(Provincial Summary)—*continued.*

Class.	Group.	Caste.	Religion.	NALDRUG. Males. Total Males.	NALDRUG. Males. Literate. Total.	NALDRUG. Males. Literate. English.	NALDRUG. Females. Total Females.	NALDRUG. Females. Literate. Total.	NALDRUG. Females. Literate. English.	BIDAR. Males. Total Males.	BIDAR. Males. Literate. Total.	BIDAR. Males. Literate. English.	BIDAR. Females. Total Females.	BIDAR. Females. Literate. Total.	BIDAR. Females. Literate. English.	PARBHANI. Males. Total Males.	PARBHANI. Males. Literate. Total.	PARBHANI. Males. Literate. English.	PARBHANI. Females. Total Females	PARBHANI. Females. Literate. Total.	PARBHANI. Females. Literate. English.
				77	78	79	80	81	82	83	84	85	86	87	88	89	90	91	92	93	94
D. Artisan and Village Menial—*contd.*	26	Kurma	Hindu ..	...	..	...	...	...	...	49	...	...	45	...	...	1	1	...	...	...	...
		Total Group 26 ...		22,113	174	..	21,236	3	...	35,845	90	...	34,701	1		33,559	120	...	32,409	1	...
	27	Gandla	Hindu ...	3,611	166	...	3,391	...	..	1,894	196	...	1,628	2	...	5,783	151	...	5,551	1	..
		Do.	Mussulman	...	...	...	...	..	...	...	...	...	...	...	...	..	...	...	...	..	...
		Total Group 27 ...		3,611	166	...	3,394	...	...	1,891	196	.	1,628	2	..	5,783	151	..	5,551	1	...
	28	Kummari	Hindu .	2,634	18	...	2,407	...	...	2,862	1	...	2,68:	...	..	2,711	18	...	2,576	...	...
		Total Group 28 ...		2,654	18	...	2,407	...	...	2,862	1	...	2,684	...	...	2 711	18	...	2,576	...	...
	29	Kachari	Hindu ...	...	...	...	...	...	..	...	..	...	...	...	...	137	8	..	135	...	...
		Gajula	" ...	...	...	.	..	...	...	...	...	...	..	..	..	...	...	...	...	...	...
		Maniari	" ...	605	54	...	552	...	...	849	14	...	887	...	...	13	.	...	10	...	...
		Do.	Mussulman	3	...	..	5	...	...	...	...	...	...	...		...	...	...	...	...	...
		Total Group 29 ...		608	54	...	557	...	...	849	14	...	887	...	..	150	8	...	145	...	...
	30	Lonari	Hindu ..	18	...		25	...	...	21	1	...	30	...	..	42	1	..	75	...	...
		Uppara	" ..	...	...	..	...	...	...	634	14	...	942	...	..	...	...	...	...	...	...
		Total Group 30 ...		18	...	..	25	...	...	655	15	...	971	...	..	42	1	...	75	...	..
	32	Zarikari	Hindu ..	...	...	...	...	...	...	...	...	...	..	...	..	..	...	...	...	...	...
		Total Group 32 ...		...	...	...	...	...	...	...	. .	...	...	...	...	...	...	...	..		..
	35	Besta	Hindu ..	..	...	.	...	...	...	...	...	...	...	...	...	..	...	...	...	...	...
		Bhoyi	" ..	381	7	...	359	...	...	330	8	...	354	...	...	832	3	...	856	...	...
		Kahar	" ...	....	...	...	...	...	...	21	...	..	15	...	...	10	2	...	10	...	...
		Do.	Sikh ...	...	..	...	...	...	...	...	...	...	..	...	...	2	...	...	...	...	...
		Malla or Mulli	Hindu ..	...	...	...	...	...	...	9	1	...	9	...	...	...	.	...	...	...	...
		Total Group 35 ...		381	7	...	359	...	...	360	9	...	378	...	...	844	5	...	866	...	
	36	Bhandari	Hindu ...	10	...	...	4	...	...	284	4	...	292	...	...	2	...	...	12	...	...
		Gaondla	" ...	...	...	...	...	...	...	298	4	...	294	...	...	10	1	...	8	..	
		Kalal	" ...	448	16	...	430	...	...	2,077	51	...	2,008	...	...	390	30	...	436	...	...

TABLE C.

Literate by Language known—(Provincial Summary)—*continued.*

Class.	Group.	Caste.	Religion.	SIRPUR TANDUR. Males. Total Males.	SIRPUR TANDUR. Males. Literate. Total.	SIRPUR TANDUR. Males. Literate. English.	SIRPUR TANDUR. Females. Total Females.	SIRPUR TANDUR. Females. Literate. Total.	SIRPUR TANDUR. Females. Literate. English.	GULBARGA. Males. Total Males.	GULBARGA. Males. Literate. Total.	GULBARGA. Males. Literate. English.	GULBARGA. Females. Total Females.	GULBARGA. Females. Literate. Total.	GULBARGA. Females. Literate. English.	RAICHUR. Males. Total Males.	RAICHUR. Males. Literate. Total.	RAICHUR. Males. Literate. English	RAICHUR. Females. Total Females.	RAICHUR. Females. Literate. Total.	RAICHUR. Females. Literate. English.
				95	96	97	98	99	100	101	102	103	104	105	106	107	108	109	110	111	112
D. Artisan and Village Menial—(*contd.*)	26	Kurma	Hindu	...	...	...	...	...	...	...	...	...	...	...	...	23,722	182	...	23,201	2	...
		Total Group 26		3,097	6	...	3,035	...	...	25,332	318	...	24,020	2	...	31,803	319	...	31,110	8	...
	27	Gandla	Hindu	1,141	19	...	1,033	...	...	1,483	140	...	1,375	4	...	1,043	143	...	1,098	4	...
		Do.	Mussulman	...	...	...	...	...	...	...	...	...	...	...	...	...	...	...	...	...	...
		Total Group 27		1,141	19	...	1,033	...	...	1,483	140	...	1,375	4	...	1,043	143		1,098	4	...
	28	Kummari	Hindu	672	..	..	660	...	...	1,987	8	...	1,869	...	...	2,300	68	...	2,098	1	...
		Total Group 28		672	...	...	660	...	...	1,987	8	...	1,859	...	...	2,300	68	...	2,098	1	...
	29	Kachari	Hindu	4	2	...	1	...	...	...	...	...	...	...	...	...	...	...	...	...	...
		Gajula	"	...	...	...	...	...	...	...	...	...	...	...	...	75	40	...	73	...	...
		Maniari	"	13	...	...	15	...	...	9	...	...	15	...	...	..	...	...	...	..	...
		Do.	Mussulman	..	...	...	...	...	...	...	...	...	...	...	...	...	...	...	...	...	..
		Total Group 29		17	2	...	16	...	...	9	...	...	15	...	...	75	40	...	73	...	..
	30	Lonari	Hindu	...	...	...	...	...	...	...	...	...	...	...	...	...	...	..	...	...	...
		Uppara	"	...	...	...	...	...	...	910	7	..	911	...	...	3,313	16	..	3 228	...	...
		Total Group 30		...	...	...	...	...	...	910	7	...	911	...	...	3,318	16	...	3,228	...	...
	32	Zarikari	Hindu	...	..	...	...	...	...	4	3	...	3	...	...	...	..	...	...	...	...
		Total Group 32		...	...	...	...	...	...	4	3	...	3	...	...	...	...	...	...	...	...
	35	Besta...	Hindu	...	...	...	...	...	...	...	...	...	...	...	...	12,321	19	...	12,233	...	...
		Bhoyi...	"	2,599	6	...	2,680	...	...	317	9	...	329	...	...	...	...	...	...	...	...
		Kahar	"	...	...	...	...	...	...	...	...	...	...	...	...	3	...	...	1	...	...
		Do.	Sikh	...	...	...	...	...	...	...	...	...	...	...	...	...	...	...	...	...	...
		Malla or Mulli	Hindu	...	...	...	...	...	...	9	1	1	8	...	...	...	...	...	...	...	..
		Total Group 35		2,599	6	...	2,680	...	...	326	10	1	337	...	...	12,324	19	...	12,234	...	...
	36	Bhandari	Hindu	...	...	...	...	...	...	45	...	...	34	...	...	...	...	...	...	...	...
		Gaondla	"	...	...	...	...	...	...	24	...	...	24	..	...	4,797	95	...	4,678	2	...
		Kalal...	"	1,006	51	...	941	...	...	3,227	27	1	3,313	1	...	352	13	...	359	...	...

TABLE C.

Literate by Language known—(Provincial Summary)—*continued.*

Class.	Group.	Caste.	Religion.	LINGSUGUR. Males. Total Males.	Males. Literate. Total.	Males. Literate. English.	Females. Total Females.	Females. Literate. Total.	Females. Literate. English.	RAILWAYS. Males. Total Males.	Males. Literate. Total.	Males. Literate. English.	Females. Total Females.	Females. Literate. Total.	Females. Literate. English.
				113	114	115	116	117	118	119	120	121	122	123	124
D. Artisan and Village Menial—(*contd.*)	26	Kurma	Hindu	48,781	301	...	48,077	5	...	2	...	...	...	...	...
		Total Group 26		51,575	317	...	50,709	5	...	103	2	...	80	...	...
	27	Gandla	Hindu	7,580	772	...	7,441	13	...	6	3	...	8	...	...
		Do.	Mussulman	...	...	...	...	...	...	...	...	...	...	...	...
		Total Group 27		7,580	772	...	7,441	13	...	6	3	...	8	...	...
	28	Kummari	Hindu	2,828	103	...	2,899	...	...	4	2	...	3	...	...
		Total Group 28		2,828	103	...	2,899	...	...	4	2	...	3	...	...
	29	Kachari	Hindu	...	...	...	...	...	...	...	...	...	...	...	...
		Gajula	"	155	36	...	190	...	...	...	...	...	...	...	...
		Maniari	"	...	...	...	...	...	...	...	...	...	...	...	...
		Do.	Mussulman	...	...	...	...	...	...	...	...	...	...	...	...
		Total Group 29		155	36	...	190	...	...	...	...	...	...	...	...
	30	Lonari	Hindu	...	...	...	...	...	...	2	...	...	...	...	...
		Uppara	"	6,748	45	...	6,685	...	...	...	...	...	...	...	...
		Total Group 30		6,748	45	...	6,685	...	...	2	...	...	...	...	...
	32	Zarikari	Hindu	11	...	...	7	...	...	...	...	...	...	...	...
		Total Group 32		11		...	7	...	...	...	...	...	...	...	...
	35	Besta	Hindu	73	1	...	70	...	...	68	...	...	10	...	...
		Bhoyi	"	...	...	...	...	...	...	...	...	...	...	...	...
		Kahar	"	...	...	...	...	...	...	3	1	...	2	...	...
		Do.	Sikh	...	...	...	...	...	...	...	...	...	...	...	...
		Malla or Mulli	Hindu	...	...	...	...	...	...	...	...	...	...	...	...
		Total Group 35		73	1	...	70	...	...	71	1	...	12	...	...
	36	Bhandari	Hindu	82	...	...	91	...	...	...	...	...	...	...	...
		Gaondla	"	2,287	29	...	2,111	...	...	1	...	...	...	...	...
		Kalal	"	46	...	...	56	...	...	3	...	...	3	...	...

TABLE C.

Literate by Language known.—(Provincial Summary)—*continued.*

Class.	Group.	Caste.	Religion.	TOTAL STRENGTH. Males. Total Males.	Males. Literate. Total.	Males. Literate. English.	Females. Total Females.	Females. Literate. Total.	Females. Literate. English.	HYDERABAD. Males. Total Males.	Males. Literate. Total.	Males. Literate. English.	Females. Total Females.	Females. Literate. Total.	Females. Literate. English.	ATRAF-I-BALDA. Males. Total Males.	Males. Literate. Total.	Males. Literate. English.	Females. Total Females.	Females. Literate. Total.	Females. Literate. English.
1	2	3	4	5	6	7	8	9	10	11	12	13	14	15	16	17	18	19	20	21	22
D. Artisan and Village Menial—(concld).	36	Kalal...	Jain	31	5	...	35	...	...	...	...	...	...	...	...	...	..	..	...	...	...
		Do.	Mussulman	7	...	..	3	...	...	...	...	...	...	.	...	...	..	...	...	...	...
		Total Group 36		1,45,333	2,800	4	1,40,830	50	...	1,602	264	2	1,509	2	..	14,336	464	.	13,978	11	..
	37	Kasai	Hindu	3,932	94	2	3,749	...	...	618	12	2	589	..	...	27[illegible]	15	...	223	...	...
		Do.	Mussulman	339	5	.	338	1	...	11	1	..	21	...	...	5	...	...	5	...	...
		Katik	Hindu	1,287	130	...	1,265	3	...	19	...	...	23	...	...	215	9	...	225	...	...
		Do.	Mussulman	57	3	...	56	...	...	12	3	...	17	...	...	...	..	...	...	...	...
		Total Group 37		5,615	232	2	5,408	4	...	660	16	2	650	...	...	495	24	...	463	...	...
	38	Chamar	Hindu	51,652	104	4	50,380	5	...	3,983	71	4	4,087	2	...	2,253	2	...	2,127	...	..
		Dhor	,,	4,645	14	...	4,510	...	...	25	2	..	31	...	...	...	...	...	...	...	...
		Dokala or Dakkala	,,	236	49	...	226	2	...	...	...	...	...	...	...	...	...	...	...	...	...
		Katari	,,	55	...	...	44	...	...	...	...	...	...	...	...	...	...	...	...	...	...
		Mochi	,,	2,454	25	1	2,019	5	...	980	14	1	717	2	...	20	3	...	8	...	...
		Soonkari	,,	56	..	...	67	...	...	...	...	...	...	...	...	...	...	...	...	.	...
		Total Group 38		59,097	282	5	57,246	12	...	4,988	87	5	4,835	4	...	2,273	5	...	2,135	...	...
	38a	Bedar or Badaru	Hindu	81,547	732	3	80,844	38	...	516	21	2	536	...	...	...	...	...	...	...	...
		Kamkoli	,,	2	1	...	...	..	...	...	...	...	...	...	...	...	...	...	...	...	...
		Mala...	,,	1,36,055	892	62	128,368	40	...	1,960	297	46	2,013	18	...	12,372	97	5	11,961	1	...
		Naik ...	,,	12,558	73	12	12,206	1	...	55	13	1	43	...	...	11	...	...	12	...	...
		Total Group 38a		2,30,162	1,699	77	221,418	79	...	2,531	331	49	2,592	18	...	12,383	97	5	11,973	1	...
	39	Chandal	Hindu	127	...	...	128	...	...	...	...	...	...	...	...	...	...	...	...	...	...
		Mehtar	,,	206	10	...	213	...	..	90	3	...	81	...	...	...	...	...	...	...	...
		Do.	Mussulman	30	2	...	35	..	...	20	1	...	23	...	...	...	...	...	...	...	...
		Do.	Sikh	18	6	...	20	..	...	...	...	...	...	...	...	...	...	...	...	...	..
		Total Group 39		381	19	...	396	...	...	110	4	...	104	...	...	..	..	...	...	...	...
		Total Class D		16,61,756	40,152	222	16,03,328	610	2	33,736	3,264	136	30,700	97	2	76,150	2,410	9	73,326	33	...

TABLE C.

Literate by Language known.—(Provincial Summary)—*continued.*

Class.	Group.	Caste.	Religion.	MAHBUBNAGAR. Males. Total Males.	MAHBUBNAGAR. Males. Literate. Total.	MAHBUBNAGAR. Males. Literate. English.	MAHBUBNAGAR. Females. Total Females.	MAHBUBNAGAR. Females. Literate. Total.	MAHBUBNAGAR. Females. Literate. English.	NALGONDA. Males. Total Males.	NALGONDA. Males. Literate. Total.	NALGONDA. Males. Literate. English.	NALGONDA. Females. Total Females.	NALGONDA. Females. Literate. Total.	NALGONDA. Females. Literate. English.	WARANGAL. Males. Total Males.	WARANGAL. Males. Literate. Total.	WARANGAL. Males. Literate. English.	WARANGAL. Females. Total Females.	WARANGAL. Females. Literate. Total.	WARANGAL. Females. Literate. English.
				23	24	25	26	27	28	29	30	31	32	33	34	35	36	37	38	39	40
D. Artisan and Village Menial—(concld.)	36	Kalal ...	Jain ...	...	...	...	...	...	...	...	...	...	...	...	...	...	...	...	...	...	...
		Do. ...	Mussulman	...	..	...	...	...	...	...	...	...	...	...	...	...	...	...	...	...	..
		Total Group 36		14 944	181	...	15,330	2	..	24,697	137	...	24 016	22	...	24,770	277	...	23 901	2	..
	37	Kasai...	Hindu ...	1 305	41	...	1,239	..	...	...	...	...	...	...	...	...	...	...	...	...	...
		Do.	Mussulman	15	...	...	15	...	...	...	...	...	...	...	...	...	...	...	...	...	...
		Katik	Hindu ...	...	...	...	...	...	...	198	6	...	194	..	...	444	105	...	371	3	...
		Do.	Mussulman	...	..	...	...	...	...	...	...	...	...	...	...	...	...	...	...	...	...
		Total Group 37		1,320	41	...	1,254	...	...	198	6	...	194	...	...	444	105	...	371	3	...
	38	Chamar	Hindu ...	...	...	...	...	..	...	...	...	...	...	...	...	...	...	...	...	...	...
		Dhor ..	" ...	...	...	...	..	...	...	...	...	...	...	...	...	...	...	...	...	...	...
		Dokala or Dakkala ...	" ...	3	2	...	1	...	...	61	18	...	55	...	...	108	22	...	105	2	...
		Katari	" ...	...	...	...	...	...	...	...	...	...	...	...	...	...	...	...	...	...	...
		Mochi	" ...	301	...	...	285	...	...	52	...	...	58	...	...	22	...	...	25	...	...
		Soonkari	" ...	1	...	...	12	...	...	...	...	...	...	...	...	...	...	...	...	...	...
		Group Total 38		305	2	...	298	...	...	113	18	...	113	...	...	130	22	...	130	2	...
	38 a	Bedar or Badaru ...	Hindu ...	2,259	4	...	2,177	1	...	4	...	...	8	...	...	49	4	...	49	...	...
		Kamkoli ...	" ...	...	...	...	..	...	...	...	...	...	...	...	...	...	...	...	...	...	...
		Mala ...	" ...	22,666	89	..	22,262	1	...	22,237	84	...	20,810	7	..	28,094	167	3	26 172	7	...
		Naik ...	" ...	...	...	...	...	...	...	71	9	...	83	...	...	5 172	26	11	4.991	1	..
		Total Group 38 a ...		24,925	93	...	24,429	2	...	22,312	93	...	20,901	7	...	33,315	197	14	31,21[illegible]	8	...
	39	Chandal	Hindu ...	127	...	...	123	...	..	...	...	...	...	...	...	...	...	...	...	...	...
		Mehtar	" ...	...	...	...	...	...	...	...	...	...	...	...	...	...	...	...	...	...	...
		Do.	Mussulman	...	...	...	...	...	...	...	...	...	...	...	..	...	...	..	...	...	...
		Do.	Sikh ...	...	...	...	...	...	..	...	...	...	...	...	...	...	...	...	...	...	...
		Total Group 39		127	...	...	128	...	...	...	...	...	...	...	...	...	...	...	...	...	...
		Total Class D.		133,789	3,670	..	131,193	59	...	138,741	2,497	9	132,644	59	...	167,325	3,716	23	159,386	75	...

TABLE C.

Literate by Language known.—(Provincial Summary)—*continued.*

Class.	Group.	Caste.	Religion.	ELGANDAL. Males. Total Males.	ELGANDAL. Males. Literate. Total.	ELGANDAL. Males. Literate. English.	ELGANDAL. Females. Total Females.	ELGANDAL. Females. Literate. Total.	ELGANDAL. Females. Literate. English.	INDUR. Males. Total Males.	INDUR. Males. Literate. Total.	INDUR. Males. Literate. English.	INDUR. Females. Total Females.	INDUR. Females. Literate. Total.	INDUR. Females. Literate. English.	MEDAK. Males. Total Males.	MEDAK. Males. Literate. Total.	MEDAK. Males. Literate. English.	MEDAK. Females. Total Females.	MEDAK. Females. Literate. Total	MEDAK. Females. Literate. English.
				41	42	43	44	45	46	47	48	49	50	51	52	53	54	55	56	57	58
D. Artisan and village Menial.—(concld.)	36	Kalal	Jain	...	...	...	...	...	...	...	...	...	...	...	...	...	...	...	...	...	...
		Do.	Mussulman	...	...	...	...	...	...	...	...	...	...	...	...	...	...	...	...	...	...
		Total Group 35		32,338	238	...	30,278	2	...	6,343	431	...	6,035	2	...	8,474	297	...	8,241	4	...
	37	Kasai	Hindu	182	7	...	170	...	...	106	2	...	95	...	...	148	8	...	142	...	...
		Do.	Mussulman	1	1	...	...	...	...	7	...	...	8	...	...	...	...	...	...	...	...
		Katik	Hindu	...	...	...	...	...	...	...	...	...	...	...	...	...	...	...	...	...	...
		Do.	Mussulman	...	...	...	...	...	...	...	...	...	...	...	...	...	...	...	...	...	...
		Total Group 37		183	8	...	170	...	...	113	2	...	103	...	...	148	8	...	142	...	...
	38	Chamar	Hindu	...	...	...	...	...	...	871	4	...	896	...	...	17,079	72	...	16,749	1	...
		Dhor	"	...	...	...	...	...	...	18	...	...	20	...	...	...	...	...	...	...	...
		Dokala or Dakkala	"	55	7	...	60	...	...	...	...	...	...	...	...	...	...	...	...	...	...
		Katari	"	...	...	...	...	...	...	...	...	...	...	...	...	...	...	...	...	...	...
		Mochi	"	31	...	...	27	...	...	...	...	...	...	...	...	180	...	...	156	...	...
		Soonkari	"	19	...	...	18	...	...	...	...	...	...	...	...	...	...	...	...	...	...
		Total Group 38		105	7	...	105	...	...	889	4	...	916	...	...	17,259	72	...	16,905	1	...
	38 a	Bedar or Badaru	Hindu	...	...	...	...	...	...	7	...	...	8	...	...	7	...	...	3	...	...
		Kamkoli	"	...	...	...	...	...	...	...	...	...	...	...	...	...	...	...	...	...	...
		Mala	"	48,239	121	1	44,668	6	...	118	1	...	114	...	...	277	13	...	280	...	...
		Naik	"	2,162	7	...	2,048	...	...	964	4	...	894	...	...	2	...	...	3	...	...
		Total Goup 38 a		50,401	128	1	46,716	6	...	1,089	5	...	1,016	...	...	286	13	...	286	...	...
	39	Chandal	Hindu	...	...	...	...	...	...	...	...	...	...	...	...	...	...	...	...	...	...
		Mehtar	"	...	...	...	...	...	...	...	...	...	...	...	...	...	...	...	...	...	...
		Do.	Mussulman	...	...	...	1	...	...	...	...	...	...	...	...	...	...	...	...	...	...
		Do.	Sikh	...	...	...	...	...	...	...	...	...	...	...	...	...	...	...	...	...	...
		Total Group 39		...	...	...	1	...	...	...	...	...	...	...	...	...	...	...	...	...	...
		Total Class D		2,54,027	4,535	9	2,37,052	55	...	82,100	2,345	...	83,407	19	...	68,051	2,033	5	66,707	21	...

TABLE C.

Literate by Language known.—(Provincial Summary)—*continued.*

Class.	Group.	Caste.	Religion.	AURUNGABAD.						BIRH.						NANDER.					
				MALES.			FEMALES.			MALES.			FEMALES.			MALES.			FEMALES.		
				Total Males.	Literate. Total.	Literate. English.	Total Females.	Literate. Total.	Literate. English.	Total Males.	Literate. Total.	Literate. English.	Total Females.	Literate. Total.	Literate. English.	Total Males.	Literate. Total.	Literate. English.	Total Females.	Literate. Total.	Literate. English.
				59	60	61	62	63	64	65	66	67	68	69	70	71	72	73	74	75	76
D. Artisan and Village Menial—(concld.)	36	Kalal ...	Jain ...	...	...	...	...	...	...	...	...	...	...	...	...	...	...	...	...	...	...
		Do. ...	Mussulman	...	...	...	...	...	...	...	...	...	...	...	...	...	...	...	...	...	...
		Total Group 36 ...		908	79	1	874	...	...	241	32	...	220	...	...	1,3[illegible]3	74	...	1,340	...	...
	37	Kasai ...	Hindu ...	...	...	...	...	...	...	3	...	...	5	...	...	34	...	...	40	...	...
		Do. ...	Mussulman	122	...	...	110	...	...	68	3	...	67	...	...	17	...	...	10	...	...
		Katik ...	Hindu ...	58	1	...	50	...	...	...	...	...	...	...	...	28	...	...	26	...	...
		Do. ...	Mussulman	41	...	...	38	...	...	...	...	...	...	...	...	1	...	...	1	...	...
		Total Group 37 ...		224	1	...	198	...	...	71	3	...	72	...	...	80	...	...	77	...	...
	38	Chamar ...	Hindu ...	6,317	12	...	6,256	2	...	4,727	12	...	4,611	...	...	1,616	5	...	1,554	...	...
		Dhor ...	"	676	1	...	673	...	...	742	3	...	698	...	...	214	1	...	210	...	...
		Dokkala or Dakkala ...	"	...	...	...	...	...	...	...	...	...	...	...	...	...	...	...	...	...	...
		Katari ...	"	45	...	...	37	...	...	10	...	...	7	...	...	...	...	...	...	...	...
		Mochi ...	"	74	5	...	36	1	...	...	...	...	...	...	...	...	...	...	2	...	...
		Soonkari ...	"	...	...	...	...	...	...	35	...	...	37	...	...	...	...	...	...	...	...
		Total Group 38 ...		7,112	18	...	7,002	3	...	5,514	15	...	5,353	...	...	1,830	6	...	1,766	...	...
	38 a	Bedar or Badaru ...	Hindu ...	140	18	...	138	...	...	67	...	...	73	...	...	61	...	...	60	1	...
		Kamkoli ...	"	...	...	...	...	...	...	...	...	...	...	...	...	2	1	...	...	...	...
		Mala ...	"	...	...	...	...	...	...	...	...	...	...	...	...	2	...	...	2	...	...
		Naik ...	"	30	1	...	28	...	...	25	...	...	20	...	...	1,932	4	...	1,935	...	...
		Total Group 38 a ...		179	19	...	166	...	...	92	...	...	93	...	...	1,997	5	...	1 997	1	...
	39	Chandal ...	Hindu ...	...	...	...	...	...	...	...	...	...	...	...	...	...	...	...	...	...	...
		Mehtar ...	"	85	4	...	93	...	...	...	...	...	...	...	...	4	2	...	7	...	...
		Do. ...	Mussulman	...	...	...	...	...	...	...	...	...	...	...	...	...	...	...	...	...	...
		Do. ...	Sikh ...	...	...	...	...	...	...	...	...	...	...	...	...	...	...	...	...	...	...
		Total Group 39 ...		85	4	...	93	...	...	...	...	...	...	...	...	4	2	...	7	...	...
		Total Class D ...		62,446	2,077	6	61,161	21	...	54,579	1,359	...	52,841	12	...	55,787	1,030	...	54,759	9	...

TABLE C.

Literate by Language known—(Provincial Summary)—*continued.*

Class.	Group.	Caste.	Religion.	NALDRUG.						BIDAR.						PARBHANI.					
				Males			Females.			Males.			Females.			Males.			Females.		
				Total Males.	Literate.		Total Females.	Literate.		Total Males.	Literate.		Total Females.	Literate.		Total Males.	Literate.		Total Females.	Literate.	
					Total.	English.		Total.	English.		Total.	English.		Total.	English.		Total.	English.		Total.	English.
				77	78	79	80	81	82	83	84	85	86	87	88	89	90	91	92	93	94
D. Artisan and Village Menial—(*concld.*)	36	Kalal ..	Jain	...	...	...	...	...	...	...	...	...	...	...	...	...	...	...	...	...	...
		Do. ...	Mussulman	...	...	...	...	...	...	7	...	...	3	...	...	...	...	...	...	...	...
		Total Group 36......		458	16	...	434	...	...	2,666	59	...	2,597	...	...	402	31	...	456	...	...
	37	Kasai ..	Hindu	7	...	...	14	...	...	83	1	...	68	...	...	38	1	...	28	...	...
		Do. ...	Mussulman	...	...	...	...	...	...	41	...	...	35	...	...	22	...	...	45	1	...
		Katik	Hindu	178	6	...	182	...	...	...	...	...	1	...	...	5	...	...	2[illegible]	...	...
		Do. ...	Mussulman	...	...	...	...	...	...	...	...	...	...	...	...	...	...	...	...	...	...
		Total Group 37......		185	6	...	195	...	...	124	1	...	104	...	...	65	1	...	99	1	...
	38	Chamar	Hindu	6,053	3	...	5,685	...	...	2,758	1	...	2,636	...	...	3,555	8	...	3,408	...	...
		Dhor	"	79[illegible]	6	...	765	...	...	1,020	...	...	917	...	...	705	1	...	759	...	...
		Dokala or Dakkala...	"	...	...	...	...	...	...	...	...	...	...	...	...	...	...	...	...	...	...
		Katari	"	...	...	...	...	...	...	...	...	...	...	...	...	...	...	...	...	...	...
		Mochi	"	34	...	...	32	...	...	36	...	...	40	...	...	209	2	...	183	2	...
		Soonkari	"	...	...	...	...	...	...	...	...	...	...	...	...	...	...	...	...	...	...
		Total Group 38.....		6,877	9	...	6,482	...	...	3,814	1	...	3,593	...	...	4,472	11	...	4,350	2	...
	38 *a*	Bedar or Badaru	Hindu	935	4	...	838	...	...	...	...	...	...	...	...	22	5	...	30	...	...
		Kamkoli	"	...	...	...	...	...	...	...	...	...	...	...	...	...	...	...	...	...	...
		Mala ...	"	...	...	...	...	...	...	...	...	...	...	...	...	...	...	...	...	...	...
		Naik ...	"	...	...	...	...	...	...	697	2	...	682	...	...	157	...	...	160	...	...
		Total Group 38 a		935	4	...	838	...	...	697	2	...	682	..	...	179	5	...	190	...	...
	39	Chandal	Hindu	...	...	...	...	...	...	...	...	...	...	...	...	...	...	...	...	...	...
		Mehtar	"	...	...	...	...	...	...	...	...	...	...	...	...	6	...	...	11	...	...
		Do.	Mussulman	...	...	...	...	...	...	...	...	...	...	...	...	...	...	...	...	...	...
		Do.	Sikh	...	...	...	...	...	...	...	...	...	...	...	...	18	6	...	20	...	...
		Total Group 39		...	...	...	...	...	...	...	...	...	...	...	...	24	6	...	31	...	...
		Total Class D		56,358	1,436	...	53,115	5	...	77,234	1,303	...	75,005	7	...	72,333	1,548	3	69,949	7	...

TABLE C.

Literate by language known—(Provincial Summary)—*continued.*

Class.	Group.	Caste.	Religion.	SIRPUR-TANDUR. Males. Total Males.	Males. Literate. Total.	Males. Literate. English.	Females. Total Females.	Females. Literate. Total.	Females. Literate. English.	GULBARGA. Males. Total Males.	Males. Literate. Total.	Males. Literate. English.	Females. Total Females.	Females. Literate. Total.	Females. Literate. English.	RAICHUR. Males. Total Males.	Males. Literate. Total.	Males. Literate. English.	Females. Total Females.	Females. Literate. Total.	Females. Literate. English.
				95	96	97	98	99	100	101	102	103	104	105	106	107	108	109	110	111	112
D. Artisan and Village Menial—(*concld.*).	36	Kalal...	Jain	31	5	..	35	...	...	...	...	...	...	...	...	...	...	...	...	...	...
		Do. ...	Mussulman	...	..	...	...	...	...	...	...	...	...	...	...	...	...	...	...	...	...
		Total Grooup 36		1,037	56	...	976	...	...	3,296	27	1	3,371	1	...	5,149	108	...	5,037	2	..
	37	Kasai	Hindu	998	2	..	988	...	...	52	...	...	54	...	...	83	5	...	84	...	...
		Do.	Mussulman	...	...	..	...	...	...	2	...	...	2	...	...	10	...	...	3	...	...
		Katik	Hindu	...	...	..	...	...	...	...	...	...	...	..	...	123	3	...	151	...	...
		Do.	Mussulman	...	...	...	...	...	...	...	...	...	...	...	...	...	...	...	...	...	...
		Total Group 21		998	2	..	988	...	...	54	...	...	56	...	...	216	8	...	238	...	...
	38	Chamar	Hindu	137	...	...	158	...	...	1,856	3	...	1,794	...	...	334	...	...	355	...	...
		Dhor	"	8	...	...	17	...	...	421	...	...	390	...	...	...	...	...	...	...	...
		Dokala or Dakkala	"	...	...	...	...	...	...	...	...	...	...	...	...	4	...	...	1	...	...
		Katari	"	...	...	...	...	...	...	...	...	...	...	...	...	...	...	...	...	...	...
		Mochi	"	...	...	...	...	...	...	2	...	...	6	...	...	18	1	...	14	...	...
		Soonkari	"	...	...	...	...	...	...	...	...	...	...	...	...	...	...	...	...	...	...
		Total Group 38		145	...	...	175	...	...	2,279	3	...	2,190	...	...	356	1	...	370	...	...
	38 a	Bedar or Badaru	Hindu	1,033	2	...	1,009	...	...	3,100	39	...	2,987	1	...	32,755	279	1	32,286	5	...
		Kamkoli	"	...	...	...	...	...	...	...	...	...	...	...	...	...	...	...	...	...	...
		Mala ...	"	...	...	...	...	...	...	...	...	...	...	...	...	67	23	7	74	...	...
		Naik ...	"	1,705	1	...	1,230	...	...	48	5	...	49	...	...	22	1	...	22	...	...
		Total Group 38 a		2,238	3	...	2,239	...	...	3,148	44	...	3,036	1	...	32,844	303	8	32,382	5	...
	39	Chandal	Hindu	...	...	...	...	...	...	...	...	...	...	...	...	...	...	...	...	..	...
		Mehtar	"	...	...	...	...	...	...	...	...	...	...	...	...	...	...	...	...	...	...
		Do.	Mussulman	...	...	...	...	...	...	...	...	...	...	...	...	6	2	...	8	..	...
		Do.	Sikh	...	...	...	...	...	...	...	...	...	...	...	...	...	...	...	...	...	...
		Total Group 39		...	...	...	...	...	...	..	...	...	...	...	...	6	2	...	8	..	...
		Total Class D		24,538	349	1	24,150	1	...	59,580	1,476	9	57,127	13	...	1,09,323	2,380	9	107,082	46	...

TABLE C.

Literate by Language known—(Provincial Summary)—*continued.*

Class.	Group.	Caste.	Religion.	LINGASUGUR. Males. Total Males.	Males. Literate. Total.	Males. Literate. English.	Females. Total Females.	Females. Literate. Total.	Females. Literate. English.	RAILWAYS. Males. Total Males.	Males. Literate. Total.	Males. Literate. English.	Females. Total Females.	Females. Literate. Total.	Females. Literate. English.
				113	114	115	116	117	118	119	120	121	122	123	124
D. Artisan and Village Menial—(*concld*).	36	Kalal...	Jain ...	...	...	...	...	...	...	...	...	...	...	...	...
		Do.	Mussulman	...	...	...	...	...	...	...	...	...	...	...	...
		Total Group 16		2,415	29	...	2,258	...	...	4	...	...	3	...	...
	37	Kasai...	Hindu ...	...	...	...	...	...	...	...	...	...	...	...	...
		Do. ...	Mussulman	18	...	...	17	...	...	...	...	...	...	...	...
		Katik	Hindu ...	18	...	...	16	...	...	1	...	...	...	...	...
		Do.	Mussulman	...	...	...	...	...	...	...	...	...	...	...	...
		Total Group 37		36	...	...	33	...	...	1	...	...	...	...	...
	38	Chamar	Hindu ...	...	...	...	...	...	...	110	1	...	64	...	...
		Dhor	"	15	...	...	29	...	...	11	...	...	1	...	...
		Dokala or Dakkala...	"	5	...	...	4	...	...	...	...	...	...	...	...
		Katari	"	...	...	...	...	...	...	...	...	...	...	...	...
		Mochi	"	490	...	...	425	...	...	5	...	...	5	...	...
		Soonkari	"	...	...	...	...	...	...	...	...	...	...	...	...
		Total Group 38		510	...	...	458	...	...	126	1	...	70	...	...
	38 *a*	Bedar or Badaru	Hindu ...	40,572	356	...	40,634	30	...	11	...	...	8	...	...
		Kamkoli	"	...	...	...	...	...	...	...	...	...	...	...	...
		Mala..	"	...	...	...	...	...	...	23	1	...	11	...	...
		Naik ...	"	...	...	...	...	...	...	5	...	...	6	...	...
		Total Group 38 *a*......		40,572	356	...	40,634	30	...	39	1	...	25	...	...
	39	Ohandal	Hindu ...	...	...	...	...	...	...	...	...	...	...	...	...
		Mehtar	"	20	1	...	21	...	...	1	...	...	...	...	...
		Do.	Mussulman	...	...	...	...	...	...	4	...	...	3	...	...
		Do.	Sikh ...	...	...	...	...	...	...	...	...	...	...	...	...
		Total Group 39		20	1	...	21	...	...	5	...	...	3	...	...
		Total Class D.		135,188	3,300	1	133,479	71	...	471	24	2	245	...	...

TABLE C.

Literate by Language known—(Provincial Summary)—*continued.*

Class.	Group.	Caste.	Religion.	TOTAL STRENGTH.						HYDERABAD.						ATRAF-I-BALDA.					
				Males.			Females.			Males.			Females.			Males.			Females		
				Total Males.	Literate. Total.	Literate. English.	Total Females.	Literate. Total.	Literate. English.	Total Males.	Literate. Total.	Literate. English.	Total Females.	Literate. Total.	Literate. English.	Total Males.	Literate. Total.	Literate. English.	Total Females.	Literate. Total.	Literate. English.
1	2	3	4	5	6	7	8	9	10	11	12	13	14	15	16	17	18	19	20	21	22
E. Vagrant Minor Artisans and Performers, &c.	40	Takari	Hindu	135	...	...	150	...	...	...	...	...	...	...	...	...	...	...	...	...	...
		Do.	Mussalman	4	...	...	3	...	...	...	...	...	...	...	...	...	...	...	...	...	...
		Waddar	Hindu	45,533	105	...	44,266	5	...	122	1	...	138	...	...	1,397	3	...	1,269	...	...
		Total Group 40		45,672	105	...	44,419	5	...	122	1	...	138	...	...	1,397	3	...	1,269	...	...
	41	Beldar	Hindu	951	6	...	1,029	...	...	...	...	...	...	...	...	...	...	...	...	...	...
		Kamati	,,	45	12	...	25	...	...	5	3	...	3	...	...	...	...	...	...	...	...
		Sangtarash	,,	967	56	...	1,017	2	...	6	...	...	1	...	...	62	6	...	67	1	...
		Total Group 41		1,963	74	...	2,071	2	...	11	3	...	4	...	...	62	6	...	67	1	...
	42	Sikalgar	Hindu	43	...	...	38	...	...	...	...	...	...	...	...	...	...	...	...	...	...
		Total Group 42		43	...	...	38	...	...	...	...	...	...	...	...	...	...	...	...	...	...
	43	Burud	Hindu	8,304	110	1	8,244	3	...	254	22	1	205	...	...	191	3	...	179	...	...
		Kaikadi	,,	4,102	7	...	4,170	...	...	138	3	...	58	...	...	...	...	...	...	...	...
		Kanjari	,,	21	1	...	14	...	...	...	...	...	...	...	...	...	...	...	...	...	...
		Korvi	,,	416	3	...	392	...	...	...	...	...	...	...	...	...	...	...	...	...	...
		Kunchawad or Kanchara	,,	45	...	...	36	...	...	...	...	...	...	...	...	...	...	...	...	...	...
		Total Group 43		12,888	121	1	12,856	3	...	392	25	1	263	...	...	191	3	...	179	...	...
	44	Erkala	Hindu	11,955	126	...	11,824	6	...	195	5	...	231	...	...	1,005	45	...	1,028	...	...
		Paradhi	,,	1,524	18	...	1,409	4	...	12	4	...	12	...	...	164	...	...	144	...	...
		Total Group 44		13,479	144	...	13,233	10	...	207	9	...	243	..	...	1,169	45	...	1,172	...	...
	45	Badamavaru	Hindu	45	...	...	40	...	...	7	...	...	9	...	...	...	...	...	...	...	...
		Balsantosh	,,	246	4	...	219	...	...	...	...	...	...	...	...	14	...	...	12	...	...
		Baniala	,,	78	9	...	67	...	...	...	...	...	...	...	...	...	...	...	...	...	...
		Bahusagar	,,	72	23	...	70	...	...	17	...	...	15	...	...	...	...	...	...	...	...

TABLE C.

Literate by Language known—(Provincial Summary)—*continued.*

Class.	Group.	Caste.	Religion.	MAHBUBNAGAR.						NALGONDA.						WARANGAL.					
				Males.			Females.			Males.			Females.			Males.			Females.		
				Total Males.	Literate. Total.	Literate. English.	Total Females.	Literate. Total.	Literate. English.	Total Males.	Literate. Total.	Literate. English.	Total Females.	Literate. Total.	Literate. English.	Total Males.	Literate. Total.	Literate. English.	Total Females.	Literate. Total.	Literate. English.
				23	24	25	26	27	28	29	30	31	32	33	34	35	36	37	38	39	40
E. Vagrant Minor Artisans and Performers, &c.	40	Takari	Hindu	1	...	..	1	...	...	...	...	...	...	...	...	...	..	...	...	...	...
		Do.	Mussulman	...	..		...	...	...	...	...	...	...	...	...	...	...	...	...	...	...
		Waddar	Hindu	4,382	10	..	4,093	3	...	7,075	9	..	7,694	..	...	6,944	8	...	6,686	1	...
		Total Group 40		4,383	10	...	4,094	3	...	7,075	9	...	7,694	..	...	6,944	8	..	6,686	1	...
	41	Beldar	Hindu	...	...	...	...	...	...	...	...	..	...	...	...	15	..	..	10	..	...
		Kamati	"	...	...	...	...	...	...	2	...	..	3	...	...	...	...	...	...	...	...
		Sangtarash	"	113	2	...	103	...	...	29	2	..	22	...	...	...	...	...	...	...	...
		Total Group 41		113	2	..	103	...	...	31	2	..	25	...	...	15	...	...	10	...	..
	42	Sikalgar	Hindu	...	...	..	..	...	...	...	...	...	...	...	...	...	...	...	...	...	...
		Total Group 42		..	...	...	...	...	...	...	...	...	..	...	...	...	...	...	..	...	...
	43	Burud	Hindu	717	2	...	658	..	...	197	2	...	238	...	...	476	4	...	537	...	...
		Kaikadi	"	...	...	...	...	...	...	2	...	...	4	...	...	...	...	...	...	...	...
		Kanjari	"	...	...	...	...	...	...	...	...	...	...	...	...	...	...	...	...	...	...
		Korvi	"	...	...	...	...	...	...	...	...	...	...	...	...	...	...	...	...	...	...
		Kanchawad or Kanchara	"	...	...	...	...	...	...	...	...	...	...	...	..	...	...	...	...	...	...
		Total Group 43		717	2	...	658	...	...	199	2	...	242	...	...	476	4	...	537	...	...
	44	Erkala	Hindu	1,298	3	...	1,209	...	...	1,438	3	...	1,414	...	...	2,270	5	...	2,107	2	..
		Paradhi	"	243	...	...	278	...	...	...	...	...	...	...	...	13	...	...	14	...	...
		Total Group 44		1,541	3	...	1,487	..	...	1,438	3	...	1,414	..	...	2,283	5	...	2,121	2	..
	45	Badamavaru	Hindu	...	...	...	...	...	...	32	...	...	29	...	...	...	...	...	...	...	...
		Balsantosh	"	30	...	...	25	...	...	18	...	...	17	...	...	120	4	...	102	...	...
		Baniala	"	...	...	...	...	...	...	...	...	...	...	...	...	53	9	...	45	...	...
		Babusagar	"	30	15	...	22	...	...	...	...	...	...	...	...	..	...	..	...	...	...

TABLE C.

Literate by Language known—(Provincial Summary)—*continued.*

Class.	Group.	Caste.	Religion.	ELGANDAL. Males. Total Males.	Males. Literate. Total.	Males. Literate. English.	Females. Total Females.	Females. Literate. Total.	Females. Literate. English.	INDUR. Males. Total Males.	Males. Literate. Total.	Males. Literate. English.	Females. Total Females.	Females. Literate. Total.	Females. Literate. English.	MEDAK. Males. Total Males.	Males. Literate. Total.	Males. Literate. English.	Females. Total Females.	Females. Literate. Total.	Females. Literate. English.
				41	42	43	44	45	46	47	48	49	50	51	52	53	54	55	56	57	58
E. Vagrant Minor Artisans and Performers, &c.	40	Takari	Hindu	...	...	...	...	...	...	...	...	...	...	...	...	...	...	...	...	...	...
		Do.	Mussalman	...	...	...	...	...	...	...	...	...	...	...	...	...	...	...	...	...	...
		Waddar	Hindu	2,618	9	...	2,372	...	...	1,307	...	...	1,177	...	...	614	1	...	535	...	...
		Total Group 40		2,618	9	...	2,372	...	...	1,307	...	...	1,177	...	...	614	1	...	535	...	...
	41	Beldar	Hindu	...	...	...	...	...	...	86	...	...	100	...	...	...	...	...	...	...	...
		Kamati	"	...	...	...	...	...	...	1	1	...	2	...	...	...	...	...	...	...	...
		Sangtarash	"	149	31	...	186	...	...	40	6	...	47	...	...	62	8	...	55	...	...
		Total Group 41		149	31	...	186	...	...	127	7	...	149	...	...	62	8	...	55	...	...
	42	Sikalgar	Hindu	...	...	...	...	...	...	...	...	...	...	...	...	...	...	...	...	...	...
		Total Group 42		...	...	...	...	...	...	...	...	...	...	...	...	...	...	...	...	...	...
	43	Burud	Hindu	1,995	7	...	1,791	...	...	1,047	8	...	1,051	2	...	368	4	...	357	...	...
		Kaikadi	"	53	...	...	49	...	...	184	...	...	204	...	...	...	...	...	...	...	...
		Kanjari	"	...	...	...	...	...	...	...	...	...	...	...	...	...	...	...	...	...	...
		Korvi	"	...	...	...	...	...	...	...	...	...	...	...	...	...	...	...	...	...	...
		Kanchawad or Kanchara	"	...	...	...	...	...	...	...	...	...	...	...	...	...	...	...	...	...	...
		Total Group 43		2,048	7	...	1,840	...	...	1,231	8	...	1,255	2	...	368	4	...	357	...	...
	44	Erkala	Hindu	834	2	...	775	...	...	370	10	...	315	...	...	549	16	...	579	...	...
		Paradhi	"	4	...	...	3	...	...	37	...	...	27	...	...	13	...	...	10	...	...
		Total Group 44		838	2	...	779	...	...	407	10	...	342	...	...	562	16	...	589	...	...
	45	Badamavaru	Hindu	6	...	...	2	...	...	...	...	...	...	...	...	...	...	...	...	...	...
		Ba'santosh	"	53	...	...	48	...	...	7	...	...	10	...	...	4	...	...	3	...	...
		Baniala	"	25	...	...	22	...	...	...	...	...	...	...	...	...	...	...	...	...	...
		Bahusagar	"	...	...	...	...	...	...	1	1	...	3	...	...	...	...	...	...	...	...

TABLE C.

Literate by Language known—(Provincial Summary)—*continued.*

Class.	Group.	Caste.	Religion.	AURUNGABAD. Males. Total Males.	AURUNGABAD. Males. Literate. Total.	AURUNGABAD. Males. Literate. English.	AURUNGABAD. Females. Total Females.	AURUNGABAD. Females. Literate. Total.	AURUNGABAD. Females. Literate. English.	BIRH. Males. Total Males.	BIRH. Males. Literate. Total.	BIRH. Males. Literate. English.	BIRH. Females. Total Females.	BIRH. Females. Literate. Total.	BIRH. Females. Literate. English.	NANDER. Males. Total Males.	NANDER. Males. Literate. Total.	NANDER. Males. Literate. English.	NANDER. Females. Total Females.	NANDER. Females. Literate. Total.	NANDER. Females. Literate. English.
				59	60	61	62	63	64	65	66	67	68	69	70	71	72	73	74	75	76
E. Vagrant Minor Artisans and Performers, &c.	40	Takari	Hindu	52	...	...	57	...	...	80	...	...	89	...	...	1	...	...	1	...	...
		Do.	Mussulman	..	...	...	...	...	...	...	...	...	...	...	...	...	...	...	...	...	...
		Waddar	Hindu	958	4	...	882	..	...	743	3	...	712	...	...	2,078	5	...	1,949	...	...
		Total Group 40		1,010	4	...	939	...	...	823	3	...	801	...	...	2,079	5	...	1,950	...	...
	41	Beldár	Hindu	160	2	...	168	...	...	121	...	...	129	...	...	73	...	...	68	...	...
		Kamati	"	...	...	...	...	...	...	...	...	...	...	...	...	...	...	...	...	...	...
		Sangtarash	"	10	...	...	11	...	...	47	...	...	48	...	...	210	...	...	213	1	...
		Total Group 41		170	2	...	179	...	...	168	...	...	177	...	...	283	...	...	281	1	...
	42	Sikalgar	Hindu	13	...	...	15	...	...	14	...	...	4	...	...	15	...	...	18	...	...
		Total Group 42		13	..	...	15	...	...	14	..	...	4	...	...	15	...	...	18	...	...
	43	Burud	Hindu	11[illegible]	8	...	147	1	...	95	...	...	91	...	...	377	...	...	395	...	...
		Kaikadi	"	363	3	...	411	...	...	483	...	...	480	...	...	358	...	...	378	...	...
		Kanjari	"	21	1	...	14	...	...	...	...	...	...	...	...	...	...	...	...	...	...
		Korvi	"	2	1	...	...	...	...	...	...	...	...	...	...	...	...	...	...	...	...
		Kanchawad or Kanchara	"	45	...	...	36	...	...	...	...	...	...	...	...	...	...	...	...	...	...
		Total Group 43		571	13	...	608	1	...	578	...	...	571	...	...	735	...	...	773	...	...
	44	Erkala	Hindu	...	...	...	...	...	...	...	...	...	...	...	...	6	...	...	6	...	...
		Paradhi	"	293	9	...	219	...	...	72	...	...	60	...	...	31	5	...	29	4	...
		Total Group 44		293	9	...	219	..	...	72	...	...	60	...	...	37	5	...	35	4	...
	45	Badamavaru	Hindu	...	...	...	...	...	...	...	...	...	...	...	...	...	...	...	...	...	...
		Balsantosh	"	...	...	...	...	...	...	...	...	...	...	...	...	...	...	...	...	...	...
		Bania'a	"	...	...	...	...	...	...	...	...	...	...	...	...	...	...	...	...	...	...
		Bahusagar	"	...	...	...	...	...	...	24	7	...	30	...	...	...	...	...	...	...	...

TABLE C.

Literate by Language known—(Provincial Summary)—*continued.*

Class.	Group.	Caste.	Religion.	NALDRUG. Males. Total Males.	NALDRUG. Males. Literate. Total.	NALDRUG. Males. Literate. English.	NALDRUG. Females. Total Females.	NALDRUG. Females. Literate. Total.	NALDRUG. Females. Literate. English.	BIDAR. Males. Total Males.	BIDAR. Males. Literate. Total.	BIDAR. Males. Literate. English.	BIDAR. Females. Total Females.	BIDAR. Females. Literate. Total.	BIDAR. Females. Literate. English.	PARBHANI. Males. Total Males.	PARBHANI. Males. Literate. Total.	PARBHANI. Males. Literate. English.	PARBHANI. Females. Total Females.	PARBHANI. Females. Literate. Total.	PARBHANI. Females. Literate. English.
				77	78	79	80	81	82	83	84	85	86	87	88	89	90	91	92	93	94
E. Vagrant Minor Artisans and Performers, &c.	40	Takari	Hindu ..	...	...	...	...	...	...	...	...	...	...	...	...	...	...	...	...	...	...
		Do.	Mussulman	...	...	...	...	...	...	...	...	...	...	...	...	4	...	...	3	...	...
		Waddar	Hindu ...	934	5	...	919	...	...	1,277	1	...	1,212	...	...	1,479	...	...	1,500	...	...
		Total Group 40......		934	5	...	919	..	...	1,277	1	...	1,212	...	...	1,483	...	...	1,503	...	...
	41	Beldar	Hindu ...	22	...	...	25	...	...	134	1	...	153	...	...	117	1	...	114	...	...
		Kamati	„ ..	...	...	...	...	...	...	...	...	...	...	...	...	37	8	...	17	...	...
		Sangtarash	„ ..	94	...	...	117	...	...	64	...	...	70	...	...	65	...	..	6	...	...
		Total Group 41... ..		116	...	...	142	...	...	198	1	...	273	...	...	219	9	...	191	...	...
	42	Sikalgar	Hindu ..	...	...	...	...	...	...	...	...	...	...	...	...	...	...	...	...	...	...
		Total Group 42......		...	...	...	...	...	...	...	...	...	...	...	...	...	...	...	...	...	...
	43	Burud	Hindu ..	212	7	...	229	...	...	512	6	...	495	...	...	347	28	...	349	...	...
		Kaikadi	„ ...	693	1	...	723	...	...	663	...	...	712	...	...	355	...	...	346	...	...
		Kanjari	„ ...	...	...	...	...	...	...	...	...	...	...	...	...	...	...	...	...	...	...
		Korvi	„ ...	...	...	...	...	...	...	...	...	...	...	...	...	...	...	...	...	...	...
		Kanchawad or Kanchara	„ ..	...	...	...	..	...	...	...	...	...	...	...	...	...	...	...	...	...	...
		Total Group 43......		905	8	...	952	...	...	1,175	6	...	1,207	...	...	702	28	...	695	...	...
	44	Erkala	Hindu ...	...	...	...	...	...	...	1	...	...	...	...	...	...	...	...	...	...	...
		Paradhi	„ ...	268	...	...	239	...	...	35	...	...	45	...	...	232	...	...	231	...	...
		Total Group 44......		268	...	...	239	...	...	36	...	...	45	...	...	232	...	...	231	...	...
	45	Badamavaru	Hindu ...	...	...	...	...	...	...	...	...	...	...	...	...	...	...	...	...	...	...
		Balsantosh	„ ...	...	...	...	...	...	...	...	...	...	...	...	...	...	...	...	...	...	...
		Baniala	„ ...	...	...	...	...	...	...	...	...	...	...	...	...	...	...	...	...	...	...
		Babusagar	„ ...	...	...	...	...	...	...	...	...	...	...	...	...	...	...	...	...	...	...

TABLE C.

Literate by Language known—(Provincial Summary)—*continued.*

Class.	Group.	Caste.	Religion.	SIRPUR-TANDUR.						GULBARGA.						RAICHUR.					
				Males.			Females.			Males.			Females.			Males.			Females.		
				Total Males.	Literate. Total.	Literate. English.	Total Females.	Literate. Total.	Literate. English.	Total Males.	Literate. Total.	Literate. English.	Total Females.	Literate. Total.	Literate. English.	Total Males.	Literate. Total.	Literate. English.	Total Females.	Literate. Total.	Literate. English.
				95	96	97	98	99	100	101	102	103	104	105	106	107	108	109	110	111	112
E. Vagrant Minor Artisans and Performers, &c.	40	Takari	Hindu	...	...	...	...	...	...	...	...	...	...	...	...	...	...	...	...	...	...
		Do.	Mussulman	...	...	...	...	...	...	...	...	...	...	...	...	...	...	...	...	...	...
		Waddar	Hindu	192	...	...	187	...	...	2,835	...	...	2,706	...	...	4,676	17	...	4,465	1	...
		Total Group 40		192	...	...	187	...	...	2,835	...	...	2,706	...	...	4,676	17	...	4,465	1	...
	41	Beldar	Hindu	176	...	...	211	...	...	47	2	...	51	...	...	...	...	...	...	...	...
		Kamati	"	...	...	...	...	...	...	...	...	...	...	...	...	...	...	...	...	...	...
		Sangtarash	"	...	...	...	...	...	...	1	...	...	2	...	...	8	1	...	7	...	...
		Total Group 41		176	...	...	211	...	...	48	2	...	53	...	...	8	1	...	7	...	...
	42	Sikalgar	Hindu	...	...	...	...	...	...	...	...	...	...	...	...	1	...	...	1	...	...
		Total Group 42		...	...	...	...	...	...	...	...	...	...	...	...	1	...	...	1	...	...
	43	Burud	Hindu	139	...	...	130	...	...	267	7	...	44[illegible]	...	...	602	1	...	595	...	...
		Kaikadi	"	72	...	...	69	...	...	511	...	...	498	...	...	116	...	...	120	...	...
		Kanjari	"	...	...	...	...	...	...	...	...	...	...	...	...	...	...	...	...	...	...
		Korvi	"	...	...	...	...	...	...	414	2	...	392	...	...	...	...	...	...	...	...
		Kanchawad or Kanchara	"	...	...	...	...	...	...	...	...	...	...	...	...	...	...	...	...	...	...
		Total Group 43		211	...	...	199	...	...	1,192	9	...	1,334	...	...	718	1	...	71[illegible]	...	...
	44	Erkala	Hindu	...	...	...	...	...	...	75	...	...	66	...	...	1,332	17	...	1,368	2	...
		Paradhi	"	27	...	...	20	...	...	77	...	...	77	...	...	...	...	...	...	...	...
		Total Group 44		27	...	...	20	...	...	152	...	...	143	...	...	1,332	17	...	1,368	2	...
	45	Badamavaru	Hindu	...	...	...	...	...	...	...	...	...	...	...	...	...	...	...	...	...	...
		Ba'santosh	"	...	...	...	...	...	...	...	...	...	2	...	...	...	...	...	...	...	...
		Baniala	"	...	...	...	...	...	...	...	...	...	...	...	...	...	...	...	...	...	...
		Bahusagar	"	...	...	...	...	...	...	...	...	...	...	...	...	...	...	...	...	...	...

TABLE C.

Literate by Language known—(Provincial Summary)—*continued.*

Class.	Group.	Caste.	Religion.	LINGASUGUR. Males. Total Males.	LINGASUGUR. Males. Literate. Total.	LINGASUGUR. Males. Literate. English.	LINGASUGUR. Females. Total Females.	LINGASUGUR. Females. Literate. Total.	LINGASUGUR. Females. Literate. English.	RAILWAYS. Males. Total Males.	RAILWAYS. Males. Literate. Total.	RAILWAYS. Males. Literate. English.	RAILWAYS. Females. Total Females.	RAILWAYS. Females. Literate. Total.	RAILWAYS. Females. Literate. English.
				113	114	115	116	117	118	119	120	121	122	123	124
E. Vagrant Minor Artisans and Performers, &c.	40	Takari	Hindu	...	...	...	...	...	...	1	...	...	2	...	...
		Do.	Mussulman	...	...	...	...	...	...	...	...	...	...	...	...
		Waddar	Hindu	5,899	29	...	5,770	...	...	3	...	...	...	...	...
		Total Group 40		5,899	29	...	5,770	...	...	4	...	...	2	...	...
	41	Beldar	Hindu	...	...	...	...	...	...	...	...	...	...	...	...
		Kanati	"	...	...	...	...	...	...	...	...	...	...	...	...
		Sangtarash	"	7	...	...	8	...	...	...	...	...	...	...	...
			"												
		Total Group 41		7	...	...	8	...	...	...	...	...	...	...	...
	42	Sikalgar	Hindu	...	...	...	...	...	...	...	...	...	...	...	...
		Total Group 42		...	...	...	...	...	...	...	...	...	...	...	...
	43	Burud	Hindu	368	1	...	353	...	...	...	...	...	...	...	...
		Kaikadi	"	106	...	...	116	...	...	5	...	...	2	...	...
		Kanjari	"	...	...	...	...	...	...	...	...	...	...	...	...
		Korvi	"	...	...	...	...	...	...	...	...	...	...	...	...
		Kanchawad or Kanchara	"	...	...	...	...	...	...	...	...	...	...	...	...
		Total Group 43		474	1	...	469	...	...	5	...	...	2	...	...
	44	Erkala	Hindu	2,582	20	...	2,725	2	...	...	...	...	...	...	...
		Paradhi	"	3	...	...	1	...	...	...	...	...	...	...	...
		Total Group 44		2,585	20	...	2,726	2	...	...	...	...	...	...	...
	45	Badamavaru	Hindu	...	...	...	...	...	...	...	...	...	...	...	...
		Balsantosh	"	...	...	...	...	...	...	...	...	...	...	...	...
		Baniala	"	...	...	...	...	...	...	...	...	...	...	...	...
		Bahusagar	"	...	...	...	...	...	...	...	...	...	...	...	...

TABLE C.

Literate by Language known—(Provincial Summary)—*continued.*

Class.	Group.	Caste.	Religion.	TOTAL STRENGTH. Males. Total Males.	Males. Literate. Total.	Males. Literate. English.	Females. Total Females.	Females. Literate. Total.	Females. Literate. English.	HYDERABAD. Males. Total Males.	Males. Literate. Total.	Males. Literate. English.	Females. Total Females.	Females. Literate. Total.	Females. Literate. English.	ATRAF-I-BALDA. Males. Total Males.	Males. Literate. Total.	Males. Literate. English.	Females. Total Females.	Females. Literate. Total.	Females. Literate. English.
1	2	3	4	5	6	7	8	9	10	11	12	13	14	15	16	17	18	19	20	21	22
E. Vagrant Minor Artisans and Performers, &c.—(concld.)	45	Budbuduki	Hindu	562	8	...	563	...	...	6	...	...	2	...	...	5	1	...	2	...	...
		Ganjakuti	„	...	...	...	2	...	...	...	...	...	...	...	...	...	...	...	...	...	...
		Kunapusala	„	84	27	...	75	...	...	...	...	...	...	...	...	...	...	...	...	...	...
		Mundi	„	72	4	...	61	...	...	5	4	...	1	...	...	8	...	...	5	...	...
		Mittulu	„	44	1	...	36	...	...	...	...	...	...	...	...	...	...	...	...	...	...
		Pandawa	„	59	...	...	40	...	...	...	...	...	...	...	...	...	...	...	...	...	...
		Pardesi	„	6,855	174	...	5,953	2	...	92	16	...	56	...	...	14	3	...	5	...	...
		Parmavaru	„	256	1	...	231	...	...	...	...	...	...	...	...	...	...	...	...	...	...
		Ramdesi	„	24	5	...	23	...	...	...	...	...	...	...	...	...	...	...	...	...	...
		Saradhi	„	109	...	...	107	...	...	...	...	...	...	...	...	24	...	...	24	...	...
		Vipravinodulu	„	46	3	...	30	...	...	...	...	...	...	...	...	...	...	...	...	...	...
		Total Group 45......		8,552	259	...	7,517	2	...	127	20	...	83	...	...	65	4	...	48	...	...
	46	Dommari	Hindu	1,835	145	...	1,676	1	...	4	...	...	...	...	...	10	...	...	32	...	...
		Gopal	„	1,489	1	...	1,335	...	...	...	...	...	...	...	...	...	...	...	...	...	...
		Jetty	„	301	33	3	318	1	...	20	9	1	13	...	...	2	...	...	3	...	...
		Total Group 46		3,625	179	3	3,329	2	...	24	9	1	13	...	...	12	...	...	35	...	...
	47	Gungadla	Hindu	96	...	...	78	...	...	...	...	...	...	...	...	8	...	...	3	...	...
		Garodi	„	41	...	...	39	...	...	...	...	...	...	...	...	...	...	...	...	...	...
		Katipapa	„	116	1	...	158	...	...	...	...	...	...	...	...	...	...	...	...	...	...
		Kalsutri	„	195	1	...	174	...	...	...	...	...	...	...	...	...	...	...	...	...	...
		Total Group 47		448	2	...	440	...	...	...	...	...	...	...	...	8	...	...	3	...	...
		Total Class E.		86,670	834	4	83,903	24	...	883	67	2	744	...	...	2,904	61	...	2,773	1	...
F. Races and Nationalities.	48	Armenian	Christian	7	3	2	1	1	1	5	1	1	1	1	1	...	...	...	...	...	...
		Arab	Mussalman	1,011	210	1	729	3	...	21	7	1	4	...	...	67	14	...	25	...	...
		Baluch	„	10	2	...	9	1	...	8	2	...	7	1	...	...	...	...	...	...	...

TABLE C.

Literate by Language known—(Provincial Summary)—*continued.*

Class.	Group.	Caste.	Religion.	MAHBUBNAGAR. Males. Total Males.	Males. Literate. Total.	Males. Literate. English.	Females. Total Females.	Females. Literate. Total.	Females. Literate. English.	NALGONDA. Males. Total Males.	Males. Literate. Total.	Males. Literate. English.	Females. Total Females.	Females. Literate. Total.	Females. Literate. English.	WARANGAL. Males. Total Males.	Males. Literate. Total.	Males. Literate. English.	Females. Total Females.	Females. Literate. Total.	Females. Literate. English.
				23	24	25	26	27	28	29	30	31	32	33	34	35	36	37	38	39	40
E. Vagrant Minor Artisan and Performer, &c.—(contd.)	45	Budubduki	Hindu	3	...	...	1	...	...	3	...	...	3	...	...	32	...	...	28	...	...
		Ganjakuti	"	...	...	...	...	...	...	...	...	...	2	...	...	...	...	...	...	...	...
		Kunapusala	"	26	3	...	18	...	...	...	...	...	...	...	...	...	...	...	...	...	...
		Mundi	"	...	...	...	...	...	...	41	...	...	38	...	...	12	...	...	12	...	...
		Mittulu	"	...	...	...	...	...	...	...	...	...	...	...	...	...	...	...	...	...	...
		Pandawa	"	...	...	...	...	...	...	...	...	...	...	...	...	39	...	...	18	...	...
		Pardesi	"	...	...	...	...	...	...	1	1	...	...	...	...	1	...	...	1	...	...
		Parmavaru	"	...	...	...	...	...	...	...	...	...	...	...	...	...	...	...	...	...	...
		Ramdesi	"	...	...	...	...	...	...	...	...	...	...	...	...	...	...	...	...	...	...
		Saradhi	"	...	...	...	...	...	...	46	...	...	40	...	...	7	...	...	8	...	...
		Vipravinodulu	"	...	...	...	...	...	...	15	2	...	13	...	...	18	1	...	9	...	...
		Total Group 45		89	18	...	66		...	156	3	...	142	...	...	282	14	...	223	...	...
	46	Dommari	Hindu	142	...	...	132	...	...	133	...	...	134	1	...	239	...	...	286	...	...
		Gopal	"	...	...	...	...	...	...	...	...	...	...	...	...	...	...	...	...	...	...
		Jetty	"	73	1	...	73	...	...	4	...	...	2	...	...	...	...	...	...	...	...
		Total Group 46		215	1	...	205	...	...	137	...	...	136	1	...	239	...	...	286	...	...
	47	Gungadla	Hindu	35	...	...	32	...	...	16	...	...	9	...	...	...	...	...	...	...	...
		Garodi	"	...	...	...	...	...	...	...	...	...	...	...	...	19	...	...	12	...	...
		Katipapa	"	...	...	...	...	...	...	2	...	...	2	...	...	8	...	...	6	...	...
		Kalsutri	"	...	...	...	...	...	...	...	...	...	...	...	...	...	...	...	...	...	...
		Total Group 47		35	...	...	32	...	...	18	...	...	11	...	...	27	...	...	18	...	...
		Total Class E		7,093	35	...	6,645	3	...	9,054	19	...	9,664	1	...	10,265	31	...	9,881	3	...
F. Races and Nationalities.	48	Armenian	Christian	...	...	...	...	...	...	...	...	...	...	...	...	...	...	...	...	...	...
		Arab	Mussalman	100	26	...	99	1	...	6	2	...	...	...	...	13	4	...	13	...	...
		Baluch	"	...	...	...	...	...	...	1	...	...	...	...	...	1	...	...	2	...	...

TABLE C.

Literate by language known—(Provincial Summary)—*continued.*

Class.	Group.	Caste.	Religion.	ELGANDAL. Males. Total Males.	Literate. Total.	Literate. English.	Females. Total Females.	Literate. Total.	Literate. English.	INDUR. Males. Total Males.	Literate. Total.	Literate. English.	Females. Total Females.	Literate. Total.	Literate. English.	MEDAK. Males. Total Males.	Literate. Total.	Literate. English.	Females. Total Females.	Literate. Total.	Literate. English.
				41	42	43	44	45	46	47	48	49	50	51	52	53	54	55	56	57	58
E. Vagrant Minor Artisans and Performers, &c.—(concld.)	45	Budbuduki	Hindu	19	...	...	8	...	...	6	...	...	2	...	...	40	1	...	31	...	...
		Ganjakuti	"	...	...	...	...	...	...	...	...	...	...	...	...	...	...	...	...	...	...
		Kunapusala	"	7	2	...	10	...	...	28	9	...	23	...	...	17	12	...	16	...	...
		Mundi	"	6	...	...	5	...	...	...	...	...	...	...	...	...	...	...	...	...	...
		Mittulu	"	...	...	...	...	...	...	...	...	...	1	...	...	1	1	...	3	...	...
		Pandawa	"	27	...	...	22	...	...	...	...	...	...	...	...	...	...	...	...	...	...
		Pardesi	"	81	...	...	75	...	...	...	...	...	...	...	...	1	...	...	...	...	...
		Parmavaru	"	...	...	...	...	...	...	256	1	...	231	...	...	...	...	...	...	...	...
		Ramdesi	"	...	...	...	...	...	...	24	5	...	23	...	...	...	...	...	...	...	...
		Saradhi	"	...	...	...	...	...	...	10	...	...	10	...	...	10	...	...	16	...	...
		Vipravinodulu	"	...	...	...	...	...	...	7	...	...	4	...	...	6	...	...	4	...	...
		Total Group 45		217	2	...	192	...	...	339	16	...	307	...	...	79	14	...	73	...	...
	46	Dommari	Hindu	144	1	...	137	...	...	63	2	...	76	...	...	49	...	...	49	...	...
		Gopal	"	...	...	...	...	...	...	...	...	...	...	...	...	...	...	...	...	...	...
		Jetty	"	1	...	...	25	...	...	...	...	...	...	...	...	5	...	...	3	...	...
		Total Group 46		145	1	...	162	...	...	63	2	...	76	...	...	54	...	...	5	...	...
	47	Gungadla	Hindu	...	...	...	...	...	...	...	...	...	...	...	...	...	...	...	...	...	...
		Garodi	"	...	...	...	...	...	...	7	...	...	11	...	...	3	...	...	1	...	...
		Katipapa	"	10	1	...	8	...	...	5	...	...	7	...	...	...	...	...	...	...	...
		Kalsutri	"	...	...	...	...	...	...	...	...	...	...	...	...	...	...	...	...	...	...
		Total Group 47		10	1	...	8	...	...	12	...	...	18	...	...	3	...	...	1	...	...
		Total Class E.		6,025	53	..	5,539	...	...	3,486	43	...	3,324	2	...	1,742	43	...	1,662	...	...
F. Rogues and Nationalities.	48	Armenian	Christian	...	...	...	...	...	...	...	...	...	...	...	...	...	...	...	...	...	...
		Arab	Mussalman	30	6	...	11	...	...	43	7	...	38	...	...	136	25	...	105	1	...
		Baluch	"	...	...	...	...	...	...	...	...	...	...	...	...	...	...	...	...	...	...

TABLE C.

Literate by Language known—(Provincial Summary)—*continued.*

AURUNGABAD.

Class.	Group.	Caste.	Religion.	Males: Total Males.	Males: Literate: Total.	Males: Literate: English.	Females: Total Females.	Females: Literate: Total.	Females: Literate: English.
				59	60	61	62	63	64
E. Vagrant Minor Artisans and Performers, &c.—(*concld*).	45	Budbuduki	Hindu	...	...	...	...	...	...
		Ganjakuti	,,	...	...	...	...	...	...
		Kunapusala	,,	...	...	...	...	...	...
		Mundi	,,	...	...	...	...	...	...
		Mittulu	,,	...	...	...	...	...	...
		Pandawa	,,	...	...	...	...	...	...
		Pardesi	,,	6,248	123	...	5,440	2	...
		Parmavaru	,,	...	...	...	...	...	...
		Ramdesi	,,	...	...	...	...	...	...
		Saradhi	,,	1	...	...	...	...	...
		Vipravinodulu	,,	...	...	...	...	...	...
		Total Group 45		6,249	123	...	5,440	2	...
	46	Dommari	Hindu	68	...	...	138	...	...
		Gopal	,,	720	...	...	600	...	...
		Jetty	,,	31	12	...	41	...	...
		Total Group 46		819	12	...	788	...	...
	47	Gungadla	Hindu	...	...	...	...	...	...
		Garodi	,,	...	...	...	...	...	...
		Katipapa	,,	...	...	...	...	...	...
		Kalsutti	,,	2	...	...	1	...	...
		Total Group 47		2	...	...	1	...	...
		Total Class E.		9,127	163	...	8,189	3	...
F. Races and Nationalities.	48	Armenian	Christian	1	1	...	...	...	...
		Arab	Mussalman	142	27	...	131	...	...
		Baluch	,,	...	...	...	...	...	...

BIRH.

Class.	Group.	Caste.	Religion.	Males: Total Males.	Males: Literate: Total.	Males: Literate: English.	Females: Total Females.	Females: Literate: Total.	Females: Literate: English.
				65	66	67	68	69	70
E. Vagrant Minor Artisans and Performers, &c.—(*concld*).	45	Budbuduki	Hindu	...	...	...	...	...	...
		Ganjakuti	,,	...	...	...	...	...	...
		Kunapusala	,,	...	...	...	...	...	...
		Mundi	,,	...	...	...	...	...	...
		Mittulu	,,	...	...	...	...	...	...
		Pandawa	,,	...	...	...	...	...	...
		Pardesi	,,	139	9	...	141	...	...
		Parmavaru	,,	...	...	...	...	...	...
		Ramdesi	,,	...	...	...	...	...	...
		Saradhi	,,	...	...	...	...	...	...
		Vipravinodulu	,,	...	...	...	...	...	...
		Total Group 45		163	16	...	171	...	...
	46	Dommari	Hindu	100	2	...	142	...	...
		Gopal	,,	107	...	...	95	...	...
		Jetty	,,	...	...	...	...	...	...
		Total Group 46		207	2	...	237	...	...
	47	Gungadla	Hindu	...	...	...	...	...	...
		Garodi	,,	...	...	...	...	...	...
		Katipapa	,,	...	...	...	...	...	...
		Kalsutti	,,	...	...	...	...	...	...
		Total Group 47		...	...	...	...	...	...
		Total Class E.		2,025	21	...	2,021	...	...
F. Races and Nationalities.	48	Armenian	Christian	...	...	...	...	...	...
		Arab	Mussalman	42	13	...	34	...	...
		Baluch	,,	...	...	...	...	...	...

NANDER.

Class.	Group.	Caste.	Religion.	Males: Total Males.	Males: Literate: Total.	Males: Literate: English.	Females: Total Females.	Females: Literate: Total.	Females: Literate: English.
				71	72	73	74	75	76
E. Vagrant Minor Artisans and Performers, &c.—(*concld*).	45	Budbuduki	Hindu	...	...	...	...	...	...
		Ganjakuti	,,	...	...	...	...	...	...
		Kunapusala	,,	6	1	...	8	...	...
		Mundi	,,	...	...	...	...	...	...
		Mittulu	,,	...	...	...	...	...	...
		Pandawa	,,	...	...	...	...	...	...
		Pardesi	,,	14	...	...	7	...	...
		Parmavaru	,,	...	...	...	...	...	...
		Ramdesi	,,	...	...	...	...	...	...
		Saradhi	,,	11	...	...	9	...	...
		Vipravinodulu	,,	...	...	...	...	...	...
		Total Group 45		31	1	...	24	...	...
	46	Dommari	Hindu	67	...	...	99	...	...
		Gopal	,,	179	...	...	141	...	...
		Jetty	,,	...	...	...	...	...	...
		Total Group 46		246	...	...	240	...	...
	47	Gungadla	Hindu	...	...	...	...	...	...
		Garodi	,,	...	...	...	...	...	...
		Katipapa	,,	...	...	...	...	...	...
		Kalsutti	,,	...	...	...	...	...	...
		Total Group 47		...	...	...	...	...	...
		Total Class E.		3,426	11	...	3,321	5	...
F. Races and Nationalities.	48	Armenian	Christian	...	...	...	...	...	...
		Arab	Mussalman	36	4	...	23	...	...
		Baluch	,,	...	...	...	...	...	...

TABLE C.

Literate by Language known—(Provincial Summary)—*continued.*

Class.	Group.	Caste.	Religion.	NALDRUG.						BIDAR.						PARBHANI.					
				Males.			Females.			Males.			Females.			Males.			Females.		
				Total Males.	Literate. Total.	Literate. English.	Total Females.	Literate. Total.	Literate. English.	Total Males.	Literate. Total.	Literate. English.	Total Females.	Literate. Total.	Literate. English.	Total Males.	Literate. Total.	Literate. English.	Total Females.	Literate. Total.	Literate. English.
				77	78	79	80	81	82	83	84	85	86	87	88	89	90	91	92	93	94
E. Vagrant Minor Artisans and Performers, &c.—(contd).	45	Budbuduki	Hindu	3	...	...	...	...	...	256	5	...	304	...	...	...	...	...	...	...	...
		Ganjakuti	„	...	...	...	...	...	...	...	...	...	...	...	...	...	...	...	...	...	...
		Konapusala	„	...	...	...	...	...	...	...	...	...	...	...	...	...	...	...	...	...	...
		Mundi	„	...	...	...	...	...	...	...	...	...	...	...	...	...	...	...	...	...	...
		Mittulu	„	...	...	...	...	...	...	...	...	...	...	...	...	...	...	...	...	...	...
		Pandawa	„	...	...	...	...	...	...	...	...	...	...	...	...	...	...	...	...	...	...
		Pardesi	„	100	4	...	117	...	...	6	...	...	1	...	...	116	11	...	69	...	...
		Parmavaru	„	...	...	...	...	...	...	...	...	...	...	...	...	...	...	...	...	...	...
		Ramdesi	„	...	...	...	...	...	...	...	...	...	...	...	...	...	...	...	...	...	...
		Saradhi	„	...	...	...	...	...	...	...	...	...	...	...	...	...	...	...	...	...	...
		Vipravinodulu	„	...	...	...	...	...	...	...	...	...	...	...	...	...	...	...	...	...	...
		Total Group 45		103	4	...	117	...	...	262	5	...	305	...	...	116	11	...	69	...	...
	46	Dommari	Hindu	37	...	...	55	...	...	6	...	...	13	...	...	462	138	...	53	...	...
		Gopal	„	53	...	...	42	...	...	...	...	...	...	...	...	406	...	...	434	...	...
		Jetty	„	...	...	...	...	...	...	103	2	...	84	...	...	...	...	...	...	...	...
		Total Group 46		90	...	...	97	...	...	109	2	...	97	...	...	868	138	...	487	...	...
	47	Gungadla	Hindu	...	...	...	...	...	...	...	...	...	...	...	...	...	...	...	...	...	...
		Garodi	„	10	...	...	5	...	...	...	...	...	...	...	...	...	...	...	...	...	...
		Katipapa	„	...	...	...	...	...	...	...	...	...	...	...	...	...	...	...	...	...	...
		Kalsutri	„	...	...	...	...	...	...	...	...	...	...	...	...	2	...	...	3	...	...
		Total Group 47		10	...	...	5	...	...	...	...	...	...	...	...	2	...	...	3	...	...
		Total Class E		2,426	17	...	2,471	...	...	3,057	15	...	3,089	...	...	3,622	186	...	3,179	...	...
F. Races and Nationalities.	48	Armenian	Christian	...	...	...	...	...	...	...	...	...	...	...	...	...	...	...	...	...	...
		Arab	Mussalman	95	10	...	34	...	...	82	14	...	75	1	...	72	16	...	42	...	...
		Baluch	„	...	...	...	...	...	...	...	...	...	...	...	...	...	...	...	...	...	...

TABLE C.

Literate by Language known—(Provincial Summary)—*continued.*

Class.	Group.	Caste.	Religion.	SIRPUR TANDUR.						GULBARGA.						RAICHUR.					
				MALES.			FEMALES.			MALES.			FEMALES.			MALES.			FEMALES.		
				Total Males.	Literate.		Total Females.	Literate.		Total Males.	Literate.		Total Females.	Literate.		Total Males.	Literate.		Total Females.	Literate.	
					Total.	English.		Total.	English.		Total.	English.		Total.	English.		Total.	English.		Total.	English.
				95	96	97	98	99	100	101	102	103	104	105	106	107	108	109	110	111	112
E. Vagrant Minor Artisans and Performers, &c.—(concld.)	45	Budbuduki	Hindu	...	...	...	...	...	...	131	...	...	130	...	...	18	1	...	16	...	...
		Ganjakuti	"	...	...	...	...	...	...	...	...	...	...	...	...	...	...	...	...	...	...
		Konapusala	"	...	...	...	...	...	...	...	...	...	...	...	...	...	...	...	...	...	...
		Mundi	"	...	...	...	...	...	...	...	...	...	...	...	...	...	...	...	...	...	...
		Mittula	"	...	...	...	...	...	...	...	...	...	...	...	...	42	...	...	32	...	...
		Pandawa	"	...	...	...	...	...	...	...	...	...	...	...	...	...	...	...	...	...	...
		Pardesi	"	38	5	...	40	...	...	1	...	...	...	...	...	...	...	...	...	...	...
		Parmavaru	"	...	...	...	...	...	...	...	...	...	...	...	...	...	...	...	...	...	...
		Ramdesi	"	...	...	...	...	...	...	...	...	...	...	...	...	...	...	...	...	...	...
		Saradhi	"	...	...	...	...	...	...	...	...	...	...	...	...	...	...	...	...	...	...
		Vipravinodulu	"	...	...	...	...	...	...	...	...	...	...	...	...	...	...	...	...	...	...
		Total Group 45		38	5	...	40	...	...	132	...	...	132	...	...	61	1	...	48	...	...
	46	Dommari	Hindu	35	...	...	44	...	...	26	...	...	25	...	...	54	...	...	66	...	...
		Gopal	"	...	...	...	...	...	...	4	1	...	1	...	...	...	...	...	...	...	...
		Jetty	"	...	...	...	...	...	...	13	4	...	22	...	...	3	...	...	1	...	...
		Total Group 46		35	...	...	44	...	...	43	5	...	48	...	...	57	...	...	67	...	...
	47	Gungadla	Hindu	...	...	...	...	...	...	...	...	...	...	...	...	37	...	...	34	...	...
		Garodi	"	...	...	...	...	...	...	2	...	...	1	...	...	...	...	...	...	...	...
		Katipapa	"	...	...	...	...	...	...	2	...	...	2	...	...	7	...	...	4	...	...
		Kalsutri	"	...	...	...	...	...	...	45	...	...	38	...	...	41	...	...	30	...	...
		Total Group 47		...	...	...	...	...	...	49	...	...	41	...	...	85	...	...	68	...	...
		Total Class E		679	5	...	701	...	...	4,451	16	...	4,457	...	...	6,938	37	...	6,739	3	...
F. Races & Nationalities.	48	Armenian	Christian	...	...	...	...	...	...	...	...	...	...	...	...	...	...	...	...	...	...
		Arab	Mussulman	16	...	...	11	...	...	74	28	...	53	...	...	...	...	...	...	...	...
		Baluch	"	...	...	...	...	...	...	...	...	...	...	...	...	...	...	...	...	...	...

TABLE C.

Literate by Language known—(Provincial Summary)—*continued.*

Class.	Group.	Caste.	Religion.	LINGASUGUR. Males. Total Males.	Males. Literate. Total.	Males. Literate. English.	Females. Total Females.	Females. Literate. Total.	Females. Literate. English.	RAILWAYS. Males. Total Males.	Males. Literate. Total.	Males. Literate. English.	Females. Total Females.	Females. Literate. Total.	Females. Literate. English.
				113	114	115	116	117	118	119	120	121	122	123	124
E. Vagrant Minor Artisans and Performers, &c.—(*concld.*)	45	Budbuduki	Hindu ...	40	...	...	36	...	...	...	...	...	...	...	...
		Ganjakuti	" ...	...	...	...	...	...	...	...	...	...	...	...	...
		Konapusala...	" ...	...	...	...	...	...	...	...	...	...	...	...	...
		Mundi	" ...	...	...	...	...	...	...	...	...	...	...	...	...
		Mittulu	" ...	...	...	...	...	...	...	...	...	...	...	...	...
		Pandawa	" ...	...	...	...	...	...	...	...	...	...	...	...	...
		Pardesi	" ...	3	2	...	1	...	...	...	...	...	...	...	...
		Parmavaru	" ...	...	...	...	...	...	...	...	...	...	...	...	...
		Ramdesi	" ...	...	...	...	...	...	...	...	...	...	...	...	...
		Saradhi	" ...	...	...	...	...	...	...	...	...	...	...	...	...
		Vipravinodulu	" ...	...	...	...	...	...	...	...	...	...	...	...	...
		Total Group 45		43	2	...	37	...	...	...	...	...	...	...	...
	46	Dommari	Hindu ...	196	2	...	195	...	...	...	...	...	...	...	...
		Gopal	" ...	20	...	...	13	...	...	...	...	...	...	...	...
		Jetty	" ...	43	2	...	50	...	...	3	3	2	1	1	...
		Total Group 46		259	4	...	258	...	...	3	3	2	1	1	...
	47	Gungadla	Hindu ...	...	...	...	...	...	...	...	...	...	...	...	...
		Garodi	" ...	...	...	...	...	...	...	...	...	...	...	...	...
		Katipapa	" ...	82	...	...	129	...	...	...	...	...	...	...	...
		Kalsutri	" ...	105	1	...	102	...	...	...	...	...	...	...	...
		Total Group 47		187	1	...	231	...	...	...	...	...	...	...	...
		Total Class E.		9,454	57	...	9,499	2	...	12	3	2	5	1	...
F. Races and Nationalities.	48	Armenian	Christian..	...	...	...	...	...	...	1	1	1	...	...	...
		Arab	Mussalman	34	6	...	31	...	...	2	1	...	...	...	...
		Baluch	" ...	...	...	...	...	...	...	...	...	...	...	...	...

TABLE C.

Literate by Language known—(Provincial Summary)—*continued.*

Class.	Group.	Caste.	Religion.	TOTAL STRENGTH. Males. Total Males.	TOTAL STRENGTH. Males. Literate. Total.	TOTAL STRENGTH. Males. Literate. English.	TOTAL STRENGTH. Females. Total Females.	TOTAL STRENGTH. Females. Literate. Total.	TOTAL STRENGTH. Females. Literate. English.	HYDERABAD. Males. Total Males.	HYDERABAD. Males. Literate. Total.	HYDERABAD. Males. Literate. English.	HYDERABAD. Females. Total Females.	HYDERABAD. Females. Literate. Total.	HYDERABAD. Females. Literate. English.	ATRAF-I-BALDA. Males. Total Males.	ATRAF-I-BALDA. Males. Literate. Total.	ATRAF-I-BALDA. Males. Literate. English.	ATRAF-I-BALDA. Females. Total Females.	ATRAF-I-BALDA. Females. Literate. Total.	ATRAF-I-BALDA. Females. Literate. English.
1	2	3	4	5	6	7	8	9	10	11	12	13	14	15	16	17	18	19	20	21	22
F. Races and Nationalities—(contd.)	48	Irani ...	Mussalman	37	18	...	12	2	...	20	14	...	7	2	...	2	2	...	2	...	...
		Jew ...	Jew ...	10	6	2	16	...	...	7	4	1	14	...	...	..	...	...	...	...	...
		Mughal ...	Mussalman	11,462	1,803	42	10 302	170	...	4,375	1,124	30	3,632	144	...	338	42	...	347	...	...
		Pathan ...	" ...	64,552	5,927	144	58,447	399	...	11,874	2,687	111	9,905	281	...	1,755	145	3	1,667	1	...
		Parsi ...	Parsi ...	628	398	164	430	205	29	372	245	107	244	119	19	2	...	...	1	11	...
		Rohilla ...	Mussalman	209	24	...	174	...	...	2	...	...	7	...	...	47	2	...	37	...	...
		Sheikh ...	" ...	435,267	29,876	628	4,20,857	1,991	12	55,691	9,439	437	54,632	1,188	6	16,435	1,167	11	15,117	...	...
		Sayyed ...	" ...	57,624	8,489	251	55,663	812	4	15,787	4,595	184	15,149	540	2	3,103	453	8	3,131	19	2
		Turk ...	" ...	20	5	...	13	...	...	1	1	...	1	...	...	...	...	...	...	35	2
		Other Mussalman ...	" ...	7,519	718	36	7,343	78	...	390	127	11	833	36	...	153	11	...	142	...	...
		Total Group 48		578,356	47,479	1,273	5,53,996	3,662	46	88,553	18,246	883	84,436	2,312	28	21,902	1,836	22	20,469	66	4
	49b	Arya ...	Hindu ...	1	1	...	1	...	...	...	...	...	...	...	...	...	...	...	...	...	...
		Dasri ...	" ...	3,301	266	1	3,372	7	...	75	7	1	60	...	...	410	19	..	447	...	...
		Jain ...	Jain ...	6,877	2,069	4	6,146	13	...	44	31	...	14	1	...	49	28	...	45	...	...
		Jenpa ...	Hindu ...	9	3	1	7	...	...	5	2	1	4	...	...	...	...	...	...	...	...
		Jauhari ...	" ...	544	24	...	496	...	...	...	...	...	...	...	...	...	...	...	...	...	...
		Kanada ...	" ...	1,140	174	3	1,043	2	1	255	65	3	204	1	1	106	50	...	84	...	...
		Nadgudda ...	" ...	4	...	...	2	...	...	...	...	...	...	...	...	...	...	...	...	...	...
		Perika ...	" ...	1,7042	362	2	16,821	4	...	...	...	...	1	...	...	350	24	...	377	...	...
		Sikh ...	Sikh ...	2,305	755	2	1,999	16	...	355	153	2	253	7	...	143	57	...	111	2	...
		Thelugu ...	Hindu ...	159,925	2,628	43	1,56,521	250	...	4,056	378	25	39,36	11	...	8,906	103	2	9,061	15	...
		Other Hindus ...	" ...	34,072	2,617	211	32,789	138	9	5,391	1,475	178	5,102	118	9	1,105	105	1	1,041	...	...
		Total Group 49b......		225,220	8,899	267	2,19,197	430	10	10,181	2,111	210	9,574	138	10	11,069	386	3	11,166	17	...
	50	Europeans ...	Christian...	4,011	3,498	3,114	1,242	836	736	3,702	3,247	2,866	1,035	705	606	3	2	2	4	4	3
		Sidhi ...	Mussalman	73	12	...	38	...	...	61	9	...	21	...	...	...	...	...	...	...	...

TABLE C.

Literate by Language known—(Provincial Summary)—*continued.*

Class.	Group.	Caste.	Religion.	MAHBUBNAGAR.						NALGONDA.						WARANGAL.					
				Males.			Females.			Males.			Females.			Males.			Females.		
				Total Males.	Literate.		Total Females.	Literate.		Total Males.	Literate.		Total Females.	Literate.		Total Males.	Literate.		Total Females.	Literate.	
					Total.	English.		Total.	English.		Total.	English.		Total.	English.		Total.	English.		Total.	English.
				23	24	25	26	27	28	29	30	31	32	33	34	35	36	37	38	39	40
F. Races and Nationalities—(*contd.*)	48	Irani ...	Mussalman	2	...	...	1	...	...	...	...	...	...	...	...	...	...	...	...	...	...
		Jew ...	Jew ...	...	...	...	...	...	...	...	...	...	...	...	...	...	...	...	...	...	...
		Mughal ...	Mussalman	305	50	4	349	4	...	110	11	...	119	...	...	306	61	1	353	...	...
		Pathan ...	" ...	1,595	148	3	1,597	9	...	766	91	3	606	2	...	1,202	147	3	1,107	10	...
		Parsi ...	Parsi ...	...	...	...	...	...	...	4	3	...	9	1	...	28	20	6	12	8	2
		Rohilla ...	Mussalman	21	1	...	26	...	...	4	1	...	5	...	...	4	...	...	...	...	...
		Sheikh ...	" ...	22,166	1,460	19	22,178	55	...	11,346	985	2	10,824	17	...	17,039	1,412	14	15,922	103	4
		Sayyed ...	" ...	2,487	295	4	2,465	21	...	1,510	178	1	1,479	12	...	2,322	412	1	2,020	53	...
		Turk ...	" ...	...	...	...	...	...	...	...	...	...	...	...	...	...	...	...	...	...	...
		Other Mussalman ...	" ...	815	41	...	776	1	...	1,484	214	12	1,486	16	...	770	83	1	639	5	...
		Total Group 48		27,491	2,021	30	27,491	91	...	15,231	1,485	18	14,528	48	...	21,685	2,139	26	20,068	179	6
	49*b*	Arya ...	Hindu ...	...	...	...	...	...	...	...	...	...	...	...	...	...	...	...	...	...	...
		Dasri ...	" ...	376	16	...	372	3	...	99	10	...	102	...	...	396	64	...	372	1	...
		Jain ...	Jain ...	4	2	...	...	...	...	...	...	...	...	...	...	2	2	...	...	...	...
		Jenpa ...	Hindu ...	...	...	...	...	...	...	...	...	...	...	...	...	...	...	...	...	...	...
		Jauhari ...	" ...	...	...	...	...	...	...	...	...	...	...	...	...	...	...	...	...	...	...
		Kanada ...	" ...	...	...	...	1	...	...	...	...	...	...	...	...	...	...	...	...	...	...
		Nadgudda ...	" ...	...	...	...	...	...	...	...	...	...	...	...	...	...	...	...	...	...	...
		Perika ...	" ...	82	1	...	93	...	...	2,906	94	...	2,970	...	...	4,513	138	2	4,534	4	...
		Sikh ...	Sikh ...	48	18	...	27	...	...	63	26	...	48	1	...	161	77	...	120	...	...
		Thelugu ...	Hindu ...	24,540	230	...	24,409	36	...	11,127	299	1	11,287	28	...	25,841	552	5	24,764	23	...
		Other Hindus ...	" ...	286	21	...	329	7	...	403	18	...	355	1	...	850	96	...	858	...	...
		Total Group 49*b*		25,336	288	...	25,231	46	...	14,598	447	1	14,762	30	...	31,763	929	7	30,648	28	...
	50	European ...	Christian.	9	5	5	11	4	4	1	1	1	1	1	1	40	30	30	22	20	20
		Sidhi ...	Mussalman	...	...	...	...	...	...	...	...	...	...	...	...	3	3	...	5	...	...

TABLE C.

Literate by Language known—(Provincial Summary)—*continued.*

Class.	Group.	Caste.	Religion.	ELGANDAL.						INDUR.						MEDAK.					
				Males.			Females.			Males.			Females.			Males.			Females.		
				Total Males.	Literate. Total.	Literate. English.	Total Females.	Literate. Total.	Literate. English.	Total Males.	Literate. Total.	Literate. English.	Total Females.	Literate. Total.	Literate. English.	Total Males.	Literate. Total.	Literate. English.	Total Females.	Literate. Total.	Literate. English.
				41	42	43	44	45	46	47	48	49	50	51	52	53	54	55	56	57	58
F. Races and Nationalities—(contd.)	48	Irani ...	Mussalman	...	...	...	...	...	...	...	...	...	...	...	...	7	...	...	...	...	...
		Jew ...	Jew ...	...	...	...	...	...	...	...	...	...	...	...	...	...	...	...	...	...	...
		Mughal ...	Mussalman	304	56	...	265	3	...	444	47	...	420	...	...	215	30	...	200	4	...
		Pathan ...	,, ...	1,541	171	...	1,414	3	...	2,406	130	...	2,349	8	...	1,124	129	1	1,054	3	...
		Parsi ...	Parsi ...	2	2	1	1	1	...	2	2	...	5	2	...	...	...	...	...	...	...
		Rohilla ...	Mussalman	5	...	...	9	...	...	18	5	...	19	...	...	8	...	...	8	...	...
		Sheikh ...	,, ...	16,659	1,332	3	157,35	47	...	19,856	1,249	2	20,351	27	...	14,995	1,245	12	14,882	49	...
		Sayyed ...	,, ...	2,800	388	7	2,824	14	...	1,800	155	1	1,806	4	...	2,231	300	4	2,244	18	...
		Turk ...	,, ...	...	...	...	...	...	...	...	...	...	...	...	...	12	...	...	6	...	...
		Other Mussulman ...	,, ...	652	40	4	604	7	...	112	4	...	98	...	...	141	25	...	150	...	...
		Total Group 48		21,993	1,995	15	20,863	75	...	24,681	1,599	3	25,086	41	...	18,859	1,754	17	18,649	75	...
	49b	Arya ...	Hindu ...	...	...	...	...	...	...	...	...	...	...	...	...	...	...	...	...	...	...
		Dasri ...	,, ...	597	99	...	597	2	...	46	1	...	29	...	...	141	18	...	167	...	...
		Jain ...	Jain ...	7	1	...	5	...	...	30	16	...	42	...	...	48	23	...	54	...	...
		Jenpa ...	Hindu ...	4	1	...	3	...	...	...	...	...	...	...	...	...	...	...	...	...	...
		Jaubari ...	,, ...	...	...	...	...	...	...	19	...	..	25	...	...	...	...	...	...	...	...
		Kanada ...	,, ...	2	...	...	...	...	...	54	...	...	58	...	...	40	11	...	48	...	...
		Nadgudda ...	,, ...	...	...	...	...	...	...	...	...	...	...	...	...	...	...	...	...	...	...
		Perika ...	,, ...	7,843	88	...	7,443	...	...	322	4	...	299	...	...	286	11	...	341	...	...
		Sikh ...	Sikh ...	182	50	...	153	2	...	273	108	...	262	2	...	121	64	...	92	2	...
		Thelugu ...	Hindu ...	42,156	525	3	40,007	61	...	12,022	92	1	12,029	4	...	17,438	240	...	17,636	14	...
		Other Hindus ...	,, ...	2,209	90	...	2,009	1	...	3,307	82	...	3,194	1	...	199	13	...	169	...	...
		Total Group 49b		53,000	854	3	50,217	66	...	16,073	303	1	15,938	7	...	18,273	380	...	18,507	16	...
	50	Europeans ...	Christian.	9	7	7	9	4	4	7	5	5	5	4	4	10	7	7	4	2	2
		Sidhi ...	Mussalman	...	...	...	...	...	...	...	...	...	...	...	...	1	...	...	5	...	...

TABLE C.

Literate by Language known—(Provincial Summary)—*continued.*

Class.	Group.	Caste.	Religion.	AURUNGABAD.						BIRH.						NANDER.					
				MALES.			FEMALES.			MALES.			FEMALES.			MALES.			FEMALES.		
				Total Males.	Literate.		Total Females.	Literate.		Total Males.	Literate.		Total Females.	Literate.		Total Males.	Literate.		Total Females.	Literate.	
					Total.	English.		Total.	English.		Total.	English.		Total.	English.		Total.	English.		Total.	English.
				59	60	61	62	63	64	65	66	67	68	69	70	71	72	73	74	75	76
F. Races and Nationalities—(*contd*).	48	Irani ...	Mussalman	6	2	...	2	...	...	...	...	...	...	...	...	...	...	...	...	...	...
		Jew ...	Jew ...	...	...	...	...	...	...	...	...	...	...	...	...	...	...	...	...	...	...
		Mughal	Mussalman	1,296	80	1	1,242	1	...	477	44	...	466	5	...	534	27	...	470	1	...
		Pathan	" ...	10,365	701	8	9,642	24	...	4,641	321	1	4,006	13	...	3,624	143	...	3,459	5	...
		Parsi ...	Parsi ...	68	43	25	62	35	...	11	7	3	8	3	...	6	5	...	1	1	...
		Rohilla	Mussalman	6	1	...	9	...	...	6	...	...	5	...	...	5	1	...	1	...	...
		Sheikh	" ...	32,574	2,082	37	31,774	83	...	19,293	867	2	18,254	56	...	22,489	868	2	21,485	90	...
		Sayyed	" ...	2,967	398	19	2,884	51	...	1,658	119	1	1,572	11	...	1,768	80	1	1,675	2	...
		Turk ...	" ...	2	1	...	3	...	...	...	...	...	...	...	...	...	...	...	...	...	...
		Other Mussulman ...	" ...	508	30	...	478	...	...	539	18	...	473	2	...	200	4	...	157	...	...
		Total Group 48......		47,935	3,366	90	46,227	194	...	26,667	1,389	7	24,818	90	...	28,662	1,132	3	27,271	99	...
	49b	Arya ...	Hindu ...	...	...	...	...	...	...	...	...	...	...	...	...	...	...	...	...	...	...
		Dasri ...	" ...	...	...	...	...	...	...	...	...	...	...	...	...	122	...	...	131	...	...
		Jain ...	Jain ...	761	222	...	739	...	...	857	299	...	732	3	...	369	133	...	362	...	...
		Jenpa ...	Hindu ...	...	...	...	...	...	...	...	...	...	...	...	...	...	...	...	...	...	...
		Jauhari	" ...	415	2	...	361	...	...	3	1	...	2	...	...	7	3	...	5	...	...
		Kanada	" ...	322	42	...	317	1	...	45	...	...	53	...	...	...	...	...	...	...	...
		Nadgudda	" ...	...	...	...	...	...	...	...	...	...	...	...	...	4	...	...	2	...	...
		Perika	" ...	...	...	...	...	...	...	...	...	...	...	...	...	333	1	...	337	...	...
		Sikh ...	Sikh ...	119	35	...	156	...	...	130	19	...	115	...	...	583	131	...	548	...	...
		Thelugu	Hindu ...	680	54	3	597	2	...	126	9	...	109	...	...	1,282	5	...	1,195	2	...
		Other Hindus	" ...	1,310	174	4	1,140	...	...	478	14	...	467	...	...	306	8	...	349	...	...
		Total Group 49b......		3,607	529	7	3,310	3	...	1,639	342	...	1,478	3	...	3,006	281	...	2,929	2	...
	50	Europeans ...	Christian.	46	36	36	3[illegible]	19	19	15	13	13	9	3	3	2	2	2	...	...	...
		Sidhi ...	Mussalman	1	...	...	4	...	...	...	...	...	...	...	...	...	...	...	...	...	...

TABLE C.

Literate by Language known—(Provincial Summary)—*continued.*

Class.	Group.	Caste.	Religion.	NALDRUG. Males. Total Males.	NALDRUG. Males. Literate. Total.	NALDRUG. Males. Literate. English.	NALDRUG. Females. Total Females.	NALDRUG. Females. Literate. Total.	NALDRUG. Females. Literate. English.	BIDAR. Males. Total Males.	BIDAR. Males. Literate. Total.	BIDAR. Males. Literate. English.	BIDAR. Females. Total Females.	BIDAR. Females. Literate. Total.	BIDAR. Females. Literate. English.	PARBHANI. Males. Total Males.	PARBHANI. Males. Literate. Total.	PARBHANI. Males. Literate. English.	PARBHANI. Females. Total Females.	PARBHANI. Females. Literate. Total.	PARBHANI. Females. Literate. English.
				77	78	79	80	81	82	83	84	85	86	87	88	89	90	91	92	93	94
F. Races and Nationalities—*contd.*	48	Irani ...	Mussalman	...	...	...	...	...	...	...	...	...	...	...	...	...	...	...	...	...	...
		Jew ...	Jew ...	...	...	...	...	...	...	...	...	...	...	...	...	...	...	...	...	...	...
		Mughal ...	Mussalman	405	16	...	353	1	...	542	55	...	532	1	...	593	49	...	501	...	...
		Pathan ...	" ...	4,260	128	...	3,875	2	...	4,968	238	...	4,593	9	...	6,306	364	3	5,837	7	...
		Parsi ...	Parsi ..	10	10	...	...	...	...	2	1	...	1	1	...	12	3	1	12	6	3
		Rohilla ...	Mussalman	20	2	...	5	...	...	9	1	...	5	...	...	27	6	...	22	...	...
		Sheikh ...	" ..	22,515	852	2	21,608	24	...	48,633	1,669	4	47,021	38	...	24,528	954	1	23,726	19	...
		Sayyed ...	" ...	2,417	124	1	2,281	9	...	3,594	204	1	3,564	13	...	1,933	110	1	1,838	3	...
		Turk ..	" ...	...	...	...	...	...	...	5	3	...	3	...	...	...	...	...	...	...	...
		Other Mussulman ...	" ..	73	5	...	62	...	...	462	18	...	482	...	...	529	14	...	485	1	...
		Total Group 48......		29,795	1,147	3	28,218	36	...	58,297	2,203	5	56,276	63	...	31,000	1,516	6	32,463	36	3
	49 b	Arya ...	Hindu ...	...	...	...	...	...	...	1	1	...	1	...	...	...	...	...	...	...	...
		Dasri ...	" ...	...	...	...	...	...	...	189	9	...	186	...	...	42	...	...	40	...	...
		Jain ...	Jain ..	1,271	377	...	1,177	2	...	902	204	...	784	...	...	1,111	267	...	1,044	2	...
		Jenpa ..	Hindu ...	...	...	...	...	...	...	...	...	...	...	...	...	...	...	...	...	...	...
		Jauhari ...	" ..	3	2	...	5	...	...	7	1	...	19	...	...	63	15	...	53	...	...
		Kanada ...	" ..	3	...	...	2	...	...	14	...	...	12	...	...	274	1	...	243	...	...
		Nadgudda ...	" ..	...	...	...	...	...	...	...	...	...	...	...	...	...	...	...	...	...	...
		Perika ...	" ..	...	...	...	...	...	...	3	1	...	4	...	...	...	...	...	...	...	...
		Sikh ...	Sikh ...	4	4	...	1	...	...	30	4	...	27	...	...	58	7	...	49	...	...
		Thelugu ...	Hindu ...	92	5	...	83	...	...	1,139	13	...	1,121	...	...	103	6	1	112	...	...
		Other Hindus ...	" ...	185	10	...	194	...	...	1,534	111	...	1,629	3	...	437	88	...	324	...	...
		Total Group 49b......		1,558	398	...	1,462	2	...	3,819	344	...	3,783	3	...	2,088	384	1	1,865	2	...
	50	Europeans ...	Christian.	...	...	...	...	...	...	2	2	2	4	2	2	15	15	15	5	4	4
		Sidhi ...	Mussalman	2	...	...	1	...	...	...	...	...	...	...	...	...	...	...	...	...	...

TABLE C.

Literate by Language known—(Provincial Summary)—*continued.*

Class.	Group.	Caste.	Religion.	SIRPUR TANDUR.						GULBARGA.						RAICHUR.					
				Males.			Females.			Males.			Females.			Males.			Females.		
				Total Males.	Literate. Total.	Literate. English.	Total Females.	Literate. Total.	Literate. English.	Total Males.	Literate. Total.	Literate. English.	Total Females.	Literate. Total.	Literate. English.	Total Males.	Literate. Total.	Literate. English.	Total Females.	Literate. Total.	Literate. English.
				95	96	97	98	99	100	101	102	103	104	105	106	107	108	109	110	111	112
F. Races and Nationalities—(*contd.*)	48	Irani ...	Mussalman	...	...	...	...	...	...	...	...	...	...	...	...	...	...	...	...	...	...
		Jew ...	Jew	...	...	...	...	...	...	...	...	...	...	...	...	...	...	...	...	...	...
		Mughal ...	Mussalman	78	12	...	51	...	...	511	50	3	478	2	...	320	32	...	263	3	...
		Pathan ...	" ...	851	61	...	751	...	...	3,553	182	4	3,214	6	...	1,339	87	4	1,235	4	...
		Parsi ...	Parsi ...	1	...	...	...	...	...	43	22	...	23	4	...	20	7	5	14	4	1
		Rohilla ...	Mussalman	3	1	...	1	...	...	19	1	...	10	...	...	3	...	...	5	...	...
		Sheikh ...	" ...	3,613	161	...	3,607	3	...	40,991	1,434	24	39,388	48	...	21,755	1,283	27	20,710	49	...
		Sayyed ...	" ...	394	19	...	462	...	...	3,330	227	9	3,186	10	...	3,093	205	6	2,969	10	...
		Turk ...	" ...	...	...	...	...	...	...	...	...	...	...	...	...	...	...	...	...	...	...
		Other Mussulman ...	" ...	90	...	...	47	...	...	157	11	...	114	...	...	36	...	...	36	...	...
		Total Group 48		5,046	254	...	4,930	3	...	48,678	4,955	40	46,466	70	...	26,566	1,614	42	25,232	70	1
	49*b*	Arya ...	Hindu ...	...	...	...	...	...	...	...	...	...	...	...	...	...	...	...	...	...	...
		Dasri ...	" ...	45	1	...	34	...	...	111	4	...	128	...	...	398	13	...	412	...	...
		Jain ...	Jain ...	97	2	...	85	...	...	762	211	4	688	4	...	72	31	...	33	1	...
		Jenpa...	Hindu ...	...	...	...	...	...	...	...	...	...	...	...	...	...	...	...	...	...	...
		Jauhari ...	" ...	27	...	...	26	...	...	...	...	...	...	...	...	...	...	...	...	...	...
		Kanada ...	" ...	...	...	...	...	...	...	15	5	...	18	...	...	6	...	...	3	...	...
		Nadgudda ...	" ...	...	...	...	...	...	...	...	...	...	...	...	...	...	...	...	...	...	...
		Perika ...	" ...	393	...	...	417	...	...	11	...	...	5	...	...	...	...	...	...	...	...
		Sikh ...	Sikh ...	22	...	...	22	...	...	5	1	...	9	...	...	3	...	...	1	...	...
		Thelugu ...	Hindu ...	505	4	...	518	...	...	5,430	43	...	5,387	...	...	4,169	49	...	4,097	53	...
		Other Hindus ...	" ...	12,010	20	...	11,769	...	...	1,547	113	1	1,531	...	...	961	101	9	966	3	...
		Total Group 49*b*		13,099	27	...	12,871	...	...	7,881	377	5	7,766	4	...	5,609	194	9	5,512	57	...
		Europeans ...	Christian.	...	...	...	...	...	...	13	10	10	6	4	4	35	26	26	26	17	17
		Sidhi ...	Mussalman	...	...	...	...	...	...	...	...	...	...	...	...	5	...	...	2	...	...

TABLE C.

Literate by Language known—(Provincial Summary)—*continued.*

Class.	Group.	Caste.	Religion.	LINGASUGAR. Males. Total Males.	LINGASUGAR. Males. Literate. Total.	LINGASUGAR. Males. Literate. English.	LINGASUGAR. Females. Total Females.	LINGASUGAR. Females. Literate. Total.	LINGASUGAR. Females. Literate. English.	RAILWAYS. Males. Total Males.	RAILWAYS. Males. Literate. Total.	RAILWAYS. Males. Literate. English.	RAILWAYS. Females. Total Females.	RAILWAYS. Females. Literate. Total.	RAILWAYS. Females. Literate. English.
				113	114	115	116	117	118	119	120	121	122	123	124
F. Races and Nationalities—(*contd.*)	48	Irani ...	Mussalman	...	...	...	...	...	...	...	...	...	...	...	...
		Jew ...	Jew ...	...	...	...	...	...	...	3	2	1	2	...	...
		Mughal	Mussalman	296	12	1	260	...	...	13	5	2	1	...	...
		Pathan	" ...	2,366	46	...	2,099	2	...	76	8	...	37	...	...
		Parsi ...	Parsi ...	8	4	1	5	2	...	37	24	15	32	18	4
		Rohilla	Mussalman	...	...	...	...	...	...	2	2	...	...	...	...
		Sheikh	" ...	24,265	1,330	11	23,428	72	...	424	87	18	215	4	...
		Sayyed	" ...	4,287	197	1	4,048	1	...	143	30	4	66	5	...
		Turk ...	" ...	...	...	...	...	...	...	...	...	...	...	...	...
		Other Mussalman ...	" ...	192	9	...	172	3	...	216	66	8	109	7	...
		Total Group 48		31,388	1,604	14	30,043	80	...	917	226	49	462	34	4
	49*b*	Arya ...	Hindu ..	...	...	...	...	...	...	...	...	...	...	...	...
		Dasri...	" ...	254	5	...	295	1	...	...	...	...	...	...	...
		Jain ...	Jain ...	491	220	...	342	...	...	...	...	...	...	...	...
		Jenpa	Hindu ...	...	...	...	...	...	...	...	...	...	...	...	...
		Jauhari	" ...	...	...	...	...	...	...	...	...	...	...	...	...
		Kanada	" ...	...	...	...	...	...	...	4	...	...	...	...	...
		Nadgudda ...	" ...	...	...	...	...	...	...	...	...	...	...	...	...
		Perika	" ...	...	...	...	...	...	...	...	...	...	...	...	...
		Sikh ...	Sikh ...	3	1	...	2	...	...	2	...	...	3	...	...
		Thelugu ...	Hindu ...	127	...	...	113	...	...	186	21	2	60	1	...
		Other Hindus	" ...	1,151	15	...	1,183	...	...	403	63	18	180	4	...
		Total Group 49*b*		2,026	241	...	1,935	1	...	595	84	20	243	5	...
	5c	Europeans ...	Christian...	13	13	13	11	7	7	89	77	74	60	36	36
		Sidhi ...	Mussulman	...	...	...	...	...	...	...	...	...	...	...	...

TABLE C.

Literate by Language known—(Provincial Summary)—*continued.*

Class.	Group.	Caste.	Religion.	TOTAL STRENGTH.						HYDERABAD.						ATRAF-I-BALDA.					
				MALES.			FEMALES.			MALES.			FEMALES.			MALES.			FEMALES.		
				Total Males.	Literate. Total.	Literate. English.	Total Females.	Literate. Total.	Literate. English.	Total Males.	Literate. Total.	Literate. English.	Total Females.	Literate. Total.	Literate. English.	Total Males.	Literate. Total.	Literate. English.	Total Females.	Literate. Total.	Literate. English.
1	2	3	4	5	6	7	8	9	10	11	12	13	14	15	16	17	18	19	20	21	22
F. Races and Nationalities—(*concld*).		Total Group 50.....		4,084	3,510	3,114	1,280	836	736	3,763	3,256	2,866	1,056	705	606	3	2	2	4	4	3
	51	Eurasians	Christian...	1,276	828	584	1,231	637	470	914	574	333	951	467	301	1	1	1	...	...	...
		Total Group 51.....		1,276	828	584	1,231	637	470	914	574	333	951	467	301	1	1	1	...	...	...
	52	Native Christians	Christian...	6,280	1,801	596	6,283	1,442	177	3,488	1,273	439	3,646	1,285	151	212	21	4	230	7	1
		Goanese	" ...	56	28	12	42	4	...	47	22	9	40	4	...	...	...	...	...	...	...
		Total Group 52 ...		6,336	1,829	608	6,325	1,446	177	3,535	1,295	448	3,686	1,289	151	212	21	4	230	7	1
		Total Class F ..		815,272	62,545	5,846	782,029	7,011	1,439	106,946	25,482	4,740	99,703	4,911	1,096	33,187	2,246	32	31,869	94	8
		Grand Total.....		5,873,128	343,441	8,054	56,63,911	11,063	1,462	216,324	45,328	6,149	198,715	5,592	1,114	198,258	14,059	64	191,526	317	8

TABLE C.

Literate by Language known—(Provincial Summary)—*continued.*

Class.	Group.	Caste.	Religion.	MAHBUBNAGAR. Males. Total Males.	MAHBUBNAGAR. Males. Literate. Total.	MAHBUBNAGAR. Males. Literate. English.	MAHBUBNAGAR. Females. Total Females.	MAHBUBNAGAR. Females. Literate. Total.	MAHBUBNAGAR. Females. Literate. English.	NALGONDA. Males. Total Males.	NALGONDA. Males. Literate. Total.	NALGONDA. Males. Literate. English.	NALGONDA. Females. Total Females.	NALGONDA. Females. Literate. Total.	NALGONDA. Females. Literate. English.	WARANGAL. Males. Total Males.	WARANGAL. Males. Literate. Total.	WARANGAL. Males. Literate. English.	WARANGAL. Females. Total Females.	WARANGAL. Females. Literate. Total.	WARANGAL. Females. Literate. English.
.				23	24	25	26	27	28	29	30	31	32	33	34	35	36	37	38	39	40
F. Races and Nationalities—(*concld.*)		Total Group 50......		9	5	5	11	4	4	1	1	1	1	1	1	43	33	30	27	20	20
	51	Eurasian	Christian ...	3	3	3	...	...	...	...	...	...	...	...	...	29	27	27	11	7	7
		Total Group 51......		3	3	3	...	...	...	...	...	...	...	...	...	29	27	27	11	7	7
	52	Native Christians	Christian.	55	12	3	43	7	1	72	16	6	61	3	...	725	86	...	657	24	...
		Goanese	" ...	...	...	...	...	...	...	...	...	...	...	...	...	...	...	...	...	...	...
		Total Group 52......		55	12	3	43	7	1	72	16	6	61	3	...	725	86	...	657	24	...
		Total Class F		52,894	2,329	41	52,776	148	5	29,902	1,949	26	29,352	82	1	54,245	3,214	90	51,411	258	33
		Grand Total		341,601	21,926	69	333,048	674	7	319,823	16,362	83	304,791	348	1	438,635	24,389	195	414,494	684	33

TABLE C.

Literate by language known—(Provincial Summary)—*continued.*

Class.	Group.	Caste.	Religion.	ELGANDAL. Males. Total Males.	ELGANDAL. Males. Literate. Total.	ELGANDAL. Males. Literate. English.	ELGANDAL. Females. Total Females.	ELGANDAL. Females. Literate. Total.	ELGANDAL. Females. Literate. English.	INDUR. Males. Total Males.	INDUR. Males. Literate. Total.	INDUR. Males. Literate. English.	INDUR. Females. Total Females.	INDUR. Females. Literate. Total.	INDUR. Females. Literate. English.	MEDAK. Males. Total Males.	MEDAK. Males. Literate. Total.	MEDAK. Males. Literate. English.	MEDAK. Females. Total Females.	MEDAK. Females. Literate. Total.	MEDAK. Females. Literate. English.
				41	42	43	44	45	46	47	48	49	59	51	53	53	54	55	56	57	58
F. Races and Nationalities—(*concld.*).		Total Grooup 50		9	7	7	9	4	4	7	5	5	5	4	4	11	7	7	9	2	2
	51	Eurasians	Christian ...	20	12	12	10	7	7	7	6	6	6	2	2	4	4	4	2	...	...
		Total Group 51		20	12	12	10	7	7	7	6	6	6	2	2	4	4	4	2	...	...
	52	Native Christians	Christian	93	27	6	52	16	...	8	1	1	7	...	...	39	13	6	47	9	4
		Goanese	„ ...	...	...	...	...	...	...	...	...	...	...	...	...	...	...	...	...	...	...
		Total Group 52		93	27	6	52	16	...	8	1	1	7	...	...	39	13	6	47	9	4
		Total Class F		75,115	2,895	43	71,151	168	11	40,776	1,914	16	41,042	54	6	37,196	2,158	34	37,214	102	6
		Grand Total......		563,845	28,535	85	530,756	633	11	319,237	16,863	28	320,361	207	6	183,908	15,101	68	180,827	251	6

TABLE C.

Literate by Language known—(Provincial Summary)—*continued.*

Class.	Group.	Caste.	Religion.	AURUNGABAD. Males. Total Males.	AURUNGABAD. Males. Literate. Total.	AURUNGABAD. Males. Literate. English.	AURUNGABAD. Females. Total Females.	AURUNGABAD. Females. Literate. Total.	AURUNGABAD. Females. Literate. English.	BIRH. Males. Total Males.	BIRH. Males. Literate. Total.	BIRH. Males. Literate. English.	BIRH. Females. Total Females.	BIRH. Females. Literate. Total.	BIRH. Females. Literate. English.	NANDER. Males. Total Males.	NANDER. Males. Literate. Total.	NANDER. Males. Literate. English.	NANDER. Females. Total Females.	NANDER. Females. Literate. Total.	NANDER. Females. Literate. English.
				59	60	61	62	63	64	65	66	67	68	69	70	71	72	73	74	75	76
F. Races and Nationalities—(*concld.*)		Total Group 50		47	36	36	34	19	19	15	13	13	9	3	3	2	2	2	...	...	...
	51	Eurasians	Christian ...	26	18	18	21	15	15	2	1	1	1	1	1	...	...	...	...	...	...
		Total Group 51		26	18	18	21	15	15	2	1	1	1	1	1	...	...	...	...	...	...
	52	Native Christians	Christian.	887	161	51	918	46	7	69	21	21	52	6	6	...	...	...	...	...	...
		Goanese	" ...	...	...	...	...	...	...	...	...	...	...	...	...	...	...	...	...	...	...
		Total Group 52		887	161	51	918	46	7	69	21	21	52	6	6	...	...	...	...	...	...
		Total Class F		52,502	4,110	202	50,510	277	41	28,392	1,766	42	26,358	102	10	31,670	1,415	5	30,200	101	...
		Grand Total		421,018	22,523	283	407,957	437	41	328,530	15,659	47	314,192	208	10	320,136	12,722	10	312,393	220	...

TABLE C.

Literate by Language known—(Provincial Summary)—*continued.*

Class.	Group.	Caste.	Religion.	NALDRUG. Males. Total Males.	NALDRUG. Males. Literate. Total.	NALDRUG. Males. Literate. English.	NALDRUG. Females. Total Females.	NALDRUG. Females. Literate. Total.	NALDRUG. Females. Literate. English.	BIDAR. Males. Total Males.	BIDAR. Males. Literate. Total.	BIDAR. Males. Literate. English.	BIDAR. Females. Total Females.	BIDAR. Females. Literate. Total.	BIDAR. Females. Literate. English.	PARBHANI. Males. Total Males.	PARBHANI. Males. Literate. Total.	PARBHANI. Males. Literate. English.	PARBHANI. Females. Total Females.	PARBHANI. Females. Literate. Total.	PARBHANI. Females. Literate. English.
				77	78	79	80	81	82	83	84	85	86	87	88	89	90	91	92	93	94
F. Races and Nationalities—(*concld.*)		Total Group 50		2	...	...	1	...	...	2	2	2	4	2	2	15	15	15	5	4	4
	51	Eurasians	Christian ...	...	...	...	...	...	...	2	2	2	2	1	1	1	1	1	...	...	...
		Total Group 51		...	...	...	...	...	...	2	2	2	2	1	1	1	1	1	...	...	...
	52	Native Christians	Christian.	107	11	4	107	4	1	8	2	2	3	...	...	25	8	3	21	...	...
		Goanese	" ...	...	...	...	...	...	...	...	...	...	...	...	...	...	...	...	...	...	...
		Total Group 52		107	11	4	107	4	1	8	2	2	3	...	...	25	8	3	21	...	...
		Total Class F.		31,462	1,556	7	29,788	42	1	62,128	2,553	11	60,068	69	3	36,129	1,922	26	34,354	42	7
		Grand Total		331,747	16,067	11	317,525	113	1	457,088	20,940	15	444,896	162	3	410,499	17,065	40	394,836	136	7

TABLE C.

Literate by Language known—(Provincial Summary)—*continued.*

Class.	Group.	Caste.	Religion.	SIRPUR TANDUR. Males. Total Males.	Males. Literate. Total.	Males. Literate. English.	Females. Total Females.	Females. Literate. Total.	Females. Literate. English.	GULBARGA. Males. Total Males.	Males. Literate. Total.	Males. Literate. English.	Females. Total Females.	Females. Literate. Total.	Females. Literate. English.	RAICHUR. Males. Total Males.	Males. Literate. Total.	Males. Literate. English.	Females. Total Females.	Females. Literate. Total.	Females. Literate. English.
				77	78	79	80	81	82	83	84	85	86	87	88	89	90	91	92	93	94
F. Races and Nationalities—(*concld.*)		Total Group 50		...	...	...	...	...	...	13	10	10	6	4	4	40	26	26	28	17	17
	51	Eurasians	Christian ...	...	...	...	...	...	..	9	7	7	21	12	12	63	43	43	55	36	36
		Total Group 51		...	...	...	...	...	...	9	7	7	21	12	12	63	43	43	55	36	36
	52	Native Christians	Christian...	...	...	...	...	...	...	128	33	13	110	4	1	79	31	6	77	8	...
		Goanese	" ...	...	...	...	...	...	...	...	...	...	...	...	...	...	...	...	...	...	...
		Total Group 52		...	...	...	...	...	...	128	33	13	110	4	1	79	31	6	77	8	...
		Total Class F.		18,145	281	...	17,801	3	...	56,709	2,382	75	54,369	94	17	32,257	1,908	126	30,934	188	54
		Grand Total		116,955	2,821	9	114,799	17	...	329,678	17,393	230	319,580	182	17	260,217	15,728	191	252,238	397	54

TABLE C.

Literate by Language known—(Provincial Summary)—*concluded.*

Class.	Group.	Caste.	Religion.	LINGSUGUR. Males. Total Males.	Lingsugur. Males. Literate. Total.	Lingsugur. Males. Literate. English.	Lingsugur. Females. Total Females.	Lingsugur. Females. Literate. Total.	Lingsugur. Females. Literate. English.	RAILWAYS. Males. Total Males.	Railways. Males. Literate. Total.	Railways. Males. Literate. English.	Railways. Females. Total Females.	Railways. Females. Literate. Total.	Railways. Females. Literate. English.
				95	96	97	98	99	100	101	102	103	104	105	106
F. Races and Nationalities—(*concld.*).		Total Group 50		13	13	13	11	7	7	89	77	74	60	36	36
	51	Eurasians	Christian...	27	18	18	16	3	3	168	111	108	135	86	85
		Total Group 51		27	18	18	16	3	3	168	111	108	135	86	85
	52	Native Christians	Christian...	163	24	...	168	11	...	122	61	31	84	12	5
		Goanese	" ...	...	...	...	...	...	...	9	6	3	2	...	...
		Total Group 52		163	24	...	168	11	...	131	67	34	86	12	5
		Total Class F.		33,617	1,900	45	32,173	102	10	1,900	565	285	986	173	130
		Grand Total		311,394	18,988	81	308,620	293	10	4,236	972	396	2,354	192	133

NOTE.—Some apparent discrepancies will be noted between the figures of Table C. and the Caste Index. These require a word of explanation. *Bhil* (Mussalman) shown in Table C. is wrong. The figures ought to have been amalgamated with *Koya*. *Otermani* is a sub-division of *Koya* and not a main caste. The figures for this sub-caste have, in the Caste Index, been amalgamated with *Koya*. *Chenai* is only another way of spelling *Sonnayi* and has therefore been included in the latter. Similarly *Kachi* and *Kutchi*. *Tonier*, *Odhmat*, *Nadgudda* and *Arya* are not main castes. They have been amalgamated under "other Hindus" in the Index.

MALES & FEMALES.

Return showing the Civil Condition Sex and Age of British born subjects found in the Cantonment and Railway Stations, &c., in H. H. the Nizam's Dominions.

MALES.

Return showing the Civil Condition Sex and Age of British born subjects found in the Cantonment and Railway Stations, &c., in H. H. the Nizam's Dominions.

District or State.	Infant.				1				2				3				4			
	Married.	Unmarried.	Widower.	Total.	Married.	Unmarried.	Widower.	Total.	Married.	Unmarried.	Widower.	Total.	Married.	Unmarried.	Widower.	Total.	Married.	Unmarried.	Widower.	Total.
1	2	3	4	5	6	7	8	9	10	11	12	13	14	15	16	17	18	19	20	21
Tolingana. Hyderabad. City	...	...	...	...	...	...	...	...	...	...	...	...	...	...	...	...	...	...	...	...
Suburbs including Secunderabad	...	2	...	2	...	1	...	1	...	5	...	5	...	8	...	8	...	11	...	11
Total......	...	2	...	2	...	1	...	1	...	5	...	5	...	8	...	8	...	11	...	11
Atraf-i-Balda District ...	...	...	...	...	...	...	...	...	...	...	...	...	...	...	...	...	...	...	...	...
Mahabubnagar (Nagar Karnul)	...	...	...	...	...	...	...	...	...	...	...	...	...	...	...	...	...	...	...	...
Nalgonda	...	...	...	...	...	...	...	...	...	...	...	...	...	...	...	...	...	...	...	...
Warangal (Khamam) ...	...	1	...	1	...	...	...	...	...	1	...	1	...	...	...	...	...	...	...	...
Elgandal	...	...	...	...	...	...	...	...	...	...	...	...	...	...	...	...	...	...	...	...
Indur	...	...	...	...	...	...	...	...	...	...	...	...	...	...	...	...	...	...	...	...
Medak	...	...	...	...	...	...	...	...	...	...	...	...	...	...	...	...	...	...	...	...
Mahratwara. Aurangabad	...	...	...	...	...	...	...	...	...	...	...	...	...	...	...	...	...	...	...	...
Birh...	...	...	...	...	...	...	...	...	...	...	...	...	...	...	...	...	...	...	...	...
Nander	...	...	...	...	...	...	...	...	...	...	...	...	...	...	...	...	...	...	...	...
Naldrug	...	...	...	...	...	...	...	...	...	...	...	...	...	...	...	...	...	...	...	...
Bidar	...	...	...	...	...	...	...	...	...	...	...	...	...	...	...	...	...	...	...	...
Parbhani	...	...	...	...	...	...	...	...	...	...	...	...	...	...	...	...	...	...	...	...
Sirpur Tandur	...	...	...	...	...	...	...	...	...	...	...	...	...	...	...	...	...	...	...	...
Karnatic or Kanada. Gulbarga	...	...	...	...	...	...	...	...	...	...	...	...	...	...	...	...	...	...	...	...
Raichur	...	...	...	...	...	...	...	...	...	...	...	...	...	...	...	...	...	...	...	...
Lingasugur	...	...	...	...	...	...	...	...	...	...	...	...	...	...	...	...	...	...	...	...
Total Districts......	...	1	...	1	...	...	...	...	...	1	...	1	...	...	...	...	...	...	...	...
Total Districts including Hyderabad......	...	3	...	3	...	1	...	1	...	6	...	6	...	8	...	8	...	11	...	11
Railways......	...	...	...	...	...	...	...	...	...	...	...	...	...	...	...	...	...	...	...	...
Grand Total......	...	3	...	3	...	1	...	1	...	6	...	6	...	8	...	8	...	11	...	11

District or State.	4—9				10—14				15—19				20—23				25—29			
	Married.	Unmarried.	Widower.	Total.	Married.	Unmarried.	Widower.	Total.	Married.	Unmarried.	Widower.	Total.	Married.	Unmarried.	Widower.	Total.	Married.	Unmarried.	Widower.	Total.
1	22	23	24	25	26	27	28	29	30	31	32	33	34	35	36	37	38	39	40	41
Tolingana. Hyderabad. City	...	...	...	...	...	...	...	...	...	...	...	...	...	...	...	...	...	...	...	...
Suburbs including Secunderabad	...	38	...	38	1	15	...	16	...	56	...	56	13	1,478	...	1,491	57	899	1	957
Total......	...	38	...	38	1	15	...	16	...	56	...	56	13	1,478	...	1,491	57	899	1	957
Atraf-i-Balda District ...	...	...	...	...	...	1	...	1	...	...	...	...	...	...	...	...	...	...	...	...
Mahabubnagar (Nagar Karnul)	...	...	...	...	...	...	...	...	...	...	...	...	...	...	...	...	...	...	...	...
Nalgonda	...	...	...	...	...	...	...	...	...	...	...	...	...	...	...	...	...	...	...	...
Warangal (Khamam) ...	...	...	...	...	...	...	...	...	...	1	...	1	...	...	...	...	...	2	...	2
Elgandal	...	...	...	...	...	...	...	...	...	...	...	...	...	1	...	1	...	1	...	1
Indur	...	...	...	...	...	...	...	...	...	...	...	...	...	...	...	...	...	...	...	...
Medak	...	...	...	...	...	...	...	...	...	...	...	...	...	2	...	2	1	1	...	2
Mahratwara. Aurangabad	...	...	...	...	...	...	...	...	...	...	...	...	...	...	...	...	...	...	...	...
Birh...	...	...	...	...	...	...	...	...	...	...	...	...	...	...	...	...	...	...	...	...
Nander	...	...	...	...	...	...	...	...	...	...	...	...	...	...	...	...	...	...	...	...
Naldrug	...	...	...	...	...	...	...	...	...	...	...	...	...	...	...	...	...	...	...	...
Bidar	...	...	...	...	...	...	...	...	...	...	...	...	...	...	...	...	...	...	...	...
Parbhani	...	...	...	...	...	...	...	...	...	...	...	...	...	...	...	...	...	...	...	...
Sirpur Tandur	...	...	...	...	...	...	...	...	...	...	...	...	...	...	...	...	...	...	...	...
Karnatic or Kanada. Gulbarga	...	...	...	...	...	...	...	...	...	...	...	...	...	...	...	...	...	...	...	...
Raichur	...	...	...	...	...	...	...	...	...	...	...	...	...	...	...	...	...	1	...	1
Lingasugur	...	...	...	...	...	...	...	...	...	...	...	...	...	...	...	...	1	1	...	2
Total Districts......	...	...	...	...	...	1	...	1	...	1	...	1	...	3	...	3	2	6	...	8
Total Districts including Hyderabad......	...	38	...	38	1	16	...	17	...	57	...	57	13	1,481	...	1,494	59	905	1	965
Railways......	...	2	...	2	...	...	...	...	...	1	...	1	1	9	...	10	2	9	...	11
Grand Total......	...	40	...	40	1	16	...	17	...	58	...	58	14	1,490	...	1,504	61	914	1	976

MALES.

RETURN showing the Civil Condition Sex and Age of British born subjects found in the Cantonment and Railway Stations, &c., in H. H. the Nizam's Dominions.—*Continued.*

District or State.	30—34				35—39				40—44				45—49				50—54				55—59				60 and over.				Unspecified.				Total.			
	Married.	Unmarried.	Widower.	Total.	Married.	Unmarried.	Widower.	Total.	Married.	Unmarried.	Widower.	Total.	Married.	Unmarried.	Widower.	Total.	Married.	Unmarried.	Widower.	Total.	Married.	Unmarried.	Widower.	Total.	Married.	Unmarried.	Widower.	Total.	Married.	Unmarried.	Widower.	Total.	Married.	Unmarried.	Widower.	Total.
	42	43	44	45	46	47	48	49	50	51	52	53	54	55	56	57	58	59	60	61	62	63	64	65	66	67	68	69	70	71	72	73	74	75	76	77
Telingana. Hyderabad. City	...	...	...	...	...	...	...	...	...	...	...	...	...	...	...	...	...	...	...	...	...	...	...	...	1	...	...	1	...	...	...	...	1	...	...	1
Suburbs including Secunderabad	90	147	3	240	53	32	2	87	33	6	1	40	32	3	...	35	22	...	2	24	5	2	...	7	9	...	2	11	...	...	...	...	315	2,703	11	3,029
Total......	90	147	3	240	53	32	2	87	33	6	1	40	32	3	...	35	22	...	2	24	5	2	...	7	10	...	2	12	...	...	...	...	316	2,703	11	3,030
Atraf-i-Balda District	...	...	...	...	...	...	...	...	...	...	...	...	...	...	...	...	...	...	...	...	...	...	1	1	...	...	...	...	...	...	...	...	...	1	1	2
Mahabubnagar (Nagar Karnul)	...	...	...	...	...	...	...	...	1	...	...	1	...	...	...	...	...	...	...	...	...	...	...	...	...	...	...	...	...	...	...	...	1	...	...	1
Nalgonda	...	...	...	...	...	...	...	...	...	...	...	...	...	...	...	...	...	...	...	...	...	...	...	...	...	...	...	...	...	...	...	...	...	...	...	...
Warangal (Khamam)	4	...	...	4	2	...	...	2	...	...	...	...	...	...	...	...	...	1	...	1	...	...	...	...	...	...	...	...	...	...	...	...	6	6	...	12
Elgandal	2	...	...	2	...	...	...	...	...	...	...	...	1	...	...	1	...	...	...	...	...	...	...	...	...	...	...	...	...	...	...	...	3	2	...	5
Indur	...	...	...	...	...	...	...	...	...	...	...	...	...	...	...	...	1	...	...	1	...	...	1	1	1	...	...	1	...	...	...	...	2	...	1	3
Medak	...	...	...	...	...	...	...	...	1	...	...	1	...	...	...	...	...	...	...	...	...	...	...	...	...	...	...	...	...	...	...	...	2	3	...	5
Mahratwara. Aurangabad	...	...	...	...	...	...	...	...	...	...	...	...	1	...	...	1	...	...	...	...	...	...	...	...	...	...	...	...	...	...	...	...	1	...	...	1
Birh	...	...	...	...	...	...	...	...	1	...	...	1	...	...	...	...	...	...	...	...	...	...	...	...	...	...	...	...	...	...	...	...	1	...	...	1
Nander	...	...	...	...	...	2	...	2	...	...	...	...	...	...	...	...	...	...	...	...	...	...	...	...	...	...	...	...	...	...	...	...	...	2	...	2
Naldrug	...	...	...	...	...	...	...	...	...	...	...	...	...	...	...	...	...	...	...	...	...	...	...	...	...	...	...	...	...	...	...	...	...	...	...	...
Bidar	...	...	...	...	...	...	...	...	...	...	...	...	...	...	...	...	...	...	...	...	...	...	...	...	...	...	...	...	...	...	...	...	...	...	...	...
Parbhani	...	...	...	...	...	...	...	...	...	...	...	...	...	...	...	...	...	...	...	...	...	...	...	...	...	...	...	...	...	...	...	...	...	...	...	...
Sirpur Tandur	...	...	...	...	...	...	...	...	...	...	...	...	...	...	...	...	...	...	...	...	...	...	...	...	...	...	...	...	...	...	...	...	...	...	...	...
Karnatic or Kanada. Gulbarga	1	...	...	1	...	...	...	...	...	...	...	...	...	...	...	...	...	...	...	...	...	...	...	...	...	...	...	...	...	...	...	...	1	...	...	1
Raichur	...	...	...	...	...	...	...	...	...	...	...	...	...	...	...	...	...	...	...	...	...	...	...	...	2	...	...	2	...	...	...	...	2	1	...	3
Lingasugur	...	...	...	...	...	...	...	...	...	...	...	...	...	...	1	1	1	...	...	1	...	...	...	...	...	...	...	...	...	...	...	...	2	1	1	4
Total Districts......	7	...	...	7	2	2	...	4	3	...	...	3	2	...	1	3	2	1	...	3	...	...	2	2	3	...	...	3	...	...	...	...	21	16	3	40
Total Districts including Hyderabad...	97	147	3	247	55	34	2	91	36	6	1	43	34	3	1	38	24	1	2	27	5	2	2	9	13	...	2	15	...	...	...	...	337	2,719	14	3,070
Railways......	3	2	...	5	2	...	...	2	1	...	...	1	...	...	...	...	3	...	...	3	...	...	...	...	...	...	...	...	...	...	...	...	12	23	...	35
Grand Total......	100	149	3	252	57	34	2	93	37	6	1	44	34	3	1	38	27	1	2	30	5	2	2	9	13	...	2	15	...	...	...	...	349	2,742	14	3,105

FEMALES.

Return showing the Civil Condition Sex and Age of British born subjects found in the Cantonment and Railway Stations, &c., in H. H. the Nizam's Dominions.

District or State.	Infant.				1				2				3				4				5–9				10–14				15–19				20–24				25–29			
	Married.	Unmarried.	Widow.	Total.	Married.	Unmarried.	Widow.	Total.	Married.	Unmarried.	Widow.	Total.	Married.	Unmarried.	Widow.	Total.	Married.	Unmarried.	Widow.	Total.	Married.	Unmarried.	Widow.	Total.	Married.	Unmarried.	Widow.	Total.	Married.	Unmarried.	Widow.	Total.	Married.	Unmarried.	Widow.	Total.	Married.	Unmarried.	Widow.	Total.
1	2	3	4	5	6	7	8	9	10	11	12	13	14	15	16	17	18	19	20	21	22	23	24	25	26	27	28	29	30	31	32	33	34	35	36	37	38	39	40	41
Telingana. Hyderabad. City	...	...	...	...	...	...	...	...	...	...	...	...	...	...	...	...	...	...	...	...	...	...	...	...	...	...	...	...	...	...	...	...	...	...	...	...	...	...	...	...
Suburbs including Secunderabad	...	2	...	2	...	1	...	1	...	4	...	4	...	5	...	5	...	1	...	1	...	34	...	34	1	9	...	10	5	5	...	10	28	2	...	30	65	8	4	77
Total......	...	2	...	2	...	1	...	1	...	4	...	4	...	5	...	5	...	1	...	1	...	34	...	34	1	9	...	10	5	5	...	10	28	2	...	30	65	8	4	77
Atraf-i-Balda District ...	...	...	...	...	...	...	...	...	...	...	...	...	...	...	...	...	...	...	...	...	...	...	...	...	...	...	...	...	...	...	...	...	...	...	...	...	...	...	...	...
Mahabubnagar (Nagar Karnul)	...	...	...	...	...	...	...	...	...	...	...	...	...	...	...	...	...	...	...	...	...	...	...	...	...	...	...	...	...	...	...	...	...	...	...	...	...	...	...	...
Nalgonda	...	...	...	...	...	...	...	...	...	...	...	...	...	...	...	...	...	...	...	...	...	...	...	...	...	...	...	...	...	...	...	...	...	...	...	...	...	...	...	...
Warangal (Khamam) ...	...	...	...	...	...	...	...	...	...	...	...	...	...	...	...	...	...	...	...	...	...	...	...	...	...	...	...	...	...	...	...	...	2	...	...	2	2	...	...	2
Elgandal	...	...	...	...	...	...	...	...	...	...	...	...	...	...	...	...	...	...	...	...	...	2	...	2	...	...	...	...	...	...	...	...	...	...	...	...	1	...	...	1
Indur	...	...	...	...	...	...	...	...	...	...	...	...	...	...	...	...	...	...	...	...	...	...	...	...	...	...	...	...	...	...	...	...	...	...	...	...	...	...	...	...
Medak...	...	...	...	...	...	...	...	...	...	...	...	...	...	...	...	...	...	...	...	...	...	...	...	...	...	...	...	...	...	...	...	...	...	...	...	...	1	...	...	1
Mahratwara. Aurangabad	...	...	...	...	...	...	...	...	...	...	...	...	...	...	...	...	...	...	...	...	...	...	...	...	...	...	...	...	...	...	...	...	...	...	...	...	...	...	...	...
Birh	...	...	...	...	...	...	...	...	...	...	...	...	...	...	...	...	...	...	...	...	...	...	...	...	...	...	...	...	...	...	...	...	...	...	...	...	...	...	...	...
Nander	...	...	...	...	...	...	...	...	...	...	...	...	...	...	...	...	...	...	...	...	...	...	...	...	...	...	...	...	...	...	...	...	...	...	...	...	...	...	...	...
Naldrug	...	...	...	...	...	...	...	...	...	...	...	...	...	...	...	...	...	...	...	...	...	...	...	...	...	...	...	...	...	...	...	...	...	...	...	...	...	...	...	...
Bidar	...	...	...	...	...	...	...	...	...	...	...	...	...	...	...	...	...	...	...	...	...	...	...	...	...	...	...	...	...	...	...	...	...	...	...	...	...	...	...	...
Parbhani	...	...	...	...	...	...	...	...	...	...	...	...	...	...	...	...	...	...	...	...	...	...	...	...	...	...	...	...	...	...	...	...	...	...	...	...	...	...	...	...
Sirpur Tandur	...	...	...	...	...	...	...	...	...	...	...	...	...	...	...	...	...	...	...	...	...	...	...	...	...	...	...	...	...	...	...	...	...	...	...	...	...	...	...	...
Karnatic or Kanada. Gulbarga	...	...	...	...	...	...	...	...	...	...	...	...	...	...	...	...	...	...	...	...	...	...	...	...	...	...	...	...	...	...	...	...	...	...	...	...	...	...	...	...
Raichur	...	...	...	...	...	...	...	...	...	...	...	...	...	...	...	...	...	...	...	...	...	1	...	1	...	...	...	...	...	...	...	...	...	...	...	...	...	...	...	...
Lingasugur	...	...	...	...	...	...	...	...	...	...	...	...	...	...	...	...	...	...	...	...	...	...	...	...	...	...	...	...	...	...	...	...	...	...	...	...	...	...	...	...
Total Districts......	...	...	...	...	...	...	...	...	...	...	...	...	...	...	...	...	...	...	...	...	...	3	...	3	...	...	...	...	...	...	...	...	2	...	...	2	4	...	...	4
Total Districts including Hyderabad...	...	2	...	2	...	1	...	1	...	4	...	4	...	5	...	5	...	1	...	1	...	37	...	37	1	9	...	10	5	5	...	10	30	2	...	32	69	8	4	81
Railways......	...	...	...	...	...	...	...	...	...	...	...	...	...	...	...	...	...	...	...	...	...	1	...	1	...	1	...	1	...	8	...	8	...	...	...	...	...	...	...	...
Grand Total......	...	2	...	2	...	1	...	1	...	4	...	4	...	5	...	5	...	1	...	1	...	38	...	38	1	10	...	11	5	8	...	13	30	2	...	32	69	8	4	81

FEMALES.

Return showing the Civil Condition Sex and Age of Bri ish born subjects found in the Cantonment and Railway Stations, &c., in H. H. the Nizam's Dominions.—*Continued.*

District or State.	30—34 Married.	Unmarried.	Widow.	Total.	35—39 Married.	Unmarried.	Widow.	Total.	40—44 Married.	Unmarried.	Widow.	Total.	45—49 Married.	Unmarried.	Widow.	Total.	50—54 Married.	Unmarried.	Widow.	Total.	55—59 Married.	Unmarried.	Widow.	Total.	60 and over. Married.	Unmarried.	Widow.	Total.	Unspecified. Married.	Unmarried.	Widow.	Total.	Total. Married.	Unmarried.	Widow.	Total.
	42	43	44	45	46	47	48	49	50	51	52	53	54	55	56	57	58	59	60	61	62	63	64	65	66	67	68	69	70	71	72	73	74	75	76	77
Telingana. Hyderabad. City	1	...	...	1	...	...	...	...	...	...	...	...	...	...	...	...	...	...	...	...	...	...	...	...	...	...	...	...	...	...	...	...	1	...	...	1
Suburbs including Secunderabad	47	2	...	49	19	2	2	23	12	...	1	13	3	...	3	6	2	...	...	2	1	...	1	2	1	...	3	4	...	...	...	...	184	75	14	278
Total......	48	2	...	50	19	2	2	23	12	...	1	13	3	...	3	6	2	...	...	2	1	...	1	2	1	...	3	4	...	...	...	...	185	75	14	274
Atraf-i-Balda District	...	...	...	...	...	...	...	...	...	...	...	...	...	...	...	...	1	...	...	1	...	...	...	...	...	...	...	...	...	...	...	...				
Mahabubnagar (Nagar Karnul) ...	...	...	...	...	...	...	...	...	...		...	...	...	...	...	...	...	...	...	...	...	...	...	...	...	...	...	...	...	...	...	...	1	...	...	1
Nalgonda	...	...	...	...	...	...	...	...	...	...	...	...	...	...	...	...	...	...	...	...	...	...	...	...	...	...	...	...	...	...	...	...	...	...	...	...
Warangal (Khamam)	1	...	...	1	...	...	...	...	...	...	...	...	...	...	...	...	...	...	...	...	...	...	...	...	...	...	...	...	...	...	...	...	...	...	...	...
Elgandal	1	...	...	1	1	...	...	1	...	...	...	...	...	...	...	...	...	...	...	...	...	...	...	...	...	...	...	...	...	...	...	...	5	...	...	5
Indur	...	...	...	...	...	...	...	...	...	...	...	...	...	...	...	...	...	...	...	...	...	...	...	...	...	...	...	...	...	...	...	...	3	2	...	5
Medak	...	...	...	...	...	...	...	...	...	...	...	...	...	...	...	...	...	...	...	...	...	...	...	...	...	...	...	...	...	...	...	...	1	...	...	1
Mahratwara. Aurangabad	...	...	...	...	...	...	...	...	...	...	...	...	...	...	...	...	...	...	...	...	...	...	...	...	...	...	...	...	...	...	...	...	...	...	...	...
Bith	...	...	...	...	...	...	...	...	...	...	...	...	...	...	...	...	...	...	...	...	...	...	...	...	...	...	...	...	...	...	...	...	...	...	...	...
Nander	...	...	...	...	...	...	...	...	...	...	...	...	...	...	...	...	...	...	...	...	...	...	...	...	...	...	...	...	...	...	...	...	...	...	...	...
Naldrug	...	...	...	...	...	...	...	...	...	...	...	...	...	...	...	...	...	...	...	...	...	...	...	...	...	...	...	...	...	...	...	...	...	...	...	...
Bidar	...	...	...	...	...	...	...	...	...	...	...	...	...	...	...	...	...	...	...	...	...	...	...	...	...	...	...	...	...	...	...	...	...	...	...	...
Parbhani	...	...	...	...	...	...	...	...	...	...	...	...	...	...	...	...	...	...	...	...	...	...	...	...	...	...	...	...	...	...	...	...	...	...	...	...
Sirpur Tandur	...	...	...	...	...	...	...	...	...	...	...	...	...	...	...	...	...	...	...	...	...	...	...	...	...	...	...	...	...	...	...	...	...	...	...	...
Karnatic or Kannada. Gulbarga	...	1		1	...	...		...	...	...	...	...	...	...	...	...			...	...	...	...	...	...	...	...	...	...	...	...	...	...	...	1	...	1
Raichur	...	...	...	...	...	...	...	...	1	...	...	1	...	...	...	...	...	...	...	...	...	...	...	...	...	...	...	...	...	...	...	...	1	1	...	2
Lingasugur	...	...		...	...	...	...	...	...	...	...	...	...	...	...	...	...	...	...	...	...	...	...	...	...	...	...	...	...	...	...	...	...	...	...	...
Total Districts......	2	1	...	3	1	...	...	1	1	...	...	1	...	...	...	...	1	...	...	1	...	...	...	...	...	...	...	...	...	...	...	...	11	4	...	15
Total Districts including Hyderabad......	50	3		53	20	2	2	24	13	...	1	14	3	...	3	6	3	...	...	3	1	...	1	2	1	...	3	4	...	...	...	...	196	79	14	289
Railways......	...	...	...	...	...	...	...	...	...	...	...	...	...	...	1	1	...	...	...	...	...	...	...	...	...	...	1	1	...	...	...	...	...	5	2	7
Grand Total......	50	3	...	53	20	2	2	24	13	...	1	14	3	...	4	7	3	...	...	3	1	...	1	2	1	...	4	5	...	...	...	...	196	84	16	296

BRITISH BORN SUBJECTS IN HIS HIGHNESS THE NIZAM'S DOMINIONS.

British born subjects in H. H. the Nizam's Dominions.

	District or State.	England.		Scotland.		Ireland.		Wales.		Jersey.	
		Males.	Females.	Males.	Females.	Males.	Females.	Males.	Females.	Males.	Females.
	1	2	3	4	5	6	7	8	9	10	11
Telingana. Hyderabad.	City	1	1	...	...	...	...	...	...	...	...
Telingana. Hyderabad.	Suburbs including Secunderabad	2,034	172	83	7	897	74	12	20	3	...
	Total......	2,035	173	83	7	897	74	12	20	3	...
Telingana.	Atraf-i-Balda District	2	...	...	1	...	...	...	...	...	...
Telingana.	Mahabubnagar (Nagar Karnul) ...	1	...	...	...	...	...	...	...	...	...
Telingana.	Nalgonda	...	...	...	...	...	...	...	...	...	...
Telingana.	Warangal (Khamam)	10	5	2	...	...	...	...	...	...	...
Telingana.	Elgandal	5	5	...	...	...	...	...	...	...	...
Telingana.	Indur	3	...	...	...	...	...	...	...	...	...
Telingana.	Medak...	4	1	1	...	...	...	...	...	...	...
Mahratwara.	Aurangabad	1	...	...	...	...	...	...	...	...	...
Mahratwara.	Birh	1	...	...	...	...	...	...	...	...	...
Mahratwara.	Nander...	2	...	...	...	...	...	...	...	...	...
Mahratwara.	Naldrug	...	...	...	...	...	...	...	...	...	...
Mahratwara.	Bidar	...	...	...	...	...	...	...	...	...	...
Mahratwara.	Parbhani	...	...	...	...	...	...	...	...	...	...
Mahratwara.	Sirpur Tandur	...	...	...	...	...	...	...	...	...	...
Karnatic or Kanada.	Gulbarga	1	1	...	...	...	...	...	...	...	...
Karnatic or Kanada.	Raichur	3	2	...	...	...	...	...	...	...	...
Karnatic or Kanada.	Lingasugur	3	...	...	...	1	...	...	...	...	...
	Total Districts......	36	14	3	1	1	...	...	...	...	...
	Total Districts including Hyderabad...	2,071	187	86	8	898	74	12	20	3	...
	Railways......	29	6	4	...	2	1	...	...	...	...
	Grand Total......	2,100	193	90	8	900	75	12	20	3	...

CASTE INDEX.

Index of Castes and Sub-Castes returned in the Dominions of H. H. the Nizam (1891.)

Index of Castes returned in the Dominions of H. H. the Nizam. (1891.)

N.B.—The Sub-divisions are shown as returned in the Schedules. M. represents Mussulman; J. Jain; S. Sikh; C. Christian.

MAIN CASET.				SUB-CASTE.		Consecutive number of Sub-caste.	Hereditary or Traditional Occupation.	CLASSIFI-CATION.		REMARKS.
Serial No.	Name.	POPULATION.		No.	Name.			Class.	Group.	
		Male.	Female.							
1	Aghori	5	6	1	Aghori	1	Devotees	B	6	
2	Agiala	4	7	1	Agiala	2	Shepherds and wool weavers.	D	26	
3	Ahir...	802	603	1	Ahir	3				
				2	Gwalbansi	4				
				3	Kapoor	5				
				4	Kishen	6				
				5	Mahratta	7				
				6	Mushtigolla	8				
				7	Nakulabandaku ...	9	Graziers	A	2b	Gaoli.
				8	Pakanati	10				
				9	Siva	11				
				10	Surat	12				
				11	Telugu	13				
				12	Varahansi	14				
4	Aiyawar	101	115	1	Aiyawar	15	Temple servants	B	7	Aiyagar.
5	Andh	9,289	8,920	1	Andh	16	Landholders	A	2a	
6	Anjanwar	314	325	1	Anjanwar	17	Do.	A	2a	Anjana.
7	Aoti...	18	17	1	Aoti	18	Traders	C	14	
				2	Aosi	19				
8	Arab... ... M	1,011	729	1	Ajfi	20				
				2	Badri	21				
				3	Balirsar	22				
				4	Basri	23				
				5	Darvan	24				
				6	Habib...	25				
				7	Hazramut	26	Non-Indian Asiatic races	F	48	
				8	Kalabtar	27				
				9	Kohavi	28				
				10	Movallad	29				
				11	Nadi	30				
				12	Rafai	31				
				13	Saori	32				
				14	Sharif	33				
9	Aradhya	14	12	1	Aradhya	34	Musicians and Ballad-reciters.	B	11	
10	Armenian ... C	7	1	1	Armenian	35	Non-Indian Asiatic races	F	48	
11	Arthi	1	2	1	Arthikulam	36	Devotees	B	6	Arthikulam.
				2	Avadhud	37				
12	Arya...	1,246	1,231	1	Arya	38	Landholders	A	2a	
13	Attar... ... H	418	384	1	Attar	39	Perfumers, drug preparers &c.	D	22b	
	M	17	12							
		2	2							
14	Ansala ... H	52,382	50,754	1	Ahib	40				
	M	...	1	2	Arava	41				
	J	56	34	3	Ansala	42				
				4	Bairagisolaru... ...	43				
				5	Cheepurrawallu ...	44				
				6	Elkatollu	45				
				7	Gujarwad	46				
				8	Kamsala	47				
				9	Kasar...	48				
				10	Lad	49				
				11	Lingavantu	50				
				12	Mahadevu	51				
				13	' aisri	52				
				14	Malkal	53				
				15	Malvi...	54	Goldsmiths	D	17	Kamsala, Sonar.
				16	Mahratta	55				
				17	Maya	56				
				18	Munnurwad	57				
				19	Nokiti...	58				
				20	Panchadai	59				
				21	Panchala	60				
				22	Paradesi	61				
				23	Rajput	62				
				24	Ramancherla ...	63				
				25	Ratod...	64				
				26	Sardha	65				
				27	Saraswat	66				
				28	Seelavantu	67				
				29	Sudra	68				
				30	Sukunati	69				

INDEX OF CASTES.—*Continued.*

MAIN CASTE.				SUB-CASTE.		Consecutive number of Sub-caste.	Hereditary or Traditional Occupation.	CLASSIFICATION.		REMARKS.
Serial No.	Name.	POPULATION.		No.	Name.			Class.	Group.	
		Males.	Females.							
14	Ausala,—*concld.* ...			31	Sunaru	70				
				32	Suvarangothram ...	71				
				33	Swami	72				
				34	Talluchu	73				
				35	Telanga	74				
				36	Tokatta	75	Goldsmiths	D	17	
				37	Vallabhachari ...	76				
				38	Vibhutidari	77				
				39	Visvabramha... ...	78				
				40	Viswakarma	79				
				41	Visvarajati	80				
15	Badamavaru... ...	45	40	1	Badamavandlu ...	81				
				2	Boochamavod	82	Miscellaneous and disreputable livers.	E	45	Padmavandlu.
				3	Dalvargodi	83				
				4	Padmavandlu... ...	84				
16	Badaru	81,547	80,844	1	Badus	85				
				2	Bahsvikulam	86				
				3	Bairut	87				
				4	Bajalooru	88				
				5	Bannyalavaru ...	89				
				6	Bantulavaru	90				
				7	Banvikulu	91				
				8	Bodaru	92				
				9	Benki	98				
				10	Bhopal	94				
				11	Bogadavaru	95				
				12	Boya	96				
				13	Changalavaru ...	97				
				14	Changodai	98				
				15	Chapalvad	99				
				16	Charvu	100				
				17	Chinnagallu	101				
				18	Dher	102				
				19	Dinnayalvaru ...	103				
				20	Elmeru	104				
				21	Gadivar	105				
				22	Gavavalai	106				
				23	Gavi	107				
				24	Goodhavati	108				
				25	Gosalavaru	109				
				26	Gujagavad	110				
				27	Gujjala	111				
				28	Gulaivaru	112				
				29	Gunjavad	113				
				30	Gurumani	114				
				31	Hathikankana... ...	115	Village watchmen ...	D	38a	Bedar.
				32	Hullamavaru... ...	116				
				33	Jakkalu	117				
				34	Jampalu	118				
				35	Japalu...	119				
				36	Javanalaru	120				
				37	Jopalu...	121				
				38	Kankaya	122				
				39	Kavalavaru	123				
				40	Kuluparu	124				
				41	Kurli	125				
				42	Kurulavad	126				
				43	Kurutalavar	127				
				44	Kusulvan	128				
				45	Lingayet	129				
				46	Madamalu	130				
				47	Majulu	131				
				48	Majuru	132				
				49	Malaiku	133				
				50	Malivalai	134				
				51	Mallabharu	135				
				52	Mammullu	136				
				53	Manakalavaru ...	137				
				54	Manakaru	138				
				55	Mang	139				
				56	Mannai	140				
				57	Masakalavar	141				
				58	Mattoru	142				
				59	Mecnagalu	143				
				60	Mugulavana	144				
				61	Mulalukara	145				

INDEX OF CASTES.—*Continued.*

MAIN CASTE.				SUB-CASTE.		Consecutive number of Sub-caste.	Hereditary or Traditional Occupation.	CLASSIFICATION.		REMARKS.
Serial No.	Name.	POPULATION.		No.	Name.			Class.	Group.	
		Males.	Females.							
16	Badaru.—*concld.* ...	......	......	62	Munnailu	146				
				63	Munnuru	147				
				64	Mupadala	148				
				65	Murayi	149				
				66	Nallavaru	150				
				67	Nallaidavaru	151				
				68	Nalugotalavaru ...	152				
				69	Namali	153				
				70	Namdari	154				
				71	Nankabidavaru ...	155				
				72	Napalvasu	156				
				73	Nayalavaru	157	Village watchmen ...	D	38a	
				74	Neelagujalu	158				
				75	Petavalku	159				
				76	Polalollu	160				
				77	Pulujalavaru	161				
				78	Sajjan...	162				
				79	Santalvaru	163				
				80	Sivamut	164				
				81	Tabakalavaru ...	165				
				82	Valmikulu	166				
				83	Voobanabagi	167				
				84	Vurubadru	168				
				85	Yoovinakalu	169				
17	Badbooj	289	202	1	Badbooj	170	Grain Parchers and confectioners.	D	22a	Bhadboonja.
				2	Bhujwa	171				
18	Bagwan ... H	7	11	1	Bagwan	172	Betel leaf dealers	D	22b	
	M	53	40							
19	Bahurupi ... H	124	160	1	Bahurupi	173		B	13	
	M	1	3	2	Parabikaya	174	Actors and Mimics ...			
20	Bahusagar	72	70	1	Bahusagar	175	Miscellaneous and disreputable livers.	E	45	Bhaosagar.
				2	Bahusar	176				
21	Bairagi	2,875	2,207	1	Ayavaru	177				
				2	Bairagi	178				
				3	Bavaji	179				
				4	Brahman	180				
				5	Dhanvayi	181				
				6	Ekari	182				
				7	Elgandal Sanyasi ...	183				
				8	Gaodbrahmana ...	184				
				9	Humshar	185				
				10	Jalandar	186				
				11	Jamunayi	187				
				12	Jumati	188				
				13	Katia	189	Devotees	B	6	
				14	Kshetri	190				
				15	Mahanandasi	191				
				16	Mattam Sanyasi ...	192				
				17	Nanati	193				
				18	Neranjan	194				
				19	Raimen	195				
				20	Ramanandu-Bairagi ...	196				
				21	Ranjit...	197				
				22	Runja...	198				
				23	Sadhu...	199				
				24	Sambhogi	200				
				25	Sanyasi	201				
				26	Sreevaishnava ...	202				
				27	Tirmali	203				
				28	Udasi	204				
22	Balija	41,548	41,386	1	Adi	205				
				2	Balija	206				
				3	Balijawad	207				
				4	Ballaiju	208				
				5	Banjara	209				
				6	Basameswar	210				
				7	Bikshavantulu ...	211				
				8	Bogam	212	Traders	C	14	
				9	Chervalu	213				
				10	Dikshavantulu ...	214				
				11	Gajula	215				
				12	Gaori	216				
				13	Gruhastulu	217				
				14	Gurudikota	218				
				15	Guru	219				
				16	Jangam	220				
				17	Kannada	221				

INDEX OF CASTES.—*Continued.*

MAIN CASTE.				SUB-CASTE.				CLASSIFICATION.		
Serial No.	Name.	POPULATION. Males.	POPULATION. Females.	No.	Name.	Consecutive number of Sub-caste.	Hereditary or Traditional Occupation.	Class.	Group.	REMARKS.
22	Balija.—*concld.*	......	......	18	Kanukuda	222				
				19	Komma	223				
				20	Lingadari	224				
				21	Lingangulu	225				
				22	Lingavantulu	226				
				23	Lingayetulu	227				
				24	Mahadevu	228				
				25	Mathamayi	229				
				26	Motabalija	230				
				27	Neerumamidi	231				
				28	Pashamnn	232				
				29	Pooja	233				
				30	Rachutla	234				
				31	Risha	235				
				32	Sajjana	236	Traders	C	14	
				33	Sarigundi	237				
				34	Savayi	238				
				35	Seelavantu	239				
				36	Setti Balija	240				
				37	Sivapuja	241				
				38	Sukhi Balija	242				
				39	Telaga	243				
				40	Thota	244				
				41	Vaishnava	245				
				42	Vibhutidaru	246				
				43	Vikshavadu	247				
				44	Virasaivam	248				
				45	Vrishabhadamsi	249				
				46	Udak	250				
23	Balsantosh	246	219	1	Balasantulu	251	Miscellaneous and disreputable livers	E	45	Balasantulu.
24	Baluch M	10	9	1	Baluch	252	Non-Indian Asiatic races	F	48	
25	Baniala	78	67	1	Baniala	253	Miscellaneous and disreputable livers	E	45	
26	Banjara	69,010	64,024	1	Badekar	254				
				2	Banjar	255				
				3	Banjarabhadekori	256				
				4	Char	257				
				5	Charana	258				
				6	Dasaru	259				
				7	Dhadi	260				
				8	Gruhastulu	261	Carriers	C	16	
				9	Ladu	262				
				10	Lingayet	263				
				11	Lingavantu	264				
				12	Lambadi	265				
				13	Mathuri	266				
				14	Seelavantu	267				
				15	Vanjari	268				
27	Begari	2,351	2,485	1	Begari	269				
				2	Bagoor	270				
				3	Bandalavaru	271				
				4	Begaru-Vaishnava	272				
				5	Belgari	273	Land holders	A	2a	
				6	Harelavaru	274				
				7	Huvinavar	275				
				8	Sayees	276				
				9	Syse	277				
28	Beldar	951	1,029	1	Beldar	278	Earth-workers and stone dressers.	E	41	
29	Besta	42,499	41,051	1	Banta	279				
				2	Berki	280				
				3	Besta	281				
				4	Bhoi	282				
				5	Botu	283				
				6	Boya	284				
				7	Chadaruboya	285				
				8	Choadri	286				
				9	Erra	287	Fishermen, Palki bearers, &c.	D	35	
				10	Gangachalaku	288				
				11	Goolla	289				
				12	Gudutela	290				
				13	Gundla	291				
				14	Halmaku	292				
				15	Karuboya	293				
				16	Katikaboya	294				
				17	Mahigeer	295				
				18	Manda	296				

INDEX OF CASTES.—*Continued.*

Serial No.	Main Caste: Name	Population: Males	Population: Females	Sub-Caste: No.	Sub-Caste: Name	Consecutive number of Sub-caste	Hereditary or Traditional Occupation	Class	Group	Remarks
29	Besta.—*concld.*	...	...	19	Mahratta	297				
				20	Metu	298				
				21	Mudalvantu	299				
				22	Mutrasi	300				
				23	Nallaboya	301				
				24	Nallaboyi	302				
				25	Neelabindai	303				
				26	Neelabandugulu	304				
				27	Parigati	305				
				28	Parikiti	306				
				29	Poda	307				
				30	Perati	308	Fishermen, Palki bearers, &c.	D	35	
				31	Perka	309				
				32	Racha	310				
				33	Rachasampradayakam	311				
				34	Rakshaswamipuravadiku	312				
				35	Sadaru	313				
				36	Sajjana	314				
				37	Tengadiboya	315				
				38	Tondalaboya	316				
				39	Valmeekulu	317				
				40	Varyki	318				
30	Bhagavatalu	38	35	1	Bhagat	319				
				2	Bhagvat	320	Actors & mimics	B	13	Bhagavat.
				3	Ganta	321				
31	Bhand	152	131	1	Bhand	322				
32	Bhandari	644	666	1	Bhandari	323	Distillers & Toddydrawers.	D	36	
33	Bhat ... H	4,118	3,753	1	Bhat	324				
	J	5	...	2	Bhatmad	325				
				3	Bhatmurthi	326				
				4	Bhatraj	327	Genealogists	B	8	
				5	Bhatti	328				
				6	Bhav	329				
				7	Bhat-Jain	330				
34	Bhattia	105	88	1	Bhattia	331	Traders	C	14	
				2	Do. Guzerati	332				
35	Bhattiara ... M	3	5	1	Bhattiara	333	Perfumers, Drug preparers, &c.	D	22b	
36	Bhil ... Bhil	235	235	1	Bhil	334				
	H	5,179	5,366	2	Bhil-Hindu	335	Forest and hill tribes	A	4	
				3	Nayakudu	336				
37	Bhoyi	24,689	25,043	1	Amalavad	337				
				2	Bhoyi	338	Fishermen, Palki bearers.	D	35	
				3	Kabe	339				
38	Bogam ... H	1,908	3,193	1	Bogam	340				
	M	94	132	2	Chirubogam	341				
	J	3	2	3	Erkalu	342				
				4	Gollapatru	343				
				5	Jangam	344				
				6	Kadavan	345				
				7	Kalavath	346				
				8	Kapu	347				
				9	Kasban	348				
				10	Korwa	349	Dancers & Singers	B	12	Kanchani.
				11	Lingayet	350				
				12	Mala	351				
				13	Munnuru	352				
				14	Mutharasi	353				
				15	Namadhari	354				
				16	Patradavaru	355				
				17	Setti Balija	356				
				18	Seelavantulu	357				
39	Bommalavaru	17	22	1	Bommalavaru	358	Actors & Mimics	B	13	
40	Borah ... M	123	105	1	Borah	359	Traders	C	14	
41	Brahman	140,884	129,548	1	Adharvanvedam	360				
				2	Adhwaitam	361				
				3	Adhya	362				
				4	Aidad	363				
				5	Andrulu	364				
				6	Ankyavate	365				
				7	Anoli	366	Priests	B	5	
				8	Apastambh	367				
				9	Apayeti	368				
				10	Aradthia	369				
				11	Aravatukkulu	370				
				12	Arva	371				
				13	Arvellu	372				

INDEX OF CASTES.—*Continued.*

Main Caste: Serial No.	Main Caste: Name	Population: Males	Population: Females	Sub-Caste: No.	Sub-Caste: Name	Consecutive number of Sub-caste	Hereditary or Traditional Occupation	Classification: Class	Classification: Group	Remarks
41	Brahman,—*contd.* ...	...	...	14	Asletu	373				
				15	Asvalain	374				
				16	Atrigotri	375				
				17	Ayavar	376				
				18	Baduri	377				
				19	Baharkath	378				
				20	Bedpar	379				
				21	Bejabargi	380				
				22	Betke	381				
				23	Beyas	382				
				24	Bhagwat	383				
				25	Bramha	384				
				26	Bhargao	385				
				27	Charakshahi	386				
				28	Chirunchee	387				
				29	Chitpavan	388				
				30	Daim	389				
				31	Dandni	390				
				32	Dasnu...	391				
				33	Dava	392				
				34	Davag	393				
				35	Daya	394				
				36	Deshust	395				
				37	Dravid	396				
				38	Duli	397				
				39	Dundval	398				
				40	Gaitri	399				
				41	Gaivadi	400				
				42	Gangotre	401				
				43	Garg	402				
				44	Good	403				
				45	Gojargoad	404				
				46	Gojrati	405				
				47	Gokudi	406				
				48	Goverdhan	407				
				49	Gujarpand	408				
				50	Gundikota	409				
				51	Harak...	410				
				52	Haridas	411	Priests	B	5	
				53	Hiras	412				
				54	Hirpati	413				
				55	Jamnath	414				
				56	Jiyangaru	415				
				57	Johi	416				
				58	Joshi	417				
				59	Kalli	418				
				60	Kalikunj	419				
				61	Kamkoti	420				
				62	Kankobj	421				
				63	Kanno...	422				
				64	Karadi	423				
				65	Kasoyap	424				
				66	Kathri	425				
				67	Katiyalani	426				
				68	Koknast	427				
				69	Kondnia	428				
				70	Krishnpukshi... ...	429				
				71	Kunojia	430				
				72	Kurvatiki	431				
				73	Laval	432				
				74	Lingdhari	433				
				75	Machuri	434				
				76	Madhianjun	435				
				77	Madhinale	436				
				78	Madhva	437				
				79	Malvi	438				
				80	Mahrashtra	439				
				81	Mekhil	440				
				82	Modanchakdu ...	441				
				83	Morkinati	442				
				84	Morti	443				
				85	Nagar...	444				
				86	Nannas	445				
				87	Neaglu	446				
				88	Pakshi	447				
				89	Panasth	448				
				90	Panchdraved	449				
				91	Panchgod	450				

INDEX OF CASTES.—*Continued.*

MAIN CASTE.				SUB-CASTE.		Consecutive number of Sub-caste.	Hereditary or Traditional Occupation.	CLASSIFICATION.		REMARKS.
Serial No.	Name.	POPULATION.		No.	Name.			Class.	Group.	
		Males.	Females.							
41	Brahman,—*concld.*...	...	...	92	Pande...	451				
				93	Parshaki	452				
				94	Pavari	453				
				95	Phatak	454				
				96	Pinda	455				
				97	Porashwar	456				
				98	Prabhu	457				
				99	Prathamshake ...	458				
				100	Puncharashtram ...	459				
				101	Radhar	460				
				102	Ramanandi	461				
				103	Ramanj	462				
				104	Rudra...	463				
				105	Rugvedi	464				
				106	Rukhe...	465				
				107	Sajgoad	466				
				108	Sakar	467				
				109	Salbar	468				
				110	Samvedi	469				
				111	Sandel	470				
				112	Sanewad	471				
				113	Sanodu	472				
				114	Sannudia	473				
				115	Sanpuj	474				
				116	Saraswut	475				
				117	Shainte	476				
				118	Shainve	477				
				119	Shawa	478				
				120	Shikwan	479				
				121	Shormati	480				
				122	Shrimali	481				
				123	Silvarta	482				
				124	Smarth	483				
				125	Sirajphur	484				
				126	Sodar	485	Priests	B	5	
				127	Sribastan	486				
				128	Sringodd	487				
				129	Srivaishnao	488				
				130	Srivardhan	489				
				131	Srivartavin	490				
				132	Srya	491				
				133	Survurya	492				
				134	Telangi	493				
				135	Tergul	494				
				136	Tertuyashaki... ...	495				
				137	Tenhala	496				
				138	Tevari...	497				
				139	Teradarti	498				
				140	Vadagalu	499				
				141	Vadahala	500				
				142	Vaidikula	501				
				143	Vaikhanas	502				
				144	Vaitrshakha	503				
				145	Vapisni	504				
				146	Varkar	505				
				147	Vasist	506				
				148	Vegunedu	507				
				149	Vrishtam	508				
				150	Vellabhacharu ...	509				
				151	Velnadeo	510				
				152	Veshnistara	511				
				153	Veshnao	512				
				154	Veshva	513				
				155	Yadostakolu	514				
				156	Yajoshakha ...	515				
				157	Yegniyatarkolu ...	516				
				158	Yegniyawalki... ...	517				
				159	Yejurvedi	518				
				160	Yellandsu	519				
				161	Yelnatte	520				
42	Brahmanjai	29	9	1	Brahmanjai	521	Writers	B	9	
43	Budbuduki	562	563	1	Bebargi	522				
				2	Boodkai	523				
				3	Budbudiki	524				
				4	Budbudukula ...	525	Miscellaneous and disreputable livers.	E	45	
				5	Burukera	526				
				6	Choodboodkai... ...	527				
				7	Hoodboodkai	258				

INDEX OF CASTES.—*Continued.*

MAIN CASTE.				SUB-CASTE.		Consecutive number of Sub-caste.	Hereditary or Traditional Occupation.	CLASSIFICATION.		REMARKS.
Serial No.	Name.	POPULATION. Males.	Females.	No.	Name.			Class.	Group.	
43	Budbuduki.—*concld.*	...	...	8	Marathi	529	Miscellaneous and disreputable livers.	E	45	
				9	Perigi...	530				
44	Bukkavaru	159	123	1	Bukkatigaru	531	Perfumers, Drug preparers, &c.	D	22b	Bhukkatgar.
				2	Bukkavandlu	532				
45	Burud	8,304	8,244	1	Barood	533	Mat makers and Cane-splitters.	E	43	
				2	Bhalavar	534				
				3	Burud...	535				
				4	Jarudan	536				
				5	Kabadayya	537				
				6	Kaikadi	538				
				7	Kosvani	539				
				8	Matarvadu	540				
				9	Medarvad	541				
				10	Mukadalad	542				
				11	Myadar	543				
				12	Nandikanti	544				
				13	Setti	545				
				14	Takalaya	546				
				15	Tivachi	547				
				16	Vudatayya	548				
46	Chakala H	98,253	95,743	1	Banda	549	Washermen	D	24	Dhobi.
	M	1	...	2	Bedaru	550				
				3	Chakala	551				
				4	Chakavad	552				
				5	Daria...	553				
				6	Dhobi...	554				
				7	Dikunada	555				
				8	Egini...	556				
				9	Kapsagaru	557				
				10	Kula...	558				
				11	Lingavantu	559				
				12	Lokabaliki	560				
				13	Madial	561				
				14	Madival	562				
				15	Maktiasalollu	563				
				16	Mala...	564				
				17	Manavar	565				
				18	Maratha	566				
				19	Munnuru	567				
				20	Parcot...	568				
				21	Perika	569				
				22	Rajput	570				
				23	Raju...	571				
				24	Reva...	572				
				25	Sangiam	573				
				26	Sati...	574				
				27	Sudra...	575				
				28	Tanugu	576				
				29	Tellakula	577				
47	Chamar	51,652	50,380	1	Ausollulu	578	Leatherworkers...	D	38	
				2	Ayavar	579				
				3	Bedaru	580				
				4	Chamar	581				
				5	Gangadhar	582				
				6	Kanada	583				
				7	Karnul Dher...	584				
				8	Madigodu	585				
				9	Mehtar	586				
				10	Malavad	587				
				11	Mochi...	588				
				12	Pavalollu	589				
				13	Sangaru	590				
				14	Seerollu	591				
				15	Telugollu	592				
48	Chandal	127	128	1	Chandal	593	Scavengers	D	39	
49	Chenewar	4,199	4,092	1	Chenewar	594	Traders	C	14	
				2	Chunaiwar	595				
50	Chentchuwad...	5,441	5,200	1	Adavi...	596	Forest and hill tribes	A	4	
				2	Chentchu	597				
				3	Deva...	598				
				4	Enadi...	599				
				5	Gondu	600				
				6	Ingi...	601				
				7	Kuria...	602				
				8	Rachagondu...	603				
				9	Ura...	604				

INDEX OF CASTES.—*Continued.*

Serial No.	Main Caste Name	Population Males	Population Females	Sub-caste No.	Sub-caste Name	Consecutive number of Sub-caste	Hereditary or Traditional Occupation	Class	Group	Remarks
51	Christian (Native) ...	6,280	6,283	1	Agnani	605	Christian converts ...	F	52	
				2	Andin...	606				
				3	Arivi	607				
				4	Christian	608				
				5	Christian Advi ...	609				
				6	Christian Gunna ...	610				
				7	Dher	611				
				8	East Indian	612				
				9	Esayee	613				
				10	Gnani...	614				
				11	Jalamani	615				
				12	Joseph	616				
				13	Kama Velama ...	617				
				14	Kanadian	618				
				15	Madgulu	619				
				16	Madoo Christian ...	620				
				17	Mulki	621				
				18	Pariah...	622				
				19	Roman Catholic ...	623				
				20	Rusitian	624				
				21	Selin Christian ...	625				
				22	Swadesa Christian ...	626				
				23	Telugu	627				
				24	Telungad	628				
				25	Yesookreestu	629				
52	Dakkala	236	226	1	Dakkala	630	Leather workers	D	38	
				2	Dubbala	631				
				3	Dugala	632				
53	Darzi ... H J	18,841 918	17,937 786	1	Adagali	633	Tailors	D	22	
				2	Balijalu	634				
				3	Chandana	635				
				4	Cheeya	636				
				5	Chippa	637				
				6	Damalia	638				
				7	Darji	639				
				8	Dasamulla	640				
				9	Gundalai	641				
				10	Harugalu	642				
				11	Jangam	643				
				12	Jhalak	644				
				13	Jingar	645				
				14	Kshetri	646				
				15	Linga...	647				
				16	Lingayet	648				
				17	Lingeetu	649				
				18	Lingavantu	650				
				19	Malakera	651				
				20	Malollu	652				
				21	Mahratta	653				
				22	Merai	654				
				23	Merai (Mahratta) ...	655				
				24	Meri	656				
				25	Mushti	657				
				26	Nagaliku	658				
				27	Nagareekulu	659				
				28	Nagasuk	660				
				29	Naglag	661				
				30	Namdev	662				
				31	Panchal	663				
				32	Sudra	664				
				33	Suyalivalai	665				
				34	Telgavadu	666				
				35	Telaga	667				
				36	Urankaru	668				
				37	Velma	669				
54	Dasari	3,301	3,372	1	Batta	670	Mixed Indian races ...	F	49b	
				2	Bayyala	671				
				3	Bhaivaru	672				
				4	Bikshagadu	673				
				5	Bukkaya	674				
				6	Channa	675				
				7	Chidimi	676				
				8	Dakada	677				
				9	Danda	678				
				10	Desari...	679				
				11	Desi	680				
				12	Dudehi	681				

INDEX OF CASTES.—*Continued.*

Main Caste: Serial No.	Main Caste: Name	Population: Males	Population: Females	Sub-Caste: No.	Sub-Caste: Name	Consecutive number of Sub-caste	Hereditary or Traditional Occupation	Classification: Class	Classification: Group	Remarks
54	Dasari.—*concld.* ...	......	......	13	Gadagalavaru ...	682				
				14	Golu	683				
				15	Govindu	684				
				16	Gudisai	685				
				17	Haridasari	686				
				18	Kantha	687				
				19	Kshetri	688				
				20	Kshavavi	689				
				21	Luhar...	690				
				22	Mala	691				
				23	Mamadeva	692				
				24	Melati...	693	Mixed Indian races ...	F	49b	
				25	Merai...	694				
				26	Mettani	695				
				27	Mitra	696				
				28	Mityulu	697				
				29	Natakani	698				
				30	Pada...	699				
				31	Padavara	700				
				32	Paga...	701				
				33	Palidasa	702				
				34	Pula	703				
				35	Salai	704				
				36	Tenugu	705				
55	Devara	1	1	1	Devara	706	Devotees	B	6	
56	Dhangar	378,212	365,106	1	Adamushki	707				
				2	Bagawat	708				
				3	Bhairathna	709				
				4	Bargi	710				
				5	Dhunger	711				
				6	Erra Golla	712				
				7	Erramushti	713				
				8	Golawar	714				
				9	Golor	715				
				10	Golla	716				
				11	Gullawar	717				
				12	Hadvai	718				
				13	Hatkar	719	Shepherds & Wool weavers.	D	26	
				14	Kareli...	720				
				15	Khandoba	721				
				16	Khandoba Bakth ...	722				
				17	Khandbad	723				
				18	Kheidari	724				
				19	Khiladi	725				
				20	Khoyar	726				
				21	Khutaikar	727				
				22	Kintari	728				
				23	Kuruvalu	729				
				24	Mandagollalu... ...	730				
				25	Mushti Gurrao ...	731				
				26	Parudwar	732				
				27	Sajjan	733				
				28	Tenugu Gollavadu ...	734				
57	Dher...	635,199	624,260	1	Abida	735				
				2	Agnani	736				
				3	Ahilavaru	737				
				4	Akalu...	738				
				5	Anamikulu	739				
				6	Anagondi	740				
				7	Arva	741				
				8	Ayavaru	742				
				9	Badamavaru	743				
				10	Badarayavaru ...	744				
				11	Badaru	745				
				12	Badasari... ...	746				
				13	Badivanu	747	Agricultural labourers ...	A	2c	
				14	Baijooloo	748				
				15	Baladai	749				
				16	Balywivarai... ...	750				
				17	Bandari	751				
				18	Bandarikaru	752				
				19	Bandetutor	753				
				20	Bandulolu	754				
				21	Baragalvaru	755				
				22	Baralvallu	756				
				23	Basarol	757				
				24	Batibalam	758				
				25	Bayavaru	759				

INDEX OF CASTES.—*Continued.*

MAIN CASTE.				SUB-CASTE.		Consecutive number of Sub-caste.	Hereditary or Traditional Occupation.	CLASSIFI-CATION.		REMARKS.
Serial No.	Name.	POPULATION.		No.	Name.			Class.	Group.	
		Males.	Females.							
57	Dher—*contd.* ...	...	...	26	Bedar	760				
				27	Beja	761				
				28	Bejulu	762				
				29	Belapavaru	763				
				30	Bennalavaru	764				
				31	Bhadari	765				
				32	Bhakthwad	766				
				33	Bhandar	767				
				34	Bhatu	768				
				35	Biavaru	769				
				36	Bidadawaru	770				
				37	Bijulavaru	771				
				38	Bojoovol	772				
				39	Bonthapallavad ...	773				
				40	Bookameri	774				
				41	Budiavaru	775				
				42	Bundololu	776				
				43	Burraipu	777				
				44	Chaobina	778				
				45	Chalavadi	779				
				46	Chalthavad	780				
				47	Chamar	781				
				48	Charma	782				
				49	Chatta	783				
				50	Chendalavam ...	784				
				51	Chethaleru	785				
				52	Chudamvad	786				
				53	Dadai...	787				
				54	Dakkala	788				
				55	Dakkalavar	789				
				56	Damluvadlu	790				
				57	Dandeluvar	791				
				58	Dankilavallu... ...	792				
				59	Darlu...	793				
				60	Darulavallu	794				
				61	Dasari	795				
				62	Davar...	796				
				63	Davarithanuvaru ...	797				
				64	Dayalvad	798				
				65	Devatwad	799	Agricultural labourers ...	A	2 c	
				66	Dhalavadi	800				
				67	Dhalthiadaru... ...	801				
				68	Dharmiavaru... ...	802				
				69	Dher	803				
				70	Dhummarwad ...	804				
				71	Dhulalvar	805				
				72	Dorubi	806				
				73	Ela Telingi	807				
				74	Gadinetu	808				
				75	Gandharia	809				
				76	Gandolavad	810				
				77	Gantanial	811				
				78	Gatalavaru	812				
				79	Gavarubansi	813				
				80	Ghathilavaru... ...	814				
				81	Gosalavaru	815				
				82	Goshiki	816				
				83	Gudakavaru	817				
				84	Gudanarai	818				
				85	Gujalavaru	819				
				86	Gujarvad	820				
				87	Gunjarwad	821				
				88	Gurliavaru	822				
				89	Gyewatmala	823				
				90	Hajjam	824				
				91	Halkiavaru	825				
				92	Hanjivaru	826				
				93	Hankumathu ...	827				
				94	Hanukupanavaru ...	828				
				95	Hanukupavaru ...	829				
				96	Hammuduvadanaru ...	830				
				97	Haravana	831				
				98	Harthivad	832				
				99	Havalaru	833				
				100	Hedapadai	834				
				101	Holair...	835				
				102	Hujama	836				
				103	Jadu	837				

INDEX OF CASTES.—*Continued.*

MAIN CASTE.				SUB-CASTE.		Consecutive number of Sub-caste.	Hereditary or Traditional Occupation.	CLASSIFICATION.		REMARKS.
Serial No.	Name.	POPULATION. Males.	Females.	No.	Name.			Class.	Group.	
57	Dher,—*contd*, ...	......	......	104	Jaginarai	838				
				105	Jalavaru	839				
				106	Jamari	840				
				107	Jamadani	841				
				108	Jamavalai	842				
				109	Jambavanthu ...	843				
				110	Jangam	844				
				111	Janukaru	845				
				112	Javamali	846				
				113	Joginavaru	847				
				114	Jolukoor	848				
				115	Juggi...	849				
				116	Julukoru	850				
				117	Kadaloodu	851				
				118	Kadarubhat	852				
				119	Kadu	853				
				120	Kakarai	854				
				121	Kalal	855				
				122	Kalinga	856				
				123	Kamadi	857				
				124	Kamati	858				
				125	Kanalvadu	859				
				126	Kandulu	860				
				127	Kangatu	861				
				128	Kankaruvadu ...	862				
				129	Kanta	863				
				130	Kantavad	864				
				131	Kanthalvallu... ...	865				
				132	Karemathi	866				
				133	Karinama	867				
				134	Karnapatah	868				
				135	Karthookam	869				
				136	Kashabbane	870				
				137	Kasusukala	871				
				138	Kathali	872				
				139	Kathevaru	873				
				140	Kathiavaru	874				
				141	Kavaladi	875				
				142	Kengarelu	876	Agricultural labourers ...	A	20	
				143	Khandoba	877				
				144	Kilkiavaru	878				
				145	Kochalagum	879				
				146	Koli	880				
				147	Kommu	881				
				148	Koorati	882				
				149	Korivi...	883				
				150	Kubalaru	884				
				151	Kunbi	885				
				152	Kuruse	886				
				153	Kuruva	887				
				154	Lingadar	888				
				155	Madiga	889				
				156	Madlodu	890				
				157	Madri...	891				
				158	Mahaliavaru... ...	892				
				159	Mahar	893				
				160	Maisamma	894				
				161	Majabudabulu ...	895				
				162	Majullollu	896				
				163	Malasabu	897				
				164	Maligadu	898				
				165	Maligi	899				
				166	Malvad	900				
				167	Manamoorvru ...	901				
				168	Mandaivad	902				
				169	Mang	903				
				170	Mangalivad	904				
				171	Mannaivad	905				
				172	Mar	906				
				173	Mahratta	907				
				174	Mahratta (Samarasi)...	908				
				175	Mashti	909				
				176	Mashtu	910				
				177	Matalu	911				
				178	Mathi	912				
				179	Matinavaru	913				
				180	Matsalavollu	914				
				181	Matungi	915				

INDEX OF CASTES.—*Continued.*

Serial No.	Main Caste: Name	Population: Males	Population: Females	Sub-Caste: No.	Sub-Caste: Name	Consecutive number of Sub-caste	Hereditary or Traditional Occupation	Classification: Class	Classification: Group	Remarks
57	Dher.—*contd.* ...	......	......	182	Matriavaru	916				
				183	Mavalkari	917				
				184	Meenagalavaru ...	918				
				185	Meenagavaru... ...	919				
				186	Meg	920				
				187	Mekalavallu	921				
				188	Minvad	922				
				189	Monlollu	923				
				190	Madva	924				
				191	Mukkaravandlu ...	925				
				192	Munnuru	926				
				193	Musali	927				
				194	Mushti	928				
				195	Muthuraju	929				
				196	Mutriavaru	930				
				197	Nokaruvallu	931				
				198	Nandadavaru ...	932				
				199	Nirmalia	933				
				200	Padaum	934				
				201	Padiavaru	935				
				202	Padukavaru	936				
				203	Panchal	937				
				204	Panchamajati ...	938				
				205	Panchamuli	939				
				206	Pandalavad	940				
				207	Parukal	941				
				208	Payaradi	942				
				209	Pinagaru	943				
				210	Pobalavaru	944				
				211	Pochamma	945				
				212	Pogahuwallu	946				
				213	Pokal	947				
				214	Potharaju	948				
				215	Pulanarai	949				
				216	Racha...	950				
				217	Rachavadu	951				
				218	Rathi	952				
				219	Royalwallu	953				
				220	Rayaru	954				
				221	Rotithupasu	955	Agricultural labourers ...	A	2c	
				222	Rubooth	956				
				223	Sadarvala	957				
				224	Sadasha					
				225	Sakurath	958				
				226	Salakachandia Bhak-	959				
					tulu	960				
				227	Salmani	961				
				228	Sandhu	962				
				229	Sankar	963				
				230	Saunkolu	964				
				231	Sataluvallu	965				
				232	Sattigotram	966				
				233	Sath	967				
				234	Savinathai	968				
				235	Sayasu	969				
				236	Sekdar	970				
				237	Sethuvad	971				
				238	Sidalvar	972				
				239	Sidhi	973				
				240	Simalvadu	974				
				241	Simpi	975				
				242	Sindhu	976				
				243	Sindi	977				
				244	Singalvaru	978				
				245	Sitalvadu	979				
				246	Sitbudai	980				
				247	Siva	981				
				248	Sivabhakta	982				
				249	Somavamsu	983				
				250	Somusi	984				
				251	Sudra...	985				
				252	Sukravarum	986				
				253	Suriavamsam ...	987				
				254	Swakulu	988				
				255	Sutar	989				
				256	Tamadevulu	990				
				257	Telinga	991				
				258	Thahudavaru ...	992				

INDEX OF CASTES.—*Continued.*

MAIN CASTE.				SUB-CASTE.				CLASSIFICATION.		
Serial No.	Name.	POPULATION. Males.	Females.	No.	Name.	Consecutive number of Sub-caste.	Hereditary or Traditional Occupation.	Class.	Group.	REMARKS.
57	Dher.—*concld.*	......	......	259	Thanuyaru	993				
				260	Tirumandar	994				
				261	Ulisithesa	995				
				262	Vagantulachuman	996				
				263	Vakhalvar	997				
				264	Vannelavaru	998				
				265	Vardhavaru	999				
				266	Vardhi	1000				
				267	Varichakavalai	1001				
				268	Varudu	1002				
				269	Vasadgasari	1003	Agricultural labourers...	A	2c	
				270	Vasaruvad	1004				
				271	Viluvallu	1005				
				272	Yadgud	1006				
				273	Yagini	1007				
				274	Yakuruvollu	1008				
				275	Yamanahi	1009				
				276	Yegni	1010				
				277	Yemlavallu	1011				
				278	Yosalavaru	1012				
58	Dhom ... M	3	6	1	Dhom	1013	Musicians and ballad-reciters.	B	11	
59	Dhor	4,645	4,510	1	Dhor	1014	Leather workers	D	38	
60	Digambar	58	46	1	Digambar	1015	Devotees...	B	6	
61	Dommari	1,835	1,676	1	Arai	1016				
				2	Dommara	1017				
				3	Dorai	1018				
				4	Elgakulu	1019				
				5	Gudisavandlu	1020	Tumblers and acrobats...	E	46	
				6	Gujjalu	1021				
				7	Kommu	1022				
				8	Koratu	1023				
				9	Reddi	1024				
62	Eginawar	26	26	1	Eginawar	1025	Traders ...	C	14	
63	Elama	47,801	46,293	1	Balijawad	1026				
				2	Bhogarna	1027				
				3	Deva	1028				
				4	Ekula	1029				
				5	Elama	1030				
				6	Elamod	1031				
				7	Elamavar	1032				
				8	Gampa	1033				
				9	Govu	1034	Military and dominant ...	A	1	
				10	Kamma	1035				
				11	Lingayeth	1036				
				12	Padma	1037				
				13	Pakanati	1038				
				14	Raja	1039				
				15	Rajubandi	1040				
				16	Tenugu	1041				
64	Elgar	2	2	1	Elgar	1042	Traders ...	C	14	
65	Erkala	11,915	11,824	1	Bandi	1043				
				2	Banavi	1044				
				3	Baragvad	1045				
				4	Bogamvandlu	1046				
				5	Butti	1047				
				6	Donta	1048				
				7	Eginwar	1049				
				8	Ergawad	1050				
				9	Erkalwad	1051				
				10	Eukalwad	1052				
				11	Ganapa	1053				
				12	Gantalu	1054				
				13	Golla	1055				
				14	Gosalu	1056	Hunters, fowlers, &c. ...	E	44	Erukalla.
				15	Gujjuloa	1057				
				16	Gulava	1058				
				17	Gummi	1059				
				18	Kedari	1060				
				19	Kanchi	1061				
				20	Kalva	1062				
				21	Kondari	1063				
				22	Koravaru	1064				
				23	Korva	1065				
				24	Kunchikorava	1066				
				25	Kurakula	1067				
				26	Mallaru	1068				
				27	Manchi	1069				

INDEX OF CASTES.—*Continued.*

MAIN CASTE.				SUB-CASTE.		Consecutive number of Sub-caste.	Hereditary or Traditional Occupation.	CLASSIFICATION.		REMARKS.
Serial No.	Name.	POPULATION. Males.	Females.	No.	Name.			Class.	Group.	
65	Erkala.—*concld.* ...	......	......	28	Meenagalu	1070				
				29	Patchi...	1071				
				30	Patchigala	1072				
				31	Samara	1073				
				32	Samudra	1074				
				33	Satuvati	1075				
				34	Sreshta	1076	Hunters, fowlers, &c. ...	E	44	
				35	Suntupadi	1077				
				36	Telaga Kuruvaru ...	1078				
				37	Ura Kuravaru ...	1079				
				38	Uri	1080				
				39	Valmeekulu	1081				
				40	Yanadi	1082				
66	Eurasian ... 0	1,276	1,231	1	Christian	1083				
				2	East Indian	1084				
				3	English	1085				
				4	Eurasian	1086				
				5	French	1087	Eurasians	F	51	
				6	Great Brittain ...	1088				
				7	Hindustani	1089				
				8	Scot	1090				
67	European ... 0	4,011	1,242	1	American	1091				
				2	Anglo-Indian... ...	1092				
				3	Austrian	1093				
				4	Church of England ...	1094				
				5	Dutch...	1095				
				6	England	1096				
				7	English	1097				
				8	European	1098	Non-Asiatic races ...	F	50	
				9	French	1099				
				10	German	1100				
				11	Italian	1101				
				12	Portuguese	1102				
				13	Protestant	1103				
				14	Roman	1104				
				15	Roman Catholic ...	1105				
68	Gadaria	3	1	1	Gadaria	1106	Devotees	B	6	
69	Gajula	363	401	1	Balgaru	1107				
				2	Balija...	1108				
				3	Gajula	1109	Glass-workers	D	29	Gajulavandlu
				4	Kojopalli	1110				
				5	Kankanala	1111				
				6	Munnuru	1112				
70	Gandaria	21	5	1	Gandaria	1113	Shepherds & Wool weavers.	D	26	
71	Gandla ... H	43,716	41,978	1	Balija...	1114				
	M	3	2	2	Bhima	1115				
				3	Chalikeswaru... ...	1116				
				4	Chaluka	1117				
				5	Cheluvala	1118				
				6	Chiluka	1119				
				7	Deva	1120				
				8	Dikshavantu	1121				
				9	Duti	1122				
				10	Egina	1123				
				11	Erra	1124				
				12	Gandla	1125				
				13	Jangam	1126				
				14	Jesuvad	1127				
				15	Karayakula	1128				
				16	Lingabalija	1129	Oil-pressers	D	27	Teli
				17	Lingayet	1130				
				18	Mahratta	1131				
				19	Panchal	1132				
				20	Panchum	1133				
				21	Paradesi	1134				
				22	Perka...	1135				
				23	Perka Salai	1¹36				
				24	Racha...	1137				
				25	Reddi...	1138				
				26	Seelavantu	1139				
				27	Setti	1140				
				28	Siniki	1141				
				29	Tega	1142				
				30	Teli	1143				
				31	Tulavai	1144				
72	Ganjakuti	... ...	2	1	Ganjakuti	1145	Miscellaneous and disreputable livers.	E	45	
73	Gaoli	7,032	6,637	1	Abiruda	1146	Graziers	A	2b	Golla

INDEX OF CASTES.—*Continued.*

MAIN CASTE.				SUB-CASTE.		Consecutive number of Sub-caste.	Hereditary or Traditional Occupation.	CLASSIFICATION.		REMARKS.
Serial No.	Name.	POPULATION.		No.	Name.			Class.	Group.	
		Males.	Females.							
73	Gaoli.—*contd.*	...	...	2	Adavigolla	1147				
				3	Ayaladavaru	1148				
				4	Ala	1149				
				5	Anelavaru	1150				
				6	Anudu	1151				
				7	Areykurabaru	1152				
				8	Arey	1153				
				9	Avar	1154				
				10	Aval	1155				
				11	Babar	1156				
				12	Badi	1157				
				13	Badiri	1158				
				14	Baladavaru	1159				
				15	Balatavaru	1160				
				16	Banagaru	1161				
				17	Bandalavaru	1162				
				18	Bandji	1163				
				19	Bannalavaru	1164				
				20	Bargi	1165				
				21	Barlavandlu	1166				
				22	Bettalavaru	1167				
				23	Bidar	1168				
				24	Bijalavaru	1169				
				25	Bijugaru	1170				
				26	Bilailavaru	1171				
				27	Bibsurgi	1172				
				28	Birathuna	1173				
				29	Hirckurubaru	1174				
				30	Boginavaru	1175				
				31	Burgi	1176				
				32	Challalavaru	1177				
				33	Chavadalavaru	1178				
				34	Checmal	1179				
				35	Chittari	1180				
				36	Chullakolu	1181				
				37	Chummalavaru	1182				
				38	Dandinakurubaru	1183				
				39	Devandra	1184				
				40	Dhivaswad	1185	Graziers	A	2b	Golla.
				41	Dollanavaru	1186				
				42	Eivya	1187				
				43	Ekkalavaru	1188				
				44	Emalavaru	1189				
				45	Entasi	1190				
				46	Garumwad	1191				
				47	Gaodi	1192				
				48	Gaoli	1193				
				49	Gavalavaru	1194				
				50	Gayagadu	1195				
				51	Gayanavaru	1196				
				52	Goli	1197				
				53	Golla	1198				
				54	Golladasaru	1199				
				55	Gollolum	1200				
				56	Gootati	1201				
				57	Gosalvaru	1202				
				58	Goudugolla	1203				
				59	Gujalavaru	1204				
				60	Gulagiri	1205				
				61	Gullum	1206				
				62	Guntalavaru	1207				
				63	Halinavaru	1208				
				64	Handevujor	1209				
				65	Hatkar	1210				
				66	Hanamagolla	1211				
				67	Handekarubaru	1212				
				68	Hathikankanam	1213				
				69	Hirekurubaru	1214				
				70	Hirckunijavaru	1215				
				71	Huggadavaru	1216				
				72	Hummal	1217				
				73	Hunnulavaru	1218				
				74	Ishtan	1219				
				75	Jainpuri	1220				
				76	Jakkalavaru	1221				
				77	Jampalavaru	1222				
				78	Jannalavaru	1223				
				79	Kadadigalla	1224				

INDEX OF CASTES.—*Continued.*

MAIN CASTE.				SUB-CASTE.		Consecutive number of Sub-caste.	Hereditary or Traditional Occupation.	CLASSIFICATION.		REMARKS.
Serial No.	Name.	POPULATION.		No.	Name.			Class.	Group.	
		Males.	Females.							
73	Gaoli.—*contd.* ...	......	......	80	Kadlailavaru... ...	1225				
				81	Kadunal	1226				
				82	Kaduvai	1227				
				83	Kakalavaru	1228				
				84	Kakanad	1229				
				85	Kakanati	1230				
				86	Kakaru	1231				
				87	Kakipadh	1232				
				88	Kakkanavaru ...	1233				
				89	Kalaivah	1234				
				90	Kali	1235				
				91	Kallailavar	1236				
				92	Kalpu...	1237				
				93	Kamma	1238				
				94	Kanati	1239				
				95	Kanchalavar... ...	1240				
				96	Kanchigolla	1241				
				97	Kandva	1242				
				98	Kannadi	1243				
				99	Kanyangolla	1244				
				100	Kapsukankunam ...	1245				
				101	Karaikurjuru ...	1246				
				102	Karelu	1247				
				103	Karidiyavaru... ...	1248				
				104	Karnal	1249				
				105	Kashtu	1250				
				106	Kasthavollu	1251				
				107	Kasvoj	1252				
				108	Katamaiya	1253				
				109	Katkaru	1254				
				110	Kavai...	1255				
				111	Kayakarasu	1256				
				112	Kempugollaru ...	1257				
				113	Khandoba	1258				
				114	Kidalayavaru ...	1259				
				115	Kirukuvadu	1260				
				116	Krishnagolla	1261				
				117	Kunbi...	1262				
				118	Kurigolla	1263	Graziers	A	2b	Golla.
				119	Kuramavallu ...	1264				
				120	Kurujuru	1265				
				121	Kurujuru Jangam ...	1266				
				122	Kurujuru Lingayet ...	1267				
				123	Kuruliavaru	1268				
				124	Kurumiyavaru ...	1269				
				125	Kuruva	1270				
				126	Kurumagolla	1271				
				127	Kushtee	1272				
				128	Lad	1273				
				129	Laldhangar	1274				
				130	Lalgond	1275				
				131	Lingavanthu... ...	1276				
				132	Lothuluyakal ...	1277				
				133	Madari	1278				
				134	Madamari	1279				
				135	Mahalolu	1280				
				136	Mamilavaru	1281				
				137	Manchalavollu ...	1282				
				138	Manda	1283				
				139	Mannelavaru ...	1284				
				140	Mannepu	1285				
				141	Manthra	1286				
				142	Manti...	1287				
				143	Mahratti	1288				
				144	Marlagollaru	1289				
				145	Masaram	1290				
				146	Mingalavaru... ...	1291				
				147	Mogathi	1292				
				148	Motati	1293				
				149	Moodoorasu	1294				
				150	Mooka	1295				
				151	Motal	1296				
				152	Muchu	1297				
				153	Mudali	1298				
				154	Mudra	1299				
				155	Munnowad	1300				
				156	Mutraju	1301				
				157	Mushtigolla	1302				

INDEX OF CASTES.—*Continued.*

MAIN CASTE.				SUB-CASTE.				CLASSIFICATION.		
Serial No.	Name.	POPULATION.		No.	Name.	Consecutive number of Sub-caste.	Hereditary or Traditional Occupation.	Class.	Group.	REMARKS.
		Males.	Females.							
73	Gaoli,—*concld.* ...	......	......	158	Nagadubedi	1303				
				159	Nalla	1304				
				160	Naranagollorn ...	1305				
				161	Nayagi	1306				
				162	Nerai	1307				
				163	Pakanati	1308				
				164	Pakanatiki	1309				
				165	Pallenavaru	1310				
				166	Panchagolla	1311				
				167	Panta	1312				
				168	Paritai	1313				
				169	Pacha...	1314				
				170	Pathi	1315				
				171	Pathikankanam ...	1316				
				172	Pavar...	1317				
				173	Pedakanti	1318				
				174	Pedata	1319				
				175	Pedati...	1320				
				176	Puja	1321				
				177	Purra	1322				
				178	Pusa	1323				
				179	Raloos	1324				
				180	Ramool	1325				
				181	Rasa	1326				
				182	Rinkankana	1327				
				183	Sadanapu	1328				
				184	Sajan	1329				
				185	Sarasivu	1330				
				186	Sathalavaru	1331				
				187	Setti	1332				
				188	Sevath	1333				
				189	Sigakaru	1334				
				190	Sila	1335				
				191	Sirigond	1336	Graziers...	A	2b	Golla.
				192	Sivabaktu	1337				
				193	Somagar	1338				
				194	Somasi	1339				
				195	Sreedhungar	1340				
				196	Suriyava	1341				
				197	Telanga	1342				
				198	Thatalavaru	1343				
				199	Theguti	1344				
				200	Thellacheeralu ...	1345				
				201	Thelagagollaru ...	1346				
				202	Thellamari	1347				
				203	Themugula	1348				
				204	Thuguru	1349				
				205	Tunti...	1350				
				206	Uthamaru	1351				
				207	Vadabhavaruthi ...	1352				
				208	Vadagalavaru ...	1353				
				209	Vanaruku	1354				
				210	Varagathavaru ...	1355				
				211	Varuasankara ...	1356				
				212	Vegina	1357				
				213	Verunla	1358				
				214	Veyee	1359				
				215	Voggu	1360				
				216	Vojee Golla	1361				
				217	Vokku	1362				
				218	Vunni...	1363				
				219	Vunnikankanam ...	1364				
				220	Vuragollaru	1365				
				221	Vupu	1366				
				222	Yadava	1367				
				223	Yanadhi	1368				
				224	Yeddi	1369				
				225	Yerravaru	1370				
74	Gaond	14,477	14,330	1	Gaondi	1371				
				2	Maistri	1372				
				3	Mathadi	1373				
				4	Od	1374	Carpenters, masons, and turners.	D	20	Gaondi.
				5	Rajalu	1375				
				6	Sagar...	1376				
				7	Sakkadi	1377				
				8	Upparu	1378				

INDEX OF CASTES.—*Continued.*

Serial No.	Main Caste: Name	Population: Males	Population: Females	Sub-Caste: No.	Sub-Caste: Name	Consecutive number of Sub-caste	Hereditary or Traditional Occupation	Classification: Class	Classification: Group	Remarks
75	Gaondla	119,944	115,718	1	Ankalavaru	1379				
				2	Baistani	1380				
				3	Benkiavaru	1381				
				4	Beta	1382				
				5	Cheluru	1383				
				6	Chaolagaondla	1384				
				7	Chikka Elygeru	1385				
				8	Daruvala	1386				
				9	Erakuladevi	1387				
				10	Erra	1388				
				11	Gaodu	1389				
				12	Gaondla	1390				
				13	Gaondlavaru	1391				
				14	Idigai	1392				
				15	Irusalaru	1393				
				16	Kallal	1394				
				17	Kalnate	1395				
				18	Kandanu	1396				
				19	Kaundinya	1397				
				20	Lad	1398				
				21	Lingayet	1399				
				22	Macharadu	1400				
				23	Mamelu	1401				
				24	Muchikulu	1402	Distillers and Toddy-drawers.	D	36	
				25	Muyyalavaru	1403				
				26	Puribhya	1404				
				27	Racha	1405				
				28	Raja	1406				
				29	Rapati	1407				
				30	Rudra	1408				
				31	Sajjana	1409				
				32	Sara	1410				
				33	Sashi	1411				
				34	Seenalavaru	1412				
				35	Sendi	1413				
				36	Setti	1414				
				37	Sipaladavaru	1415				
				38	Solibasu	1416				
				39	Sunkadavaru	1417				
				40	Suntalavaru	1418				
				41	Surabandesavaram	1419				
				42	Telaga	1420				
				43	Tenugu Idigaru	1421				
				44	Tenugu Kallal	1422				
				45	Thalla	1423				
				46	Vibhuti	1424				
				47	Vintalavaru	1425				
76	Garodi	41	30	1	Garodi	1426	Jugglers, snake charmers, &c.	E	47	
77	Gayansagar	3	5	1	Gayansagar	1427	Devotees	B	6	
78	Ghasi H	15	6	1	Ghasi	1428	Traders.	C	14	
	J	13	13							
79	Ghisadi	770	792	1	Ghisadi	1429	Blacksmiths	D	19	
80	Goanese O	56	42	1	Goanese	1430	Christian converts	F	52	
81	Golak	90	118	1	Golak	1431	Writers	B	9	
82	Gond Gond	14,637	14,023	1	Assaigond	1432				
	H	4,737	4,598	2	Charadeo	1433				
				3	Darwe	1434				
				4	Gondmali	1435				
				5	Gondwar	1486				
				6	Goliwar	1437				
				7	Gondur	1438				
				8	Gori	1439				
				9	Kaplai	1440				
				10	Khathu	1441	Forest and hill tribes	A	4	
				11	Kolam	1442				
				12	Koilabhuti	1443				
				13	Korku	1444				
				14	Panchalu	1445				
				15	Pradhan	1446				
				16	Rajgond	1447				
				17	Sagaihar	1448				
				18	Sahadev	1449				
				19	Satdev	1450				
83	Gondarvandlu	4	6	1	Gondarvandlu	1451	Devotees	B	6	

INDEX OF CASTES.—*Continued.*

Serial No.	MAIN CASTE. Name.	Population. Males.	Population. Females.	SUB-CASTE. No.	SUB-CASTE. Name.	Consecutive number of Sub-caste.	Hereditary or Traditional Occupation.	Classification. Class.	Classification. Group.	Remarks.
84	Gondhadi	2,428	2,507	1	Govavud	1452				
				2	Gol	1453				
				3	Gondlavadu	1454	Musicians and ballad-reciters.	B	11	Gondhle.
				4	Idgaru	1455				
				5	Itaga	1456				
				6	Itgar	1457				
85	Gopal	1,489	1,335	1	Gopal	1458	Tumblers and acrobats ...	E	46	
86	Gosain	14,971	12,171	1	Anath	1459				
				2	Aradhana	1460				
				3	Aranana	1461				
				4	Badubhoonja... ...	1462				
				5	Barasgari	1463				
				6	Bhaelarji	1464				
				7	Bharatawaru ...	1465				
				8	Bharathi	1466				
				9	Bharatiwandlu ...	1467				
				10	Bhasmadari	1468				
				11	Brahma	1469				
				12	Daori	1470				
				13	Dharad	1471				
				14	Garan...	1472				
				15	Gari	1473				
				16	Giri	1474				
				17	Girihari	1475				
				18	Gorakh	1476				
				19	Gokurnath	1477				
				20	Gosain	1478				
				21	Gosayi	1479				
				22	Gudisala	1480				
				23	Jomul...	1481				
				24	Jongudi	1482				
				25	Kanphadai	1483				
				26	Katnataka	1484	Devotees	B	6	
				27	Kathri	1485				
				28	Kshatri	1486				
				29	Mahanth	1487				
				30	Mahedru	1488				
				31	Malduru	1489				
				32	Maletu	1490				
				33	Mehanat	1491				
				34	Nath	1492				
				35	Palaknad	1493				
				36	Panpat	1494				
				37	Paramahans	1495				
				38	Pari	1496				
				39	Paruvi	1497				
				40	Purangir	1498				
				41	Purani	1499				
				42	Puri	1500				
				43	Raghuvansi	1501				
				44	Sabaru	1502				
				45	Sadalu	1503				
				46	Sadanand	1504				
				47	Sadhu...	1505				
				48	Sahadev	1506				
				49	Siddulu	1507				
				50	Sundarya	1508				
				51	Thakurkund Gosain...	1509				
				52	Udasi	1510				
87	Gosika	734	666	1	Gosika...	1511	Devotees...	B	6	Gosiga, Gosigi.
88	Gotralavaru	4	3	1	Gotralavaru	1512				
89	Gujar ... H	775	729	1	Gujar	1513	Landholders	A	2a	
	J	270	243							
90	Gangadia	96	78	1	Gangadia	1514	Jugglers, snake charmers, animal exhibitors.	E	47	
				2	Puja	1515				
91	Gurao ... H	8,896	8,724	1	Gurao	1516	Temple servants ...	B	7	
	J	11	6							
92	Guruvaria	16	26	1	Guruvaria	1517				
93	Guzerati	302	237	1	Baleva	1518				
				2	Bhaisapuravaru ...	1519				
				3	Bhoyi...	1520	Traders	C	14	
				4	Guzerati	1521				
				5	Mahratti	1522				
				6	Moduni	1523				

INDEX OF CASTES.—*Continued.*

MAIN CASTE.				SUB-CASTE.						
Serial No.	Name.	Population. Males.	Population. Females.	No.	Name.	Consecutive number of Sub-caste.	Hereditary or Traditional Occupation.	Classification. Class.	Classification. Group.	Remarks.
94	Halgar	3	...	1	Halgar	1524	Musicians and ballad-reciters.	B	11	
95	Halwai	453	406	1	Halwai	1525	Grain parchers and confectioners.	D	22a	
				2	Parubiah	1526				
96	Hammal	108	70	1	Dhangar	1527	Carriers (1527–1529)	C	16	
				2	Hammal	1528				
				3	Pakanati	1529				
97	Hanigevaru	22	14	1	Hanigevaru	1530	Carpenters and turners	D	20	
98	Hatkar	8,843	3,706	1	Devangulu	1531	Weavers, calenderers, and dyers. (1531–1533)	D	23	
				2	Garukula	1532				
				3	Hatkar	1533				
99	Hindu (other)	34,124	32,798	1	Adiobaya	1534	Mixed Indian races (1534–1597)	F	49b	
				2	Agini	1535				
				3	Agra	1536				
				4	Ajajama	1537				
				5	Ajam	1538				
				6	Ajmere	1539				
				7	Akusi	1540				
				8	Anamtailu	1541				
				9	Analu	1542				
				10	Anayi	1543				
				11	Andara	1544				
				12	Arva	1545				
				13	Arialu	1546				
				14	Arkati	1547				
				15	Arutur	1548				
				16	Arya	1549				
				17	Asayun	1550				
				18	Atrasulu	1551				
				19	Avaduth	1552				
				20	Ayisli	1553				
				21	Babidi	1554				
				22	Baduga	1555				
				23	Bajarwad	1556				
				24	Baura	1557				
				25	Bajati	1558				
				26	Bajurangama	1559				
				27	Bakiri	1560				
				28	Balai	1561				
				29	Balaji	1562				
				30	Balumma	1563				
				31	Balvaha	1564				
				32	Balvanlu	1565				
				33	Banasi	1566				
				34	Bandi	1567				
				35	Barawadu	1568				
				36	Barusanayee	1569				
				37	Basva	1570				
				38	Bavudidaru	1571				
				39	Bedaru	1572				
				40	Bengali	1573				
				41	Besho	1574				
				42	Bhalwa	1575				
				43	Bhurati	1576				
				44	Bikari	1577				
				45	Bikshakulu	1578				
				46	Bolanadhu	1579				
				47	Boria	1580				
				48	Buthubaru	1581				
				49	Chakuli	1582				
				50	Chamulollu	1583				
				51	Chaorai	1584				
				52	Cheli	1585				
				53	Chikkalavadlu	1586				
				54	Chillarla	1587				
				55	Chiranjeevi	1588				
				56	Chirumjee	1589				
				57	Choudri	1590				
				58	Dagulu	1591				
				59	Dali	1592				
				60	Danamma	1593				
				61	Dara	1594				
				62	Daramsa	1595				
				63	Dasari	1596				
				64	Dasi	1597				

INDEX OF CASTES.—*Continued.*

MAIN CASTE.				SUB-CASTE.		Consecutive number of Sub-caste.	Hereditary or Traditional Occupation.	CLASSIFICATION.		REMARKS.
Serial No.	Name.	Population. Males.	Population. Females.	No.	Name.			Class.	Group.	
99	Hindu (other).—*contd.*	......	......	65	Davudi	1598				
				66	Deccani	1599				
				67	Deegarusar	1600				
				68	Dejakani	1601				
				69	Devasidhi	1602				
				70	Dhadaru	1603				
				71	Dhakarya	1604				
				72	Dhanikulam	1605				
				73	Dhokaru	1606				
				74	Dhohi	1607				
				75	Dobiri...	1608				
				76	Dokal	1609				
				77	Doraivadu	1610				
				78	Ellapula	1611				
				79	Erukati	1612				
				80	Erushakulu	1613				
				81	Eupra...	1614				
				82	Gadaba	1615				
				83	Gadarulu	1616				
				84	Gadaparuvalu ...	1617				
				85	Gadda...	1618				
				86	Gadli	1619				
				87	Gadumoru	1620				
				88	Ganam	1621				
				89	Gatraliya	1622				
				90	Gujuruvad	1623				
				91	Gajasi...	1624				
				92	Gajulollu	1625				
				93	Gajumeen	1626				
				94	Galawar	1627				
				95	Gathari	1628				
				96	Gamin	1629				
				97	Ganum	1630				
				98	Gaoral	1631				
				99	Garga...	1632				
				100	Garudvar	1633				
				101	Garya...	1634				
				102	Gatralya	1635				
				103	Gharavadu	1636	Mixed Indian races ...	F	49b	
				104	Gnanasagar	1637				
				105	Godaru	1638				
				106	Gonvaru	1639				
				107	Gorvi	1640				
				108	Gosangi	1641				
				109	Gotalvadu	1642				
				110	Gotunarai	1643				
				111	Govahari	1644				
				112	Gudidai	1645				
				113	Gudla...	1646				
				114	Gurumukhi	1647				
				115	Gurunanak	1648				
				116	Hajari	1649				
				117	Hakimdevi	1650				
				118	Hamandev	1651				
				119	Harihar	1652				
				120	Harimat	1653				
				121	Harkari	1654				
				122	Hela	1655				
				123	Helavadu	1656				
				124	Helavaru	1657				
				125	Hindivi Madrasi ...	1658				
				126	Hindu...	1659				
				127	Hindustani	1660				
				128	Jagar...	1661				
				129	Jakkani	1662				
				130	Jalla	1663				
				131	Jamani	1664				
				132	Janudari	1665				
				133	Jangaru	1666				
				134	Jantavala	1667				
				135	Jarubashu	1668				
				136	Jentu	1669				
				137	Jesvadu	1670				
				138	Jhatgaru	1671				
				139	Jikki	1672				
				140	Jikkulu	1673				
				141	Jogi	1674				
				142	Juttu	1675				

INDEX OF CASTES.—*Continued.*

Main Caste: Serial No.	Main Caste: Name.	Population: Males.	Population: Females.	Sub-Caste: No.	Sub-Caste: Name.	Consecutive number of Sub-caste.	Hereditary or Traditional Occupation.	Classification: Class.	Classification: Group.	Remarks.
99	Hindu (other),—*contd.*	......	......	143	Kachar	1676				
				144	Kadam	1677				
				145	Khiavatuli	1678				
				146	Kaiyagadi	1679				
				147	Kakar	1680				
				148	Kakaria	1681				
				149	Kakkila	1682				
				150	Kakonja	1683				
				151	Kalbaru	1684				
				152	Kallar	1685				
				153	Kaluju	1686				
				154	Kamal	1687				
				155	Kamlar	1688				
				156	Kanilavala	1689				
				157	Kandagoora	1690				
				158	Kankan	1691				
				159	Karagiru	1692				
				160	Karancha	1693				
				161	Karagulu	1694				
				162	Karaguru	1695				
				163	Karwali	1696				
				164	Karayet	1697				
				165	Karnataku	1698				
				166	Karuka	1699				
				167	Kasa	1700				
				168	Kashiri	1701				
				169	Kathri	1702				
				170	Kattakulam	1703				
				171	Katoli...	1704				
				172	Kavala	1705				
				173	Kayadi	1706				
				174	Keevatu	1707				
				175	Khatia	1708				
				176	Kodipilaya	1709				
				177	Kojya...	1710				
				178	Kooka	1711				
				179	Korakunadhu ...	1712				
				180	Koral...	1713				
				181	Kotia...	1714				
				182	Kunupasayce... ...	1715	Mixed Indian races ...	F	49b	
				183	Kunapuli	1716				
				184	Ladri	1717				
				185	Lagarubhu	1718				
				186	Lakari	1719				
				187	Landri	1720				
				188	Mabasugoti	1721				
				189	Mahabiru	1722				
				190	Mahajawa	1723				
				191	Mahindru	1724				
				192	Maheswara	1725				
				193	Malgaru	1726				
				194	Malyatan	1727				
				195	Mankabavalu ...	1728				
				196	Mara	1729				
				197	Mari	1730				
				198	Marli	1731				
				199	Masi	1732				
				200	Maspi...	1733				
				201	Medaru	1734				
				202	Mirajan	1735				
				203	Monda	1736				
				204	Mushini	1737				
				205	Nadgudda	1738				
				206	Nagaralu	1739				
				207	Nagiri...	1740				
				208	Nagasam	1741				
				209	Naguru	1742				
				210	Nalasha	1743				
				211	Namadari	1744				
				212	Namberu	1745				
				213	Nanakshah	1746				
				214	Nanjabi	1747				
				215	Nanuk	1748				
				216	Navidan	1749				
				217	Neelabandukulam ...	1750				
				218	Neevari	1751				
				219	Noyini	1752				
				220	Odhmat	1753				

INDEX OF CASTES.—*Continued.*

MAIN CASTE.				SUB-CASTE.		Consecutive number of Sub-caste.	Hereditary or Traditional Occupation.	CLASSIFICATION.		REMARKS.
Serial No.	Name.	POPULATION.		No.	Name.			Class.	Group.	
		Males.	Females.							
99	Hindu (other).—*contd.*	......	......	221	Padavakulam ...	1754				
				222	Pajagaru	1755				
				223	Palahar	1756				
				224	Panchan	1757				
				225	Pandaram	1758				
				226	Panjamaru	1759				
				227	Panvari	1760				
				228	Panvaru	1761				
				229	Paramgandi	1762				
				230	Pathiwad	1763				
				231	Pariki...	1764				
				232	Parra	1765				
				233	Parukatuwadu ...	1766				
				234	Pasi	1767				
				235	Payasu	1768				
				236	Perika	1769				
				237	Phakira	1770				
				238	Pharamur	1771				
				239	Pochal	1772				
				240	Podapatri	1773				
				241	Pujari	1774				
				242	Puloosu	1775				
				243	Rabhi...	1776				
				244	Rahurasu	1777				
				245	Rajulu	1778				
				246	Ralitu...	1779				
				247	Ravatu	1780				
				248	Rayalooroo	1781				
				249	Rayudu	1782				
				250	Sadarahu	1783				
				251	Sadi	1784				
				252	Sagarlu	1785				
				253	Sakta	1786				
				254	Sakusati	1787				
				255	Sala	1788				
				256	Samali	1789				
				257	Sampenga	1790				
				258	Sanadu	1791				
				259	Sangari	1792				
				260	Sangopi	1793	Mixed Indian races ...	F	49b	
				261	Sanguadi	1794				
				262	Sarabjee	1795				
				263	Saradi	1796				
				264	Saravala	1797				
				265	Sarla	1798				
				266	Sarrapu	1799				
				267	Savakulu	1800				
				268	Sayaru	1801				
				269	Sejeel	1802				
				270	Sejlda	1803				
				271	Shadaru	1804				
				272	Shahiri	1805				
				273	Sheerni	1806				
				274	Sheevukani	1807				
				275	Shiri	1808				
				276	Sidhihamsi	1809				
				277	Siranai	1810				
				278	Siva	1811				
				279	Sivabaktulu	1812				
				280	Sivamatum	1813				
				281	Sivi	1814				
				282	Sivu	1815				
				283	Sivudarsi	1816				
				284	Somasi	1817				
				285	Somatu	1818				
				286	Sreemankasakoti ...	1819				
				287	Sudaruvadu	1820				
				288	Sudra	1821				
				289	Taljari	1822				
				290	Tamilparaya	1823				
				291	Tandi...	1824				
				292	Tandra	1825				
				293	Tanugan	1826				
				294	Tarumal	1827				
				295	Tattu	1828				
				296	Tellageera	1829				
				297	Tirumalavaru ...	1830				
				298	Tirumandara... ...	1831				

INDEX OF CASTES.—*Continued.*

MAIN CASTE.				SUB-CASTE.				CLASSIFICATION.		
Serial No.	Name.	Population. Males.	Females.	No.	Name.	Consecutive number of Sub-caste.	Hereditary or Traditional Occupation.	Class.	Group.	Remarks.
99	Hindu (other).—*concld.*	...	...	299	Tivari... ...	1832				
				300	Tonara ...	1833				
				301	Tondamandal	1834				
				302	Tonier ...	1835				
				303	Totula... ...	1836				
				304	Usirai... ...	1837				
				305	Vagaryavu ...	1838				
				306	Valisugriva ...	1839				
				307	Valuru ...	1840	Mixed Indian races ...	F	49b	
				308	Varia	1841				
				309	Vatuni ...	1842				
				310	Vayateeru ...	1843				
				311	Veladivandlu	1844				
				312	Venki... ...	1845				
				313	Voshukal ...	1846				
				314	Vuradi ...	1847				
				315	Yadagiri ...	1848				
				316	Yenkutramulu	1849				
100	Irani	37	12	1	Ajami ...	1850				
				2	Irani	1851	Non-Indian Asiatic races.	F	48	
				3	Shia	1852				
101	Jain...	6,877	6,146	1	Asaival ...	1853				
				2	Avusa ...	1854				
				3	Bari	1855				
				4	Baroval ...	1856				
				5	Bedagaru ...	1857				
				6	Bijalajapu ...	1858				
				7	Bogaru ...	1859				
				8	Desalakshanam	1860				
				9	Devabrahmana	1861				
				10	Digambar ...	1862				
				11	Duruvaru ...	1863				
				12	Haru	1864				
				13	Jagnivandlu ...	1865	Mixed Indian races ...	F	49b	
				14	Jain	1866				
				15	Kamboji ...	1867				
				16	Kshatri ...	1868				
				17	Kuruvad ...	1869				
				18	Naramani ...	1870				
				19	Paraval ...	1871				
				20	Pratuvadu ...	1872				
				21	Puruvaru ...	1873				
				22	Pusalavandlu	1874				
				23	Satanaru ...	1875				
				24	Somavamsa ...	1876				
				25	Sravaku ...	1877				
102	Janapa	9	7	1	Janapa ...	1878	Mixed Indian races ...	F	49b	
103	Jangam	52,684	52,688	1	Abidar ...	1879				
				2	Achariapatha...	1880				
				3	Aigodu ...	1881				
				4	Apaiwar ...	1882				
				5	Balija	1883				
				6	Balijar ...	1884				
				7	Banya ...	1885				
				8	Basaru ...	1886				
				9	Boda	1887				
				10	Budigai ...	1888				
				11	Damgari ...	1889				
				12	Desanti ...	1890				
				13	Deva	1891				
				14	Devangulu ...	1892	Priests	B	5	
				15	Dkshabaliki ...	1893				
				16	Dishahotai ...	1894				
				17	Gnanajungam	1895				
				18	Gruhastulu ...	1896				
				19	Gudisa ...	1897				
				20	Hulkani ...	1898				
				21	Iswara ...	1899				
				22	Jodunalingi ...	1900				
				23	Jakari ...	1901				
				24	Jangamagruhastulu...	1902				
				25	Jangam ...	1903				
				26	Jurli... ...	1904				

INDEX OF CASTES.—*Continued.*

MAIN CASTE.				SUB-CASTE.		Consecutive number of Sub-caste.	Hereditary or Traditional Occupation.	CLASSIFICATION.		REMARKS.
Serial No.	Name.	POPULATION. Males.	POPULATION. Females.	No.	Name.			Class.	Group.	
103	Jangam.—*concld.*	......	......	27	Khadavavolai	1905				
				28	Khalgari	1906				
				29	Kharja	1907				
				30	Langadi Ayalu	1908				
				31	Lingajee Iyalu	1909				
				32	Lingam	1910				
				33	Lingavantulu	1911				
				34	Lingayet	1912				
				35	Madhuwats	1913				
				36	Madugari	1914				
				37	Madurey	1915				
				38	Maheswarulu	1916				
				39	Malachi	1917				
				40	Mathastulu	1918				
				41	Malajangam	1919				
				42	Malibaji	1920				
				43	Malivalbhakt	1921				
				44	Malpathi	1922				
				45	Maratha	1923				
				46	Matapathi	1924				
				47	Matavanmala	1925				
				48	Matamaiya	1926				
				49	Mattajungam	1927				
				50	Magisari	1928				
				51	Mrigendra	1929				
				52	Mudugari	1930				
				53	Muthanakadi	1931				
				54	Namadhari	1932				
				55	Namachagi	1933				
				56	Padadabaji	1934				
				57	Padadi	1935				
				58	Padavadabaji	1936				
				59	Parika	1937				
				60	Patki	1938				
				61	Phadal	1939				
				62	Rambagi	1940				
				63	Rasavaru	1941	Priests	B	5	
				64	Rasut	1942				
				65	Reddi	1943				
				66	Rudra	1944				
				67	Sanadoom	1945				
				68	Salai	1946				
				69	Sangeth	1947				
				70	Sankaraparai	1948				
				71	Sankarupadai	1949				
				72	Sangaduval	1950				
				73	Seelabadiki	1951				
				74	Seelavantulu	1952				
				75	Singadarwad	1953				
				76	Singadoolam	1954				
				77	Sistri	1955				
				78	Siryangam	1956				
				79	Sivabakht	1957				
				80	Sivadevangulu	1958				
				81	Sivajangam	1959				
				82	Sivamath	1960				
				83	Srijangam	1961				
				84	Sthalamu	1962				
				85	Sthavara	1963				
				86	Sukapathrai	1964				
				87	Sungadoom	1965				
				88	Surabhi	1966				
				89	Surali	1967				
				90	Surigivatu	1968				
				91	Surthi	1969				
				92	Survi	1970				
				93	Talunga	1971				
				94	Urijangam	1972				
				95	Vaduvaliki	1973				
				96	Vaishnava	1974				
				97	Vibhutidar	1975				
				98	Virabhadra	1976				
				99	Virasaivam	1977				
104	Jat ... H	188	107	1	Jat	1978	Landholders	A	2a	
	S	173	88	2	Jav	1979				
				3	Vahanhill	1980				
105	Jauhari	544	496	1	Jauhari	1981	Mixed Indian races	F	49b	Johari.

INDEX OF CASTES.—*Continued.*

Serial No.	MAIN CASTE. Name.	Population. Males.	Population. Females.	SUB-CASTE. No.	SUB-CASTE. Name.	Consecutive number of Sub-caste.	Hereditary or Traditional Occupation.	Classification. Class.	Classification. Group.	Remarks.
106	Jayarkhani	202	214	1	Jalgar	1982	Traders	C	14	
				2	Jangar	1983				
				3	Jari	1984				
				4	Jasoo	1985				
107	Jetty	301	318	1	Jatigaru	1986				
				2	Jetty	1987				
				3	Mallu	1988				
				4	Pahilvan	1989				
				5	Sadhanasu	1990				
108	Jew	10	16	1	Jew	1991	Non-Indian Asiatic races ...	F	48	
109	Jogi...	2,917	2,922	1	Jogeru...	1992	Devotees...	B	6	
				2	Jogi	1993				
				3	Kankop	1994				
				4	Meenagalavaru ...	1995				
				5	Mopaka Jogi	1996				
				6	Ramajogi	1997				
110	Josaputri	8	4	1	Josaputri	1998	Traders	C	14	
111	Joshi	966	955	1	Joshi	1999	Astrologers...	B	10	
112	Kachari	591	551	1	Kachari	2000	Glassworkers	D	29	
113	Kahar ... H	519	457	1	Basaloorn	2001	Fishermen, boatmen, Palki bearers, cooks, &c.	D	35	
	S	2	...	2	Basavapuri	2002				
				3	Basalorn	2003				
				4	Boyi	2004				
				5	Gaval	2005				
				6	Gondu	2006				
				7	Kahar H. S.	2007				
				8	Koli	2008				
				9	Lingayet	2009				
				10	Mahigir	2010				
				11	Mallavadu	2011				
				12	Mutrasi	2012				
				13	Neela...	2013				
				14	Parkati	2014				
				15	Parusukulu	2015				
				16	Sanni	2016				
				17	Vasthavad	2017				
114	Kaikadi	4,102	4,170	1	Boryavalai	2018	Mat-makers & cane splitters.	E	43	
				2	Barwal Vayuvad ...	2019				
				3	Chukkabotla... ...	2020				
				4	Chukkavandlu ...	2021				
				5	Gyavari	2022				
				6	Kaikadi	2023				
				7	Kaikavad	2024				
				8	Kalai	2025				
				9	Kamkai	2026				
				10	Kankayi	2027				
				11	Karasu	2028				
				12	Korusaru	2029				
				13	Kuruchala	2030				
				14	Kusari	2031				
				15	Masakavaru	2032				
				16	Paruverivad	2033				
				17	Sukkabuvad	2034				
115	Kallal ... H	24,757	24,408	1	Akularusha	2035	Distillers & Toddydrawers	D	36	
	J	31	37	2	Banwa	2036				
	M	7	8	3	Boodollu	2037				
				4	Charucharustaru ...	2038				
				5	Darmagaoda	2039				
				6	Ellagaondla	2040				
				7	Godu	2041				
				8	Jeeval	2042				
				9	Jeevaru	2043				
				10	Kadari	2044				
				11	Kallwar	2045				
				12	Kallal	2046				
				13	Kalvar	2047				
				14	Kapuskallal	2048				
				15	Katamayya	2049				
				16	Khilasaru	2050				

INDEX OF CASTES.—*Continued.*

MAIN CASTE.				SUB-CASTE.		Consecutive number of Sub-caste.	Hereditary or Traditional Occupation.	CLASSIFICATION.		REMARKS.
Serial No.	Name.	POPULATION, Males.	Females.	No.	Name.			Class.	Group.	
115	Kallal.—*concld.* ...	......	......	17	Kuruvagaondla ...	2051	Distillers & Toddydrawers	D	36	
				18	Lad	2052				
				19	Mahadevu	2053				
				20	Mamalairu	2054				
				21	Mamasula	2055				
				22	Matakanalu	2056				
				23	Munda	2057				
				24	Munnurwad	2058				
				25	Nakkavandlu... ...	2059				
				26	Padagal	2060				
				27	Paradesi	2061				
				28	Purubhla	2062				
				29	Rankallal	2063				
				30	Rudragaondla ...	2064				
				31	Sajjanapu	2065				
				32	Sativalai	2066				
				33	Setti	2067				
				34	Sikkolu	2068				
				35	Sindivalai	2069				
				36	Sivagaondla	2070				
				37	Smarthu	2071				
				38	Sudra	2072				
				39	Telanga	2073				
				40	Thagavalai	2074				
116	Kalsutri	195	174	1	Kalsutri	2075	Jugglers, snake charmers, and animal exhibitors.	E	47	
117	Kamati	45	25	1	Kamati	2076	Earth workers and stone-dressers.	E	41	
118	Kam Koli	2	......	1	Kam Koli	2077	Village watchmen ...	D	38a	
119	Kanchara	45	36	1	Bogar...	2078	Mat-makers and cane splitters.	E	43	Kanchawad.
				2	Bogur	2079				
				3	Chencharawad ...	2080				
				4	Kandagar	2081				
				5	Kanchari	2082				
				6	Mutrasi	2083				
				7	Kasar...	2084				
				8	Panchadai	2085				
				9	Panchal	2086				
120	Kannada	1,140	1,043	1	Balijavad	2087	Mixed Indian races ...	E	49b	
				2	Kannada	2088				
				3	Lingayet	2089				
				4	Pujari...	2090				
				5	Rajput	2091				
121	Kanjari	21	14	1	Kanjari	2092	Mat-makers and cane splitters.	D	43	
122	Kapu	626,539	607,391	1	Abadvad	2093	Landholders	A	2a	Kunbi.
				2	Achchhao	2094				
				3	Adava	2095				
				4	Adi	2096				
				5	Adkapu	2097				
				6	Adle	2098				
				7	Ahal	2099				
				8	Ahervad	2100				
				9	Ahnale	2101				
				10	Aide	2102				
				11	Akramase	2103				
				12	Alivad	2104				
				13	Anjulvad	2105				
				14	Ansitivar	2106				
				15	Aogi	2107				
				16	Apar	2108				
				17	Arayatha	2109				
				18	Are	2110				
				19	Arote	2111				
				20	Asal	2112				
				21	At	2113				
				22	Athva...	2114				
				23	Autad...	2115				
				24	Aval	2116				
				25	Awat	2117				
				26	Badeole	2118				
				27	Baglo	2119				
				28	Bairaval	2120				

INDEX OF CASTES.—*Continued.*

MAIN CASTE.				SUB-CASTE.		Consecutive number of Sub-caste.	Hereditary or Traditional Occupation.	CLASSIFICATION.		REMARKS.
Serial No.	Name.	POPULATION.		No.	Name.			Class.	Group.	
		Males.	Females.							
122	Kapu.—*contd.*	......	......	29	Balwantvad	2121				
				30	Banavad	2122				
				31	Barsevad	2123				
				32	Basiput	2124				
				33	Basmad	2125				
				34	Begvad	2126				
				35	Bhadge	2127				
				36	Bhairkapu	2128				
				37	Bhajgod	2129				
				38	Bhamat	2130				
				39	Bhanor	2131				
				40	Bharadi	2132				
				41	Bharol	2133				
				42	Bhatvad	2134				
				43	Bhavane	2135				
				44	Bhavesal	2136				
				45	Bhaval	2137				
				46	Bhavle	2138				
				47	Bhayadvad	2139				
				48	Bhimle	2140				
				49	Bhishia	2141				
				50	Bhitur	2142				
				51	Bhopi	2143				
				52	Bhororvad	2144				
				53	Bhoroti	2145				
				54	Bhosar	2146				
				55	Bhoval	2147				
				56	Bhuno	2148				
				57	Bhuti	2149				
				58	Bondhle	2150				
				59	Bukalvar	2151				
				60	Chakradavaru	2152				
				61	Chari	2153				
				62	Charkli	2154				
				63	Chatamata	2155				
				64	Chausari	2156				
				65	Chikde	2157				
				66	Chinakanti	2158				
				67	Chitapvad	2159				
				68	Chitkod	2160	Landholders	A	2a	Kunbi.
				69	Chitlavad	2161				
				70	Chitpal	2162				
				71	Chorvaonshi	2163				
				72	Chubal	2164				
				73	Dag	2165				
				74	Dagi	2166				
				75	Dakakar	2167				
				76	Dalve	2168				
				77	Dandinoru	2169				
				78	Dhamgear	2170				
				79	Dawau	2171				
				80	Dayayad	2172				
				81	Deore	2173				
				82	Deosal	2174				
				83	Devangi	2175				
				84	Devaraju	2176				
				85	Devatgeru	2177				
				86	Dhad	2178				
				87	Dhadalvad	2179				
				88	Dhadang	2180				
				89	Danoji	2181				
				90	Dhanor	2182				
				91	Dhapesi	2183				
				92	Dhatta	2184				
				93	Dhavai	2185				
				94	Dhulpavad	2186				
				95	Dhulwandar	2187				
				96	Dhumal	2188				
				97	Dilarvad	2189				
				98	Dimarvad	2190				
				99	Dinkar	2191				
				100	Dinkeli	2192				
				101	Divarle	2193				
				102	Dugal	2194				
				103	Gadanol	2195				
				104	Gantelavaru	2196				
				105	Gaoja	2197				
				106	Garasi	2198				

INDEX OF CASTES.—*Continued.*

MAIN CASTE.				SUB-CASTE.				CLASSIFICATION.		
Serial No.	Name.	POPULATION.		No.	Name.	Consecutive number of Sub-caste.	Hereditary or Traditional Occupation.	Class.	Group.	REMARKS.
		Males.	Females.							
122	Kapu.—*contd.* ...	......	......	107	Gatatri	2199				
				108	Gayavad	2200				
				109	Ghadge	2201				
				110	Gharpat	2202				
				111	Ghotole	2203				
				112	Ghatlavad	2204				
				113	Ghogri	2205				
				114	Ghosavad	2206				
				115	Gilvani	2207				
				116	Girali	2208				
				117	Girne	2209				
				118	Godadi...	2210				
				119	Golas	2211				
				120	Godekari	2212				
				121	Godloi	2213				
				122	Gogbanle	2214				
				123	Golkapu	2215				
				124	Golkor	2216				
				125	Golait...	2217				
				126	Gotar	2218				
				127	Gone Kapu	2219				
				128	Gonpat...	2220				
				129	Goralvad	2221				
				130	Gorati	2222				
				131	Gorevad	2223				
				132	Govar	2224				
				133	Gosani...	2225				
				134	Gurido...	2226				
				135	Gurka	2227				
				136	Guvadvad	2228				
				137	Hachal...	2229				
				138	Hadguralkar	2230				
				139	Haindri	2231				
				140	Haral	2232				
				141	Hardi	2233				
				142	Hatkakne	2234				
				143	Hazari	2235				
				144	Hingle	2236				
				145	Hitle	2237	Landholders	A	2a	Kunbi.
				146	Hugano	2238				
				147	Idle	2239				
				148	Idve	2240				
				149	Ingle......	2241				
				150	Irpael	2242				
				151	Ityal	2243				
				152	Jalai	2244				
				153	Jadval...	2245				
				154	Jagadmal	2246				
				155	Javar	2247				
				156	Jagdund	2248				
				157	Kabeli	2249				
				158	Kabhar	2250				
				159	Kadai	2251				
				160	Kadkar	2252				
				161	Kadle	2253				
				162	Kadse	2254				
				163	Kadu	2255				
				164	Kakde	2256				
				165	Kakne	2257				
				166	Kakvat...	2258				
				167	Kalyane	2259				
				168	Kamar...	2260				
				169	Kamo...	2261				
				170	Kanale...	2262				
				171	Kanavad	2263				
				172	Kanchi...	2264				
				173	Kanda	2265				
				174	Kandvi...	2266				
				175	Kanthibagi	2267				
				176	Kaple	2268				
				177	Karikal...	2269				
				178	Karku	2270				
				179	Katali	2271				
				180	Katati	2272				
				181	Katilkute	2273				
				182	Kathwas	2274				
				183	Khadalvar	2275				
				184	Khade	2276				

INDEX OF CASTES.—*Continued.*

MAIN CASTE.				SUB-CASTE.		Consecutive number of Sub-caste.	Hereditary or Traditional Occupation.	CLASSIFICATION.		REMARKS.
Serial No.	Name.	POPULATION.		No.	Name.			Class.	Group.	
		Males.	Females.							
122	Kapu.—*contd.*	......	......	185	Khalipo	2277				
				186	Khaludak	2278				
				187	Khandan	2279				
				188	Kharari	2280				
				189	Khaud	2281				
				190	Khel	2282				
				191	Khumal	2283				
				192	Kirikola	2284				
				193	Kisalvar	2285				
				194	Kobsadvaru	2286				
				195	Kodael	2287				
				196	Kodhle	2288				
				197	Kodide	2289				
				198	Kodikal	2290				
				199	Kodvakal	2291				
				200	Kolkadgi	2292				
				201	Kondalwaru	2293				
				202	Kouri	2294				
				203	Kopaskaute	2295				
				204	Kotlad	2296				
				205	Korudvad	2297				
				206	Kulwe	2298				
				207	Kunepal	2299				
				208	Kunkar	2300				
				209	Kurausheti	2301				
				210	Kurni	2302				
				211	Kurniyavaru	2303				
				212	Kushal	2304				
				213	Kutebal	2305				
				214	Kuveban	2306				
				215	Ladvan	2307				
				216	Lagad	2308				
				217	Laghaun	2309				
				218	Lakhe	2310				
				219	Lakmari	2311				
				220	Lalgoudu	2312				
				221	Loate	2313				
				222	Lokabadki	2314				
				223	Madak	2315	Landholders	A	2a	Kunbi.
				224	Made	2316				
				225	Madge	2317				
				226	Madhukar	2318				
				227	Madke	2319				
				228	Magli	2320				
				229	Mahevad	2321				
				230	Mahud	2322				
				231	Maikot	2323				
				232	Mairal	2324				
				233	Maitrani	2325				
				234	Makni	2326				
				235	Malbegi	2327				
				236	Malhari	2328				
				237	Manale	2329				
				238	Mane	2330				
				239	Manedvad	2331				
				240	Maneve	2332				
				241	Manod	2333				
				242	Maole	2334				
				243	Masevad	2335				
				244	Mashau	2336				
				245	Matmatkai	2337				
				246	Milbadki	2338				
				247	Mochal	2339				
				248	Mond	2340				
				249	Mondbal	2341				
				250	Motadvad	2342				
				251	More	2343				
				252	Motati	2344				
				253	Mothri	2345				
				254	Mule	2346				
				255	Mukhadi	2347				
				256	Munati	2348				
				257	Munnurvad	2349				
				258	Mushti	2350				
				259	Muttinipende	2351				
				260	Nagdad	2352				
				261	Nagri	2353				
				262	Nakarle	2354				

INDEX OF CASTES.—*Continued.*

Main Caste: Serial No.	Main Caste: Name	Population: Males	Population: Females	Sub-Caste: No.	Sub-Caste: Name	Consecutive number of Sub-caste	Hereditary or Traditional Occupation	Classification: Class	Classification: Group	Remarks
122	Kapu.—*contd*, ...	......	......	263	Nakod...	2355				
				264	Narda ...	2356				
				265	Narwal	2357				
				266	Nati Kunbi	2358				
				267	Naur ...	2359				
				268	Neyapu	2360				
				269	Nidole ...	2361				
				270	Nilevar	2362				
				271	Nilkantnoda	2363				
				272	Nirvate	2364				
				273	Odkari	2365				
				274	Pachhte	2366				
				275	Pàchikadvad	2367				
				276	Padad	2368				
				277	Padamvad	2369				
				278	Padwalbagi	2370				
				279	Pairadu	2371				
				280	Paknati	2372				
				281	Palamunural	2373				
				282	Pangal	2374				
				283	Panmod	2375				
				284	Paralwal	2376				
				285	Pasodni	2377				
				286	Parkevar	2378				
				287	Parmavad	2379				
				288	Parvad	2380				
				289	Patal ...	2381				
				290	Patansetti	2382				
				291	Patkar	2383				
				292	Patti ...	2384				
				293	Patyar	2385				
				294	Pedakanti	2386				
				295	Phadao	2387				
				296	Phadsi...	2388				
				297	Phaked	2389				
				298	Phakre	2390				
				299	Pikarad	2391				
				300	Pile ...	2392				
				301	Rahidvad	2393				
				302	Rajgona	2394	Landholders	A	2a	Kunbi.
				303	Ranal ...	2395				
				304	Rane ...	2396				
				305	Ranke	2397				
				306	Raol ...	2398				
				307	Raot ...	2399				
				308	Reddi ...	2400				
				309	Rogari...	2401				
				310	Rohidas	2402				
				311	Salonke	2403				
				312	Saghban	2404				
				313	Saitvar	2405				
				314	Sakri ...	2406				
				315	Sanam	2407				
				316	Sanami	2408				
				317	Sangalvad	2409				
				318	Sangpal...	2410				
				319	Sankar...	2411				
				320	Sarke ...	2412				
				321	Sarsude	2413				
				322	Satar ...	2414				
				323	Satkut...	2415				
				324	Savan	2416				
				325	Savli ...	2417				
				326	Serol ...	2418				
				327	Setsainavad	2419				
				328	Shetve...	2420				
				329	Sigarvad	2421				
				330	Silbadki	2422				
				331	Sirsat ...	2423				
				332	Sirmani	2424				
				333	Sirur ...	2425				
				334	Sodle ...	2426				
				335	Sogal ...	2427				
				336	Sokal ...	2428				
				337	Sond ...	2429				
				338	Surialad	2430				
				339	Sutni ...	2431				
				340	Suvase	2432				
				341	Tal ...	2433				

INDEX OF CASTES.—*Continued.*

Serial No.	Main Caste Name		Population Males	Population Females	Sub-caste No.	Sub-caste Name	Consecutive number of Sub-caste	Hereditary or Traditional Occupation	Class	Group	Remarks
122	Kapu.—*concld.* ...		......	......	342	Tarti	2434	Landholders	A	2a	
					343	Tatavad	2435				
					344	Thating	2436				
					345	Tidan...	2437				
					346	Tidbuj	2438				
					347	Tilvar	2439				
					348	Tilvan	2440				
					349	Tikhali	2441				
					350	Tikun...	2442				
					351	Tilane...	2443				
					352	Tirad	2444				
					353	Tirak	2445				
					354	Todwe	2446				
					355	Tolse	2447				
					356	Urauseti	2448				
					357	Vadkar	2449				
					358	Vadmayad	2450				
					359	Vadud	2451				
					360	Vaghe	2452				
					361	Vahilevar	2453				
					362	Vakkalgri	2454				
					363	Valbalkri	2455				
					364	Valvale	2456				
					365	Vange	2457				
					366	Vanjal	2458				
					367	Vansri	2459				
					368	Vari	2460				
					369	Vartad	2461				
					370	Vashadu	2462				
					371	Vatwan	2463				
					372	Yadao...	2464				
					673	Yaravar	2465				
					374	Yara Kunbi	2466				
					375	Yeradvar	2467				
123	Kapur		7	5	1	Kapur	2468	Traders	C	14	
124	Kasai ...	H	3,932	3,749	1	Arai	2469	Butchers...	D	87	
		M	339	338	2	Araikatika	2470				
					3	Bakar...	2471				
					4	Bakrakasai	2472				
					5	Bakrahsabu	2473				
					6	Gonkaru	2474				
					7	Kasai	2475				
					8	Katak...	2476				
					9	Katikai	2477				
					10	Kathikelu	2478				
					11	Lad	2479				
					12	Ladkasab	2480				
					13	Madia	2481				
					14	Mahratha	2482				
					15	Marikudi	2483				
					16	Sara	2484				
					17	Tandi...	2485				
125	Kasar ...	H	9,174	8,666	1	Janjarwar	2486	Brass & copper smiths ...	D	21	
		J	842	820	2	Kasaivad	2487				
					3	Kasar	2488				
					4	Kanjarvar	2489				
					5	Loga	2490				
					6	Phairkasar	2491				
					7	Vathari	2492				
126	Kassad		393	358	1	Kassad	2493	Traders	C	14	
127	Katari		55	44	1	Katari	2494	Leather workers	D	28	
128	Katchigandi		128	123	1	Dan	2495	Perfumers, drug preparers, betel-leaf sellers.	D	22b	
					2	Dayala	2496				
					3	Katchigandi	2497				
					4	Karnasindhulu ...	2498				
					5	Maridulvadu... ...	2499				
					6	Mundulvad	2500				
					7	Vayi	2501				
129	Katik ...	H	1,287	1,265	1	Katkar	2502				
		M	57	56	2	Katkod	2503				
					3	Kathodvad	2504				
					4	Katik	2505				

INDEX OF CASTES.—*Continued.*

MAIN CASTE.				SUB-CASTE.		Consecutive number of Sub-caste.	Hereditary or Traditional Occupation.	CLASSIFICATION.		REMARKS.
Serial No.	Name.	POPULATION.		No.	Name.			Class.	Group.	
		Males.	Females.							
130	Katipapa	116	158	1	Kallapulu	2506	Jugglers, snake charmers, and animal exhibitors.	E	47	
				2	Katipapa	2507				
				3	Katisidaru	2508				
131	Kayasth	1,697	1,536	1	Bhatubai	2509	Writers	B	9	
				2	Godu	2510				
				3	Kayasth	2511				
				4	Maskani	2512				
				5	Mathur	2513				
				6	Pharkayesth	2514				
				7	Sakseni	2515				
				8	Sribasha	2516				
				9	Sribashthum	2517				
				10	Srivayastam	2518				
132	Khatri ... H	4,769	4,330	1	Basana	2519	Weavers, calenderers and dyers.	D	23	
	J	1	...	2	Bidaruvanu	2520				
	S	15	4	3	Hari	2521				
				4	Jopudi	2522				
				5	Kapuru	2523				
				6	Khathri	2524				
				7	Lingayet	2525				
				8	Muttaladasari ...	2526				
				9	Patukaru	2527				
				10	Rajput	2528				
				11	Rangureju	2529				
				12	Raya	2530				
				13	Talakuchandu ...	2531				
133	Kinnara	9	11	1	Kinnara	2532	Musicians and ballad reciters.	B	11	
134	Kirajgar	110	103	1	Kirajgar	2533	Blacksmiths	D	19	
135	Koli	135,297	134,911	1	Adari Bhoyi	2534	Graziers	A	2b	Kohli.
				2	Adhavan	2535				
				3	Adubhogu	2536				
				4	Agiavaru	2537				
				5	Agiwalla	2538				
				6	Akuvaru	2539				
				7	Annasathru	2540				
				8	Balubanadhu... ...	2541				
				9	Banalavaru	2542				
				10	Banovaru	2543				
				11	Barabadunulu ...	2544				
				12	Baruvana	2545				
				13	Biluvaru	2546				
				14	Bamalavaru	2547				
				15	Boyi	2548				
				16	Budilavaru	2549				
				17	Chagalaru	2550				
				18	Chalamanavaru ...	2551				
				19	Chaliavaru	2552				
				20	Chatalavaru	2553				
				21	Chiginivaru	2554				
				22	Chinagalavaru ...	2555				
				23	Dabiri...	2556				
				24	Dadiganavaru ...	2557				
				25	Dagidavalai	2558				
				26	Danaibilavaru ...	2559				
				27	Danasabaru	2560				
				28	Dasari...	2561				
				29	Devaku	2562				
				30	Dhobi	2563				
				31	Diogihogi	2564				
				32	Elijogi	2565				
				33	Gadalakoru	2566				
				34	Gadivadivi	2567				
				35	Gahavaru	2568				
				36	Galewar	2569				
				37	Gangapathru... ...	2570				
				38	Gasavagaru	2571				
				39	Gatal	2572				
				40	Gatalakoru	2573				
				41	Gataroola	2574				
				42	Gatasalaru	2575				
				43	Gatithivaru	2576				
				44	Gayar	2577				
				45	Godanavaru	2578				

INDEX OF CASTES.—*Continued.*

MAIN CASTE.				SUB-CASTE.		Consecutive number of Sub-caste.	Hereditary or Traditional Occupation.	CLASSIFICATION.		REMARKS.
Serial No.	Name.	POPULATION.		No.	Name.			Class.	Group.	
		Males.	Females.							
135	Koli.—*contd.* ...	......	......	46	Gollaru	2579	Graziers	A	2b	Kohli.
				47	Gosalavaru	2580				
				48	Govurdhanagni ...	2581				
				49	Gujalavaru	2582				
				50	Gungaval	2583				
				51	Guntalavaru	2584				
				52	Hagabali	2585				
				53	Hagadu	2586				
				54	Hagavaru	2587				
				55	Haggadavaru ...	2588				
				56	Hojamajal	2589				
				57	Halsethbil	2590				
				58	Hanakaru	2591				
				59	Hankooroo	2592				
				60	Harubahuru	2593				
				61	Hatkar	2594				
				62	Inchivalai	2595				
				63	Irilaru...	2596				
				64	Javaku	2597				
				65	Kabelu	2598				
				66	Kaduvanthi	2599				
				67	Kalanian	2600				
				68	Kalan	2601				
				69	Kallati	2602				
				70	Kamadijavalu ...	2603				
				71	Kanchani	2604				
				72	Karadalavadu ...	2605				
				73	Karadevru	2606				
				74	Karwan	2607				
				75	Karwankaru	2608				
				76	Kasthurivadu ...	2609				
				77	Kathalaru	2610				
				78	Kayabu	2611				
				79	Kenchalavaru ...	2612				
				80	Keru	2613				
				81	Khasaru	2614				
				82	Kolamvadu	2615				
				83	Kolan	2616				
				84	Koli...	2617				
				85	Kolum	2618				
				86	Korai	2619				
				87	Kshatri	2620				
				88	Kshatrivaru	2621				
				89	Kumbar	2622				
				90	Kurusaleru	2623				
				91	Lovaru	2624				
				92	Lingayet	2625				
				93	Madhunaku	2626				
				94	Mahadeva	2627				
				95	Malavaru	2628				
				96	Masavivaru	2629				
				97	Moogithi	2630				
				98	Munnurwad	2631				
				99	Muthrasi	2632				
				100	Namadaru	2633				
				101	Naravaru	2634				
				102	Navadivaru	2635				
				103	Nilabhoyi	2636				
				104	Pachana	2637				
				105	Padathinavaru ...	2638				
				106	Pagalavaru	2639				
				107	Pagarevaru	2640				
				108	Pashkali	2641				
				109	Patunar	2642				
				110	Patuvatiru	2643				
				111	Pomavaru	2644				
				112	Rabathuvanthu ...	2645				
				113	Rajamathi	2646				
				114	Sakanavaru	2647				
				115	Samalavaru	2648				
				116	Sanvaru	2649				
				117	Seduganagaru ...	2650				
				118	Setalu...	2651				
				119	Sindhivalai	2652				
				120	Singeru	2653				
				121	Sivamatham	2654				
				122	Sudalavanalu ...	2655				
				123	Sulthama	2656				

INDEX OF CASTES.—*Continued.*

Serial No.	Main Caste Name.	Population Males.	Population Females.	Sub-caste No.	Sub-caste Name.	Consecutive number of Sub-caste.	Hereditary or Traditional Occupation.	Class.	Group.	Remarks.
135	Koli.—*concld.* ...	......	......	124	Suthunalaga	2657	Graziers	A	2b	Kohli.
				125	Tayanaku	2658				
				126	Telagakabiru... ...	2659				
				127	Telanga	2660				
				128	Tiathalavaru... ...	2661				
				129	Tukaru	2662				
				130	Vakalathasi	2663				
				131	Vathuni	2664				
136	Komati	108,111	104,754	1	Adgota	2665	Traders	C	14	
				2	Adhor...	2666				
				3	Adi	2667				
				4	Agar	2668				
				5	Alesbaie	2669				
				6	Apitdar	2670				
				7	Are	2671				
				8	Arva	2672				
				9	Atralkar	2673				
				10	Badavar	2674				
				11	Balevar	2675				
				12	Balvant	2676				
				13	Bandhuvad	2677				
				14	Banma	2678				
				15	Balurvad	2679				
				16	Bejabargi	2680				
				17	Bekadvad	2681				
				18	Bekam	2682				
				19	Bhanni Komti ...	2683				
				20	Bheri	2684				
				21	Butekar	2685				
				22	Chadarvad	2686				
				23	Chilkul	2687				
				24	Chitawbari	2688				
				25	Dadulvar	2689				
				26	Dagam	2690				
				27	Davasar	2691				
				28	Deochar	2692				
				29	Dikshavant	2693				
				30	Duvar	2694				
				31	Ganevar	2695				
				32	Ganti	2696				
				33	Ghisadvad	2697				
				34	Goara...	2698				
				35	Gojrati	2699				
				36	Gopevad	2700				
				37	Goshevad	2701				
				38	Goth	2702				
				39	Hari	2703				
				40	Jaisvar	2704				
				41	Janga	2705				
				42	Javari	2706				
				43	Jodevar	2707				
				44	Jovarpai	2708				
				45	Jutipao	2709				
				46	Kachevar	2710				
				47	Kadavatar	2711				
				48	Kadhurti	2712				
				49	Kalakomti	2713				
				50	Kauvant	2714				
				51	Kardani	2715				
				52	Karlevar	2716				
				53	Karve...	2717				
				54	Katepar	2718				
				55	Kochu	2719				
				56	Kokalvar	2720				
				57	Kokuti	2721				
				58	Korgir	2722				
				59	Kotulvar	2723				
				60	Kuchi...	2724				
				61	Lingayet	2725				
				62	Lovdnar	2726				
				63	Madana	2727				
				64	Mahasvas	2728				
				65	Maisri...	2729				
				66	Mamadvar	2730				
				67	Margalvad	2731				
				68	Mirvar	2732				
				69	Modgujrati	2733				

INDEX OF CASTES.—*Continued.*

MAIN CASTE.				SUB-CASTE.		Consecutive number of Sub-caste.	Hereditary or Traditional Occupation.	CLASSIFICATION.		REMARKS.
Serial No.	Name.	POPULATION.		No.	Name.			Class.	Group.	
		Males.	Females.							
136	Komati.—*concld.* ...	......	......	70	Mogunia	2734				
				71	Molbar	2735				
				72	Monevad	2736				
				73	Muratvan	2737				
				74	Neti	2738				
				75	Nakahat	2739				
				76	Padamvar	2740				
				77	Parakh	2741				
				78	Parasvar	2742				
				79	Paravar	2743				
				80	Patekar	2744				
				81	Pechari	2745				
				82	Peshtevar	2746				
				83	Piancvar	2747				
				84	Pichchu	2748				
				85	Pinnadvad	2749				
				86	Pimparvar	2750				
				87	Pitgol	2751				
				88	Paya	2752				
				89	Rajupa	2753				
				90	Raspak	2754				
				91	Rudrakanthi	2755				
				92	Saraji	2756				
				93	Saramvar	2757				
				94	Satgulvar	2758				
				95	Soevar	2759				
				96	Sojue	2760				
				97	Somasvar	2761				
				98	Somashetti	2762				
				99	Telang	2763	Traders	C	14	
				100	Tilevari	2764				
				101	Trivar	2765				
				102	Vadukal	2766				
				103	Vagan	2767				
				104	Vaghote	2768				
				105	Vahevar	2769				
				106	Vahit	2770				
				107	Vaisarga	2771				
				108	Vaishatvar	2772				
				109	Vakevar	2773				
				110	Varamvar	2774				
				111	Varde...	2775				
				112	Vasnaw	2776				
				113	Vatil	2777				
				114	Veshamma	2778				
				115	Virasevad	2779				
				116	Yaguvar	2780				
				117	Yallavar	2781				
				118	Yalgavia	2782				
				119	Yalni	2783				
				120	Yanna	2784				
				121	Yapakvar	2785				
				122	Yastasri	2786				
				123	Yeginavar	2787				
				124	Yeralshakh	2788				
				125	Yesakvar	2789				
				126	Yesan	2790				
137	Kommu	31	12	1	Kommu	2791	Weavers, calenderers and dyers.	D	23	
				2	Singadi	2792				
138	Korivi	416	392	1	Korivi...	2793	Mat-makers and cane splitters.	E	43	
139	Koya...	30,763	30,134	1	Alikoya	2794				
				2	Bunakoya	2795				
				3	Koya	2796	Forest and hill tribes. ...	A	4	
				4	Racha...	2797				
				5	Toolookoya	2798				
140	Kshatri ... H	10,006	9,047	1	Agarubansi	2799				
	S	22	8	2	Alevar	2800				
				3	Araku...	2801				
				4	Arya	2802				
				5	Babaniah	2803	Military and dominant...	A	1	
				6	Balharu	2804				
				7	Bharatha	2805				
				8	Bisan	2806				
				9	Bondaivandlu ...	2807				

INDEX OF CASTES.—*Continued.*

MAIN CASTE.				SUB-CASTE.		Consecutive number of Sub-caste.	Hereditary or Traditional Occupation.	CLASSIFICATION.		REMARKS.
Serial No.	Name.	POPULATION.		No.	Name.			Class.	Group.	
		Males.	Females.							
140	Kshatri.—*concld.* ...	......	......	10	Bondili	2808				
				11	Brahma Kshatri ...	2809				
				12	Chalaman	2810				
				13	Chandravamsi ...	2811				
				14	Chanbana Vaisya Thakur	2812				
				15	Chashu	2813				
				16	Chowsar	2814				
				17	Dalusingara	2815				
				18	Dhanuvar	2816				
				19	Dharum	2817				
				20	Dhilvar	2818				
				21	Gantama	2819				
				22	Gantama Thakur ...	2820				
				23	Gosaria	2821				
				24	Isapu	2822				
				25	Jeshtak	2823				
				26	Jivuvar	2824				
				27	Kachitakum	2825				
				28	Kadamba	2826				
				29	Kusalia	2827				
				30	Kshatri	2828				
				31	Lakuvar	2829				
				32	Mahadevu	2830				
				33	Maheri	2831				
				34	Mahratta	2832	Military and dominant ...	A	1	
				35	Namdeo	2833				
				36	Pesapur	2834				
				37	Rachu...	2835				
				38	Raghuvamsi	2836				
				39	Raja...	2837				
				40	Raja Bhattu	2838				
				41	Rajabonasi	2839				
				42	Rajakulam	2840				
				43	Rajapuvar	2841				
				44	Rajatoor	2842				
				45	Rajput	2843				
				46	Rakur	2844				
				47	Sanooran	2845				
				48	Soma	2846				
				49	Somak	2847				
				50	Somakshatri	2848				
				51	Somasi	2849				
				52	Somavamsam ...	2850				
				53	Suam	2851				
				54	Suryabansi	2852				
				55	Suria	2853				
				56	Swajabin	2854				
				57	Taluchand	2855				
				58	Talukchand	2856				
				59	Vaishnava	2857				
141	Kulugapiyar ...	7	9	1	Kulugapiyar	2858	Temple servants	B	7	
142	Kulpand	6	4	1	Kulpand	2859	Priests	B	6	
143	Kummari	54,709	52,306	1	Basamadari	2860				
				2	Chakimahana ...	2861				
				3	Cheetu	2862				
				4	Chilka	2863				
				5	Darusarulollu ...	2864				
				6	Deekshap	2865				
				7	Golconda	2866				
				8	Gori	2867				
				9	Gundala	2868				
				10	Jagumbansu	2869				
				11	Julai	2870				
				12	Kandulu	2871	Potters	D	28	Kumbar.
				13	Katapatta	2872				
				14	Kalalavad	2873				
				15	Kummari	2874				
				16	Lad	2875				
				17	Lingayet	2876				
				18	Lookabaliki	2877				
				19	Madda...	2878				
				20	Marikidi	2879				
				21	Matti	2880				
				22	Parudesi	2881				

INDEX OF CASTES.—*Continued.*

INDEX OF CASTES.—*Continued.*

MAIN CASTE.				SUB-CASTE.		Consecutive number of Sub-caste.	Hereditary or Traditional Occupation.	CLASSIFICATION.		REMARKS.
Serial No.	Name.	POPULATION.		No.	Name.			Class.	Group.	
		Males.	Females.							
148	Lamani.—*contd.* ...	......	......	42	Bookia	2955	Carriers	C	16	Lambadi.
				43	Boopia	2956				
				44	Boosia...	2957				
				45	Borata	2958				
				46	Budata	2959				
				47	Budia...	2960				
				48	Budbida	2961				
				49	Bukia...	2962				
				50	Bukka...	2963				
				51	Bukkermavati ..	2964				
				52	Burai	2965				
				53	Burujala	2966				
				54	Chadavat	2967				
				55	Chakamuda	2968				
				56	Charan	2969				
				57	Chatavat	2970				
				58	Chavan	2971				
				59	Choorvam	2972				
				60	Dachat	2973				
				61	Danavantu	2974				
				62	Dari	2975				
				63	Delavatu	2976				
				64	Denakavatu	2977				
				65	Desavantu	2978				
				66	Dharavatu	2979				
				67	Devastu	2980				
				68	Devavatu	2981				
				69	Dikshavantu	2982				
				70	Doravat	2983				
				71	Dulparajullatu ...	2984				
				72	Ebavari	2985				
				73	Ekuman	2986				
				74	Elavati	2987				
				75	Elavat	2988				
				76	Gangamomu	2989				
				77	Gogulat	2990				
				78	Gogulati	2991				
				79	Golavath	2992				
				80	Gomat	2993				
				81	Goosuladu	2994				
				82	Gujiyadi	2995				
				83	Gugulavat	2996				
				84	Gujulaya	2997				
				85	Gulavat	2998				
				86	Gundaro'u	2999				
				87	Gumulavat	3000				
				88	Hajam	3001				
				89	Harabathu	3002				
				90	Hingulavatu	3003				
				91	Inavat	3004				
				92	Indavatu	3005				
				93	Isulavatu	3006				
				94	Jakia	3007				
				95	Jaivantu	3008				
				96	Jalavat	3009				
				97	Janasavaru	3010				
				98	Janavantu	3011				
				99	Janavaru	3012				
				100	Jandaworu	3013				
				101	Jarujala	3014				
				102	Jhatavat	3015				
				103	Jhatod...	3016				
				104	Jojhavat	3017				
				105	Kadabayya	3018				
				106	Kadvaru	3019				
				107	Kadavat	3020				
				108	Kalavant	3021				
				109	Kannojia	3022				
				110	Karraya	3023				
				111	Kasamar	3024				
				112	Katavaru	3025				
				113	Katavat	3026				
				114	Katravatu	3027				
				115	Katuroju	3028				
				116	Kayaruvat	3029				
				117	Kedavat	3030				
				118	Ketuvarum	3031				
				119	Koraivad	3032				

INDEX OF CASTES.—*Continued.*

MAIN CASTE.				SUB-CASTE.				Classification.		
Serial No.	Name.	Population. Males.	Females.	No.	Name.	Consecutive number of Sub-caste.	Hereditary or Traditional Occupation.	Class.	Group.	Remarks.
148	Lamani.—*contd.* ...	...	...	120	Kosi ...	3033				
				121	Kotra ...	3034				
				122	Kusari	3035				
				123	Labalyava	3036				
				124	Lagavatu	3037				
				125	Lakavantu	3038				
				126	Lamani	3039				
				127	Lambadi	3040				
				128	Lavalia	3041				
				129	Lavonvatu	3042				
				130	Lavudia	3043				
				131	Lavuria	3044				
				132	Letavatu	3045				
				133	Mabhavatu	3046				
				134	Madhagat	3047				
				135	Madhumati	3048				
				136	Maluvai	3049				
				137	Manasavanta...	3050				
				138	Maulan	3051				
				139	Masala	3052				
				140	Meenavatu	3053				
				141	Meghavatu	3054				
				142	Modavantu	3055				
				143	Mood ...	3056				
				144	Moodha	3057				
				145	Moodigee	3058				
				146	Mooshu	3059				
				147	Motayat	3060				
				148	Mudya	3061				
				149	Mukkedoya	3062				
				150	Mulki ...	3063				
				151	Munavat	3064				
				152	Nanavatu	3065				
				153	Naorat	3066				
				154	Navaniya	3067				
				155	Padumalaya	3068				
				156	Pahatura	3069				
				157	Pamar	3070				
				158	Pohar ...	3071				
				159	Paomat	3072	Carriers	C	16	Lambadi.
				160	Pavasath	3073				
				161	Peishumar	3074				
				162	Peshavatu	3075				
				163	Pitugeru	3076				
				164	Pohar ...	3077				
				165	Poru ...	3078				
				166	Raboti...	3079				
				167	Radhavatu	3080				
				168	Rahabevadu	3081				
				169	Rajput	3082				
				170	Rama ...	3083				
				171	Ramagolu	3084				
				172	Ramava	3085				
				173	Ramavat	3086				
				174	Rambuvar	3087				
				175	Ransooru	3088				
				176	Rateli ...	3089				
				177	Rathod	3090				
				178	Relmath	3091				
				179	Rogavatu	3092				
				180	Sabhabhatu	3093				
				181	Sadavatu	3094				
				182	Sakavat	3095				
				183	Saknvantu	3096				
				184	Samvant	3097				
				185	Samyaru	3098				
				186	Sapavat	3099				
				187	Saravatu	3100				
				188	Saruagalu	3101				
				189	Saryi ...	3102				
				190	Sarvokal	3103				
				191	Seelavanthu	3104				
				192	Seerimandu	3105				
				193	Senayatu	3106				
				194	Sukalai	3107				
				195	Tandi ...	3108				
				196	Tejavatu	3109				
				197	Tejovatu	3110				

INDEX OF CASTES.—*Continued.*

Serial No.	Main Caste: Name.	Population: Males.	Population: Females.	Sub-Caste: No.	Sub-Caste: Name.	Consecutive number of Sub-caste.	Hereditary or Traditional Occupation.	Classification: Class.	Classification: Group.	Remarks.
148	Lamani.—*concld.* ...	...	...	198	Thavadu	3111				
				199	Thopiya	3112				
				200	Totubanjaru	3113				
				201	Tulija...	3114				
				202	Vacha...	3115				
				203	Vadia	3116				
				204	Vadili	3117				
				205	Vaditha	3118				
				206	Vadta	3119				
				207	Vadthia	3120				
				208	Vadutia	3121				
				209	Vániladu	3122	Carriers	C	16	Lambadi.
				210	Vanivaru	3123				
				211	Varathothu	3124				
				212	Varjia	3125				
				213	Vartan	3126				
				214	Varti	3127				
				215	Vartia...	3128				
				216	Varuvemavatu ...	3129				
				217	Vidukananevaru ...	3130				
				218	Visalayan	3131				
				219	Vuditiyan	3132				
149	Lingayet	49,055	48,477	1	Banjari	3133				
				2	Bargi	3134				
				3	Basavanasampradaya-ka	3135				
				4	Bejabali	3136				
				5	Bejabargi	3137				
				6	Bhasmadari	3138				
				7	Bhoswa	3139				
				8	Bijapali	3140				
				9	Cheelavantu	3141				
				10	Darji	3142				
				11	Devateli	3143				
				12	Dhobi	3144				
				13	Dikshvanth	3145				
				14	Gruhastulu	3146				
				15	Gujuvar	3147				
				16	Guru	3148				
				17	Hajam	3149				
				18	Hoosoova	3150				
				19	Jangam	3151				
				20	Kanada	3152				
				21	Karikula	3153				
				22	Karisatti	3154				
				23	Koosawa	3155				
				24	Kunbi...	3156				
				25	Lingadhari	3157				
				26	Lingangulu	3158				
				27	Lingaemgler	3159	Traders	C	4	
				28	Lingavanth	3160				
				29	Lingayet	3161				
				30	Lingayari	3162				
				31	Lingi	3163				
				32	Lokabadiki	3164				
				33	Maheswarulu... ...	3165				
				34	Malibagi	3166				
				35	Matumatu	3167				
				36	Matumatu Reddy ...	3168				
				37	Munnurvad	3169				
				38	Nagni...	3170				
				39	Padam	3171				
				40	Pakanati	3172				
				41	Palubagi	3173				
				42	Panchamasali ...	3174				
				43	Panchavani	3175				
				44	Pulari...	3176				
				45	Rachotu	3177				
				46	Reddi	3178				
				47	Sahari...	3179				
				48	Saivam	3180				
				49	Sajjan...	3181				
				50	Seelavantu	3182				
				51	Simpi	3183				
				52	Siva...	3184				
				53	Sivamatam	3185				
				54	Sivi	3186				

INDEX OF CASTES.—*Continued.*

MAIN CASTE.				SUB-CASTE.		Consecutive number of Sub-caste.	Hereditary or Traditional Occupation.	CLASSIFICATION.		REMARKS.
Serial No.	Name.	POPULATION. Males.	Females.	No.	Name.			Class.	Group.	
149	Lingayet.—*concld.* ...	......	......	55	Tandi	3187				
				56	Teli	3188				
				57	Upanabagi	3189				
				58	Vani	3190				
				59	Variku	3191				
				60	Varaswa	3192	Traders...	C	14	
				61	Vaswakangam ...	3193				
				62	Vasvakankam ...	3194				
				63	Virasaiva	3195				
				64	Zatvant	3196				
150	Lodha	1,968	1,851	1	Chakatukumodha ...	3197				
				2	Chareebha	3198				
				3	Gavalbansi	3199				
				4	Jahria...	3200				
				5	Jaria...	3201				
				6	Katia	3202	Military and dominant...	A	1	
				7	Lodha...	3203				
				8	Mahratta	3204				
				9	Naidu...	3205				
				10	Rajput	3206				
151	Lohar	30,708	29,196	1	Avatai	3207				
				2	Bailkadmar	3208				
				3	Bailu	3209				
				4	Baitu	3210				
				5	Dumalur	3211				
				6	Eginavar	3212				
				7	Guggila	3213				
				8	Jaria	3214				
				9	Kammari	3215				
				10	Kambar	3216				
				11	Kyada	3217				
				12	Lingayet	3218				
				13	Lohar...	3219				
				14	Manubrahmana ...	3220				
				15	Mattulantu	3221				
				16	Murakari	3222	Blacksmiths	D	19	Kammari.
				17	Panchadai	3223				
				18	Panchal	3224				
				19	Panchalaru	3225				
				20	Panchama	3226				
				21	Paradesi	3227				
				22	Pittalollu	3228				
				23	Rayi	3229				
				24	Saivam	3230				
				25	Siva	3231				
				26	Smarthu	3232				
				27	Ura	3233				
				28	Varnasunthari ...	3234				
				29	Viswabrahmana ...	3235				
				30	Viswakarma	3236				
				31	Yagilavar	3237				
152	Lonari	183	220	1	Lonari	3238	Salt, &c., workers... ...	D	30	
153	Manbhao ... H J	1,230 1	1,086 2	1	Manbhao	3239	Devotees	B	6	
154	Mahratta ... H J	494,710 5	474,630 4	1	Abidar	3240				
				2	Adhve	3241				
				3	Agadhi	3242				
				4	Agli	3243				
				5	Ahair	3244				
				6	Ahlo	3245				
				7	Alitikar	3246				
				8	Andhvan	3247				
				9	Angarvaha	3248				
				10	Anim...	3249	Military and dominant...	A	1	
				11	Anvar	3250				
				12	Are	3251				
				13	Arge	3252				
				14	Arya	3253				
				15	Asal	3254				
				16	Atri	3255				
				17	Anchekar	3256				
				18	Avali	3257				
				19	Babre	3258				

INDEX OF CASTES.—*Continued.*

Serial No.	MAIN CASTE. Name.	Population. Males.	Population. Females.	SUB-CASTE. No.	SUB-CASTE. Name.	Consecutive number of Sub-caste.	Hereditary or Traditional Occupation.	Classification. Class.	Classification. Group.	Remarks.
154	Mahratta.—*contd.* ...	......	......	20	Badgur	3259	Military and dominant ...	A	1	
				21	Badvan	3260				
				22	Bagar...	3261				
				23	Bagle	3262				
				24	Bahare	3263				
				25	Bakre...	3264				
				26	Bal	3265				
				27	Bale	3266				
				28	Balgoti	3267				
				29	Balkar	3268				
				30	Balve	3269				
				31	Baude...	3270				
				32	Baoli	3271				
				33	Baore	3272				
				34	Baphale	3273				
				35	Baramase	3274				
				36	Bardare	3275				
				37	Bargale	3276				
				38	Barkat	3277				
				39	Basar	3278				
				40	Basett...	3279				
				41	Basgad	3280				
				42	Basve...	3281				
				43	Bateri...	3282				
				44	Bavagre	3283				
				45	Bavapura	3284				
				46	Bekar...	3285				
				47	Belladoulu	3286				
				48	Bhadao	3287				
				49	Bhaire...	3288				
				50	Bhale	3289				
				51	Bhalke	3290				
				52	Bhaoke	3291				
				53	Bhaorak	3292				
				54	Bharave	3293				
				55	Bharvad	3294				
				56	Bhavale	3295				
				57	Bhavesi	3296				
				58	Bhavechar	3297				
				59	Bhosagar	3298				
				60	Bhosle...	3299				
				61	Bhubhal	3300				
				62	Bhugod	3301				
				63	Bhuke...	3302				
				64	Bhupal	3303				
				65	Bhupevar	3304				
				66	Bhusmat	3305				
				67	Bhutale	3306				
				68	Biltani	3307				
				69	Bimat...	3308				
				70	Birhadi	3309				
				71	Bokt	3310				
				72	Budhle	3311				
				73	Chadukal	3312				
				74	Changle	3313				
				75	Changul	3314				
				76	Chanhal	3315				
				77	Chankal	3316				
				78	Chaodhari	3317				
				79	Chaple	3318				
				80	Chapsinge	3319				
				81	Charvangi	3320				
				82	Chatai...	3321				
				83	Chaval	3322				
				84	Chavan	3323				
				85	Chhapre	3324				
				86	Chinchole	3325				
				87	Chitki...	3326				
				88	Chohan	3327				
				89	Dadge...	3328				
				90	Dagan	3329				
				91	Dagde...	3330				
				92	Dakar...	3331				
				93	Dakhne	3332				
				94	Dangve	3333				
				95	Daore...	3334				
				96	Davagir	3335				
				97	Daske...	3336				

INDEX OF CASTES.—*Continued.*

MAIN CASTE.				SUB-CASTE.		Consecutive number of Sub-caste.	Hereditary or Traditional Occupation.	CLASSIFICATION.		REMARKS.
Serial No.	Name.	POPULATION.		No.	Name.			Class.	Group.	
		Males.	Females.							
154	Mahratta.—*contd.*	......	......	98	Daree	3337				
				99	Davalkar	3338				
				100	Dayal	3339				
				101	Dhahanker	3340				
				102	Dhandi	3341				
				103	Dhanuj	3342				
				104	Dhaole	3343				
				105	Dhaonare	3344				
				106	Dhape	3345				
				107	Dharoti	3346				
				108	Dhasim	3347				
				109	Dhavan	3348				
				110	Dhomale	3349				
				111	Dokre	3350				
				112	Dongre	3351				
				113	Doshant	3352				
				114	Dubad	3353				
				115	Gabad	3354				
				116	Gade	3355				
				117	Gadike	3356				
				118	Gadvine	3357				
				119	Gaike	3358				
				120	Galkaput	3359				
				121	Galve	3360				
				122	Gangotri	3361				
				123	Gania	3362				
				124	Gaone	3363				
				125	Gaosi	3364				
				126	Garad	3365				
				127	Garikad	3366				
				128	Gayakvad	3367				
				129	Ghadge	3368				
				130	Ghagar	3369				
				131	Ghastsise	3370				
				132	Ghatte	3371				
				133	Ghatvale	3372				
				134	Ghoped	3373				
				135	Ghotak	3374				
				136	Giaramasi	3375	Military and dominant...	A	1	
				137	Gingne	3376				
				138	Gokule	3377				
				139	Gole	3378				
				140	Gotkar	3379				
				141	Goone	3380				
				142	Gorpade	3381				
				143	Gorud	3382				
				144	Got	3383				
				145	Gote	3384				
				146	Had	3385				
				147	Haladjole	3386				
				148	Halve	3387				
				149	Handelawaru	3388				
				150	Hare	3389				
				151	Hartake	3390				
				152	Hartal	3391				
				153	Havanjat	3392				
				154	Hendri Marathi	3393				
				155	Hingnere	3394				
				156	Holkar	3395				
				157	Icge	3396				
				158	Iche	3397				
				159	Ingle	3398				
				160	Isve	3399				
				161	Jabande	3400				
				162	Jabute	3401				
				163	Jadalval	3402				
				164	Jadho	3403				
				165	Jagdal	3404				
				166	Jagnab	3405				
				167	Jagtal	3406				
				168	Jagtap	3407				
				169	Jagthale	3408				
				170	Jakate	3409				
				171	Jakhle	3410				
				172	Jamale	3411				
				173	Janesari	3412				
				174	Janvare	3413				
				175	Jaole	3414				

INDEX OF CASTES.—*Continued.*

Serial No.	Main Caste: Name.	Population: Males.	Population: Females.	Sub-Caste: No.	Sub-Caste: Name.	Consecutive number of Sub-caste.	Hereditary or Traditional Occupation.	Classification: Class.	Classification: Group.	Remarks.
154	Mahratta,—*contd.*	...	...	176	Jaosagar	3415				
				177	Japete	3416				
				178	Japhasan	3417				
				179	Jarbad	3418				
				180	Jate	3419				
				181	Jatpati	3420				
				182	Jasvan	3421				
				183	Jhamble	3422				
				184	Jhoned	3423				
				185	Jotvad	3424				
				186	Kadam	3425				
				187	Kadap	3426				
				188	Kaddar	3427				
				189	Kadade	3428				
				190	Kadgar	3429				
				191	Kadikod	3430				
				192	Kadkan	3431				
				193	Kadsal	3432				
				194	Kaduri	3433				
				195	Kahankar	3434				
				196	Kaka	3435				
				197	Kakde	3436				
				198	Kakse	3437				
				199	Kalanki	3438				
				200	Kale	3439				
				201	Kalleyan	3440				
				202	Kamle	3441				
				203	Kansale	3442				
				204	Kanshia	3443				
				205	Kaolibar	3444				
				206	Kar	3445				
				207	Karanwar	3446				
				208	Karle	3447				
				209	Karnag	3448				
				210	Karod	3449				
				211	Kasdi	3450				
				212	Katvat	3451				
				213	Kavi Mahratti	3452				
				214	Kedar	3453	Military and dominant ...	A	1	
				215	Keni	3454				
				216	Khalbhangi	3455				
				217	Khamunsar	3456				
				218	Khaole	3457				
				219	Kharale	3458				
				220	Kharde	3459				
				221	Khare	3460				
				222	Kharkhod	3461				
				223	Khatvan	3462				
				224	Khedkar	3463				
				225	Khodke	3464				
				226	Khoshi	3465				
				227	Khutevat	3466				
				228	Kokar	3467				
				229	Konher	3468				
				230	Kor	3469				
				231	Korsale	3470				
				232	Kote	3471				
				233	Kotle	3472				
				234	Lad	3473				
				235	Lagaya	3474				
				236	Lalsi	3475				
				237	Lamara	3476				
				238	Lasupne	3477				
				239	Lugde	3478				
				240	Mabhal	3479				
				241	Madan	3480				
				242	Magtol	3481				
				243	Mahave	3482				
				244	Mainavat	3483				
				245	Maine	3484				
				246	Maki	3485				
				247	Malve	3486				
				248	Mandria	3487				
				249	Mane	3488				
				250	Manjre	3489				
				251	Maoge	3490				
				252	Marul	3491				
				253	Masik	3492				

INDEX OF CASTES.—*Continued.*

Serial No.	Main Caste Name.	Population Males.	Population Females.	Sub-Caste No.	Sub-Caste Name.	Consecutive number of Sub-caste.	Hereditary or Traditional Occupation.	Classification Class.	Classification Group.	Remarks.
154	Mahratta.—*contd.* ...	......	......	254	Maske	3493				
				255	Mate	3494				
				256	Mathsar	3495				
				257	Medhavant	3496				
				258	Meher	3497				
				259	Mogal	3498				
				260	Mogan	3499				
				261	More	3500				
				262	Mundkar	3501				
				263	Musle	3502				
				264	Mutali	3503				
				265	Nadri	3504				
				266	Nagedhar	3505				
				267	Nagre	3506				
				268	Nagtidke	3507				
				269	Nague	3508				
				270	Naikbhosle	3509				
				271	Nalvade	3510				
				272	Namdeo	3511				
				273	Narbi	3512				
				274	Nari	3513				
				275	Nastabi	3514				
				276	Nimalvar	3515				
				277	Nirali	3516				
				278	Nirgud	3517				
				279	Nod	3518				
				280	Nundoba	3519				
				281	Opmane	3520				
				282	Padhand	3521				
				283	Padri	3522				
				284	Padval	3523				
				285	Pakhre	3524				
				286	Pakiram	3525				
				287	Palantia	3526				
				288	Palas	3527				
				289	Palayan	3528				
				290	Palre	3529				
				291	Pandovai	3530				
				292	Paore	3531				
				293	Paose	3532	Military and dominant ...	A	1	
				294	Papjadho	3533				
				295	Parvas	3534				
				296	Pasale	3535				
				297	Pathar	3536				
				298	Pathore	3537				
				299	Pavar	3538				
				300	Pavasre	3539				
				301	Phaonar	3540				
				302	Pharate	3541				
				303	Pinglo	3542				
				304	Pisali	3543				
				305	Pudan	3544				
				306	Pure	3545				
				307	Puvad	3546				
				308	Raghe	3547				
				309	Rainand	3548				
				310	Rajade	3549				
				311	Rajut	3550				
				312	Ramathar	3551				
				313	Ramnoe	3552				
				314	Ramraj	3553				
				315	Rankham	3554				
				316	Raokad	3555				
				317	Rasan	3556				
				318	Ravat	3557				
				319	Sajpan	3558				
				320	Sakul	3559				
				321	Salunke	3560				
				322	Sanam	3561				
				323	Sangjate	3562				
				324	Saole	3563				
				325	Sarangi	3564				
				326	Saraswat	3565				
				327	Sare	3566				
				328	Sarga	3567				
				329	Sarosi	3568				
				330	Satvan	3569				
				331	Savi	3570				

INDEX OF CASTES.—*Continued.*

Serial No.	Main Caste Name	Population Males	Population Females	Sub-caste No.	Sub-caste Name	Consecutive number of Sub-caste	Hereditary or Traditional Occupation	Class	Group	Remarks
154	Mahratta.—*concld*...	......	......	332	Savase	3571	Military and dominant ...	A	1	
				333	Savat	3572				
				334	Sekpao	3573				
				335	Seone	3574				
				336	Shahadesi	3575				
				337	Shilko...	3576				
				338	Shalu	3577				
				339	Sidalke	3578				
				340	Silil	3579				
				341	Sinde	3580				
				342	Sirpevar	3581				
				343	Sirsait...	3582				
				344	Sirsale...	3583				
				345	Sivije	3584				
				346	Somavamshi	3585				
				347	Songre	3586				
				348	Sonsal...	3587				
				349	Sri	3588				
				350	Sudhri	3589				
				351	Sukarvale	3590				
				352	Suratyari	3591				
				353	Suria	3592				
				354	Suriked	3593				
				355	Suror	3594				
				356	Survani	3595				
				357	Surve	3596				
				358	Tajavar	3597				
				359	Talkar	3598				
				360	Taluk...	3599				
				361	Tapakur	3600				
				362	Tara	3601				
				363	Thanar	3602				
				364	Thorat	3603				
				365	Vadne	3604				
				366	Vaghmar	3605				
				367	Vaher	3606				
				368	Vakal...	3607				
				369	Vale	3608				
				370	Valkhed	3609				
				371	Valvane	3610				
				372	Vardhan	3611				
				373	Varval	3612				
				374	Vasai	3613				
				375	Vasekari	3614				
				376	Vasudeo	3615				
				377	Vatake	3616				
				378	Vatyal	3617				
				379	Vavangi	3618				
				380	Vavre	3619				
				381	Vichsi	3620				
				382	Vighal	3621				
				383	Vikrama	3622				
				384	Vishva	3623				
				385	Vottam	3624				
				386	Yalechore	3625				
				387	Yadukal	3626				
				388	Yaoda...	3627				
				389	Yaolo...	3628				
				390	Yapugalewar... ...	3629				
				391	Yasde	3630				
				392	Yedke	3631				
155	Mala	136,055	128,368	1	Arava	3632	Village watchmen ...	D	38a	
				2	Agavaru	3633				
				3	Bainani	3634				
				4	Bala	3635				
				5	Banani	3636				
				6	Bandala	3637				
				7	Bandari	3638				
				8	Bathnekud	3639				
				9	Batwad	3640				
				10	Bayasunaikulu ...	3641				
				11	Battini	3642				
				12	Baynidla	3643				
				13	Bedaru	3644				
				14	Begari...	3645				
				15	Buttekulu	3646				
				16	Buthani	3647				

INDEX OF CASTES.—*Continued.*

MAIN CASTE.				SUB-CASTE.				CLASSIFICATION.		
Serial No.	Name.	Population. Males.	Population. Females.	No.	Name.	Consecutive number of Sub-caste.	Hereditary or Traditional Occupation.	Class.	Group.	Remarks.
155	**Mala.**—*concld.* ...	......	......	17	Chamaru	3648				
				18	Dasari	3649				
				19	Devalavandlu ...	3650				
				20	Devatalu	3651				
				21	Gagara	3652				
				22	Gampa	3653				
				23	Gantha	3654				
				24	Gunta	3655				
				25	Jangam	3656				
				26	Kantha	3657				
				27	Kanoji	3658				
				28	Karina	3659				
				29	Kolatalavandlu ...	3660				
				30	Kommumuttai ...	3661				
				31	Konanga	3662				
				32	Konda	3663				
				33	Kotagaru	3664				
				34	Kotakarug	3665				
				35	Korivi	3666				
				36	Majalvad	3667				
				37	Mala	3668				
				38	Malu	3669				
				39	Mannaipu	3670				
				40	Mashti	3671	Village watchmen ...	D	38a	
				41	Mitti	3672				
				42	Mogga	3673				
				43	Mushti	3674				
				44	Netakani	3675				
				45	Neelabundulu ...	3676				
				46	Neeradu	3677				
				47	Nityulu	3678				
				48	Paria	3679				
				49	Potaraju	3680				
				50	Saladadi	3681				
				51	Sarangi	3682				
				52	Satani...	3683				
				53	Setti	3684				
				54	Siri	3685				
				55	Siva	3686				
				56	Sivakantha	3687				
				57	Somani	3688				
				58	Talari...	3689				
				59	Tarkasi	3690				
				60	Thabadi	3691				
				61	Thota	3692				
				62	Veena...	3693				
156	Mali...	50,290	49,693	1	Hindu Bagian ...	3694				
				2	Malan	3695				
				3	Malavedi	3696				
				4	Mali	3697	Landholders	A	2a	
				5	Malvedi	3698				
				6	Pancham	3699				
157	Mang	156,134	156,988	1	Abada	3700				
				2	Ahalavaru	3701				
				3	Akusara	3702				
				4	Alaseelu	3703				
				5	Arki	3704				
				6	Athanathavad ...	3705				
				7	Autugaru	3706				
				8	Avaneeru	3707				
				9	Avuli	3708				
				10	Babood	3709				
				11	Badari	3710				
				12	Badaru	3711				
				13	Badidi	3712	Agricultural labourers ...	A	2c	
				14	Badugaru	3713				
				15	Bailama	3714				
				16	Bajod	3715				
				17	Bakalvaru	3716				
				18	Balagaru	3717				
				19	Balaney	3718				
				20	Balvadu	3719				
				21	Banavaru	3720				
				22	Bandari	3721				
				23	Banivaru	3722				
				24	Bayalijalai	3723				

INDEX OF CASTES.—*Continued.*

Serial No.	MAIN CASTE. Name.	Population. Males.	Population. Females.	SUB-CASTE. No.	SUB-CASTE. Name.	Consecutive number of Sub-caste.	Hereditary or Traditional Occupation.	Classification. Class.	Classification. Group.	Remarks.
157	Mang.—*contd.* ...	......	......	25	Bandararu	3724				
				26	Bandivalai	3725				
				27	Basiti	3726				
				28	Bedaru	3727				
				29	Bhadaru	3728				
				30	Bhadugaru	3729				
				31	Bhavadevti	3730				
				32	Bhaluti	3731				
				33	Bhadeti	3732				
				34	Bhattaru	3733				
				35	Bhanali	3734				
				36	Bhalijagili	3735				
				37	Budaban	3736				
				38	Chalvaru	3737				
				39	Dadadavaru	3738				
				40	Darji	3739				
				41	Dasana	3740				
				42	Dasannohla	3741				
				43	Dasari...	3742				
				44	Devasari	3743				
				45	Dhadavalai	3744				
				46	Dhaduvai	3745				
				47	Durli	3746				
				48	Erumaru	3747				
				49	Gabareema	3748				
				50	Gangavelu	3749				
				51	Gapaliginavaru ...	3750				
				52	Gathnlai	3751				
				53	Giaralavallu	3752				
				54	Godavaru	3753				
				55	Golu	3754				
				56	Gududavaru	3755				
				57	Gurunvaru	3756				
				58	Gurutia	3757				
				59	Guruvaru	3758				
				60	Halavagaru	3759				
				61	Haliavaru	3760				
				62	Halimani	3761				
				63	Hansutaru	3762	Agricultural labourers ...	A	2c	
				64	Hanugudi	3763				
				65	Helabastu	3764				
				66	Hubiliyavaru	3765				
				67	Idalavaru	3766				
				68	Jadulai	3767				
				69	Jagili	3768				
				70	Janakoya	3769				
				71	Jangam	3770				
				72	Jangili	3771				
				73	Jarikai	3772			...	
				74	Kakareevaru	3773				
				75	Kakaili	3774				
				76	Kalalyadu	3775				
				77	Kaliju...	3776				
				78	Kamalaru	3777				
				79	Kapatvaru	3778				
				80	Karevaru	3779				
				81	Kari	3780				
				82	Kathri	3781				
				83	Kayitar	3782				
				84	Kokavaru	3783				
				85	Kokirai	3784				
				86	Koru	3785				
				87	Koshti	3786				
				88	Kovalivaru	3787				
				89	Kulasava	3788				
				90	Kulitu...	3789				
				91	Ladhi	3790				
				92	Mahiti...	3791				
				93	Makaki	3792				
				94	Malatanabadu ...	3793				
				95	Malava	3794				
				96	Maliji	3795				
				97	Mandari	3796				
				98	Mang	3797				
				99	Mantri	3798				
				100	Mahratta	3799				
				101	Marojavaru	3800				
				102	Masalavaru	3801				

INDEX OF CASTES.—*Continued.*

Serial No.	MAIN CASTE. Name.	Population. Males.	Population. Females.	SUB-CASTE. No.	SUB-CASTE. Name.	Consecutive number of Sub-caste.	Hereditary or Traditional Occupation.	Classification. Class.	Classification. Group.	Remarks.
157	Mang.—*concld.* ...	......	......	103	Masanaku	3802				
				104	Masunavaku	3803				
				105	Matangi	3804				
				106	Matanagolaru ...	3805				
				107	Matiyalam	3806				
				108	Maturiyavaru ...	3807				
				109	Mavlai	3808				
				110	Mayanakaru	3809				
				111	Metri	3810				
				112	Mookasu	3811				
				113	Moolavaru	3812				
				114	Morewar	3813				
				115	Mutinavaru	3814				
				116	Myanavaru	3815				
				117	Neethalakulam ...	3816				
				118	Padamamaligy ...	3817				
				119	Palag	3818				
				120	Pamalavaru	3819				
				121	Panchamulu	3820				
				122	Pandari	3821				
				123	Panivala	3822				
				124	Pativaru	3823				
				125	Pattigangali	3824				
				126	Pattivalai	3825				
				127	Potharaj	3826				
				128	Pujaijangali	3827				
				129	Pulanavaru	3828				
				130	Pulasi...	3829	Agricultural labourers ...	A	2c	
				131	Puthangu	3830				
				132	Racha	3831				
				133	Raitala	3832				
				134	Ramosi	3833				
				135	Sadabharu	3834				
				136	Sadalvadalu	3835				
				137	Sajjan...	3836				
				138	Sakaru	3837				
				139	Sakki...	3838				
				140	Salama	3839				
				141	Sangetu	3840				
				142	Sankaru	3841				
				143	Saradu	3842				
				144	Sidalavar	3843				
				145	Sidol	3844				
				146	Sipalaru	3845				
				147	Sirali...	3846				
				148	Siya	3847				
				149	Tabasi	3848				
				150	Talanu	3849				
				151	Tarimin	3850				
				152	Toolukoya	3851				
				153	Upalavaru	3852				
				154	Vadavi	3853				
				155	Vinvaru	3854				
				156	Vudukad	3855				
				157	Yababaru	3856				
158	Mangala ... H J	60,455 20	58,320 8	1	Adabhanari	3857				
				2	Aisuru	3858				
				3	Barkaru	3859				
				4	Belkamanjala ...	3860				
				5	Bhasamdhari... ...	3861				
				6	Daraku	3862				
				7	Dari	3863				
				8	Deva	3864				
				9	Dikshabaliki	3865				
				10	Garigai	3866				
				11	Hajam	3867	Barbers	D	18	
				12	Hindustani	3868				
				13	Kalialapu	3869				
				14	Kalsanum	3870				
				15	Kargai	3871				
				16	Konda	3872				
				17	Linga	3873				
				18	Lingayet	3874				
				19	Maisri...	3875				
				20	Malibagi	3876				
				21	Mangali	3877				
				22	Muturasi	3878				

INDEX OF CASTES.—*Continued.*

MAIN CASTE.				SUB-CASTE.		Consecutive number of Sub-caste.	Hereditary or Traditional Occupation.	CLASSIFICATION.		REMARKS.
Serial No.	Name.	POPULATION. Males.	Females.	No.	Name.			Class.	Group.	
158	Mangala.—*concld.* ...	......	......	23	Naludaru	3879				
				24	Nari	3880				
				25	Navi	3881				
				26	Nayakulu	3882				
				27	Nayardu	3883				
				28	Nayi	3884				
				29	Pata	3885				
				30	Sajjan...	3886				
				31	Sanaiya	3887	Barbers	D	18	
				32	Sarva	3888				
				33	Sevakudu	3889				
				34	Seelavantu	3890				
				35	Sree	3891				
				36	Sreemangal	3892				
				37	Sreebastum	3893				
				38	Telangi	3894				
				39	Varik	3895				
159	Maniari ... H	1,781	1,729	1	Balgar	3896				
	M	3	5	2	Balgaru	3897				
				3	Badgaru	3898				
				4	Bangaluhar	3899				
				5	Bangadhar	3900	Glass-workers	D	29	
				6	Chudifarash	3901				
				7	Gajubali	3902				
				8	Ganjawad	3903				
				9	Kankanala	3904				
				10	Manniari	3905				
160	Mannaivar	10,719	10,230	1	Auanthapu	3906				
				2	Gollalu	3907				
				3	Gollavallu	3908				
				4	Gundai	3909				
				5	Kanchivalu	3910				
				6	Kantha	3911				
				7	Karamulavallu ...	3912				
				8	Karumen	3913				
				9	Kattulu	3914	Military and dominant ...	A	1	
				10	Konda...	3915				
				11	Kunta	3916				
				12	Madilavallu	3917				
				13	Mannai	3918				
				14	Mannaivar	3919				
				15	Muddailollu	3920				
				16	Puntai...	3921				
				17	Telaga	3922				
161	Mehtar ... H	206	213	1	Bhangi	3923				
	S	18	20	2	Chandal	3924				
	M	30	35	3	Chudra	3925				
				4	Chod	3926				
				5	Halalkor	3927	Scavengers	D	39	
				6	Khakrob	3928				
				7	Koransa	3929				
				8	Kornees	3930				
				9	Lalbegi	3931				
				10	Mehtar	3932				
162	Memon ... M	42	3	1	Memon	3933	Traders	C	14	
163	Mittulu	44	36	1	Mittulu	3934	Miscellaneous and disreputable livers	E	45	
164	Mochi	2,454	2,019	1	Chamar	3935				
				2	Kanada	3936				
				3	Mahratti	3937				
				4	Mochi	3938	Leather workers ...	D	38	
				5	Muchakoti	3939				
				6	Muchi...	3940				
				7	Samugar	3941				
				8	Thogiveru	3942				
165	Momin ... M	96	118	1	Momin	3943	Weavers, calenderers, and			
				2	Vinkari	3944	dyers	D	23	
166	Moraya	9	5	1	Moraya	3945	Landholders	A	2a	
167	Mudliyar	333	301	1	Arava	3946				
				2	Mudelli	3947	Writers	B	9	
				3	Mudliyar	3948				

INDEX OF CASTES.—*Continued.*

MAIN CASTE.				SUB-CASTE.				CLASSIFICATION.		
Serial No.	Name.	POPULATION. Males.	Females.	No.	Name.	Consecutive number of Sub-caste.	Hereditary or Traditional Occupation.	Class.	Group.	REMARKS.
168	Mughal ... M	11,462	10,302	1	Ahl-i-Koreish ...	3949	Non-Indian Asiatic races..	F	48	
				2	Barmas ...	3950				
				3	Behar ...	3951				
				4	Bujur ...	3952				
				5	Buranpuri ...	3953				
				6	Chaglailu ...	3954				
				7	Irani ...	3955				
				8	Laddaf ...	3956				
				9	Mughal ...	3957				
				10	Razavi ...	3958				
				11	Turani ...	3959				
169	Mulla	236	238	1	Amboli ...	3960	Fishermen, boatmen, palki bearers, cooks, &c.	D	35	Malli.
				2	Kishtichalevenar	3961				
				3	Malla ...	3962				
				4	Mulli ...	3963				
				5	Thari ...	3964				
				6	Tharu...	3965				
170	Mundi	72	61	1	Madava ...	3966	Miscellaneous and disreputable livers.	E	45	Mondi.
				2	Mundi...	3967				
171	Munnurwar... ...	60,772	61,211	1	Ahkamsetti ...	3968	Landholders	A	2a	
				2	Barisetti ...	3969				
				3	Bedalvad ...	3970				
				4	Chilka... ...	3971				
				5	Kanchani ...	3972				
				6	Kapu ...	3973				
				7	Kattai ...	3974				
				8	Kunbi Telangi	3975				
				9	Kuppai ...	3976				
				10	Madyemu ...	3977				
				11	Mamilla ...	3978				
				12	Manumádi ...	3979				
				13	Mathulu ...	3980				
				14	Munnura ...	3981				
				15	Munnurwad ...	3982				
				16	Muthila ...	3983				
				17	Namdhari ...	3984				
				18	Neeradi ...	3985				
				19	Pagadigothram	3986				
				20	Panwala ...	3987				
				21	Paralvad ...	3988				
				22	Peraka ...	3989				
				23	Piliga... ...	3990				
				24	Reddi	3991				
				25	Saivam ...	3992				
				26	Saukarajatti ...	3993				
				27	Satvad ...	3994				
				28	Sunvar ...	3995				
				29	Telanga ...	3996				
				30	Thota	3997				
				31	Thotabalija ...	3998				
				32	Vandelu ...	3999				
				33	Varala ...	4000				
				34	Varalavad ...	4001				
				35	Vishnu ...	4002				
				36	Yalugalu ...	4003				
				37	Yoga	4004				
172	Mushti	4,763	4,554	1	Danavalu ...	4005	Landholders	A	2a	
				2	Mushti ...	4006				
173	Mussulman (other) ...	7,519	7,343	1	Asukaru ...	4007	Non-Indian Asiatic races.	F	48	
				2	Bahadur ...	4008				
				3	Bayasur ...	4009				
				4	Bishthi ...	4010				
				5	Bogam ...	4011				
				6	Budbuduka ...	4012				
				7	Dakkani ...	4013				
				8	Dasi	4014				
				9	Dastagiru ...	4015				
				10	Gairumabadi ...	4016				
				11	Ganum ...	4017				
				12	Gulki	4018				
				13	Hamal... ...	4019				
				14	Jalar	4020				
				15	Kabeerru ...	4021				

INDEX OF CASTES.—*Continued.*

MAIN CASTE. Serial No.	MAIN CASTE. Name.	Population. Males.	Population. Females.	SUB-CASTE. No.	SUB-CASTE. Name.	Consecutive number of Sub-caste.	Hereditary or Traditional Occupation.	Classification. Class.	Classification. Group.	Remarks.
173	Mussulman.—*concld.*	......	......	16	Kajsjondi	4022				
				17	Kanjadu	4023				
				18	Kasai	4024				
				19	Kasim	4025				
				20	Koja...	4026				
				21	Majai	4027				
				22	Maniar	4028				
				23	Mujavaru	4029				
				24	Mulla	4030				
				25	Musulman	4031				
				26	Nakali	4032				
				27	Pakiru	4033	Non-Indian Asiatic races.	F	48	
				28	Pandrakulam ...	4034				
				29	Paraishi	4035				
				30	Pirojee	4036				
				31	Sounanalmin... ...	4037				
				32	Rayeesu	4038				
				33	Saku	4039				
				34	Shahsabu	4040				
				35	Sidulu...	4041				
				36	Sindhi	4042				
				37	Sunni...	4043				
174	Mutrasa	93,365	89,195	1	Balijavallu	4044				
				2	Bhattu	4045				
				3	Bogam	4046				
				4	Chulakalavadu ...	4047				
				5	Gaodu	4048				
				6	Kammakatti	4049				
				7	Karadi	4050				
				8	Koli	4051				
				9	Koli Telaga Mutrasa...	4052	Landholders	A	2a	
				10	Mahratta	4053				
				11	Maresha	4054				
				12	Munnuroo	4055				
				13	Mutraji	4056				
				14	Neolubin	4057				
				15	Padava	4058				
				16	Telanga	4059				
				17	Teluguvad	4060				
				18	Vyapakula	4061				
175	Naidu	297	258	1	Naidu	4062				
				2	Tanda	4063	Landholders	A	2a	
				3	Velkasusalu	4064				
176	Naik	12,558	12,206	1	Bandutor	4065				
				2	Bantu	4066				
				3	Dikhalewar	4067				
				4	Elari	4068				
				5	Gavatkari	4069				
				6	Kavali	4070				
				7	Kolar	4071				
				8	Mushtivad	4072				
				9	Naik	4073				
				10	Naika	4074				
				11	Naikaman	4075				
				12	Naikvad	4076				
				13	Namadi	4077				
				14	Neemat	4078	Village watchmen ...	D	38a	
				15	Neeradi	4079				
				16	Nirthadi	4080				
				17	Padmanaik	4081				
				18	Parka...	4082				
				19	Piada	4083				
				20	Ramosi	4084				
				21	Setusindi	4085				
				22	Talari	4086				
				23	Talvari	4087				
				24	Telaga	4088				
				25	Thalgari	4089				
				26	Thulvari	4090				
				27	Vuradi	4091				
177	Nakashgar ... H	431	444	1	Chathur	4092				
	J	3	1	2	Chitragaru	4093	Carpenters and Turners...	D	20	Chitrakar.
				3	Chitragar	4094				
				4	Kshetri	4095				

INDEX OF CASTES.—*Continued.*

MAIN CASTE.				SUB-CASTE.				CLASSIFICATION.		REMARKS.
Serial No.	Name.	Population. Males.	Population. Females.	No.	Name.	Consecutive number of Sub-caste.	Hereditary or Traditional Occupation.	Class.	Group.	
177	Nakashgar.—*concld* ..	......	......	5	Nakashgar	4096	Carpenters and Turners...	D	20	
				6	Nakashkal	4097				
				7	Nakashkaru	4098				
				8	Nakashu	4099				
				9	Nalshukuru	4100				
				10	Sitari	4101				
				11	Soyakshetri	4102				
178	Nalband	6	5	1	Nalband	4103	Carpenters and Turners ...	D	20	
179	Nanakshai	37	22	1	Nanakshai	4104	Devotees	B	6	
180	Nilgar	612	577	1	Mallai...	4105	Weavers, calenderers, and dyers.	D	23	
				2	Niligaru	4106				
				3	Neeligoti	4107				
				4	Neela	4108				
				5	Nilguni	4109				
181	Panasa	23	29	1	Panasa	4110	Devotees	B	6	
182	Panchala ... H	8,385	8,193	1	Avaragaori	4111	Goldsmiths	D	17	
	J	41	37	2	Devaru	4112				
				3	Kammara	4113				
				4	Kamsala	4114				
				5	Kasara	4115				
				6	Maya	4116				
				7	Pachor	4117				
				8	Panchalabaligi ...	4118				
				9	Panchadai	4119				
				10	Panchadani	4120				
				11	Panchal	4121				
				12	Panchala	4122				
				13	Panchalabaduki ...	4123				
				14	Smardhu	4124				
				15	Sunaru	4125				
				16	Viswa	4126				
				17	Viswabramha ...	4127				
				18	Viswakarma	4128				
				19	Vyshnava	4129				
183	Pandawa	59	40	1	Pandawa	4130	Miscellaneous and disreputable livers.	E	45	
184	Paradhi	1,524	1,409	1	Karath	4131	Hunters, fowlers, &c. ...	E	44	
				2	Paradhi	4132				
				3	Phasaiparadhi ...	4133				
				4	Pitalvadalu	4134				
185	Parbhu	265	276	1	Barai	4135	Military and dominant ...	A	1	
				2	Basiri	4136				
				3	Byhsavar	4137				
				4	Kosabarai	4138				
				5	Parbhu	4139				
				6	Pari	4140				
				7	Pavada	4141				
				8	Yothari	4142				
186	Pardesi	6,855	5,953	1	Jangam	4143	Miscellaneous and disreputable livers.	E	45	
				2	Paradesi	4144				
				3	Paradasun	4145				
				4	Paravastu	4146				
				5	Purasi	4147				
				6	Sanchari	4148				
187	Pardhan	2,079	2,148	1	Pardhan	4149	Weavers, calenderers, and dyers.	D	23	
				2	Pardhani	4150				
188	Paramavaru... ...	256	231	1	Parmavar	4151	Miscellaneous and disreputable livers.	E	45	
189	Parsi	628	430	1	Kadim	4152	Non-Indian Asiatic races.	F	48	
				2	Shah-in-Shahi ...	4153				
190	Pathan ... M	64,552	58,447	1	Afghan	4154	Non-Indian Asiatic races.	F	48	
				2	Afridi...	4155				
				3	Ahlikoreish	4156				
				4	Akbari	4157				
				5	Aliboshu	4158				
				6	Amarthi	4159				

INDEX OF CASTES.—*Continued.*

MAIN CASTE.				SUB-CASTE.				CLASSIFICATION.		
Serial No.	Name.	Population. Males.	Population. Females.	No.	Name.	Consecutive number of Sub-caste.	Hereditary or Traditional Occupation.	Class.	Group.	Remarks.
190	Pathan.—*contd.*	......	......	7	Badakshani	4160				
				8	Bahtu	4161				
				9	Bakar	4162				
				10	Balalzai	4163				
				11	Baluchi	4164				
				12	Bangashu	4165				
				13	Barlash	4166				
				14	Boozizai	4167				
				15	Chaghatai	4168				
				16	Charia	4169				
				17	Chariari (Sunni)	4170				
				18	Chinzai	4171				
				19	Chogu	4172				
				20	Chogathalibon	4173				
				21	Chohan	4174				
				22	Dapulkhi	4175				
				23	Dariazai	4176				
				24	Davoodi	4177				
				25	Dilzai	4178				
				26	Dowlatzai	4179				
				27	Emamzai	4180				
				28	Faminzai	4181				
				29	Firdousi	4182				
				30	Gani	4183				
				31	Gori	4184				
				32	Hashami	4185				
				33	Japperzai	4186				
				34	Jeenai	4187				
				35	Kabal	4188				
				36	Kabuli	4189				
				37	Kadalzai	4190				
				38	Kadarkhani	4191				
				39	Kaipi	4192				
				40	Kakar	4193				
				41	Kamalzai	4194				
				42	Kangali	4195				
				43	Kari	4196				
				44	Karwan	4197				
				45	Kasai	4198				
				46	Kashti	4199	Non-Indian Asiatic races.	F	48	
				47	Katik	4200				
				48	Kayamkhani	4201				
				49	Khaibari	4202				
				50	Khalai	4203				
				51	Khokar	4204				
				52	Kharasani	4205				
				53	Kirmani	4206				
				54	Kithabi	4207				
				55	Kizilbash	4208				
				56	Kokal	4209				
				57	Kokani	4210				
				58	Kotah	4211				
				59	Kotumbi	4212				
				60	Kukkini	4213				
				61	Kuraishi	4214				
				62	Kutumbi	4215				
				63	Lodi	4216				
				64	Lukmanzai	4217				
				65	Mahmanzai	4218				
				66	Mohunzai	4219				
				67	Mawal	4220				
				68	Malasaru	4221				
				69	Manduzai	4222				
				70	Manuzai	4223				
				71	Mayani	4224				
				72	Meena	4225				
				73	Memon	4226				
				74	Moghulkhani	4227				
				75	Mudularu	4228				
				76	Nagad	4229				
				77	Naik	4230				
				78	Noorbhasha	4231				
				79	Noori	4232				
				80	Omarzai	4233				
				81	Oorakzai	4234				
				82	Patan	4235				
				83	Pushtho	4236				
				84	Rohilla	4237				
				85	Saroni	4238				

INDEX OF CASTES.—*Continued.*

MAIN CASTE.				SUB-CASTE.				CLASSIFICATION.		
Serial No.	Name.	Population. Males.	Females.	No.	Name.	Consecutive number of Sub-caste.	Hereditary or Traditional Occupation.	Class.	Group.	Remarks.
190	Pathan.—*concld.* ...	...	...	86	Shadizai	4239				
				87	Shahzai	4240				
				88	Shirazi	4241				
				89	Sulamani	4242				
				90	Sulemanzai	4243				
				91	Surak	4244				
				92	Syrian	4245				
				93	Tajik	4246	Non-Indian Asiatic races	F	48	
				94	Timurzai	4247				
				95	Turani	4248				
				96	Turki	4249				
				97	Turkzai	4250				
				98	Usmanzai	4251				
				99	Yusufzai	4252				
				100	Zari	4253				
191	Patiki	112	121	1	Patiki	4254	Writers	B	9	
192	Patkari	420	396	1	Patkari	4255	Weavers, calenderers and dyers.	D	23	Palkari.
				2	Satigaodu	4256				
193	Patwegar ... H	320	266	1	Lingayet	4257	Weavers, calenderers, and Dyers.	D	23	
	M	10	4	2	Patwegar	4258				
	J	85	77							
194	Perika	17,042	16,821	1	Boya	4259				
				2	Chittu...	4260				
				3	Gonai	4261				
				4	Janapa	4262				
				5	Kavadi	4263				
				6	Paraika	4264				
				7	Perka	4265	Mixed Indian races ...	F	49b	
				8	Racha...	4266				
				9	Sankara	4267				
				10	Setti	4268				
				11	Somsetti	4269				
				12	Tukka...	4270				
195	Pitchiguntla ... H	2,634	2,462	1	Chittnapachara ...	4271				
				2	Gampa	4272				
				3	Kodisai	4273				
				4	Mooparapatti	4274				
				5	Neelakanta	4275	Landholders	A	2a	
				6	Nilakat	4276				
				7	Pitchiguntla	4277				
				8	Sardha Pichikuntla ...	4278				
				9	Thamboora	4279				
196	Pinjari ... H	289	274	1	Dudaikula	4280				
	M	2,811	2,700	2	Ladaf	4281				
				3	Nadaf	4282	Cotton cleaners	D	25	
				4	Noorbash	4283				
				5	Pinjari	4284				
197	Pulari	860	815	1	Pulari	4285	Musicians and ballad reciters.	B	11	
198	Purbhaiya	1,526	1,311	1	Ayimoon	4286				
				2	Ayadhya	4287				
				3	Bhaisan	4288				
				4	Bhaisavar	4289				
				5	Bhyan	4290				
				6	Daruwala	4291				
				7	Devia...	4292				
				8	Dhalakubansi... ...	4293				
				9	Dommaru	4294				
				10	Gaolbansi	4295				
				11	Jahuri	4296	Military and dominant ...	A	1	
				12	Jayeesa	4297				
				13	Kalu	4298				
				14	Khilvoyee	4299				
				15	Kolaha	4300				
				16	Kusubi	4301				
				17	Pardesi	4302				
				18	Purbhia kaben ...	4303				
				19	Purubhia	4304				
				20	Tharu...	4305				
				21	Zingar	4306				

INDEX OF CASTES.—*Continued.*

MAIN CASTE.				SUB-CASTE.		Consecutive number of Sub-caste.	Hereditary or Traditional Occupation.	CLASSIFICATION.		REMARKS.
Serial No.	Name.	POPULATION. Males.	POPULATION. Females.	No.	Name.			Class.	Group.	
199	Pusala	980	948	1	Kasikavali	4307				
				2	Musali	4308				
				3	Pusaperla	4309	Pedlars	C	15	
				4	Pusakasikavidi	4310				
				5	Pusala	4311				
				6	Suderlu	4312				
200	Rajput H	25,279	23,192	1	Ahir	4313				
	J	7	...	2	Aindar	4314				
	S	21	12	3	Babadi	4315				
				4	Bad-thela	4316				
				5	Baharugi	4317				
				6	Bairagi	4318				
				7	Baisu	4319				
				8	Baithubansi	4320				
				9	Baneusi	4321				
				10	Bapahel	4322				
				11	Bas	4323				
				12	Bavanadhu	4324				
				13	Bavasadhu	4325				
				14	Bayin	4326				
				15	Bedbansi	4327				
				16	Bharumanar	4328				
				17	Bhatch	4329				
				18	Bhiman	4330				
				19	Bhuthu	4331				
				20	Bodhlai	4332				
				21	Bodumasi	4333				
				22	Bondili	4334				
				23	Bundalai	4335				
				24	Bundela	4336				
				25	Chakubinsu	4337				
				26	Chandrabansi	4338				
				27	Chandrarai	4339				
				28	Chandrasen	4340				
				29	Chauban	4341				
				30	Chavan	4342				
				31	Chuban	4343				
				32	Dandabansi	4344				
				33	Dunasen Bhat	4345				
				34	Daravadu	4346				
				35	Darkath	4347				
				36	Dhakooth	4348	Military and dominant	A	1	
				37	Dhobi	4349				
				38	Dooli	4350				
				39	Garuval	4351				
				40	Gasugotu	4352				
				41	Gautam Thakur	4353				
				42	Gesi	4354				
				43	God	4355				
				44	Gopalbansi	4356				
				45	Gwalasubban	4357				
				46	Jadubansi	4358				
				47	Jaharu	4359				
				48	Jambavanthu	4360				
				49	Janapuvaru	4361				
				50	Jat	4362				
				51	Kachi	4363				
				52	Kahar	4364				
				53	Kalmia	4365				
				54	Kanoji Bondu	4366				
				55	Kanowjia	4367				
				56	Karchi	4368				
				57	Kathri	4369				
				58	Kayakathri	4370				
				59	Kayeth	4371				
				60	Kod	4372				
				61	Kshatri	4373				
				62	Kunbi	4374				
				63	Lamani	4375				
				64	Lodha	4376				
				65	Mahratha	4377				
				66	Munadu	4378				
				67	Naisthulakuch	4379				
				68	Namadaru	4380				
				69	Paradesi	4381				
				70	Pariathakur	4382				
				71	Pathri	4383				
				72	Pohar	4384				

INDEX OF CASTES.—*Continued.*

Main Caste: Serial No.	Main Caste: Name	Population: Males	Population: Females	Sub-Caste: No.	Sub-Caste: Name	Consecutive number of Sub-caste	Hereditary or Traditional Occupation	Classification: Class	Classification: Group	Remarks
200	Rajput.—*concld.* ...	......	......	73	Raghuvamsi	4385	Military and dominant ...	A	1	
				74	Rajjut ...	4386				
				75	Raju	4387				
				76	Rasavadu	4388				
				77	Ratoo	4389				
				78	Saigavanthoo... ...	4390				
				79	Sankarasu	4391				
				80	Sarakir	4392				
				81	Singudaram	4393				
				82	Suryabansi	4394				
				83	Suriaavamsam ...	4395				
				84	Suvre	4396				
				85	Talu Vukuchandi ...	4397				
				86	Telanga	4398				
				87	Thakur	4399				
				88	Thamurutakulu ...	4400				
				89	Thilakuchandan ...	4401				
				90	Thirumandar... ...	4402				
				91	Udasi	4403				
201	Ramdasi	24	23	1	Ramdesi	4404	Miscellaneous and disreputable livers.	E	45	
202	Rangres ... H	8,278	7,794	1	Adakapu	4405	Weavers, calenderers, and dyers.	D	23	
	J	5	5	2	Adakum	4406				
				3	Avujasari	4407				
				4	Dhanuvant	4408				
				5	Dinkar	4409				
				6	Koleckaru	4410				
				7	Mahratha Sudra ...	4411				
				8	Nagaleeku	4412				
				9	Namadevu	4413				
				10	Naru	4414				
				11	Petudhari	4415				
				12	Rangari	4416				
				13	Rangaruvandlu ...	4417				
				14	Ranguerzu	4418				
				15	Vannekaru	4419				
203	Rinja	8	7	1	Rinja	4420	Devotees	B	6	
204	Ratod	264	196	1	Bhai	4421	Military and dominant ...	A	1	Rahtore.
				2	Dakri	4422				
				3	Kshatri	4423				
				4	Ratod	4424				
				5	Vankri	4425				
205	Reddi	27,268	26,976	1	Arey	4426	Landholders	A	2a	
				2	Dikshavanth	4427				
				3	Gonai	4428				
				4	Gunjakaru	4429				
				5	Kamore	4430				
				6	Hanuba	4431				
				7	Kuruvai	4432				
				8	Makkaru	4433				
				9	Mathivan	4434				
				10	Matumutu	4435				
				11	Mudelliar	4436				
				12	Munnuru	4437				
				13	Namdev	4438				
				14	Nandevu	4439				
				15	Naruvar	4440				
				16	Padam	4441				
				17	Pakanati	4442				
				18	Patu	4443				
				19	Reddi	4444				
				20	Reddikapu	4445				
				21	Reddivar	4446				
				22	Suruvan	4447				
				23	Vakiligaru	4448				
206	Rohilla ... M	209	174	1	Pathan	4449	Non-Indian Asiatic races.	F	48	
				2	Rohilla	4450				
				3	Yusoof zai	4451				
207	Saiti	744	811	1	Saiti	4452	Traders	C	14	
				2	Satu	4453				

INDEX OF CASTES.—*Continued.*

Serial No.	Main Caste Name	Population Males	Population Females	Sub-caste No.	Sub-caste Name	Consecutive number of Sub-caste	Hereditary or Traditional Occupation	Class	Group	Remarks
208	Salai	162,111	153,954	1	Abidaru	4454	Weavers, calenderers, and dyers.	D	23	Julaha.
				2	Arokani	4455				
				3	Bangar	4456				
				4	Bannakani	4457				
				5	Basarapuli	4458				
				6	Batti	4459				
				7	Beesagaru	4460				
				8	Bidijadaru	4461				
				9	Chikkukurinajadru ...	4462				
				10	Chikkusalai	4463				
				11	Dalgotam	4464				
				12	Dendra	4465				
				13	Devagani	4466				
				14	Dinar	4467				
				15	Dinkarvad	4468				
				16	Divalvad	4469				
				17	Erramoolam	4470				
				18	Hadanda	4471				
				19	Hirekurnijadaru ...	4472				
				20	Inkar	4473				
				21	Isukali	4474				
				22	Jadaru	4475				
				23	Julaha	4476				
				24	Julai	4477				
				25	Jandra	4478				
				26	Kabeeru	4479				
				27	Kabekadasi	4480				
				28	Kabiru Vargati ...	4481				
				29	Kannapori	4482				
				30	Kashi	4483				
				31	Kondasalai	4484				
				32	Korai	4485				
				33	Koshti...	4486				
				34	Kurinajadru	4487				
				35	Kurudati	4488				
				36	Kurleedavaru ...	4489				
				37	Kurusalai	4490				
				38	Kuruvanasetti ...	4491				
				39	Kusarai	4492				
				40	Lalgondu	4493				
				41	Lingavantu	4494				
				42	Mahratti	4495				
				43	Markandaya	4496				
				44	Miru	4497				
				45	Mutrasi Sudra ...	4498				
				46	Naitakani	4499				
				47	Naka	4500				
				48	Naksadi	4501				
				49	Namadaru	4502				
				50	Naruganda	4503				
				51	Neelakantu	4504				
				52	Neelkaru	4505				
				53	Nesukar	4506				
				54	Netakani	4507				
				55	Padmasalai	4508				
				56	Panchamasale ...	4509				
				57	Panti	4510				
				58	Parudhani	4511				
				59	Paruspudar	4512				
				60	Rashmiavaru ...	4513				
				61	Sagar...	4514				
				62	Sakunu	4515				
				63	Salaiwad	4516				
				64	Salayi...	4517				
				65	Sankar	4518				
				66	Sarakondlu	4519				
				67	Satti	4520				
				68	Shalu	4521				
				69	Sivamat	4522				
				70	Sunkari	4523				
				71	Tabagari	4524				
				72	Tadotaru	4525				
				73	Tenugu	4526				
				74	Thakutgurao	4527				
				75	Togata	4528				
				76	Vanivu	4529				
				77	Veenakar	4530				
				78	Vinkari	4531				
				79	Vishnumata	4532				

INDEX OF CASTES.—*Continued.*

MAIN CASTE.				SUB-CASTE.				CLASSIFICATION.		
Serial No.	Name.	Population. Males.	Population. Females.	No.	Name.	Consecutive number of Sub-caste.	Hereditary or Traditional Occupation.	Class.	Group.	Remarks.
209	Sangtarash	967	1,017	1	Kachivar	4533	Earthworkers and Stone-dressers.	E	41	
				2	Kasaikar	4534				
				3	Kasaivar	4535				
				4	Kasi	4536				
				5	Kasi Raj	4537				
				6	Phatharud	4538				
				7	Panchala	4539				
				8	Ravatu	4540				
				9	Sangtrash	4541				
				10	Viswabramha ...	4542				
210	Saradhi	109	107	1	Saradha	4543	Miscellaneous and disreputable livers.	E	45	
				2	Sharagadu	4544				
211	Satani	6,105	5,907	1	Aiyavaru	4545	Landholders	A	2a	
				2	Boda	4546				
				3	Bukka	4547				
				4	Madi	4548				
				5	Nambulu	4549				
				6	Nami	4550				
				7	Natholu	4551				
				8	Nithzulu	4552				
				9	Ramajal	4553				
				10	Ramanjulu	4554				
				11	Reddi	4555				
				12	Sadgal	4556				
				13	Sanan	4557				
				14	Santhankulam ...	4558				
				15	Satani...	4559				
				16	Telugabooka	4560				
				17	Tenugu	4561				
				18	Vadagala	4562				
				19	Vadhanambi	4563				
				20	Vaishnava	4564				
				21	Yadava	4565				
212	Sayyed ... M	57,624	55,663	1	Alvi	4566	Non-Indian Asiatic races.	F	48	
				2	Bakari	4567				
				3	Hasni	4568				
				4	Hasan-ul-Husaini ...	4569				
				5	Husaini	4570				
				6	Jafari	4571				
				7	Mahdvi	4572				
				8	Musavi	4573				
				9	Nakvi...	4574				
				10	Razvi...	4575				
				11	Zaidi	4576				
213	Sheikh ... M	435,267	420,857	1	Abbasi	4577	Non-Indian Asiatic races.	F	48	
				2	Ansari	4578				
				3	Askari	4579				
				4	Faruki	4580				
				5	Kureshi	4581				
				6	Osmani	4582				
				7	Sharif...	4583				
				8	Siddiki	4584				
				9	Tarkash	4585				
214	Sidhi ... M	73	38	1	Habshi	4586	Non-Asiatic races.	F	50	
				2	Nabi	4587				
				3	Sidhi	4588				
215	Sikalgar	43	38	1	Sikalgar	4589	Knife Grinders	E	42	
216	Sikh... ... S	2,305	1,999	1	Lahir	4590	Mixed Indian races ...	F	49b	
				2	Modu	4591				
				3	Rahaba	4592				
				4	Sahcji	4593				
				5	Sikh	4594				
217	Singadi	157	131	1	Singadi	4595	Musicians and ballad reciters.	B	11	
				2	Singnavaz	4596				
218	Sonnayi	324	295	1	Bajantri	4597	Musicians and ballad reciters.	B	11	
				2	Peraka	4598				
				3	Battulu	4599				
				4	Gurigodu	4600				
				5	Sambhad	4601				
				6	Sannayee	4602				

INDEX OF CASTES.—*Continued.*

MAIN CASTE.				SUB-CASTE.				CLASSIFICATION.		
Serial No.	Name.	POPULATION. Males.	POPULATION. Females.	No.	Name.	Consecutive number of Sub-caste.	Hereditary or Traditional Occupation.	Class.	Group.	REMARKS.
218	Sonnayi—*concld.* ...	......	......	7	Sonnayee	4603	Musicians and ballad reciters.	B	11	
				8	Vadulu	4604				
219	Sunkari	55	67	1	Sunkari	4605	Leather workers	D	38	
220	Sutar ... H J	52,803 2	50,614	1	Abari	4606	Carpenters and Turners.	D	20	
				2	Ajalollu	4607				
				3	Badai	4608				
				4	Badihi	4609				
				5	Balgaru	4610				
				6	Bhagumatu	4611				
				7	Dhangi	4612				
				8	Gurupancha	4613				
				9	Kai	4614				
				10	Kamsala	4615				
				11	Karma	4616				
				12	Kasa	4617				
				13	Kayasth	4618				
				14	Khanai	4619				
				15	Koli	4620				
				16	Kshetri	4621				
				17	Lingayet	4622				
				18	Luvaru	4623				
				19	Maichari	4624				
				20	Madhwalu	4625				
				21	Magabrahma ...	4626				
				22	Mulavatai	4627				
				23	Nagalecha	4628				
				24	Najara	4629				
				25	Najarbad	4630				
				26	Najarabramha ...	4631				
				27	Panchadai	4632				
				28	Panchal	4633				
				29	Pancham	4634				
				30	Sarada	4635				
				31	Savana	4636				
				32	Seelavantam	4637				
				33	Sigar	4638				
				34	Silpi	4639				
				35	Smardhu	4640				
				36	Sutar	4641				
				37	Telanga	4642				
				38	Vadla...	4643				
				39	Vasishta	4644				
				40	Visivabrahma ...	4645				
				41	Viswakarma	4646				
				42	Vishnavantu	4647				
221	Takari ... H M	135 4	150 3	1	Takari	4648	Grindstone makers and stone quarriers.	E	40	
222	Tambatgar	368	346	1	Takitigaru	4649	Brass and Copper-smiths.	D	21	
				2	Tamatgar	4650				
				3	Tavatigar	4651				
223	Tamboli ... H M J	199 15 3	202 12 4	1	Deva	4652	Perfumers, drug preparers, &c.	D	22b	
				2	Eligar...	4653				
				3	Enavadi	4654				
				4	Guravaru	4655				
				5	Hoogar	4656				
				6	Munjivandlu... ...	4657				
				7	Nayad...	4658				
				8	Panchadagi	4659				
				9	Poolkari	4660				
				10	Pujari...	4661				
				11	Pulari...	4662				
				12	Siva	4663				
				13	Sivabaliga	4664				
				14	Sivabrahmana ...	4665				
				15	Sudra	4666				
				16	Tahodari	4667				
				17	Tamali	4668				
				18	Tamboli	4669				
				19	Tapodhama	4670				
				20	Teli	4671				
				21	Viswabrahma... ...	4672				
224	Thakur	1,756	1,732	1	Chohan	4673	Military and dominant ...	A	1	
				2	Chohan Thakur ...	4674				
				3	Gautama	4675				

INDEX OF CASTES.—*Continued.*

Serial No.	Main Caste: Name.	Population: Males.	Population: Females.	Sub-Caste: No.	Sub-Caste: Name.	Consecutive number of Sub-caste.	Hereditary or Traditional Occupation.	Classification: Class.	Classification: Group.	Remarks.
224	Thakur.—*concld.* ...	......	......	4	Jaswa...	4676				
				5	Jivathakur	4677				
				6	Janva...	4678				
				7	Kabi	4679	Military and dominant ...	A	1	
				8	Kachi	4680				
				9	Pardesi	4681				
				10	Thakur	4682				
225	Thammadi	5,934	5,972	1	Daphnavaz	4683				
				2	Ghadasi	4684				
				3	Guru	4685				
				4	Jilari	4686				
				5	Hooja...	4687				
				6	Nyad	4688	Musicians and ballad reciters.	B	11	
				7	Palasingi	4689				
				8	Pulari...	4690				
				9	Pushkari	4691				
				10	Thammadi	4692				
				11	Vayantu	4693				
226	Telugu	159,925	156,521	1	Agarwal	4694				
				2	Aiyawar	4695				
				3	Arai	4696				
				4	Avushkar	4697				
				5	Avvunavar	4698				
				6	Badai	4699				
				7	Batri	4700				
				8	Bedaru	4701				
				9	Bemboo	4702				
				10	Bhoyi	4703				
				11	Bhumandal	4704				
				12	Bobbili	4705				
				13	Brahmin	4706				
				14	Budodh	4707				
				15	Butta	4708				
				16	Chalka	4709				
				17	Chittaipu	4710				
				18	Darzi	4711				
				19	Deshumar	4712				
				20	Dhangar	4713				
				21	Dher	4714				
				22	Dhobi...	4715				
				23	Gadithulgi	4716				
				24	Gaoli	4717				
				25	Gaori	4718				
				26	God	4719				
				27	Gopi	4720				
				28	Gumpa	4721				
				29	Gutham	4722				
				30	Guzerathi	4723	Mixed Indian races ...	F	49b	
				31	Hajam	4724				
				32	Illuvellani	4725				
				33	Jangam	4726				
				34	Jetti	4727				
				35	Jogi	4728				
				36	Julaha	4729				
				37	Juttu	4730				
				38	Kani	4781				
				39	Kalal	4732				
				40	Kalani	4733				
				41	Kalanwad	4734				
				42	Kalkatha	4735				
				43	Kaloor	4736				
				44	Kalthi...	4737				
				45	Kammaravallu ...	4738				
				46	Kannada	4739				
				47	Kanapu	4740				
				48	Kapu	4741				
				49	Koli	4742				
				50	Komati	4743				
				51	Konda mangali ...	4744				
				52	Kothamadduvalu ...	4745				
				53	Kurchithelaga ...	4746				
				54	Ladkassab	4747				
				55	Lingayeth	4748				
				56	Lingavanthu	4749				
				57	Madar	4750				
				58	Madhvancha	4751				
				59	Madrasi	4752				
				60	Malapu	4753				

INDEX OF CASTES.—*Continued.*

MAIN CASTE.				SUB-CASTE.				CLASSIFICATION.		
Serial No.	Name.	POPULATION.		No.	Name.	Consecutive number of Sub-caste.	Hereditary or Traditional Occupation.	Class.	Group.	REMARKS.
		Males.	Females.							
226	Telugu.—*concld.* ...	......	......	61	Mallawad	4754				
				62	Manna Bhattu ...	4755				
				63	Mahratta	4756				
				64	Minagalavaru ...	4757				
				65	Moodelliar	4758				
				66	Moodoorash	4759				
				67	Motati...	4760				
				68	Munnurvad	4761				
				69	Nagarikulu	4762				
				70	Naik	4763				
				71	Nanduvad	4764				
				72	Neelabandhulu ...	4765				
				73	Pakanati	4766				
				74	Peria	4767				
				75	Prabhu	4768				
				76	Rainavaru	4769				
				77	Raja Bhatti	4770				
				78	Rajput	4771				
				79	Ramjayi	4772				
				80	Ranivasam	4773				
				81	Rayanavaru	4774				
				82	Rayuda	4775				
				83	Rela	4776	Mixed Indian races ...	F	49b	
				84	Sajjana	4777				
				85	Sankaram	4778				
				86	Sannapalli	4779				
				87	Separiputhrudu ...	4780				
				88	Settisarvala	4781				
				89	Shamboo	4782				
				90	Sirabaji	4783				
				91	Siria	4784				
				92	Sirimangali	4785				
				93	Som	4786				
				94	Sonar	4787				
				95	Tarasi...	4788				
				96	Telanga	4789				
				97	Theerthamamidi ...	4790				
				98	Thota	4791				
				99	Tirumandar	4792				
				100	Vaishnav	4793				
				101	Velnati	4794				
				102	Waddi	4795				
				103	Wod	4796				
				104	Yaramasi	4797				
				105	Yeri	4798				
227	Tirumalai	405	426	1	Tirumalai	4799	Landholders	A	2a	
228	Turk ... M	20	13	1	Turk	4800	Non-Indian Asiatic races ...	F	48	
229	Uppara	11,625	11,786	1	Agasana	4801				
				2	Aiduvaraha	4802				
				3	Akavamaneru ...	4803				
				4	Alapeeru	4804				
				5	Badai	4805				
				6	Badukulagondu ...	4806				
				7	Baladavar	4807				
				8	Balsatali	4808				
				9	Batadavaru	4809				
				10	Batupar	4810				
				11	Begaru	4811				
				12	Beldar...	4812				
				13	Bhagaduvad	4813				
				14	Bhattupar	4814				
				15	Chadaru	4815	Salt, &c., workers. ...	D	30	
				16	Chakra	4816				
				17	Channalavaru ...	4817				
				18	Chalukinai	4818				
				19	Chantu	4819				
				20	Chilavalai	4820				
				21	Chilkvasa	4821				
				22	Chiniavaru	4822				
				23	Chisi...	4823				
				24	Digunesaru	4824				
				25	Eduvara	4825				
				26	Gatalavaru	4826				
				27	Gaondi	4827				
				28	Goda	4828				
				29	Gujalavaru	4829				
				30	Gutaivaru	4830				

INDEX OF CASTES.—*Continued.*

MAIN CASTE.				SUB-CASTE.		Consecutive number of Sub-caste.	Hereditary or Traditional Occupation.	CLASSIFICATION.		REMARKS.
Serial No.	Name.	POPULATION.		No.	Name.			Class.	Group.	
		Males.	Females.							
229	Uppara.—*concld.* ...	......	......	31	Halabatiyaru ...	4831				
				32	Jambavar	4832				
				33	Jillavaru	4833				
				34	Jisavalai	4834				
				35	Kamakavasa	4835				
				36	Kambali	4836				
				37	Karadanavar... ...	4837				
				38	Kari	4838				
				39	Katal	4839				
				40	Katiledi	4840				
				41	Katukulai	4841				
				42	Kharau	4842				
				43	Koli	4843				
				44	Kshetri	4844				
				45	Kupati	4845				
				46	Kurliavaru	4846				
				47	Lunari	4847				
				48	Machirelu	4848				
				49	Mantrivaru	4849				
				50	Moti	4850				
				51	Munnuru	4851				
				52	Mutrasi	4852				
				53	Nagarudavaru ...	4853				
				54	Namadavaru	4854				
				55	Neelavaru	4855	Salt, &c., workers ...	D	30	
				56	Negari...	4856				
				57	Od	4857				
				58	Padamasetti	4858				
				59	Panchalavaru ...	4859				
				60	Panchamabalki ...	4860				
				61	Panchamavaru ...	4861				
				62	Para	4862				
				63	Punaruvaru	4863				
				64	Puri	4864				
				65	Rajanaru	4865				
				66	Rajanooroo	4866				
				67	Ramanjam	4867				
				68	Sabiravalall	4868				
				69	Sagara	4869				
				70	Sagarudavaru ...	4870				
				71	Salavaru	4871				
				72	Samutaru	4872				
				73	Sayalavaru	4873				
				74	Sidabad	4874				
				75	Sonkudavaru ...	4875				
				76	Telanga	4876				
				77	Thota	4877				
				78	Uppari	4878				
				79	Vaddai	4879				
				80	Vemaru	4880				
230	Vaidya	5	8	1	Vaidya	4881	Astrologers...	B	10	Baidya.
231	Vidur	3,844	3,906	1	Davilai	4882				
				2	Gujala	4883				
				3	Kalagidi	4884				
				4	Koolagedi	4885	Writers	B	9	
				5	Lalabey	4886				
				6	Sankara	4887				
				7	Vidur	4888				
232	Vipravinodulu ...	46	30	1	Vipravinodulu ...	4889	Miscellaneous and disreputable livers.	E	45	
233	Waddar	45,533	44,266	1	Alipati...	4890				
				2	Arusalaku	4891				
				3	Bandi	4892				
				4	Bantu...	4893				
				5	Barjivalu	4894				
				6	Bhumadar	4895				
				7	Bisukalu	4896				
				8	Chalka	4897				
				9	Challurga	4898	Grindstone makers and stone quarriers.	E	40	
				10	Chuttari	4899				
				11	Dandail	4900				
				12	Davara	4901				
				13	Ella	4902				
				14	Etaravaru	4903				
				15	Etravalai	4904				
				16	Gada	4905				
				17	Gadavalai	4906				

INDEX OF CASTES.—*Continued.*

MAIN CASTE.				SUB-CASTE.		Consecutive number of Sub-caste.	Hereditary or Traditional Occupation.	CLASSIFICATION.		REMARKS.
Serial No.	Name.	POPULATION. Males.	POPULATION. Females.	No.	Name.			Class.	Group.	
233	Waddar.—*concld.* ...	......	......	18	Gampa	4907				
				19	Gandikota	4908				
				20	Godarla	4909				
				21	Golela...	4910				
				22	Gudisa	4911				
				23	Gujjalu	4912				
				24	Iragakuligi	4913				
				25	Jadi	4914				
				26	Jampalu	4915				
				27	Jani	4916				
				28	Kallu	4917				
				29	Kasa	4918				
				30	Kavaragustu	4919				
				31	Konda...	4920				
				32	Kuchphalai	4921				
				33	Malatavaru	4922				
				34	Mallaru	4923				
				35	Mannailu	4924				
				36	Mati	4925				
				37	Mavalu	4926				
				38	Meenagalu	4927				
				39	Mummudala	4928	Grindstone makers and stone quarriers.	E	40	
				40	Mundala	4929				
				41	Murangala	4930				
				42	Pallapaila	4931				
				43	Pallavaru	4932				
				44	Panalavaru	4933				
				45	Paru	4934				
				46	Racha...	4935				
				47	Rathi	4936				
				48	Samapaba	4937				
				49	Sanyasi	4938				
				50	Sivamatam	4939				
				51	Swarnamali	4940				
				52	Telugu	4941				
				53	Uppara	4942				
				54	Ura	4943				
				55	Vadari	4944				
				56	Wadde	4945				
				57	Waddewar	4946				
				58	Waldar	4947				
				59	Walkodai	4948				
				60	Warasu	4949				
				61	Yaragadindla... ...	4950				
234	Wani ... H J	207,820 5,511	197,733 4,437	1	Adi	4951				
				2	Agarval	4952				
				3	Aghati	4953				
				4	Agea	4954				
				5	Andbadki	4955				
				6	Balkevar	4956				
				7	Bamlachinivar ...	4957				
				8	Baturate	4958				
				9	Bejabargi	4959				
				10	Bhadao	4960				
				11	Bhasamdhani... ...	4961				
				12	Bilenai...	4962				
				13	Birhamshetti	4963				
				14	Bondus	4964				
				15	Chad	4965				
				16	Chaikri	4966				
				17	Chatur	4967				
				18	Cheri	4968	Traders	C	14	
				19	Chilvant	4969				
				20	Chilvar	4970				
				21	Deogana	4971				
				22	Dhabu...	4972				
				23	Dhase	4973				
				24	Diksut...	4974				
				25	Dikshbadki	4975				
				26	Dikshpaneban... ...	4976				
				27	Dikshvant	4977				
				28	Govardan	4978				
				29	Govhar	4979				
				30	Gujrati	4980				
				31	Gurastulu	4981				
				32	Gursal	4982				
				33	Gulalbansi	4983				
				34	Hanjan	4984				
				35	Hatvan	4985				

INDEX OF CASTES.—*Continued.*

MAIN CASTE.				SUB-CASTE.		Consecutive number of Sub-caste.	Hereditary or Traditional Occupation.	CLASSIFICATION.		REMARKS.
Serial No.	Name.	POPULATION. Males.	Females.	No.	Name.			Class.	Group.	
234	Wani—*concld.* ...	......	......	36	Huper	4986				
				37	Jangam	4987				
				38	Janu	4988				
				39	Jasval...	4989				
				40	Jathvani	4990				
				41	Johari...	4991				
				42	Kadhar	4992				
				43	Kakangar	4993				
				44	Kalji	4994				
				45	Kandi	4995				
				46	Kavlekar	4996				
				47	Kasid	4997				
				48	Khadalvar	4998				
				49	Khadkar	4999				
				50	Kulne	5000				
				51	Kumnvat	5001				
				52	Kuvar...	5002				
				53	Lingait	5003				
				54	Maisri	5004				
				55	Majun	5005				
				56	Malesar	5006				
				57	Malseti	5007				
				58	Manad	5008				
				59	Mantri	5009				
				60	Mutijpati	5010				
				61	Natkar	5011				
				62	Oparak	5012				
				63	Osval	5013				
				64	Padsagar	5014				
				65	Panchambalki ...	5015	Traders	C	14	
				66	Panchamvar	5016				
				67	Pardesi	5017				
				68	Parvar	5018				
				69	Phalbad	5019				
				70	Pindari	5020				
				71	Purvant	5021				
				72	Rai	5022				
				73	Rasphal	5023				
				74	Rasvat	5024				
				75	Rudra...	5025				
				76	Sajan	5026				
				77	Saraogi	5027				
				78	Saravan	5028				
				79	Sargoingnath ...	5029				
				80	Sarsetti	5030				
				81	Seoti	5031				
				82	Setval	5032				
				83	Sheobalki	5033				
				84	Sheodas	5034				
				85	Sikmepancham ...	5035				
				86	Sikshivant	5036				
				87	Simeseti	5037				
				88	Sirul	5038				
				89	Somale	5039				
				90	Vashe	5040				
				91	Vibhutidar	5041				
				92	Virpankh	5042				
				93	Virsheo	5043				
				94	Zangriwar	5044				
235	Wanjari	3,430	3,380	1	Bara	5045				
				2	Bedar	5046				
				3	Gaodu	5047				
				4	Gonai	5048				
				5	Kanukadi	5049				
				6	Kharwai	5050	Landholders	A	2a	
				7	Kundaraidu	5051				
				8	Marwari	5052				
				9	Ramojee	5053				
				10	Telinga	5054				
				11	Wanjara	5055				
236	Zarkari	69	56	1	Jalgar...	5056				
				2	Jangar	5057				
				3	Jari	5058	Goldsmiths' refuse collectors.	D	42	
				4	Jasoo	5059				
				5	Zarkari	5060				
237	Zingar	2,377	2,330	1	Kshetrapani	5061				
				2	Kshetri	5062				
				3	Lingayet	5063	Tailors	D	22	Jingar.
				4	Panchaboi	5064				
				5	Zingar	5065				